LAND-USE PLANNING

Editorial Advisory Board
Little, Brown and Company
Law Book Division

Richard A. Epstein
James Parker Hall Professor of Law
University of Chicago

E. Allan Farnsworth
Alfred McCormack Professor of Law
Columbia University

Geoffrey C. Hazard, Jr.
Sterling Professor of Law
Yale University

James E. Krier
Earl Warren DeLano Professor of Law
University of Michigan

Bernard Wolfman
Fessenden Professor of Law
Harvard University

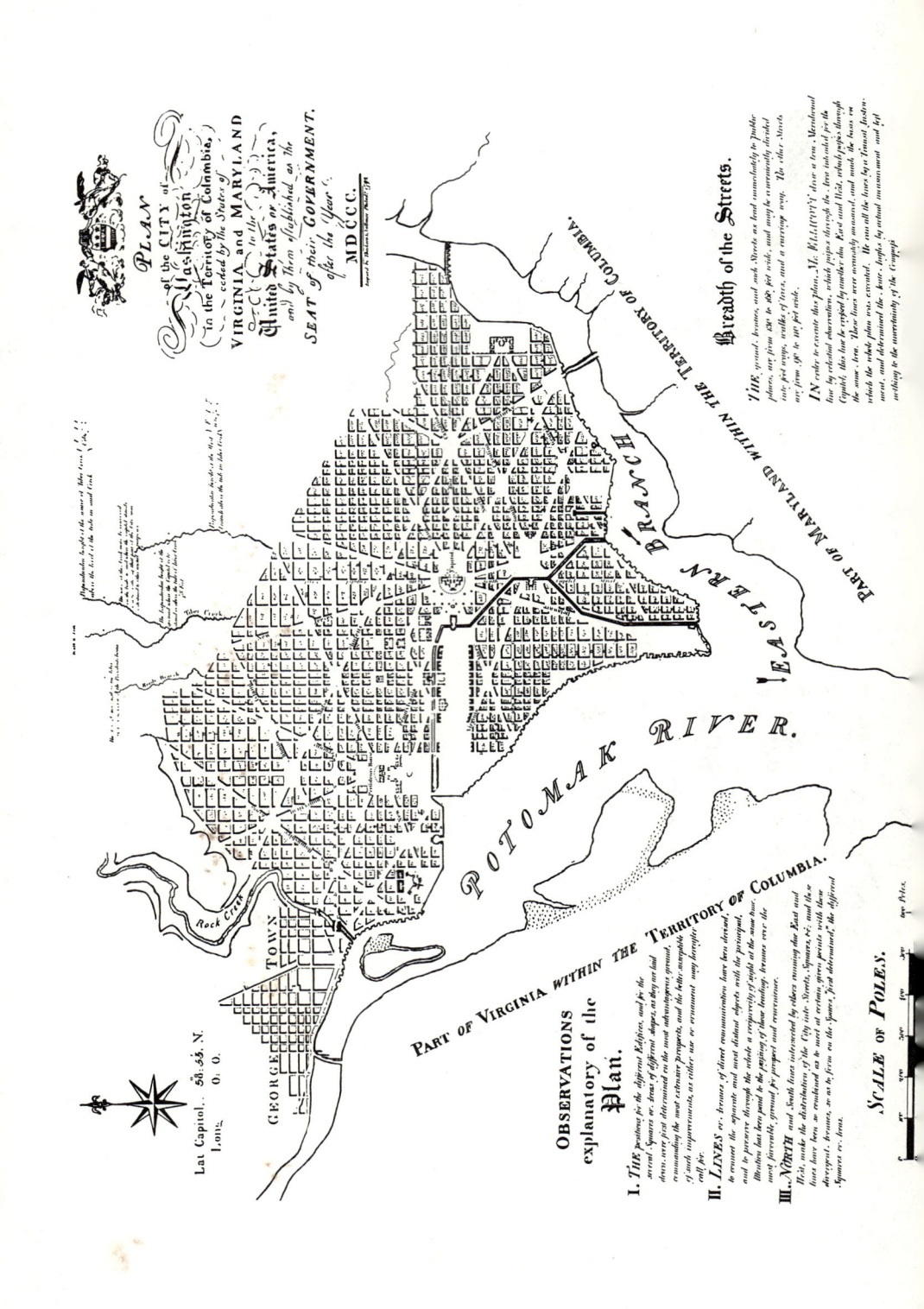

PLAN of the CITY of Washington in the Territory of Columbia, ceded by the States of VIRGINIA and MARYLAND to the United States of America, and by them established as the SEAT of their GOVERNMENT, after the Year MDCCC.

Breadth of the Streets.

THE grand Avenues, and such Streets as lead immediately to public places, are from 130 to 160 feet wide, and may be conveniently divided into foot ways, walks of trees, and a carriage way. The other Streets are from 90 to 110 feet wide.

IN order to execute this plan, Mr. ELLICOTT'S drew a true Meridional line by celestial observation, which passes through the Area intended for the Capitol; this line he crossed by another due East and West, which passes through the same Area. These lines were accurately measured, and made the bases on which the whole plan was executed. He ran all the lines by a Transit Instrument, and determined the Acute Angles by actual measurement, and left nothing to the uncertainty of the Compass.

OBSERVATIONS explanatory of the Plan.

I. THE positions for the different Edifices, and for the several Squares or Areas of different shapes, as they are laid down, were first determined on the most advantageous ground, commanding the most extensive prospects, and the better susceptible of such improvements as either use or ornament may hereafter call for.

II. LINES or Avenues of direct communication have been devised, to connect the separate and most distant objects with the principal, and to preserve through the whole a reciprocity of sight at the same time. Attention has been paid to the passing of those leading Avenues over the most favorable ground for prospect and convenience.

III. NORTH and South lines intersected by others running due East and West, make the distribution of the City into Streets, Squares, &c. and those lines have been so combined as to meet at certain given points with those divergent Avenues, so as to form on the Spaces first determined, the different Squares or Areas.

SCALE OF POLES.

Lat. Capitol. 38.53. N.
Long. 0.0.

LAND-USE PLANNING

A Casebook on the Use, Misuse, and Re-use of Urban Land

Fourth Edition

CHARLES M. HAAR
Louis D. Brandeis Professor of Law
Harvard University

MICHAEL ALLAN WOLF
Associate Professor of Law
University of Richmond

LITTLE, BROWN AND COMPANY
Boston   Toronto   London

Copyright © 1989 by Charles M. Haar and Michael Allan Wolf

All rights reserved. No part of this book may be reproduced in any form or by any electronic or mechanical means including information storage and retrieval systems without permission in writing from the publisher, except by a reviewer who may quote passages in a review.

Library of Congress Catalog Card No. 88-80706

ISBN 0-316-33677-7

Fourth Edition

Third Printing

MV NY

**Published simultaneously in Canada
by Little, Brown & Company (Canada) Limited**

Printed in the United States of America

To our children:
> Jeremy, Susan, and Jonathan
> Daniel and Rachel

"Happy is the man that hath his quiver full of them."
Psalm 127

Summary of Contents

Contents	*xi*
Illustrations and Tables	*xxvii*
Preface to the Fourth Edition	*xxxi*
Preface to the First Edition	*xxxv*
Acknowledgments	*xxxix*
Special Notice	*xlvii*

I.	The Land Around Us: The Environment of City Planning	1
II.	"Sic Utere Tuo . . .": Reconciliation by the Judiciary of Discordant Land Uses	89
III.	Legislative Districting of Permissible Land Uses — "Euclidean" Zoning and Beyond	163
IV.	The Four Seeds Sown by *Euclid*: The Control of Metropolitan Configuration	371
V.	Regulating the Tempo and Sequence of Growth	599
VI.	Protecting the Environment: The "No Choice" Doctrine	701
VII.	Government as Landowner and Redistributor: Comprehensive Planning as the Public Use	777
VIII.	Government as Joint Venturer: Evolution and Evaluation of Public/Private Partnerships	925

IX. Planning for What, How, and by Whom? The Sources of Decision-Making for the Urban Environment   1045

Table of Cases   *1129*
Index   *1139*

Contents

Illustrations and Tables	*xxvii*
Preface to the Fourth Edition	*xxxi*
Preface to the First Edition	*xxxv*
Acknowledgments	*xxxix*
Special Notice	*xlii*

I

The Land Around Us: The Environment of City Planning — 1
A. Some Basic Data on Trends in Urban Society — 1
    Report of the President's Commission for a National Agenda for the Eighties — 4
    Committee for Economic Development, Reshaping Government in Metropolitan Areas — 5
B. An Historical Excursion — 12
   1. The Impact of the Frontier on Land Use — 12
      Story, Commentaries on the Constitution of the United States — 15

		An Ordinance for Ascertaining the Mode of Disposing of Lands in the Western Territory	21
		The Public Domain	24
		An Act to Amend the Act Entitled "An Act Providing for the Sale of the Lands of the United States in the Territory Northwest of the Ohio, and Above the Mouth of Kentucky River"	25
		An Act Making Further Provision for the Sale of the Public Lands	28
		An Act to Appropriate the Proceeds of the Sales of the Public Lands, and to Grant Pre-emption Rights	28
		An Act to Secure Homesteads to Actual Settlers on the Public Domain	29
		An Act to Provide for the Sale of Desert Lands	31
		An Act Appropriating the Receipts from the Sale and Disposal of Public Lands in Certain States and Territories to the Construction of Irrigation Works for the Reclamation of Arid Lands	32
		Water Pollution Control Act	33
		National Environmental Policy Act of 1969	33
		Federal Land Policy and Management Act of 1976	36
	2.	Planning the Nation's Capital	39
C.	Meaning and Means of Planning		45
	1.	The City Planning Commission	45
	2.	The Structure of State Land-Use Planning	48
	3.	The Plan	48
		Goodman and Kaufman, City Planning in the Sixties	48
		Chicago Department of Development and Planning, The Comprehensive Plan	51
		New York City Planning Commission, Plan for New York City	53
		Berkeley People's Architecture, The Recovery of Cities	56
		American Land Institute, A Model Land Development Code	58
		Montgomery County, MD Planning Board, Growth Policy Report	59

■ Contents   xiii

	Salt Lake County, Utah Planning Commission, A Master Plan for Salt Lake County	62
D.	Tools and Techniques	63
	1. Urban Design	63
	Descartes, Discourse on the Method of Rightly Conducting the Reason	63
	2. Planning for People	67
	Mumford, The Social Foundations of Post-War Building	67
	Moynihan, Urban Conditions: General	71
	Peattie, Reflections on Advocacy Planning	73
	Mazziotti, The Underlying Assumptions of Advocacy Planning: Pluralism and Reform	74
	Munoz-Mendoza v. Pierce	76
	Rohe and Gates, Planning with Neighborhoods	80
	Problem	82
	Note: The Lawyer's Role	85

II

"Sic Utere Tuo . . .": Reconciliation by the Judiciary of Discordant Land Uses   89

A.	The Use and Enjoyment of Private Land	91
	Trespass on the Case in Regard to Certain Mills	91
	Holgate, What Is a "Rival Market"?	94
	Raising a Covert to the Nuisance	95
	Notes	95
	Rose v. Socony-Vacuum Corp.	95
	Notes	101
	Alevizos v. Metropolitan Airports Commission of Minneapolis & St. Paul	104
	Rodrigue v. Copeland	109
	Notes	112
	Powell v. Taylor	113
	Notes	116
	Boomer v. Atlantic Cement Co.	120
	Notes	124
	Prah v. Maretti	130
	California Solar Shade Control Act	135

		Notes	136
		Ellickson, Alternatives to Zoning: Covenants, Nuisance Rules, and Fines as Land Use Controls	137
	B.	An Annoyance to All the King's Subjects	139
		Rex v. White and Ward	*139*
		Notes	141
	C.	Statutory Preemption and Alternatives to Adjudication	152
		Notes on Preemption	153
		Holznagel, Negotiation and Mediation: The Newest Approach to Hazardous Waste Facility Siting	154
		Notes	156

III

Legislative Districting of Permissible Land Uses — "Euclidean" Zoning and Beyond   163

	A.	The Power to Zone	166
		Respublica v. Philip Urbin Duquet	*166*
		Notes	167
		Kline v. City of Harrisburg	*168*
		Frug, The City as a Legal Concept	*175*
		Village of Euclid v. Ambler Realty Co.	*178*
		Notes	187
		Nectow v. City of Cambridge	*190*
		Notes	193
		Arverne Bay Construction Co. v. Thatcher	*195*
		Vernon Park Realty, Inc. v. City of Mount Vernon	*201*
		Rockhill v. Chesterfield Township	*206*
		Eves v. Zoning Board of Adjustment of Lower Gwynedd Township	*211*
		Note: An English View Town and Country Planning Act, 1971	217
	B.	The Zoning Trio — Height, Bulk, and Use	220
		1. Building Size, Shape, and Placement: Density of Occupation	220
		Clemons v. City of Los Angeles	*220*
		Notes	226
		Norwood Heights Improvement Association v. Mayor and City Council of Baltimore	*226*

Contents

	Ronda Realty Corp. v. Lawton	229
	Note	232
2.	Land Use: Classification and Segregation	236
	Katobimar Realty Co. v. Webster	*236*
	Notes	242
	Record on Appeal in *Corthouts v. Town of Newington*	244
	Wiles, The Use of Expert Witnesses in Litigation	246
	Village of Belle Terre v. Boraas	*248*
	Notes	253
C.	Post-Euclidean Modifications of the Zoning Ordinance	255
1.	Incentive Zoning	256
	Kayden, Incentive Zoning in New York City: A Cost-Benefit Analysis	260
	Notes	265
2.	Transferable Development Rights	269
	Fred F. French Investing Co. v. City of New York	*269*
	Haar, Horowitz, and Katz, Transfer of Development Rights: A Primer	273
3.	Performance Standards	276
	Notes	276
4.	Planned Unit Development	279
	Notes	279
5.	Mixed-Use Development	283
6.	Contract and Conditional Zoning	283
	Collard v. Incorporated Village of Flower Hill	*283*
D.	Departures from the Zoning Ordinance: The Extent of Discretion	289
1.	Nonconforming Uses: Preexisting Uses That Won't Fade Away	290
	City of Los Angeles v. Gage	*290*
	Notes	297
	Notes on Retroactivity and Building Permits	308
	Town and Country Planning Act of 1971	311
2.	Amendments: Legislating (or Adjudicating?) Small-Scale Changes	313
	Kuehne v. Town Council of East Hartford	*313*
	Haar, Sawyer, and Cummings, Computer Power and Legal Reasoning: A Case Study of Judicial Decision Prediction in Zoning Amendment Cases	317
	MacDonald v. Board of Commissioners	*319*

			Notes and Problems	327
			Fasano v. Board of Commissioners of Washington County	*330*
			Notes and Problems	336
	3.		Variances and Special Exceptions: From "Safety Valves" to "Steady Leaks"	343
			Williams, The Law on Variances	343
			De Simone v. Greater Englewood Housing Corp. No. 1	*344*
			Kisil v. City of Sandusky	*349*
			Notes	351
			City of Cleburne v. Cleburne Living Center	*357*
			Notes	359
E.	Voices in Opposition: Champions of De- and Re-regulation			363
			Siegan, Non-Zoning in Houston	363
			Kmiec, The Role of the Planner in a Deregulated World	365
			The Report of the President's Commission on Housing	368

IV
■

The Four Seeds Sown by Euclid: *The Control of Metropolitan Configuration* — *371*

A.	Exclusion			372
	1.	Excluding People		376
			CASE STUDY # 1:	376
		a.	Experimenting in the State Laboratories — A View from the *Mount*	376
			Lionshead Lake, Inc. v. Wayne Township	*377*
			Notes and Problems	383
			Oakwood at Madison, Inc. v. Township of Madison (1971)	*386*
			Notes	391
			Southern Burlington County NAACP v. Township of Mount Laurel (1974)	*398*
			Notes	400
			Southern Burlington County NAACP v. Township of Mount Laurel (1975) [*Mount Laurel I*]	*402*

■ **Contents** xvii

	Notes	409
	Oakwood at Madison, Inc. v. Township of Madison (1977)	*414*
	Home Builders League of South Jersey v. Township of Berlin	*415*
	Notes	417
	Southern Burlington County NAACP v. Township of Mount Laurel (1983) [*Mount Laurel II*]	*420*
	Note on Inclusionary Zoning	431
	Notes	435
	Hills Development Co. v. Township of Barnards [*Mount Laurel III*]	*441*
	Notes	445
b.	Running the Federal Gauntlet	445
	Warth v. Seldin	*446*
	Notes	449
	Village of Arlington Heights v. Metropolitan Housing Development Corp.	*450*
	Notes	456
	Scott v. Greenville County	*462*
	Notes on §1983	466
	A Comparative Note: The Common Law, Equity, and the Demise of Racially Restrictive Covenants	470
	Drinan, Untying the White Noose	475
2.	Excluding Uses: Things Profane, Sacred, and In-Between	476
	Young v. American Mini Theatres, Inc.	*478*
	Notes	480
	Schad v. Borough of Mount Ephraim	*484*
	Notes	488
	Larkin v. Grendel's Den, Inc.	*492*
	Notes	495
	Grosz v. City of Miami Beach	*498*
	Notes	502
B. Anticompetitiveness		504
	Scott v. City of Sioux City	*507*
	Notes	511
C. Urban Design		518
	Scenic Hudson Preservation Conference v. Federal Power Commission (1965)	*520*
	Scenic Hudson Preservation Conference v. Federal Power Commission (1971)	*522*
	Notes	524

			Lutheran Church in America v. City of New York	527
			Notes	531
			Penn Central Transportation Co. v. New York City	537
			Notes	544
			Minister of Housing and Local Government, Design	550
			Urban Design	551
D.	Parochialism			555
	1.	The Puzzle of Comprehensiveness		557
			Borough of Cresskill v. Borough of Dumont	558
			Fairlawns Cemetery Association v. Zoning Commission of Bethel	560
			Connor v. Township of Chanhassen	560
			Udell v. Haas	561
			Baker v. City of Milwaukie (1974)	562
			Baker v. City of Milwaukie (1975)	563
			Bell v. City of Elkhorn	563
			United States Department of Commerce, A Standard City Planning Enabling Act	564
	2.	Community Growth Policies		567
			Meier, Planning for Tomorrow's World	567
			Ministry of Housing and Local Government, Circular No. 42/55	567
			Golden v. Planning Board of Town of Ramapo	570
			Notes	578
			Construction Industry Association v. City of Petaluma	583
			Notes	588
			California Government Code	593
			California Evidence Code	594
			Notes	594

V

Regulating the Tempo and Sequence of Growth — 599

A.	Conflict at the Rural-Urban Fringe: The Developer's "Own Sweet Will"			601
	1.	Enabling Legislation for Subdivision Control		601
		a.	Definitions	603

■ Contents   xix

		United States Department of Commerce,	
		A Standard City Planning Enabling Act	603
		Wisconsin Statutes Annotated	603
		Massachusetts General Laws Annotated	604
	b.	Governmental Organization	605
		New Jersey Statutes Annotated	605
		Texas Property Code Annotated	607
		Maryland Annotated Code	608
	c.	Jurisdiction	608
		United States Department of Commerce,	
		A Standard City Planning Enabling Act	608
		Indiana Code Annotated	609
	d.	Standards and Requirements	610
		Revised Statutes of Ontario	610
		Washington Revised Code Annotated	611
	e.	Sanctions	612
		New Jersey Statutes Annotated	612
		Washington Revised Code Annotated	612
		Pennsylvania Statutes Annotated	613
	f.	Exactions	614
		California Government Code	614
		Problems	616
2.		Authorizing Dealmaking: Development Agreements	617
B. The Attitude of the Judiciary			621
1.		Scrutinizing the Dealmaking Process	621
		Ayres v. City Council of Los Angeles	*621*
		Home Builders and Contractors Association of Palm Beach County v. Board of County Commissioners	*629*
		Notes	632
		Nollan v. California Coastal Commission	*636*
		Notes	644
		CASE STUDY # 2:	647
2.		Mandating the Provision of Services	647
	a.	*Hawkins* and Hope	647
		Hawkins v. Town of Shaw (1969)	*647*
		Hawkins v. Town of Shaw (1971)	*654*
		Notes	655
	b.	Federal Bars	657
		Beal v. Lindsay	*657*
		Notes	659
	c.	Tracing the Common Law Duty to Serve	660
		Bracton, "De Adquirendo Rerum Dominio" (Of Acquiring the Dominion of Things)	660

		Trespass on the Case in Regard to Certain Mills	*661*
		Haar and Fessler, The Wrong Side of the Tracks	661
		White and Snoak and His Wife v. Porter	*663*
		Messenger v. Pennsylvania Railroad	*664*
		State ex rel. Webster v. Nebraska Telephone Co.	*666*
		Questions	667
		Reid Development Corp. v. Parsippany-Troy Hills Township	*667*
		Notes	670
		Questions	672
	3.	Private Subdivision Controls: The Lawyer as Urban (and Suburban) Planner	673
		Harrod v. Rigelhaupt	*676*
		Notes	682
		Notes on Enforcement and Administration	684
C.	The Official Map Technique: The "Dead Hand" of the Future		687
		Headley v. City of Rochester	*687*
		Notes	693
D.	Limitations on Local Discretion		696
		Interstate Land Sales Full Disclosure Act	697
		Notes	698
		Fuller, Freedom — A Suggested Analysis	699

VI

■

Protecting the Environment: The "No Choice" Doctrine — 701

A.	Preserving the Hydrologic Cycle ("Only Preserving Nature from Despoilage")		702
		Flood Plain Conservation and Protection	702
		Dooley v. Town of Fairfield	*704*
		Notes	707
		Delaware Wetlands Act	709
		Notes	711
		Just v. Marinette County	*712*
		Notes	718
		Internal Revenue Code §170(h)	722
		Treasury Regulations §1.170A-14	723
		Notes	724
B.	Environmental Policy Acts: Controlling the		

		"Destructive Engine of Material 'Progress'"	727
		Coalition for Los Angeles County Planning in the Public Interest v. Board of Supervisors	729
		H.O.M.E.S. v. New York State Urban Development Corp.	732
		Notes	735
		Keystone Bituminous Coal Association v. DeBenedictus	736
		Notes	742
C.	Takeover by the States?		743
	1.	Goals and Purposes	744
		Maine Site Location of Development Law	745
		Florida Environmental Land and Water Management Act of 1972	746
		Hawaii Quality Growth Act of 1972	746
		Oregon Land Use Law	747
	2.	Definitions	748
		Maine Site Location of Development Law	748
		Florida Environmental Land and Water Management Act of 1972	748
		Florida Environmental Land and Water Management Act of 1972	749
		Oregon Land Use Law	749
		Florida Environmental Land and Water Management Act of 1972	750
	3.	Standards	751
		Florida Environmental Land and Water Management Act of 1972	751
		Maine Site Location of Development Law	752
	4.	State Land-Use Districts	752
		Hawaii Land Use Law	752
		Notes	754
D.	Politics, Economics, and the Limits of Legalism		756
	1.	Coastal New Federalism	756
		Nollan v. California Coastal Commission	756
		Wolf, Accommodating Tensions in the Coastal Zone: An Introduction and Overview	756
		Notes	761
		CASE STUDY # 3:	761
	2.	The Judicial Role in Complex Environmental Disputes: The Case of Boston Harbor	761
		Griffin. The Politics and Litigation of Boston Harbor: From Superior Court to Beacon Hill	762
		Notes	773

VII

Government as Landowner and Redistributor: Comprehensive Planning as the Public Use — 777

A. From Blackstone to *Berman*'s Progeny: Redefining the Public Use Requirement	780
Blackstone, Commentaries	780
Schlesinger, Soviet Legal Theory	780
Chief Joseph	781
State Constitutional Provisions	781
Kaskel v. Impellitteri	*784*
Jacobs, The Death and Life of Great American Cities	787
Berman v. Parker	*788*
Notes	794
Poletown Neighborhood Council v. City of Detroit	*798*
Notes	805
City of Oakland v. Oakland Raiders	*809*
Notes	813
Hawaii Housing Authority v. Midkiff	*816*
Notes	820
Mosley, Disney's World	822
Caro, The Power Broker: Robert Moses and the Fall of New York	824
B. Land Banks	826
Note	830
Problem	830
C. The Riddle of Just Compensation	831
Blackstone, Commentaries	831
Horwitz, The Transformation of American Law, 1780–1860	831
State Constitutional Provisions	832
1. Fair Market Value	834
Riley v. District of Columbia Redevelopment Land Agency	*834*
Note on Valuation Formulas	840
Notes and Problems	845
2. Injurious Affection: Incidental, Consequential, and Severance Damages	855
In re Water Front in City of New York	*855*
Notes	860
Notes on Goodwill and Relocation	864

		Commons, Institutional Economics	867
		New York City Housing Authority v. Muller	*867*
		Epstein, Takings: Private Property and the Power of Eminent Domain	868
D.	An Experiment in Finance: The British Town and Country Planning Acts		869
		Report of the Expert Committee on Compensation and Betterment	870
		Haar, Land Planning Law in a Free Society	871
		Town and Country Planning Act, 1947	872
		McAuslan, Compensation and Betterment	874
E.	Regulation versus Taking		875
	1.	The Supreme Court's Decisional Labyrinth: A Conservation among the Justices	879
	2.	Of Bright Lights and Balancing: The Commentators Respond	888
		a. Can We Meaningfully Distinguish between the Police Power and Eminent Domain?	891
		b. When (If Ever) Is Compensation Appropriate?	894
		c. How Much Compensation?	898
		d. Are We Asking the Right Questions?	900
	3.	Ending the Procedural Tango	902
		San Diego Gas & Electric Co. v. City of San Diego	*903*
		Notes	910
		First English Evangelical Lutheran Church of Glendale v. County of Los Angeles	*913*
		Notes	921

VIII
■
Government as Joint Venturer: Evolution and Evaluation of Public/Private Partnerships   **925**

A.	Variations on a Theme: Federal Attempts to Spur Economic Redevelopment and Neighborhood Revitalization		930
	1.	Model Cities	930
		Demonstration Cities and Metropolitan Development Act of 1966	930
		Notes	932

	2.	New Communities	933
		Housing and Urban Development Act of 1970	933
		Notes	936
	3.	Community Development Block Grants (CDBG)	942
		Housing and Community Development Act of 1974	942
		Notes	945
		24 C.F.R. §570.424	951
	4.	Urban Development Action Grants (UDAG)	952
		Housing and Community Development Act of 1977	952
		Notes	954
	5.	Federal Enterprise Zones (EZ)	958
		Housing and Community Development Act of 1987	958
		Notes	962
B.	Replication and Innovation: The State and Local Experience		964
	1.	The New Urban Alphabet Soup: IRB, TIF, UDC, EDC, and the Like	965
	2.	Public Purpose Redux: Tax Incentives before the Bench	971
		Florida Constitutional Provisions	973
		State v. Clay County Development Authority	*975*
		State v. Housing Finance Authority	*977*
		State v. City of Miami	*979*
		State v. Miami Beach Redevelopment Agency	*981*
		Notes	986
	3.	On the Impact of Redevelopment Partnerships	986
		Jackson v. New York State Urban Development Corporation	*986*
		Notes	989
		CASE STUDY # 4:	992
	4.	Maryland Enterprise Zones	992
		Greater Baltimore Committee, Inc., Report of the Enterprise Zone Subcommittee	992
		Funkhouser and Saquella, Establishing Enterprise Zones in Maryland	994
		Maryland Annotated Code	998
		Baltimore Economic Development Corp. (BEDCO), Enterprise Zone Annual Report	1001

■ Contents

	Maryland Division of Local Government Assistance, Maryland's Enterprise Zone Program: A Third Year Report	1004
	Questions	1005
C.	Housing the Deserving and Undeserving Poor	1005
1.	Alternative Paths to Affordable Housing	1007
	Mitchell, The Historical Context for Housing Policy	1007
	Notes	1009
	Massachusetts Housing Finance Agency v. New England Merchants National Bank	*1019*
	Notes	1022
2.	Site Selection for Federally Subsidized Housing	1025
	Gautreaux v. Chicago Housing Authority	*1025*
	Notes	1028
3.	"The Best Laid Schemes . . .": Implementing and Enforcing Desegregation	1037
	Young v. Pierce	*1037*
	Notes	1040

IX
■

Planning for What, How, and By Whom? The Sources of Decision-Making for the Urban Environment   *1045*

A.	The Master Plan: An Impermanent Constitution	1046
	Bassett, The Master Plan	1047
	American Law Institute, A Model Land Development Code	1050
	Ayres v. City Council of Los Angeles	*1052*
	Coalition for Los Angeles County Planning in the Public Interest v. Board of Supervisors	*1052*
	Kozesnik v. Township of Montgomery	*1052*
	Board of County Commissioners of Cecil County v. Gaster	*1053*
	Notes	1054
	Rider, Transition from Land Use to Policy Planning: Lessons Learned	1056
B.	Planning Process, Market Mechanism, and Administrative Controls	1058
1.	The Efficacy and Desirability of Land-Use	

			Controls in Achieving Values	1058
			Polanyi, The Logic of Liberty	1058
			Tugwell, The Fourth Power	1059
			Fuller, Freedom — A Suggested Analysis	1063
			Keller, The Planning of Communities: Anticipations and Hindsights	1065
			Lock, Planning: The Future	1070
	2.		How Should a Land-Use Decision Be Made?	1071
			Cross v. Bilett	*1071*
			Notes on Private Restrictions	1075
			City of Eastlake v. Forest City Enterprises, Inc.	*1078*
			Notes	1082
			City of Cleburne v. Cleburne Living Center	*1085*
			Hendricks and Alexander, Subculture Cells	1089
			CASE STUDY # 5:	1090
	3.		Neighborhood Buyouts of Zoning "Rights"	1090
		a.	The Context: New Forms of Metropolitan Growth and the Buyout Phenomenon	1091
			Haar and Lindsay, Business and the Revolution in Land Use Planning: New Private Sector Roles and New Suburban Forms	1092
			Clary and Rasmussen, The Buyout Phenomenon	1094
		b.	The Lake Hearn Assemblage: Neighborhood Mobilization and County Opposition	1096
			DeKalb County Planning Department Recommendation, Denial Justification	1099
		c.	The Buyout in Court	1101
			Dekalb County v. Albritton Properties	*1101*
			Notes	1105
C.			The Master Plan: An Inquiry in Dialogue Form	1108

Table of Cases   *1129*
Index   *1139*

Illustrations and Tables

Plan for Washington, D.C.	Frontispiece
The Rural-Urban Contrast	2
Percent of Local Governments by Type in SMSA's: 1962 to 1982	7
Percent of Population in Central Cities and Rings of Metropolitan Areas, and Urban and Rural Portions of Nonmetropolitan Areas: 1900–1980	8
One Out of Every Five Persons Moves Each Year	9
Personal Income per Capita in Constant 1972 Dollars: 1970 to 1980	10
Resident Population 1970 to 1980	10
Population 55 Years and Over, by Age: 1900 to 2050	11
Poverty Rate in 1981 of Persons 60 Years and Over, by Age, Race, and Sex	11
Estimates and Projections of Total Population: 1950 to 2080	13
Components of Population Growth in the United States: 1900 to 1983	14
Population Changes by Residence and Race: 1982 and 1970	16
Percent Change in Employment, by Major Industry Groups: 1972 to 1982	17

Median Family Income by Place of Residence, 1970–76	18
U.S., Central City, Suburban, and Nonmetropolitan Unemployment Rates, 1973–77	18
Change in Central City Retail Markets, 1970 to 1980	18
Distribution of the White, Black, and Spanish-Origin Populations, by Metropolitan-Nonmetropolitan Residence: 1982	19
Increase in Black Population in Central Cities and Suburbs in Metropolitan Areas of 1 Million or More	20
The Purposes for Which Urban Land Is Used	26
Use of Land Downtown, Washington, D.C. — 1980	27
Land Area, Population, and Density: 1970–1980	27
Principal Means of Transportation to Work — Selected Metropolitan Areas: 1980	30
Young and Elderly Support Ratios: 1900 to 2050	34
Ratio of Residential Capital Formation to Gross National Product and to Total Consumption	35
Evolution of the National Capital	41
The L'Enfant Plan	42
The McMillan Plan of 1901, Showing the Mall	43
Government Employment Centers	43
Jurisdictional Boundaries	44
Participants in Planning in the Municipality of Los Angeles	45
City Planning Agency Organizational Chart	46
The Place of the City Planning Commission	47
Organizational Structure for Implementation of Florida's Environmental Land and Water Management Act of 1972	49
Administrative Structure of Land-Use Agencies in Hawaii	50
Wright, Broadacre City	65
Le Corbusier, Ville Radieuse and the City-Squares of Sitte	65
Goodman, Consumer City	65
Soleri, Babel IIB	66
Typical Funeral Parlor Litigations	115
Spur Industries, Inc. v. Del E. Webb Development Co.	128
Village of Euclid v. Ambler Realty Co.	179
Nectow v. City of Cambridge	192
Daylight Factor	235
Comparison of Bonused Building Z and Unbonused Building UZ's Financial Statements	263
Comparison of Bonused Building Z and Unbonused Building UZ's Simple Rates of Return	264

■ Illustrations and Tables   xxix

Parkchester, New York City	280
Midtown Plaza, Rochester, New York	284
Amortization of Nonconforming Uses	299
Parkview Associates Building, New York City	310
Summary of Regression Analysis for Zoning Amendment Litigation Study	318
Typical Spot-Zoning Cases	322
Summary Classification of Problems and Proposed Reforms	339
Survey of Big City Zoning Boards of Appeals	360
Mount Laurel Cost for Moderate Income Housing	437
Mount Laurel Cost for Low Income Housing	437
Borough of Cresskill v. Borough of Dumont	559
Community Direct Cost Analysis	568
Neighborhood Direct Cost Analysis	569
Development Point System	580
Requesting Subdivision Approval in Henrico County, Virginia	606
Summary of Santa Monica Development Agreements	618
Ayres v. City Council of Los Angeles	623
Harrod v. Rigelhaupt	677
"As soon as things pick up a little we're going to have it landscaped."	720
Pogo on Pollution	759
Captain America: "A Nefarious Urban-Demolition Scheme."	791
Acquisition of Land for Improvements in the Future	829
Typical Expressway Problems	862
Garden City	937
Stevenage New Town	937
CDBG Housing Assistance Plan	948
CDBG Grantee Performance Report	949
Doonesbury on Gentrification	991
Incentives Available in Existing State and Local EZ Programs	996
Enterprise Zones in Maryland	999
Maryland Tax Form 500Z	1003
Federal Role in Residential Mortgage Markets	1011
Gautreaux v. Chicago Housing Authority	1026
Four Policymaking Styles	1066
O'Brian Cartoon	1090
Washington, D.C.	1127

Preface to the Fourth Edition

That the pendulum swings should neither surprise nor disappoint us. We would be foolish to ignore the signs of public dissatisfaction with the retreat of government from the planning sphere. The past decade was marked by widespread displeasure with government intervention and a fascination with market solutions. In large part this reshuffling of the American political agenda was fostered by suspicion of the competency of the public sector in affording society a productive environment. There is now a growing awareness of the twin legacy of extreme privatization: an endangered environment and a crumbling infrastructure. Zealousness, even greed, has destroyed skylines, lakes, and broad shorelines; private developers seeking a smooth canvas upon which to realize their vision are frustrated by rubble, decay, and disrepair.

Land use is an ever-evolving, provocative, even exciting area that continues to tap the ingenuity of legal and planning practitioners and to challenge the hypotheses of social scientists. Land-use planning reflects the general ideals and aspirations of a society, as we strive to create a physical environment that satisfies the Aristotelian desire for the good life. The principles and conflicts derived from feudal relationships that form the core of the basic property course are raised again in the modern context, as the law reflects and anticipates technological, social, and political change.

The 1970s and 1980s have witnessed impressive shifts in the theory and practice of land-use planning and law, often paralleling modifications in the development and taxation of real estate. In addition to new cases, statutes, and regulations, three major conditions most immediately prompted this revision: (1) The withdrawal of federal funding has resulted in the flowering of local governmental creativity. Incentives, exactions, and linkages — the public share of the modern joint venture — have leveraged impressive developments. In a growing number of instances, however, frustrated participants (and courts) have voiced concern over the potential for abuse and unfairness to the new. The search for a comfortable and effective conjunction of public and private goes on. (2) Litigants and commentators have waged a counter-revolution, a multi-front attack on the underside of traditional height, area, and use zoning: its anticompetitiveness, socioeconomic exclusionary potential, rejection of a regional approach to land-use decision-making, and emphasis on subjective (particularly aesthetic) considerations. (3) The United States Supreme Court has displayed a curiously bifurcated approach to land-use dilemmas — choosing to address and resolve problems arising when ordinances and regulations touch on constitutionally protected interests (for example, religious practice and free speech), while only incrementally confronting the Achilles heel of land-use planning: the determination of whether and when a regulation can amount to a taking. Even as the Court rendered three important regulatory takings decisions in the 1986-1987 Term (*Keystone*, *First English*, and *Nollan*), it was evident that many more questions regarding the availability and amount of compensation remain unresolved.

There have also been alterations in the legal education menu, shifts brought about by changing student appetites, career paths, and perceptions. The focus in land-use law — not unlike a major concern of modern tort, contract, and antitrust law — is on the provision of late twentieth century necessities (in this case, decent housing, adequate employment, and a safe neighborhood) in the face of financial shortfalls and government shortcomings. Moreover, students are increasingly concerned with the practical side of law, the hands-on experience that is often ignored in course materials and lectures. The ideas presented in this casebook seek to tap into both sets of developments within the law and the law school. To highlight these and other areas of inquiry, we have included five Case Studies, each designed to immerse the class in the facts, issues, and practical nuances of areas on the cutting edge of the law. We see no reason why the business school should claim a monopoly over this provocative teaching tool.

While the basic structure of *Land-Use Planning* has proven to be an excellent framework for study and discussion of new developments — legal and extra-legal — over the past several years, there has naturally been a good deal of reworking of cases and topics. Data are updated, obsolete opinions are replaced, and two new chapters are included: one surveying the rich legacy of *Euclid v. Ambler* (Chapter IV), the other devoted primarily to environmental issues (Chapter VI). In addition, Chapter VIII, concerned with public-private joint ventures, combines new and revised materials on government-sponsored redevelopment efforts with a set of readings on lower-income housing. The materials on private land-use devices such as covenants and easements no longer warrant a discrete chapter, particularly in light of the increased attention paid in first-year property courses; readings on these topics serve instead as useful contrasts to the prevailing regime of public regulation. The authors have shaped chapters (and organized major divisions therein) to stand as distinct treatments of such major topics as eminent domain, nuisance, and subdivision law. This allows the individual instructor to design a course that best meets her interests and expertise. Yet no matter the arrangement selected, certain themes recur throughout the text, and students are directed to pursue the interdependent rules and principles that shape land-use regulation.

Despite these modifications, the fundamental approach of the first three editions is retained — that is, basically a recognition of the idealistic and realistic potential of comprehensive land-use planning. This tenor prevails despite the provocative challenges posed by champions of the free market (many of whose writings are included in the casebook) and the disturbing mistakes that have resulted from the application of the latest planning trends. While one should not ignore the demands and limitations of the market, there are also pitfalls in failing to regard the underlying public interest that always has influenced and reflected decisions made in the public and private sectors regarding the use, development, and preservation of real property. The presentation of arguments from more than one side enables teachers — through a dialectic process — to pursue the strengths and weaknesses of competing theories. Ours is not (and has never been) an unyielding dedication to government planning. Instead we recognize the centrality of comprehensive planning — especially on the state and local levels — and choose to compare and contrast other systems (or nonsystems) with that reality.

What follows then, we trust, is a stimulating and instructive collection of cases and materials in the area of land-use law — a casebook that provides the student with a wide-ranging and up-to-date compilation of common law, constitutional, legislative, and administrative source materials; an introduction to the most provocative legal scholarship in this area; a strong foundation in the relevant theory, philosophy, and history of land-use planning; and a glimpse of the notions and developments on the horizon of land-use planning, development, and finance.

This new edition could not have been completed without the assistance of a number of people, to whom the authors are most grateful: Shirley Bitts, Vickey Cannady, Jerold Kayden, Jonathan Lindsay, George Marek, Kate Porter, Tony Ratner, Jeff Sharp, Anne Smith, Stuart Strasner, Rebecca Weinreich, and Barbara West. Several classes full of students in Cambridge, Oklahoma City, and Richmond aided the process of revising drafts. At Little, Brown and Company Sandra Doherty and Maureen Kaplan, and Rick Heuser and Betsy Kenny helped us craft a challenging, student-friendly volume. Our special appreciation goes to Professor Robert A. Williams, Jr., whose contributions, insights, and criticisms improved the quality and sharpened the clarity of our final product. Others assist by keeping perspectives fresh, spirits up, and distractions at a distance, particularly when the work is most demanding. In these and countless other ways, Betty Morganstern Wolf proved an invaluable partner. We also thank our teaching colleagues and the many practitioners — lawyers and planners — who encouraged us to update and reinvigorate the book they first used in class and continue to consult for their work in the field.

Charles M. Haar
Michael Allan Wolf

January 1989

Preface to the First Edition

"Regard of the law for private property," wrote Blackstone, "is so great . . . that it will not authorize the least violation of it, not even for the general good of the whole community"; and in the eighteenth century, the elder Pitt declaimed that "the poorest man in his cottage could defy the King — storms may enter; the rain may enter — but the King of England cannot enter." In sharp contrast, the United States Supreme Court, by upholding in sweeping terms urban redevelopment legislation, has ruled in effect that the King not only may enter, but may remain, in the name of the general good, indeed for the very purpose of keeping the rain out.

It is to the exploration and analysis of the evolution of property law marked by these conflicting statements that this volume is primarily devoted. It examines the assumptions, doctrines, and implications of city planning law. It considers the impact of planning on the common law of property rights, on the operation of the land market in a constitutional democratic state, and on the lawyer's role in real estate transactions — be he representative of landowner, government, or financial institution. This book therefore attempts to place property law in its contemporary setting. The aim is to produce an interpretive organization of materials which will enable students and practitioners of law and planning to analyze effectively the legal and administrative problems of allocating and developing that increasingly scarce resource — urban land in metropolitan areas.

The transformation in the way men live in an industrialized society, the shift from the feudal manor and a rural society to the city and suburb of the metropolitan area, outmode old ways and, with them, accepted legal doctrines and administrative techniques. In particular, the rules of land law have been subjected to massive pressures. Since the end of World War II the statute books and judicial opinions have reflected the attempts to provide a new synthesis for the law governing property.

The impact of taxation on conveyancing is now appreciated; other aspects of the intervention of government in the real estate market and in land development have yet to be fully absorbed into the thinking of the bar. Yet a lawyer, whether he represents a client purchasing a home in the latest subdivision or an insurance company projecting a downtown commercial redevelopment, cannot do an adequate job without an understanding — and one predicated on something more than being a participant in the twentieth century — of the changes the urban revolution has produced in his client's expectations, of society's demands in fashioning the physical environment, and of the reshaping of the entrepreneur's role in the allocation of land resources. Moreover, the indications already are that lawyers of the next generation will be even more concerned with the competition and coordination of private rights and public values in urban land: the metropolitan area is increasingly the most pressing American domestic problem. Accordingly, the law schools cannot effectively discharge their educational task without an attempt to analyze and synthesize in their curricula these profound alterations in thought and outlook. And practitioners, both of planning and of law, need further awareness of their import.

This is not to deny the wisdom of intensive study of ancient legal doctrine; the ingenuity of the past in dealing with the demands of population upon limited resources provides insights which, when modified for present conditions or adapted for contemporary issues, can help in dealing with new crises. The fourteenth-century Pakenham's Case, holding that the promise of a prior to sing in a chapel on the covenantee's manor runs with the land, may seem a far chant indeed from the laying out of a new town for the production of aluminum for a world market. Yet the draftsman of each of these arrangements found common legal problems. That ancient legal tools acquire new vitality in a contemporary setting comes as no surprise to students of property law. While it is the field par excellence of certainty — for men and governments must arrange their affairs on the basis of expectations that will be honored — the law of property has proved over the centuries a marvelously flexible and supple instrument in accommodating new interests and wants. The subtle confluence of modification and invention has permitted society to realize important land policies and objectives. Law must preserve the investments of the past at the

Preface to the First Edition

same time that it accommodates current and anticipated needs. As perhaps the most planned sector of the American economy, the land-use area contains in microcosm the broader issues of freedom and planning. Here, at the juncture of property law and constitutional law, stand the often conflicting loyalties of "master plan" and "rights in land."

This book is divided into eight chapters:

1. An introduction to the goals and assumptions (remedial, utopian, and emergent) of land-use planning, and the interaction of American history, planning theory and land policies.

2. Judicial determinations of conflicting land uses in the law of nuisance, and the relation of private to public nuisance.

3. Legislative districting of permissible land use through zoning, the most extensively employed city planning tool.

4. Subdivision and street controls, including a more intensive study of the regional framework for land planning already implicit in the zoning materials.

5. The use of eminent domain by government as landowner and redistributor, stressing the issues of public use and just compensation, as well as the English experience with compensation.

6. The private planning of land use through covenants, conditions, defeasible estates, easements, and other devices having their roots in feudal times, but now utilized in urban renewal.

7. The role of the federal government in land-use policies, and the indirect restraints and inducements through housing, credit, fiscal, and tax policies.

8. Land-use planning by whom, how, and for whom — the role of the master plan, and the desirability and efficacy of urban planning.

In each chapter I have attempted to clarify a number of issues underlying the land-use field. What is the social function of private property, the relation of individual to public decision-making and the process by which land-use decisions are made? What are the alternative agencies for settling disputes? How is urban land different from other types of resources or economic activities? What are the relative benefits and disadvantages of competing modes of land allocation and development which legal and planning inventiveness can devise? What legal powers and institutions are available under a constitutional system? How can legal and property institutions be molded into a more rational and effective organization of the land resource?

As will be seen, this volume attempts to view American legal policies for urban land against a broad background. In order to shed a different light on property and planning concepts, materials are included which often fall into a twilight zone between courses, such as just compensation in eminent domain and the law of public nuisance. Since English experience has gone furthest in the manipulation of the land market, and in the reduction of the fee simple, it seemed relevant to incorporate part of that experience. It is also necessary to reach out beyond the library to gain a full understanding of the issues involved. Promulgated decisions frequently lag behind practice; and many of the influences affecting zoning, subdivision, eminent domain, and the other controls are simply not available in published literature. Discussions with administrators, lawyers, and planners have proved helpful in the isolation and formulation of problems which do arise in practice.

To adjust community and private interest in the urban environment requires the sympathetic, albeit not uncritical, alliance of planners and lawyers. I hope, therefore, that this volume will be of interest to the planner as well as the lawyer and that it will stimulate the introduction into both law and planning schools of courses on the legal and administrative problems of land-use planning. Experience has indicated that the case method is a vivid way of introducing the planner to the legal and institutional implications of a conscious fashioning of the physical environment; and an understanding of the legal background may call for a reconsideration of some aspects of planning theory. Planners, it is hoped, will not be discouraged by the legal apparatus of the book; the use of the materials in temporary form seems to justify this expectation. To the degree planners can grasp planning issues in legal terms, they can help assure that the legal organization and system will properly reflect planning terms.

Fundamental in the arrangement of the materials has been a conception of the book as a teaching instrument. I have tried to place differing and inconsistent opinions (judicial or planning) in juxtaposition so as to encourage a critical and closely analytical approach. Only by weaving his own way through diverse situations of fact and opinion, and subjecting them to as precise reasoning as possible, can the student of law or planning strike his own determinations. As Proust reminds us, "That which we have not been forced to decipher, to clarify by our own personal effort, that which was made clear before, is not ours."

Charles M. Haar

July 1, 1958

Acknowledgments

The authors acknowledge the permissions kindly granted to reproduce the materials indicated below.

Abeles Schwartz Associates, Inc., *Mount Laurel* Cost Tables. Reprinted with permission.
A Model Land Development Code. Copyright © 1976 by the American Law Institute. Reprinted with the permission of the American Law Institute.
Baltimore Economic Development Corp., Enterprise Zone Annual Report 1-4 (1984). Reprinted with permission.
Bartholomew, Land Use in American Cities 121 (1955) (table). Reprinted with permission of Harvard University Press.
Bassett, The Master Plan: With a Discussion of the Theory of Community Land Planning Legislation, © 1938 by Edward M. Bassett, Russell Sage Foundation, New York.
Berry, The Question of Policy Alternatives, Four Policymaking Styles (table), in The Good Earth of America: Planning Our Land Use 159 (Harris ed. 1973). Reprinted with permission of The American Assembly.
Bogue, The Population of the United States 13, 21, 130. Reprinted with permission of The Free Press, a Division of MacMillan, Inc., from The Population of the United States: Historical Trends and

Future Projections by Donald J. Bogue. Copyright © 1985 by The Free Press.
Bracton, 2 De Legibus et Consuetudinibus Angliae 166-167 (Thorne trans. 1968). Reprinted with permission of Harvard University Press.
Branch, Continuous City Planning: Integrating Municipal Management and City Planning 66 (Los Angeles planning chart). Reprinted with permission of John Wiley & Sons, Inc., copyright © 1981.
Brazil, Special Masters in Complex Cases, 53 University of Chicago Law Review 394, 414, 416, 422 (1986). Reprinted with permission.
Breitel, A Judicial View of Transferable Development Rights, Land Use Law and Zoning Digest, February 1978, at 5, 5-6. Reprinted with permission from the American Planning Association. Copyright © 1978 by the American Planning Association, 1313 E. 60th St., Chicago, IL 60637.
Bryden, A Phantom Doctrine: The Origins and Effects of Just v. Marinette County, 1978 American Bar Foundation Research Journal 397, 434-437. Reprinted with permission.
Calabresi, Some Thoughts on Risk Distribution and the Law of Torts. Reprinted by permission of The Yale Law Journal Company and Fred B. Rothman & Co. from The Yale Law Journal, Vol. 70, pp. 499, 517-518 (1961).
Captain America cartoon. Copyright © 1989, Marvel Entertainment Group, Inc. Reprinted with permission.
Caro, The Power Broker: Robert Moses and the Fall of New York. Copyright © 1975 by Robert Caro. Reprinted by permission of Alfred A. Knopf, Inc.
Clary and Rasmussen, The Buyout Phenomenon. Reprinted with permission from Planning, copyright © 1985 by the American Planning Association, 1313 E. 60th St., Chicago, IL 60637.
Committee for Economic Development, Reshaping Government in Metropolitan Areas 19-20 (1970).
Cook, Zoning for Downtown Urban Design 88 (1980). Reprinted with permission of D.C. Heath and Company.
Costonis, "Fair" Compensation and the Accommodation Power: Antidotes for the Taking Impasses in Land Use Controversies, 75 Columbia Law Review 1021, 1022-1023, 1052 (1975). Copyright © 1980 by the Directors of the Columbia Law Review Association. All Rights Reserved. This article originally appeared at 75 Col. L. Rev. 1975. Reprinted by permission.
Costonis, Presumptive and Per Se Takings: A Decisional Model for the Taking Issue, 58 New York University Law Review 465, 468-469 (1983). Reprinted with permission.
DeGrove and Stroud, State Land Planning and Regulation: Innovative Roles in the 1980s and Beyond. Reprinted with permission from

■ Acknowledgments   xli

   Land Use Law and Zoning Digest, copyright © 1987 by the American Planning Association, 1313 E. 60th St., Chicago, IL 60637.
Descartes, Discourse on the Method of Rightly Conducting the Reason, in Philosophical Works 87-88 (Haldane & Ross trans. 1931). Reprinted with permission of copyright holder, Cambridge University Press.
Development in Barsetshire, 1950 Journal of Planning Law 26. Reprinted with permission of Sweet & Maxwell Ltd.
Drinan, Untying the White Noose. Reprinted by permission of The Yale Law Journal Company, Fred B. Rothman & Company, and the author, Vol. 94, pp. 435, 441-443 (1984).
Ellickson, Alternatives to Zoning: Covenants, Nuisance Rules, and Fines as Land Use Controls, 40 University of Chicago Law Review 681, 748, 761-764, 772 (1973). Reprinted with permission of the University of Chicago Law Review and the author.
Epstein, Takings: Private Property and the Power of Eminent Domain 102-104, 196-198 (1985). Reprinted with permission of Harvard University Press.
Frug, The City as a Legal Concept, 93 Harvard Law Review 1057, 1105-1108 (1980). Copyright © 1980 by the Harvard Law Review Association. Reprinted with permission.
Fuller, Freedom — A Suggested Analysis, 68 Harvard Law Review, 1305, 1316-1320, 1324-1325 (1955). Copyright © 1955 by the Harvard Law Review Association. Reprinted with permission.
Funkhouser and Saquella, Establishing Enterprise Zones in Maryland 3-7, Lincoln Institute of Land Policy, Basic Concept Series No. 106 (1984). Reprinted with permission.
Gallion, The Urban Pattern 171 (1930), Parkchester, New York City (diagrams) (1930). Van Nostrand, New York. Courtesy The Architectural Forum.
Gillette, Equality and Variety in the Delivery of Municipal Services, 100 Harvard Law Review 946, 955-957 (1987). Copyright © 1987 by the Harvard Law Review Association. Reprinted with permission.
Goodman and Freund, Principles and Practices of Urban Planning, 1968 (chart at 537). Reprinted with permission of the International City Management Association, 1120 G Street, N.W., Washington, D.C. 20005. All rights reserved.
Goodman and Kaufman, City Planning in the Sixties 4-7 (1965).
Greater Baltimore Committee, Inc., Report of the Enterprise Zone Subcommittee 1-3, 8, 10, 20-22 (July 10, 1981). Reprinted with permission.
Grebler, Blank, and Winnick, Capital Formation in Residential Real Estate, Ratio of Residential Capital Formation to Gross National Product and to Total Consumption (chart), p. 135 (1956). Reprinted by permission of the National Bureau of Economics.

Griffin, The Politics and Litigation of Boston Harbor: From Superior Court to Beacon Hill. Reprinted with permission of the author and the Harvard Law School Program on the Legal Profession.

Haar, The Joint Venture Approach to Urban Renewal: From Model Cities to Enterprise Zones. From Brooks, Liebman, and Schelling's Public-Private Partnership: New Opportunities for Meeting Social Needs, Copyright © 1984 by the American Academy of Arts and Science. Reprinted by permission of Ballinger Publishing Company.

Haar, Land Planning Law in a Free Society 100-101 (1951). Reprinted with permission of Harvard University Press.

Haar and Fessler, The Wrong Side of the Tracks 21-23, 183 (1986). Copyright © 1986 by Charles M. Haar and Daniel Wm. Fessler. Reprinted by permission of Simon & Schuster, Inc.

Haar, Horwitz, and Katz, Transfer of Development Rights: A Primer 11-13, 16-17, Lincoln Institute of Land Policy, Policy Analysis Series No. 206 (1980). Reprinted with permission.

Haar and Lindsay, Business and the Revolution in Land Use Planning: New Private Sector Roles and New Suburban Forms 1-4, 6-7, Lincoln Institute of Land Policy, Policy Analysis Series No. 213 (1987). Reprinted with permission.

Haar, Sawyer, and Cummings, Computer Power and Legal Reasoning: A Case Study of Judicial Prediction in Zoning Amendment Cases, 1977 American Bar Foundation Research Journal 655, 657, 742-745. Reprinted with permission.

Hagman and Misczynski, Executive Summary. Reprinted with permission from Windfall for Wipeouts, by Donald G. Hagman and Dean J. Misczynski, published 1978 by the American Planning Association.

Henrico County Planning Office, ... so you need to subdivide your property? Reprinted with permission of the Planning Office, County of Henrico, Virginia.

Highway Research Board, Special Report 26 (1957) (charts). Reprinted with permission of Transportation Research Board, National Research Council, Washington, D.C.

Holgate, What Is a "Rival Market"?, 1985 Journal of Planning and Environmental Law 759, 760, 764-765. Reprinted with permission of Sweet & Maxwell Ltd.

Holznagel, Negotiation and Mediation: The Newest Approach to Hazardous Waste Facility Siting, 13 Boston College Environmental Affairs Law Review 329, 329-330, 357-358, 364-365, 378 (1986). Reprinted with permission.

Horwitz, The Transformation of American Law, 1780-1860, at 63-64 (1977). Reprinted with permission of Harvard University Press.

Houston Adopts Limited Development Controls. Reprinted with permission from Land Use Law and Zoning Digest, copyright © 1982

■ **Acknowledgments** xliii

by the American Planning Association, 1313 E. 60th St., Chicago, IL 60637.

Jacobs, The Death and Life of Great American Cities 9-10. Copyright © 1961 by Jane Jacobs. Reprinted by permission of Random House, Inc.

Jost, The Defeasible Fee and the Birth of the Modern Residential Subdivision, 49 Missouri Law Review 695, 708-709, 728, 735 (1984). Reprinted with permission.

Kayden, Incentive Zoning in New York City: A Cost-Benefit Analysis, Lincoln Institute of Land Policy, Policy Analysis Series No. 201 (1978). Reprinted with permission.

Keller, The Planning of Communities: Anticipations, Hindsights, in The Idea of Social Structure (Coser ed. 1975).

Kmiec, The Role of the Planner in a Deregulated World. Reprinted with permission from Land Use Law and Zoning Digest, copyright © 1982 by the American Planning Association, 1313 E. 60th St., Chicago, IL 60637.

Laitos and Westfall, Government Interference with Private Interests in Public Resources, 11 Harvard Environmental Law Review, 1, 4-5, 74-75 (1987). Reprinted with permission. Copyright © 1987 by the President and Fellows of Harvard College.

Langendorf, Computers and Decision Making, at 422, 422-423, 428. Reprinted with permission of the author and the Journal of the American Planning Association, volume 51 (1985).

McAuslan, Compensation and Betterment, in Cities, Law, and Social Policy: Learning from the British 77, 86-87 (1984). Reprinted with permission of Lexington Books. Copyright © 1984 D.C. Heath & Co.

McGivern, Putting a Speed Limit on Growth. Reprinted with permission from Planning, copyright © 1972 by the American Planning Association, 1313 E. 60th St., Chicago, IL 60637.

McReynolds, Enterprise Zones: Are They Working?, Baltimore Business Journal, April 2-8, 1984, at 12. Reprinted with permission of the Baltimore Business Journal.

Mazzioti, The Underlying Assumptions of Advocacy Planning: Pluralism and Reform. Reprinted by permission of the Journal of the American Institute of Planners, Vol. 40, No. 1, January 1974, and the American Planning Association.

Meier, Planning for Tomorrow's World. Reprinted with permission from Planning, copyright © 1956 by the American Planning Association, 1313 E. 60th St., Chicago, IL 60637.

Michelman, Property, Utility and Fairness, 80 Harvard Law Review 1165, 1212-1215 (1967). Copyright © 1967 by the Harvard Law Review Association. Reprinted with permission.

Minister of Housing and Local Government, Design, 3 Encyclopedia of Urban Planning 4535 (1974).

Mitchell, The Historical Context for Housing Policy, in Federal Housing Policy and Programs (1985). Reprinted with permission of the Center for Urban Policy Research.

Mosley, Disney's World 280-283 (1985). Copyright © 1985 by Leonard Mosley. From the book Disney's World. Reprinted with permission of Stein and Day Publishers.

Moynihan, Urban Conditions: General, 37 Annals of the American Academy of Political and Social Science 159, 160-162 (1967). Reprinted with permission of the American Academy of Political and Social Science.

Mumford, The Social Foundations of Post-War Building 9-13, 24-32 (1943). Reprinted by permission of the author.

Nelson, A Breath of Free Markets in Zoning, Wall Street Journal, May 22, 1985, at 32. Reprinted with permission of the author.

Nelson, A Property Right Theory of Zoning. Reprinted by permission of The Urban Lawyer, the national quarterly journal of the American Bar Association, Section of Urban, State and Local Government Law, as it appeared in Volume 11, Number 4 (Fall 1979).

Newark Star-Ledger, *Mount Laurel* article, May 21, 1987. Reprinted from The Star-Ledger with permission.

Niedercorn & Hearle, Recent Land-Use Trends in Forty-Eight Large American Cities (RM-3664-1-FF), September 1963 (Table 2). The Rand Corporation, 1700 Main Street, P.O. Box 2138, Santa Monica, CA 90406-2138. Reprinted with permission.

Peattie, Reflections on Advocacy Planning. Reprinted by permission of the Journal of the American Institute of Planners, Vol. 34, No. 2, March 1968, and the American Planning Association.

Polanyi, The Logic of Liberty 134-135 (1951). Reprinted with permission of The University of Chicago Press.

Reischauer, The Economy, the Federal Budget and Prospects for Urban Aid, in The Fiscal Outlook for Cities 95-96 (Bahl ed. 1978) (tables). Reprinted with permission of Syracuse University Press.

Rider, Transition from Land Use to Policy Planning: Lessons Learned, 44 Journal of the American Institute of Planners 25 (1978). Reprinted by permission of the American Planning Association.

Rose, How Will New Jersey Municipalities Comply? Reprinted with permission from Land Use Law & Zoning Digest, copyright © 1983 by the American Planning Association, 1313 E. 60th St., Chicago, IL 60637.

Rose, *Mahon* Reconstructed: Why the Taking Issue Is Still a Muddle, 57 Southern California Law Review 561, 596-599 (1984). Reprinted with the permission of the Southern California Law Review.

Rose, Planning and Dealing: Piecemeal Land Controls as a Problem of Local Legitimacy. © 1983 by the California Law Review, Inc.

Acknowledgments

Reprinted from California Law Review Vol. 71, No. 3, May 1983, pp. 837-912, by permission of publisher and author.

Salmons, Petaluma's Experiment in Growth Management, Urban Land, September 1986, at 7, 8-9. Reprinted with permission from Urban Land, published by ULI — The Urban Land Institute, 1090 Vermont Ave., N.W., Washington, D.C. 20005.

Sax, Takings and the Police Power. Reprinted by permission of The Yale Law Journal, Fred B. Rothman & Company, and the author from The Yale Law Journal Company, Vol. 74, pp. 36, 62-63 (1964).

Sax, Takings, Private Property and Public Rights. Reprinted by permission of The Yale Law Journal, Fred B. Rothman & Company, and the author from The Yale Law Journal, Vol. 81, pp. 149, 161, 164 (1971).

Schnidman, So You Think You Have Problems? Antiquated Subdivisions in Florida, in Antiquated Subdivisions: Beyond Lot Mergers and Vested Rights 63, 65 (Glickfeld ed. 1984) (Lincoln Institute of Land Policy Conference Proceedings). Reprinted with permission.

Siegan, Non-Zoning in Houston, 13 Journal of Law and Economics 71, concluding at 141-143 (1970). Reprinted with permission of The University of Chicago Press.

Silvern, Negotiating the Public Interest: California's Development Agreement Statute, Land Use Law and Zoning Digest, October 1985, at 3, 7-8. Reprinted with permission from the American Planning Association. Copyright © 1985 by the American Planning Association, 1313 E. 16th St., Chicago, IL 60637.

Stevenage Development Corporation, Building the New Town of Stevenage (1954) (drawing).

Stoebuck, Police Power, Takings, and Due Process, 37 Washington and Lee Law Review 1057, 1093 (1980). Reprinted with permission of the Washington and Lee Law Review and the author.

Survey of Big City Zoning Boards of Appeals (table). Reprinted with permission from Zoning News copyright © 1985 by the American Planning Association, 1313 E. 60th St., Chicago, IL 60637.

Talbot, Settling Things: Six Case Studies in Environmental Mediation 8-11, 24 (1983). Reprinted with permission of The Conservation Foundation.

Tugwell, The Fourth Power 1-4, 6-9, 16-17, 21-22. Reprinted by permission of Planning and Civic Comment, Washington, D.C. Printed by Mount Pleasant Press, The McFarland Company, Harrisburg, Pennsylvania.

Urban Design, 37 Progressive Architecture August, 1956, at 97.

Urban Land Institute, Downtown Retail Development: Conditions for Success and Project Profiles 6 (1983) (Table 1). Reprinted with permission of ULI — The Urban Land Institute.

Wiles, The Use of Expert Witnesses in Litigation, in Handling Zoning and Land Use Litigation: A Practical Guide 158-159, 165-167 (Peterson and McCarthy eds. 1982). Reprinted with permission of The Michie Company.

Williams, The Law on Variances 2, 5, Lincoln Institute of Land Policy, Policy Analysis Series No. 207 (1982). Reprinted with permission.

Williams, On the Inclination of Developers to Help the Poor 24, Lincoln Institute of Land Policy, Policy Analysis Series No. 211 (1985). Reprinted with permission.

Williams, State and Local Government Incentives for Successful Enterprise Zone Initiatives, 14 Rutgers Law Journal 41 (1982). Reprinted with Permission of the Rutgers Law Journal. Copyrighted 1982 by Rutgers School of Law-Camden.

Witherspoon, Alpert, and Gladstone, Mixed-Use Development Handbook 18 (1987) (Chart 1-11). Reprinted with permission of the ULI — The Urban Land Institute.

Wolf, Accommodating Tensions in the Coastal Zone: An Introduction and Overview, 25 Natural Resources Journal 7, 7-10, 14-19 (1985). Reprinted with permission.

Wolf, Potential Legal Pitfalls Facing State and Local Enterprise Zones, 8 Urban Law and Policy 77, 119-120 (1986-1987). Reprinted with permission.

Special Notice

Throughout this book, where there are footnotes in quoted material — that is, cases, articles, and so forth — the original numbers have been maintained. Editors' notes are numbered beginning with 1 at the start of each chapter. Whenever these notes are keyed to quoted material they are signed "EDS." Citations and footnotes have been omitted from quoted material, unless otherwise indicated.

LAND-USE PLANNING

I

The Land Around Us: The Environment of City Planning

A. SOME BASIC DATA ON TRENDS IN URBAN SOCIETY

Time, technology, and the changing needs and aspirations of human beings produce stresses upon existing legal institutions and doctrines. Interspersed throughout this chapter are tables and charts that attempt to outline a few of the salient facts about the conditions of land interdependence in the United States that have intensified ancient conflicts or spawned new problems. Central to these statistics is change — and the scale and pattern of growth of the urban community. They illustrate in essence the startling transformation in the outward face of society over the past few decades. It is the impact of these forces that underlies those efforts to arrive at a new synthesis of framework and function commonly subsumed under the title of city planning law.

A major question for the lawyer is the type of data necessary for an effective presentation of the client's side of a land dispute. In Pennsylvania v. Lynn, 501 F.2d 848 (D.C. Cir. 1974), in determining that the suspension of funding of subsidized housing was within the discretion of the Secretary of Housing and Urban Development, the court gave controlling weight to the department's factual and policy study, Housing in the Seventies. And of equal importance is an acquaintance with the limitations of such materials: some figures require

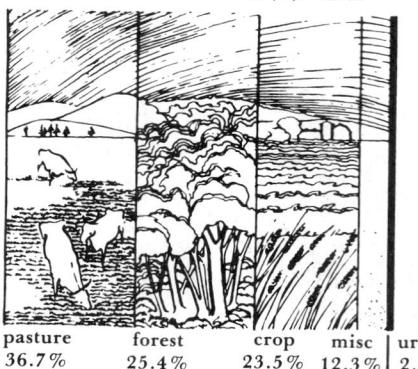

The Rural-Urban Contrast*

LAND AREA
97.9% rural   2.1% urban

pasture	forest	crop	misc	urban
36.7%	25.4%	23.5%	12.3%	2.1%

POPULATION
26.3% rural   73.7% urban

REAL ESTATE VALUE
11% rural   89% urban

---

* The figures on land use and population are taken from the Department of the Census, Statistical Abstract of the United States, Population Table 24 (1984). Of the total land area of 3,539,289 square miles, 73,930 square miles are classified as urban areas;

A. Some Basic Data on Trends in Urban Society

as much reading between the columns as down the columns. It is on these same raw statistics — although with a different orientation and purpose — that the judge, legislator, administrator, planner, entrepreneur, and all concerned with land development base their decisions.

The following questions should be borne in mind in analyzing the charts and in discerning underlying themes, if any, and their significance for property, land law, and the existing institutions of private and public ordering of development. How can the organization of land uses maximize the satisfaction of "valid" human wants? What are the land-use patterns and problems peculiar to the metropolitan environment?[1] Which are those interactions of living patterns and physical environment most crucial for the shaping of property policies and the legal processes affecting land-use planning and development?[2] And how fixed are these forces — what, for example, are the effects of innovations in transportation such as DIAL-A-BUS? What is the significance of the growing minority presence in suburbia and of gentrification in the inner city? What effects will the aging of the population have on the provision of metropolitan services? How are land patterns shaped by alternative forms of financing land development, or, on the level of government intervention, by the withdrawal of federal funding for urban and suburban programs? What dynamics are introduced by shifts in social norms and in attitudes toward the relative roles of different levels of government such as are exemplified in "new federalism" and in "creative federalism"?

Today, fundamental questions are being raised over adequacy of the institutional response to serious urban ills — indeed about the very future of American cities and the metropolitan areas in which they are located.

18,876 square miles are classified as central city. The Census classification divides land use into five major categories: cropland, pasture land, forest land, special uses (including urban, transportation, recreation, wildlife, national defense, and industrial areas; and farmsteads, farm roads and lanes) and "other" (including marshes, open swamps, bare rock area, deserts, and tundra). Estimates of the annual conversion of rural land to nonagricultural uses run as high as 2 million acres, of which 420,000 are devoted to urban development; 160,000 to airports and highways; 420,000 to reservoirs and flood control; and 1 million to wilderness, park, recreation, or wildlife uses. Council on Environmental Quality Annual Report (1983).

1. Today, ironically, many inner-ring suburbs are facing problems traditionally associated with the central city at the same time exurban growth is booming. See Herbers, The New Heartland (1986); Increasing Number of Suburbs Face Problems Once Confined to Cities, Wall St. J., Feb. 27, 1985; Now Even the Suburbs Have Suburbs, N.Y. Times, May 5, 1985.

Do metropolitan-wide plans hold any promise for dealing with these problems?

2. See Reich, The Greening of America (1970); Boyer, Dreaming the Rational City: The Myth of American City Planning (1983); McDougal, The Influence of the Metropolis on Concepts, Rules, and Institutions Relating to Property, 4 J. Pub. L. 93 (1955); Cribbett, Concepts in Transition: The Search for a New Definition of Property, 1986 U. of Ill. L. Rev. 1. For a contrasting approach, see Frankfurter, The Public and Its Government 8-35 (1930).

■ REPORT OF THE PRESIDENT'S COMMISSION FOR A NATIONAL AGENDA FOR THE EIGHTIES
165 (1980)

Until 50 years ago, the proper federal role vis-à-vis the nation's cities was easily summarized. Because the Constitution had not explicitly specified otherwise, the responsibility for cities devolved to state governments. With the onslaught of the Depression, the federal government began for the first time to consider cities as national, rather than merely state, assets. Accordingly, New Deal recovery policies included federal assistance for both distressed people and beleaguered local governments. This national economic calamity henceforth legitimized the appropriateness of a general federal urban policy presence, even though a commitment to continuing federal involvement in the functioning of local economies was never intended.

The New Deal emphasis on helping distressed people in cities directly has evolved into an emphasis on helping distressed places (local business and government) directly for the purpose of helping people indirectly. Today, most federal funds aimed at urban problems go to "place" recipients rather than distressed people. In the late 1970s, a social sensitivity developed during the previous decade appears to have been overtaken in large part by a spatial sensitivity as illustrated by the dominant thrusts, particularly during the last 4 years, of the national urban policy and executive orders devoted to urban impact analysis, Federal facility, siting, and targeted procurement. Politically, this shift is justified by the assertion that aiding places with problems is easier than aiding people with problems. Economically, this shift is justified by the assertion that direct aid to local economies multiplies its impact so that benefits reverberate throughout the economy in ways that direct aid to people does not.

The 1980s may well require a new perspective on aiding distressed people in urban America. Unlike a half-century ago, contemporary urban economies are no longer confined within the political jurisdictions of cities. Modern urban economies have an expanded scope that integrates central city, suburban, and nonmetropolitan economies.

Today it may be in the best interest of the nation to commit itself to the promotion of locationally neutral economic and social policies rather than spatially sensitive urban policies that either explicitly or inadvertently seek to preserve cities in their historical roles. A federal policy presence that allows places to transform and assists them in adjusting to difficult circumstances can justify shifting greater explicit emphasis to helping directly those people who are suffering from the transformation process.

Our cities are truly national assets. As such, cities and their residents

A. Some Basic Data on Trends in Urban Society

are the responsibilities of us all during their adjustment to their new functions for the larger society in the postindustrial era.[3]

■ COMMITTEE FOR ECONOMIC DEVELOPMENT, RESHAPING GOVERNMENT IN METROPOLITAN AREAS
19-20 (1970)

In principle a governmental system for America's metropolitan areas must recognize the need for both a community level and a metropolitan level of government. There are many different governmental arrangements which will meet this need. As long as legitimate demands for centralization and decentralization are met, the specific arrangements may vary to fit the economic, cultural, and political characteristics of each area. Some may require greater emphasis on consolidation of local units; others may require greater emphasis on creating units which will enhance community participation.

Therefore, in the following proposals to achieve the dual advantages of a combined community-metropolitan governmental system, we would expect variations in application. In some areas a comprehensive solution may be feasible at an early date. In other areas achievement of an effective two-level system may require several steps over a period of time.

To gain the advantages of both centralization and decentralization, we recommend as an ultimate solution a governmental system of two levels. Some func-

---

3. Recent changes in the institutional relationship between the federal government and municipalities have led to repercussions and reverberations in the relationship between the public and private sectors within cities:

> Mayors and municipal officials across the country share a common nightmare as they gaze into the future. . . . City sidewalks are overrun by the homeless. Streets are pocked with potholes. Bridges are tumbling down. Water supplies are contaminated. And the federal government doesn't seem to care. . . . Complaints from local officials that they are not getting enough federal funds are hardly novel. But the magnitude of the recent federal cutbacks, coupled with new challenges ranging from drugs to illiteracy to new immigration populations, signals the beginning of a new era in which municipalities will be forced to redefine their working relationship with, and reliance on, the federal government. And officials say that the cities that handle it best will be more self-reliant and entrepreneurial than cities have ever been before.
>
> Already new strategies are being phased in across the country. Five years ago municipalities nationwide paid $67 billion to private firms for city services; today that figure is more than $100 billion. The city of Atlanta is helping local companies find new international markets; San Antonio offers tax breaks to encourage economic development; Boston forces developers to contribute to neighborhood housing; and Indianapolis has an intensive goals-and-measurement program for its work force.

Frisby, Nation's Mayors Share Urban Nightmare, Boston Globe, Dec. 7, 1986. For analysis of the fiscal arrangements under federalism, see Barfield, Rethinking Federalism: Block Grants and Federal, State and Local Responsibilities (1981); Brezic, Financing Government in a Federal System (1980).

tions should be assigned in their entirety to the area-wide government, others to the local level, but most will be assigned in part to each level. More important than the division of functions is the *sharing of power.* Local communities will be assigned some power over functions placed at the area-wide level of government. Further, state and federal governments must be involved in most functions. This two-level system will not provide neatness and symmetry, but effectiveness, responsiveness, and adequate resources.

In those situations where the metropolitan area is contained within one county, a reconstituted county government should be used as the basic framework for a new area-wide government. This may, but need not, include consolidation of a large dominant central city with the county government in which it is located. If there are two or more sizable cities in the county, consolidation may not be appropriate. Counties in some states already have very wide powers. An indispensable requirement is the restructuring of such counties with a suitable legislative organ, a strong chief executive, and modern management.

In cases where the metropolitan area spreads over several counties or towns, a new jurisdiction should be created which embraces all of its territory. Although a federation of existing counties and towns might be considerably easier to implement, it is clear that rapid metropolitan growth makes a stronger jurisdiction considerably more appropriate, especially for purposes of long-range planning.

In addition to an area-wide level, modern metropolitan government should contain a community-level government system comprised of "community districts." These units might consist of existing local governments with functions readjusted to the two-level system, together with new districts in areas where no local unit exists. The new community districts should not be imposed from without, but created through local initiative by the simplest possible methods. A state boundary commission or similar body might be established to begin the process of delineating new districts. Citizen groups which seek community-district status might first make their appeal to this body if it is established.

In some cities there are areas which already possess strong community identity and these could become the new community districts. But in many cities, particularly the big cities, the sense of community is diminishing. Isolation and alienation, on the other hand, are increasing. Once the smaller political units are created — units with genuine power — a stronger sense of community is bound to emerge. In the suburbs, existing municipalities are likely to be retained as the community districts. Except in the most recently settled suburbs, these municipalities tend not only to represent "natural areas," but also to have well-developed community identities. Thus, local communities in both cities and suburbs can be guaranteed full participation within the metropolitan system.

Percent of Local Governments by Type in SMSA's: 1962 to 1982*

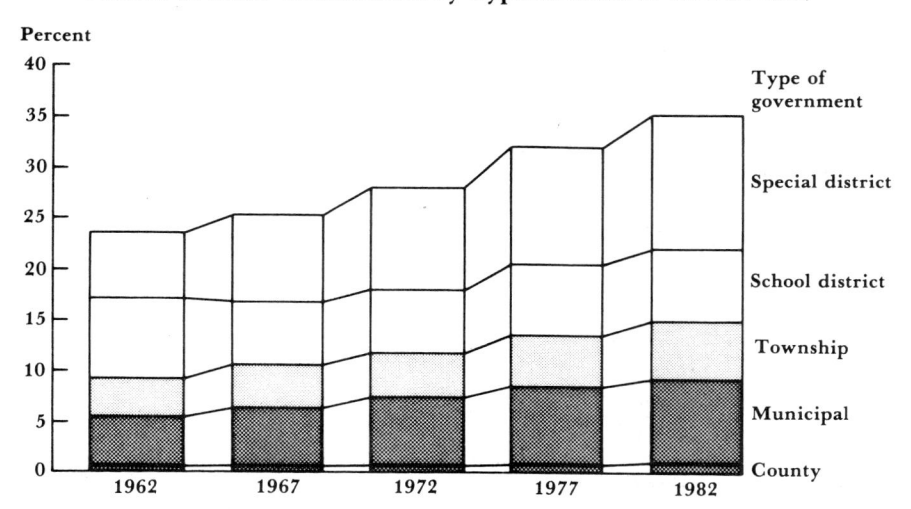

Source: U.S. Bureau of the Census, Census of Governments, vol. 6, no. 5, at 11 (1982). "Nearly 30,000 (about 36 percent) of the nation's local governments are located within 289 SMSA's [Standard Metropolitan Statistical Areas] and 16 New England county metropolitan areas (NECMA's). These 305 areas in 1980 contained a population of 170.5 million — slightly over 75 percent of the nationwide total of 226.5 million." Id. at 11. Since 1983, the Census terminology has changed somewhat. Metropolitan areas are now generally referred to as MSAs (Metropolitan Statistical Areas); an MSA is "a large population nucleus together with adjacent communities which have a high degree of social and economic integration with that nucleus." Statistical Abstract of the United States: 1986, at 2 (1985).

Percent of Population in Central Cities and Rings of Metropolitan Areas, and Urban and Rural Portions of Nonmetropolitan Areas: 1900-1980*

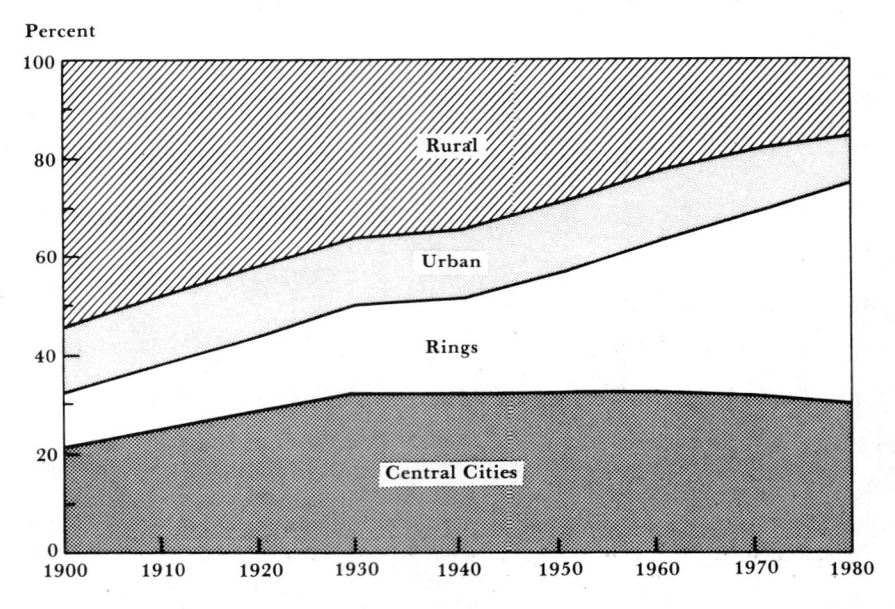

Source: Bogue, The Population of the United States: Historical Trends and Future Projections 130 (1985). Is low-density urban development, like that found in suburbia, becoming the new American concept of "city living"? How do suburban and exurban development affect the traditional dichotomy between urban and rural land use?

One Out of Every Five Persons Moves Each Year*

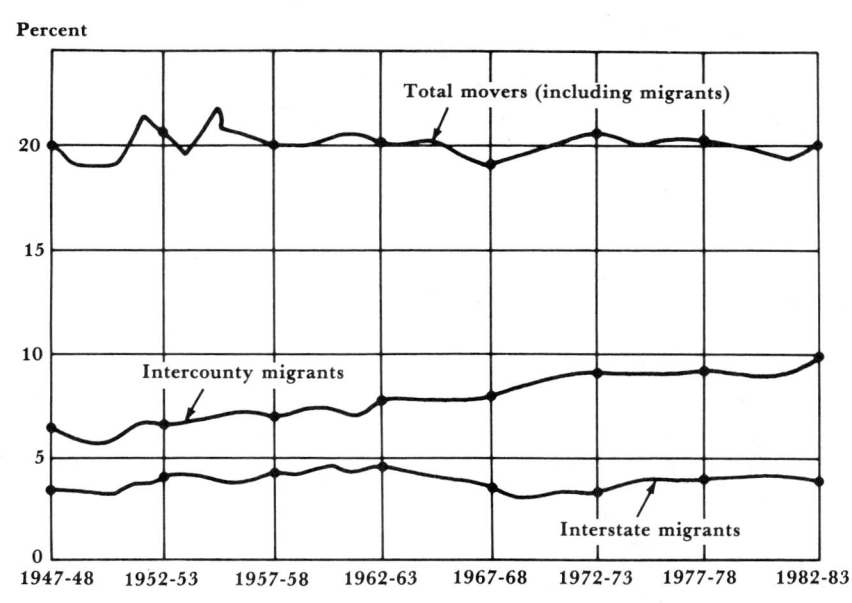

[Graph showing three lines from 1947-48 to 1982-83:
- Total movers (including migrants): around 20%
- Intercounty migrants: rising from about 6% to about 10%
- Interstate migrants: around 3-4%]

*From 1984 to 1985, 16.8 percent of the total population moved; 6.4 percent of the population made intercounty moves and 2.8 percent made interstate moves. Department of the Census, Statistical Abstract of the United States, Population Graph no. 16 (1986). See generally Sacks, Central City-Suburban Fiscal Disparity and City Distress (1977); Sternlieb, Hughes & Hughes, Demographic Trends and Economic Reality (1982); Roseman, Cities in Flux: Migration, Mobility and Political Change, in Modern Metropolitan Systems (Christian & Harper eds. 1982).

Personal Income per Capita in Constant 1972 Dollars: 1970 to 1980

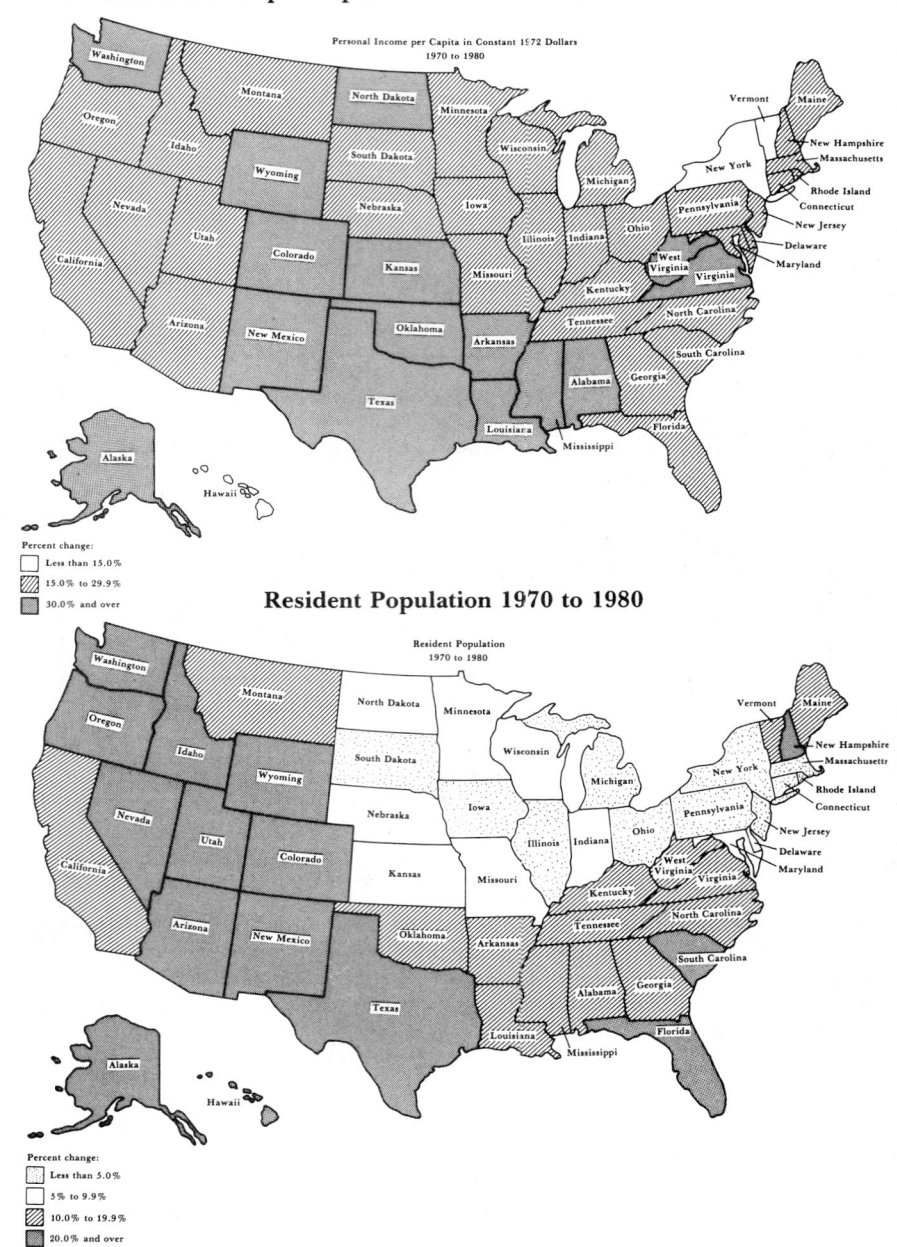

Percent change:
- Less than 15.0%
- 15.0% to 29.9%
- 30.0% and over

Resident Population 1970 to 1980

Percent change:
- Less than 5.0%
- 5% to 9.9%
- 10.0% to 19.9%
- 20.0% and over

Source: Department of the Census, State and Metropolitan Area Data Book, at xxx, xxxv (1982). On regional shifts in economic activity, see Sunbelt/Snowbelt: Urban Development and Regional Restructuring (Sawers & Tabb eds. 1984); Clark, Interregional Migration, National Policy and Social Justice (1983).

Population 55 Years and Over, by Age: 1900 to 2050

Population in millions

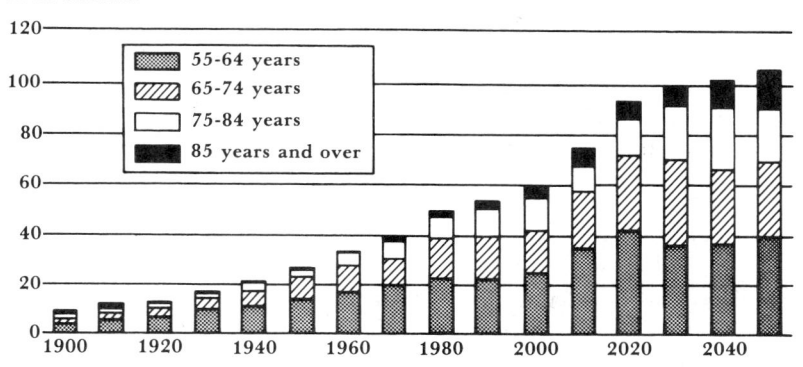

- 55-64 years
- 65-74 years
- 75-84 years
- 85 years and over

Poverty Rate in 1981 of Persons 60 Years and Over, by Age, Race, and Sex

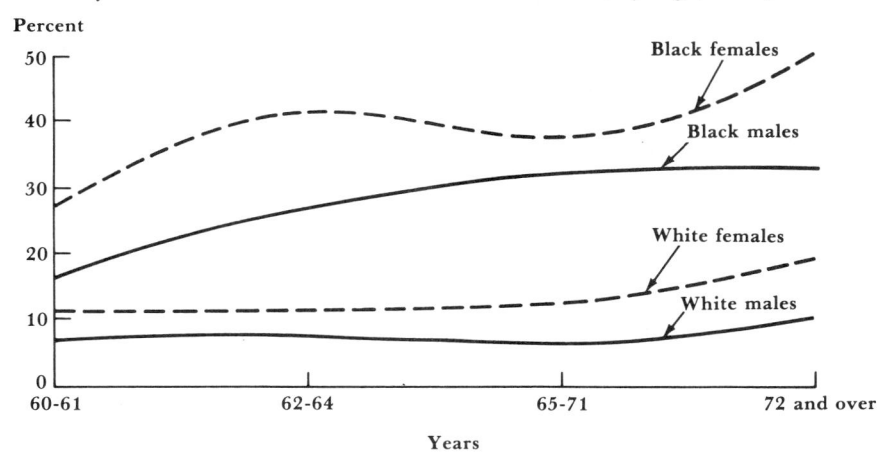

Percent

Years

Source: Bureau of the Census, America in Transition: An Aging Society, Current Population Reports, Special Study, P-23, No. 128, Figs. 1, 14 (1985).

B. AN HISTORICAL EXCURSION

1. The Impact of the Frontier on Land Use

Restructuring the physical environment with ancient legal tools is a further complicating factor in an already overcomplex picture. The imprint of government on land comes primarily through the law of real property — a law rooted in the land policies of feudal England. Yet the current problems of land use stem from the industrial and technological revolutions of the twentieth century. However, it would be an oversimplification to blame this heritage of property prescriptions and institutions for the acute dilemmas in metropolitan areas; worse, like most laments, it is not particularly productive. The true inquiry for the lawyer is how best to change, adapt, invent — to preserve in the Burkean sense — within this framework.

The following material outlines the evolution of United States land policies over a period of 200 years.

"The chief circumstance which has favored the establishment and maintenance of a democratic system in the United States is the nature of the territory which the Americans inhabit. Their ancestors gave them the means of remaining equal and free by placing them on a boundless continent." de Tocqueville, Democracy in America 301 (Vintage ed. 1945). The Revolution brought a sharp break in the continuity of land practices, as of other political and economic institutions. With one sweep the tenure system and other major remnants of feudalism were banished, and a radical experiment of a free land system in a market economy was innovated.[4] This measure is partly responsible for the great release of energy and enterprise that characterized this country's expansion from a colony to its present position. A nation without a city of 50,000 in 1790 witnessed a population growth that attained over 200 million in 1970. Primitive areas were developed; resources discovered and harnessed; millions of immigrants absorbed. New towns burgeoned, older cities expanded; and an agricultural economy was transformed into an industrial workshop and a commercial entrepôt for the world.

---

4. "Comment on the following: 'Under the feudal system the Crown was the universal landlord. The modern socialist dream is to make the state the universal landlord. Thus, in a strange way, William the Conqueror is the ideological forerunner of Deng Xiaoping.'" Harvard Law School Examination, Property I, June 1985.

Estimates and Projections of Total Population: 1950 to 2080*

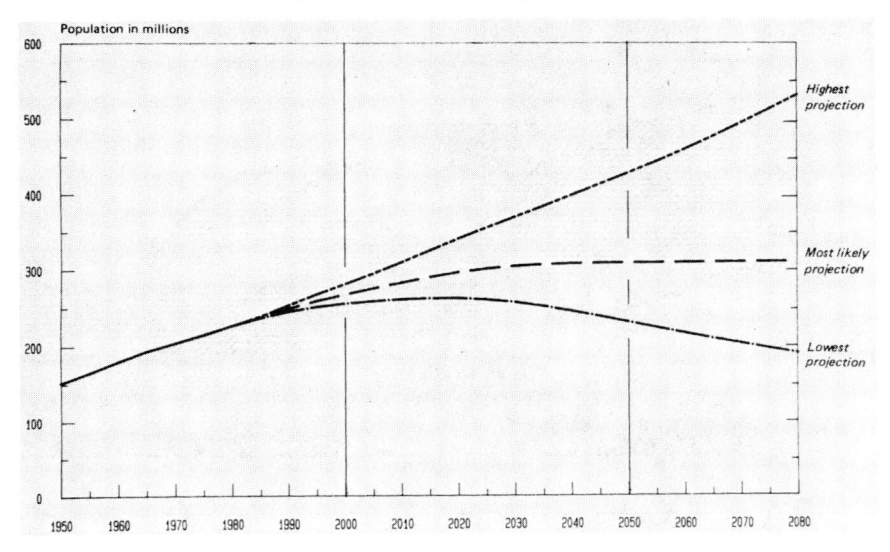

Population in millions

[Graph showing population projections from 1950 to 2080, with three projection curves labeled "Highest projection" (rising to above 500 million), "Most likely projection" (leveling around 300 million), and "Lowest projection" (declining after peaking around 250 million).]

* *Source:* Bogue, The Population of the United States: Historical Trends and Future Projections 21 (1985). The "future course of fertility" causes the greatest variations in the projections. For example, the "most likely projection" is based on U.S. Bureau of the Census estimates of fertility rates of 15-16 per 1,000 until the 1990s, then declining to 11 by 2080. Id. at 20-21.

This background of colonization and settlement is a key to an understanding of the urban land problems and policies in the United States. Today the old system of landholding and land commerce is being reexamined. Contemporary urban land policies result in part from the recognition of inadequacies both in the operation of this market system and in its institutional framework. Yet the advantages of the entrepreneurial economy and the resulting strong attachments have led to certain types of solution. Similar loyalties have shaped the approach to major institutional difficulties.

A possible approach to this statutory material is that of the legal archaeologist. Assume these writings were the only artifacts left of this civilization — what generalizations could be drawn as to the type of society? A few questions suggest themselves. What were the roles of government, of large aggregates of capital, and of individual ownership? What was the prevailing attitude toward this land resource? How did these legislative policies reflect and affect the law of real property? What were the competing social forces, and their relative strengths, as revealed within each particular enactment and by the sequence of acts? Did the acts serve as a reasonable accommodation of these conflicts? What were the systems of transfer of land and of recording of title,

Components of Population Growth in the United States: 1900 to 1983

Rate per 1,000 Population

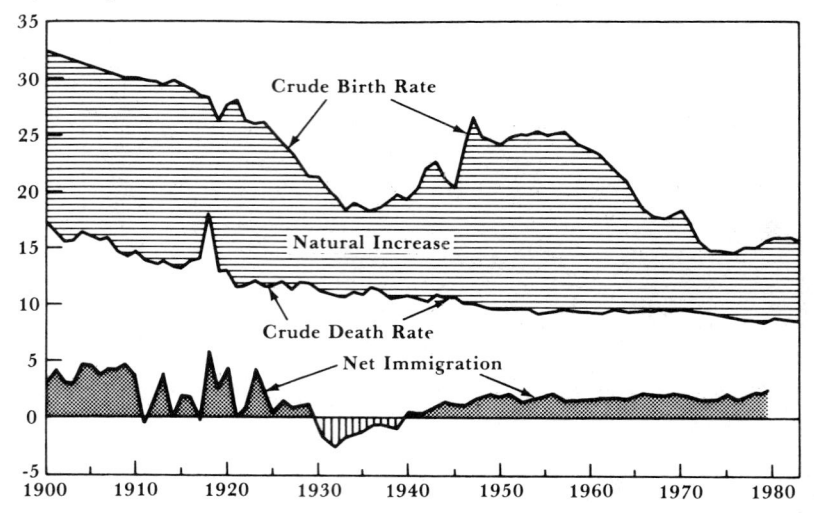

Source: Bogue, The Population of the United States: Historical Trends and Future Projections 13 (1985).

The four general methods [for making population projections] are:
1. Graphical or mathematical projections of the curve of past population growth.
2. Projections based on relationships of population growth in an area to that in other areas.
3. Projections of net immigration and of natural increases.
4. Forecasts based on specific estimates of future employment.

Stanbery, Better Population Forecasting for Areas and Communities 17 (1952).

At what point do the unarticulated assumptions of the forecaster enter into each case? Would a combined method increase reliability? Cf. Urban Systems Laboratory, MIT Systems Analysis of the Primary Water Distribution Network of New York City 11 (1969). Consider the following:

> A striking decline in birth rates during the late nineteen-sixties will mean 100 million fewer Americans in the year 2000 than previously projected, the Census Bureau said today. There will be between 266 and 320 million Americans by 2000 ... compared with the current ... population of about 205 million.

N.Y. Times, Aug. 13, 1970.

and were they adequate to meet the needs of the day? What elements of stability and instability were built into the land structure? What was the attitude toward the future of land values, and toward speculation? Did these policies put land at a competitive advantage or disadvantage with other enterprises seeking investment funds? Was there any provision for a land-credit policy? What was the relation of government policy to the security of real estate loans? Can you isolate from these acts any conscious attempt to plan — on either the social, economic, or physical plane — or to control the use of land? What significance do these nineteenth-century attempts to handle land development hold for twentieth-century lawyers and planners? Do the concepts of ownership and property attendant upon an apparently inexhaustible supply of land make an effective and desirable law of real property today? What is the possible application of this experience to other countries? If called on to advise a developing nation, what features of the American experience would you stress, and which would you think transplantable? Is the recent program for selling off "surplus" federal lands a minor correction after decades of conservation, or a determined return to earlier disposition policies?

■ STORY, COMMENTARIES ON THE CONSTITUTION OF THE UNITED STATES
159-161, 165-169 (1833)

Sec. 172. (3) In all the colonies, the lands within their limits were by the very terms of their original grants and charters to be holden of the crown in free and common socage, and not in capite, or by knight's service. They were all holden either as of the manor of East Greenwich in Kent, or of the manor of Hampton Court in Middlesex, or of the castle of Windsor in Berkshire. All the slavish and military part of the ancient feudal tenures was thus effectually prevented from taking root in the American soil; and the colonists escaped from the oppressive burdens, which for a long time affected the parent country, and were not abolished until after the restoration of Charles the Second. Our tenures thus acquired a universal simplicity; and it is believed that none but freehold tenures in socage ever were in use among us. No traces are to be found of copyhold, or gavelkind, or burgage tenures. In short, for most purposes, our lands may be deemed to be perfectly allodial, or held of no superior at all; though many of the distinctions of the feudal law have necessarily insinuated themselves into the modes of acquiring, transferring, and transmitting real estates. One of the most remarkable circumstances in our colonial history is the almost total absence of leasehold estates. The erection of manors with all their attendant privileges, was, indeed, provided for in several of the charters. But it was so little congenial with the feelings, the wants, or the interests of the people, that after their erection they gradually fell into desuetude; and the few remaining in our day are but shadows of the past, the relics of faded grandeur in the last steps of decay, enjoying no privileges, and conferring no power.

Sec. 173. In fact, partly from the cheapness of land, and partly

Population Changes by Residence and Race: 1982 and 1970*
(Numbers in Thousands)

	1982	1970	Percent change 1970–82	Percent change 1960–70
ALL RACES				
Total	227,375	199,819	13.8	13.3
Metropolitan areas	153,763	137,058	12.2	16.6
In central cities	62,370	62,876	−0.8	6.5
Outside central cities	91,393	74,182	23.2	26.7
Nonmetropolitan areas	73,612	62,761	17.3	6.8
WHITE				
Total	194,647	175,276	11.1	11.9
Metropolitan areas	128,855	118,938	8.3	14.0
In central cities	45,463	48,909	−7.0	0.1
Outside central cities	83,393	70,029	19.1	26.1
Nonmetropolitan areas	65,792	56,338	16.8	7.8
BLACK				
Total	26,896	22,056	21.9	19.7
Metropolitan areas	20,415	16,342	24.9	31.6
In central cities	14,717	12,909	14.0	33.2
Outside central cities	5,697	3,433	65.9	26.4
Nonmetropolitan areas	6,481	5,714	13.4	−5.3
SPANISH ORIGIN				
Total	14,043	8,988	56.2	(NA)
Metropolitan areas	11,894	7,409	60.5	(NA)
In central cities	6,890	4,646	48.3	(NA)
Outside central cities	5,004	2,764	81.0	(NA)
Nonmetropolitan areas	2,149	1,578	36.2	(NA)

* *Source:* Bureau of the Census, Population Profiles of the United States, Current Population Reports, Special Study, P-23, No. 160, Table 6 (1986). For major implications of this territorial division see Report of the National Advisory Commission on Civil Disorders 1-29, 389-482 (Bantam ed. 1968). But cf. Birch, The Economic Future of City and Suburb 28-33 (1970). As to an earlier study of the distribution of poor white families in the metropolitan area, see President's Task Force on Suburban Problems, Final Report 20-23 (1968).

The meaning of these changes is disputed. Compare Sternlieb, The City as a Sandbox, Public Interest, Fall 1971 at 15-19 with Gans, Our Large Cities: New Light on Their Recent Transformation (1972). See The State and the Poor in the 1980s (Carballo & Bane eds. 1983).

from an innate love of independence, few agricultural estates in the whole country have at any time been held on lease for a stipulated rent. The tenants and occupiers are almost universally the proprietors of the soil in fee simple. The estates of a more limited duration are principally those arising from the acts of the law, such as estates in dower, and in curtesy. Strictly speaking, therefore, there has never been in this country a dependent peasantry. The yeomanry are absolute owners of the soil,

Percent Change in Employment, by Major Industry Groups: 1972 to 1982*

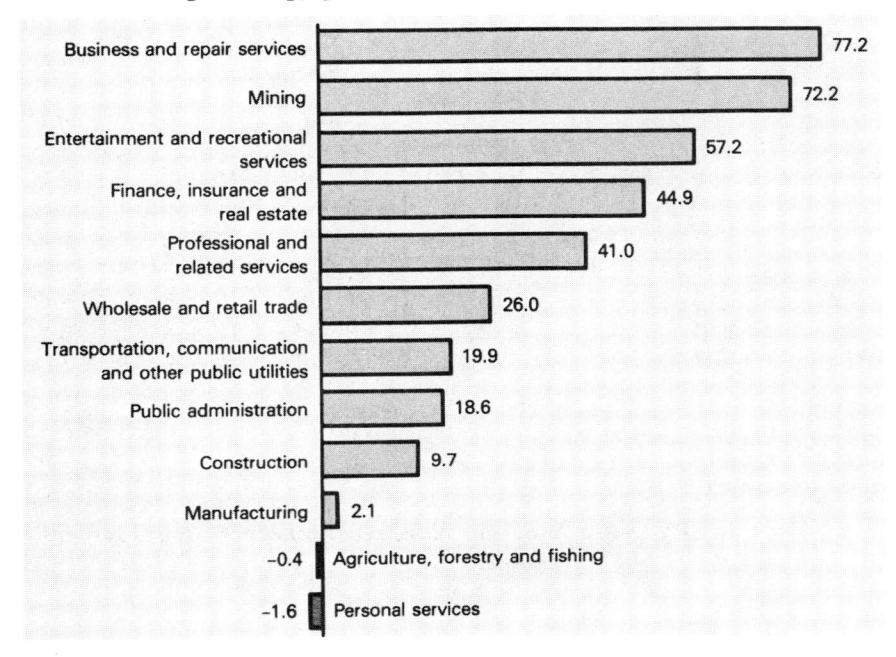

Industry	Percent Change
Business and repair services	77.2
Mining	72.2
Entertainment and recreational services	57.2
Finance, insurance and real estate	44.9
Professional and related services	41.0
Wholesale and retail trade	26.0
Transportation, communication and other public utilities	19.9
Public administration	18.6
Construction	9.7
Manufacturing	2.1
Agriculture, forestry and fishing	-0.4
Personal services	-1.6

* *Source:* Bureau of the Census, Population Profiles of the United States, Current Population Reports, Special Study, P-23, No. 130, Fig. 26, at 29 (1982).

on which they tread; and their character has from this circumstance been marked by a more jealous watchfulness of their rights, and by a more steady spirit of resistance against every encroachment, than can be found among any other people, whose habits and pursuits are less homogeneous and independent, less influenced by personal choice, and more controlled by political circumstances.

Sec. 174. (4) Connected with this state of things, and, indeed, as a natural consequence flowing from it, is the simplicity of the system of conveyances, by which the titles to estates are passed, and the notoriety of the transfers made. From a very early period of their settlement the colonies adopted an almost uniform mode of conveyance of land, at once simple and practicable and safe. The differences are so slight that they became almost evanescent. All lands were conveyed by a deed, commonly in the form of a feoffment, or a bargain and sale, or a lease and release, attested by one or more witnesses, acknowledged or proved before some court or magistrate, and then registered in some public registry. When so executed, acknowledged, and recorded, it had full effect to convey the estate without any livery of seisin, or any other act or ceremony whatsoever. This mode of conveyance prevailed, if not in

Median Family Income by Place of Residence, 1970–76

	Total U.S.	SMSAs over one million Central city	Suburbs	SMSAs under one million Central city	Suburbs	Non-metropolitan areas
1976	$14,958	$13,700	$18,419	$14,198	$15,908	$12,831
1975	13,719	12,957	17,156	13,031	14,859	11,600
1974	12,902	12,341	16,206	12,202	13,839	11,057
1973	12,051	11,440	14,945	11,314	12,845	10,366
1972	11,116	11,548	13,995	11,361	12,090	9,841
1971	10,285	10,100	12,696	9,953	10,884	8,605
1970	9,867	9,900	12,425	9,477	10,599	8,348

U.S., Central City, Suburban, and Nonmetropolitan Unemployment Rates, 1973–77

Year	Total U.S.	Central city	Central city poverty areas	Suburbs	Non-metropolitan
1977	7.0	8.7	14.9	6.3	6.6
1976	7.7	9.2	14.7	7.1	7.0
1975	8.5	9.6	15.1	8.0	8.0
1974	5.6	6.5	10.6	5.3	5.1
1973	4.9	5.9	9.8	4.6	4.4

Source: Reischauer, The Economy, the Federal Budget and Prospects for Urban Aid, in The Fiscal Outlook for Cities 95-96 (Bahl ed. 1985).

Change in Central City Retail Markets, 1970 to 1980

Item	1970	1980	% Change
Total Population (millions)	63.8	59.9	(−6.1)
Total Households (millions)	21.4	23.4	9.3
Total Income ($ billions constant 1979)	$412.6	$434.8	5.4

Source: Urban Land Institute, Downtown Retail Development: Conditions for Success and Project Profiles 6 (1983). It further notes that "the suburban retail market in some metropolitan areas may be saturated or even over-built while downtown, with its unique characteristics, may offer new opportunities."

Distribution of the White, Black, and Spanish-Origin Populations, by Metropolitan-Nonmetropolitan Residence: 1982*

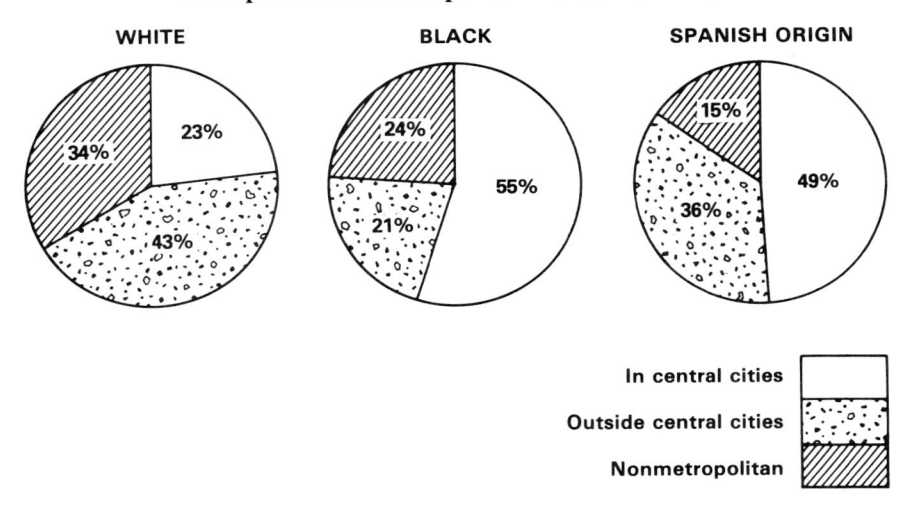

WHITE: 23%, 34%, 43%
BLACK: 24%, 55%, 21%
SPANISH ORIGIN: 15%, 49%, 36%

- In central cities
- Outside central cities
- Nonmetropolitan

* *Source:* Bureau of the Census, Population Profiles of the United States, Current Population Reports, Special Study, P-23, No. 130, Fig. 5, at 10 (1982).

Black suburbanization became so great during the 1970s that it brought about a deconcentration of the black population. While the number of blacks living in central cities and the percentage of the central city population which was black went up during the 1970s, the proportion of the total black population living in the central cities declined for the first time in many decades.

Long and DeAre, The Suburbanization of Blacks, 44 American Demographics 16 (1981). See Grier & Grier, Black Suburbanization in the 1970s: An Analysis of Census Results (1983); Schafer & Ladd, Discrimination in Mortgage Lending (1981).

Increase in Black Population in Central Cities and Suburbs in Metropolitan Areas of 1 Million or More*
[Numbers in Thousands]

	1977	1970	Numerical change 1970 to 1977	Percent change 1970 to 1977
Total	11,819	10,715	1,104	10.3
Central Cities	8,863	8,664	199	2.3
Suburbs	2,956	2,051	905	44.1

* *Source:* Bureau of the Census, Social and Economic Characteristics of the Metropolitan and Nonmetropolitan Population, P-23, No. 75 (1978).

In one view, the accelerated movement of blacks to the suburbs does not necessarily indicate desegregation and upward economic mobility. "Suburbanization, per se is neither synonymous with equal housing opportunity nor will it automatically serve the wealth accumulative function it has provided for previous suburbanizing ethnic groups." Lake, Racial Transition and Black Ownership in American Suburbs, America's Housing 436 (Sternlieb and Hughes eds. 1980).

all, in nearly all the colonies from a very early period; and it has now become absolutely universal. It is hardly possible to measure the beneficial influences upon our titles arising from this source, in point of security, facility of transfer, and marketable value. . . .

Sec. 180. In all the colonies, where the rule of partible inheritance prevailed, estates were soon parcelled out into moderate plantations and farms; and the general equality of property introduced habits of industry and economy, the effects of which are still visible in their local customs, institutions, and public policy. The philosophical mind can scarcely fail to trace the intimate connection which naturally subsists between the general equality of the apportionment of property among the mass of a nation, and the popular form of its government. The former can scarcely fail, first or last, to introduce the substance of a republic into the actual administration of the government, though its forms do not bear such an external impress. Our Revolutionary statesmen were not insensible to this silent but potent influence; and the fact, that at the present time the law of divisible inheritances pervades the Union, is a strong proof of the general sense, not merely of its equity, but of its political importance. . . .

Sec. 182. (2) . . . [W]e may notice the strong tendency of the colonies to make lands liable to the payment of debts. In some of them, indeed, the English rule prevailed of making lands liable only to an extent upon an elegit. But in by far the greatest number, lands were liable to be set off upon appraisement, or sold for the payment of debts. And lands were also assets, in cases of a deficiency of personal property, to

B. An Historical Excursion

be applied in the course of administration to discharge the debts of the party deceased. This was a natural result of the condition of the people in a new country, who possessed little monied capital; whose wants were numerous; and whose desire of credit was correspondently great. The true policy in such a state of things was to make land, in some degree, a substitute for money, by giving it all the facilities of transfer, and all the prompt applicability of personal property. It will be found that the growth of the respective colonies was in no small degree affected by this circumstance. Complaints were made, and perhaps justly, that undue priorities in payment of debts were given to the inhabitants of the colony over all other creditors; and that occasional obstructions were thrown in the way of collecting debts. But the evil was not general in its operation; and the policy, wherever it was pursued, retarded the growth, and stinted the means of the settlements. For the purpose, however, of giving greater security to creditors, as well as for a more easy recovery of debts due in the plantations and colonies in America, the statute of 5 Geo. 2, ch. 7 (1732), among other things declared, that all houses, lands, negroes, and other hereditaments and real estates in the plantations should be liable to, and chargeable with the debts of the proprietor, and be assets for the satisfaction thereof, in like manner as real estates are by the law of England liable, to the satisfaction of debts due by bond or other specialty, and shall be subject to like remedies in courts of law and equity, for seizing, extending, selling, and disposing of the same, toward satisfaction of such debts, in like manner as personal estates in any of such plantations are seized, extended, sold, or disposed of, for satisfaction of debts. This act does not seem to have been resisted on the part of any of the colonies to whom it peculiarly applied.

■ AN ORDINANCE FOR ASCERTAINING THE MODE OF DISPOSING OF LANDS IN THE WESTERN TERRITORY
28 J. Cont. Cong. 375 (1785)

... [T]he territory ceded by individual States to the United States, which has been purchased of the Indian inhabitants, shall be disposed of in the following manner:

A surveyor from each State shall be appointed by Congress, or a Committee of the States, who shall take an oath for the faithful discharge of his duty, before the geographer of the United States, who is hereby empowered and directed to administer the same; and the like oath shall be administered to each chain carrier, by the surveyor under whom he acts....

The Surveyors, as they are respectively qualified, shall proceed to divide the said territory into townships of six miles square, by lines running due north and south, and others crossing these at right angles, as near as may be, unless where the boundaries of the late Indian purchases may render the same impracticable, and then they shall depart from this rule no farther than such particular circumstances may require; and each surveyor shall be allowed and paid at the rate of two dollars for every mile in length he shall run, including the wages of chain carriers, markers, and every other expense attending the same.

The first line, running north and south as aforesaid, shall begin on the Ohio river, at a point that shall be found to be due north from the western termination of a line which has been run as the southern boundary of the State of Pennsylvania; and the first running east and west shall begin at the same point, and shall extend throughout the whole territory. Provided, That nothing herein shall be construed as fixing the western boundary of the State of Pennsylvania. The geographer shall designate the townships or fractional parts of townships by numbers, progressively, from south to north, always beginning each range with No. 1; and the ranges shall be distinguished by their progressive numbers to the westward — the first range, extending from the Ohio to the Lake Erie, being marked No. 1. The geographer shall personally attend to the running of the first east and west line, and shall take the latitude of the extremes of the first north and south line, and of the mouths of the principal rivers.

The lines shall be measured with a chain; shall be plainly marked by chaps on the trees, and exactly described on a plat; whereon shall be noted by the surveyor, at their proper distances, all mines, salt springs, salt licks, and mill seats, that shall come to his knowledge; and all watercourses, mountains, and other remarkable and permanent things, over or near which such lines shall pass, and also the quality of the lands.

The plats of the townships respectively, shall be marked by subdivisions into lots of one mile square, or 640 acres,[5] in the same direction as the external lines, and numbered from 1 to 36; always beginning the succeeding range of the lots with the number next to that with which the preceding one concluded. And where, from the causes before mentioned, only a fractional part of a township shall be surveyed, the lots protracted thereon shall bear the same numbers as if the township had been entire. And the surveyors, in running the external lines of the townships, shall, at the interval of every mile, mark corners for the lots which are adjacent, always designating the same in a different manner from those of the townships. . . .

---

5. An attempt to reduce the minimum to 320 acres was beaten down. Hibbard, A History of the Public Land Policies 39 (1924) — Eds.

B. An Historical Excursion 23

As soon as seven ranges of townships and fractional parts of townships, in the direction from south to north, shall have been surveyed, the geographer shall transmit plats thereof to the Board of Treasury, who shall record the same, with the report, in well bound books to be kept for that purpose. And the geographer shall make similar returns, from time to time, of every seven ranges, as they may be surveyed. The Secretary of War shall have recourse thereto, and shall take by lot therefrom, a number of townships and fractional parts of townships, as well from those to be sold entire as from those to be sold in lots, as will be equal to one seventh part of the whole of such seven ranges, as nearly as may be, for the use of the late continental army; . . . The Board of Treasury shall, from time to time, cause the remaining numbers, as well those to be sold entire, as those to be sold in lots, to be drawn for, in the name of the thirteen states respectively, according to the quotas in the last preceding requisition on all the states; Provided, That in case more land than its proportion is allotted for sale in any State at any distribution, a deduction be made therefor at the next.

The Board of Treasury shall transmit a copy of the original plats, previously noting thereon the townships and fractional parts of townships which shall have fallen to the several states by the distribution aforesaid, to the Commissioners of the loan office of the several states, who, after giving notice of not less than two nor more than six months, by causing advertisements to be posted up at the court houses or other noted places in every county, and to be inserted in one newspaper published in the States of their residence respectively, shall proceed to sell the townships or fractional parts of townships, at public vendue, in the following manner, viz.: the township or fractional part of a township No. 1, in the first range, shall be sold entire; and No. 2, in the same range, by lots; and thus in alternate order through the whole of the first range. The township or fractional part of a township No. 1, in the second range, shall be sold by lots; and No. 2, in the same range, entire; and so in alternate order through the whole of the second range; and the third range shall be sold in the same manner as the first, and the fourth in the same manner as the second, and thus alternately throughout all the ranges; Provided, That none of the lands within the said territory be sold under the price of one dollar the acre. . . .

There shall be reserved for the United States, out of every township, the four lots, being numbered 8, 11, 26, 29, and out of every fractional part of a township, so many lots of the same numbers as shall be found thereon, for future sale. There shall be reserved the lot No. 16, of every township, for the maintenance of public shools within the said township; also one third part of all gold, silver, lead, and copper mines, to be sold, or otherwise disposed of, as Congress shall hereafter direct.[6]

■ THE PUBLIC DOMAIN
198 (Donaldson ed. 1881)

TREASURY DEPARTMENT
July 20, 1790

In obedience to the order of the House of Representatives . . . the Secretary of the Treasury respectfully reports:

That in the formation of a plan for the disposition of the vacant lands of the United States there appear to be two leading objects of consideration: one, the facility of advantageous sales, according to the probable course of purchases; the other the accommodation of individuals now inhabiting the western country, or who may hereafter emigrate thither. The former, as an operation of finance, claims primary attention; the latter is important as it relates to the satisfaction of the inhabitants of the western country. It is desirable, and does not appear impracticable, to conciliate both. Purchasers may be contemplated in three classes: moneyed individuals and companies who will buy to sell again; associations of persons who intend to make settlements themselves; single persons or families, now resident in the western country, or who may emigrate thither hereafter. The two first will be frequently blended, and will always want considerable tracts. The last will generally purchase small quantities. Hence a plan for the sale of the western lands, while it may have due regard for the last, should be calculated to obtain all the advantages which may be derived from the two first classes. For this reason it seems requisite that the General Land Office should be established at the seat of Government. It is there that the principal purchasers, whether citizens or foreigners, can most easily find proper agents and that contracts for large purchases can be best adjusted. But the accommodation of the present inhabitants of the western territory and of unassociated persons and families who may emigrate thither seems to require that one office, subordinate to that at the seat of Congress, should be opened in the Northwestern and another in the Southwestern government. . . .

All of which is humbly submitted.

ALEXANDER HAMILTON
Secretary of the Treasury

6. The first land law of the Confederation was the Ordinance of 1784, 26 J. Cont. Cong. 275 (Fitzpatrick ed. 1928), for the Northwest Territory. No settlement of territory was made under that act, however. The Ordinance of 1787, 2 Federal and State Constitutions 957 (Thorpe ed. 1909), which superseded it, dealt with the entire structure of government for the territory. — EDS.

AN ACT TO AMEND THE ACT ENTITLED "AN ACT PROVIDING FOR THE SALE OF THE LANDS OF THE UNITED STATES IN THE TERRITORY NORTHWEST OF THE OHIO, AND ABOVE THE MOUTH OF KENTUCKY RIVER"
2 Stat. 73 (1800)

Sec. 1. There shall be four land offices established in the ... territory: one at Cincinnati ... one at Chilicothe ... one at Marietta ... and one at Steubenville. ... Each of the said offices shall be under the direction of an officer, ... who shall be appointed by the President of the United States, by and with the advice and consent of the Senate. ...

Sec. 3. The surveyor-general shall cause the townships west of the Muskingum, which, by the above-mentioned act are directed to be sold in quarter townships, to be subdivided into half sections of three hundred and twenty acres each,[7] as nearly as may be. ...

Sec. 5. No lands shall be sold by virtue of this act, at either public or private sale, for less than two dollars per acre, and payment may be made for the same by all purchasers, either in specie, or in evidences of the public debt of the United States ... and shall be made in the following manner, and under the following conditions, to wit:

1. At the time of purchase, every purchaser shall, exclusively of the fees hereafter mentioned, pay six dollars for every section, and three dollars for every half section, he may have purchased, for surveying expenses, and deposit one twentieth part of the amount of purchase money, to be forfeited, if, within forty days one fourth part of the purchase money, including the said twentieth part, is not paid.

2. One fourth part of the purchase money shall be paid within forty days after the day of sale as aforesaid; another fourth part shall be paid within two years; another fourth part within three years; and another fourth part within four years after the day of sale.

3. Interest, at the rate of six per cent. a year from the day of sale shall be charged upon each of the three last payments. ...

Sec. 15. The lands of the United States reserved for future disposition, may be let upon leases by the surveyor-general, in sections or half sections, for terms not exceeding seven years, on condition of making such improvements as he shall deem reasonable.

---

7. In 1804, this was halved to 160 acres. 2 Stat. 281 (1804). — Eds.

The Purposes for Which Urban Land Is Used*
[Expressed in percentages of total land]

Type of use	Proportion of total land
Total developed	78.4
Residential	31.0
Industrial	8.5
Commercial	4.0
Road and highway	19.8
Other public	15.2
Total undeveloped	21.6
Vacant	20.4
Underwater	1.2

* This table is adapted from Niedercorn and Hearle, Recent Land-Use Trends in Forty-Eight Large American Cities, Table 2 (Rand Memorandum RM-3664-1-FF, 1963). Compare the earlier figures set forth in Bartholomew, Land Uses in American Cities 121 (1955):

	53 Central cities	33 Satellite cities	11 Urban areas
Public and semi-public	45.77	42.97	57.50
Streets	*28.10*	*27.67*	*27.61*
Parks and playgrounds	*6.74*	*4.37*	*4.59*
Other public and semi-public	*10.93*	*10.93*	*25.30*
Residential	39.61	41.98	27.99
Single-family dwellings	*31.81*	*36.18*	*25.05*
Two-family dwellings	*4.79*	*3.31*	*1.63*
Multi-family dwellings	*3.01*	*2.49*	*1.31*
Railroad property	4.86	4.65	6.22
Heavy industry	3.60		3.77
Light industry	2.84	7.86	1.87
Commercial areas	3.32	2.54	2.65
Total developed area	100.0	100.0	100.0

"The term 'central city' here refers to the municipality in which is centered the major social and economic activities of an urban area.... The 'satellite city' is a community adjacent to a larger municipality. While the satellite city has a separate political existence, it is in one degree or another dependent on the central city for its economic and cultural well-being.... The 'urban area,' on the other hand, is not a political or governmental unit, but includes the central city, any satellite community, and all developed area within the urban fringe." Id. at 8. Cf. 2 National Resources Committee, Urban Planning and Land Policies 261 (1939).

Use of Land Downtown, Washington, D.C. — 1980*

Land use	Area (in acres)	Percent
Total Land Area	658	100.0
Less: Streets	320	48.6
Less: Alleys	11	1.7
Less: Parks and Open Space	19	2.9
Equals: Net Development Area	308	46.8
Net Downtown Area	308	100.0
Retail	42	13.6
Private Office	56	18.2
Hotels	9	2.9
Industry and Wholesale	13	4.2
Private Institutions	10	3.2
Residential	24	7.8
District Government	35	11.4
Federal Government	39	12.7
Parking Garages	8	2.6
Parking Lots and Vacant Land	66	21.4
Other	8	2.0

* *Source:* Washington, D.C., Department of Planning, 1982 Master Plan (1982).

Land Area, Population, and Density: 1970–1980†

Metropolitan	16.0	74.8	300
Nonmetropolitan	84.0	25.2	19
Total	100.0	100.0	64
1970 (243 SMSAs):			
Metropolitan	10.9	68.6	360
Nonmetropolitan	89.1	31.4	20
Total	100.0	100.0	57

† *Source:* Bureau of the Census, Statistical Abstract of the United States, No. 18, at 15 (1982).

■ AN ACT MAKING FURTHER PROVISION FOR THE SALE OF THE PUBLIC LANDS
3 Stat. 566 (1820)

Sec. 1. All the public lands of the United States, the sale of which is, or may be authorized by law, shall, when offered at public sale, to the highest bidder, be offered in half quarter sections; and when offered at private sale, may be purchased, at the option of the purchaser, either in entire sections, half sections, quarter sections, or half quarter sections; . . . but fractional sections containing less than one hundred and sixty acres shall not be divided, but shall be sold entire: Provided, That this section shall not be construed to alter any special provision made by law for the sale of land in town lots.

Sec. 2. Credit shall not be allowed for the purchase-money on the sale of any of the public lands . . . but every purchaser of land sold at public sale . . . shall, on the day of purchase, make complete payment therefor; and the purchaser at private sale shall produce to the register of the land office a receipt from the Treasurer of the United States, or from the receiver of public moneys of the district, for the amount of the purchase money on any tract, before he shall enter the same at the land office. . . .[8]

■ AN ACT TO APPROPRIATE THE PROCEEDS OF THE SALES OF THE PUBLIC LANDS, AND TO GRANT PRE-EMPTION RIGHTS
5 Stat. 453 (1841)

Sec. 8. There shall be granted to [Ohio, Indiana, Illinois, Alabama, Missouri, Mississippi, Louisiana, Arkansas, and Michigan] five hundred thousand acres of land for purposes of internal improvement: . . . the selections in all of the said States, to be made within their limits

---

8. See An Act Supplementing to the Several Laws for the Sale of the Public Lands, 4 Stat. 503 (1832):

> [N]o person shall be permitted to enter more than one half-quarter section of land under this act, in quarter-quarter sections, in his own name, or in the name of any other person, and in no case unless he intends it for cultivation, or for the use of his improvement.

From 1809 to 1832, fully twenty-three relief acts were passed. Sato, History of the Land Question in the United States 407 (1886). See, for example, An Act for the Relief of the Purchasers of Public Lands, and for the Suppression of Fraudulent Practices at the Public Sales of the Lands of the United States, 4 Stat. 390 (1830). — EDS.

respectively in such manner as the Legislatures thereof shall direct; and located in parcels conformably to sectional divisions and subdivisions, of not less than three hundred and twenty acres in any one location, on any public land except such as is or may be reserved from sale by any law of Congress or proclamation of the President of the United States, which said locations may be made at any time after the lands of the United States in said States respectively, shall have been surveyed according to existing laws. . . .

Sec. 9. The lands herein granted to the States above named shall not be disposed of at a price less than one dollar and twenty-five cents per acre, until otherwise authorized by a law of the United States; and the net proceeds of the sale of said lands shall be faithfully applied to objects of internal improvement within the States aforesaid, respectively, namely: Roads, railways, bridges, canals and improvement of water-courses, and draining of swamps; and such roads, railways, canals, bridges and water-courses, when made or improved, shall be free for the transportation of the United States mail, and munitions of war, and for the passage of their troops, without the payment of any toll whatever.

■ AN ACT TO SECURE HOMESTEADS TO ACTUAL SETTLERS ON THE PUBLIC DOMAIN
12 Stat. 392 (1862)

Sec. 1. Any person who is the head of a family, or who has arrived at the age of twenty-one years, and is a citizen of the United States, or who shall have filed his declaration of intention to become such, as required by the naturalization laws of the United States, and who has never borne arms against the United States Government or given aid and comfort to its enemies, shall . . . be entitled to enter one quarter section or a less quantity of unappropriated public lands, upon which said person may have filed a pre-emption claim, or which may, at the time the application is made, be subject to pre-emption at one dollar and twenty-five cents, or less, per acre; or eighty acres or less of such unappropriated lands, at two dollars and fifty cents per acre, to be located in a body, in conformity to the legal subdivisions of the public lands, and after the same shall have been surveyed: Provided, That any person owning and residing on land may . . . enter other land lying contiguous to his or her said land, which shall not, with the land so already owned and occupied, exceed in the aggregate one hundred and sixty acres.

Sec. 2. The person applying for the benefit of this act shall, upon

Principal Means of Transportation to Work—Selected Metropolitan Areas: 1980

Metropolitan area	Workers (1,000)	Drive alone	Carpool	Public transportation	Other means
Anaheim-Santa Ana-Garden Grove, Calif.	948	75.1	16.1	1.9	6.9
Atlanta, Ga.	955	69.5	18.9	7.4	4.2
Baltimore, Md.	959	60.4	22.4	10.6	6.7
Boston, Mass.	1,285	55.3	17.6	15.8	11.3
Chicago, Ill.	3,114	57.8	16.8	17.6	7.7
Cleveland, Ohio	822	67.9	15.7	10.7	5.7
Dallas-Fort Worth, Tex.	1,464	71.2	20.2	3.6	5.0
Denver-Boulder, Colo.	803	65.1	20.1	6.9	7.9
Detroit, Mich.	1,662	74.8	16.9	3.5	4.8
Houston, Tex.	1,405	69.5	22.6	2.8	5.1
Indianapolis, Ind.	524	71.7	20.4	2.9	5.0
Kansas City, Mo.-Kans.	621	69.8	21.1	4.4	4.7
Los Angeles-Long Beach, Calif.	3,395	68.7	17.5	6.3	7.5
Miami, Fla.	715	67.8	18.9	6.4	7.0
Milwaukee, Wis.	639	66.2	18.8	7.2	7.8
Minneapolis-St. Paul, Minn.-Wis.	1,048	63.8	19.2	8.2	8.8
Nassau-Suffolk, N.Y.	1,157	63.4	18.1	12.2	6.3
New Orleans, La.	477	62.1	21.1	10.5	6.3
New York, N.Y.-N.J.	3,764	31.0	11.8	43.5	13.8
Philadelphia, Pa.-N.J.	1,934	59.2	17.7	14.4	8.8
Phoenix, Ariz.	663	71.1	18.8	1.9	8.2
Pittsburgh, Pa.	922	61.0	18.7	11.7	8.6
Portland, Oreg.-Wash.	573	65.4	17.9	8.4	8.4
St. Louis, Mo.-Ill.	1,011	67.1	21.2	6.0	5.7
San Antonio, Tex.	444	66.9	20.4	5.1	7.7
San Diego, Calif.	865	63.3	17.8	3.1	15.8
San Francisco-Oakland, Calif.	1,549	56.9	16.0	17.1	10.0
Seattle-Everett, Wash.	774	64.1	18.6	10.1	7.2
Tampa-St. Petersburg, Fla.	602	71.9	18.3	1.6	8.2
Washington, D.C.-Md.-Va.	1,562	52.6	23.3	15.9	8.1

Source: Bureau of the Census, 1980 Census of Population and Housing, Supplementary Report, series PHC 80-S1-1.

The impact of limited-access road construction on metropolitan land development has been well documented. See Poulton, The Relationship Between Transportation and the Viability of Central and Inner Urban Areas, 14 J. Trans., Econ. & Poly. 249 (1980). The consequences of a drastic increase in the price of motor fuel — ground transportation consumes some 45 percent of total oil-produced energy — and on land use is the next guessing game. Responses can reorder existing technology, such as improvising the demonstration bus line, begun in July 1966, linking Watts to areas of industrial employment. Haar, Transportation and Economic Opportunity, 21 Traffic Q. 521 (1967). Responses can also include new transportation technologies, such as integrating light rail transit with downtown pedestrian malls as part of downtown redevelopment. Cervero, Light Rail Transit and Urban Development, 50 J. Am. Plan. Assn. 133 (1984). One final question is to whom should such policy responses be targeted. Again, responses in land-use patterns can affect automobile pollution, energy consumption, and the very feasibility of mass transit. — Eds.

application to the register of the land office in which he or she is about to make such entry, make affidavit . . . that such application is made for his or her exclusive use and benefit, and that said entry is made for the purpose of actual settlement and cultivation, and not either directly or indirectly for the use or benefit of any other person or persons whomsoever; and upon filing the said affidavit with the register or receiver, and on payment of ten dollars, he or she shall thereupon be permitted to enter the quantity of land specified: Provided, however, That no certificate shall be given or patent issued therefor until the expiration of five years from the date of such entry; and if, at the expiration of such time, or at any time within two years thereafter, the person making such entry; or, if he be dead, his widow; or in case of her death, his heirs or devisee; or in case of a widow making such entry, her heirs or devisee, in case of her death; shall prove by two credible witnesses that he, she, or they have resided upon or cultivated the same for the term of five years immediately succeeding the time of filing the affidavit aforesaid, and shall make affidavit that no part of said land has been alienated, and that he has borne true allegiance to the Government of the United States; then in such case, he, she, or they, if at that time a citizen of the United States, shall be entitled to a patent. . . .

Sec. 4. No lands acquired under the provisions of this act shall in any event become liable to the satisfaction of any debt or debts contracted prior to the issuing of the patent therefor.

. . . [N]o person who has served, or may hereafter serve, for a period of not less than fourteen days in the army or navy of the United States, either regular or volunteer, under the laws thereof, during the existence of an actual war, domestic or foreign, shall be deprived of the benefits of this act on account of not having attained the age of twenty-one years.

■ AN ACT TO PROVIDE FOR THE SALE OF DESERT LANDS
19 Stat. 377 (1877)

Sec. 1. It shall be lawful for any citizen of the United States, . . . upon payment of twenty-five cents per acre — to file a declaration under oath with the register and the receiver of the land district in which any desert land is situated, that he intends to reclaim a tract of desert land not exceeding one section, by conducting water upon the same, within the period of three years thereafter, Provided however That the right to the use of water by the person so conducting the same, on or to any tract of desert land of six hundred and forty acres shall depend upon bona fide prior appropriation: and such right shall not exceed the amount of water actually appropriated, and necessarily used for the purpose of irrigation and reclamation. . . .[9]

■ AN ACT APPROPRIATING THE RECEIPTS FROM THE SALE AND DISPOSAL OF PUBLIC LANDS IN CERTAIN STATES AND TERRITORIES TO THE CONSTRUCTION OF IRRIGATION WORKS FOR THE RECLAMATION OF ARID LANDS
32 Stat. 388 (1902)

Sec. 1. [A]ll moneys received from the sale and disposal of public lands in Arizona, California, Colorado, Idaho, Kansas, Montana, Nebraska, Nevada, New Mexico, North Dakota, Oklahoma, Oregon, South Dakota, Utah, Washington, and Wyoming . . . including the surplus of fees and commissions in excess of allowances to registers and receivers, and excepting the five per centum of the proceeds of the sales of public lands in the above States set aside by law for educational and other purposes shall be, and the same are hereby, reserved, set aside, and appropriated as a special fund in the Treasury to be known as the "reclamation fund," to be used in the examination and survey for and the construction and maintenance of irrigation works for the storage, diversion, and development of waters for the reclamation of arid and semiarid lands in the said States and Territories, and for the payment of all other expenditures provided for in this act. . . .[10]

---

9. See Stegner, Beyond the Hundredth Meridian 223-231 (1954). Also see An Act to Repeal Timber-Culture Laws, and for Other Purposes, 26 Stat. 1095 (1891) ("The President . . . may . . . set apart and reserve, in any State or Territory having public land bearing forests, in any part of the public lands wholly or in part covered with timber or undergrowth, whether of commercial value or not, as public reservations . . .").

Provisions for the administration and protection of the forest reserves were not made until An Act Making Appropriations for Sundry Civil Expenses of the Government, 30 Stat. 11, 34-36 (1897), was passed. President Cleveland's attempt to create thirteen reserves unleashed a storm of protest from the West. See Ise, The United States Forest Policy (1920). As to the "cowboy mentality," see Boulding, The Economics of Coming Spaceship Earth, in The Environmental Handbook 96 (DeBell ed. 1970). — Eds.

10. Section 3 of 37 Stat. 265, 266 (1912) reads in part as follows:

Provided, That no person shall at any one time or in any manner . . . acquire, own, or hold irrigable land for which entry or water right application shall have been made . . . before final payment in full of all installments of building and betterment charges shall have been made on account of such land in excess of one farm unit as fixed by the Secretary of the Interior as the limit of area per entry of public land or per single ownership of private land for which a water right may be purchased respectively, nor in any case in excess of one hundred and sixty acres, nor shall water be furnished . . . nor a water right sold or recognized for such excess; but any such excess land acquired at any time in good faith by descent, by will, or by foreclosure of any lien may be held for two years and no longer after its acquisition; and every excess holding prohibited as aforesaid shall be forfeited

■ WATER POLLUTION CONTROL ACT
62 Stat. 1155 (1948)

... That in connection with the exercise of jurisdiction over the waterways of the Nation and in consequence of the benefits resulting to the public health and welfare by the abatement of stream pollution, it is hereby declared to be the policy of Congress to recognize, preserve, and protect the primary responsibilities and rights of the States in controlling water pollution, to support and aid technical research to devise and perfect methods of treatment of industrial wastes which are not susceptible to known effective methods of treatment, and to provide Federal technical services to State and interstate agencies and to industries, and financial aid to State and interstate agencies and to municipalities, in the formulation and execution of their stream pollution abatement programs....

Sec. 2. (a) The Surgeon General shall, after careful investigation, and in cooperation with other Federal agencies, with State water pollution agencies and interstate agencies, and with the municipalities and industries involved, prepare or adopt comprehensive programs for eliminating or reducing the pollution of interstate waters and tributaries thereof and improving the sanitary condition of surface and underground waters. In the development of such comprehensive programs due regard shall be given to the improvements which are necessary to conserve such waters for public water supplies, propagation of fish and aquatic life, recreational purposes, and agricultural, industrial, and other legitimate uses....

■ NATIONAL ENVIRONMENTAL POLICY ACT OF 1969
83 Stat. 852 (1970)

Sec. 101. (a) The Congress, recognizing the profound impact of man's activity on the interrelations of all components of the natural

---

to the United States ... and this proviso shall be recited in every patent and water-right certificate issued by the United States under the provisions of this Act.

Taylor, The Excess Land Law, 64 Yale L.J. 477 (1955), is a stimulating discussion. See also Mayer & Riley, Public Domain, Private Dominion: A History of Public Mineral Policy in America (1985).

During the Great Depression, Congress responded to natural disaster with An Act to Stop Injury to the Public Grazing Lands by Preventing Overgrazing and Soil Deterioration, to Provide for Their Orderly Use, Improvement, and Development, to Stabilize the Livestock Industry Dependent upon the Public Range, and for Other Purposes, 48 Stat. 1269 (1934). This has been called "perhaps the greatest contribution of the New Deal administration to the history of the old public domain." Robbins, Our Landed Heritage 421 (1950). See also Peffer, The Closing of the Public Domain (1951); Johnson & Barlowe, Land Problems and Policies 15-98 (1954); Clawson & Held, The Federal Lands (1957); Rethinking the Federal Lands (Brubaker ed. 1984). — EDS.

environment, particularly the profound influences of population growth, high-density urbanization, industrial expansion, resource exploitation, and new and expanding technological advances and recognizing further the critical importance of restoring and maintaining environmental quality to the overall welfare and development of man, declares that it is the continuing policy of the Federal Government, in cooperation with State and local governments, and other concerned public and private organizations, to use all practicable means and measures, including financial and technical assistance, in a manner calculated to foster and promote the general welfare, to create and maintain conditions under which man and nature can exist in productive harmony, and fulfill the social, economic, and other requirements of present and future generations of Americans.

(b) In order to carry out the policy set forth in this Act, it is the continuing responsibility of the Federal Government to use all practicable means, consistent with other essential considerations of national policy, to improve and coordinate Federal plans, functions, programs, and resources to the end that the Nation may —

(1) fulfill the responsibilities of each generation as trustee of the environment for succeeding generations;

(2) assure all Americans safe, healthful, productive, and esthetically and culturally pleasing surroundings;

(3) attain the widest range of beneficial uses of the environment without degradation, risk to health or safety, or other undesirable and unintended consequences;

(4) preserve important historic, cultural and natural aspects of our national heritage, and maintain, wherever possible, an environment which supports diversity and variety of individual choice;

(5) achieve a balance between population and resource use which

Young and Elderly Support Ratios: 1900 to 2050*

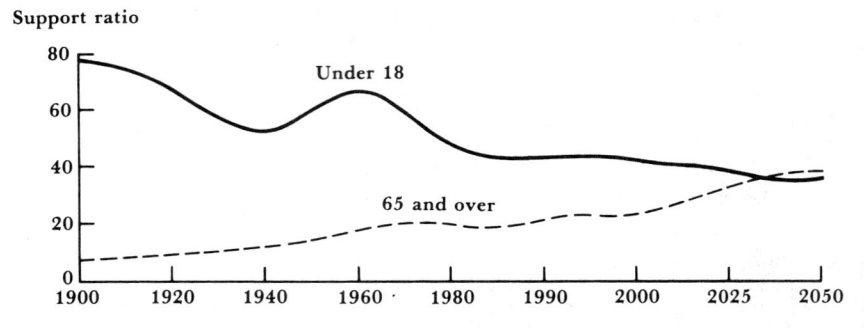

* *Source:* Bureau of the Census, America in Transition: An Aging Society, Current Population Reports, Special Study, P-23, No. 128, Fig. 6 (1985).

Ratio of Residential Capital Formation to Gross National Product and to Total Consumption*

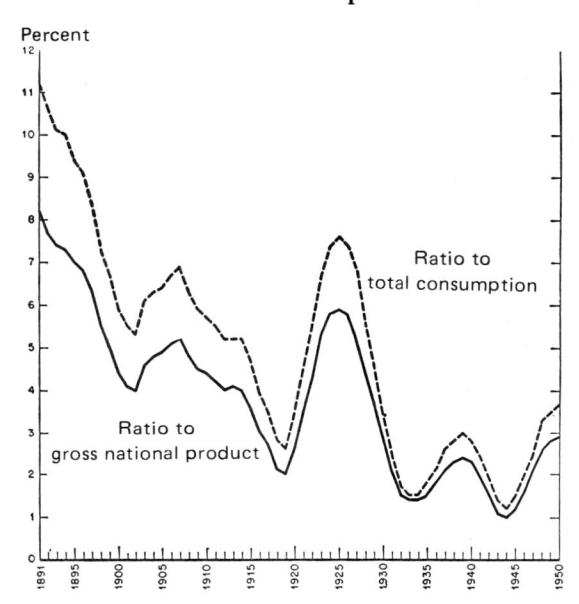

Source: Grebler, Blank & Winnick, Capital Formation in Residential Real Estate 135 (1956). What does this chart indicate about the dependence of capital formation on national economic, as compared to national housing, policies? If extrapolated to the present, do you think there are some surprises for the decision maker? Cf. de Jouvenal, The Art of Conjecture (1966). In 1983, Professor Grebler brought these figures up to date: for the period 1976-1980, residential construction totaled $100.6 billion, while the GNP leapt to $2166.4 billion. Grebler, Inflation: Blessing or Curse?, 465 Annals Am. Acad. 21 (1983). For a discussion of the unpredictable variables, see Urban Housing 127-307 (Wheaton, Milgram and Meyerson eds. 1966).

will permit high standards of living and a wide sharing of life's amenities; and

(6) enhance the quality of renewable resources and approach the maximum attainable recycling of depletable resources.

(c) The Congress recognizes that each person should enjoy a healthful environment and that each person has a responsibility to contribute to the preservation and enhancement of the environment.

Sec. 102. The Congress authorizes and directs that, to the fullest extent possible: (1) the policies, regulations, and public laws of the United States shall be interpreted and administered in accordance with the policies set forth in this Act, and (2) all agencies of the Federal Government shall —

. . . (C) include in every recommendation or report on proposals for legislation and other major Federal actions significantly affecting the quality of the human environment, a detailed statement by the responsible official on —

(i) the environmental impact of the proposed action,

(ii) any adverse environmental effects which cannot be avoided should the proposal be implemented,

(iii) alternatives to the proposed action,

(iv) the relationship between local short-term uses of man's environment and the maintenance and enhancement of long-term productivity, and

(v) any irreversible and irretrievable commitments of resources which would be involved in the proposed action should it be implemented.[11]

■ FEDERAL LAND POLICY AND MANAGEMENT ACT OF 1976
90 Stat. 2743 (1976)

Sec. 102. (a) The Congress declares that it is the policy of the United States that —

(1) the public lands be retained in Federal ownership, unless as a result of the land use planning procedure provided for in this Act, it is determined that disposal of a particular parcel will serve the national interest;

(2) the national interest will be best realized if the public lands and their resources are periodically and systematically inventoried

---

11. See President Nixon's Message to Congress, 116 Cong. Rec. S12996 (daily ed. Aug. 10, 1970):

> We have treated our land as if it were a limitless resource. Traditionally, Americans have felt that what they do with their own land is their own business. This attitude has been a natural outgrowth of the pioneer spirit. Today, we are coming to realize that our land is finite, while our population is growing. The uses to which our generation puts the land can either expand or severely limit the choices our children will have. The time has come when we must accept the idea that none of us has a right to abuse the land, and that on the contrary society as a whole has a legitimate interest in proper land use. There is a national interest in effective land use planning all across the nation.
>
> I believe that the problem of urbanization which I have described, of resource management, and of land and water use generally can only be met by comprehensive approaches which take into account the widest range of social, economic, and ecological concerns. I believe we must work toward development of a National Land Use Policy to be carried out by an effective partnership of Federal, State and local governments together, and, where appropriate, with new regional institutional arrangements.

See also Waite, Problems of National Land Use Planning, 20 Catholic U.L. Rev. 702 (1971), and also the series of bills, H.R. 19250, H.R. 16647, and H.R. 19106 (91st Cong., 2d Sess.), all introduced in 1970, all aimed at establishing a national urban growth policy. — Eds.

B. An Historical Excursion

and their present and future use is projected through a land use planning process coordinated with other Federal and State planning efforts;

(3) public lands not previously designated for any specific use and all existing classifications of public lands that were effected by executive action or statute before the date of enactment of this Act be reviewed in accordance with the provisions of this Act;

(4) the Congress exercise its constitutional authority to withdraw or otherwise designate or dedicate Federal lands for specified purposes and that Congress delineate the extent to which the Executive may withdraw lands without legislative action;

(5) in administering public land statutes and exercising discretionary authority granted by them, the Secretary be required to establish comprehensive rules and regulations after considering the views of the general public; and to structure adjudication procedures to assure adequate third party participation, objective administrative review of initial decisions, and expeditious decisionmaking;

(6) judicial review of public land adjudication decisions be provided by law;

(7) goals and objectives be established by law as guidelines for public land use planning, and that management be on the basis of multiple use and sustained yield unless otherwise specified by law;

(8) the public lands be managed in a manner that will protect the quality of scientific, scenic, historical, ecological, environmental, air and atmospheric, water resource, and archeological values; that, where appropriate, will preserve and protect certain public lands in their natural condition; that will provide food and habitat for fish and wildlife and domestic animals; and that will provide for outdoor recreation and human occupancy and use;

(9) the United States receive fair market value of the use of the public lands and their resources unless otherwise provided for by statute; . . .

(11) regulations and plans for the protection of public land areas of critical environmental concern be promptly developed; . . .

Sec. 103. . . .

(a) The term "areas of critical environmental concern" means areas within the public lands where special management attention is required (when such areas are developed or used or where no development is required) to protect and prevent irreparable damage to important historic, cultural, or scenic values, fish and wildlife resources or other natural systems or processes, or to protect life and safety from natural hazards. . . .

(c) The term "multiple use" means the management of the public lands and their various resource values so that they are utilized in the combination that will best meet the present and future needs of the

American people; making the most judicious use of the land for some or all of these resources or related services over areas large enough to provide sufficient latitude for periodic adjustments in use to conform to changing needs and conditions; the use of some land for less than all of the resources; a combination of balanced and diverse resource uses that takes into account the long-term needs of future generations for renewable and nonrenewable resources, including, but not limited to, recreation, range, timber, minerals, watershed, wildlife and fish, and natural scenic, scientific and historical values; and harmonious and coordinated management of the various resources without permanent impairment of the productivity of the land and the quality of the environment with consideration being given to the relative values of the resources and not necessarily to the combination of uses that will give the greatest economic return or the greatest unit output....

(h) The term "sustained yield" means the achievement and maintenance in perpetuity of a high-level annual or regular periodic output of the various renewable resources of the public lands consistent with multiple use....

(j) The term "withdrawal" means withholding an area of Federal land from settlement, sale, location, or entry, under some or all of the general land laws, for the purpose of limiting activities under those laws in order to maintain other public values in the area or reserving the area for a particular public purpose or program; or transferring jurisdiction over an area of Federal land ... from one department, bureau or agency to another department, bureau or agency....

Sec. 202. (a) The Secretary shall, with public involvement and consistent with the terms and conditions of this Act, develop, maintain, and, when appropriate, revise land use plans which provide by tracts or areas for the use of the public lands. Land use plans shall be developed for the public lands regardless of whether such lands previously have been classified, withdrawn, set aside, or otherwise designated for one or more uses.[12]

---

12. See Policy and Management Act, Pub. L. No. 94-579, 6176 House Report No. 94-1163 (1976):

> The underlying mission proposed for the public lands is the multiple use of resources on a sustained-yield basis. Corollary to this is the selective transfer of public lands to other ownership where the public interest will be served thereby. The proper multiple use mix of retained public lands is to be achieved by comprehensive land use planning, coordinated with state and local planning. Planning decisions are to be made only after full opportunity for public involvement in the planning process. Management and disposal of the public lands are to be consistent with land-use plans so developed.

See Executive Order No. 12348, 47 Fed. Reg. 8547 (1982):

> ... in order to improve management of Federal Real Property, it is hereby ordered as follows:

B. An Historical Excursion   39

2. Planning the Nation's Capital

Inevitably the design of a nation's capital captures the attention of planners; a capital reflects the culture, resources, and achievements of the people that it represents. The plans for Washington are a basis of city planning in the United States; indeed, the organization of the National Conference on City Planning in 1907 was inspired by the work of the McMillan Commission of 1901. Here are a series of plans from the inception of Washington's and Jefferson's dreams to the present.[13]

> Section 1. (a) There is hereby established a Property Review Board. . . .
> Section 2. The Board shall perform such functions as may be directed by the President, including the following:
> (a) Develop and review Federal real property acquisition, utilization, and disposal policies with respect to their relationship to other Federal policies;
> (b) Advise the Administrator of General Services with respect to such standards and procedures for executive agencies that are necessary to ensure that real property holdings no longer essential to their activities and responsibilities are promptly identified and released for appropriate disposition;
> (c) Review and examine prior disposals of surplus property for public benefit discount conveyances to ensure that the property is being used and maintained for the purpose for which it was conveyed; . . .

In Conservation Law Foundation v. Harper, 587 F. Supp. 357 (D. Mass. 1984), the court upheld in part the motion to dismiss:

> Plaintiffs claim that defendants have developed a "comprehensive new program administered by the Property Review Board and carried out by the other defendants" to change dramatically the federal government's disposal of public property. They allege that the PRB and other defendants "have begun to carry out their new duties and implement [a] massive new program of land sales."
> Under this "program," the PRB would direct a concerted effort to improve Federal asset management and to dispose of unneeded Federal property. The program allegedly calls for discontinuance of free land transfers to Federal agencies and the "phasing out" of discounted and no-cost conveyances to state and local governments. It allegedly requires that conveyances to state and local governments be made "as a rule . . . only at fair market value," with limited exceptions. Excess properties will be offered for sale first to state and local governments. If state and local governments are unwilling to pay fair market value, the properties will be offered for sale to the general public. Proceeds from such sales would be used "to begin retiring the national debt."

Cf. Urban Park and Recreation Recovery Act of 1978, 92 Stat. 3538 (1978):

> The purpose of this chapter is to authorize the Secretary to establish an urban park and recreation recovery program which would provide Federal grants to economically hard-pressed communities specifically for the rehabilitation of critically needed recreation areas, facilities, and development of improved recreation programs for a period of five years.

13. Observers have reflected upon the gap between official Washington (the gleaming city of monuments), the traditional focus of expenditures, and the relatively impoverished downtown neighborhoods that are increasingly the target of modern planning efforts. From George Washington to the present, presidents have given personal twists to planning: President Kennedy, disturbed during his inaugural parade by the deterioration of the north side of Pennsylvania Avenue, created the Pennsylvania Avenue Commission that has so enhanced the beauty of the city, while President Johnson's concerns emphasized design review, historic and open space preservation. Yet extensive deterioration and

40 I ■ The Land Around Us: The Environment of City Planning

See if you can isolate differing planning conceptions and goals, as they have evolved over time, and their likely impact on individual parcels and on property rights.[14]

---

slums persist within sight of the Capitol Dome. (See the redevelopment cases, infra page 788.) The neglect of local living conditions within the District (typical of older central areas), exacerbated by the flood of suburban expansion that competed for new shopping and office centers, exploded in the riots of 1968 and still underlies modern efforts at improving neighborhood life.

For a recent congressional attempt to "protect and preserve views to and from the historic monuments and buildings," see the National Preservation Act of 1986 (S. 2537). The Act, cosponsored by Senators Cranston and Moynihan, would have imposed special taxes on buildings exceeding certain heights, including a "52-story glass tower ellipsis to be built in the midst of the Washington panorama, nearly 200 feet higher than the Monument, and 15 times more massive." Senator Cranston observed:

> Washington is a city in which sky and land and air are treated as partners in a landscape masterpiece.... What a tragedy if what the future holds for this enchanting Federal city is relegation to a few acres of land surrounded by a forest of tall buildings like New York with its Central Park.

14. There is not one, but a plethora of initial Washington plans. It is not altogether clear whether the so-called L'Enfant Plan, as it has come down to posterity (in the possession of the Map Division of the Library of Congress), is his original proposal.

The Residence Act of 1790, 1 Stat. 130, instructed the president to approve a plan for the capital. On December 13, 1791, Washington sent a L'Enfant scheme to Congress, as "a delineation of a grand plan for the local distribution of the city." Later, L'Enfant's unconventional behavior brought about his dismissal. For one thing, out of fear of speculation, he opposed the commissioners' decision for quick disposal of lots; at the sale he refused to show his plan. A commissioner complained to Washington, "Could we have exhibited a general plan, I believe it would have aided the sale considerably." Washington replied, "There has been something very unaccountable in the conduct of the engraver, yet I cannot be of opinion the delays were occasioned by L'Enfant." Caemmerer, The Life of L'Enfant 175 (1950). The archives reveal a letter from L'Enfant to Tobias Lear, Washington's private secretary, on the day of the sale.

> Happily the few squares where the lots have been sold . . . are so situated as to lessen . . . the inconveniency of their remaining . . . for ages unimproved . . . their local [sic] being wholly owing to the care I took to prevent the exhibition of the general plan at the spot where the sale is made.... [T]he judiciousness of my measure makes me hope the Commissioners would themselves acknowledge the propriety of it were not a mistaken motive for resentment in my opposition to them to interest their selling contrary to their better judgment.

L'Enfant and Washington 76, 77 (Kite ed. 1929).

In 1792, Washington sent the commissioners a different plan, in the form of an engraved map by Andrew Ellicott. Since L'Enfant had refused to make his own plan available to Ellicott (who had worked under him as a surveyor), this second plan is presumably different in many details. (L'Enfant refers to this Ellicott draft as "most unmercifully spoiled and altered . . . to a degree indeed evidently tending to disgrace me and ridicule the very undertaking." Id. at 142.)

On March 2, 1797, a third plan appeared on the stage; Washington sent a letter to the commissioners stating that he was enclosing a plan, on the basis of which land was to be conveyed. Unfortunately, someone forgot to enclose a plan. President Adams corrected the omission on July 23, 1798, by attaching a plan drawn by one Dermott. This was popularly known as the Tin Case Map, because the original was thus found preserved some fifty years later.

Dispute arose later as to whether the plan which Washington intended to annex was that of Dermott or Ellicott. The Attorney General in 1820 thought it was Ellicott's plan, and that hence Adams had lacked the power to annex a different plan. In Van Ness v.

Evolution of the National Capital

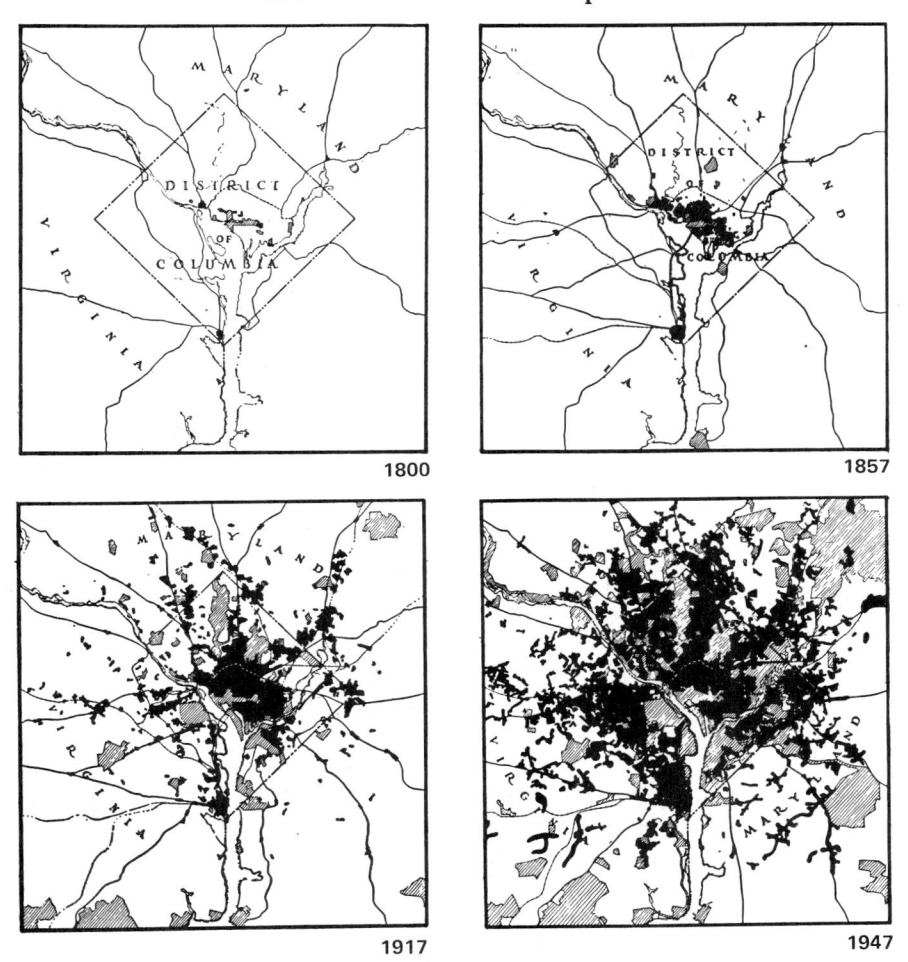

1800

1857

1917

1947

City of Washington, 29 U.S. (4 Pet.) 232, 233 (1830), the Supreme Court assumed it was L'Enfant's, "improved and matured by Ellicott." Counsel urged in Morris v. United States, 174 U.S. 196 (1899), that the decision in Potomac Steamboat Co. v. Upper Potomac Steamboat Co., 109 U.S. 672 (1883), had been incorrectly decided because the Court did not have the Dermott map before it; the Supreme Court concluded that it was the Dermott plan that Washington had in mind, although this made no difference in the final outcome.

When, in President Jefferson's phrase, is a plan "final"? What is the legal significance of the plan? For what activities is it important? At what decision-makers is it aimed? Nicholas King, surveyor of Washington, who himself had prepared a city plan in 1803, stated, "If this decision [perfecting the plan] is left to a future period and our courts of law, they can only have a partial view of the subject, and any general rule they adopt may be attended with serious disadvantages."

The L'Enfant Plan

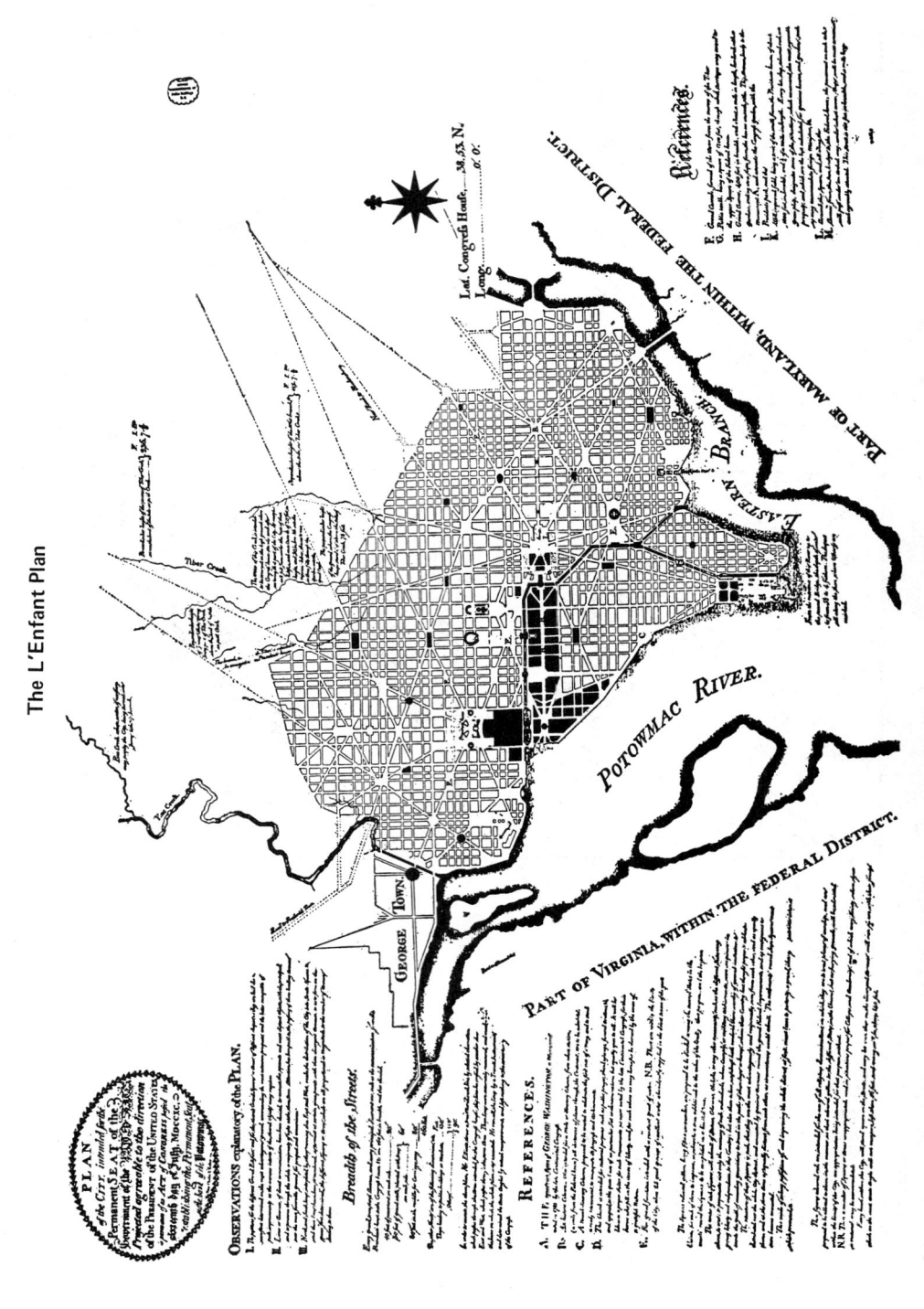

The McMillan Plan of 1901, Showing the Mall

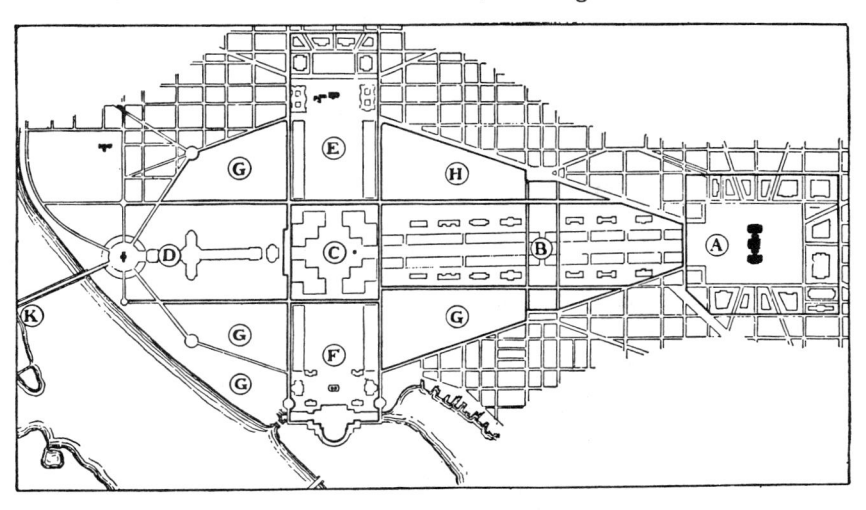

KEY TO THE MALL SYSTEM.

A—Capitol Division.
B—The Mall.
C—Monument Section.
D—Lincoln Division.
E—White House Division.
F—Washington Common.
GG—Park Spaces.
H—Section south of Pennsylvania Avenue.
K—Memorial Bridge.

Government Employment Centers

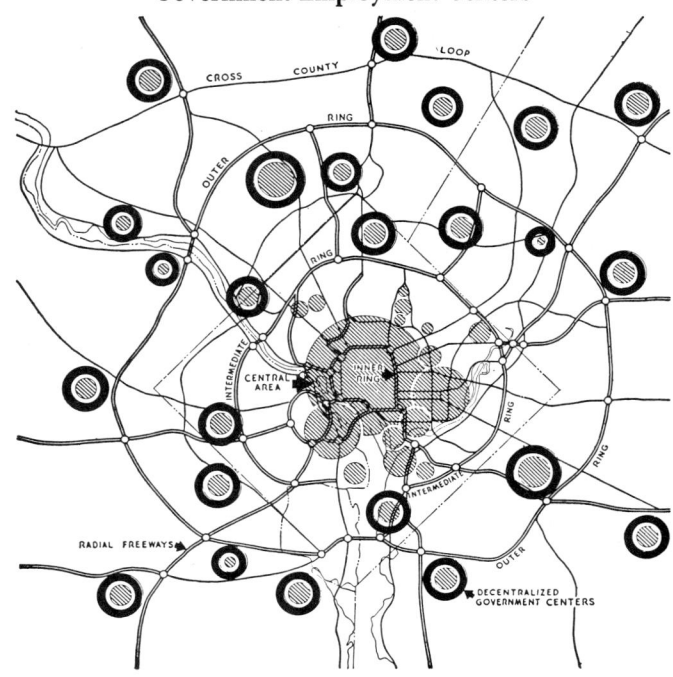

43

Jurisdictional Boundaries

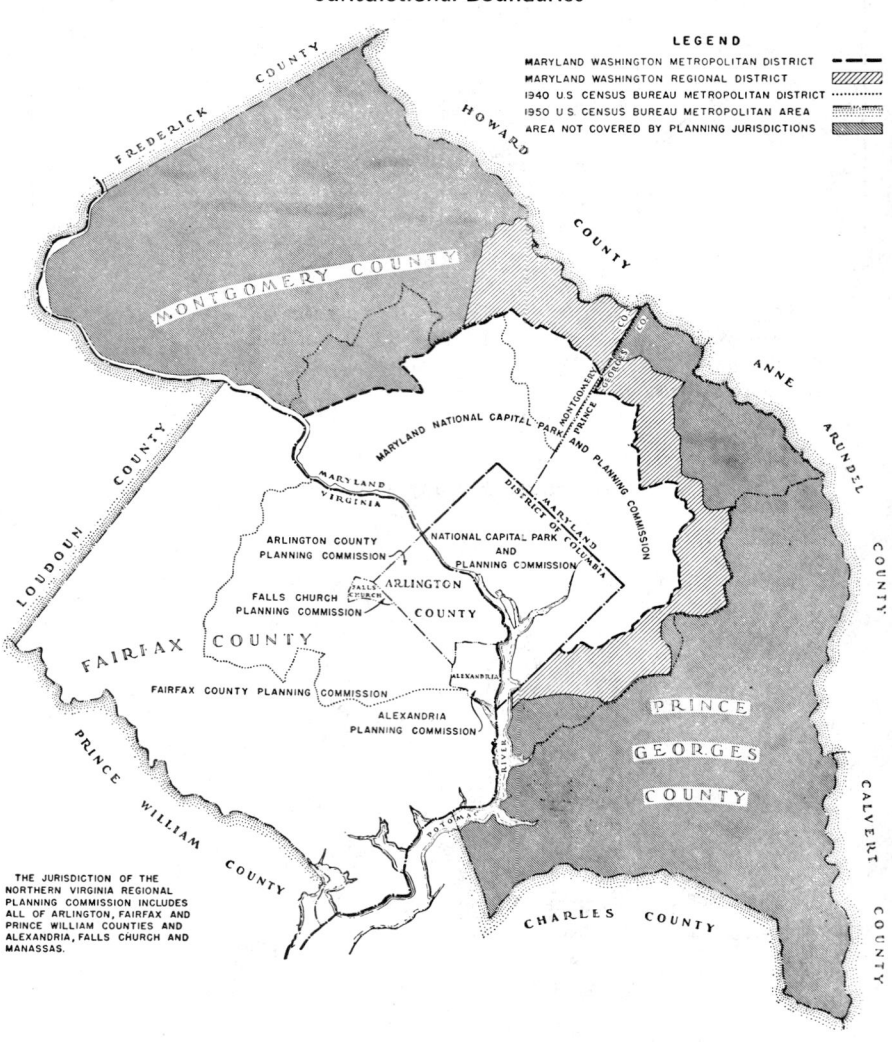

LEGEND
- MARYLAND WASHINGTON METROPOLITAN DISTRICT
- MARYLAND WASHINGTON REGIONAL DISTRICT
- 1940 U.S. CENSUS BUREAU METROPOLITAN DISTRICT
- 1950 U.S. CENSUS BUREAU METROPOLITAN AREA
- AREA NOT COVERED BY PLANNING JURISDICTIONS

THE JURISDICTION OF THE NORTHERN VIRGINIA REGIONAL PLANNING COMMISSION INCLUDES ALL OF ARLINGTON, FAIRFAX AND PRINCE WILLIAM COUNTIES AND ALEXANDRIA, FALLS CHURCH AND MANASSAS.

C. MEANINGS AND MEANS OF PLANNING

1. *The City Planning Commission*

Participants in Planning in the Municipality of Los Angeles*

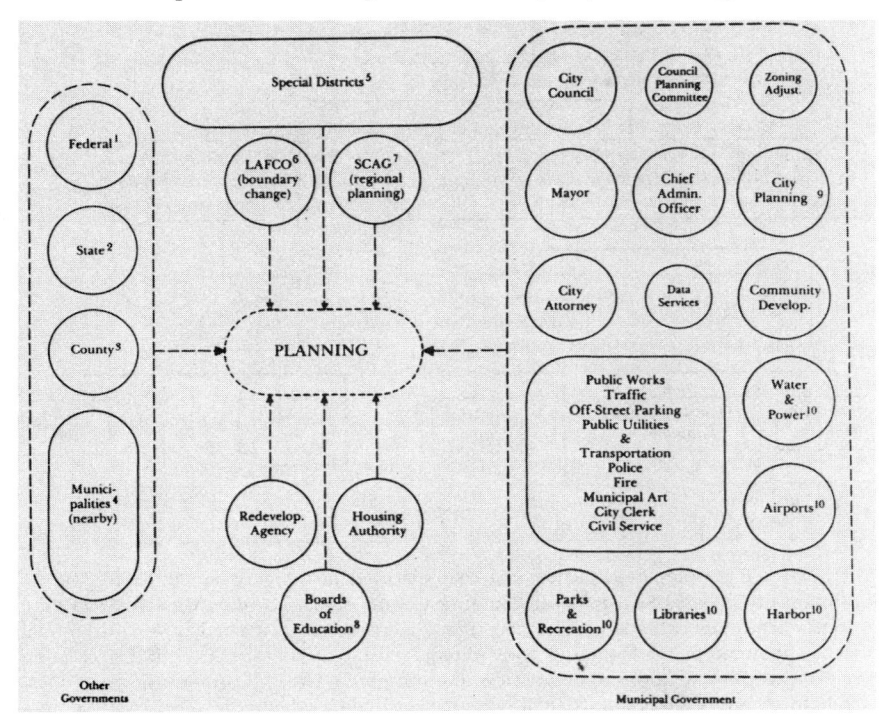

[Diagram: Participants in Planning in the Municipality of Los Angeles. Other Governments side includes: Federal[1], State[2], County[3], Municipalities[4] (nearby), Special Districts[5], LAFCO[6] (boundary change), SCAG[7] (regional planning), Redevelop. Agency, Housing Authority, Boards of Education[8], all connecting to central PLANNING node. Municipal Government side includes: City Council, Council Planning Committee, Zoning Adjust., Mayor, Chief Admin. Officer, City Planning[9], City Attorney, Data Services, Community Develop., Public Works, Traffic, Off-Street Parking, Public Utilities & Transportation, Police, Fire, Municipal Art, City Clerk, Civil Service, Water & Power[10], Airports[10], Parks & Recreation[10], Libraries[10], Harbor[10].]

* *Source:* Branch, Continuous City Planning: Integrating Municipal Management and City Planning 66 (1981). Frank So points out the rapid increase in the power and presence of the professional planning staffs and has challenged the traditional role of the planning commission. He notes that the traditional planning agency focused upon long-range physical development under the oversight of the citizen board that acted "much as a corporate board of directors, establishing policy and hiring capable managers to oversee operations." So, Practice of Local Government Planning 64, 65 (1979). As planning work has become more closely related to the administrative and political functions of governing the city, he notes there has been increased criticism that the planning commission is being inappropriately called upon to act as a body of experts rather than for "purposes of representation and policy review." Id. at 72-73. Increasingly, the power of the planning commission has been circumscribed and the role of the professional staff enlarged.

As to the continuing debate over the place of the city planner in the local government structure, see Tugwell and Banfield, The Planning Function Reappraised, 17 J. Am. Inst. Planners 46 (1951); Benveniste, The Politics of Expertise (1972); Jones, Do Planning Boards Need a Shot in the Arm?, Planning News, Jan.-Feb. 1975, at 1. For a first-hand account of the political dimensions of planners' practice, see Jacobs, Making City Planning Work 53-68 (1978), particularly the account of the interaction with other branches of city government in the development of San Francisco's waterfront.

City Planning Agency Organizational Chart*

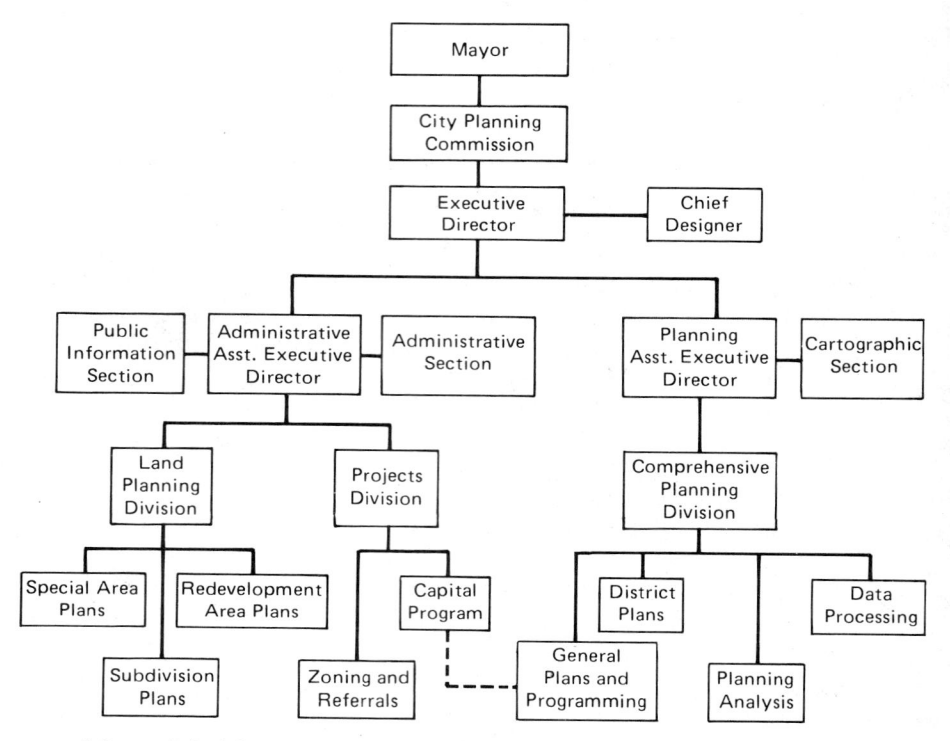

```
                            Mayor
                              |
                     City Planning
                       Commission
                              |
                        Executive ─────── Chief
                        Director          Designer
                              |
     ┌────────────┬───────────┴──────────┬──────────────┐
  Public    Administrative        Administrative     Planning        Cartographic
Information  Asst. Executive        Section       Asst. Executive     Section
  Section      Director                              Director
                  |                                     |
        ┌─────────┴─────────┐                   Comprehensive
      Land              Projects                  Planning
    Planning            Division                  Division
    Division
        |                   |                        |
  ┌─────┴──────┐            |              ┌─────────┼──────────┐
Special Area  Redevelopment Capital     District              Data
   Plans       Area Plans   Program      Plans              Processing
        |                   |
  Subdivision        Zoning and        General         Planning
    Plans             Referrals        Plans and       Analysis
                                       Programming
```

Source: Principles and Practices of Urban Planning 537 (Goodman ed. 1968). Jerome Kaufman, in Changes Sweep Local Planning Commissions, 48 Pub. Mgmt. 221 (1966), contrasts planning commissions of the past ("a group of respected, often influential citizens appointed by the legislative body to mold, cushion, and ram through the planning program with few weapons and even less ammunition") with the present; he concludes: "While the commission is still there, it is being crowded by other groups who want a piece of the planning limelight — citizen planning associations, technical advisory committees, city development co-ordinators, private development corporations, and urban renewal agencies. In cities where the planning staff is organized into a planning department under the locality's chief executive, the planning commission is frequently relegated to a minor advisory role. In a few cities, the planning commission has been stripped of virtually all its authority and serves merely as window dressing." Id. at 222. The author also comments that the main criticisms leveled at planning commissions are: the commission does not spend enough time on planning; even if they had the time, planning commission members are not really qualified to plan; since the commission is a semi-independent agency and not an integral part of local government, it is not actively sought out for advice on local development matters. How do you evaluate these criticisms? It has been suggested that the multipurpose planning commission be replaced by specialized task forces for each problem area; the old commission would then be a long-range advisory board of equal rank with all other task forces. See Nash and Durden, A Task Force Approach to Replace the Planning Board, 30 J. Am. Inst. Planners 10 (1964). The views of planning commission members are surveyed in ASPO Planning Advisory Service, Rep. No. 200, The Planning Commission as Viewed by the Planning Directors (July 1965); Rabinowitz and Pottinger, Organization for Local Planning: The Attitude of Directors, J. Am. Inst. Planners, Jan. 1967, at 27. See The American Planner: Biographies and Recollections (Kruecheberg ed. 1983).

The Place of the City Planning Commission

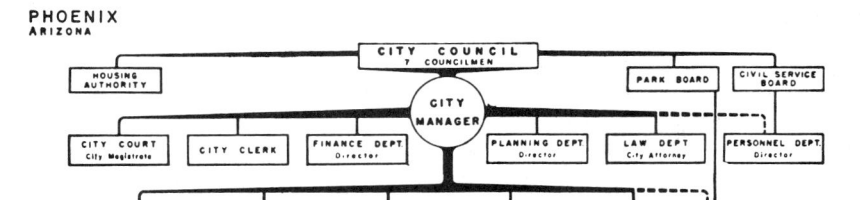

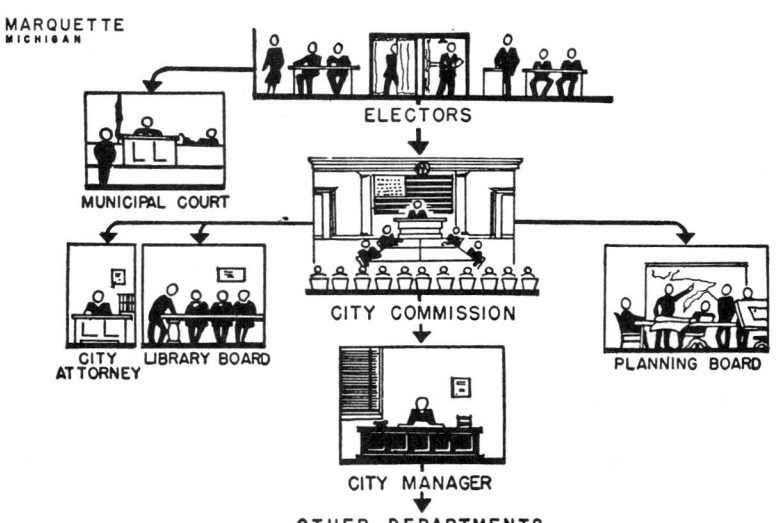

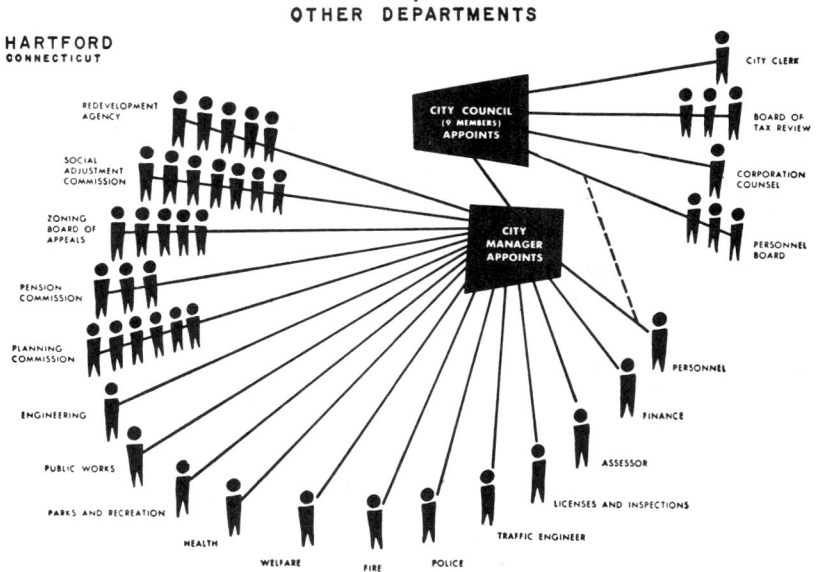

PHOENIX
ARIZONA

MARQUETTE
MICHIGAN

HARTFORD
CONNECTICUT

47

2. The Structure of State Land-Use Planning

Location within the bureaucratic structure is frequently indicative of the importance attached to an agency's responsibilities, and determines the agency's influence with the executive, legislature, and other agencies. Compare the structures utilized in Florida and Hawaii [see infra pages 49-50] . Are land-use decisions "better" when made by an independent commission, a governor's cabinet, or a committee of the state legislature?

3. The Plan

■ GOODMAN AND KAUFMAN, CITY PLANNING IN THE SIXTIES
4-7 (1965)

Comprehensive planning is generally considered to be divided into four working processes:

1. *Survey and analysis,* or collection of basic data related to physical, economic, and social conditions.
2. *Goal formulation,* or identification of and agreement upon social and economic objectives.
3. *Plan making,* or determination of suitable uses and densities for specific areas and for the circulation system and public facilities.
4. *Plan effectuation,* or legal and administrative tools to carry out the plan and to coordinate decisions.

Those objectives that are considered desirable can be specifically incorporated in the comprehensive plan in several ways: through establishing norms, such as the assignment of desirable population densities to particular areas; through qualitative determinations, such as the type of school plants to be built; through expression of standards, such as the acreage to be allotted for recreational areas or the range of facilities to be included in these areas; through area plans, indicating the physical relationships between residential and other facilities; and through three-dimensional representations, showing building types that would be appropriate in the municipality. . . . [The plan's] range of subject matter and its expression are as broad as the opportunities available to the community.

The scope and content of the plan largely determine its functions and objectives as a document for the citizens of the community. If well-drawn, it will contribute significantly in these directions:

Organizational Structure for Implementation of Florida's Environmental Land and Water Management Act of 1972*

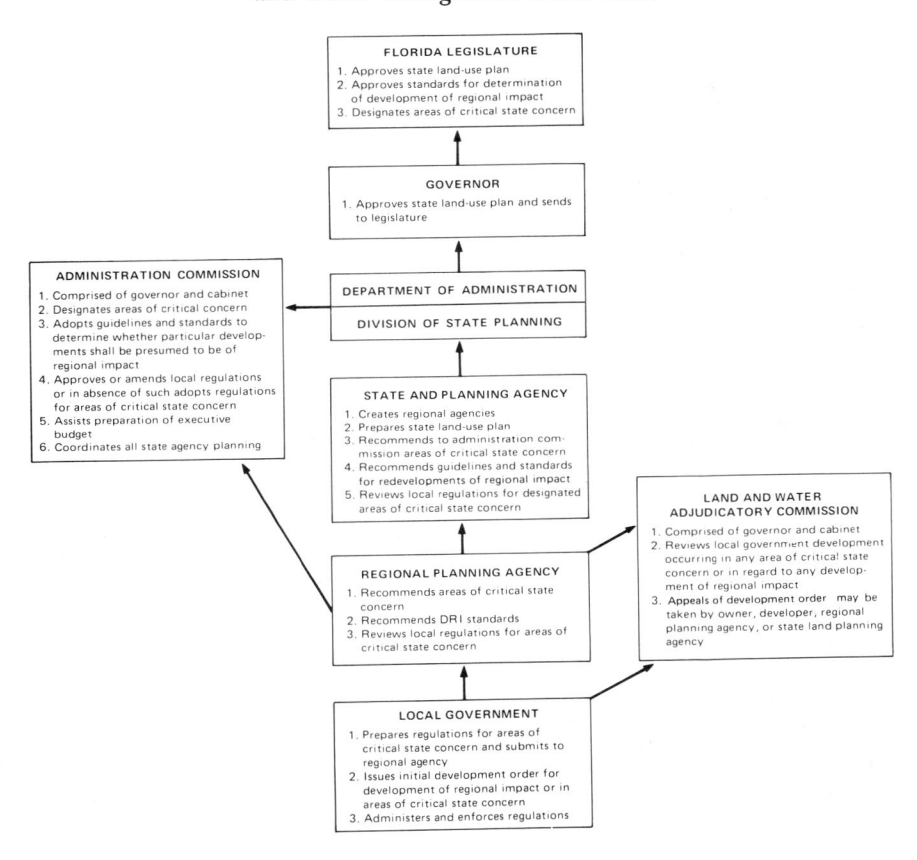

```
                        FLORIDA LEGISLATURE
                        1. Approves state land-use plan
                        2. Approves standards for determination
                           of development of regional impact
                        3. Designates areas of critical state concern
                                    ↑
                             GOVERNOR
                        1. Approves state land-use plan and sends
                           to legislature
                                    ↑
ADMINISTRATION COMMISSION    DEPARTMENT OF ADMINISTRATION
1. Comprised of governor and cabinet ←
2. Designates areas of critical concern   DIVISION OF STATE PLANNING
3. Adopts guidelines and standards to
   determine whether particular develop-
   ments shall be presumed to be of
   regional impact
4. Approves or amends local regulations   STATE AND PLANNING AGENCY
   or in absence of such adopts regulations  1. Creates regional agencies
   for areas of critical state concern    2. Prepares state land-use plan
5. Assists preparation of executive       3. Recommends to administration com-
   budget                                    mission areas of critical state concern
6. Coordinates all state agency planning  4. Recommends guidelines and standards
                                             for redevelopments of regional impact
                                          5. Reviews local regulations for designated
                                             areas of critical state concern
                                                                        LAND AND WATER
                                                                        ADJUDICATORY COMMISSION
                                                                        1. Comprised of governor and cabinet
                                                                        2. Reviews local government development
                             REGIONAL PLANNING AGENCY                      occurring in any area of critical state
                        1. Recommends areas of critical state              concern or in regard to any develop-
                           concern                                         ment of regional impact
                        2. Recommends DRI standards                     3. Appeals of development order may be
                        3. Reviews local regulations for areas of          taken by owner, developer, regional
                           critical state concern                          planning agency, or state land planning
                                                                           agency
                                    ↑
                             LOCAL GOVERNMENT
                        1. Prepares regulations for areas of
                           critical state concern and submits to
                           regional agency
                        2. Issues initial development order for
                           development of regional impact or in
                           areas of critical state concern
                        3. Administers and enforces regulations
```

* The bureaucratic placement and composition of land-use agencies also frequently reveals a state's priorities in pursuing (or not pursuing) land-use planning. Maine has established overlapping review authority in two separate agencies: one, in the Department of Conservation, is charged with land-use regulation in all unincorporated areas and is to include individuals knowledgeable about Maine's major industries, Maine Land Use Law (1979), Me. Rev. Stat. Ann. tit. 12, §§681 to 685, and the other, in the Department of Environmental Protection, is authorized specifically to monitor the environmental consequences of development, Maine Site Location of Development Law (1979), Me. Rev. Stat. Ann. tit. 38, §§481-486. Nevada, by way of contrast, limits the state's land-use planning function to coordination of local efforts and adds that responsibility to the other functions of the Department of Conservation and Natural Resources. Nev. Rev. Stat. §321 (1982).

Administrative Structure of Land-Use Agencies in Hawaii*

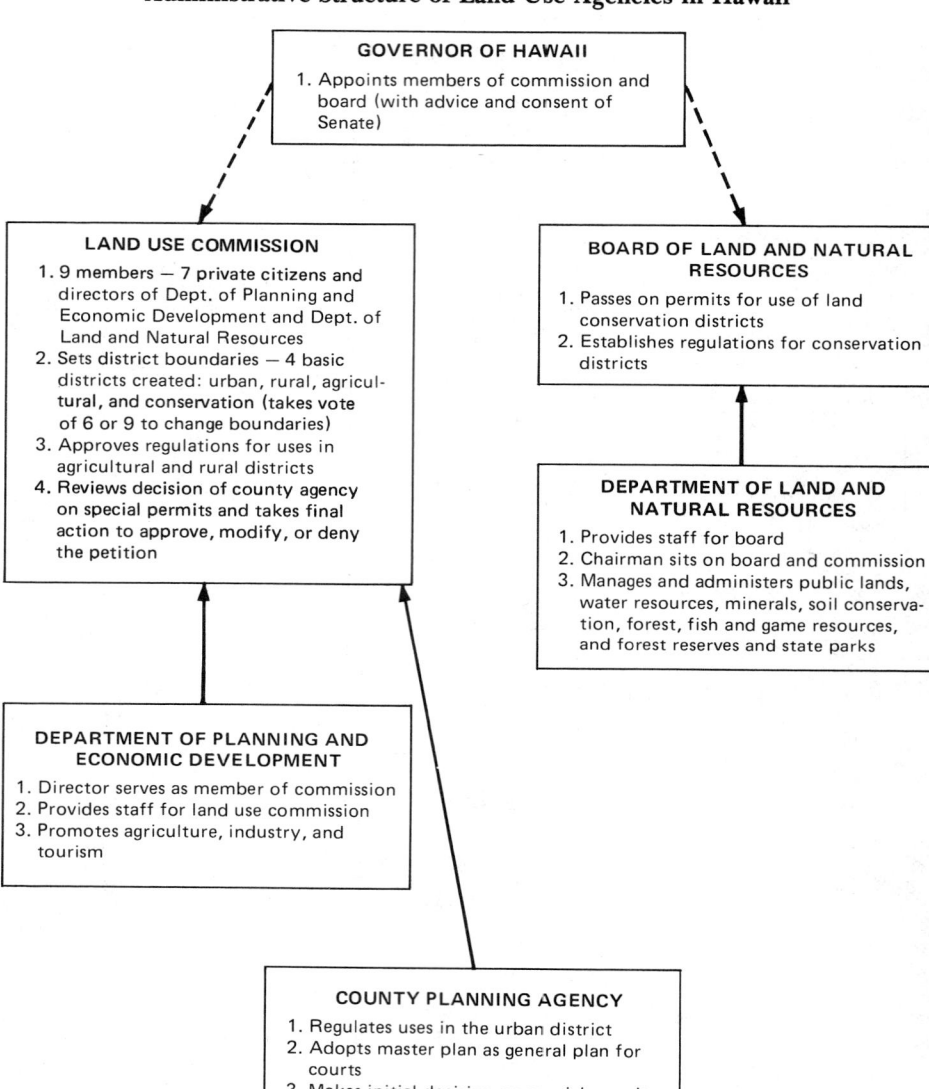

GOVERNOR OF HAWAII
1. Appoints members of commission and board (with advice and consent of Senate)

LAND USE COMMISSION
1. 9 members — 7 private citizens and directors of Dept. of Planning and Economic Development and Dept. of Land and Natural Resources
2. Sets district boundaries — 4 basic districts created: urban, rural, agricultural, and conservation (takes vote of 6 or 9 to change boundaries)
3. Approves regulations for uses in agricultural and rural districts
4. Reviews decision of county agency on special permits and takes final action to approve, modify, or deny the petition

BOARD OF LAND AND NATURAL RESOURCES
1. Passes on permits for use of land conservation districts
2. Establishes regulations for conservation districts

DEPARTMENT OF LAND AND NATURAL RESOURCES
1. Provides staff for board
2. Chairman sits on board and commission
3. Manages and administers public lands, water resources, minerals, soil conservation, forest, fish and game resources, and forest reserves and state parks

DEPARTMENT OF PLANNING AND ECONOMIC DEVELOPMENT
1. Director serves as member of commission
2. Provides staff for land use commission
3. Promotes agriculture, industry, and tourism

COUNTY PLANNING AGENCY
1. Regulates uses in the urban district
2. Adopts master plan as general plan for courts
3. Makes initial decision on special permit requests in agricultural and rural zones
4. Enforcement of district regulations is responsibility of agency which enforces county zoning laws

*To what extent is land-use planning affected by the other functions of the administrative agency by which it is performed? Should it be carried out exclusively by a professional bureaucracy or monitored, if not performed, by a citizen commission? See Nev. Rev. Stat. §321 (1982) that creates an advisory commission of local elected officials, N.H. Rev. Stat. Ann. ch. 12-A (1985) that creates a general citizen advisory panel, and Colo. Rev. Stat. ch. 106 (1970) that sets up a commission including at least one member from each congressional district.

C. Meanings and Means of Planning

1. To provide information about the present status and resources of the community; to make citizens aware of how the community is constituted.
2. To chart the future growth of the municipality and to outline the goals and objectives publicly agreed upon; to provide a clue to the character and quality of the area that might be anticipated at some later date.
3. To serve as a rallying point for worthy proposals and as a test of the validity of development schemes.
4. To act as a framework of the kinds of tools required to carry out the plan.
5. To stimulate understanding and support among the citizenry, and so to elicit the necessary fiscal resources and legal tools.
6. To put property interests on notice as to the intent of the city to take action in various locations and in regard to specific projects.[15]

■ CHICAGO DEPARTMENT OF DEVELOPMENT AND PLANNING, THE COMPREHENSIVE PLAN
104 (1966)

The six "strategic objectives" of the Comprehensive Plan are described in the first section on the Quality of Life:

1. Family Life and the Environment
2. Expanded Opportunities for the Disadvantaged
3. Economic Developments and Job Opportunities
4. Moving People and Goods
5. The Proper Allocation of Land
6. Unified City Development

These are the main elements of the plan's strategy — the particular components of the city's over-all objectives which are most critical at the present time and which should be emphasized in the allocation of resources. Generally, the first three strategic objectives represent the "ends" of the plan, while the second three represent "means."

The first three objectives reflect the three main goals of the plan — improving the environment, enlarging human opportunities, and strengthening and diversifying the economy.

---

15. See Haar, The Master Plan: An Impermanent Constitution, 20 Law & Contemp. Probs. 353 (1955); Kent, The Urban General Plan (1964); Castells, The City and the Grass Roots (1983). — Eds.

Functional, physical, and managerial capability is also necessary if the city is to attain its basic goals. The fourth and fifth objectives are directed toward efficient operation and development of the city, and the sixth has to do with the effectiveness of administrative organization. To achieve these objectives, the Improvement Plan calls for detailed analysis and programming of the following activities.

For *moving people and goods,* strategic concerns at this time are transit in the central area, the development of high accessibility corridors, and the effects that technological change will have on air and rail transportation.

For *the proper allocation of land,* the strategic concerns include future land requirements for parks and schools, lakefront development, and the use of the Zoning Ordinance to achieve land development policies most effectively.

The sixth strategic objective — *unified city development* — recognizes the fact that social development programs, economic development programs, and physical development programs must all be aimed at the same strategic objectives. The Development Area procedure is designed to facilitate joint public and private efforts and to coordinate public agency actions. Project review conducted by the Chicago Plan Commission under the referral procedure is the statutory means of coordinating public actions toward the objectives of the Comprehensive Plan.[16]

16. As part of the Comprehensive Plan, the planning commission has devised the Improvement Plan. The Improvement Plan, while not setting definite priorities for specific projects (this is left to other procedures such as the five-year Capital Improvements Program) does determine "specific targets for the seven planning systems . . . Residence, Recreation, Education, Safety and Health, Industry, Business, and Transportation." The targets are summarized below in outline form:

Improvement Targets

Residence
    Maintain sound residential areas by establishing a system of neighborhood service centers and by expanding community facilities and services.
    Improve or replace all deficient units through redevelopment, rehabilitation, and code enforcement programs.

Expand the housing supply by:
    Rebuilding 2500 acres of severely blighted housing with 100,000 new homes.
    Developing four central opportunity areas with new housing for 200,000 people.
    Increasing the supply of public housing by 35,000 units through leasing, rehabilitation, and new construction.

Recreation
    Bring all neighborhoods to minimum standards for local recreation space (add 1800 acres).
    Expand lakefront parks by two square miles of landfill.
    Modernize regional inland parks.
    Coordinate park and school site programs for maximum efficiency and beautification.

Education
    Expand University of Illinois and develop three senior colleges.
    Develop system of eight to twelve junior colleges.

C. Meanings and Means of Planning

■ NEW YORK CITY PLANNING COMMISSION, PLAN FOR NEW YORK CITY
Vol. 1, at 7-20 (1969)

SUMMARY

National Center. We strongly favor expansion of the national center. There is room for growth — in the underused area of west midtown, on new landfill along the river in lower Manhattan — and the growth can be shaped in a way that will make the center a far more amenable place than ever before. But the city must take the initiative.... We ... think that the city can help developers in land assembly by applying its power of eminent domain to holdouts; and are recommending legislation that would carefully define the requirements for such action....

Our plan for lower Manhattan combines the whole arsenal of [land-use] tools and incentives. The key to it is the decking of peripheral highways and the creation of new land around the entire southern end of Manhattan out to the pierhead line. Downtown will stay open after five. Battery Park City and the other waterfront communities ... will mix office towers with housing for every income range, a wide variety of commercial activities, museums, parks and marinas. Other major elements of the plan are three urban renewal projects on the edge of

---

> Provide school capacity for 35,000-50,000 more high school students and 65,000-100,000 more elementary students with major emphasis on park-school arrangements.
> Build new library branches to serve all sections of city.
>
> *Safety and Health*
> Provide needed police headquarters and training academy and expanded personnel.
> Complete system of fire stations.
> Develop system of community and neighborhood health centers.
> Continue intensive air and water pollution abatement program.
> Expand incinerator system and use controlled lakefill disposal system.
>
> *Industry*
> Strengthen sound industrial districts with transportation and other public services.
> Rebuild nearly 1000 acres of industrial land with public renewal assistance.
> Stimulate and support private redevelopment of 1200 more acres of industrial land.
>
> *Business*
> Support Central Business District growth, especially with transportation and environmental improvements.
> Rehabilitate regional and other centers.
> Develop special districts for offices and other special business functions.
> Rebuild strip business in conjunction with residential and street improvements.
>
> *Transportation*
> Construct Crosstown Expressway and Franklin Street Connector.
> Expand Loop subway facilities and pedestrian connections.
> Improve capacity of 200 to 250 miles of major streets in conjunction with urban renewal and beautification programs.
> Develop additional rapid transit routes and expand park-and-ride and transfer terminals — EDS.

the district, expansion of the civic center, improved pedestrian and traffic circulation and expanded subway service....

Transportation. New York can function as a national center because it has the best mass transit system in America. Yes, the subways are grossly overburdened during the rush hour and they are hideous and uncomfortable at all hours. The buses are noisy and their schedules erratic. It is astonishing that we have managed to create a system that is such an affront to the senses. But it works. For all its discomforts, the subway system is a far more efficient way of moving people than automobiles, and the improvement of it is the core of the City's transportation effort....

Highways. In planning for highways one thing is clear. They should not be routed toward Manhattan's business district.... We believe that the use of cars in the business districts should be limited to the few people for whom they are a necessity, and to those who are willing to pay handsomely for the privilege. The proposals that have been made for cut-rate municipal garages in the business district are completely inadvisable; such garages belong in the peripheral areas....

Noise and air pollution caused by trucks has been a problem and so has their size. Street loading and unloading has clogged traffic.... New measures to increase off-street loading facilities are needed. Another possibility that must be explored is the provision of truck terminals on the periphery....

The Port. The startling growth of containerization has revolutionized shipping.... The Manhattan waterfront cannot compete for containership freight. There is not enough back-up space. The old freight piers should be used as long as there is demand for them, but further investments in them would be a waste of money. New container freight terminals within the City should be in Brooklyn and Staten Island. Manhattan is still the place for passenger liners.... The new superliner terminal should encourage this trade. The Manhattan waterfront is a priceless asset. Instead of being wasted on obsolete functions, it should be opened up for recreation, commerce and housing....

Job Development. The City's economy has its own dynamics and there is only so much the government can do to shape it. But that margin is critically important. If the City uses its points of leverage it can generate a large number of jobs — and good jobs, jobs that lead to advancement.... As a major purchaser of goods and services, the City can stimulate business enterprise in the ghetto. The growth of black and Puerto Rican firms will produce more local jobs; it will also create the kind of managerial talent the ghetto needs.... The point of such policies is not to create an independent ghetto economy. It is to do jobs that desperately need doing, and to make ghetto people better able to do jobs anywhere....

Welfare. The present system of welfare is inadequate, inequitable

C. Meanings and Means of Planning 55

and degrading. It is also costly to the City.... The big changes must come in Federal policy. What is needed is a national program that will radically overhaul the present welfare system and eventually replace it with a new system of Social Security.... For the long term the nation must seek a form of guaranteed minimum income. One way to achieve this would be a negative income tax.... Payment would be in relation to need, yet the incentive to work would not be destroyed. Such a program would not cost a great deal more than the present welfare system. It has been estimated that the cost in New York City would be about $2 billion a year versus the present $1.5 billion....

Environment. Neighborhood change is at the bottom of the tensions of this City. But it is a dynamic and it cuts both ways. Many once fine neighborhoods are deteriorating at an alarming rate. Others that were slums are being transformed into good places.... We reject the concept of wholesale demolition and barrack-like projects. Instead of clearing away neighborhoods, we must work with the fabric of them and put as much emphasis on maintenance and rehabilitation as on new construction. Instead of one fixed static plan, we must follow an incremental, step-by-step approach and involve the people of the neighborhoods from the first steps on.... We recommend a strengthening of incentive approaches: establishment of local nonprofit maintenance corporations, tenant and community cooperatives, private lending consortiums backed up by public guarantees, increased loans to property owners....

Crime. Procedures [of the City's courts] are obsolete, justice is so slow as to be injustice.... The adoption of a master calendar office, for example, could as much as double available judge time. Pretrial detention, which helps overcrowd our jails, could be sharply reduced. Bail procedures which unfairly discriminate against the poor should be liberalized....

It is the losers of the City who are its scourge. Out of all proportion, street crimes are committed by boys and young men of the slums. Simply locking them up will not meet the issues. Unless the conditions that bred them are changed, there will be more like them to come. In the long run, the most important programs to curb crime will be our programs to improve education, job training, incomes; to make neighborhoods fit to live in and grow up in....

Government. To realize the goals of this Plan, New York City must have an administrative structure that works efficiently and a bureaucracy that is responsible to elected officials and to the citizens.... The budget system must be reformed.... Another thing that needs changing is the City's cumbersome apparatus for reviewing and auditing contracts.... The personnel system is archaic.... The Civil Service system is much to blame. Set up, like the anti-graft measures, for what were once the best of reasons, it has become sufficient unto itself, insulated not only from politicians but from the political process and from people....

The City government must be more responsive to the needs of the local neighborhoods. The City's man in charge of the local operations of a department must be given more on-the-spot authority. Most important, the people of the community must be able to participate in the decisions that affect them. . . .

The relationship between the City and the State and Federal government must be changed. The City is not allowed to be master in its own house. . . . Many of the City's most difficult problems transcend its boundaries. . . . [T]here is as yet no agency with authority and jurisdiction for the broader social and economic problems. . . . Our slum problem, for example, is greatly influenced by the suburbs. . . .

We pursue no illusory Utopia. New York could never be an ideal city. It has too great a dynamism and its problems are immense because they are in part the consequence of it. . . . The fierce competition for land, the crowding, the dislocations of demolition and rebuilding are vexing problems but they are also problems of vitality. . . .[17]

■ BERKELEY PEOPLE'S ARCHITECTURE, THE RECOVERY OF CITIES
The Environmental Handbook 234, 238-239 (1970)

[T]here is no legitimate reason why there should be any more downtown office space. Communications technology now permits a geographically decentralized association of people who are engaged in

---

17. See N.Y. Times, June 26, 1974:

> A new concept in neighborhood planning, epitomized by a series of "miniplans" tailored to the needs of individual communities, is being inaugurated by the City Planning Commission.
> The approach is in marked contrast to the master plan for New York City, drawn up with much fanfare six years ago but shelved by the commission last year as little more than a handy reference tool.
> "This, we think, is planning for the seventies," said John E. Zuccotti, the commission"s chairman, in making public the first three miniplans — for the Kingsbridge, Soundview and Hunts Point sections of the Bronx.
> "The glossy-covered brochures may have had their place," Mr. Zuccotti said, referring to the expensively produced volumes of the citywide master plan, complete with elaborate graphics. "But times have changed. With a city the size of New York, in a democratic society that is as diverse as ours, there is clearly a need for more attention to local needs and desires."
> Mr. Zuccotti, who became a member of the commission in 1971 and took over as chairman a year ago last February, has fostered the neighborhood approach in planning. He has sought greater involvement by the 62 community boards and local civic organizations in the planning process.
> Abandonment of the master plan does not mean that controls on development in the city will be diminished, but rather that they will be reoriented toward community participation. Under the city's zoning resolution, the Planning Commission has continuing responsibility for balancing local and citywide priorities and its approval is required for all zoning changes and for major new projects. — EDS.

C. Meanings and Means of Planning

information processing. Even now most lessees of space in highrise downtown buildings don't share anything with their neighbors except the crowded elevators, inadequate sidewalk space, and the six-lane freeway on the way home.

The present form of downtown growth represents massive profits to the big building interests (banks, realtor-developers, insurance companies, big corporations). Clean monumental space, undefiled by non-commercial realities of the funky diversity of true community, is the jealously guarded status image of downtown territory. Highrise office buildings are designed more to advertise the prestige of large corporations, to announce their arrival in the world of downtown, than as a response to any real corporate need for ten thousand people working in the same building.

PROGRAM FOR DOWNTOWN RECOVERY

1. Freeze downtown highrise development. *There is no need for any new highrise structures.*

2. Selectively dismantle whole buildings and parts of buildings; save materials for reuse.

3. Close off streets for orchards, vegetable gardens, parks, market places. Close the city center to private automobiles. Buses and other service transit only.

4. Rebuild southern exposures for hydroponic gardens.

5. Renovate office space for multiple use — housing, community marketing, meeting places, schools and other much needed things for the surrounding communities. *Diversify and decentralize downtown. . . .*

Of the three areas — downtown, the suburbs, and the middle city — it is the middle city which is the only matrix for new culture.[18] Downtown does not create new culture; it merely markets it to the suburbs. The middle city will be the first to reclaim its environment, the suburbs second, the downtown last. The downtown environment will be reclaimed when the middle city defeats the bid of downtown for its territory and when suburbia becomes self-supporting communities.

FACTORIES: THE MATERIAL OF "PROGRESS"

Developing neighborhood communities as ecologically balanced, self-managing entities appeals to underemployed ghetto dwellers, the

---

18. The middle city, "the colonized culture," is the ghetto. "The middle city has the longest history of unbroken social growth . . . the street is still a meeting place for people not merely a transportation artery for somewhere else, neighborhood grocery stores still exist. Neighbors are often relatives and religious and social life is centered in the neighborhood. The middle city has been the source of most urban American culture." The Environmental Handbook, at 238-239. — EDS.

"new earth" counterculture, and disillusioned school-age suburban youth as they are the least integrated into the centralized system of production. But for millions of Americans who are plugged in to the system through a forty-hour-a-week job and credit payments, the decentralized vision is seen as a threat to industrial workers. . . .

The factory worker, whose life is tied completely to his job and who has no time to see his neighborhood as his "community," will be initially unreceptive to geographically-based community action for recovery of the environment. This means that the factory itself must be thought of as a potential community, from which working people can begin the job of dismantling centralized corporate control and reassembling geographically decentralized work places. . . .

■ AMERICAN LAW INSTITUTE, A MODEL LAND DEVELOPMENT CODE
(1975)

Section 3-101. (1) [A] local government may adopt a Local Land Development Plan which shall be a statement (in words, maps, illustrations or other media of communication) setting forth its objectives, policies and standards to guide public and private development of land within its planning jurisdiction and including a short-term program of public actions. . . .

Section 3-102. The purposes of preparing a Local Land Development Plan are:

(1) to initiate comprehensive studies of factors relevant to development;

(2) to recognize and state major problems and opportunities concerning development and the social and economic effects of development;

(3) to set forth the desired sequence, patterns, and characteristics of future development and its probable environmental, economic and social consequences;

(4) to provide a statement of programs to obtain the desired sequence, patterns, and characteristics of development; and

(5) to determine the probable environmental, economic and social consequences of the desired development and the proposed programs.

As the legal tools for managing growth control work their way into judicial acceptability, more and more governments — even at the regional level — are embarking on this ambitious joint venture of the

C. Meanings and Means of Planning

public and private sectors to solve land-use problems. A good example follows:

■ MONTGOMERY COUNTY, MD PLANNING BOARD, GROWTH POLICY REPORT
(1979)

CHAPTER 1 — FRAMEWORK

Chapter 1 outlines a narrative argument that includes the following major points. Prior to 1970, urban planning was based largely on the implicit concept of growth "accommodation." Since 1970, planning has been shifted to a growth "management" approach, in response to public demand. The growth management approach requires use of the police power to limit growth, and requires a way of making judgments about when to exercise it. The police power is a limited power, constrained by constitutional limitations enforced by the courts. Successful exercise of the police power for growth management requires an explicit "public purpose rationale."

The term "carrying capacity" embodies the ideas from which such a rationale may be drawn. By dividing total growth into its private sector and public sector components, it is possible to portray the capacity of the public sector, to carry the weight of the private sector, in terms of an equation:

$$\frac{\text{Public}}{\text{Private}} = \text{Level of Public Service}$$

By developing a level-of-public-service measuring technique, it is possible to translate this general equation into a specific tool for growth management.

In Montgomery County, this process is used to implement an "Adequate Public Facilities" Ordinance, which is an adjunct to the Subdivision Regulations. It requires that no subdivision be approved, if the total public facilities available under the adopted Capital Improvements Program (CIP) are not adequate to the task. Eight specific facilities are identified. Administration of this Ordinance has revealed technical difficulties that are characterized by the term, "a scale dilemma."

To improve the County's ability to manage growth through the adequate public facilities method, a revised approach is recommended, called the "Comprehensive Staging Plan" approach. This involves the adoption of a Comprehensive Staging Plan (CSP), as an amendment to the County's General Plan; and its subsequent monitoring and updating on a periodic basis. This Plan establishes interim thresholds of private sector growth, that are keyed to incremental additions of public facility projects in the Capital Improvements Program.

These thresholds would constitute binding ceilings on the regulatory approval process for private development projects, until such time as the plan is amended. The plan also would provide guidance to the capital programming process, through its background information on facility impacts, fiscal impacts, and private sector growth forecasts.

This information would be portrayed in a simple format, called the "staging chart technique," which displays in graphic, mapped, and tabulated form, the interplay of forecasts, facilities, and threshold levels. A staging chart is prepared for each of a number of subareas of the County, called "Policy Areas," so that different threshold levels can be established, in accordance with the unique conditions that relate to each area....

An analysis of the sensitivity of stress of the various public systems in the County concluded that the order of priority was as follows: (1) sewerage, (2) transportation, (3) fiscal, (4) schools, and (5) stream valley parks.

Chapter 2 — Facilities

Chapter 2 describes the technical background to the development of computerized simulation models for the sewerage and transportation network systems of the County. Geographic areas that act as data containers, related to the branches of these networks, are described under the terms "sewer sheds" and "traffic sheds." A geographic cross-reference file is described, that permits the conversion of impact assessment analysis from one system to another....

Chapter 3 — Forecast

This chapter describes the methodology and results of a forecasting process that draws on the perspective of the planning staffs in other jurisdictions within the metropolitan area. Under a process called "Cooperative Forecasting," developed under the auspices of the Metropolitan Washington Council of Governments, the planning staffs of the various jurisdictions meet collectively to review and critique individual forecasts, prepared within their jurisdictions, and to contrast these with a single regional forecast, prepared through a simulation modelling process called the regional model.

The results of the most recent forecast, adopted in 1978, show a slight decline in the forecasted levels of growth, over the previous forecast adopted in 1976. Steeper reductions have been made in the forecast for Prince George's County, Fairfax County, and the District

C. Meanings and Means of Planning 61

of Columbia, than for Montgomery County, possibly reflecting a more consistent view of the future among all the jurisdictions in the 1978 cycle.

An important feature of the 1978 forecast is its recognition of the uncertainty inherent in such forecasting. This uncertainty is expressed by producing not just a single forecast number, but rather a range with a high, low, and most probably intermediate set of numbers. It has now become explicitly understood that the use of such forecast ranges, in the planning process, requires the additional step of performing a "risk analysis," which involves using both the high and the low ends of the range, to test for carrying capacity impact, before a final planning judgment is reached.

CHAPTER 4 — FISCAL

This chapter describes a computerized simulation model for assessing the fiscal impact of growth, in either, or both, of the private and public sectors. It outlines the assumptions used in applying this model to testing the fiscal impacts of the new growth forecast, and their relationships to the private sector growth thresholds proposed in the Comprehensive Staging Plan. It concludes that all of the three growth forecasts should produce incremental revenues that slightly exceed the incremental costs associated with servicing them, provided that the incoming growth continues to share the current characteristics of the growth the County has been receiving over the past decade. The fiscal surplus, however, is only marginal, and is not large enough to make any significant contribution towards lowering the County's tax rate. The impact of growth on the County's budget, therefore, can be considered essentially neutral under these conditions.

Since any fiscal simulation is highly dependent on the subtleties of the revenue assumptions made, as well as the details of the expenditure categories, it is pointed out that one of the major uses of this fiscal model can be to play "what-if" games about specific questions (i.e., if such-and-so develops, what is the fiscal impact?). Similarly, it is pointed out that the model offers the opportunity to further analyze the fiscal conditions of the County, and possibly to develop normative standards that could influence the private growth threshold levels, if such were deemed acceptable as a policy decision. In this way, the model offers the opportunity for further elaboration of the Comprehensive Staging Plan approach. . . .[19]

19. See Dawson, No Little Plans: Fairfax County's PLUS Program for Managing Growth (1977).

■ SALT LAKE COUNTY, UTAH PLANNING COMMISSION, A MASTER PLAN FOR SALT LAKE COUNTY
28 (1986)

The Salt Lake Valley Master Plan is designed to serve as a base of reference to which both public and private groups can refer and on which they can rely in making future plans. The Plan covers the urban and rural areas of Salt Lake Valley and refers to the mountain and desert areas of the County only in general terms.

The following are the major policies and proposals in the Master Plan.

- Residential uses are considered in three density categories: high density residence, close to major business districts; medium density residence, adjacent to and surrounding high density residence; and low density residence, filling in the balance of the proposed living areas.
- Central Business Districts are encouraged to grow and develop to provide a range and depth of services. Regional shopping centers are proposed for each urban planning area. Commercial districts providing general commercial and service activities are encouraged to expand in areas with adequate transportation facilities and in locations convenient to their needs.
- Dispersal of industrial activity is a key recommendation of the Plan. Existing industrial districts are enlarged to fill in presently vacant land and to encourage the transition of nonindustrial uses to industry. Industrial development is proposed at the intersection of the Bonneville and Valley Central Freeways in the cities of Murray and Midvale. Industrial and research parks are also proposed in the vicinity of Sandy and the University of Utah. Thus, industrial and related employment opportunities will be conveniently available to all urban sections of the Valley.
- Recreation areas are greatly expanded. The Jordan River complex is proposed to be the major focus of park and lake development in the Valley. The Wasatch and Oquirrh Mountains are proposed for continued recreational development.
- Junior colleges and suburban hospitals are proposed for each of the three urban planning districts. All other facilities, though not shown, are to be provided in relation to the population to be served.
- An integrated transportation system is proposed. The interstate freeways would be linked by a belt route freeway and comprehensive network of expressways and major arterials.

D. Tool and Techniques

- A broad agricultural belt is proposed for the southern part of the Valley to protect the productive soils and prosperous farms from urbanization.

D. TOOLS AND TECHNIQUES

1. Urban Design

■ DESCARTES, DISCOURSE ON THE METHOD OF RIGHTLY CONDUCTING THE REASON
Philosophical Works 87, 88 (Haldane & Ross trans. 1931)

I was then in Germany, to which country I had been attracted by the wars which are not yet at an end. And as I was returning from the coronation of the Emperor to join the army, the setting in of winter detained me in a quarter where, since I found no society to divert me, while fortunately I had also no cares or passions to trouble me, I remained the whole day shut up alone in a stove-heated room, where I had complete leisure to occupy myself with my own thoughts. One of the first of the considerations that occurred to me was that there is very often less perfection in works composed of several portions, and carried out by the hands of various masters, than in those on which one individual alone has worked. Thus we see that buildings planned and carried out by one architect alone are usually more beautiful and better proportioned than those which many have tried to put in order and improve, making use of old walls which are built with other ends in view. In the same way also, those ancient cities which, originally mere villages, have become in the process of time great towns, are usually badly constructed in comparison with those which are regularly laid out on a plain by a surveyor who is free to follow his own ideas. Even though, considering their buildings each one apart, there is often as much or more display of skill in the one case than in the other, the former having large buildings and small buildings indiscriminately placed together, thus rendering the streets crooked and irregular, so that it might be said that it was chance rather than the will of men guided by reason that led to such an arrangement. And if we consider that this happens despite the fact that from all time there have been certain officials who have had the special duty of looking after the buildings of private individuals in order that they may be public ornaments, we shall understand how difficult it is to bring about much that is satisfactory in operating only upon the works of others.[20]

Le Corbusier, in Concerning Town Planning 67-68 (1948), condemns the phrase "family house" as touching and admirable, but one which no longer applies in reality, since the family "melts" in the course of twenty years and the family house has no duration. While the stability on which it is founded has been upset, "A society seeking to defend an equilibrium which it has already lost, looks for means of tying down the nomadic elements of a society which is in need of a new and harmonious organization of its life." The result, to paraphrase him, is a universal wasteland of garden cities. The solution he advances is the vertical garden city.[21]

The illustrations on the following pages present in diagram form the visions of some outstanding physical planners. In examining the

20. This metaphor of interdependency recurs in urban design, looked at from the outside. Thus, Pigou states: "It is as idle to expect a well-planned town to result from the independent activities of isolated speculators as it would be to expect a satisfactory picture to result if each separate square would be painted by an independent artist." Economics of Welfare 194-195 (4th ed. 1962). See also Pigou, The Economics of Welfare 182-186 (4th ed. 1952):

> [T]he essence of the matter is that one person A, in the course of rendering some service, for which payment is made, to a second person B, incidentally also renders services or disservices to other persons (not producers of like services), of such a sort that payment cannot be exacted from the benefited parties or compensation enforced on behalf of the injured parties. . . . Among these examples we may set out first a number of instances in which marginal private net product falls short of marginal social net product, because incidental services are performed to third parties from whom it is technically difficult to exact payment. . . . Corresponding to the above investments in which marginal private net product falls short of marginal social net product, there are a number of others, in which, owing to the technical difficulty of enforcing compensation for incidental disservices, marginal private net product is greater than marginal social net product. Cf. Wendt, Theory of Urban Land Values, 33 Land Econ. 228 (1957).
>
> It is believed that the inclusion or exclusion of a particular kind of shop should be decided not by planners but rather by the economics of the particular situation. . . . Obviously those which are needed will survive while those for which there is little demand will be forced to locate elsewhere. Metropolitan Association of Real Estate Boards, Critical Analysis of the Plan for Rezoning New York 3 (1951). And if the price system is not doing it [putting land to its best use], is that not evidence that we in aggregate do not want it done? This is the crux of the problem, and however it may be proper to dress it up in public, this is the question that the economist must privately answer for himself. Robinson, The Scott and Uthwatt Reports on Land Utilisation, 13 Econ. J. 28, 31 (1943).

For a critical analysis of Pigou's famous thesis, see Coase, The Problem of Social Cost, 3 J. Law & Econ. 1 (1960). See Public Enterprise (Turvey ed. 1968). — Eds.

21. "I said: 'The sky-scrapers of New York are too small.' And the New York Herald Tribune made a headline of it." Le Corbusier, When the Cathedrals Were White 187 (1947).

> [C]ities are freezing on a design for living ideally calculated to keep everybody in

Wright, Broadacre City

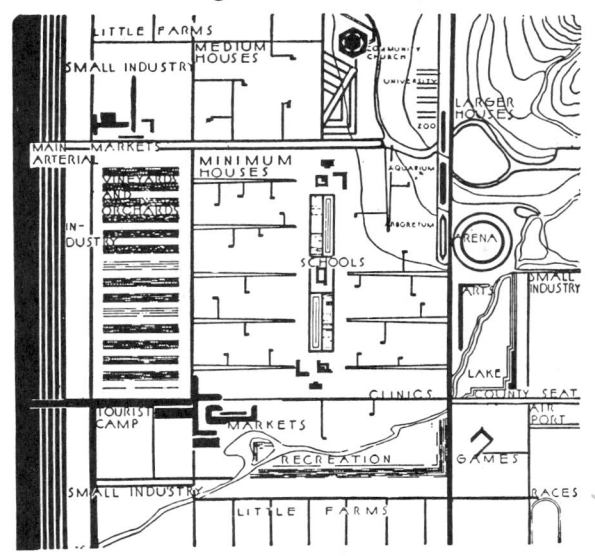

Le Corbusier, Ville Radieuse and the City-Squares of Sitte

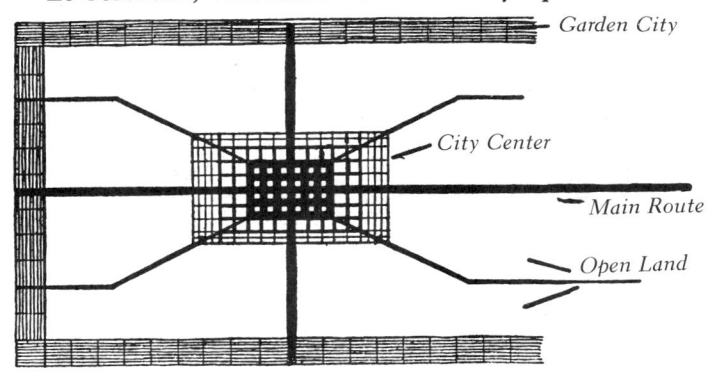

Goodman, Consumer City

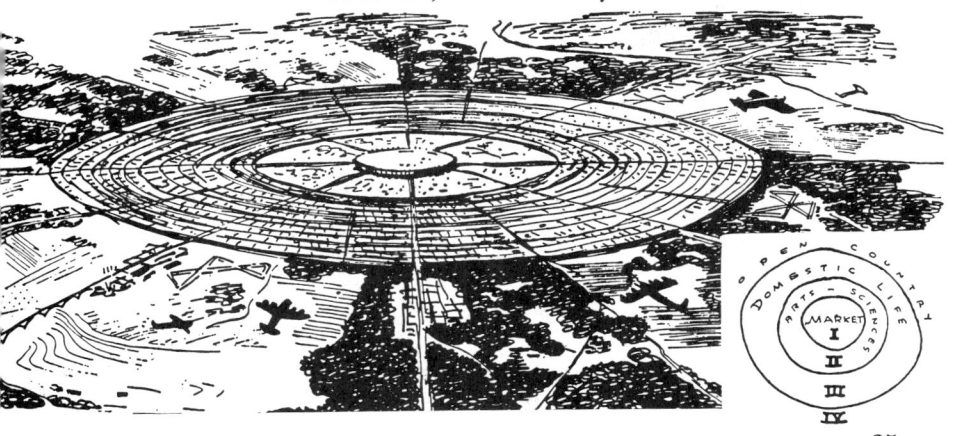

Soleri, Babel IIB

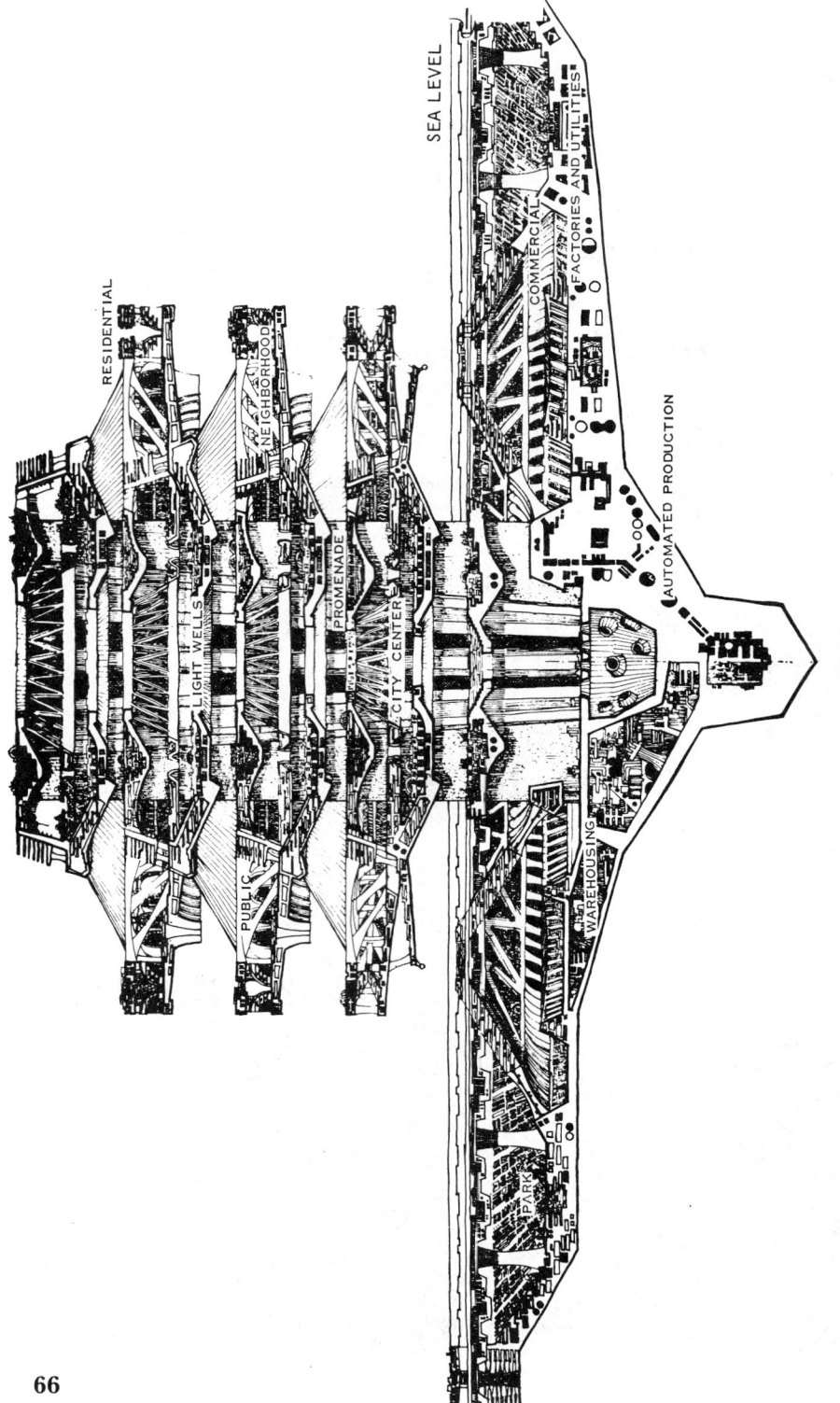

D. Tools and Techniques 67

plans with a view to their implementation in the real world, consider the new and broader planning controls, the reevaluation of the social role of land, and the realignment of property rights that each of them may entail.[22]

In examining these striking city planning diagrams, it is quickly apparent that land-use decisions have become increasingly complex with the confrontation of their social and economic impact. Today "planning" has expanded far beyond the technical issue of physical interfaces between uses into the very quality of urban life. Professor Keller's The Urban Neighborhood (1968) is a sparkling effort to reduce the gap "between analytic social science and practical planning." Id. at 9. With the broadened perspective, planners, lawyers, and politicians are faced with a mutual dilemma which Alexander describes in Notes on the Synthesis of Form (1964):

> Today functional problems are becoming less simple all the time. But designers rarely confess their inability to solve them. Instead, when a designer does not understand a problem clearly enough to find the order it really calls for, he falls back on some arbitrarily chosen formal order. The problem, because of its complexity, remains unsolved. Id. at 1.

2. Planning for People

■ MUMFORD, THE SOCIAL FOUNDATIONS OF POST-WAR BUILDING
9-13, 24-32 (1943)

In our anticipations of post-war planning, perhaps the most important thing to remember is that our task is not the simple one of rebuilding demolished houses and ruined cities. If only the material shell of our society needed repair, our designs might follow familiar patterns. But the fact is our task is a far heavier one; it is that of replacing an outworn civilization. The question is not how much of the

---

suburbia. Look at the project below [multi-story units set in a park]. These vast, barracks-like superblocks are not designed for people who *like* cities, but for people who have no other choice.... The institutional approach is dominant, and unless the assumptions embalmed in it are re-examined the city is going to be turned into a gigantic bore.

Whyte, Are Cities Un-American?, Fortune, Sept. 1957, at 125. Among the first major attacks on modern architecture's orthodoxy is Venturi, Complexity and Contradiction in Architecture (1967); Moore, Allen & Lyndon, The Place of Houses (1974), continues the assaults on the formal goals, dealing with the order of rooms, the order of machines, and the order of dreams.

22. For further imaginative environmental schemes which will require adjustment of property rights, see McHarg, Design with Nature (1969).

superstructure should be replaced, but how much of the foundations can be used for a new set of purposes and for a radically different mode of life. . . .

Western man has exhausted the possibilities of the dream of mechanical power, which has so long dominated his imagination; he is now the self-betrayed victim of those who would utilize that power for the fulfillment of debased and irrational purposes, barbarizing man instead of subduing and humanizing nature. We live in a world given over to devitalized mechanisms, desocialized organisms, and depersonalized societies; a world that has lost its sense of the ultimate dignity of the person as completely as the Roman Empire did, at the height of its military greatness and technical facility. The farther we follow this road, the more hopelessly we shall be lost. . . .

If the old plot has become meaningless, the scenery against which the action has taken place is even more irrelevant. The great capital cities of the last four hundred years, in which military might and social luxury were massed, can no longer be the ultimate expression of human desire. In the universal products of our mechanical civilization, like the radio, the telephone, and the cinema, they share their proudest achievements with the meanest village; their very size, moreover, has reduced the opportunity of their inhabitants to participate in the parade of fashion and taste. As for the great industrial towns of the last two centuries, in which people swarmed together in grimy regimented streets, to take part in the daily battle of production — these cities were the stage of ambitions that have ceased to be real and of achievements that have become increasingly hollow. No money income could make amends for a life-confinement in these dreary infernos: counter-irritants, narcotics, aphrodisiacs, mechanized fantasies only increase the debasement they seek to alleviate.

Once, perhaps, the blight and misery of these cities could be speciously justified: they were symbols of enterprise; they were monuments to mechanical ingenuity in which the age rejoiced; they were, at the lowest, a source of vast profits to ground landlords, speculative builders, industrial enterprisers, and small groups or classes gained, even if the general good was ruthlessly sacrificed and the entire environment befouled. More hopefully, under the doctrine of progress, they were steps to a better society.

But even these narrow private gains are no longer in prospect: Private enterprise, still hoping for past gains, prevents the centers of our cities from being adequately rebuilt; and as a result, those who wish better conditions find a temporary surcease, if not an effective permanent solution, on the outskirts. Where the automobile has been most freely used, the disorganization and disruption of our urban centers is most marked; Los Angeles and Detroit, both largely the creations of this new machine, are also its most conspicuous victims.

D. Tools and Techniques

But in one degree or another, the tendency to planless dispersion is world-wide; in a hundred futile ways people seek an individual solution for their social problem, and so ultimately create a second social problem.

The prewar migration to suburban cottages, to week-end huts, to rural estates, was a recognition of the fact that our typical urban environments no longer offer the possibility of a significant or healthy life. Something more genial to the human soul is desired: contact with the soil, the discipline of manual labor, more intimate companionship with one's fellows, the esthetic joys of sunrise and sunset, of passing cloud and rising moon; and in the search for these fundamental qualities many people temporarily forget that social intercourse and social cooperation are no less important. Biologically, the rural scene is more adequate; but the invasions and perversions of a dying civilization contaminate even the countryside; roadside slums are reminders of the social insufficiency of mere escapism.

In America, where in some respects the mischiefs of contemporary urban civilization have been carried farthest, the greater part of our overgrown metropolises are, in strict economic terms, bankrupt: their dwindling taxes cannot support the load of debt incurred through growth, disorganization, and blight; and their urgent repair awaits a systematic deflation of the still absurd structure of values that was created in the past, in anticipation of further growth. The "increase of population and wealth" has become a purely ironic term; depopulation and bankruptcy are indicated. . . .

Such city planning as has existed during the last generation has started mainly from certain narrow physical, technical, and economic assumptions. The planner studied the site, made a canvass of industrial needs, measured the flow of traffic, and laid out plans for future roads or future water mains. One would have thought from the bulk of city plans, whether theoretical essays like Le Corbusier's or practical expedients like that of the local municipal engineer, that city life existed for the purpose of multiplying the mechanical means of existence. Even plans that stressed the idea of relationship, confined themselves, as a rule, to the physical terms of relationship: roads, highways, avenues, terminals, airports, shopping centers, factory districts.

In most countries, housing and city planning have been treated as separate departments of human effort. Yet even housing has taken place within the same general framework of ideas; most of the improvements in housing have been conceived in a purely mechanical fashion, in terms of experiments with materials and methods of building, of quantitative increase in equipment, of cheapening costs so as to make housing economically more available to lower income groups. As a result, the design and layout of the latest Federal housing development in the United States show no substantial improvement over the design and layout of the housing of the mill workers in Lowell, Massachusetts, more than a hundred years ago. Nothing has changed because the ideal behind housing has not changed; the worker's life in mill, office, or factory is still taken to be the central term of his existence; and improvement in the form and layout of dwellings is still conceived in mechanical or economic terms, not social and personal terms.

Now, just as our age has already seen, although mainly in a base form, the subordination of economics to politics, so it must see, in the transition to a more stable order, the subordination of the machine to the human personality, and economic needs to social needs. The technical and economic studies that have engrossed city planners to the exclusion of every other element in life, must in the coming era take second place to primary studies of the needs of persons and groups. Subordinate questions — the spatial separation of industry and domestic life, or the number of houses per acre — cannot be settled intelligently until more fundamental problems are answered: What sort of personality do we seek to foster and nurture? What kind of common life? What is the order of preference in our life-needs? Do we place babies above motor cars or vice versa? Do we place schools staffed by able teachers above schools that have expensively equipped shops and laboratories, gymnasiums and swimming pools? Or, even more fundamentally, do we want schools or do we want clover-leaf road-junctions? . . .

The task for our age is to decentralize power in all its manifestations and to build up balanced personalities, capable of utilizing all our immense resources of energy, knowledge, and wealth without being demoralized by them. Our job is to repair the mistakes of a one-sided specialization that has disintegrated the human personality, and of a pursuit of power and material wealth that has crippled Western man's capacity for life-fulfillment. We must provide an environment and a routine in which the inner life can flourish, no less than the outer life; in which fantasies will not be wholly dependent upon the film, in which the need for song will not depend wholly upon the radio or the gramophone; in which men and women will have a going personal life that is central to all their associated activities. We must create conditions of living in which the life of a parent will be as momentous and as full of interest and as valid as any other sphere of activity: a life with its own center of gravity. We must offer more physical outlets, not merely for aimless play, but for sober manual activities: the work of the gardener, smith, carpenter, weaver, no less than potter, painter, or sculptor. Ironically, the introduction of these salutary arts is now delayed until a neurosis appears; whereas in a well-balanced life they are ways of guarding against a breakdown. All these needs must be expressed in our designs and embodied in our structures. . . .

In short, the balanced personality needs a balanced environment to support it, to encourage it, to give it the variety of stimuli and interests it needs in order to grow steadily and to maintain its equilibrium during this process. In purely urban terms — hence *un*balanced in terms of man's fuller life-needs — the great metropolis provided this essential variety for man's occupational, professional, and political interests; and because of that fact the metropolis has played an indispensable part in the human economy since the seventeenth century. Now that the metropolis can no longer serve the new economy, except by helping to direct in the decentralization of its own power and authority, we must utilize the organizing and planning ability of the metropolis to achieve a much more comprehensive balance.

■ MOYNIHAN, URBAN CONDITIONS: GENERAL
371 Annals Am. Acad. 159, 160-162 (1967)

THREE GENERAL PROPOSITIONS

. . . First of all, it is essential that all concerned with the development of a system of urban social indicators be prepared in advance to find themselves accused of having betrayed some of those very causes with which they have been most allied. Concern about urban affairs derives directly from concern about urban problems: it involves the statement by certain persons that certain things are not as they ought to be, and must be changed for the better. Such attitudes are almost always minority views, at least in the beginning. As a group, however, American social scientists are peculiarly prone to sharing and even to creating such concerns. They are problem-prone and reform-minded, and inevitably come to be seen as allies by those about whose problems they are most concerned. . . . Knowledge is power, and in contemporary society social scientists are often in the position of handing power about in an almost absent-minded way. Professional ethics, at least as ideally defined, can lead them to hand out the very best arguments to those whom they would consider the very worst contenders. This is a dilemma not yet well understood, and certainly not resolved. For the moment, the most that can be done is to be forewarned.

The second proposition is that the way in which urban indicators are developed is likely to have considerable influence on the level of government — and of abstraction — at which the problems are dealt with. Specifically, if urban indicators remain for the most part "national" statistics, a powerful built-in tendency to seek "national" solutions will emerge. . . .

A third generation consideration may be termed a matter of temperament. It has to do with the fact that urban social indicators are almost certainly going to be developed by professors and government executives who will be far more concerned with what is bad about cities than with what is good about them. These men will judge good and bad in terms of their own rather special values acquired in the course of family, religious, educational, and occupational experiences that, by and large, are quite different from those of the urban masses whose condition they will seek to measure. The idea of social indicators, and of an urban subset, is pre-eminently a product of the American intellectual world, although, of course, with a whole European tradition behind it. But the particular quality of the American intellectual — quite distinct from his European counterpart — has been the tendency to view cities with alarm, fear, and distaste, a history which Morton and Lucia White have summed up as "one of adverse metaphysical speculation and bad dreams about urban life, of aesthetic and moral recoil from the American city's ugliness, commercialism, and crime." Surely some measure of the present concern with ugliness, commercialism, and crime is simply an inversion of the earlier views: precisely the same judgment about cities is handed down, with only a gloss of compassion and concern that things might somehow be made otherwise. The view that when one is tired of London one is tired of life is not one that has met much favor on American campuses — nor yet the proposition put to Hennessy by Dooley that while the country might be where the good things in life come from, it is the city that they go *to*. Neither the great Tory nor the Chicago saloon-keeper spoke with the accents of liberal academia: the one too confident, the other too clever for that special world.

The task, then, is to make the most of the special kinds of sensibility that will be brought to bear on cities by this group, including one of its most attractive qualities, the awareness that tastes differ and a willingness to allow, even to encourage, them to do so.[23]

23. Is Moynihan's approach here consistent with his approach in Maximum Feasible Misunderstanding (1969)? See Report of the National Goals Research Staff, Toward Balanced Growth, Quantity with Quality (1970). A perceptive analysis can be found in Henriot, Political Questions about Social Indicators, 23 W. Pol. Q. 235 (1970). The collection of data with a metropolitan focus poses some obvious, but unsolved, problems:

> A high flying reconnaissance plane is cruising over 26 American cities this summer, taking photographs to develop an early warning system for urban change. When this program is developed, the photography will be taken over by orbiting satellites that will pass over every point in the country more than once a month and be able to see details as small as a house trailer.... [The program] is a part of the Interior Department's earth resources observation program, called Eros for short.

N.Y. Times, Aug. 7, 1970. — Eds.

D. Tools and Techniques

■ PEATTIE, REFLECTIONS ON ADVOCACY PLANNING
34 J. Am. Inst. Planners 80 (1968)

The concept of "advocacy planning" can only be understood in the context of the management of modern American cities. In ancient cities, planning was primarily a function of individual leaders and of relatively small social groups — families, guilds, religious fraternities, and the like. The "squatter settlements" surrounding cities of the developing countries suggest the degree to which public policy and official planning still control only a relatively limited part of urban life. Our cities are more and more publicly managed environments. Private actions take place within a generally narrowing network of public intervention, public policy, and public planning. . . .

But as a consequence, we have developed a set of bureaucratic management institutions which often seem impersonal and alien to human feelings. "Our technological civilization . . . seems to overtake and overwhelm us as though it were something foreign coming in on us. . . ." People may respond to this sense of being overwhelmed by political apathy and disengagement or they may protest. It is interesting to see how the polemic literature against urban renewal and against fluoridation of drinking water share the angry suspicion that something has been "put over" on ordinary people by the experts. . . .

The shift from politics to expertise changes the rules for exercising power, as well as the structure of effective power. The result may entail a cost in equity, since it can well be argued that those most disadvantaged will be the people at the bottom of the system — those who are, through lack of education and of technical sophistication, particularly ill-prepared to deal with the presentation of issues in a technical framework. Such groups tend to be disadvantaged in the traditional political framework, and still more so when it comes to dealing with those who speak the language of maps, diagrams, and statistical tables. Advocacy planning has its origins initially in the perception that such groups need planners to make their case, to express their interests. Therefore, it represents a search by planners for new kinds of clientele.

Advocate planners take the view that any plan is the embodiment of particular group interests, and therefore they see it as important that any group which has interests at stake in the planning process should have those interests articulated. In effect, they reject both the notion of a single "best" solution and the notion of a general welfare which such a solution might serve. Planning in this view becomes pluralistic and partisan — in a word, overtly political.[24]

---

24. See Keyes and Teitcher, Limitations on Advocacy Planning: A View from the Establishment, 35 J. Am. Inst. Planners 225 (1970):

[T]he advocacy road is becoming overcrowded with students fresh from planning school. . . . Our main problem with advocacy is that it tends to encourage

■ MAZZIOTTI, THE UNDERLYING
ASSUMPTIONS OF ADVOCACY PLANNING:
PLURALISM AND REFORM
40 J. Am. Inst. Planners 38, 45 (1974)

Since the inception of the concept of advocacy planning in 1965, the modus operandi of this new planning technique was based upon an analogy drawn between the role and function of the legal advocate and the role and function of the advocate planner. The planner-advocate would plead for his or her client's point of view: furthermore, the planner would provide more than information, analysis, and simulations — specific substantive solutions would be argued. Davidoff's analogy between lawyer and planner was stated specifically in his classic article, "Advocacy and Pluralism in Planning": "Thus, the advocate's plan might have some characteristics of a legal brief. It would be a document presenting the facts and reasons for supporting one set of proposals, and facts and reasons indicating the inferiority of counter-proposals." . . .

The argument made here with respect to the analogy between the advocate lawyer and planner is that the uncritical acceptance of such a comparison assumes that the adoption of the legal-advocate model will somehow establish an effective urban democracy, one in which citizens may be able to play an active role in the process of deciding public policy. The analogy is an extension of the pluralist faith that given the opportunity to be heard, the demands of competing groups will go through an adversary process through which the best decisions concerning planned community change will result.

There is substantial danger in using analogy carelessly, i.e., using only logical rationalizations and never resorting to testing or making a discovered induction without proving the degrees of similarity. In this case, the danger of drawing an analogy between the legal-advocate and the planner-advocate has materialized into another unrealistic guidepost. A fair test of the analogy is to examine the nature of legal advocacy and whether that model, in fact, maximizes citizen participation or access into the realm of decisionmaking, results in the best or most justified decision, or arrives at a truth which is the synthesis of groups

---

what might be called the "exhortation" side of the planning profession — that concerned with values, goals, and issues focused on the rights of the poor — rather than to promote the "nuts and bolts" side of planning — specifically, how to get complex tasks accomplished under the appalling organizational and political conditions of metropolitan America.

But see Deasy, When Architects Consult People, Psychology Today, Mar. 1970, for a discussion of the results obtained when community surveys were conducted in connection with the design of three projects (an urban shopping plaza, a ghetto school, and a college campus). — EDS.

D. Tools and Techniques 75

competing equally before public tribunals (given the opportunity to be heard).

As the socioeconomic organization of American society is based upon property rights and the balancing of public and private relations, so the law serves the most powerful property interests; as argued in the section dealing with the myth of pluralism, the masses of people and interest groups who have no direct connection to the bases of power are governed by rules intended to maintain and fortify existing power relationships. To the assertion that the adversary process establishes equality before the law, a radical critique of such a sweeping statement can be placed with a well-constructed and documented syllogism: law serves power, the law is made by those holding power, it perpetuates those in power, it decides what the tolerable limits of justice are — law is made by the power elite to protect and enshrine its own interests.

The good liberal, particularly the good liberal lawyer, will respond to the radical critique by pointing to the host of legal decisions which have expanded the civil rights of men and women, the extensive social welfare system which has been constructed to help, not control, the economically disadvantaged. They may well allude to, as do the pluralist-advocate planners, the "guarantees of fair notice and hearings, production of supporting evidence, cross examination, reasoned decision(s)."

The ostensible goal of the advocate planner is, through the use of advocacy, to meet the "just demand for political and social equality on the part of the Negro and the impoverished" to provide social change which will benefit "those who are, through lack of education and of technical sophistication, particularly ill-prepared to deal with the presentation of issues in a technical framework" and "defend or prosecute the interests of his clients." The critical issue is whether the superimposition of the legal-advocate model upon the planner will work to achieve these goals. Clearly, recent court decisions, based upon an expanded theory of equal protection, used very broad egalitarian rhetoric in the criminal law area, encouraging attorneys for the poor to apply this same argument to other social problems, e.g., inequality in education and the unequal provision of state and municipal services. Again, the problem of myth versus reality rolls into operation; the general public, including naive planners, assume that headline cases mark "high impact" social decisions which serve to ameliorate the position of the poor and disenfranchised. The analysis of the impact of a visible social decision, however, falls short of examining anything but the outcome, without asking whether the process of decisionmaking has been materially affected.

A critical view of the process would reveal that legal advocacy, like planning, has severe institutional restraints imposed upon it. . . .

That persons occupying positions of control over capital are among the key wielders of local influence and control has long been one of the most commonplace assumptions of American sociologists and, more recently, planners. While it is clear that to ignore particularly local configurations of economic and political power in developing strategies for advocacy planning efforts would be inappropriate, this analysis has attempted to suggest that there are clear and growing indicators of power concentrations which are apart from the local community. Furthermore, the development of capital concentration within a growing corporate structure imposes rather substantial external controls over local decision-making. There is increasing evidence which suggests that local planning decisions are becoming the function of private market decisions and that this characteristic is an inherent component of the way corporate capitalism has developed in the United States.

This analysis does not suggest that elitism and concentration of power is an inherent element of capitalism — anymore than to suggest, for example, that a socialized economy would be inherently free of such control. What is specifically suggested is that the evolution of capitalism in the United States has developed into a system with inherent defects which can be modified only by changes in the nature of that system per se. The analysis raises significant implications for both planning education and planning practice.

From a conceptual and theoretical standpoint, the great majority of commentators on advocacy planning either explicitly or implicitly make inaccurate, misleading, and incongruent assumptions regarding the political economy within which advocacy must be made operational. Acceptance of the assumptions discussed here requires an endorsement of the political myth of pluralism, a posture which must ultimately embrace the status quo or the liberal-reformist approach to solving complex social problems, and the adoption of a set of tactical strategies which emulate existing professions so as to preserve centers of power and frustrate the notion of participatory democracy. . . .

■ MUNOZ-MENDOZA v. PIERCE
711 F.2d 421 (1st Cir. 1983)

BREYER, Circuit Judge. . . .

The following facts are not in dispute. In April 1980, the city of Boston asked HUD for an Urban Development Action Grant ("UDAG") to help it and private developers build Copley Place. This $450 million commercial project in downtown Boston will contain three million square feet of space, and will include a 712-room luxury hotel, a 960-room convention hotel, retail facilities, office space, parking facilities, and 100 to 150 units of housing, 25 percent of which will be subsidized

D. Tools and Techniques 77

and reserved for low-income tenants. The project is being built on 9.5 acres of previously vacant land next to the Massachusetts Turnpike, near the neighborhoods of Back Bay, Fenway, the South End, South Cove, and Chinatown.

As part of its application for the UDAG, Boston presented a study of the project's likely impact on local housing demand. It estimated that the project would generate increased demand for residential space that would in turn displace several hundred families. Soon thereafter, several neighborhood organizations, including the Chinatown Housing Task Force, a plaintiff here, complained to HUD's Boston area Division of Fair Housing and Equal Opportunity that the project would limit housing opportunities for low-income and minority residents in nearby neighborhoods. The Division considered the complaint; its director concluded that the minority displacement problem was serious; and further meetings were held with the complainants and others in Washington. HUD eventually decided to provide a $19 million grant. While that grant was not conditioned precisely in the manner that the complainants had requested, HUD allowed the city to use the loan repayments (amounting to roughly $40 million) for various neighborhood development projects, including at least $2.5 million for low and moderate income residents. HUD concluded that the grant, in light of these terms, did not violate any civil rights laws or regulations.

In November 1980, six weeks after HUD announced the grant, the Task Force and seven individuals brought this suit. Six of the seven individual plaintiffs are black or Puerto Rican residents of the South End. The seventh is a Chinese resident of South Cove. The Task Force is a community advocacy organization, 75 percent of whose members are Chinese. The plaintiffs' primary legal claim is that Title VI of the Civil Rights Act of 1964, Title VIII of the Civil Rights Act of 1968, and various related HUD regulations required HUD to conduct a more thorough study of the impact of Copley Place on the racial integration of nearby neighborhoods. They point to several statutes, regulations, and cases that, they claim, support them: 42 U.S.C. §§2000d, 3608(d)(5); 24 C.F.R. §§1.1-1.12, 570.450-570.466; Otero v. New York City Housing Authority, 484 F.2d 1122 (2d Cir. 1973); Shannon v. HUD, 436 F.2d 809 (3d Cir. 1970); Marin City Council v. Marin County Redevelopment Agency, 416 F. Supp. 700 (N.D. Cal. 1975).

The defendants, officials of HUD and the City of Boston, asked the district court to dismiss the complaint summarily on the ground that the action complained of — the decision to provide the grant — did not cause the harm that the plaintiffs allegedly will suffer. The defendants argued that the independent actions of private landlords and homebuyers, not the grant, would "cause" the rent increases, tenant displacement, and loss of integrated neighborhoods of which the plaintiffs complained. They added that, since other private and public development would continue in the absence of the grant, "gentrification" would occur regardless of whether Copley Place were built.

Initially, the district court ruled against the defendants. But one year later, after additional discovery and the submission of considerable evidence through affidavits, the court held that the plaintiffs had not successfully shown that the HUD grant would cause the injuries of which they complained. Munoz-Mendoza v. Pierce, No. 80-2589-C (D. Mass. June 28, 1982). The court added that, in any event, conducting the residential impact study now would not provide the plaintiffs with meaningful relief, for withdrawal of HUD funding would not lead to abandonment of the project. The district court therefore dismissed the suit. . . .

Applying a "clearly erroneous" standard, we agree that the plaintiffs have failed to show an adequate causal connection between HUD's action — the award of the UDAG — and *one* alleged injury, the risk that the plaintiffs will have to pay increased rents or move from their homes. The district court reasoned that the causal linkage involved — from the grant to the building of Copley Place, to increased demand for housing in nearby neighborhoods, to private landlords' decisions to raise the rent in the units occupied by the plaintiffs themselves, to the eventual need to find new housing — was simply too speculative.

The plaintiffs, however, also allege another, and different, sort of injury. They claim that the grant will increase racial segregation in nearby neighborhoods, and that as a result, they will lose the advantage of living in an integrated local community. There is no question that this *type* of injury is sufficient under Article III to allow standing to contest the legality of conduct that causes it, for the Supreme Court has specifically so held. Gladstone, Realtors v. Village of Bellwood, 441 U.S. at 112, 99 S. Ct. at 1614 (deprivation of "the social and professional advantages of living in an integrated community" is "sufficient to satisfy the constitutional standing requirement of actual or threatened harm"); Trafficante v. Metropolitan Life Insurance Co., 409 U.S. 205, 93 S. Ct. 364, 34 L. Ed. 2d 415 (1972); see Fox v. HUD, 416 F. Supp. 954 (E.D. Pa.1976). The issue therefore is whether the plaintiffs have proved a sufficient causal connection between the grant and the harm to allow them to contest the lawfulness of the grant procedure. We believe that they have. . . .

. . . The Copley Place project is a $450 million undertaking, which its developers expect will create over 6,000 permanent jobs in downtown Boston. It cannot seriously be contended that a commercial complex of this scale will not create a material impact on housing demand in

D. Tools and Techniques

neighborhoods adjacent to it. It is also impossible for us to believe — without record evidence — that, had the HUD grant been denied, some other project or set of projects, waiting in the wings, would soon have stepped forward and taken its place. The record does suggest that $450 million projects in a midtown urban area take considerable time and effort to assemble — in this case, at least five years. The record provides no suggestion that a project similar to Copley Place could have been put together in less than five years. We do not see how to avoid the conclusion that Copley Place at least will cause several additional years of higher rents and more displacement than would have occurred in its absence.

... [T]he link between higher rents and less residential integration is not seriously disputed with respect to the six individual plaintiffs who reside in the South End. The district court found in a prior opinion, and the defendants do not contest, that the South End is "a fully integrated residential neighborhood." Munoz-Mendoza v. Pierce, 520 F. Supp. 180, 182 (D.Mass.1981). According to the most recent census data, while non-whites made up 33.6 percent of Boston's families in 1979, they accounted for 38.4 percent of families earning from 10 to 15 thousand dollars, 43.4 percent of those earning from 5 to 10 thousand, and 54.8 percent of those earning less than 5 thousand. Bureau of the Census, U.S. Dept. of Commerce, 1980 Census of Population and Housing — Supplementary Report: Advance Estimates of Social, Economic and Housing Characteristics — Massachusetts 35 (1982). Given this racial stratification, and given the present racial balance in the South End, the displacement of low income residents in favor of more wealthy residents will disproportionately displace minorities and increase racial segregation in the South End. This is the plaintiffs' view, and it is nowhere denied. Therefore, even if rising rents do not displace the South End plaintiffs themselves, those plaintiffs can be expected to suffer the constitutionally material harm of residential racial segregation....

... [W]e reassert our view that there remain several difficult issues in this case. The plaintiffs must show that their substantive view of the statutes and regulations is a correct one. They must also show that Congress intended the courts, at the risk of interrupting or seriously delaying multi-million dollar projects aimed at helping distressed areas, to review agency "study" decisions *of the sort here at issue* in order to correct the type of abuse of discretion that the plaintiffs here allege. See 5 U.S.C. §701(a)(2); Hahn v. Gottlieb, 430 F.2d 1243 (1st Cir. 1970). Finally, they must prove that there was such an abuse of discretion. Because these issues have not been argued clearly before us, even though the first two are issues of law, we remand to the district court, which will have the first opportunity to decide them in light of the facts and arguments to be adduced....

■ ROHE AND GATES, PLANNING WITH NEIGHBORHOODS
3-5 (1985)

Contemporary neighborhood planning programs represent attempts to address the quality of life in neighborhoods. . . .

Currently three forms of neighborhood planning are being practiced in the United States. The first involves independently organized efforts sponsored by indigenous neighborhood organizations. Although these organizations may receive grants from public agencies or private foundations, they are not sanctioned or controlled by them. These efforts typically aim to address a perceived problem or set of problems in the neighborhood through self-help or advocacy efforts.

The second form of contemporary neighborhood planning consists of federally sponsored community development programs. Planners employed by local municipalities are charged with identifying problem areas, called neighborhood strategy areas (NSAs), developing a comprehensive rehabilitation program, and administering the implementation of that program. Although citizens have opportunities to comment at several public hearings required by federal regulations, their involvement in designing and implementing improvements is often limited. Furthermore, program activities are typically limited to a relatively small number of neighborhoods compared to the total number in any city.

The third form comprises locally sponsored, city-wide neighborhood planning programs. These programs seek to involve all neighborhoods in public planning and municipal affairs. They are sponsored by municipal government, although federal funds are often used to subsidize their operation. Participating neighborhood groups become involved in a wide variety of issues, including zoning changes, evaluation of local service delivery, comprehensive planning, and local problem solving. . . .[25]

The issue, then, is to develop a procedural framework for synthesizing interrelated problems in a manner that lends itself to under-

25. The thorny issues of citizen participation are not new:

A large crowd of Queens property owners cheered, stamped and at times jeered during a hearing in City Hall yesterday to punctuate their insistence that their home areas were not slums.

The demonstrations enlivened proceedings before the City Planning Commission as it heard a score of Astoria and Rockaway spokesmen in opposition to the Queens master plan for slum clearance in five areas.

At one point an excited speaker . . . shouted: "This City Planning Commission has become a roosting place for tired politicians."

. . . [M]embers of the Planning Commission sought to reassure the Queens property owners that approval of the master plan would not mean an immediate

D. Tools and Techniques 81

standing and, ultimately, solution. When confronted with a land-use plan, a capital budget, or a new community development, how does one even begin to analyze its content, direction, and focus? What are the strengths or weaknesses of the proposal? Which elements are omitted or overemphasized? In Man and His Urban Environment Project, A Manual of Specific Considerations for the Seventies and Beyond 1 (1972), the problem of creating a city "to accommodate the nature of man" was explored. Before elaborating on the potential of new towns to meet the demands of the 1970s, the minimum requirements of man in an urban system were postulated. The social scientists, anthropolo-

---

change in the status of their homes. But spokesmen shouted back that they faced ultimate loss of their properties and were being made "guinea pigs" of the Housing Redevelopment Law. . . .

Those opposing the plan were supported by a letter to the commission from Borough President James A. Lundy of Queens. He wrote that "a grave injustice is being wrought upon the residents of the Astoria section."

N.Y. Times, Nov. 11, 1954.

Citizen participation has undergone similar transformations in England. In May 1946, the Minister of Town and Country Planning addressed a public meeting in Stevenage Town Hall, called to consider the designation of part of the community as a New Town site. Amid jeers, boos, and applause he stated:

Local authorities will be consulted all the way through. But we have a duty to perform, and I am not going to be deterred from that duty. While I will consult as far as possible all the local authorities, at the end, if people become fractious and unreasonable, I shall have to carry out my duty — (Voice: *Gestapo!*).

Franklin v. Minister of Town and Country Planning, [1948] A.C. 87, [1947] 2 All E.R. 289 (H.L.). Compare Part 1 of the Town and Country Planning Act (1971). The government's White Paper, "Town and Country Planning," which preceded the 1968 legislation, states: "One of the . . . main aims . . . is to ensure . . . greater opportunities for the discussion of important changes while they are still at the formative stage and can be influenced by the people whose lives they will affect." Committee on Public Participation in Planning, Ministry of Housing and Local Government, People and Planning 7 (London 1969). See also Altshuler, The City Planning Process (1965), and Urban Renewal: People, Politics and Planning 274-313 (Bellush & Hausknecht eds. 1967); Gans, People and Plans (1968). For a striking illustration of Florida's Sunshine Law, see IDS Properties, Inc. v. Palm Beach, 279 S.2d 353 (Fla. 4th Dist. Ct. 1973); Hammersley, Plans, Policies and the Local Omsbudsman, J. Plan & Envtl. L. 101-105 (Feb. 1987); Cf. Turton, The Planner and the Politician, Planner 68 (Feb. 1984):

- It is important to accept that local planning activity, whether plan making or development control decision making, is a local political activity. Thus far the system has not fallen prey to the tentacles of central government. We must keep it so. The fact that it may be capricious, or messy, uncomfortable or difficult for the professionals is, perhaps, not too important.
- We must accept that political involvement in what have hitherto been regarded as professional activities will increase. We must accept that this may push plan making activities, especially, into areas of social policy making.
- The professional town planners must find a place for themselves in this activity. They must consider their own particular stance. I suggest there will be a variety of responses from retreat into the professional standard and the mystique of objectivity, to a viewpoint that sees the professional adviser as the enabler, promoter and supporter of those who represent the community interest. — EDS.

gists, and political leaders who worked on the report agreed that "[t]he physical attributes of the city, the design of its institutions and the pattern of its management should have these nine concerns at the heart of their specification":

1. Livable shelter, planned and designed for people,
2. Effective urban services, from basic urban utilities to police protection and law enforcement,
3. Reasonable security: this permeates the other issues and includes spiritual and social security as well as protection from physical harm or damage to personal property,
4. Hope for personal and community improvement,
5. A source of income and sense of belonging,
6. Reduction of waste that increases living costs and frustrates citizens,
7. Cultural and recreation facilities,
8. An integrated transportation system,
9. Minimization of pollution and ecological disruption.

Is such an inventory of minimum needs for an urban environment useful in analyzing land-use issues? Can it be used by the planner, the politician, the judge, the neighborhood council, the lawyer or the individual citizen as a starting point for analysis?

How would you develop such a list of minimum needs? Is there a common set of needs on which all could agree? Are disagreements over the basic elements, or, rather, are they over the priority and means of providing for these needs? What would you add or subtract from this list?

Reexamine the statistical data presented in Section A, with this list of minimum needs in mind. Are problem areas more recognizable? Are the statistics more manageable? Using such a list, can you synthesize the statistics into a more meaningful statement about trends in our urban society?

Problem

Take the land-use plan or the budget prepared for your hometown and analyze it in light of this concept of minimum needs.

1. Evaluate the status of the community in regard to these nine minimum needs. How many homes are without sewers? How are neighborhood parks distributed? How well integrated is the transportation system?
2. Identify the problems disclosed under each appropriate category.

D. Tools and Techniques

3. Where cost estimates are given for correction of a problem, list these in the appropriate category.

4. Break down the budget into corresponding categories so that you can compare the expenditures with the problems as identified.

5. Since not all problems are amenable to monetary solutions, see what laws are designed to focus on these problems, or on the provision of the minimum needs themselves.

6. In reviewing the above materials, consider which level of government is the most appropriate unit to provide for the minimum needs in each area, and which needs should be met by private enterprise rather than by government.

A prerequisite to any attempt to change urban conditions is some model of the consequences that will be produced by different sets of actions. This "model" can range from a simple set of intuitions accumulated during years of experience to a sophisticated set of equations whose solution taxes the efforts of the latest products of IBM. However, the growing experience with the limits of simple models carried around in individuals' heads and an increasing respect for the complexity of the interactions governing urban development are making the more formal mathematical models an increasingly important tool for urban planners.

The urban highway program provides one example of the fallacies in the too-simple approach — if the roads are too crowded, then build more of them! Because of the interactions among the existence of roads, the relocation decisions of both people and industry, and the demand for use of those roads, the construction of new roads initiated reactions that resulted in further dispersal of homes and employment and a need for automobile access even greater than the original increase in road capacity.

Urban housing programs provide a second example. After its review of urban housing needs, the Douglas Commission recommended that in addition to new housing being constructed to meet the low-income housing needs identified in the report, there be a specific linkage of urban renewal and other federal or federally assisted programs involving demolition of residences, to federal programs providing new housing in the areas affected, so "that sufficient new housing available to low income households (including but not limited to those displaced) is constructed in these areas to offset the market pressures created by the demolition of existing residences." National Commission on Urban Problems, Recommendation No. 25(c) (1968).

However, using a computer simulation model of urban development, Professor Jay Forrester found that a program for construction of low-cost housing in urban areas brings additional pressure on the land area. It attracts people in the underemployed category, making the population proportions within the urban area even more unfavorable than in the normal stagnant condition. The higher land occupancy, unfavorable population ratio, and rising tax rate all combine to reduce the kinds of new construction the city needs most. An examination shows remarkably large changes in an unfavorable direction. In comparison to what sounds like an innocuous 2.5% housing-construction rate for the underemployed, the results are unfavorable for all categories of population. The housing program, aimed at ameliorating conditions for the underemployed, has increased unemployment and has reduced upward economic mobility both in absolute numbers and as a percentage of population. Upward mobility as a percentage of the underemployed has decreased from 1.5% in the normal stagnant city to 1% after inauguration of the low-cost housing program.

Urban Dynamics 69 (1969). As a result, one of Forrester's primary recommendations is a program of low-cost housing *demolition*.

The difficulty is that the present state of understanding of the processes governing urban development in general and the response to specific policies in particular still leaves much to be desired. Even with extensive experience with the results of urban highway programs and major efforts at attempting to model the full consequences of those programs — financed largely by federal grants — the value of urban development models in designing highway programs remains small. While state of the art of the modeling of transportation programs is the most advanced of all urban policy areas, considerable controversy rages over the importance, existence, and formulation of interactions among such variables as accessibility and location, housing demand, and changes in housing supply. For example, Hester, Systems Analysis for Social Policies, 168 Science 674 (May 1970), challenges Forrester's conclusions because "Forrester's mechanisms for both industrial growth and population migration strongly contradict existing theories, and he offers no empirical evidence to support his divergent formulation." For the foreseeable future, then, planners and others setting urban policy must continue to examine closely the results of the computer models, while continuing to carefully challenge the assumptions which are implicit in the equations which have produced those results.[26]

26. The analysis went worldwide with Forrester's colleague, Dennis Meadows, in the Club of Rome study, Limits to Growth. This, too, has roused controversy as to methodology. One specialist, according to Time (Oct. 15, 1973), found that the number concerning the rate of pollution generated by industrial output is ten times as large as it should have been to be located where it is in the sequence; beyond this, he "shares the view of many computer experts that so many factors are involved in mathematical modeling on a global scale that even the best computer programs are still far too crude to make really accurate predictions." See also Lee, Requiem for Large Scale Models, 39 J. Am. Inst. Planners 3 (1973), and the responses thereto, 40 id. 52 (1974). See Wheaton, Operations Research for Metropolitan Planning, 29 id. 250 (1963); Webber, The Roles of Intelligence Systems

D. Tools and Techniques

Note: The Lawyer's Role

The objectives of a legal system may complement or conflict with those of a land-use planning system. A most distinguished planner, Dennis O'Harrow, once wrote in the official newsletter of the American Society of Planning Officials:

> It is my belief, based on bitter experience, that (a) with few exceptions, attorneys have not the faintest knowledge of zoning theory; and (b) with the exception of those cities that have had the foresight to assign a special

---

in Urban-Systems Planning, 31 id. 289 (1965). See also Langendorf, Computers and Decision Making, 51 J. Am. Plan. Assn. 422, 422-423, 428 (1985):

> In the past twenty-five years planners have been taken on a roller coaster ride regarding the promise of computers for urban and regional planning. The Journal of the American Institute of Planners has provided an accurate barometer of these changes. In 1959 and again in 1965, special issues of the Journal were devoted to the subject of computer models in planning. . . . In 1968, the Highway Research Board published the proceedings of a conference on urban development models. . . . During that period, most of the emphasis was on the development and use of large-scale transportation or land use models. For the most part, these early efforts were costly and failed to produce usable computer models. By the early 1970s these failures were increasingly recognized, and in 1973 a Journal article aptly titled "Requiem for Large-Scale Models" documented that recognition for the profession at large. . . . Although the article was not a blanket condemnation of quantitative methods or the use of computers in planning, it nevertheless reflected and legitimated the loss of enthusiasm for computers as decision-making aids to planners.
>
> During the 1970s computing underwent a quiet revolution. By the early 1980s it erupted into a not-so-quiet computer revolution, widely heralded in books, professional journals, and the popular news media. By 1984 interest in computers was rekindled among planners, as evidenced in the 1984 annual conference of the American Planning Association, whose theme was computers and planning.
>
> Today, in contrast to a decade ago, many examples of computer models are available to planners. . . . These models are capable of producing reliable answers to the problems they are designed to address. Nevertheless, for many years now observers have noted that even when computer models have been available, they have not been used often in decision making. . . . There often are problems with data and technical aspects of model design and calibration; but even when those problems are satisfactorily resolved, decision makers often resist using such models. The literature provides many explanations:
>
> - decision makers do not understand and trust the models;
> - decision makers often cannot specify in advance what they want — that is, they require a trial-and-error and sequential decision-making process that the models typically do not accommodate;
> - decision-making needs change, and the models often lack the flexibility to respond to changing needs;
> - decision making often involves judgmental and other "soft" criteria, multiple criteria or objectives, and individual or group preferences that the formal models typically do not accommodate.
>
> In short, it is often perceived that computer-based decision aids may not be well suited to decision-making styles or to the nature of the problems urban decision makers confront. Although such a perception may often be correct, it reflects historical circumstances more than current possibilities.

assistant corporation counsel to the planning and zoning department, the chief planner in a city is much more familiar with zoning law than the corporation counsel's office. So don't let yourself be pushed around.[27]

On the other hand, Harlan Bartholomew, for many years the head of one of the largest planning firms, could say:

> Most of the favorable decisions on zoning appear to me to be the result of a clear expression of ideas and the principles in the minds of city planners by competent lawyers. I should like to cite two illustrations. Two years ago the Ware case in Wichita, Kansas, was decided by the Supreme Court in favor of the constitutionality of zoning. More recently Mr. Ware brought a whole series of cases involving practically every phase of zoning. When these cases came before the court, the city was represented by an exceedingly able city attorney who presented to the courts the broader aspects of zoning and only ten days ago one of the most clean-cut and remarkable decisions in favor of zoning was handed down. . . .[28]

Undoubtedly the interdisciplinary and intractable nature of land-use problems will necessitate the perseverance of this close but uneasy alliance. At this point, we can close by presenting for evaluation and criticism the following excerpt from a Harvard Law School Catalogue, introducing Urban Legal Studies:

> In a nation permeated by law and legal institutions, the legal profession has an inescapable responsibility to participate in the solution of problems that are an intrinsic part of the nature of our society. The very terms in which we describe the problems of metropolitan areas — from issues of land use, transportation, taxation and local government structure to those of civil rights, crime and the deficiencies of welfare and housing programs — emphasize the role of law and lawyers in establishing the existing institutions and distributions of rights and powers, and the roles they must play in revising, reforming and redefining them. This is true for all kinds of lawyers, whether they represent individual interests, large corporations or financial institutions, governmental agencies at the local,

---

27. Editorial, 19 ASPO Newsletter (1953). In 1964, a suit by the Illinois State Bar Association against a planning consulting firm resulted in a consent decree which provided

> [t]hat the Defendant . . . shall in connection with providing professional planning consultant services . . . restrict themselves [sic] solely and completely to the preparation and recommendation of technical planning standards which may be embodied in a subsequent draft of a zoning ordinance, it being understood that the preparation of the draft of such zoning ordinance shall be the responsibility of a member of the Bar.

See Care, The City Planner and the Unauthorized Practice of Law, 34 Urban Planning News 25—Eds. (1968).

28. Planning Problems of Town, City, and Region 201 (1925). Cf. Mandelker, The Role of Law in the Planning Process, 30 Law & Contemp. Probs. 20 (1965); Dluhy & Chen, Interdisciplinary Planning: A Perspective for the Future—Eds. (1986).

D. Tools and Techniques

state, federal or international levels, community organizations, or, in some now unforeseeable way, "the public interest." Law Schools are increasingly responsible for attracting and training able people for the conduct of urban affairs, both as an avenue for professional practice on behalf of private and governmental clients, and as an aspect of business careers and public service as well.

II

"Sic Utere Tuo...": Reconciliation by the Judiciary of Discordant Land Uses

No plot of land is "intire of itselfe." Its value depends upon its physical location with respect to other land, and upon the line drawn by society between the privilege of use and the interest of surrounding owners in the untrammeled use of *their* land. Nuisance doctrines, which have evolved case by case over the centuries, reveal those limitations on a landowner's freedom that the equal (and potentially competitive) rights of his or her neighbors impose.[1]

The "law" of nuisance may be treated under categories of tort or of land law. The tort concept stresses the wrongfulness of conduct and the relation of nuisance to intentional, negligent, or ultrahazardous behavior. The property concept emphasizes the private interest — the use and enjoyment of land — to which the courts have accorded legal protection. From either viewpoint courts may be seen as pricking out the scope and extent of interests in land: delimiting at the same time

---

1. Or, as Professor Cohen has phrased the converse,

> To permit anyone to do absolutely what he likes with his property in creating noise, smells, or danger of fire, would be to make property in general valueless. To be really effective, therefore, the right of property must be supported by restrictions or positive duties on the part of the owners, enforced by the state as much as the right to exclude others which is the essence of property.

Property and Sovereignty, 13 Cornell L.Q. 8, 21 (1927).

both the owner's power of free use and the neighbors' power to veto such use.

Where competing land interests vie to dominate, the court is the traditional forum for decision. Realistically evaluated within the framework of the conventional syntax in which the courts operate, such decisions may be regarded as planning and zoning by the judiciary. The history of this process — one of the earliest forms of land-use regulation in our legal system — should afford insight into the attempt by society to develop a coherent and efficient ordering of land uses. In this field of sharp human conflict arising out of the interdependence of land, the contributions, as well as the limitations, of the judicial process can be appreciated.

The primary concern of this chapter, then, is to illustrate the judicial treatment of conflicts arising from unplanned urban life, when an increasing population presses on diminishing quantities of land. How useful in practice is the law of nuisance to a contemporary lawyer? How does it dovetail with other techniques of land-use planning now available? Of what relevance are these doctrines, given the extensive body of federal and state administrative law mandating protection of the environment and preservation of scenic beauty?

Consider the problems raised in the following questions: How does a court evaluate the pertinent factors in land-use disputes? How does it ascertain the value placed by the community on a particular land use, in comparison with other uses? Are these factors largely extraneous to legal syntax? Is there a generally accepted scale of social values relating to land uses to which courts can refer? Can some land-use activities be said to produce a direct public benefit, others to be carried on primarily for the benefit of the individual? Does judicial resolution of conflicts here reflect, in its results, the social, economic, and political convictions of the dominant class?[2]

How does a court become informed of the bases of competing claims? How can it ascertain the existing land-use pattern, or likely future development, or the ideal development? How can it determine the suitability of a particular activity to a locality, or the size of the neighborhood with which a use should be compatible? How often, in fact, have judges' decisions coincided with "good" land-use planning? How does the process of judicial decision-making differ from that of the city planner?

What is now called "public" or "common" nuisance — where control by the sovereign for a public purpose is involved[3] — is also considered in this chapter. True, the law here has developed along

---

2. For an interesting contrast, compare Bohlen, The Rule in Rylands v. Fletcher, 59 U. Pa. L. Rev. 298 (1911) with Pound, Economic Interpretation of Torts, 53 Harv. L. Rev. 365 (1940).

3. 8 Holdsworth, History of English Law 424, 425 (2d ed. 1937).

A. The Use and Enjoyment of Private Land

different lines from private nuisance, and the two are far apart conceptually.[4] Yet historically there has been an overlap between the class of crimes known as purprestures and cases covered by the thirteenth-century assize of nuisance. The interplay is often crucial in the relations of landowners. Courts still weave the terms together. An action may exist for both a public and private nuisance at one and the same time. Factors of contemporary litigation, such as the granting of individual rights to sue in regulatory ordinances, and the joining of as many as 190 plaintiffs in one action, cause even further blurring.[5] Moreover, the contrasting aspects of public nuisance law cast a critical light on the adequacies of private nuisance doctrine in coping with the problems of municipal growth.

Granting the difficulties, in our society where courts are traditionally the first-line institutions for adjusting disputes, are there real alternatives? Should the vagaries and ambiguities of the common law yield to the relative certainty of administrative rules and regulations? Are the problems instead attributable to the adversarial *mode* of resolution? The materials that close this chapter raise these and other inquiries in the context of disputes regarding competing uses of property.

A. THE USE AND ENJOYMENT OF PRIVATE LAND

■ TRESPASS ON THE CASE IN REGARD TO CERTAIN MILLS
Y.B. 22 Hen. 6, F. 14 (C.P. 1444)[6]

The Prior of S. Nedeport brought a writ of trespass on the case against J. Weston, and alleged through Bingham, his counsel, that he

---

4. Garrett & Garrett, Law of Nuisance 1 (3d ed. 1908); Paton, Liability for Nuisance, 37 Ill. L. Rev. 1, 9 (1942); Newark, Boundaries of Nuisance, 65 L.Q. Rev. 480 (1949).

5. According to Dean Prosser, judges, practitioners, and students who confuse concepts and terms are in good company:

> There is perhaps no more impenetrable jungle in the entire law than that which surrounds the word "nuisance." It has meant all things to all men, and has been applied indiscriminately to everything from an alarming advertisement to a cockroach baked in a pie. There is general agreement that it is incapable of any exact or comprehensive definition. Few terms have afforded so excellent an illustration of the familiar tendency of the courts to seize upon a catchword as a substitute for any analysis of a problem; the defendant's interference with the plaintiff's interests is characterized as a "nuisance," and there is nothing more to be said.

W. Prosser, Law of Torts 571 (4th ed. 1971).

6. Professor John P. Dawson has graciously translated this case for use in these materials.

was the Lord of S. Nede, and that he and all the previous lords of that vill had had three mills in that vill since a time to which memory of man runs not to the contrary, and no one other than the Prior and predecessors had had any mill there since time immemorial, and that all the tenants of the said Prior and all other residents of right should grind and from time immemorial have been accustomed to grind at the said mills, and that the said defendant, one of the tenants of the said Prior, has erected a mill at which the residents of the said vill grind grain and will in future grind grain wrongfully and to the damage of the plaintiff.

PRISOT (counsel for defendant). Judgment of the writ, for the writ is founded on a title by prescription and the prescription is both in the affirmative and in the negative, and I claim that one cannot prescribe in the negative. . . .

MARKHAM, Justice. A usage or custom cannot be binding if it relates only to a vill, but must be followed in a large area, like a county.

PASTON, Justice. Prescription both in the affirmative and in the negative and prescription such as that invoked in the case at bar can be good. . . .

NEWTON, Justice. . . . Even though he has such mills from time immemorial and his tenants and all other residents have been accustomed to grind at the said mills, nevertheless he who has a freehold within a vill can erect a mill on his own land and this is not a wrong to anyone. For if there are two lords in a vill and their lands extend along the banks of a river and one of them has had a mill on the river from time immemorial and the other has not, and he who has had no mill erects one on his own land next to the river, if he does not obstruct or reduce the flow of water to the other mill the other is without remedy against him; but he will have his remedy against those who owe a legal duty to grind at this mill and nevertheless commence to go to the other.

PRISOT (counsel for defendant). . . . If two persons are seised of 100 acres of land in a vill and one of them and his ancestors have had a house on the land from time immemorial, and the other has not, does this prevent the other from erecting a house on his own land? I understand the law is otherwise. And, Sir, a case like the one at bar is reported in our books, a case in which a schoolhouse was claimed to be held in a vill by prescription so that no one else was allowed to have a school in the vill and it was shown that the defendant had erected a schoolhouse in the vill, but the writ was abated.

BINGHAM (counsel for plaintiff). It seems to me that we should have this action or otherwise we are without remedy. For we cannot have an action against those who grind at this new mill and who of right should grind at our mill; the writ secta facienda ad molendinum does not lie except where one by tenure owes suit to the mill and here suit is owed by virtue of residence and not by virtue of tenure. . . .

A. The Use and Enjoyment of Private Land 93

PASTON, Justice. . . . If one of his own free will has been accustomed from time immemorial to grind at my mill, he can change this will as he pleases. If the case were that one person had had from time immemorial a mill next to a certain stream and the stream divided into two branches and then another person erected another mill on the other branch of the divided stream, the old mill is not impaired by this. But if he causes the men who ought to use and have used the old mill to go to the new mill, so that the profit of the old mill is impaired, perhaps some would say that no action lies against him who erects the mill, but I think that if I have a market or fair on Saturday and another person creates a market or fair on the same day in a town that is near my market so that my market or fair is impaired, I will have against him an assize of nuisance of an action on the case. And the rule is the same if I have from time immemorial a ferry in a town and another builds another ferry on the same river near mine so that the profits of my ferry are interfered with, I will have against him an action on the case. So perhaps in the present case.

NEWTON, Justice. Your case of the ferry differs from the case at bar, for in your case, you are required to maintain the ferry and to operate it and repair it for the convenience of the common people; if you fail you will be subject to money fines and this is inquirable by the sheriff in his tourn as well as before the justices in eyre. But in the case at bar if the lord of the mills allows them to go into ruin or even destroys them he is not punishable. And your case of a market or fair cannot arise, for the grant from the king of the right to hold a market or fair will include a clause: "provided nevertheless that this be no nuisance to any other markets or fairs," so that erecting the market is in itself a nuisance. . . .

PASTON, Justice. Let us suppose that the king grants to me a market without any proviso of the kind mentioned. If one thereafter erects a market which is a nuisance to it, I shall have an assize of nuisance against him.

FULTHORPE, Justice. It seems that he is limited in the case at bar to an assize of nuisance and cannot have this action.

MARKHAM, Justice. No, Sir, but if one builds a house which cuts off light from my house or causes rain to run down onto my house or does anything that interferes with my freehold, I will have an assize against him; but in this case and in the case that is put of a ferry, my freehold is not impaired and for this reason I am left to an action on the case. . . .

MOILE (counsel for plaintiff). If I have a roadway appurtenant to my land over your land, if you make a barrier on the land so that I am prevented from using my road, I will have an assize of nuisance against you. But if a stranger without your consent makes such a barrier I will not have an assize but an action on the case.

And then at the end of the term the defendant traversed the statement in the writ and they were at issue. And then for the reasons given above and also for other reasons the plaintiff abandoned the writ and purchased a new one.

■ HOLGATE, WHAT IS A "RIVAL MARKET"?
1985 J. Plan. & Envt. L. 759, 760, 764-765

The question of what constitutes a rival market was considered afresh in Kingston Upon Hull City Council v. Greenwood. There, the council, who owned the market rights, operated a market through a licensee three times a week. The defendant proposed to take a licence of ground floor premises about half-a-mile from the council's market site, intending to operate part of the premises as a market to be occupied by individual traders. The premises were to be open for a week over Christmas. The council informed the defendant that the letting of part of the premises to other traders would constitute a rival market and warned him that they would seek an injunction if the proposals were carried out. The defendant took legal advice and informed the council that he was proposing to set up a shopping arcade with separate self-contained units and that these proposals would not give rise to a concourse of buyers and sellers, and that this would not infringe the council's market rights. On November 3 the defendant obtained a licence to use the premises from November 1 until December 31, 1983, and thereafter until terminated by two weeks' notice. On November 11 he granted sub-licences to the various traders who occupied the individual units which were determinable by either side on one week's notice, but which were not to extend beyond December 30, 1983. The council commenced proceedings for an injunction on November 18 to restrain the defendant from levying a rival market. . . .

. . . Nourse J. concluded that, firstly, the defendant, by means of the advertisements placed in the local and trade press, had invited a sufficiently wide section of the public to come and sell in the arcade. Secondly, he was satisfied that the defendant had retained a sufficient degree of control which enabled him from time to time to maintain or renew his invitation to other members of the public to come and sell. Thirdly, the defendant's contention that practically all the purchases were made from inside separate and self-contained units of a fairly solid, semi-permanent construction which, for the purpose of the law of markets, may well be shops and not stalls, could be of no assistance to him. . . .

That being so, the defendant was levying a rival market. The buyers and sellers had ". . . passed the test prescribed by Lord Keith o⌊

A. The Use and Enjoyment of Private Land

Avonholm. There is a coming together of both. They are gathered together in one place for a common purpose."

■ RAISING A COVERT TO THE NUISANCE
Y.B. 33-35 Edw. 1 (R.S.) 258 (C.P. 1306)

A. has complained to us that B. has raised a certain covert to the nuisance &c. And tortiously for this that whereas the said A. has his land adjoining to B.'s land on the north, B. has planted in his soil trees so that by reason of the shade &c. the corn of A. can not ripen. — *Toudeby.* Any one can make a covert except for birds, judgment of the writ.

Notes

1. No judgment appears in the report of this case; what should the judgment be? What result if *B* raises a dam and floods *A*'s field; where smoke from *B*'s dyehouse reduces the yield of *A*'s cornfield?

2. Should the result differ if the covert were for birds? Serjeant Toudeby's argument is somewhat incorrect: a lord of the manor, by customary law, could erect such a covert on his parcel of land. See Viner's Abridgment, Nuisance §F.2 (2d ed. 1793). A tenant also could purchase a license from his lord to keep a covert for birds. If *L* erects a covert for birds could *T* set off his crop damage against his rent? What if *T* held of another lord?

3. Polanyi writes that "money-making organizes those aspects of economic life which are atomistic, localizable and additive, and leaves uncontrolled its 'diffuse' or 'social' aspects. Wherever these repercussions become prominent, there is a case for action by the public authorities, who are ultimately responsible for social welfare." The Logic of Liberty 148 (1951). Yet, for all this, he continues, the major portion of production and consumption must remain under the control of an economic system that ignores the "diffuse" results of its own action.[7]

■ ROSE v. SOCONY-VACUUM CORP.
54 R.I. 411, 173 A. 627 (1934)

MURDOCK, Justice. These cases, described in the writs as trespass on the case for causing a nuisance, were heard together for the reason

---

7. See also Hayek, Individualism and Economic Order 113 (1949); Kapp, The Social Costs of Private Enterprise (1950); Pollock, The Law of Torts 149-159 (12th ed. 1923).

that the same questions of law are involved in each case. They are here on plaintiffs' exceptions to a ruling of the superior court sustaining demurrers to the declarations which are summarized in plaintiffs' brief as follows:

> The plaintiff (Manuel Rose) for thirty years prior to and in June 1930, owned a farm in East Providence, bounding southerly on the state highway known as the Wampanoag Trail, comprising fifty-seven acres with a dwelling house, large barn and other out buildings thereon, and occupied by him and his family. On the farm was a well of pure water used for drinking purposes, and on the westerly part of the farm was a stream in part fed by percolations of water in and under the land of the defendant and said highway and into said stream. On the farm was a large piggery and a hennery, the hens supplied by water from the well, and the pigs supplied by water of the stream. On the southerly side of and bounding northerly on said highway and opposite said farm the defendant had a large tract of land at a higher elevation than the farm.
>
> Years before 1930, the defendant acquired said tract of land and built upon it a large oil refinery and a large number of tanks for storing petroleum, gasoline and other petroleum products, and operated the same and from time to time suffered and permitted to be discharged on its land and into settling basins, bodies of water and natural ponds and ways thereon large quantities of petroleum, gasoline, petroleum products and waste substances from its refinery and tanks with the result that large parts of its said land, basins, bodies of water and natural water ponds and ways became impregnated, and polluted by the same, and that it was the duty of the defendant to confine to its said land said polluting matters and substances and said waters in their polluted condition and not suffer or permit the same to be discharged or escape from its land to, in, under and on any adjoining or neighboring land, and thereby create a nuisance thereon to its injury, but the defendant disregarding its duty wrongfully and injuriously suffered and permitted large quantites of said polluting matters and substances and said waters in their polluted condition to escape from time to time from its land by means of percolations thereof in, under and through its land to, in, under and through said highway and to, in, under, on and through said farm and parts thereof and to and into said well and said stream, with the direct result that in said June, 1930, said well became polluted by the same and especially by gasoline and rendered unfit as drinking water for use by man or beast, and also said stream theretofore fit for use then became polluted and unfit for use by man or beast with the direct result the plaintiff in June, 1930, and until the present time was deprived of the use of said well and stream and obliged since to obtain water from other sources off his farm for the supply of his house for drinking and domestic uses and watering his hens and for watering his hogs and pigs and other uses for which the stream was available.
>
> Further the declaration sets forth that because of the pollution of the stream 136 of his hogs and pigs died from drinking the waters,

A. The Use and Enjoyment of Private Land   97

including 75 breeding sows, and because of the pollution of the well about 700 of his hens died from drinking the well waters, and that because of a lack of a wholesome water supply the plaintiff has been deprived of raising on his farm as large a number of pigs and hens as theretofore and his business in raising and selling the same interfered with and greatly reduced in amount to his monetary damage and loss. The declaration concludes with a general allegation as to other damages from said nuisance caused by the defendant.

The declarations allege no negligent act, and recovery is sought principally on the ground that the acts set forth in the declarations have resulted in a nuisance for which defendant is liable even though not negligent. The assertion that the acts of the defendant complained of have resulted in a nuisance is petitio principii.

There is no wholly satisfactory definition of what constitutes a nuisance, but it is generally agreed that a nuisance has its origin in the invasion of a legal right. In Cooley on Torts, vol. 3 (4th Ed.) §398, it is said that "An actionable nuisance may, therefore, be said to be anything wrongfully done or permitted which injures or annoys another in the enjoyment of his legal rights," and in Joyce on Nuisances, §29, that "a nuisance does not necessarily exist even though one may by the use of his property cause an injury or damage to another." The plaintiffs must therefore go further to establish liability than the mere assertion that a nuisance exists on their land by reason of the acts of the defendant.

The plaintiffs' cases rest on the proposition that they have a cause of action from the fact that contaminating and deleterious substances have escaped from the land of the defendant through the medium of percolating waters to their land. The plaintiffs rely on the much-discussed case of Rylands v. Fletcher, L.R. 3 H.L. 330, where the following rule laid down by Mr. Justice Blackburn in Fletcher vs. Rylands, L.R. 1 Ex. 265, was approved:

> We think that the true rule of law is, that the person who, for his own purposes, brings on his land and collects and keeps there anything likely to do mischief if it escapes, must keep it in at his peril, and if he does not do so, is prima facie answerable for all the damage which is the natural consequence of its escape. He can excuse himself by showing that the escape was owing to the plaintiff's default; or, perhaps that it was the consequence of vis major, or the act of God; but as nothing of this sort exists here, it is unnecessary to inquire what excuse would be sufficient. The general rule, as above stated, seems on principle just . . . and it seems but reasonable and just that the neighbour who has brought something on his own property (which was not naturally there), harmless to others so long as it is confined to his own property, but which he knows will be mischievous if it gets on his neighbour's, should be obliged to

make good the damage which ensues if he does not succeed in confining it to his own property.

This rule is a radical departure from the commonly accepted doctrine of the law of torts that liability is predicated on fault. It has not found general acceptance in this country, and in England it has been greatly modified by later decisions.

A profound criticism of the rule is found in the opinion of Mr. Justice Doe in Brown v. Collins, 53 N.H. 442, at page 448, 16 Am. Rep. 372, where it is said:

> Everything that a man can bring on his land is capable of escaping, — against his will, and without his fault, with or without assistance, in some form, solid, liquid, or gaseous, changed or unchanged by the transforming processes of nature or art, — and of doing damage after its escape. Moreover, if there is a legal principle that makes a man liable for the natural consequences of the escape of things which he brings on his land, the application of such a principle cannot be limited to those things; it must be applied to all his acts that disturb the original order of creation; or, at least, to all things which he undertakes to possess or control anywhere, and which were not used and enjoyed in what is called the natural or primitive condition of mankind, whatever that may have been. This is going back a long way for a standard of legal rights, and adopting an arbitrary test of responsibility that confounds all degrees of danger, pays no heed to the essential elements of actual fault, puts a clog upon natural and reasonably necessary uses of matter, and tends to embarrass and obstruct much of the work which it seems to be man's duty carefully to do.

Losee v. Buchanan, 51 N.Y. 476, 10 Am. Rep. 623; Burdick, Law of Torts (4th Ed.) §12: "The rule in Rylands v. Fletcher, even with the recognized limitations, finds no favor even in England, and American courts have generally refused to follow it." See, also, Bohlen, Studies in the Law of Torts, p. 421.

We think, therefore, that reason and the great weight of authority in this country sustain us in refusing to adopt the rule of absolute liability as stated in Rylands v. Fletcher, supra.

The plaintiffs lean heavily on the maxim sic utere tuo ut alienum non laedas. This maxim, so often cited as the governing principle of decisions, affords little, if any, aid in the determination of the rights of parties in litigation. If it be taken to mean any injury to another by the use of one's own, it is not true, and, if it means legal injury, it is simply a restatement of what has already been determined.

> The maxim, sic utere tuo ut alienum non laedas, is mere verbiage. A party may damage the property of another where the law permits; and

A. The Use and Enjoyment of Private Land 99

he may not where the law prohibits: so that the maxim can never be applied till the law is ascertained; and, when it is, the maxim is superfluous.

Erle, J., in Bonomi v. Backhouse, El. Bl. & El. 622, 643; 2 Austin, Jur. (3rd.) 795, 829. The maxim is undoubtedly a sound moral precept expressing an ideal never fully attained in the social state.

We must therefore look for some fault on the part of the defendant. It is well-settled law that one who accumulates filth or other deleterious matter on his land must confine it there and not allow it to spread over the surface of his land to the surface of the land of another. "Where one has filth deposited on his premises, he whose dirt it is must keep it that it may not trespass." Tenant v. Goldwin, 1 Salk. 360. And this rule will apply where the objectional matter permeates the soil superficially and by the action of the elements reaches the soil of another. Liability in this class of cases sounds in trespass.

The owner of land bounding on a surface stream may not pollute the same to the impairment of the use and enjoyment of the stream by other riparian owners; and this rule applies to subterranean streams following a known or readily ascertainable and well-defined course. 27 R.C.L. p. 1170. Liability for the pollution of a surface stream or subterranean stream following a well-defined course is predicated on the invasion of a correlative right of the injured party in such waters. This leads to an inquiry into the nature and extent of the right of a landowner in the waters beneath the soil which pass from his land, not in a well-defined stream, but by percolation or seepage.

The leading case on this question is Acton v. Blundell, 12 Mees. & Wels. Rep. 324, decided in 1843. In that case it was held that the right to the waters in the soil was not governed by the rule applicable to surface streams. . . .

In England this right to underground waters has been held to be absolute, and the motive of the owner in appropriating or diverting the same is immaterial. Mayor of Bradford v. Pickles, [1895] App. Cas. 587. In this country the authorities are in conflict as to the nature of the right in underground waters. Some jurisdictions follow the English rule and others modify the rule to the extent that the owner of land may not through malice or negligence deprive the adjoining owner of percolating waters. To this extent in the latter jurisdictions the right is not absolute but relative.

In this state the right to subterranean waters appears to be relative to the extent that they may not be purposely or negligently diverted. . . .

While the defendant could appropriate to its own use the percolating waters under its soil, providing that in so doing it was not actuated by an improper motive and was not negligent, can it, by the use to which it puts its land, deprive the plaintiffs of such waters by rendering them unfit for plaintiffs' use by contamination? Authorities, few in number, which bear directly on this question, are in conflict. . . .

Dillon v. Acme Oil Co., 49 Hun 565, 2 N.Y.S. 289, 291, is strikingly similar in many particulars to the instant case. In that case the plaintiff owned land on which there were two wells; twenty rods away, and separated therefrom by a public street and a railroad with several tracks, defendant conducted an oil refinery. Plaintiff's wells were polluted by oil from this refinery which had percolated through the earth and was carried by some subterranean stream to plaintiff's wells. It was held that the law controlling the rights of the parties to surface streams had no application to subterranean waters running through unknown channels and that, "In the absence of negligence and of knowledge as to the existence of such subterranean water-courses, when the business is legitimate, and conducted with care and skill, there can be no liability if such subterranean courses become contaminated."

In Upjohn v. Richland Board of Health, 46 Mich. 542, 9 N.W. 845, 848, relief, by way of injunction to restrain the board of health in said township from extending its cemetery so as to bring it closer to complainant's premises was denied. The opinion in this case is of particular interest for the reason that it was written by that distinguished commentator on the law, Mr. Justice Cooley. While relief appears to have been denied in part on other grounds, the opinion discusses at length the law pertaining to percolating waters. After stating the distinction between surface streams and percolating waters, the opinion proceeds:

> But if withdrawing the water from one's well by an excavation on adjoining lands will give no right of action, it is difficult to understand how corrupting its waters by a proper use of the adjoining premises can be actionable, when there was no actual intent to injure, and no negligence. The one act destroys the well, and the other does no more; the injury is the same in kind and degree in the two cases.

The rationale of these opinions is that the courses of subterranean waters are as a rule indefinite and obscure, and therefore the rights relating to them cannot well be defined as in the case of surface streams. To give to others a right in such waters may subject a landowner to liability for consequences, arising from a legitimate use of his land, which he did not intend and which he could not foresee. Contra are Kinnaird v. Standard Oil Co., 89 Ky. 468, 12 S.W. 937; Beatrice Gas Co. v. Thomas, 41 Neb. 662, 59 N.W. 925; Berger v. Minneapolis Gaslight Co., 60 Minn. 296, 62 N.W. 336, Gilmore v. Royal Salt Co., 84 Kan. 729, 115 P. 541; Masten v. Texas Co., 194 N.C. 540, 140 S.E. 89. . . .

A query arises as to whether the divergence of views expressed in

A. The Use and Enjoyment of Private Land

these cases is not due to the influence of the predominating economic interests of the jurisdictions to which these apply; in other words, whether these opinions do not rest on public policy rather than legal theory. On the question of public policy as a ground of judicial decision, see an article by Mr. Justice Holmes in 8 Harvard Law Review, 1.

It will be observed that in jurisdictions holding that, even though there is no negligence, there is liability for the pollution of subterranean waters, the predominating economic interest is agricultural.

Defendant's refinery is located at the head of Narragansett Bay, a natural waterway for commerce. This plant is situated in the heart of a region highly developed industrially. Here it prepares for use and distributes a product which has become one of the prime necessities of modern life. It is an unavoidable incident of the growth of population and its segregation in restricted areas that individual rights recognized in a sparsely settled state have to be surrendered for the benefit of the community, as it develops and expands. If, in the process of refining petroleum, injury is occasioned to those in the vicinity, not through negligence or lack of skill or the invasion of a recognized legal right, but by the contamination of percolating waters whose courses are not known, we think that public policy justifies a determination that such harm is damnum absque injuria.

The plaintiff's exceptions in each case are overruled, and each case is remitted to the superior court for further proceedings.

Notes

1. After this decision, if you had been representing the plaintiff, what other proceedings would you have taken and on what basis? See Rose v. Socony-Vacuum Corp., 56 R.I. 272, 185 A. 251 (1936). Cf. King v. Columbian Carbon Co., 152 F.2d 636 (5th Cir. 1945); Phillips v. Sun Oil Co., 307 N.Y. 328, 121 N.E. 2d 249 (1954). If a similar case arose and you were the trial judge, how would you charge the jury?

2. How does Rose's action in this case differ from one framed in trespass? Compare Judson v. Los Angeles Suburban Gas Co., 157 Cal. 168, 106 P. 581 (1910) with Karnoff v. Kingsburg Cotton Oil Co., 45 Cal. 2d 265, 288 P.2d 507 (1955). In negligent conduct? Cf. Longhurst v. Metropolitan Water Board, [1948] 2 All E.R. 834 (H.L.). In ultrahazardous activity? Does it make any difference where the forms of action are abolished? See Kenworthey, The Private Nuisance Concept in Pennsylvania: A Comparison with the Restatement, 54 Dick. L. Rev. 109 (1949). See also Note, 14 B.U.L. Rev. 865, 887 (1934):

> In conclusion it is submitted that the Rhode Island court erred in sustaining defendant's demurrers, and in holding that it was necessary to

allege and prove a negligent, or intentional or malicious act in order to find for the plaintiff. Liability should have been imposed on the defendant on the ground that the pollution of the percolating waters, stream, and well constituted a nuisance.

Overcoming the psychological hazard of reviewing that final arbiter of the law — the Review Note — how do you appraise the validity of this criticism? Is this statement an unconscious crystallization of what some courts, in fact, are doing? See Prosser, Nuisance Without Fault, 20 Tex. L. Rev. 399 (1942). Cf. R. L. Renken v. Harvey Aluminum, Inc., 226 F. Supp. 169 (D. Or. 1963) (burden of proof).

3. Stammler, The Theory of Justice 243-244 (Husik trans. 1925):

In the celebrated lawsuit of the miller Arnold under Frederick the Great, the question under discussion was whether the neighbor of a miller may construct fish-ponds and fill them from the water of the mill-stream if the miller is prevented thereby from getting enough water to drive his mill. The neighbor, who was the defendant, maintained his absolute right to do this; and in his examination gave expression to the following view: "That since he was merely exercising his right, he was not concerned about the water being withdrawn from the plaintiff; that this is the dictate of good common sense; else there would arise the greatest injustice, and he would be deprived of what was evidently his property and well-authenticated right."

The supreme court adopted this view and rejected the charge on the ground, "That the defendant can not be prevented from constructing the pond; and that he also has the right to use the water of the river to fill his pond. For as long as the river flows through his grounds, it belongs to him; and a person who exercises a right that is his does no injustice to another."

The king was highly wrought up about this judgment. He felt that a grievous injustice had been committed against the miller. A charge was brought against the judges who rendered the decision. But the senate of the supreme court expressed itself as follows concerning the vexatious decision participated in by the accused: ". . . [E]very proprietor or owner of real property may upon his own ground and estate build and lay out as he pleases, and that consequently he may use and apply the water of a river flowing through his estate in any way he sees fit, without concerning himself about the convenience of his neighbors, so far as he is not restrained by police laws or by contracts and agreements with his neighbors. . . . He only exercises his right; and, according to the law of nature and the statutes, the following principle is valid that a person who exercises his right does no injustice to any one."

But Frederick the Great decided otherwise. He rejected the judgment of the supreme court, removed the members of the council who were responsible for it and sent them to the fortress for a year. The mill was

A. The Use and Enjoyment of Private Land   103

again put in order and Arnold's loss was reimbursed from the private property of the judges. The ponds that caused the damage were destroyed.

4. Consider the approach of the Second Restatement of Torts:

§822. General Rule

One is subject to liability for a private nuisance if, but only if, his conduct is a legal cause of an invasion of another's interest in the private use and enjoyment of land, and the invasion is either
    (a) intentional and unreasonable, or
    (b) unintentional and otherwise actionable under the rules controlling liability for negligent or reckless conduct, or for abnormally dangerous conditions or activities.

§828. Utility of Conduct — Factors Involved

In determining the utility of conduct that causes an intentional invasion of another's interest in the use and enjoyment of land, the following factors are important:
    (a) the social value that the law attaches to the primary purpose of the conduct;
    (b) the suitability of the conduct to the character of the locality; and
    (c) the impracticability of preventing or avoiding the invasion.

See Wheeling Bridge Co. v. State of Pennsylvania, 54 U.S. (13 How.) 519 (1851). Compare Justice McLean's analysis at 568 to Justice Daniel's dissent at 602-612.

5. Compare this definition, by Blackstone, of private nuisance, with that of the court: "anything done to the hurt or annoyance of the lands, tenements, or hereditaments of another." 3 Blackstone, Commentaries *216. Cal. Civ. Code §3479 (West 1970) provides: "Anything which is injurious to health, or is indecent or offensive to the senses, or an obstruction to the free use of property, so as to interfere with the comfortable enjoyment of life or property . . . is a nuisance." See Smith's discussion of definition-making in this context, Torts Without Particular Names, 69 U. Pa. L. Rev. 91 (1921). What framework would be more helpful (or should the inquiry be phrased differently)? See Restatement (Second) of Torts §822 Comment b (1977):

> Failure to recognize that private nuisance has reference to the interest invaded and not to the type of conduct that subjects the actor to liability has led to confusion. Thus, in respect to an interference with the use and enjoyment of land, attempts are made to distinguish between private nuisance and negligence, overlooking the fact that private nuisance has reference to the interest invaded and negligence to the conduct that subjects the actor to liability for the invasion. Similar distinctions are

attempted between private nuisance and abnormally dangerous activities for the same reason.

See also 6A American Law of Property §28.24 (1954); 5 Powell, Real Property, ch. 64 (1986).

On the adequacy of the conventional terminology, see Seavey, Nuisance: Contributory Negligence and Other Mysteries, 65 Harv. L. Rev. 984 (1952). In Patterson v. Peabody Coal Co., 3 Ill. App. 2d 311, 318, 122 N.E.2d 48, 52 (1954), the defendant complained of an instruction to the jury using the word "nuisance." The court agreed with him. Cf. Walling v. City of Fremont, 138 Neb. 399, 293 N.W. 226 (1940).

6. Suppose two other refineries operated and drained onto Rose's land. Is this a proper defense? See Slater v. Pacific American Oil Co., 212 Cal. 648, 300 P. 31 (1931). It is stipulated that the emission of dense smoke from the defendant's factory in and of itself is harmless and would cause no inconvenience or damage to the public. However, when added to the smoke of five other neighboring factories, a nuisance condition exists. Any liability? Ingram v. City of Gridley, 100 Cal. App. 2d 815, 224 P.2d 798 (1950). How should damages, if granted, be apportioned? Compare Key v. Armour Fertilizer Works, 18 Ga. App. 472, 89 S.E. 593 (1916) with Spiker v. Eikenberry, 135 Iowa 79, 110 N.W. 457 (1907).

In Holman v. Athens Empire Laundry Co., 149 Ga. 345, 100 S.E. 207 (1919), a verdict was directed for the defendant on the ground that equity should not undertake to regulate smoke in populous communities. On appeal, what result?

■ ALEVIZOS v. METROPOLITAN AIRPORTS COMMISSION OF MINNEAPOLIS & ST. PAUL
298 Minn. 471, 216 N.W.2d 651 (1974)

KELLY, Justice. . . .

This action was commenced by a group of property owners who reside under or near the take-off and landing flight paths for the Minneapolis-St. Paul International Airport. The 100 petitioners-appellants reside in the area of the city of Minneapolis, Hennepin County, generally referred to as South Minneapolis. They sought to bring this action as a class action on behalf of themselves and all others similarly situated. An affidavit filed in behalf of petitioners' motion before the district court indicates that the property affected would include approximately 27,565 homes, apartments, churches, places of business, and other buildings located in Hennepin, Ramsey, and Dakota counties.

A. The Use and Enjoyment of Private Land 105

Petitioners compose a community cross section which includes the following occupations: A dentist, doctor, minister, lawyer, law professor, clerical and executive employees, a real estate appraiser, retired persons, a personnel manager, and a court reporter.

The class encompasses owners of all properties located within four corridors or sound cones emanating from the airport. These corridors extend generally northwest, northeast, southwest, and southeast from the airport. . . .

Petitioners allege that MAC [Metropolitan Airport Commission] in the operation and use of the Minneapolis-St. Paul International Airport has interfered with the use and enjoyment of their property to such an extent as to amount to a taking, requiring compensation under the Constitution of the State of Minnesota. Minn. Const. art. 1, §13. In support of this contention, petitioners have alleged that respondent's operation has interfered with their use of the property in a number of ways. In their complaint, it is alleged, inter alia:

> By reason of defendant's use and operation of the Minneapolis-St. Paul International Airport, aircraft take off and land in great numbers at said airport, at irregular intervals at all hours of the day and night. Said aircraft fly at low altitudes within the airspace immediately above or in close proximity to the property of the plaintiffs.
> Such activity of the defendant has caused and is causing air and noise pollution to invade the property of the plaintiffs to such a degree that physical damage to such property has resulted and to such an extent that plaintiffs have been deprived of the free and unmolested use, possession and quiet enjoyment of their property.
> The activity of the defendant creates deafening, disturbing and frightening noises and vibrations to intrude upon the property of the plaintiffs, and causes dust and oily grime to pass over and to settle upon plaintiffs' property and in the homes and other structures located thereon.
> Defendant, by such activity, is perpetuating a continuing trespass and maintaining a continuing nuisance to such an unreasonable degree that plaintiffs have been greatly molested and annoyed thereby.
> Such acts of the defendant disrupt sleep, interfere seriously with entertainment and normal peaceful enjoyment and use of the property of the plaintiffs; interrupt and prevent normal conversation and communication, use and enjoyment of the telephone, television and radio; and create fear, nervousness and apprehension on the part of the plaintiffs and others lawfully in and upon the property of the plaintiffs.
> The defendant, by such activity, has caused depreciation and diminution of the market value of the property of the plaintiffs, has confiscated and condemned such property, has interfered with the ownership, possession, enjoyment and value of such property and has caused a taking or damaging of the property of the plaintiffs for its use, without just compensation having been paid, without due process of law, and contrary to the Constitution and the Laws of the State of Minnesota and the Constitution of the United States of America.

Petitioners contend that all of these interferences have resulted in a substantial detrimental effect upon the market value of the properties under and near the aircraft flight paths. One property owner estimated his property decreased 20 percent in value. Four professional real estate appraisers filed affidavits in which they stated their belief that the property below and near the flight paths had been substantially and measurably decreased in value.

Because of the posture of this appeal, this court must assume that all of the foregoing allegations and contentions are true and base its decisions on that assumption.

Does mandamus lie against MAC to compel inverse condemnation? . . .

The trial court, in its memorandum supporting the dismissal of this action, analyzed the existing case law in inverse condemnation by airplane overflight. Citing Batten v. United States, 306 F.2d 580 (10 Cir. 1962), it concluded that a physical trespass is required.

In the development of the common law, courts have attempted to place their decisions in legal pigeonholes sometimes described as legal fictions. These legal fictions and theories have undergone not only minor changes, but also drastic changes to meet the varying contemporary needs of society and to improve our system of justice. The courts which have ordered inverse condemnation based upon overflights of airplanes have done so, in general, either on the theory of trespass or on the theory of nuisance. Perhaps at one time in the history of common law, a direct overflight by an airplane would unquestionably have been a trespass, as ownership of land included ownership of the airspace directly above to the periphery of the universe. In United States v. Causby, 328 U.S. 256, 260 (1946), the Supreme Court of the United States stated:

> It is ancient doctrine that at common law ownership of the land extended to the periphery of the universe — Cujus est solum ejus est usque ad coelum. But that doctrine has no place in the modern world. The air is a public highway, as Congress has declared. Were that not true, every transcontinental flight would subject the operator to countless trespass suits. Common sense revolts at the idea. To recognize such private claims to the airspace would clog these highways, seriously interfere with their control and development in the public interest, and transfer into private ownership that to which only the public has a just claim.

In determining whether or not inverse condemnation should be ordered as to landowners near airports, some courts, following the trespass theory, have insisted upon direct overflights before permitting recovery. Other courts have permitted inverse condemnation on the nuisance theory without requiring a direct overflight. Mr. Chief Justice Kenneth J. O'Connell of the Oregon Supreme Court, in questioning

A. The Use and Enjoyment of Private Land

the need for the distinction between nuisance and trespass, has written "Why not simply declare that henceforth all invasions of interest in land, whether affecting the interest of exclusive possession or the interest in use and enjoyment, are to be embraced in one tort?" O'Connell, Streamlining Appellate Procedures, 56 J. Am. Jud. Soc. 234, 238. . . .

Any discussion of whether inverse condemnation should be anchored to a nuisance theory, a trespass theory, a trespass theory with a new look, or on some combination of these theories should be preceded by a summary of United States Supreme Court decisions dealing with inverse condemnation, i.e., United States v. Causby, 328 U.S. 256 (1946); and Griggs v. Allegheny County, 369 U.S. 84 (1962).

The *Causby* case involved an action by the owner of property located directly below the take-off and landing glide path of an airport used extensively by military aircraft. No actual touching of the property's surface was found. Aircraft passing as low as 67 feet above his house cause[d] the plaintiff much anxiety and discomfort in addition to ruining his chicken raising business. The Supreme Court initially brushed aside the argument based on the common-law principle that ownership of property extends to the periphery of the universe and held that Causby had suffered a compensable taking under the Fifth Amendment. While not defining precisely what elements are necessary for a taking by overflight, the court indicated several of the factors it found significant in reaching its decision. It thereby created confusion, however, because it used concepts of nuisance and trespass alternatively as the bases for the holding. Elements of trespass were relied upon by the court when it stated that although a direct touching of the property was not necessary, an invasion of that airspace above the ground which the landowner can occupy and use in connection with the land would be a taking. The court then went on to indicate that factors such as inconvenience, frequency, interference, and rights to the enjoyment and use of land played a significant role in reaching its decision — concepts normally associated with nuisance actions. Thus, if a trespass is required, may only those people affected by direct overflight to their property recover? If a nuisance concept may be applied, then may all those whose use and enjoyment of their property is substantially interfered with recover regardless of the flightpath's location? . . .

The lower Federal courts which have dealt with this issue have almost unanimously allowed recovery only to those property owners located directly below the flight path. This approach more nearly resembles the trespass theory rather than the nuisance theory and for ease in reference, we refer to it as such.

The state court decisions have largely deviated from the Federal court pattern by allowing recovery both to those property owners directly beneath the flightpath and to those near the flightpath. . . .

... It should be pointed out initially that the Minnesota Constitution requires compensation where private property is taken, destroyed, or damaged.... Petitioners in this case do not allege that they have been dispossessed by MAC's operations. They allege that their right to use the property without undue interference has been infringed and the decrease in market value due to defendant's operations has deprived them of their right to dispose of their property for a fair price. The right to use one's property in relative freedom from irritating noise and interference can hardly be disputed in view of present-day living conditions where a great deal of governmental and private effort is spent on planning and zoning our cities in an effort to improve the quality of life. These societal efforts to protect certain land uses from irritating interferences, then, indicate that the use and enjoyment of one's property without unduly irritating noise, vibrations, and gaseous fumes have arisen to the status of a property right for which a property owner may demand compensation when it is denied to him by governmental activity.

This does not mean that every noise or interference with a property owner's use and enjoyment thereof constitutes a taking. Every landowner must continue to endure that level of inconvenience, discomfort, and loss of peace and quiet which can be reasonably anticipated by any average member of a vibrant and progressive society. But when those interferences reach the point where they cause a measurable decrease in property market value, it is reasonable to assume that, considering the permanency of the air flights, a property right has been, if not "taken or destroyed," at the very least "damaged," for which our constitution requires that compensation be paid. This will not give relief to the unusually sensitive person because the measure of recovery is decrease in market value of the property due to its decreased desirability in the general market place rather than the amount of discomfort to the individual.

We recognize that most property in a metropolitan area would have a higher value if it were completely free of any noise, smog, or other undesirable features, provided the same conveniences were available. We are sure that if the metropolitan area had no airports, freeways, buses, trucks, trains, ambulances, and many other conveniences that are sources of noise, fumes, and whatnot, that property values would be substantially reduced. Property owners cannot — and we are sure they do not expect to — have the advantages created by conveniences and yet be paid for the undesirable effects created by the same conveniences unless those effects adversely affect their property so directly and so substantially that it is manifestly unfair to require them to sustain a measurable loss in market value which the property-owning public in general does not suffer. Thus, not every inconvenience,

A. The Use and Enjoyment of Private Land   109

annoyance, or loss of peace and quiet caused by air flights will give rise to a cause of action in inverse condemnation against an airport operator.

The test, then, that we prescribe will give relief to any property owner who can show a direct and substantial invasion of his property rights of such a magnitude he is deprived of the practical enjoyment of the property and that such invasion results in a definite and measurable diminution of the market value of the property.

To justify an award of damages it must be proved that these invasions of property rights are not of an occasional nature, but are repeated and aggravated, and that there is a reasonable probability that they will be continued in the future. . . .

Reversed and remanded for proceedings consistent with this decision.[8]

■ **RODRIGUE v. COPELAND**
475 So. 2d 1071 (La. 1985)

DIXON, Chief Justice.

Plaintiffs, three residents of the Pontchartrain Shores Subdivision in Jefferson Parish, instituted this action to enjoin defendant, Alvin C. Copeland, from erecting and operating his annual Christmas display. The plaintiffs sought injunctive relief under C.C. 667-669 due to problems associated with an enormous influx of visitors to their limited access, residential neighborhood. . . .

Since 1977 defendant has annually maintained a Christmas display on his premises at 5001 Folse Drive. The display has grown in size and popularity since the year of its inception. The display consists of an extravagant array of lights and lighted figures accompanied by traditional Christmas music.[9]

The neighborhood is a limited access area which is zoned solely for single family residences. Defendant's premises, which front on Folse Drive, are bounded to the north by the Lake Pontchartrain levee, to

---

[8]. In this connection see Vittek, Airport Noise Control — Can Communities Live Without It? Can Airlines Live With It?, 385 J. Air Law & Commerce 473 (1972); Haar, Airport Noise and the Urban Dwellers: A Proposed Solution, 159 N.Y.L.J. No. 101, at 4 (1968), No. 102, at 4 (1968): Spater, Noise and the Law, 63 Mich. L. Rev. 1375 (1965); and Hearings on Noise: Its Effect on Man and Machine, Before the Special Investigating Subcommittee of the House Committee on Science and Astronautics, 86th Cong., 2d Sess. (1960). As Chapter VII indicates, courts continue to wrestle with the problem of condemnation accomplished by means other than outright physical occupation by the state. Compare the struggles of the Minnesota court with the "easy" solution in Loretto v. Teleprompter Manhattan CATV Corp., 458 U.S. 419 (1982). — EDS.

[9]. Copeland testified "that the cost of the display, $30,000-$50,000, has been borne by his business, A. Copeland Enterprises, Inc., since 1980. Defendant owns 100% of the stock in A. Copeland Enterprises, Inc. This corporation is the parent company of Popeye's Famous Fried Chicken, Inc." 475 So. 2d at 1076. — EDS.

the east by a public right-of-way and to the west by the residence of plaintiff Mary Borrell. . . .

Since 1982 defendant's exhibition has drawn numerous spectators to the neighborhood during the hours while the display is in operation. The spectators view the display either from their automobiles or on foot after parking their vehicles in the surrounding neighborhood. The increased congestion in the neighborhood has created numerous problems for some of the defendant's neighbors such as restricted access to their homes, noise, public urination, property damage and a lack of on-street parking. . . .

Owners of immovable property are restrained in the use of their property by certain obligations. These obligations include the responsibilities imposed by articles 667-669 of the Civil Code:

> Although a proprietor may do with his estate whatever he pleases, still he can not make any work on it, which may deprive his neighbor of the liberty of enjoying his own, or which may be the cause of any damage to him. C.C. 667.
>
> Although one be not at liberty to make any work by which his neighbor's buildings may be damaged, yet every one has the liberty of doing on his own ground whatsoever he pleases, although it should occasion some inconvenience to his neighbor.
>
> Thus he who is not subject to any servitude originating from a particular agreement in that respect, may raise his house as high as he pleases, although by such elevation he should darken the lights of his neighbor's house, because this act occasions only an inconvenience, but not a real damage. C.C. 668.
>
> If the works or materials for any manufactory or other operation, cause an inconvenience to those in the same or in the neighboring houses, by diffusing smoke or nauseous smell, and there be no servitude established by which they are regulated, their sufferance must be determined by the rules of the police, or the customs of the place. C.C. 669.

These obligations of vicinage are legal servitudes imposed on the owner of property. These provisions embody a balancing of rights and obligations associated with the ownership of immovables. As a general rule, the landowner is free to exercise his rights of ownership in any manner he sees fit. He may even use his property in ways which ". . . occasion some inconvenience to his neighbor." However, his extensive rights do not allow him to do "real damage" to his neighbor.

At issue in this case is whether Copeland's light and sound display has caused a mere inconvenience or real damage to his neighbors and their right to enjoy their own premises.

In determining whether an activity or work occasions real damage or mere inconvenience, a court is required to determine the reasonableness of the conduct in light of the circumstances. This analysis

A. The Use and Enjoyment of Private Land 111

requires consideration of factors such as the character of the neighborhood, the degree of the intrusion and the effect of the activity on the health and safety of the neighbors.

In the past, this court has borrowed from the common law of nuisance in describing the type of conduct which violates the pronouncements embodied in C.C. 667-669. . . .

Defendant's exhibition constitutes an unreasonable intrusion into the lives of his neighbors when considered in light of the character of the neighborhood, the degree of the intrusion and its effect on the use and enjoyment of their properties by his neighbors. . . .

The damage suffered by plaintiffs during the operation of defendant's display is extensive, both in terms of its duration and its size. Defendant's display becomes operative in early December and remains in operation until January 5. During this period, plaintiffs are forced to contend with a flow of bumper to bumper traffic through their limited access neighborhood. In addition, they must endure the noise and property abuse associated with the crowd of visitors who congregate near the display.

The display begins operation at dusk each evening and continues until 11:00 p.m. on weekdays and 12:00 midnight on weekends. The display is occasionally operational beyond midnight. While in operation, it features an extravagant display of lights which are located across the front of defendant's residence, on the roof and in the enclosed yard to the west of the residence. Some of the lights comprising the display are shaped into figures such as a star, a reindeer, a snowman, three angels and a depiction of Santa and his reindeer. Lights are also located in the trees and shrubs. In addition to the lights, the display features a tapestry proclaiming "Glory to God in the Highest" and a creche.

Noise emanates from the display and from the visitors. The display is accompanied by traditional Christmas music which is amplified through loudspeakers located on the second floor of defendant's residence. The music is audible inside the home of Mary Borrell. The plaintiffs also complain of noise emanating from car engines, car horns, the slamming of car doors and police whistles. . . .

The increased traffic attracted to the display has some impact on the health and safety of the residents. The response time for emergency services is increased due to the traffic congestion. However, the record indicates that this danger was minimized under the sheriff's plan through the creation of an emergency lane on Transcontinental and the presence of two motor scooters to be used in medical emergencies. If the physical health and safety of the plaintiffs had been the only factor to consider, we would not have deemed it necessary to restrain defendant's display. However, in consideration of all the factors, the district court committed clear error in failing to find that plaintiffs suffered damage under C.C. 667-669 and irreparable injury. Likewise, the court of appeal erred in affirming the district court.

Plaintiffs' injury stems from the nature and size of the display which render it incompatible with the restricted access, residential neighborhood. Defendant is enjoined from erecting and operating a Christmas exhibition which is calculated to and does attract an unusually large number of visitors to the neighborhood.

In complying with our order, defendant is specifically enjoined from placing oversized lighted figures, such as the reindeer and snowman, in his yards or upon the roof of his residence. The proper place for these "commercial size" decorations is not within a quiet, residential neighborhood. Defendant is also specifically ordered to reduce the volume of any sound accompanying the display so that it is not audible from within the closest homes of his neighbors.

In limiting his display, the burden is placed on defendant to reduce substantially the size and extravagance of his display to a level at which it will not attract the large crowds that have been drawn to the neighborhood in the past.

Of course, defendant is free to maintain his display unrestricted, at a location which is appropriate. The injunction granted herein is limited to activity at defendant's premises on Folse Drive. . . .

In consideration of defendant's right of religious expression, he is free to retain the religious symbols which are included in his display, that is, the Star of Bethlehem, nativity scene, religious tapestry and oversized lighted angels. The limitations on defendant's activity do not extend to the content of the display. . . .

Notes

1. The plaintiff operates an outdoor motion picture theater. He built high fences to prevent the lights of automobiles on the public highway from interfering with the performance, and a shadow box over the screen to exclude the light of the moon and stars. The defendant constructed a racetrack on adjoining property. Brilliant floodlights from the racetrack shine with the approximate intensity of full moonlight upon the screen, and by dimming the pictures exhibited by the plaintiff, cause him considerable financial loss. The plaintiff brings an action for damages, claiming a nuisance. The trial court directs a verdict for the defendant. On appeal, what result? Amphitheaters, Inc. v. Portland Meadows, 184 Or. 336, 198 P.2d 847 (1948). Cf. Gronn v. Rogers Construction, Inc., 221 Or. 226, 350 P.2d 1086 (1960); Martin v. Reynolds Metal Co., 221 Or. 86, 342 P.2d 790 (1960) (especially the concurring opinion, dissenting from attempt to reconcile holding with that of *Amphitheaters*).

A. The Use and Enjoyment of Private Land

2. The plaintiff is an oculist. The floor above his consulting rooms is occupied by a dancing school. He sues the school for damages caused by noise and vibration. What result? See Whycer v. Urry, [1956] J. Plan. & Prop. L. 365 (A.C. 1955).

3. The defendant public utility constructed a spring pond as a part of its plant for the generation of electric current. The plaintiff charged that mist and vapors were precipitated upon his property, depreciating its value and causing annoyance, discomfort, and inconvenience to himself and his family during the two years immediately preceding the filing of his action. The defendant demurred on the ground that the plaintiff's action is barred by the statute of limitations. What ruling? Consumers' Light & Power Co. v. Holland, 118 Okla. 132, 247 P. 50 (1926). What are the pertinent factors in determining whether the nuisance is of a permanent or temporary character? See Kentucky-Ohio Gas Co. v. Bowling, 264 Ky. 470, 95 S.W.2d 1 (1936); cf. Harnik v. Levine, 281 App. Div. 878, 120 N.Y.S.2d 62 (1st Dept. 1953) (double parking). What is the measure of damages when the defendant has modified the activity by more careful procedures by the time the action is brought? Walling v. City of Fremont, 138 Neb. 399, 293 N.W. 226 (1940). See McCormick, Damages for Anticipated Injury to Land, 37 Harv. L. Rev. 574 (1924).

4. Suppose the plaintiff — or a predecessor in title — purchases land with full knowledge of the existence of the defendant's conflicting use of land. See Note, 41 Cal. L. Rev. 148, 148-149 (1953): "Although a few courts apparently still follow Rex v. Cross [2C. & P. 483, 172 Eng. Rep. 219 (1826)], the overwhelming majority of American and English courts have rejected the doctrine. A host of cases emphatically declare that 'coming to the nuisance' is not a defense either in an action for damages or in a suit for an injunction." See also Riblet v. Spokane-Portland Cement Co., 41 Wash. 2d 249, 248 P.2d 380 (1952). Can one acquire a prescriptive right to maintain a nuisance? See Russell Transport Ltd. v. Ontario Malleable Iron Co., [1952] Ont. 621.

■ POWELL v. TAYLOR
22 Ark. 896, 263 S.W.2d 906 (1954)

GEORGE ROSE SMITH, Justice. This is a suit brought by six residents of Gurdon to enjoin the appellees from establishing a funeral home in a residential district within the city. The defendants intend to remodel a dwelling known as the Taylor place and to use it as a combined residence and undertaking parlor. The plaintiffs, who own homes nearby, objected to the proposal and offered to reimburse the defendants for the preliminary expenses already incurred. This effort to dissuade the defendants having failed, the present suit was filed. The chancellor denied relief upon the ground that the neighborhood is not exclusively residential.

On this particular subject the law has undergone a marked change in the past fifty years. Until about the end of the nineteenth century the only limitation upon one's right to use his property as he pleased was the prohibition against inflicting upon his neighbors injury affecting the physical senses. Hence the older cases went no farther than to exclude as nuisances, in residential districts, such offensive businesses as slaughterhouses, livery stables, blasting operations, and the like.

Today this narrow view prevails, if at all, in a few jurisdictions only. It is now generally recognized that the inhabitants of a residential neighborhood may, by taking prompt action before a funeral home has been established therein, prevent its intrusion. In 1952 the Supreme Court of Louisiana reviewed the more recent decisions in twenty-two States and found that nineteen prohibit the entry of a mortuary into a residential area, while only three courts adhered to the older view. Frederick v. Brown Funeral Homes, Inc., 222 La. 57, 62 So. 2d 100. In a casenote the matter is summed up in these words: "The modern tendency to expand equity's protection of aesthetics and mental health has led the majority of jurisdictions to bar funeral homes or cemeteries from the residential sanctuaries of ordinarily sensitive people." 4 Ark. L. Rev. 483. These decisions rest not upon a finding that an undertaking parlor is physically offensive but rather upon the premise that its continuous suggestion of death and dead bodies tends to destroy the comfort and repose sought in home ownership.

. . . It is our conclusion in the case at bar that the neighborhood in question is so essentially residential in character as to entitle the appellants to the relief asked. The Taylor place is situated at the corner of Eighth and East Main Streets, and the testimony is largely directed to the area extending for two blocks in each direction, or a total of sixteen city blocks. In a relatively small city an area of this size may well be treated as a district in itself, else there might be no residential districts in the whole community. Gurdon is a city of the second class, having had a population of 2,390 in the year 1950. It is not shown to have adopted a zoning ordinance.

This square of sixteen blocks is bounded on the west by a public highway which is bordered by commercial establishments, their exact nature not being shown in detail. Otherwise the neighborhood is exclusively residential in appearance and almost so in its actual use. A seamstress living two doors east of the Taylor place earns some income by sewing at home. The couple in the house just south of the Taylor place rent rooms to elderly people and take care of them when they are ill. J. T. McAllister lives diagonally across the intersection from the Taylor place. He is in the wholesale lumber business and uses one room as an office, keeping books there and transacting business by telephone

Typical Funeral Parlor Litigations

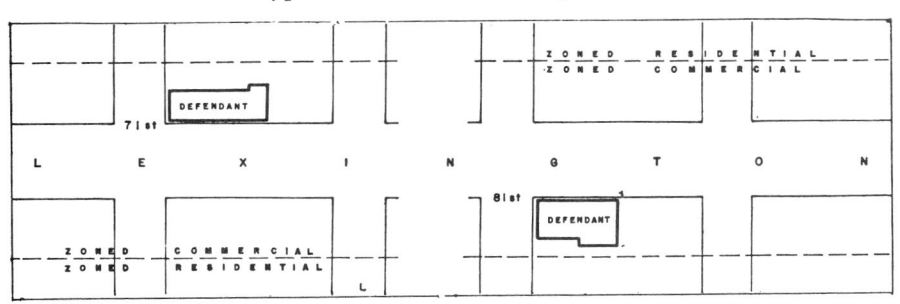

Jones v. Chapel Hill, Inc., 273 App. Div. 510, 77 N.Y.S.2d 867 (Sup. Ct. 1948)

Devereux v. Grand-Americas Junior Corp. 85 N.Y.S.2d 783 (Sup. Ct. 1949)

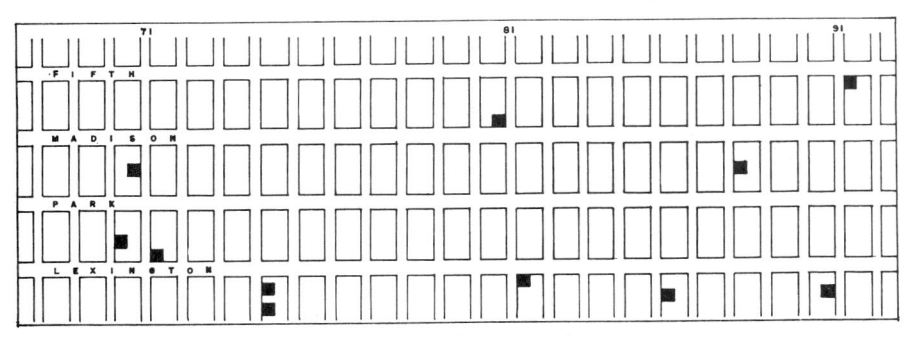

Funeral Parlor Locations in *Jones* and *Devereux* Area

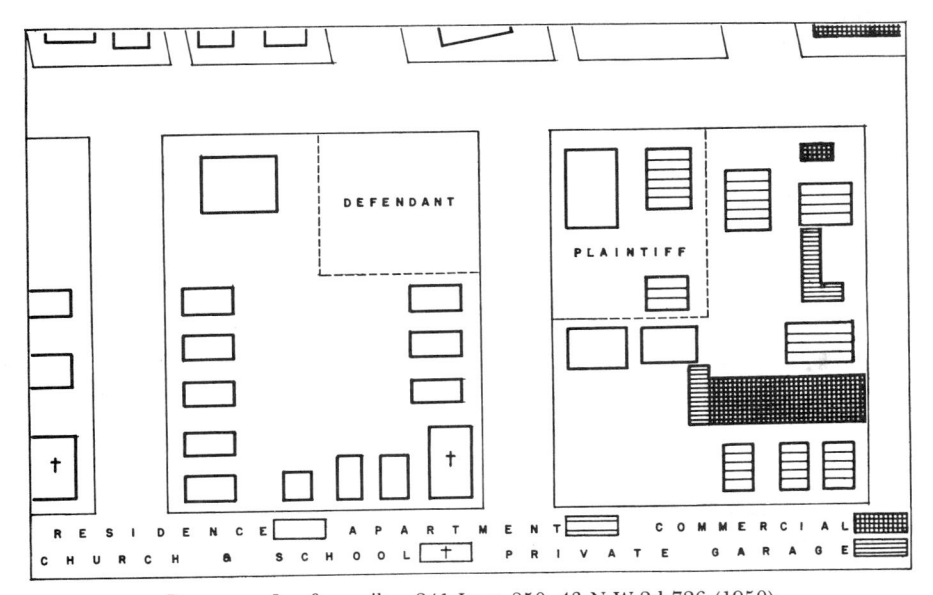

Dawson v. Laufersweiler, 241 Iowa 850, 43 N.W.2d 726 (1950)

115

and with persons who call. A photograph of this home shows that there is no sign or anything else to indicate that business is carried on there. Farther up the street an eighty-year-old dentist has a small office in his yard and occasionally treats patients. The testimony discloses no other commercial activity within the area.

On the other hand, the residential quality of the neighborhood is convincingly shown. A real estate dealer describes it as the best residential section in Gurdon. Estimates as to the value of various homes range from $15,000 to $35,000. Many inhabitants of the area confirm its residential character and earnestly protest the entry of the mortuary. One, whose wife suffered a mental illness some years ago, says that he will be forced to move away if the funeral home is established. Another testifies that he will not build a home on his vacant lots across the street from the Taylor place if it is converted to a funeral parlor. A third testifies that she lost interest in buying the house next to the Taylor place when she learned of the defendants' plans. It is true that other witnesses state that they have no objection to the proposal, and the chancellor found that property values will not be adversely affected. But we regard the residential character of the vicinity as the controlling issue, and the evidence upon that question preponderates in favor of the appellants.

Reversed.

MILLWEE, Justice (dissenting). As I read the opinion of the majority, it is now the law in Arkansas that the operation of a modest undertaking parlor in a mixed residential and business area of a city of the second class constitutes a nuisance per se and may be abated as such by injunction. This holding is so foreign to the traditional attitude of this court and the general legislative policy of this state that I must respectfully dissent. . . .

About the only businesses or operations which this court has seen fit to enjoin as nuisances per se are: a gaming house, Vandeworker v. State, 13 Ark. 700; a bawdy house, State v. Porter, 38 Ark. 637; and the standing of a stallion or jackass within the limits of a municipality, Ex parte Foote, 70 Ark. 12, 65 S.W. 706. To this select group must now be added the operation of a modest undertaking parlor, where no funerals are to be held, in an area of a city of the second class which is "essentially" but not "actually" or "exclusively" residential. . . .[10]

Notes

1. A dairy farmer seeks to enjoin the use of adjoining land as a cemetery site. The land is underlaid with cavernous limestone and the

---

10. In Wescott v. Middleton, 43 N.J. Eq. 478, 483, 11 A. 490, 493 (1887), the court stated: "It is not within the judicial scheme of things to make things pleasant or agreeable for all the citizens of the State." In general, see Note, 39 A.L.R.2d 1000 (1955). Cf. Mathewson v. Primeau, 64 Wash. 2d 929, 395 P.2d 183 (1964). — EDS.

A. The Use and Enjoyment of Private Land

topsoil is shallow; therefore, it is alleged, wells in the area will be contaminated by the bacteria from dead human bodies. "A cemetery does not constitute a nuisance merely because it is a constant reminder of death and has a depressing influence on the minds of persons who observe it, or because it tends to depreciate the value of property in the neighborhood, or is offensive to the aesthetic sense of an adjoining proprietor." McCaw v. Harrison, 259 S.W.2d 457, 458 (Ky. 1953). See Noel, Unaesthetic Sights as Nuisances, 25 Cornell L.Q.1 (1939).

2. Defendants operate a halfway house for parolees and ex-convicts in a mixed business-residential area. Plaintiffs present testimony of law enforcement officers that "criminal activity originates where criminals congregate," and evidence contradicting defendants' alleged exclusion of alcoholics and sexual offenders. The lower court holds that the halfway house constitutes a private nuisance in fact and issues an injunction. On appeal, what result? Compare Arkansas Release Guidance Foundation v. Needler, 252 Ark. 194, 477 S.W.2d 821 (1972) with Nicholson v. Connecticut Halfway House, 153 Conn. 507, 218 A.2d 383 (1966).

3. In Yeager v. Traylor, 306 Pa. 530, 535, 160 A. 108, 109 (1932), the court ruled:

> This right [to build], however, is not to be exercised without limitations, which must be under supervision of the proper court. The proposed building [a garage] . . . if erected, must be enclosed entirely and conform in architectural design to the building to which it is attached. Ramps and other devices having a tendency to disturb the peace and quiet of the neighborhood must be avoided, and all means for raising and lowering cars must be within the walls of the building. If it is proposed to supply parking space upon the roof, an effective screen must be provided by means of a suitable balustrade or other device to hide the unsightly appearance which would be the result of such practice.

Cf. Livingston v. Davis, 243 Iowa 21, 50 N.W.2d 592 (1951); see Comments, 59 W. Va. L. Rev. 92 (1956); 20 Syracuse L. Rev. 45 (1968).

An injunction sought by the chairman of the English department at Bard College to stop La Goulue Restaurant from emitting nuisances was refused. "Those weren't nuisances," the court ruled, but "the redolent odors of garlic . . . the wafted odors of sauces and stews." Man with No Nose for French Cuisine Lectured by Judge, N.Y. Times, Dec. 28, 1974. In Louisville v. Munro, 475 S.W.2d 479 (Ky. 1971), an award of damages for depreciation of residential property resulting from the establishment of a city zoo was reversed; the court found no validity in the proposition that the zoo was a nuisance per se.

4. See Krebs v. Hermann, 90 Colo. 61, 65, 6 P.2d 907, 908 (1931):

> The trial judge in his opinion said: "The barking of a dog ought not to

disturb an ordinary person. That is a common sound heard in every community. To some ears the barking of a dog, especially on the person's own premises, is a sound that is pleasing, and one which tends to make him feel secure." Counsel for the defendants in his brief in discussing this subject, refers to the eulogy of the late Senator Best of Missouri upon a dog. The Senator, however, was speaking only of one dog and not of a collection of forty or ninety dogs, all of whom were continuously howling and yelping at the same time under his window in the night time while he was unsuccessfully trying to sleep and get repose of body and mind. If the Senator had been in his home, trying to obtain sleep and the chorus of forty to ninety dogs had been continuously howling and yelping under his window, we might conjecture, although we do not attempt to state, the blistering language which he probably would have employed because of his inability to sleep.

5. In American Smelting & Refining Co. v. Godfrey, 158 F. 225, 229 (8th Cir. 1907), the court stated: "The rights of habitation are superior to the rights of trade, and whenever they conflict, the rights of trade must yield to the primary or natural right."

The court in Stevens v. Rockport Granite Co., 216 Mass. 486, 489, 104 N.E. 371, 374 (1914), said:

The neighborhood in question is of a mixed character. It is adjacent to the sea, with inlets upon a somewhat bold and rocky shore. On this account it has become increasingly attractive for summer residence. The plaintiffs and others nearby, and more at a greater distance, have estates for this purpose. Nature also has planted valuable stone quarries in the vicinity, which have been opened and worked, and are useful not only to their owners but also in centers of population where they give beauty and strength to public buildings. This circumstance renders apposite the words of James, L.J., in Salvin v. North Brancepeth, L.R. 9 Ch. App. 705, at 709: "If some picturesque haven opens its arms to invite the commerce of the world, it is not for this court to forbid the embrace, although the fruit of it should be the sights and sounds and smells of a common seaport and shipbuilding town, which would drive the Dryads and their masters from their ancient solitudes." Both these uses, commencing about the same time, have grown together in the same village. It cannot be said upon the evidence or upon the findings of the master that either has become so dominant as to impress its special character upon the community. The village is not given over exclusively to the granite industry, nor has the summer resident so overwhelmed it as to have become its distinctive feature. Therefore, each must yield something to the presence of the other. The plaintiffs cannot demand the quiet of a remote cove far distant from any industry. The defendant cannot insist upon conducting its business in disregard of those who seek some degree of rest and refreshment by the ocean side. The standard of comfort for the one is affected by the reasonable business needs of the other, and the same is true conversely.

A. The Use and Enjoyment of Private Land 119

Compare Adams v. Snouffer, 88 Ohio App. 79, 85, 87 N.E.2d 484, 488 (1949):

> The plaintiffs proceed upon the theory that their homes are in a residential section and therefore the relief sought is peculiarly applicable. It is the contention of the appellants that the section involved is not residential but open country. They point to the fact that the residences are widely separated, some are of little value; that the terrain in the vicinity of the properties involved is rough and rocky, and, in all, the presence of the quarry, because of these physical conditions, and particularly because of its distance from the homes of the plaintiffs, is not a nuisance. It is true that the district in which plaintiffs' homes are located is not closely built up but the parcels of land in which they live have been and are used exclusively for residential purposes. The section involved may be designated as the highest type of exclusive residential territory. Manifestly, it is a modern development where those who can afford it and care for that manner of living move where they may have spacious grounds upon which their homes are built and the opportunity for rustic environment where in part, at least, natural beauty is found in a somewhat wild and uncultivated state.

Cf. Ballstadt v. Pagel, 202 Wis. 484, 232 N.W. 862 (1930) (residential area bordered by business district not in transitional stage in view of lack of population growth over twenty-year period).

In Bove v. Donner-Hanna Coke Corp., 236 App. Div. 37, 41, 258 N.Y.S. 229, 233 (Sup. Ct. 1932), the court stated:

> With all the dirt, smoke and gas which necessarily come from factory chimneys, trains and boats, and with full knowledge that this region was especially adapted for industrial rather than residential purposes, and that factories would increase in the future, plaintiff selected this locality as the site of her future home. She voluntarily moved into this district, fully aware of the fact that the atmosphere would constantly be contaminated by dirt, gas and foul odors; and she could not hope to find in this locality the pure air of a strictly residential zone. She evidently saw certain advantages in living in this congested center. This is not the case of an industry, with its attendant noise and dirt, invading a quiet, residential district. It is just the opposite. Here a residence is built in an area naturally adapted for industrial purposes and already dedicated to that use. Plaintiff can hardly be heard to complain at this late date that her peace and comfort have been disturbed by a situation which existed, to some extent at least, at the very time she bought her property, and which condition she must have known would grow worse rather than better as the years went by.

See Fuchs v. Curran Carbonizing and Engineering Co., 279 S.W.2d 211 (Mo. 1955).

6. Gases from the defendant's factory spread into the rooms of the house where *H* and *W* live, subjecting them and their children to substantial discomfort. The title to the house is recorded in *W*'s name. *H* sues to recover damages for a nuisance. What result? Compare Kavanagh v. Barber, 131 N.Y. 211, 30 N.E. 235 (1892) with Towaliga Falls Power Co. v. Sims, 6 Ga. App. 749, 65 S.E. 844 (1909). *A*, claiming title to his home on what, at trial, turns out to be a forged deed, sues *B* to recover damages for the harm caused by *B*'s riveting process. What result?

7. In Giles v. Walker, 24 Q.B.D. 656, 657 (1890), in reversing a finding that the defendant had been negligent in failing to mow land on which thistles had sprung up after cultivation had ceased, the court, in a two-sentence opinion, stated: "I never heard of such an action as this. There can be no duty as between adjoining occupiers to cut the thistles, which are the natural growth of the soil." Compare the doctrine of nonliability for the spreading of surface water. 3 Tiffany, Real Property §742 (3d ed. 1939). Roots of a black Italian poplar growing on the defendant's land extended under the plaintiff's land, causing the subsidence of the plaintiff's house by undermining the foundation. The defendant's house had been built in 1904 and the plaintiff's in 1912. In 1950, the plaintiff brings an action for damages "for trespass and nuisance" and for an injunction. What result? McCombe v. Read, [1955] 2 All E.R. 458 (Q.B.). As to the rationale, see Bohlen, Studies in Torts 47 (1926). But see Goodhart, Liability for Things Naturally on the Land, 4 Camb. L.J. 13 (1930). Are there considerations with respect to city property that make this an unsatisfactory rule? See Prosser & Keeton, Torts 390-391 (5th ed. 1984). If liability is to be imposed for natural conditions, is it wiser to accomplish this result by statute or by judicial decision? Does this rule aid or hinder land from receiving its optimum use? See Noel, Nuisances from Land in Its Natural Condition, 56 Harv. L. Rev. 722 (1943).

■ BOOMER v. ATLANTIC CEMENT CO.
26 N.Y.2d 219, 257 N.E.2d 870, 309 N.Y.S.2d 312 (1970)

[Action for injunction and damages for injury to property from dirt, smoke, and vibration emanating from defendant's cement plant. The trial court determined that defendant maintained a nuisance, awarded temporary damages, but denied an injunction. The appellate division affirmed. The court of appeals affirmed the denial of a permanent injunction expressly because of the "large disparity in economic consequences of the nuisance and the injunction,"[11] but

---

11. Investment in the plant was in excess of $45 million, and it employed over 300 people; the trial court found plaintiffs had suffered permanent damages of $185,000. — EDS.

A. The Use and Enjoyment of Private Land 121

reversed and remitted the case to the trial court "to grant an injunction which shall be vacated upon payment . . . of amounts of permanent damage to respective plaintiffs."

Portions of the majority opinion, per Justice BERGAN, follow.]

A court performs its essential function when it decides the rights of parties before it. Its decision of private controversies may sometimes greatly affect public issues. Large questions of law are often resolved by the manner in which private litigation is decided. But this is normally an incident to the court's main function to settle controversy. It is a rare exercise of judicial power to use a decision in private litigation as a purposeful mechanism to achieve direct public objectives greatly beyond the rights and interests before the court.

Effective control of air pollution is a problem presently far from solution even with the full public and financial powers of government. In large measure adequate technical procedures are yet to be developed and some that appear possible may be economically impracticable.

It seems apparent that the amelioration of air pollution will depend on technical research in great depth; on a carefully balanced consideration of the economic impact of close regulation; and on the actual effect on public health. It is likely to require massive public expenditure and to demand more than any local community can accomplish and to depend on regional and interstate controls.

A court should not try to do this on its own as a by-product of private litigation and it seems manifest that the judicial establishment is neither equipped in the limited nature of any judgment it can pronounce nor prepared to lay down and implement an effective policy for the elimination of air pollution. This is an area beyond the circumference of one private lawsuit. It is a direct responsibility for government and should not thus be undertaken as an incident to solving a dispute between property owners and a single cement plant — one of many — in the Hudson River valley. . . .

If the injunction were to be granted unless within a short period — e.g., 18 months — the nuisance be abated by improved methods, there would be no assurance that any significant technical improvement would occur.

The parties could settle this private litigation at any time if defendant paid enough money and the imminent threat of closing the plant would build up the pressure on defendant. If there were no improved techniques found, there would inevitably be applications to the court at Special Term for extensions of time to perform on showing of good faith efforts to find such techniques.

Moreover, techniques to eliminate dust and other annoying by-products of cement making are unlikely to be developed by any research the defendant can undertake within any short period, but will depend on the total resources of the cement industry nationwide and throughout the world. The problem is universal wherever cement is made.

For obvious reasons the rate of the research is beyond control of defendant. . . .

JASEN, Judge (dissenting). I agree with the majority that a reversal is required here, but I do not subscribe to the newly enunciated doctrine of assessment of permanent damages, in lieu of an injunction, where substantial property rights have been impaired by the creation of a nuisance.

It has long been the rule in this State, as the majority acknowledges, that a nuisance which results in substantial continuing damage to neighbors must be enjoined. (Whalen v. Union Bag & Paper Co., 208 N.Y. 1, 101 N.E. 805; Campbell v. Seaman, 63 N.Y. 568; see, also, Kennedy v. Moog Servocontrols, 21 N.Y.2d 966, 290 N.Y.S.2d 193, 237 N.E.2d 356.) To now change the rule to permit the cement company to continue polluting the air indefinitely upon the payment of permanent damages is, in my opinion, compounding the magnitude of a very serious problem in our State and Nation today.

In recognition of this problem, the Legislature of this State has enacted the Air Pollution Control Act (Public Health Law, Consol. Laws, c. 45, §§1264 to 1299-m) declaring that it is the State policy to require the use of all available and reasonable methods to prevent and control air pollution (Public Health Law §1265).

The harmful nature and widespread occurrence of air pollution have been extensively documented. Congressional hearings have revealed that air pollution causes substantial property damage, as well as being a contributing factor to a rising incidence of lung cancer, emphysema, bronchitis and asthma.

The specific problem faced here is known as particulate contamination because of the fine dust particles emanating from defendant's cement plant. The particular type of nuisance is not new, having appeared in many cases for at least the past 60 years. (See Hulbert v. California Portland Cement Co., 161 Cal. 239, 118 P. 928 [1911].) It is interesting to note that cement production has recently been identified as a significant source of particulate contamination in the Hudson Valley. This type of pollution, wherein very small particles escape and stay in the atmosphere, has been denominated as the type of air pollution which produces the greatest hazard to human health. We have thus a nuisance which not only is damaging to the plaintiffs, but also is decidedly harmful to the general public.

I see grave dangers in overruling our long-established rule of granting an injunction where a nuisance results in substantial continuing damage. In permitting the injunction to become inoperative upon the payment of permanent damages, the majority is, in effect, licensing a continuing wrong. It is the same as saying to the cement company, you

A. The Use and Enjoyment of Private Land 123

may continue to do harm to your neighbors so long as you pay a fee for it. Furthermore, once such permanent damages are assessed and paid, the incentive to alleviate the wrong would be eliminated, thereby continuing air pollution of an area without abatement.

It is true that some courts have sanctioned the remedy here proposed by the majority in a number of cases, but none of the authorities relied upon by the majority are analogous to the situations before us. In those cases, the courts, in denying an injunction and awarding money damages, grounded their decision on a showing that the use to which the property was intended to be put was primarily for the public benefit. Here, on the other hand, it is clearly established that the cement company is creating a continuing air pollution nuisance primarily for its own private interest with no public benefit.

This kind of inverse condemnation (Ferguson v. Village of Hamburg, 272 N.Y. 234, 5 N.E.2d 801) may not be invoked by a private person or corporation for private gain or advantage. Inverse condemnation should only be permitted when the public is primarily served in the taking or impairment of property.

The promotion of the interests of the polluting cement company has, in my opinion, no public use or benefit.

Nor is it constitutionally permissible to impose servitude on land, without consent of the owner, by payment of permanent damages where the continuing impairment of the land is for a private use. This is made clear by the State Constitution (art. I, §7, subd. [a]) which provides that "[p]rivate property shall not be taken for *public use* without just compensation" (emphasis added). It is, of course, significant that the section makes no mention of taking for a *private use*. . . .

It is not my intention to cause the removal of the cement plant from the Albany area, but to recognize the urgency of the problem stemming from this stationary source of air pollution, and to allow the company a specified period of time to develop a means to alleviate this nuisance.

I am aware that the trial court found that the most modern dust control devices available have been installed in defendant's plant, but, I submit, this does not mean that *better* and more effective dust control devices could not be developed within the time allowed to abate the pollution.

Moreover, I believe it is incumbent upon the defendant to develop such devices, since the cement company, at the time the plant commenced production (1962), was well aware of the plaintiffs' presence in the area, as well as the probable consequences of its contemplated operation. Yet, it still chose to build and operate the plant at this site.

In a day when there is growing concern for clean air, highly developed industry should not expect acquiescence by the courts, but should, instead, plan its operations to eliminate contamination of our air and damage to its neighbors.

Accordingly, the orders of the Appellate Division, insofar as they denied the injunction, should be reversed, and the actions remitted to Supreme Court, Albany County to grant an injunction to take effect 18 months hence, unless the nuisance is abated by improved techniques prior to said date.

Notes

1. The paper plant involved in the *Whalen* case (decided in 1913), cited by Justice Jasen, cost $1 million and employed over 400 people; plaintiff's operation of a 255-acre farm was damaged $100 a year by water pollution. The plant involved in the *Hulbert* case had a monthly payroll of $35,000 but emitted a contaminant which coated the oranges of a small grower with a cement-like crust. What result, on appeal, when the grower obtains an injunction?

The result reached in *Boomer* bears the imprimatur of two of America's leading jurists. When defendant's stone-crushing mill, worth $1 million, damaged plaintiff's summer residence, variously valued from $10,000 to $40,000, by air pollution and blasting vibrations, Judge Hand, while stating that there was a violation of a legal right, found the situation required "a quantitative compromise between two conflicting interests" to be settled by balancing the conveniences. Smith v. Staso Milling Co., 18 F.2d 736 (2d Cir. 1927). See also the opinion of Brandeis, J., in City of Harrisonville v. W. S. Dickey Clay Manufacturing Co., 289 U.S. 334 (1933).

Should employment of the most approved and skilled methods in the construction and operation of defendant's plant, or other facts, such as the relative utility and social value of the conflicting uses, relieve defendant of damage liability as well? Compare Jost v. Dairyland Power Cooperative, 45 Wis. 2d 164, 172 N.W.2d 647 (1970); Watts v. Parma Manufacturing Co., 256 N.C. 611, 124 S.E.2d 809 (1962); and Ryan v. City of Emmetsburg, 232 Iowa 600, 4 N.W.2d 435 (1942). See Roberts, The Right to a Decent Environment; $E = MC^2$: Environment Equals Men Times Courts Redoubling Their Efforts, 55 Cornell L. Rev. 674 (1970).

2. Debate surrounding injunctive relief in nuisance actions is rooted in part in the entwined, yet distinct, histories of nuisance adjudication and equity jurisprudence. The remedy of the medieval assize of nuisance was judicial abatement, but this action had fallen into disuse by Blackstone's time. Blackstone reports that Action on the Case for Nuisance, for which damages were granted, was considered sufficient

A. The Use and Enjoyment of Private Land

to compel voluntary abatement, for a neighbor would need be "ill-natured" to continue a nuisance knowing he would be liable for further injury. 3 Blackstone, Commentaries *221. Bush v. Western, Prec. in Ch. 530 (1720) is the first reported case to enjoin a nuisance; exercise of this power remained infrequent until Lord Eldon sat on the woolsack from 1801 to 1827. Concerns over the power of the injunctive remedy resulted in two doctrines, evolved in both England and America, limiting its use. First, but not relevant since the merger of law and equity, was the doctrine that the plaintiff could appeal to the chancellor only after his "right" had been determined in a law court. See Chaffee, Cases on Equitable Relief Against Tort 55-60 (1924). Second was an attempt to limit the discretionary power of the chancellor — the doctrine that when a suitor brings his cause within the rules of equity jurisprudence the relief he asks is "demandable ex debito justitiae, and needs not be implored ex gratia." Walters v. McElroy, 151 Pa. 549, 25 A. 125, 127 (1892). Consider the differing approaches one court, the Supreme Court of Pennsylvania, has used in attempting to settle this issue:

> It seems to be supposed that, as at law, whenever a case is made out of wrongful acts on the one side and consequent injury on the other, a decree to restrain the act complained of, must as certainly follow, as a judgment would follow a verdict at common law. This is a mistake. It is elementary law, that in Equity a decree is never of right, as a judgment at law is, but of grace. Hence the chancellor will consider whether he would not do a greater injury by enjoining than would result from refusing, and leaving the party to his redress at the hands of a court and a jury. If in conscience the former should appear, he will refuse to enjoin.

Richards's Appeal, 57 Pa. 105, 113, 98 Am. Dec. 202, 205 (1868).
See Walters v. McElroy, 151 Pa. 549, 557, 25 A. 125, 127 (1892):

> The phrase "of grace," predicated of a decree in equity, had its origin in an age when kings dispensed their royal favors by the hands of their chancellors, but, although it continues to be repeated occasionally, it has no rightful place in the jurisprudence of a free commonwealth, and ought to be relegated to the age in which it was appropriate. It has been somewhere said that equity has its laws, as law has its equity. This is but another form of saying that equitable remedies are administered in accordance with rules as certain as human wisdom can devise, leaving their application only in doubtful cases to the discretion, not the unmerited favor or grace, of the chancellor.... And as to the principle invoked, that a chancellor will refuse to enjoin when greater injury will result from granting than from refusing an injunction, it is enough to observe that it has no application where the act complained of is in itself, as well as in its incidents, tortious. In such case it cannot be said that injury would result from an injunction, for no man can complain that he is injured by

being prevented from doing, to the hurt of another, that which he has no right to do.

Compare the discussion of the chancellor's discretion in Hennessey v. Carmony, 50 N.J. Eq. 616, 625, 25 A. 374, 379 (1892).

Sullivan v. Jones & Laughlin Steel Co., 208 Pa. 540, 554, 57 A. 1065, 1071 (1904), involved the operations of the Eliza Blast Furnaces, then the largest in the United States. One of the plaintiffs removed three barrels of dust weighing 1200 pounds from his porch roof, and there was testimony that the corrosive effect of the dust would rot cloth on contact. In granting an injunction, the court said:

> A chancellor does act as of grace, but that grace sometimes becomes a matter of right to the suitor in his court, and, when it is clear that the law cannot give protection and relief — to which the complainant in equity is admittedly entitled — the chancellor can no more withhold his grace than the law can deny protection and relief, if able to give them.

Four years later the plaintiff asked the court to find the defendant in contempt of the prior order. The defendant had spent $285,000 in alterations of the furnaces. See Sullivan v. Jones & Laughlin Steel Co., 222 Pa. 72, 70 A. 775 (1908). As to the interesting development of Pennsylvania law, see also Pennsylvania Coal Co. v. Sanderson, 113 Pa. 126, 6 A. 453 (1886); Berkey v. Berwind-White Coal Mining Co., 220 Pa. 65, 69 A. 329 (1908); Elliott Nursery Co. v. Du Quesne Light Co., 281 Pa. 166, 126 A. 345 (1924).

Does equity imply a peculiar system of executive justice — can the chancellor more than the judge follow his "conscience" to the disregard of other interests? Is there an additional factor owing to the uniqueness of land? Does this mean there is a "right" but no remedy; if so, is this the "white" rose of the fairy tale, which whenever gazed on appears red? Is this an example of "judicial" legislation? Does it mark the end of predictability in this type of case? For an interesting juxtaposition of this problem with facts analogous to the *Rose* case, see K.V.P. Co. v. McKie, [1949] 4 D.L.R. 497 (Ont.), and its follow-up by the Ontario legislature in enacting the KVP Company Limited Act, 1950, 14 Geo. VI. ch. 33 (Ont.).

Lord Cairns' Act, 1858, 21 & 22 Vict., ch. 27, allows courts to grant damages either in addition to or substitution for injunctive relief; it is interesting to speculate on the relationship between Lord Cairns' sponsorship of the act, and his opinion in Rylands v. Fletcher, cited in the *Rose* case, page 97 supra. As to the subsequent narrow reading of the act, see Wood v. Conway Corp., [1914] 2 Ch. 47, 83 L.J. Ch. 498.

Would the "narrow" rule in fact limit the exercise of free decision

A. The Use and Enjoyment of Private Land

by the courts? Is a rule requiring an unconditional injunction in all nuisance cases desirable? What effect does such a doctrine have on the concept of private property? How would you draft a statute incorporating the narrow rule? The "broad" rule?

Is the injunction, in the context of private nuisance, an effective way to prevent pollution? See Coase, The Problem of Social Cost, 3 J.L. & Econ. 1 (1960); Calabresi, Transaction Costs, Resource Allocation and Liability Rules — A Comment, 11 J.L. & Econ. 67 (1968); Note, 21 Stan. L. Rev. 293 (1968); Posner, Economic Analysis of Law 42-48, 56-57 (3d ed. 1986); Posner, Tort Law: Cases and Economic Analysis ch. 10 (1982). Professor Calabresi writes (at 67-68):

> [I]f we assume that the cost of factory smoke which destroys neighboring farmers' wheat can be avoided more cheaply by a smoke control device than by growing a smoke resistant wheat, then, even if the loss is left on the farmers they will, under the assumptions made, pay the factory to install the smoke control device. This would . . . result in more factories relative to farmers and lower relative farm output than if the liability rule had been reversed. But if, as a result of this liability rule, farm output is too low relative to factory output those who lose from this "misallocation" would have every reason to bribe farmers to produce more and factories to produce less. This process would continue until no bargain could improve the allocation of resources. . . . We can, therefore, state as an axiom the proposition that all externalities can be internalized and all misallocations, even those created by legal structures, can be remedied by the market, except to the extent that transactions cost money or the structure itself creates some impediments to bargaining.

What values, other than optimum resource allocation, is nuisance doctrine designed to foster? If some of them are regarded as dearer than resource allocation, can you suggest how the legal system should impede the bargaining process? For an extended analysis of internalization of external costs through tort liability, see Katz, The Function of Tort Liability in Technology Assessment, 38 U. Cin. L. Rev. 587 (1969).

Regan, The Problem of Social Cost Revisited, 15 J.L. & Econ. 427 (1972), has seriously questioned the proposition that liability rules will not affect resource allocation. The debate continues. Demsetz, What Does the Rule of Liability Matter?, 1 J. Legal Stud. 13 (1972); Cooter, The Cost of Coase, 11 J. Legal Stud. 1 (1982); Hoffman & Spitzer, The Coase Theorem: Some Experimental Tests, 25 J.L. & Econ. 73 (1982). For an intriguing discussion of common lawyers' intuitive resistance to Coase and his followers, see Gjerdingen, The Coase Theorem and the Psychology of Common-Law Thought, 56 S. Cal. L. Rev. 711 (1983).

Calabresi and Melamed, in Property Rules, Liability Rules, and Inalienability: One View of the Cathedral, 85 Harv. L. Rev. 1089, 1115-

1124 (1972), suggest four possible rules: plaintiff is entitled to enjoin the nuisance; plaintiff is entitled to damages but not to an injunction; plaintiff may neither enjoin the defendant nor collect damages; finally, plaintiff may enjoin but only if he compensates the defendant for defendant's losses flowing from the injunction.

3. Farming started in an area some fifteen miles west of Phoenix in 1911. By 1950, the only urban areas were agriculturally related communities. In 1954, the retirement community of Youngstown was begun. In 1956, Spur Industries' predecessor developed feedlots, and by 1959, there were twenty-five cattle feeding pens within a seven-mile radius.

In May 1959, Del E. Webb Development Co. began to plan the

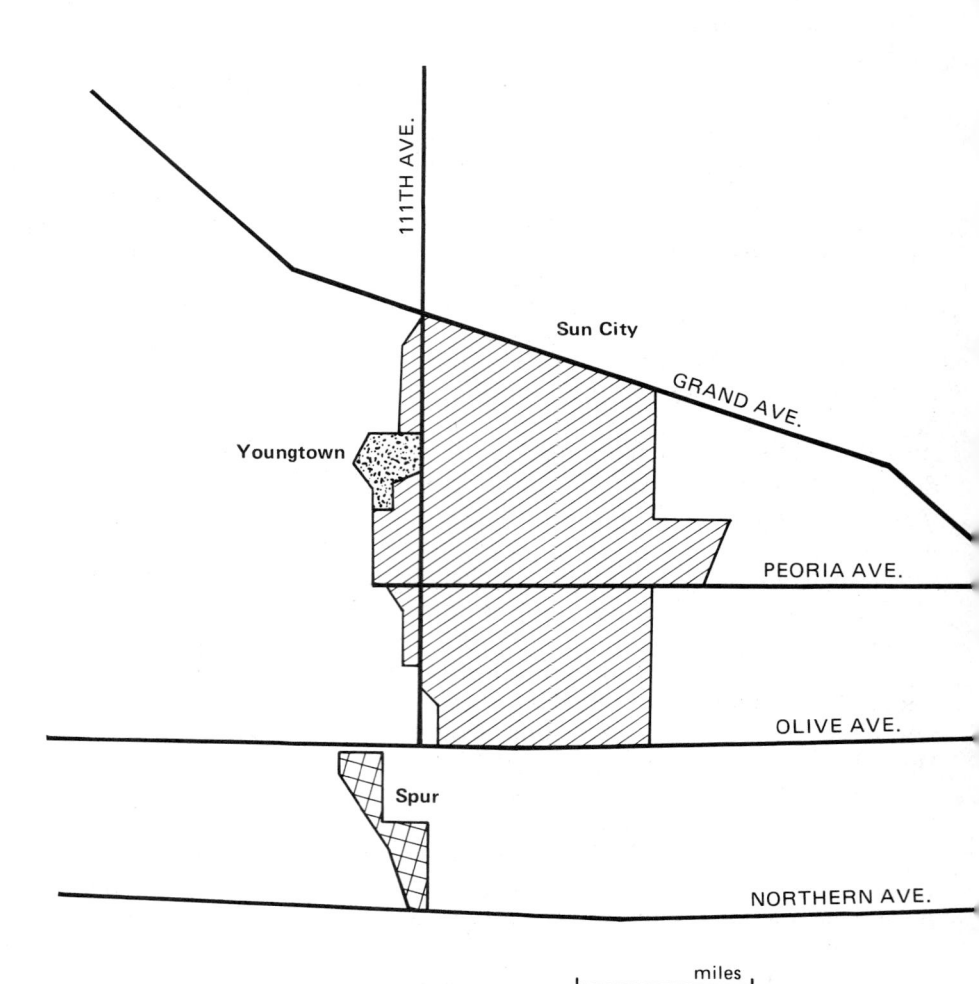

A. The Use and Enjoyment of Private Land 129

development of Sun City. For this purpose, some 20,000 acres of farmland were purchased for $15,000,000, or $750 per acre, a price considerably less than the price of land located near Phoenix. By September 1959, it started construction of a golf course south of Grand Avenue, and Spur's predecessor started to level ground for more feedlots. In 1960, Spur began a rebuilding and expansion program extending both to the north and south of the original facilities; by 1962, its expansion program was completed and occupied 114 acres.

Originally, Del Webb did not consider odors from the Spur feed pens a problem and it continued to develop in a southerly direction, until sales resistance became so great that the parcels became impossible to sell. At the time of the suit by Del Webb, Spur was feeding between 20,000 and 30,000 head of cattle; testimony indicated that cattle in a commercial feedlot will produce thirty-five to forty pounds of wet manure per day, per head, or over a million pounds per day for 30,000 head of cattle, and that despite the admittedly good feedlot management and housekeeping practices by Spur, the resulting odor and flies produced an annoying if not unhealthy situation so far as the senior citizens of southern Sun City were concerned.

For the state supreme court's creative resolution, see Spur Industries, Inc., v. Del E. Webb Development Co., 108 Ariz. 178, 494 P.2d 700 (1972):

> It is clear that as to the citizens of Sun City, the operation of Spur's feedlot was both a public and a private nuisance. They could have successfully maintained an action to abate the nuisance. Del Webb, having shown a special injury in the loss of sales, had a standing to bring suit to enjoin the nuisance. The judgment of the trial court permanently enjoining the operation of the feedlot is affirmed. . . .
>
> Having brought people to the nuisance to the foreseeable detriment of Spur, Webb must indemnify Spur for a reasonable amount of the cost of moving or shutting down. It should be noted that this relief to Spur is limited to a case wherein a developer has, with foreseeability, brought into a previously agricultural or industrial area the population which makes necessary the granting of an injunction against a lawful business and for which the business has no adequate relief.
>
> It is therefore the decision of this court that the matter be remanded to the trial court for a hearing upon the damages sustained by the defendant Spur as a reasonable and direct result of the granting of the permanent injunction.

See also Spur Feeding Co. v. Superior Court of Maricopa County, 109 Ariz. 105, 505 P.2d 1377 (1973) (*Spur Industries* holding not res judicata as to issue presented by feedlot operator in third party claim seeking indemnity against Webb for liability to property owners).

As the cases and materials that follow suggest, perhaps the new frontier for nuisance law is the accommodation of alternative forms of providing energy in the wake of fossil fuel shortages. Have the common law principles been stretched too far beyond their intended uses? Do statutes and ordinances do a better job of reflecting modern norms and expectations? Consider Chief Justice Shaw's famous observation:

> It is one of the great merits and advantages of the common law, that ... when the practice and course of business ... should cease or change, the common law consists of a few broad and comprehensive principles, founded on reason, natural justice, and enlightened public policy, modified and adapted to the circumstances of all particular cases which fall within it.

Norway Plains Co. v. Boston & Maine R.R., 67 Mass. (1 Gray) 263, 267 (1854).

■ PRAH v. MARETTI
108 Wis. 2d 223, 321 N.W.2d 182 (1982)

SHIRLEY S. ABRAHAMSON, J. . . . This case . . . involves a conflict between one landowner (Glenn Prah, the plaintiff) interested in unobstructed access to sunlight across adjoining property as a natural source of energy and an adjoining landowner (Richard D. Maretti, the defendant) interested in the development of his land. . . .

According to the complaint, the plaintiff is the owner of a residence which was constructed during the years 1978-1979. The complaint alleges that the residence has a solar system which includes collectors on the roof to supply energy for heat and hot water and that after the plaintiff built his solar-heated house, the defendant purchased the lot adjacent to and immediately to the south of the plaintiff's lot and commenced planning construction of a home. The complaint further states that when the plaintiff learned of defendant's plans to build the house he advised the defendant that if the house were built at the proposed location, defendant's house would substantially and adversely affect the integrity of plaintiff's solar system and could cause plaintiff other damage. Nevertheless, the defendant began construction. The complaint further alleges that the plaintiff is entitled to "unrestricted use of the sun and its solar power" and demands judgment for injunctive relief and damages.

. . . Plaintiff's home was the first residence built in the subdivision, and although plaintiff did not build his house in the center of the lot it was built in accordance with applicable restrictions. Plaintiff advised

A. The Use and Enjoyment of Private Land 131

defendant that if the defendant's home were built at the proposed site it would cause a shadowing effect on the solar collectors which would reduce the efficiency of the system and possibly damage the system. To avoid these adverse effects, plaintiff requested defendant to locate his home an additional several feet away from the plaintiff's lot line, the exact number being disputed. Plaintiff and defendant failed to reach an agreement on the location of defendant's home before defendant started construction. The Architectural Control Committee of the subdivision and the Planning Commission of the City of Muskego approved the defendant's plans for his home, including its location on the lot. After such approval, the defendant apparently changed the grade of the property without prior notice to the Architectural Control Committee. The problem with defendant's proposed construction, as far as the plaintiff's interests are concerned, arises from a combination of the grade and the distance of defendant's home from the defendant's lot line. . . .

The private nuisance doctrine has traditionally been employed in this state to balance the conflicting rights of landowners, and this court has recently adopted the analysis of private nuisance set forth in the Restatement (Second) of Torts. The Restatement defines private nuisance as "a nontrespassory invasion of another's interest in the private use and enjoyment of land." Restatement (Second) of Torts Sec. 821D (1977). The phrase "interest in the private use and enjoyment of land" as used in sec. 821D is broadly defined to include any disturbance of the enjoyment of property. . . .

Although the defendant's obstruction of the plaintiff's access to sunlight appears to fall within the Restatement's broad concept of a private nuisance as a nontrespassory invasion of another's interest in the private use and enjoyment of land, the defendant asserts that he has a right to develop his property in compliance with statutes, ordinances and private covenants without regard to the effect of such development upon the plaintiff's access to sunlight. In essence, the defendant is asking this court to hold that the private nuisance doctrine is not applicable in the instant case and that his right to develop his land is a right which is per se superior to his neighbor's interest in access to sunlight. This position is expressed in the maxim "cujus est solum, ejus est usque ad coelum et ad infernos," that is, the owner of land owns up to the sky and down to the center of the earth. The rights of the surface owner are, however, not unlimited. U.S. v. Causby, 328 U.S. 256, 260-1 (1946).

The defendant is not completely correct in asserting that the common law did not protect a landowner's access to sunlight across adjoining property. At English common law a landowner could acquire a right to receive sunlight across adjoining land by both express agreement and under the judge-made doctrine of "ancient lights."

Under the doctrine of ancient lights if the landowner had received sunlight across adjoining property for a specified period of time, the landowner was entitled to continue to receive unobstructed access to sunlight across the adjoining property. Under the doctrine the landowner acquired a negative prescriptive easement and could prevent the adjoining landowner from obstructing access to light.

Although American courts have not been as receptive to protecting a landowner's access to sunlight as the English courts, American courts have afforded some protection to a landowner's interest in access to sunlight. American courts honor express easements to sunlight. American courts initially enforced the English common law doctrine of ancient lights, but later every state which considered the doctrine repudiated it as inconsistent with the needs of a developing country. Indeed, for just that reason this court concluded that an easement to light and air over adjacent property could not be created or acquired by prescription and has been unwilling to recognize such an easement by implication.

Many jurisdictions in this country have protected a landowner from malicious obstruction of access to light (the spite fence cases) under the common law private nuisance doctrine. If an activity is motivated by malice it lacks utility and the harm it causes others outweighs any social values. . . . This court's reluctance in the nineteenth and early part of the twentieth century to provide broader protection for a landowner's access to sunlight was premised on three policy considerations. First, the right of landowners to use their property as they wished, as long as they did not cause physical damage to a neighbor, was jealously guarded.

Second, sunlight was valued only for aesthetic enjoyment or as illumination. Since artificial light could be used for illumination, loss of sunlight was at most a personal annoyance which was given little, if any, weight by society.

Third, society had a significant interest in not restricting or impeding land development. . . .

. . . These three policies are no longer fully accepted or applicable. They reflect factual circumstances and social priorities that are now obsolete.

First, society has increasingly regulated the use of land by the landowner for the general welfare. Euclid v. Ambler Realty Co., 272 U.S. 365 (1926); Just v. Marinette, 56 Wis. 2d 7, 201 N.W.2d 761 (1972).

Second, access to sunlight has taken on a new significance in recent years. In this case the plaintiff seeks to protect access to sunlight, not for aesthetic reasons or as a source of illumination but as a source of energy. Access to sunlight as an energy source is of significance both

A. The Use and Enjoyment of Private Land 133

to the landowner who invests in solar collectors and to a society which has an interest in developing alternative sources of energy.

Third, the policy of favoring unhindered private development in an expanding economy is no longer in harmony with the realities of our society. State v. Deetz, 66 Wis. 2d 1, 224 N.W.2d 407 (1974). The need for easy and rapid development is not as great today as it once was, while our perception of the value of sunlight as a source of energy has increased significantly.

Courts should not implement obsolete policies that have lost their vigor over the course of the years. The law of private nuisance is better suited to resolve landowners' disputes about property development in the 1980's than is a rigid rule which does not recognize a landowner's interest in access to sunlight. . . .

Private nuisance law, the law traditionally used to adjudicate conflicts between private landowners, has the flexibility to protect both the landowner's right of access to sunlight and another landowner's right to develop land. Private nuisance law is better suited to regulate access to sunlight in modern society and is more in harmony with legislative policy and the prior decisions of this court than is an inflexible doctrine of non-recognition of any interest in access to sunlight across adjoining land.

We therefore hold that private nuisance law, that is, the reasonable use doctrine as set forth in the Restatement, is applicable to the instant case. Recognition of a nuisance claim for unreasonable obstruction of access to sunlight will not prevent land development or unduly hinder the use of adjoining land. It will promote the reasonable use and enjoyment of land in a manner suitable to the 1980's. That obstruction of access to light might be found to constitute a nuisance in certain circumstances does not mean that it will be or must be found to constitute a nuisance under all circumstances. The result in each case depends on whether the conduct complained of is unreasonable.

Accordingly we hold that the plaintiff in this case has stated a claim under which relief can be granted. Nonetheless we do not determine whether the plaintiff in this case is entitled to relief. In order to be entitled to relief the plaintiff must prove the elements required to establish actionable nuisance, and the conduct of the defendant herein must be judged by the reasonable use doctrine. . . .

For the reasons set forth, we reverse the judgment of the circuit court dismissing the complaint and remand the matter to circuit court for further proceedings not inconsistent with this opinion. . . .

WILLIAM G. CALLOW, J. (dissenting). . . .

. . . I firmly believe that a landowner's right to use his property within the limits of ordinances, statutes, and restrictions of record where such use is necessary to serve his legitimate needs is a fundamental precept of a free society which this court should strive to uphold. . . .

Regarding the third policy the majority apparently believes is obsolete (that society has a significant interest in not restricting land development) . . . I concede the law may be tending to recognize the value of aesthetics over increased volume development and that an individual may not use his land in such a way as to harm the *public*. The instant case, however, deals with a *private* benefit. . . . I find it significant that community planners are dealing with this country's continued population growth and building revitalization where "[t]he number of households is expected to reach almost 100 million by the end of the decade; that would be 34 percent higher than the number in 1970." F. Strom, 1981 Zoning and Planning Law Handbook, sec. 22.02[3], 396 (1981). It is clear that community planners are acutely aware of the present housing shortages, particularly among those two groups with limited financial resources, the young and the elderly. Id. While the majority's policy arguments may be directed to a cause of action for public nuisance, we are presented with a private nuisance case which I believe is distinguishable in this regard. . . .

I conclude that plaintiff's solar heating system is an unusually sensitive use. In other words, the defendant's proposed construction of his home, under ordinary circumstances, would not interfere with the use and enjoyment of the usual person's property. "The plaintiff cannot, by devoting his own land to an unusually sensitive use, such as a drive-in motion picture theater easily affected by light, make a nuisance out of conduct of the adjoining defendant which would otherwise be harmless." Id. at 579 (footnote omitted). . . .

I believe the facts of the instant controversy present the classic case of the owner of a solar collector who fails to take any action to protect his investment. There is nothing in the record to indicate that Mr. Prah disclosed his situation to Mr. Maretti prior to Maretti's purchase of the lot or attempted to secure protection for his solar collector prior to Maretti's submission of his building plans to the architectural committee. Such inaction should be considered a significant factor in determining whether a cause of action exists.

The majority's failure to recognize the need for notice may perpetuate a vicious cycle. Maretti may feel compelled to sell his lot because of Prah's solar collector's interference with his plans to build his family home. If so, Maretti will not be obliged to inform prospective purchasers of the problem. Certainly, such information will reduce the value of his land. If the presence of collectors is sufficient notice, it cannot be said that the seller of the lot has a duty to disclose information peculiarly within his knowledge. I do not believe that an adjacent lot owner should be obliged to experience the substantial economic loss resulting from the lot being rendered unbuildable by the contour of the land as it relates to the location and design of the adjoining home using solar collectors.[12]

■ CALIFORNIA SOLAR SHADE CONTROL ACT
Cal. Pub. Res. Code (West 1986)

§25980

This chapter shall be known and may be cited as the Solar Shade Control Act. It is the policy of the state to promote all feasible means of energy conservation and all feasible uses of alternative energy supply sources. In particular, the state encourages the planting and maintenance of trees and shrubs to create shading, moderate outdoor temperatures, and provide various economic and aesthetic benefits. However, there are certain situations in which the need for widespread use of alternative energy devices, such as solar collectors, requires specific and limited controls on trees and shrubs.

§25982

After January 1, 1979, no person owning, or in control of a property shall allow a tree or shrub to be placed, or, if placed, to grow on such property, subsequent to the installation of a solar collector on the property of another so as to cast a shadow greater than 10 percent of the collector absorption area upon that solar collector surface on the property of another at any one time between the hours of 10 a.m. and 2 p.m., local standard time; provided, that this section shall not apply to specific trees and shrubs which at the time of installation of a solar collector or during the remainder of that annual solar cycle cast a shadow upon that solar collector. For the purposes of this chapter, the location of a solar collector is required to comply with the local building and setback regulations, and to be set back not less than five feet from the property line, and no less than 10 feet above the ground. A collector

---

12. The Supreme Court of New Hampshire, in Tenn v. 889 Associates, 500 A.2d 366 (N.H. 1985), cited *Prah* with approval and stated that "there is no reason in principle why the law of nuisance should not be applied to claims for the protection of a property owner's interests in light and air." Id. at 370. Still, the court upheld the superior court's dismissal of plaintiff's bill in equity, for she failed to demonstrate that the defendant company's planned six-story building would unreasonably interfere with the use and enjoyment of property by blocking the windows and the walls of the light shaft in plaintiff's neighboring structure. — EDS.

may be less than 10 feet in height, only if in addition to the five feet setback, the collector is set back three times the amount lowered.[13]

Notes

1. In Rose v. Chaikin, 187 N.J. Super. 210, 453 A.2d 1378 (Super. Ct. Ch. Div. 1982), neighbors sought to enjoin the operation of a windmill (atop a sixty-foot tower) on residential property:

> [D]efendants' windmill constitutes an actionable nuisance. As indicated, the noise produced is offensive because of its character, volume and duration. It is a sound which is not only distinctive, but one which is louder than others and is more or less constant. Its intrusive quality is heightened because of the locality. The neighborhood is quiet and residential. It is well separated, not only from commercial sounds, but from the heavier residential traffic as well. Plaintiffs specifically chose the area because of these qualities and the proximity to the ocean. Sounds which are natural to this area — the sea, the shore birds, the ocean breeze — are soothing and welcome. The noise of the windmill, which would be unwelcome in most neighborhoods, is particularly alien here. . . .
>
> When consideration is given to the social utility of the windmill and the availability of reasonable alternatives, the conclusion supporting an injunction is the same. Defendants' purpose in installing the windmill was to conserve energy and save on electric bills. Speaking to the latter goal first, clearly the court can take judicial notice that alternative devices are available which are significantly less intrusive. As to its social utility, a more careful analysis is required. Defendants argue that the windmill furthers the national need to conserve energy by the use of an alternate renewable source of power. See, generally, Wind Energy Systems Act of 1980, 42 U.S.C.A., §§9201-13, and Public Utility Regulatory Policies Act of 1978, 16 U.S.C.A., §824a-3. The social utility of alternate energy sources cannot be denied; nor should the court ignore the proposition that scientific and social progress sometimes reasonably require a reduction in personal comfort. On the other hand, the fact that a device represents a scientific advance and has social utility does not mean that it is permissible at any cost. Such factors must be weighed against the quantum of harm the device brings to others.
>
> In this case the activity in question substantially interferes with the health and comfort of plaintiffs. In addition to the negative effect on their health, their ability to enjoy the sanctity of their homes has been significantly reduced. The ability to look to one's home as a refuge from the noise and stress associated with the outside world is a right to be jealously guarded. Before that right can be eroded in the name of social progress, the benefit to society must be clear and the intrusion must be

---

13. See Sher v. Herbert, 181 Cal. App. 3d 867, 226 Cal. Rptr. 698 (Cal. Ct. App. 1986) (Act not intended to apply to "exclusively passive" solar homes). — EDS.

A. The Use and Enjoyment of Private Land

warranted under all of the circumstances. Here, the benefits are relatively small and the irritation is substantial.

2. Sometimes the complaint about a neighbor's intrusive use of state-of-the-art technology asserts a violation of covenants entered into by the defendant or a predecessor in interest. See, for example, DeNina v. Bammel Forest Civic Club, Inc., 712 S.W.2d 195 (Tex. Ct. App. 1986), in which the court affirmed "a temporary injunction enjoining [the DeNinas] from maintaining their thirteen-foot diameter satellite disc at their home in the Brammel Forest subdivision." The failure to secure "prior architectural approval" for installing the "disc" "constitute[d] substantial violations of the deed restrictions," notwithstanding the plaintiffs' failure to demonstrate "actual damages or irreparable injury. But cf. 47 C.F.R. §25.104 (1986):

> State and local zoning or other regulations that differentiate between satellite receive-only antennas and other types of antenna facilities are preempted unless such regulations:
> (a) Have a reasonable and clearly defined health, safety or aesthetic objective; and
> (b) Do not operate to impose unreasonable limitations on, or prevent, reception of satellite delivered signals by receive-only antennas or to impose costs on the users of such antennas that are excessive in light of the purchase and installation cost of the equipment.
>
> Regulation of satellite transmitting antennas is preempted in the same manner except that state and local health and safety regulation is not preempted.

■ ELLICKSON, ALTERNATIVES TO ZONING: COVENANTS, NUISANCE RULES, AND FINES AS LAND USE CONTROLS
40 U. Chi. L. Rev. 681, 748, 761-764, 772 (1973)

The prima facie nuisance case can . . . be summarized as follows:

A landowner who intentionally carries out activities, or permits natural conditions to develop, that are perceived as unneighborly under contemporary community standards shall be liable for all damages (measured by the diminution in the market value of plaintiff's land plus bonuses for diminutions in widely held subjective values) to all parties who are thereby substantially injured, and continuation of the activity may be enjoined by any party willing to compensate the landowner for any losses he suffers from that injunction. . . .

... This article proposes that private nuisance remedies become the exclusive remedy for "localized" spillovers — that is, those that concern no more than several dozen parties. Private nuisance remedies, however, are not the optimal internalization system for all types of harmful spillovers from land use activity; in particular private remedies are likely to be an inefficient means of handling insubstantial injuries from "pervasive" nuisances that affect many outsiders. More centralized systems for internalizing pervasive harms may be capable of achieving savings in administrative costs that outweigh the inevitable allocative inefficiencies of collective regulation. This article will suggest that fines be assessed by a public authority to internalize insubstantial injuries from those pervasive nuisances that present a reasonably objective index of noxiousness. These fines would complement the nuisance remedies that would remain available to persons able to show substantial injury from the pervasive problem. Lack of an objective index of noxiousness may justify imposition of mandatory standards on pervasive nuisance activity, but such an approach is usually justified only when the public authority is willing to impose standards retroactively. To develop and administer these systems, this article proposes creation of a specialized metropolitan body....

1. *Nuisance Boards.* The following administrative structure would be a good start. First, the state would enact the nuisance rules suggested above. The state would then establish metropolitan Nuisance Boards and grant them primary jurisdiction over nuisance cases and exclusive rule making power over land use problems in their metropolitan area. Each Nuisance Board would then use this power principally (a) to publish regulations stating with considerable specificity which land use activities are considered unneighborly by that metropolitan population at that time, (b) to identify hypersensitive uses with similar specificity, (c) to establish threshold levels of "substantial harm," and (d) to promulgate schedules of bonus payments for losses of common non-fungible consumer surplus. By thus clarifying entitlements, the Board would assist the private settlement of disputes and thus lower administrative costs....

The proposed Nuisance Boards would not be wholly immune from the evils of ineptness, corruption, and discrimination often characteristic of zoning administration. The nuisance approach, however, does correct the three major flaws of zoning.... In Professor Calabresi's terminology, private nuisance actions for damages are a system of general deterrence and avoid the high prevention costs of specific deterrence systems like zoning. Second, largely because the standards of conduct are not mandatory, nuisance law can be more efficiently applied to preexisting land uses than any system of mandatory regulation. In addition, the suggested nuisance approach is a system of uniform regulation that avoids variation of standards from zone to

B. An Annoyance to All the King's Subjects

zone, thus eliminating a primary source of the discrimination and corruption typically found in zoning systems. Although Nuisance Boards will probably not be models of honest government, nuisance cases, unlike zoning changes, present readily reviewable legal issues and thus are more amenable to effective judicial scrutiny. . . .

. . . [I]n many instances fines should be tried in the place of mandatory standards and prohibitions as a means of regulating pervasive nuisances.

1. *Uniform Standards Enforced Solely through Fines.* Welfare economists have historically favored fines as solutions to problems of external cost. Unlike mandatory standards and prohibitions, fines can be applied retrospectively to existing nuisances without imposing the drastic prevention costs that deter many zoning administrators from eliminating nonconforming uses. Fines are also more flexible than mandatory regulations since a landowner is free to buy, in effect, the right to violate an inefficient standard. A system of fines requires establishment of standards for imposition of the fines, rules for calculating their amounts and an administrative structure for assessment and collection. . . .

Do we sacrifice Justice Shaw's beloved "reason, natural justice, and enlightened public policy" if we move to such a scheme? Note that Professor Ellickson's recipe for relief from centralized regulation has a definite Coasean flavor. For Ellickson's recent reconsideration of transaction costs and rules of liability, see Ellickson, Of Coase and Cattle: Dispute Resolution Among Neighbors in Shasta County, 38 Stan. L. Rev. 623 (1986).

Is private nuisance a blunderbuss, or can it be made into a more precise tool? Or is there some advantage to the ambiguity Prosser noted, in that judges can massage the facts and craft remedies to resolve property disputes more equitably? In considering the role of private nuisance in the continuing battle against ecological decay, keep in mind the alternative of public nuisance as well as the role of nonnuisance techniques such as positive or negative inducements specially tailored by the legislature.

B. AN ANNOYANCE TO ALL THE KING'S SUBJECTS

■ REX v. WHITE AND WARD
1 Burr. Rep. 333, 97 Eng. Rep. 338 (K.B. 1757)

The defendants had been convicted of a nuisance in erecting and continuing their works at Twickenham, for making acid spirit of sulphur, oil of vitriol, and oil of aqua fortis. The indictment runs thus, viz. that

> at the parish of Twickenham, &c. near the King's common highway there, and near the dwelling-houses of several of the inhabitants, the defendants erected twenty buildings for making noisome, stinking and offensive liquors; and then and there made fires of sea-coal and other things, which sent forth abundance of noisome, offensive and stinking smoke, and made, &c. great quantities of noisome, offensive, stinking liquors, called, &c.; whereby and by reason of which noisome, offensive and stinking, &c. the air was impregnated with noisome and offensive stinks and smells; to the common nuisance of all the King's liege subjects inhabiting, &c. and travelling and passing the said King's common highway; and against the peace, &c. . . .

. . . Mr. Just. DENISON reported the evidence; which was of great length he said, there being about seventy-five witnesses on each side: however, he collected the substance of it together in his report. It appeared to be very strong on the part of the prosecution: and he declared himself satisfied with the verdict. And it appeared upon his report, that the smell was not only intolerably offensive, but also noxious and hurtful, and made many persons sick, and gave them head-achs. . . .

Lord MANSFIELD thought there was nothing in the objections: which, he said, are reducible to three heads; viz.

1st. That there is no sufficient charge of the hurtfulness;

2dly. That it is not precisely charged, "to whom" the hurt is done;

3dly. That it only laid generally, "in the parish of Twickenham."

First — The jury have found "that it is to the common nuisance of the King's subjects dwelling, &c. and travelling, &c."

And the word "noxious" not only means "hurtful and offensive to the smell;" but it is also the translation of the very technical term "nocivus;" and has been always used for it, ever since the Act, for the proceedings being in English.

But it is not necessary that the smell should be unwholesome: it is enough, if it renders the enjoyment of life and property uncomfortable.

Secondly — The persons incommoded are sufficiently described: and the offence is charged to be to the common nuisance of persons inhabiting and travelling near, &c. And unless they had been so near as to be hurt by it, the indictment could not have been proved. Whereas in the case of Wilkes and Broadbent, it was quite uncertain how near the rubbish might be laid.

Thirdly — It is sufficiently laid, and in the accustomed manner. The very existence of the nuisance depends upon the number of houses and concourse of people: and this is a matter of fact, to be judged of by the jury. And in the very cases in Tremaine 195, of a glasshouse,

B. An Annoyance to All the King's Subjects 141

and 298, of a soap-boiler's furnace, — they are laid in parishes "apud paroch' &c." Therefore there is no foundation for the objections. . . .

On Thursday 5th May 1757, on a motion for the judgment (or rather sentence) of the Court upon the defendants, for the offence whereof they stood convicted, — it appearing that the nuisance was absolutely removed; (the works being demolished, and the materials, utensils and instruments, all sold and parted with;) they were, upon entering (each for himself only, and for such as acted for or under him) into a rule "not to renew them," only fined 6s. 8d. each. But on a dispute afterwards arising, how the rule should be drawn up, it was on Friday 20th May settled by the Court to be thus —

> By consent of counsel on both sides, it is ordered that, upon the defendant Ward's undertaking that neither he nor any other person by his consent or direction or for his use or benefit, shall for the future make or cause to be made in the works lately carried on by the defendant White at Twickenham, mentioned in the indictment in this cause, any acid spirit of sulphur, or preparations of vitriol, or oil of aqua fortis; a fine of 6s. 8d. be set upon the said defendant Ward, for the nuisance of which he has been convicted.

And
  The defendant White entered into a like rule, mutatis mutandis.

Notes

1. Lawton v. Steele, 152 U.S. 133 (1894), is the classic case. It involved the constitutionality of two New York statutes which provided that

> [a]ny net, pound, or other means or device for taking or capturing fish, or whereby they may be taken or captured, set, put, floated, had, found, or maintained, in or upon any of the waters of this State, or upon the shores of or islands in any of the waters of this State, in violation of any existing or hereafter enacted statutes or laws for the protection of fish, is hereby declared to be, and is, a public nuisance, and may be abated and summarily destroyed by any person, and it shall be the duty of each and every protector aforesaid and of every game constable to seize and remove and forthwith destroy the same . . . and no action for damages shall lie or be maintained against any person for or on account of any such seizure or destruction.

In upholding the law, the court said:

> The extent and limits of what is known as the police power have been a

fruitful subject of discussion in the appellate courts of nearly every State in the Union. It is universally conceded to include everything essential to the public safety, health, and morals, and to justify the destruction or abatement, by summary proceedings, of whatever may be regarded as a public nuisance. Under this power it has been held that the State may order the destruction of a house falling to decay or otherwise endangering the lives of passers-by; the demolition of such as are in the path of a conflagration; the slaughter of diseased cattle; the destruction of decayed or unwholesome food; the prohibition of wooden buildings in cities; the regulation of railways and other means of public conveyance, and of interments in burial grounds; the restriction of objectionable trades to certain localities; the compulsory vaccination of children; the confinement of the insane or those afflicted with contagious diseases; the restraint of vagrants, beggars, and habitual drunkards; the suppression of obscene publications and houses of ill fame; and the prohibition of gambling houses and places where intoxicating liquors are sold. Beyond this, however, the State may interfere wherever the public interests demand it, and in this particular a large discretion is necessarily vested in the legislature to determine, not only what the interests of the public require, but what measures are necessary for the protection of such interests. . . . To justify the state in thus interposing its authority in behalf of the public, it must appear, first, that the interests of the public generally, as distinguished from those of a particular class, require such interference; and, second, that the means are reasonably necessary for the accomplishment of the purpose, and not unduly oppressive upon individuals. . . .

It is evident that the efficacy of this statute would be very seriously impaired by requiring every net illegally used to be carefully taken from the water, carried before a court or magistrate, notice of the seizure to be given by publication, and regular judicial proceedings to be instituted for its condemnation.

Four years later, the New York court invalidated a statute authorizing the seizure and sale of boats used in disturbing oyster beds. Colon v. Lisk, 153 N.Y. 188, 47 N.E. 302 (1897). See C. J. Hendry Co. v. Moore, 318 U.S. 133 (1943).

2. The early utilization of public nuisance power can be seen in Acts and Resolves of the Province of Massachusetts Bay (Province Laws, 1692-1693), ch. 23:

An Act for Prevention of Common Nusances [sic] Arising By Slaughter-Houses, Still-Houses, &c., Tallow Chandlers, and Curriers . . .

Sec. 1. That the selectmen of the towns of Boston, Salem and Charlestown [sic] respectively, or other market towns in the province, with two or more justices of the peace dwelling in the town, or two of the next justices in the county, shall at or before the last day of March, one thousand six hundred ninety-three, assign some certain places in each of said towns (where it may be least offensive) for the erecting or setting up of slaughter-houses for the killing of all meat, still-houses, and houses for

B. An Annoyance to All the King's Subjects 143

trying of tallow and currying of leather (which houses may be erected of timber, the law referring to building with brick or stone notwithstanding), and shall cause an entry to be made in the townbook of what places shall be by them so assigned, and make known the same by posting it up in some publick places of the town; at which houses and places respectively, and no other, all butchers and slaughtermen, distillers, chandlers and curriers shall exercise and practice their respective trades and mysteries; on pain that any butcher or slaughterman transgressing of this act by killing of meat in any other place, for every conviction thereof before one or more justices of the peace, shall forfeit and pay the sum of twenty shillings; and any distiller, chandler or currier offending against this act, for every conviction thereof before their majesties' justices at the general sessions of the peace for the county, shall forfeit and pay the sum of five pounds; one-third part of said forfeitures to be the use of their majesties for the support of the government of the province and the incident charges thereof, one-third to the poor of the town where such offence shall be committed, and the other third to him or them that shall inform and sue for the same.

3. When the defendants in Town of Preble v. Song Mountain, Inc., 62 Misc. 2d 353, 308 N.Y.S.2d 1001 (Sup. Ct. 1970), proposed an "open-air concert" featuring a "name band" and "five or six lesser name bands," the Town objected, invoking the public safety horrors of the Woodstock Festival held the summer before. While the court noted "numerous dissimilarities" between the two events, it concluded:

In balancing the equities there must be considered the rights and the interests of the defendants in conducting the proposed event, on the one hand, and, on the other hand, the serious consequences of permitting the defendants to conduct the proposed event in the particular surroundings and location they have chosen; the inconvenience and danger imposed upon the community by having important roads and highways blocked with crowds of people; the potential drain upon hospital personnel and facilities; the potential drain upon medical personnel and upon sheriffs' personnel, of men needed throughout the counties for the performance of their regular duties. The potential for harm to the community, the public, far outweighs any good which might be derived from such an event.[14]

4. Can "public nuisance" be brought within any of the definitions considered supra at pages 103-104? If so, for what purposes?

5. "The court found special damages because the smoke, soot, etc.

---

14. The case does not seem to have been appealed; appeals would surely have failed in view of N.Y. Public Health Law §225(4)(o) (McKinney 1971) (authorizing regulations necessary for the security of life and health of mass gatherings). Cf. County of Sullivan v. Filippo, 64 Misc. 2d 533, 315 N.Y.S.2d 519 (Sup. Ct. 1970); Bauman v. County of Schuyler, 84 Misc. 2d 775, 374 N.Y.S.2d 903 (1975) (county and town defendants not liable for allowing rock concert that allegedly constituted public nuisance). — EDS.

thrown upon plaintiffs' property were in excess of that thrown upon other property in the vicinity of plaintiffs' home and premises. That excess was due to two elements present in the situation: first, the proximity of plaintiffs' house to the railroad tracks; and, second, the use of the track nearest the house, that is, the scale track, by the defendant as a convenient place to spot its engines for necessary purposes, when, as claimed by plaintiffs and found by the court, they might have been spotted elsewhere." On appeal, what result? Thompson v. Kimball, 165 F.2d 677, 681 (8th Cir. 1948). See Commonwealth ex rel. Shumaker v. New York & Pennsylvania Corp., 65 Dauph. 118 (Pa. C.P. 1953). On the rule of "special damage" to support the private action, compare Smith, Private Action for Obstruction to Public Right of Passage, 15 Colum. L. Rev. 1, 149 (1915), with Beuscher, Roadside Protection Through Nuisance and Property Law, Highway Research Bd. Bull. No. 113, at 66 (1956).

Compare Soap Corp. of America v. Reynolds, 178 F.2d 503, 506 (5th Cir. 1949). The City of Wichita Falls was denied an injunction against the defendant as a public nuisance. Thereafter the defendant proceeded with the construction of his soap factory. Homeowners in the vicinity now seek an injunction restraining the defendant from operating it as a nuisance. What result?

6. The trial judge addressed Mrs. Nation and the other defendants:

> I want to say to you people who appear charged with having aided and abetted her that this is a court of law, and not one of sentiment. Having broken the law, you have no more rights in this court than the jointist. Your contempt of the law is as great as his. Mrs. Nation and her followers made an attack Sunday upon a perfectly legitimate business in which $100,000 is invested. They have repeatedly broken the law and destroyed property and gone unhindered and unpunished. The time has come in this community when people are demanding that something be done. I want to say to you that this unwarranted destruction of property must stop. Have people no rights that a crazy woman and her deluded followers are bound to respect? There is not a lawyer in this room who will not tell you that you have no right under the law to do these things.... You have no right to attempt to abate a nuisance except through the regular channels. Reputable men in this community have given sanction to a movement that has led to riot and may lead to bloodshed. I want to say to you people who have been placed under bond that if you go out on any more raids your bondsmen will be compelled to forfeit the amount to the last penny. I want to make this proposition clear to you. Property must and will be defended.

Offer of proof that the prosecuting witness was the keeper of a place where intoxicating liquors were sold in violation of law was rejected, and the testimony excluded. By Kansas statute all places where intoxi-

B. An Annoyance to All the King's Subjects 145

cating liquors are sold are declared to be common nuisances. On appeal, what result? State v. Stark, 63 Kan. 529, 530, 66 P. 243 (1901).

7. Section 330.313 of the Jacksonville City Ordinances read,

> It shall be unlawful and it is hereby declared a public nuisance for any ticket seller, ticket taker, usher, motion picture projection machine operator, manager, owner, or any other person, connected with or employed by any drive-in theater in the City to exhibit, aid or assist in exhibiting, any motion picture, slide, or other exhibit in which a human male or female bare buttocks, human female bare breasts, or human bare pubic areas are shown, if such motion picture, slide, or other exhibit is visible from any public street or public place.

The manager of the University Drive-In Theatre was charged with violating the ordinance, because of his showing of the R-rated movie "Class of '74," featuring female buttocks and bare breasts. On appeal, Justice Powell, for six members of the Court, found that the statute was facially invalid:

> A State or municipality may protect individual privacy by enacting reasonable time, place, and manner regulations applicable to all speech irrespective of content. But when the government, acting as censor, undertakes selectively to shield the public from some kinds of speech on the ground that they are more offensive than others, the First Amendment strictly limits its power.

Erznoznik v. City of Jacksonville, 422 U.S. 205, 209 (1975). The majority rejected the city's proffered reasons for the ordinance — to protect children (overbroad) and to regulate traffic (underinclusive) — and concluded that "the deterrent effect of this ordinance is both real and substantial." Id. at 217.

Chief Justice Burger, joined by Justice Rehnquist, dissented, noting that the public nuisance law, "although no model of draftsmanship, is narrowly drawn to regulate only certain unique public exhibitions of nudity; it would be absurd to suggest that it operates to suppress expression of *ideas*." Id. at 205 (Burger, C.J., dissenting). Justice White also dissented.

Eleven years later, in one of the final opinions penned by Chief Justice Burger, the Court upheld against a first amendment challenge the use of a state nuisance statute to close an adult bookstore in which prostitution and other illicit sexual activity were occurring. Arcara v. Cloud Books, Inc., 478 U.S. 697 (1986). Section 2320 of the New York Public Health Law reads, "1. Whoever shall erect, establish, continue, maintain, use, own, or lease any building, erection, or place used for the purpose of lewdness, assignation, or prostitution is guilty of maintaining a nuisance."

Justice Blackmun, joined by Brennan and Marshall, took exception, reasoning that "[t]he State's purpose in stopping public lewdness cannot justify such a substantial infringement on First Amendment rights. First Amendment interests require the use of more 'sensitive tools.'" Id. at 3180 (Blackmun, J., dissenting).

Is the apparent inconsistency of these two cases explainable on grounds other than a shift in Court membership? Does the Court do a better job of reconciling the first amendment and land-use regulations? See the *Young* and *Schad* cases in Chapter IV.

8. What Professor Gaus has called the catastrophe theory of planning is borne out in the history of air pollution control. Much of the legislation can be analyzed as a direct response to dramatic incidents. (And, indeed, a correlation can be made between such events and the contents of law reviews: Note, 1 Stan. L. Rev. 452 (1949) followed the Donora disaster, while 27 S. Cal. L. Rev. 347-414 (1954) manifested the interest of the legal profession in the Los Angeles smog.) One such case occurred in Donora:

> The American Steel and Wire Company made an out-of-court settlement of about 130 damage suits that asked $4,643,000 as a result of the 1948 Donora smog disaster in which 22 persons died and 5,190 were made ill. The settlement was understood to be $235,000. In a statement confirming the settlement, the company did not admit that fumes from its plant caused the fatalities. According to the State Tax Equalization Board's survey, the market value of Donora property, principally residential, had declined after the disaster $9\frac{1}{2}$ per cent from $34,000,000 to approximately $30,800,000.

N.Y. Times, April 18, 1951. For further details, see Schrenk and others, Air Pollution in Donora, U.S. Pub. Health Bull. No. 306 (1949).

Pollution of the atmosphere by people is an ancient problem. The first smoke abatement law was apparently passed in 1273. In 1307, a Royal Proclamation prohibited the use of coal in furnaces; the following year a person was executed for this offense. Steer, The Law of Smoke Nuisances (2d ed. 1945). And, reinverting the proverb, in 1648 Londoners petitioned Parliament to prohibit the importation of coal from Newcastle.

A typical "primitive type" ordinance seeking to control air pollution reads:

> The emission of dense smoke from the smokestack of any locomotive or engine, or from the smokestack of any stationary engine, or from the smokestack, chimney or fireplace of any building or plant anywhere within the corporate limits of the City of Lorain, Ohio, shall be deemed, and is hereby declared to be a public nuisance and is hereby prohibited except as hereafter provided.

B. An Annoyance to All the King's Subjects 147

Ord. No. 4991, §1 (1941). See Williams, Implications of the Franklin Institute Study for Planning and Zoning, 18 J. Am. Inst. Planners 181 (1952). Had your opinion been asked, would you so have framed the ordinance? Cf. Board of Health of Weehawken Township v. New York Central R.R., 10 N.J. 294, 90 A.2d 729 (1952). What of the Sacramento ordinance tested in In re Junqua, 10 Cal. App. 602, 604, 103 P. 159, 160 (1909): "It shall be unlawful for any person . . . to permit any soot to escape from the smokestack or from the chimney of any furnace . . . in which distillate or crude oil is consumed as fuel." See also Department of Health v. Ebling Brewing Co., 38 Misc. 537, 78 N.Y.S. 11 (N.Y. Mun. Ct., 1902) (construing ordinance reading, "Nor shall any . . . person . . . allow any smoke . . . to escape . . . from any . . . building . . . and every furnace employed shall be so constructed as to consume or burn the smoke arising therefrom"). Contrast the two opinions in Atlantic City v. France, 74 N.J.L. 389, 65 A. 894 (Sup. Ct. 1907), aff'd, 75 N.J.L. 910, 70 A. 163 (Ct. Err. & App. 1908). As to constitutionality, see Penn-Dixie Cement Corp. v. Kingsport, 189 Tenn. 450, 225 S.W.2d 270 (1949). Northwestern Laundry v. Des Moines, 239 U.S. 486 (1916), is an early leading federal case. Assuming its legal validity, how adequate is this for a successful control program? On statewide control, see the discussion in Moran, The Air Pollution Control Act and Its Administration, 9 Rutgers L. Rev. 640 (1955).

The Federal Clean Air Act (42 U.S.C. §7401 et seq.) continues to raise the issue of whether the best government technique for cleaning up the nation's air is that of source or of land-use control. The act sets up primary (to protect public health) and secondary (to protect general welfare) national ambient air standards and emission standards by new sources. While ambient air quality (affected both by stationary and mobile sources) is measured by stations spaced throughout a metropolitan area, new source standards are monitored at the site. See White, The Auto Pollution Muddle, 32 Pub. Interest 97 (Summer 1973). Within nine months after a new or revised national ambient air quality standard is promulgated, each state must adopt "a plan which provides for implementation, maintenance, and enforcement of such . . . standard in each air quality control region (or portion thereof) within such State." §7410 (a) (1). Failure to prepare a satisfactory plan could result in the Administrator of the EPA preparing a plan or in the withholding of federal funds for highways or other projects. See NRDC v. EPA, 475 F.2d 968 (D.C. Cir. 1973). To some degree unforeseen, the act has evolved into a tool to control land use and future development. See Note, 12 Harv. J. on Legis. 111 (1974).

In calling for a state air quality-control strategy, the regulations issued by EPA require that it must provide for the "degree of emission reduction necessary to offset emission increases . . . reasonably expected . . . to result from projected growth of population, industrial activity, motor vehicle traffic, or other factors." See Mandelker and Rothschild, The Role of Land-Use Controls in Combating Air Pollution under the Clean Air Act of 1970, 3 Ecology L.Q. 235 (1973); Batchelder, Land Use Transportation Controls for Air Quality, 6 Urb. Law. 235 (1974); Ferrante & Capello, A Look at the Regulation of Two Urban Environmental Problems: Solid Waste Management and Air Pollution Control, 11 Urb. Law. 515, 520-528 (1979). Will indirect source standards and traffic restrictions force development into suburbia, driving one more nail into the central city coffin?

EPA's backdoor approach to land-use controls usually left to local determination can have extraordinary consequences. Presumably, cities will be making land-use decisions based predominantly on air pollution, not on the social, economic, and environmental factors usually entering into good planning. The ramifications of potential federal effect on land-use controls come to a head in the vague "nondegradation" policy — a requirement that air quality should not be made worse in areas already within federal minimums. See Fri v. Sierra Club, 412 U.S. 541 (1973).

9. See Robinson v. Indianola Municipal Separate School District, 467 So. 2d 911 (Miss. 1985):

> Appellants Robinson and Gardner requested the Chancery Court of Sunflower County to enjoin the Indianola Municipal Separate School District from constructing a high school gymnasium across the street from their homes on the ground that it would constitute a public nuisance. . . .
> The question becomes whether this non-compliance with the off-street parking ordinance is a public nuisance which the appellants, as abutting landowners, are entitled to enjoin. While it is generally acknowledged that the violation of a municipal ordinance does not constitute a public nuisance, the continuing violation of a valid ordinance may constitute a nuisance. A private individual cannot ordinarily maintain an action with respect to the enforcement of a zoning regulation, except where the use constitutes a nuisance per se or the individual has suffered or is threatened with special damage, i.e., injury or threat of injury of a special or peculiar nature amounting to a private wrong affecting his personal or property rights. . . .
> . . . [A]ppellants have alleged the existence of a public nuisance in the form of obstruction of Battle Street by traffic. This condition is directly traceable to the school district's non-compliance with the Indianola off-street parking ordinance. While it is true that ordinarily a private individual may not maintain a suit to enforce a zoning ordinance, nor may he enjoin what is in essence a public nuisance, where, as here, the condition obstructs an abutting landowner's right of ingress and egress, an injunction will lie. Under the established law, we are required to reverse the chancellor and issue an injunction barring the school district from proceeding with the construction of the Gentry High School

B. An Annoyance to All the King's Subjects

gymnatorium unless and until it complies with the Indianola off-street parking ordinance....

10. In Weltshe v. Graf, 323 Mass. 498, 82 N.E.2d 795 (1948), the court concludes:

> The hotel and the freight terminal are located at the boundaries of a district zoned for business and adjoin a district zoned for residences in which all the plaintiffs have their homes. The fact that the operation of certain kinds of commercial enterprises is permitted under a zoning ordinance is an important factor in determining whether the use being made of the land in conducting a particular enterprise goes beyond what is reasonable in view of the nature and character of the locality, the effect of the use upon those who live in the neighborhood, and the strength and force appropriately due to the various conflicting interests usually involved in the subject matter. But a zoning ordinance affords no protection to one who uses his land in such a manner as to constitute a private nuisance.

Cf. Robinson Brick Co. v. Luthi, 115 Colo. 106, 169 P.2d 171 (1946); see Note, 52 Colum. L. Rev. 781 (1952). In Kirk v. Mabis, 215 Iowa 769, 246 N.W. 759 (1933), an owner of an adjoining residence sought to enjoin an undertaking establishment located in a district zoned as commercial. See also Rockenbach v. Apostle, 330 Mich., 338, 47 N.W.2d 636 (1951).

In Davis v. Sawyer, 133 Mass. 289 (1882), the ringing of a bell at an early hour to arouse employees of the defendant's plant was enjoined as a private nuisance as to those deprived of sleep. Thereafter, a statute was passed allowing local governments to license employers to ring the call to work. The selectmen of Plymouth gave the defendant a license. In an action to dissolve the injunction, what result? See Sawyer v. Davis, 136 Mass. 239 (1884). See Note, 54 Mich. L. Rev. 266 (1955).

11. Pendoley v. Ferreira, 342 Mass. 309, 187 N.E.2d 142 (1963), enjoined a piggery (emanating a garbagey, nauseating, obnoxious odor) which had not been assigned as a piggery location under Mass. Gen. Laws ch. 111, §143. Licenses granted under §143 are not vested rights and may be revoked "whenever in the opinion of the board of health the continuance of such a trade or employment has become hurtful to the inhabitants, injurious to their estates, dangerous to the public health or is attended by noisome and injurious odors." Revere v. Riceman, 280 Mass. 76, 181 N.E. 716 (1932). Mass. Gen. Laws ch. 111, §144, which has not yet been interpreted by the court, provides:

> If a place or building so assigned becomes a nuisance by reason of offensive odors or exhalations therefrom, or is otherwise hurtful or dangerous to the neighborhood or to travelers, the superior court may,

on complaint of any person, revoke such assignment, prohibit such further use of such place or building, and cause the nuisance to be removed or prevented.

How would you interpret the phrase "any person" in light of the fact that its use in the statute antedates the broadened conception of standing exemplified by Scenic Hudson Preservation Conference v. FPC, infra page 520, or the Michigan Environmental Protection Act of 1970, Mich. Comp. Laws Ann. §691.1201, granting residents standing to sue on environmental issues:

> Sec. 2. (1) The attorney general, any political subdivision of the state, any instrumentality or agency of the state or of a political subdivision thereof, any person, partnership, corporation, association, organization, or other legal entity may maintain an action in the circuit court having jurisdiction where the alleged violation occurred or is likely to occur for declaratory and equitable relief against the state, any political subdivision thereof, any instrumentality or agency of the state or of a political subdivision thereof, any person, partnership, corporation, association, organization or other legal entity for the protection of the air, water and other natural resources and the public trust therein from pollution, impairment or destruction.
>
> (2) In granting relief provided by subsection (1) where there is involved a standard for pollution or for an anti-pollution device or procedure, fixed by rule or otherwise, by an instrumentality or agency of the state or a political subdivision thereof, the court may:
>
> (a) Determine the validity, applicability and reasonableness of the standard.
>
> (b) When a court finds a standard to be deficient, direct the adoption of a standard approved and specified by the court.

Contrast Cal. Civ. Pro. Code §731a (1980):

> Whenever any city, city and county, or county shall have established zones or districts under authority of law wherein certain manufacturing or commercial or airport uses are expressly permitted, except in an action to abate a public nuisance brought in the name of the people of the State of California, no person or persons, firm or corporation shall be enjoined or restrained by the injunctive process from the reasonable and necessary operation in any such industrial or commercial zone or airport of any use expressly permitted therein, nor shall such use be deemed a nuisance without evidence of the employment of unnecessary and injurious methods of operation. . . .

When the forum is an administrative tribunal, rules of evidence are relaxed. FTC v. Cement Institute, 333 U.S. 683, 705-706 (1948). What are the factors to be considered in determining the res judicata

B. An Annoyance to All the King's Subjects 151

effect of an environmental agency's prior determination favorable to the defendant? See City of Fond du Lac v. Department of Natural Resources, 173 N.W.2d 605 (Wis. 1970); 4 Davis, Administrative Law Treatise §21.1 et seq. (1983). As defendant's attorney, how would you develop the law of estoppel?

12. The administrative agency increasingly is the first line decisionmaker in the environmental area, in part because of the spate of public nuisance-type statutes enacted in recent years. Interspersed among the many carrots in the federal arsenal are several sticks. The Water Quality Act of 1965 provided:

> If a State does not . . . establish water quality standards in accordance with . . . this subsection, or if the Secretary . . . desires revision in such standards, the Secretary may, after reasonable notice and a conference of representatives of Federal departments and agencies, interstate agencies, States, municipalities and industries involved, prepare regulations setting forth standards of water quality to be applicable to interstate waters or portions thereof.

33 U.S.C. §466g(c)(2).

The Water Pollution Control Act of 1972 calls for water quality standards and goals,[15] and under §208 authorizes a state areawide planning process which includes regulating "the location, modification, and construction of any facilities within such an area which may result in any discharge in such area." Throughout, the act seems to call for sophisticated trade-offs between structural solutions (e.g., waste treatment facilities), and nonstructural solutions (e.g., land-use controls). 33 U.S.C. §1288 — Areawide Waste Treatment Management. In general, see Note, 1973 Wis. L. Rev. 893. Regulations require a continuing planning process to coordinate water treatment plans with other state and local plans.

A harsh appraisal of the congressional process from the academic halls, on cost and efficiency grounds, can be found in Kneese & Schultze, Pollution, Prices and Public Policy (1975). For further exploration of environmental issues, see infra, Chapter VI.

---

15. Two national goals are enunciated: "that the discharge of pollutants into the navigable waters be eliminated by 1985" (33 U.S.C. §1251(a)(1)); and "that wherever attainable, an interim goal of water quality which provides for the protection and propagation of fish, shellfish, and wildlife and provides for recreation in and on the water to be achieved by July 1, 1983" (33 U.S.C. §1251(a)(2)). The most recent amendments to the Clean Water Act added a new goal: "(7) it is the national policy that programs for the control of nonpoint sources of pollution be developed and implemented in an expeditious manner so as to enable the goals of this chapter to be met through the control of both point and nonpoint sources of pollution." Water Quality Act of 1987, Pub. L. No. 100-4, §316(b), 101 Stat. 60 (1987).

C. STATUTORY PREEMPTION AND ALTERNATIVES TO ADJUDICATION

The traditional adjudicatory mode for resolving disputes has yielded recently to two competitors — comprehensive regulation, often accomplished through preemptive state and federal legislation; and forms of alternative dispute resolution (ADR) such as mediation and arbitration, encouraged if not mandated by legislation as well. Both of these trends should be familiar to you, particularly because you have moved "beyond" the study of private law systems that dominates the first-year classroom. Consider whether there are any special attributes of the law regarding the use and enjoyment of private property that should insulate nuisance law from these "intrusions."

The occupation, by statutes and administrative regulations, of the former common-law domains of private and public nuisance is by no means complete. Indeed, rules are only as strong and influential as the bureaucrats responsible for day-to-day enforcement and the political officials who shape overriding policies. Potential litigants fall into the gaps (intended or unavoidable) that exist in the administration of federal and state laws regarding noxious and dangerous use of property. Yet the doctrine of preemption — to some an essential component of federalism, to others a threat — may serve to block access to injunctive or compensatory relief. Can and should courts respond to these inevitable gaps and governmental shortfalls by reviving common-law causes of action? Do we step backward and risk nonuniformity with such an approach? Are frustrated victims the price we pay for our modern, "comprehensive" approach to environmental disasters?

Some of that frustration is shared by individual litigants who lose in the winner-take-all adjudicatory arena. ADR, a phenomenon that seems to have captured the imagination and energy of a generation of lawyers and laypersons, has a rich American heritage reaching centuries back.[16] While it is beyond the scope of this casebook to capture the debate over the advantages and pitfalls of alternative systems,[17] the materials included here should raise certain questions in your mind concerning the feasibility and desirability of ADR to resolve or head off nuisance disputes. For example, who should be entrusted with the responsibility of negotiating on behalf of the community at risk? Can elected officials meaningfully represent the often conflicting needs of

---

16. See Auerbach, Justice Without Law? (1983); Wolf, Of Devils and Angels, Lawyers and Communities (Book Review), 97 Harv. L. Rev. 607 (1983).
17. See, e.g., Fuller, The Forms and Limits of Adjudication, 92 Harv. L. Rev. 353 (1978); Burger, Isn't There a Better Way?, 68 A.B.A. J. 274 (1982); Fiss, Against Settlement, 93 Yale L.J. 1073 (1984). Cf. Galanter, Reading the Landscape of Disputes: What We Know and Don't Know (And Think We Know) About Our Allegedly Contentious and Litigious Society, 31 ULCA L. Rev. 4 (1983).

C. Statutory Preemption and Alternatives to Adjudication 153

neighborhood residents, local businesses, and the public coffers? Should dissenters be able to preserve their rights to object by bringing lawsuits? Can mediators and arbitrators (even those trained as lawyers) meaningfully consider the legal rights of the parties? Can settlements bind future residents of the affected area? What about unborn children whose parents accepted payment in return for their legal right to object? If the technological bases for an agreement are later proved inaccurate, is litigation foreclosed?

Notes on Preemption

1. See Chappell v. SCA Services, Inc., 540 F. Supp. 1087 (1982):

> The suit is a class action brought on behalf of the residents of the Village of Wilsonville, seeking damages for property losses and personal injury which resulted from the creation, maintenance and operation of a hazardous-chemical-waste landfill containing polychlorinated byphenyls (PCB's), together with other toxic waste substances, near Wilsonville. The Macoupin County Circuit Court, after 104 days of trial, concluded that the hazardous waste landfill constituted both a private and public nuisance. The court enjoined defendant SCA Services, Inc. from operating the landfill and ordered SCA to remove all toxic waste buried there and to restore and reclaim the site. . . .
>
> Defendant SCA . . . seeks to remove the action on the basis that Count IV can be characterized as stating a federal cause of action pursuant to the Toxic Substances Control Act (TSCA), 15 U.S.C. §2601 et seq. Defendant SCA contends that the plaintiffs have disguised their complaint so that it hides a claim within the exclusive jurisdiction of the federal courts. Defendant also argues that the federal Act preempts state law on these issues. . . .
>
> The face of plaintiffs' complaint clearly reveals an action for damages grounded upon the state common law of nuisance. Generally, a plaintiff is free to ignore a federal question and pitch his claim on a state ground, so long as no fraud is involved, thus defeating removal to the federal courts. . . .
>
> . . . [I]t would appear that a state common law nuisance action may be the only way plaintiffs can recover for any damages which have accrued to them. In sum, it appears to the court that the TSCA does not preempt state common law nuisance actions for damages.

The case made its way through the state courts and, in Village of Wilsonville v. SCA Services, 86 Ill. 2d 1, 426 N.E.2d 824 (1981), the Supreme Court of Illinois upheld the trial court that had "concluded that the site constitutes a [public] nuisance and enjoined the defendant from operating its hazardous-chemical-waste landfill in Wilsonville."

SCA was ordered to remove all buried toxic waste and contaminated soil, and "to restore and reclaim the site."

2. Anheuser-Busch, Inc., owners of a brewery in Merrimack, New Hampshire, objected to a proposed waste treatment and disposal facility in the town, fearing "that sales of its products could be harmed if consumers learn of the proximity of the treatment facility." In Applied Chemical Technology, Inc. [ACT] v. Town of Merrimack, 490 A.2d 1348 (N.H. 1985), the state supreme court found that the town's denial of a site application permit to ACT was preempted by state law. While certain local activities are excluded from preemption (regulations pertaining to traffic, garbage removal, signs, and the like), "the denial of the site plan has a direct 'exclusionary effect' on the siting of the ACT facility and thereby has a 'frustrating' effect on the State regulation of this matter." Id. at 1349 (quoting Stablex Corp. v. Town of Hookset, 122 N.H. 1091, 456 A.2d 94 (1982)).

3. One weakness with the nuisance action in this context is the remedy: the Supreme Court has indicated that a property owner has no constitutional right to any particular remedy so long as the available relief does not deny due process. Duke Power Co. v. Carolina Environmental Study Group, 438 U.S. 59 (1978). If local property owners are limited to a damage remedy, who should set the amount of damages? Should the property owners be able to recover for the depreciation in the value of their property? If legislation were to prevent such a recovery would it run afoul of the fifth and fourteenth amendments?

Utah has legislatively preempted the common law nuisance action in the case of legislatively approved construction or operation of a hazardous waste facility. (See Utah Code Ann. §26-14a-7.) Does that legislation violate constitutional strictures?

■ HOLZNAGEL, NEGOTIATION AND MEDIATION: THE NEWEST APPROACH TO HAZARDOUS WASTE FACILITY SITING
13 B.C. Envtl. Aff. L. Rev. 329, 329-330, 357-358, 364-365, 378 (1986)

Consensual approaches to resolving environmental disputes have now been used for a decade. At first, mediators were employed on a case-by-case basis to resolve disputes involving the siting of flood control dams, highways, public parks, and transportation terminals. Recently, several federal agencies, including the Environmental Protection Agency (EPA), have experimented with mediation and negotiation in the administrative rule-making process. Statutes in Massachusetts, Rhode Island, Wisconsin, and Connecticut authorize, or even require, negoti-

C. Statutory Preemption and Alternatives to Adjudication 155

ation and mediation of waste facility siting disputes. While the techniques used in environmental mediation extend far beyond the methods employed for mediation in the private sector, however, mediation should be viewed as a supplement to, rather than a replacement for, traditional adjudicatory procedures. . . .

Pursuant to the Massachusetts Hazardous Waste Facility Siting Act [Mass. Gen. Laws Ann. ch. 210 (West 1981)], a developer must obtain several licenses and permits prior to the construction of a facility. The operating license must be obtained from the State Department of Environmental Quality Engineering (DEQE); the site assignment must be obtained from the local board of health; and siting agreement must be signed with the local assessment committee (LAC), which is a representative body of the host community. The siting agreement, which describes the facility construction and monitoring procedures, as well as the mitigation and compensation efforts of the developer, is the new statute's most important departure from the former Massachusetts statute. . . .

Formal negotiations take place between the LAC and the developer. The negotiations are intended to result in a siting agreement that must be signed before the developer is permitted to construct the facility. It is worth noting here that the basic environmental and public health protection provided for by state and the federal laws are not subject to negotiation. Bargaining is only over the stricter, or supplementary, standards. The parties thus negotiate over measures that are specially tailored to alleviate the community's particular concerns about environmental and socio-economic impacts. The resulting siting agreement is a nonassignable contract, and is enforceable in court against the parties.

The Massachusetts statute lists a number of issues that must be addressed in any siting agreement, including: facility construction and maintenance procedures; facility design and operation procedures; monitoring procedures; services provided by the developer to the community; compensation provided by the developer to the community; services and benefits provided by the state agencies to the community; provisions for pre-payments, accelerated tax payments, or payment in lieu of taxes; provisions for renegotiating, amending, or extending the agreement; provisions for resolving disagreements; and compensation to be provided to abutting communities.

Before the initiation of formal negotiations, the developer and the community may agree to employ a mediator at their own expense. If the parties refuse a mediator, or if the HWFSSC [Hazardous Waste Facility Site Safety Council] determines that the negotiations are not progressing satisfactorily, then the HWFSSC may require the parties to employ a mediator. In such a case, the mediator is selected and compensated by the HWFSSC. The mediator aids the parties in executing a siting agreement, and holds meetings at times and places convenient to both parties. The mediator notifies both the HWFSSC and the DEM [Department of Environmental Management] as to the time and place of the meetings and of any progress in the negotiations.

If no siting agreement is reached within sixty days of a determination that the socio-economic appendix is adequate, the parties are required to submit a negotiation status report to the HWFSSC and to the DEM. The report identifies unresolved issues and suggests whether and when negotiations are expected to be completed. At any time subsequent to the submission of the report, the developer or the LAC may notify the HWFSSC that an impasse in the negotiations has been reached. The HWFSSC then determines whether an extension is warranted, whether an impasse actually exists, and when final binding arbitration will begin. . . .

On balance, . . . when compared to the former Massachusetts approach, or to the strict preemption approach, the use of negotiation and mediation in the siting of new facilities has several advantages. The availability of compensatory payments addresses the underlying causes of public opposition. Communities remain continuously involved in the siting process, and the required agreement between a developer and a community provides the opportunity for more alternatives than simply the approval or disapproval of a particular project. Technical assistance grants provided by the state allow the community to develop its own position for negotiation with the developer. The Massachusetts statute provides further for the involvement of the general public and the abutting communities in the decision-making process, thus permitting them to influence the final result.

Notes

1. The Massachusetts legislation survived a constitutional challenge in Town of Warren v. Hazardous Waste Facility Site Safety Council, 392 Mass. 107, 466 N.E.2d 102 (1984):

> St. 1980, c. 508, §8, does not unconstitutionally delegate legislative power to the council. The plaintiffs contend that the council has improperly been delegated legislative power because the Legislature failed to enact adequate standards to guide the council in arriving at its feasibility determination. In effect, according to the argument, by making an unguided determination that a proposal for a hazardous waste facility is feasible and deserving of State assistance, the council may arbitrarily force the town to establish a committee to negotiate a siting agreement and to accept binding arbitration contrary to the town's constitutional right of self-government. The plaintiffs' argument that the Legislature has not provided sufficient standards to guide the council is combined with an attack on the statute as being void for vagueness. . . .

C. Statutory Preemption and Alternatives to Adjudication 157

Although the statute does not expressly provide standards to guide the council's feasibility determination, those standards may nevertheless be found in the statute's "necessary implications. The purpose, to a substantial degree, sets the standards. A detailed specification of standards is not required. The Legislature may delegate to a board or officer the working out of the details of a policy adopted by the Legislature.". . . It is apparent from the nature of the information that is required to be included in the notice of intent filed with the council, and from the clear purpose of the statute, what considerations should guide the council in making its determination of feasibility and worthiness of State assistance. By making that determination the council does not make laws but rather implements the policies of the Legislature.

2. Is it only during a period of lax enforcement of environmental laws that conservationists agree to sit down at the table to "work out" differences with developers and energy concerns? See Reilly, Cleaning Our Chemical Waste Backyard, Wall St. J., May 31, 1984:

At a press conference in Washington today, a coalition of chemical industry executives and leaders in the environmental community will announce the creation of a nonprofit organization, Clean Sites, Inc. The new, totally private group will clean up hazardous waste dumps throughout the U.S. Its goal eventually is to clean up 60 such sites a year. By comparison, during the four years since the nation made a priority of cleaning up hazardous waste sites and enacted the federal Superfund law, the Environmental Protection Agency has cleaned up only a handful of sites. . . .

One benefit of experience with environmental laws is that we know better the limitations of the adversarial model on which so much governmental regulation relies: staff up with a large number of lawyers, fill the Federal Register with detailed regulations, every one the subject of prolonged consultations, public hearings, revisions and court challenges, and then flood the federal courts' already crowded dockets with complaints. Building a structure of environmental protection that is more effective, that will not be frustrated or delayed by endless litigation and prolonged conflict, may require the creation of new kinds of consensus-building institutions. Such new institutions will need to be designed to fit into the interstices of public policy, relying on a mix of regulation on the one hand and incentives on the other. . . .

3. The field of hazardous waste offers interesting examples of the boundaries of the local government's exclusionary rights in the nuisance field. Any decision to locate a hazardous waste management facility necessarily balances two opposing interests: society's interest in providing safe storage for waste and the local interest in protecting the health of those who will be most directly exposed to the facility. Society at large will tend to have a higher tolerance for safety trade-offs; the local

government unit will have little economic incentive to adopt the facility because it is capital-intensive and does not make a substantial contribution to local taxes. Traditionally the bargaining process has been tilted in favor of the local government. Because of the necessity of establishing waste sites, the central government has had to shift the balance of rights away from the local government unit while still maintaining local participation in the siting process. See O'Hare, Bacow & Sanderson, Facility Siting and Public Opposition (1983).

4. One controversial variation on this theme has occurred in the debate between the federal government and several states concerning the siting of nuclear waste repositories. Discussion has focused on the right of a state legislature to veto the federal government's decision to build a site within that state's boundaries. With the availability of such a veto it is unlikely that state lawmakers would allow the facility; without the veto little serious bargaining power would be left to the states.

After several proposed bills were defeated, the Nuclear Waste Policy Act of 1982 gave individual states a right to veto a location suggested by the Department of Energy. However, the bill also gave Congress the right, through a joint resolution, to override that veto (see 42 U.S.C. §10,135(c). In an earlier version the bill stated that the veto could be overridden on the vote of one house of Congress. The last-minute change was produced when Senator William Proxmire, whose home state of Wisconsin contains rock formations that are of interest to the Department of Energy, threatened a filibuster. Idaho Senator James McClure, Chair of the Energy and National Resources Committee, gave in, rather than see the bill die as previous ones had. See Carter, The Radwaste Paradox, 219 Science 33, 34 (Jan. 1983). For a discussion of the other options available to Congress at the time, see Hart and Glaser, A Failure to Enact: A Review of Radioactive Waste Issues and Legislation Considered by the 96th Congress, 32 S.C.L. Rev. 641, 717-740 (1981). For a discussion of the scientific difficulties of predicting the risks involved and some legal ramifications, see Symposium on the Management of Nuclear Wastes, 21 Nat. Resources J. 693 (1981). See also Woychik, California's Nuclear Disposal Law Confronts the Nuclear Waste Management Dilemma, 14 Envtl. L. 358 (1984).

5. See Suits Filed by Western Candidate States over High-Level Nuclear Waste Repository, [17 Current Developments] Envt. Rep. (BNA) 144 (June 6, 1986):

> Less than a week after President Reagan's approval of sites in three Western states for further detailed study in the search for the first permanent, high level nuclear waste repository in the United States, two states have filed several suits challenging the decision and the process which brought it about.
> Nevada and Texas filed suits, and Washington is expected to, after

C. Statutory Preemption and Alternatives to Adjudication 159

sites within their boundaries were recommended to the President by the Department of Energy May 28 for further site characterization work that may take five years and cost nearly $1 billion each.

The sites were Yucca Mountain, Nev., Deaf Smith County, Texas, and Hanford, Wash....

6. Another field that has recently emerged as a focal point of environmental litigation involves the clean-up of existing hazardous waste sites. The area is dominated by two federal statutes: the Resource Conservation and Recovery Act (RCRA, 42 U.S.C. §§6901 et seq.) and the Comprehensive Environmental Response, Compensation and Liability Act (CERCLA or Superfund, 42 U.S.C. §§9601 et seq.). The acts were designed by Congress to place the burden of hazardous waste site cleanup on those who had any kind of involvement in the dumping.

RCRA regulates solid and hazardous waste disposal nationwide and prohibits the operation of hazardous waste disposal sites without federally authorized permits. In a recent case, the West Virginia Supreme Court found that the "savings clause" of RCRA, 42 U.S.C. §6972(f), preserved a city's right to prohibit permanent hazardous waste disposal facilities through a public nuisance ordinance. Sharon Steel Corp. v. City of Fairmont, 334 S.E.2d 616 (W. Va. 1985), appeal dismissed, 474 U.S. 1098 (1986). Nor did the West Virginia Hazardous Waste Management Act preempt the local ordinance.

CERCLA governs the cleanup of abandoned sites, giving the federal government considerable leverage to deal with those involved in hazardous waste dumping. The act has an expansive definition of those who can be held liable for cleanup costs. With only limited exceptions, liability can extend to the present owner or operator of the facility, any person who at the time of disposal owned or operated the facility, and any party who arranged for the disposal or transport of the substance to the disposal or treatment facility, in cases in which the facility was chosen by such a person. Because few hazardous waste facilities maintained adequate records of who contributed to a specific site and how much waste they contributed, the result is that the statute may translate into liability for companies that merely had indirect involvement with the actual disposal (e.g., ownership or contractual relationships). Does this mean that the statute is effectively legislating strict liability? The act also provides for joint and several liability.

For a good example of the factual and procedural intricacies of CERCLA litigation, see United States v. Wade, 577 F. Supp. 1326 (E.D. Pa. 1983). The statute also makes it possible to collect cleanup costs from a later purchaser of the property. In United States v. Maryland Bank and Trust Company, 632 F. Supp. 573 (D. Md. 1986), the court was presented with "the novel question of whether a bank, which formerly held a mortgage on a parcel of land at a foreclosure sale and continues to own it, must reimburse the United States for the cost of cleaning up hazardous wastes on the land, when those wastes were dumped prior to the bank's purchase of the property." Id. at 574. The court denied the bank's motion for summary judgment, noting that "defendant's position would convert CERCLA into an insurance scheme for financial institutions, protecting them against possible losses due to security of loans with polluted properties. Mortgagees, however, already have the means to protect themselves, by making prudent loans." Id. at 580. For a different view of lender liability, see United States v. Mirabile, 15 E.L.R. 20992 (E.D. Pa. Sept. 4, 1985).

Should it make a difference that when the dumping was initially done there was no law forbidding it and little social concern over the environmental effects of such waste?

The federal government also has the right to levy treble damages (§9607(c)(3)) and fines of up to $25,000 per day for a refusal to comply with an order under the act, and up to $75,000 per day for a subsequent violation.[18]

What can the planner and the lawyer contribute to the adjudication of nuisance cases? How can they provide more precise and more equitable means of deciding such disputes? What planning criteria should be advanced by the lawyer? What use can the courts make of

18. For recent Superfund developments, see Hayes & MacKerron, Superfund II: A New Mandate 1-5 (1987) (BNA Special Report):

 An arduous three-year process of reauthorizing the superfund hazardous waste site cleanup law ended Oct. 17, 1986, when President Reagan signed the Superfund Amendments and Reauthorization Act of 1986 (PL99-499) (SARA). It provides $8.5 billion over five years to the Environmental Protection Agency and other federal agencies for the cleanup of abandoned and inoperative waste sites, an enormous, fivefold increase in the funds available under the original 1980 law.
 The amendments make major changes to the original law . . . (CERCLA). The revisions add strict cleanup standards strongly favoring permanent remedies at waste sites, stronger EPA control over the process of reaching settlement with parties responsible for waste sites, a mandatory schedule for initiation of cleanup work and studies, individual assessments of the potential threat to human health posed by each waste site, and increased state and public involvement in the cleanup decision-making process, including the right of citizens to file lawsuits for violations of the law.
 The amended superfund law retains the concept of strict, joint and several liability, which EPA has found to be its most powerful enforcement tool in inducing responsible parties to clean up waste sites. It also codifies many existing agency enforcement practices that evolved under the first five years of CERCLA. . . .
 The amendments also provide for significantly increased criminal and civil penalties for violations of CERCLA and provide an administrative enforcement mechanism for rapid action against violators.

C. Statutory Preemption and Alternatives to Adjudication 161

performance standards in fact determinations?[19] Is there, for instance, a method of stimulating interest in the possibility of new industrial techniques that might lessen nuisance conditions?[20]

The interplay between private actions and public laws can be extremely fertile. Is nuisance law a forgotten tool in modern land-use control? Can it be revamped into contemporary usefulness? In examining the subsequent programs for land-use planning and control, consider the advantages that may lie in the nuisance device and how they could be reclaimed.

---

19. *"Wrong Note Struck As Bells Drown Out Antinoise Defender.*

"The bells were right on cue today at the antinoise trial of the Tompkins County Savings Bank carillon. . . .

"The trial was held before City Court Judge James J. Clynes Jr. to take evidence for and against the chimes, which ring at 9 A.M., noon and 5 P.M. and follow up with about 3½ minutes of melody after heralding the time.

"At noon, the carillon chimed the hour, then went into the melody. W. Robert Farnsworth, president of the bank and owner of the bells, was on the stand. Bruce Dean, a defense lawyer, thought it would be the perfect time to drive home a point.

"'Does the sound of those bells interfere with your hearing the testimony that's being presented in this room?' Mr. Dean asked.

"Mr. Farnsworth replied: 'What?'

"Both sides were given a week in which to file briefs after testimony ended." N.Y. Times, Jan. 29, 1970.

20. Here is some Monday morning quarterbacking aided by field research compiled by Harvard law and planning students:

Immediately after World War I, Beacon Oil started operations of an admittedly crude and dangerous nature on a favorite picnicking and recreation spot on the waterfront. Also close at hand was the Congregational Church, then a focal point of local community social life. Strachan v. Beacon Oil Co., 251 Mass. 479, 146 N.E. 787 (1925). Using a new technology which eliminates odor and air pollution, Beacon Oil expanded into the largest refinery in New England. The cigar factory, absolved from responsibility for "irritability and headaches" in Tortorella v. H. Traiser & Co., 284 Mass. 497, 188 N.E. 254 (1933), no longer exists, while the milk plant involved in Kasper v. H. P. Hood & Sons, Inc., 291 Mass. 24, 196 N.E. 149 (1935), has replaced horse-drawn wagons and noisy cans with trucks and cartons.

III

Legislative Districting of Permissible Land Uses — "Euclidean" Zoning and Beyond

The most widely employed land-use control today is zoning; it is in fact the workhorse of the planning movement in this country. That it has gained acceptance as an indispensable tool of planning may be seen from the figures: by 1967, over 9000 governments employed zoning powers; it is all-dominant — used by over 97 percent of cities having a population over 5000.[1] Since zoning has achieved such general application, it is clearly the legislative process most worthy of detailed consideration in this field.

To formulate a practical system of zoning for American municipalities and to present a legal theory to sustain such an exercise of power was a major creative achievement of the American bar. This was no easy task. And, as with all social engineering, considerable ingenuity was required to convert philosophy into legislation. An illuminating insight into the strategy of litigation is provided by the annual discussions at the National Conference on City Planning.[2] What alternative systems of land-use control could have been devised, and what rationales might have been woven from existing legal doctrines and precedents?

1. Manvel, Local Land and Building Regulations 24 (National Commission on Urban Problems, Research Report No. 6, 1968); see Toll, Zoned American (1969).
2. See Bettman, Discussion, National Conference on City Planning 111 (1914); Bassett, Legal Aspects of Zoning, id. at 193 (1919); Freund, Discussion, id. at 62 (1913); Freund, Discussion, id. at 73 (1926).

During the decade preceding 1926, the advocates of zoning fought a vigorous battle for its judicial recognition. Throughout this period courts were loath to sustain any legislative attempt to restrict or regulate the free exercise of what were then deemed the rights of property. Indeed, many states considered, and a few adopted,[3] constitutional amendments to permit zoning. But there always remained the very real possibility that the Supreme Court would interpret this as an unconstitutional use of state power under the fourteenth amendment.

Zoning received only passing attention at the first City Planning Conference in 1909.[4] Although in 1911 the Committee on Legislative and Administrative Methods presented model acts for other aspects of city planning, it suggested no comprehensive zoning act; the reason given for this omission was that the views of conference members were as yet too undecided on the subject.[5] However, a paper the following year, The Control of Municipal Development by the "Zoning System" and Its Application in the United States,[6] was followed up, in 1913, by the Report, "Districting," by the Height of Buildings Commission.[7] New York City is generally credited with enacting the first comprehensive zoning ordinance, in 1916. Prior to this time, height restrictions had been enacted in Washington, D.C., in 1889,[8] and upheld in Boston in 1909,[9] while use restrictions were upheld in California in 1886.[10]

The movement in favor of zoning took on the aspects of a fervid crusade.[11] Whereas, in 1916, Lawrence Veiller had announced that

3. E.g., Ga. Const. art. 3, §2-1923 (1945); La. Const. art. 14, §29 (1921); Mass. Const. art. 60, §190 (1918); N. J. Const. art. 4. §6, par. 2 (1928).
4. See Ford, The Scope of City Planning in the United States, S. Doc. No. 422, Hearing on City Planning, 61st Cong., 2d Sess. 70 (1910); Morgenthau, A National Constructive Programme for City Planning, id. at 59.
5. See Crawford, Certain Principles of a Uniform City Planning Code, National Conference on City Planning 231, 239 (1911). And see the comments by Ernst Freund, and the reactions thereto, id. at 241, 258.
6. By Halderman. Id. at 173 (1912).
7. Reprinted in Commission on Building Districts and Restrictions, Final Report, App. III, 51 (1916).
8. On October 17, 1791, President Washington issued a regulation "that the wall of no House shall be higher than forty feet to the Roof, in any part of the City, nor shall any be lower than thirty-five feet on any of the avenues." In order to attract the settlement of "Mechanics and others whose Circumstances did not admit of erecting Houses authorized by the said Regulations," they were suspended in 1796. See Thomas Jefferson and the National Capital 197 (Padover ed. 1946).
9. Welch v. Swasey, 214 U.S. 91 (1909); cf. 122 Main Street Corp. v. Brockton, 323 Mass. 646, 84 N.E.2d 13 (1949).
10. In re Hang Kie, 69 Cal. 149, 10 P. 327 (1886); Ex parte Quong Wo, 161 Cal. 220, 118 P. 714 (1911). In general, see Commission on Building Districts and Restrictions, Final Report 59-72 (1916); Pomeroy, Zoning: How Far Have We Come? How Far Can We Go?, Natl. Conf. Plan. 70 (1940); Pollard, Outline of Zoning in the United States, 155 Annals 15 (May 1931); Adams, Review: Williams, The Law of City Planning and Zoning, 12 Natl. Mun. Rev. 395 (1923).
11. Metzenbaum, the attorney for the Village of Euclid, expounds on "the great sacrifice and efforts on the part of many noble men who consecrated themselves." 1 Law of Zoning 52 (2d ed. 1955).

III ■ Legislative Districting of Permissible Land Uses

zoning "sounds like a beautiful dream,"[12] by the following year George Ford was able to state that, as a result of the success in New York, zoning was being organized, actively promoted, or actually carried on in twenty municipalities.[13] In 1922, Frank B. Williams published The Law of City Planning and Zoning, the first comprehensive American work in the field. The same year Theodora Kimball could write that "Zoning has taken the country by storm"; she reported twenty enabling acts, nearly fifty ordinances, and about one hundred zone plans in progress.[14] Perhaps the most noteworthy advance in zoning in the pre-*Euclid* period was the appointment, by Secretary of Commerce Herbert Hoover, of an Advisory Committee on Building Codes and Zoning. The committee published much valuable material designed to acquaint interested parties with sound zoning techniques and related legal issues. It drafted a Standard State Zoning Enabling Act which was adopted, in whole or in part, by nineteen states in 1925, and which is still the model for much state enabling legislation.

The readings in this chapter are concerned with the legislative and administrative structure of Euclidean zoning and of some of the alternative land-use regulatory structures proffered by planners and lawmakers. While the primary emphasis in the preceding chapter was on the active formulation and adaptation of common-law rules and principles by members of the judiciary, the cases and materials that follow reflect a more discreet, interpretive mode of decision-making, as judges subject the work of the co-equal branches to a mild degree of judicial scrutiny, in harmony with the deferential tone set by the Supreme Court's holding in Village of Euclid v. Ambler Realty Co.

Before one can evaluate in a meaningful way the criticisms of zoning — raised by those who would have us return to something approaching a free market in land values as well as by those who propose stricter state and federal oversight of permissive local authorities — we must first understand the structure of height, bulk, and use regulation; the relationship of zoning to comprehensive planning; the mechanisms for modifying or avoiding the initial assignment of categories; and the avenues of judicial relief should local decision-makers fail to perform their tasks satisfactorily. Likewise, before we study the increasingly active role recent courts have taken in the area of planning and zoning (the focus of Chapter IV), we need to understand the statutes and ordinances by which significant public control of land

---

12. Districting by Municipal Regulation, National Conference on City Planning 147 (1916).
13. What Has Been Accomplished in City Planning During the Past Year, 6 Natl. Mun. Rev. 346 (1917).
14. Review of Planning in the United States, 1920-1921, at 11 Natl. Mun. Rev. 27, 32 (1922).

development was attempted and, despite some pockets of resistance, achieved.

A. THE POWER TO ZONE

■ RESPUBLICA v. PHILIP URBIN DUQUET
2 Yeates 493 (Pa. 1799)

SHIPPEN, C.J., pronounced the opinion of the court.

The questions in this case are principally two: 1st, Whether the corporation of the city of Philadelphia have passed such an ordinance under the powers vested in them by act of assembly, as by law they might do, both with respect to the mode of punishment, and the court in which the offender is to be tried. And 2d, If they have passed a valid ordinance according to the act, is that act a constitutional one?

The material objection to the ordinance is, that they have directed a prosecution by indictment, whereas it is contended, that a corporation has only power to inflict pecuniary penalties to be levied by distress, or recovered by action of debt. This is undoubtedly true, with regard to ordinances founded on no authority but their own; but in this case they are vested with extraordinary powers by the acknowledged legislature of the state. By the act of assembly of 11th March 1789, §20, the corporation have power to make bye laws, &c. for the well governing and welfare of the city, and to try and determine certain specified offences named, as larcenies, forgeries, &c. and likewise all offences which shall be committed within the said city, against the laws, ordinances, regulations or constitutions, that shall be made, ordained or established in pursuance of that act, and to punish the offenders as by the said laws or ordinances shall be prescribed. 2dly, By the act of 18th April 1795, the legislature enacts, that the mayor, aldermen and common council shall be empowered to pass ordinances to prevent any person or persons, from erecting or causing to be erected, any wooden mansion house, shop, ware house, store, carriage house, or stable, within such part of the city of Philadelphia, as lies to the eastward of Tenth street from the river Delaware, "as they may judge proper." So that the state legislature have exercised their judgment upon the subject matter, and directed by law, that every person should be prevented from erecting wooden buildings within certain populous parts of the city; and the mode of preventing such an evil is left to the mayor, aldermen and common council, by very general words, "as they may judge proper."

This act, connected with the former act, giving the Mayor's Court

A. The Power to Zone 167

power to try all offences against the laws and ordinances which the said corporation shall make in pursuance of the former act, and to punish the offences as by the said laws and ordinances shall be prescribed, appears to us *decisive*, that they may punish offenders against the ordinance, by indictment in the Mayor's Court.

It is not sufficient to say, that the corporation could not of their own authority pass ordinances to punish by indictment or imprisonment, because they are expressly authorized to try and punish offenders against their ordinances in the same court and in the same manner as larcenies, forgeries, and other such offences as are directed to be punished. And although corporations cannot of themselves make ordinances to punish offenders by imprisonment, yet the law cases are express, that if such a power is founded on the custom, they may; and surely an act of the legislature is as effectual as any custom can be.

As to the constitutionality of these laws, a breach of the constitution by the legislature, and the clashing of the law with the constitution, must be evident indeed, before we should think ourselves at liberty to declare a law void and a nullity on that account; yet if a violation of the constitution should in any case be made by an act of the legislature, and that violation should unequivocally appear to us, we shall think it our duty not to shrink from the task of saying such law is void. We however see no such violation in the present case, and therefore give judgment for the commonwealth.

Notes

1. Not all ordinances regulating wooden structures passed judicial scrutiny, nor were all motivated solely by public safety concerns. In Yick Wo v. Hopkins, 118 U.S. 356 (1886), the Supreme Court, having granted writs of habeas corpus, ordered the release from custody of two Chinese immigrants who had been imprisoned for violating an 1880 San Francisco ordinance that outlawed wooden laundries, unless permission had first been obtained from the board of supervisors. Despite the apparently legitimate exercise of the police power in a city with a history of devastating fires, the Court held that the officials' race-based selective enforcement of the ordinance (two hundred Chinese applicants were denied permission, while eight non-Chinese were allowed "to carry on their business under similar conditions") amounted to a constitutional violation.

2. In May 1985, ground was broken in Philadelphia for One Liberty Place, featuring "a 60-story skyscraper that is shattering Philadelphia tradition. The post-modern shaft of blue-and-gray granite, designed by Chicago architect Helmut Jahn, will be the first Philadelphia

building to rise higher than the Quaker hat on the statue of William Penn atop City Hall's bell tower." N.Y. Times, May 4, 1986. Thus was the "gentlemen's agreement" regarding the height of buildings in the City of Brotherly Love dissolved: "The height limit wasn't a city ordinance or a zoning law; the only place it appeared was in the code of the city's redevelopment authority. But generations of Philadelphians accepted it as a 'moral consensus, more powerful than the law,' says Edmund N. Bacon, director of the city planning commission in the 1950s and 1960s." White, Putting William Penn in the Shade, Wall St. J., May 15, 1985.

■ KLINE v. CITY OF HARRISBURG
362 Pa. 438, 68 A.2d 182 (1949)

The following is the opinion of Judge WOODSIDE in the court below:

The plaintiffs here are seeking to restrain the City of Harrisburg and certain of its officials from enforcing the provisions of what is sometimes called an "interim" zoning ordinance, and to direct the proper city officials to issue a building permit to the plaintiffs authorizing the construction of five apartment buildings in the city.

It is admitted by the defendants that the application, drawing and specifications and statement on the basis of which the building permit was requested conform in all respects to the requirements of the Building Code of the City of Harrisburg, and that the permit was refused by the defendants because of the aforesaid ordinance. . . .

One of the plaintiffs who owns a four acre tract of land in the City of Harrisburg entered into an agreement with the other two plaintiffs whereby a business corporation is to be formed and five garden-type apartment buildings are to be erected on said tract and financed in the manner provided by the National Housing Act, 12 U.S.C.A. §1701 et seq. . . .

On April 25, the plaintiffs applied to the Building Inspector of the City of Harrisburg, requesting the issuance of a building permit authorizing the construction of the apartment building, and as required by the Building Code a fee of $1300 was tendered.

On May 6, 1949, Ordinance No. 153 Session of 1948-49 was read and placed before the Council of the City of Harrisburg and was passed finally on May 10 and, if valid, became effective May 20.

The following preamble is in the Ordinance:

> Whereas, the City Planning Commission of the City of Harrisburg, has for several years been studying the details of a comprehensive zoning ordinance for the City, and

A. The Power to Zone

Whereas, the various zoning districts together with the regulations and restrictions to be imposed therein, have in a large part been reduced to writing, but the work has not matured to the point where public hearings can be had, and

Whereas, in the opinion of City Council it will take additional time to work out the details of a zoning plan, and, further, that it will be destructive of the plan if before the date of its final completion the status quo of the residential districts as contemplated by the plan should not be preserved, and

Whereas, it is the desire of City Council in order to promote the general welfare of the community to preserve the status quo of the residential districts of the City until the final zoning ordinance can be completed and adopted.

The Ordinance then provides:

that the erection or construction within the residential districts of the City of Harrisburg as hereinafter defined, of any building or premises which shall be used for, or designed for other than a single family detached dwelling, together with its usual accessories, or the alteration within the said residential districts of any existing single family detached dwelling for any other purpose be and the same is hereby prohibited. . . .

The land on which the plaintiffs propose to erect the apartment lies wholly within one of the two residential areas described in Ordinance No. 153.

The City Planning Commission, which has been in existence since 1923, recommended the employment of a zoning specialist, who was employed by the City on about May 15, 1945.

On July 12, 1945 the City Planning Commission directed the office of the City Engineer to which the zoning specialist was assigned, to make a complete study of the problems arising in the preparation of a zoning ordinance and to present a zoning plan. Such plan was submitted to the City Planning Commission in 1946 and contained two residential areas known as "R-1" areas, which are the same areas as set forth in Ordinance No. 153. These areas accommodate in the main, single family detached dwellings. The final details of the comprehensive zoning plan and the regulations and restrictions to be imposed in the various districts have not as yet been approved by the said City Planning Commission. . . .

The only question argued and submitted to us is

whether Ordinance No. 153 is ultra vires and invalid in that:

(a) its enactment was contrary to the express provisions of subheading "(b) Zoning" of Article XLI of the Third Class City Law [53 P.S. §12198-4101 et seq.];

(b) its enactment was not within any power, implied or inherent, under the provisions of said sub-heading "(b) Zoning" of Article XLI of the Third Class City Law;

(c) its enactment was contrary to the provisions of said sub-heading "(b) Zoning" of Article XLI of the Third Class City Law, since no comprehensive zoning plan was adopted by said Ordinance; and

(d) its enactment was not within any general police power, or any other power, either express, implied or inherent, other than that expressly provided for by said sub-heading "(b) Zoning" of Article XLI of the Third Class City Law?

Municipalities are not sovereigns. Their powers are limited. It has been said that:

Nothing is better settled than that a municipal corporation does not possess and cannot exercise any other than the following powers: (1) those granted in express words; (2) those necessarily or fairly implied in or incident to the powers expressly granted; (3) those essential to the declared objects and purposes of the corporation, not simply convenient but indispensable. Any fair, reasonable doubt as to the existence of power is resolved by the courts against its existence in the corporation, and therefore denied.

Express authority is given to Third Class Cities to enact zoning ordinance[s] under Sections 4110-4113 of The Third Class City Law of June 23, 1931, P.L. 932, 53 P.S. §§12198-4110 to 4113, inclusive.

The Act provides as follows: . . .

Section 4110. Cities may, by ordinance, regulate and restrict the height, number of stories, bulk, and size of buildings and other structures, the percentage of lots that may be occupied, the size, depth, and width of yards, courts, and other open spaces, the density of population, and the location and use of buildings, structures and land for trade, industry, residents, or other purposes, and may make different regulations for different districts thereof, and may alter the same; but no alteration of such regulations may be made, except by the affirmative vote of not less than four of the members of council. Such regulations shall provide that a board of appeals may determine and vary their application in harmony with their general purpose and intent, and in accordance with general or specific rules therein contained. . . .

. . . It is to be noted that Section 4111 provides that:

(1) The City Planning Commission shall recommend to Council the boundaries and appropriate regulations and restrictions to be imposed therein; (2) shall make a tentative report and hold public meetings thereon before submitting its final report; (3) Council shall specify in a notice to be published for ten consecutive days in a daily

A. The Power to Zone 171

newspaper a time and place of hearing; (4) Council shall afford persons affected an opportunity to be heard after the aforesaid final report.

Council is specifically prohibited from imposing any regulation or restriction until after the final report and after said hearing.

It is agreed that none of these things was done prior to the passage of the Ordinance in question. Furthermore, no Board of Appeals has been appointed as required by Sec. 4113.

The defendants admit that they did not comply with the above provisions of the statute, and cannot rely upon the expressed authority to zone contained therein, but contend

> that such provisions carry with them the implied or inherent power to pass an interim ordinance to give effect to the power expressly granted in said sub-heading in order to prevent the defeat of the legislative intent of the expressed powers thus granted. And, furthermore, it is contended that the said Ordinance No. 153 was within the express grant of the police power as provided in Section 2403 of The Third Class City Law, 53 P.S. §12198-2403.

Section 2403 of The Third Class City Law, supra, provides as follows:

> Specific powers. In addition to other powers granted by this act, the council of each city shall have power, by ordinance:
> (then after 53 paragraphs)
> 54. Local Self-Government. — In addition to the powers and authority vested in each city by the provisions of this act, to make and adopt all such ordinances, by-laws, rules and regulations, not inconsistent with or restrained by the Constitution and laws of this Commonwealth, as may be expedient or necessary for the proper management, care and control of the city and its finances, and the maintenance of the peace, good government, safety and welfare of the city, and its trade, commerce and manufactures; and also all such ordinances, by-laws, rules and regulations as may be necessary in and to the exercise of the powers and authority of local self-government in all municipal affairs; . . .

We cannot agree that the above provision authorizes a city to enact a zoning ordinance without following the provisions of Article XLI of the same act which relate to zoning, nor that said zoning provisions carry with them the implied or inherent power to pass an interim zoning ordinance.

It is settled in Pennsylvania that in the absence of the granting of specific power from the Legislature municipalities do not have the authority to pass zoning ordinances.

Pennsylvania has had what today would be called "zoning" since the days of George Washington. The City of Philadelphia adopted an

Ordinance on June 6, 1796, prohibiting the erection of wooden buildings in a specifically described area of the city. The Ordinance however was adopted under authority given to the City by the Act of April 18, 1795, 3 Dall. St. Laws 771, which empowered it to pass ordinances to prevent persons from erecting wooden mansion houses, etc., within such part of the city "as lies to the eastward of Tenth Street from the River Delaware as they may judge proper." In Respublica v. Duquet, 1799, 2 Yeates 493, the Supreme Court declared the Act and the Ordinance constitutional.

Nearly a century later when the Borough of Norristown attempted to limit the construction of frame buildings without express legislative authority the Supreme Court pointed out that the above Philadelphia Ordinance rested upon specific legislative authority and said:

> The Charter of the Borough of Norristown contains no authority to the Council to enact ordinances prohibiting the erection of wooden buildings. Nor is there anything in the grant of general powers conferred upon the borough from which such an authority can be necessarily inferred or to which it is indispensable. Lacking these requirements the qualities necessary to create the power in question are not present.

Kneedler v. Borough of Norristown, 1882, 100 Pa. 368, 371, 45 Am. Rep. 384.

In Junge's Appeal (No. 2), 1926, 89 Pa. Super. 548, 556, Judge Keller said:

> It may be admitted that such zoning ordinance without a statute authorizing it would be void in this state. Whatever may be the law in other states the decisions of our Supreme Court make it clear that in the absence of a grant of power from the Legislature the municipalities of this Commonwealth do not possess the authority to pass such Ordinance. . . .

The legislature was clear and explicit in its language. Note the "may"s and the "shall"s. Cities "may" regulate and restrict, and "may" make different regulations for different districts, and "may" alter them. But the regulation "shall" provide that a board of appeals "may" vary their application. Note that the legislature says the planning commission (or other body) "shall" recommend to council, "shall" make a tentative report and hold public hearings, council "shall" afford persons an opportunity to be heard. And then to make doubly sure that the procedure outlined in the section would be followed the legislature provided that

> Council shall not determine the boundaries of any district, nor impose any regulations or restrictions, until after the final report and after said hearing.

A. The Power to Zone

It is contended by the defendants that without the power to enact such an interim ordinance as is here in question it would be possible for an owner of land to proceed with the erection of an undesirable building in a residential section immediately before the enactment of a zoning ordinance which would prohibit such building, and thus defeat what the city was attempting to establish after years of deliberation and study. There are two answers to this. In the first place, although the argument is not entirely without merit, it is one which must be directed to the legislature and not to the courts. If the legislature wishes to authorize the enactment of a "temporary" or "interim" ordinance to maintain the status quo it can so provide by legislation with proper safeguards. In the second place, apparently experience has not indicated that the failure to pass a "temporary" or "interim" ordinance has been any substantial menace to zoning.

... Although there are scores and possibly hundreds of municipalities in Pennyslvania which have enacted zoning ordinances in accordance with the expressed provisions of the relevant statutes, all of which are similar in nature, there is no indication that we could find either by proposed legislation or by cases in any of the courts of this state that these municipalities have suffered from inability to maintain the status quo during the enactment of zoning ordinances. . . .

A few states have approved temporary zoning ordinances. Cases of each jurisdiction, of course, rest upon the constitution, statutes and decisions of the particular state, as well as the peculiar facts of the particular case, and are not satisfactory authority for our determination of the matter before us. . . .

The leading case cited by the defendants is Miller v. Board of Public Works, 1925, 195 Cal. 477, 234 P. 381, 38 A.L.R. 1479, in which the Supreme Court of California upheld a temporary zoning ordinance passed by the City of Los Angeles. This case dealt primarily with the question of whether zoning directed solely to use and occupancy is a rightful exercise of the police power conferred upon municipalities. Although the Ordinance in question was a temporary Ordinance, the temporary nature of it was not the issue before the Court, nor was the failure of the City to comply with any legislative mandate as to procedure. . . .

In Fowler v. Obier, 1928, 224 Ky. 742, 7 S.W.2d 219 the Supreme Court of Kentucky upheld the power of the City of Louisville to pass a zoning ordinance. The question was whether the City had authority to pass any zoning ordinance because at the time no specific statutory authority existed. The Court held it did. Again there was no question of compliance with statutory regulations or proceedings, for none existed. . . .

McCurley v. City of El Reno, 1929, 138 Okl. 92, 280 P. 467 is in our opinion the only case which supports the contention of the defendants. The Oklahoma Court relied upon the Miller and Fowler cases, supra, which as stated are not authority for the proposition here advanced. As pointed out in State ex rel. Kramer v. Schwartz, 1935, 336 Mo. 932, 82 S.W.2d 63 these cases although relied upon by the Oklahoma Court did not lend support to the views expressed by that court.

The Oklahoma case is not in accord with the prevailing views as reference to the cases of many other jurisdictions will show.

We think it is not necessary to demonstrate that the Ordinance before us is a zoning ordinance. It may be intended to be a temporary or interim one but a zoning ordinance nevertheless.

The defendants admit that the Ordinance before us could not "permanently" restrict the use or erection of the forbidden buildings in the described areas. Yet the Ordinance is drafted to do just that. There is nothing in it limiting the time when it shall be effective. In this respect it differs from the temporary ordinances referred to in the Kentucky and Oklahoma cases where the time the ordinance was to be effective was limited by the ordinance itself.

It is contended by the defendants that the Ordinance will remain in effect until the passage of another zoning ordinance, or for a "reasonable time." If there have been ordinances or statutes, which have been adopted without any provisions limiting their effective time, and which are admittedly illegal except for a "reasonable time," we have no recollection of ever having heard of such.

We have here the anomalous situation of an Ordinance providing an absolute prohibition without limit of time which the defendants admit cannot be valid for an unlimited time.

The record of the case indicates that the City has been in the process of preparing a zoning ordinance since May 15, 1945, a period of over four years, and that "the work has not matured to the point where public hearings can be had" before the City Planning Commission. As a matter of fact a "final" zoning ordinance may never be enacted. There is no duty upon the Council to enact any zoning Ordinance. There is nothing contained in the so-called interim Ordinance by which the present Council even pledges itself to the enactment of a "final" Ordinance. . . .

In summarizing we point out that we start in this case with the proposition that before specific legislative authority to zone was given municipalities, they did not have the authority under their general powers to enact zoning ordinances; that the legislature then gave them power to enact zoning ordinances but specifically set forth what they shall do before they impose any regulations or restrictions. It is our opinion that the municipalities must comply with the provisions of the statute relating to zoning before they can enact any restrictions. The Ordinance before us containing restrictions was not enacted in accord-

A. The Power to Zone 175

ance with the provisions of the statute relating to zoning and is therefore void, and the defendants must be restrained from enforcing it. As the building permit would be issued except for the Ordinance the building inspector must be directed to issue it. . . .

MAXEY, Chief Justice. . . . [I]t is Ordered that the decree of the court below in the above entitled case be affirmed on the opinion of Judge Robert E. Woodside. . . .[15]

■ FRUG, THE CITY AS A LEGAL CONCEPT
93 Harv. L. Rev. 1057, 1105-1108 (1980)

It is by no means self-explanatory why, once corporate property rights were protected, early nineteenth century writers like Chancellor Kent seemed to think it obvious that the other functions of cities would be subordinate to state power. Cities, like other corporations, had never based their resistance to state control simply on the protection of property. Freedom of association and the exercise of self-government had always been values sought to be protected by the defense of the corporation. It did not, therefore, follow from the need to protect property that property alone needed protection and that these other values could be sacrificed to state domination. Indeed, even at the time, these other values were seen as part of the definition of liberty, their defense being most clearly articulated in the defense of state power against federal control encapsulated in the doctrine of federalism.[188]

---

15. Cf. Aberman, Inc. v. City of New Kensington, 377 Pa. 520, 105 A.2d 586 (1954); Kelly v. City of Philadelphia, 382 Pa. 459, 115 A.2d 238 (1955); see Note, 18 Syracuse L. Rev. 837 (1967). See Cappture Realty Corp. v. Borough of Elmwood Park, 126 N.J. Super. 200, 313 A.2d 624 (Law Div. 1973); State v. Snohomish County, 79 Wash. 2d 619, 488 P.2d 511 (1971) ("holding zones").

Some states have legislated permission for limited interim zoning. See, e.g., Colo. Rev. Stat. §30-28-121 (1973):

> **Temporary Regulations.** The board of county commissioners of any county, after appointment of a county or district planning commission and pending the adoption by such commission of a zoning plan, where in the opinion of the board conditions require such action, may promulgate, by resolution without a public hearing, regulations of a temporary nature, to be effective for a limited period only and in any event not to exceed six months, prohibiting or regulating in any part or all of the unincorporated territory of the county or district the erection, construction, reconstruction, or alteration of any building or structure used or to be used for any business, residential, industrial, or commercial purpose.

As to the analogous problem of rights attaching to a building permit, see Penn Township v. Yecko Bros., 420 Pa. 386, 217 A.2d 171 (1966); Heeter, Zoning Estoppel, 1971 Urb. L. Ann. 63; Witt, Vested Rights in Land Uses, 21 Real Prop., Prob. & Tr. J. 317 (1986). — EDS.

188. See e.g., The Federalist No. 51 (J. Madison). To the modern reader, American states seem to be, like cities, entities that are intermediate between the central (federal) government and the individual. It therefore seems odd that the city's subordination to an American state could be understood as limiting the power of intermediate entities

In addition, such a notion of subordination would turn the political world as it then existed upside down. New England towns had controlled state legislatures since prior to the Revolution, and the move in other sections of the country to end aristocratic city governance in favor of democracy was not made with the intention of establishing state control over cities. Nor could subservience to the state be considered an inevitable product of liberal thought. The proper relationship of city to state was instead a hotly contested political issue. Some argued that the sovereignty of the people required control at the local level, but others feared the power of democratic cities over the allocation of property in America. Aristotle, Montesquieu, and Rousseau could be invoked in favor of power at the local level, while Madison and Hume could be cited to show the danger of local self-government. Thus, it is necessary to explain how legal theorists could classify cities as public corporations and thereby subject them to state control. . . .

Once the cities became synonymous with the people within them, one could acknowledge city rights only if one were willing to recognize the right of association and self-determination for any group of people, however large. Such a recognition would threaten many other important values. It would limit the nation's ability to establish a unified political system under the Federal Constitution, preventing the needed centralization of authority and perpetuating the idea that the nation was merely a loose federation of localities. Moreover, these groups, particularly small groups, could be seen as "factions" dangerous to the individuals within them, inhibiting the individual's free development and threatening his property rights. In other words, recognizing the rights of the city as an exercise of the freedom of association would frustrate both the interests of the state and the individual and would defy the liberal attempt to dissolve the power of groups in favor of the state and the individual. . . .

The amount of emphasis to put on the fear of democratic power in explaining the judicial decision to limit the power of cities is, of course, a matter of conjecture. Such fear plainly existed, however, even in the minds of such champions of local power as Jefferson and de Tocqueville. While Jefferson saw towns as the "elementary republics"

---

rather than merely as a transfer from one intermediate entity to another. To the 19th century thinker, however, an American state was sovereign; it wielded ultimate governmental power and not just the power of an intermediate entity. While the federal government was absolute in its sphere, that sphere at the time was limited. Of course, the dividing line between federal and state power was often in dispute, as demonstrated by the advocacy of states' rights in opposition to Jacksonian programs in the 1820's and 1830's, and in support of slavery in the Nullification controversy. See, e.g., M. Peterson, The Jeffersonian Image in the American Mind 36-66 (1960). It was not until the 20th century, however, that an American state could be understood as an intermediate entity superior to the individual but subordinate to federal power. Once this occurred, of course, the liberal undermining of this new intermediate entity has proceeded apace.

A. The Power to Zone

of the nation that must be preserved so that "the voice of the whole people would be fairly, fully, and peaceably expressed ... by the common reason" of all citizens, he also saw them as objects to be feared: "The mobs of great cities add just so much to the support of pure government, as sores do to the strength of the human body." For de Tocqueville, "the strength of free people resides in the local community," giving them both the "spirit of liberty" and the ability to withstand the "tyranny of the majority"; but the size of American cities and the nature of their inhabitants were also so threatening to the future of the republic that they required "an armed force which, while remaining subject to the wishes of the national majority, is independent of the peoples of the towns and capable of suppressing their excesses." Indeed, the vision of cities as being the home of "mobs," the working class, immigrants, and, finally, racial minorities, is a theme that runs throughout much of nineteenth and twentieth century thought....

... [T]he classification of American cities as corporations mattered; it can be understood as helping to repress the notion that associational rights were being affected in defining the laws governing city rights. No rights of association needed to be articulated when discussing the rights of "private" corporations, since property rights were sufficient to protect them against state power, and there was nothing that required rights of association to be imagined in discussing the subordination of "public" corporations. Yet, if no rights of association were recognized, cities, increasingly deprived of their economic character — the basis of their power for hundreds of years — had little defense against the reallocation of their power to the individual and to the state. There was nothing left that seemed to demand protection; therefore, nothing could prevent the control of the cities by the state.[16] ...

---

16. See also Hartog, Public Property and Private Power: The Corporation of the City of New York in American Law, 1730-1870, at 1 (1983):

> For the past 150 years American lawyers and judges have used the term "municipal corporation" to characterize the legal existence of a city. In doing so they have pictured urban government in ways that might surprise those not fully acculturated into legal ways of thinking. American courts do not usually regard a municipal corporation as the embodiment of a local political community. To the contrary, a municipal corporation is said to be a public corporation created by a state legislature solely for the purpose of providing subordinate administration. In legal theory, cities, towns, counties, and villages exist only because they serve as useful agencies of state power. No local government has any natural or inherent rights or constitutional authority. A municipal corporation is whatever the state legislature says it is, and it does whatever the state legislature and the state courts say it can do. As John Dillon insisted in the famous "Rule" proclaimed in his treatise of 1872 (which remained for many years the definitive legal source in all matters local governmental), unless municipal authority was expressly granted, necessarily implied, or crucial to the accomplishment of a legislatively defined goal, its legitimacy would not be recognized by an American court. "Any fair, reasonable (substantial) doubt concerning the existence of power is resolved by the courts against the municipal corporation, and the power is denied." — EDS.

■ VILLAGE OF EUCLID v. AMBLER REALTY CO.
272 U.S. 365 (1926)

Mr. Justice SUTHERLAND delivered the opinion of the Court.

The Village of Euclid is an Ohio municipal corporation. It adjoins and practically is a suburb of the City of Cleveland. Its estimated population is between 5,000 and 10,000, and its area from twelve to fourteen square miles, the greater part of which is farm lands or unimproved acreage. It lies, roughly, in the form of a parallelogram measuring approximately three and one-half miles each way. East and west it is traversed by three principal highways: Euclid Avenue, through the southerly border, St. Clair Avenue, through the central portion, and Lake Shore Boulevard, through the northerly border in close proximity to the shore of Lake Erie. The Nickel Plate railroad lies from 1,500 to 1,800 feet north of Euclid Avenue, and the Lake Shore railroad 1,600 feet farther to the north. The three highways and the two railroads are substantially parallel.

Appellee is the owner of a tract of land containing 68 acres, situated in the westerly end of the village, abutting on Euclid Avenue to the south and the Nickel Plate railroad to the north. Adjoining this tract, both on the east and on the west, there have been laid out restricted residential plats upon which residences have been erected.

On November 13, 1922, an ordinance was adopted by the Village Council, establishing a comprehensive zoning plan for regulating and restricting the location of trades, industries, apartment houses, two-family houses, single family houses, etc., the lot area to be built upon, the size and height of buildings, etc.

The entire area of the village is divided by the ordinance into six classes of use districts, denominated U-1 to U-6, inclusive; three classes of height districts, denominated H-1 to H-3, inclusive; and four classes of area districts, denominated A-1 to A-4, inclusive. The use districts are classified in respect of the buildings which may be erected within their respective limits, as follows: U-1 is restricted to single family dwellings, public parks, water towers and reservoirs, suburban and interurban electric railway passenger stations and rights of way, and farming, noncommercial greenhouse nurseries and truck gardening; U-2 is extended to include two-family dwellings; U-3 is further extended to include apartment houses, hotels, churches, schools, public libraries, museums, private clubs, community center buildings, hospitals, sanitariums, public playgrounds and recreation buildings, and a city hall and courthouse; U-4 is further extended to include banks, offices, studios, telephone exchanges, fire and police stations, restaurants, theatres and moving picture shows, retail stores and shops, sales offices, sample rooms, wholesale stores for hardware, drugs and groceries, stations for gasoline and oil (not exceeding 1,000 gallons storage) and for ice delivery, skating rinks and dance halls, electric substations, job and newspaper printing, public garages for motor vehicles, stables and wagon sheds (not exceeding five horses, wagons or motor trucks) and distributing stations for central store and commercial enterprises; U-5 is further extended to include billboards and advertising signs (if permitted), warehouses, ice and ice cream manufacturing and cold storage plants, bottling works, milk bottling and central distribution stations, laundries, carpet cleaning, dry cleaning and dyeing establishments, blacksmith, horseshoeing, wagon and motor vehicle repair shops, freight stations, street car barns, stables and wagon sheds (for more than five horses, wagons or motor trucks), and wholesale produce markets and salesrooms; U-6 is further extended to include plants for sewage disposal and for producing gas, garbage and refuse incineration, scrap iron, junk, scrap paper and rag storage, aviation fields, cemeteries, crematories, penal and correctional institutions, insane and feeble minded institutions, storage of oil and gasoline (not to exceed 25,000 gallons), and manufacturing and industrial operations of any kind other than, and any public utility not included in, a class U-1, U-2, U-3,

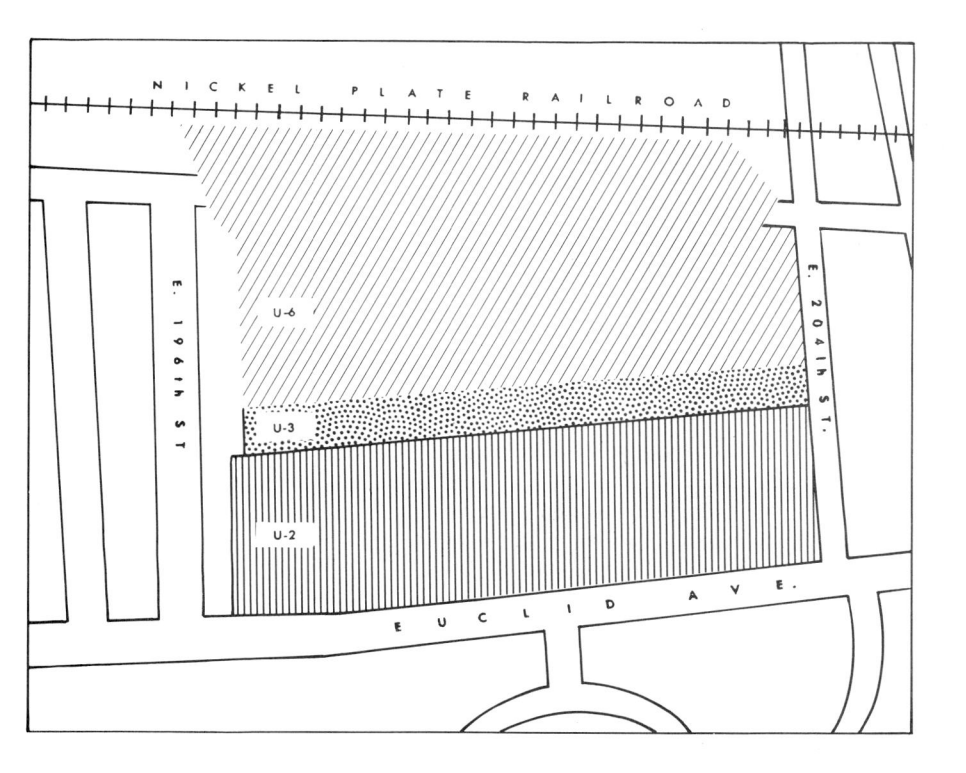

U-4, or U-5 use. There is a seventh class of uses which is prohibited altogether.

Class U-1 is the only district in which buildings are restricted to those enumerated. In the other classes the uses are cumulative; that is to say, uses in class U-2 include those enumerated in the preceding class, U-1; class U-3 includes uses enumerated in the preceding classes, U-2 and U-1; and so on. In addition to the enumerated uses, the ordinance provides for accessory uses, that is, for uses customarily incident to the principal use, such as private garages. Many regulations are provided in respect of such accessory uses.

The height districts are classified as follows: In class H-1, buildings are limited to a height of two and one-half stories or thirty-five feet; in class H-2, to four stories or fifty feet; in class H-3, to eight feet. To all of these, certain exceptions are made, as in the case of church spires, water tanks, etc.

The classification of area districts is: In A-1 districts, dwellings or apartment houses to accommodate more than one family must have at least 5,000 square feet for interior lots and at least 4,000 square feet for corner lots; in A-2 districts, the area must be at least 2,500 square feet for interior lots, and 2,000 square feet for corner lots; in A-3 districts, the limits are 1,250 and 1,000 square feet, respectively; in A-4 districts, the limits are 900 and 700 square feet, respectively. The ordinance contains, in great variety and detail, provisions in respect of width of lots, front, side and rear yards, and other matters, including restrictions and regulations as to the use of bill boards, sign boards and advertising signs.

A single family dwelling consists of a basement and not less than three rooms and a bathroom. A two-family dwelling consists of a basement and not less than four living rooms and a bathroom for each family; and is further described as a detached dwelling for the occupation of two families, one having its principal living rooms on the first floor and the other on the second floor.

Appellee's tract of land comes under U-2, U-3 and U-6. The first strip of 620 feet immediately north of Euclid Avenue falls in class U-2, the next 130 feet to the north, in U-3, and the remainder in U-6. The uses of the first 620 feet, therefore, do not include apartment houses, hotels, churches, schools, or other public and semi-public buildings, or other uses enumerated in respect of U-3 to U-6, inclusive. The uses of the next 130 feet include all of these, but exclude industries, theatres, banks, shops, and the various other uses set forth in respect of U-4 to U-6, inclusive.

Annexed to the ordinance, and made a part of it, is a zone map, showing the location and limits of the various use, height and area districts, from which it appears that the three classes overlap one another; that is to say, for example, both U-5 and U-6 use districts are

A. The Power to Zone 181

in A-4 area districts, but the former is in H-2 and the latter in H-3 height districts. The plan is a complicated one and can be better understood by an inspection of the map, though it does not seem necessary to reproduce it for present purposes.

The lands lying between the two railroads for the entire length of the village area and extending some distance on either side to the north and south, having an average width of about 1,600 feet, are left open, with slight exceptions, for industrial and all other uses. This includes the larger part of appellee's tract. Approximately one-sixth of the area of the entire village is included in U-5 and U-6 use districts. That part of the village lying south of Euclid Avenue is principally in U-1 districts. The lands lying north of Euclid Avenue and bordering on the long strip just described are included in U-1, U-2, U-3 and U-4 districts, principally in U-2.

The enforcement of the ordinance is entrusted to the inspector of buildings, under rules and regulations of the board of zoning appeals. Meetings of the board are public, and minutes of its proceedings are kept. It is authorized to adopt rules and regulations to carry into effect provisions of the ordinance. Decisions of the inspector of buildings may be appealed to the board by any person claiming to be adversely affected by any such decision. The board is given power in specific cases of practical difficulty or unnecessary hardship to interpret the ordinance in harmony with its general purpose and intent, so that the public health, safety and general welfare may be secure and substantial justice done. Penalties are prescribed for violations, and it is provided that the various provisions are to be regarded as independent and the holding of any provision to be unconstitutional, void or ineffective shall not affect any of the others.

The ordinance is assailed on the grounds that it is in derogation of §1 of the Fourteenth Amendment to the Federal Constitution in that it deprives appellee of liberty and property without due process of law and denies it the equal protection of the law, and that it offends against certain provisions of the Constitution of the State of Ohio. The prayer of the bill is for an injunction restraining the enforcement of the ordinance and all attempts to impose or maintain as to appellee's property any of the restrictions, limitations or conditions. The court below held the ordinance to be unconstitutional and void, and enjoined its enforcement. 297 Fed. 307.

Before proceeding to a consideration of the case, it is necessary to determine the scope of the inquiry. The bill alleges that the tract of land in question is vacant and has been held for years for the purpose of selling and developing it for industrial uses, for which it is especially adapted, being immediately in the path of progressive industrial development; that for such uses it has a market value of about $10,000 per acre, but if the use be limited to residential purposes the market value is not in excess of $2,500 per acre; that the first 200 feet of the parcel back from Euclid Avenue, if unrestricted in respect of use, has a value of $150 per front foot, but if limited to residential uses, and ordinary mercantile business be excluded therefrom, its value is not in excess of $50 per front foot.

It is specifically averred that the ordinance attempts to restrict and control the lawful uses of appellee's land so as to confiscate and destroy a great part of its value; that it is being enforced in accordance with its terms; that prospective buyers of land for industrial, commercial and residential uses in the metropolitan district of Cleveland are deterred from buying any part of this land because of the existence of the ordinance and the necessity thereby entailed of conducting burdensome and expensive litigation in order to vindicate the right to use the land for lawful and legitimate purposes; that the ordinance constitutes a cloud upon the land, reduces and destroys its value, and has the effect of diverting the normal industrial, commercial and residential development thereof to other and less favorable locations.

The record goes no farther than to show, as the lower court found, that the normal, and reasonably to be expected, use and development of that part of appellee's land adjoining Euclid Avenue is for general trade and commercial purposes, particularly retail stores and like establishments, and that the normal, and reasonably to be expected, use and development of the residue of the land is for industrial and trade purposes. Whatever injury is inflicted by the mere existence and threatened enforcement of the ordinance is due to restrictions in respect of these and similar uses; to which perhaps should be added — if not included in the foregoing — restrictions in respect of apartment houses. Specifically, there is nothing in the record to suggest that any damage results from the presence in the ordinance of those restrictions relating to churches, schools, libraries and other public and semi-public buildings. It is neither alleged nor proved that there is, or may be, a demand for any part of appellee's land for any of the last named uses; and we cannot assume the existence of facts which would justify an injunction upon this record in respect of this class of restrictions. For present purposes the provisions of the ordinance in respect of these uses may, therefore, be put aside as unnecessary to be considered. It is also unnecessary to consider the effect of the restrictions in respect of U-1 districts, since none of appellee's land falls within that class.

We proceed, then, to a consideration of those provisions of the ordinance to which the case as it is made relates, first disposing of a preliminary matter.

A motion was made in the court below to dismiss the bill on the ground that, because complainant [appellee] had made no effort to obtain a building permit or apply to the zoning board of appeals for relief as it might have done under the terms of the ordinance, the suit

A. The Power to Zone

was premature. The motion was properly overruled. The effect of the allegations of the bill is that the ordinance of its own force operates greatly to reduce the value of appellee's lands and destroy their marketability for industrial, commercial and residential uses; and the attack is directed, not against any specific provision or provisions, but against the ordinance as an entirety. Assuming the premises, the existence and maintenance of the ordinance, in effect, constitutes a present invasion of appellee's property rights and a threat to continue it. Under these circumstances, the equitable jurisdiction is clear. See Terrace v. Thompson, 263 U.S. 197, 215; Pierce v. Society of Sisters, 268 U.S. 510, 535.

It is not necessary to set forth the provisions of the Ohio Constitution which are thought to be infringed. The question is the same under both Constitutions, namely, as stated by appellee: Is the ordinance invalid in that it violates the constitutional protection "to the right of property in the appellee by attempted regulations under the guise of the police power, which are unreasonable and confiscatory?"

Building zone laws are of modern origin. They began in this country about twenty-five years ago. Until recent years, urban life was comparatively simple; but with the great increase and concentration of population, problems have developed, and constantly are developing, which require, and will continue to require, additional restrictions in respect of the use and occupation of private lands in urban communities. Regulations, the wisdom, necessity and validity of which, as applied to existing conditions, are so apparent that they are now uniformly sustained, a century ago, or even half a century ago, probably would have been rejected as arbitrary and oppressive. Such regulations are sustained, under the complex conditions of our day, for reasons analogous to those which justify traffic regulations, which, before the advent of automobiles and rapid transit street railways, would have been condemned as fatally arbitrary and unreasonable. And in this there is no inconsistency, for while the meaning of constitutional guaranties never varies, the scope of their application must expand or contract to meet the new and different conditions which are constantly coming within the field of their operation. In a changing world, it is impossible that it should be otherwise. But although a degree of elasticity is thus imparted, not to the *meaning*, but to the *application* of constitutional principles, statutes and ordinances, which, after giving due weight to the new conditions, are found clearly not to conform to the Constitution, of course, must fall.

The ordinance now under review, and all similar laws and regulations, must find their justification in some aspect of the police power, asserted for the public welfare. The line which in this field separates the legitimate from the illegitimate assumption of power is not capable of precise delimitation. It varies with circumstances and conditions. A regulatory zoning ordinance, which would be clearly valid as applied to the great cities, might be clearly invalid as applied to rural communities. In solving doubts, the maxim sic utere tuo ut alienum non laedas, which lies at the foundation of so much of the common law of nuisances, ordinarily will furnish a fairly helpful clew. And the law of nuisances, likewise, may be consulted, not for the purpose of controlling, but for the helpful aid of its analogies in the process of ascertaining the scope of, the power. Thus the question whether the power exists to forbid the erection of a building of a particular kind or for a particular use, like the question whether a particular thing is a nuisance, is to be determined, not by an abstract consideration of the building or of the thing considered apart, but by considering it in connection with the circumstances and the locality. Sturgis v. Bridgeman, L.R. 11 Ch. 852, 865. A nuisance may be merely a right thing in the wrong place, — like a pig in the parlor instead of the barnyard. If the validity of the legislative classification for zoning purposes be fairly debatable, the legislative judgment must be allowed to control. Radice v. New York, 264 U.S. 292, 294.

There is no serious difference of opinion in respect of the validity of laws and regulations fixing the height of buildings within reasonable limits, the character of materials and methods of construction, and the adjoining area which must be left open, in order to minimize the danger of fire or collapse, the evils of overcrowding, and the like, and excluding from residential sections offensive trades, industries and structures likely to create nuisances. See Welch v. Swasey, 214 U.S. 91; Hadacheck v. Los Angeles, 239 U.S. 394; Reinman v. Little Rock, 237 U.S. 171; Cusack Co. v. City of Chicago, 242 U.S. 526, 529-530.

Here, however, the exclusion is in general terms of all industrial establishments, and it may thereby happen that not only offensive or dangerous industries will be excluded, but those which are neither offensive nor dangerous will share the same fate. But this is no more than happens in respect of many practice-forbidding laws which this Court has upheld although drawn in general terms so as to include individual cases that may turn out to be innocuous in themselves. Hebe Co. v. Shaw, 248 U.S. 297, 303; Pierce Oil Corp. v. City of Hope, 248 U.S. 498, 500. The inclusion of a reasonable margin to insure effective enforcement, will not put upon a law, otherwise valid, the stamp of invalidity. Such laws may also find their justification in the fact that, in some fields, the bad fades into the good by such insensible degrees that the two are not capable of being readily distinguished and separated in terms of legislation. In the light of these considerations, we are not prepared to say that the end in view was not sufficient to justify the general rule of the ordinance, although some industries of an innocent character might fall within the proscribed class. It can not be said that the ordinance in this respect "passes the bounds of reason and assumes

A. The Power to Zone 185

the character of a merely arbitrary fiat." Purity Extract Co. v. Lynch, 226 U.S. 192, 204. Moreover, the restrictive provisions of the ordinance in this particular may be sustained upon the principles applicable to the broader exclusion from residential districts of all business and trade structures, presently to be discussed.

It is said that the Village of Euclid is a mere suburb of the City of Cleveland; that the industrial development of that city has now reached and in some degree extended into the village and, in the obvious course of things, will soon absorb the entire area for industrial enterprises; that the effect of the ordinance is to divert this natural development elsewhere with the consequent loss of increased values to the owners of the lands within the village borders. But the village, though physically a suburb of Cleveland, is politically a separate municipality, with powers of its own and authority to govern itself as it sees fit within the limits of the organic law of its creation and the State and Federal Constitutions. Its governing authorities, presumably representing a majority of its inhabitants and voicing their will, have determined, not that industrial development shall cease at its boundaries, but that the course of such development shall proceed within definitely fixed lines. If it be a proper exercise of the police power to relegate industrial establishments to localities separated from residential sections, it is not easy to find a sufficient reason for denying the power because the effect of its exercise is to divert an industrial flow from the course which it would follow, to the injury of the residential public if left alone, to another course where such injury will be obviated. It is not meant by this, however, to exclude the possibility of cases where the general public interest would so far outweigh the interest of the municipality that the municipality would not be allowed to stand in the way.

We find no difficulty in sustaining restrictions of the kind thus far reviewed. The serious question in the case arises over the provisions of the ordinance excluding from residential districts, apartment houses, business houses, retail stores and shops, and other like establishments. This question involves the validity of what is really the crux of the more recent zoning legislation, namely, the creation and maintenance of residential districts, from which business and trade of every sort, including hotels and apartment houses, are excluded. Upon that question this Court has not thus far spoken. The decisions of the state courts are numerous and conflicting; but those which broadly sustain the power greatly outnumber those which deny altogether or narrowly limit it; and it is very apparent that there is a constantly increasing tendency in the direction of the broader view. . . .

The matter of zoning has received much attention at the hands of commissions and experts, and the results of their investigations have been set forth in comprehensive reports. These reports, which bear every evidence of painstaking consideration, concur in the view that the segregation of residential, business, and industrial buildings will make it easier to provide fire apparatus suitable for the character and intensity of the development in each section; that it will increase the safety and security of home life; greatly tend to prevent street accidents, especially to children, by reducing the traffic and resulting confusion in residential sections; decrease noise and other conditions which produce or intensify nervous disorders; preserve a more favorable environment in which to rear children, etc. With particular reference to apartment houses, it is pointed out that the development of detached house sections is greatly retarded by the coming of apartment houses, which has sometimes resulted in destroying the entire section for private house purposes; that in such sections very often the apartment house is a mere parasite, constructed in order to take advantage of the open spaces and attractive surroundings created by the residential character of the district. Moreover, the coming of one apartment house is followed by others, interfering by their height and bulk with the free circulation of air and monopolizing the rays of the sun which otherwise would fall upon the smaller homes, and bringing, as their necessary accompaniments, the disturbing noises incident to increased traffic and business, and the occupation, by means of moving and parked automobiles, of larger portions of the streets, thus detracting from their safety and depriving children of the privilege of quiet and open spaces for play, enjoyed by those in more favored localities, — until, finally, the residential character of the neighborhood and its desirability as a place of detached residences are utterly destroyed. Under these circumstances, apartment houses, which in a different environment would be not only entirely unobjectionable but highly desirable, come very near to being nuisances.

If these reasons, thus summarized, do not demonstrate the wisdom or sound policy in all respects of those restrictions which we have indicated as pertinent to the inquiry, at least, the reasons are sufficiently cogent to preclude us from saying, as it must be said before the ordinance can be declared unconstitutional, that such provisions are clearly arbitrary and unreasonable, having no substantial relation to the public health, safety, morals, or general welfare.

It is true that when, if ever, the provisions set forth in the ordinance in tedious and minute detail, come to be concretely applied to particular premises, including those of the appellee, or to particular conditions, or to be considered in connection with specific complaints, some of them, or even many of them, may be found to be clearly arbitrary and unreasonable. But where the equitable remedy of injunction is sought, as it is here, not upon the ground of a present infringement or denial of a specific right, or of a particular injury in process of actual execution, but upon the broad ground that the mere existence and threatened enforcement of the ordinance, by materially and adversely affecting

A. The Power to Zone

values and curtailing the opportunities of the market, constitute a present and irreparable injury, the court will not scrutinize its provisions, sentence by sentence, to ascertain by a process of piecemeal dissection whether there may be, here and there, provisions of a minor character, or relating to matters of administration, or not shown to contribute to the injury complained of, which, if attacked separately, might not withstand the test of constitutionality. In respect of such provisions, of which specific complaint is not made, it cannot be said that the land owner has suffered or is threatened with an injury which entitles him to challenge their constitutionality. . . .

The relief sought here is of the same character, namely, an injunction against the enforcement of any of the restrictions, limitations or conditions of the ordinance. And the gravamen of the complaint is that a portion of the land of the appellee cannot be sold for certain enumerated uses because of the general and broad restraints of the ordinance. What would be the effect of a restraint imposed by one or more of the innumerable provisions of the ordinance, considered apart, upon the value or marketability of the lands is neither disclosed by the bill nor by the evidence, and we are afforded no basis, apart from mere speculation, upon which to rest a conclusion that it or they would have any appreciable effect upon those matters. Under these circumstances, therefore, it is enough for us to determine, as we do, that the ordinance in its general scope and dominant features, so far as its provisions are here involved, is a valid exercise of authority, leaving other provisions to be dealt with as cases arise directly involving them.

And this is in accordance with the traditional policy of this Court. In the realm of constitutional law, especially, this Court has perceived the embarrassment which is likely to result from an attempt to formulate rules or decide questions beyond the necessities of the immediate issue. It has preferred to follow the method of a gradual approach to the general by a systematically guarded application and extension of constitutional principles to particular cases as they arise, rather than by out of hand attempts to establish general rules to which future cases must be fitted. This process applies with peculiar force to the solution of questions arising under the due process clause of the Constitution as applied to the exercise of the flexible powers of police, with which we are here concerned.

Decree reversed.

Mr. Justice VAN DEVANTER, Mr. Justice MCREYNOLDS and Mr. Justice BUTLER, dissent.

Notes

1. The lower court in Ambler Realty Co. v. Village of Euclid, 297 F. 307, 313, 316 (N.D. Ohio 1924), reasoned:

The argument supporting this ordinance proceeds, it seems to me, both on a mistaken view of what is property and of what is police power. Property, generally speaking, defendant's counsel concede, is protected against a taking without compensation, by the guaranties of the Ohio and United States Constitutions. But their view seems to be that so long as the owner remains clothed with the legal title thereto and is not ousted from the physical possession thereof, his property is not taken, no matter to what extent his right to use it is invaded or destroyed or its present or prospective value is depreciated. This is an erroneous view. The right to property, as used in the Constitution, has no such limited meaning. As has often been said is substance by the Supreme Court: "There can be no conception of property aside from its control and use, and upon its use depends its value." . . .

The plain truth is that the true object of the ordinance in question is to place all the property in an undeveloped area of 16 square miles in a strait-jacket. The purpose to be accomplished is really to regulate the mode of living of persons who may hereafter inhabit it. In the last analysis, the result to be accomplished is to classify the population and segregate them according to their income or situation in life. The true reason why some persons live in a mansion and others in a shack, why some live in a single-family dwelling and others in a double-family dwelling, why some live in a two-family dwelling and others in an apartment, or why some live in a well-kept apartment and others in a tenement, is primarily economic. It is a matter of income and wealth, plus the labor and difficulty of procuring adequate domestic service. Aside from contributing to these results and furthering such class tendencies, the ordinance has also an esthetic purpose; that is to say, to make this village develop into a city along lines now conceived by the village council to be attractive and beautiful.

District Judge Westenhaver, whose disapproval of Euclid's zoning ordinance was reversed by the Supreme Court, was a long-time personal friend and professional associate of Ambler counsel Newton D. Baker, former Cleveland mayor and Secretary of War in the Wilson Administration.

2. The history of the *Euclid* case is the story of the adoption of zoning in this country. Two opposing lines of decision in the state courts were presented to the Supreme Court. The cases are compiled in Bettman's amicus brief at 15 et seq. (1926). See also Note, 72 U. Pa. L. Rev. 421 (1924). After the first argument, a majority of the Court apparently concluded that zoning was an unconstitutional interference with property. See McCormack, A Law Clerk's Recollections, 46 Colum. L. Rev. 710 (1946). However, a dramatic reversal of the vote followed an equally dramatic rehearing. See Metzenbaum, The Law of Zoning 108 et seq. (1930). If you like so to express things, "Smug reaction gave way before the enlightened forces of social advancement." Isaacs, The Place of Municipal Attorneys in City Planning, Institute of Municipal Law Officers 126, 127 (1930).

A. The Power to Zone

By the end of 1927, zoning laws had been enacted by some forty-five states. United States Department of Commerce, Survey of Zoning Laws and Ordinances 2 (1928). At the close of 1930, authority for the adoption of zoning ordinances had been extended to municipalities in forty-seven states, and in the forty-eighth, the general home rule provisions of the constitution had been judicially construed to grant authority for the adoption of zoning ordinances by cities of the first class. United States Department of Commerce, Survey of Zoning Laws and Ordinances Adopted During 1930, 2-3 (1931). At the close of 1930, zoning ordinances were in effect in 981 municipalities throughout the United States, representing a population of more than 46 million, some 67 percent of the urban population. United States Department of Commerce, Zoned Municipalities in the United States 1 (1931). See also National Resources Planning Board, State Legislation on Planning, Zoning and Platting xii (rev. ed. 1941).

3. Appropriately enough the subject of a biography subtitled "A Man Against the State," Justice Sutherland is, of course, noted for the conservative views he espoused on the Court. In the famous Adkins v. Children's Hospital, 261 U.S. 525, 560, 561 (1923), he wrote the opinion invalidating a minimum wage law for women. While acknowledging the "mass of reports, opinions of special observers and students of the subject," the Court found the data "interesting but only mildly persuasive" and overruled the legislature. "To sustain the individual freedom of action contemplated by the Constitution," wrote Justice Sutherland, "is not to strike down the common good, but to exalt it; for surely the good of society as a whole cannot be better served than by the preservation against arbitrary restraint of the liberties of its constituent members."

4. See State ex rel. Lieux v. Village of Westlake, 154 Ohio St. 412, 417, 96 N.E.2d 414, 416 (1951):

> Our conclusion is that an applicant for a building permit, whose application is refused because of the provisions of a zoning ordinance, cannot secure a writ of mandamus, compelling the issuance of such permit on the ground that the ordinance as a whole is unconstitutional, without first exhausting administrative remedies provided by such ordinance, if such remedies might enable her to secure such a permit.

5. See 1 Metzenbaum, The Law of Zoning 60 (2d ed. 1955):

> Euclid has not been hampered, as was predicted by those opposed to the zoning.
> On the contrary, it has enjoyed what is said to have been one of the most singular ratios of growth, among all municipalities in this land, from 1940 to 1950; then numbering more than 42,000 population. It has become the third largest of the municipalities in its county. . . .

It is believed that its Zoning Ordinance — early enacted — has played no inconspicuous part in this almost unmatched development, for homes have felt safe against intrusion of factories and business; great industrial plants have abundant acreage for their fine buildings; retail business is advantageously situated.

Is this valid evidence of the efficacy of zoning? Since 1926, industrial growth in Cleveland has extended largely along the railroad lines, and the area between the Nickel Plate and New York Central tracks is almost wholly industrialized. The Ambler Realty Company property is today zoned for industry. (Letter from Regional Planning Commission to Professor Haar, Nov. 22, 1954.) The plot is now occupied by General Motors' Inland Plant, with two gas stations, a restaurant, and a medical center nearby.

6. As you read the zoning cases that take up much of the remainder of this volume, it should strike you that the nature of the typical land-use case differs very little from *Euclid*. Disgruntled property owners (sometimes developers, at other times their neighbors) seek access to the courts to redress the negative economic and social consequences of local decision-makers' acts or omissions. Litigants and their advocates call on courts to draw useful lines between the valid exercise of the police power and confiscatory or arbitrary regulations that amount to due process violations, if not compensable takings. Members of the judiciary still wrestle with the appropriate level of deference to state and local legislators and administrators.

The Euclidean model of judicial discretion, not the activism of the *Nectow* case that follows, remains ascendant for the most part, despite the occasional flexing of judicial activism as outlined in Chapter IV. Once you have studied Justice Sutherland's words from just two years later, consider how flexible and responsive Euclidean zoning would have been if it had been subjected to such judicial oversight over the succeeding six decades.

■ NECTOW v. CITY OF CAMBRIDGE
277 U.S. 183 (1928)

Mr. Justice SUTHERLAND delivered the opinion of the Court.

A zoning ordinance of the City of Cambridge divides the city into three kinds of districts: residential, business and unrestricted. Each of these districts is subclassified in respect of the kind of buildings which may be erected. The ordinance is an elaborate one, and of the same general character as that considered by this Court in Euclid v. Ambler

A. The Power to Zone

Co., 272 U.S. 365. In its general scope it is conceded to be constitutional within that decision. The land of plaintiff in error was put in district R-3, in which are permitted only dwellings, hotels, clubs, churches, schools, philanthropic institutions, greenhouses and gardening, with customary incidental accessories. The attack upon the ordinance is that, as specifically applied to plaintiff in error, it deprived him of his property without due process of law in contravention of the Fourteenth Amendment.

The suit was for a mandatory injunction directing the city and its inspector of buildings to pass upon an application of the plaintiff in error for a permit to erect any lawful buildings upon a tract of land without regard to the provisions of the ordinance including such tract within a residential district. The case was referred to a master to make and report findings of fact. After a view of the premises and the surrounding territory, and a hearing, the master made and reported his findings. The case came on to be heard by a justice of the court, who, after confirming the master's report, reported the case for the determination of the full court. Upon consideration, that court sustained the ordinance as applied to plaintiff in error, and dismissed the bill. 260 Mass. 441.

A condensed statement of facts, taken from the master's report, is all that is necessary. When the zoning ordinance was enacted, plaintiff in error was and still is the owner of a tract of land containing 140,000 square feet, of which the locus here in question is a part. The locus contains about 29,000 square feet, with a frontage on Brookline street, lying west, of 304.75 feet, on Henry street, lying north, of 100 feet, on the other land of the plaintiff in error, lying east, of 264 feet, and on land of the Ford Motor Company, lying southerly, of 75 feet. The territory lying east and south is unrestricted. The lands beyond Henry street to the north and beyond Brookline street to the west are within a restricted residential district. The effect of the zoning is to separate from the west end of plaintiff in error's tract a strip 100 feet in width. The Ford Motor Company has a large auto assembling factory south of the locus; and a soap factory and the tracks of the Boston & Albany Railroad lie near. Opposite the locus, on Brookline street, and included in the same district, there are some residences; and opposite the locus, on Henry street, and in the same district, are other residences. The locus is now vacant, although it was once occupied by a mansion house. Before the passage of the ordinance in question, plaintiff in error had outstanding a contract for the sale of the greater part of his entire tract of land for the sum of $63,000. Because of the zoning restrictions, the purchaser refused to comply with the contract. Under the ordinance, business and industry of all sorts are excluded from the locus, while the remainder of the tract is unrestricted. It further appears that provision has been made for widening Brookline street, the effect of which, if carried out, will be to reduce the depth of the locus to 65 feet. After a statement at length of further facts, the master finds "that no practical use can be made of the land in question for residential purposes, because among other reasons herein related, there would not be adequate return on the amount of any investment for the development of the property." The last finding of the master is:

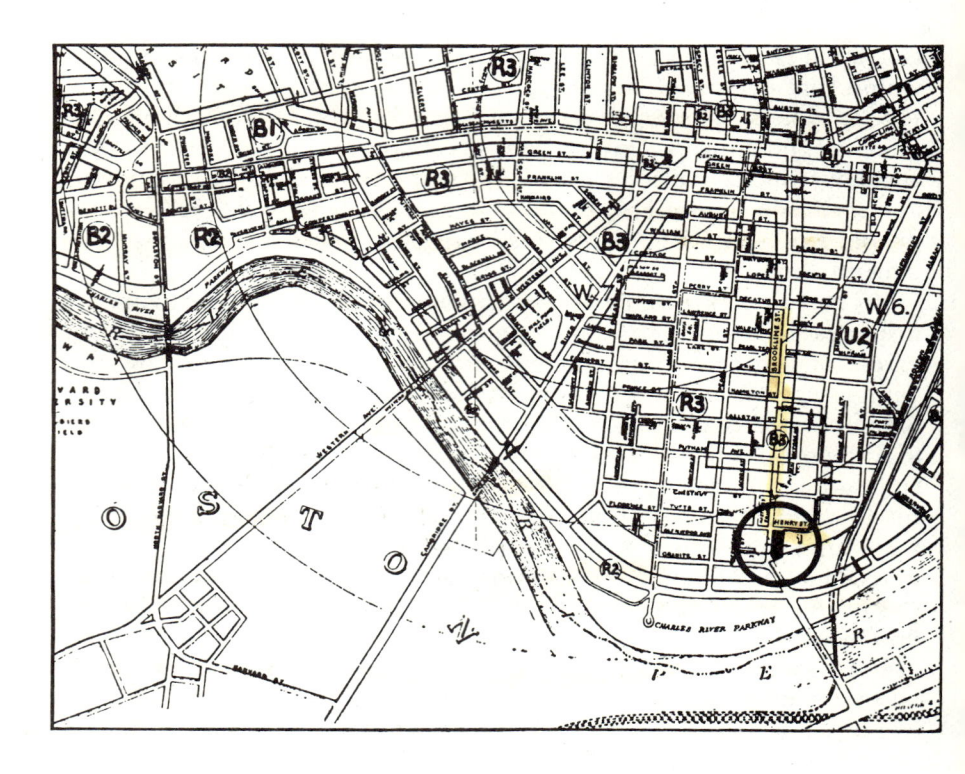

> I am satisfied that the districting of the plaintiff's land in a residence district would not promote the health, safety, convenience and general welfare of the inhabitants of that part of the defendant City, taking into account the natural development thereof and the character of the district and the resulting benefit to accrue to the whole City and I so find.

It is made pretty clear that because of the industrial and railroad purposes to which the immediately adjoining lands to the south and east have been devoted and for which they are zoned, the locus is of comparatively little value for the limited uses permitted by the ordinance.

We quite agree with the opinion expressed below that a court should not set aside the determination of public officers in such a

A. The Power to Zone

matter unless it is clear that their action "has no foundation in reason and is a mere arbitrary or irrational exercise of power having no substantial relation to the public health, the public morals, the public safety or the public welfare in its proper sense." Euclid v. Ambler Co., supra, p. 395.

An inspection of a plat of the city upon which the zoning districts are outlined, taken in connection with the master's findings, shows with reasonable certainty that the inclusion of the locus in question is not indispensable to the general plan. The boundary line of the residential district before reaching the locus runs for some distance along the streets, and to exclude the locus from the residential district requires only that such line shall be continued 100 feet further along Henry street and thence south along Brookline street. There does not appear to be any reason why this should not be done. Nevertheless, if that were all, we should not be warranted in substituting our judgment for that of the zoning authorities primarily charged with the duty and responsibility of determining the question. Zahn v. Bd. of Public Works, 274 U.S. 325, 328, and cases cited. But that is not all. The governmental power to interfere by zoning regulations with the general rights of the land owner by restricting the character of his use, is not unlimited, and other questions aside, such restriction cannot be imposed if it does not bear a substantial relation to the public health, safety, morals, or general welfare. Euclid v. Ambler Co., supra, p. 395. Here, the express finding of the master, already quoted, confirmed by the court below, is that the health, safety, convenience and general welfare of the inhabitants of the part of the city affected will not be promoted by the disposition made by the ordinance of the locus in question. This finding of the master, after a hearing and an inspection of the entire area affected, supported, as we think it is, by other findings of fact, is determinative of the case. That the invasion of the property of plaintiff in error was serious and highly injurious is clearly established; and, since a necessary basis for the support of that invasion is wanting, the action of the zoning authorities comes within the ban of the Fourteenth Amendment and cannot be sustained.

Judgment reversed.

Notes

1. In the *Nectow* decision, the Supreme Court seems to enunciate what had been foreshadowed in *Euclid* — a close supervision of the recently validated zoning power. Yet you will note in the subsequent cases that the Court has consistently refused to pass judgment in zoning cases. During the six terms of the Court from 1949-1950 to 1954-1955,

appeals were dismissed or petitions for certiorari denied in twenty-one cases involving zoning and local planning matters. Johnson, Constitutional Law and Community Planning, 20 Law & Contemp. Probs. 199, 208 (1955). As many of the cases in Chapter IV illustrate, the Burger Court, despite some failures to resolve such nagging questions as the remedy for regulatory takings (see infra page 875), put an end to the period of nonintervention.

2. Zahn v. Board of Public Works, 274 U.S. 325, 327-328 (1927), cited by the *Nectow* Court, offered the following scenario:

> The property of plaintiffs in error adjoins Wilshire Avenue, a main artery of travel through and beyond the city; and if such property were available for business purposes its market value would be greatly enhanced. The lands within the district were, when the ordinance was adopted, sparsely occupied by buildings, those in which business was carried on being limited to a few real estate offices, a grocery store, a market, a fruit stand, and a two-story business block. Much of the land adjoining the boulevard within the restricted district had already been sold with restrictions against buildings for business purposes, although the property of plaintiffs in error and the adjacent property had not been so restricted. The effect of the evidence is to show that the entire neighborhood, at the time of the passage of the zoning ordinance, was largely unimproved, but in course of rapid development. The Common Council of the city, upon these and other facts, concluded that the public welfare would be promoted by constituting the area, including the property of plaintiffs in error, a zone "B" district; and it is impossible for us to say that their conclusion in that respect was clearly arbitrary and unreasonable. The most that can be said is that whether that determination was an unreasonable, arbitrary or unequal exercise of power is fairly debatable. In such circumstances, the settled rule of this court is that it will not substitute its judgment for that of the legislative body charged with the primary duty and responsibility of determining the question.

3. In Nectow v. City of Cambridge, 260 Mass. 441, 447, 448, 157 N.E. 618, 620 (1927), the court stated:

> If there is to be zoning at all, the dividing line must be drawn somewhere. There cannot be a twilight zone. If residence districts are to exist, they must be bounded. In the nature of things, the location of the precise limits of the several districts demands the exercise of judgment and sagacity. There can be no standard susceptible of mathematical exactness in its application. Opinions of the wise and good well may differ as to the place to put the separation between different districts. . . . Courts cannot set aside the decisions of public officers in such a matter unless compelled to the conclusion that it has no foundation in reason and is a mere arbitrary or irrational exercise of power having no substantial relation to

A. The Power to Zone

the public health, the public morals, the public safety or the public welfare in its proper sense. These considerations cannot be weighed with exactness. That they demand the placing of the boundary of a zone 100 feet one way or the other in land having similar material features would be hard to say as matter of law.... The case at bar is close to the line. But we do not feel justified in holding that the zoning line established is whimsical and without foundation in reason.

See also Gleason v. Keswick Improvement Association, 197 Md. 46, 78 A.2d 164 (1951). Suppose the line between two districts runs right through plaintiff's building? See City of Everett v. Capitol Motor Transport Co., 330 Mass. 417, 114 N.E.2d 547 (1953). ("There is nothing to show that peculiar significance should be attached to the division of the premises.")

Those state and lower federal court judges evaluating zoning and planning schemes who were looking for guidance from the United States Supreme Court were thus left with two conflicting messages: the extreme deference of *Euclid* and the stern warning of *Nectow*. For the most part, Sutherland's initial word has been heeded and in the great majority of cases judges have given planners and local legislators a great amount of leeway. Nevertheless, as the four cases that follow illustrate, there is a limit to a court's patience with a zoning scheme that proves confiscatory or arbitrary, and thus violates federal and state constitutional notions of due process. Even without a detailed Supreme Court blueprint, notice how judges — inspired and instructed by the legal commentators — moved from a visceral reaction to local regulatory abuse toward a studious inquiry as to the existence of a meaningful nexus between a single zoning act and the demands of comprehensive planning.

■ ARVERNE BAY CONSTRUCTION CO. v. THATCHER
278 N.Y. 222, 15 N.E.2d 587 (1938)

LEHMAN, Judge. The plaintiff is the owner of a plot of vacant land on the northerly side of Linden boulevard in the borough of Brooklyn. Until 1928 the district in which the property is situated was classified as an "unrestricted" zone, under the Building Zone Resolution of the city of New York (New York Code of Ordinances, Appendix B). Then, by amendment of the ordinance and the "Use District Map," the district was placed in a residence zone. The plaintiff, claiming that its property could not be used properly or profitably for any purpose permitted in a residence zone and that, in consequence, the zoning ordinance imposed unnecessary hardship upon it, applied to the Board of Standards and Appeals, under section 21 of the Building Zone Resolution, for a variance which would permit the use of the premises for a gasoline service station. The application was denied, and, upon review in certiorari proceedings, the courts sustained the determination of the board. People ex rel. Arverne Bay Construction Co. v. Murdock, 247 App. Div. 889, 286 N.Y.S. 785; affirmed, 271 N.Y. 631, 3 N.E.2d 457.

Defeated in its attempt to obtain permission to put its property to a profitable use, the plaintiff has brought this action to secure an adjudication that the restrictions placed upon the use of its property by the zoning ordinance result in deprivation of its property without due process of law and that, in so far as the ordinance affects its property, the ordinance violates the provisions of the Constitution of the United States and the Constitution of the State of New York. U.S.C.A. Const. Amend. 14; Const. N.Y. art. 1, §6. In this action it demands as a right what has been refused to it as a favor. . . .

The amendment to the zoning ordinance, about which complaint is made, changed from an unrestricted zone to a residential district the property abutting on Linden boulevard for a distance of four miles, with the exception of a small section at a railroad crossing. The district is almost undeveloped. There had been no building construction in that area for many years prior to the amendment. The chairman of the building zone commission which drafted the zoning ordinance, testifying as an expert witness for the defendant, described the district as in a "transition state from the farms as I knew them thirty and forty years ago south of this location." There are some old buildings used for non-conforming purposes, left from the days when the district was used for farming. There are only three buildings in Linden boulevard in a distance of about a mile. One of these buildings is a cow stable and a second building is used as an office in connection with the dairy business conducted there. A gasoline station erected on that boulevard would, it is plain, not adversely affect the health, morals, safety or general welfare of the people who now live in that neighborhood. Justification, if any, for the ordinance restricting the use of the property on Linden boulevard to residential purposes must be found in the control over future development which will result from such restrictions.

Without zoning restrictions, the self-interest of the individual property owners will almost inevitably dictate the form of the development of the district. The plaintiff claims, and has conclusively shown at the trial, that at no time since the amendment of the zoning resolution could its property be profitably used for residential purposes. The expert witness for the city, to whose testimony we have already referred and whose qualifications are universally recognized, admits that such a

A. The Power to Zone

residential improvement would, even now after the lapse of ten years, be "premature." The property, then, must for the present remain unimproved and unproductive, a source of expense to the owner, or must be put to some non-conforming use. In a district otherwise well adapted for residences a gasoline station or other non-conforming use of property may render neighboring property less desirable for use as a private residence. The development of a district for residential purposes might best serve the interests of the city as a whole and, in the end, might perhaps prove the most profitable use of the property within such district. A majority of the property owners might conceivably be content to bear the burden of taxes and other carrying charges upon unimproved land in order to reap profit in the future from the development of the land for residential purposes. They could not safely do so without reasonable assurance that the district will remain adapted for residence use and will not be spoilt for such purpose by the intrusion of structures used for less desirable purposes. The zoning ordinance is calculated to provide such assurance to property owners in the district and to constrain the property owners to develop their land in manner which in the future will prove of benefit to the city. Such considerations have induced the Appellate Division to hold that the ordinance is valid.

There is little room for disagreement with the general rules and tests set forth in the opinion of the Appellate Division. The difficulty arises in the application of such rules and tests to the particular facts in this case. We are not disposed to define the police power of the State so narrowly that it would exclude reasonable restrictions placed upon the use of property in order to aid the development of new districts in accordance with plans calculated to advance the public welfare of the city in the future. We have said that "the need for vision of the future in the governance of cities has not lessened with the years. The dweller within the gates, even more than the stranger from afar, will pay the price of blindness." Hesse v. Rath, 249 N.Y. 436, 438, 164 N.E. 342. We have, indeed, recognized that long-time planning for zoning purposes may be a valid exercise of the police power, but at the same time we have pointed out that the power is not unlimited.

> We are not required to say that a merely temporary restraint of beneficial enjoyment is unlawful where the interference is necessary to promote the ultimate good either of the municipality as a whole or of the immediate neighborhood. Such problems will have to be solved when they arise. If we assume that the restraint may be permitted, the interference must be not unreasonable, but on the contrary must be kept within the limits of necessity.

People ex rel. St. Albans-Springfield Corporation v. Connell, 257 N.Y.

73, 83, 177 N.E. 313, 316.[17] The problem presented upon this appeal is whether or not the zoning ordinance as applied to the plaintiff's property is unreasonable.

Findings of the trial judge, sustained by evidence presented by the plaintiff, establish that, in the vicinity of the plaintiff's premises, the city operates an incinerator which "gives off offensive fumes and odors which permeate plaintiff's premises." About 1,200 or 1,500 feet from the plaintiff's land, "a trunk sewer carrying both storm and sanitary sewage empties into an open creek. . . . The said creek runs to the south of plaintiff's premises and gives off nauseating odors which permeate the said property." The trial judge further found that other conditions exist which, it is plain, render the property entirely unfit, at present, for any conforming use. Though the defendant urges that the conditions are not as bad as the plaintiff's witnesses have pictured, yet as the Appellate Division has said: "It must be conceded, upon the undisputed facts in this case, that this property cannot, presently or in the immediate future, be profitably used for residential purposes." 253 App. Div. 285, 286, 2 N.Y.S.2d 112, 114.

We may assume that the zoning ordinance is the product of far-sighted planning calculated to promote the general welfare of the city at some future time.

The warning of Mr. Justice Holmes [in Pennsylvania Coal Co. v. Mahon, 260 U.S. 393, 415 (1922)] should perhaps be directed rather

---

17. In this case, the plaintiff owned a vacant lot in a rural section of Queens, New York. In the words of the court:

> While some of the property has been laid out in building lots, almost the entire section consists of vacant land, there being only six buildings in the entire area extending 400 feet from the premises in each direction. Four of these are brick buildings, with stores in the ground floor and apartments for dwelling purposes overhead, which cannot be rented for enough to bring in a reasonable return upon the investment. As transit facilities do not reach this territory, it has been slow in development; the few families who do live in the neighborhood being transported by bus or in their own automobiles.

The plaintiff's property was placed in a business district. Finding that it could not profitably dispose of the property either for residential or business purposes, it applied to the Board of Standards and Appeals to permit the construction of a gasoline station. The application was denied. On appeal, the special referee found "that the site in question is not suitable for the erection of a business building of any character whatever, and that a gasoline-selling station is the only available use to which the property in question can be put." The lower court then directed the Board of Appeals to grant the relief. On appeal it was held:

> The order, therefore, of the court below, which authorizes and permits the erection and use of this gasoline station, must be modified by a direction that when the circumstances so change by the development of the city that the property is reasonably susceptible of being applied to business uses, then, upon the application of the authorities or any one interested, the gasoline station must be removed.

257 N.Y. at 83, 177 N.E. at 316. See also People ex rel. Arseekay Syndicate v. Murdock, 265 N.Y. 158, 191 N.E. 871 (1934). — Eds.

A. The Power to Zone

to Legislatures than to courts; for the courts have not hesitated to declare statutes invalid wherever regulation has gone so far that it is clearly unreasonable and must be "recognized as [a] taking"; and unless regulation does clearly go so far the courts may not deny force to the regulation. We have already pointed out that in the case which we are reviewing, the plaintiff's land cannot at present or in the immediate future be profitably or reasonably used without violation of the restriction. An ordinance which *permanently* so restricts the use of property that it cannot be used for any reasonable purpose goes, it is plain, beyond regulation, and must be recognized as a taking of the property. The only substantial difference, in such case, between restriction and actual taking, is that the restriction leaves the owner subject to the burden of payment of taxation, while outright confiscation would relieve him of that burden.

The situation, of course, might be quite different where it appears that within a reasonable time the property can be put to a profitable use. The temporary inconvenience or even hardship of holding unproductive property might then be compensated by ultimate benefit to the owner or, perhaps, even without such compensation, the individual owners might be compelled to bear a temporary burden in order to promote the public good. We do not pass upon such problems now, for here no inference is permissible that within a reasonable time the property can be put to a profitable use or that the present inconvenience or hardship imposed upon the plaintiff is temporary. True, there is evidence that the neighborhood is improving and that some or all of the conditions which now render the district entirely unsuitable for residence purposes will in time be removed. Even so, it is conceded that prognostication that the district will in time become suited for residences rests upon hope and not upon certainty, and no estimate can be made of the time which must elapse before the hope becomes fact.

During the nine years from 1928 to 1936, when concededly the property was unsuitable for any conforming use, the property was assessed at $18,000, and taxes amounting to $4,566 were levied upon it, in addition to assessments of several thousand dollars; yet, so far as appears, the district was no better suited for residence purposes at the time of the trial in 1936 than it was when the zoning ordinance was amended in 1928. In such case the ordinance is clearly more than a temporary and reasonable restriction placed upon the land to promote the general welfare. It is in substance a taking of the land prohibited by the Constitution of the United States and by the Constitution of the State.

We repeat here what under similar circumstances the court said in People ex rel. St. Albans-Springfield Corporation v. Connell, supra, page 83, 177 N.E. page 316: "we are not required to say that a merely temporary restraint of beneficial enjoyment is unlawful where the interference is necessary to promote the ultimate good either of the municipality as a whole or of the immediate neighborhood." There the court held that the "ultimate good" could be attained and a "productive use" allowed by a variation of the zoning ordinance that "will be temporary and provisional and readily terminable." Here the application of the plaintiff for any variation was properly refused, for the conditions which render the plaintiff's property unsuitable for residential use are general and not confined to plaintiff's property. In such case, we have held that the general hardship should be remedied by revision of the general regulation, not by granting the special privilege of a variation to single owners. Levy v. Board of Standards and Appeals of City of New York, 267 N.Y. 347, 196 N.E. 284. Perhaps a new ordinance might be evolved by which the "ultimate good" may be attained without depriving owners of the productive use of their property. That is a problem for the legislative authority, not for the courts. Now we hold only that the present regulation as applied to plaintiff's property is not valid.

The judgment of the Appellate Division should be reversed and that of the Special Term affirmed, with costs in this court and in the Appellate Division.[18]

---

18. Cf. Devore v. Blake, 260 App. Div. 1050, 24 N.Y.S.2d 524 (2d Dept. 1940), rev'd mem., 285 N.Y. 826, 35 N.E.2d 499 (1941).

Consider the following extract from the report of the New York City Board of Standards and Appeals, No. 740-38-BZ (Feb. 11, 1939):

> It is apparent that the question of the then existing nuisances played a large part in the consideration of the Courts in both Arverne Bay Construction Co. v. Thatcher and Arverne Bay Construction Co. v. Murdock. The applicant in this present application, two blocks away to the east on the same side of Linden boulevard, claims that his hardship consists of the same nuisance conditions which persuaded the Court of Appeals in their decision on the question of constitutionality. He mentioned the incinerator and garbage disposal plant, the trunk and open sewer, the dumping ground for depositing and burning garbage, the cow shed, as among the nuisances still existing. That he is incorrect in these statements is evident from the testimony of nearby owners at the hearing and from the exhaustive inspection made by the Committee of the Board of the extensive area between Linden boulevard and Jamaica Bay and from reports requested by the Board from the Borough President of Brooklyn, the Department of Public Works, the Department of Parks and the Department of Sanitation. By these reports, confirming the inspection by a Committee of the Board, it is shown that the main nuisances referred to have been entirely abated by the construction and extension of a large sewer for 2500 feet southerly and the filling in of the meadow lands adjoining Fresh Creek Basin, by the filling in and grading by a W.P.A. project of vacant plots formerly used for dumping and burning garbage, by chlorination, and by discontinuance of the incinerator formerly used by the Sanitation Department. . . . The Committee found that no non-conforming uses existed in the area of notification, other than the gasoline station on the northerly side of Linden boulevard diagonally opposite and the pocket book factory at 818 Pennsylvania avenue. . . . While the immediate area adjacent to the plot under appeal and to the south of Linden boulevard, is not greatly developed, west thereof and across Linden boulevard, is largely developed. This photograph does not show. . . . the

A. The Power to Zone

■ **VERNON PARK REALTY, INC. v. CITY OF MOUNT VERNON**
307 N.Y. 493, 121 N.E.2d 517 (1954)

DYE, Judge. The City of Mount Vernon appeals as of right on constitutional grounds from a judgment declaring invalid and void insofar as they affected the plaintiff's property, the City Zoning Ordinance and Zoning Map of the City of Mount Vernon, enacted and adopted March 22, 1927, as amended March 9, 1949, and the amendment thereto, chapter 4A, enacted and adopted January 16, 1952.

The subject premises are known locally as the "Plaza," consisting of an open area containing approximately 86,000 square feet adjacent to the New York, New Haven & Hartford Railroad station. It is in the middle of a highly developed Business "B" district (Zoning Ordinance, 1927, ch. 12) and as such constitutes an island completely surrounded by business buildings. It has always been used by the patrons of the railroad and others for the parking of private automobiles. When the city first enacted a zoning ordinance, the Plaza was placed in a Business "B" district (Zoning Ordinance adopted 1922), later being changed without objection to a Resident "B" district (Zoning Ordinance adopted 1927), following which the parking of automobiles was continued as a valid nonconforming use. In 1932, upon the application of the railroad and its then tenant, the city granted a variance to permit the installation of a gasoline filling station. Later and in 1951 the railroad sold the premises to the plaintiff, the title being closed June 21, 1951. The purchaser applied without success for a variance to permit the erection of a retail shopping center, a prohibited use as the zoning ordinance then read (Zoning Ordinance adopted 1927, chs. 9-10).

The plaintiff then commenced this action for a judgment declaring the 1927 ordinance unconstitutional, unreasonable, and void and not binding on the plaintiff insofar as the same pertains to the use of plaintiff's premises, and for injunctive relief. After joinder of issue and on January 16, 1952, the common council amended the zoning ordi-

---

new public school now being erected on Pennsylvania avenue, approximately three hundred feet distant from the plot under appeal. Air-view Exhibit A-1 does not correctly show present conditions or the street and sewer development that has since taken place. Pennsylvania avenue southerly from Linden boulevard is a wide paved avenue to Fairfield avenue, which is an extension of Flatlands avenue and is used largely as a short cut for traffic from South Brooklyn. When the Circumferential Highway is completed, the entire area between it and Linden boulevard should be immediately available for development. . . .

For other views as to the permissible period of prediction, see Acker v. Baldwin, 18 Cal.2d 341, 344, 115 P.2d 455, 457 (1941); Frederick v. Jackson County, 197 Miss. 293, 20 So. 2d 92 (1944); Padover v. Township of Farmington, 374 Mich. 622, 132 N.W.2d 687 (1965); Golden v. Planning Board of Town of Ramapo, 30 N.Y.2d 359, 285 N.E.2d 291, 324 N.Y.S.2d 190 (1972). — EDS.

nance by adding thereto a new district to be known as "D.P.D." (Designed Parking District). In substance, the effect of this amendment was to prohibit the use of the property for any purpose except the parking and storage of automobiles, a service station within the parking area and the continuance of prior non-conforming uses (Zoning Ordinance as amended January 16, 1952, ch. 4A). Faced with this change in classification, the plaintiff amended its complaint so as to include an attack on both the zoning ordinance and the 1952 amendment. The amended complaint alleges that the ordinance and its 1952 amendment, as pertaining to the plaintiff's property, work an undue hardship as to use, destroy the greater part of its value, are discriminatory as a denial of the equal protection of the law, and amount to a taking of private property without just compensation contrary to due process and, as such, are constitutionally invalid and void. The city justifies the ordinance and its amendment by reason of the congested traffic and parking conditions now existing in Mount Vernon which, it says, have become so acute as to reach a strangulation point. However compelling and acute the community traffic problem may be, its solution does not lie in placing an undue and uncompensated burden on the individual owner of a single parcel of land in the guise of regulation, even for a public purpose. True it is that for a long time the land has been devoted to parking, a non-conforming use, but it does not follow that an ordinance prohibiting any other use is a reasonable exercise of the police power. While the common council has the unquestioned right to enact zoning laws respecting the use of property in accordance with a well-considered and comprehensive plan designed to promote public health, safety and general welfare, General City Law, Consol. Laws, c. 21, §83, such power is subject to the constitutional limitation that it may not be exerted arbitrarily or unreasonably, Nashville, C. & St. L. Ry. v. Walters, 294 U.S. 405; Brous v. Smith, 304 N.Y. 164, 106 N.E.2d 503, and this is so whenever the zoning ordinance precludes the use of the property for any purpose for which it is reasonably adapted. Arverne Bay Construction Co. v. Thatcher, 278 N.Y. 222, 15 N.E.2d 587, 117 A.L.R. 1110. By the same token, an ordinance valid when adopted will nevertheless be stricken down as invalid when, at a later time, its operation under changed conditions proves confiscatory. . . .

On this record, the plaintiff, having asserted an invasion of his property rights, cf. Rodgers v. Village of Tarrytown, 302 N.Y. 115, 96 N.E.2d 731, has met the burden of proof by establishing that the property is so situated that it has no possibilities for residential use and that the use added by the 1952 amendment does not improve the situation but, in fact, will operate to destroy the greater part of the value of the property since, in authorizing its use for parking and incidental services, it necessarily permanently precludes the use for which it is most readily adapted, i.e., a business use such as permitted

A. The Power to Zone 203

and actually carried on by the owners of all the surrounding property. Under such circumstances, the 1927 zoning ordinance and zoning map and the 1952 amendment, as they pertain to the plaintiff's property, are so unreasonable and arbitrary as to constitute an invasion of property rights, contrary to constitutional due process and, as such, are invalid, illegal and void enactments.

Mention should be made of appellant's contention that plaintiff has no right to bring this action because it has not shown good faith in that the contract of purchase provided for a reconveyance of the premises to the seller, at the option of the purchaser, in the event that, within one year from the date of closing title, the purchaser was unable to obtain from the city or through court action a change of zoning so as to permit use of the premises for a business purpose, and, in that it purchased the property with knowledge of the zoning restrictions. There is no merit to this claim of lack of good faith. The plaintiff took title to the property by deed prior to the enactment of the 1952 amendment and could not very well have known or anticipated that the city, under the guise of regulating traffic, would permanently limit the use of the property to the parking of automobiles and incidental services, such as we have said constituted an illegal invasion of the plaintiff's property rights. Under such circumstances, the validity of the zoning ordinance and its zoning map may be attacked at any time and at any stage of the proceedings. . . .

Purchase of property with knowledge of the restriction does not bar the purchaser from testing the validity of the zoning ordinance since the zoning ordinance in the very nature of things has reference to land rather than to owner (Bassett on Zoning, p. 177). Knowledge of the owner cannot validate an otherwise invalid ordinance. The owner's right to attack the validity of a zoning ordinance is not waived by the circumstance that he has on a previous occasion applied for a variance. Such an application is, primarily, an appeal to the discretion of the board and, for that purpose, the validity of the ordinance is assumed[;] but that does not operate to confer validity if, in fact, as here, the zoning ordinance is clearly confiscatory. Cf. Arverne Bay Construction Co. v. Thatcher, supra. Conversely, an attack on the legality of a zoning ordinance prior to any request for a variance has long been accepted as proper procedure. . . .

The judgment appealed from should be affirmed, with costs.

FULD, Judge (dissenting). I cannot agree that the zoning ordinance of the City of Mount Vernon here under attack is unconstitutional.

A zoning ordinance is confiscatory and, hence, unconstitutional only when it "so restricts the use of property that it cannot be used for any reasonable purpose," Arverne Bay Construction Co. v. Thatcher, 278 N.Y. 222, 232, 15 N.E.2d 587, 592, 117 A.L.R. 1110, or when it restricts it "to a use for which the property is not adapted." Dowsey v.

Village of Kensington, 257 N.Y. 221, 231, 177 N.E. 427, 430, 86 A.L.R. 642. But, if "the validity of the legislative classification for zoning purposes be fairly debatable, the legislative judgment must be allowed to control." Euclid, Ohio v. Ambler Co., 272 U.S. 365, 388; see, also, Shepard v. Village of Skaneateles, 300 N.Y. 115, 118, 89 N.E.2d 619, 620. It seems to me that neither the 1927 ordinance nor its 1952 amendment is so unreasonable as to permit us to interfere with the judgment of Mount Vernon's Common Council.

In the present case, although the 1927 ordinance placed the property in a residential zone, all of the area was in fact employed for parking purposes since 1922. That being so we may not ignore realities and say that the ordinance was invalid because it singled out a small area in the midst of a large business zone for residential use. For all practical purposes, the district continued, as it had been, zoned for parking. Adjacent to the New York, New Haven & Hartford Railroad, the area served the community's obvious need for parking facilities. Accordingly, the continuance — indeed, even the creation — of a special parking zone was more than warranted. Serving, as it did, the parking needs of railroad passengers, permitting easier access to the trains and reducing congestion in the crowded business section, the ordinance not only afforded the owner an entirely reasonable use for his property, but advanced the public good and well-being.

Nor may the ordinance be condemned because it affected but a small area. It has long been recognized that, if it is done for the general welfare of the community as a whole, a municipality may, as part of a comprehensive zoning plan, set aside even a single plot in the center of a large zone devoted to a different use. See, e.g., Rodgers v. Village of Tarrytown, 302 N.Y. 115, 124, 96 N.E.2d 731, 734; Nappi v. LaGuardia, 295 N.Y. 652, 64 N.E.2d 716; Higbee v. Chicago, B. & Q.R. Co., 235 Wis. 91, 292 N.W. 320, 128 A.L.R. 734. And land adjacent to a railroad station has been regarded as a particularly appropriate subject for such treatment. See Higbee v. Chicago, B. & Q.R. Co., supra, 235 Wis. 91, 292 N.W. 320.

The ordinance being valid in 1927, it is valid today unless conditions have changed. Not even respondent claims that they have, and the fact is that, except for the erection of a gas station on part of the space involved, neither the area nor the surrounding business district has undergone any alteration. There has, of course, been an increase in population and in the number of automobiles, but that — a general and widespread change affecting all of Mount Vernon — only serves to render the long-continued parking use still more suitable and necessary. It is, perhaps, true, that a parking lot may not afford a purchaser as great a return on his money as a shopping center, but that circumstance, standing alone, does not justify invalidation of the ordinance. . . .

A. The Power to Zone

There is at least one other reason for upholding the 1927 ordinance. While mere acquiescence in an unconstitutional ordinance cannot serve to validate it, see, e.g., Wuttke v. O'Connor, 306 N.Y. 677, 117 N.E.2d 128, the fact that for over twenty-five years the owner railroad actually occupied the property satisfactorily as a parking space — without objection or the slightest claim that it effected a confiscation — cannot be overlooked. Since an ordinance is unconstitutional only if it bars "any reasonable" use of property, it is difficult to see how it may be attacked successfully as confiscatory or invalid where it appears that the land was put to a "reasonable" use for a quarter of a century under conditions which have up to the present remained unchanged. And, that being so, a vendee, such as respondent, who buys with full knowledge of the applicable zoning regulations, certainly stands in no better or stronger position than his predecessor in title. Cf., e.g., Wuttke v. O'Connor, 306 N.Y. 677, 117 N.E.2d 128, supra; People ex rel. Arseekay Syndicate v. Murdock, 265 N.Y. 158, 191 N.E. 871.

The 1927 law, being, as I believe, constitutional, no fault may be found with the 1952 amendment. That merely brought about by enactment what had previously been accomplished by a nonconforming use and is no more subject to attack than the 1927 ordinance. . . .

I would reverse the judgment rendered below.

LEWIS, Ch. J., and CONWAY, DESMOND, FROESSEL and VAN VOORHIS, J.J., concur with DYE, J.; FULD, J., dissents in opinion.

Judgment affirmed.[19]

---

19. In McCarthy v. City of Manhattan Beach, 41 Cal. 2d 879, 264 P.2d 932 (1953), the plaintiffs owned three-fifths of a mile of sandy beach frontage, varying in width from 174 to 186 feet. In 1924, the city brought a quiet-title action, claiming that the land had been dedicated for public use. Judgment went against the city. Thereafter the plaintiffs and the city cooperated in various unsuccessful efforts to persuade the county or the state to acquire the land for a public beach.

In 1940, the plaintiffs began to construct a fence in the hope of charging admission for the property's use. It was never fully completed, as parts of it were destroyed by the public. The plaintiffs demanded police protection, and stated their intention of holding the city responsible for all damage suffered.

Later the plaintiffs requested rezoning of the property, which had been classified single-family residential under a 1929 ordinance, for business purposes. This was denied. In 1941, the city council adopted a zoning ordinance providing for ten zoning districts. The plaintiffs' property was placed in a "beach recreation district" and could be used only for the operation of beach facilities for an admission fee; the only structures permitted were lifeguard towers, open smooth wire fences, and small signs. The plaintiffs made no use of their property as permitted by the 1941 zoning ordinance. They paid taxes ranging from $4200 in 1940 to $9000 in 1950. In 1950, they applied to the city for a zoning amendment to reclassify the property to a single-family residence district. This being denied they brought an action for declaratory relief. At the time of the action, the plaintiffs' land was the only privately owned property falling within the beach recreation zone.

The trial court found that the plaintiffs' property was, from time to time, subject to erosion and replacement by reason of storms and wave action of the Pacific Ocean; that any residences upon the property would necessarily be erected on pilings; that reasonable minds might differ as to the safety of residences so constructed; that such construction

ROCKHILL v. CHESTERFIELD TOWNSHIP
23 N.J. 117, 128 A.2d 473 (1956)

HEHER, J. The issue here concerns the legal sufficiency of an ordinance of the defendant Township of Chesterfield adopted October 1, 1955, entitled "An ordinance regulating and restricting the location, the size and use of buildings and structures and the use of land in the Township of Chesterfield in the County of Burlington, providing for [its] administration and enforcement . . . fixing penalties for the violation thereof and establishing a zoning board of adjustment."

The regulation is denominated a "zoning ordinance"; and its "purpose" is declared to be: ". . . lessening congestion in the streets; securing safety from fire, panic and other dangers; promoting health, morals or the general welfare; providing adequate light, air and sanitation; preventing the overcrowding of land or buildings; and avoiding undue concentration of population . . .," the statutorily-enumerated consideration of policy involved in use zoning. R.S. 40:55-32, N.J.S.A.

---

might also create police problems by reason of possible uses of the areas underneath the residences for immoral purposes; that one of the principal characteristics of the city was its beach location; that at all times since adoption of the 1941 ordinance, the plaintiffs' property had been suitable for use and had been used for beach recreational purposes; that it was not true that the city, through its mayor and councilmen, or otherwise, had conceived any scheme designed to keep the property unimproved so that it could be used as a public beach recreation area or to depreciate the value of the property so as to enable the public authorities to acquire it at the lowest possible price.

> The court also found that "reasonable minds might reasonably differ and might have in the year 1941 reasonably differed" as to the following matters: whether the property is or was suitable for residential or commercial development; whether the city would be subjected to liability by reason of the necessity of employing lifeguards, wrecking crews and salvage employees to protect the property and installations thereon from the ravages of high tides and frequent storms; the propriety of the enactment of the zoning restriction declared in the 1941 ordinance; and the proper classification of the property as being within a beach recreational district. Upon such findings the court concluded that the zoning restriction is a valid enactment within the city's police power; that it does not deprive plaintiffs of their property without due process of law or deny them the equal protection of the laws; that it has a foundation in reason and is not a mere arbitrary or irrational exercise of power; and that the scheme of classification and districting followed in the ordinance has been applied fairly and impartially in the instance of plaintiffs' property.

41 Cal. 2d at 885, 264 P.2d at 935. The Supreme Court affirmed. Cf. King v. Incorporated Village of Ocean Beach, 207 Misc. 100, 136 N.Y.S.2d 690 (Sup. Ct. 1954); Westwood Forest Estates, Inc. v. Village of South Nyack, 23 N.Y.2d 424, 244 N.E.2d 700, 297 N.Y.S.2d 129 (1969); New Products Corp. v. North Miami, 241 So. 2d 451 (Fla. 3d Dist. 1970).

The Supreme Court's recent intervention in Nollan v. California Coastal Commission, infra page 636, should have an impact for years to come on judicial scrutiny of not only such creative coastal zoning, but also of the popular practice of conditioning development approval on certain concessions extracted by the permitting agency. See infra page 614 — EDS.

A. The Power to Zone 207

But the zoning scheme laid down in the ordinance is not in the conventional pattern; and the inquiry is whether it conforms to the constitutional and statutory principle and policy.

Land and building uses, Article III, shall be "in conformance with the provisions" of the ordinance and the attached "schedule of regulations" entitled "Schedule of Permitted Uses and General Regulations"; and "In addition, certain uses may be permitted and certain modification of requirements may be made in accordance with the special provisions" of the ordinance. "Normal agricultural uses shall be permitted in accordance with the general standards set forth in the schedule." . . .

"Residential uses shall be permitted in accordance with the general standards set forth in the schedule," Article V, including certain "Accessory uses on the same lot and customarily incidental to the permitted dwelling unit," provided that (a) "No dwelling unit shall be located within 250 feet of, or between buildings of an existing or permitted light industrial activity"; (b) where a dwelling unit is located on a corner lot, there shall be a side yard as therein prescribed; and (c) there shall be "off-street parking for all residences," as set down in the schedule.

Provision is then made, Article VI, for "Special Uses"; and this is the declared "Purpose": "In view of the rural characteristics of the Township, it is deemed desirable to permit certain structures and uses but only after investigation has shown that such structures and uses will be beneficial to the general development"; and "In order to assure that such structures and uses meet all requirements and standards, all applications for zoning permits shall be referred to the Planning Board for review in accordance with Revised Statutes 40:55-1.13 [N.J.S.A.]." The planning board is directed to "investigate the matter in accordance with the standards herein provided and submit its recommendations in writing to the Governing Body within 45 days after the filing of the application with the Zoning Officer." . . . And the governing body "shall, no later than the second regularly scheduled meeting after the receipt" of the board's report, "either approve or disapprove the application by resolution based on the standards as set forth" in the ordinance; and "if approved, the necessary zoning permit shall then be issued."

These are the stated "special structures and uses which may be permitted only in keeping with the special standards herein listed," Article VI: (a) an "existing one-family dwelling may be converted into multi-family dwelling units," subject to certain conditions and specifications and the submission of the plans to the planning board "prior to approval or disapproval"; (b) "Neighborhood business" may be permitted subject to prescribed physical conditions . . .; (c) "Designed shopping center units may be permitted" subject to specified conditions, and "Any business use that is not specifically prohibited within the

Township and not included in Section 3, paragraph b, of Article VI may be considered to be a permitted business use if the Planning Board deems such business use to be desirable and to the best interests of the Township," provided that "An area at least five feet in width and following the lot lines of the business property if adjacent to residential properties shall be properly landscaped to form a buffer screen between residential and business uses," and the required illumination during evening business periods "shall be shielded from adjacent residential properties and public roads or streets"; (d) "Gasoline and Filling stations may be permitted" if certain requirements are met . . .; (e) "Restaurants and roadside refreshment uses may be permitted," at the same distances from other land uses prescribed in (d) supra, and provided, inter alia, that parking space "shall be available to adequately meet maximum capacity conditions," and parking areas shall be illuminated during evening business operations and "shielded from adjacent residential properties and public roads or streets"; (f) "Light industrial uses and other similar facilities having no adverse effect on surrounding property and deemed desirable to the general economic well-being of the Township may be permitted," and "Included among such uses may be administrative offices, laboratories, research offices and light manufacturing or processing," provided that the "industrial activity shall not by its own inherent characteristics or industrial processes be noxious or injurious to the adjacent properties by reason of the production or emission of dust, smoke, refuse matter, odor, gas, fumes, noise, vibration, unsightly conditions, or other similar conditions," also that certain sanitation requirements shall be met, and that no "building or structure" shall be located within 1,000 feet of an "existing or proposed school or public facility" or 250 feet from the "adjoining lot line of any existing dwelling unit" or 200 feet from the "adjoining lot line of any business use"; and (g) "Public utility uses such as distribution lines, towers, substations and telephone exchanges but no service or storage yards may be permitted," provided the planning board finds that the "design of any structure in connection with [the] facility conforms to the general character of the surrounding area and will in no way adversely affect the safe and comfortable enjoyment of property rights of the Township," and there is provision for "adequate and attractive fences and other safety devices" and "sufficient landscaping . . . periodically maintained.". . .

Certain uses are prohibited altogether, Article IX . . . these among others: "Commercial or periodic auction sales"; "Used car lots or used car sales"; "Tourist cabins, motels and trailer camps"; "Manufacture or sale of pottery and cast stone decorations"; "Drive-in theatres"; "Slaughter houses and abattoirs"; "Junk yards and scrap reclamation"; "Garbage-fed piggeries"; "Billboards and advertising of products not for sale on the premises"; "Salvage and wrecking activities"; and "Multi-

A. The Power to Zone

family dwelling units, other than permitted conversions; and similar types of uses of land, structures and buildings so adjudged by the Zoning Board of Adjustment." . . .

The Law Division of the Superior Court set aside Article VI, section 3(c) iv, of the ordinance providing that "any business use . . . not specifically prohibited" within the township, and not included in section 3, paragraph B of that Article, "may be considered to be a permitted business use," if the planning board deems such use "to be desirable and to the best interest of the township," as a regulation wanting in "proper constitutional standards to guide the administrative action" of the board and the township committee, but sustained the ordinance otherwise; and we certified here plaintiff's appeal from so much of the judgment as affirms the ordinance in part. There was no cross-appeal. . . .

The constitutional and statutory zoning principle is territorial division according to the character of the lands and structures and their peculiar suitability for particular uses, and uniformity of use within the division. And the legislative grant of authority has the selfsame delineation. R.S. 40:55-30, as amended by L. 1948, c. 305, p. 1221, N.J.S.A.

The local governing body is empowered, R.S. 40:55-31, as amended by L. 1948, c. 305, N.J.S.A., to divide the municipality into districts of such number, shape, and area as may be deemed best suited to carry out the statutory policy, and to regulate and restrict the construction and use of buildings and other structures and the use of land within such districts, provided that "All such regulations shall be uniform for each class or kind of buildings or other structures or uses of land throughout each district, but the regulations in one district may be different from those in other districts." And such regulations shall be, R.S. 40:55-32, N.J.S.A., in accordance with a "comprehensive plan and designed" to subserve the public welfare in one or more of the enumerated particulars involving the public health, safety, morals, or the general welfare, and "shall be made with reasonable consideration, among other things, to the character of the district and its peculiar suitability for particular uses, and with a view of conserving the value of property and encouraging the most appropriate use of land throughout such municipality." And thus it is basic to the local exercise of the power that the use restrictions be general and uniform in the particular district, delimited in keeping with the constitutional and statutory considerations; otherwise, there would be the arbitrary discrimination at war with the substance of due process and the equal protection of the laws.

The scheme of the ordinance is the negation of zoning. It overrides the basic concept of use zoning by districts, that is to say, territorial division according to the character of the lands and structures and their peculiar use suitability and a comprehensive regulatory plan to advance the general good within the prescribed range of the police power. The local design is "normal agricultural" and residence uses and the specified "special uses" by the authority of the planning board and the local governing body, generally where "investigation has shown that such structures and uses will be beneficial to the general development," and "light industrial uses and other similar facilities having no adverse effect on surrounding property and deemed desirable to the general economic well-being of the Township," terms hardly adequate to channel local administrative discretion but, at all events, making for the "piecemeal" and "spot" zoning alien to the constitutional and statutory principle of land use zoning by districts and comprehensive planning for the fulfillment of the declared policy. The fault is elementary and vital; the rule of the ordinance is ultra vires and void. See Raskin v. Town of Morristown, 21 N.J. 180, 121 A.2d 378 (1956).

Reserving the use of the whole of the municipal area for "normal agricultural" and residence uses, and then providing for all manner of "special uses," "neighborhood" and other businesses, even "light industrial" uses and "other similar facilities," placed according to local discretion without regard to districts, ruled by vague and illusive criteria, is indeed the antithesis of zoning. It makes for arbitrary and discriminatory interference with the basic right of private property, in no real sense concerned with the essential common welfare. The statute, N.J.S.A. 40:55-39, provides for regulation by districts and for exceptions and variances from the prescribed land uses under given conditions. The course taken here would flout this essential concept of district zoning according to a comprehensive plan designed to fulfill the declared statutory policy. Comprehensive zoning means an orderly and coordinate system of community development according to socioeconomic needs. See Professor Haar's exposition of the relation between planning principles and the exercise of the zoning power, "In Accordance With a Comprehensive Plan," 68 Harv. L. Rev. 1154, and the comment, p. 1170, that the phrase "in accordance with a comprehensive plan" apparently had its origin in section 3 of the Standard State Zoning Enabling Act, accompanied by this explanatory note: "This will prevent haphazard or piecemeal zoning." . . .

Zoning and planning are not identical in concept. Mansfield & Swett, Inc., v. Town of West Orange, 120 N.J.L. 145, 198 A. 225 (Sup. Ct. 1938). Zoning is a separation of the municipality into districts for the most appropriate use of the land, by general rules according to a comprehensive plan for the common good in matters within the domain of the police power. And, though the landowner does not have a vested right to a particular zone classification, one of the essential purposes of zoning regulation is the stabilization of property uses. Investments are made in lands and structures on the faith of district use control having some degree of permanency, a well considered plan that will stand until changing conditions dictate otherwise. Such is the nature of use zoning by districts according to a comprehensive plan. The regulations here are in contravention of the principle.

The ordinance is vacated as ultra vires the enabling statute; and the cause is remanded for judicial action accordingly. . . .[20]

■ EVES v. ZONING BOARD OF ADJUSTMENT OF LOWER GWYNEDD TOWNSHIP
401 Pa. 211, 164 A.2d 7 (1960)

COHEN, Justice. These appeals, involving specifically the validity of two ordinances which amend respectively the general zoning ordinance and the zoning map of Lower Gwynedd Township, present the problem of the validity of a method of zoning aptly termed by the appellants as "flexible selective zoning."

On April 28, 1958 the Board of Supervisors of Lower Gwynedd Township adopted Ordinance 28 which officially amended the General Zoning Ordinance of the township to provide for the new zoning district known as "F-1" Limited Industrial District. This ordinance sets forth in detail the requirements, conditions and restrictive uses for an "F-1" classification, including the requirements that any proposed development be constructed in accordance with an overall plan; that any plan shall be designed as a single architectural scheme with appropriate common landscaping and shall provide a minimum size of 25 acres; that adequate parking space shall be provided for all employees and visitors' vehicles; that parking, loading or service areas used by motor vehicles shall be located within the lot lines of the Limited Industrial District, and shall be physically separated from the public streets by a buffer strip; that no building or other permanent structure, nor parking lot, shall be located within 200 feet of a public street, right-of-way, or property line; and that the area of land occupied by the buildings shall not exceed 10% of each site within the Limited Industrial District. The ordinance reserves the right in the board of supervisors to prescribe particular requirements or any further reasonable conditions deemed appropriate with respect to the suitability of the Limited Industrial District in the neighborhood.

Ordinance 28, however, does not itself delineate the boundaries of

---

20. The ordinance defines a "residence district" as "a territory or district within 1000 feet in a direct line in every direction from the nearest part of a building proposed or intended to be located, built, constructed or used for the purpose of a factory or manufacturing plant, in which territory or district more than half of the existing buildings are used wholly or partly for residential purposes." Are there any problems raised by this draft? See Matter of Kensington-Davis Corp. v. Schwab, 239 N.Y. 54, 145 N.E. 738 (1924) ("This is not a division into districts, within the meaning of the [state] statute.") — EDS.

those specific areas which are to be classified as "F-1" districts. Instead, the ordinance outlines a procedure whereby anyone may submit to the board an application requesting that his land be rezoned to "F-1" limited industrial, together with plans showing the nature of the industry the applicant wishes to establish and the conformity of any proposed construction with the requirements of the district as enumerated in the ordinance. The supervisors must in turn refer the application and plans to the Planning Commission of Lower Gwynedd Township, which is to review them and then return them to the supervisors accompanied by its recommendations within 45 days. The board of supervisors must then hold public hearings and finally decide whether or not to reject or approve the application and accordingly amend the zoning map. The ordinance finally provides that should any successful applicant fail to undertake substantial construction of any proposed building within 18 months after the rezoning, or after the issuance of a permit for an area previously zoned "F-1" Limited Industrial District, the area is to revert to its former zoning classification.

Pursuant to the terms of Ordinance 28, on September 11, 1958, the Moore Construction Company, a Pennsylvania corporation desiring to construct an industrial plant and a sewage treatment plant in Lower Gwynedd Township, applied for a rezoning of a 103 acre tract of land known as the "Hardwick Tract" from "A" residential to "F-1" Limited Industrial. A public hearing was held by the supervisors to consider the rezoning on September 20, 1958, at which time a petition signed by 300 residents, all property owners, who opposed the change, was filed. On January 5, 1959, the supervisors adopted Ordinance 34 which rezoned the area in question to the requested "F-1" classification (although it reduced the area rezoned from 103 acres to 86 acres). On January 14, 1959, a certificate of conformity (building permit) was issued to the Moore Products Company. Schuyler Eves, a resident of the township, and the Sisters of Mercy appealed to the zoning board, challenging the validity of the two ordinances on the grounds that they were unconstitutional and that they failed to conform to the enabling legislation. Sustaining the validity of the ordinances, the board dismissed the appeal. The Court of Common Pleas of Montgomery County affirmed and these appeals followed.

The authority of a municipality to enact zoning legislation must be strictly construed. "Any fair, reasonable doubt as to the existence of power is resolved by the courts against its existence in the corporation, and therefore denied." Kline v. City of Harrisburg, 1949, 362 Pa. 438, 443, 68 A.2d 182, 185. Appellants' principal contention is that the zoning scheme as contemplated by ordinances 28 and 34 fails to comport with the same enabling legislation from which the township derives its power to zone. After having thoroughly examined the relevant portions of that statute, we are in complete accord.

A. The Power to Zone

"Zoning is the legislative division of a community into areas in each of which only certain designated uses of land are permitted so that the community may develop in an orderly manner in accordance with a comprehensive plan." Best v. Zoning Board of Adjustment, 1958, 393 Pa. 106, 110, 141 A.2d 606, 609. The zoning regulations of a second class township, by legislative edict, must be the implementation of such a comprehensive plan. Just what the precise attributes of a comprehensive plan must be, or the extent to which the plan must approach a development plan for the township formulated by a planning commission should one exist is not now before us. See Haar, In Accordance With a Comprehensive Plan, 68 Harv. L. Rev. 1154 (1955), Kozesnik v. Township of Montgomery, 1957, 24 N.J. 154, 131 A.2d 1. For present purposes, it is only important to point out that the focus of any plan is land use, and the considerations in the formulation of a plan for the orderly development of a community must be made with regard thereto. This positive focus is thrust upon the township supervisors by the enabling legislation itself, for their "purpose in view" in fulfilling their zoning functions must be to enact regulations

> designed to lessen congestion in the roads and highways; to secure safety from fire, panic and other dangers; to promote health and the general welfare; to provide adequate light and air; to prevent the overcrowding of land; to avoid undue congestion of the population; to facilitate the adequate provision of transportation, water, sewerage, schools, parks and other public requirements. Such regulations shall be made with reasonable consideration, among other things, to the character of the district and its peculiar suitability for particular uses, and with a view to conserving the value of buildings and encouraging the most appropriate use of land throughout such municipality.

Second Class Township Code, §2003, 53 P.S. §67003. And since any zoning ordinance must be enacted in accordance with the comprehensive plan, the plan itself, embodying resolutions of land use and restrictions, must have been at the point of enactment a final formulation.

The role of the township supervisors in the field of zoning, as contemplated by the enabling legislation, emerges quite clearly upon consideration of the powers granted the supervisors and the duties they are bound to perform. Their duty is to implement the comprehensive plan by enacting zoning regulations in accordance therewith. Section 2003, 53 P.S. §67003. They are to shape the land uses "into districts of such number, shape and area as may be deemed best suited to carry out the purpose of this article . . .," Section 2002, 53 P.S. §67002, which "purpose in view" is set out above in Section 2003. They may regulate or restrict "the erection, construction, reconstruction, alteration, repair or use of buildings, structures or land" within any district, and may regulate one district differently from the next, but all "such regulations shall be uniform for each class or kind of buildings throughout each district. . . ." Section 2002, 53 P.S. §67002. All such regulations are to be embodied initially in a general zoning ordinance for the township, which may be subsequently amended, supplemented or repealed by the supervisors as conditions require, Section 2004, 53 P.S. §67004, although again such alterations must be "in accordance with a comprehensive plan."

The zoning scheme as outlined by Ordinances 28 and 34 is at variance with these legislative directives for second class townships in two objectionable ways: (1) The ordinances were not enacted "in accordance with a comprehensive plan" and (2) they devolve upon the township supervisors duties quite beyond those duties outlined for them in the enabling legislation. Accordingly, the ordinances are invalid and the certificates of conformity (building permits) were improperly issued.

The adoption of a procedure whereby it is decided which areas of land will eventually be zoned "F-1" Limited Industrial Districts on a case by case basis patently admits that at the point of enactment of Ordinance 28 there was no orderly plan of particular land use for the community. Final determination under such a scheme would expressly await solicitation by individual landowners, thus making the planned land use of the community dependent upon its development. In other words, the development itself would become the plan, which is manifestly the antithesis of zoning "in accordance with a comprehensive plan."

Several secondary evils of such a scheme are cogently advanced by counsel for the appellants. It would produce situations in which the personal predilections of the supervisors or the affluence or political power of the applicant would have a greater part in determining rezoning applications than the suitability of the land for a particular use from an overall community point of view. Further, while it may not be readily apparent with a minimum acreage requirement of 25 acres, "flexible selective zoning" carries evils akin to "spot zoning," for in theory it allows piecemeal placement of relatively small acreage areas in differently zoned districts. Finally, because of the absence of a simultaneous delineation of the boundaries of the new "F-1" district, no notice of the true nature of his vicinity or its limitations is afforded the property owner or the prospective property owner. While it is undoubtedly true that a property owner has no vested interest in an existing zoning map and, accordingly, is always subject to the possibility of a rezoning without notice, the zoning ordinance and its accompanying zoning maps should nevertheless at any given time reflect the current planned use of the community's land so as to afford as much notice as possible.

Appellees vigorously contend that a comprehensive plan does exist

A. The Power to Zone

for the Township of Lower Gwynedd and is set forth in the record. Essentially, appellees argue, the plan contemplates a "greenbelt" township predominately residential in character with a certain amount of compatible non-residential occupancy consisting of shopping centers, research and engineering centers and limited industrial uses. It also contemplates that these non-residential uses shall be strictly controlled as to setback, building area, noise, smoke, sewage disposal, etc., and that the means of such control shall be vested in the supervisors through strict ordinances of general application such as Ordinance 28, supra, setting up the requirements and limitations on limited industrial uses. In turn, these tools of control and minimum standards are to be the polestars (along with other factors, such as the proximity of through highways, availability of adequate streams for effluent disposal, etc.), in any further consideration to be given by the planning commission and the supervisors to applications for specific locations or areas. By adopting this approach, the appellees have confused comprehensive planning with a comprehensive plan. The foregoing are certainly the rudiments and fundamentals which enter into the promulgation of a planned zoning scheme for the township. They are, however, only the most preliminary and basic considerations from which the ultimate decision[s] of selective land uses are to be made. Until such time, no final formulation exists which satisfies the "comprehensive plan" requirement within the meaning of the enabling legislation.

As to the second objection, the township supervisors have gone beyond their function of implementing a comprehensive plan with zoning regulations: they are to analyze on a case by case basis for rezoning purposes individual applications and accompanying technical plans for structure and development to determine their suitability and compliance with the standards they themselves established in the ordinance.

In the enabling legislation, only the specialized township board of adjustment was empowered to permit deviations from the prevailing zoning regulations on a case by case basis, and then only by means of two detailed procedures — variances and special exceptions. §2007, 53 P.S. §67007. To obtain either, a petitioner must follow a system specifically devised to give certain protection to any affected property owners. To obtain a variance, a petitioner must convince the board of adjustment that "owing to special conditions a literal enforcement of the provisions of the ordinance will result in unnecessary hardship, and . . . that the spirit of the ordinance shall be observed and substantial justice done." Section 2007, 53 P.S. §67007. The board's determination is then subject to careful review by our courts to assure that in exercising its discretion in these matters the board of adjustment has adhered to the statutory standards. And in reviewing such matters, this Court has been quite demanding. See, e.g., Luciany v. Zoning Board of Adjustment, 1960, 399 Pa. 176, 159 A.2d 701; Springfield Township Zoning Case, 1960, 399 Pa. 53, 159 A.2d 684. Those who protest against the variance are allowed to resist any change both before the board and in the courts. Section 2007, 53 P.S. §67007.

Special exceptions are handled somewhat differently, but similar safeguards are still provided. In planning the original comprehensive ordinance, the supervisors may anticipate that certain special uses for particular districts may become desirable, even though, to some extent, they should be in derogation of the character of the district. The ordinance will then provide that an exceptional use may exist within a particular district if the board of adjustment determines its availability. Such uses are thus made available as a privilege, assuming that the requisite facts and conditions detailed in the ordinance are found to exist. See Devereux Foundation, Inc., Zoning Case, 1945, 351 Pa. 478, 41 A.2d 744. Again, there is scrutinizing court review to assure that the board has not overstepped its boundaries of prudent discretion. See, e.g., Kotzin v. Plymouth Twp. Zoning Board of Adjustment, 1959, 395 Pa. 125, 149 A.2d 116. Importantly, all property owners are put on notice of the possibility of an exceptional use within their district because such use is set out originally as part of the district's scheme in the ordinance.

Under the "flexible selective zoning" scheme here under attack, changes in the prevailing zoning regulations are to be made on a case by case basis, not, however, by a specialized body such as the zoning board of adjustment, but by the legislative body, without rigid statutory standards and without any scintilla of notice of potential change as in the case of special exceptions. The standard review by the courts, as indeed the appellees argue we should adopt herein, would be nothing more than to assure ourselves that each legislative act of amending the zoning map by the township supervisors was not "arbitrary, capricious, or unreasonable." If the legislature contemplated such a novel scheme of zoning, withdrawing as it does a close standard of court review in the very delicate area of protecting property rights, and shifting as it does the focus from planned use to individual solicitation, we are convinced it would have said so in more clear and exact terms than are found anywhere in the enabling legislation.

Order reversed.

[Concurring opinion of BELL, J., omitted.][21]

21. The Supreme Court of Maryland, in upholding the use of floating zones, states: "A zoning plan does not cease to be a comprehensive plan because it looks to reasonably foreseeable potential uses of land which cannot be precisely determined when the zoning is passed." Huff v. Board of Zoning Appeals, 214 Md. 48, 133 A.2d 83 (1957). Do you agree? See Haar and Hering, The *Lower Gwynedd Township* Case: Too Flexible Zoning or an Inflexible Judiciary?, 74 Harv. L. Rev. 1552 (1961); Reno, Non-Euclidian Zoning: The Use of the Floating Zone, 23 Md. L. Rev. 105 (1963). Cf. Knudsen v. Montgomery County Council, 241 Md. 436, 217 A.2d 97 (1966).

A. The Power to Zone 217

Note: An English View

■ TOWN AND COUNTRY PLANNING ACT, 1971
ch. 78 (as amended by Local Government Act, 1972, and Local Government, Planning and Land Act, 1980)

22. — (1) In this Act, except where the context otherwise requires, "development", subject to the following provisions of this section, means the carrying out of building, engineering, mining or other operations in, on, over or under land, or the making of any material change in the use of any buildings or other land. . . .

23. — (1) [P]lanning permission is required for the carrying out of any development of land. . . .

24. — (1) The Secretary of State shall by order (in this Act referred to as a "development order") provide for the granting of planning permission.

(2) A development order may either —

(*a*) itself grant planning permission for development specified in the order, or for development of any class so specified; or

(*b*) in respect of development for which planning permission is not granted by the order itself, provide for the granting of planning permission by the local planning authority (or, in the cases hereinafter provided, by the Secretary of State) on an application in that behalf made to the local planning authority in accordance with the provisions of the order.

(3) A development order may be made either as a general order applicable (subject to such exceptions as may be specified therein) to all land, or as a special order applicable only to such land or descriptions of land as may be so specified.

(4) Planning permission granted by a development order may be granted either unconditionally or subject to such conditions or limitations as may be specified in the order.

(5) Without prejudice to the generality of subsection (4) of this section —

(*a*) where planning permission is granted by a development order for the erection, extension or alteration of any buildings, the order may require the approval of the local planning authority to be obtained with respect to the design or external appearance of the buildings;

(*b*) where planning permission is granted by a development order for development of a specified class, the order may enable the Secretary of State or the local planning authority to direct that the permission shall not apply either in relation to development in a particular area or in relation to any particular development . . .

29. — (1) [W]here an application is made to a local planning authority for planning permission, that authority, in dealing with the application, shall have regard to the provisions of the development plan, so far as material to the application, and to any other material considerations, and —

(*a*) . . . may grant planning permission, either unconditionally or subject to such conditions as they think fit; or

(*b*) may refuse planning permission . . .

30. — (1) [C]onditions may be imposed on the grant of planning permission thereunder —

(*a*) for regulating the development or use of any land under the control of the applicant (whether or not it is land in respect of which the application was made) or requiring the carrying out of works on any such land, so far as appears to the local planning authority to be expedient for the purposes of or in connection with the development authorised by the permission;

(*b*) for requiring the removal of any buildings or works authorised by the permission, or the discontinuance of any use of land so authorised, at the end of a specified period, and the carrying out of any works required for the reinstatement of land at the end of that period. . . .

31. — (1) . . . [P]rovision may be made by a development order for regulating the manner in which applications for planning permission to develop land are to be dealt with by local planning authorities, and in particular —

(*a*) for enabling the Secretary of State to give directions restricting the grant of planning permission by the local planning authority, either indefinitely or during such period as may be specified in the directions, in respect of any such development, or in respect of development of any such class, as may be so specified;

(*b*) for authorising the local planning authority . . . to grant planning permission for development which does not accord with the provisions of the development plan;

(*c*) for requiring the local planning authority, before granting or refusing planning permission for any development, to consult with such authorities or persons as may be prescribed by the order or by directions given by the Secretary of State thereunder;

(*d*) for requiring the local planning authority to give to any applicant for planning permission, within such time as may be prescribed by the order, such notice as may be so prescribed as to the manner in which his application has been dealt with;

(*dd*) for requiring the local planning authority to give any applicant for any consent, agreement or approval required by a condition imposed on a grant of planning permission notice of their decision on his application, within such time as may be so prescribed;

A. The Power to Zone

(*e*) for requiring the local planning authority to give to the Secretary of State, and to such other persons as may be prescribed by or under the order, such information as may be so prescribed with respect to applications for planning permission made to the authority, including information as to the manner in which any such application has been dealt with. ...

180. — (1) Where, on an application for planning permission to develop any land, permission is refused or is granted subject to conditions, then if any owner of the land claims —

(*a*) that the land has become incapable of reasonably beneficial use in its existing state; and

(*b*) in a case where planning permission was granted subject to conditions, that the land cannot be rendered capable of reasonably beneficial use by the carrying out of the permitted development in accordance with those conditions; and

(*c*) in any case, that the land cannot be rendered capable of reasonably beneficial use by the carrying out of any other development for which planning permission has been granted or for which the local planning authority or the Secretary of State has undertaken to grant planning permission,

he may, within the time and in the manner prescribed by regulations under this Act, serve on the council of the London borough or county district in which the land is situated a notice requiring that council to purchase his interest in the land in accordance with the following provisions of this Part of this Act.

(2) Where, for the purpose of determining whether the conditions specified in subsection (I) (*a*) to (*c*) of this section are fulfilled in relation to any land, any question arises as to what is or would in any particular circumstances be a reasonably beneficial use of that land, then, in determining that question for that purpose, no account shall be taken of any prospective use of that land which would involve the carrying out of new development. ...

183. — (1) [I]f the Secretary of State is satisfied that the conditions specified in section 180 (1) (*a*) to (*c*) of this Act are fulfilled in relation to a purchase notice, he shall confirm the notice.

(2) If it appears to the Secretary of State to be expedient to do so, he may, in lieu of confirming the purchase notice, grant planning permission for the development in respect of which the application was made, or, where planning permission for that development was granted subject to conditions, revoke or amend those conditions so far as appears to him to be required in order to enable the land to be rendered capable of reasonably beneficial use by the carrying out of that development.

(3) If it appears to the Secretary of State that the land, or any part of the land, could be rendered capable of reasonably beneficial use within a reasonable time by the carrying out of any other development

for which planning permission ought to be granted, he may, in lieu of confirming the purchase notice, or in lieu of confirming it so far as it relates to that part of the land, as the case may be, direct that planning permission for that development shall be granted in the event of an application being made in that behalf. . . .[22]

B. THE ZONING TRIO — HEIGHT, BULK, AND USE

1. Building Size, Shape, and Placement: Density of Occupation

■ CLEMONS v. CITY OF LOS ANGELES
36 Cal. 2d 95, 222 P.2d 439 (1950)

SPENCE, Justice. . . .

It appears from the agreed statement of facts that within two years prior to the commencement of this action on December 12, 1946, plaintiff purchased the property in question, a bungalow court of nine units which had been built some twenty years previously and had been used continuously for residential purposes. Located in zone C-2 on Beverly Boulevard, the property was subject to section 12.21-C of the Los Angeles Municipal Code (Ordinance No. 77,000 adopted September 28, 1936, as amended by Ordinance No. 90,500, adopted March 7, 1946) providing that no lot "held under separate ownership" at the law's effective date and "used . . . for dwelling purposes" shall be "reduced in any manner below the minimum lot area, size or dimensions" prescribed — "a minimum average width of fifty (50) feet and a minimum area of five thousand (5000) square feet."

Following his purchase, plaintiff subdivided the property into nine separate parcels, each averaging 925 square feet (25' × 37') and having a bungalow thereon. Through sale or 99-year lease arrangements plaintiff conveyed eight of these parcels to various individuals — transactions contrary to the minimum lot area and width requirements of the ordinance as a zoning regulation. Each parcel was conveyed with an easement to Beverly Boulevard over the walkways within the bungalow court. Two of the parcels had no frontage on any street or alley. The entire property was serviced by only one incinerator and two sewer connections.

Threatened with arrest and prosecution for violation of the ordi-

---

22. Cf. the definitions of "development" in §1-202 of the Model Land Development Code (1975). — EDS.

B. The Zoning Trio — Height, Bulk, and Use

nance, plaintiff instituted this action for declaratory and injunctive relief from the enforcement of such municipal regulation against him as a property owner, charging that it transcended the legitimate scope of the exercise of the police power and constituted "an unwarranted and arbitrary interference with [his] constitutional rights." . . .

Zoning is an essential part of a city's overall master plan for community development, Planning Act of 1929, Stats. 1929, p. 1805, as amended, 2 Deering's Gen. Laws, Act 5211b; later superseded by Conservation and Planning Act, Stats. 1947, ch. 807, p. 1909, as amended, 2 Deering's Gen. Laws, Act 5211c, and a city is vested with control of "the design and improvement of subdivisions," subject to judicial review as to reasonableness. Subdivision Map Act, Stats. 1937, p. 1864, as amended, now Bus. & Prof. Code, sec. 11500 et seq.; sec. 11525. The word "design" is defined in the latter Act to include, among other things, provision for "minimum lot area and width," Bus. & Prof. Code sec. 11510, by "local ordinance." Ibid. secs. 11506, 11526. Consistent with this state recognition of municipal functions and in line with its autonomous character, Cal. Const. art. XI, sec. 6; West Coast Advertising Co. v. San Francisco, 14 Cal. 2d 516, 519-521, 96 P.2d 138, the city of Los Angeles adopted the zoning ordinance prohibiting the reduction of residential lots below the specified minimum of 5,000 square feet in area and 50-foot frontage. The city's charter expressly contemplates the adoption of regulations pursuant to the authority granted by the Subdivision Map Act, charter, sec. 95(g), and on this point the trial court found that the ordinance

> constitutes an essential part of the master plan for the comprehensive development of the City of Los Angeles in that it is designed to prevent the cutting up of lots into unduly small areas and into parcels of economically unusable widths; that the ordinance . . . supplements the California Subdivision Map Act in that it prevents lots sold pursuant to said Act from being further subdivided, and in so doing, the ordinance prevents or diminishes the possibility of circumvention of [said] Act.

In support of its view that the "ordinance is an important factor in the orderly development of the city," the trial court found that the "attempted cutting up" of such property as plaintiff's bungalow court would "tend to create and accelerate the creation of slum conditions" and "overcrowd[ing]," thus "militating against orderly, quiet and peaceful living"; that "health and sanitary regulations and laws would be more difficult to enforce" if the bungalow units "were sold to various separate owners"; and that therefore "said ordinance has a reasonable relation to the public health, safety and general welfare, and was enacted for the public good."

Where from a consideration of the evidence the trial court has found certain physical facts and conditions to exist in relation to the particular property restriction involved as would justify regulation by the city through the exercise of its police power, all intendments must be indulged to sustain such findings and resulting judgment. Ayres v. City Council of Los Angeles, 34 Cal. 2d 31, 39, 207 P.2d 1. So significant are these factors in accord with the objectives found by the trial court to be within the design of the ordinance. The benefits of the Subdivision Map Act would be of little practical value in aid of desirable community planning if following the subdivider's compliance for the terms of the initial sale, the purchasers of the lots could erect multiple dwellings thereon according to authorized specifications and then "cut up" the units for separate sale. In this regard the ordinance clearly appears to supplement the state act and to operate in avoidance of its circumvention as the trial court found. Likewise appropriate for consideration here is the memorandum opinion filed by the trial judge and included in the record . . . as bearing on the interpretation of the findings. The comment is there made that according to the view of experts in the field of community development, the subdivision of "bungalow courts into separate parcels" tends "to create slum conditions" because it would be unlikely that a uniform state of repair would be maintained by the various owners and a "hodge-podge appearance" would result, with a consequent depreciation in value of the entire property; "overcrowding" develops because where it is "a common practice for landlords to limit the number of people who may occupy a bungalow in a court," such restriction would not apply under separate ownership of the various units, and the probable increase and concentration of people within the limited area would "add to the noise and other irritations that militate against orderly, quiet and peaceful living"; "health and sanitary regulations" become "more difficult to provide for and enforce," and particularly where such "close living" in separately owned bungalow units contemplates "each person . . . constantly making use of easements over the others' property, and where there is no one to make or enforce any rules touching items of common necessity to all, such as, for example, use of incinerators or other disposal of trash, and keeping clean the common walkways," the situation could create disturbing tensions. As is further there said, the "City Council may well have had all these matters in mind in passing the ordinance here under attack and may have concluded that it was necessary in furtherance of the general welfare of the city and its orderly development." . . .

Plaintiff argues that the zoning ordinance prohibiting his conveyance of the bungalow units in separate parcels to individuals as he chooses encroaches upon constitutional guarantees attaching to the ownership of property and securing him in his right to contract concerning the use, enjoyment, and disposition of his property. U.S. Const., Fourteenth Amend., sec. 1; Cal. Const., art. I, secs. 1, 13, and

14. But the fact that the ordinance so restricts plaintiff in his right to dispose of his property is not determinative of its invalidity, for in innumerable situations the sale of various types of property has been subject to regulation by public authority. . . . Likewise here the zoning ordinance as above considered in relation to the city's accomplishment of a comprehensive and systematic plan of community development shows the challenged regulation to have been reasonably adopted in furtherance of the "general welfare," and plaintiff's individual liberty in the disposition of his property may be curtailed to that extent in the public interest. Moreover, it should be noted that plaintiff still has the right to sell the property as he bought it — the bungalow court as a single entity — and he has only been deprived of his right to "cut it up" into individual units for conveyance to separate individuals, to what reasonably appears would be to the public detriment and at variance with the dictates of the city's overall plan of community design.

Plaintiff further argues that the zoning ordinance is unreasonable and arbitrary in its application to his property because his subdivision and separate conveyance of the bungalow units to various individuals would effect only a change in ownership, and not a change in their use for dwelling purposes. In this connection reliance is placed on these factors: that the bungalow units were constructed on plaintiff's property some twenty years before the adoption of the ordinance in question; that the city laws do not purport to require the removal of these improvements nor cessation of the present use thereof; that the property would remain exactly as it has been in the past, without a change in its improvements, its use or its existing yard areas, and the sole difference would be the circumstance of single ownership of the bungalow units through the respective conveyances; and that the city manifestly does not consider such bungalow courts a nuisance, for the very ordinance here considered permits the present construction of just such improvements on 5,000-square-foot lots held under single ownership in the C-2 zone (where plaintiff's property is situated), with a requirement of only 800 square feet of lot area per dwelling unit — while each of the parcels into which plaintiff has subdivided his property contains approximately 925 square feet. But the mere fact that the property in its existing condition is not deemed a nuisance per se nor objectionable as a "near-nuisance" in constituting a menace to health, safety or morals in the strict sense of the phrase does not strengthen plaintiff's position. . . .

. . . The various factors above reviewed as found by the trial court to be possible motivating forces in the city's adoption of the ordinance show it to have a reasonable relation to the interests of the community as a whole in establishing a recommended residential pattern through regulation of minimum lot areas under single ownership. . . .

The purported appeal from the court denying a new trial is dismissed. The judgment is affirmed.

GIBSON, C. J., and SHENK, EDMONDS, and TRAYNOR, J. J., concur.

CARTER, Justice. I dissent. . . .

It would seem that the ordinance here involved is not the usual type of zoning ordinance, nor does it fall within the definitions given above insofar as it applied to the *ownership* of lots of certain size. By it a restriction is placed on the ownership, *not the use*, of parcels of land below a certain specified area.

I concede that the objectives of zoning are within the police power — that the public health, safety, morals and general welfare must be safeguarded. *But* there must be a rational connection between the means used and the end result to be attained. The majority opinion sets forth the reasons why this ordinance providing for single ownership of the units, rather than individual ownership, is a rational basis for the ordinance enacted under the police power of the municipalities. These reasons would have validity if, and only if, the ordinance prohibited more than a single dwelling or two on each 5000 square foot parcel of land (which was heretofore used by the occupants of the nine bungalows). These reasons are: (1) Avoidance of congestion in the streets. The absurdity of this is apparent — because a man owns his own home, does he tend to make for greater congestion in the streets? (2) Prevention of overcrowding the land — because a man owns his land, does he tend to have more children, more guests, more relatives? (3) Facilitation in furnishing transportation, water, light, sewer and other public necessities — I may be obtuse, but it appears that this reason is less than valid. In bungalow courts, unfurnished apartments, and the like, each tenant usually pays for his own water, light, and public utilities — these facilities are furnished to him as an individual tenant, and have nothing whatsoever to do with his ownership of the property. The transportation argument seems so ridiculous as to require no answer. (4) Provision of recreational space for children to play — how can individual ownership of the various units have the slightest bearing on such space? (5) Encouragement of the cultivation of flowers, shrubs, vegetables — it has been my experience that individual ownership tends toward the encouragement of interest in the land, rather than tending to diminish it, and the same argument applies so far as the upkeep of property is concerned. Tenants are only too willing to let the landlord take care of any repairs, and if the landlord fails to do so, the tenant is not willing to expend his funds on someone else's property. (6) As another reason we are told that a "probable increase in occupancy" would add to the noise and other irritations which militate against orderly, quiet and peaceful living. As I have pointed out previously, this is a valid argument if we are to prohibit absolutely such bungalow courts, but, in the very nature of things, can have no validity when we take into consideration the fact that these units will be occupied in the same manner whether or not they are individually owned. (7) Health and Sanitary regulations — this argument is equally delusive. There is one incinerator and two sewer connections servicing the nine units and it would seem that individual ownership would not make these services less adequate. There are common walkways which will need to be cleaned, we are told, and there are easements over other property which will need to be regulated. And on these very speculative and improbable future neighborhood squabbles, we are asked to say that the ordinance has a reasonable basis in that it will tend to promote the public health, welfare, safety and general well-being! A corollary of finding this ordinance a sound and rational exercise of the police power of the municipality is to restrain the free alienation of property. . . .

When the Constitution is disregarded we reach the perimeter of the police state. True, city councilmen are elected, but what chance has a property owner who may be in the minority to protect himself against arbitrary and unreasonable action by a city council who may see fit to zone his property for a use for which it is wholly unsuited? This Court has said it will not interfere with such action. Of what value to him is the inalienable right guaranteed by the Constitution to acquire, possess and protect property when a city council or board of supervisors tells him he can only use his property for a purpose dictated by whim or caprice and the courts refuse to grant him relief? The instant case is a shining example of such arbitrary action. The bungalow units were legally constructed and have been legally occupied, but they cannot be legally sold in separate units. Does this really make sense? Is there a scintilla of reason or logic behind such a rule? If there is, it is not apparent to me, and I doubt that it would be to any unprejudiced mind.

[The dissenting opinion of SCHAUER, J., is omitted.][23]

---

23. In Morris v. City of Los Angeles, 116 Cal. App. 2d 856, 254 P.2d 935 (1953), the plaintiffs owned a corner lot with a frontage of 45 feet on Pennsylvania Avenue and a depth of 120.9 feet on Fickett Street. There are two houses and a double garage on the lot; one house faces Fickett and the other faces Pennsylvania. The area is a multiple-dwelling zone, within which "every lot shall have a minimum width of fifty (50) feet and a minimum area of five thousand (5,000) square feet." Although the lot is nonconforming as to minimum area, this does not constitute a violation, since it antedates the ordinance. However, the zoning ordinance further provides: "No lot or parcel of land held under separate ownership at the time this Article became effective shall be separated in ownership or reduced in size below the minimum lot width or lot area required by this Article." The plaintiffs sold the northerly forty feet and the house fronting on Fickett Street. After the sale, a criminal prosecution was commenced against them.

The plaintiffs brought an action seeking to enjoin prosecution of the municipal court action and for a declaratory judgment that the zoning was invalid. The trial court found that both residences had been on the property for more than twenty-five years, as was true of most of the buildings in the neighborhood, and that practically all of the corner lots in the area had more than one dwelling unit. The court further found that each of

Notes

1. By Pa. Stat. Ann. tit. 21, §§611-615 (Purdon Supp. 1986), sellers of real property are required at or before settlement to show to the purchaser "a use registration permit showing the legal use and zoning classification of such property." The agreement of sale must also state whether the present use is in compliance with or in violation of the zoning ordinance. Applied at first only to multiple-residence and commercial establishments with one or more dwelling units, it was extended in 1957 to all uses except one- and two-family residences. In general, see Dunham, Effect on Title of Violations of Building Covenants and Zoning Ordinances, 27 Rocky Mt. L. Rev. 255 (1955).

2. A consolidated mortgage covers the ten buildings erected on a five-acre parcel by the Associated Veterans' Cooperative. A prospective purchaser of one house consults you. Of what relevance is the *Clemons* decision in determining the advice you give him?

3. How would the *Clemons* facts be affected by §1370 of the California Civil Code, enacted in 1963 (currently codified in slightly amended form as §1372): "Unless a contrary intent is clearly expressed, local zoning ordinances shall be construed to treat like structures, lots, or parcels in like manner regardless of whether the ownership thereof is divided by sale of condominiums or into community apartments . . . rather than by lease of apartments, offices, or stores."?

■ NORWOOD HEIGHTS IMPROVEMENT ASSOCIATION v. MAYOR AND CITY COUNCIL OF BALTIMORE
191 Md. 155, 60 A.2d 192 (1948)

COLLINS, Judge. This is an appeal by Norwood Heights Improvement Association, Inc., appellant, from a decision of the Baltimore

---

the dwelling units had separate utility connections and that:

> Corner lots having thereon two or more separate and unconnected dwelling units, when such lots are divided and sold, together with a residence, to separate owners who occupy the same, are better kept, maintained or occupied by a better type of occupant and have fewer occupants than those which are tenant occupied, and neither public health or sanitary regulations are adversely affected where such corner lots are sold and the residences thereon are occupied by separate owners.

The court concluded that the ordinance, "as applied under the evidence in this case to the subject property, [is] invalid, arbitrary, discriminatory and unconstitutional and [is] not a reasonable use of the police power." The court permanently enjoined the city from prosecuting or bringing any civil or criminal action against the plaintiffs by reason of the accomplished sale of the northerly forty feet or by reason of the maintenance or future sale of the southerly eighty feet. From this judgment the defendant city appeals. On appeal, it was the defendant's contention that "all the issues of this case were settled adversely to the plaintiffs by Clemons v. City of Los Angeles," and that "the trial court erroneously refused to follow that decision." The District Court of Appeals disagreed, noting that "[t]he conditions in the *Clemons* case were novel and . . . extreme." — EDS.

B. The Zoning Trio — Height, Bulk, and Use 227

City Court affirming a resolution of the Board of Municipal and Zoning Appeals approving an application for a permit by the Stulman Building Company, Inc., one of the appellees, (hereinafter known as appellee), to erect on a 15 acre tract, 10 apartment buildings made up of 34 units containing 168 suites and open parking spaces for 168 cars thereon. . . .

The plan of the development in this case shows a tract of land, after the area for streets is deducted, of 9.3 acres located partly in E-area and partly in C-area districts, where row houses are prohibited. 80 familes are to be housed on the 5.2 acres which constitute the E-area, which is within the limit under the zoning law. 88 families are to be housed on the 4.1 acres which comprise the C-area, which is well within the limit provided by the zoning ordinance. The project calls for a garden apartment development. There are 168 open-air off-street parking spaces for the use of tenants. The apartment houses are comprised of groups of two-story units containing varying numbers of apartments. The apartments are of four and five rooms. 34 such units are grouped into the 10 apartment buildings. These units are planned to over-lap and connect at the corners, leaving them separate fronts, sides and backs, except for the corner connections, where the foundation walls and roofs are to be continuous, as in the case of Akers v. City of Baltimore, 179 Md. 448, 20 A.2d 181. Each apartment building is heated by a common heating plant from a central boiler. Each group has its own water and sewage pipes and playground facilities. Each unit is to be encompassed by a firewall. There is a continuous foundation for each group and each group constitutes one building under one roof. The appellee claims that none of the apartment buildings are to be sold separately, nor can any of the units be separated from the apartment group of which they are a part. It claims that no basements are to be put under most of the units, no places for separate heating and other facilities are provided, and the cost of excavating basements would be costly and difficult. It is contended that the project is to remain as an entity under the ownership and control of the appellee which will manage it, rent out individual apartments, and collect the rents. The open-air parking spaces and playground are for the common use of all tenants and are not to be rented to anyone. There is only one gas meter, one water meter and one electric meter for the entire project. It is all financed by one mortgage on the entire development. The appellee strenuously contends that the project is designed and will always remain as one unit. It is admitted, however, by the appellee, that there are no "lot lines" laid out on the project for each building.

The primary question for us in this case is whether the present application violates the area and yard provisions of Paragraphs 21 and 24 of Ordinance No. 1247. . . . Paragraph 44(b) provides: "Lot. A lot is a parcel of land now or hereafter laid out and occupied by one building and the accessory buildings or uses customarily or necessarily incident to it, including such open spaces as are required by this ordinance."

Paragraph 44(l) defines a yard as: "The clear, unoccupied space on the same lot with a building required by the provisions of this ordinance."

Paragraph 44(m) defines a front yard as: "A clear, unoccupied space on the same lot with a building, extending across the entire width of the lot and situated between the front line of the building and the front line of the lot."

Paragraph 44(n) defines a rear yard as: "A clear, unoccupied space on the same lot with a building, extending across the entire width of the lot and situated between the rear line of the building and the rear line of the lot."

Paragraph 44(o) defines a side yard as: "A clear, unoccupied space on the same lot with a building and extending for the full length of the building between the building and the side lot line."

Paragraph 44(u) defines a group house as: "Not less than three and not more than six single family habitations, designed and erected as a unit on a lot."

Appellee relies strongly on the case of Akers v. City of Baltimore, 179 Md. 448, 20 A.2d 181, supra, which involved a permit for a more or less similar type of garden apartments. However, the six separated buildings or groups containing 27 units and housing 108 families in that case, were on separate lots. It was said there, 179 Md. at page 451, 20 A.2d 182: "The six separated buildings or groups, on separated lots, are to contain twenty-seven units in all, housing one hundred and eight families." The zoning ordinance #1247, supra, in Paragraphs 21 and 24, sets up the percentage of area of lot, rear yards, side yards and population density. The definitions in Paragraph 44, supra, seem to make it clear that "lots" and "buildings" are the units of zoning. The opinion in Akers v. City of Baltimore, supra, 179 Md. at pages 450, 451, 452, and 453, 20 A.2d 181, 182, 183, emphasizes the fact that there are lots for each building in that case. Chief Judge Bond, who wrote that opinion, carefully considered whether an aggregation of garden type apartments constituted six buildings, "on separate lots," or 27 buildings. Nothing in that opinion remotely suggested that the whole "development" could be regarded as one building. See also Colati v. Jirout, 186 Md. 652, 47 A.2d 613.

Perhaps a surveyor or an advanced mathematician might keep the score of percentages of the whole, though this would be difficult and not worth doing. A wilderness at the rear of the whole might furnish percentages for row houses where row houses are prohibited. Unless lots are defined in advance, sales of parts might leave a crazy-quilt of remnants and force the zoning authorities either (a) to rezone and thereby remove restrictions or else (b) to block further sales — or even use of the property — by maintaining restrictions that have become unworkable. "Yard" requirements, however, expressed not in percentages but in feet, mean nothing at all except with reference to defined "lots" and "buildings."

To disregard "lot lines" and treat an entire development as a unit would seem to disregard the plain words of the zoning ordinance. It is, of course, true that it is undoubtedly the intention of the present owners to keep this whole project as a single unit and under one ownership and, if that is done, compliance with the zoning laws as to "lot lines" will not embarrass the owner. However, if because of voluntary, or even forced sale by reason of financial difficulties, the buildings in the project hereafter become separately owned and changes in lines then become necessary, that will be the owner's problem, as it should be. This possibility, however, does not seem to justify the ignoring of the plain requirements in the zoning laws requiring division into lots. It is, of course, possible that the plans for this project might be revised to provide for "lot lines" for each building.

The order affirming the decision and resolution of the Board of Municipal and Zoning Appeals in this case must therefore be reversed.

Order reversed, with costs.

[The dissenting opinion of HENDERSON, J., is omitted.][24]

■ RONDA REALTY CORP. v. LAWTON
414 Ill. 313, 111 N.E.2d 310 (1953)

DAILY, Justice. This is an appeal from a judgment of the circuit court of Cook County which found subparagraph (2) of section 8 of the Chicago zoning ordinance (Municipal Code of Chicago, sec. 194A-8(2)), to be unconstitutional and void. The trial court has certified that the validity of a municipal ordinance is involved and, that in its opinion, the public interest requires a direct appeal to this court.

The leading facts show that appellee, which is the Ronda Realty Corporation, applied to the commissioner of buildings in the city of

---

24. Subsequently an ordinance was passed by the city of Baltimore to the effect that garden-type apartments are permitted "without providing a separate lot for each structure . . . provided the area of such project shall cover at least five acres of land." Thereafter, an application to erect three apartment houses, to contain nine houses in all, to house forty-five families on less than five acres was approved by the Board of Municipal and Zoning Appeals. A neighboring homeowners association objected, pointing out that "the units are connected — and separated — at the sides by a solid wall, and . . . the roof lines are, for sake of appearance broken." The Court of Appeals, upholding the permit, observed, "By the latter test presumably the House of the Seven Gables would not be one house but several." See Windsor Hills Improvement Assn. v. Mayor and City Council of Baltimore, 195 Md. 383, 73 A.2d 531 (1950). Cf. Note, 10 Wm. & Mary L. Rev. 739 (1969). — EDS.

Chicago, for a permit to remodel appellee's apartment building at 4201-15 North Sheridan Road, from twenty-one to fifty-three apartments. Accompanying the application was a certificate, by the secretary of the appellee, to the effect that on the premises there would be off-street facilities for parking eighteen automobiles. The commissioner issued the permit, whereupon thirteen tenants of the building, who are some of the appellants here, appealed to the zoning board of appeals seeking to reverse the action of the commissioner. The ground of the appeal was that the remodeling would result in the creation of fifty-three apartments; that section 194A-8(2) of the Municipal Code of Chicago requires an apartment building to provide off-street automobile parking facilities on the lot where the apartment building is maintained at the ratio of one automobile for each three apartments, that there is only space on appellee's lot for parking eight automobiles; that fifty-three apartments would require eighteen parking spaces and therefore the commissioner should not have issued the permit.

A hearing was held before the zoning board of appeals, which body, after hearing evidence and viewing the premises, concluded that there were not enough off-street parking facilities on appellee's property to comply with the ordinance and entered an order reversing the action of the commissioner and revoking the permit. Appellee then filed a complaint in the circuit court for review under the provisions of the Administrative Review Act (Ill. Rev. Stat. 1951, chap. 110, pars. 264-279) setting forth the facts and pleading the invalidity of the ordinance relied upon by the board. On the hearing for review, the court stated that it was deciding the case purely on a question of law and not on questions of fact, and entered its judgment that the section of the ordinance relied upon was unconstitutional and void in that it discriminated against appellee and deprived it of equal protection of the law. The order of the zoning board of appeals was reversed and the issuance of the building permit sustained. The tenants, the commissioner of buildings, the zoning board of appeals and the city of Chicago have perfected the appeal to this court.

The errors assigned in this court present but one decisive issue, namely, whether subparagraph (2) of section 8 of the zoning ordinance is invalid because it creates an unlawful classification, discriminatory in its nature. The complete provisions of section 8 of the ordinance are as follows:

> 194A-8. (Section 8.) Apartment House Districts. Permitted uses in Apartment House districts are:
> (1) Any use permitted in a Family Residence district without restrictions except such as are applicable to auxiliary uses and any other use permitted in a Duplex Residence or Group House district;
> (2) Apartment house, provided that where there are more than two

apartments in the building a private garage or automobile compound for the storage of one passenger automobile for each of 33 per cent of the number of apartments shall be erected or established and maintained on the lot used for the apartment house;

(3) Boarding or lodging house, hotel, hospital, home for dependents or nursing home;

(4) Boarding school, vocational school, college or university, when not operated for pecuniary profit;

(5) Club, fraternity or sorority house, when not operated for pecuniary profit;

(6) Public art gallery, library or museum;

(7) Auxiliary uses . . .

. . . Laws will not be regarded as special or class legislation merely because they affect one class and not another, provided they affect all members of the same class alike. A classification which is not purely arbitrary and is reasonably adapted to secure the purpose for which it was intended will not be disturbed by the courts unless it can be clearly seen that there is no fair reason for the distinction made. Stearns v. City of Chicago, 368 Ill. 112, 13 N.E.2d 63. Also, in this regard, we have held that even though a zoning ordinance be based upon proper statutory authority and is reasonably designed to protect the public health or safety, it cannot, in such guise, under the rights guaranteed by the Illinois and Federal constitutions, effect an arbitrary discrimination against the class on which it operates by omitting from its coverage persons and objects similarly situated. Statutory classifications can only be sustained where there are real differences between the classes, and where the selection of the particular class, as distinguished from others, is reasonably related to the evils to be remedied by the statute or ordinance.

Tested in the light of these established rules of law, we believe it is manifest that subparagraph (2) of section 8 creates an unlawful classification, both arbitrary and discriminatory in its nature. Of all the different types of structures upon which the section is made to operate, it is only apartment buildings that are required to furnish off-street parking facilities. The evils to be remedied on crowded city streets are well known, but we do not see that the singling out of apartment buildings from the other types of buildings embraced by the ordinance is reasonably related to the elimination of those evils. Appellants urge that the classification is not discriminatory because it applies to all apartment buildings equally and because it is apartment buildings, more than any other type structure permitted, which contribute the most to street congestion caused by parked automobiles. We see neither a fair nor reasonable basis for such classification nor its reasonable relation to the object and purpose of the ordinance. The street congestion problems created by boarding or rooming houses, hotels, and the like, are not essentially different from those caused by apartment buildings. All are similarly situated in their relation to the problems of congestion that are caused by parking cars in the street, and all contribute proportionately to the evil sought to be remedied. Indeed, we think it not unreasonable to say that the scope and nature of the congestion may be greater in the case of large rooming houses and hotels than in the case of apartment houses. First, due to the comparative number of persons accommodated and, second, because the apartment dweller suggests a resident of some permanency who would seek to alleviate the problem of parking on the street, whereas the hotel or rooming house guest suggests a transient who makes no effort to solve his parking problem. It is our conclusion that the differences in kind between apartment buildings and numerous of the other structures upon which the section is made to operate are not such as to warrant the distinction made by subparagraph (2). Relieving congestion in the streets is no doubt a proper legislative purpose, but imposing the burden on one kind of property, while excepting other kinds not significantly different, is not a valid means for its accomplishment. A statute or ordinance cannot be sustained which applies to some cases and does not apply to other cases not essentially different in kind. Josma v. Western Steel Car & Foundry Co., 249 Ill. 508, 94 N.E. 945. . . .

Judgment affirmed.[25]

Note

The existing technique of controlling intensity of use by means of height limitation and yard and setback requirements is largely a geometric control, or, as many consultants complain, a "zoning envelope" that dictates the shape of the building by prescribing its outer measurements. Modern zoning ordinances are trying to break through

---

25. Cf. Roselle v. Wright, 21 N.J. 400, 122 A.2d 506 (1956) (ordinance prohibited storage garages in business districts, but permitted other public and private garages), and Jefferson National Bank v. Miami Beach, 267 So. 2d 100 (Fla. 3d Dist. 1972) (public parking lot permitted).

In August 1953, the Chicago City Council adopted an amendment to the zoning ordinance, listing twenty-six property uses for which off-street parking facilities are required. For the background of the new approach, see Kelly, Zoning Approach to the Parking Problem, Highway Research Board Bull. No. 101, at 61 (1955).

Another solution looking toward the efficient and convenient movement of people and goods is that of Moses, How to Plan and Pay for the Safe and Adequate Highways We Need (1953) (General Motors Contest prize essay). A broader recognition of the relationship between streets, traffic, and land use is advocated in Mitchell & Rapkin, Urban Traffic: A Function of Land Use (1954); Owen, The Metropolitan Transportation Problem (1956); Meyer, Kain & Wohl, The Urban Transportation Problem (1965); Lane, Analytical Transport Planning (1973); Stone, Beyond the Automobile, Reshaping the Transportation Environment (1971); and Robinson, Highways and Our Environment (1971). — Eds.

B. The Zoning Trio — Height, Bulk, and Use 233

this rigid dictation of size in order to permit the greatest possible flexibility in protecting neighborhood character and in satisfying individual needs and architectural design.

You should reexamine your local zoning ordinance. What are the purposes of bulk controls, and which techniques can most readily foster them? For whose guidance are the various regulations framed? In what way do they stimulate the construction of certain types of buildings? In general, what are the relative advantages of regulations based on requirements regarding height, setback, yard, court, coverage, lot area per family, dwelling unit or room, cubage, floor area ratio?[26] Note, to take one instance, that the minimum dimension for a yard could be set according to different principles: an absolute dimension; one that is related to the height of the nearest outside wall of the building; one which increases with the height of the wall above the ground. For what purpose should any be used, and what combinations might be most effective?

Floor area ratio. The relating of floor area in the building to the lot area has become a popular zoning device; "FAR" gives the multiple by which the maximum permitted floor area may be calculated.[27] While this formula can be applied to all types of buildings, regardless of the shape of lot, and does not restrict the building to a specific shape or location, it is nevertheless subject to certain defects.[28] Consider, for example, its efficiency in retaining a balance between bulk and open space; one illustration, which may suggest others, is the case where the first story covers 100 percent of the site, and the remaining permitted bulk goes into a tower set upon this "pedestal."[29]

---

26. See Comment, 60 Yale L.J. 506 (1951); Agle, A New Kind of Zoning, Arch. Forum, July 1951, at 176.

27. Some illustrations may be helpful: the Empire State Building has a floor area ratio of 25:1; Radio City and Stuyvesant Town, 3.13:1 each.

28. Even in its definition: floor area is "the sum of the gross horizontal area of the several floors of a building, including interior balconies and mezzanines but excluding garage area and basement and cellar floor areas not devoted to residence use. All horizontal dimensions are to be measured between the exterior faces of walls, including the walls of roofed porches." N.Y.C. Zoning Res. §1(u). The impact of modern architecture is apparent. Even a simple and concrete word like "room" becomes difficult to define; folding walls, space dividers, and movable partitions are becoming commonplace, while areas within the dwelling place often overlap and even blend into the outdoors.

This difficulty applies equally to standard techniques. Consider typical yard requirements: is not the concept related to a home as consisting of a group of rooms clearly defined by walls and surrounded by four unrelated yard segments? In some areas cantilevered second-story decks and sun porches are used to maximize space — could their projection into a required yard be allowed under the usual ordinance? How would a "finger plan" fit into the yard requirements? The ranch-type house, by incorporating the garage, may provide more effective insulation (and privacy) than do side yards.

29. Some ordinances attempt to provide open space by increasing side yard requirements as the number of families in the building increases. Is this a wise regulation? Compare the concept of "usable open space" found in Harrison, Ballard & Allen, Plan for Rezoning the City of New York 197 (1950), which allows up to 25 percent of such space to be on roofs, balconies, and areas other than the ground itself. Moerder v. City

Daylight. To fill the gap caused by rejection of the English "ancient lights" doctrine, and to supplement other bulk controls, "daylighting" techniques are now employed. The usual device is a regulation based on "angle of light" of structure; an early Denver zoning ordinance is typical:

> No part of any structure ... (except church spires, church towers, flagpoles, antennas, chimneys, flues, vents, or accessory water tanks) shall project up through bulk limits which are defined by planes starting at the center lines of all streets within and abutting the district and extending up over the Zone Lot at an angle of 75 degrees and 4 minutes with respect to the horizontal (a pitch of 3.75 feet additional rise for each foot additional setback).

§612.10-4(2) (1957).[30]

A further refinement of this method is the averaging device.[31]

> *Averaging Light Angles.* In any district, along the street frontage or along the rear lot line of any zoning lot, the angles of light obstruction whose inclined planes pass unobstructed over each building (or other structure or part thereof) may be averaged, provided that:
> a. The weighted average of such angles shall not exceed the angle of light obstruction specified in the district regulations. ...

A type of control frequently used to supplement this device is the "area of light access" or "wedge for light" technique. The English Daylight Code, developed for use in replanning the city of London, is a more complex formula. It is based on the "daylight factor," which measures the percentage of total light (assuming a clear sky)[32] available in any building; credit is thus given for light coming around the side of an obstruction as well as over it.[33]

---

of Moscow, Idaho, 78 Idaho 246, 300 P.2d 808 (1956), dealt with a regulation that a new house must be set back from the street as far as the average of the other houses then in existence on the block. Is this a proper bulk control?

30. "To insure enough light and air," writes Mumford, "the distance between buildings should increase with their length. Our municipal setback regulations make a hypocritical acknowledgment of this principle, but since they were framed to keep land values high rather than buildings low or widely spaced, they have never come within shooting distance of achieving an ideal." From the Ground Up 117 (1956).

31. Harrison, Ballard & Allen, supra note 29, at 193.

32. Studies of office-work efficiency in relation to the degree of daylight produced a "recommended" standard (1 percent daylight factor at a distance of 12 feet from the external wall, at a height of 2 feet 9 inches from the floor).

33. Ministry of Town and Country Planning, Redevelopment of Central Areas (1947). Much of this legislation developed out of the experience of experts in easements of light litigation. See 1 Swarbrick, Easements of Light 16, 18, 65 (1931).

In evaluating such light and air provisions, consider the statement in Sheffield

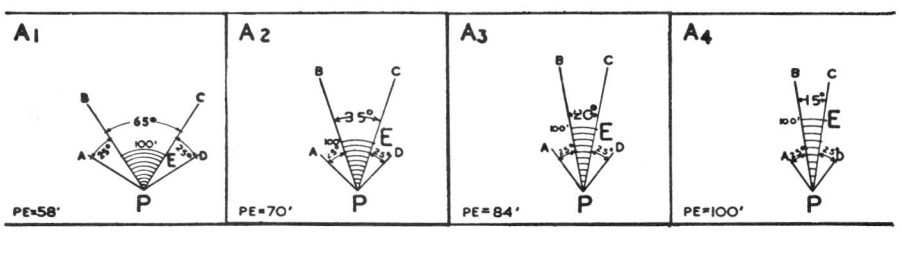

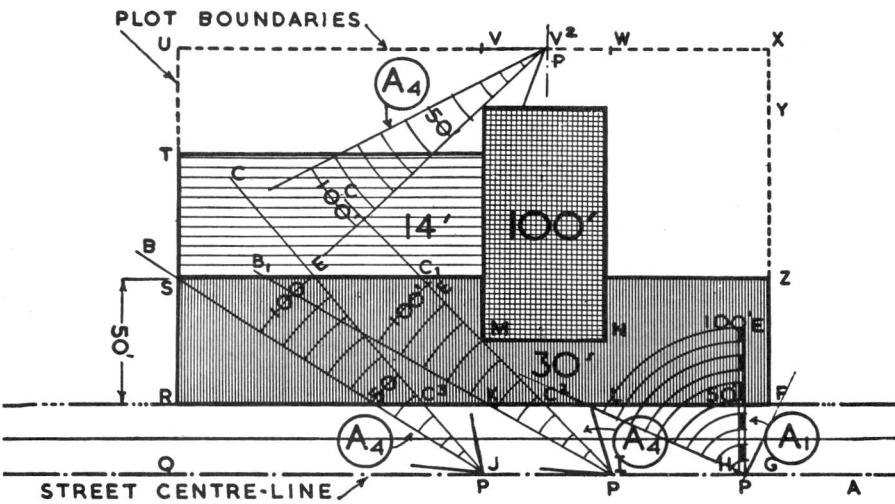

Heights of proposed buildings are tested by "permissible height indicators." Four transparent fan-shaped wedges are placed along the plot boundaries or center of streets; these show allowable construction height for all points. If any one of the four is satisfied, the new building is permitted, for, in theory, all guarantee the minimum standard in terms of the daylight factor (some giving vertically narrow but tall

---

Masonic Hall Co. v. Sheffield Corp., [1932] 2 Ch. 17, 23-24:

> There is one other thing which I think it my duty to say, and that is with reference to the value of expert evidence in cases of this kind. I do not desire to minimize the value of that evidence, or to intimate a doubt that the lines on which it has recently been given are far more useful to the Court than they used to be before ... experts devised a new method of measuring the amount of obscuration of light caused by a new building. But I do think I ought to say that, in my opinion, it is possible to exaggerate that evidence in a particular case. The question to be solved by the Court is not really a question which can always be fairly decided by the amount of direct sky which will reach a hypothetical table two feet nine inches high in a particular room. I think it is safer ... to consider whether, as a matter of common sense, there is such a deprivation of light as to render the occupation of the house uncomfortable in accordance with the ordinary ideas of mankind.

segments of lights, as A_4; or others, horizontally narrow but wide segments of light, as A_1).

Elasticity. British experience has shown that in some cases controls that are flexible in concept nevertheless produce uniformity of construction because of the dictates of building costs that rule out alternative shapes and sizes allowed by the law. For example, a floor area ratio of 3.0 permits a three-story building to cover all of the lot, or a six-story building to cover 50 percent of the lot (or endless permutations of coverages and stories). The economics of building, however, may overwhelmingly favor a three-story structure. In this case, a floor area ratio may produce a spate of buildings of uniform height, and the net effect will not differ from a rigid three-story height "envelope," the very result that the floor area ratio was designed to prevent.

The idea has therefore evolved of introducing "situations of choice" into the investment decision. If, for example, high-rise building (to follow the illustration) is more costly than low-rise, why not permit an additional floor area where the developer chooses a "50 percent coverage — six story" as opposed to "100 percent coverage — three story" construction? The additional rentable floor area will thus offset, to some degree, the additional cost. The floor area ratio itself can thus be put on a sliding scale, increasing as the amount of usable open space is increased. Once this basic incentive principle is brought into play, all sorts of modifications suggest themselves: rewards for front rather than rear open space (if such is desired), varying incentives for ground open space, for space on the first- or second-story roof, for arcaded space (e.g., Lever House), and for experiments which introduce amenities judged to be socially desirable. Can such incentives be calculated with sufficient finesse to offset the market pressures toward a given type of structure under given regulations? Are there any abuses inherent in such devices? How far can judicial review go in assessing the reasonableness of such mechanisms?[34]

2. Land Use: Classification and Segregation

■ KATOBIMAR REALTY CO. v. WEBSTER
20 N.J. 114, 118 A.2d 824 (1955)

HEHER, J. At issue here is the legal sufficiency of an amendment to the zoning ordinance of the Borough of New Providence providing

---

34. Compare this statement by H.M. Lewis:

> [T]here is no convincing evidence available to show that there is damage to the health of workers whose offices and shops have windows on the existing narrow alleys and courts. There are, in fact, thousands of persons who work in interior

B. The Zoning Trio — Height, Bulk, and Use

that "No lands or structures shall be used, nor shall any structures be erected, altered or used within the Industrial Zone" delineated by the ordinance "for any residential, or retail commercial purpose," and "Only industrial uses which are not detrimental to health, safety or property shall be permitted, and in no event" shall leave be given to conduct storage yards for òil, coal, lumber, junk, certain "noxious and deleterious manufacturing," or "any other use or purpose which in the opinion of the Mayor and Borough Council is detrimental to health, safety, or property, or to property values."

The proceeding is in lieu of mandamus to compel the issuance of a building permit for the construction in the industrial zone of nine retail commercial stores, to constitute a "shopping center." Plaintiffs' plot comprises 5.14 acres fronting 425 feet on Central Avenue and extending back a depth of 537 feet, the whole being within the industrial zone. The individual plaintiff, Thompson, acquired the land by deed dated June 25, 1953, recorded the ensuing September 14. He is the principal stockholder of the plaintiff corporation, which seems to be a family enterprise. The formal application for the building permit was made October 19, 1954. The building inspector deferred action pending submission of the plans and specifications for the project to the mayor and council. But negotiations began the prior April for the construction on the land of a "small shopping center consisting of nine to eleven stores in one continuous front." Then came the introduction, September 27, 1954, of the later-adopted supplement to the zoning ordinance now under attack. On October 25, the application for a building permit was renewed before the council and was "tabled until after hearing on the ordinance revising rules and regulations of the Industrial Zone is held on November 8, 1954." Upon the adoption of the supplement, the building inspector advised plaintiffs by letter dated November 15 that the proposed use "is forbidden by the Zoning Ordinance, as amended." Thereupon the complaint in this proceeding, filed the prior November 3, was amended to allege that the supplement to the ordinance is unreasonable, arbitrary and capricious and deprives plaintiffs of their property without due process of law, and, moreover, it was "enacted contrary to the statute and is null and void."

There was summary judgment for defendants on a stipulation of facts and affidavits; and the case is here by certification on our own

---

spaces with only artificial light and ventilation. On the other hand, office space on the upper floors of tall buildings with exterior windows commonly pay a premium rent over those that are lower and darker. This is partly due to a reduction of noise and dust, and to a traditional prestige which has become associated with "a view," as well as to the higher level of light available in such situations.

A New Zoning Plan for the District of Columbia 55 (1956). See Cribbet, Changing Concepts in the Law of Land Use, 50 Iowa L. Rev. 45 (1965).

motion of plaintiffs' pending appeal to the Appellate Division of the Superior Court. . . .

Plaintiffs' lands are situate in the southwesterly quarter of the borough, near the Murray Hill station of the Delaware, Lackawanna & Western Railroad's line running from Gladstone, Bernardsville, and Summit to New York City, in an area having several wholesale commercial greenhouses and connected boiler plants. The plot abuts on the south the zone in which business is a permissible use. Central Avenue is one of the borough's main thoroughfares, running generally east to west; the particular plot is just west of South Street, also a main highway. In the immediate vicinity are located the Bell Laboratories, the Air Reduction Laboratories, and an office building of the All-State Insurance Company; and the construction of an office building for the American Mineral Spirits Company and a 172-suite garden apartment structure are in prospect. Due north is the plant and office building of a manufacturer of diamond drills and mining equipment; northwest a factory of the Garden Mower Company, a subsidiary of U.S. Hammered Piston Ring Company, is under construction; due west, contiguous to the plaintiffs' lands, are three separate greenhouses and the boiler rooms, heating plants and smokestacks of wholesale florists and flower growers, and to the southwest there is another such plant. Due south is a business area and 11 multiple family dwellings and stores and outbuildings of the Baldwin Company, dealers in fuel oil, coal and building materials and supplies, and retail hardware. Bordering the Baldwin property, and along the railroad, are a freight station and public and private track sidings, and to the south of the tracks are the railroad station, the federal post-office, two coal pockets, one privately owned and the other the railroad's. Due east of plaintiffs' lands is an office building of the New York Life Insurance Company, used also for the filing and storing of records and archives, and to the southeast are commercial greenhouses and boiler rooms. . . .

The more exclusive use is justified as the most appropriate use of the land in the given district, e.g., residence use, and by the same token such use is ordinarily permissible in districts set apart for the less exclusive uses. Such is in common understanding the essence of use classification, so much so as to have evoked little or no dissent, a principle comporting with the constitutional rights of person and of property. Generally, the higher uses are allowable in the less limited use districts, normally so when account is taken of the nature and design of the inherent limitations of the zoning process. But, by the same reasoning, the general rule has its exceptions; and the higher use may be forbidden in the less restricted districts where such exclusion bears a real and substantial relation to the general good and welfare in the areas of service peculiar to zoning. The considerations governing residence, business and industrial uses differ in their very nature; and

B. The Zoning Trio — Height, Bulk, and Use

where the exclusion has a rational relation to the field of police action comprehended in zoning, there is no transgression upon constitutional right. And where the sufficiency of the classification and the exclusions, so measured, are fairly debatable, the local legislative judgment prevails. The inquiry in the given case necessarily depends upon the particular circumstances. . . .

An eminent authority on the subject has this to say:

"Use districts are ordinarily residential, business, and industrial. The district of less restrained use always admits the uses of the more restricted ones. Perhaps the only exceptions to this statement are in a few cities where dwellings are excluded from industrial districts." Bassett, Zoning 63.

The principles thus obtaining to sustain the higher residential use in a "heavy" industrial zone are a fortiori applicable to the proposed retail commercial use in the "light" industrial zone of the ordinance under review. It is difficult to perceive a rational distinction referable to the fulfillment of the statutory zoning considerations, all or any of them, between the contemplated shopping center and the uses permissible in the limited industrial district now before us. Is the shopping center proposed here less acceptable than the business center allowed in a residence district in Ward v. Scott, 16 N.J. 16, 105 A.2d 851 (1954)? It does not matter that there the retail shopping concession was the subject of a variance. The principle invocable is much the same, certainly so where the landowner asserts an intrusion upon his basic right of property. Here, "noxious and deleterious manufacturing" and uses "detrimental to health, safety or property" are forbidden in the industrial zone as finally constituted. . . .

The projected business center and light industrial uses are not incompatible in nature; they are generally, so far as zoning policy goes, wholly congruous uses, and if in special circumstances a distinction may reasonably be made to serve an overriding public interest, such showing is not made here. There was no such finding below. The conclusion there was that the "exclusion of retail commercial uses from such light industrial zone has in fact a reasonable bearing upon the health, safety, morals and welfare of the community, including the exclusion of traffic hazards, the establishment of aesthetic levels and like elements." There is no reasonable basis for the classification. Retail commercial uses would not conflict with industrial uses. There must be a reasonable exercise of the grouping power; such is of the essence of comprehensive zoning.

But however this may be, a shopping center here would be the use most compatible with its surroundings, more in harmony with the setting of its environment; and the exclusion of such use would be unreasonable, arbitrary and capricious. . . .

This conclusion is plainly not in conflict with . . . Pierro v. Baxendale, 20 N.J. 17, 118 A.2d 401 (1955), barring motels from the municipality. We are here concerned with the exclusion of a retail commercial use from a light industrial zone, in an area where such use is in keeping with the environment, if not indeed with the permissible light industrial uses. This is not a question of "liberal" zoning, but of zoning comporting with the constitutional rights of private property and the equal protection of the laws.

The judgment is reversed and the cause is remanded for proceedings conforming to these conclusions.

For reversal: Chief Justice VANDERBILT and Justices HEHER, WACHENFELD and BURLING — 4.

For affirmance: Justices OLIPHANT, JACOBS and BRENNAN — 3.

WILLIAM J. BRENNAN, JR., J. (dissenting). New Jersey has witnessed a marked and salutary change in the judicial attitude toward municipal zoning over the past decade. Long overdue recognition of the legitimate aspirations of the community to further its proper social, economic and political progress, and of the propriety of requiring individual landowners to defer to the greater public good, have replaced the narrow concepts held by former courts. Present-day decisions rightly give maximum play to the philosophy underlying our constitutional and statutory zoning provisions that localities may decide for themselves what zoning best serves and furthers the local public welfare, subject only to the rule of reason forbidding arbitrary and capricious action. . . .

The instant decision not only departs from [this policy] in its application of the law to the facts but, of graver concern, does so in language, substantially in haec verba, which did not command majority support in *Pierro* and appears only in the *Pierro* dissent. Local governing bodies and their advisors must surely be troubled to know which — the *Pierro* majority opinion or the *Pierro* dissent — expresses the prevailing view in this court. And the bewilderment will be the greater because this opinion is filed but a few weeks after *Pierro* was decided. . . .

The motivation for the prohibition was the desire to attract non-nuisance industries to the borough to increase tax ratables and support the expanded school needs and greater municipal services incident to the rapid residential growth of the community. The borough emerged after World War II from a primarily rural and farm economy into a fast-growing suburban community of modest homes. From its 1950 population of 3,500 it has grown to a 1955 population of 6,000. It was feared, and with good reason, that taxes to be realized on modest residential properties would be insufficient to support the mounting cost of schooling and borough government without undue hardship to the individual home owner.

Faced with that situation, the governing body intelligently and responsibly gave consideration to ways and means to increase tax

B. The Zoning Trio — Height, Bulk, and Use

revenues without impairment of the essentially residential character of the borough. They hit upon a program of attracting new non-nuisance industries, thereby augmenting ratables without incurring heavy additional expenses for municipal service. . . .

This type of program as part of a comprehensive zoning plan for communities of the character of New Providence is customarily recommended by professional planners. There was expert evidence that not only are residences incompatible in such a zone but that general retail and commercial business should also be recognized as incompatible with a well planned district designed for non-nuisance industries. Numerous disadvantages from such an intermixture are referred to in the evidence. . . .

Upon this set of facts I find it impossible to square the majority's holding with the sustaining . . . in *Pierro* of an ordinance excluding motels although the ordinance allowed boarding and rooming houses. Commercial shopping centers are not wholly banned from New Providence. Provision is made for them in the business districts contiguous to residential areas, where they rightly belong. In forbidding them in the district in question, the conclusion is inescapable that New Providence evolved a sound long-range policy designed to achieve a well balanced local economy and in nowise exceeded the zoning authority so to do acknowledged in the cited cases. . . .

. . . If well-conceived and carefully thought out zoning plans such as this, so obviously and peculiarly appropriate to further the well-being of the community of New Providence, are to be struck down in this fashion, a grievous blow will be dealt the forward progress of zoning as an instrument for the enhancement of the overall social and economic welfare of our municipalities.

I vote to affirm.

This dissent is joined in by Mr. Justice JACOBS.[35]

---

35. Pierro v. Baxendale, cited in both opinions above, was decided the same term, with Jacobs, J., writing for the majority, and with Heher, J., in dissent. The case involved the exclusion of motels from the Borough of Palisades Park, a municipality of one square mile located a mile and a half from the George Washington Bridge. Plaintiff had applied to the borough building inspector for a permit to construct a twenty-seven-unit motel in a Residence District A (one- and two-family dwellings and apartment houses) where motels were not expressly permitted. The permit was denied, and, six days after plaintiff made application, the borough adopted a supplemental zoning ordinance expressly prohibiting motels anywhere within the municipal limits. Plaintiff filed suit seeking to set aside the supplemental ordinance and compel issuance of a building permit. The court upheld the ordinance; upon what rationale? See also City of Miami Beach v. Arthree, Inc., 269 So. 2d 699 (Fla. Dist. Ct. App. 1972), cert. denied, 276 So. 2d 166, cert. denied, 414 U.S. 859 (1973) (apartment hotels); Bennett M. Lifter, Inc. v. Metropolitan Dade County, 482 So. 2d 479 (Fla. Dist. Ct. App. 1986) (condominium conversions); Schad v. Borough of Mount Ephraim, infra page 484 (live entertainment). — EDS.

Notes

1. (a) The telephone company wishes to extend its facilities. Part of the block on which it is located is zoned Business A, on which it proposes to erect an office building, a permitted use; on the other portion, zoned Residence B, it proposes to build a telephone exchange, also a permitted use. Adjacent to the exchange and within the Residence B district the company wishes to establish a parking lot for use by its employees working in both buildings and by its customers. May it do so?

The zoning ordinance provides that within any residence district no building or premises shall be used other than for nine specified classes of purpose. A parking lot is not one of the nine. The ordinance further provides: "Accessory uses, customary with or incidental to any of the aforesaid permitted uses, including private garages and private stables" shall be permitted. See Application of Emmett S. Hickman Co., 49 Del. 13, 108 A.2d 667 (1954) ("the company was attempting to do indirectly that which it could not do directly — use residential property as an accessory to a business use in a business district.") Cf. Premium Point Park Association v. Polar Bar, 306 N.Y. 507, 119 N.E.2d 360 (1954) (refreshment stand occupying a small portion of a plot — the remainder is devoted to a free parking lot for customers — did not violate a covenant against use of the land for a "commercial garage, or automobile parking lot").

(b) *P* maintains an office as an accountant; he brings home work in the evening, which he attends to in a room containing ordinary household furniture, a desk, typewriter, and adding machine. During the busiest time of the year — naturally that between January 2 and April 15 — no more than sixty of his clients come to his residence and then they come singly and not in groups. *P* has no assistants in his employ at the house. The zoning ordinance provides that "no lot or premises shall be used for any purpose, except as hereinafter specifically provided and allowed in this section." Nothing in this provision specifically allows the business of accounting to be carried on at a residence. In an action by *P* to enjoin the city from enforcing the zoning ordinance, what result? See Kort v. City of Los Angeles, 52 Cal. App. 2d 804, 127 P.2d 66 (2d Dist. 1942) ("the limitations upon the use of property are not unreasonable or oppressive").

Suppose that the record reveals that *P*'s home is in a zone in which property may be used for single-family dwellings, private garages, hotels, apartments, rooming and boarding houses, private clubs, public dining rooms, and restaurants, with their usual "accessories" and garage accommodations. The office of a minister of religion, physician, dentist, or healer is also lawful, provided the room used as an office "constitutes an integral part of the dwelling" and that it is not used for the conduct

B. The Zoning Trio — Height, Bulk, and Use 243

of the general practice of medicine, surgery, dentistry, or healing other than as a religious vocation. What result? Is a "beauty salon" a "customary home occupation"? Jantausch v. Borough of Verona, 41 N.J. Super. 89, 124 A.2d 14 (Law Div. 1956) (yes — court takes judicial notice of Small Business Administration bulletin that includes "beauty-parlors" among "home businesses"). Is a dance studio a proper "accessory use" for an artist? Stewart v. Humphries, 132 N.E.2d 758 (Ohio Ct. App. 1955) (yes — court cites Plato for conclusion that "dancing is an art"). What about a karate school? Carbonara v. Sacca, 45 A.D.2d 1006, 385 N.Y.S.2d 82 (App. Div. 1974) (court rejected homeowner's claim that his pursuit was sufficiently "similar" to "[t]eaching with musical instruction").

(c) "Guppy Fancier Put on Trial as Zoning Violator" was the headline in the N.Y. Herald Tribune, May 10, 1951. In People v. Glettner, the defendant was charged with using his home for the business of breeding guppies in contravention of zoning laws. Mr. Glettner told reporters that the trial evolved from a situation in which male admirers of his bitch, Lucky, trampled his neighbor's hyacinths. In offering to make reparations, he happened to remark, "My hobby . . . is breeding fish." Three days later a cease and desist order was served on Mr. Glettner, whose guppies, ignorant of the village ordinance, continued to breed. An expert for the defendant "testified that with enthusiastic hobbyists 'they want a little privacy for breeding.' Judge Berman was puzzled. 'Are you talking about fish or hobbyists?' he asked. 'Fish,' said [the expert]. 'To do guppies right, you might need 1,000 tanks.' Judge Berman appeared enraptured." There was further testimony that fish fanciers must give away, sell, or kill surplus fish, or risk driving their spouses from the home.

(d) Jean Client has recently purchased a parcel of land containing a house and a substantial building formerly used as a barn. Both of the buildings are situated within an A-zone under the following zoning bylaw: "In an A-zone, no building, structure, or premises shall be erected, altered, or used for any purpose except one or more of the following: (1) a single-family or two-family detached dwelling. . . . (8) the use of a room or rooms in a dwelling as an office or studio or for customary home occupation by a person residing in the dwelling."

Client wishes to use the barn as a real estate office and as an antique shop. Client's request for a building permit has been denied, and she has applied to the Board of Appeals. The notice of public hearing reads: "The Zoning Board of Appeals will hold a hearing in the High School cafeteria on Thursday, June 18, 1990, at 8:00 P.M., to act upon the appeal of Jean Client from the refusal of the building commissioner to grant a permit to make certain alterations on a dwelling at No. 2 Countryway for the purpose of using the building as a real-estate office and antique shop." How would you advise Client?

2. Dearborn Township has passed an amendment to its zoning ordinance as follows: "It shall be unlawful for any person within any part of the unincorporated areas of the township to in any manner use or carry any gun, weapon or any firearm within said unincorporated areas for the purpose of hunting any wild game or fowl or for shooting at targets." Your opinion is requested by the Director of the State Department of Conservation as to the validity of the ordinance. See Mich. Atty. Gen. Rep. 72 (1947-1948). Cf. Quilici v. Village of Morton Grove [Illinois], 532 F.2nd 1166 (7th Cir. 1982), cert. denied, 464 U.S. 863 (1983) (no constitutional violation in prohibition of handgun possession within Village's borders).

3. The classification of the permitted use raises a host of definitional problems at which the property owner may clutch for respite. A typical problem is that of Sioux Falls v. Cleveland, 75 S.D. 548, 70 N.W.2d 62 (1955): Is a mobile home permitted in a district that allows "every use as a dwelling house, double house, or duplex house"? Compare Rundell v. May, 258 So. 2d 90 (La. App. 1972), with Town of Greenland v. Hussey, 110 N.H. 269, 266 A.2d 122 (1970). In Application of Laporte, 2 App. Div. 2d 710, 152 N.Y.S.2d 816 (2d Dept. 1956), a dormitory for sixty students was held to be a "one-family dwelling."

The Spencerian law of evolution from the simple to the complex is certainly illustrated in the multiplication of zoning districts. To take an isolated example, Libertyville, Illinois, divided the village in 1925 into three residence zones, one business zone, and one manufacturing zone; the 1952 revision divided the village into five residential districts, two commercial districts, two manufacturing districts, and one agricultural district. Babcock, Classification and Segregation Among Zoning Districts, 1954 U. Ill. L. Forum 186, 187.[36] In City of Los Altos v. Silvey, 206 Cal. App. 2d 606, 24 Cal. Rptr. 200 (1st Dist. 1964), change of factory from wine bottling to boat manufacturing was prohibited.

■ RECORD ON APPEAL IN CORTHOUTS v. TOWN OF NEWINGTON
140 Conn. 284, 99 A.2d 112 (1953)

The Court: Of course, I can go along with the witness as I look at the map and he looks at the town — If you were zoning the town,

---

[36]. For the additional curlicue of "material change of use" under the English system, see Haar, Land Planning Law in a Free Society 70-72 (1951). As to the draftsman's problem, see City of Tulsa v. Mizel, 265 P.2d 496 (Okla. 1953) ("Commercial District" permitted "Retail and Wholesale Business: . . . oil well supplies"; "Industrial District" permitted "Pipe and Oil Field Supply Yard"). People v. Kasold, 153 Cal. App. 2d 891, 314 P.2d 241 (Cal. Super. 1957), considered whether keeping bees was permitted in a zone allowing "domestic animals" in conjunction with a residential use. For an interesting criticism of the vague language employed in an ordinance ("similar business"), see People v. Binzley, 146 Cal. App. 2d Supp. 889, 303 P.2d 903 (1956). See Sears, Roebuck & Co. v. Power, 390 Pa. 206, 134 A.2d 659 (1957) (passage of title concept in the Uniform Commercial Code to determine if structure is a "warehouse" for zoning purposes).

B. The Zoning Trio — Height, Bulk, and Use 245

where would you put industry? You would put it along the railroad, as he suggests. At least, he would say to the people, That is where we hope to channel industry; it is the natural place for industry, where they can have sidings, opportunity to load and unload heavy material, and so forth. It is on the outskirts of the built up section. You attack simply this — that within this industrial zone they have excluded a use that is permitted in what I called the highest zone.

Mr. Francis: Yes, and they have gone too far and taken too much for that use also.

The Court: That is the novel problem in this whole case, it seems to me, and I confess I have never heard it mentioned before until today — that it would be proper to exclude the use which, it seems to me, we have considered the highest use in the A Residence from the lowest zone, which has the usual nuisance and noxious odors exceptions, and so forth. . . .

The Court: You both seem to be willing to let the gentleman rest on his statement that it is good zoning as a matter of opinion. Nobody seems to see fit to ask him why he feels it is good zoning.

The Witness: Why?

The Court: Yes.

The Witness: I think it is good zoning because it is principally protection to people and the public welfare. If you let people move into and have houses in industrial zones, you subject them to the very things that people have zoning for — the impact of industry on homes. What difference does it make if you exclude industry from residence areas or allow residences to come into industrial areas? The incompatibility is the thing we believe, as zoners, should be knocked out. Homes suffer just as much from industry, whether they are in industrial areas or in residential areas.

The Court: I would like to test your conclusion by this, if I may? If we have the area X, which is an area occupied by single family homes, the things that are permitted in almost an accepted pattern of A zone across the country, if industry moved into that zone and acquired some of the houses and tore them down, or some land, and built a manufacturing plant, of course, the impact of the industry on all the homes in the area would be, I think, no doubt, to depreciate them in value.

A: Yes.

Q: (By the Court) So, generally speaking, where the planners and zoners are confronted with an un-zoned area like that, they properly protect it and the people with residences by zoning that area and excluding business and industry from that zone or area. That protects all those people from the so-called impact of industry, the depreciation of their property; it protects them from the noises and smoke and all the incidents of industry.

Now, in the same community, if there is a railroad line and

some shore line with wharves and docks and the beginnings of industry, the planners seem to canvass the situation and say that and the adjoining and contiguous area are the areas to presently zone for industry, looking ahead to endeavor to channel industry, as it grows, into that neighborhood. So they zone that to industry and exclude therefrom only the very objectionable businesses that everybody wants to have in somebody else's yard and not in their own. But they generally permit, as this ordinance did up until the time of the most recent amendment, in the industrial zone, all the uses which have been permitted in the so-called higher zones.

A: Yes.

Q: So that John Doe comes along and buys his strip of land in the industrial zone at a point where there is no industry, where he can look around and see the rolling countryside, maybe the river, maybe the railroad — So he buys it, knowing it is an industrial zone, and that in the course of time the smokestacks and the factory walls and the traffic and noise will creep nearer and nearer to him. But he decides he would like to build a residence on his holdings. When the industry does come to him, he is going to be subjected to the noise all right; he is going to have to put up with the incidental smells, the smoke, the increase in traffic and the fact that it may depreciate his property in value, but unless he is prevented by a restriction of the nature called for here, he has a right to exercise that dominion over his land and build his house there and run the risk that before he dies or sells he will be exposed to these troubles.

   Now I think that is a different proposition from the first one we discussed. That is why I say this whole proposition seems too novel to me.

Mr. Francis: Isn't the answer "Yes" as far as that is concerned?

The Court: Well the witness, I have inferred, takes the position that good zoning requires that this particular property holder in the suppositious case I have made should be protected against himself.

The Witness: That is exactly it — protected against himself.

The Court: Whether that is valid is the point we have to decide in this case.

■ WILES, THE USE OF EXPERT WITNESSES IN LITIGATION
Peterson & McCarthy, Handling Zoning and Land Use Litigation: A Practical Guide §4-1, at 158-159, 165-167 (1982)

A key decision in the litigation process is whether expert testimony is required; what kind of expert witnesses will be necessary; and the

B. The Zoning Trio — Height, Bulk, and Use

level of involvement desired of the expert. These decisions should be made early in the litigation process so that experts can become fully involved in trial preparation. . . .

The expert witness should not be a "professional witness." The attorney should interview prospective expert witnesses carefully to make sure they are not professional witnesses. The professional witness is one who appears in court one month extolling the evils of commercial shopping centers and the next month telling the judge that if the shopping center is not approved the city will suffer greatly. Witnesses who appear in court on any side of any issue eventually lose their credibility. A true professional will not be afraid to decline to testify in matters of questionable merit.

Staff witnesses should be screened. It is difficult for a public-sector planner to decline to act as an expert witness on behalf of the agency. However, there can be problems if a planner who recommended against the decision at the staff level appears in court in support of the action.

The expert should be truly convinced of the merits of the case. An expert who thinks the case is without merit should withdraw. Sincerity is apparent in the courtroom. The expert should make a preliminary analysis of the issues prior to agreeing to act as the expert.

The expert should have strong practical experience in the field. Occasionally, the situation may require academic opinions instead of facts; but, as a rule, depth in the field of testimony is required. There is an old adage that says opposing attorneys never ask witnesses any questions they think the witness can answer. The classic question opposing attorneys use to trap unwary planning witnesses, of course, is whether planning is an art or a science.

The expert's testimony should be confined to his/her field of expertise. In other words, don't ask an architect to testify about traffic. Increasingly, attorneys are becoming highly experienced in technical fields, like planning, traffic, and economics. It does not take long to strip away the superficial answers of experts who testify outside their field.

The expert should have experience in both the public and the private sector. Neither the consultant with no practical experience in a public agency nor the planner who has never worked for private interests makes a good witness. . . .

The expert should deal with facts. Although opinions are often required in testimony, they are more reliable if supported by factual information. The expert who tries to support his/her position solely with opinions or theories eventually runs into trouble.

The expert should be able to explain and present technical information in a logical and comprehensive manner. A primary purpose of the expert is to assist the court in the deliberation of factual issues. Technical jargon, abstract theories, and unsubstantiated opinions are detrimental to this function.

The expert witness should provide the attorney and client with information on both the positive and negative aspect of findings. Often it is important to understand the weaker arguments in order to devise appropriate strategy prior to courtroom testimony.

The expert should be able to work effectively with other specialists and should not hesitate to recommend the use of additional expert witnesses. If more than one expert is used, their efforts must be closely coordinated. It can be extremely damaging if experts give conflicting testimony or if experts testify beyond their field of knowledge.[37]

■ VILLAGE OF BELLE TERRE v. BORAAS
416 U.S. 1 (1974)

Mr. Justice DOUGLAS delivered the opinion of the Court.

Belle Terre is a village on Long Island's north shore of about 220 homes inhabited by 700 people. Its total land area is less than one square mile. It has restricted land use to one-family dwellings excluding lodging houses, boarding houses, fraternity houses, or multiple dwelling houses. The word "Family" as used in the ordinance means, "One or more persons related by blood, adoption, or marriage, living and cooking together as a single housekeeping unit, exclusive of household servants. A number of persons but not exceeding two (2) living and cooking together as a single housekeeping unit though not related by blood, adoption, or marriage shall be deemed to constitute a family."

Appellees (Dickmans) are owners of a house in the village and leased it in December, 1971 for a term of 18 months to Michael Truman. Later Bruce Boraas became a colessee. Then Anne Parish moved into

---

37. See also Pomeroy, Preparation and Trial of Zoning and Zoning and Planning Cases as Viewed by the Expert Witness, 21st Annual Conference, National Institute of Municipal Law Officers (Mimeo. 1956):

> The witness should endeavor to be a good psychologist with respect to the temperament and attitudes of the particular judge. This isn't a case of trying to be "clever" — which can discount the effectiveness of a witness probably more quickly than anything else except a display of sheer ignorance — but of appraising, if possible, those things about which the court is particularly concerned and of endeavoring to supply information that will be of value to him in reaching a decision.
>
> Sometimes a judge will actually explore with a witness some interesting point of zoning philosophy. Recently I was testifying before a judge in New Jersey who is one of the most erudite scholars of zoning I have ever seen on the bench. He permitted a full development of the points I was making with respect to some of the newer applications of zoning. At times he went off the record to discuss some question with me and with counsel, who are themselves able students of zoning. In contrast, I have appeared before another judge in the same state who characterizes planners, from the bench, as "pseudo-experts" and is eager to get the expert witness off the stand so as to hasten the recording of the substitution of his own judgment for that of the legislative body. — EDS.

B. The Zoning Trio — Height, Bulk, and Use 249

the house along with three others. These six are students at nearby State University at Stony Brook and none is related to the other by blood, adoption, or marriage. When the village served the Dickmans with an "Order to Remedy Violations" of the ordinance, the owners plus three tenants thereupon brought this action under 42 U.S.C. §1983 for an injunction declaring the ordinance unconstitutional. The District Court held the ordinance constitutional and the Court of Appeals reversed, one judge dissenting. 2 Cir., 476 F.2d 806. . . .

This case brings to this Court a different phase of local zoning regulations than we have previously reviewed. Village of Euclid v. Ambler Realty Co., 272 U.S. 365, involved a zoning ordinance classifying land use in a given area into six categories. . . .

The Court sustained the zoning ordinance under the police power of the State, saying that the line "which in this field separates the legitimate from the illegitimate assumption of power is not capable of precise delimitation. It varies with circumstances and conditions." 272 U.S., at 387. . . . The ordinance was sanctioned because the validity of the legislative classification was "fairly debatable" and therefore could not be said to be wholly arbitrary. Id., at 388. . . .

The present ordinance is challenged on several grounds: that it interferes with a person's right to travel; that it interferes with the right to migrate to and settle within a State; that it bars people who are uncongenial to the present residents; that the ordinance expresses the social preferences of the residents for groups that will be congenial to them; that social homogeneity is not a legitimate interest of government; that the restriction of those whom the neighbors do not like trenches on the newcomers' rights of privacy; that it is of no rightful concern to villagers whether the residents are married or unmarried; that the ordinance is antithetical to the Nation's experience, ideology and self-perception as an open, egalitarian, and integrated society.

We find none of these reasons in the record before us. It is not aimed at transients. Cf. Shapiro v. Thompson, 394 U.S. 618. It involves no procedural disparity inflicted on some but not on others such as was presented by Griffin v. Illinois, 351 U.S. 12. It involves no "fundamental" right guaranteed by the Constitution, such as voting, the right of association, the right of access to the courts, or any rights of privacy. We deal with economic and social legislation where legislatures have historically drawn lines which we respect against the charge of violation of the Equal Protection Clause if the law be "reasonable, not arbitrary" (quoting F. S. Royster Guano Co. v. Virginia, 253 U.S. 412, 415) and bears "a rational relationship to a [permissible] state objective." Reed v. Reed, 404 U.S. 71, 76.

It is said, however, that if two unmarried people can constitute a "family," there is no reason why three or four may not. But every line drawn by a legislature leaves some out that might well have been included.[5] That exercise of discretion, however, is a legislative not a judicial function.

It is said that the Belle Terre ordinance reeks with an animosity to unmarried couples who live together.[6] There is no evidence to support it; and the provision of the ordinance bringing within the definition of a "family" two unmarried people belies the charge.

The ordinance places no ban on other forms of association, for a "family" may, so far as the ordinance is concerned, entertain whomever they like.

The regimes of boarding houses, fraternity houses, and the like present urban problems. More people occupy a given space; more cars rather continuously pass by; more cars are parked; noise travels with crowds.

A quiet place where yards are wide, people few, and motor vehicles restricted are legitimate guidelines in a land use project addressed to family needs. This goal is a permissible one within Berman v. Parker [348 U.S. 26 (1954)]. The police power is not confined to elimination of filth, stench, and unhealthy places. It is ample to lay out zones where family values, youth values, and the blessings of quiet seclusion, and clean air make the area a sanctuary for people.

The suggestion that the case may be moot need not detain us. A zoning ordinance usually has an impact on the value of the property which it regulates. But in spite of the fact that the precise impact of the ordinance sustained in *Euclid* on a given piece of property was not known, 272 U.S., at 397, the Court, considering the matter a controversy in the realm of city planning, sustained the ordinance. Here we are a step closer to the impact of the ordinance on the value of the lessor's property. He has not only lost six tenants and acquired only two in their place; it is obvious that the scale of rental values rides on what we decide today. When *Berman* reached us it was not certain whether an entire tract would be taken or only the buildings on it and a scenic easement. 348 U.S., at 36. But that did not make the case any the less a controversy in the constitutional sense. When Mr. Justice Holmes said

---

5. Mr. Justice Holmes made the point a half century ago.

> When a legal distinction is determined, as no one doubts that it may be, between night and day, childhood and maturity, or any other extremes, a point has to be fixed or a line has to be drawn, or gradually picked out by successive decisions, to mark where the change takes place. Looked at by itself without regard to the necessity behind it the line or point seems arbitrary. It might as well or nearly as well be a little more to one side or the other. But when it is seen that a line or point there must be, and that there is no mathematical or logical way of fixing it precisely, the decision of the legislature must be accepted unless we can say that it is very wide of any reasonable mark.

Louisville Gas & Electric Co. v. Coleman, 277 U.S. 32, 41 (dissenting).

6. U.S. Dept. of Agriculture v. Moreno, 413 U.S. 528 (1973), is therefore inapt as there a household containing anyone unrelated to the rest was denied food stamps.

B. The Zoning Trio — Height, Bulk, and Use 251

for the Court in Block v. Hirsh, 256 U.S. 135, 155, "property rights may be cut down, and to that extent taken, without pay," he stated the issue here. As is true in most zoning cases, the precise impact on value may, at the threshold of litigation over validity, not yet be known.

Reversed.

Mr. Justice BRENNAN, dissenting.

The constitutional challenge to the village ordinance is premised *solely* on alleged infringement of associational and other constitutional rights of *tenants*. But the named tenant appellees have quit the house, thus raising a serious question whether there now exists a cognizable "case or controversy" that satisfies that indispensable requisite of Art. III of the Constitution. Existence of a case or controversy must of course appear at every stage of review. . . . In my view it does not appear at this stage of this case.

Mr. Justice MARSHALL, dissenting. . . .

Appellees, the two owners of a Belle Terre residence, and three unrelated student tenants challenged the ordinance on the grounds that it establishes a classification between households of related and unrelated individuals, which deprives them of equal protection of the laws. In my view, the disputed classification burdens the students' fundamental rights of association and privacy guaranteed by the First and Fourteenth Amendments. Because the application of strict equal protection scrutiny is therefore required, I am at odds with my brethren's conclusion that the ordinance may be sustained on a showing that it bears a rational relationship to the accomplishment of legitimate governmental objectives.

I am in full agreement with the majority that zoning is a complex and important function of the State. It may indeed be the most essential function performed by local government, for it is one of the primary means by which we protect that sometimes difficult to define concept of quality of life. I therefore continue to adhere to the principle of Village of Euclid v. Ambler Realty Co., 272 U.S. 365 (1926), that deference should be given to governmental judgments concerning proper land use allocation. That deference is a principle which has served this Court well and which is necessary for the continued development of effective zoning and land use control mechanisms. Had the owners alone brought this suit alleging that the restrictive ordinance deprived them of their property or was an irrational legislative classification, I would agree that the ordinance would have to be sustained. Our role is not and should not be to sit as a zoning board of appeals. . . .

My disagreement with the Court today is based upon my view that the ordinance in this case unnecessarily burdens appellees' First Amendment freedom of association and their constitutionally guaranteed right to privacy. Our decisions establish that the First and Fourteenth

Amendments protect the freedom to choose one's associates. NAACP v. Button, 371 U.S. 415, 430 (1963). Constitutional protection is extended not only to modes of association that are political in the usual sense, but also to those that pertain to the social and economic benefit of the members. . . . The selection of one's living companions involves similar choices as to the emotional, social, or economic benefits to be derived from alternative living arrangements. . . .

This is not a case where the Court is being asked to nullify a township's sincere efforts to maintain its residential character by preventing the operation of rooming houses, fraternity houses or other commercial or high-density residential uses. Unquestionably, a town is free to restrict such uses. Moreover, as a general proposition, I see no constitutional infirmity in a town limiting the density of use in residential areas by zoning regulations which do not discriminate on the basis of constitutionally suspect criteria. This ordinance, however, limits the density of occupancy of only those homes occupied by unrelated persons. It thus reaches beyond control of the use of land or the density of population, and undertakes to regulate the way people choose to associate with each other within the privacy of their own homes.

It is no answer to say, as does the majority that associational interests are not infringed because Belle Terre residents may entertain whomever they choose. Only last Term Mr. Justice Douglas indicated in concurrence that he saw the right of association protected by the First Amendment as involving far more than the right to entertain visitors. He found that right infringed by a restriction on food stamp assistance, penalizing households of "unrelated persons." As Mr. Justice Douglas there said, freedom of association encompasses the "right to invite a stranger into one's home" not only for "entertainment" but to join the household as well. Moreno v. Department of Agriculture, 413 U.S. 528, 538-545 (1973, Douglas, J., concurring). I am still persuaded that the choice of those who will form one's household implicates constitutionally protected rights.

Because I believe that this zoning ordinance creates a classification which impinges upon fundamental personal rights, it can withstand constitutional scrutiny only upon a clear showing that the burden imposed is necessary to protect a compelling and substantial governmental interest, Shapiro v. Thompson, 394 U.S. 618 (1969). And, once it be determined that a burden has been placed upon a constitutional right, the onus of demonstrating that no less intrusive means will adequately protect the compelling state interest and that the challenged statute is sufficiently narrowly drawn, is upon the party seeking to justify the burden. . . .

By limiting unrelated households to two persons while placing no limitation on households of related individuals, the village has embarked upon its commendable course in a constitutionally faulty vessel. I would

B. The Zoning Trio — Height, Bulk, and Use

find the challenged ordinance unconstitutional. But I would not ask the village to abandon its goal of providing quiet streets, little traffic, and a pleasant and reasonably priced environment in which families might raise their children. Rather, I would commend the town to continue to pursue those purposes but by means of more carefully drawn and even-handed legislation.

I respectfully dissent.

Notes

1. Cabbott House is a nonprofit corporation licensed by the state to care for neglected and abandoned children. The group home consists of a married couple, their two children, and ten foster children. Abutters argue that the group home does not constitute a single-family unit under the zoning requirement of an R-2 single-family zone. In representing Cabbott House, what would you argue and how would you distinguish *Belle Terre*? Is the fact that the owner receives compensation from government and private sources relevant? What if the group home is a neighborhood alternative to institutionalization for the mentally retarded? City of White Plains v. Ferrailoli, 34 N.Y.2d 300, 313 N.E.2d 756 (1974) ("Zoning is intended to control types of housing and living and not the genetic or intimate internal family relations of human beings."). Cf. Seaton v. Clifford, 24 Cal. App. 3d 46, 100 Cal. Rptr. 779 (1972). See also Lauber & Bangs, Zoning for Family and Group Care Facilities, ASPO PAS Rep. No. 300 (Mar. 1974); City of Cleburne v. Cleburne Living Center, infra page 357.

In State v. Baker, 81 N.J. 99, 405 A.2d 368 (1979), in a 5-2 holding, the New Jersey court struck down a zoning ordinance that prohibited more than four persons who were "not related by blood, marriage or adoption" from occupying a single-family unit. As long as a group bore the "generic character of a family unit as a relatively permanent household," it should be treated similarly to "its biologically related neighbors." Can this be squared with the Supreme Court's holding? The New Jersey Supreme Court thought not:

> ... *Belle Terre* is at most dispositive of any federal constitutional question here involved. We, of course, remain free to interpret our constitution and statutes more stringently. We find the reasoning of *Belle Terre* to be both unpersuasive and inconsistent with the results reached by this Court in [previous opinions]. Hence we do not choose to follow it.

Jackson v. Williams, 714 P.2d 1917 (Okla. 1985), held that use of a residence as a group home for five mentally handicapped women and their housekeeper did not violate a covenant restricting use to a "single-family dwelling."

2. Section 1341.08 of the Codified Ordinances of the City of East Cleveland, Ohio, read:

> "Family" means a number of individuals related to the nominal head of the household or to the spouse of the nominal head of the household living as a single housekeeping unit in a single dwelling unit, but limited to the following:
> (a) Husband or wife of the nominal head of the household.
> (b) Unmarried children of the nominal head of the household or of the spouse of the nominal head of the household, provided, however, that such unmarried children have no children residing with them.
> (c) Father or mother of the nominal head of the household or of the spouse of the nominal head of the household.
> (d) Notwithstanding the provisions of subsection (b) hereof, a family may include not more than one dependent married or unmarried child of the nominal head of the household or of the spouse of the nominal head of the household and the spouse and dependent children of such dependent child. For the purpose of this subsection, a dependent person is one who has more than fifty percent of his total support furnished for him by the nominal head of the household and the spouse of the nominal head of the household.
> (e) A family may consist of one individual.

In Moore v. City of East Cleveland, 431 U.S. 94 (1977), the Court considered the following facts:

> Appellant, Mrs. Inez Moore, lives in her East Cleveland home together with her son, Dale Moore Sr., and her two grandsons, Dale, Jr., and John Moore, Jr. The two boys are first cousins rather than brothers; we are told that John came to live with his grandmother and with the elder and younger Dale Moores after his mother's death.
> In early 1973, Mrs. Moore received a notice of violation from the city, stating that John was an "illegal occupant" and directing her to comply with the ordinance. When she failed to remove him from her home, the city filed a criminal charge. Mrs. Moore moved to dismiss, claiming that the ordinance was constitutionally invalid on its face. Her motion was overruled, and upon conviction she was sentenced to five days in jail and a $25 fine. The Ohio Court of Appeals affirmed after giving full consideration to her constitutional claims, and the Ohio Supreme Court denied review.

Justice Powell, writing for a plurality, reluctantly unsheathed substantive due process in order to rescue Mrs. Moore from her criminal predicament. The "one overriding factor" distinguishing this case from *Belle Terre* was that the

> ordinance there affected only *unrelated* individuals. It expressly allowed

C. Post-Euclidean Modifications of the Zoning Ordinance

all who were related by "blood, adoption, or marriage" to live together, and in sustaining the ordinance we were careful to note that it promoted "family needs" and "family values." East Cleveland, in contrast, has chosen to regulate the occupancy of its housing by slicing deeply into the family itself. . . .

When a city undertakes such intrusive regulation of the family, neither *Belle Terre* nor *Euclid* governs; the usual judicial deference to the legislature is inappropriate. "This Court has long recognized that freedom of personal choice in matters of marriage and family life is one of the liberties protected by the Due Process Clause of the Fourteenth Amendment." . . .

Justice Stevens, concurring in the judgment and noting state decisions in this troublesome area, found that the ordinance failed even the limited standard of review articulated in *Euclid*. Four Justices dissented.

3. In McMinn v. Town of Oyster Bay, 105 A.D. 46, 482 N.Y.S.2d 773 (App. Div. 1984), the challenged ordinance "define[d] 'family' as 'any number of persons related by blood, marriage or legal adoption, living and cooking on the premises together as a single nonprofit housekeeping unit' or any two persons not so related who are 62 years of age or over and live and cook together on the premises as a single nonprofit housekeeping unit." 482 N.Y.S.2d at 775. The ordinance did not survive the court's scrutiny, for its arbitrariness amounted to a denial of due process:

> The fact that restrictions in the Oyster Bay ordinance are arbitrary and unreasonable does not imply that single-family zoning is an unsound concept. What it does indicate, however, is something that other states and many municipalities in New York recognize — the viability of single-family zoning restrictions no longer depends on biological or legal relationships but on the single housekeeping unit which reflects a certain level of stability.

Id. at 782.

The Wall Street Journal, May 1, 1985, reported that nine Greenwich, Connecticut, property owners who could not stop a home for former psychiatric patients from occupying a neighboring house found another avenue of attack: they persuaded the town Board of Tax Review to trim their assessed valuations by 5 percent to 10 percent.

C. POST-EUCLIDEAN MODIFICATIONS OF THE ZONING ORDINANCE

Height, bulk, and use zoning has not remained static during the six decades following *Euclid*. As part of the ongoing process of state and local experimentation with regulation generally, and in response specifically to the critics of "traditional" zoning and to the demands and needs of each separate locality, lawmakers and planners have crafted variations from the Euclidean pattern, while retaining the heart of comprehensive, governmental land-use planning: the recognition that the public holds the development rights for each separate parcel in excess of the reasonable limitations set by a properly promulgated land-use plan.

The new planning and zoning tools discussed in this section have been used to make the applicable regulations more responsive to the desires of private and public actors. These approaches often involve landowners and regulators in a bargaining process that results in permission to develop above and beyond established limits (TDR, conditional zoning), the provision of public amenities (incentive zoning), the elimination of harmful spillovers and unimaginative rigidity (performance standards), and the integration of traditionally segregated uses (mixed-use development, PUD).

Do you think these modifications do enough to redress the inadequacies of the Euclidean scheme? Are these signs of weakness or adaptability? Is it time to move to a system of stronger judicial (Chapter IV) or legislative (Chapter VI) control from on high, or should we, as some of the critics in the final section of this chapter argue, reconsider the Taft Court's redistribution of development rights and return to a pre-Euclidean regime in which the property holder is limited only by the vagaries of the market, the constraints of common law nuisance, and the requirements listed in enforceable agreements between neighbors? Or do we need a bolder vision for shaping the metropolitan area of the future?

1. Incentive Zoning

Zoning incentive devices are not new. New York City's comprehensive zoning ordinance of 1916, which attempted to control development through maximum height and minimum setback requirements, allowed builders to increase height when additional open space was provided.[38] This provided considerable incentive for more walking space at street level, because a thin slab of volume off the front of a building could be traded for additional floors. On a street 100 feet wide, a building 250 feet tall could be constructed; with a base of 200 ft. × 100 ft., a

38. In a two and one-half times district no building shall be erected to a height in excess of two and one-half times the width of the street, but for each one foot that the building or a portion of it sets back from the street line five feet shall be added to the height limit of such building or portion thereof. New York City Zoning Resolution of 1916, §8 (f).

C. Post-Euclidean Modifications of the Zoning Ordinance 257

building of box shape could have a volume of 5 million cubic feet; but if the building were set back an additional 4 feet from the street line, the allowed height would be 270 feet, with a resulting volume of 5.184 million cubic feet ($V_1 = 100 \times 200 \times 250 = 5 \times 10^6$; $V_2 = 96 \times 200 \times 270 = 5.184 \times 10^6$).

When does the trade-off between additional height and setback become unattractive for a builder? Should the ordinance set an absolute maximum on height, inclusive of bonuses? How can the relative values of additional open space and reduced light and air be measured? Keep these questions in mind when reading the provisions of modern ordinances.

The ordinance of 1916 (even with amendments) proved inadequate to control New York's expanding population. By one estimate it would have allowed the city's residential districts to house 77 million people, and the working population to total 344 million. Rodgers, New York Plans for the Future 176 (1943). Such high figures were possible under the old ordinance partly because the height and setback restrictions, while controlling to some extent the form of buildings, could not effectively control density of occupants. Nor were the old controls and incentives sufficient to provide adequate open space, daylight, and natural air ventilation. As a result, the 1916 ordinance, which had become complicated by a three-map system with over 2500 amendments to the maps and text, was replaced in 1961.

A post-Euclidean technique is the creation of a floor area bonus in return for building features with public advantages. In 1961, New York City granted a 20 percent floor area bonus where a "plaza" was provided in certain high-density districts. When theaters were threatened by an office building boom, the city created a district wherein developers were granted a discretionary bonus fixed by the city planning commission, subject to a 20 percent limit, if they built a legitimate theater as a part of the building. See Comment, 21 Syracuse L. Rev. 895 (1970). Under the unintended-consequences-of-reform column, note that the New York Port Authority's World Trade Center (authorized as a proper use of eminent domain power in Courtesy Sandwich Shop, Inc. v. Port of New York Authority, 12 N.Y.2d 379, 190 N.E.2d 402, 240 N.Y.S.2d 1 (1963)) meets the FAR requirements by a large open plaza, which Ada Louise Huxtable foresaw as being "vast, desolate, dull, windswept and empty most of the time." N.Y. Times, April 16, 1967, §D. "Even as the $700 million World Trade Center was being dedicated on April 5, 1973, questions remained about the open space and environment around the huge building complex." N.Y. Times, April 5, 1973.

In relation to housing, the 1961 resolution created a new set of use districts and a series of detailed bulk regulations. Chapter 1, §21-00 of the resolution announced the following purposes, among others, in creating the new residence districts:

(a) To provide sufficient space in appropriate locations for residential development to meet the housing needs of the city's present and expected future population, with due allowance for the need for choice sites.

(d) To protect residential areas against congestion, as far as possible, by regulating the density of population and the bulk of buildings in relation to the land around them and to one another, and by providing for off-street parking spaces; to require the provision of open space in residential areas wherever practicable; and to encourage the provision of additional open space by permitting moderately higher bulk and density with better standards of open space, in order to open up residential areas to light and air, to provide open areas for rest and recreation, and to break the monotony of continuous building bulk, and thereby provide a more desirable environment for urban living in a congested metropolitan area.

(e) To provide for access of light and air to windows and for privacy, as far as possible, by controls over the spacing and height of building and other structures.[39]

To accomplish these purposes, the 1961 resolution added new controls on the development of residence districts — floor area ratios, defined as "the total floor area on a zoning lot, divided by the lot area of that zoning lot," and open space ratios, defined as "the number of square feet of open space on the zoning lot, expressed as a percentage of the floor area on that zoning lot."[40]

It has been suggested that floor area ratio regulations tend to encourage the building of small apartments — a builder faced with a set amount of floor area can derive a higher return from many small apartments than from a few large ones. Citizens' Housing Council, Densities in New York City 21-22 (1944). On the other hand, it is reasonable to assume that controls on minimum lot area per room or dwelling unit would encourage the construction of large, costly apart-

---

39. Similarly, the announced general purposes in establishing residential bulk regulations were to protect residential areas against congestion and to encourage the development of desirable and stable residential neighborhoods. In order to achieve these purposes, a direct control of density as well as the physical volume of buildings was established. In order to open up residential areas to light and air and encourage better standards of open space, moderately higher levels of density and of buildings volume were permitted when greater amounts of open space were provided. Ch. 3, §23-02.

40. Section 23-11. Note that height factor (H.F.) of a building is the total floor area of the building divided by its lot coverage, where lot coverage is that portion of a zoning lot which, when viewed directly from above, would be covered by a building or any part of a building. Ch. 3, §23-11.

23-141:

Minimum required open space ratio	Maximum floor area ratio				
150.00	0.50	R1	R2	R3	
80.0	0.75				R4

23-142:

C. Post-Euclidean Modifications of the Zoning Ordinance 259

ments. Does the presence of both types of controls in the 1961 ordinance cancel these suggested effects of zoning requirements on the kind of apartments built? If there is such a cancellation effect, wouldn't the elimination of the requirement on minimum lot area per room or dwelling unit be advisable for encouraging construction of needed reduced-rent apartments for the city's low-income families?[41]

Minimum Required Open Space Ratio and Maximum Floor Area Ratio, R5 Through R9 Districts

	In R5 districts		In R6 districts		In R7 districts		In R8 districts		In R9 districts	
For buildings with a height factor of	Min. required open space ratio	Max. floor area ratio	Min. required open space ratio	Max. floor area ratio	Min. required open space ratio	Max. floor area ratio	Min. required open space ratio	Max. floor area ratio	Min. required open space ratio	Max. floor area ratio
1	47.0	0.68	27.5	0.78	15.5	0.87	5.9	0.94	1.0	0.99
5	59.0	1.26	30.0	2.02	17.5	2.67	7.1	3.69	2.6	4.42
10	74.0	1.19	32.0	2.38	20.0	3.33	8.3	5.38	4.6	6.85
15	89.0	1.04	34.5	2.43	22.5	3.42	10.1	5.95	6.6	7.52
20	104.0	0.92	37.0	2.38	25.0	3.33	11.6	6.02	8.6	7.35

23-15. In the [R10] district, the *floor area ratio* for any *building* on a *zoning lot* shall not exceed 10.0, except as provided in the [bonus provisions below].

23-16. In the [R10] district for each square foot of a *plaza* or portion of a *plaza* provided on a *zoning lot*, the total *floor area* permitted on that *zoning lot* under the provisions of Section 23-15 (Maximum Floor Area Ratio in R10 Districts) may be increased by six square feet.

23-17. In the [R10] district for each square foot of open area unobstructed from its lowest level to the sky, which has a minimum dimension of 40 feet and which connects two *plazas* or a *plaza* with a *street*, the total *floor area* permitted in a *zoning lot* under the provisions of Section 23-15. . . may be increased by six square feet.

23-18. In the [R10] district for each square foot of *arcade* provided on a *zoning lot*, the total *floor area* permitted on that *zoning lot* under the provisions of Section 23-15. . . may be increased by three square feet.

41. On January 29, 1969, the New York City Planning Commission proposed that seventeen acres of commercial land along Second Avenue from Thirty-third to Thirty-seventh Street, Third Avenue from Eighth to Fifteenth Street, and the Avenue of the Americas from Fourteenth to Twenty-third Street be remapped from the existing zoning designation of C6-1 (FAR 6) and from R7 (FAR 2.80-3.40) to R10, with a maximum floor area ratio, inclusive of bonuses, of 12. The ordinance describes R10 as "a special, very confined, high-rise apartment house district in Manhattan where greater densities are permitted than would otherwise be desired."

On February 13, 1969, however, the planning commission withdrew the proposal to remap the nine commercially mapped blocks on the Avenue of the Americas. Chairman Elliott gave no reason for backing down on the proposal, except to say that more information was needed. The other two areas were retained, and a hearing was scheduled for February 19. At the hearing there was strong community opposition claiming that the proposed remapping would lead to the demolition of needed low-rent housing. The proposal's effects on public facilities, the nearby Cooper Square urban renewal area, and on congestion were raised. Most embarrassingly, members of the city planning commission's professional staff accused the commission of disregarding planners' findings and of yielding to powerful real estate speculators.

The day after the hearing, Mayor Lindsay said that the commission and he were in entire accord. But the commission took no action on the proposal. Instead, it undertook a study to review the basic issues raised at the public hearing.

Ada Louise Huxtable called the controversy "only the tip of the zoning iceberg."

■ KAYDEN, INCENTIVE ZONING IN NEW YORK CITY: A COST-BENEFIT ANALYSIS
Lincoln Institute of Land Policy, Policy Analysis Series No. 201 (1978)

In reviewing the incentive zoning mechanisms that were developed first in the 1961 (New York City) Resolution, and subsequently as amendments to it during the late 1960's and early 1970's, they can be

---

"Under the muddy political waters," she continued in an article entitled Pressing the Panic Button on City Zoning, "lie three intimately related issues: the present insolubility of the city's housing needs by any currently available methods, the political implications of the unsolved housing crisis for the Lindsay administration seeking reelection, and the question of whether the proposed zoning changes will ease the crisis."

Neil Gold and Paul Davidoff, of Planners for Equal Opportunity, presented a memorandum to the city planning department. They proposed utilizing the city's zoning laws "to develop low and moderate income housing at no capital cost to the City or to the Federal Government." They took the point of view that "if it was proper to demand that developers in the Lincoln Center District include arcades, plazas and galleries in return for an increase in floor area, then it was also proper to demand that these same developers lease a portion of their units to the City Housing Authority in return for a similar increase in floor area." Such units could be provided either in the development or elsewhere in the special district.

On April 13, 1970, the commission announced details of a proposal for a Special Lower Third Avenue Development District. It scheduled a public hearing for May 13, 1970. According to Commissioner Beverly Spatt, the plan was apparently revived as the result of private meetings held by Elliott with "those people interested" in the zoning change. Ms. Spatt said the commissioners did not attend these meetings and were not "privy" to what occurred at them; she had asked to attend, but the "request was not honored."

Under the plan, developers would have to choose between two options in order to obtain R10 mapping: reserve part of their units for low- or moderate-income tenants; or contribute to a special fund for acquiring two designated low-income housing sites on the west side of Third Avenue between Tenth and Twelfth Streets. Under the first option, the developer might include in his development "low- and moderate-income housing units" occupying at least 15 percent of the development's residential floor area. Under the second option, the developer was to pay the city a percentage of the estimated cost of acquiring the two sites within the special district, on which the New York City Housing Authority was to construct a public housing project; the "public housing site's acquisition contribution" was to be equal to twice the combined assessed valuation of the two sites multiplied by the ratio which the portion of the lot area bore to the special district, but excluding the public housing.

On August 12, over protests against "selling zoning" and "deforming the city physically and socially," the City Planning Commission, in an unusually close 4 to 3 vote, approved the Special Lower Third Avenue Development District. Commissioner McQuade voiced a dissent: "Zoning should not be bent to solve what is really a cost problem; there is the danger of deforming the city physically and/or socially. I do not believe the big dumbly designed new apartment houses now conventional to R10 improve most New York neighborhoods physically, or in spirit. I share the reaction of other middle class people to these high undistinguished cliffs filled with apartments renting for nearly a thousand dollars a month. These buildings are excessive with their rooftop swimming pools and saunas, their pretentious little curved driveways, interfering with pedestrians and street traffic. We are told eloquently these buildings are essential to house the executives of the businesses which make Manhattan prosper. I don't believe that. Most of the executives I know avoid them. Instead you find squadrons of airline hostesses, which is fine, and less

C. Post-Euclidean Modifications of the Zoning Ordinance

divided into five major categories: (1) the "as of right" plaza and arcade bonuses; (2) the Special Districts; (3) the Special Permits; (4) the Incentive Rezonings; and (5) the Incentive Variances. Each one of these mechanisms has been applied to the development community in order to obtain different kinds of amenities or more simply to attain urban design or planning objectives. In the 91 buildings that have taken advantage of one or more of these incentive devices as of 1975, the aggregate figure for bonus floor area used as leverage to obtain public amenities from private developers was 12,547,375 sq. ft. . . .

1. PLAZA AND ARCADE BONUSES

The first type of incentive zoning, and by far the most popular if judged by frequency of use, is the "as of right" bonus for plazas and arcades, incorporated in the original 1961 Zoning Resolution. The plaza bonus has provided 7,940,792 sq. ft. of floor area to the office market, while the arcade, used more occasionally, has added 496,918 sq. ft. In the maximum 15 FAR districts, the developer receives 10 square feet of bonus floor area for every square foot of plaza, and three square feet for every square foot of arcade, up to a 20% maximum. A plaza is principally defined as "an open area accessible to the public at all times . . . not less than 10 feet deep measured from the front lot line . . . not at any point more than five feet above nor more than twelve feet below the curb level of the adjoining street . . . and unobstructed from its lowest level to the sky. . . ." An arcade is "a continuous area open to a street or to a plaza, which is open and unobstructed to a height of not less than 12 feet . . . is accessible to the public at all times . . ." (pre-1976 amendment definitions).

The two bonuses are considered "as of right" because no special action is required by the CPC to take advantage of them. Instead, the developer submits a series of zoning computations to the Department of Buildings, which, in turn, theoretically checks to make sure the plans conform to the requirements of the ordinance. The floor area bonus is automatically awarded when the "New Building" number is given, indicating approval of initial filing plans. The plaza provisions were meant to open up ground space at street level for the pedestrian, removing bulky building facades from the street line, and allowing greater access of light and air. Yet, from a design and use viewpoint, many feel they have been less than successful.

---

good, hardpressed families, who cannot really afford these rents."

Finally, on October 8, 1970, over the opposition of Mayor Lindsay, the Board of Estimate voted 18 to 4 against the plan; the mayor's stand-in, Edward A. Morrison, voted for the plan "as the only way to get low-income housing built in this area." Chairman Elliott, in expressing his disappointment at the board's decision, described the plans as "an unprecedented opportunity to create new housing at a range of income levels in an area where land costs are high."

2. Special Districts

The second incentive zoning mechanism, responsible for 1,690,071 sq. ft. of bonus floor area, is the Special District approach. It was conceived as a legally sound method of circumventing the "uniform, reasonable and non-arbitrary" requirements of zoning by declaring that certain areas, because of peculiar and unique circumstances, required special zoning. Through 1975, the CPC had created 17 of these districts, of which four have effectively used the incentive system to gain different public amenities in new development. The four are the Special Theatre District, the Special Lincoln Square District, the Special Greenwich Street District, and the Special Fifth Avenue District. For each one, a single developer's request for special dispensations in the form of FAR increases and height and setback waivers seems to have stimulated a codification of planning principles. . . .

3. Special Permits

The third category of incentive zoning devices is the "Special Permit" powers granted by the "Administration" section of the Zoning Resolution. These special permit authorities were added to the original ordinance because the Planning Commission desired more flexibility in its bargaining position with developers. Under Section 74 of the Resolution, 996,138 sq. ft. of bonus floor area have been given to the development community in return for various amenities. The most widely-used "Special Permit" incentive, Section 74-72, provides a bonus in the form of increased tower coverage, and height and setback waivers, instead of increased FAR, for lots having a minimum area of 40,000 sq. ft. . . .

Through block arcades, authorized under Section 74-82, are approved only when they "result in substantial improvement of pedestrian circulation" and "provide appropriate secondary commercial frontage along the through block arcade such as small shops and restaurants." Strategic use of these pedestrian circulation amenities can reduce walking distances, provide shelters from poor weather, and create alternate pedestrian flows to relieve existing sidewalk congestion. . . .

Section 74-87 provides for a "Covered Pedestrian Space," to be encouraged by a basic bonus of 11 sq. ft. and a maximum of 14 sq. ft. for an enclosed air-conditioned space. . . .

From the City of New York's point of view, the primary expected benefit of incentive zoning is increasing tax revenues derived from the extra office floor area. . . . Expected costs can be ascribed to the necessary concomitant increases in municipal services. . . .

The principal anticipated benefit is the marginal real estate tax revenue generated from 10,977,145 sq. ft. of extra office floor area.

C. Post-Euclidean Modifications of the Zoning Ordinance

One would intuitively expect the real estate tax net benefit to equal average total assessed valuation per square foot of office building multiplied by the extra floor area, and finally multiplied by the tax rate. Upon closer examination, however, it seems that the extra floor area has actually contributed to an erosion of the entire office building tax base, resulting in a total revenue loss that more than offsets the incremental tax revenue gain. To express this syllogistically:

Part 1: Incentive zoning has contributed more than 10 million sq. ft. to the substantial oversupply of office space caused by overbuilding, causing a dramatic increase in the vacancy rates, and a resulting drastic decrease in rental prices per square foot. These two factors are the principal reasons behind the unhealthy condition of 1973 office buildings' financial statements.

Part 2: Assessed valuation of all real property reflects the depressed state of the real estate sector, with little or no change in office building assessments.

Part 3: Therefore, incentive zoning has contributed to unchanged assessments, representing a slippage of valuation in real terms, and this has resulted in a loss of potential tax revenue for the City. . . .

The following analysis will attempt to ascertain incentive zoning costs and benefits for the incentive zoning development community. Although benefits derived by the developer also accrue to society at large, the policy-maker would undoubtedly be interested in determining which sectors of society receive the benefits. Only by separating the development community from the rest of society can its actual net benefits and costs be ascribed. . . .

Comparison of Bonused Building Z and Unbonused Building UZ's Financial Statements

	Building Z	Building UZ
Zoning Floor Area	955,000	795,000
Land	$10,280,545	$10,280,545
Building and Equipment	$40,044,379	$32,682,450
Total	$50,324,924	$42,962,995
Average Construction Cost Per Sq. Ft.	$41.93	$41.11
Total Income	$10,799,126	$ 8,745,000
Average Income Per Sq. Ft.	$11.31	$11.00
Operating Expenses	$ 6,231,244	$ 5,207,250
Average Operating Expense Per Sq. Ft.	$ 6.52	$ 6.55
Net Income Before Financing	$ 4,567,882	$ 3,537,750
Capitalized @ 9%	$50,754,244	$39,308,333

	Building Z	Building UZ
Less Building and Equipment	$40,044,379	$32,682,450
Total Land Residual	$10,709,865	$ 6,625,883

Capitalized Value of 160,000 Sq. Ft. of Bonus Office Space	$ 4,083,982
Less Construction Cost of Bldg. Z Plaza Saved by Developer of Bldg. UZ @ $5 Per Sq. Ft.	−$ 80,000
Less Additional Equity Retained by Developer of Bldg. UZ	−$ 185,251
Net Capitalized Value of Bonus Office Space to Developer of Bldg. Z	$ 3,818,731
Average Net Capitalized Value of Bonus Office Space Per Sq. Ft.	$23.87

Comparison of Bonused Building Z and Unbonused Building UZ's Simple Rates of Return

Building Z

Land, Building, Equipment	$50,324,924
Mortgages:	
First Mortgage @ 6% Interest	34,854,562
Second Mortgage @ 6% Interest	5,600,000
Purchase Money Mortgage @ 5% Interest	5,169,209
Fourth Mortgage @ 13.6% Interest	3,484,790
Total Mortgage (97.6% of Total)	49,108,561
Equity of Owner in Property	1,216,363
Interest Paid @ 6.7%	3,288,493
Amortization Paid @ .6%	292,268
Debt Service	3,574,761
Net Income Before Financing	4,567,882
Debt Service	−3,574,761
Net Income After Financing	993,121

Simple Rate of Return $\dfrac{993,121}{1,216,363} = 81.6\%$

Building UZ

Land, Building, Equipment	$42,962,995
Mortgage (97.6% of total)	41,931,883
Equity of Owner in Property	1,031,112
Interest Paid @ 6.7%	2,809,436
Amortization paid @ .6%	251,591
Debt Service	3,061,027
Net Income Before Financing	3,537,750

C. Post-Euclidean Modifications of the Zoning Ordinance

Debt Service $\quad -3,061,027$
Net Income After Financing $\quad \overline{476,723}$

Simple Rate of Return $\dfrac{476,723}{1,031,112} = 46.2\%$

Notes

1. As the above analysis suggests, at least some developers appear to have made substantial profits under New York's incentive zoning system. How would you calculate the value of the total bonus floor area given to the development community in New York City? What assumptions and qualifications would you offer in regard to any specific dollar value calculated?

2. The article criticizes the "as-of-right" portion of New York's incentive zoning system. What arguments can be made in support of the "as-of-right" system? Do you see any method whereby the "as-of-right" and "discretionary" systems can be usefully merged?

3. See Cook, Zoning for Downtown Urban Design 88 (1980):

> Experience with the plaza bonus illustrates some of the pitfalls of a predetermined, as-of-right bonus feature. As originally enacted in 1961, the zoning did not contain a detailed description of a plaza's necessary design features. Consequently, it was possible for a development to qualify for the bonus with a design feature that lived up to the letter but not the spirit of the law. Either through ignorance or indifference about what design characteristics made a plaza usable, or because the owner wanted to discourage public use to avoid maintenance, liability, and image problems, architects designed many spaces whose design said "keep out." After scores of plazas had been built and the questionable results were on public display, the city commissioned urbanologist William H. Whyte to study plaza usage in order to recommend design changes.[42] ...

42. See Whyte, How to Make Midtown Livable, New York, Mar. 9, 1981, at 24-29:

> When my research group studied plazas in the early seventies, we found that even at lunchtime on a pleasant day, most of them would have precious few people sitting in them. (One reason: no place to sit.) Based on this and other elemental findings, the urban-design group of the Planning Commission drew up new standards for open spaces, and these were adopted as zoning amendments in 1975. The principal provisions included plenty of sitting space, close relationship to the sidewalk, more trees, food facilities, and stores on building frontage. Similar standards for residential plazas were adopted in 1977.
>
> By then, however, plazas were old-hat. Planners were pushing *internal* spaces, such as arcades and through-block areas and atriums. These were to be substitute streets. Planners had developed an overriding concern with pedestrian congestion in midtown, and they saw in these spaces the way to relief. They would save people from the crowded streets by enticing them off the sidewalks.
>
> The strategy has proved wrong because the premise is wrong. Most of midtown's streets are *not* crowded. They may seem to be, but the perception is due largely to

A more fundamental problem with the plaza bonus transcends the question of how the zoning could anticipate design problems and describe desired results. The problem is that plaza location can be controlled only in a limited way; it is primarily determined by the random actions of the real estate market rather than by urban open-space needs. The principal determinant of a plaza's location is the "softness," or developability, of a site. As a result, one plaza may provide a welcome break in a building-wall line as well as a needed outdoor space, while another, next to it, may be visually disruptive and functionally redundant. In the absence of an overall plan for public open space that would specify the location of bonused pedestrian features, the contribution of such plazas to the quality of the pedestrian environment is spotty. Whatever its merits, however, the plaza bonus has become an entrenched part of the zoning game in New York, which, in the absence of an upward revision of base densities, developers now have a vested interest in maintaining.

4. See San Francisco Master Plan — Excerpts from the Plan for the Downtown Area, in 6 Rohan, Zoning and Land Use Controls (1986) (Appendix 42-2):*

> This is the Plan for downtown San Francisco. The Plan grows out of an awareness of the public concern in recent years over the degree of change occurring downtown — and of the often conflicting civic objectives between fostering a vital economy and retaining the urban patterns and structures which collectively form the physical essence of San Francisco.
>
> The Plan foresees a downtown known the world over as a center of ideas, services and trade and as a place for stimulating experiences. In essence, downtown San Francisco should encompass a compact mix of activities, historical values, and distinctive architecture and urban forms that engender a special excitement reflective of a world city.
>
> Principal Features:
>
> - The Plan controls the overall scale and intensity of downtown building by:
>   reducing the overall allowable density downtown through lowered base floor area ratios (FARs). . . .
>
> - The Plan redirects downtown office expansion south of Market Street by:
>   establishing a Special Development District between Howard and Folsom Streets east of YBC;
>   reducing the area of the highest permitted heights and shifting

---

the intense crowding on two avenues — Lexington and Madison — and to the choke points in the subway stations. Action is certainly in order to clear these up. On most streets, however, what the planners term congestion is a bustle that people enjoy; it is, indeed, one of the great amenities of the city. — Eds.

*Copyright © 1986 by Matthew Bender & Co., Inc., and reprinted with permission from Zoning and Land Use Controls.

C. Post-Euclidean Modifications of the Zoning Ordinance 267

it to include the south side of Mission Street near the Transbay Terminal; lowering heights significantly in areas north of Market, where significant groupings of smaller buildings, such as those on Belden and Front Streets, are located within the highrise office core.

- The Plan requires smaller, thinner, and more finely detailed buildings by:
  lowering the overall maximum permitted heights in nearly all of the C-3 district;
  requiring new bulk controls that taper buildings at the upper levels;
  requiring more expressive, sculptured building tops;
  requiring design review of all major projects.
- The Plan preserves architecturally significant buildings. . . .
- The Plan creates a new open space and public arts program by:
  requiring open space to be provided for many types of new developments in proportion to the size of the building. . . .
- The Plan preserves sunlight access to selected streets and open spaces by:
  adopting height limits and solar access standards to assure direct sunlight during the critical times of the day to important public open spaces and sidewalks in areas with smaller buildings.
- The Plan proposes new areas of housing within and near the downtown. . . .
- The Plan improves circulation within the downtown environment by:
  expanding the system of transit preferential streets for movement of buses downtown;
  requiring sufficient off-street loading and service vehicle parking for new developments including tour bus loading for hotels.[43]

43. See Vettel, San Francisco's Downtown Plan: Environmental and Urban Design Values in Central Business District Regulation, 12 Ecology L.Q. 511-512 (1985):

Although San Francisco, like most cities, has encouraged downtown development in order to reap economic and other benefits, the city has made concerted efforts to control the social and environmental costs of growth. In response, San Francisco has adopted numerous land use regulations which, taken as a whole, may be more stringent than those in any other major city in the United States. San Francisco's regulations, however, have been enacted largely on a piecemeal basis and, as a result, have not comprised a coherent, comprehensive package of regulatory tools, nor have they protected the unique urban character of downtown San Francisco. Even projects that have been constructed in compliance with all current regulations have proved to be environmentally and aesthetically harmful. Moreover, there is currently no cogent means of managing the cumulative effects of downtown growth in San Francisco.

Recognizing the need for comprehensive development guidelines, the city's Planning Commission, on November 29, 1984, adopted a new downtown regulatory system, known as the Downtown Plan. The Downtown Plan and the proposed Planning Code Amendments, when finally adopted, will implement a more demanding and innovative downtown land use scheme than ever before proposed by a major American city. Growth will continue under the Plan, but at a slower pace, and at a significantly reduced cost to the city's environment. Not only does the

See Williams, On the Inclination of Developers to Help the Poor 22-24, Lincoln Institute of Land Policy, Policy Analysis Series No. 211 (1985):

> The most far reaching of these programs to date is administered by San Francisco. Faced with perhaps the nation's most critical housing crisis, while at the same time enjoying an unprecedented office construction boom, San Francisco devised a program in 1981 whereby office developers are required to build, rehabilitate, sponsor, or finance housing in order to receive a building permit.
>
> The program, called the Office/Housing Production Program (OHPP), is administered by the Mayor's Office of Housing and Community Development, and applies to developers of large office complexes of greater than 50,000 square feet. The program's purpose, as defined by the City's Planning Department, "is to assure that developers of new office buildings, as employment generators, share the responsibility of increasing and preserving the City's housing stock, particularly affordable housing."
>
> The developer's responsibility for increasing and preserving the City's housing stock is based on a complex formula developed from a study prepared for the Planning Department. The study found that office use generates one employee per 250 gross square feet of office space; that 40% of all office workers choose to live within San Francisco's borders; and that the average residential unit in the city is occupied by 1.8 working adults.
>
> Based on these findings, the Planning Department calculates the housing requirements of a developer's office proposal according to the following formula:
>
> Housing units = gross sq. ft. of office space × (1 worker/250 sq. ft.) × .40 × (1 unit/1.8 workers).
>
> Under OHPP, the developer can meet his calculated housing share by providing new units or substantially rehabilitating vacant units through one of three methods. The developer can (1) serve as an equity or development partner of a housing project; (2) assist in the financing of a project, so long as the assistance is not used solely to reduce the sale price of units already under construction; or, (3) contribute to a pool of funds (the Home Mortgage Assistance Trust) to be used for reducing the monthly mortgage payments of lower income households, at the rate of $6,000 per required unit. . . .

For more on linking commercial and other development to the provision of low- and moderate-income housing, see infra page 431. See also Major, Linkage of Housing and Commercial Development: The Legal Issues, 15 Real Est. L.J. 328 (1987). Would the San Francisco

---

Downtown Plan attempt to prevent the construction of environmentally destructive individual projects, but it also strives to control the cumulative effects of growth.

approach pass the Supreme Court's exaction test as enunciated by the majority in Nollan v. California Coastal Commission, infra page 636?

2. Transferable Development Rights

The rational strength of the common law and its adaptability in transforming fundamental principles concerning property to accord with modern needs is evidenced by its treatment of the three-dimensional zoning envelope. "For what is the land," Coke once asked, "but the profits thereof?" One imaginative device to increase the scarce urban space within the framework of existing zoning laws is that of conveying unused potential capacity. Thus, the New York plan permitted a transfer of unused development rights from landmark sites across adjacent lot lines and to lots across the street; in 1969, the concept was further expanded to lots within a chain of common ownership extending to the landmark lot. See Morris, Air Rights Transfers in New York City, 36 Law & Contemp. Probs. 372 (1971). Professor Costonis has recommended a "zoning bank" where unused air rights over buildings are sold to developers to increase their zoned bulk, thereby allowing a burdened landowner to recoup his losses as balanced against the development benefits conferred upon another. Developments Rights Transfer, 83 Yale L.J. 75 (1973). See also Carmichael, Transferable Development Rights as a Basis for Land Use Controls, 2 Fla. St. U.L. Rev. 35 (1974), and Note, 84 Yale L.J. 1101 (1975).

■ **FRED F. FRENCH INVESTING CO. v. CITY OF NEW YORK**
39 N.Y.2d 587, 350 N.E.2d 381, 385 N.Y.S.2d 5 (1976)

BREITEL, Chief Judge. . . .

Tudor City is a four-acre residential complex built on an elevated level above East 42nd Street, across First Avenue from the United Nations in mid-town Manhattan. Planned and developed as a residential community, Tudor City consists of 10 large apartment buildings housing approximately 8,000 people, a hotel, four brownstone buildings, and two 15,000 square-foot private parks. The parks, covering about $18\frac{1}{2}\%$ of the area of the complex, are elevated from grade and located on the north and south sides of East 42nd Street, with a connecting viaduct.

On September 30, 1970, plaintiff sold the Tudor City complex to defendant Ramsgate Properties for $36,000,000. In addition to cash, plaintiff took back eight purchase money mortgages, two of which covered in part the two parks. Payment of the mortgage interest for three years was personally guaranteed by defendant Helmsley. Ramsgate thereafter conveyed, subject to plaintiff's mortgages, properties including the north and south parks to defendants, North Assemblage Co. and South Assemblage Co. Each of the mortgages secured in part by the parks has been in default since December 7, 1972.

Soon after acquiring the Tudor City property, the new owner announced plans to erect a building, said to be a 50-story tower, over East 42nd Street between First and Second Avenues. This plan would have required New York City Planning Commission approval of a shifting of development rights from the parks to the proposed adjoining site and a corresponding zoning change. Alternatively, the owner proposed to erect on each of the Tudor City park sites a building of maximum size permitted by the existing zoning regulations.

There was immediately an adverse public reaction to the owner's proposals, especially from Tudor City residents. After public hearings, the City Planning Commission recommended, over the dissent of one commissioner, and on December 7, 1972 the Board of Estimate approved, an amendment to the zoning resolution establishing Special Park District "P". By contemporaneous amendment to the zoning map, the two Tudor City parks were included within Special Park District "P".

Under the zoning amendment, "only passive recreational uses are permitted" in the Special Park District and improvements are limited to "structures incidental to passive recreational use". When the Special Park District would be mapped, the parks are required to be open daily to the public between 6:00 A.M. and 10:00 P.M.

The zoning amendment permits the transfer of development rights from a privately owned lot zoned as a Special Park District, denominated a "granting lot", to other areas in midtown Manhattan, bounded by 60th Street, Third Avenue, 38th Street and Eighth Avenue, denominated "receiving lots". Lots eligible to be receiving lots are those with a minimum lot size of 30,000 square feet and zoned to permit development at the maximum commercial density. The owner of a granting lot would be permitted to transfer part of his development rights to any eligible receiving lot, thereby increasing its maximum floor area up to 10%. Further increase in the receiving lot's floor area, limited to 20% of the maximum commercial density, is contingent upon a public hearing and approval by the City Planning Commission and the Board of Estimate. Development rights may be transferred by the owner directly to a receiving lot or to an individual or organization for later disposition to a receiving lot. Before development rights may be transferred, however, the Chairman of the City Planning Commission must certify the suitability of a plan for the continuing maintenance, at the owner's expense, of the granting lot as a park open to the public.

C. Post-Euclidean Modifications of the Zoning Ordinance 271

It is notable that the private parks become open to the public upon mapping of the Special Park District, and the opening does not depend upon the relocation and effective utilization of the transferable development rights. Indeed, the mapping occurred on December 7, 1972, and the development rights have never been marketed or used. . . .

The broad police power of the State to regulate the use of private property is not unlimited. Every enactment under the police power must be reasonable. An exercise of the police power to regulate private property by zoning which is unreasonable constitutes a deprivation of property without due process of law.

What is an "unreasonable" exercise of the police power depends upon the relevant converging factors. Hence, the facts of each case must be evaluated in order to determine the private and social balance of convenience before the exercise of the power may be condemned as unreasonable. . . .

In this case, the zoning amendment is unreasonable and, therefore, unconstitutional because, without due process of law, it deprives the owner of all his property rights, except the bare title and a dubious future reversion of full use. The amendment renders the park property unsuitable for any reasonable income productive or other private use for which it is adapted and thus destroys its economic value and deprives plaintiff of its security for its mortgages.

It is recognized that the "value" of property is not a concrete or tangible attribute but an abstraction derived from the economic uses to which the property may be put. Thus, the development rights are an essential component of the value of the underlying property because they constitute some of the economic uses to which the property may be put. As such, they are a potentially valuable and even a transferable commodity and may not be disregarded in determining whether the ordinance has destroyed the economic value of the underlying property.

Of course, the development rights of the parks were not nullified by the city's action. In an attempt to preserve the rights they were severed from the real property and made transferable to another section of mid-Manhattan in the city, but not to any particular parcel or place. There was thus created floating development rights, utterly unusable until they could be attached to some accommodating real property, available by happenstance of prior ownership, or by grant, purchase, or devise, and subject to the contingent approvals of administrative agencies. In such case, the development rights, disembodied abstractions of man's ingenuity, float in a limbo until restored to reality by reattachment to tangible real property. Put another way, it is a tolerable abstraction to consider development rights apart from the solid land from which as a matter of zoning law they derive. But severed, the development rights are a double abstraction until they are actually attached to a receiving parcel, yet to be identified, acquired, and subject to the contingent future approvals of administrative agencies, events which may never happen because of the exigencies of the market and the contingencies and exigencies of administrative action. The acceptance of this contingency-ridden arrangement, however, was mandatory under the amendment.

The problem with this arrangement, as Mr. Justice Waltemade so wisely observed at Special Term, is that it fails to assure preservation of the very real economic value of the development rights as they existed when still attached to the underlying property. By compelling the owner to enter an unpredictable real estate market to find a suitable receiving lot for the rights, or a purchaser who would then share the same interest in using additional development rights, the amendment renders uncertain and thus severely impairs the value of the development rights before they were severed (see Note, The Unconstitutionality of Transferable Development Rights, 84 Yale L.J. 1101, 1110-1111). Hence, when viewed in relation to both the value of the private parks after the amendment, and the value of the development rights detached from the private parks, the amendment destroyed the economic value of the property. It thus constituted a deprivation of property without due process of law.

None of this discussion of the effort to accomplish the highly beneficial purposes of creating additional park land in the teeming city bears any relation to other schemes, variously described as a "development bank" or the "Chicago Plan" (see Costonis, The Chicago Plan: Incentive Zoning and the Preservation of Urban Landmarks, 85 Harv. L. Rev. 574; Costonis, Development Rights Transfer: An Exploratory Essay, 83 Yale L.J. 75, 86-87). For under such schemes or variations of them, the owner of the granting parcel may be allowed just compensation for his development rights, instantly and in money, and the acquired development rights are then placed in a "bank" from which enterprises may for a price purchase development rights to use on land owned by them. Insofar as the owner of the granting parcel is concerned, his development rights are taken by the State, straightforwardly, and he is paid just compensation for them in eminent domain. The appropriating governmental entity recoups its disbursements, when, as, and if it obtains a purchaser for those rights. In contrast, the 1972 zoning amendment short-circuits the double-tracked compensation scheme but to do this leaves the granting parcel's owner's development rights in limbo until the day of salvation, if ever it comes. . . .

Solutions must be reached for the problems of modern zoning, urban and rural conservation, and last but not least landmark preservations, whether by particular buildings or historical districts. Unfortunately, the land planners are now only at the beginning of the path to solution. In the process of traversing that path further, new ideas and new standards of constitutional tolerance must and will evolve. It is enough to say that the loose-ended transferable development rights in this case fall short of achieving a fair allocation of economic burden. Even though the development rights have not been nullified, their severance has rendered their value so uncertain and contingent, as to deprive the property owner of their practical usefulness, except under rare and perhaps coincidental circumstances. . . .[44]

■ HAAR, HOROWITZ AND KATZ, TRANSFER OF DEVELOPMENT RIGHTS: A PRIMER
11-13, 16-17, 32, Lincoln Institute of Land Policy, Policy Analysis Series No. 206 (1980)

While TDR schemes can serve a variety of goals, they all demand that certain structural elements be well conceived. The principal requirements are elucidated by Costonis:

> The typical TDR program proceeds in four phases. First, the administering authority must pinpoint the sites from which development rights may be transferred.
> Second, the authority must identify correlative "transfer districts,"

---

44. The New York TDR story continues with Penn Central Transportation Co. v. City of New York, infra page 537. The year after his opinion in *Fred French* was announced, Chief Judge Breitel, at a TDR seminar, offered the following observations concerning the controversial land-use device:

> I would say that the most important part of what we are considering is the social ingredient that we find in property values. At the very root of value in society was land, which was not produced by any man or men but was there. Within the social order and the organized society that permitted man to function, he was able to occupy land and exploit it; and, if he had any idea that he, alone, was responsible for that, he of course was in error.
> This, I think, is one of the fundamentals that we have to treat when we deal with the problem of transferable development rights, because under no analysis could TDRs possibly give an owner of the original site the full value of that property interest, in the classic sense, that is now severed from the land from which the TDR originates.
> Immediately two propositions became critical if this kind of land use and planning is to be accomplished: first, we have to abandon the fiction or pretense that we are going to give the owner of the original site full value of that part which we take away from him, let alone the full fee interest; and, second, that the TDR is not even going to come anywhere close to the exploitive value of the air rights over his land. . . .
> The next problem, of course, is that if you do have TD rights, in limiting the TDRs only to the neighboring properties owned by the same owner, you prevent their valuable use in other transfer districts. In the *Fred F. French* case, the owner at one point had been offered a tremendous price for those development rights somewhere else in mid-Manhattan. But by the time the case was decided, mid-Manhattan was terribly overbuilt and the value of the TDRs had dropped. That really isn't an accidental circumstance. This is the nature of our economy.

Breitel, A Judicial View of Transferable Development Rights, Land Use L. & Zoning Dig., Feb. 1978, at 5, 5-6.

areas to which the rights may be transferred. These districts must be appropriate receiving areas for added density both in light of the community's over-all planning goals and of the capacity of the districts' physical and service infra-structures to absorb the density. Next, machinery for the actual transfer of rights must be set in motion. Under some schemes, transfers occur exclusively between private landowners subject to general public supervision. Under others, only government can transfer the rights, and the resulting income is used to create an "Environmental Trust Fund" from which cash awards are made to resource owners. A mixed pattern of private and governmental transfers is prescribed by a third variant; here, government makes the transfer only if the resource owner declines to do so. Again, the income generated through public sale is used to cancel the costs to government of compensating affected owners. . . .

Lastly, criteria must be devised to determine exactly what the owner ought to receive for his losses under the program, whether payment is made in development rights or in dollars. Two patterns prevail. One determines the compensation by measuring the difference between the quantity of rights actually used at the resource site and the total quantity of rights authorized for the site by existing zoning. . . . The second pattern, on the other hand, entitles the resource owner to transfer only that quantity of rights — or to receive its cash equivalent — required to take up the slack between the economic return possible at his site under the Resource Protection zoning and the return under zoning fixed at the Reasonable Beneficial Use level. If a marginal increase in development potential would not endanger the protected resource, government may alternatively increase the site's development potential to the latter level, much as it does when it grants a variance under traditional zoning procedures.[32]

Every TDR scheme must initially designate which locations are to be preserved, generally called preservation zones or granting zones, and thus eligible for development rights transfers. The identification of these zones must be closely linked to the planning process. In landmark preservation programs, such areas may be no larger than a specific landmark site, and the identification process can simply track the process for designation of landmarks by an existing agency, as in New York City's Zoning Resolution:

> A "landmark building" shall include any structure designated as a landmark by the Landmarks Preservation Commission and the Board of Estimate pursuant to Chapter 8-A of the New York City Charter and Chapter 8-A of the New York City Administrative Code.

In contrast, preservation zones may be created by new zoning

---

32. Costonis II ["Fair" Compensation and the Accommodation Power: Antidotes for the Taking Impasse in Land Use Controversies, 75 Colum. L. Rev. 1021 (1975)], at 1061.

C. Post-Euclidean Modifications of the Zoning Ordinance

classifications to be superimposed on those already existing, as in the Collier County, [Florida] and Scottsdale, [Arizona] ordinances. Ordinances will vary in the specificity with which they try to define preservation zones, but typically only broad guidelines are provided in the ordinances, as in this model TDR ordinance developed for South Brunswick, New Jersey:

> The Preservation Zone shall be composed of five districts designated on the zoning map as PD 1 through PD 5, corresponding to the purpose for which the land in the particular district is being preserved. PD 1 district shall consist primarily of aquifer recharge areas; PD 2 districts shall consist primarily of flood plains, swamp, and surface water; PD 3 districts shall consist primarily of farmland in production; PD 4 districts shall consist primarily of woodland; and PD 5 districts shall consist primarily of prime agricultural land not in agricultural production.

After defining the preservation zone, the ordinance should specify which locations are eligible to receive transferred development rights, generally called receiving or development zones. These zones may be coterminous with or independent of the granting zones. However, these zones must of course be capable of absorbing the extra density, a quality which will depend on a variety of political, economic, and planning characteristics. . . .

Most TDR plans propose transfers between private parties. These private market plans exist in two varieties. One enables a private developer to purchase rights from another private property owner whose land has been subjected to restrictions or otherwise declared eligible for TDR. The second, embodied in the TDR programs of New York City, Chesterfield Township and Hillsborough Township, New Jersey, requires that both the property to be preserved and that to be developed be under common ownership. Naturally, the latter type of plan places an obstacle in the path of many desirable transfers and prevents the system from achieving its goals as fully as it might under the former type of plan.

Public market TDR schemes, as mentioned previously, involve the government as a buyer and/or seller of development rights. If the government buys rights from a landowner, it can choose to bank them, which has the effect of reducing allowable density in the overall area covered by the TDR scheme. Alternatively, the government may act as a broker and resell the rights in an eligible receiving district, as Costonis proposed in the Chicago and Puerto Rico plans. Such sales produce income which can be used to finance more purchases, the government assuming a role of real estate banker. A final role which the government may play is that of owner of a landmark or other property from which development rights may be transferred. One such proposed transfer involved the U.S. Customs House in New York City. In these cases, the development rights are granted to a private owner in exchange for money or a public amenity.[45]

3. Performance Standards

Notes

1. It was an accepted tenet of city planners, and one adopted by the courts, that industry must be separated from housing. The converse proposition, however, was not embraced until a later period. Although "the surroundings are unhealthful and residences in such locations are almost sure to become neglected and unsanitary," Bassett wrote, yet "the residences do not hurt the neighboring factories, and the grounds of prohibition cannot be based on the maxim that one should so use his own as not to injure another." Zoning, 9 Natl. Mun. Rev. 315, 325 (1920). What are the economic, social, and municipal service factors that make a site appropriate for industrial development? Consider the reasons why factories should be confined to industrial zones, insulated

---

45. See Richards, Downtown Growth Control Through Development Rights Transfer, 21 Real Prop., Prob. & Tr. J. 435 (1986); Pedowitz, TDR (The Demise of the Fee Simple), 19 Real Prop., Prob. & Tr. J. 604 (1984); Delaney, Kommiers, and Gordon, TDR Redux: A Second Generation of Practical Legal Concerns, 15 Urb. Law. 593 (1983); Richards, Transferable Development Rights: Corrective, Catastrophe, or Curiosity?, 12 Real Est. L.J. 26 (1983); Marcus, A Comparative Look at TDR, Subdivision Exactions and Zoning as Environmental Preservation Panaceas, 13 Land Use & Envtl. L. Rev. 231 (1982).

New York Times architectural critic Paul Goldberger offers the following critique of TDR in use:

> [T]hese are strange times. There seems to be a tower proposed for every block in Manhattan, and the city Government is coming to look as if it were less interested in guiding and directing private development than in cheering it on. At a time when the city is actively selling or leasing its own properties . . . for mega-size office development, what is to distinguish the attitude of the city from that of the average private developer? . . .
>
> Nowhere has the city's willingness to play handmaiden to overdevelopment been more clear than at Columbus Circle, where the city, in cooperation with the Metropolitan Transportation Authority, sold the site of the obsolete New York Coliseum for private development. . . .
>
> The city is no longer our protector, but a full-fledged participant in the orgy of Manhattan real-estate development. This is the sad truth — that the municipal Government which at its best should be a moral force for good development, has shown so little interest in anything except accommodation. It is not the job of private developers to set limits; it is their job to make money. It is the function of the city to represent the public interest and forge into the building process the values that matter, which often means drawing the line. And that is just what the city has chosen *not* to do. . . .

Goldberger, The City's Birthright Sold for Air Rights, N.Y. Times, May 31, 1987. — Eds.

C. Post-Euclidean Modifications of the Zoning Ordinance 277

from residential areas by belts of open space. Is this dogmatism or a recognition of the facts of life? Or is it impossible to generalize in view of the divergencies among industries? See Logie, Industry in Towns (1952); Krasnowiecki, Ownership and Development of Land 491-492 (1965).

The planner can never overlook the fact that economic progress is an essential concomitant of improvements in the physical environment. An acceptance of the legitimate claims of industry is essential if land-use planning is to achieve respectability — or even receive a fruitful trial — in a society that entrusts the dynamics of land development to private enterprise. In many of the master plans and comprehensive zoning ordinances the needs of industry still tend to get less consideration than do those of housing, schools, and shopping centers. In postwar England, where the term "productivity" was a magic password, industry was given pride of place, both in redevelopment and in the planning of new communities. Some American commentators were sympathetic. See Urban Land Institute, Planned Industrial Districts, Tech. Bull. No. 19 (1952); Muncy, Land for Industry — A Neglected Problem, Harv. Bus. Rev., March-April 1954, at 51.

Shannon v. Building Inspector of Woburn, 328 Mass. 633, 637, 105 N.E.2d 192, 194 (1952), upheld a rezoning from residential to industrial of a district along a new circumferential highway, stating, "Woburn, with its leather trade gone, needs new industries to increase property valuations, decrease taxes, and provide employment." Cf. Lockard v. City of Los Angeles, 33 Cal. 2d 453, 202 P.2d 38, cert. denied, 337 U.S. 939 (1949) (germ of the right to walk to work?). Clearly, contemporary industry is in a position to make a bid for higher status in the zoning social register. See National Industrial Zoning Committee, Principles of Industrial Zoning (1951); O'Harrow, Performance Standards in Industrial Zoning, Planning 42 (1951); Gillespie, Industrial Zoning and Beyond: Compatibility Through Performance Standards, 46 J. Urb. L. 723 (1969).

2. By analogy to building codes, which have abandoned the "specifications standards" approach for regulations that judge materials and structural soundness by performance, the use of performance standards (especially for industrial districts) is on the increase in zoning. Appraise this proposed draft:

> All industrial operations in any industrial district shall, as a condition of permitted use, emit no obnoxious, hazardous or annoying odors, but shall, by the installation and operation of suitable deodorizing equipment, totally eliminate or diminish such odors to the highest possible degree. Where odor threshold jury standards and measurements have been expertly determined for particular odor-generating substances, and are available for references and use, the building commissioner, in his

discretion, may employ such standards and measurements, or any other reasonable standards, in determining compliance with this subsection.

Odor threshold. The minimum, measurable concentration of odor required to give the first sensation of odor to a substantial majority of members of a twelve person jury of average odor sensitivities at any boundary line of property used for industrial purposes.

Of similar character are provisions for smoke, noise and sound, industrial waste, and electromagnetic interference. Cf. Newark Milk and Cream Co. v. Township of Parsippany-Troy Hills, 47 N.J. Super. 306, 135 A.2d 682 (Law Div. 1957).

In State v. Zack, 138 Ariz. 266, 674 P.2d 329 (1983), the court let stand a provision of the Phoenix Zoning Code that read: "No use is permitted [in the Heavy Industrial district] which will emit any offensive odor, dust, noxious gas, noise, vibration, smoke, heat or glare beyond the boundaries of the lot on which such use is conducted." The court rejected the contention of appellants (operators of a scrap metal processing plant) that the use of the ambiguous term "offensive" rendered the penal statute void for vagueness. After consulting Webster's New Collegiate dictionary, the court opined,

> we cannot accept appellants' position that a person of ordinary intelligence would fail to understand what is proscribed by the terms of the zoning ordinance. The term "offensive vibration" connotes a vibration emanating beyond the boundaries of the authorized lot which, applying a reasonable man standard, would be unpleasant to a person of ordinary sensibilities.

See also Rose v. Chaikin, 187 N.J. Super. 210, 453 A.2d 1378 (N.J. Super. Ct. Ch. Div. 1982) (included, in part, in Chapter II, supra at 136):

> Defendants' violation of the zoning ordinance is uncontroverted. At all times the windmill operated in violation of the 50 dBA standard. Defendants' response is that the ordinance is arbitrary and unreasonable. . . .
>
> Pursuant to a police power statute, the Brigantine ordinance legitimately protects public health and welfare by proscribing excessive noise. Limiting noise from windmills indisputably advances that legitimate purpose and does so in a reasonable way. The claim that "other ambient sounds" may exist above 50 dBA ignores the distinction between noise (unwanted sound) and natural ambient sounds. It is not unreasonable for Brigantine to classify a windmill's sound "noise" and thus limit it. Nor is it unreasonable for the city to attack the noise problem "one step at a time," beginning, with windmills, "addressing itself to the phase of the problem which seems most acute to the legislative mind." Williamson v. Lee Optical Co., 348 U.S. 483, 489 (1955). Defendant's constitutional claims are thus without merit.

C. Post-Euclidean Modifications of the Zoning Ordinance

3. Two helpful resources on performance zoning — a practice in use in Bucks County, Pennsylvania; King County, Washington; and Lake County, Illinois, among other places — are Kendig, Performance Zoning (1980) (featuring a highly detailed Model Ordinance in Part Two), and McDougal, Performance Standards: A Viable Alternative to Euclidean Zoning?, 47 Tul. L. Rev. 255 (1973). Kendig's working definition follows:

> Performance zoning is based on the use of a density factor which applies only to buildable land. The intensity of use on any piece of buildable land within a zoning district is held constant, although the gross density may vary depending on the characteristics of the individual property.
>
> Performance zoning protects the environment by specifying developmental limits on a resource-by-resource basis. For example, no disturbance of a very unstable or rare resource is permitted, whereas some level of disturbance of a less sensitive feature may be allowed. This approach avoids the device of numerous, small zoning districts to provide different levels of resource protection. By setting a maximum use intensity (density factor) on the buildable portion of a site, this approach ameliorates conflict between that portion of the site and less intensely developed neighboring property. It is a rational system in which value relates to the physical characteristics of the site, not just to a page in the zoning ordinance.

4. Planned Unit Development

Notes

1. In 1963, the Borough of New Hope, Pennsylvania, adopted the New Hope Comprehensive Plan, containing a detailed projection of future land uses; two years later, the borough council, at the urging of a developer, amended the township zoning ordinance, creating a Planned Unit Development (PUD) district (permitted uses include single-family dwellings, apartments, golf courses, ski slopes, a school, art galleries, professional offices, a theater, hotels), and amended the Borough Zoning Map, rezoning a tract of land, envisioned in the plan as containing only low-density single-family dwellings, to PUD. Neighboring property owners brought suit claiming, in part, that the PUD is not "in accordance with [the] comprehensive plan." The court in the leading PUD case, Cheney v. Village 2 at New Hope, Inc., 429 Pa. 626, 241 A.2d 81 (1968), observed:

> The ultimate goal of this so-called density or cluster concept of zoning is achieved when an entire self-contained little community is permitted to

Parkchester, New York City*

Development of site as permitted by the zoning ordinance

Development of site as built by the Metropolitan Life Insurance Company (Courtesy The Architectural Forum)

*Gallion, The Urban Pattern 171 (1930).

be built within a zoning district, with the rules of density controlling not only the relation of private dwellings to open space, but also the relation of homes to commercial establishments such as theaters, hotels, restaurants, and quasi-commercial uses such as schools and churches.

Despite the appellee's contention that the *Eves* holding (supra page 211) mandated a conclusion of "spot zoning," the court reasoned:

In *Eves*, the municipality created a limited industrial district, F-1, which, by explicit legislative pronouncement, was not to be applied to any particular tract until the individual landowner requested that his own tract be so rezoned. The obvious evil in this procedure did *not* lie in the fact that a limited industrial district might be placed in an area previously zoned, for example, residential. The evil was the *preordained* uncertainty as to where the F-1 districts would crop up. The ordinance all but invited spot zoning where the legislature could respond to private entreaties from landowners and rezone tracts F-1 without regard to the surrounding community. In *Eves*, it was almost impossible for the F-1 districts to conform to a comprehensive plan since tracts would be rezoned on a strictly ad hoc basis.

Quite to the contrary, no such "floating zone" exists in the present case. On the very day that the PUD district was created by ordinance 160,

C. Post-Euclidean Modifications of the Zoning Ordinance 281

it was brought to earth by ordinance 161; and ... this *was* done "in accordance with a comprehensive plan."

Are you satisfied with the court's efforts to distinguish *Eves*?

2. One of the difficult problems involved in PUD (or "cluster development," as preferred by Orinda Homeowners Committee v. Board of Supervisors, 11 Cal. App. 3d 768, 90 Cal. Rptr. 88 (1st Dist. 1970)), is the definition of standards by which administrators will review proposed uses and densities. The Pennsylvania PUD-enabling statute, Pa. Stat. Ann. tit. 53, §10701 (1972), contains a provision, derived from the Model State Statute offered as part of the Symposium on PUD, 114 U. Pa. L. Rev. 3-170 (1965):

> 3(f) Other Standards and Conditions. An ordinance adopted pursuant to this Act shall set forth the standards and criteria by which the design, bulk, and location of buildings shall be evaluated, and all standards and criteria for any feature of a Planned Unit Development shall be set forth in such ordinance with sufficient certainty to provide reasonable criteria by which specific proposals can be evaluated.

Commentary on this paragraph states that compelling the local ordinance to "speak to policy and objectives with clarity sufficient to permit a reviewer of a local decision to determine whether that decision was consistent with the stated policy" is the solution to the dilemma of departing from detailed regulations and risking reliance on local discretion.

PUD can be said to reflect an attitudinal change toward the developer: "The basic philosophy of PUD is to substitute flexibility, creativity, and variety for the inflexibility and lack of variety which conventional zoning often imposes on the developer." Planned Unit Development, 35 Mo. L. Rev. 27 (1970). Will courts permit planning commissions to require originality? How would you word a local ordinance, authorizing aesthetic control, but with "standards and criteria" meeting the requirements of the model act? See Pacesetter Homes v. Village of Olympia Fields, 104 Ill. App. 2d 218, N.E.2d 369 (1968). Warth v. Seldin, 422 U.S. 490 (1975) (infra page 446), involved an attack on an ordinance requiring a substantial part of each PUD unit .o be reserved for single-family dwellings with specified minimum acreages.

3. See Frankland v. City of Lake Oswego, 517 P.2d 1042, 1048-1052 (Or. 1973):

> Section 53.330 of the PUD ordinance requires, inter alia, a developer to submit architectural sketches showing the type of buildings to be constructed, their prospective locations in the development, and their general height and bulk characteristics.
>
> Implicit in this requirement is that the developer build in accordance

with these sketches so that the City's approval of the sketches acts as a device to control development. Thus, if a developer fails to comply with the sketches he has submitted, he is in noncompliance with the final plan and the zoning ordinance which was passed to implement that final plan. . . .

The sketches submitted to the Planning Commission and the City Council, Exhibits 3 and 5, bear no resemblance, either generally or specifically, to the apartment building constructed. Exhibit 5 is a sketch showing a portion of a three-story apartment building on the right, a smaller portion of a similar building on the left, and in the center a two-story apartment building consisting of three apartments on each floor, the buildings having been separated by open space and a pool. Exhibit 3 shows an apartment building apparently five stories high at one end which resembles a tower, with the remainder of the apartments being substantially lower and more elongated, with only two levels.

The apartment actually constructed is a monolithic, large, gray rectangular building 375 feet long and 75 feet wide, with five stories at one end and four stories at the other.

The witnesses agreed that the apartment constructed was a departure from the sketches submitted. . . .

A requirement in a PUD ordinance that a developer submit final plans showing with some particularity the various features involved in his planned unit development, and that thereafter he is bound to these plans, serves at least two desirable purposes. First, it gives the planning authorities and the City Council full knowledge of what they are asked to approve before they grant a zone change. Secondly, it gives any opponent complete information about the project. It serves no worthwhile purpose for an ordinance to allow a full public hearing on a proposed planned unit development and zone change if the facts are not available. There is nothing to debate. Neither the opponents nor the proponents would know the issues, and the governing body charged with making a decision would be doing so in a vacuum. In so holding, we are aware of the need for flexibility in planning, but flexible planning does not, in our view, justify delegation of the planning function to a private developer, nor does it allow a developer to build without regard to plans as presented to the appropriate planning authorities. . . .

While it might be said that the term "sketches" in the ordinance should not be read so expansively, we note that this is the only tool which the City can use to oversee the type, height, and bulk of structures to be built in advance of construction and thus has enhanced importance under the scheme of development envisaged by the general Lake Oswego PUD ordinance.

Therefore, because the Christensen apartment did not comply with the sketches submitted, that structure violated the final plan and the zoning ordinance which implemented that plan. . . .

4. Hayek, in The Road to Serfdom 74 (1956), writes:

The distinction . . . between formal law or justice and substantive rules is very important and at the same time most difficult to draw precisely in

C. Post-Euclidean Modifications of the Zoning Ordinance

practice. Yet the general principle involved is simple enough. The difference between the two kinds of rules is the same as that between laying down a Rule of the Road, as in the Highway Code, and ordering people where to go; or, better still, between providing signposts and commanding people which road to take. The formal rules tell people in advance what action the state will take in certain types of situations, defined in general terms, without reference to time and place or particular people. They refer to typical situations into which anyone may get and in which the existence of such rules will be useful for a great variety of individual purposes. The knowledge that in such situations the state will act in a definite way, or require people to behave in a certain manner, is provided as a means for people to use in making their own plans.

5. Mixed-Use Development

See drawing on page 284.[46]

6. Contract and Conditional Zoning

■ **COLLARD v. INCORPORATED VILLAGE OF FLOWER HILL**
52 N.Y.2d 594, 421 N.E.2d 818, 439 N.Y.S.2d 326 (1981)

JONES, Judge . . .

Appellants now own improved property in the Village of Flower Hill. In 1976, the then owners of the subject premises and appellants'

---

46. From Witherspoon, Alpert & Gladstone, Mixed-Use Development Handbook: 18 (1987). The authors cite the following examples of "MXDs": Houston's Galleria, San Francisco's Embarcadero Center, Washington's Watergate, New York City's Rockefeller Center, and Baltimore's Charles Center, among several other projects that fit this working definition:

A "mixed use development" means a relatively large-scale real estate project characterized by:

- three or more significant revenue-producing uses (such as retail, office, residential, hotel/motel, and recreation — which in well-planned projects are mutually supporting);
- significant functional and physical integration of project components (and thus a highly-intensive use of land), including uninterrupted pedestrian connections; and
- development in conformance with a coherent plan (which frequently stipulates the type and scale of uses, permitted densities, and related items).

This definition clearly differentiates mixed use developments from other forms of land use and also identifies "common denominator" characteristics of mixed use projects with a minimum number of criteria.

Are the economies of scale advantages of mixed-use offset by the complexity in running such large-scale plans through governmental procedures designed for much simpler projects? See, for example, the legal and practical difficulties posed by the Admiral Thomas development in Honolulu, the focus of Life of the Land v. City Council, 61 Haw. 390, 606 P.2d 866 (1980).

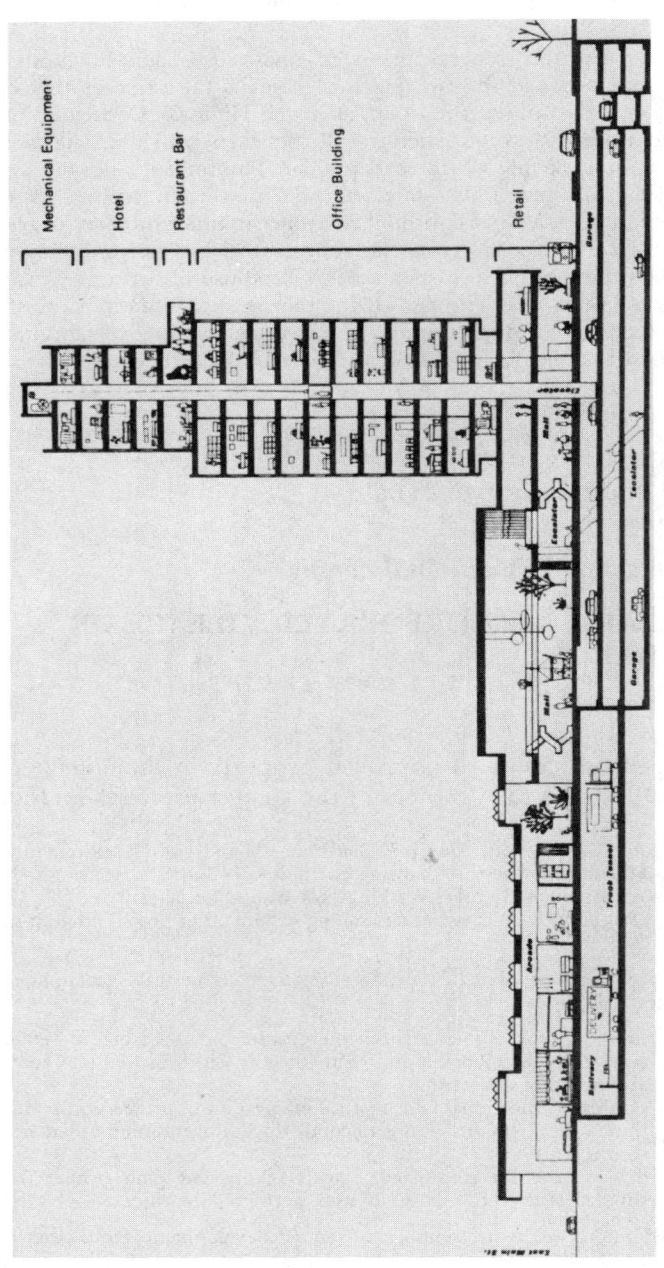

Section drawing of Midtown Plaza, Rochester, New York, illustrates the important characteristics of mixed use development. The three uses contained within the complex include hotel, office, and retail. The 18-story tower's first 13 floors house offices; the 14th floor is occupied by a restaurant offering a view of Rochester, and the three top floors are devoted to a hotel. The tower rises above a portion of the parking garage and the climate-controlled shopping mall.

C. Post-Euclidean Modifications of the Zoning Ordinance

predecessors in title, applied to the village board of trustees to rezone the property from a General Municipal and Public Purposes District to a Business District.[1] On October 4 of that year the village board granted the rezoning application by the following resolution:

> RESOLVED that the application of Ray R. Beck Company for a change of Zone of premises known and designated as Section 6, Block 73, Lots 9, 12 and 13 on the land and tax maps of Nassau County from General Municipal and Public Purposes District be and the same hereby is granted upon the following conditions:
> (a) The Subject Premises and any buildings, structures and improvements situated or to be situated thereon, will be erected, altered, renovated, remodelled, used, occupied and maintained for the following purposes and no other;
> (i) Offices for the practice of the professions of medicine, dentistry, law, engineering, architecture or accountancy;
> (ii) Executive offices to be used solely for the management of business concerns and associations. . . .
> (d) No building or structure situated on the Subject Premises on the date of this Declaration of Covenants will be altered, extended, rebuilt, renovated or enlarged without the prior consent of the Board of Trustees of the Village. . . .

Subsequently, appellants' predecessors in title entered into the contemplated declaration of covenants which was recorded in the office of the Clerk of Nassau County on November 29, 1976. . . .

Appellants, after acquiring title, made application in late 1978 to the village board for approval to enlarge and extend the existing structure on the premises. Without any reason being given that application was denied. Appellants then commenced this action to have the board's determination declared arbitrary, capricious, unreasonable, and unconstitutional and sought by way of ultimate relief an order directing the board to issue the necessary building permits.

Asserting that the board's denial of the application was beyond review as to reasonableness, respondent moved to dismiss the complaint for failure to state a cause of action. Special Term denied the motion,

---

1. Prior to 1964 the subject premises, then vacant, had been zoned for single-family dwellings with a minimum lot size of 7,500 square feet. In that year the then owners applied to the village board to rezone a portion of the property and place it in the General Municipal and Public Purposes District so that a private sanitarium might be constructed. Concurrently with that application a declaration of covenants restricting the use of the property to a sanitarium was recorded in the county clerk's office. The village board then granted the rezoning application, but limited the property's use to the purposes set forth in the declaration of covenants. The 1976 rezoning application, which as conditionally granted is the subject of this suit, was made because the private sanitarium had fallen into disuse and it was asserted that without rezoning the property could neither be sold nor leased.

equating appellants' allegation that the board's action was arbitrary and capricious with an allegation that such action was lacking in good faith and fair dealing — an allegation which it found raised triable issues of fact. The Appellate Division, 75 A.D.2d 631, 427 N.Y.S.2d 301, reversed and dismissed the complaint, holding that the allegation of arbitrary and capricious action by the board was not the equivalent of an allegation that the board breached an implied covenant of fair dealing and good faith. . . .

. . . Prior to our decision in Church v. Town of Islip, 8 N.Y.2d 254, 203 N.Y.S.2d 866, 168 N.E.2d 680 in which we upheld rezoning of property subject to reasonable conditions, conditional rezoning had been almost uniformly condemned by courts of all jurisdictions — a position to which a majority of States appear to continue to adhere. Since *Church*, however, the practice of conditional zoning has become increasingly widespread in this State, as well as having gained popularity in other jurisdictions.

Because much criticism has been mounted against the practice, both by commentators and the courts of some of our sister States,[3] further exposition is in order.

Probably the principal objection to conditional rezoning is that it constitutes illegal spot zoning, thus violating the legislative mandate requiring that there be a comprehensive plan for, and that all conditions be uniform within, a given zoning district. When courts have considered the issue, the assumptions have been made that conditional zoning benefits particular landowners rather than the community as a whole and that it undermines the foundation upon which comprehensive zoning depends by destroying uniformity within use districts. Such unexamined assumptions are questionable. First, it is a downward change to a less restrictive zoning classification that benefits the property rezoned and not the opposite imposition of greater restrictions on land use. Indeed, imposing limiting conditions, while benefiting surrounding properties, normally adversely affects the premises on which the conditions are imposed. Second, zoning is not invalid per se merely because only a single parcel is involved or benefited; the real test for spot zoning is whether the change is other than part of a well-considered and comprehensive plan calculated to serve the general welfare of the community. Such a determination, in turn, depends on the reasonableness of the rezoning in relation to neighboring uses — an inquiry

---

3. (See, e.g., Babcock, The Zoning Game, chs. 1, 3; Basset, Zoning, ch. 9; Crolly, The Rezoning of Properties Conditioned on Agreements with Property Owners — Zoning by Contract, N.Y. L. J., March 9, 1961, p. 4, col. 1; Scott, Toward a Strategy for Utilization of Contract and Conditional Zoning, 51 J. Urban L. 94; Trager, Contract Zoning, 23 Md. L. Rev. 121; Note, Three Aspects of Zoning: Unincorporated Areas — Exclusionary Zoning — Conditional Zoning, 6 Real Prop., Prob. & Tr. J. 178 (1971). Comment, The Use and Abuse of Contract Zoning, 12 UCLA L. Rev. 897. . . .)

C. Post-Euclidean Modifications of the Zoning Ordinance

required regardless of whether the change in zone is conditional in form. Third, if it is initially proper to change a zoning classification without the imposition of restrictive conditions notwithstanding that such change may depart from uniformity, then no reason exists why accomplishing that change subject to condition should automatically be classified as impermissible spot zoning.

Both conditional and unconditional rezoning involve essentially the same legislative act — an amendment of the zoning ordinance. The standards for judging the validity of conditional rezoning are no different from the standards used to judge whether unconditional rezoning is illegal. If modification to a less restrictive zoning classification is warranted, then a fortiori conditions imposed by a local legislature to minimize conflicts among districts should not in and of themselves violate any prohibition against spot zoning.

Another fault commonly voiced in disapproval of conditional zoning is that it constitutes an illegal bargaining away of a local government's police power. Because no municipal government has the power to make contracts that control or limit it in the exercise of its legislative powers and duties, restrictive agreements made by a municipality in conjunction with a rezoning are sometimes said to violate public policy. While permitting citizens to be governed by the best bargain they can strike with a local legislature would not be consonant with notions of good government, absent proof of a contract purporting to bind the local legislature in advance to exercise its zoning authority in a bargained-for manner, a rule which would have the effect of forbidding a municipality from trying to protect landowners in the vicinity of a zoning change by imposing protective conditions based on the assertion that that body is bargaining away its discretion, would not be in the best interests of the public. The imposition of conditions on property sought to be rezoned may not be classified as a prospective commitment on the part of the municipality to zone as requested if the conditions are met; nor would the municipality necessarily be precluded on this account from later reversing or altering its decision.

Yet another criticism leveled at conditional zoning is that the State enabling legislation does not confer on local authorities authorization to enact conditional zoning amendments. On this view any such ordinance would be ultra vires. While it is accurate to say there exists no explicit authorization that a legislative body may attach conditions to zoning amendments, neither is there any language which expressly forbids a local legislature to do so. Statutory silence is not necessarily a denial of the authority to engage in such a practice. . . .

One final concern of those reluctant to uphold the practice is that resort to conditional rezoning carries with it no inherent restrictions apart from the restrictive agreement itself. This fear, however, is justifiable only if conditional rezoning is considered a contractual relationship between municipality and private party, outside the scope of the zoning power — a view to which we do not subscribe. When conditions are incorporated in an amending ordinance, the result is as much a "zoning regulation" as an ordinance, adopted without conditions. Just as the scope of all zoning regulation is limited by the police power, and thus local legislative bodies must act reasonably and in the best interests of public safety, welfare and convenience, the scope of permissible conditions must of necessity be similarly limited. If, upon proper proof, the conditions imposed are found unreasonable, the rezoning amendment as well as the required conditions would have to be nullified, with the affected property reverting to the preamendment zoning classification. . . .

The focus of appellants' assault is the provision of the declaration of covenants that no structure may be extended or enlarged "without the prior consent of the Board of Trustees of the Village". Appellants would have us import the added substantive prescription — "which consent may not be unreasonably withheld". Their argument proceeds along two paths: first, that as a matter of construction the added prescription should be read into the provision; second, that because of limitations associated with the exercise of municipal zoning power the village board would have been required to include such a prescription.

Appellants' construction argument must fail. The terminology employed in the declaration is explicit. The concept that appellants would invoke is not obscure and language to give it effect was readily available had it been the intention of the parties to include this added stipulation. Appellants point to no canon of construction in the law of real property or of contracts which would call for judicial insertion of the missing clause. Where language has been chosen containing no inherent ambiguity or uncertainty, courts are properly hesitant, under the guise of judicial construction, to imply additional requirements to relieve a party from asserted disadvantage flowing from the terms actually used. . . .

For the reasons stated the Board of Trustees of the incorporated Village of Flower Hill may not now be compelled to issue its consent to the proposed enlargement and extension of the existing structure on the premises or in the alternative give an acceptable reason for failing to do so. Accordingly, the order of the Appellate Division should be affirmed, with costs.[47]

47. See Kramer, Contract Zoning — Old Myths and New Realities, Land Use L. & Zoning Dig., Aug. 1982, at 4 (reviewing the status of contract and conditional zoning on a state-by-state basis):

The term contract zoning had achieved a secondary meaning not unlike "spot zoning." . . . As a result, a new term — conditional zoning — was coined so that the same technique might be utilized without the court's invalidating it.
This contract-conditional zoning dichotomy is little more than a semantic

D. DEPARTURES FROM THE ZONING ORDINANCE: THE EXTENT OF DISCRETION

No zoning scheme, Euclidean or post-Euclidean, can anticipate every change in technology, demographics, and economics; nor can its drafters be error-free in evaluating past trends, present capabilities, and future needs. These inevitable shortcomings have given rise to the doctrine of nonconforming use to allow for past development, and have led to amendments, special use permits, exceptions, variances, and the other "zoning forms of action," to use Professor Hagman's coinage:

> As with common law forms of action, the choice of a form may or will dictate the allegations to be made, decision makers involved, subject matter jurisdiction of the decision makers, evidence to be presented, parties who have standing to be proponents or opponents, scope of relief and routes of appeal.[48]

As you study the complaints of frustrated developers and disgruntled neighbors, compare the methods the courts employ to resolve these disputes to the common-law forms you confronted in your first year of law study, and to the quasi-judicial mode of resolution found in the realm of "public law." By requiring the court to find a significant mistake or change in circumstances are we unnecessarily restricting judicial discretion and creativity? Does the difference between implementing a general program for land use and deciding what is appropriate for a particular parcel justify varying levels of scrutiny? Is deference to lawmakers, particularly local decision-makers who are too easily tempted by the promise of political and financial rewards, an outmoded and stultifying concept, or a sure path to domination by the "least dangerous" (judicial) branch? What are the factors that would lead you to pursue one course of conduct rather than another? In

---

game. In many cases, courts have labeled unilateral promises as contract zoning and bilateral promises as conditional zoning. To state that conditional zoning is valid because only the developer is bound, while contract zoning is invalid because the local legislative body is also bound, sheds more light than heat.

See also Va. Code Ann. §15.1-491.1 (1981): "It is the purpose of §§15.1-491.1 through 15.1-491.4 to provide a more flexible and adaptable zoning method . . . whereby a zoning classification may be allowed subject to certain conditions proffered by the zoning applicant for the protection of the community that are not generally applicable to land similarly zoned." See also the materials on development agreements, infra page 617.

For a detailed analysis of experimentation with "contingent zoning," see Wegner, Moving Toward the Bargaining Table: Contract Zoning, Development Agreements, and the Theoretical Foundations of Government Land Use Deals, 65 N.C.L. Rev. 957, 977-994 (1987). For more on spot zoning and rezonings, see infra page 313. — EDS.

48. Hagman, Urban Planning and Land Development Control Law 190 (1975).

addition to different procedures — in initiation, publication, hearing, and agency — what sort of arguments would have to be advanced, and what is their likelihood of success in particular fact situations?[49]

1. Nonconforming Uses: Preexisting Uses That Won't Fade Away

■ CITY OF LOS ANGELES v. GAGE
127 Cal. App. 2d 442, 274 P.2d 34 (2nd Dist. 1954)

VALLEE, Justice. . . .

In 1930 Gage acquired adjoining lots 220 and 221 located on Cochran Avenue in Los Angeles. He constructed a two-family residential building on lot 221 and rented the upper half solely for residential purposes. He established a wholesale and retail plumbing supply business on the property. He used a room in the lower half of the residential building on lot 221 as the office for the conduct of the business, and the rest of the lower half for residential purposes for himself and his family; he used a garage on lot 221 for the storage of plumbing supplies and materials; and he constructed and used racks, bins, and stalls for the storage of such supplies and materials on lot 220. Later Gage incorporated defendant company. . . .

In 1930 the two lots and other property facing on Cochran Avenue in their vicinity were classified in "C" zone by the zoning ordinance then in effect. Under this classification the use to which Gage put the property was permitted. Shortly after Gage acquired lots 220 and 221, they were classified "C-3" zone and the use to which he put the property was expressly permitted. In 1936 the city council of the city passed Ordinance 77,000 which contained a comprehensive zoning plan for the city. Ordinance 77,000 re-enacted the prior ordinances with respect to the use of lots 220 and 221. In 1941 the city council passed Ordinance 85,015 by the terms of which the use of a residential building for the conduct of an office in connection with the plumbing supply business

---

49. See, e.g., Conlon v. Board of Public Works, 11 N.J. 363, 94 A.2d 660 (1953). For a typical case distinguishing between a special exception and a variance, see Carson v. Board of Appeals of Lexington, 321 Mass. 649, 75 N.E.2d 116 (1947). For the difference in result between rezoning and the grant of a special exception permit, compare Smith v. Board of Appeals of Salem, 313 Mass. 622, 48 N.E.2d 620 (1943) with Lambert v. Board of Appeals of Lowell, 295 Mass. 224, 3 N.E.2d 784 (1936).

For the confusing terminology with respect to variances and exceptions in Delaware, see In the Matter of Emmett S. Hickman Co., 49 Del 13, 108 A.2d 667 (1954); Searles v. Darling, 46 Del. 263, 83 A.2d 96 (1951). Compare Josephson v. Autrey, 96 So. 2d 784 (Fla. 1957) with Kaeslin v. Adams, 97 So. 2d 461 (Fla. 1957). Mitchell Land Co. v. Planning and Zoning Board of Appeals, 140 Conn. 527, 532, 102 A.2d 316, 319 n. 2 (1953), lists "[c]ases in which a variance has been sought, although in certain instances the owner was actually, though unwittingly, seeking an exception."

D. Departures from the Zoning Ordinance 291

was permitted. Ordinance 85,015 prohibited the open storage of materials in zone "C-3" but permitted such uses as had been established to continue as nonconforming uses. The use to which lots 220 and 221 was put by defendants was a nonconforming use that might be continued. In 1946 the city council passed Ordinance 90,500. This ordinance reclassified lots 220 and 221 and other property fronting on Cochran Avenue in their vicinity from zone "C-3" to zone "R-4" (Multiple dwelling zone). Use of lots 220 and 221 for the conduct of a plumbing business was not permitted in zone "R-4." At the time Ordinance 90,500 was passed, and at all times since, the Los Angeles Municipal Code (§12.23 B & C) provided:

> (a) The nonconforming use of a conforming building or structure may be continued, except that in the "R" Zones any nonconforming commercial or industrial use of a residential building or residential accessory building shall be discontinued within five (5) years from June 1, 1946, or five (5) years from the date the use becomes nonconforming, whichever date is later. . . .
>
> (a) The nonconforming use of land shall be discontinued within five (5) years from June 1, 1946, or within five (5) years from the date the use became nonconforming, in each of the following cases: (1) where no buildings are employed in connection with such use; (2) where the only buildings employed are accessory or incidental to such use; (3) where such use is maintained in connection with a conforming building.

Prior to the passage of Ordinance 90,500 about 50% of the city had been zoned. It was the first ordinance which "attempted to zone the entire corporate limits of the city." Prior to its passage, several thousand exceptions and variances were granted from restrictive provisions of prior ordinances, some of which permitted commercial use of property zoned for residential use, "and in some cases permitted the use of land for particular purposes like or similar to use of subject property which otherwise would have been prohibited." Under Ordinance 90,500, the uses permitted by these exceptions and variances that did not carry a time limit may be continued indefinitely.

The business conducted by Gage on the property has produced a gross revenue varying between $125,000 and $350,000 a year. If he is required to abandon the use of the property for his business, he will be put to the following expenses:

> (1) The value of a suitable site for the conduct of its business would be about $10,000; which would be offset by the value of $7,500 of the lot now used. (2) The cost incident to removing of supplies to another location and construction of the necessary racks, sheds, bins and stalls which would be about $2,500. (3) The cost necessary to expend to advertise a new location. (4) The risk of a gain or a loss of business while moving, and

the cost necessary to reestablish the business at a new location, the amount of which is uncertain.

The noise and disturbance caused by the loading and unloading of supplies, trucking, and the going and coming of workmen in connection with the operation of a plumbing business with an open storage yard is greater than the noise and disturbance that is normal in a district used solely for residential purposes. . . .

The fact that various exceptions and variances were granted under zoning ordinances prior to Ordinance 90,500, and that some of them permitted the use of land for particular purposes like or similar to the use of defendants' property which otherwise would have been prohibited, presents a question for the zoning authorities of the city. They are the persons charged with the duty of deciding whether the conditions in other parts of the city require like prohibition. The mere fact that a prior ordinance excepts a parcel of land in a residential district does not give the owner thereof a vested right to have the exception continued so as to entitle him, on that ground, to attack the validity of a later ordinance repealing the former. . . .

The right of a city council, in the exercise of the police power, to regulate or, in proper cases, to prohibit the conduct of a given business, is not limited by the fact that the value of investments made in the business prior to any legislative actions will be greatly diminished. A business which, when established, was entirely unobjectionable, may, by the growth or change in the character of the neighborhood, become a source of danger to the public health, morals, safety, or general welfare of those who have come to be occupants of the surrounding territory. . . .

No case seems to have been decided in this state squarely involving the precise question presented in the case at bar. Until recently zoning ordinances have made no provision for any systematic and comprehensive elimination of the nonconforming use. The expectation seems to have been that existing nonconforming uses would be of little consequence and that they would eventually disappear. The contrary appears to be the case. It is said that the fundamental problem facing zoning is the inability to eliminate the nonconforming use. The general purpose of present-day zoning ordinances is to eventually end all nonconforming uses. There is a growing tendency to guard against the indefinite continuance of nonconforming uses by providing for their liquidation within a prescribed period. It is said, "The only positive method of getting rid of nonconforming uses yet devised is to amortize a nonconforming building. That is, to determine the normal useful remaining life of the building and prohibit the owner from maintaining it after the expiration of that time." Crolly and Norton, Termination of

D. Departures from the Zoning Ordinance 293

Nonconforming Uses, 62 Zoning Bulletin 1, Regional Plan Assn., June 1952.

    Amortization of nonconforming uses has been expressly authorized by recent amendments to zoning enabling laws in a number of states. Ordinances providing for amortization of nonconforming uses have been passed in a number of large cities. The length of time given the owner to eliminate his nonconforming use or building varies with the city and with the type of structure. . . .

    In State ex rel. Dema Realty Co. v. McDonald, 168 La. 172, 121 So. 613, the defendants had used their property as a retail grocery store for a great many years prior to 1927. In 1927 the city passed a zoning ordinance which established the area in which the property was located as a residential district and provided that all businesses then in operation within that area should be liquidated within one year from the passage of the ordinance. It was contended that this provision was unconstitutional as being arbitrary and unreasonable, and that it amounted to a taking of the defendants' property without due process of law. . . . [T]he court stated, 121 So. 617:

> It is to be observed, too, that the ordinance there under consideration provided for the establishment and maintenance of residential districts from which every kind of business was excluded. The ordinance did not deal specially with any already established business in the zoned district. But, if the village had the authority to create and to maintain a purely residential district, which the court held it did have, and if such an ordinance was not arbitrary and unreasonable, it follows necessarily that the village was vested with the authority to remove any business or trade from the district and to fix a limit of time in which the same shall be done.

The Supreme Court of the United States denied certiorari. 280 U.S. 556. . . .

    In Standard Oil Co. v. City of Tallahassee, 5 Cir., 183 F.2d 410 the plaintiff was operating a motor vehicle service station at the time the area in which it was located was, by a zoning ordinance, made a residence district. The ordinance, adopted in April 1948, provided that all locations then used for motor vehicle service stations should be discontinued as such on and after January 1, 1949. In upholding the validity of the ordinance the court stated, 183 F.2d at page 413:

> The power of a municipality to require by ordinance the discontinuance of an existing property use also appears to be well established law in Florida. Here, plaintiff's service station is near the State Capitol and the State Supreme Court Building, as well as several other state office buildings and a public school. It therefore becomes manifest that its discontinuance under the ordinance cannot be viewed as arbitrary and unreasonable, or

as having no relation to the safety and general welfare of the community affected. We find no merit in appellant's contention that enforcement of this ordinance would entail any unjust discrimination, or would be tantamount to depriving it of its property without due process merely because the site was acquired and improved at considerable expense before the zoning ordinance was enacted. The general rule here applicable is that considerations of financial loss or of so-called "vested rights" in private property are insufficient to outweigh the necessity for legitimate exercise of the police power of a municipality.

The Supreme Court of the United States denied certiorari. 340 U.S. 892. . . .

Jones v. City of Los Angeles, 211 Cal. 304, 295 P. 14, relied on by Gage, held unconstitutional, as applied to existing establishments, an ordinance making it unlawful to erect, operate, or maintain, in certain residential areas, a sanitarium for the treatment of persons suffering from mental or nervous diseases. The *Jones* case was distinguished in the recent case of Livingston Rock, etc., Co. v. County of Los Angeles, 43 Cal. 2d 121, 272 P.2d 4. In the *Livingston* case an ordinance of the county of Los Angeles allowed certain existing nonconforming uses to continue for 20 years unless such exception should be revoked as provided in the ordinance. One ground of revocation specified was if the use was so exercised "as to be detrimental to the public health or safety, or so as to be a nuisance." Distinguishing the *Jones* case the court said, 43 Cal. 2d 126, 272 P.2d 8:

> Moreover, the ordinance under consideration in the Jones case differed materially from the one here involved. There the ordinance, cast in the form of a penal statute rather than in the form of comprehensive zoning law, prohibited the maintenance of sanitariums of a certain type in designated districts. By its terms the ordinance, unlike the ordinary zoning laws, purported to have both a retroactive as well as a prospective effect, thereby automatically prohibiting the continued maintenance of several established sanitariums representing large investments. In other words, no provision was made for any automatic exception for existing nonconforming uses. In the present case, the zoning ordinance does provide for automatic exceptions of reasonable duration for existing nonconforming uses, subject, however, to earlier revocation of the automatic exception if the use for which approval was granted is so exercised "as to be detrimental to the public health or safety, or so as to be a nuisance" (§649 . . .); and the power to determine, upon notice, the question of whether the property was being so used was vested in the Regional Planning Commission.

Assuming, as suggested by Gage, that the foregoing was dictum, we think it a correct statement of the distinction between the *Jones* case and the case at bar. There are other differences between *Jones* and the present case. There the regulation was of one type of commercial use.

D. Departures from the Zoning Ordinance 295

Here the regulation is of all commercial uses. There the ordinance affected a substantial investment in land and special buildings designed and built for the use to which they were being put. Here the ordinance affects only the use of land and the nonconforming use of a conforming building. The building has been, and may continue to be, used for the purpose for which it was designed and built. There the property could not have been used immediately for other purposes. Here the property can be used immediately for the uses for which it is zoned. In the *Jones* case the court said, 211 Cal. at pages 319, 321, 295 P. at page 21:

> We do not mean to hold that those engaged in the zoning of cities must always be faced with the impossibility of eradicating the nonconforming uses.... Our conclusion is that where, as here, a retroactive ordinance causes *substantial* injury and the prohibited business is not a nuisance, the ordinance is to that extent an unreasonable and unjustifiable exercise of police power. (Italics added.)

The theory in zoning is that each district is an appropriate area for the location of the uses which the zone plan permits in that area, and that the existence or entrance of other uses will tend to impair the development and stability of the area for the appropriate uses.... The presence of any nonconforming use endangers the benefits to be derived from a comprehensive zoning plan. Having the undoubted power to establish residential districts, the legislative body has the power to make such classification really effective by adopting such reasonable regulations as would be conducive to the welfare, health, and safety of those desiring to live in such district and enjoy the benefits thereof. There would be no object in creating a residential district unless there were to be secured to those dwelling therein the advantages which are ordinarily considered the benefits of such residence. It would seem to be the logical and reasonable method of approach to place a time limit upon the continuance of existing nonconforming uses, commensurate with the investment involved and based on the nature of the use; and in cases of nonconforming structures, on their character, age, and other relevant factors....

The distinction between an ordinance restricting future uses and one requiring the termination of present uses within a reasonable period of time is merely one of degree, and constitutionality depends on the relative importance to be given to the public gain and to the private loss. Zoning as it affects every piece of property is to some extent retroactive in that it applies to property already owned at the time of the effective date of the ordinance. The elimination of existing uses within a reasonable time does not amount to a taking of property nor does it necessarily restrict the use of property so that it cannot be used for any reasonable purpose. Use of a reasonable amortization scheme provides an equitable means of reconciliation of the conflicting interests in satisfaction of due process requirements. As a method of eliminating existing nonconforming uses it allows the owner of the nonconforming use, by affording an opportunity to make new plans, at least partially to offset any loss he might suffer. The loss he suffers, if any, is spread out over a period of years, and he enjoys a monopolistic position by virtue of the zoning ordinance as long as he remains. If the amortization period is reasonable the loss to the owner may be small when compared with the benefit to the public. Nonconforming uses will eventually be eliminated. A legislative body may well conclude that the beneficial effect on the community of the eventual elimination of all nonconforming uses by a reasonable amortization plan more than offsets individual losses.

The ordinance in question provides, according to a graduated periodic schedule, for the gradual and ultimate elimination of all commercial and industrial uses in residential zones. These provisions require the discontinuance of nonconforming uses of land within a five-year period, and the discontinuance of nonconforming commercial and industrial uses of residential buildings in the "R" zones within the same five-year period. These provisions are the only ones pertinent to the decision in this case. However, it may be noted that other provisions of the ordinance require the discontinuance of nonconforming billboards and, in residential zones, the discontinuance of nonconforming buildings and of nonconforming uses of nonconforming buildings, within specified periods running from 20 to 40 years according to the type of building construction.

We have no doubt that Ordinance 90,500, in compelling the discontinuance of the use of defendants' property for a wholesale and retail plumbing and plumbing supply business, and for the open storage of plumbing supplies within five years after its passage, is a valid exercise of the police power. Lots 220 and 221 are several blocks from a business center and it appears that they are not within any reasonable or logical extension of such a center. The ordinance does not prevent the operation of defendants' business; it merely restricts its location. Discontinuance of the nonconforming use requires only that Gage move his plumbing business to property that is zoned for it. Such property can be found within a half mile of Gage's property. The cost of moving is $5,000, or less than 1% of Gage's minimum gross business for five years, or less than half of 1% of the mean of his gross business for five years. He has had eight years within which to move. The property is usable for residential purpose. Since 1930 lot 221 has been used for residential purposes. All of the land within 500 feet of Gage's property is now improved and used for such purposes. Lot 220, now unimproved, can be improved for the same purposes.

We think it apparent that none of the agreed facts and none of the

D. Departures from the Zoning Ordinance 297

ultimate facts found by the court justify the conclusion that Ordinance 90,500, as applied to Gage's property, is clearly arbitrary or unreasonable, or has no substantial relation to the public's health, safety, morals, or general welfare, or that it is an unconstitutional impairment of his property rights. . . .

The judgment is reversed, and the superior court is directed to render judgment for plaintiff as prayed for in the complaint.[50]

Notes

1. The corner grocery store in the midst of a neighborhood about to be zoned residential attracted relatively little attention from the advocates of zoning in 1913. The spirit of the times is typified by Bassett's statement: "Zoning has sought to safeguard the future, in the expectation that time will repair the mistakes of the past." Zoning 105 (1936). But in 1990 the store may still be there — and even joined by other nonresidential uses whose existence it encourages. Nonconforming uses seldom die — nor do they fade away. Consider the testimony of a well-known planner, Harland Bartholomew:

> The thesis of this paper is that in the now familiar "non-conforming use" is found one of the most potent factors — if not the principal factor — which cause prospective home builders and buyers to seek newly developing suburban areas.
>
> At a public hearing called to consider the adoption of a zoning ordinance one citizen stated that during his lifetime his family had built six homes, each successive home being farther removed from the city's

---

50. City of La Mesa v. Tweed & Gambrell Planing Mill, 146 Cal. App. 2d 762, 304 P.2d 803 (1956), held a five-year period for amortization of a nonconforming use unconstitutional as applied to a planing mill that had twenty-one years of economic life remaining. (The *Gage* case was distinguished.) See, in general, Norton, Elimination of Incompatible Uses and Structures, 20 Law & Contemp. Probs. 305 (1955). An amendment to the Monterey County zoning ordinance reclassifies certain land as N-district (rural area) in which billboards are not permitted subject to a one-year amortization period for existing signs. Plaintiff, who owns forty-two billboards within the new N-district, seeks to enjoin their removal. Eleven of the signs have unamortized lives, under the applicable federal tax regulations, of five to eleven years; and thirty-one, although fully amortized, have a present value in excess of $10,000 owing to maintenance repairs (allowed by the zoning ordinance) and existing three- and four-year contracts (under which no profit is usually made until the final year). What result under *Gage*? See National Advertising Co. v. County of Monterey, 1 Cal. 3d 875, 464 P.2d 33, 83 Cal. Rptr. 577 (1970).

Despite "the greater weight of authority" supporting amortization of nonconforming uses, the Supreme Court of Indiana recently held that "an ordinance prohibiting any continuation of an existing lawful use within a zoned area regardless of the length of time given to amortize that use is unconstitutional as the taking of property without due process of law and an unreasonable exercise of the police power." Appellants-petitioners were thus allowed to continue to operate junkyards at their residences. Ailes v. Decatur County Area Planning Commn., 448 N.E.2d 1057 (Ind. 1983), cert. denied, 465 U.S. 1100 (1984). — Eds.

center than the last, that each home had been well built but had to be abandoned because the environment of the neighborhood became objectionable as the result of the intrusion of non-residential uses. Each of the old homes was sold at a small sum compared with its original cost, and all but one were still standing.

This story caused the city plan commission to make an exhaustive study of non-conforming uses throughout the city's area. The study revealed a definite pattern. The older the neighborhood the higher the percentage of non-conforming uses. The oldest centrally located neighborhoods contained non-residential uses occupying approximately 15% of net block area. Midtown districts contained about 5% of net block area. As outlying districts were approached, non-conforming uses occupied less than 1% of net block area, while the newest subdivisions usually contained no non-conforming uses.

The history of property development and of trends in property values in American cities is thus illustrated. It is a record of gradual abandonment and loss caused by inadequate protection of home environment. . . .

Bartholomew, Non-Conforming Uses Destroy the Neighborhood, 15 J. Land & Pub. Util. Econ. 96 (1939). For a discussion of the nonconforming use problem in an Indiana community, see Note, 30 Ind. L.J. 521 (1955).

2. A zoning ordinance provides: "A nonconforming use is a use that now exists and does not comply with the regulations for the use district in which it is established." It continues: "Nothing contained in this ordinance shall be construed to prevent the continuance of any use which now legally exists." The Pimlico Race Track purchased land before the passage of the ordinance. It intended to acquire the adjoining land, and then use all the land for stables. The area is now zoned residential. The adjoining land has just been acquired. On application by the owners of a nearby dwelling for an injunction to restrain the erection of the stables, what result? See Chayt v. Board of Zoning Appeals, 117 Md. 426, 9 A.2d 747 (1939) ("The ordinance deals with uses made of land, not with businesses and their needs or plans."). On discontinuance or abandonment of a nonconforming use, see McLay v. Maryland Assemblies, Inc., 269 Md. 465, 306 A.2d 524 (1973).

3. While it is generally in its use that a nonconforming building offends, it may also be its height or bulk which does not meet the requirements of a new zoning ordinance. Should these different types of nonconformity receive different treatment? Cf. Peirce Appeal, 384 Pa. 100, 119 A.2d 506 (1956) (existing nonconforming use of land includes right to enclose the lot with a building). Compare Article 4 of the Model Land Development Code.

4. A zoning ordinance passed in 1928 contained a common provision: "Whenever a nonconforming use of a building has been changed

Use amortized	Time period	Case
Signs	5 years	National Advertising Co. v. County of Monterey, 27 Cal. Rptr. 136, 211 Cal. App. 2d 375 (1962)
Junkyards	1 years	McKinney v. Riley, 105 N.H. 249, 197 A.2d 218 (1964)
Dog kennels	7 years	Wolf v. City of Omaha, 177 Neb. 545, 129 N.W.2d 501 (1964)
"Check cashing and money changing or similar types of agencies"	18 months	Eutaw Enterprises, Inc. v. City of Baltimore, 241 Md. 686, 217 A.2d 348 (1966)
Junkyards	1 year	Lachapelle v. Town of Goffstown, 107 N.H. 485, 225 A.2d 624 (1967)
Junkyards	2 years	Shifflett v. Baltimore County, 247 Md. 151, 230 A.2d 310 (1967)
Billboards and signs	3 years	Naegele Outdoor Advertising Co. v. Minnetonka, 281 Minn. 492, 162 N.W.2d 206 (1968)
Gasoline station	25 years	Swain v. Board of Adjustment, 433 S.W.2d 727 (Tex. Civ. App., 1968) error ref n r e, appeal dismissed and cert. denied, 396 U.S. 277
Automobile wrecking yard	5 years	Board of Supervisors v. Miller, 170 N.W.2d 358 (Iowa 1969)
Billboards	1 year	National Advertising Co. v. County of Monterey, 1 Cal. 3d 875, 83 Cal. Rptr. 577, 464 P.2d 33 (1970), cert. denied, 398 U.S. 946
Advertising signs	unstated	Asia v. City of Seattle, 4 Wash. App. 530, 482 P.2d 810 (1971)
Billboards	5 years	Western Outdoor Advertising Co. v. City of Miami, 256 So. 2d 556 (Fla. App. 1972)
Business Signs	2 years	People v. Goodman, 31 N.Y.2d 262, 338 N.Y.S.2d 97, 290 N.E.2d 139 (1972)
Self-service Gasoline Station	1 year	Garland v. Valley Oil Co., 482 S.W.2d 342 (Tex. Civ. App. 1972) error ref n r e, cert. denied, 411 U.S. 933 (1973)
Commercial Buildings	25 years	City of University Park v. Benners, 485 S.W.2d 773 (Tex. 1972), appeal dismissed, 411 U.S. 901 (1973)
Signs	5 years	Art Neon Co. v. City & County of Denver, 488 F.2d 118 (1973), cert. denied, 417 U.S. 932 (1974)
Salvage yard	3 years	State v. Joyner, 208 S.E.2d 233 (N.C. App. 1974)

From Model Land Dev. Code art. 4 commentary at 148 (1975).

to a more restricted use or to a conforming use, such use shall not thereafter be changed to a less restricted use." A building constructed and especially adapted for use as a fraternity house was so used before the ordinance zoned its district for single-family residences. The building was occupied as a fraternity house up to 1932, when the defendant took possession under a mortgage. From 1932 to 1934, the building was operated as a rooming house. From 1934 to 1938, it was leased and used as a single-family residence; the lease provided that the premises were to be "used for the purpose of residence only." No major structural changes in the house have been made. In 1938, a college fraternity wanted to purchase it, if a ruling could be obtained allowing the building to revert to its earlier use. What result? See State ex rel. Morehouse v. Hunt, 235 Wis. 358, 291 N.W. 745 (1940) (no intent to abandon nonconforming use). Had you been the draftsman of the zoning ordinance, what changes in language would you have recommended in the provision quoted above? See Wis. Laws 1941, ch. 203, codified at Wis. Stat. Ann. §62.23(7)(h) (1957). See also O'Neill v. Philadelphia Zoning Board of Adjustment, 384 Pa. 379, 120 A.2d 901 (1956). For a case in which wartime gasoline rationing impelled the closing of a nonconforming filling station, see Franmor Realty Co. v. LeBoeuf, 201 Misc. 220, 104 N.Y.S.2d 247 (Sup. Ct. 1951). See Rudnick v. Mayers, 387 Mich. 368, 196 N.W.2d 770 (1972).

5. From the 1920s to the mid-1950s, the hotel then known as the Terrace Gables was the "'center of social life'" in the Falmouth Heights section of Falmouth, Massachusetts:

> Guests were required to "dress" for dinner. There were no separate bars or cocktail lounges, although drinks were available in the dining room at tables and at a small bar on one side of the dining room. A piano player or trio occasionally provided music during the dinner hour. A range of entertainment was provided in the evenings. These activities, including cards, bingo, and movies, were generally concluded by 10 P.M.

In the 1980s, the facility, now called Brothers Four and operated by Cape Resort Hotels, Inc., is billed as "the largest entertainment complex on Cape Cod," boasting "Three Clubs under One Roof" (the "pub," the "show lounge," and the "disco"). Special events at the Brothers Four include "summer, Halloween and New Year's Eve parties, 'beat the clock' nights during which drinks become progressively more expensive, and audience participation shows such as a 'gong show,' 'creative goldfish eating' and pie-eating contests, and talent shows, for which the winners are awarded prizes."

The trial court held that, although the original hotel "was a nonconforming use under the original Falmouth zoning by-law" the changes made by Cape Resort constituted "such a 'change or substantial

D. Departures from the Zoning Ordinance 301

extension' of that [prior] use that the current operation of the hotel is no longer protected ... as a valid continuation of the 1926 nonconforming use."

Cape Resort was partially rescued, however, by the court's more liberal interpretation of another regulation, as the proprietors were permitted to continue to operate the show lounge. A previous owner (in 1961) had received a building permit to construct the frolic room, and since more than six years had passed during which time no objections had been raised to that improvement, the statute of limitations barred the challenge. Because the show lounge "is being used for the same purposes as it [sic] predecessor, the frolic room, was used, i.e., afternoon 'happy hours' and dancing, drinking, and entertainment in the evening. . . . Cape Resort meets the requirement that the space be 'used in accordance with the terms of the original building permit.'" Cape Resort Hotels v. Alcoholic Licensing Board of Falmouth, 431 N.E. 2d 213 (Mass. 1982).

6. Ordinances commonly restrict the extension, repair, and alteration of nonconforming structures. The provisions naturally vary a good deal. Thus the percentage of destruction beyond which rebuilding is prohibited averages 60 percent, but may be as high as 75 percent or as low as 20 percent. The base on which the percentage of damage is computed is perhaps the most difficult problem. In one case, the ordinance provided that structural alterations to a nonconforming building would be permitted only if the building were thereby made to conform. The operator of a nonconforming greenhouse tears down some buildings so as to build entirely new ones — which all agree are more efficient and more aesthetically pleasing than the existing ones. May he do this? Cole v. City of Battle Creek, 298 Mich. 98, 298 N.W. 466 (1941) (no — erection of additions not structural alteration of existing building). Consider the case of the owner of a nonconforming building who wishes to repair it following an order of the building inspector. See Weyls v. Zoning Board of Appeals, 161 Conn. 416, 290 A.2d 350 (1971) (winterizing a nonconforming summer cabin without changing exterior appearance).

An owner of a nonconforming factory installed a sprinkler system. Since the municipality had no public water supply, it was necessary to construct a 250,000 gallon water tank. A permit was secured, $85,000 spent, and the tank erected. Should an injunction directing the dismantling of the tank be granted? Borough of Rockleigh v. Astral Industries, Inc., 23 N.J. Super. 255, 92 A.2d 851 (Ch. 1952), rev'd, 29 N.J. Super. 154, 102 A.2d 84 (App. Div. 1953) ("no right can derive from the permit and ... no estoppel can arise from it").

Mary Chess, Inc. v. City of Glen Cove, 18 N.Y.2d 205, 219 N.E.2d 406, 273 N.Y.S.2d 46 (1966), in a result it forthrightly conceded as "anomalous if not absurd," dealt with a change of zone that made factory buildings nonconforming. Cf. De Forrest & Hotchkiss Co. v. Town of Madison, 152 Conn. 262, 205 A.2d 774 (1964).

The difference between the "parking" and "storage" of automobiles was the difference between winning and losing the appeal brought by Eberhard and Anita Pfitzner. The couple was not allowed to continue to "store" wrecked or severely damaged vehicles on the lot adjacent to their nonconforming auto body repair shop. However, vehicles with only minor damage that were awaiting repair could remain "parked" on the lot, for this practice would not amount to an expansion of the nonconforming use. St. Louis County v. Pfitzner, 657 S.W.2d 262 (Mo. App. 1983).

7. The city of Moscow, Idaho, adopted an ordinance making it unlawful to open or operate on First Street any new or additional place of business in which any pool, billiard, card, or dice game is played, or in which draft beer or liquor by the drink is sold. The ordinance states: "Any change of ownership of an existing business of the type herein defined shall be deemed a new or additional business." For the past ten years, the plaintiff has been operating a combined pool hall, card room, and retail beer parlor. He brings suit for a declaratory judgment to void the ordinance. What result? See O'Connor v. City of Moscow, 69 Idaho 37, 202 P.2d 401 (1949) (provision void — "use, not ownership, is the concern of this type of zoning"). How would it differ if the case arose in California after the *Clemons* decision?

8. In People v. Miller, 304 N.Y. 105, 109, 106 N.E.2d 34, 36 (1952), the defendant appealed on the ground that his preexisting use of the premises for harboring pigeons rendered a regulation unenforceable against him. Upholding the conviction, Judge Fuld said:

> [E]xisting non-conforming uses will be permitted to continue, despite the enactment of a prohibitory zoning ordinance, if, and only if, enforcement of the ordinance would, by rendering valueless substantial improvements or business built up over the years, cause serious financial harm to the property owner. This rule, with its emphasis upon pecuniary and economic loss, is clearly inapplicable to a purely incidental use of the property for recreational or amusement purposes only. Such an inconsequential use as that here involved — the harboring of pigeons as a hobby — does not amount to a "vested right," and "Depriving [defendant] of this pastime does not affect substantially [his] property rights . . . in the use of the premises, which are otherwise undisturbed and unimpaired."

Can you formulate an operational definition of "vested right"? The one consideration common to all retroactive pronouncements is the destruction of a major assumption of the affected person: namely, that he may order his affairs within the limits fixed by law at the time he acts. Where a person invests in land, what assumptions as to existing or future use of her property are disrupted by forbidding a use formerly

D. Departures from the Zoning Ordinance

in conformity with the zoning laws? Which are disrupted by a provision prohibiting extension of such a use? Does it make any difference if it is the mortgagee of the nonconforming property who is complaining? How do these enactments differ from the ordinary zoning ordinance "looking only to the future"? Is the British distinction between "existing use value" and "development value" of any utility in this situation? Is the holding in the *Miller* case a victory for city planners, since it eliminates a nonconforming use? Are the "rights" referred to in the nonconforming use cases synonymous with "rights" as used in the variance cases? (See discussion at page 343 infra.) See University Park v. Benners, 485 S.W.2d 773 (Tex. 1972).

The defendant's premises (about fifty-five acres) are used as a source of sand and gravel. In 1945, a zoning ordinance was adopted, placing the property in a residential zone but providing for the continuance of nonconforming uses. In 1953, the zoning ordinance was amended to provide that permits for removing sand and gravel "shall be for a period of not to exceed one year," and that structures and improvements should be removed at the termination of the approval period. What do you think Judge Fuld had in mind when, in dissenting from an opinion declaring the amendment unconstitutional, he wrote: "While the effect of the court's decision will not, of course, toll the death knell of zoning, it certainly ushers in a sad day for sound, wise and adequate municipal planning"? Town of Somers v. Camarco, 308 N.Y. 537, 541, 127 N.E.2d 327, 329 (1955).

When the fourteen-acre Hollow Pines farm was placed in an "open lands" zone as part of a comprehensive zoning ordinance in 1955, the automobile junkyard that occupied two acres of the farm became a nonconforming use. The owners continued to use the property as a junkyard, and the automobile corpses spread so that the junk now covers a substantial part of the farm. Does this constitute a violation of the ordinance? See Breed v. Town of Clay, 201 N.Y.S.2d 939 (Sup. Ct. 1959) ("no vested right . . . to use the entire farm for auto junking").

9. The city of Boston, the cradle of liberty, is the one major American city (apart from Washington, D.C.) in which zoning is not entrusted to the local legislature. Here, zoning is accomplished by direct act of the state legislature, rather than by the usual procedure of a state enabling act followed by local legislation. Mass. Acts of 1924, ch. 488. In 1941 the legislature amended the zoning law and provided: "No use of a building or premises, or part thereof, which does not conform to the [height, area, or use provisions] of this act, shall be continued after April 1, 1961." Acts of 1941, ch. 373, §8. This amended the legislation of 1932. Can you guess the contents of the earlier section thus amended? In some cases where planners have taken a rigid stand on nonconforming uses, the result has been strong political pressure to redistrict the area so as to "eliminate" the element of nonconformity. On this and

other practical problems, see Planning Advisory Service Rep. No. 280 (May 1972).

10. The Standard State Zoning Enabling Act made no attempt to protect nonconforming uses. That this omission was a calculation rather than an oversight seems clear from the explanatory note stating:

> It is recognized that there may arise local conditions of a peculiar character that make it necessary and desirable to deal with some isolated case by means of a retroactive provision affecting that case only. For this reason, it does not seem wise to debar the local legislative body from dealing with such a situation.

For more recent legislative activity, see the footnotes accompanying 6 Rohan, Zoning and Land Use Controls §41.01[4] (1986):

> Enabling acts of a number of states authorize limitations on the alteration, extension or change of nonconforming uses. Some statutes also provide for the restoration of nonconforming uses or structures or for termination after a specified period of discontinuance or after the buildings or structures have been destroyed or substantially damaged. Specific authority may be granted to terminate non-conforming uses through such methods as amortization and condemnation.

See Housing and Home Finance Agency, Comparative Digest of Municipal and County Zoning Enabling Statutes (1953); Wood, Zoning Ordinances Requiring the Termination of a Non-Conforming Use, 1973 Sw. Inst. on Plan., Zoning & Eminent Domain 65; Comment, Conforming the Nonconforming Use: Proposed Legislative Relief for a Zoning Dilemma, 33 S.W. L.J. 855 (1979).

In United Advertising Corp. v. Raritan, 11 N.J. 144, 93 A.2d 362 (1952), an ordinance providing for a two-year amortization period for the elimination of billboards in certain zones was held ultra vires; no holding issued, however, on the constitutionality of such an ordinance had the power been delegated to municipalities. As a result of this decision, the following was proposed as an amendment to the enabling act:

> Any nonconforming use or structure existing at the time of passage of an ordinance may be continued upon the lot or in the building so occupied. But reasonable provisions may be adopted for the gradual elimination of such nonconforming uses or structures, including but in no way limited to, reasonable provisions for:
>   a. amortization over a period of time;
>   b. elimination of nonconforming uses of unimproved land;
>   c. elimination of nonconformances upon termination of the rental period of the person in possession;

D. Departures from the Zoning Ordinance 305

      d. elimination of nonconforming uses located in structures adaptable to conforming uses;
      e. elimination of nonconformances upon discontinuance, abandonment or destruction.

Comment on the wisdom of this proposal. See Note, 27 Stan. L. Rev. 1325 (1975).

11. A zoning ordinance passed in 1922 placed the defendant's property, operated as a junkyard since 1916, in the residential district. The ordinance further provided that any nonconforming use was to be discontinued whenever the city council determined that a "reasonable time" had elapsed. In 1950, the council passed another ordinance giving the defendant approximately one year in which to discontinue his nonconforming use. The state supreme court, finding that the 1950 ordinance violated "the due process clauses of the state and federal Constitutions," denied the city injunctive relief. Akron v. Chapman, 160 Ohio St. 382, 116 N.E.2d 697 (1953). There is an interesting comment on this case in Grant v. Mayor of Baltimore, 212 Md. 301, 309, 129 A.2d 363, 366 n.2 (1957).

12. Consider the following provision in Mich. Comp. Laws Ann. §125.583a(3) (West 1986):

> [A] city or village may acquire by purchase, condemnation, or otherwise private property or an interest in private property for the removal of nonconforming uses and structures. . . . The elimination of nonconforming uses and structures in a zoned district as provided in this act is declared to be for a public purpose and for a public use.

In this connection, it might be well to examine the nature of the legislative weapons that have been employed for the purpose of zoning. The historical choice has been that of the police power. However, there were early attempts to zone entirely by eminent domain. In State ex rel. Twin City Building and Investment Co. v. Houghton, 144 Minn. 1, 19, 20, 176 N.W. 159, 162 (1920), the court said in upholding such an enabling law:

> . . . In large cities, where the lots for residences must necessarily be of the minimum size, especially where the man of small means must dwell, it is readily seen that if a home is built on such a lot, and thereafter three-story apartments extending to the lot line are constructed on both sides of the home, it becomes almost unlivable and its value utterly destroyed. Not only that, but the construction of such apartments or other like buildings in a territory of individual homes depreciates very much the values in the whole territory. The loss is not only to the owners, but to the state and municipality, by reason of the diminished taxes resulting from diminished values.

The absence of restrictions of use also gives occasion for extortion. The occurrences have been common in our large cities of unscrupulous and designing persons securing lots in desirable residential districts and then passing the word that an apartment or other objectionable structure is to be erected thereon. In order to protect themselves against heavy loss and bitter annoyance, the adjacent owners, or parties interested in property in the neighborhood, are forced to buy the lots so held at exorbitant price. The well-to-do may in this way be able by financial sacrifice to protect their homes against undesirable invasions. But when this occurs in territory occupied by people of modest homes and moderate means, where all they have is represented by the home, and that, perhaps, not free of mortgage lien, there is nothing to do but to submit to the loss and the injustice. There should be a lawful way to forestall such wrongs. Courts have often resorted to the rule, "Sic utere tuo ut alienum non laedas," in administering justice between property owners. Why should not the Legislature also make use of this rule?

Another reason is that giving the people a means to secure for that portion of a city, wherein they establish their homes, fit and harmonious surroundings, promotes contentment, induces further efforts to enhance the appearance and value of the home, fosters civic pride, and thus tends to produce a better type of citizen. It is time that courts recognized the aesthetic as a factor in life. . . . The act in question responds to this call and should be deemed to provide for a taking for a public use.

While exercise of the power of eminent domain for the purpose of zoning was thus held valid, it has not achieved any popularity. Under this statute Minneapolis zoned less than 1 percent of its area, St. Paul only 1.22 percent, and Duluth less than 0.05 percent.[51] As Bassett put it:

No effective zoning plan could be accomplished by the exercise of eminent domain. If there were some diminution of the full use of property, the city would need to pay the loss to the private owner. This would mean a laborious and expensive proceeding for almost every parcel of land. Since the city could not afford to pay this cost out of public funds, but would need to assess the awards on the property benefited, the cost of the process would be enormous. The restrictions would consist of public easements of a permanent nature. But as every living organism grows and changes, these easements would have to be changed from time to time by successive applications of condemnation. The method would be

---

51. In 1921, another enabling act that based zoning on the police power was passed. Minn. Laws 1921, ch. 217. Its validity was upheld in State ex rel. Beery v. Houghton, 164 Minn. 146, 204 N.W. 569 (1925). See also State ex rel. Sheffield v. City of Minneapolis, 235 Minn. 174, 50 N.W.2d 296 (1951); Naegele Outdoor Advertising Co. v. Minnetonka, 281 Minn. 492, 162 N.W.2d 206 (1968). For other instances imposing restrictions upon use of property by means of eminent domain, see Attorney General v. Williams, 174 Mass. 476, 55 N.E. 77 (1899); Kansas City v. Liebi, 298 Mo. 569, 252 S.W. 404 (1923). But see Pontiac Improvement Co. v. Board of Commissioners, 104 Ohio St. 447, 135 N.E. 635 (1922).

D. Departures from the Zoning Ordinance 307

clumsy and ineffective. Some states in their zoning enabling acts have tried to provide for the employment of eminent domain in whole or part, but the attempts have never been successful.

Zoning 27 (1936). Are there any reasons for utilizing public purchase as a device to eliminate nonconforming uses in view of this experience? If the legislative determination is to apply eminent domain in solving this planning problem, how would it fare constitutionally? See Goldblatt v. Town of Hempstead 368 U.S. 892 (1962) (memorandum opinion).

13. A county zoning ordinance forbids clay mining in the district, but the defendant's mining operation is permitted as a nonconforming use. The plaintiff, a greenhouse operator, sues for an injunction on the ground that the defendant's operations constitute a nuisance in that the dust, among other injurious effects, "spoiled his baby-breath plants growing in the open." What result? Robinson Brick Co. v. Luthi, 115 Colo. 106, 169 P.2d 171 (1946) (injunction denied — nominal damages ($10) awarded); see Willis, The Elimination of Non-conforming Uses, 1951 Wis. L. Rev. 685; Noel, Retroactive Zoning and Nuisances, 41 Colum. L. Rev. 457 (1941).

14. Sound physical planning may require the removal of some nonconforming structures. The economist may well argue that this will represent a loss not only to the individual owner but to the community as a whole. British planners have evolved a theory to confound this argument. Planning, they claim, does not destroy land values; it merely redistributes them or "shifts" them. If development is prohibited on one piece of land it will rise up triumphant on another. (Some such reasoning was presumably a premise for the *Euclid* decision — that the industrial development prohibited on the company's land would materialize elsewhere.) A second prong in this defense of planning is the assumption that the loss in value to the nonconforming owner is offset by increases in value to the surrounding properties.

The theory of "shifting value" appeals to some, since it parallels the findings of the natural sciences. Cf. Northrop, The Meeting of East and West 66-72 (1946). (You will recall the strange aberrations that befell Henry Adams' thought when the law of thermodynamics swam into his ken). It postulates a law of conservation of land value similar to the physical law of conservation of energy — that matter can be neither created nor destroyed. But what proof is there that development prohibited on one site will nevertheless erupt automatically on another? There is the further consideration that, even if planning merely causes a shift in land values, these shifts may jump the boundaries of local planning areas. Thus the elimination of nonconforming uses in one area may bring increased land value — but only in another. And does not the individual landowner deserve individual treatment irrespective of the overall sum of land values? For a practical application of the concept of shifting values, see Hagman, Zoning by Special Assessment Financed Eminent Domain (ZSAFED), 28 U. Fla. L. Rev. 655 (1976).

If, owing to such economic arguments and to the American tradition of nonretroactive regulation, the community decides to compensate for the elimination of nonconforming uses, either by outright payment from the public treasury or by permitting the landowner to amortize his capital investment over some period of time, problems still remain. Compensation to the private property owner does not obviate the loss to the community; it merely transfers it from the individual owner to the general taxpayer. Moreover, what is the effect of this elimination of nonconforming use on the capital venturer? Having once discovered the caprice of the law, will he not be far more reluctant to risk his capital?

Planners advocate the elimination of nonconforming uses but do not always consider what will occur subsequently. If the building is readily adaptable to a conforming use, there may be no problem. If, however, it has no alternative use within the prescriptions of the zoning law, the result may be to "sterilize" the land. Most nonconforming uses occur in the older and more depressed neighborhoods, and these are precisely the areas least attractive to real estate investors. The owner of the land may find herself unable to finance the redevelopment of her land, and the community may find itself with parcels of land which are unused and unproductive of tax revenue.

How would you reply to these arguments?

Notes on Retroactivity and Building Permits

1. In Queenside Hills Realty Co. v. Saxl, 328 U.S. 80 (1946), the appellant had operated a lodging house since 1940. It was constructed in compliance with all existing laws, but in 1944 New York amended its Multiple Dwelling Law, and provided that lodging houses "of non-fireproof construction existing prior to the enactment of this subdivision" should comply with new requirements. These included the installation of an automatic wet pipe sprinkler system. The court held that "in no case does the owner of property acquire immunity against exercise of the police power because he constructed it in full compliance with the existing laws." Id. at 83. Cf. O'Daniel v. Barach, 1 Ill. App. 2d 157, 116 N.E.2d 912 (1954). How do you explain the different attitude toward an old-law tenement building and a nonconforming gas station?

The question of retroactive operation of a zoning ordinance has also been litigated in connection with buildings in process of construction when the ordinance is passed. In these cases the courts usually sustain the revocation of a building permit issued before the enactment of a

D. Departures from the Zoning Ordinance 309

zoning ordinance, provided there has been no "material" reliance on the permit. Brett v. Building Commissioner of Brookline, 250 Mass. 73, 145 N.E. 269 (1924), is the classic case.

2. A developer had purchased land in the Nukolii area of the Hawaiian island of Kauai, and had successfully sought amendments to both the county general plan and the comprehensive zoning code to change the zoning designation from "open space/agriculture" to "resort." When the developer began building the resort, the Committee to Save Nukolii circulated a petition calling for repeal of the rezoning and eventually collected enough signatures to place a referendum question on the 1980 general election ballot. The committee finally won voter approval — by a 2 to 1 margin — to repeal the zoning ordinance. In the interim, however, the developer, not having been required by the courts to halt construction, had completed 150 condominium units (priced at $185,000 each) and had begun work on a 350-room hotel. A total of $50 million had been sunk into the project.

Kauai County filed a lawsuit to determine the rights of the parties involved. The circuit court ruled that, because the zoning ordinance had not been suspended, the building permits had been validly issued. The developer had acquired "vested rights" by the time of the election, and the county was equitably estopped from prohibiting the developer from completing the project.

The Hawaii Supreme Court reversed, ruling that the developer had acquired "vested rights" only if final discretionary action on the project had taken place before the referendum petition was certified. The court then reasoned that because the referendum itself constituted a development approval, the vesting of rights had not occurred. The court restrained further construction and instructed the trial court to order the building permits revoked. County of Kauai v. Pacific Standard Life Insurance Co., 65 Haw. 318, 653 P.2d 766 (1982), appeal dismissed sub nom. Pacific Standard Life Insurance Co. v. Committee to Save Nukolii, 460 U.S. 1077 (1983).

In February 1984 a special election, $50,000 of the cost of which was paid for by the resort developer, was held on Kauai to decide whether to allow completion of the Nukolii project. This time the voters chose to restore resort zoning to the development site, allowing the developer to complete construction of the project. N.Y. Times, Feb. 6, 1984.

3. The Department of Buildings erroneously interpreted a zoning map outlining the boundaries of a Special Park Improvement District (P.I.D.) — within which new buildings are limited to the lesser of nineteen stories or 210 feet — and granted a building permit to Parkview Associates on November 21, 1985. Nearly eight months later, after having been alerted by an Upper East Side community group that the structure appeared to be too tall, the Department issued a stop

The Parkview Associates Building towering over its neighbors. Wide World Photos.

D. Departures from the Zoning Ordinance

order for construction over nineteen stories. Recognizing their error, officials then partially revoked the building permit.

Parkview, having lost before the Board of Standards and Appeals, took its case to the courts. In Parkview Associates v. City of New York, 71 N.Y.2d 274, 519 N.E.2d 1372 (1988), a unanimous Court of Appeals disposed of the landowner's claim "that its reliance on the permit caused substantial and irreparable harm requiring that the City be estopped from revoking the permit":

> Insofar as estoppel is not available to preclude a municipality from enforcing the provisions of its zoning laws and the mistaken or erroneous issuance of a permit does not estop a municipality from correcting errors, even where there are harsh results, the City should not be estopped here from revoking that portion of the building permit which violated the long-standing zoning limits imposed by the applicable P.I.D. resolution. Even if there was municipal error in one map and in the mistaken administrative issuance of the original permit, those factors would be completely outweighed in this case by the doctrine that reasonable diligence would have readily uncovered for a good-faith inquirer the existence of the unequivocal limitations . . . in the original metes and bounds description of the enabling legislation, and that this boundary has never been changed by the Board of Estimate. The policy reasons which foreclose estoppel against a governmental entity in all but the rarest cases thus have irrefutable cogency in this case.

As a result, Parkview has been left with a partially completed thirty-one-story apartment building, of which twelve floors are "illegal." On the day the opinion was released, Buildings Commissioner Charles Smith "ordered the architects to modify the building: 'They are required to file engineering documents on how they plan to remove the top 12 stories and how they are going to protect the adjacent buildings while the demolition is going on.'" Washington Post, Feb. 10, 1988. On October 3, the Supreme Court dismissed Parkview's appeal and denied certiorari. 109 S. Ct. 30 (1988). As you read the remainder of this chapter, consider whether there are any judicial or administrative paths to relief left for Parkview.

■ TOWN AND COUNTRY PLANNING ACT OF 1971
ch. 78, §94 (as amended by The Local Government and Planning (Amendment) Act of 1981)

(1) For the purposes of this Part of this Act, a use of land is established if —
    (a) it was begun before the beginning of 1964 without planning

permission in that behalf and has continued since the end of 1963; or

(b) it was begun before the beginning of 1964 under a planning permission in that behalf granted subject to conditions or limitations, which either have never been complied with or have not been complied with since the end of 1963; or

(c) it was begun after the end of 1963 as the result of a change of use not requiring planning permission and there has been, since the end of 1963, no change of use requiring planning permission.

(2) Where a person having an interest in land claims that a particular use of it has become established, he may apply to the local planning authority for a certificate (in this Act referred to as an "established use certificate") to that effect.[52]

Provided that no such application may be made in respect of the use of land as a single dwelling-house, or of any use not subsisting at the time of the application. . . .

(4) On an application to them under this section, the local planning authority shall, if and so far as they are satisfied that the applicant's claim is made out, grant to him an established use certificate accordingly. . . .

(7) An established use certificate shall, as respects any matters stated therein, be conclusive for the purposes of an appeal to the Secretary of State, against an enforcement notice a copy of which has been served in respect of any land to which the certificate relates, but only where the copy of the notice is served after the date of the application on which the certificate was granted.

(8) If any person, for the purpose of procuring a particular decision on an application (whether by himself or another) for an established use certificate or on an appeal arising out of such an application, —

(a) knowingly or recklessly makes a statement which is false in a material particular; or

(b) with intent to deceive, produces, furnishes, sends or otherwise makes use of any document which is false in a material particular; or

(c) with intent to deceive, withholds any material information,

he shall be guilty of an offence and liable on summary conviction to a fine not exceeding £400 or, on conviction on indictment, to imprisonment for a term not exceeding two years or a fine, or both.[53]

---

52. Section 87 provides that an established use certificate serves as conclusive evidence against the issuance of an enforcement notice. — EDS.

53. The following conversation may be supposed to have taken place between S, a solicitor, and C, his client.

C. I got your letter saying there was a hitch over the sale. What has gone wrong?

S. The solicitors who are acting for Jones, your purchaser, have sent me a letter to say that your planning permission is to be revoked.

D. Departures from the Zoning Ordinance 313

2. Amendments: Legislating (or Adjudicating?) Small-Scale Changes

■ KUEHNE v. TOWN COUNCIL OF EAST HARTFORD
136 Conn. 452, 72 A.2d 474 (1950)

MALTBIE, Chief Justice. The plaintiffs, certain property owners, appealed to the Court of Common Pleas from the granting by the defendant of an application for a change in the zoning of a piece of property owned by Wilfred H. Langlois from an A residence to an A

C. Well, it's the first I've heard of it.
S. Apparently what has happened is this: the solicitors, on getting the draft contract of sale, very properly made some searches before contract. They sent the usual form to the county council, and about a week later they got a letter from the clerk of the county council, a copy of which has been sent to me.
C. Does this letter say why they are going to revoke my permission? I've had it since 1947 and no one has ever mentioned this possibility before.
S. The letter is in rather guarded terms, but what it says briefly is that, at their next meeting, the County Planning Committee will be asked to revoke your permission to use the building as a fish and chip saloon. The grounds are that this use would be detrimental to the amenities of this good class residential area.
C. In these days of rationed cooking fat, even good class residents patronize fish and chip shops! Anyway, we're in the clear. They have not made the order yet and you can push the sale through before they do.
S. Yes, but only if I can persuade the purchaser's solicitors that they have nothing to lose by so doing. . . .
C. You don't think then that there's much hope of pushing the sale through before the meeting of the planning committee.
S. A quick sale is not the key to the situation. The point is, that a revocation order can only be made *before* the change of use to a fish and chip shop takes place. I've found out that the County Planning Committee doesn't meet for eight days.
C. No good, I'm afraid. Although the structural alterations are finished, and I've passed my order for equipment to Jones, the manufacturers cannot promise delivery till next month. . . .
C. If Jones and I could have three weeks we could get the business started.
S. You can rely on at least four weeks before the Minister confirms the order. The point is whether the revocation order operates from the date it is made by the county council or not. If it does, our only hope is to put your case to the planning authority and to the Minister, and if we fail then to claim compensation.
C. Compensation will be no good, they had better buy the building and land off me.
S. Assuming, which I suppose is possible, that there isn't any other reasonable beneficial use for this narrow strip of land or for your shelter, we can force a purchase, besides claiming for abortive expenditure and loss directly due to the revocation. The fact, too, that there is no other beneficial use will be a useful ground of objection to the revocation.
C. Jones and a lot of other people who like fish and chips in that area would prefer to see you put salt on the tail of the planning authority!
S. Well, I shall do my best. We may succeed in persuading the planning authority or the Minister to drop the whole thing of course. If only we could effect our change of use *before* the order is made no one could touch us. I must get down to it and see if there is nothing I can put before the county council on this point. If I persuade them that both legally and in equity it is too late to stop us, we'll all be saved a lot of

business zone. The trial court dismissed the appeal and the plaintiffs have appealed. . . .

Main Street in East Hartford runs substantially north and south. The petitioner before the town council, Langlois, owned a piece of land on the east side of it which he had been using for growing fruit and vegetables, and he has had upon it a greenhouse and a roadside stand for the sale of products of the land. The premises, ever since zoning was established in East Hartford in 1927, had been in an A residence district. Langlois made an application to the town council to change to an A business district a portion of the tract fronting on Main Street for about 500 feet and extending to a depth of 150 feet. He intended, if the application was granted, to erect upon the tract a building containing six or eight stores, apparently in the nature of retail stores and small business establishments calculated to serve the needs of residents in the vicinity. Starting at a business district to the north and extending for almost three miles to the town boundary on the south, the land along Main Street and extending to a considerable depth on each side of it has been, ever since zoning was established in the town, in an A residence district, with certain exceptions hereinafter described. Seven hundred feet north of the Langlois property is a small business district lying on both sides of Main Street; the land on the east side is used for a fruit and vegetable stand, a milk bar and a garage and gas station; and the land on the west side, with an area a little larger than the Langlois tract in question, is now unoccupied. About 500 feet south of the Langlois property is another small business district in which is located a grill and restaurant, a drugstore, a cleaning and dyeing business and a large grocery and meat market. Formerly the land about the tract in question was used quite largely for agricultural purposes, but within the last few years a large residential community, comprising some one thousand houses, has grown up in the vicinity.

The application to the town council was based upon the claim that residents in the vicinity need the stores and services which could be located in the building Langlois proposed to erect. There was, for example, a petition filed with the council in support of the application signed by fifty-one of those residents which asked it to allow such a change as might be necessary to permit for their benefit a shopping center on the property. None of the signers, however, owned property on Main Street or in the immediate vicinity of the Langlois property. On the other hand, the application was opposed by the owner of

---

trouble.

C. Well, good luck to you. You can drop me a line later to say how things are getting on.

1950 J. Plan. L. 26.

Section 41 of the Town and Country Planning Act, 1971, makes it unlikely this conversation would take place today. — Eds.

D. Departures from the Zoning Ordinance 315

property directly opposite the tract in question and by the owners of the two properties fronting on Main Street immediately south of the Langlois land.

The council voted that the application "be granted for the general welfare and the good of the town in that section." In Bartram v. Zoning Commission, 136 Conn. 89, 68 A.2d 308, we recently had before us an appeal from the granting by a zoning commission of an application to change a lot in Bridgeport even smaller than the tract here in question from a residence to a business zone, and we sustained the action of the commission. We said:

> A limitation upon the powers of zoning authorities which has been in effect ever since zoning statutes were made applicable generally to municipalities in the state is that the regulations they adopt must be made "in accordance with a comprehensive plan." Public Acts, 1925, c. 242, §3, Rev. 1949, §837. . . . Action by a zoning authority which gives to a single lot or a small area privileges which are not extended to other land in the vicinity is in general against sound public policy and obnoxious to the law. It can be justified only when it is done in furtherance of a general plan properly adopted for and designed to serve the best interests of the community as a whole. The vice of spot zoning lies in the fact that it singles out for special treatment a lot or a small area in a way that does not further such a plan. Where, however, in pursuance of it, a zoning commission takes such action, its decision can be assailed only on the ground that it abused the discretion vested in it by law. To permit business in a small area within a residence zone may fall within the scope of such a plan, and to do so, unless it amounts to unreasonable or arbitrary action, is not unlawful.

It appeared in that case that the change was granted by the commission in pursuance of a policy to encourage decentralization of business in the city and to that end to permit neighborhood stores in outlying districts. It is true that we said in that opinion, 136 Conn. at page 94, 68 A.2d at page 311, that if the commission decided,

> on facts affording a sufficient basis and in the exercise of a proper discretion, that it would serve the best interests of the community as a whole to permit a use of a single lot or small area in a different way than was allowed in surrounding territory, it would not be guilty of spot zoning in any sense obnoxious to the law.

We meant by that statement to emphasize the fact that the controlling test must be, not the benefit to a particular individual or group of individuals, but the good of the community as a whole, and we did not mean in any way to derogate from our previous statement that any such change can only be made if it falls within the requirements of a comprehensive plan for the use and development of property in the municipality or a large part of it.

In the case before us it is obvious that the council looked no further than the benefit which might accrue to Langlois and those who resided in the vicinity of his property, and that they gave no consideration to the larger question as to the effect the change would have upon the general plan of zoning in the community. In fact, the controlling consideration seems to have been that Langlois intended to go ahead at once with his building rather than any consideration of the suitability of the particular lot for business uses, because there is no suggestion in the record that the council considered the fact that only some 700 feet away was a tract of land already zoned for business which, as appears from the zoning map in evidence, was more easily accessible to most of the signers of the petition than was the Langlois land.

In Strain v. Mims, 123 Conn. 275, 287, 193 A. 754, 759, we said "One of the essential purposes of zoning regulations is to stabilize property uses." In this case it is significant that the change was opposed by the owners of three properties so situated as to be most affected by it, while those who supported it were the owner of the tract and residents who did not live in its immediate vicinity. It should also be noted that the petition they signed contained a provision that it should not be construed as supporting permission for the use of the premises as a liquor outlet, but at the hearing before the council the attorney for Langlois in effect conceded that the zoning regulations permitted such a use in an A business district; and if that is so and the change were granted, it is quite possible that the premises would be sooner or later converted to such a use.

The action of the town council in this case was not in furtherance of any general plan of zoning in the community and cannot be sustained. . . .

There is error, the judgment is set aside and the case is remanded to be proceeded with according to law.[54]

---

54. For interesting developments in the Connecticut law see Eden v. Zoning Commission of Bloomfield, 139 Conn. 59, 89 A.2d 746 (1952) (change of residence to business to establish an ice-cream bar with fifty-one stools; expert city planner had prepared comprehensive plan); Hills v. Zoning Commission of Newington, 139 Conn. 603, 96 A.2d 212 (1953) (extending industrial zone; "mere lack of a town plan cannot have the effect of preventing a change of zone"); Kutcher v. Town Planning Commission of Manchester, 138 Conn. 705, 88 A.2d 538 (1952) (creation of small industrial zone in a town where all land is not otherwise zoned was incorporated in a rural residence zone). An apparent reversal of the trend is pointed out in the dissenting opinion in Town of Lebanon v. Woods, 153 Conn. 182, 215 A.2d 112 (1965). A more recent trend upholding the decision of the initial administrator is reflected in First Hartford Realty v. Planning and Zoning Commn. of Hartford, 165 Conn. 470, 338 A.2d 490 (1973) (change from business to residence), and Lathrop v. Planning and Zoning Commn. of Trumbull, 164 Conn. 215, 319 A.2d 376 (1973) (change from residential to commercial use). — Eds.

D. Departures from the Zoning Ordinance

Under the title, "A Thinking Machine Can Think Like a Judge, 99 Percent of the Time," the New York Times, July 15, 1979, went on to report that "computers are taking degrees in the law." A study for the American Bar Association and the National Science Foundation programmed a computer with more than 1,200 zoning amendment appeals cases recorded by the supreme courts of six states; the study was able to reduce the relevant considerations to 204 variables. An earlier study focusing on the state of Connecticut, in which the *Bartram* and the *Kuehne* cases were decided, offered the following conclusions:

■ HAAR, SAWYER, AND CUMMINGS, COMPUTER POWER AND LEGAL REASONING: A CASE STUDY OF JUDICIAL DECISION PREDICTION IN ZONING AMENDMENT CASES
1977 Am. B. Found. J. 651, 742-744

In the final analysis, the statistical research seems to have managed to identify and, roughly, to quantify crucial issues in the zoning amendment litigation in Connecticut. One of the important questions of this study was whether the articulated rule of decision (found in the court opinions) corresponded to the unarticulated rule of decision (the relationship of the actual facts to the outcome). While verifying many traditional rules, we found important discrepancies. The tentative and confused use of the concept of the "comprehensive plan" remained elusive even when examined by a molecular approach, which did not employ general principles or statements or expound on legal doctrines but which, using the information gleaned by traditional legal analysis, isolated factors important to outcome and weighted them according to the court's analyses.

How does this "computerized restatement" of the law differ from a traditional legal analysis? Both identify the crucial issues in the zoning amendment litigation in Connecticut. The computer restatement also quantifies the effect of the various factors on the outcome of the decisions and, in so doing, assigns them relative weights. The legal analysis is drawn from the court's explanation of its reasoning process; the computer-aided statistical analysis is drawn from a comparison of the facts of the case with its outcome. There is a large residue of legal analysis in the statistical model, nevertheless, because all the "facts" in the latter analysis (with the exception of the census data) were gleaned from the court's opinions by the conventional legal approach to case analysis, that is, were derived from the court's interpretation of the evidence.

Summary Table

	Value[b]
Constant[a]	.57
Variables:	
Zoning authority denies zone change (Var. 012)	−.55
Court of common pleas approves zone change (Var. 011)	.16
Not a departure from large uniform blocks (from Scale 8)	.62
Streets inadequate (from Scale 7)	−.39
Adverse impact on value of adjacent lots (from Scale 6)	−.35
Physical hazard created (from Scale 7)	−.30
Area relatively large (from Scale 11)	.25
Completion of necessary improvements unlikely (from Scale 7)	−.24
Character of area improving (from Scale 6)	−.23
Character of area deteriorating (from Scale 10)	.13
Other municipal services adequate (from Scale 10)	.10
Retention of control (from Scale 4)	.07
Proposed use aesthetically compatible (from Scales 5 & 8)	.06[c]
Common zoning technique (from Scale 11)	.06
Specific, detailed limits in zoning ordinances (from Scale 4)	.05
More flexible land-use controls (from Scale 4)	.04
Adequate buffer (from Scale 4)	.02
Proposed use needed in neighborhood (from Scale 10)	.02
Existing zoning line a natural boundary (from Scale 8)	−.02

[a] The constant term is the intercept a of the regression equation $y = a + b_1x_1 + b_2x_2 + \ldots b_nx_n$. For simplicity, the lawyer can consider it the initial probability of approval when no other information is known; all other variables change the probability from this starting point.

[b] The sum of all relevant decision variables determines the prediction. A sum close to one predicts approval of the zone change by the court; a net value close to zero implies denial.

[c] From this point in the Summary Table the variables add only marginally to the predictive capability of the model.

The degree of court deference to the administrative process has been quantified — the decision tree indicates the overwhelming significance given to the decision of the initial trier, the zoning agency. The nature of the plaintiff also is highly significant. Other key factors are size of the subject parcel, capacity of municipal services to support the proposed use, presence of hazardous conditions, and economic impact on adjacent lots. . . .

In the zoning amendment cases, the concept of change "in accordance with a comprehensive plan" lacks the specificity of a workable legal doctrine; like substantive due process, equal protection, and police power, its bounds can be circumscribed only by references to specific factual circumstances where its limits have been tested by the parties and the court has rendered a verdict. The doctrine sets the tone, but it provides no operational guidelines; often it merely sweeps up loose, perhaps troubling, facts after the conclusion has been reached in a case. To get the broom to sweep in the client's direction, however, the lawyer needs to focus on the specific factors given and refined by the computer.

The lawyer must concentrate on preparing his client's case within the constraints of limited time and money. Computer analysis of the cases can help make the decisions of the court more predictable. In preparing his case, the lawyer must try to create a record that establishes that the proposed development either avoids or creates the problems designated as crucial in the Summary Table. The computer analysis has clarified the issues that have sufficient impact to convince the court to overturn the initial decision of the zoning authority. This clear focus can save research and preparation, for the lawyer then knows where to direct his energies and available resources.

In advising his client, the lawyer can use such research as a concrete basis for discussing the risks and costs of litigation and as a more objective standard against which to review the strengths and weaknesses of the case.

■ MacDONALD v. BOARD OF COMMISSIONERS
238 Md. 549, 210 A.2d 325 (1965)

OPPENHEIMER, J. Adjacent property owners appeal from an order of the Circuit Court for Prince George's County affirming a zoning action of the Board of County Commissioners for Prince George's County, sitting as a District Council for the Prince George's portion of the Maryland-Washington Regional District (the Council). The Council had approved applications of the Isle of Thye Land Company, one of the appellees (the Land Company), to reclassify three tracts of land all zoned R-R (Rural Residential). Two tracts of approximately nine and three acres respectively were rezoned to C-2 (General Commercial) and the third, of about 29 acres, to R-H (Multiple Family, High Rise Residential).

The three tracts are part of a larger area of 655 acres owned by the Land Company, called Tantallon on the Potomac, located in the southwestern portion of the County on Swan Creek, which empties into the Potomac. The Woodrow Wilson Bridge and the Capital Beltway are four or five miles to the north. Fort Washington National Park, a 341 acre reservation is adjacent to the area on the south and Mount Vernon is across the Potomac River to the west. . . .

The technical staff of the Planning Commission recommended denial of all three applications. Its amended report stated, in part:

> The staff, in its review of this application, concludes that the granting of any zone on this property other than the existing R-R Zone, would be spot zoning. The development which has occurred in the area has been that of single family dwellings on larger than minimum lot size standards, and, the changes which have occurred in this area, the Tantallon community included, are a continuation and solidification of this pattern. . . .

The Planning Board recommended denial of the R-H rezoning for the reasons given by its technical staff. . . .

At the hearing before the Council, the expert witnesses of the Land Company offered voluminous and plausible testimony as to the attractive nature of the plans for the area which it owns. It claimed but offered no evidence to support a mistake in the Master Zoning Map. It relied, instead, upon claimed substantial changes in the area since the adoption of the comprehensive zoning map. The nature of the alleged changes will be considered hereafter. The Chief Engineer of the Planning Commission elaborated upon the reports of the technical staff, and testified that the changes that had occurred in the area of the Land Company's property were oriented towards low density, single family development. Neighboring and adjacent property owners, including the appellants, presented testimony in opposition to the reclassifications, with letters from other protestants, including Secretary of the Interior Udall.

The Council, one of the Commissioners dissenting, approved all three of the Land Company's applications for rezoning. The formal notice of the Council gave no reasons for its decision. The only statement in the nature of reasons is contained in what appears to be a press release on behalf of the Council. This release, apart from some extraneous remarks, contained the following statements:

> Commissioner Brooke, in making his motion, pointed out that the several proposed 20-story apartments would be 3400 feet back from the river, "in a natural valley which would keep them screened from view from the river and the Virginia shore."
> He also noted expanded highway development in the general area

D. Departures from the Zoning Ordinance

and that neither the Board of Education nor the National Capital Planning Commission opposed the planned community. . . .

It was also stated that the Chairman of the Council, who votes only in case of tie, had declared himself in sympathy with the zoning request. Commissioner Gladys Spellman, who dissented, in a separate announcement, said in part:

> The changes which have taken place in the area are not sufficient to warrant rezoning from a low density, single family category. . . . No need has been established for high density apartments in the middle of an area of extremely low density, other than that of remunerative return for the applicant. . . . No proof of error in the original zoning was presented.
>
> The Isle of Thye Land Company plans high rise apartments on approximately 29 acres, and accordingly requests a change to R-H zoning. However, the use of this zone category in a low-density setting is *totally at variance* with the *purpose* of R-H zoning as set forth in the text of the classification. . . . We must recognize that the District Council is concerned for the County as a whole and not merely 650 acres of the county. It is certainly not reasonable to assume that because a community is well-planned and well-balanced, it may be set down at any point in the County without doing violence to the surrounding areas. Planning must extend beyond the borders of individual communities and encompass the larger areas of the County in order that communities may complement each other rather than inflict harm upon one another.

There was a hearing on the Petition for Review of the Council's order before Judge Loveless. In his opinion affirming the order, the Judge pointed out that the Land Company had not contended there had been a mistake in the original zoning, and that the court had no alternative other than to say that no mistake had been shown. Judge Loveless referred to the 14 items relied upon by the Land Company as changes in the area since the original zoning was made and held they were sufficient evidence to justify a reclassification if the Council, in its legislative discretion, so decided. He held, further, that the issues were fairly debatable, and that the Board's action in approving the applications was not arbitrary or capricious. We disagree in respect of the Board's order granting the application to rezone the 29 acres for high-rise apartments.

We have repeatedly held that there is a strong presumption of the correctness of original zoning, and that to sustain a piecemeal change therefrom, there must be strong evidence of mistake in the original zoning or else of a substantial change in conditions. The Land Company contends that here comprehensive rezoning is involved, because of the extent of its entire acreage and the nature of its plans for the development of that acreage. However, as Commissioner Spellman points

Typical Spot-Zoning Cases

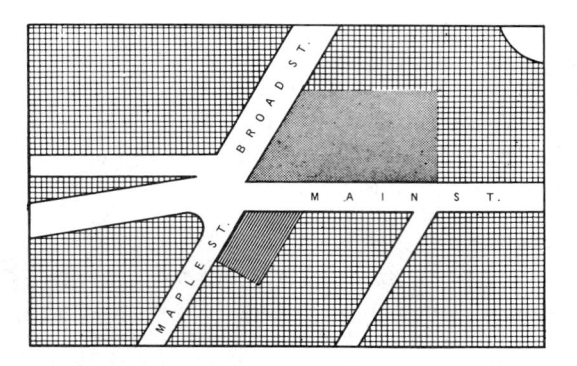

Chouinard v. Zoning Commission
of East Hartford,
139 Conn. 728, 97A.2d 562 (1953)

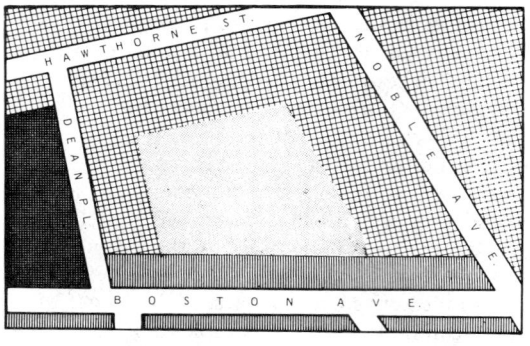

Levinsky v. Zoning Commission
of Bridgeport, 144 Conn. 117,
127 A.2d 822 (1956)

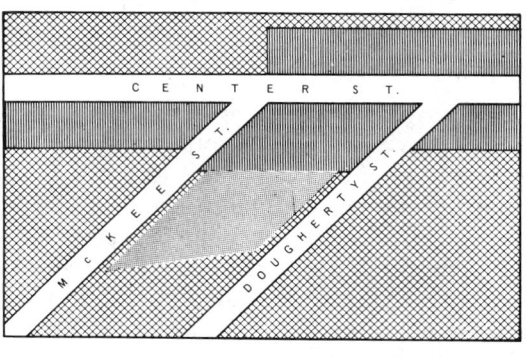

Miller v. Town Planning Commission
of Manchester, 142 Conn. 265,
113 A.2d 504 (1955)

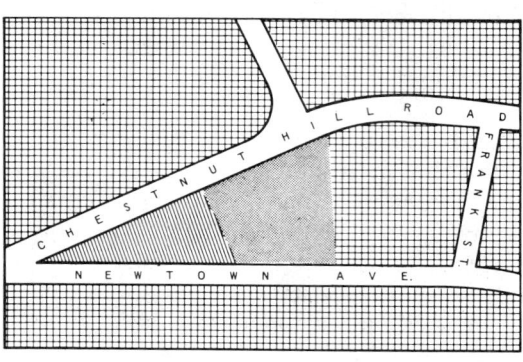

Anderson v. Zoning Commission
of Norwalk, 157 Conn. 285,
253 A.2d 16 (1968)

RESIDENTIAL   INDUSTRIAL   COMMERCIAL   PROPOSED COMM.

D. Departures from the Zoning Ordinance 323

out in her dissent from the Council's order, it is not the proposed treatment of a particular tract within the broad territory encompassed by the original zoning plan which governs; the impingement of the proposed rezoning upon the general plan is the criterion. We hold that, in this case, it is proposed piecemeal rezoning which is involved and that the strong presumption of the correctness of the original comprehensive zoning prevails.

The majority of the Council, in effect, gave no reasons for its order. The alleged changes of conditions in the immediate area adduced by the Land Company to support their application to rezone the 29 acres for high-rise apartments, in our opinion, do not constitute evidence sufficient to make the facts fairly debatable. A number of these changes have taken place, or are contemplated, within the Tantallon tract itself. The building of a golf course, the dredging of Swan Creek, the reservation of a school site within the tract, and the authorization of public utility services for the Tantallon enterprise are as consistent with increased rural residential development as they are with the building of high-rise apartments. The characterization by the appellants of these alleged changes as "bootstrap" arguments, in our opinion, is appropriate. The report of the technical staff of the Planning Commission states that the development which has occurred within the area, including the Tantallon tract, has been a continuation and solidification of the single family dwelling pattern, with lots larger than the minimum standard, and this statement was not contradicted. The road improvements referred to by the Land Company do not change the character of the neighborhood; as the technical staff pointed out, "[t]he character of the surrounding area is reflected in the road network which consists of generally narrow, winding two-lane pavements designed to serve traffic volumes generated by low density, large lot development." The completion of the Woodrow Wilson Bridge and Anacostia Freeway listed as additional changes presumably were envisaged in the comprehensive zoning plan, adopted by the legislative body only a little less than five years before the Land Company's application. In any event, the Bridge and Freeway are some miles away.

The Planning Board, as well as its technical staff, recommended that the applications for the high-rise apartment rezoning be denied. The majority of the Council refused to accept the Board's recommendations, without substantive evidence to support its actions. In similar circumstances, although on varying facts, we have held that an order of the lower court affirming the Board's action must be reversed.

The Land Company does not contend that denial of the application would preclude the use of its property for any purpose to which it is reasonably adapted. On the contrary, it admitted it would be practical, although from its point of view not as satisfactory, to continue the development of Tantallon without high-rise apartments. The developer's desire to make additional profits is a legitimate motive, but not sufficient to justify a rezoning.

BARNES, J. (dissenting)....

[T]he majority's statement that the population boom, together with the new highways and bridges some miles away "presumably were envisaged in the comprehensive plan," does not seem justified to me. There is no evidence that they were so envisaged and the probabilities are strong that they were not. The situation in Prince George's County is too volatile to attribute such prophetic powers to those who prepared the "comprehensive" plan. It should be kept in mind that the Tantallon area was virgin territory and, with most of such territory in this area, was all put in the R-R area in order to cover this area with this general type of zoning restriction. The plan was "comprehensive" only in that it covered all areas in the County. There have been no detailed plans in this area promulgated by the County; the only detailed plan is the October 1961 development plan of Tantallon prepared by Mr. Robinson. Then too, what physical changes occurring after the promulgation of the "comprehensive" plan in 1957 by the County might not be said to have been "presumably envisaged" in that plan and thus be made to disappear, as it were, from consideration as subsequent changes? There is far too much room here for the operation of subjective considerations....

Commissioner Gladys Spellman, the single Councilman who failed to concur in the granting of the R-H rezoning request, based her dissent largely on the basis of the presumed effect of the proposed apartments on the Potomac shoreline and skyline, and the deleterious effect upon the view from Mount Vernon and Fort Washington. Secretary of the Interior Udall also expressed these sentiments in a letter to the Council which prophesied that the apartments might become "dominant." The appellant MacDonald, a historian by profession, voiced his fear that the apartments would be "shockingly visible." But opposed to these opinions was an overwhelming mass of evidence to the effect that Secretary Udall's fears had little chance of materializing. It was testified that the proposed luxury apartments would be some 3400 feet back from the Potomac, on the south side of Swan Creek, approximately in the center of the 650-acre parcel of land. Indeed Councilman Sutphin stated he would have opposed R-H rezoning had they not been. The apartments would be screened from view by trees, already in place, 60 feet in height, surrounded by a high ridge on the south, southwest, and southeast....

The majority states, in effect, that rezoning can only be sustained when there is "strong evidence of mistake" in the original zoning or where there is "a substantial change in conditions" in the neighborhood. This "mistake-change in conditions" rule came into the Maryland law by way of dicta of our predecessors and in a rather oblique way.... It was entirely judicially conceived and delivered. It had no legislative assistance. It has had a rapid and, to my mind, unhealthy growth in the Maryland law. The formulae have become talismanic phrases now applied with Draconian severity to the rezoning efforts of the local legislative bodies, with unfortunate results. In my opinion, the time to re-examine the entire doctrine and its premises is long overdue. As it is entirely "judge-made," a change in, or broadening of, the doctrine would operate only prospectively and it would no way impair vested rights, inasmuch as it is not a rule of property. Under these circumstances, the doctrine of stare decisis is not a substantial obstacle in effecting a much-needed change. If my Brethren are reluctant to overrule or modify the "mistake-change" doctrine, I suggest with great respect, that the Legislative Council and ultimately the General Assembly give serious thought to a change by appropriate legislation.

Let us examine the syllogisms upon which this "change-or-mistake" rule rests. As I see them they are:

Major premise: The comprehensive zoning plan was a good plan when enacted; the plan is good today, if physical conditions have not changed.

Minor premise: Physical conditions have not changed.

Conclusion: The plan is good today.

The "mistake" part of the "change-or-mistake" rule is founded on another such syllogism, equally grim, which goes like this:

Major premise: Today's plan is a good plan, but differs from the original plan; if physical conditions have not changed, the original plan must have been bad.

Minor premise: Physical conditions have not changed.

Conclusion: The original plan must have been bad.

The difficulty lies in the dependence upon the terms "good" — "bad" — "conditions", and the interpretation to be placed on each. Or, to put the matter a different way, the defect may lie in confining the term "conditions" to the connotation of "physical conditions." As a cursory glance at the Index to Legal Periodicals and to other compilations of journal topics will show, the ideas of planning and zoning, for the modern urban complex, have come a long way since that day in 1926 when Euclid, Ohio v. Ambler Realty Company first upheld the idea and practical application of zoning.

The "change-or-mistake" rule derived from the syllogisms above set forth is rendered erroneous by the simple truth: "Ideas change."

In my opinion, the correct rule in considering the validity of rezoning ordinances is whether or not the ordinance is unreasonable, arbitrary or capricious. . . .

There is a strong presumption in favor of the reasonableness of a zoning ordinance, but we have indicated that this presumption of reasonableness does not apply with the same weight or "with as great force" to a rezoning ordinance.... In my opinion, the presumption of reasonableness is just as strong in support of the rezoning ordinance as it was in support of the original zoning ordinance. This seems to be the general rule....

... As above indicated, ideas change. They particularly change in considering zoning reclassifications in a volatile situation and particularly in an area of rural virgin territory in the process of change to urban or suburban development. The syllogisms of the "mistake-change in condition" rule applied by the majority give no place to these new ideas. As I see the matter, it is entirely possible that the original zoning viewed in the light of conditions existing at the time of the formulation of the original comprehensive plan might have been proper and in accordance with the then recognized zoning concepts, and, with no change in physical conditions in the meantime, a new subdivision, prepared in accordance with more modern and more enlightened zoning ideas, be proper a relatively short time later. If we broadened our perspective and raised our sights in the "change in conditions" portion of the rule to include changes in zoning concepts and philosophy and did not limit it to a change in physical conditions merely, the problem would be largely solved. The people's representatives would then be free to give effect to the new ideas and concepts; they would arise from the present Procrustean bed upon which we have placed them, with renewed vigor, to advance the public interest. The case at bar is an excellent example of the unfortunate effect of the presently restricted rule....[55]

---

55. McCahill, Stealing: A Primer on Zoning Corruption, Planning Dec. 1973, at 6, writes:

> There were enough tips of icebergs to indicate to the editorial writers at the Wall Street Journal that the Agnew mess was a revolution in government: now even those in "planning . . . and other respectable-looking gents in business suits" who steal might get caught. The U.S. Attorney's office in Baltimore concurred. When Planning asked how there could be so much kickback money floating around without some zoning corruption, too, a spokesman noted dryly: "Everything in Baltimore County is for sale. We just haven't had time to get into it yet." Planning also called four members of the Baltimore County Planning Department who had been fired last year when they spoke out publicly against the real estate interests who were ripping up the county. Some said they often wondered whether or not their firing had to do with some of the real estate corruption. They all lamented the fact that the department, which has a planning commission noted for its progressiveness, now seemed to have a taint to it. (The man who fired the planners, County Administrative Officer William E. Fornoff, pleaded guilty to an income tax charge early in the Agnew affair.) In a kind of epitaph for Baltimore County, Fornoff told Planning in June 1972, "I'm getting out of here in the next two or three years. You've got to be loyal to the administration, but I don't think you should break yourself in half." He also notes that Spiro Agnew and John Ehrlichman began their public careers as zoning lawyers.

See also Building in Ft. Lee, One Way or Another, N.Y. Times, Sept. 15, 1974, §IV ($1.4 million to public officials in return for variances). A witness told how two men chased the mayor through city hall in an attempt to bribe him, with one of them screaming: "Pay

D. Departures from the Zoning Ordinance

Notes and Problems

1. Beall v. Montgomery County Council, 240 Md. 77, 212 A.2d 751 (1965), decided only a few months after *MacDonald* and by the same court, sustains a zoning ordinance creating a similar multiple-family, high-rise planned residential zone. The court distinguishes *MacDonald* on the facts: "[T]he factual situation there differed materially from that here presented. In the case at bar, there is an 'island' of land completely surrounding R-60 land. This situation did not exist in *MacDonald*." 212 A.2d at 761.

Jane Doe, a developer, consults you about 500 acres of land in Montgomery County, now zoned for single-family use, on which she plans to build a complex of apartment towers, townhouses, and recreational facilities. She asks you what rule of law will govern her petition for rezoning. What answer will you give her?

2. What is the quantum of evidence necessary to show a "change in conditions"? The appellee in Wells v. Pierpont, 253 Md. 554, 253 A.2d 749 (1969), bought his home in 1918; in 1965, "having reached the age of 81," he sold the property to a supermarket concern, conditioned on reclassification from Residence-6 (residence, one- and two-family) to Business-Local. Between 1962, when the property was zoned R-6, and 1965, one road on which the property abutted had been widened and "is . . . a major highway in [the] County"; the neighboring volunteer fire company's building was rebuilt with new kitchen facilities that accommodate 140 people at crab feasts and other social functions; a twenty-two-acre tract a half mile west of the property had been reclassified from R-6 to Residence-Apartments. The zoning board of appeals granted the reclassification and the trial court affirmed; the court of appeals reversed, "since Pierpont has failed to sustain his 'onerous' burden of proof" that substantial change occurred. But see Wier v. Witney Land Co., 263 A.2d 833 (Md. 1970); Hillelheber v. Charnock, No. 435 (Md. Ct. App., July 8, 1970); cf. Germenko v. County Board of Appeals, 264 A.2d 825 (Md. 1970). As to how the "Virginia rule" differs from that of Maryland, see Board of Supervisors v. Snell Construction Corp. 202 S.E. 2d 889 (Va. 1974). Does a showing of special damages have to be made in challenging a rezoning? Renard v. Dade County, 261 So. 2d 832 (Fla. 1972) (special damages rule appropriate for cases brought "to enforce valid zoning ordinance," but inappropriate when attacking ordinance). Can the zoning amendment be challenged in the voting booth? Coral Gables v. Carmichael, 256 So. 2d 404 (Fla. 3d Dist. 1972) ("referendum . . . represents alternative

---

him a million dollars!" N.Y. Times, March 19, 1975. Six in Fort Lee Bribery Case Draw Five-Year Prison Terms, N.Y. Times, June 4, 1975, is the end of the sad story. — EDS.

legislative action on the ordinance by vote of the electors"). (See also the discussion of referendum zoning, infra page 1078.)

3. For a recent example of an appellate court wrestling with the interstices of the change-mistake rule, see Cardon Investments v. Town of New Market, 466 A.2d 504 (Md. Ct. Spec. App. 1983). The trial court held (and the appellate court agreed) that the town was correct when it asserted that the key date from which alleged changes should be measured was 1977, when a comprehensive rezoning ordinance was adopted in Frederick County, not, as Cardon asserted, 1959, the year "[t]he Board of County Commissioners adopted its first comprehensive zoning ordinance" and the year designated by the 1977 ordinance "for determining any changes or mistakes required to be shown for purposes of rezoning." Because there was no "substantial change in the character of the neighborhood" (as required by Maryland statute) since 1977, the courts' refusal to use 1959 was fatal to Cardon's efforts to sustain the Board's approval of a rezoning that would have permitted the company to use the property, located just outside New Market's town limits, as a truck stop. See also Burke, The Change-Mistake Rule and Zoning in Maryland, 25 Am. U.L. Rev. 631 (1976); Gladden, The Change or Mistake Rule: A Question of Flexibility, 50 Miss. L.J. 375 (1979).

4. The Maryland Jockey Club used a lot contiguous to its Pimlico Race Track as a parking area. A comprehensive zoning ordinance placed the lot in a residential zone, but it was allowed to continue as a nonconforming use. The neighboring area developed as a residential district. Ten years after the original ordinance was passed, the club secured from the zoning commission a reclassification of the lot to commercial in order to build a stable thereon. This amendment was unsuccessfully attacked as "spot zoning." Chayt v. Maryland Jockey Club, 179 Md. 390, 18 A.2d 856 (1941).

a. Comment on one portion of the court's reasoning:

> [S]pot zoning . . . signifies a carving out of one or more properties located in a given use district and reclassifying them in a different use district. While it is true that in one sense this definition is gratified by the present ordinance, such an argument . . . disregards the fact that Pimlico . . . was not disturbed by the passage of [the ordinance], because of the nonconforming use provisions of the Zoning Ordinance. It is thus seen that while that ordinance in general classified the property of the Maryland Jockey Club as a residential use district, yet the effect of [the exemption for nonconforming uses] was such as to place it in a first commercial classification, and this being true we have the same result as if it had originally been classified as a first commercial use district.

179 Md. at 393-394, 18 A.2d at 858: Cf. Rathkopf, Law of Zoning and Planning ch. 26 (3d ed. 1969).

b. Suppose a private covenant permitted the erection of a stable

D. Departures from the Zoning Ordinance

on the lot in question. What effect on the question of spot zoning? Suppose a private covenant prohibited the erection of a stable on the lot in question. What effect on the question of spot zoning?

c. In Hartnett v. Austin, 93 So. 2d 86 (Fla. 1956), an attack was made upon a rezoning for shopping center use, which provided that it was "dependent upon the full and complete observance" of the following conditions: a wall be built around the property; a forty-foot setback area be landscaped and maintained; and the property owner pay for police protection. The supreme court disapproved of the amendment and noted, "Any contrary rule would condone a violation of the long established principle that a municipality cannot contract away the exercise of its police powers." Review the *Collard* case, supra page 283, and consider whether this principle is or should remain respected.

5. In invalidating an ordinance amending the General Plan of the City and County of Honolulu by changing a forty-seven-acre area from residential and agricultural uses to medium-density apartment use, the court conceded that the power to amend did not confront the same procedural hurdles placed before the adoption of the general plan, but concluded

> that the better and correct interpretation . . . requires that . . . not only a public hearing is necessary but the council, the planning commission and the planning director are required to follow a course of conduct consistent with the safeguards that were required in the initial adoption of the general plan. This interpretation will not only meet the spirit of the law but fulfill the true intent of the laws covering the general plan.

Dalton v. City and County of Honolulu, 462 P.2d 199 (Haw. 1969). As to how fared an objection to a combination of two proceedings to amend the comprehensive plan and the implementing zoning controls, see Chrobuck v. Snohomish County, infra page 341.

6. See Stein & Bauer, Store Buildings and Neighborhood Shopping Centers 1, 2-3, 13-14 (1934):

> To plan a successful neighborhood shopping center, we must first know what to plan for, how many stores and what kind. Numerous painstaking surveys of existing conditions have been made for the purpose of setting up a basis for future planning. These have attempted to find the number and kinds of stores that would be needed by counting the number of existing stores or measuring the number of front feet occupied by existing stores and comparing that with the neighboring population. All these studies serve but one purpose: they show us what not to do, for any one who looks around his own neighborhood knows that there are too many stores. And so we can only use most of these analyses of existing conditions as a warning. They show why the great majority of shopkeepers make something less than the barest living and die off like flies before

they even get started. They explain the long rows of empty stores in every neighborhood. They explain the enormous and expensive turnover in store property. They explain decreased values, empty lots, blighted streets and uncollected taxes. . . .

What is the use of developing a scientific method of store planning? None whatever, if present methods of subdivision and chaotic development are allowed to continue. None whatever, unless the complete, planned neighborhood is accepted as the minimum unit of development. No scientific store-planning method can be applied to speculative methods of development. But, on the other hand, one of the basic reasons for the acceptance of the neighborhood unit is the *necessity* for economic planning, for the preservation for the benefit of the community of the value increment which the community itself brings to its property. And this real increment (as opposed to inflated speculative expectation-value) which must be planned for, guarded and permanently preserved, occurs in store properties.

In such a shopping center, who is to determine which of a number of competing stores should receive space? Are planned shopping centers "the cartels of suburbia"? Cf. In re Lieb's Appeal, 179 Pa. Super. 318, 116 A.2d 860 (1955); Forte v. Borough of Tenafly, 106 N.J. 346, 55 A.2d 804 (1969).

Interesting cases reflecting the traffic-generating considerations of shopping centers are Temmink v. Board of Zoning Appeals of Baltimore County, 212 Md. 6, 128 A.2d 256 (1957) (reversing rezoning on basis of favorable report of planning commissioner), and City and County of San Francisco v. Safeway Stores, 150 Cal. App. 2d 327, 310 P.2d 68 (1st Dist. 1957) (access to supermarket through easement over land zoned residential). See Beman, Appraising Shopping Centers, 25 Appraisal J. 251 (1957). For the anticompetitive implications of shopping centers, see infra page 511.

■ FASANO v. BOARD OF COMMISSIONERS OF WASHINGTON COUNTY
264 Or. 574, 507 P.2d 23 (1973)

HOWELL, Justice.

The plaintiffs, homeowners in Washington County, unsuccessfully opposed a zone change before the Board of County Commissioners of Washington County. Plaintiffs applied for and received a writ of review of the action of the commissioners allowing the change. The trial court found in favor of plaintiffs, disallowed the zone change, and reversed the commissioners' order. The Court of Appeals affirmed, 489 P.2d 693 (1971), and this court granted review.

The defendants are the Board of County Commissioners and

D. Departures from the Zoning Ordinance 331

A.G.S. Development Company. A.G.S., the owner of 32 acres which had been zoned R-7 (Single Family Residential), applied for a zone change to P-R (Planned Residential), which allows for the construction of a mobile home park. The change failed to receive a majority vote of the Planning Commission. The Board of County Commissioners approved the change and found, among other matters, that the change allows for "increased densities and different types of housing to meet the needs of urbanization over that allowed by the existing zoning."

The trial court, relying on its interpretation of Roseta v. County of Washington, 254 Or. 161, 458 P.2d 405, 40 A.L.R. 3d 364 (1969), reversed the order of the commissioners because the commissioners had not shown any change in the character of the neighborhood which would justify the rezoning. The Court of Appeals affirmed for the same reason, but added the additional ground that the defendants failed to show that the change was consistent with the comprehensive plan for Washington County.

According to the briefs, the comprehensive plan of development for Washington County was adopted in 1959 and included classifications in the county for residential, neighborhood commercial, retail commercial, general commercial, industrial park and light industry, general and heavy industry, and agricultural areas.

The land in question, which was designated "residential" by the comprehensive plan, was zoned R-7, Single Family Residential.

Subsequent to the time the comprehensive plan was adopted, Washington County established a Planned Residential (P-R) zoning classification in 1963. The P-R classification was adopted by ordinance and provided that a planned residential unit development could be established and should include open space for utilities, access, and recreation; should not be less than 10 acres in size; and should be located in or adjacent to a residential zone. The P-R zone adopted by the 1963 ordinance is of the type known as a "floating zone," so-called because the ordinance creates a zone classification authorized for future use but not placed on the zoning map until its use at a particular location is approved by the governing body. The R-7 classification for the 32 acres continued until April 1970 when the classification was changed to P-R to permit the defendant A.G.S. to construct the mobile home park on the 32 acres involved. . . .

Any meaningful decision as to the proper scope of judicial review of a zoning decision must start with a characterization of the nature of that decision. The majority of jurisdictions state that a zoning ordinance is a legislative act and is thereby entitled to presumptive validity. . . .

At this juncture we feel we would be ignoring reality to rigidly view all zoning decisions by local governing bodies as legislative acts to be accorded a full presumption of validity and shielded from less than constitutional scrutiny by the theory of separation of powers. Local and small decision groups are simply not the equivalent in all respects of state and national legislatures. There is a growing judicial recognition of this fact of life:

> It is not a part of the legislative function to grant permits, make special exceptions, or decide particular cases. Such activities are not legislative but administrative, quasi-judicial, or judicial in character. To place them in the hands of legislative bodies, whose acts as such are not judicially reviewable, is to open the door completely to arbitrary government.

Ward v. Village of Skokie, 26 Ill. 2d 415, 186 N.E.2d 529, 533 (1962) (Klingbiel, J., specially concurring).

The Supreme Court of Washington, in reviewing a rezoning decision, recently stated:

> Whatever descriptive characterization may be otherwise attached to the role or function of the planning commission in zoning procedures, e.g., advisory, recommendatory, investigatory, administrative or legislative, it is manifest . . . that it is a public agency, . . . a principle [sic] and statutory duty of which is to conduct public hearings in specified planning and zoning matters, enter findings of fact — often on the basis of disputed facts — and make recommendations with reasons assigned thereto. Certainly, in its role as a hearing and fact-finding tribunal, the planning commission's function more nearly than not partakes of the nature of an administrative, quasi-judicial proceeding. . . .

Chrobuck v. Snohomish County, 78 Wash. 2d 884, 480 P.2d 489, 495-496 (1971).

Ordinances laying down general policies without regard to a specific piece of property are usually an exercise of legislative authority, are subject to limited review, and may only be attacked upon constitutional grounds for an arbitrary abuse of authority. On the other hand, a determination whether the permissible use of a specific piece of property should be changed is usually an exercise of judicial authority and its propriety is subject to an altogether different test. An illustration of an exercise of legislative authority is the passage of the ordinance by the Washington County Commission in 1963 which provided for the formation of a planned residential classification to be located in or adjacent to any residential zone. An exercise of judicial authority is the county commissioners' determination in this particular matter to change the classification of A.G.S. Development Company's specific piece of property. The distinction is stated, as follows, in Comment, Zoning Amendments — The Product of Judicial or Quasi-Judicial Action, 33 Ohio St. L.J. 130 (1972):

D. Departures from the Zoning Ordinance

> ... Basically, this test involves the determination of whether action produces a general rule on policy which is applicable to an open class of individuals, interests, or situations, or whether it entails the application of a general rule or policy to specific individuals, interests, or situations. If the former determination is satisfied, there is legislative action; if the latter determination is satisfied, the action is judicial.

33 Ohio St. L.J. at 137.

We reject the proposition that judicial review of the county commissioners' determination to change the zoning of the particular property in question is limited to a determination whether the change was arbitrary and capricious.

In order to establish a standard of review, it is necessary to delineate certain basic principles relating to land use regulation.

The basic instrument for county or municipal land use planning is the "comprehensive plan." Haar, In Accordance with a Comprehensive Plan, 68 Harv. L. Rev. 1154 (1955); 1 Yokley, Zoning Law and Practice, §3-2 (1965); 1 Rathkopf, The Law of Zoning and Planning §9-1 (3d ed. 1969). The plan has been described as a general plan to control and direct the use and development of property in a municipality. Nowicki v. Planning and Zoning Board, 148 Conn. 492, 172 A.2d 386, 389 (1961).

In Oregon the county planning commission is required by ORS 215.050 to adopt a comprehensive plan for the use of some or all of the land in the county. Under ORS 215.110 (1), after the comprehensive plan has been adopted, the planning commission recommends to the governing body of the county the ordinances necessary to "carry out" the comprehensive plan. The purpose of the zoning ordinances, both under our statute and the general law of land use regulation, is to "carry out" or implement the comprehensive plan. 1 Anderson, American Law of Zoning, §1.12 (1968). Although we are aware of the analytical distinction between zoning and planning, it is clear that under our statutes the plan adopted by the planning commission and the zoning ordinances enacted by the county governing body are closely related; both are intended to be parts of a single integrated procedure for land use control. The plan embodies policy determinations and guiding principles; the zoning ordinances provide the detailed means of giving effect to those principles.

ORS 215.050 states county planning commissions "shall adopt and may from time to time revise a comprehensive plan." In a hearing of the Senate Committee on Local Government, the proponents of ORS 215.050 described its purpose as follows:

> ... The intent here is to require a basic document, geared into population, land use, and economic forecasts, which should be the basis of any zoning or other regulations to be adopted by the county. ...

In addition, ORS 215.055 provides:

> 215.055 Standards for plan. (1) The plan and all legislation and regulations authorized by ORS 215.010 to 215.233 shall be designed to promote the public health, safety and general welfare and shall be based on the following considerations, among others: The various characteristics of the various areas in the county, the suitability of the areas for particular land uses and improvements, the land uses and improvements in the areas, trends in land improvement, density of development, property values, the needs of economic enterprises in the future development of the areas, needed access to particular sites in the areas, natural resources of the county and prospective needs for development thereof, and the public need for healthful, safe, aesthetic surroundings and conditions.

We believe that the state legislature has conditioned the county's power to zone upon the prerequisite that the zoning attempt to further the general welfare of the community through consciousness, in a prospective sense, of the factors mentioned above. In other words, except as noted later in this opinion, it must be proved that the change is in conformance with the comprehensive plan.

In proving that the change is in conformance with the comprehensive plan in this case, the proof, at a minimum, should show (1) there is a public need for a change of the kind in question, and (2) that need will be best served by changing the classification of the particular piece of property in question as compared with other available property.

In the instant case the trial court and the Court of Appeals interpreted prior decisions of this court as requiring the county commissions to show a change of conditions within the immediate neighborhood in which the change was sought since the enactment of the comprehensive plan, or a mistake in the comprehensive plan as a condition precedent to the zone change....[56]

However, *Roseta* [v. County of Washington, which the court discussed above in an omitted portion of its opinion] should not be interpreted as establishing a rule that a physical change of circumstances within the rezoned neighborhood is the only justification for rezoning. The county governing body is directed by ORS 215.055 to consider a number of other factors when enacting zoning ordinances, and the list there does not purport to be exclusive. The important issues, as *Roseta* recognized, are compliance with the statutory directive and consideration of the proposed change in light of the comprehensive plan.

Because the action of the commission in this instance is an exercise of judicial authority, the burden of proof should be placed, as is usual in judicial proceedings, upon the one seeking change. The more drastic

---

56. The court also referred to the Maryland line of decisions. How do you think they were distinguished? — EDS.

D. Departures from the Zoning Ordinance

the change, the greater will be the burden of showing that it is in conformance with the comprehensive plan as implemented by the ordinance, that there is a public need for the kind of change in question, and that the need is best met by the proposal under consideration. As the degree of change increases, the burden of showing that the potential impact upon the area in question was carefully considered and weighed will also increase. If other areas have previously been designated for the particular type of development, it must be shown why it is necessary to introduce it into an area not previously contemplated and why the property owners there should bear the burden of the departure.

Although we have said in *Roseta* that zoning changes may be justified without a showing of a mistake in the original plan or ordinance, or of changes in the physical characteristics of an affected area, any of these factors which are present in a particular case would, of course, be relevant. Their importance would depend upon the nature of the precise change under consideration.

By treating the exercise of authority by the commission in this case as the exercise of judicial rather than of legislative authority and thus enlarging the scope of review on appeal, and by placing the burden of the above level of proof upon the one seeking change, we may lay the court open to criticism by legal scholars who think it desirable that planning authorities be vested with the ability to adjust more freely to changed conditions. However, having weighed the dangers of making desirable change more difficult against the dangers of the almost irresistible pressures that can be asserted by private economic interests on local government, we believe that the latter dangers are more to be feared.

What we have said above is necessarily general, as the approach we adopt contains no absolute standards or mechanical tests. We believe, however, that it is adequate to provide meaningful guidance for local governments making zoning decisions and for trial courts called upon to review them. With future cases in mind, it is appropriate to add some brief remarks on questions of procedure. Parties at the hearing before the county governing body are entitled to an opportunity to be heard, to an opportunity to present and rebut evidence, to a tribunal which is impartial in the matter — i.e., having had no pre-hearing or ex parte contacts concerning the question at issue — and to a record made and adequate findings executed.

When we apply the standards we have adopted to the present case, we find that the burden was not sustained before the commission. The record now before us is insufficient to ascertain whether there was a justifiable basis for the decision. The only evidence in the record, that of the staff report of the Washington County Planning Department, is too conclusory and superficial to support the zoning change. It merely states:

The staff finds that the requested use does conform to the residential designation of the Plan of Development. It further finds that the proposed use reflects the urbanization of the County and the necessity to provide increased densities and different types of housing to meet the needs of urbanization over that allowed by the existing zoning. . . .

Such generalizations and conclusions, without any statement of the facts on which they are based, are insufficient to justify a change of use. Moreover, no portions of the comprehensive plan of Washington County are before us, and we feel it would be improper for us to take judicial notice of the plan without at least some reference to its specifics by counsel.

As there has not been an adequate showing that the change was in accord with the plan, or that the factors listed in ORS 215.055 were given proper consideration, the judgment is affirmed.[57]

Notes and Problems

1. Not surprisingly for a case that challenged nearly a half-century of judicial noninterference, *Fasano* received a mixed reception. Some courts have accepted and cited the Oregon justices' characterization of small-scale rezonings as "quasi-judicial." For example, the Colorado high court, in Snyder v. City of Lakewood, 189 Colo. 421, 542 P.2d 371 (1975), upheld a challenge brought by neighboring residential landowners to the grant of a rezoning to a church: "[T]he enactment

---

57. In his specially concurring opinion, Justice Bryson wrote:

The basic facts in this case exemplify the prohibitive cost and extended uncertainty to a homeowner when a governmental body decides to change or modify a zoning ordinance or comprehensive plan affecting such owner's real property.

This controversy has proceeded through the following steps:

1. The respondent opposed the zone change before the Washington County Planning Department and Planning Commission.
2. The County Commission, after a hearing, allowed the change.
3. The trial court reversed (disallowed the change).
4. The Court of Appeals affirmed the trial court.
5. We ordered reargument and additional briefs.
6. This court affirmed.

The principal respondent in this case, Fasano, happens to be an attorney at law, and his residence is near the proposed mobile home park of the petitioner A.G.S. No average homeowner or small business enterprise can afford a judicial process such as described above nor can a judicial system cope with or endure such a process in achieving justice. The number of such controversies is ascending.

In this case the majority opinion, in which I concur, adopts some sound rules to enable county and municipal planning commissions and governing bodies, as well as trial courts, to reach finality in decision. However, the procedure is no panacea and it is still burdensome.

It is solely within the domain of the legislative branch of government to devise a new and simplified statutory procedure to expedite finality of decision. — Eds.

D. Departures from the Zoning Ordinance 337

of a rezoning ordinance pursuant to the statutory criteria, after notice and a public hearing, constituted a quasi-judicial function subject to certiorari review. This rule is in accord with the modern trend in zoning law" (citations, including *Fasano*, omitted).

The framers of the Model Land Development Code endorsed the spirit, and much of the substance, of *Fasano*. See, e.g., §2-312(2) and note.

Even a landowner frustrated by the city council's *refusal* to rezone for a more lucrative use has been able to take advantage of the court's heightened scrutiny. Golden v. City of Overland Park, 224 Kan. 591, 584 P.2d 130 (1978). Does such a holding make sense, given one of the prime motivations for judicial inquiry: the suspicion that the *grant* of a controversial zoning change is a result of undue economic influence?

Other states have resisted the movement. In State v. City of Rochester, 268 N.W.2d 885 (Minn. 1978), owners of residences surrounding the rezoned property challenged the action, relying on *Fasano*. The court's rejection was explicit:

> We decline to follow the rule applied in those jurisdictions, for we have consistently held that when a municipality adopts or amends a zoning ordinance, it acts in a legislative capacity under its delegated police powers. . . . Our narrow scope of review reflects a policy decision that a legislative body can best determine which zoning classifications best serve the public welfare.

The Michigan Supreme Court, in Sabo v. Monroe Township, 394 Mich. 531, 232 N.W.2d 584 (1975), leapt onto the *Fasano* bandwagon. A year later, a more deferential court reconsidered the leap:

> Upon reflection, it does not seem wise as *Sabo* did to attempt to engraft upon the established legislative scheme of zoning and rezoning, a new system which admittedly requires new legislative action to operate optimally. Should the Legislature choose to revise the approach to zoning amendments in our state, this Court would, of course, view matters differently.

Kirk v. Township of Tyrone, 398 Mich. 427, 247 N.W.2d 848 (1976).

Oregon legislators complemented the work of their co-equal branch by enacting §§227.160-.180 of the Oregon Revised Statutes (Planning and Zoning Hearings and Review).

2. See Rose, Planning and Dealing: Piecemeal Land Controls as a Problem of Local Legitimacy, 71 Calif. L. Rev. 837, 853-857 (1983):

> One reason that a local representative body is not a legislature is the mere fact of its subordination to a state government. Municipalities, after all, are creatures of the state rather than independent "sovereigns." But this answer is too easy. *Fasano* may have cited administrative law cases,

but local governments are not merely administrative bodies that fill in the interstices of statutes passed by state legislatures, or that carry out preestablished state policies. Rather, they exercise wide police powers within their jurisdictions, at least insofar as state legislation is not preemptive. Indeed, many state constitutions guarantee the local powers of home rule against state legislative incursions. Moreover, local governing councils, like larger legislatures, are composed of elected representatives for fixed terms of office. Why, then, even despite subordination to state government, are local governments not "legislative" bodies?

As one pair of administrative law authors has said, the American understanding of governance through separate branches was "developed by Locke and Montesquieu and refined by Madison."[57] Madison's chief refinement has to do precisely with the legislature, and with the qualities that make a legislature's decisions fair and reliable. His celebrated The Federalist No. 10 merits study here, for it suggests why a local elected government should not always be seen as a legislature.

Madison's essay begins with the argument that the chief obstacle to fairness in a legislative body is "faction": the tendency of one interest group to impose its will at the expense of others. The antidote to faction, Madison says, lies in a constituency of sufficient size and variety; The Federalist No. 10 argued that the great advantage of the "extended republic" (i.e., the proposed national government) was that it would contain such a variety of interests that no one "faction" could tyrannize the others. Where the constituency is large, action is possible only through persuasion and coalitions of interest groups. Through a pattern of shifting alliances and vote trading, every interest can obtain at least partial satisfaction in the legislature of the "extended republic."

That all of the participating parties can expect some satisfaction of at least some of their desires is one assurance of fairness in legislation. Fairness is also advanced by the conditions that attend coalition-building itself: no interest group can safely go for the jugular of another, because all know that they may need to call on each other in different coalitions. Thus the very expectations built into the coalition-building process impose a modicum of mutual forbearance on the various interest groups.

Hannah Pitkin, in her analysis of The Federalist No. 10, has stressed a second characteristic of its legislature, one that assures due consideration of the public interest: the clash of multiple interests prevents hasty and ill-considered decisions and forces the legislators to take the time to reflect on the true public welfare.[62] Because of these factors, then, the courts can safely trust the larger legislature to make fair and careful decisions under most circumstances, and can give broad leeway to those decisions.

But this justification of large legislatures' decisions contains an implicit criticism of small-scale government: A legislative body drawn from too small or too homogeneous a constituency may be dominated by a single interest or faction. Factional domination may take varying forms. One is sheer corruption, made possible in smaller representative bodies because

---

57. S. Breyer & R. Stewart, Administrative Law and Regulatory Policy 37 (1979). See also D. Walker, Toward a Functioning Federalism 23-43, 227-228 (1981).
62. H. Pitkin, The Concept of Representation 195-196 (1967).

Summary Classification of Problems and Proposed Reforms*

Secrecy and Lack of Accountability
Separate administrative from legislative roles; set up proper procedures.
Pass related legislation:
- Sunshine laws
- Financial disclosure law
- Freedom of information law
- Conflict of interest law
- Sunset laws.

Complexity of Procedures
Establish hearing examiners
Set up land-use task force
Define administrative procedures
Clarify ordinances
Divide political decision-making from technical decision-making.

Lack of Standards
Establish mandatory planning
Make zoning dependent on plans
Use appropriate technological approaches.

Land Speculation
Remove zoning altogether
Establish windfall and wipeout provisions
Buy and sell zoning
Establish a government land bank.

* *Source:* National Institute of Law Enforcement and Criminal Justice, An Analysis of Zoning Reforms: Minimizing the Incentive for Corruption vi (1979).[58]

---

58. "Every proposed reform has its advantages and drawbacks. It is our conclusion that the best hope for zoning reform which touches the underlying issues involved in zoning corruption lies in the procedural safeguards suggested in the *Fasano* decision and the ALI code. Strict procedures, if followed, will have the additional effect of putting pressure on legislative bodies to provide clearer and more definite standards. Though the other methods of reform offer promise, the institution of procedural reforms directly reaches into the zoning process and appears to be the broadest reform and the one most likely to be accepted by the public at this time. Public scrutiny and public participation is the best protection against corruption, and strict procedures for reviewing and administering zoning appear to offer the best support for these activities." Id. How realistic are the proposed reforms? Is municipal corruption — the stuff of movies (*Chinatown, Against All Odds*, to name but two) — an inevitable byproduct of local democracy? Would private sector exchanges of development rights be any less fraught with intimidation and graft?

a limited number of persons have influence which must be bought. Another possibility is domination by a few who are perceived by others as the powerful. The decisions of these few can affect many within the community; others must curry their favor, and even larger interests find difficulty in organizing against their "cabals." Finally, and perhaps most feared by Madison, is the factional domination created by a popular "passion" — sometimes a sudden whim, sometimes a longstanding prejudice — that carries a majority before it. Under any of these various forms of factional domination, all of which are far more likely to occur in a smaller legislature than in a larger one, a dominant group may subject others to sudden destruction or to permanent political disability....

However much or little local governments may structurally resemble the Federalist legislature in general, they are very unlikely to be restrained by the Federalist safeguards in making specific piecemeal land decisions. In making these decisions, which involve only a few interested parties meeting only on single issues, legislatures are restrained neither by a coalition-building process that assures the fairness of the decisions, nor by a clash of interests that gives time for sober consideration. Courts should therefore not assume that these safeguards have worked. If these decisions are to be found reasonable, the finding requires some alternative source of fairness and due consideration.

It seems, then, that any model suggesting that local governments are just like larger legislative bodies is unrealistic. It follows that courts should not give local governments' ad hoc land decisions the deference they accord to measures taken by state legislatures. *Fasano*'s plan jurisprudence attempts to solve the problem by agreeing that the local government is not a true legislature; rather, it is more like a court, and its decisions should therefore be made according to judicial standards. The substantive standards for these adjudicative decisions derive from the locality's own plan; the procedures derive from the courts.

3. **The Miami Beach City Council** voted to change the zoning on an extensive area fronting on the Atlantic Ocean from a private residence or estate district to a multiple-family or hotel district. One of the affirmative votes was cast by a councilman holding a personal interest in some of the property affected, which would be increased in value by more than $500,000 as a result of this change in zoning. Is the rezoning valid? Does it matter whether or not the councilman's vote was necessary to pass the rezoning motion? City of Miami Beach v. Schauer, 104 So. 2d 129 (Fla. App. 1958) (city council acting in legislative capacity — "motives of the governing body ... will not be the subject of judicial inquiry," even though vote was necessary). But see Aldom v. Borough of Roseland, 42 N.J. Super. 495, 127 A.2d 190 (App. Div. 1956) (quasi-judicial activity — measure voided despite sufficient remaining affirmative votes — borough councilman violated public trust). What if the councilmember made full disclosure of a financial interest

D. Departures from the Zoning Ordinance

to the council and proceeded to vote only after the council granted informed consent to the member's participation?

4. Draft a statute for your state to deal with this problem. Consider the following sentence from such a statute in Connecticut:

> No member of any zoning commission or board and no member of any zoning board of appeals shall participate in the hearing or decision of the board or commission of which he is a member upon any matter in which he is directly or indirectly interested in a personal or financial sense.

Conn. Gen. Stat. §8-11 (1971). Can a board member participate in a decision affecting the property of her brother-in-law? Her employer? A small client of the board member's larger law firm? A potential employer? A friend with whom the board member sometimes plays golf? Consider these words from a court construing the Connecticut statute:

> Local governments would ... be seriously handicapped if any conceivable interest, no matter how remote and speculative, would require the disqualification of a zoning official. If this were so, it would not only discourage but might even prevent capable men and women from serving as members of the various zoning authorities.

Anderson v. Zoning Commission of Norwalk, 157 Conn. 285, 283 A.2d 16 (1968). Compare Kremer v. City of Plainfield, 101 N.J. Super. 346, 244 A.2d 335 (Law Div. 1968).

5. Does a planning board member who is a lawyer have a special obligation to withdraw from proceedings whenever a question of personal interest may arise? Canon 9 of the ABA's Code of Professional Responsibility states: "A lawyer should avoid even the appearance of professional impropriety." See also Disciplinary Rule 8-101 ("Action as a Public Official"). What if the board member is a planner? See American Institute of Planners, Code of Professional Responsibility 1.1(f): "A planner shall avoid even the appearance of improper professional conduct." Draft disciplinary rules to guide the legal and planning professions in applying the canons to this problem.

6. Chrobuck v. Snohomish County, 78 Wash. 858, 865, 480 P.2d 489, 494 (1971) narrates these interesting facts:

> Sometime prior to the hearings before the planning commission, the chairman of the planning commission and the chairman of the board of county commissioners made a trip to Los Angeles, California, for the purpose of inspecting an Atlantic Richfield refinery there located.... [T]hey were met by representatives of Atlantic Richfield, ... who accompanied them on a tour of the refinery site and facilities, provided hotel

accommodations and some meals, and attended a big league baseball game with them. The expense of the trip was borne by Atlantic Richfield, although the county sometime later reimbursed Atlantic Richfield for the transportation costs. Following their return, and before the hearings commenced, the chairman of the board of county commissioners publicly announced his support of Atlantic Richfield's proposal to locate a refinery at Kayak Point. When the matter of this trip was raised by counsel for plaintiffs at the hearings, the chairman of the planning commission refused to permit any discussion concerning it. However, his deposition was taken later and entered as an exhibit in these proceedings.

Mr. Lewis A. Bell, a respected and reputable attorney practicing in Everett, was a member of the planning commission. He, during the period in 1950 when Atlantic Richfield was acquiring its property around Kayak Point, on one occasion carried on negotiations with Atlantic Richfield concerning property belonging to one of his clients and on another occasion represented Atlantic Richfield in a lien foreclosure proceeding incident to the acquisition by it of a different piece of property. During the course of these relationships, Mr. Bell became acquainted with an Atlantic Richfield vice-president, which acquaintanceship continued on a social basis and was implemented by several fishing excursions, one of which occurred in the fall of 1967. In the summer of 1967, when Atlantic Richfield announced its proposal to construct an oil refinery on its property, the vice-president queried Mr. Bell concerning legal representation for Atlantic Richfield during the procedures for reclassifying the property involved, at which time Mr. Bell informed [him that] he was on the planning commission and recommended the retention of Mr. Joseph Meagher, Atlantic Richfield's present counsel. Mr. Bell thereafter continued as a member of the planning commission, participated in the comprehensive plan change hearing and in the decision emanating therefrom.

In January, 1968, after the planning commission had delivered its findings and recommendations concerning the comprehensive plan change to the county commissioners but before the county commissioners had rendered their decision . . . , plaintiffs sought a public hearing before the county commissioners concerning the foregoing circumstances but their request was refused.

At about this time, Mr. Bell resigned from the planning commission and Mr. Edward Jones, attorney for the town of Stanwood, and a trustee for the Sno-Isl Regional Library District, was appointed to succeed him. Prior to the comprehensive plan change hearing, Mr. Jones had signed an advertisement in the Stanwood newspaper in support of Atlantic Richfield's proposed refinery and during the course of the hearing before the planning commission appeared as a witness favoring the refinery, at which time he emphasized the benefits that would flow to the Stanwood area and the library district if the refinery project was approved. Plaintiffs' objections to Mr. Jones sitting as a member of the planning commission during the subsequent rezone hearings were denied. Mr. Jones, then, sat as a member of the planning commission during the public hearings on the rezoning issue, and participated to some extent in executive sessions of the planning commission, but disqualified himself from taking part in the planning commission's decision and recommendations concerning the proposed rezone.

There is a strong dissent to reliance on the "appearance of unfairness" doctrine.

6. Are there "preferred" uses in rezoning cases? See Bronstein and Erickson, Zoning Amendments in Michigan — Two Recent Developments, 50 J. Urb. L. 729 (1973). Rumblings to the effect that the usual presumption of validity would not apply to public interest uses seem to be stilled (temporarily, at least) in Kropf v. City of Sterling Heights, 391 Mich. 139, 215 N.W.2d 179 (1974). Cf. Rodo Land, Inc. v. Board of Community Commissioners, 517 P.2d 873 (Colo. 1974).

3. Variances and Special Exceptions: From "Safety Valves" to "Steady Leaks"

■ WILLIAMS, THE LAW ON VARIANCES
2, 5, Lincoln Institute of Land Policy, Policy Analysis Series No. 207 (1982)

The grant of a variance by a zoning board of appeals (hereinafter referred to as the "board") authorizes a property owner to depart from the literal requirements of a zoning ordinance. The grant of the variance is proper where strict application of the ordinance works a hardship to the individual landowner while the benefit to the community of enforcing the ordinance is slight.

In granting a right to develop land for a purpose or in a manner otherwise prohibited by law, the variance differs from a special permit or an amendment to the zoning ordinance. A special permit (also called a special exception or use) allows a permitted use, but only upon a showing by the applicant that conditions specified in the ordinance have been met. An amendment involves an appeal to the legislature for a change in the law.

Generally, the variance offers more immediate and less complicated relief than the amendment process. And where a type of use is not designated under special permit provisions, the variance may be the only alternative for a property owner suffering undue hardship by literal enforcement of zoning regulations. Attacks on the constitutionality of the zoning ordinance itself, claiming that the regulation as applied deprives a landowner of all reasonable use of his property, have had little success in American jurisdictions.

Most states follow the wording and structure of the Standard State

Zoning Enabling Act, §7, in providing for a board of adjustment with the power to grant variances. Under the Act, the board has the power:

> To authorize upon appeal in specific cases such variance from the terms of the ordinance that will not be contrary to the public interest where owing to specific conditions, a literal enforcement of the ordinance will result in unnecessary hardship and so that the spirit of the ordinance shall be served and substantial justice done.

The enabling acts of most states maintain the substance if not the exact language of the model act. . . .

The classic formulation outlining the criteria which a zoning board must follow in deciding whether to grant or deny a variance is stated in the oft-cited case of Otto v. Steinhilber.[28] In order to prove that the zoning ordinance works an unnecessary hardship, the landowner must demonstrate that:

1. The land in question cannot yield a reasonable return if used only for a purpose allowed in that zone.
2. The plight of the owner is due to unique circumstances and not to general conditions in the neighborhood which may reflect the unreasonableness of the zoning ordinance itself.
3. The use to be authorized by the variance will not alter the essential character of the locality.[29]

■ DeSIMONE v. GREATER ENGLEWOOD HOUSING CORP. NO. 1
56 N.J. 428, 267 A.2d 31 (1970)

HALL, J.

These consolidated appeals stem from Law Division judgments in five actions in lieu of prerogative writ sustaining the actions of administrative and legislative bodies of the city of Englewood in connection with a low and moderate income housing project being undertaken by defendant Greater Englewood Housing Corporation No. 1 (GEHC).

The project comprises 146 units of cluster-type, two-story apartments to be constructed on a 10 acre tract of city-owned land, leased to GEHC, in the Second Ward of the city (the Trumbull Park site), a district zoned for one-family dwellings and primarily white in population. GEHC is an approved non-profit housing sponsor, organized by the city's Galilee United Methodist Church and incorporated under the

---

28. Otto v. Steinhilber, 282 N.Y. 71, 24 N.E.2d 851 (1939).
29. Id. at 78, 24 N.E.2d at 853.

D. Departures from the Zoning Ordinance 345

Limited-Dividend Nonprofit Housing Corporations or Associations Law, N.J.S.A. 55:16-1 et seq., as amended L. 1967, c. 112. The purpose of the project, which is to receive state and federal financial assistance, is to aid in the clearance and reconstruction of blighted areas in the predominantly black Fourth Ward of the city, necessitating relocation of many slum residents, and to provide low and moderate income families with safe, sanitary and decent living accommodations outside of that area. GEHC is also the sponsor of a companion project within the Fourth Ward (the Lafayette site), likewise in a one-family residential zone, as to which the municipal authorities acted similarly and contemporaneously and which has not been the subject of any litigation. Plaintiffs are taxpayer-residents of the Second Ward and representatives of a local organization know as FACT (First Association of Citizens and Taxpayers)....

The basic case in this panoply of litigation is that involving the use variance. The background and setting of GEHC's Trumbull Park project is thoroughly elucidated in the voluminous testimony and extensive exhibits presented to the Board of Adjustment. From that mass of evidence the following picture emerges.

Englewood, like many others, is a city of striking constrasts. It is five square miles in area and lies on the western slope of the Palisades in eastern Bergen County. The population of about 28,000 is 20% to 25% black. It is one of the older suburban residential communities adjacent to New York City, its white population is generally affluent, and its Master Plan described it in 1959 as almost wholly built up, with an exceedingly low housing vacancy rate.

By far the greater part of the black population lives in the Fourth Ward (the southwestern quadrant of the city), literally and figuratively "on the other side of the tracks", and a very high percentage of housing there is substandard, much of it not capable of rehabilitation. The trial judge found:

> ... [F]or a considerable period the need for low and moderate income housing in the City of Englewood has not only been set forth and stated by government agencies and private citizens, but has been readily apparent to anyone viewing the Englewood scene. Down through the years an inevitable racial polarization of the inhabitants of Englewood has come into being. Of the City's four wards the First [northeast quadrant] and Second [southeast quadrant] are generally developed with expensive homes inhabited by Caucasians ranging from the more modest at the southern end of the Second Ward to impressive estates as one goes northward into the First Ward....
>
> ... [T]he Third Ward [northwest quadrant] can be generally characterized as one made up of modest one family structures on smaller lots predominately white with some degree of integration effected in recent years. The Fourth Ward, generally down hill from the First and Second

Wards, is practically all black and can truly and accurately be characterized as a ghetto, a blighted and racially impacted area of the City. For some time the City of Englewood has passed resolutions and ordinances, it has conducted surveys and has issued reports in great number demonstrating the need for razing the ghetto area and building new housing.

(Plaintiffs expressly concede the need for low and moderate income housing in the Fourth Ward.)

Numerous prior efforts to provide some decent housing for the city's blacks have all failed. Not a single governmentally sponsored or assisted housing accommodation has been constructed. By reason of a racial disturbance in the city in July 1967, it became one of the communities scrutinized by the Governor's Select Commission on Civil Disorder. The Commission's "Report for Action" (February 1968) commented cogently on the housing situation, pointing out that prior efforts had foundered, in a sharply divided community, on the issue "whether to build within the Fourth Ward only, or whether to spread renewal beyond the ghetto."...

As has been indicated, the Trumbull Park site project in question is being undertaken by GEHC simultaneously with the Lafayette site project in the Fourth Ward. They will make possible redevelopment and renewal plans in the Fourth Ward by providing relocation homes for families to be displaced thereby. Construction of both is to be financed by an already committed $5.4 million, 100% mortgage granted by the State Housing Financing Agency. Mortgage interest subsidy, as well as rent supplements to qualifying occupants, are to be provided by appropriate federal agencies. Federal regulations require, in such a situation, that new housing be built outside a ghetto area on at least a one for one basis with respect to that constructed within it. As the Board of Adjustment put it in its resolution recommending the use variance:

> It is said, in short, that slum clearance cannot proceed without relocation housing; that low and/or moderate-income housing cannot be constructed without federal subsidies; that federal subsidies will not be forthcoming in the absence of provisions for balancing new units within the area of racial concentration with new units outside the area....

The Board went on to remark that the Trumbull Park site is "the only available tract of suitable size in the City outside the racially-impacted area."

The site is, as the Board of Adjustment found, isolated from existing residential uses. Located in the extreme southeasterly end of the city, it is part of a slightly larger area, laid out in lots and paper streets on a filed map in the 30's and acquired by the city for non-

D. Departures from the Zoning Ordinance 347

payment of taxes some years later. The area is hilly, wooded and unimproved except for Trumbull Park, a neighborhood recreation facility created by the city in the 50's, fronting on the easterly sideline of Broad Avenue, a main thoroughfare, approximately 450 feet and about 330 feet deep. The easterly boundary of the park forms the westerly line of the project site. The site is further bounded on the north by city-owned parkland in a natural state and beyond that by State Highway Route 4; on the east by a steep buffer area and beyond by Jones Road; and on the south by the golf course of the Englewood Country Club which is bisected by the Englewood-Leonia line and Interstate Highway Route 95. The closest houses are at a considerable distance — on the east side of Broad Avenue, beyond Route 4 and on the east side of Jones Road — only one or two of which will even be able to see the project buildings. The cluster-type development is designed to take advantage of the topography, sloping upward rather sharply to the east. The proposed design of the several buildings seeks to create a pleasing single family dwelling, rather than institutional, atmosphere. . . .

The one issue which is novel and important is the basis for the grant of the use variance.

The pertinent section of the zoning enabling act, N.J.S.A. 40:55-39(d) authorizes the grant of a use variance upon an affirmative finding of "special reasons" "in particular cases", together with the negative findings, applicable in all zoning relief situations, that the "relief can be granted without substantial detriment to the public good and will not substantially impair the intent and purpose of the zone plan and zoning ordinance."

It is long settled law in this state that this unique provision does not require that the particular premises cannot feasibly be used for a permitted use or that other hardship exists. "Special reasons" is a flexible concept; broadly speaking, it may be defined by the purposes of zoning set forth in N.J.S.A. 40:55-32, which specifically include "promotion of health, morals or the general welfare." Ward v. Scott, 11 N.J. 117, 93 A.2d 385 (1952). So variances have been approved for many public and semi-public uses because they significantly further the general welfare. See, e.g., Andrews v. Board of Adjustment of the Township of Ocean, 30 N.J. 245, 152 A.2d 580 (1959) (parochial school in residential zone); Black v. Montclair, 34 N.J. 105, 167 A.2d 388 (1961) (additional parochial school building in residential zone); Burton v. Montclair, 40 N.J. 1, 190 A.2d 377 (1963) (private school in residential zones); Yahnel v. Board of Adjustment of Jamesburg, 79 N.J. Super. 509, 192 A.2d 177 (App. Div. 1963), cert. denied, 41 N.J. 116, 195 A.2d 15 (1963) (telephone equipment building in residential zone); Kunzler v. Hoffman, 48 N.J. 277, 225 A.2d 321 (1966) (private hospital for emotionally disturbed in residential zone). . . .

The conclusions of the Board of Adjustment and the governing body in this regard are fully supported by the very comprehensive proofs before the Board, and are worthy of full quotation. The Board said:

> Without regard, however, to any official federal or state requirements, the Board finds and concludes that the demand of public policy cannot be satisfied by continued confinement of non-white families in the Fourth Ward area, and that breaking the long-standing patterns of racial segregation in this city will promote the general welfare of the community. The Board further finds and concludes that the program in question will serve to alleviate urban blight; to promote the health, morals and general welfare of the residents of this City; and to encourage appropriate land use throughout the City....

Plaintiffs challenge these conclusions as insufficient to constitute "special reasons." Judge Trautwein held that they were legally adequate and we thoroughly concur. We specifically hold, as matter of law in the light of public policy and the law of the land, that public or, as here, semi-public housing accommodations to provide safe, sanitary and decent housing, to relieve and replace substandard living conditions or to furnish housing for minority or underprivileged segments of the population outside of ghetto areas is a special reason adequate to meet that requirement of N.J.S.A. 40:55-39(d) and to ground a use variance.

Plaintiffs also challenge the agencies' findings that the negative criteria were not factually and legally met. The Board found that,

> by reason of the location, topography and isolation of the tract in question, as well as the design and layout of the structures proposed to be erected, such adverse effect as the proposed multi-family use may have on nearby one-family uses will be minimal, and that the relief requested may, accordingly, be granted without substantial detriment to the public good and without substantial impairment of the intent or purpose of the zone plan or zoning ordinance.

The governing body concluded that this finding was supported by the evidence. The trial court agreed and we think the conclusion is irresistible in the light of the proofs.

Indeed, we should observe, parenthetically, that courts rarely find land use cases where the evidence before local bodies is as comprehensive and as thoroughly presented and where, procedurally, hearings and other proceedings are as fairly, fully and meticulously conducted and resolutions and ordinances as well prepared as was done in the instant situation.

Finally, plaintiffs urge that the use variance is invalid as constituting rezoning without legislative action. Stress is laid on the 10 acre size of

D. Departures from the Zoning Ordinance

the tract. While a zoning amendment specifically changing the use of the site (some of the zoning ordinance's multi-family districts appear to be no larger) or providing for the use as a special exception under N.J.S.A. 40:55-39(b) would have been appropriate as well, the size of the site does not preclude a use variance under the circumstances. . . . At that time (d) of section 39 had not been enacted in its present form and a use variance applicant had to establish hardship.

In sum, the use variance was properly granted. In fact, a denial of it under the circumstances and proofs could not well be sustained.[59]

■ KISIL v. CITY OF SANDUSKY
12 Ohio St. 3d 30, 465 N.E.2d 848 (1984)

C. F. BROWN, Justice. . . .

The parcel of land located at 508 Huron Avenue, Sandusky, Ohio, is a single-family residence which was erected before the 1956 enactment of the Sandusky city zoning ordinances. The area in which the property is situated was designated R2F by the 1956 ordinance. R2F zoning allows two-family dwellings and single-family dwellings. When plaintiff-appellant purchased the property in question in 1981, he did so for investment purposes with the idea of renting the residence. Appellant testified before the commission and board that he desired to convert the residence from a single-family to a two-family residence so as to make the rental property profitable.

The conversion of appellant's property to a duplex would not need the approval of the commission but for the fact that the lot on which the residence is situated is below the minimum area and yard requirements contained in the city zoning provisions. Appellant, therefore, sought a variance to allow the conversion of the residence. Such a variance is not a pure use variance. The variance sought by appellant is merely an area variance. It has been noted by other jurisdictions that

---

59. For the troubled, but typical line of Massachusetts decisions, see Pendergast v. Board of Appeals of Barnstable, 331 Mass. 55, 120 N.E.2d 906 (1954); Devine v. Board of Appeals of Lynn, 332 Mass. 319, 125 N.E.2d 131 (1955); Lawrence v. Board of Appeals of Lynn, 336 Mass. 87, 142 N.E.2d 378 (1957); Sullivan v. Board of Appeals of Belmont, 346 Mass. 81, 190 N.E.2d 83 (1963); Garfield v. Board of Appeals of Rockport, 356 Mass. 37, 247 N.E.2d 720 (1969); City Council of Waltham v. Vinciullo, 364 Mass. 624, 307 N.E.2d 316 (1974). On the strained New Jersey cases, see Ward v. Scott, 18 N.J. Super. 36, 86 A.2d 613 (Super. Ct. Law Div.) (grant of variance upheld), 11 N.J. 117, 93 A.2d 385 (1952) (insufficient findings by board of adjustment, reversed and remanded), 16 N.J. 16, 105 A.2d 851 (1954) (variance upheld again, no abuse of discretion — J. Heher, dissenting); Ramney v. Instituto Pontificio Delle Maestre Fillippini, 20 N.J. 189, 119 A.2d 142 (1955); Moriarty v. Pozner, 21 N.J. 199, 121 A.2d 527 (1956); Commons v. Westwood Zoning Board of Adjustment, 81 N.J. 597, 410 A.2d 1138 (1980); Nash v. Board of Adjustment of Township of Morris, 96 N.J. 97, 474 A.2d 241 (1984). — EDS.

the standard for granting a variance which relates to area requirements only should be a lesser standard than that applied to use variances.

The New York Court of Appeals when faced with a case quite similar to the present action explained, "[a]n applicant for an area variance need not establish special [unnecessary] hardship. It is sufficient to show practical difficulties. . . ." Matter of Hoffman v. Harris (1966), 17 N.Y.2d 138, 144, 269 N.Y. Supp. 2d 119, 123, 216 N.E.2d 326, 329. The court went on to cite the reason for such distinctions between use and area variances as being, ". . . [w]hen the variance is one of area only, there is no change in the character of the zoned district and the neighborhood considerations are not as strong as in a use variance."

In this case the grant of a variance to appellant will not alter the character of the surrounding neighborhood. The record reveals that a vast majority of the surrounding neighborhood is at the present time being used as two-family residential rental property. In fact the lot directly north of appellant's property was granted a variance by the commission to be used as a multifamily residence, which is not only an area but a use variance. The residence granted this variance is on a lot which is smaller in area than the appellant's lot.

This court has recently addressed the issue of variances in Consolidated Mgmt., Inc. v. Cleveland (1983), 6 Ohio St. 3d 238, 452 N.E.2d 1287. In that case the plaintiff sought a variance to convert his commercial property to a use which was outside the use permitted by the zoning ordinance. This court held that the requirement of an unnecessary hardship suffered by a landowner seeking a variance could not be met when the landowner purchased the property with knowledge of the zoning restrictions.

The instant case is a different situation. While appellant had prior knowledge of the commission's denial of a variance requested by the previous landowner, the decision entered by the commission at that time was never appealed. The granting of a variance to the appellant should not be judged on the traditional showing of an "unnecessary hardship" but on the lesser standard of a "practical difficulty." Because the standard which is used to guide the decision of the reviewing authorities is different in this action, the value of the precedent enunciated in *Consolidated Mgmt., Inc.* is minimal.

We are further persuaded that the common pleas court was correct when it found that the denial of the variance by the commission and board was unreasonable and arbitrary. An examination of the record reveals that the neighborhood in which appellant's parcel of land is situated contains many duplex residences.[3] A significant number of

---

3. Appellant requested an appraisal of the property located at 508 Huron Avenue from the independent professional appraisal service of Reynolds and Associates. In its report the firm found eighty percent of the neighborhood in which the residence is located consists of two- to four-family residences.

these residences are on lots insufficient in size, according to the zoning ordinances. Even more persuasive is the fact that the lot north of appellant's lot was recently granted a variance for a multifamily residence. The allowance of other duplexes on lots insufficient in size and the granting of a multifamily variance to a neighboring landowner, while denying appellant's request for a variance, is unreasonable and arbitrary enforcement of the zoning ordinances. . . .

Since the standard for granting a variance which relates solely to area requirements should be a lesser standard than that applied to variances which relate to use, an application for an area variance need not establish unnecessary hardship. It is sufficient the application show practical difficulties. Having examined the record, this court concludes that the court of common pleas did not abuse its discretion in reaching its judgment. The judgment of the court of appeals is therefore reversed. . . .

LOCHER, Justice, dissenting. . . .

In effect, the majority today finds a difference between commercial property and residential property for variance purposes. Appellant readily admits to having knowledge of the zoning restrictions applicable to his residential property when he purchased it in 1981 for investment purposes, yet is now permitted to ignore such restrictions. . . .

The majority makes much of the fact that a neighboring landowner to appellant was granted a multifamily variance from a previous commercial use. This commercial use, however, was a *nonconforming* use that was eliminated by the variance. Hence, the present use of that property is more restricted than its previous use, and is now more closely tailored to the zoning plan than before. Thus, the neighborhood was *upgraded* by the granting of that variance. This is far different from what has occurred in the case herein: appellant is permitted to vary his previously conforming use into a downgrading use outside the bounds of the zoning code.

Notes

1. An article that contrasts the theory of the variance power with its practice states "the board of appeals variance procedure, conceived as the 'safety valve' of the zoning ordinance, has ruptured into a steady leak." Shapiro, The Zoning Variance Power, 29 Md. L. Rev. 1 (1969). In general, see Makieski, Zoning: Legal Theory and Political Practice, 45 J. Urb. L. 1 (1967); Wexler, "A Zoning Ordinance Is No Better Than Its Administration" — A Platitude Proved, 1 John Marshall J. Prac. & Proc. 74 (1967).

That the reports, year after year, contain numerous cases dealing with variances is itself an indication that all is not well in the administration of zoning. To take one rough figure: out of the 248 appellate cases reported in 1953 that could be classified as zoning-type cases, forty-eight dealt with variances. Haar, Emerging Legal Issues in Zoning, in Planning 138 (1954). In Cincinnati, during the period 1926–1937, out of 1940 applications, 1493 variances were granted; in Philadelphia from 1933 to 1937, 4000 variances were granted out of 4800 requests. ASPO, Zoning Changes and Variances, Bull. No. 43, at 3, 5 (April 1938); Administration of Zoning Variances in 20 Cities, 30 Pub. Mgmt. 70 (1948). In Chicago, some 4260 variances were granted from 1923 to 1953. Comment, 48 Nw. U.L. Rev. 470, 481 (1953). During the year 1952, Cambridge granted forty-eight use variances, denied nine; granted fifty-one bulk variances, denied eight. (Incidentally, no decision, either affirming or denying a grant, made any mention of the reasons for the board's action.) From 1949 to 1963, only twenty-nine variance decisions were appealed to the Massachusetts Supreme Court. In Baltimore, only fifteen of 464 zoning variance cases were appealed to the city court. Shapiro, supra, at n.89. See also Dukeminier and Stapleton, The Zoning Board of Adjustment: A Case Study in Misrule, 50 Ky. L.J. 273, 320 (1962) (70 percent of variance petitions granted by Lexington Board — "seems generally in line with the percentage granted by boards elsewhere"); Note, Zoning Variance Administration in Vermont, 8 Vt. L. Rev. 371, 388, 391, 393 (1983) (Brattleboro: fifty-seven of eighty-eight area variances granted, Montpelier: fifty-one of seventy-one granted, East Montpelier: forty-four of fifty-nine granted); Bryden, The Impact of Variances: A Study of Statewide Zoning, 61 Minn. L. Rev. 769 (1977).

See Heady v. Zoning Board of Appeals for Milford, 139 Conn. 463, 467, 94 A.2d 789, 791 (1953):

> [U]nless great caution is used and variations are granted only in proper cases, the whole fabric of town- and city-wide planning will be worn through in spots and raveled at the edges until its purpose in protecting property values and securing an orderly development of the community is completely thwarted.

See also Pomeroy, Losing the Effectiveness of Zoning Through Leakage, 7 Plan. & Civic Comment 13 (Oct. 1941). One expert estimates that 50 percent of all rulings of the zoning boards of appeal are illegal usurpations of power. See Blucher, Is Zoning Wagging the Dog?, Planning 96, 100 (1956). A detailed account of the situation in one American city is given in Note, 103 U. Pa. L. Rev. 516 (1955). See Green, The Power of the Zoning Board of Adjustment to Grant Variances from the Zoning Ordinance, 29 N.C.L. Rev. 245 (1951).

An analysis of two proposals designed to secure legal recognition of the "discretionary function" concludes: "Ultimately, the courts should

D. Departures from the Zoning Ordinance

recognize that political safeguards constitute the only possible defense against the abuse of zoning discretion." Note, Administrative Discretion in Zoning, 82 Harv. L. Rev. 668, 685 (1969). The proposals discussed therein, modeled on the British experience, vest "significant discretionary authority" in a politically sensitive agency, which would operate under a zoning code drawn up in terms of either a purposive description of existing regulations or an enumeration of future desired land uses. Decisions would be reviewable by the judiciary or a state agency (in which case judicial scrutiny would be limited to procedural matters).

2. The zoning ordinance provided that the board of review, after notice and hearing,

> may in a specific case and subject to appropriate conditions and safeguards, determine and vary the application of the regulations herein established in harmony with their general purposes and intent as follows.... (8) Approve in any district an application for any use of building deemed by the said Board to be in harmony with the character of the neighborhood and appropriate to the uses of buildings permitted in such district.

This section was held illegal as an improper delegation of legislative power. Flynn v. Zoning Board of Review of Pawtucket, 77 R.I. 118, 73 A.2d 808 (1950).[60]

---

60. Cf. Harrison v. Zoning Board of Review of Pawtucket, 74 R.I. 135, 59 A.2d 361 (1948) (three-family house in a two-family zone). See also Abbott v. Zoning Board of Review of Warwick, 78 R.I. 84, 79 A.2d 620 (1951) (drive-in theater in undeveloped residential zone).

In another Rhode Island municipality, the local ordinance provided that the board of review has the power "In appropriate cases and subject to appropriate conditions and safeguards to make special exceptions to the terms of this Ordinance where the exception is reasonably necessary for the convenience and welfare of the public." Upon application for a variance to establish a funeral home in a residence district, what result? See Woodbury v. Zoning Board of Review of Warwick, 78 R.I. 319, 321, 82 A.2d 164, 165 (1951) (grant of variance upheld). Compare Welton v. Hamilton, 344 Ill. 82, 92, 176 N.E. 333, 337 (1931) ("practical difficulties or unnecessary hardship in the way of carrying out the strict letter of such ordinance . . . so that the spirit of the ordinance shall be observed") with Heath v. Mayor and City Council of Baltimore, 187 Md. 296, 49 A.2d 799 (1946), and Johnston v. Board of Supervisors of Marin County, 31 Cal. 2d 66, 187 P.2d 686 (1947). See Freund, Zoning — Power of Board to Vary, 26 Ill. L. Rev. 575 (1932). How serious would be the effect on planning of the invalidation of such an ordinance?

How would you recommend the legislation be amended? See Ill. Laws 1933, at 288, §1 (substituting "particular hardship" for "unnecessary hardship," among other changes); Downey v. Grimshaw, 410 Ill. 21, 101 N.E.2d 275 (1951). See also Dallstream and Hunt, Variations, Exceptions and Special Uses, 1954 U. Ill. L.F. 213; Reps, Discretionary Powers of the Board of Zoning Appeals, 20 Law & Contemp. Probs. 280 (1955). Compare Underhill v. Board of Appeals of Oyster Bay, 72 N.Y.S.2d 588, 593 (Sup. Ct. 1947), aff'd mem., 297 N.Y. 937, 80 N.E.2d 342 (1948) (when "public convenience and welfare will be substantially served [and] the appropriate use of neighboring property will not be substantially or permanently injured") with Aloe v. Dassler, 278 App. Div. 975, 106 N.Y.S.2d 24, 25 (2d Dept. 1951), aff'd, 303 N.Y. 878, 105 N.E.2d 104 (1952) ("taking into consideration the public health, safety and general welfare, and subject to appropriate conditions and safeguards").

3. A theater is located on the corner of Broadway within the district zoned for business. The owner applies for permission to erect a gasoline station in place of the theater. There are presently gasoline stations on the two other corners, but no gasoline station exists on the west side of Broadway for ten blocks. The land and building are assessed at $110,000, and the owner of the theater is losing $200 to $300 per week. It is agreed that the neighborhood has deteriorated within the past ten years. The board of standards and appeals grants the application. Upon appeal, what determination by the court? See In the Matter of Young Women's Hebrew Association v. Board of Standards and Appeals of City of New York, 266 N.Y. 270, 194 N.E. 751 (1935) (reversed — no unnecessary hardship found). See Note, 8 Syracuse L. Rev. 85 (1956).

4. Application was granted to change a private home to doctors' offices. Two such nonconforming uses and two variances have been granted in the same block. "The facts before the board indicate that the whole area is changing. It is becoming a medical center." Parsons v. Board of Zoning Appeals of New Haven, 140 Conn. 290, 295, 99 A.2d 149, 151 (1953). Contrast Paul v. Board of Zoning Appeals, 142 Conn. 40, 110 A.2d 619 (1955).

5. A large hotel applied for a permit to use a recently purchased lot, 100 feet from the hotel, zoned in a general residence district, for the parking of automobiles of its patrons without charge. The board of appeals reversed a denial of permit by the building inspector. It made a finding that a serious parking problem, incidental to the operation of the hotel, had arisen; that public necessity and public safety would be served by affording the requested off-street parking facilities, which would relieve dangerous traffic congestion and benefit the neighborhood by preserving real estate values; and that the restriction of the premises to a residential district would not promote the health, safety, morals, and welfare of that part of the city. On appeal, what result? See Brackett v. Board of Appeal, 311 Mass. 52, 39 N.E.2d 956 (1942) (variance inappropriate — "plight of premises" not "unique").

6. The British Minister of Housing and Local Government on July 9, 1952, allowed an appeal against the condition imposed by a city council in granting permission for the erection of a dwelling house and garage. The condition read: "[T]he development shall be so executed as to avoid any disruption thereby, whether at the time of the development or subsequently, of sewerage arrangements in the area by reason of damage to public sewers which cross the land." 1952 J. Plan. & Prop. L. 639. Compare Besselman v. Moses Lake, 46 Wash. 2d 279, 280 P.2d 689 (1955) with State ex rel. Myhre v. Spokane, 70 Wash. 2d 207, 422 P.2d 790 (1967).

The British Town and Country Planning Act originally provided that the local planning authority, in dealing with individual applications

D. Departures from the Zoning Ordinance

to the planning commission, shall have regard both to the provisions of the development plan "and to any other material considerations." The minister issued the Town and Country Planning (Development Plans) Regulation, June 25, 1954, by which a local planning authority is authorized to grant permission for development of land that does not accord with the development plan in any case where the development "would neither involve a substantial departure from the provisions of the Plan nor injuriously affect the amenity of adjoining land." The regulations have been revoked, but the conferred power is still held by local planning authorities. Departures are classified into three types: not substantial departures from the plan; contrary to expressed government views or which would affect the whole neighborhood; others.

7. The owner of a large country home remodeled the upstairs and rented it. Two neighbors did the same. The corporate authorities charged all three with violating the zoning ordinances. After many continuances, the defendants assured the court they would remove the separate facilities, cancel the leases with their tenants, and revert to single-family occupancy. Thereupon the court dismissed the proceedings. Without complying with his representations to the court, one violator (who has since moved from the state) sold his property to a couple, who, relying upon the rental income to maintain a large family, paid a price far in excess of the value of the property as a single-family dwelling. They cannot meet the mortgage payments without rental income. They now apply for a variance. Should it be granted? See Dallstream and Hunt, Variations, Exceptions and Special Uses, 1954 U. Ill. L. Forum 213, 233, 234; Prusik v. Board of Appeal, 262 Mass. 451, 160 N.E. 312 (1928). In L. M. Pike & Son, Inc. v. Town of Waterford, 130 Vt. 432, 296 A.2d 262 (1972), petitioner failed to locate the town boundaries correctly, and was denied a variance. The court, noting that "[t]he heart of any variance to a zoning ordinance is the factor of imposing unnecessary hardship upon the owner of the land," nevertheless denied relief, for "[a]ppellant's hardship, if any, was not created by the zoning ordinance . . . but by the very acts of the appellant."

8. The petitioner, a neighboring landowner, wishes to protest the grant of a variance. Although the ordinance appears to allow an appeal, the state statute indicates otherwise. In Tranfaglia v. Building Commissioner of Winchester, 306 Mass. 495, 28 N.E.2d 537 (1940), the court heard the neighbor's petition for a writ of mandamus, but ultimately upheld the variance. See also 222 East Chestnut Street Corp. v. Board of Appeals of Chicago, 10 Ill. 2d 132, 139 N.E.2d 218 (1956) (narrow definition of party aggrieved).

An oral contract for the purchase of a tract of land zoned residential has been entered into by the petitioner. He requests a variance for a commercial use. What result? Marinelli v. Board of Appeal, 275 Mass. 169, 175 N.E. 479 (1931) (even though agreement not enforceable, "there is no reason why their purpose to execute an obligation of honor and fair dealing should not be respected"); Carson v. Board of Appeal, 321 Mass. 649, 75 N.E.2d 116 (1947). But cf. Lee v. Board of Adjustment, 226 N.C. 107, 37 S.E.2d 128 (1946). *A*, the owner of a grocery store located in the commercial district, wishes to protest the proposed grant of a variance to *B* permitting him to open a grocery store in a residential district. What result? Circle Lounge and Grille, Inc. v. Board of Appeal, 324 Mass. 427, 86 N.E.2d 920 (1949) (zoning regulations not intended "to protect business from competition"). Cf. Smith v. Board of Review, 103 R.I. 328, 237 A.2d 551 (1968).

The petitioner is notified that the properties considered to be affected by his petition to erect a filling station in a single-family residence district are those within 200 feet of the property. Determining the owners from the most recent tax list, the petitioner notifies them by registered mail of the date of the hearing on his request for a "variance . . . as applied to the erection of alterations in a proposed building." The variance is later granted. Any possible attack? Kane v. Board of Appeal, 273 Mass. 97, 173 N.E. 1 (1930) (notice "contained no adequate intimation of the subject-matter of the petition").

Section 267 of the Town Law allows any "aggrieved person" to bring an appeal before the Zoning Board of Appeals of the Town of Salina. According to the New York Court of Appeals, this included a commercial tenant seeking variances, apparently without the consent of its landlord:

> In this case, where the evidence before the Board showed that Mobil was the tenant, had paid the property taxes, and had made prior applications to the Board on its own, and on one occasion with the support of the owner, it cannot be said that the Board acted unreasonably in considering and granting its application for the zoning variances.

Emmi v. Zoning Board of Appeals, 482 N.Y.S.2d 263 (Ct. App. 1984).

9. As to the interesting problem of the board of appeals reversing a prior decision, see Sipperley v. Board of Appeals on Zoning, 140 Conn. 164, 98 A.2d 907 (1953). See also Maltbie, The Legal Background of Zoning, 22 Conn. B.J. 2-9 (1948). For a case holding that the reversal rule should apply differently to the case of the special exception, see Mitchell Land Co. v. Planning and Zoning Board of Appeals, 140 Conn. 527, 102 A.2d 316 (1953).

10. After a period of trial and error, and having gained experience with the problem, the board of appeals formally announced that henceforth all applications for two-family houses in Single-Family Residence-A District will be granted. Is this proper?

11. In Plumb v. Board of Zoning Appeals of New Haven, 141

D. Departures from the Zoning Ordinance 357

Conn. 595, 602, 108 A.2d 899, 902 (1954), the board granted a variance allowing the use of property in a residential zone as a lumber yard. In reversing the lower court that had overruled the board, the court stated: "Moreover, the variance asked was one which was in harmony with the fundamental purposes of the zoning regulations. Those purposes are to promote public safety, to avoid traffic hazards and to stabilize property values."

12. One particularly persistent property owner not only won his variance after bringing his case before the state supreme court, but also later convinced an appellate court to uphold $125,000 in damages from the Zoning Administrator for the official's refusal to grant the variance after the city's board of permit appeals decided in the landowner's favor. Associate Justice Scott was not persuaded by the administrator's assertion of governmental immunity. The California Supreme Court denied review and "ordered that the opinion be not officially published." Edwards v. Steele, 216 Cal. Rptr. 283 (Ct. App. 1985).

■ CITY OF CLEBURNE v. CLEBURNE LIVING CENTER
473 U.S. 432 (1985)

Justice WHITE delivered the opinion of the Court. . . .

In July, 1980, respondent Jan Hannah purchased a building at 201 Featherston Street in the city of Cleburne, Texas, with the intention of leasing it to Cleburne Living Centers, Inc. (CLC) for the operation of a group home for the mentally retarded. It was anticipated that the home would house 13 retarded men and women, who would be under the constant supervision of CLC staff members. The house had four bedrooms and two baths, with a half bath to be added. CLC planned to comply with all applicable state and federal regulations.

The city informed CLC that a special use permit would be required for the operation of a group home at the site, and CLC accordingly submitted a permit application. In response to a subsequent inquiry from CLC, the city explained that under the zoning regulations applicable to the site, a special use permit, renewable annually, was required for the construction of "[h]ospitals for the insane or feeble-minded, or alcoholic [sic] or drug addicts, or penal or correctional institutions."[3]

---

3. The site of the home is an area zoned "R-3," an "Apartment House District." App. 51. Section 8 of the Cleburne zoning ordinance, in pertinent part, allows the

The city had determined that the proposed group home should be classified as a "hospital for the feebleminded." After holding a public hearing on CLC's application, the city council voted three to one to deny a special use permit.

CLC then filed suit in Federal District Court against the city and a number of its officials, alleging, *inter alia,* that the zoning ordinance was invalid on its face and as applied because it discriminated against the mentally retarded in violation of the equal protection rights of CLC and its potential residents. The District Court found that "[i]f the potential residents of the Featherston Street home were not mentally retarded, but the home was the same in all other respects, its use would be permitted under the city's zoning ordinance," and that the city counsel's decision "was motivated primarily by the fact that the residents of the home would be persons who are mentally retarded." App. 93, 94. Even so, the District Court held the ordinance and its application constitutional. Concluding that no fundamental right was implicated and that mental retardation was neither a suspect nor a quasi-suspect classification, the court employed the minimum level of judicial scrutiny applicable to equal protection claims. The court deemed the ordinance, as written and applied, to be rationally related to the City's legitimate interests in "the legal responsibility of CLC and its residents, . . . the safety and fears of residents in the adjoining neighborhood," and the number of people to be housed in the home. Id., at 103.

The Court of Appeals for the Fifth Circuit reversed, determining that mental retardation was a quasi-suspect classification and that it should assess the validity of the ordinance under intermediate-level scrutiny. 726 F.2d 191 (1984). . . .

---

following uses in an R-3 district:
1. Any use permitted in District R-2.
2. Apartment houses, or multiple dwellings.
3. Boarding and lodging houses.
4. Fraternity or sorority houses and dormitories.
5. Apartment hotels.
6. Hospitals, sanitariums, nursing homes or homes for convalescents or aged, *other than for the* insane or *feeble-minded* or alcoholics or drug addicts.
7. Private clubs or fraternal orders, except those whose chief activity is carried on as a business.
8. Philanthropic or eleemosynary institutions, other than penal institutions.
9. Accessory uses customarily incident to any of the above uses. . . . Id., at 60-61 (emphasis added).

Section 16 of the ordinance specifies the uses for which a special use permit is required. These include "[h]ospitals for the insane or feebleminded, or alcoholic or drug addicts, or penal or correctional institutions." Id., at 63. Section 16 provides that a permit for such a use may be issued by "the Governing Body, after public hearing, and after recommendation of the Planning Commission." All special use permits are limited to one year, and each applicant is required "to obtain the signatures of the property owners within two hundred (200) feet of the property to be used." Ibid.

D. Departures from the Zoning Ordinance

[For the United States Supreme Court's reaction to the city's employment of the special use permit provision, see infra page 1085.]

Notes

1. Under the *Nectow* approach, does the absence of a provision for exceptions and variances render an ordinance constitutionally infirm? Compare Bolduc v. Pinkham, 148 Me. 17, 88 A.2d 817 (1952) with Florentine v. Town of Darien, 142 Conn. 415, 423-427, 115 A.2d 328, 332-333 (1955).

2. Who sits on the board of adjustment and what is the extent of their knowledge concerning the (often-confusing) state of the law? Consider the results of one comprehensive study of rural boards in Iowa:

> Obviously, the requirement that a majority of the board be comprised of residents of unincorporated areas makes likely that farmers will be chosen to serve on the board. Over one-half of the board members responding to the Project questionnaire were people engaged in farming or spouses of farmers. Also, most board of adjustment members are long-time residents of their counties. Only two percent have lived in their counties for less than ten years, while over eighty percent have resided in their counties for more than thirty years.
>
> A clear majority of county board of adjustment members have high school degrees; only six and one-half percent have less than a high school education. Board members rarely possess any formal education related to land use planning, however. Although one-third of all county board of adjustment members in Iowa have some education beyond high school, only four percent have a formal education related to land use planning.

Contemporary Studies Project, Rural Land Use Regulation in Iowa: An Empirical Analysis of County Board of Adjustment Practices, 68 Iowa L. Rev. 1083, 1146-1147 (1983).

3. Environmental control invokes the powers of many agencies at different levels of government.

> A Zoning Commission should be brave, and forthrightly declare all permitted uses and all prohibited uses, and leave to the Zoning Board of Appeals its basic function of granting hardship variances and nothing more. The Board of Appeals is constantly face to face with the public, bearing the brunt of all criticisms of zoning, listening to personal abuse and incurring the hostility of the losers. It is little enough to ask that their pathway to correct and just decisions be kept clear and straight, and that their guides be kept free from perplexities and ambiguities.

Survey of Big City Zoning Boards of Appeals
(Boards hearing variances, appeals, and special exceptions)

City	No. of Board Members	Frequency of Meeting	1984 Zoning Caseload	Qualifications	Compensation
Atlanta[a]	5	2/month	330	At least two members must be drawn from the professions of law, planning, or engineering	$25/meeting
Baltimore[b]	5	1/week	637	—	Chair $8,600/yr; Others $8,000/yr.
Birmingham, Alabama	5 plus 2 alternates	2/month	139	One licensed architect, one engineer, one building contractor, one real estate broker, and three representatives of the community at large	Gratis
Boston	5 plus 3 alternates	1/week	790 (7/1/83-6/30/84)	One appointed by mayor, one by board of architects or engineers, one by board of Realtors, one by building trades union, one by central labor union; three alternates appointed by mayor	$100/meeting

360

Louisville/ Jefferson Co., Kentucky	7	2/month	210	Two county residents; two city residents; three residents of fourth-class cities	$40/meeting
New York City[c]	6	1/week	200	Two licensed engineers (civil and mechanical) with 10 years experience; two registered architects with 10 years experience; one urban planner with 10 years experience; and one lay person	Chair $71,000; Vice-Chair $64,473; Others $58,161
Norfolk, Virginia[d]	5	1/month	49	Appointed by circuit court	—
Phoenix	7	1/month	180	—	Gratis

The APA survey also found that Cincinnati, Long Beach, Los Angeles, Portland, San Diego, San Francisco, and Seattle either don't have a zoning board of appeals or have a board with limited duties. In these cities, either the zoning administrator, planning director, director of building inspections, or hearings officer handles many of the duties (e.g., variance decisions) normally handled by a zoning board of appeals.

[a] A separate zoning review board holds hearings on rezoning and use permits.
[b] Referred to as "Board of Municipal Appeal"; handles building code appeals.
[c] The New York City Board of Standards and Appeals also makes decisions related to the city building code, fire code, multiple dwelling law, and other development codes (e.g., loft conversion laws). Board members may not hold other jobs and are expected to devote themselves full time to their duties. The chair and vice-chair must be professional.
[d] State law strictly limits the board's authority; the board does not issue use permits but grants dimensional variances.

Source: Zoning News, June 1985, at 2-3 (selections).

Crawford, Special Exceptions Prove to Be the Rule, 26 Conn. B.J. 172, 182 (1952).

Many cities are delegating regulatory functions to zoning commissioners, administrators, or examiners, who undertake functions traditionally exercised by planning commissions or boards of appeals. The zoning administrator of Los Angeles described his duties as follows:

> The original charter amendment ... also gave the administrator control of and responsibility for the administration and enforcement of the zoning ordinances. As is customary in all well devised zoning ordinances, our ordinance provides that any permit or license issued for uses of land or buildings that does not conform in every respect with the zoning regulations is null and void. We have installed a system that requires every city department with authority to issue any kind of permit or license involving any use of land or buildings to have applications for such permits checked for zoning compliance before they are issued or rejected. This system removes the embarrassment of one department issuing a permit or certificate that violates an ordinance enforced by another department....
>
> There are many other duties assigned to him by the ordinance that further relieve the commission and others could be assigned. Some of the other duties and matters over which he has authority are as follows:
>
> 1. To hear and determine appeals from orders and decisions of the building department in its zoning administration and enforcement activities.
>
> 2. To determine the proper zone allocation of uses not mentioned or specifically classified in the ordinance.
>
> 3. To adopt general interpretations determining the proper application of the yard regulations to groups of lots located in hillside districts or affected by common problems.
>
> 4. To permit higher walls or fences in front yards in developments of suburban or estate character.
>
> 5. To perform all administrative acts required of the planning commission or city council under old zone variance ordinances, such as approval of plans and signs.
>
> 6. To determine and prescribe conditions and methods of operation to be employed for each oil drilling enterprise in the various oil drilling districts created by ordinance and for each animal slaughtering enterprise to be established or enlarged in the few animal slaughtering districts.

Smutz, Is the Zoning Tail Wagging the Dog?, in Planning 102, 109, 110 (1956). See The Position of the Zoning Administrator, ASPO, June 1970; Washington State Land Planning Commission, Land Planning for our Future (1973).

E. VOICES IN OPPOSITION: CHAMPIONS OF DE- AND RE-REGULATION

The assault on the Euclidean citadel did not end with Newton D. Baker's unsuccessful foray. Lately, as part of a growing dissatisfaction with nearly all forms of public regulation, a number of commentators have proffered alternative development rights transfer and control systems. As you study these proposals consider whether the system under attack is as unresponsive and inflexible as the critics assume. Is Houston still a valid model of nonzoning, given the city's recent experimentation with land-use regulation?[61] Does Kmiec's alternative system suffer from the same potential complications as the Ellickson proposal previewed in Chapter II? How much of the solution to the "zoning problem" is to be found in the sort of judicial scrutiny favored by a majority of the President's Commission? As you read the activist cases and protective legislation in Chapter IV, keep in mind the cries for devolution to the private sector as well as the Commission's suggestions concerning heightened scrutiny and responsive statutes.

■ SIEGAN, NON-ZONING IN HOUSTON
13 J. L. & Econ. 71, 141–143 (1970)

These in brief are the conclusions drawn from this examination of Houston's system of non-zoning, with appropriate comparisons with, and conclusions about zoning.

---

61. See Houston Adopts Limited Development Controls, Land Use L. & Zoning Dig., Aug. 1982, at 3:

> Houston has long prided itself on rejecting public land use controls, primarily zoning, to control growth and segregate different land uses. Instead, it has relied on restrictive covenants and other private agreements to regulate development. Developer opposition and voter rejection of past zoning proposals have inspired diverse commentaries on the city's land use management, ranging from Bernard Siegan's endorsement in his 1972 treatise, Land Use Without Zoning, to Richard Babcock's more critical evaluation, "Houston: Unzoned, Unfettered, and Mostly Unrepentant," in the March 1982 issue of Planning magazine.
>
> On June 22, however, the Houston city council adopted Ordinance 82-1010 — Houston's first limited development control ordinance. The ordinance requires city planning commission approval of all commercial and residential development plats and establishes development standards for frontage, offstreet parking, common open space, block length, and building setbacks as conditions for plat approval. In substance, the ordinance is more like a subdivision regulation than a zoning ordinance: it does not segregate various land uses into districts and it does not establish standards for each district. But the ordinance indicates a new willingness on the part of the city to take some tentative steps toward applying the police power in an effort to alleviate some of the transportation-related effects of rapid growth.
>
> Formerly, the city could review the provision of public streets only in residential subdivisions. Now the review process has been extended to nonresidential projects as well. The ordinance requires city approval of all development plats, both inside the city limits and within five miles of its border.

1. Economic forces tend to make for a separation of uses even without zoning. Business uses will tend to locate in certain areas, residential in others, and industrial in still others. Apartments, however, may be built in almost any area except within an industrial one. There is also a tendency for further separation within a category; light industrial uses do not want to adjoin heavy industrial uses, and vice versa. Different kinds of business uses require different locations. Expensive homes will separate from less expensive ones, townhouses, duplexes, etc. It is difficult to assess the effectiveness of zoning in furthering this process. It is highly successful in this respect in the "bedroom" suburbs, but much less so in the larger cities.

2. When these economic forces do not guarantee that there will be a separation, and separation is vital to maximize profits (or promote one's tastes and desires), property owners will enter into agreements to provide such protection. The restrictive covenants covering home and industrial subdivisions are the most prominent example of this. Adjoining property owners (such as those on a strip location) can also make agreements not to sell for a use that will be injurious to one or both.

3. Because many of the early restrictive covenants in Houston were (a) limited in duration, or (b) legally insufficient, or (c) not enforced by owners, zoning would have kept more areas as strictly single-family. The covenants created subsequent to 1950 were more durable and as a practical matter will remain in force for long periods. They may be as effective as zoning in maintaining single-family homogeneity.

4. When covenants expire, land and properties will be used as economic pressures dictate. Most business uses will not locate on interior streets because they require favorable traffic conditions available only on major thoroughfares. Within recent years, the most important factor influencing diversity in nonrestricted interior areas is the strong demand for multiple-family accommodations. But this demand does not extend to all sections of the city. Accordingly, some areas fronting on interior streets will remain relatively free of diverse uses after their covenants expire.

5. A non-zoned city is a cosmopolitan collection of property uses. The standard is supply and demand, and if there is economic justification for the use, it is likely to be forthcoming. Zoning restricts the supply of some uses, and thereby prevents some demands from being satisfied. It may likewise impede innovation. However, in general, zoning in the major cities, which contain diverse life styles, has responded and accommodated to most consumer demands. This has not occurred usually in the more homogeneous suburbs.

6. Zoning is a legislative function. As such, political, economic, and social pressures of many, or even a relatively few, often influence or control zoning decisions. These pressures may even be more important

than the provisions of the zoning ordinance. Such forces play no part in a non-zoned city.

7. The most measurable influence of zoning is its effect on multiple-family dwellings. If Houston had adopted zoning in 1962, this would probably have resulted in higher rents and a lesser number and variety of apartments and, in consequence, some tenants would have been priced out of the new apartment market. Most adversely affected would be tenants of average incomes.

8. The experience of the FHA suggests that the appreciation over the years in values of new and existing single-family homes has not differed in Houston from those of zoned cities.

9. The role of planning under zoning is a curious one. The original zoning ordinance will largely freeze the existing pattern of land use. All subsequent decisions on the ordinance will be made through the legislative process, which would seem inherently more responsive to political and economic opinion and pressures than the recommendations of the planners. As one result, changes in zoning in the major cities seem to follow a more chaotic than orderly pattern.

10. In Houston, the level of control over land use and development has not increased appreciably over the years. The most significant policy adopted in recent years has been the city's enforcement since 1965 of the restrictive covenants in residential subdivisions. By contrast, zoning has tended to give the municipality greater and more minute control. One reason is that the failure of existing controls has usually led to more severe controls, not lesser ones.[62]

■ KMIEC, THE ROLE OF THE PLANNER IN A DEREGULATED WORLD
Land Use L. & Zoning Dig., June 1982, at 4-6

[T]he existing system is procedurally unfair because it unjustifiably accords substantial weight to self-selected samples of neighbors to the detriment of the landowner and the consumers he represents; distributionally unfair because it arbitrarily favors some landowners while burdening others; inefficient as a mechanism for internalizing spillovers because it relies upon a system of specific deterrence; inefficient as a mechanism of public control because it is fractured among numerous agencies and legislative bodies; inflexible because it is founded upon predetermined, crude categories of permitted uses unable to accom-

---

62. The thesis is developed at fuller length in Siegan's book, Land Use Without Zoning (1972). For a startlingly contrasting vision of how Houston has developed without public land-use regulation, see Feagin, Free Enterprise City: Houston in Political-Economic Perspective (1988). — EDS.

modate new development techniques; and uncertain because it is subject to changes granted without standards or without adherence to announced standards and without sufficient or consistent regard for investments made in reliance thereon. . . .

To clean the slate, zoning and subdivision controls as presently applied to undeveloped land should be repealed and replaced by an alternative free enterprise development system ("alternative system") that would allow private decisions to determine the desired use, location, and design of land development.

To illustrate, the alternative system can be set out in a step-by-step format using as an example a landowner who voluntarily decides to develop his land into a mixed residential/commercial project.

Step 1. All undeveloped land is reclassified agricultural/open space.

Step 2. The local legislative body, after consultation with planners and the public specifies the maximum permissible land use intensity (LUI) in each of four separate schedules for residential, commercial, industrial, and mixed-use projects.

Step 3. The landowner notifies an administrative Land Use Control Agency (LUCA) of his decision to build a residential/commerical project at or below the density permitted under the mixed-use schedule.

Step 4. An appraiser determines the difference in land value (the unearned increment) between the agricultural/open space use and the selected mixed use.

Step 5. On the basis of the landowner's private improvement plans, LUCA specifies in the Public Improvement Contract the nature of the public improvements to be constructed with the recaptured unearned increment. (If private improvement plans materially change thereafter, the landowner is required to negotiate an Intensity Modification Contract to reflect corresponding changes in public improvements.)

Step 6. The landowner constructs private improvements as desired and public improvements as required by the Public Improvement Contract.

Step 7. The subdivision plat is recorded for the purpose of accurate title description. . . .

Fundamentally, the alternative system assumes that public regulation should not define how land is to be used specifically, but should instead articulate general standards ensuring that land will be used — without regard to its specific use — in a manner that is safe and healthful. From the land development standpoint, safety and health issues relate

E. Voices in Opposition

to matters of population density and the quantity and quality of public improvements. The alternative system articulates safety and health standards through the determination of land use intensity (LUI) schedules and the supervision and specification of public improvements. Thus, the alternative system establishes a general framework for guiding private development and a mechanism for supplying complementary public improvement. . . .

Beyond the initial collectivized statement of normalcy (in the form of an overall limit on density), the alternative system favors individual freedom and less collectivized methods of control. For example, the individual landowner selects the type and location of use. In addition, the landowner determines, in reference to market demand, unit size and building and site design. This freedom opens up possibilities for architectural competition and supplies flexibility to meet changing consumer preferences for units of different sizes.[63]

63. See also Kmiec, Deregulating Land Use: An Alternative Free Enterprise Development System, 130 U. Pa. L. Rev. 28 (1981); Delogu, Local Land Use Controls: An Idea Whose Time Has Passed, 36 Me. L. Rev. 261 (1984).
Cf. Nelson, A Property Right Theory of Zoning, 11 Urb. Law. 713, 725-727 (1979):

In light of the popularity of zoning in existing neighborhoods, the American public clearly appears to prefer fairly tight collective control by local residents over their immediate environment; this might also be described as a preference for collective possession by neighborhood residents of the specific bundle of property rights pertaining to new uses as well as to those relating to major alterations in existing neighborhood properties. Furthermore, the public seems to regard the neighborhood environment as essentially a private rather than a public good, and the collective property rights held by the local residents, therefore, are expected to be exercised according to the standards of an ordinary private property owner.

If these demonstrated popular preferences are accepted as valid, a first step in a new tenure system would be to recognize and give a more formal status to the collective property rights of neighborhoods. In existing neighborhoods such a step would involve the establishment of a new neighborhood legal entity to which the collective rights created by zoning would be transferred from their current lodging at the municipal level. This new neighborhood entity — it could be called a "neighborhood association" — would have a private legal status. It would also be necessary to specify the precise division between individual and collective property rights in each neighborhood, or perhaps to develop a mechanism for determining such a division differently on a neighborhood-by-neighborhood basis. Collective decision-making rules and procedures for the exercise of neighborhood property rights would also be required. Another important need would be a method for determining neighborhood boundaries — perhaps superimposed by a state or municipal body or perhaps left more to citizens to work out through local negotiations.

An important issue in this process is whether the new collective private property rights should be saleable. The idea of selling permission to enter a neighborhood naturally violates existing zoning theories and may also appear unethical. It should be kept in mind, however, that social attitudes vary greatly and often change significantly concerning the transactions which can be legitimately undertaken in the market. In feudal society many current property rights were not considered legitimately saleable, and the modern capitalist system evolved as these sanctions were dropped and the market place became the accepted mechanism for the exchange of property rights.

If the sale of collective property rights by neighborhood residents is treated

■ THE REPORT OF THE PRESIDENT'S COMMISSION ON HOUSING
200-202 (1982)

To protect property rights and to increase the production of housing and lower its cost, all State and local legislatures should enact legislation providing that no zoning regulations denying or limiting the development of housing should be deemed valid unless their existence or adoption is necessary to achieve a vital and pressing governmental interest. In litigation, the governmental body seeking to maintain or impose the regulation should bear the burden for proving it complies with the foregoing standard.

Under the Federal system, States have primary responsibility for zoning regulation. Virtually all States, however, have chosen to delegate this authority to local governments, and many municipalities have used this power in ways that unnecessarily restrict the production of housing and increase its costs.

To correct improper use of this power, States should adopt constitutional or legislative enabling provisions that prohibit restrictive local zoning — except where land-use regulation is necessary to satisfy a "vital and pressing" governmental interest. Where States fail to act, localities should enact their own ordinances to correct improper zoning.

Generally, a vital and pressing governmental interest will involve protecting health and safety, remedying unique environmental problems, preserving historic resources, or protecting investments in existing public infrastructure resources.[5] This new standard for zoning is intended to limit substantially the imposition of exclusionary land-use policies, since exclusion is clearly not an acceptable governmental interest.

---

as a practical rather than an ethical question, there are good reasons to allow it. Sale of entry rights would greatly increase the range of siting opportunities for new land uses in metropolitan areas. At present only those uses which tend to enhance the neighborhood environment are likely to be granted permission to enter by local residents. Other less attractive uses, however, might well be willing to offer neighborhood residents more than sufficient financial compensation for any adverse impacts which might arise from their introduction to the area. If the neighborhood residents are fully compensated financially and the new use is thereby able to obtain a superior location, there would seem to be little reason to object to such a sale of zoning rights.

See also Nelson, Zoning and Property Rights (1977), as well as the readings on the sale of neighborhood zoning "rights" in Chapter IX. — Eds.

5. Vital and pressing governmental interests that zoning ordinances should serve include adequate sanitary sewer and water services; flood protection; topographical conditions that permit safe construction and accommodate septic tank effluence; protection of drinking-water aquifers; avoidance of nuisance or obnoxious uses; off-street parking; prohibition of residential construction amidst industrial development; and avoidance of long-term damage to the vitality of historically established neighborhoods.

E. Voices in Opposition

In enacting the proposed new standard, the States should give this standard specific content to assure it is not abused. State statutes (or local ordinances, where applicable) should specifically define what constitutes vital and pressing governmental interests, thereby leaving to the genius of federalism the ultimate contours of this standard. However, a locality should have the burden of proving that any zoning restriction it imposes on housing meets the new standard in later judicial review.

The Commission's proposed standard would apply only to housing. Thus, all decisions related to size of lot, size or type of housing, percentage of multifamily, or other housing types and locations would be left to the market, unless government intervention is justified by the locality as serving a vital and pressing governmental interest. . . .

The President should direct the Attorney General to analyze the constitutional validity and jurisprudential ramifications of the "vital and pressing" standard for judicially determining the validity of zoning ordinances and related standards that strike a balance between legitimate governmental interest and individuals' rights to property; if the Attorney General then concludes that a change should be sought in the existing *Euclid* standard, he should seek an appropriate case for urging the Supreme Court to adopt a new test.

The Commission believes that in recent years our legal system has weakened the property rights of owners of real property and largely ignored the implicit rights of newcomers deprived of affordable housing by excessive or exclusionary zoning. This imbalance should be redressed by State legislatures. But there is another potential source of protection — the courts.

In the past 25 years, the courts and legislatures have expanded the traditional meanings of property in applying due process protections. Yet the ownership of real property continues to be governed by a 50-year-old precedent that constitutes a significant departure from the traditional judicial role of protecting such property rights against government interference. . . .

Euclid was controversial in its day and still has critics. Experience indicates that the broad land-use charter it afforded localities has been abused — often at the expense of housing. . . .

The Commission believes the pendulum has swung too far away from the right to enjoy the ownership of real property and the important societal interests of increasing mobility and access to housing opportunities. Accordingly, the Commission believes the *Euclid* doctrine should be reexamined. The Commission recommends that the Attorney General seek an appropriate case in which to request review of the *Euclid* docrine in the context of modern land-use issues and the due process protections afforded other property rights in the 50 years since *Euclid* was decided.

Efforts to eliminate zoning have been successful, if at all, solely on an academic level. The reality is that communities continue to utilize height, area, and use regulations in order to plan (or control) land development and use. The healthy dose of experimentation we call post-Euclidean zoning has an impact on the way zoning is perceived and performed. How do the sweeping schemes of the de- and re-regulators hold up to the increased complexity of metropolitan life, the fragile interdependence of land uses, and the competing claims on the environment made by an ever-growing number of interest groups? Barring wholesale abandonment of *Euclid*, what role can the courts and state legislatures play in fine-tuning land-use devices to respond to the societal and constitutional demands of the next few decades?

IV

The Four Seeds Sown by Euclid: The Control of Metropolitan Configuration

The written judicial opinion, the lifeblood of the Anglo-American system of common law, on occasion is imbued by jurists, teachers, and scholars with the trappings and influence of symbol. There lies within the body of cases studied in nearly each American legal discipline one opinion from which the careful reader may perceive the dominant themes, the pervasive pattern of decision-making, the extralegal underpinnings, or the operative vocabulary of the pertinent area of the law.

So, for example, the torts student struggles with Benjamin Cardozo's daedal text in *Palsgraf*,[1] hoping to be rewarded with a fundamental appreciation of foreseeability. Every exercise of judicial review, the essential tool of constitutional litigation, is justified or criticized in Chief Justice John Marshall's terms, derived from his jurisprudential and political coup in Marbury v. Madison.[2] Justice Louis Brandeis, in his *Erie*[3] and *Chicago Board of Trade*[4] offerings, set the tone for generations of opinion writers and litigants immersed in federal choice of law and antitrust. To practitioners, students, and other interested

---

1. Palsgraf v. Long Island R.R., 248 N.Y. 339, 162 N.E. 99 (1928).
2. 5 U.S. (1 Cranch) 137 (1803).
3. Erie R.R. v. Tompkins, 304 U.S. 64 (1938).
4. Board of Trade v. United States, 246 U.S. 231 (1918).

observers, the names *Clifford*[5] and *Miranda*[6] conjure up not only esoteric legal images and nuances, but also practices and policies with significant "real-world" implications.

Land-use law has its central opinion as well, rendered in a case known by a geographical name, *Euclid*, that suggests to the layperson the lines, points, and planes of elementary geometry. The importance of Justice George Sutherland's nineteen-page opinion is undisputed. Sixty years after the Court's approval of zoning, *Euclid* endures as substance and symbol, despite waves of demographic, economic, and political change. The tools of the land-use lawyer and planner have indeed changed since the 1920s, as professionals have sought to match the socioeconomic intricacy and technological sophistication of urban and suburban life in the 1980s and beyond. Given this profound temporal and developmental gap, it is easy to dismiss *Euclid* as relevant only to a Model-T, "Lochnerian" universe. Such a dismissal, however, would ignore one of the opinion's most important aspects: the manner in which the Court's words and phrases anticipate four principal "modern" objections to Euclidean zoning and comprehensive governmental land-use regulation. In fact, to study Euclidean and post-Euclidean zoning absent some appreciation of the "four seeds" planted in Sutherland's opinion — exclusion, anticompetitiveness, urban design, and parochialism — is a shallow exercise for the modern land-use attorney who hopes to be not only fully prepared but sensitive as well to the wider implications of her or his practice.

A. EXCLUSION

> The serious question in the case arises over the provisions of the ordinance excluding from residential districts, apartment houses, business houses, retail stores and shops, and other like establishments. This question involves the validity of what is really the crux of the more recent zoning legislation, namely, the creation and maintenance of residential districts, from which business and trade of every sort, including hotels and apartment houses, are excluded.
>
> — *Euclid v. Ambler*, 272 U.S. at 390.

Exclusion is the essence of Euclidean zoning. Structures and lots are classified according to the height, area, and use deemed appropriate for the specific location. The Court had no trouble with the Village's segregation of residential and industrial uses, a course of separation in

---

5. Helvering v. Clifford, 309 U.S. 331 (1940).
6. Miranda v. Arizona, 348 U.S. 436 (1966).

A. Exclusion

accordance with and abetted by the then-current state of nuisance law. Exclusion of apartment houses and hotels posed the "serious question" left unresolved in "numerous and conflicting" state court decisions. In the name of health, safety, morals, and general welfare — the legitimate goals of the police power — and with the blessings of "commissions and experts," Sutherland and his brethren refused to find that setting apart single-family housing, in theory, necessarily violated fourteenth amendment due process strictures.

The insulation of single-family residences that was approved in *Euclid* was an attempt to use the power of the state (or city) to regulate land uses more rigidly and effectively than had been the case with private devices (particularly covenants and defeasible fees) that ran the risk of unreasonably restricting the essential right of alienation. No longer, it was hoped, would the character of a neighborhood depend on the whims of developers or the insistence of neighbors. Officers of local government — planners, commissioners, inspectors — would devise and enforce a properly legislated zoning plan.

The solution — governmental regulation — was so simple that one wonders why it took until the second decade of the twentieth century for comprehensive land-use planning to appear. There are two basic explanations. First, America had only recently turned the corner on urbanization. Second, it must be remembered that, although state encouragement of private enterprise is as old as the Republic,[7] it was not until the Progressive era of American history that widespread tampering with the market was broadly accepted, even encouraged by politicians and judges.[8] Even the more conservative members of the Supreme Court, during the initial two decades of the twentieth century, allowed some experimentation under the rubric of the police power, despite some negative impact on cherished constitutional liberties.[9]

By the early 1920s, however, when Sutherland and Pierce Butler joined James C. McReynolds and Willis Van Devanter to form the conservative bloc we know as the "Four Horsemen," the period of judicially approved experimentation swiftly drew to a close.[10] *Euclid v. Ambler*, a case that split Sutherland from the remaining three (dissenting) "horsemen," was a glaring exception to the pervasive pattern of judicial activism.

In many ways Euclidean zoning is a quintessential Progressive concept. Several of the key components are present: the reliance on

---

7. See Handlin & Handlin, Commonwealth: A Study of the Role of Government in the American Economy: Massachusetts, 1774-861 (rev. ed. 1969).

8. See, e.g., Hofstadter, The Age of Reform 227-256 (1955); Kolko, The Triumph of Conservatism: A Reinterpretation of American History, 1900-1916, at 2-3 (1963).

9. See Warren, The Progressiveness of the United States Supreme Court, 13 Colum. L. Rev. 294 (1913).

10. See, e.g., Adkins v. Children's Hospital, 261 U.S. 525 (1923).

experts to craft and enforce a regulatory scheme;[11] the belief that a pleasant environment would foster healthy, responsible citizens;[12] and the trust in decentralized control, a belief in what Frederic Howe called The City: The Hope of Democracy.[13] But there was another sentiment shared by many active in the Progressive movement that underlay zoning and contributed to its approval and popularity in the conservative climate of the 1920s: a decidedly negative view of the immigrants, particularly Southern and Eastern Europeans, who from the 1880s to the mid-1920s poured into America's cities in "alarming" numbers.[14]

The less than holy alliance between zoning as a particular land-use planning tool and anti-immigration sentiment dates back to the birthplace of American height, area, and use zoning — New York City. As demonstrated by Seymour Toll in his insightful Zoned American,[15] one of the driving forces behind passage of New York's 1916 ordinance was a coalition of Fifth Avenue retailers. The garment industry that had worked its way up the avenue over the past few decades, with its mass of Eastern European workers, posed a serious threat to the future of high-class retailing:

What was coming up the avenue in hot pursuit was the garment industry.

11. See Hofstadter, supra note 8, at 155:

Reform brought with it the brain trust. In Wisconsin even before the turn of the century there was an intimate union between the La Follette regime and the state university at Madison that foreshadowed all later brain trusts. National recognition of the importance of the academic scholar came in 1918 under Woodrow Wilson, himself an ex-professor, when the President took with him as counselors to Paris that grand conclave of expert advisers from several fields of knowledge which was known to contemporaries as The Inquiry.

12. See, e.g., Ekirch, Progressivism in America 77-78 (1974).
13. Howe, The City: The Hope of Democracy (1909); see also Hofstadter, supra note 8, at 175:

Even with the best traditions of public administration, the complex and constantly changing problems created by city growth would have been enormously difficult. Cities throughout the industrial world grew rapidly, almost as rapidly as those in the United States. But a great many of the European cities had histories stretching back hundreds of years before the founding of the first white village in North America, and therefore had traditions of government and administration that predated the age of unrestricted private enterprise. While they too were disfigured and brutalized by industrialism, they often managed to set examples of local administration and municipal planning that American students of municipal life envied and hoped to copy.

14. See, e.g., Mowry, The Era of Theodore Roosevelt and the Birth of Modern America, 1900-1912, at 91-94 (1958); Solomon, Ancestors and Immigrants: A Changing New England Tradition (1956). Of course, there were many reformers who were dedicated to "Americanizing" the nation's newcomers, and others who, "[l]ike the rest of their generation, . . . felt little enmity toward the immigrants but little identification with them either." Higham, Strangers in the Land: Patterns of American Nativism 1860-1925, at 118 (2d ed. 1977).

15. Toll, Zoned American (1969).

A. Exclusion

It sought the same thing as the carriage trade merchant — gain — but its route was lower Fifth Avenue, its great weapon was the tall loft building, its generals were real estate speculators, and its troops were lower East Side immigrants.[16]

That the Justices who participated in the *Euclid* case (at least those who studied the lower court opinion) were aware of the socioeconomic ramifications of their holding is undeniable. As the members of the Court reviewed Judge Westenhaver's opinion in Ambler Realty Co. v. Village of Euclid, they should have pondered this direct allusion to the exclusionary purpose and potential of land-use controls:

> The purpose to be accomplished [by Euclid's zoning ordinance] is really to regulate the mode of living of persons who may hereafter inhabit [the village]. In the last analysis, the result to be accomplished is to classify the population and segregate them according to their income or situation in life. The true reason why some persons live in a mansion and others in a shack, why some live in a single-family dwelling and others in a double-family dwelling, why some live in a two-family dwelling and others in an apartment, or why some live in a well-kept apartment and others in a tenement, is primarily economic.

Indeed, Westenhaver provided his reader with an important clue as to zoning's exclusionary potential:

> [I]t is equally apparent that the next step in the exercise of this police power would be to apply similar restrictions for the purpose of segregating in like manner various groups of newly arrived immigrants. The blighting of property values and the congesting of population, whenever the colored or certain foreign races invade a residential section, are so well known as to be within the judicial cognizance.

In 1926, despite this warning, the Supreme Court allowed the bold experiment in urban and suburban planning to continue.

The careful student of the Court's opinion in *Euclid* should not be surprised at the most recent developments described in the following section — efforts (primarily by courts, with the occasional legislative encouragement) to sanction the abusive use of ostensibly neutral zoning and planning tools to exclude the poor, minorities, and other "undesirable" groups and uses. For the potential use of governmental property restrictions to exclude those "not like us" — not unlike private restrictions before Shelley v. Kraemer.[17] — is one of the seeds of *Euclid*.

---

16. Id. at 110.
17. 334 U.S. 1 (1948).

1. Excluding People

CASE STUDY #1

a. Experimenting in the State Laboratories — A View from the *Mount*

Nearly five decades after the Supreme Court approved the work of Euclid's planners, the New Jersey Supreme Court dropped a bombshell on the law and planning community. In their 1975 opinion in Southern Burlington County NAACP v. Township of Mount Laurel, infra page 402, the justices recognized and attacked the link between land-use restrictions and socioeconomic segregation, a tie that was particularly distasteful because of the state's "crisis" — "a desperate need for housing, especially of decent living accommodations economically suitable for low and moderate income families." To commentators who had perceived this connection two decades before,[18] *Mount Laurel* was an appropriate, if somewhat delayed, judicial response. To a number of critics, particularly local and state legislators and skeptical jurists from other jurisdictions, those who sat on New Jersey's high court were mistaken arbiters at best, socialist usurpers at worst.

During the subsequent decade, the legacy of *Mount Laurel* has been impressive: some corrective legislation, replication and modification in a number of state courts, oceans of ink in planning and law journals, and stubborn resistance leading to a second (more restrictive and demanding) supreme court decision in New Jersey. Even if one opposed the court's activism and social tampering, it was now evident that zoning and socioeconomic exclusion were intertwined.

Just as earlier chapters follow the decisional path from nuisance law to zoning, these materials trace the steps that led up to (and far beyond) the New Jersey court's dramatic stand. But first this caveat is offered: For many first-year property students the revolution in landlord-tenant law,[19] though national in scope and far from uniform in substance, is identified with the name *Javins*[20] — one case, from one court, in one jurisdiction.[21] Likewise, exclusionary zoning and *Mount Laurel* are commonly uttered in the same breath, despite the fact that the judicial attack has not been confined to one jurisdiction, or even to

---

18. See, e.g., Williams, Planning Law and Democratic Living, 20 Law & Contemp. Probs. 316 (1955).
19. See, e.g., Symposium: The Revolution in Landlord-Tenant Law: Causes and Consequences, 69 Cornell L. Rev. 517 (1984).
20. Javins v. First National Realty Corp., 428 F.2d 1071 (D.C. Cir. 1970).
21. See, e.g., Rabin, The Revolution in Landlord-Tenant Law, 69 Cornell L. Rev. 517, 522: "Although there were precursors, *Javins* . . . is the leading case establishing the implied warranty of habitability."

A. Exclusion

the northeastern region of the country. Still, even for one studying or practicing law in a jurisdiction not yet within the *Mount Laurel* fold, and thus not subject to rules regarding "fair share" and "developing communities," the extensive (and somewhat organic) New Jersey experience offers an instructive perspective on the adaptability of the common law to changing social patterns; on the shifting responsibilities of judges (on trial and appellate courts), legislators, and local residents; and on the efficacy of judicially imposed solutions to decades-old problems of segregation.

By the time the journey down this path concludes, the reader will be well acquainted with many of the ostensibly neutral devices employed by municipalities to help create or maintain a livable community, as well as with the substantive and procedural rules governing the exclusionary zoning challenge to those devices in New Jersey and beyond. Moreover, as in our appreciation of the efforts of courts in the District of Columbia and elsewhere to fashion and enforce a warranty of habitability for lower-income urban tenants, several important inquiries warrant careful consideration: When, if ever, does judicial impatience with legislative and administrative dilatoriness or even obstructionism warrant an activist role? How convincing, in political and economic terms, are the court's justifications for imposing extraordinary remedies? Are judges who have taken on the responsibilities of mandating and overseeing large-scale real estate development decision-making equipped for the task, even when special masters and court-appointed experts serve to fill any expertise gap? What alternatives to such activism does our political and legal system offer? How responsive are state legislatures and administrative agencies? Would general education of the electorate make judicial excesses unnecessary? Without the judge operating the balance, how can the essential goods of affordable housing and the conservation of a fragile environment be reconciled?

■ LIONSHEAD LAKE, INC. v. WAYNE TOWNSHIP
10 N.J. 165, 89 A.2d 693 (1952), appeal dismissed, 344 U.S. 919 (1953)

VANDERBILT, C. J. The plaintiff, the owner and developer of a large tract of land in the defendant township, commenced this action in lieu of a prerogative writ challenging the validity of the defendant's zoning ordinance in fixing the minimum size of dwellings and in placing certain of its properties in a residential district. On the plaintiff's motion the trial court entered summary judgment in its favor on the first count, setting aside the provisions of the ordinance fixing the minimum size of dwellings, Lionshead Lake, Inc. v. Wayne Tp., 8 N.J. Super. 468, 73

A.2d 287 (Law Div. 1950). On appeal this judgment was reversed by the Appellate Division of the Superior Court because of the existence of a factual question and the case was remanded for trial, Lionshead Lake, Inc. v. Wayne Tp., 9 N.J. Super. 83, 74 A.2d 609 (App. Div. 1950).

The Township of Wayne is the most extensive municipality in Passaic County. It covers 25.34 square miles in comparison with the 23.57 square miles of Newark. It has a population of 11,815 in comparison with Newark's 437,857. Only 12% of the total area of the township has been built up. Included within its borders are several sizable lakes (the one located within the plaintiff's development, e.g., having an area of about 145 acres) and as a result a considerable number of its residences have been built for summer occupancy only. Although a political entity it is in fact a composite of about a dozen widely scattered residential communities, varying from developments like the plaintiff's where the average home costs less than $10,000, to more expensive sections where the homes cost from $35,000 to $75,000. It has but little business or industry.

On July 12, 1949, four years after the plaintiff had commenced the development of its Lionshead Lake properties and after over a hundred houses had been constructed there, the defendant adopted a revised zoning ordinance dividing the entire township into four districts; residence districts A and B, a business district and an industrial district, the last two comprising but a very small proportion of the township's total area. In section 3 of the ordinance pertaining to residence A districts it was provided that:

> (d) Minimum Size of Dwellings:
> Every dwelling hereafter erected or placed in a Residence A District shall have a living-floor space, as herein defined,
> of not less than 768 square feet for a one story dwelling;
> of not less than 1000 square feet for a two story dwelling having an attached garage;
> of not less than 1200 square feet for a two story dwelling not having an attached garage.

... [T]he same minimum size requirements for dwellings prevail throughout the entire township.

Within the entire township only about 70% of all the existing dwellings meet the minimum requirements of the ordinance; in some sections of the township as few as 20% of the existing dwellings comply with the ordinance requirements, in others (among them the plaintiff's Lionshead Lake development) only about 50% are above the prescribed minimum, while in other areas the percentage of compliance is far greater, reaching 100% in some of the more exclusive sections. The

A. Exclusion 379

low percentage of compliance in certain areas is not particularly significant, however, for the reason that the township is as yet substantially undeveloped. Compliance with the requirements of the ordinance in the future will undoubtedly result in the nonconforming houses comprising but a small minority even in those areas where they are now in the majority. There was testimony to the effect that to build a house for year-round occupancy having the minimum 768 square feet of living space would cost from $10,000 to $12,000, if mass produced, and that only about 30% of the population were financially able to afford such homes. The plaintiff's witness who so testified, a builder and developer, was hardly qualified, however, to express an opinion as to the financial ability of present and potential residents of the township and his opinion as to construction costs was considerably out of line with that of the defendant's expert who testified that homes complying with the ordinance could be and were built at a cost of $8,500 to $9,200 if for year-round occupancy and $7,500 to $8,200 if for seasonal use only.

To meet the plaintiff's attack on the reasonableness of the ordinance the defendant produced a recognized public health expert, who testified that the living-floor space in a dwelling had a direct relation to the mental and emotional health of its occupants and that he had developed scientific standards for different size families: 400 square feet for one person, 750 square feet for two persons, 1,000 square feet for three persons, 1,150 square feet for four persons, 1,400 square feet for five persons and 1,550 square feet for six persons. These the witness considered as desirable goals rather than legal standards. He conceded that the housing standards prescribed by the agencies of the Federal Government are below those written into the ordinance, as are those of the New Jersey Code of Minimum Construction Requirements for One and Two Family Dwellings, prepared by the Department of Economic Development, Division of Planning and Engineering (1946), which, however, does not have the force of law but is merely advisory. . . .

The zoning powers of municipalities have been extended by Art. IV, Sec. VI, par. 2 of the Constitution of 1947:

> The Legislature may enact general laws under which municipalities, other than counties, may adopt zoning ordinances limiting and restricting to specified districts and regulating therein, buildings and structures, according to their construction, and the nature and extent of their use, *and the nature and extent of the uses of land,* and the exercise of such authority shall be deemed to be within the police power of the State. . . .

The zoning statutes then in effect were amended by Chapter 305 of the Laws of 1948 to give effect to the expansion of the zoning power contemplated by the addition of the italicized words to the corresponding provision of the 1844 Constitution (Art. IV, Sec. VI, par. 5). Moreover, by Art. IV, Sec. VII, par. 11 of the Constitution of 1947, which had no counterpart in the 1844 Constitution, we are required to construe the constitutional and statutory provisions pertaining to zoning liberally in favor of a municipality. . . .

When the enabling zoning statutes are read in the light of the constitutional mandate to construe them liberally, there can be no doubt that a municipality has the power by a suitable zoning ordinance to impose minimum living-floor space requirements for dwellings. N.J.S.A. 40:55-30 provides:

> Any municipality may by ordinance, limit and restrict to specified districts and may regulate therein, buildings and structures according to their construction, and the nature and extent of their use, and the nature and extent of the uses of land, and the exercise of such authority, subject to the provisions of this article, shall be deemed to be within the police power of the State. . . .
>
> The authority conferred by this article shall include the right to regulate and restrict the height, number of stories, and size of buildings, and other structures, the percentage of lot that may be occupied, the sizes of yards, courts, and other open spaces, the density of population, and the location and use and extent of use of buildings and structures and land for trade, industry, residence, or other purposes. . . .

In Duffcon Concrete Products, Inc. v. Borough of Cresskill, 1 N.J. 509, 513, 64 A.2d 347, 349 we said:

> What may be the most appropriate use of any particular property depends not only on all the conditions, physical, economic and social, prevailing within the municipality and its needs, present and reasonably prospective, but also on the nature of the entire region in which the municipality is located and the use to which the land in that region has been or may be put most advantageously.

The Township of Wayne is still for the most part a sparsely settled countryside with great natural attractions in its lakes, hills and streams, but obviously it lies in the path of the next onward wave of suburban development. Whether that development shall be "with a view of conserving the value of property and encouraging the most appropriate use of land throughout such municipality" and whether it will "prevent the overcrowding of land or buildings" and "avoid undue concentration of population" depends in large measure on the wisdom of the governing body of the municipality as expressed in its zoning ordinance. It requires as much official watchfulness to anticipate and prevent suburban blight as it does to eradicate city slums.

Has a municipality the right to impose minimum floor area re-

A. Exclusion

quirements in the exercise of its zoning powers? Much of the proof adduced by the defendant township was devoted to showing that the mental and emotional health of its inhabitants depended on the proper size of their homes. We may take notice without formal proof that there are minimums in housing below which one may not go without risk of impairing the health of those who dwell therein. One does not need extensive experience in matrimonial causes to become aware of the adverse effect of overcrowding on the well-being of our most important institution, the home. Moreover, people who move into the country rightly expect more land, more living room, indoors and out, and more freedom in their scale of living than is generally possible in the city. City standards of housing are not adaptable to suburban areas and especially to the upbringing of children. But quite apart from these considerations of public health which cannot be overlooked, minimum flow-area standards are justified on the ground that they promote the general welfare of the community and, as we have seen in Schmidt v. Board of Adjustment of the City of Newark, 9 N.J. 405, 88 A.2d 607 (1952) . . . the courts in conformance with the constitutional provisions and the statutes hereinbefore cited take a broad view of what constitutes general welfare. The size of the dwellings in any community inevitably affects the character of the community and does much to determine whether or not it is a desirable place in which to live. It is the prevailing view in municipalities throughout the State that such minimum floor-area standards are necessary to protect the character of the community. A survey made by the Department of Conservation and Economic Development in 1951 disclosed that 64 municipalities out of the 138 reporting had minimum dwelling requirements. In the light of the Constitution and of the enabling statutes, the right of a municipality to impose minimum floor-area requirements is beyond controversy.

With respect to every zoning ordinance, however, the question remains as to whether or not in the particular facts of the case and in the light of all of the surrounding circumstances the minimum floor-area requirements are reasonable. Can a minimum of living floor space of 768 square feet for a one-story building; of 1,000 square feet for a two-story dwelling having an attached garage; and of 1,200 square feet for a two-story dwelling not having an attached garage be deemed unreasonable in a rural area just beginning to change to a suburban community? It is significant that the plaintiff admits that of the 100 houses in its development 30 met the minimum requirements when constructed and 20 more by voluntary additions of the owners to meet their individual needs have been enlarged to conform to the minimum requirements of the ordinance, and while this litigation has been pending 20 others have been constructed conforming to the ordinance. If some such requirements were not imposed there would be grave danger in certain parts of the township, particularly around the lakes which attract summer visitors, of the erection of shanties which would deteriorate land values generally to the great detriment of the increasing number of people who live in Wayne Township the year round. The minimum floor-area requirements imposed by the ordinance are not large for a family of normal size. Without some such restrictions there is always the danger that after some homes have been erected giving a character to a neighborhood others might follow which would fail to live up to the standards thus voluntarily set. This has been the experience in many communities and it is against this that the township has sought to safeguard itself within limits which seem to us to be altogether reasonable. . . .

OLIPHANT, J. (dissenting). I find I must dissent from the philosophy and the result arrived at in the majority opinion. Zoning has its purposes, but as I conceive the effect of the majority opinion it precludes individuals in those income brackets who could not pay between $8,500 and $12,000 for the erection of a house on a lot from ever establishing a residence in this community as long as the 768 square feet of living space is the minimum requirement in the zoning ordinance. A zoning provision that can produce this effect certainly runs afoul of the fundamental principles of our form of government. It places an unnecessary and severe restriction upon the alienation of real estate. It is not necessary, it seems to me, in order to meet any possible threat to the general health and welfare of the community.

It should be borne in mind that the threat to the general welfare and health of the community usually springs from the type of home that is maintained within the house rather than the house itself. Certain well-behaved families will be barred from these communities, not because of any acts they do or conditions they create, but simply because the income of the family will not permit them to build a house at the cost testified to in this case. They will be relegated to living in the large cities or in multiple-family dwellings even though it be against what they consider the welfare of their immediate families. . . .

My views on this particular phase of zoning do not prohibit minimum floor space in a house in particular districts or a proper correlation of minimum floor space in the house and the area of the lot or lots in question, but I cannot agree with the majority when they state with respect to this minimum square footage requirement that "whether it will 'prevent the overcrowding of land or buildings' and 'avoid undue concentration of the buildings' depends in large measure on the wisdom of the governing body of the municipality." This is clearly indicative of a lack of standard with respect to this particular phase of zoning in the Zoning Act itself and it assumes that the discretion of the zoning board or governing body of a municipality amounts to wisdom. To buttress their position the majority further states: "We may take notice without formal proof that there are

A. Exclusion

minimums in housing below which one may not go without risk of impairing the health of those who dwell therein." In so stating they inferentially approve certain theories advanced to sustain this ordinance by text writers and certain reports of the Department of Conservation and Economic Development. But it seems to me that the decision as to what the minimum square footage in a particular house should be is essentially within the legislative province, and the Legislature not having spoken it is not within the power of this court or the Department of Conservation and Economic Development to attempt to supply the deficiency in the statute.[22]

Notes and Problems

1. Justice Oliphant's discomfort with the social implications of zoning practices was shared, nine years after *Lionshead Lake*, by dissenting Justice Hall, in Vickers v. Township Committee of Gloucester Township, 37 N.J. 233, 81 A.2d 129 (1962). The majority held "that the township zoning ordinance amendment barring trailer camps from its industrial district was a valid exercise of its zoning power and was

---

22. A requirement of a minimum floor area of 1800 square feet was upheld in Flower Hill Building Corp. v. Village of Flower Hill, 199 Misc. 344, 100 N.Y. S.2d 903 (Sup. Ct. 1950). Senefsky v. Lawler, 307 Mich. 728, 12 N.W.2d 387 (1943), held unreasonable a minimum of 1300 square feet for all residences, and Hitchman v. Township of Oakland, 329 Mich. 331, 45 N.W.2d 306 (1951), held an ordinance to be unreasonable that required 800 square feet or more of floor area per family at the first floor level, or not less than 10,000 cubic feet of content. Fischer v. Bedminster Township, 11 N.J. 194, 93 A.2d 378 (1952), upheld a zoning provision requiring a minimum lot size of five acres in a semirural residence district as furthering "the advancement of a community as a social, economic and political unit." Du Page County v. Halkier, 1 Ill. 2d 491, 115 N.E.2d 635 (1953), invalidated a two and one-half acre requirement of an "Estate" zone; cf. Young v. Town Planning and Zoning Commission, 151 Conn. 235, 196 A.2d 427 (1963). See also Gignoux v. Village of Kings Point, 199 Misc. 485, 99 N.Y.S.2d 280 (Sup. Ct. 1950), and Scheve v. Township of Freehold, 119 N.J. Super. 433, 292 A.2d 35 (App. Div. 1972) (both cases, 40,000 sq. ft.); Dilliard v. Village of North Hills, 276 App. Div. 969, 94 N.Y.S.2d 715 (2d Dept. 1950) (two acres); Flora Realty and Investment Co. v. City of Ladue, 362 Mo. 1025, 246 S.W.2d 771, appeal dismissed, 344 U.S. 802 (1952) (three acres); Honek v. Cook County, 12 Ill. 2d 257, 146 N.E.2d 35 (1957) (five acres). For a poetic view (with an occasional fling at economics), see Whyte, The Last Landscape (1968) (proposing ordinances for *maximum* lot sizes).

See Haar, Zoning for Minimum Standards: The *Wayne Township* Case, 66 Harv. L. Rev. 1051 (1953); Nolan and Horack, How Small a House? — Zoning for Minimum Space Requirements, 67 id. 967 (1954); Haar, *Wayne Township*: Zoning for Whom? — In Brief Reply, 67 id. 986 (1954); Schaffer, Small Homes and Community Growth (1954); Isard & Coughlin, Municipal Costs and Revenues Resulting from Community Growth (1957); Urban Land Institute, Do Single Family Homes Pay Their Way? (1968); Note, 106 U. Pa. L. Rev. 292 (1957); Zoning and Planning Notes, Am. City 129 (Feb. 1951), id. 130 (Oct. 1951), id. 131 (Nov. 1951); for further background, see Warner, American Life: Dream and Reality (1953); Williams and Wacks, Segregation of Residential Areas Along Economic Lines: *Lionshead Lake* Revisited, 1969 Wis. L. Rev. 827. For further developments in New Jersey, see infra page 415. — EDS.

adopted in conformity with the statutory requirements." Law review articles were cited in support of the proposition that "[t]railer camps, because of their particular nature and relation to the public health, safety, morals and general welfare, present a municipality with a host of problems, and these problems persist wherever such camps are located."

Justice Hall offered the following observations:

> In my opinion legitimate use of the zoning power by such municipalities does not encompass the right to erect barricades on their boundaries through exclusion or too tight restriction of uses where the real purpose is to prevent feared disruption with a so-called chosen way of life. Nor does it encompass provisions designed to let in as new residents only certain kinds of people, or those who can afford to live in favored kinds of housing, or to keep down tax bills for present property owners. When one of the above is the true situation deeper considerations intrinsic in a free society gain the ascendency and courts must not be hesitant to strike down purely selfish and undemocratic elements. I am not suggesting that every such municipality must endure a plague of locusts or suffer transition to a metropolis overnight. I suggest only that regulation rather than prohibition is the appropriate technique for attaining a balanced and attractive community.

Despite wider acceptance of mobile and manufactured housing by consumers, planners, and lawmakers, prejudices still persist. See Brown and Sellman, Manufactured Housing: The Invalidity of the "Mobility" Standard, 19 Urb. Law. 367 (1987):

> While most state governments acknowledge a "duty to accommodate" manufactured housing within their communities, the controversy surrounding this issue is the precise nature of this duty and what has been described as "actual adherence and enthusiasm" of state and local governments in implementing this duty. Despite the number of state and local governments which now have progressive laws on their books reflecting an enlightened perception of manufactured housing, this attempt to accommodate may be "illusory unless manufactured homes are permitted by right in residential districts and not by special or conditional use permit."

2. In 1960, 80 percent of the vacant land zoned for residential use within fifty miles of Manhattan was subject to minimum lot requirements of one-half acre or more; over half was zoned for single-family dwellings on lots of at least one acre. See Regional Plan Association, Spread City 40 (1962); cf. ASPO, New Directions in Connecticut Planning Legislation 186 (1967). When faced with a large-lot case, most courts accord the regulation less of a presumption of validity, but restrict their inquiry to factors internal to the defendant municipality.

A. Exclusion

See Fulling v. Palumbo, 21 N.Y.2d 30, 233 N.E.2d 272, 286 N.Y.S.2d 249 (1967). What basic purposes of zoning tend to justify large-lot zoning?

3. In Medinger Appeal, 377 Pa. 217, 104 A.2d 118 (1954), the zoning ordinance prescribed a different requirement as to minumum habitable floor area in the several districts. Two-story houses were provided for as follows: AA — minimum habitable floor area, 1800 square feet; A — 1400; B — 1125; C — 1000; D — 1000. Is this a valid ordinance? See also American Veterans Housing Cooperative, Inc. v. Zoning Board of Adjustment, 69 Pa. D. & C. 449 (C.P. 1949). The ordinance in De Mars v. Zoning Commission, 19 Conn. Supp. 24, 109 A.2d 876 (1954), fixed the following minima: 860 square feet for a single-story dwelling; 1000 square feet for a one-and-one-half- or two-story dwelling, with the ground floor area to be no less than 720 square feet. Is this a valid ordinance?

4. Consider the following three cases: (a) A community passes a zoning ordinance to the effect that no person with an income of less than $20,000 per annum may establish his residence there. (b) A community passes a zoning ordinance to the effect that only single-family dwellings costing at least $60,000 may be erected there. (c) A community passes a zoning ordinance to the effect that only single-family dwellings may be erected, and (1) must be constructed of stone, brick, or other nonflammable material, (2) must contain 1500 square feet of inside floor space on the ground floor, and (3) must be sited on a lot a half acre in area or more. In each instance, assume an individual earning less than $20,000 yearly, who plans to build a $48,000 house of wood. Can he successfully allege the invalidity of any of the foregoing provisions? See Durkin Lumber Co. v. Fitzsimmons, 106 N.J.L. 183, 147 A. 555 (Ct. Err. & App. 1929); Stein v. Long Branch, 2 N.J. Misc. 121 (Sup. Ct. 1924); Guaclides v. Borough of Englewood Cliffs, 11 N.J. Super. 405, 78 A.2d 435 (App. Div. 1952).

5. Cities also added housing codes which establish minimum standards for all housing within the municipality to the more familiar regulatory measures such as building codes and zoning ordinances. In general, the standards cover three main aspects of housing quality: required facilities (bathrooms, toilets, sinks), maintenance of dwelling units and equipment, and occupancy limitation. The fact that a housing code was required to satisfy the workable program necessary to obtain federal aid for urban renewal no doubt helps to explain the increased popularity of this measure.

A city which chooses to enact a minimum housing code for its slum areas would prefer a higher standard in areas not yet blighted, to head off the cumulative cycle of decay. A single city-wide standard, such as the one adopted by the model ordinance of the American Public Health Association, requires a choice between slum prevention and slum amelioration, or an unhappy compromise; however, it raises no serious constitutional issues. A "zoned" housing code has been suggested, prescribing different standards for dwellings in different areas within the city. In Milwaukee, such a bill was not presented to the legislature on the advice of the corporation counsel that it would be unconstitutional. In Brennan v. City of Milwaukee, 265 Wis. 52, 60 N.W.2d 704 (1953), a provision that two apartments of not more than three rooms each could share a single bathtub or shower, while larger apartments had to have their own bathing facility, was held to deny equal protection. However, in Givner v. Commissioner of Health, 207 Md. 184, 113 A.2d 899 (1955), a provision requiring every dwelling unit to provide a private bathroom with hot and cold water, but exempting "any two story dwelling which contains not more than two dwelling units" was upheld. See Note, 69 Harv. L. Rev. 1115 (1956). On the proliferation of housing and building codes following passage of the Housing Act of 1954, see Hagman & Juergensmeyer, Urban Planning and Land Development Control Law §8.2 (2d ed. 1986).

The pattern was now well established: for every municipality asserting a right to "orderly and sound planning" there was a developer crying arbitrariness or discrimination. Until the balance of the supreme court shifted, Justice Hall's skepticism in *Vickers* about the motives of local officials (like the concerns of dissenting Justice Oliphant a decade before) was outvoted by a majority not yet ready to abandon its accustomed deferential posture in land-use litigation. As the next pair of cases indicates, however, lower court judges — disturbed by exclusionary practices and encouraged by developments in other jurisdictions — were not about to await a change in the attitude of the high court. Do the courts reveal the reasons why deference is no longer in order? Are we now entering a period of special sensitivity to the detrimental effects of separating those diverse groups that make up our expanding community?

■ OAKWOOD AT MADISON, INC. v. TOWNSHIP OF MADISON
117 N.J. Super. 11, 283 A.2d 353 (Law Div. 1971)

FURMAN, J.S.C.

This prerogative writ action challenges the constitutionality of the Zoning Act, N.J.S.A. 40:55-30 et seq., and the validity under that act of the Madison Township zoning ordinance adopted on September 25, 1970. Plaintiffs are two developers, who own vacant and developable

A. Exclusion

land in Madison Township, and six individuals, all with low income, representing as a class those who reside outside the township and have sought housing there unsuccessfully because of the newly adopted zoning restrictions, including one and two-acre minimum lot sizes.

Madison Township is 42 square miles in the southeast corner of Middlesex County, extending from Raritan Bay westward. In two decades of explosive growth from 1950 to 1970, paralleling the trend in the county and region, its population mounted from 7,366 to 48,715. Most of the new housing was single-family in developments on 15,000 square foot or smaller lots, and since 1965 multi-family in garden apartments. Reflecting school construction and other expanded costs of government, the real property tax rate increased from one of the lowest in 1950 to the highest in 1970 in the county.

Despite this population surge much of the township, approximately 30% of its land area, excluding Cheesequake State Park, is vacant and developable. A member of the planning firm which submitted a new master plan in May 1970 testified that the township could hold a population of 200,000 without overcrowding.

A new township administration in 1970 determined to curb population growth significantly and thus to stabilize the tax rate. The township was to "catch its breath," a phrase recurrent in the testimony. Because of exigencies of time arising from a court order in other litigation, the planning firm which was retained early in 1970 was given only two months within which to submit its proposal for a master plan. The deadline was met. The master plan proposal relied in part upon the studies of the township's previous planning consultant. It purported to represent a shift in approach, from explosive growth on a patchwork basis to orderly growth in densely developed areas and the preservation of open areas. . . .

The attack on the constitutionality of the Zoning Act is novel. By way of background plaintiffs suggest that the purposes of zoning, which were enacted in 1928, a time of relatively static population, are not commensurate with the general welfare today, a time of rapid population expansion. Specifically plaintiffs contend that the declared zoning purposes are fatally defective, thwarting the general welfare, because they fail to encompass housing needs. . . .

About 55% of the land area of the township is zoned R40 or R80. The R80 zone is new, the R40 zone expanded. Minimum lot size is one acre in R40 and two acres in R80. Minimum floor space is 1500 square feet in R40 and 1600 square feet in R80. According to the former township engineer, 80% of R40 (or about 5500 acres) and 30% of R80 (or about 2500 acres) is vacant and developable. Minimal acreage is vacant and developable in the R7, R10 and R20 zones. Since the 1930s there has not been a development on two-acre lots within the township. Since 1964 only one subdivision plan for one-acre lots has been proposed. Land and construction costs are such that the minimum purchase price in R40 would be $45,000 and in R80 $50,000. Only those with incomes in the top 10% of the nation and county could finance new housing in R40; an even smaller percentage in R80.

The multi-family zones, which are scattered through the township, are so restricted in land area that no more than 500 to 700 additional units can be built in all. Three or more bedroom units are not permitted. Two bedroom units must be limited to 20% of the total units in any apartment development. New units must not exceed 200 in any year.

Madison Township, among other municipalities, is encouraging new industry. Industry is moving into the county and region from the central cities. Population continues to expand rapidly. New housing is in short supply. Congestion is worsening under deplorable living conditions in the central cities, both of the county and nearby. The ghetto population to an increasing extent is trapped, unable to find or afford adequate housing in the suburbs because of restrictive zoning. See N.J.S.A. 55:16-2 (L. 1967, c. 112): "It is hereby declared that there is a severe housing shortage in the State...."

The township concedes the invalidity of the limitation to 200 new multi-family units per year but defends all other provisions of the zoning ordinance which are challenged. Its contentions are that it is seeking a balanced community, encouraging high income and moderate income housing to balance its predominant low income housing, and protecting drainage systems where high density residential development might result in floods and surface drainage problems and interfere with and imperil underground water resources.

As recently stated by the Supreme Court in Harvard Enterprises, Inc. v. Bd. of Adj., Madison Tp., 56 N.J. 362, 266 A.2d 588 (1970), litigation arising out of prior zoning provisions in Madison Township:

> ... [I]t should be noted that the judicial role in reviewing a zoning ordinance is tightly circumscribed. There is a strong presumption in favor of its validity, and the court cannot invalidate it, or any provision thereof, unless this presumption is overcome by a clear showing that it is arbitrary or unreasonable. [at 368, 266 A.2d at 592]

The underlying objective of the ordinance under attack was fiscal zoning, zoning as a device to avoid school construction and other governmental costs incident to population expansion. Housing needs of the region were not taken into consideration in its enactment, according to several members of the township council and planning board....

Fiscal zoning per se is irrelevant to the statutory purposes of zoning. But the Supreme Court in Gruber v. Mayor, etc., Raritan Tp., 39 N.J. 1, 9, 186 A.2d 489 (1962) recognized that "alleviating the tax burden

A. Exclusion

and the harmful school congestion" was a permissible zoning purpose if done reasonably and in furtherance of a comprehensive zoning plan. Gruber and the antecedent Newark, etc., Cream Co. v. Parsippany-Troy Hills Tp., 47 N.J. Super. 306, 135 A.2d 682 (Law Div. 1957), may be distinguished because they dealt with the pursuit of tax revenues through zoning for new industry, not the stabilization of the tax rate through zoning to exclude new low and moderate income housing.

In any event, the Madison Township zoning ordinance must stand or fall not as fiscal zoning. The test must be whether it promotes reasonably a balanced and well ordered plan for the entire municipality.

Several decisions have recognized balance within a municipality, which is in part undeveloped, as a valid zoning purpose. . . .

. . . [T]he highest courts of Pennsylvania and Virginia have struck down two, three, and four-acre minimum lot requirements in undeveloped areas as invalid zoning, without reasonable relation to the general welfare. Appeal of Kit-Mar Builders, Inc., 439 Pa. 466, 268 A.2d 765 (Sup. Ct. 1970); National Land and Investment Co. v. Kohn, 419 Pa. 504, 215 A.2d 597 (Sup. Ct. 1965); Board of County Sup'rs of Fairfax County v. Carper, 200 Va. 653, 107 S.E.2d 390 (Sup. Ct. App. 1959).

The Pennsylvania Supreme Court commented in *National Land*:

> . . . Four acre zoning represents Easttown's position that it does not desire to accommodate those who are pressing for admittance to the township unless such admittance will not create any additional burdens upon governmental functions and services. The question posed is whether the township can stand in the way of the natural forces which send our growing population into hitherto undeveloped areas in search of a comfortable place to live. We have concluded not. A zoning ordinance whose primary purpose is to prevent the entrance of newcomers in order to avoid future burdens, economic and otherwise, upon the administration of public services and facilities can not be held valid. [215 A.2d at 612.] . . .

In Madison Township's approach to the objective of balance, its attempted cure is a worse malady than whatever imbalance existed. About 8000 acres of land, apparently prime for low or moderate income housing development, have been taken out of the reach of 90% of the population, prohibitive in land and construction costs. The acreage available for multi-family apartments units is minuscule. Families with more than one child are barred from multi-family apartments because of the one and two bedroom restrictions, restrictions without any guise of a health or safety purpose.

The exclusionary approach in the ordinance under attack coincides in time with desperate housing needs in the county and region and expanding programs, federal and state, for subsidized housing for low income families.

Regional needs are a proper consideration in local zoning.

In pursuing the valid zoning purpose of a balanced community, a municipality must not ignore housing needs, that is, its fair proportion of the obligation to meet the housing needs of its own population and of the region. Housing needs are encompassed within the general welfare. The general welfare does not stop at each municipal boundary. Large areas of vacant and developable land should not be zoned, as Madison Township has, into such minimum lot sizes and with such other restrictions that regional as well as local housing needs are shunted aside. Vickers v. Tp. Com., Gloucester Tp., 37 N.J. 232, 181 A.2d 129 (1962), upholding a prohibition against trailer camps anywhere within a municipality, is not to the contrary.

The ordinance under attack must be held invalid because it fails to promote reasonably a balanced community in accordance with the general welfare, unless it is defensible on some other ground. Such other ground is urged, namely that low population density zoning provides protection against floods and other surface drainage problems and against diversion of water from an aquifer, an underground water resource. . . .

Only engineering data and expert opinion and, it may be, ecological data and expert opinion could justify the ordinance under attack. These were lacking both in the legislative process and at the trial. The record fails to substantiate that safeguarding against flood and surface drainage problems and protection of the Englishtown aquifer would be reasonably advanced by the sweeping zoning revision into low population density districts along the four water courses and elsewhere or the exclusionary limitations on multi-family apartment units.

For all the foregoing reasons the Madison Township zoning ordinance of September 15, 1970 is held to be invalid in its entirety.[23]

---

23. Steel Hill Development, Inc. v. Town of Sanbornton, 469 F.2d 956 (1st Cir. 1972), presents an interesting variant:

> Located in the rolling hills of Belknap County, New Hampshire is the tiny town of Sanbornton with a year-round population of approximately 1,000 persons living in some 330 regular homes. Long popular as a major recreational and resort area, Belknap County commenced to share its rural beauty with visitors in considerably greater degree with the opening in the 1960's of Interstate Highway 93 which funneled droves of touring urbanites from the Boston area, one hundred miles away, into towns like Sanbornton. . . . In short, as the district court stated, "this case reflects the current clash between those interested in opening up new and hitherto undeveloped land for sale and profit and those wishing to preserve the rural character of Northern New England and shield it from the relentless pressure of an affluent segment of our society seeking new areas for rest, recreation and year round living." Steel Hill Development, Inc. v. Town of Sanbornton, 338 F. Supp. 301, 302 (D.N.H. 1972).
>
> Steel Hill acquired its 510 acres in December 1969 and immediately began surveying the land, mapping the topography and creating plans for conventional and "cluster" development. At that time and until March 9, 1971 the entire Steel

A. Exclusion

Notes

1. By what right could Oakwood at Madison, Inc. and the nonresident plaintiffs maintain a cause of action against the township? See N.J. Stat. Ann. §§40-55D-4, -18 (West Supp. 1987):

> "Interested party" means: . . . (b) in the case of a civil proceeding in any court or in an administrative proceeding before a municipal agency, any person, whether residing within or without the municipality, whose right to use, acquire, or enjoy property is or may be affected by any action taken under this act, or whose rights to use, acquire, or enjoy property under this act, or under any other law of this State or of the United States have been denied, violated or infringed by an action or a failure to act under this act. . . .
>
> . . . In case any building or structure is erected, constructed, altered, repaired, converted, or maintained, or any building, structure or land is used in violation of this act or any ordinance or other regulation made under authority conferred hereby, the proper local authorities of the municipality or an interested party, in addition to other remedies, may institute any appropriate action or proceedings to prevent such unlawful erection, construction, reconstruction, alteration, repair, conversion, maintenance or use, to restrain, correct or abate such violation, to prevent the occupancy of said building, structure or land, or to prevent any illegal act, conduct, business or use in or about such premises.

Compare the United States Supreme Court's restrictive view of standing in Warth v. Seldin, infra page 446. See also Comment, 22 Syracuse L. Rev. 598 (1971); Branfman, Cohen, and Trubek, Measuring the Invis-

---

Hill tract was zoned as General Residence and Agricultural, requiring a minimum lot size of 35,000 square feet, or about three-fourths of an acre. . . . Because public interest had been heightened in preserving Sanbornton's "charm as a New England small town," the planning board then proposed amendments to the zoning ordinance designed to enlarge the Forest Conservation areas, and to establish separate General Residential Districts and Agricultural Districts, with increased minimum acreage requirements in these districts and in the Historical Preservation and the Recreational Districts. These were passed.

As a result of the re-zoning, approximately 70 per cent of appellant's land is in the Forest Conservation District and 30 per cent in the Agricultural District. Clearly, its plans for "cluster" or conventional development are inconsistent with the new zoning ordinance. Appellant filed suit in the district court alleging that the three and six acre minimum lot size requirements are unconstitutional.

The appellant, who relied heavily on the Pennsylvania line of decisions and on *Madison Township*, was turned back once again by the court of appeals who noted: "These different problems of suburban and rural expansion, their scientific and legal analyses, and their appropriate solutions, cannot so easily be equated." For Steel Hill's subsequent court tries, see 392 F. Supp. 1144 (D.N.H. 1974) (claim based on denial of new proposal for mobile home development dismissed by reason of collateral estoppel).

See infra page 725 for the question of large-lot zoning for the preservation of agricultural land. — EDS.

ible Wall: Land Use Controls and the Residential Patterns of the Poor, 82 Yale L.J. 483 (1973).

2. Judge Furman's citation of the *National Land* (1965) and *Kit-Mar* (1970) cases suggests the lead role Pennsylvania courts assumed in attacking socioeconomic exclusion by means of large-lot zoning. In the latter case, the court held unconstitutional Concord Township's two- and three-acre minimums. Citing the court's recent approval of the PUD approach in *Village 2 at New Hope,* supra page 279, Justice Roberts offered the following suggestion and warning to municipal officials:

> New and exciting techniques are available to the local governing bodies of this Commonwealth for dealing with problems of population growth. Neither Concord Township nor Easttown Township nor any other local governing unit may retreat behind a cover of exclusive zoning. . . . The power currently resides in the hands of each local governing unit, and we will not tolerate their abusing that power in attempting to zone out growth at the expense of neighboring communities.

268 A.2d at 769.

Not all observers of this pattern of judicial intolerance have been as admiring as Judge Furman, however. The Suburban and Wayne Times, in its November 18, 1968 edition, criticized the Pennsylvania Supreme Court for having "issued a sociological ukase, following in the steps of the U.S. Supreme Court. As with the parent body, the State Court has thumbed its nose at Constitutions, while eyeing the political returns." For a discussion of more recent encounters with exclusionary zoning in Pennsylvania courts, see infra page 411.

3. At the same time some states chose the legislative route to negate or override local impediments to the development of lower income housing units. In the "Anti-Snob Zoning Act," Mass. Gen. Laws Ann. ch. 40B §§20-23 (West 1979), Massachusetts lawmakers took the following approach:

> §21. Any public agency or limited dividend or nonprofit organization proposing to build low or moderate income housing may submit to the board of appeals, established under section twelve of chapter forty A, a single application to build such housing in lieu of separate applications to the applicable local boards. The board of appeals shall forthwith notify each such local board, as applicable, of the filing of such application by sending a copy thereof to such local boards for their recommendations and shall, within thirty days of the receipt of such application, hold a public hearing on the same. The board of appeals shall request the appearance at said hearing of such representatives of said local boards as are deemed necessary or helpful in making its decision upon such application and shall have the same power to issue permits or approvals as any local board or official who would otherwise act with respect to

A. Exclusion

such application, including but not limited to the power to attach to said permit or approval conditions and requirements with respect to height, site plan, size or shape, or building materials as are consistent with the terms of this section. The board of appeals, in making its decision on said application, shall take into consideration the recommendations of the local boards and shall have the authority to use the testimony of consultants. . . .

The board of appeals shall render a decision, based upon a majority vote of said board, within forty days after the termination of the public hearing and, if favorable to the applicant, shall forthwith issue a comprehensive permit or approval. If said hearing is not convened or a decision is not rendered within the time allowed, unless the time has been extended by mutual agreement between the board and the applicant, the application shall be deemed to have been allowed and the comprehensive permit or approval shall forthwith issue. Any person aggrieved by the issuance of a comprehensive permit or approval may appeal to the court. . . .

How should the state committee weigh certain traditional local planning criteria such as the protection of health and safety, the preservation of open space, and the maintenance of uniformity in applying construction regulations? What risks of expensive and extensive litigation does a developer run when using the act? What are the possible consequences of these risks? As a Massachusetts legislator, what changes in the act would you propose? Should the state "impose" its policy on local communities? The constitutionality of this act was upheld by the Massachusetts Supreme Judicial Court in Board of Appeals of Hanover v. Housing Appeals Committee in the Department of Community Affairs, 363 Mass. 339, 294 N.E.2d 393 (1973).[24]

24. It took a long time to establish procedures, hear appeals, test the constitutionality of the Act, and make decisions. In the first five years under the Act, after many delays, there were twenty decisions involving 2905 units, overturning nineteen local decisions, and ordering the issuance of comprehensive permits on 2873 units. Developers in eight communities involving 2986 proposed units at some point in their appeals withdrew their petitions; these included several particularly large developments, such as a controversial multiple-site proposal in Newton. See Haar & Iatridis, Housing the Poor in Suburbia 25-132 (1975).

The process can be laborious, eating up valuable time and money for the developer. The Newton hearings, for example, dragged on for well over one year as the lawyer fighting the development called a seemingly endless list of witnesses. There was Joe Fitzsimmons, a Newton fireman. Al Schiavone, the city engineer, was asked to give his views. So was Janice Cadwell, a housewife. And Alfonso Mascia, a police captain. And Henry Murphy, the assistant fire chief. And James Hinkle, former assistant school superintendent. And Helene Ryan, another housewife, and many more.

The tactics of the lawyer prolonged the hearings from the predicted three or five sessions to forty-two sessions, beginning in July of 1971 and recessing in June of 1972; at that time, he said that he had enough additional witnesses to keep the hearings going at least another six months; he said he was not stalling but was merely trying to make sure the law was interpreted correctly. Mark Slotnick, head of the Newton Community Development Corporation (NCDF), said, "the whole purpose is to wear us down so we will run out of time and money." See Wall St. J., Oct. 17, 1972. NCDF was forced to pay for extended options on land, and eventually withdrew its appeal. How would you propose to eliminate or reduce delays?

4. In New York, the Urban Development Corporation (UDC) was granted the following powers:

> (3) After consultation with local officials, ... the corporation and any subsidiary thereof shall, in constructing, reconstructing, rehabilitating, altering or improving any project, comply with the requirements of local laws, ordinances, codes, charters or regulations applicable to such construction, reconstruction, rehabilitation, alteration or improvement, provided however, that when, in the discretion of the corporation, such compliance is not feasible or practicable, the corporation and any subsidiary thereof shall comply with the requirements of the state building construction code, ... applicable to such construction, reconstruction, rehabilitation, alteration or improvement. No municipality shall have power to modify or change the drawings, plans or specifications for the construction, reconstruction, rehabilitation, alteration or improvement of any project of the corporation or of any subsidiary thereof, or the construction, plumbing, heating, lighting or other mechanical branch of work necessary to complete the work in question, nor to require that any person, firm or corporation employed on any such work shall perform any such work in any other or different manner than that provided by such plans and specifications, nor to require that any such person, firm or corporation obtain any other or additional authority, approval, permit or certificate from such municipality in relation to the work being done, and the doing of any such work by any person, firm or corporation in accordance with the terms of such drawings, plans, specifications or contracts shall not subject said person, firm or corporation to any liability or penalty, civil or criminal, other than as may be stated in such contracts or incidental to the proper enforcement thereof; nor shall any municipality have power to require the corporation of any subsidiary thereof, or lessee therefrom or successor in interest thereto, to obtain any other or additional authority, approval, permit, certificate or certificate of occupancy from such municipality as a condition of owning, using, maintaining, operating or occupying any project acquired, constructed, reconstructed, rehabilitated, altered or improved by the corporation or by any subsidiary thereof.

N.Y. Unconsol. Laws §6266(3) (McKinney 1979).

This provision withstood a constitutional challenge in a zoning context in Floyd v. New York State Urban Development Corp., 33 N.Y.2d 1, 300 N.E.2d 704, 347 N.Y.S.2d 161 (1973). In the meantime, however, popular and legislative opposition led to curtailment of this preemptive power. See §6265(5) (authorized by L. 1973, ch. 466, §3).[25]

---

25. The New York Urban Development Corporation (UDC) used its power to override local zoning regulations rarely and reluctantly during its first four years. In April 1972, the New York State Legislature voted to take the power away, but Governor Rockefeller vetoed the bill. Two months later, the UDC announced that it was prepared to preempt local zoning regulations to build 100 units of low- and moderate-income housing in each of nine Westchester County towns. Supervisors of several of the selected towns were in the audience at the formal announcement and took the opportunity to

A. Exclusion

5. The National Commission on Urban Problems proposed action by the states to assure strict review of any local zoning decision of building permits for the construction of any private place of employment that will employ a substantial number of employees, for the purpose of determining whether adequate housing is available in or near the locality for persons of all income levels to be employed by the installation. Building the American City 243 (1968). The movement of jobs in private industry from the cities to the suburbs has made it difficult for the urban poor to get to work.

Isn't it in the corporation's best interests to ensure that there is adequate housing nearby for its workers? When the Ford Motor Company located a major factory in Mahwah, N.J., it had to organize car pools to bring in workers from center city areas, often more than an hour's trip; this led to high absenteeism. Consider a news release from the company in support of a plan to build a fully integrated new community of 19,000 people in Mahwah:

> Ford Motor Company management in New Jersey believes that all citizens are entitled to have access to housing at a reasonable price within reasonable reach of their places of employment.... We believe that such a development would be good for the community, for our employees and for Ford Motor Company. Zoning that precludes local housing opportunities for large numbers of our work force imposes hardships on them and raises the cost of doing business. When employees are forced to travel great distances to their jobs, absenteeism and turnover go up, and morale and productivity decline.

Ford Motor Company news release, Dec. 11, 1972.

Consider also the following statement (Newsweek, Jan. 16, 1971), and assess the possibility of a new coalition between excluded groups and private industry:

> Builders, especially, are actively supporting suits to break down zoning

---

pass out press releases of their own denouncing the UDC and threatening to bring the agency before "the highest courts." N.Y. Times, June 21, 1972. See N.Y. Times, June 8, 1973:

> On June 7, Governor Rockefeller signed into law a bill that curbs some of the power of the state Urban Development Corporation, one of the Governor's pet agencies.
> In signing the bill, Governor Rockefeller, noted that, except for towns and villages, the UDC authority "to waive compliance with local zoning and other local laws and regulations will be unimpaired."
> The Governor also noted that the law increased the agency's authority to increase bonds to $2 billion from $1.5 billion, and he said the added borrowing capacity is "most important" because of the withdrawal of Federal housing subsidies by President Nixon's Administration.

For more on the history and functions of the UDC, see infra page 989.

and other barriers. Their interest is obvious: About one-third of their housing starts are "government-assisted AAA," the classification for federally subsidized low- and middle-income housing.

Big employers, which have been ignoring the issue, may be starting to side with the excluded groups. McDonnell Douglas Corp., which has a major plant near Black Jack, kicked in $30,000 in "seed money" to help the blacks get housing.

That company's support reflects a critical problem confronting the many companies that have moved to the suburbs. Many moved into exclusive communities, which welcomed the plants as taxpayers but did nothing to modify barriers to housing. So the workers stayed in the cities, and turnover accelerated because of the lack of fast, cheap public transportation.

See also §7-305 of the Model Land Development Code (Additional Standards Applicable to Development of Regional Impact Substantially Increasing Employment).

7. How would you vote on the following bill?

Limitations on the Power of Local Government to Control Development

(1) No local government may

(a) exclude from any part of its jurisdiction or otherwise discriminate against any class of persons by reason of race, color, religion, national origin, or income; or

(b) exclude any charitable, educational, or religious institution from the use of any location at which it would be entitled to exemption from real property tax under the laws of this state and at which it proposes in good faith to locate, unless such use would cause a substantial detriment more onerous in kind or degree than that which is ordinarily associated with location of such uses; or

(c) prohibit the construction of dwelling units for less than a stated minimum cost; or

(d) restrict the location, density, or rate of residential development of any area within its jurisdiction primarily for the purpose of avoiding the expenses of providing additional public community facilities, except where such restriction furthers the scheduled expansion of public community facilities as stated in the land development plan; or

(e) regulate the use of land at or near state facilities such as freeway and highway interchanges, public buildings, or recreational and scenic areas developed or maintained by the state, so as to impose a burden on the facility contrary to a specific policy promulgated by the state planning agency; or

(f) exclude from its jurisdiction any commercial or industrial development, if the exclusion is in substantial conflict with a specific policy promulgated by the state planning agency; or

(g) exclude from its jurisdiction a type of residential development if the exclusion unreasonably restricts the range of choice of housing,

A. Exclusion

as to type and location, which is available to the residents of the state. An exclusion is unreasonable if it is not

(i) necessary to public health or safety; or

(ii) necessary to the preservation of an established physical character of the area affected; or

(iii) affirmatively authorized by an officially adopted metropolitan land development plan; or

(iv) necessary for accomplishing a program of expansion pursuant to clause (d) of this section.

(2) In determining the reasonableness of any regulation under this part by a local government, a reviewing body shall give due weight to all adjoining and nearby uses which may be relevant to the determination, without regard to whether such uses are within the jurisdiction or outside its boundaries.

(3) All public development shall conform to the local land development plan for the area in which it is to be located and to the related ordinances, unless the plan or one or more such ordinances is clearly inconsistent with state law authorizing such development, or, in the case of development by a body having powers of eminent domain or licensed or specially authorized by a state utility commission, would substantially increase the cost or decrease the efficiency of the development.

8. Norman Williams has called the *Madison Township* decision "clearly the right decision in the wrong place." He observed that the township had no history of exclusion and had been one of the few towns in the region to accept large quantities of multiple dwellings; he also noted that the actual site entailed in the litigation involves "serious ecological questions." 23 Zoning Dig. 473 (1971).

Precisely five months after the *Madison Township* decision, the governor of New Jersey delivered a special message to the legislature, saying in part: "It must be apparent to members of this Legislature that the courts already have acted decisively in this area. Unless we act together to help open the way for needed housing, the courts will do it for us and will continue to move strongly in the direction of bypassing home rule by judicial process." Special message from Governor William T. Cahill, New Horizons in Housing, March 27, 1972. The governor pointed out the decision in *Madison Township* and cited no fewer than seven significant challenges to local exclusionary zoning ordinances pending in the New Jersey courts. Nevertheless, his proposal for a voluntary balanced housing plan won no support in the legislature.

The state's highest court remanded the case after the township amended its zoning ordinance; the amended ordinance reduced the extent of large lot zoning and increased the amount of land available for apartments. Thereafter, the superior court struck down the amended ordinance in a second opinion, 128 N.J. Super. 438, 320 A.2d 223 (Law Div. 1974), finding that "an elite community of high income families with few children is maintained by the 1973 amendments." The court offered the following standard:

> Without the rigidity of a mathematical formula this court holds that Madison Township's obligation to provide its fair share of housing needs of its region is not met unless its zoning ordinance approximates in additional housing unit capacity the same proportion of low income housing as its present low income population, about 12%, and the same proportion of moderate income housing as its present moderate income population, about 19%.

Do you agree with that standard and, if not, what principle would you offer? Consider the following response of another New Jersey superior court judge.

■ SOUTHERN BURLINGTON COUNTY NAACP v. TOWNSHIP OF MOUNT LAUREL
119 N.J. Super. 164, 290 A.2d 465 (Law Div. 1974)

MARTINO, J. . . .

The patterns and practice clearly indicate that defendant municipality through its zoning ordinances has exhibited economic discrimination in that the poor have been deprived of adequate housing and the opportunity to secure the construction of subsidized housing, and has used federal, state, county and local finances and resources solely for the betterment of middle and upper-income persons. The zoning ordinance is, therefore, declared invalid.

Plaintiffs, in seeking declaratory and injunctive relief, argue that even if the zoning ordinance were declared invalid, the injury they suffer will not afford a remedy. They argue there is a desperate need for affirmative municipal action within parameters established by the court.

In Hawkins v. Shaw, 437 F.2d 1286, 1293 (5 Cir. 1971), the court declared that a municipality cannot discriminate in the use of municipal services and said that a town could be required to submit a plan for the equitable distribution of such services.

This court agrees with plaintiffs and, therefore, orders that defendant municipality shall, upon the entry of a judgment to conform with these findings and conclusions of law, immediately undertake a study to identify:

a. The existing sub-standard dwelling units in the township and the number of individuals and families, by income and size, who would be displaced by an effective code-enforcement program;

b. The housing needs for persons of low and moderate income:

A. Exclusion

1. Residing in the township;
2. Presently employed by the municipality or in commercial and industrial uses in the township;
3. Expected or projected to be employed by the municipality or in commercial and industrial uses, the development of which can reasonably be anticipated in the township.

Defendant shall, upon completion of the investigation referred to in the preceding paragraph, establish, to the extent possible, an estimated number of both low and moderate income units which should be constructed in the township each year to provide for the needs as identified in the preceding paragraph.

Defendant shall, upon completion of the analysis set forth in the preceding paragraphs, develop a plan of implementation, that is, an affirmative program, to enable and encourage the satisfaction of the needs as previously set forth. That plan shall include an analysis of the ways in which the township can act affirmatively to enable and encourage the satisfaction of the indicated needs and shall include a plan of action which the township has chosen for the purposes of implementing this program. The adopted plan shall encompass the most effective and thorough means by which municipal action can be utilized to accomplish the goals set forth above.

If for any reason the township shall find that circumstances exist which in any way interfere with or bar the implementation of the plan chosen, it shall set forth in explicit detail:

a. Each and every factor;
b. The way in which each factor interferes with or bars implementation of the plan;
c. Possible alternative plans or municipal action which temporarily or permanently, wholly or in part, eliminate the indicated factor or factors, and
d. The reason why the alternative plans have not been adopted.

To the extent possible, the aforementioned analyses, studies and plans shall be undertaken with the cooperation and participation of plaintiffs and their representatives.

The aforementioned analyses, studies, development of plans and other action shall be completed within 90 days from the date of judgment. The township shall serve copies of the analyses, studies and plans on plaintiffs' attorney and this court within 90 days. The parties shall appear before this court no later than ten days, or on a date set by this court, after service of said papers for a determination of whether defendants have complied with the order of this court and whether further action is necessary.

The judgment entered in this matter as to the invalidity of the zoning ordinance shall not become effective until this court shall decide that sufficient time has elapsed to enable the municipality to enact new and proper regulations for the municipality. Morris County Land, etc. v. Parsippany-Troy Hills, 40 N.J. 539, 193 A.2d 232 (1963).

This court retains jurisdiction until a final order issues requiring implementation of the plan as agreed upon.

Notes

1. How do the theories on which *Mount Laurel* and *Madison Township* were decided differ? How do the remedies differ? Is the *Mount Laurel* judge ordering the township to build houses? How many houses? How would you go about answering item (b)(3) in the study ordered by the judge?

2. Has the *Mount Laurel* judge proclaimed a "right to housing"? Consider the implications of the following language contained in Lindsey v. Normet, 405 U.S. 56 (1972), in which the Supreme Court upheld the constitutionality of an Oregon statute authorizing swift eviction procedures for residential tenants who fall behind in their rent payments: "We do not denigrate the importance of decent, safe, and sanitary housing. But the Constitution does not provide judicial remedies for every social and economic ill. We are unable to perceive in that document any constitutional guarantee of access to dwellings of a particular quality." 406 U.S. at 74. Suppose the ordinance excluded commercial facilities? Pure Oil Division v. Brook Park, 26 Ohio App. 2d 153, 269 N.E.2d 853 (1971) (ordinance limiting competition with existing commercial uses unconstitutional).

3. After holding an ordinance invalid and after the town fails to respond in good faith with a new ordinance to meet the standards laid down by the court, what should a judge do? Overturn the second ordinance and leave the town without zoning? Say this is not a matter for the courts and let the second ordinance stand? Appoint expert advisors to the court to evaluate the second ordinance and, if necessary, to make a new zoning ordinance? See Pascack Association, Ltd. v. Mayor and Council of Township of Washington, 131 N.J. Super. 195, 329 A.2d 89 (Law Div. 1974). Professors Melvin Levin and Jerome Rose of the Rutgers University department of urban planning, serving as advisors to the court, submitted their report to the court on January 9, 1974. The advisors determined the second ordinance did not comply with the court order and recommended rezoning to expand the multiple-dwelling district, reduce off-street parking restrictions for multiple-dwelling units, modify bedroom percentage limitations, modify density requirements, and adopt a planned unit development ordinance. The court ordered that the parties share the cost of hiring the consultants. The developer delayed construction, in large measure

A. Exclusion 401

because it believed the new restrictions still left the venture unprofitable. Is this an effective judicial response and, if not, what should the court do? For later legal developments in Washington Township, see infra page 417.

4. The New Jersey Supreme Court heard five hours of oral argument in *Madison Township* and *Mount Laurel* on March 5, 1973. Consider the following excerpts from two arguments reported in The Evening Times, Trenton, N.J., March 6, 1973:

> A township attorney Monday told the State Supreme Court that to require local zoning codes to meet regional low income housing needs "just moves the ghetto around."
>
> Madison Township Atty. Richard Plechner said, "I don't see how you can compel a community to provide any kind of housing."
>
> Mrs. Lois Thompson, attorney for the Suburban Action Institute, an opponent of the Madison zoning ordinance, contended that "the issue is whether zoning is going to be used by a private club to determine who is going to live in a community, or for the public welfare.". . .
>
> Plechner said if the court upheld Furman's ruling "then the court becomes a great zoning board in Trenton . . . when the solution belongs rightly in the Legislature.". . .
>
> "We've got everything but ratables . . . Striking down the ordinance only aggravates the problem without offering us a solution," he said. . . .
>
> Mrs. Thompson said that every community has a responsibility to do its "fair share" in providing housing for the poor.
>
> Her assertion brought this question from Chief Justice Joseph Weintraub: "By fair share you mean a responsibility for a community that welcomes industry to provide housing within the means of its workers, or in other words, providing the bedrooms for your own enterprises?"
>
> Mrs. Thompson agreed and the chief justice commented that it would be hard for the court to determine what a community's "fair share" would be. "Send us a proposal." Weintraub told her. . . .
>
> Justice Frederick Hall asked Mount Laurel attorney John W. Trimble if he felt the township had any responsibility to meet the housing needs of the area outside the community.
>
> Trimble replied no, and Hall commented. "That's really what this case is all about."

5. In June 1973, the New Jersey Supreme Court ordered a rehearing of the *Madison Township* and *Mount Laurel* cases after three new justices joined the court in the fall. The retiring Chief Justice, Joseph Weintraub, stated, "Cases of this magnitude should be decided by those who will have to live with the decisions." Bergen Evening Record, July 3, 1973. On January 8, 1974, the court devoted a morning to the rearguments.

■ SOUTHERN BURLINGTON COUNTY NAACP v. TOWNSHIP OF MOUNT LAUREL
67 N.J. 151, 336 A.2d 713, appeal dismissed and cert. denied, 423 U.S. 808 (1975)

[Mount Laurel I]

The opinion of the Court was delivered by HALL, J. . . .

Plaintiffs represent the minority group poor (black and Hispanic) seeking such [affordable] quarters. But they are not the only category of persons barred from so many municipalities by reason of restrictive land use regulations. We have reference to young and elderly couples, single persons and large, growing families not in the poverty class, but who still cannot afford the only kinds of housing realistically permitted in most places — relatively high-priced, single-family detached dwellings on sizeable lots and, in some municipalities, expensive apartments. We will, therefore, consider the case from the wider viewpoint that the effect of Mount Laurel's land use regulation has been to prevent various categories of persons from living in the township because of the limited extent of their income and resources. In this connection, we accept the representation of the municipality's counsel at oral argument that the regulatory scheme was not adopted with any desire or intent to exclude prospective residents on the obviously illegal bases of race, origin or believed social incompatibility.

As already intimated, the issue here is not confined to Mount Laurel. The same question arises with respect to any number of other municipalities of sizeable land area outside the central cities and older built-up suburbs of our North and South Jersey metropolitan areas (and surrounding some of the smaller cities outside those areas as well) which, like Mount Laurel, have substantially shed rural characteristics and have undergone great population increase since World War II, or are now in the process of doing so, but still are not completely developed and remain in the path of inevitable future residential, commercial and industrial demand and growth. Most such municipalities, with but relatively insignificant variation in details, present generally comparable physical situations, courses of municipal policies, practices, enactments and results and human, governmental and legal problems arising therefrom. It is in the context of communities now of this type or which become so in the future, rather than with central cities or older built-up suburbs or areas still rural and likely to continue to be for some time yet, that we deal with the question raised. . . .

The legal question before us . . . is whether a developing municipality like Mount Laurel may validly, by a system of land use regulation, make it physically and economically impossible to provide low and

A. Exclusion

moderate income housing in the municipality for the various categories of persons who need and want it and thereby, as Mount Laurel has, exclude such people from living within its confines because of the limited extent of their income and resources. Necessarily implicated are the broader questions of the right of such municipalities to limit the kinds of available housing and of any obligation to make possible a variety and choice of types of living accommodations.

We conclude that every such municipality must, by its land use regulations, presumptively make realistically possible an appropriate variety and choice of housing. More specifically, presumptively it cannot foreclose the opportunity of the classes of people mentioned for low and moderate income housing and in its regulations must affirmatively afford that opportunity, at least to the extent of the municipality's fair share of the present and prospective regional need therefor. These obligations must be met unless the particular municipality can sustain the heavy burden of demonstrating peculiar circumstances which dictate that it should not be required so to do.

We reach this conclusion under state law and so do not find it necessary to consider federal constitutional grounds urged by plaintiffs. We begin with some fundamental principles as applied to the scene before us. . . . It is required that, affirmatively, a zoning regulation, like any police power enactment, must promote public health, safety, morals or the general welfare. (The last term seems broad enough to encompass the others.) Conversely, a zoning enactment which is contrary to the general welfare is invalid. . . .

This court . . . has plainly warned, even in cases decided some years ago sanctioning a broad measure of restrictive municipal decisions, of the inevitability of change in judicial approach and view as mandated by change in the world around us.

The warning implicates the matter of *whose* general welfare must be served or not violated in the field of land use regulation. Frequently the decisions in this state . . . have spoken only in terms of the interest of the enacting municipality, so that it has been thought, at least in some quarters, that such was the only welfare requiring consideration. It is, of course, true that many cases have dealt only with regulations having little, if any, outside impact where the local decision is ordinarily entitled to prevail. However, it is fundamental and not to be forgotten that the zoning power is a police power of the state and the local authority is acting only as a delegate of that power and is restricted in the same manner as is the state. So, when regulation does have a substantial external impact, the welfare of the state's citizens beyond the borders of the particular municipality cannot be disregarded and must be recognized and served. . . .

It is plain beyond dispute that proper provision for adequate housing of all categories of people is certainly an absolute essential in promotion of the general welfare required in all local land use regulation. Further, the universal and constant need for such housing is so important and of such broad public interest that the general welfare which developing municipalities like Mount Laurel must consider extends beyond their boundaries and cannot be parochially confined to the claimed good of the particular municipality. It has to follow that, broadly speaking, the presumptive obligation arises for each such municipality affirmatively to plan and provide, by its land use regulations, the reasonable opportunity for an appropriate variety and choice of housing, including, of course, low and moderate cost housing, to meet the needs, desires and resources of all categories of people who may desire to live within its boundaries. Negatively, it may not adopt regulations or policies which thwart or preclude the opportunity.

It is also entirely clear, as we pointed out earlier, that most developing municipalities, including Mount Laurel, have not met their affirmative or negative obligations, primarily for local fiscal reasons. . . .

In sum, we are satisfied beyond any doubt that, by reason of the basic importance of appropriate housing and the long-standing pressing need for it, especially in the low and moderate cost category, and of the exclusionary zoning practices of so many municipalities, conditions have changed, and consistent with the warning in *Pierro*, judicial attitudes must be altered from that espoused in that and other cases cited earlier, to require, as we have just said, a broader view of the general welfare and the presumptive obligation on the part of developing municipalities at least to afford the opportunity by land use regulations for appropriate housing for all.

We have spoken of this obligation of such municipalities as "presumptive." The term has two aspects, procedural and substantive. Procedurally, we think the basic importance of appropriate housing for all dictates that, when it is shown that a developing municipality in its land use regulations has not made realistically possible a variety and choice of housing, including adequate provision to afford the opportunity for low and moderate income housing or has expressly prescribed requirements or restrictions which preclude or substantially hinder it, a facial showing of violation of substantive due process or equal protection under the state constitution has been made out and the burden, and it is a heavy one, shifts to the municipality to establish a valid basis for its action or non-action. . . . The substantive aspect of "presumptive" relates to the specifics, on the one hand, of what municipal land use regulation provisions, or the absence thereof, will evidence invalidity and shift the burden of proof and, on the other hand, of what bases and considerations will carry the municipality's burden and sustain what it has done or failed to do. Both kinds of specifics may well vary between municipalities according to peculiar circumstances. . . .

A. Exclusion

Without further elaboration at this point, our opinion is that Mount Laurel's zoning ordinance is presumptively contrary to the general welfare and outside the intended scope of the zoning power in the particulars mentioned. A facial showing of invalidity is thus established, shifting to the municipality the burden of establishing valid superseding reasons for its action and non-action. We now examine the reasons it advances.

The township's principal reason in support of its zoning plan and ordinance housing provisions, advanced especially strongly at oral argument, is the fiscal one previously adverted to, i.e., that by reason of New Jersey's tax structure which substantially finances municipal governmental and educational costs from taxes on local real property, every municipality may, by the exercise of the zoning power, allow only such uses and to such extent as will be beneficial to the local tax rate. In other words, the position is that any municipality may zone extensively to seek and encourage the "good" tax ratables of industry and commerce and limit the permissible types of housing to those having the fewest school children or to those providing sufficient value to attain or approach paying their own way taxwise.

We have previously held that a developing municipality may properly zone for and seek industrial ratables to create a better economic balance for the community vis-à-vis educational and governmental costs engendered by residential development, provided that such was ". . . done reasonably as part of and in furtherance of a legitimate comprehensive plan for the zoning of the entire municipality." Gruber v. Mayor and Township Committee of Raritan Township, 39 N.J. 1, 9-11 (1962). We adhere to that view today. But we were not there concerned with, and did not pass upon, the validity of municipal exclusion by zoning of types of housing and kinds of people for the same local financial end. We have no hesitancy in now saying, and do so emphatically, that, considering the basic importance of the opportunity for appropriate housing for all classes of our citizenry, no municipality may exclude or limit categories of housing for that reason or purpose. While we fully recognize the increasingly heavy burden of local taxes for municipal governmental and school costs on homeowners, relief from the consequences of this tax system will have to be furnished by other branches of government. It cannot legitimately be accomplished by restricting types of housing through the zoning process in developing municipalities.

The propriety of zoning ordinance limitations on housing for ecological or environmental reasons seems also to be suggested by Mount Laurel in support of the one-half acre minimum lot size in that very considerable portion of the township still available for residential development. It is said that the area is without sewer or water utilities and that the soil is such that this plot size is required for safe individual lot sewage disposal and water supply. The short answer is that, this being flat land and readily amenable to such utility installations, the township could require them as improvements by developers or install them under the special assessment or other appropriate statutory procedure. The present environmental situation of the area is, therefore, no sufficient excuse in itself for limiting housing therein to single-family dwellings on large lots. Cf. National Land and Investment Co. v. Kohn, 419 Pa. 504, 215 A.2d 597 (1965). This is not to say that land use regulations should not take due account of ecological or environmental factors or problems. Quite the contrary. Their importance, at least being recognized, should always be considered. Generally only a relatively small portion of a developing municipality will be involved, for, to have a valid effect, the danger and impact must be substantial and very real (the construction of every building or the improvement of every plot has some environmental impact) — not simply a makeweight to support exclusionary housing measures or preclude growth — and the regulation adopted must be only that reasonably necessary for public protection of a vital interest. Otherwise difficult additional problems relating to a "taking" of a property owner's land may arise. . . .

By way of summary, what we have said comes down to this. As a developing municipality, Mount Laurel must, by its land use regulations, make realistically possible the opportunity for an appropriate variety and choice of housing for all categories of people who may desire to live there, of course including those of low and moderate income. It must permit multi-family housing, without bedroom or similar restrictions, as well as small dwellings on very small lots, low cost housing of other types and, in general, high density zoning, without artificial and unjustifiable minimum requirements as to lot size, building size and the like, to meet the full panoply of these needs. Certainly when a municipality zones for industry and commerce for local tax benefit purposes, it without question must zone to permit adequate housing within the means of the employees involved in such uses. (If planned unit developments are authorized, one would assume that each must include a reasonable amount of low and moderate income housing in its residential "mix," unless opportunity for such housing has already been realistically provided for elsewhere in the municipality.) The amount of land removed from residential use by allocation to industrial and commercial purposes must be reasonably related to the present and future potential for such purposes. In other words, such municipalities must zone primarily for the living welfare of people and not for the benefit of the local tax rate.[20]

20. This case does not properly present the question of whether a developing municipality may time its growth and, if so, how. See, e.g., Golden v. Planning Board of the Town of Ramapo, 30 N.Y.2d 359, 285 N.E.2d 291 (1972), appeal dismissed, 409 U.S. 1003 (1972); Construction Industry Association of Sonoma County v. City of Petaluma,

A. Exclusion

We have earlier stated that a developing municipality's obligation to afford the opportunity for decent and adequate low and moderate income housing extends at least to ". . . that municipality's fair share of the present and prospective regional need therefor." Some comment on that conclusion is in order at this point. Frequently it might be sounder to have more of such housing, like some specialized land uses, in one municipality in a region than in another, because of greater availability of suitable land, location of employment, accessibility of public transportation or some other significant reason. But, under present New Jersey legislation, zoning must be on an individual municipal basis, rather than regionally. So long as that situation persists under the present tax structure, or in the absence of some kind of binding agreement among all the municipalities of a region, we feel that every municipality therein must bear its fair share of the regional burden. (In this respect our holding is broader than that of the trial court, which was limited to Mount Laurel-related low and moderate income housing needs.)

The composition of the applicable "region" will necessarily vary from situation to situation and probably no hard and fast rule will serve to furnish the answer in every case. Confinement to or within a certain county appears not to be realistic, but restriction within the boundaries of the state seems practical and advisable. (This is not to say that a developing municipality can ignore a demand for housing within its boundaries on the part of people who commute to work in another state.) Here we have already defined the region at present as "those portions of Camden, Burlington and Gloucester Counties within a semicircle having a radius of 20 miles or so from the heart of Camden City." The concept of "fair share" is coming into more general use and, through the expertise of the municipal planning adviser, the county planning boards and the state planning agency, a reasonable figure for Mount Laurel can be determined, which can then be translated to the allocation of sufficient land therefor on the zoning map. . . .

There is no reason why developing municipalities like Mount Laurel, required by this opinion to afford the opportunity for all types of housing to meet the needs of various categories of people, may not become and remain attractive, viable communities providing good living and adequate services for all their residents in the kind of atmosphere which a democracy and free institutions demand. They can have industrial sections, commercial sections and sections for every kind of housing from low cost and multi-family to lots of more than an acre

---

375 F. Supp. 574 (N.D. Cal. 1974), appeal pending (citation of these cases is not intended to indicate either agreement or disagreement with their conclusions). [See infra page 570. — EDS.] We now say only that, assuming some type of timed growth is permissible, it cannot be utilized as an exclusionary device or to stop all further development and must include early provision for low and moderate income housing.

with very expensive homes. Proper planning and governmental cooperation can prevent over-intensive and too sudden development, insure against future suburban sprawl and slums and assure the preservation of open space and local beauty. We do not intend that developing municipalities shall be overwhelmed by voracious land speculators and developers if they use the powers which they have intelligently and in the broad public interest. Under our holdings today, they can be better communities for all than they previously have been. . . .

We are of the view that the trial court's judgment should be modified in certain respects. We see no reason why the entire zoning ordinance should be nullified. Therefore we declare it to be invalid only to the extent and in the particulars set forth in this opinion. The township is granted 90 days from the date hereof, or such additional time as the trial court may find it reasonable and necessary to allow, to adopt amendments to correct the deficiencies herein specified. It is the local function and responsibility, in the first instance at least, rather than the court's, to decide on the details of the same within the guidelines we have laid down. If plaintiffs desire to attach such amendments, they may do so by supplemental complaint filed in this cause within 30 days of the final adoption of the amendments.

We are not at all sure what the trial judge had in mind as ultimate action with reference to the approval of a plan for affirmative public action concerning the satisfaction of indicated housing needs and the entry of a final order requiring implementation thereof. Courts do not build housing nor do municipalities. That function is performed by private builders, various kinds of associations, or, for public housing, by special agencies created for that purpose at various levels of government. The municipal function is initially to provide the opportunity through appropriate land use regulations and we have spelled out what Mount Laurel must do in that regard. It is not appropriate at this time, particularly in view of the advanced view of zoning law as applied to housing laid down by this opinion, to deal with the matter of the further extent of judicial power in the field or to exercise any such power. . . . The municipality should first have full opportunity to itself act without judicial supervision. We trust it will do so in the spirit we have suggested, both by appropriate zoning ordinance amendments and whatever additional action encouraging the fulfillment of its fair share of the regional need for low and moderate income housing may be indicated as necessary and advisable. (We have in mind that there is at least a moral obligation in a municipality to establish a local housing agency pursuant to state law to provide housing for its resident poor now living in dilapidated, unhealthy quarters.) The portion of the trial court's judgment ordering the preparation and submission of the aforesaid study, report and plan to it for further action is therefore vacated as at least premature. Should Mount Laurel not perform as we expect,

A. Exclusion

further judicial action may be sought by supplemental pleading in this cause.

The judgment of the Law Division is modified as set forth herein. . . .

PASHMAN, J. (concurring).

With this decision, the Court begins to cope with the dark side of municipal land use regulation — the use of zoning power to advance the parochial interests of the municipality at the expense of the surrounding region and to establish and perpetuate social and economic segregation. . . .

It is not the business of this Court or any member of it to instruct the municipalities of the State of New Jersey on the good life. Nevertheless, I cannot help but note that many suburban communities have accepted at face value the traditional canard whispered by the "blockbuster": "When low income families move into your neighborhood, it will cease being a decent place to live." But as there is no difference between the love of low income mothers and fathers and those of high income for their children, so there is no difference between the desire for a decent community felt by one group and that felt by the other. Many low income families have learned from necessity the desirability of community involvement and improvement. At least as well as persons with higher incomes, they have learned that one cannot simply leave the fate of the community in the hands of the government, that things do not run themselves, but simply run down.

Equally important, many suburban communities have failed to learn the lesson of cultural pluralism. . . .

The people of New Jersey should welcome the result reached by the Court in this case, not merely because it is required by our laws, but, more fundamentally, because the result is right and true to the highest American ideals.

Notes

1. Not surprisingly, the popular, expert, and judicial reactions to the *Mount Laurel I* decision were swift and at times furious. See, for example, the New York Daily News for March 30, 1975: "At one stroke, the court yanked out the cornerstone of home rule, removed the basis for orderly and regulated development of available land, and usurped a traditionally legislative function. To conform to the social doctrines of a few judges, New Jersey must now have homogenized communities."

Before Volume 336 of the Atlantic Reporter 2d was shelved, one symposium had already been assembled. A review of the titles provides a good introduction to the immediate (and in some cases lasting) concerns of several astute observers of land-use planning and law:

Delogu, On the Choice of Remedies, at 6; Babcock, On the Choice of Forum, at 7; Franklin, The Commandments from *Mount Laurel*: New Route to the Unpromised Land, at 9; Fessler, *Mt. Laurel*: A Note to *Petaluma*, at 10; Kushner, Land Use Litigation and Low-Income Housing: Mandating Regional Fair Share Plans, at 12; Slade, *Mt. Laurel*: A View from the Bridge, at 15; Rose, *Mt. Laurel*: Is It Based on Wishful Thinking?, at 18; Keene, What's the Next Step After *Mt. Laurel*?, at 22; Anderson, *Mt. Laurel*: A Move in the Right Direction, at 25; Scott, Beyond 'Sic Utere. . .' to the Regional General Welfare, at 27; Rahenkamp, Fair Share Housing for Managed Growth, at 30; Williams, *Mt. Laurel*: A Major Transition in American Planning Law, at 33.

Land Use L. & Zoning Dig., June, 1975. These early attempts to interpret the procedural and substantive contributions of Justice Hall and his fellow justices — as well as the political, economic, and jurisprudential ramifications — were replicated, augmented, and re-argued in a wide range of fora.[26]

2. The anti-exclusionary trend spread rapidly in state courts. A number of other jurisdictions have adopted portions of the *Mount Laurel I* doctrine, often with variations reflecting local concerns and limitations. The New York Court of Appeals declared, in Berenson v. Town of New Castle, 38 N.Y.2d 102, 341 N.E.2d 236 (1975), that a valid zoning ordinance must provide adequately for regional needs. The court put forth a two-part test:

---

26. Oakwood at Madison, Inc. v. Township of Madison, 72 N.J. 481, 371 A.2d 1192, 1198-1199 n.3 (1977):

Mount Laurel has been the subject of extensive discussion in the literature. See Ackerman, The *Mount Laurel* Decision: Expanding the Boundaries of Zoning Reform, 1976 U. Ill. Law Forum 1; Payne, Delegation Doctrine in the Reform of Local Government Law: The Case of Exclusionary Zoning, 29 Rutgers L. Rev. 803, 805-819, 859, 866 (1976); Williams, American Land Planning Law (1975) Addendum Ch. 66; Rose, The *Mount Laurel* Decision: Is It Based on Wishful Thinking?, 4 Real Estate L.J. 61 (1975); Mytelka and Mytelka, Exclusionary Zoning: A Consideration of Remedies, 7 Seton Hall L. Rev. 1, 3-4 (1975); Kushner, Land Use Litigation and Low Income Housing: Mandating Regional Fair Share Plans, 9 Clearinghouse Rev. 10 (1975) (terming *Mount Laurel* the "Magna Carta of suburban low and moderate income housing"); Rohan, Property Planning and the Search for a Comprehensive Housing Policy — The View from *Mount Laurel*, 49 St. Johns L. Rev. 653 (1975); Williams and Doughty, Studies on Legal Realism: *Mount Laurel, Belle Terre* and *Berman*, 29 Rutgers L. Rev. 73 (1975) (calling *Mount Laurel* a "major turnaround on a major current problem"); Mallach, Do Law Suits Build Housing? The Implications of Exclusionary Zoning Litigation, 6 Rutgers-Camden L.J. 653 (1975); Rose, Exclusionary Zoning and Managed Growth: Some Unresolved Issues, 6 Rutgers-Camden L.J. 689 (1975); 6 Powell, Real Property, §872.1[2][g] (1975); Rose and Levin, What is a "Developing Municipality" Within the Meaning of the *Mount Laurel* Decision?, 4 Real Estate L.J. 359 (1976). See also Berger, Land Ownership and Use 790-799 (2d ed. 1975). For a journalistic appraisal, see U.S. Journal: Mount Laurel, N.J. — Some Thoughts on Where Lines Are Drawn, New Yorker, Feb. 2, 1976, at 69. See also Note, The Inadequacy of Judicial Remedies in Cases of Exclusionary Zoning, 74 Mich. L. Rev. 760 (1976).

A. Exclusion

the first branch of the test . . . is simply whether the board has provided a properly balanced and well ordered plan for the community. . . . Secondly, in enacting a zoning ordinance, consideration must be given to regional needs and requirements. . . . There must be a balancing of the local desire to maintain the *status quo* within the community and the greater public interest that regional needs be met.[27]

341 N.E.2d at 242.

In Associated Home Builders v. City of Livermore, 18 Cal. 3d 582, 557 P.2d 473, 135 Cal. Rptr. 41 (1976), the court refused to apply the *Mount Laurel I* standard of review, as urged by the plaintiff, and "reaffirm[ed] the established constitutional principle that a local land use ordinance falls within the authority of the police power if it is reasonably related to the public welfare." Still, the court held open one strategy for overcoming this burden:

> When we inquire whether an ordinance reasonably relates to the public welfare, inquiry should begin by asking *whose* welfare must the ordinance serve. . . . If [the challenged ordinance's] impact is limited to the city boundaries, the inquiry may be limited accordingly; if, as alleged here, the ordinance may strongly influence the supply and distribution of housing for an entire metropolitan region, judicial inquiry must consider the welfare of that region.

557 P.2d at 487. This time the California court cited their New Jersey counterparts approvingly for the notion of regional obligation. Id. at 488.

An interesting wrinkle was added by the Supreme Court of Washington in Save a Valuable Environment v. City of Bothell, 89 Wash. 2d 862, 576 P.2d 401 (1978), a challenge mounted by a nonprofit group against the rezoning of farmland for a major regional shopping center. The court noted that California, New Jersey, and New York "have imposed a duty to serve regional welfare when considering adequate housing. . . . We find such a duty to exist when the interest at stake is the quality of the environment." 576 P.2d at 406.

The Pennsylvania Supreme Court, with its own approach toward striking down exclusionary ordinances (supra page 392), explicitly adopted the "fair share" doctrine in Surrick v. Zoning Hearing Board

---

27. In 1983, a New York appellate court considered landowners' challenge to a New Castle zoning ordinance enacted in response to the *Berenson* opinion. Although the town had replaced its prior ban on multi-family dwellings with "five provisions for the construction of multi-family housing in New Castle," the plaintiffs alleged that the two-part test devised by the court of appeals was not met and that the effect of the new ordinance was confiscatory. Blitz v. Town of New Castle, 94 A.D.2d 92, 463 N.Y.S.2d 832, 833 (App. Div. 1983). The court disagreed, finding the town's changes acceptable. — EDS.

of Upper Providence Township, 476 Pa. 182, 382 A.2d 105, 110-111 (1977), setting forth an "analytical matrix" to be applied to the facts of exclusionary zoning cases:

> The initial inquiry must focus upon whether the community in question is a logical area for development and population growth. . . .
>
> Having determined that a particular community is in the path of urban-suburban growth, the present level of development within the particular community must be examined. Population density data and the percentage of total undeveloped land and the percentage available for the development of multi-family dwellings are factors highly relevant to this inquiry.
>
> Assuming that a community is situated in the path of population expansion and is not already highly developed, this Court has, in the past, determined whether the challenged zoning scheme effected an exclusionary result or, alternatively, whether there was evidence of a "primary purpose" or exclusionary intent to zone out the natural growth of population. . . .
>
> In analyzing the effect of a zoning ordinance, the extent of the exclusion, if any, must be considered. Is there *total* exclusion of multi-family dwellings, which we disapproved in *Girsh Appeal* [437 Pa. 237, 263 A.2d 395 (1970)], or is the exclusion *partial*? If the zoning exclusion is partial, obviously the question of the ordinance's validity is more difficult to answer. In resolving this issue, once again the percentage of community land available under the zoning ordinance for multi-family dwellings becomes relevant. This percentage must be considered in light of current population growth pressure, within the community as well as the region, and in light of the total amount of undeveloped land in the community. Where the amount of land zoned as being available for multi-family dwellings is disproportionately small in relation to these latter factors, the ordinance will be held to be exclusionary.

In three post-*Surrick* cases, however, a sharply divided supreme court struggled with the implications and scope of its fair share mandate. In In re Appeal of M. A. Kravitz Co., 501 Pa. 200, 460 A.2d 1075 (1983), the plurality found that the Board of Supervisors for the Wrightstown Township — given the absence of major employers within the township, the lack of major highway links with Trenton and Philadelphia, and expert testimony that the "area has experienced little growth in the past and is designated as an area slated for little growth in the future" — had legitimately denied a zoning amendment to allow plaintiff to create a townhouse development on its ninety-six-acre parcel. Justice Hutchinson, one of three dissenters, was disturbed by the township's "total exclusion of townhouses."

Two days later the court decided In re Appeal of Elocin, Inc., 501 Pa. 348, 461 A.2d 771 (1983). In another plurality opinion, Justice Zappala wrote:

> We do not agree that a municipality must necessarily provide for every

A. Exclusion

conceivable use. Where a municipality provides for a reasonable share of multi-family dwellings [semi-detached homes, two-family homes, and apartment homes with up to four units] as Springfield has done [12 percent of its housing units], it need not provide for every conceivable subcategory of such dwellings.

461 A.2d at 773. Thus, the rejection of Elocin's proposal "to construct 567 mid- or high-rise apartment units and 305 townhouse units" was not unconstitutional. See Note, The Pennsylvania Supreme Court and the Exclusionary Zoning Dilemma, 29 Vill. L. Rev. 477 (1983-1984).

Two years after this apparent shift from the activism of the 1970s, in Fernley v. Board of Supervisors of Schuylkill Township, 509 Pa. 413, 502 A.2d 585 (1985), a four-member majority decided an issue that lay unresolved since *Surrick*: "We are now confronted with the question of whether a fair share analysis must be employed to assess the exclusionary impact of zoning regulations which totally prohibit a basic type of housing. We hold that the fair share analysis is inapplicable to this Schuylkill Township ordinance which absolutely prohibits apartment buildings." 502 A.2d at 587. The balancing test appropriate for de facto exclusion was found inappropriate for municipalities engaged in de jure bans, even if the municipality could demonstrate that it projected little or no growth in the future. Predictably, there were dissents, objecting to the reformulation of the court's strategy and to the extreme remedy ordered by the majority: "remand . . . to the Court of Common Pleas for approval of appellants' proposed development [245 acres with garden apartments, townhouses, and quadraplexes] unless the appellee can show that appellants' plan is incompatible with the site or reasonable, pre-existing health and safety codes and regulations." Id. at 591.

Some of the Pennsylvania decisional shifts, as in the New Jersey line of cases, can be attributed to changes in court membership. How well have these courts balanced the desire to fine-tune doctrines with the need for predictability and continuity? What are the benefits of trial and appellate judges working out the nuances of reform on a case-by-case basis, as opposed to the wholesale change ushered in by comprehensive legislation? How do the efforts of the courts in these two key jurisdictions to correct the injustices they perceived, to draw meaningful distinctions (de facto versus de jure, developing versus developed, etc.), and to craft effective remedies, compare with the efforts of the Supreme Court in Brown v. Board of Education (I and II), 347 U.S. 483 (1954), 349 U.S. 294 (1955), and their controversial, often-complicated progeny? Cf. Tribe, American Constitutional Law 1488-1501 (2d ed. 1988).

As the supreme court rode out the controversy (and on occasion basked in the admiration) wrought by their decision, much work remained for lower courts and the municipal officials involved in or anticipating exclusionary zoning litigation. What follows is a sampling of judicial and nonjudicial attempts to articulate and implement the "fair share" mandate, and to determine the geographical and demographic scope of the holding. There also remained some troublesome vestiges of the preactivist regime — such as minimum floor area ordinances — and the nagging fear that, for some dilatory or obstinate municipalities, one stern warning would not suffice.

■ OAKWOOD AT MADISON, INC. v. TOWNSHIP OF MADISON
72 N.J. 481, 371 A.2d 1192 (1977)

CONFORD, P. J. A. D., Temporarily Assigned. . . .
. . . [T]he prime question before us, in *Mount Laurel* terms, is whether the trial court has correctly found that Madison's zoning ordinance does not provide the opportunity to meet a fair share of the regional burden for low and moderate income housing needs. We have seen that the trial court did not specify the precise boundaries of the applicable region nor fix an absolute number of appropriate housing units to be provided. It merely described the pertinent region as the area from which the population of the township would be drawn, absent exclusionary zoning. . . .

. . . [W]e do not regard it as mandatory for developing municipalities whose ordinances are challenged as exclusionary to devise specific formulae for estimating their precise fair share of the lower income housing needs of a specifically demarcated region. Nor do we conceive it as necessary for a trial court to make findings of that nature in a contested case. Firstly, numerical housing goals are not realistically translatable into specific substantive changes in a zoning ordinance by any technique revealed to us by our study of the data before us. There are too many imponderables between a zone change and the actual production of housing on sites as zoned, not to mention the production of a specific number of lower cost units in a given period of time. Municipalities do not themselves have the duty to build or subsidize housing. Secondly, the breadth of approach by the experts to the factor of the appropriate region and to the criteria for allocation of regional housing goals to municipal "subregions" is so great and the pertinent economic and sociological considerations so diverse as to preclude judicial dictation or acceptance of any one solution as authoritative. For the same reasons, we would not mandate the formula approach as obligatory on any municipality seeking to correct a fair share deficiency. . . .

A. Exclusion

The trial court specified that for Madison to meet its fair share of the housing needs of the region its zoning ordinance must approximate "in additional housing unit capacity the same proportion of low-income housing as its present low-income population, about 12%, and the same proportion of moderate-income housing as its moderate-income population, about 19%". The 1973 ordinance was held "palpably short" of these requirements. 128 N.J. Super. at 447, 320 A.2d 223....

Based upon our analysis and findings ... the 1973 ordinance is clearly deficient in meeting Madison's obligation to share in providing the opportunity for lower cost housing needed in the region, whether or not the specific fair share estimates submitted by defendant are acceptable. Those estimates are, in any event, defective at least in not including prospective need beyond 1975....

We herewith modify the judgment entered in the Law Division to hold, as we did in *Mount Laurel* as to the ordinance there involved, that the 1973 zoning ordinance is invalid, not *in toto*, but only "to the extent and in the particulars set forth in this opinion". *Mount Laurel*, 67 N.J. at 191, 336 A.2d at 734. For the reasons elaborated above the ordinance is presumptively contrary to the general welfare and beyond the scope of the zoning power in the particulars mentioned. *Mount Laurel*, 67 N.J. at 185, 336 A.2d 713. The municipality has not borne its consequent burden of establishing valid reasons for the deficiencies of the ordinance. Id. at 185, 336 A.2d 713. It is obvious that a revision of the residential provisions of the ordinance is called for in order to provide the opportunity for that amount of least-cost housing in the township which will comply with the directions contained in this opinion.

■ HOME BUILDERS LEAGUE OF SOUTH JERSEY v. TOWNSHIP OF BERLIN
81 N.J. 127, 405 A.2d 381 (1979)

SCHREIBER, J.

At issue in this case is the validity of provisions in a municipal zoning ordinance which impose minimum floor area requirements for residential dwellings irrespective of the number of occupants living in the home and unrelated to any other factor, such as frontage or lot size....

Voorhees Township is located within the Philadelphia-Camden area, less than 15 miles southeast of Camden. It is a developing municipality. Its population grew from 3784 in 1960 to 6214 in 1970, and 7320 in 1976. The Camden County Planning Board has projected an increase in population to 23,458 by 1990, and the Township's master plan estimates population at full development to be 37,627....

The bases which Voorhees has advanced are that the minima will (1) promote public health and safety and (2) maintain the nature of residential neighborhoods and conserve property values. . . .

We agree with the trial court's factual findings that minimum floor area requirements are not *per se* related to public health, safety or morals. The record contains substantial evidence in this respect. Dr. Eric Mood, Associate Clinical Professor of Public Health in the Department of Epidemiology and Public Health in the Yale School of Medicine, testified that the Voorhees floor space requirements were not related to and did not serve the public health, safety and welfare. In his opinion such criteria could be so related only if they were based on occupancy. . . .

Professor Haar has noted the irrelevance of minimum dwelling size to the traditional zoning concerns of safety and health:

> Prescribing minimum standards for size of a land parcel will indirectly but effectively control bulk and the density of population, thus securing light, air, and open space. In addition to preventing overcrowding of land and undue concentrations of people, the minimum land requirement secures safety from fire, panic, contagions, and other dangers. And further, the maintenance of large and open areas free from noise and bustle and the preservation of natural surroundings may be legitimate planning purposes in themselves. *Minimum requirements as to dwelling size, however, accomplish none of the traditional purposes of the zoning power.* Where the problem is size of the building occupying the land, the goals of physical planning can be achieved only in terms of maximums. Thus building bulk regulations are almost invariably formulated in such terms (height, cubage, percentage of lot coverage, floor area ratio). [Haar, Zoning for Minimum Standards, 66 Harv. L. Rev. at 1060-1061; emphasis supplied; footnotes omitted]

The ratio of occupants to space obviously can affect public health, family stability and emotional well being. This interrelationship is found in standards fixed by the American Public Health Association which set a minimum residency requirement of 150 square feet for one person and 100 square feet for each additional occupant. These criteria are currently recommended by the U.S. Department of Housing and Urban Development (HUD). HUD has always prescribed occupancy-based standards in relation to space.

We have previously adverted to the different area minima in Voorhees' various residential zones. Since the minima necessary for public health, safety and morals in the R.R., RD-2 and other zones are unquestionably the same, it follows that the Township was not considering health, safety and morals when it enacted these provisions. As the trial court aptly commented, "It is ridiculous to suggest that an

A. Exclusion

1,100 square foot house may be 'healthful' in one part of town and not another." 157 N.J. Super. at 601, 385 A.2d at 302.

Nor can minimum floor areas be utilized to prevent over-crowding. In the absence of some relationship between living areas and the number of occupants, unless there is a ratio between the space and inhabitants, obviously the problem is not being alleviated. . . .

The majority opinion in Lionshead Lake, Inc. v. Tp. of Wayne, although referring to the fact that there are minima in housing below which the health of the occupants might be impaired, rested its conclusion in upholding several minimum living areas in the zoning ordinance on the protection of land values generally and of the character of the community. . . . The opinion did not discuss the impact of economic segregation, although Justice Oliphant in dissent referred to that factor. . . .

Shortly after *Lionshead*, the Court acknowledged in Pierro v. Baxendale, 20 N.J. 17, 118 A.2d 401 (1955), that when conditions change, the dangers of economic segregation may warrant a reexamination of *Lionshead*. . . .

We have experienced that change in conditions which has been reflected in pertinent legislative and judicial attitudes. Zoning which excludes for fiscal purposes has been condemned as contrary to the general welfare. *Mount Laurel*; Oakwood at Madison, Inc. v. Tp. of Madison, 72 N.J. 481, 371 A.2d 1192 (1977). As we have stated previously, once it is demonstrated that the ordinance excludes people on an economic basis without on its face relating the minimum floor area to one or more appropriate variables, the burden of proof shifts to the municipality to show a proper purpose is being served. This was a burden Wayne was not called upon to meet and Voorhees is. It is a burden which Voorhees has failed to meet.

Notes

1. In Pascack Association, Ltd. v. Mayor and Council of Township of Washington, 74 N.J. 470, 379 A.2d 6 (1977), the supreme court determined that the *Mount Laurel* obligations were not binding "on the part of a small municipality, developed substantially fully upon detached single-family dwellings and restricted accordingly in the residential provisions of its zoning ordinance." The township (1970 population of 10,577), occupied $3\frac{1}{4}$ square miles of Bergen County, with 94.5 percent of its property residential, and merely 2.3 percent vacant. The court agreed with the decision of the appellate division to set aside a trial court's finding that the township's denial of permission to rezone plaintiff's thirty-acre tract for multi-family residential use was illegal.

Appellate Judge Conford, temporarily assigned to the high court, noted that "[t]here is no *per se* principle in this state mandating zoning for multi-family housing by every municipality regardless of its circumstances with respect to degree or nature of development."

Justice Pashman's dissent was impassioned and pessimistic:

> The Court's characterization of some communities as "developed" allows municipalities which have already attained "exclusionary bliss" to forever absolve themselves of any obligation for correcting the racial and economic segregation which their land use controls helped to create. By rewarding the past unlawful use of the zoning power to accomplish racially and economically discriminatory planning, we encourage future abuse of land use planning controls. The existence of developed, insular communities which are allowed to reap the benefits of their illegality without being required to share in the costs is a constant reminder to developing communities of the benefits to be gained from illegal and exclusionary zoning. Similarly, remaining communities and inner cities will be required by today's decision to take more than their "fair share" of low and middle-income multi-housing; that specter can only encourage municipalities to avoid the label of "developing."...
>
> ... Society as a whole suffers the failure to solve the economic and social problems which exclusionary zoning creates; we live daily with the failure of our democratic institutions to eradicate class distinctions. Inevitably, the dream of a pluralistic society begins to fade.[28]

2. The *Mount Laurel* parties found themselves before Superior Court Judge Wood in 1978, 161 N.J. Super. 317, 391 A.2d 935. This time the plaintiffs — now including Davis Enterprises, a developer seeking to develop a mobile home community — challenged the township's compliance with the supreme court's decision. The plaintiff's expert witnesses (including urban planning and development specialists Allan Mallach and Peter Abeles) challenged the township's determination of fair share: 515 units by the year 2000.

Judge Wood was not amused, or persuaded:

> What was engaged in in this trial was just the sort of statistical warfare which the court in *Madison* said should be avoided. This court is unable from the plethora of figures and formulae produced and propounded by the witnesses to make a determination of Mount Laurel's "fair share" of housing needs.
>
> ... I cannot say that the conclusions adopted by Mount Laurel as to its

---

28. See also Buchsbaum, The Irrelevance of the "Developing Municipality" Concept — A Reply to Professors Rose and Levin, 5 Real Est. L.J. 280 (1977); Housing for All Under Law (Fishman ed. 1978). — Eds.

Should the *Mount Laurel I* doctrines apply to middle-income housing? See Swiss Associates v. Wayne Township, 162 N.J. Super. 138, 392 A.2d 596 (1978) (ordinance disallowing construction of high-rise apartment buildings withstood challenge). — Eds.

A. Exclusion

fair share of low and moderate-income housing opportunities are unreasonable simply because others disagree with them. The determination is, as stated, a legislative function. I am convinced that Mount Laurel has sought to exercise that function in good faith and with the express intent of compliance with the requirements of the court.[29]

The good faith that Judge Wood perceived in Mount Laurel's efforts to comply with the 1975 mandate did not bring the desired results. On October 20-22, and December 15, 1980, the New Jersey Supreme Court — frustrated by the refusal or inability of local officials throughout the state to allow for the provision of low-cost housing — once again heard oral argument, this time with an eye toward framing an effective remedy to realize the ambitious fair share goals of *Mount Laurel I*. Twenty-five more months would pass before the court announced its dramatic opinion, running nearly 250 pages. By January 1983, as national attention once again turned to the South Jersey flatlands, not much had changed:

> Despite the order's potential for broad social and economic change, Mount Laurel's landscape remains dominated by horse farms, orchards, farms, woods and back-country roads, even though it is a 15-minute drive east of Philadelphia. None of the 515 new housing units that the Planning Board in 1976 thought would satisfy the court's dictate were ever built. . . .
>
> Mount Laurel's response to the 1975 holding — the action that drew the court's wrath in the ruling Thursday — was to rezone three widely scattered plots for low-income housing. Together, the three parcels contain 33 of the 14,176 predominantly rural acres in the town. . . .
>
> The 33 acres set aside years ago remain as they did then. One plot of 13 acres is a field on the fringe of an apple orchard. . . .
>
> Another plot has 13 acres of idle land at the rear of the Moorestown Shopping Mall. Another Philadelphia company, the Binswanger Management Corporation, which plans and manages office buildings, owns it. Binswanger has never proposed construction of housing on the site, . . . although Binswanger attempted to win approval for an industrial park on adjacent land it owns. . . .
>
> The third designated low-income housing plot, with seven acres, has for years been a farm for Christmas trees owned by Alfred DiPietro, an engineer for RCA, who lives in Guam. His nephews run the farm.
>
> Mr. Godfrey, the owner of the country store and a friend of Mr. DiPietro, said, "Until he gets a fortune for the land, he'll never sell it for any housing."

N.Y. Times, Jan. 22, 1983.

---

29. The Township did not score a total victory, however, as the court found Mount Laurel's total exclusion of mobile homes to be "arbitrary, capricious and unreasonable." — EDS.

Could the court fashion affirmative remedies and create incentives strong enough to overcome such recalcitrance? How sincere is the court in its repeated entreaties for legislative assistance (even preemption)? Had the inflation and high interest rates of the hiatus between opinions I and II, coupled with housing program budget cuts out of Washington, D.C., eliminated any real hope for large-scale real estate development for low- and moderate-income buyers and renters? Could the court avoid complicating even further the process by which municipalities calculated their regional obligations? Despite their repeated protests, were not the justices indeed trying to "build houses"?

■ SOUTHERN BURLINGTON COUNTY NAACP v. TOWNSHIP OF MOUNT LAUREL
92 N.J. 158, 456 A.2d 390 (1983)

[MOUNT LAUREL II]

The opinion of the Court was delivered by WILENTZ, C. J.

This is the return, eight years later, of Southern Burlington County N.A.A.C.P. v. Township of Mount Laurel, 67 N.J. 151, 336 A.2d 713 (1975) (*Mount Laurel I*). We set forth in that case, for the first time, the doctrine requiring that municipalities' land use regulations provide a realistic opportunity for low and moderate income housing. The doctrine has become famous. The *Mount Laurel* case itself threatens to become infamous. After all this time, ten years after the trial court's initial order invalidating its zoning ordinance, Mount Laurel remains afflicted with a blatantly exclusionary ordinance. Papered over with studies, rationalized by hired experts, the ordinance at its core is true to nothing but Mount Laurel's determination to exclude the poor. Mount Laurel is not alone; we believe that there is widespread non-compliance with the constitutional mandate of our original opinion in this case.

To the best of our ability, we shall not allow it to continue. This Court is more firmly committed to the original *Mount Laurel* doctrine than ever, and we are determined, within appropriate judicial bounds, to make it work. The obligation is to provide a realistic opportunity for housing, not litigation. We have learned from experience, however, that unless a strong judicial hand is used, *Mount Laurel* will not result in housing, but in paper, process, witnesses, trials and appeals. We intend by this decision to strengthen it, clarify it, and make it easier for public officials, including judges, to apply it.

This case is accompanied by five others, heard together and decided

A. Exclusion

in this opinion.[1] All involve questions arising from the *Mount Laurel* doctrine. They demonstrate the need to put some steel into that doctrine. The deficiencies in its application range from uncertainty and inconsistency at the trial level to inflexible review criteria at the appellate level. The waste of judicial energy involved at every level is substantial and is matched only by the often needless expenditure of talent on the part of lawyers and experts. The length and complexity of trials is often outrageous, and the expense of litigation is so high that a real question develops whether the municipality can afford to defend or the plaintiffs can afford to sue. . . .

These six cases not only afford the opportunity for, but demonstrate the necessity of reexamining the *Mount Laurel* doctrine. We do so here. The doctrine is right but its administration has been ineffective. . . .

. . . [W]hile we have always preferred legislative to judicial action in this field, we shall continue — until the Legislature acts — to do our best to uphold the constitutional obligation that underlies the *Mount Laurel* doctrine. That is our duty. We may not build houses, but we do enforce the Constitution.[7]

We note that there has been some legislative initiative in this field. We look forward to more. The new Municipal Land Use Law explicitly recognizes the obligation of municipalities to zone with regional consequences in mind, N.J.S.A. 40:55D-28(d); it also recognizes the work of the Division of State and Regional Planning in the Department of Community Affairs (DCA), in creating the State Development Guide Plan (1980) (SDGP), which plays an important part in our decisions today. Our deference to these legislative and executive initiatives can be regarded as a clear signal of our readiness to defer further to more substantial actions.

The judicial role, however, which could decrease as a result of legislative and executive action, necessarily will expand to the extent

---

1. . . . Because these cases raised many similar issues concerning the *Mount Laurel* doctrine, they were argued together and have been disposed of in this single opinion.

We would prefer that our opinion took less time and less space. The subject is complex, highly controversial, and obviously of great importance. We have not one, but six cases before us that raise practically all of the major questions involved in the *Mount Laurel* doctrine; furthermore we have dealt with other questions that, strictly speaking, might not be necessary for resolving these cases, since we thought it important to settle them as well. Unfortunately, as the history of the *Mount Laurel* doctrine proves, the clear resolution of issues of this kind requires extensive time and extensive discussion. . . .

7. In New Jersey, it has traditionally been the judiciary, and not the Legislature, that has remedied substantive abuses of the zoning power by municipalities. A review of zoning litigation and legislation since the enactment of the zoning enabling statute in the 1920's shows that the Legislature has confined itself largely to regulating the procedural aspects of zoning. The judiciary has at the same time invalidated or modified zoning ordinances that violated constitutional rights or failed to serve the general welfare. . . . Although the complexity and political sensitivity of the issue now before us make it especially appropriate for legislative resolution, we have no choice, absent that resolution, but to exercise our traditional constitutional duty to end an abuse of the zoning power.

that we remain virtually alone in this field. In the absence of adequate legislative and executive help, we must give meaning to the constitutional doctrine in the cases before us through our own devices, even if they are relatively less suitable. That is the basic explanation of our decisions today....

The following is a summary of the more significant rulings of these cases:

(1) *Every* municipality's land use regulations should provide a realistic opportunity for decent housing for at least some part of its resident poor who now occupy dilapidated housing. The zoning power is no more abused by keeping out the region's poor than by forcing out the resident poor. In other words, each municipality must provide a realistic opportunity for decent housing for its indigenous poor except where they represent a disproportionately large segment of the population as compared with the rest of the region. This is the case in many of our urban areas.

(2) The existence of a municipal obligation to provide a realistic opportunity for a fair share of the region's present and prospective low and moderate income housing need will no longer be determined by whether or not a municipality is "developing." The obligation extends, instead, to every municipality, any portion of which is designated by the State, through the SDGP as a "growth area." This obligation, imposed as a remedial measure, does not extend to those areas where the SDGP discourages growth — namely, open spaces, rural areas, prime farmland, conservation areas, limited growth areas, parts of the Pinelands and certain Coastal Zone areas. The SDGP represents the conscious determination of the State, through the executive and legislative branches, on how best to plan its future. It appropriately serves as a judicial remedial tool. The obligation to encourage lower income housing, therefore, will hereafter depend on rational long-range land use planning (incorporated into the SDGP) rather than upon the sheer economic forces that have dictated whether a municipality is "developing." Moreover, the fact that a municipality is fully developed does not eliminate this obligation although, obviously, it may affect the extent of the obligation and the timing of its satisfaction. The remedial obligation of municipalities that consist of both "growth areas" and other areas may be reduced, based on many factors, as compared to a municipality completely within a "growth area."

There shall be a heavy burden on any party seeking to vary the foregoing remedial consequences of the SDGP designations.

(3) *Mount Laurel* litigation will ordinarily include proof of the municipality's fair share of low and moderate income housing in terms of the number of units needed immediately, as well as the number needed for a reasonable period of time in the future. "Numberless" resolution of the issue based upon a conclusion that the ordinance

A. Exclusion

provides a realistic opportunity for *some* low and moderate income housing will be insufficient. Plaintiffs, however, will still be able to prove a *prima facie* case, without proving the precise fair share of the municipality, by proving that the zoning ordinance is substantially affected by restrictive devices, that proof creating a presumption that the ordinance is invalid.

The municipal obligation to provide a realistic opportunity for low and moderate income housing is not satisfied by a good faith attempt. The housing opportunity provided must, in fact, be the substantial equivalent of the fair share.

(4) Any future *Mount Laurel* litigation shall be assigned only to those judges selected by the Chief Justice with the approval of the Supreme Court. The initial group shall consist of three judges, the number to be increased or decreased hereafter by the Chief Justice with the Court's approval. The Chief Justice shall define the area of the State for which each of the three judges is responsible: any *Mount Laurel* case challenging the land use ordinance of a municipality included in that area shall be assigned to that judge.

Since the same judge will hear and decide all *Mount Laurel* cases within a particular area and only three judges will do so in the entire state, we believe that over a period of time a consistent pattern of regions will emerge. Consistency is more likely as well in determinations of regional housing needs and allocations of fair share to municipalities within the region. Along with this consistency will come the predictability needed to give full effect to the *Mount Laurel* doctrine. While determinations of region and regional housing need will not be conclusive as to any municipality not a party to the litigation, they shall be given presumptive validity in subsequent litigation involving any municipality included in a previously determined region. . . .

(5) The municipal obligation to provide a realistic opportunity for the construction of its fair share of low and moderate income housing may require more than the elimination of unnecessary cost-producing requirements and restrictions. Affirmative governmental devices should be used to make that opportunity realistic, including lower-income density bonuses and mandatory set-asides. Furthermore the municipality should cooperate with the developer's attempts to obtain federal subsidies. For instance, where federal subsidies depend on the municipality providing certain municipal tax treatment allowed by state statutes for lower income housing, the municipality should make a good faith effort to provide it. Mobile homes may not be prohibited, unless there is solid proof that sound planning in a particular municipality requires such prohibition.

(6) The lower income regional housing need is comprised of both low and moderate income housing. A municipality's fair share should include both in such proportion as reflects consideration of all relevant

factors, including the proportion of low and moderate income housing that make up the regional need.

(7) Providing a realistic opportunity for the construction of least-cost housing will satisfy a municipality's *Mount Laurel* obligation if, and only if, it cannot otherwise be satisfied. In other words, it is only after *all* alternatives have been explored, *all* affirmative devices considered, including, where appropriate, a reasonable period of time to determine whether low and moderate income housing is produced, only when everything has been considered and tried in order to produce a realistic opportunity for low and moderate income housing that least-cost housing will provide an adequate substitute. Least-cost housing means what it says, namely, housing that can be produced at the lowest possible price consistent with minimal standards of health and safety.

(8) Builder's remedies will be afforded to plaintiffs in *Mount Laurel* litigation where appropriate, on a case-by-case basis. Where the plaintiff has acted in good faith, attempted to obtain relief without litigation, and thereafter vindicates the constitutional obligation in *Mount Laurel*-type litigation, ordinarily a builder's remedy will be granted, provided that the proposed project includes an appropriate portion of low and moderate income housing, and provided further that it is located and designed in accordance with sound zoning and planning concepts, including its environmental impact.

(9) The judiciary should manage *Mount Laurel* litigation to dispose of a case in all of its aspects with one trial and one appeal, unless substantial considerations indicate some other course. This means that in most cases after a determination of invalidity, and prior to final judgment and possible appeal, the municipality will be required to rezone, preserving its contention that the trial court's adjudication was incorrect. If an appeal is taken, all facets of the litigation will be considered by the appellate court including both the correctness of the lower court's determination of invalidity, the scope of remedies imposed on the municipality, and the validity of the ordinance adopted after the judgment of invalidity. The grant or denial of a stay will depend upon the circumstances of each case. The trial court will appoint a master to assist in formulating and implementing a proper remedy whenever that course seems desirable.

(10) The *Mount Laurel* obligation to meet the prospective lower income housing need of the region is, by definition, one that is met year after year in the future, throughout the years of the particular projection used in calculating prospective need. In this sense the affirmative obligation to provide a realistic opportunity to construct a fair share of lower income housing is met by a "phase-in" over those years; it need not be provided immediately. Nevertheless, there may be circumstances in which the obligation requires zoning that will provide an immediate opportunity — for instance, zoning to meet the

A. Exclusion

region's present lower income housing need. In some cases, the provision of such a realistic opportunity might result in the immediate construction of lower income housing in such quantity as would radically transform the municipality overnight. Trial courts shall have the discretion, under those circumstances, to moderate the impact of such housing by allowing even the present need to be phased in over a period of years. Such power, however, should be exercised sparingly. The same power may be exercised in the satisfaction of prospective need, equally sparingly, and with special care to assure that such further postponement will not significantly dilute the *Mount Laurel* obligation....

The initial question in every *Mount Laurel* case is whether the municipality is subject to the *Mount Laurel* obligation. In its initial formulation in *Mount Laurel I*, this Court described the characteristics of Mount Laurel, implying that any municipality with similar characteristics would have the obligation announced in that opinion. *Mount Laurel I*, 67 N.J. at 160, 336 A.2d 713. Those municipalities are referred to as "developing municipalities."...

Lacking any official guidance ... as to the state's plans for its own future, its own determination of where development should occur and where it should not, and what kind of development, this Court fashioned its own remedial planning guide in the form of a definition of "developing." It was obvious to anyone who studied the matter that such definition of the *Mount Laurel* responsibility furnished no guarantee that if lower income housing resulted, it would be built where it should be built, i.e., where a comprehensive plan for the State of New Jersey might indicate such development was desirable. We proceeded in spite of this drawback since, given the constitutional requirement and the lack of any assurance that such a statewide plan would be forthcoming, there appeared no justification for delay.

We now have a satisfactory alternative. The State Development Guide Plan (May 1980) promulgated pursuant to N.J.S.A. 13:1B-15.52, provides a statewide blueprint for future development. Its remedial use in *Mount Laurel* disputes will ensure that the imposition of fair share obligations will coincide with the State's regional planning goals and objectives....

The SDGP divides the state into six basic areas: growth, limited growth, agriculture, conservation, pinelands and coastal zones (the pinelands and coastal zones actually being the product of other protective legislation).... By clearly setting forth the state's policy as to where growth should be encouraged and discouraged, these maps effectively serve as a blueprint for the implementation of the *Mount Laurel* doctrine.[30] Pursuant to the concept map, development (including

---

30. Not all concerned were as comfortable with the suitability of the SDGP for the

residential development) is targeted for areas characterized as "growth." The *Mount Laurel* obligation should, as a matter of sound judicial discretion reflecting public policy, be consistent with the state's plan for its future development....

As noted before, *all* municipalities' land use regulations will be required to provide a realistic opportunity for the construction of their fair share of the region's present lower income housing need generated by present dilapidated or overcrowded lower income units, including their own. Municipalities located in "growth areas" may, of course, have an obligation to meet the present need of the region that goes far beyond that generated in the municipality itself; there may be some municipalities, however, in growth areas where the portion of the region's present need generated by that municipality far exceeds the municipality's fair share. The portion of the region's present need that must be addressed by municipalities in growth areas will depend, then, on conventional fair share analysis, some municipalities' fair share being more than the present need generated within the municipality and in some cases less. In non-growth areas, however (limited growth, conservation, and agricultural), no municipality will have to provide for more than the present need generated within the municipality, for to require more than that would be to induce growth in that municipality in conflict with the SDGP....

There are two basic types of affirmative measures that a municipality can use to make the opportunity for lower income housing realistic: (1) encouraging or requiring the use of available state or federal housing subsidies, and (2) providing incentives for or requiring private developers to set aside a portion of their developments for lower income housing. Which, if either, of these devices will be necessary in any particular municipality to assure compliance with the constitutional mandate will be initially up to the municipality itself. Where necessary, the trial court overseeing compliance may require their use. We note again that least-cost housing will not ordinarily satisfy a municipality's fair share obligation to provide low and moderate income housing unless and until it has attempted the inclusionary devices outlined below or otherwise has proven the futility of the attempt....

---

purposes the court had in mind:

> George Sternlieb, Director of the Center for Urban Policy Research at Rutgers University, has called the entire document "poorly done." The administration of Governor Kean, openly opposed to the mandate because of what the Governor has called "overly aggressive judicial action," has refused to endorse it on the ground the plan is not sufficient as a statewide zoning map.
>
> "It's a good plan for the purpose for which it was written — to help with new infrastructure projects," said W. Cary Edwards, the Governor's chief counsel. "It simply is not a very accurate tool for the purposes the court wants it used."

De Palma, N.J. Housing Woes Are All Over the Map, N.Y. Times, Apr. 17, 1983. — Eds.

A. Exclusion

There are several inclusionary zoning techniques that municipalities must use if they cannot otherwise assure the construction of their fair share of lower income housing. Although we will discuss some of them here, we in no way intend our list to be exhaustive; municipalities and trial courts are encouraged to create other devices and methods for meeting fair share obligations.[28]

The most commonly used inclusionary zoning techniques are incentive zoning and mandatory set-asides. The former involves offering economic incentives to a developer through the relaxation of various restrictions of an ordinance (typically density limits) in exchange for the construction of certain amounts of low and moderate income units. The latter, a mandatory set-aside, is basically a requirement that developers include a minimum amount of lower income housing in their projects.

In addition to the mechanisms we have just described, municipalities and trial courts must consider such other affirmative devices as zoning substantial areas for mobile homes and for other types of low cost housing and establishing maximum square footage zones, i.e., zones where developers cannot build units with *more* than a certain footage or build anything other than lower income housing or housing that includes a specified portion of lower income housing. In some cases, a realistic opportunity to provide the municipality's fair share may require over-zoning, i.e., zoning to allow for *more* than the fair share if it is likely, as it usually is, that not all of the property made available for lower income housing will actually result in such housing.

Although several of the defendants concede that simply removing restrictions and exactions is unlikely to result in the construction of lower income housing, they maintain that requiring the municipality to use affirmative measures is beyond the scope of the courts' authority. We disagree. . . .

The specific contentions are that inclusionary measures amount to a taking without just compensation and an impermissible socio-economic use of the zoning power, one not substantially related to the use of land. Reliance is placed to some extent on Board of Supervisors v. DeGroff Enterprises, Inc., 214 Va. 235, 198 S.E. 2d 600 (1973), to that effect. We disagree with that decision. We now resolve the matter that

---

28. For useful discussions of how inclusionary techniques have been utilized in New Jersey municipalities see . . . Department of Community Affairs, The Princeton Housing Proposal: A Strategy to Achieve Balanced Housing without Government Subsidy (1977) (Housing Proposal). See also Oakwood at Madison, Inc. v. Township of Madison, 72 N.J. 481, 611-616, 371 A.2d 1192 (1977) (Pashman, J., concurring and dissenting); Fox & Davis, Density Bonus Zoning to Provide Low and Moderate Cost Housing, 3 Hastings Const L.Q. 1015 (1977); Kleven, Inclusionary Ordinances — Policy and Legal Issues in Requiring Private Developers to Build Low Cost Housing, 21 UCLA L. Rev. 1432 (1974); H. Franklin, D. Falk, A. Levin, In-Zoning: A Guide for Policy Makers on Inclusionary Land Use Programs (1974).

we left open in *Madison,* 72 N.J. at 518-519, 371 A.2d 1192. We hold that where the *Mount Laurel* obligation cannot be satisfied by removal of restrictive barriers, inclusionary devices such as density bonuses and mandatory set-asides keyed to the construction of lower income housing, are constitutional and within the zoning power of a municipality. . . .

The contention that generally these devices are beyond the municipal power because they are "socio-economic" is particularly inappropriate. The very basis for the constitutional obligation underlying *Mount Laurel* is a belief, fundamental, that excluding a class of citizens from housing on an economic basis (one that substantially corresponds to a socio-economic basis) distinctly disserves the general welfare. That premise is essential to the conclusion that such zoning ordinances are an abuse of the zoning power and are therefore unconstitutional.

It is nonsense to single out inclusionary zoning (providing a realistic opportunity for the construction of lower income housing) and label it "socio-economic" if that is meant to imply that other aspects of zoning are not. Detached single family residential zones, high-rise multi-family zones of any kind, factory zones, "clean" research and development zones, recreational, open space, conservation, and agricultural zones, regional shopping mall zones, indeed practically any significant kind of zoning now used, has a substantial socio-economic impact and, in some cases, a socio-economic motivation. It would be ironic if inclusionary zoning to encourage the construction of lower income housing were ruled beyond the power of a municipality because it is "socio-economic" when its need has arisen from the socio-economic zoning of the past that excluded it. . . .

Townships such as Mount Laurel that now ban mobile homes do so in reliance upon Vickers v. Gloucester, 37 N.J. 232, 181 A.2d 129 (1962), in which this Court upheld such bans. *Vickers,* however, explicitly recognized that changed circumstances could require a different result. Id. at 250, 181 A.2d 129. We find that such changed circumstances now exist. As Judge Wood found in *Mount Laurel II,* mobile homes have since 1962 become "structurally sound [and] attractive in appearance." 161 N.J. Super. at 357, 391 A.2d 935. Further, since 1974, the safety and soundness of mobile homes have been regulated by the National Mobile Home Construction and Safety Standards Act, 42 U.S.C. 5401 (1974). *Vickers,* therefore, is overruled; absolute bans of mobile homes are no longer permissible on the grounds stated in that case. . . .

Lest we be misunderstood, we do *not* hold that every municipality must allow the use of mobile homes as an affirmative device to meet its *Mount Laurel* obligation, or that any ordinance that totally excludes mobile homes is *per se* invalid. Insofar as the *Mount Laurel* doctrine is concerned, whether mobile homes must be permitted as an affirmative device will depend upon the overall effectiveness of the municipality's

A. Exclusion

attempts to comply: if compliance can be just as effectively assured without allowing mobile homes, *Mount Laurel* does not command them; if not, then assuming a suitable site is available, they must be allowed.

There may be municipalities where special conditions such as extremely high land costs make it impossible for the fair share obligation to be met even after all excessive restrictions and exactions, i.e., those not essential for safety and health, have been removed and all affirmative measures have been attempted. In such cases, *and only in such cases*, the *Mount Laurel* obligation can be met by supplementing whatever lower income housing can be built with enough "least cost" housing to satisfy the fair share. Least cost housing does not, however, mean the most inexpensive housing that developers will build on their own; it does not mean $50,000-plus single family homes and very expensive apartments. Least cost housing means the least expensive housing that builders can provide after removal by a municipality of *all* excessive restrictions and exactions and after thorough use by a municipality of all affirmative devices that might lower costs. Presumably, such housing, though unaffordable by those in the lower income brackets, will be inexpensive enough to provide shelter for families who could not afford housing in the conventional suburban housing market. At the very minimum, provision of least cost housing will make certain that municipalities in "growth" areas of this state do not "grow" only for the well-to-do....

... We hold that where a developer succeeds in *Mount Laurel* litigation and proposes a project providing a substantial amount of lower income housing, a builder's remedy should be granted unless the municipality establishes that because of environmental or other substantial planning concerns, the plaintiff's proposed project is clearly contrary to sound land use planning. We emphasize that the builder's remedy should not be denied solely because the municipality prefers some other location for lower income housing, even if it is in fact a better site. Nor is it essential that considerable funds be invested or that the litigation be intensive....

... Trial courts should guard the public interest carefully to be sure that plaintiff-developers do not abuse the *Mount Laurel* doctrine. Where builder's remedies are awarded, the remedy should be carefully conditioned to assure that in fact the plaintiff-developer constructs a substantial amount of lower income housing. Various devices can be used for that purpose, including prohibiting construction of more than a certain percentage of the non-lower income housing until a certain amount of the lower income housing is completed....

The scope of remedies authorized by this opinion is similar to those used in a rapidly growing area of the law commonly referred to as "institutional litigation" or "public law litigation."[43] While it may not

---

43. These cases have involved school desegregation, prison overcrowding, reappor-

have been appropriate at the time of *Mount Laurel* to employ those remedies, regularly used in such public law litigation, we clearly recognized "the further extent of judicial power in the field" by citing the lower court's decision in *Pascack*, 131 N.J. Super. 195, 329 A.2d 89 (Law Div. 1974), a case in which the panoply of remedies appropriate in institutional litigation was used. What we said in *Mount Laurel* in reference to remedy eight years ago was that such remedies were "not appropriate at this time, particularly in view of the advanced view of zoning law as applied to housing laid down by this opinion. . . ." 67 N.J. at 192, 336 A.2d 713. That view is no longer "advanced," at least not in this state. It is eight years old. . . .

The provision of decent housing for the poor is not a function of this Court. Our only role is to see to it that zoning does not prevent it, but rather provides a realistic opportunity for its construction as required by New Jersey's Constitution. The actual construction of that housing will continue to depend, in a much larger degree, on the economy, on private enterprise, and on the actions of the other branches of government at the national, state and local level. We intend here only to make sure that if the poor remain locked into urban slums, it will not be because we failed to enforce the Constitution.[31]

---

tionment and, significantly, housing. In them the courts, and they are usually federal courts, have found that the scope of a particular constitutional obligation, and the resistance to its vindication, are such as to require much more active judicial involvement in the remedial stage of litigation than is conventional if the constitutional obligation is to be satisfied. Federal district courts have retained particular school desegregation disputes for many years, fashioning remedies year after year as the circumstances seem to require; in some, they have actually taken over school districts, administered prisons, hospitals, and other institutions, ordered housing authorities to build housing in certain areas, in some cases even outside of the municipality involved. The authorities, both case and comment, are unanimous in their conclusion that exclusionary zoning cases fall within this category, that they are "institutional litigation" or "public law litigation" for the purpose of determining what kinds of procedures, including remedies, are appropriate. . . .

31. Once again the New Jersey court's bold move inspired reactions pro and con. The January 30, 1983, editorial in the New York Times was supportive, but tempered with caution:

> Will the opinion prevail? The answer isn't clear. Aware of the radical implications, the court called for gradual implementation. The troubles of the housing market and shrinking funds for subsidies may frustrate this ruling even more than legal battles frustrated the first. Over time, however, some change seems inevitable — and highly desirable.

This time the "instant symposium" — entitled *"Mount Laurel II*: A Case of National Significance," featured the following contributions: Davidoff and Tegeler, *Mount Laurel II*: Well Worth the Wait; Washburn, Some Unresolved Issues in *Mount Laurel II*; Mandelker, Fair Share and Set-Aside Issues; Siemon, Remedies Under *Mount Laurel II*; Rose, How Will New Jersey Municipalities Comply?, Land Use L. & Zoning Dig., March 1983. See also the Symposium in 14 Seton Hall L. Rev. 829 (1984); Williams, The Background and Significance of *Mount Laurel II*, 26 Wash. U.J. Urb. & Contemp. L. 3 (1984); Rose, The *Mount Laurel II* Decision: Is It Based on Wishful Thinking?, 12 Real Est. L.J. 115 (1983). — Eds.

Note on Inclusionary Zoning

In large part, the court staked the ultimate success or failure of its revised mandate on the effectiveness of a set of devices collectively labeled "inclusionary zoning." The two methods singled out by the court — density bonus zoning and mandatory set-asides — had been the subject of some experimentation in New Jersey and other jurisdictions and the target of critics concerned with constitutional deprivation and misguided income distribution. In addition to the sources cited by the court at note 28, see Williams, On the Inclination of Developers to Help the Poor, Lincoln Institute of Land Policy, Policy Analysis Series No. 211 (1985); Mallach, Inclusionary Housing Programs: Policies and Practices (1984); Mallach, The Fallacy of Laissez-Faire: Land Use Deregulation, Housing Affordability, and the Poor, 30 Wash. U.J. Urb. & Contemp. L. 35 (1986); Ellickson, The Irony of "Inclusionary" Zoning, 54 S. Cal. L. Rev. 1167 (1981).

The nascent inclusionary zoning movement suffered its first serious setback before the Supreme Court of Virginia in Board of Supervisors of Fairfax County v. DeGroff Enterprises, 214 Va. 235, 198 S.E.2d 600 (1973). On June 30, 1971, the Board had adopted amendment 156 of the Fairfax County Zoning Ordinance. Key language from the section labeled "Required Use: Low and Moderate Income Dwelling Units" follows:

> Except as otherwise provided herein, every planned development of a PDH district shall provide dwelling units for families of low and moderate income. An applicant for PDH zoning . . . shall provide or cause others to provide under the development plan, low income dwelling units which shall be not less (and may be more) than six per cent (6%) of the total number of dwelling units in the development. The applicant shall also provide, or cause others to provide, the number of moderate income dwelling units which, when added to the number of low income dwelling units, shall be not less (and may be more) than fifteen per cent (15%) of the total number of dwelling units in the development.

The court invalidated the amendment, holding that the state legislators intended "to permit localities to enact only traditional zoning ordinances directed to physical characteristics and having the purpose neither to include nor exclude any particular socio-economic group." In addition, the 15 percent set-aside was an illegal attempt "to control the compensation for the use of land and the improvements thereon." Finally, the state constitution's takings clause was invoked to strike down the confiscatory scheme.

Legislators in other jurisdictions pressed on undaunted by this judicial warning. See, for example, Cal. Gov't Code §65915 (West Supp. 1987):

(a) When a developer of housing agrees to construct at least (1) 25 percent of the total units of a housing development for persons and families of low or moderate income, as defined in Section 50093 of the Health and Safety Code, or (2) 10 percent of the total units of a housing development for lower-income households, as defined in Section 50079.5 of the Health and Safety Code, or (3) 50 percent of the total dwelling units of a housing development for qualifying residents, as defined in Section 51.2 of the Civil Code, a city, county, or city and county shall either (1) grant a density bonus or (2) provide other incentives of equivalent financial value. . . .

(c) For the purposes of this chapter, "density bonus" means a density increase of at least 25 percent of the otherwise maximum allowable residential density under the applicable zoning ordinance and land use element of the general plan. The density bonus shall not be included when determining the number of housing units which is equal to 10 or 25 percent of the total. The density bonus shall apply to housing developments consisting of five or more dwelling units.

In May 1977, Newton, Massachusetts, a middle-class suburb of Boston, adopted the following modification to the city ordinances:

"Whenever a request under this Section for permission of the Board of Aldermen seeks to increase the density of residential development for apartment houses, apartment hotels, garden apartments, or attached dwellings to a level greater than that permissible without said permit, the Board of Aldermen shall require as a condition of any such grant of permission, the provision, within the development, of low income family and/or elderly housing units amounting to ten percent (10%) of the development's total number of dwelling units."

Iodice v. City of Newton, 397 Mass. 329, 491 N.E.2d 618, 620 (1986) (quoting §24-29(b) of Newton revised ordinances). This set-aside program was enacted pursuant to Mass. Gen. L. ch. 40A §9 (West 1979), enacted in 1975, which reads in pertinent part,

Zoning ordinances or by-laws may also provide for special permits authorizing increases in the permissible density of population or intensity of a particular use in a proposed development; provided that the petitioner or applicant shall, as a condition for the grant of said permit, provide certain open space, housing for persons of low or moderate income, traffic or pedestrian improvements, installation of solar energy systems, protection for solar access, or other amenities. Such zoning ordinances or by-laws shall state the specific improvements or amenities or locations of proposed uses for which the special permits shall be granted, and the maximum increases in density of population or intensity of use which may be authorized by such special permits.

On two occasions the Supreme Judicial Court heard challenges to

A. Exclusion

the Newton "ten-percent program." In Middlesex & Boston St. Ry. v. Aldermen of Newton, 371 Mass. 849, 359 N.E.2d 1279 (1977), the court invalidated a conditional permit based on a *pre-1975* city set-aside program. In the *Iodice* case, the court did not reach the question of the constitutionality of the now state-authorized scheme, as the plaintiff's appeal was not timely brought.

The question of the constitutionality of inclusionary zoning programs in New Jersey gave the *Mount Laurel II* court little pause. In their unanimous opinion, the justices "disagreed" with their Virginia counterparts (supra page 427). A few months later, in In the Matter of Egg Harbor Associates, 94 N.J. 358, 464 A.2d 1115 (1983), the court turned down a challenge to ten percent low-income and ten percent moderate-income set-asides required of a residential community developer in the Atlantic City area. Complicating the matter was the fact that the state entity that conditioned the approval was the Division of Coastal Resources of the Department of Environmental Protection (DEP), an agency empowered by the Coastal Area Facility Review Act (CAFRA), N.J. Stat. Ann. §§13:19-1 to -21 (West 1979), to impose "fair share" provisions.

The supreme court first rejected the developer's narrow characterization of CAFRA's purpose: "Although CAFRA is principally an environmental protection statute, the powers delegated to DEP extend well beyond the protection of the natural environment. Succinctly stated, the delegated powers require DEP to regulate land use within the coastal zone for the general welfare." 464 A.2d at 1118. Next the justices concluded that the legislature had delegated to DEP the power to condition development approval in the coastal zone on a commitment to provide a set percentage of low- and moderate-income units. At the end of the opinion, the court held that the developer had failed to carry its burden of proving "by clear and convincing evidence" that a confiscatory taking had occurred. Id. at 1123.

When you read the Supreme Court's recent opinion in Nollan v. California Coastal Commission, infra page 636, consider whether takings and due process challenges directed toward linkage programs in use in New Jersey and elsewhere can still be so readily dismissed. Even if such programs pass constitutional muster, are they poorly targeted and economically inefficient tools that rarely lead to the desired results? In a detailed study based primarily on the experience of California municipalities, Professor Ellickson arrives at these disturbing conclusions:

> The costs of inclusionary zoning . . . are large and tangible. Inclusionary zoning involves in-kind housing subsidies, a method increasingly viewed as one of the most inefficient forms of income redistribution. Inclusionary zoning can also constitute a double tax on new housing

construction — first, through the burden of its exactions; and second, through the "undesirable" social environment it may force on new housing projects. In the sorts of housing markets in which inclusionary zoning has been practiced, this double tax is likely to push up housing prices across the board, often to the net injury of the moderate-income households inclusionary zoning was supposed to help. The irony of inclusionary zoning is thus that, in the places where it has proven most likely to be adopted, its net effects are apt to be the opposite of the ones advertised.

Ellickson, supra at 1215-1216.

For more positive assessments of inclusionary zoning in action and in theory, see Williams, On the Inclination, supra; and Mallach, The Fallacy, supra. Williams recommends (at 24) linking lower income housing programs with nonresidential real estate development by means of mandatory set-asides combined with density bonuses, as in San Francisco's Office/Housing Production Program (OHPP):

> Numerous advantages are presented by making such a program applicable to all forms of real estate development generating increased housing demand. First, such a strategy avoids the weakness inherent in most mandatory set aside programs that rely upon only one sector of the real estate development economy. By focusing upon a broad spectrum of development activity, structural imperfections in one sector of the market will not necessarily destroy the total effectiveness of a program, so long as other segments demonstrate a relative degree of strength.
>
> Second, such a strategy assures that all forms of real estate development "pay their way" with respect to the housing externalities created by a particular project. Simple equity as well as efficiency considerations argue strongly against any strategy that singles out one class of developers to carry the entire burden of providing low and moderate income housing within a municipality. Spreading relative burdens also lessens disincentive impacts upon any one development sector.
>
> Finally, with respect to judicial adoption of such a strategy as a remedial affirmative measure in fair share litigation, a non-residentially linked lower income housing provision program assures that municipalities cannot avoid lower income housing obligations without also sacrificing all other forms of real estate development within their borders. Mandating such a strategy as an affirmative measure assures that office, commercial and industrial development in a municipality will also be accompanied by lower income housing construction. The historical craving by municipalities for these types of favorable tax ratables indicates that few municipalities would willingly sacrifice promoting all forms of non-residential real estate development as the cost for continuing in their attempts to exclude the poor. Linking a fair share obligation to desired types of real estate development, rather than non-desired types, is simply a far more sensible way to effectuate a judicial fair share remedy from a strategic viewpoint.

A. Exclusion

Mallach emphasizes the increased importance of creative programs for inducing private sector participation in the low- and moderate-income market, given significant cutbacks in federal housing subsidy programs. He also questions (at 65) some of Ellickson's suppositions concerning increased costs attributed to incentive programs:

> To determine, however, who bears those costs is a complex and highly variable matter. To assert that the developer must therefore reduce his profit or, in the alternative, pass the cost on to the buyers of market units is simplistic. Indeed, Ellickson argues that in many cases, the landowner will end up bearing much of the cost in the form of a reduction in land value on his property. Where Ellickson errs, however, is in suggesting that such an outcome is necessarily unfair or unreasonable. Indeed, it generally is recognized that government can and does affect land values in the interest of public policy. The broad discretion permitted in this area, short of a taking, has been affirmed by a long line of cases throughout the modern history of land use law.
>
> Beyond that, there is the underlying issue that value both is created and removed by public action and rarely by the landowner. The degree to which many commentators are upset by the unfairness of the distribution of the costs of inclusionary housing programs appears to be vastly out of proportion to the dimensions of the issue. Indeed, from an economic standpoint, the imposition of an inclusionary requirement readily can be compared either to the downzoning of land, . . . or to the imposition of an exaction.

As a legislator how would you balance the equities of an inclusionary zoning proposal? Would your answer depend on whether you represented an urban, suburban, or rural constituency? Might there be a disincentive for the inner-city lawmaker to support such efforts to relocate the voters responsible for his or her (re-)election? Or do notions of "fair share" supersede legislative district and political party lines? Upon which principle should the conservative lawmaker from the white-collar suburb act: the protection of the landowner/developer's private property rights or the opposition to regulating even further the real estate market? What about his or her liberal counterpart, forced to choose between the desire to aid members of minority groups excluded by zoning and planning barriers, and the instinct to resist large-scale development in environmentally sensitive regions? As a judge, how would your responses differ?

Notes

1. One of the more challenging legacies of *Mount Laurel II* was the proliferation of complicated quantitative studies and complex formulas

that were devised, criticized and reformulated to respond to the court's demands. For example, the tables entitled *Mount Laurel* Cost for Moderate Income Housing and *Mount Laurel* Cost for Low Income Housing were prepared by one group of planning and development consultants (Abeles Schwartz Associates) to counter the data used by a developer as the basis for a decision not to complete its acquisition of property in Princeton, New Jersey, for a large-scale project. According to Abeles, the developer had overestimated the total subsidy required for a projected 2000 units by $1.7 million dollars.

The private sector did not have a monopoly on statistical analysis by any means, however. For example, here are Judge Serpentelli's calculations for one township's fair share of the present and prospective regional need:

a. Present Need

Using the 11-county present need region, Warren's fair share of the reallocation pool of 35,014 is 162 for the decade of 1980-1990 based on the following calculation.

Warren's present need percentage of the present regional need is 1.126%. That figure is arrived at as follows:

Growth Area = 1.780%
Present Employment = .179%
Median Income Ratio = 1.45

$$\frac{1.780 + .179}{2} = .9795\% \times 1.45 = 1.420\%$$ (represents the percentage modified by the ratio)

$$\frac{1.780 + .179 + 1.420}{3} = 1.126\%$$

Reallocation Excess Pool = 35,014
× 1.126 (Fair Share %)
Municipal Share = 394
Phased in by one third (394/3) = 131
Additional 20% reallocation (131 × 1.2) = 157
Vacancy allowance (157 × 1.03) = 162
Total Present Need is:
Indigenous 52
Reallocated Present 162
214

b. Prospective Need

Warren's fair share of the prospective regional need of 49,004 is 732 units for the decade of 1980-1990.

Mount Laurel Cost for Moderate Income Housing

Persons in family per unit size	Annual income at 90%	28% for housing	Monthly housing allocation	Operating cost excluding utilities	Balance for housing	30 Year mortgage @ 30%	Sales price of house	Cost of average unit including cost of land	(Loss) or profit
One Bedroom, 1-2 Persons	$17,955	$5,027	$418	($120)	$298	$27,029	$30,000	$47,000	($17,000)
Two Bedroom, 2-4 Persons	22,450	6,286	523	(120)	403	36,513	40,600	47,000	(6,400)
Three Bedroom, 5-6 Persons	25,245	7,068	589	(120)	469	42,409	47,100	47,000	100
								Average Loss	$7,767

Mount Laurel Cost for Low Income Housing

Persons in family per unit size	Annual income at 90%	28% for housing	Monthly housing allocation	Operating cost excluding utilities	Balance for housing	30 Year mortgage @ 30%	Sales price of house	Cost of average unit including cost of land	(Loss) or profit
One Bedroom, 1-2 Persons	$11,200	$3,136	$261	($100)	$161	$14,550	$16,170	$47,000	($30,830)
Two Bedroom, 2-4 Persons	14,000	3,920	326	(100)	226	20,490	22,760	47,000	(24,230)
Three Bedroom, 5-6 Persons	16,200	4,536	376	(100)	276	25,131	27,920	47,000	(19,000)
								Average Loss	$24,720

Source: Abeles Schwartz Associates, Inc. (April 4, 1985).

Warren's prospective need percentage of the prospective regional need is 1.208%. That figure is arrived at as follows:

Growth Area	= 2.556%
Present Employment	= .304%
Employment Growth	= .428%
Median Income Ratio	= 1.41
$\dfrac{2.556 + .304 + .428}{3} = 1.096\% \times 1.41$	= 1.545% (represents the percentage modified by the ratio)
$\dfrac{2.556 + .304 + .428 + 1.545}{4}$	= 1.208%
Prospective Regional Need	= 49,004
	× 1.208 (Fair Share %)
Municipal Share	= 592
Additional 20% reallocation (592 × 1.2)	= 710
Vacancy Allowance (710 × 1.03)	= 732
Summary	
Total Present Need	= 214
Total Prospective Need	= 732
Total Fair Share	= 946

AMG Realty Co. v. Warren Township, 207 N.J. Super. 388, 504 A.2d 692, 703-704 (N.J. Super. L. 1984). For an insider's view of the development, intricacies, and drawbacks of the "*Urban League* formula" used by the special *Mount Laurel II* courts, see Payne, Rethinking Fair Share: The Judicial Enforcement of Affordable Housing Policies, 16 Real Est. L.J. 20, 22-29 (1987).

2. Like its precursor, *Mount Laurel II* has inspired judicial responses in other jurisdictions. In Asian Americans for Equality v. Koch, 129 Misc. 2d 67, 492 N.Y.S.2d 837 (Sup. Ct. 1985), plaintiffs were challenging a 1981 New York City zoning amendment, creating the Special Manhattan Bridge District,

> as part of a plan of gentrification to specifically exclude minority and low-income people from New York City, and Chinatown in particular. . . . Here, the plaintiffs do not wish to relocate to the suburbs (the normal situation in exclusionary zoning cases) but rather state that they are compelled by their jobs, cultures and family ties to remain in the inner city region of Chinatown. While the zoning amendment here is not exclusionary as classically defined, if as alleged, it will result in displacement of Chinatown's low-income residents, then, its effect is the same. Accordingly, the proper scope of inquiry for analysis is that line of cases involving exclusionary zoning. . . .
> While New York courts have previously been hesitant to adopt the *Mount Laurel Doctrine* because it places a heavier burden on municipalities, upon consideration of the important constitutional considerations at stake, it is my opinion that it is now appropriate to adopt the *Mount Laurel*

A. Exclusion

Doctrine as the law of New York. Moreover, at the time *Berenson* was decided by the Court of Appeals, *Mount Laurel II* had not yet been decided. The *Mount Laurel II* decision not only expands upon the reasoning initially set forth in *Mount Laurel I*, but also discusses its application within the urban setting.

492 N.Y.S.2d at 846, 848. Because the plaintiffs contended that the city failed "to affirmatively provide a reasonable opportunity for the construction of low-income housing," despite the availability of density bonuses to developers who include lower-income units, the court found that a *"Mount Laurel Doctrine"* cause of action had been stated. Id. at 849. See also Dobkin, Smith, & Tockman, Zoning for the General Welfare: A Constitutional Weapon for Lower-Income Tenants, 13 N.Y.U. Rev. L. & Soc. Change 911 (1984-1985).

On appeal, a divided court emphatically rejected the lower court's reliance on New Jersey law: "Not by the widest stretch of the imagination could the fact pattern in *Mount Laurel* be applicable to New York City's record for providing low and moderate income housing." 514 N.Y.S.2d 939, 950 (App. Div. 1987). See also Suffolk Housing Services v. Town of Brookhaven, 109 A.2d 323, 491 N.Y.S.2d 396, 402 (App. Div. 1985), aff'd, 70 N.Y.2d 122, 517 N.Y.S.2d 924 (1987) ("present acceptance of the legal theories advanced by the plaintiffs [adopting New Jersey law] would require us to work a change of historic proportions in the development of New York zoning law, a step we respectfully decline to take").

3. Following the line of predecessors occupying his position, New Jersey Governor Thomas H. Kean was less than pleased with what he perceived as intrusions by a co-equal branch:

> Kean, in his Annual Message to the New Jersey State Legislature, delivered on January 10, 1984, acknowledged the tremendous impact this decision has had on housing development in the state and invited the legislature to come up with a more efficient and less disruptive way of satisfying the constitutional mandate. Among other things, the governor said the following about that decision:
>
>> The decision by our State Supreme Court in the case known as *Mount Laurel II* has caused a significant change in the law with respect to the obligation of various municipalities to provide a "fair share" of low and moderate income housing. Because of the novel and far-reaching implications of the Supreme Court's decision in this case, my Administration has been carefully monitoring efforts of municipalities, builders, land use planners and other groups and individuals affected by the decision. . . .
>>   I will be glad to cooperate with you in the design of legislation that would encourage municipalities to assume this responsibility voluntarily rather than leave to the judiciary the task of redesigning zoning ordinances throughout the State of New Jersey.

Hill, Proposed Legislation in Response to *Mount Laurel II*, 13 Real Est. L.J. 170, 170-171 (1984).

On March 7, 1985, the state legislature passed the Fair Housing Act (S. 2046, S. 2334); the governor, displeased with some components of the legislation, exercised a conditional veto. The lawmakers then responded with an amended proposal and the bill was signed into law on July 3, 1985. The Act, codified at N.J. Stat. Ann. §§52:27D-301 to -329 (West 1986), includes these legislative findings:

§52:27D-302. The Legislature finds that:

a. The New Jersey Supreme Court, through its rulings in South Burlington County NAACP v. Mount Laurel, 67 N.J. 151 (1975) and South Burlington County NAACP v. Mount Laurel, 92 N.J. 158 (1983), has determined that every municipality in a growth area has a constitutional obligation to provide through its land use regulations a realistic opportunity for a fair share of its region's present and prospective needs for housing for low and moderate income families.

b. In the second *Mount Laurel* ruling, the Supreme Court stated that the determination of the methods for satisfying this constitutional obligation "is better left to the Legislature," that the court has "always preferred legislative to judicial action in their field," and that the judicial role in upholding the *Mount Laurel* doctrine "could decrease as a result of legislative and executive action."

c. The interest of all citizens, including low and moderate income families in need of affordable housing, would be best served by a comprehensive planning and implementation response to this constitutional obligation.

d. There are a number of essential ingredients to a comprehensive planning and implementation response, including the establishment of reasonable fair share housing guidelines and standards, the initial determination of fair share by officials at the municipal level and the preparation of a municipal housing element, State review of the local fair share study and housing element, and continuous State funding for low and moderate income housing to replace the federal housing subsidy programs which have been almost completely eliminated.

e. The State can maximize the number of low and moderate income units provided in New Jersey by allowing its municipalities to adopt appropriate phasing schedules for meeting their fair share, so long as the municipalities permit a timely achievement of an appropriate fair share of the regional need for low and moderate income housing as required by the *Mt. Laurel I* and *II* opinions.

f. The State can also maximize the number of low and moderate income units by rehabilitating existing, but substandard, housing in the State, and, in order to achieve this end, it is appropriate to permit the transfer of a limited portion of the fair share obligations among municipalities in a housing region, so long as the transfer occurs on the basis of sound, comprehensive planning, with regard to an adequate housing financing plan, and in relation to the access of low and moderate income households to employment opportunities.

g. Since the urban areas are vitally important to the State, construction,

A. Exclusion

conversion and rehabilitation of housing in our urban centers should be encouraged. However, the provision of housing in urban areas must be balanced with the need to provide housing throughout the State for the free mobility of citizens.

h. The Supreme Court of New Jersey in its *Mount Laurel* decisions demands that municipal land use regulations affirmatively afford a reasonable opportunity for a variety and choice of housing including low and moderate cost housing, to meet the needs of people desiring to live there. While provision for the actual construction of that housing by municipalities is not required, they are encouraged but not mandated to expend their own resources to help provide low and moderate income housing.

See also Rose, New Jersey Enacts a Fair Housing Law, 14 Real Est. L.J. 195 (1985).

On November 15, 1985, Stephen Townsend, Clerk of the Supreme Court of New Jersey, notified counsel in twelve pending cases that the court had granted leave to appeal, and included a one and a half page list of "Issues to Be Addressed," questions raised by the long-awaited legislative (and executive) contribution to the exclusionary zoning debate. Oral arguments followed on January 6 and 7 and the decision was announced February 20, 1986. As you read *Mount Laurel III*, not only the court's summary of the Fair Housing Act but also the justices' determination of the validity and efficacy of the new regime, consider whether the judiciary should feel vindicated or corrected. Is the survival of the fair share doctrine, given the legislature's modification of remedies and the authorization of contribution agreement transfers, victory enough? In repeatedly reminding its audience that the legislative branch had an important role to play, was the court protesting too much?

■ HILLS DEVELOPMENT CO. v. TOWNSHIP OF BARNARDS
103 N.J. 1, 510 A.2d 621 (1986)

[MOUNT LAUREL III]

The opinion of the Court was delivered by WILENTZ, C.J.

In this appeal we are called upon to determine the constitutionality and effect of the "Fair Housing Act" (L. 1985, c. 222), the Legislature's response to the *Mount Laurel* cases. The Act creates an administrative agency (the Council on Affordable Housing) with power to define housing regions within the state and the regional need for low and moderate income housing, along with the power to promulgate criteria and guidelines to enable municipalities within each region to determine their fair share of that regional need. The Council is further empowered, on application, to decide whether proposed ordinances and related measures of a particular municipality will, if enacted, satisfy its *Mount Laurel* obligation, i.e., will they create a realistic opportunity for the construction of that municipality's fair share of the regional need for low and moderate income housing. Southern Burlington County N.A.A.C.P. v. Mount Laurel, 92 N.J. 158, 208-09, 456 A.2d 390 (1983). The agency's determination that the municipality's *Mount Laurel* obligation has been satisfied will ordinarily amount to a final resolution of that issue; it can be set aside in court only by "clear and convincing evidence" to the contrary. §17a. The Act includes appropriations and other financial means designed to help achieve the construction of low and moderate income housing.

In order to assure that the extent and satisfaction of a municipality's *Mount Laurel* obligation are decided and managed by the Council through this administrative procedure, rather than by the courts, the Act provides for the transfer of pending and future *Mount Laurel* litigation to the agency. Transfer is required in all cases except, as to cases commenced more than 60 days before the effective date of the Act (July 2, 1985), when it would result in "manifest injustice to any party to the litigation." §16.

The statutory scheme set forth in the Act is intended to satisfy the constitutional obligation enunciated by this Court in the *Mount Laurel* cases. . . .

The Council will determine the total need for lower income housing, the regional portion of that need, and the standards for allocating to each municipality its fair share. The Council is charged by law with that responsibility, imparting to it the legitimacy and presumed expertise that derives from selection by the Governor and confirmation by the Senate, in accordance with the will of the Legislature. Instead of varying and potentially inconsistent definitions of total need, regions, regional need, and fair share that can result from the case-by-case determinations of courts involved in isolated litigation, an overall plan for the entire state is envisioned, with definitions and standards that will have the kind of consistency that can result only when full responsibility and power are given to a single entity. . . .

There are other significant provisions of the Act. One allows municipalities to share *Mount Laurel* obligations by entering into regional contribution agreements. §12. This device requires either Council or court approval to be effective. Under this provision, one municipality can transfer to another, if that other agrees, a portion, under 50%, of its fair share obligation, the receiving municipality adding that to its

A. Exclusion 443

own. The Act contemplates that the first municipality will contribute funds to the other, §12d, presumably to make the housing construction possible and to eliminate any financial burden resulting from the added fair share. The provisions seem intended to allow suburban municipalities to transfer a portion of their obligation to urban areas (see §2g, evincing a legislative intent to encourage construction, conversion, or rehabilitation of housing in urban areas), thereby aiding in the construction of decent lower income housing in the area where most lower income households are found, provided, however, that such areas are "within convenient access to employment opportunities," and conform to "sound comprehensive regional planning." §12c. . . .

The main challenges to the Act's constitutionality are based on a measurement of the Act against the *Mount Laurel* constitutional obligation. It is also asserted that this legislation impermissibly interferes with the Court's exclusive power over prerogative writ actions. We hold that the Act, as interpreted herein, is constitutional.

A major claim is that the Act is unconstitutional because it will result in delay in the satisfaction of the *Mount Laurel* obligation. That claim is based on a totally false premise, namely, that there is some constitutional timetable implicit in that obligation. . . .

The next claim is that the builder's remedy moratorium is unconstitutional since that remedy is part of the constitutional obligation. This claim suffers from two deficiencies. First, the moratorium on builder's remedies imposed by section 28 is extremely limited; our courts have, in analogous contexts, upheld the power to enact a reasonable moratorium. Second, and more significant, the builder's remedy itself has never been made part of the constitutional obligation. In *Mount Laurel II* we noted that the concept of a "developing municipality," whereby only municipalities so characterized had a *Mount Laurel* obligation, was not of constitutional dimension. It was simply a method for achieving the "constitutionally mandated goal" of providing a realistic opportunity for lower income housing needed by the citizens of this state. . . .

By virtue of the Act, the three branches of government in New Jersey are now committed to a common goal: the provision of a realistic opportunity for the construction of needed lower income housing. It is a most difficult goal to achieve. It is pursued within an even larger context, for the implications of the State Development and Redevelopment Plan legislation indicate significant movement by the State in the direction of regional planning. . . .

Mount Laurel II will result in a fair amount of low and moderate income housing. When various settlements are implemented, the effectiveness of the decision will become more apparent. As of the time we entertained oral argument on the cases before us (January 6 and 7, 1986), some twenty-two *Mount Laurel* cases had reached virtually final settlement. The total fair share under those settlements was in excess of 14,000 units: given the terms of these settlements, it is highly probable that a substantial portion will be built. . . .

No one should assume that our exercise of comity today signals a weakening of our resolve to enforce the constitutional rights of New Jersey's lower income citizens. The constitutional obligation has not changed; the judiciary's ultimate duty to enforce it has not changed; our determination to perform that duty has not changed. What *has* changed is that we are no longer alone in this field. The other branches of government have fashioned a comprehensive statewide response to the *Mount Laurel* obligation. This kind of response, one that would permit us to withdraw from this field, is what this Court has always wanted and sought. It is potentially far better for the State and for its lower income citizens.[32]

---

32. Consider the following:

> Ten municipalities proposing to build 932 housing units for lower-income families yesterday became the first in the state to have their *Mt. Laurel* plans approved by the Council on Affordable Housing (COAH).
>
> "The process is working," said COAH Chairman Arthur Kondrup, defending the affordable housing program created two years ago by the Legislature in response to the state Supreme Court's *Mt. Laurel* rulings. . . .
>
> COAH last year calculated how many affordable housing units would be needed in each municipality by 1993 and gave the municipalities until January to submit plans detailing how they intended to provide the housing. The 123 municipalities that responded have been shielded from further *Mt. Laurel* litigation.
>
> Of the 10 municipalities whose plans were approved yesterday, four had their quotas cut to zero by persuading COAH they had provided sufficient affordable housing since 1980. South Brunswick, meanwhile, agreed to plan for 590 affordable housing units, 15 more than called for by COAH. . . .
>
> Nearly all the municipalities will apply for state and federal assistance to help subsidize the cost of the new housing. . . .
>
> The Public Advocate's Office, which was active in prior *Mt. Laurel* litigation, had objected to several of the plans approved yesterday and will continue to file formal objections, according to Steve Eisdorfer, an assistant deputy public advocate. Eisdorfer declined comment on the COAH process.

Newark Star Ledger, May 21, 1987.

> Warren's housing obligation . . . has been more than halved, to 367 homes, by the state's Council on Affordable Housing. In addition, the township is negotiating to pay the city of New Brunswick to assume the obligation for construction of 166 of those homes.
>
> Warren is attempting to comply with the *Mount Laurel* doctrine. But nearly 80 percent of the state's municipalities have ignored the housing council, which the Kean administration and the Legislature created in 1985 to enforce the law.
>
> By law, the nine-member council has virtually no enforcement powers. Its emphasis is on using the *Mount Laurel* doctrine to rebuild inner-city housing, a Kean administration tactic that some suggest is overly ambitious, underfinanced and a reversal of Mount Laurel's spirit.

N.Y. Times, June 1, 1987 (Metro News section).

Reports of dissatisfaction with the legislative solution — from opponents and defenders of the Mount Laurel doctrines — suggest that Professor Rose was something

Notes

1. Is the transfer of fair-share obligations allowed by the New Jersey Fair Housing Act a good-faith effort to rebuild decayed urban neighborhoods or the legislative embodiment of the NIMBY (not in my backyard) syndrome?

2. N.Y. Times, June 18, 1987:

> Calling it "an extremely difficult decision," a key lawmaker agreed today not to block Governor Kean's renomination of Justice Stewart G. Pollock of the New Jersey Supreme Court.
>
> The lawmaker, State Senator John H. Dorsey of Mountain Lakes in Morris County, approved the nomination, which a home county senator must do before the State Judiciary Committee will consider it. But he said he would publicly oppose Judge Pollock's confirmation because of the judge's concurrence in the landmark *Mount Laurel* decisions attacking exclusionary zoning.

b. Running the Federal Gauntlet

Although the United States Supreme Court declined to hear a number of state exclusionary zoning cases — including *Mount Laurel I* — it seemed but a matter of time before the Justices would hold forth on whether the Constitution's equal protection and due process protections, so greatly expanded in the area of personal liberties during the years of the Warren Court, would extend to reach persons shut out from the modern American dream of suburban life. In two cases from the mid-1970s an answer did come from the Court; but for observers anxious for replication of the New Jersey and Pennsylvania experiences on the federal level, the answer was disappointing. Two formidable barriers — a restrictive formulation of standing and the need to demonstrate discriminatory intent — were placed before many potential

---

of a seer when he wrote in 1983:

> What is a municipality to do
> To comply with *Mount Laurel Two*?
>
> What are the issues to be
> In the *Case of Mount Laurel Three*?
>
> What new pronouncements of law
> Will be left for *Mount Laurel Four*?
>
> What questions will our children contrive
> To be solved in *Mount Laurel Five*?

Rose, How Will New Jersey Municipalities Comply?, Land Use L. & Zoning Dig., March 1983, at 12. — Eds.

litigants eager to air Constitution-grounded complaints in federal court. Yet there remained some hope for injunctive, even monetary relief, at least according to some lower federal judges who turned to two federal statutes — one enacted following the Civil War, the other a product of the civil rights struggles nearly one hundred years later.

■ WARTH v. SELDIN
422 U.S. 490 (1975)

Mr. Justice POWELL delivered the opinion of the Court.

Petitioners, various organizations and individuals resident in the Rochester, N. Y., metropolitan area, brought this action in the District Court for the Western District of New York against the town of Penfield, an incorporated municipality adjacent to Rochester, and against members of Penfield's Zoning, Planning, and Town Boards. Petitioners claimed that the town's zoning ordinance, by its terms and as enforced by the defendant board members, respondents here, effectively excluded persons of low and moderate income from living in the town, in contravention of petitioners' First, Ninth, and Fourteenth Amendment rights and in violation of 42 U. S. C. §§1981, 1982, 1983. The District Court dismissed the complaint and denied a motion to add petitioner Housing Council in the Monroe County Area, Inc., as party-plaintiff and also a motion by petitioner Rochester Home Builders Association, Inc., for leave to intervene as party-plaintiff. The Court of Appeals for the Second Circuit affirmed, holding that none of the plaintiffs, and neither Housing Council nor Home Builders Association, had standing to prosecute the action....

Petitioners further alleged certain harm to themselves. The Rochester property owners and taxpayers — Vinkey, Reichert, Warth, Harris, and Ortiz — claimed that because of Penfield's exclusionary practices, the city of Rochester had been forced to impose higher tax rates on them and others similarly situated than would otherwise have been necessary. The low- and moderate-income, minority plaintiffs — Ortiz, Broadnax, Reyes, and Sinkler — claimed that Penfield's zoning practices had prevented them from acquiring, by lease or purchase, residential property in the town, and thus had forced them and their families to reside in less attractive environments. To relieve these various harms, petitioners asked the District Court to declare the Penfield ordinance unconstitutional, to enjoin the defendants from enforcing the ordinance, to order the defendants to enact and administer a new ordinance designed to alleviate the effects of their past actions, and to award $750,000 in actual and exemplary damages....

In its constitutional dimension, standing imports justiciability: whether the plaintiff has made out a "case or controversy" between

A. Exclusion

of occupancy because of its plan to exhibit adult films. Both theaters were located within 1,000 feet of two other regulated uses and the Pussy Cat was less than 500 feet from a residential area. The respondents brought two separate actions against appropriate city officials, seeking a declaratory judgment that the ordinances were unconstitutional and an injunction against their enforcement. Federal jurisdiction was properly invoked and the two cases were consolidated for decision. . . .

II

Petitioners acknowledge that the ordinances prohibit theaters which are not licensed as "adult motion picture theaters" from exhibiting films which are protected by the First Amendment. Respondents argue that the ordinances are therefore invalid as prior restraints on free speech. . . .

. . . The city's interest in planning and regulating the use of property for commercial purposes . . . is clearly adequate to support that kind of restriction applicable to all theaters within the city limits.

III . . .

. . . Whether political oratory or philosophical discussion moves us to applaud or to despise what is said, every schoolchild can understand why our duty to defend the right to speak remains the same. But few of us would march our sons and daughters off to war to preserve the citizen's right to see "Specified Sexual Activities" exhibited in the theaters of our choice. Even though the First Amendment protects communication in this area from total suppression, we hold that the State may legitimately use the content of these materials as the basis for placing them in a different classification from other motion pictures.

The remaining question is whether the line drawn by these ordinances is justified by the city's interest in preserving the character of its neighborhoods. On this question we agree with the views expressed by District Judges Kennedy and Gubow. The record discloses a factual basis for the Common Council's conclusion that this kind of restriction will have the desired effect. It is not our function to appraise the wisdom of its decision to require adult theaters to be separated rather than concentrated in the same areas. In either event, the city's interest in attempting to preserve the quality of urban life is one that must be accorded high respect. Moreover, the city must be allowed a reasonable opportunity to experiment with solutions to admittedly serious problems.

Since what is ultimately at stake is nothing more than a limitation on the place where adult films may be exhibited, even though the determination of whether a particular film fits that characterization turns on the nature of its content, we conclude that the city's interest in the present and future character of its neighborhoods adequately supports its classification of motion pictures. We hold that the zoning ordinances requiring that adult motion picture theaters not be located within 1,000 feet of two other regulated uses does not violate the Equal Protection Clause of the Fourteenth Amendment.

The judgment of the Court of Appeals is

Reversed....

Mr. Justice STEWART, with whom Mr. Justice BRENNAN, Mr. Justice MARSHALL, and Mr. Justice BLACKMUN join, dissenting....

This case does not involve a simple zoning ordinance, or a content-neutral time, place, and manner restriction, or a regulation of obscene expression or other speech that is entitled to less than the full protection of the First Amendment. The kind of expression at issue here is no doubt objectionable to some, but that fact does not diminish its protected status any more than did the particular content of the "offensive" expression in Erznoznik v. City of Jacksonville, 422 U. S. 205....

What this case does involve is the constitutional permissibility of selective interference with protected speech whose content is thought to produce distasteful effects. It is elementary that a prime function of the First Amendment is to guard against just such interference. By refusing to invalidate Detroit's ordinance the Court rides roughshod over cardinal principles of First Amendment law, which require that time, place, and manner regulations that affect protected expression be content neutral except in the limited context of a captive or juvenile audience. In place of these principles the Court invokes a concept wholly alien to the First Amendment. Since "few of us would march our sons and daughters off to war to preserve the citizen's right to see 'Specified Sexual Activities' exhibited in the theaters of our choice," the Court implies that these films are not entitled to the full protection of the Constitution.... For if the guarantees of the First Amendment were reserved for expression that more than a "few of us" would take up arms to defend, then the right of free expression would be defined and circumscribed by current popular opinion. The guarantees of the Bill of Rights were designed to protect against precisely such majoritarian limitations on individual liberty....

Notes

1. During oral argument, the Court was interested in the reasons Detroit chose to scatter adult uses throughout the city, abandoning the cluster approach used in Baltimore's Block and Boston's Combat Zone:

Question: The category of regulated uses had been one that was part of

A. Exclusion

> the Detroit zoning pattern for many years, hadn't it been there for some time?
>
> *Mrs. Reilly* [counsel for Young]: Yes, your Honor. The idea, the concept of regulated uses so far as I know was a new concept of inverse zoning adopted by the city in 1962. The city found out that certain uses when clustered together caused a downgrading of a neighborhood.
>
> *Question:* Pool halls and shoeshine parlors and —
>
> *Mrs. Reilly:* Motels, bars, those businesses which catered to transient type patrons.
>
> *Question:* As contrasted with a neighborhood patronage.
>
> *Mrs. Reilly:* That's right, your Honor.
>
> It seemed only proper that the adult businesses be included in the regulated use category because they follow the same pattern. They cluster together, they drew patrons who were not members of the immediate neighborhood but from the surrounding community, and had operational characteristics which set them apart from other types of theaters and bookstores.
>
> Those theaters and bookstores which offered — a substantial portion of their stock in trade or their films were sexually stimulating on the spot. It was not like a drugstore which would offer a pill and you go home and five hours later you feel sexually stimulated. Whether you walk into the theater and watch the film on the screen or you walk into the bookstore and review the material there, the immediate reaction was sexual stimulation. I think this Court can almost take judicial notice of that. . . .
>
> *Question:* I take it, or have you suggested, that one of the purposes of these restrictions is to maintain property values, like zoning sometimes is aimed at that.
>
> *Mrs. Reilly:* It is very definitely directed to preserve property values, yes, your Honor. . . .
>
> *Question:* It's an environmental problem which has an incidental impact on property values, is that not a fair way to say it?
>
> *Mrs. Reilly:* Yes, your Honor.
>
> *Question:* They didn't set out in the first place to try to hold up property values; they set out to try to, as you describe it in your briefs, they set out to try to preserve a decent environment in the city and one of the consequences of that is it will also help the property values.

Based on this and other information, the plurality was convinced that, despite the dissent's concerns about interference with protected speech, there was a "factual basis" for the city's regulation.

2. How far can a city take this scattering approach before the court will step in? Although many such ordinances, inspired by Detroit's victory in *Young*, have been approved, there is a limit to the exclusionary effect they may produce. See, for example, Alexander v. City of Minneapolis, 698 F.2d 936 (8th Cir. 1983), in which the city's Zoning Supervisor testified that five of thirty existing adult uses would be

allowed to remain under Minneapolis's 500-foot radius ordinance. The appellate court, citing an exception in *Young* for regulations "greatly restricting access," affirmed the district court's holding that the ordinance violated the first and fourteenth amendments. See also Christy v. The City of Ann Arbor, 824 F.2d 489 (6th Cir. 1987) (plaintiff asserted that under challenged ordinance only .23 of 1 percent of city was available for location of adult bookstore).

3. How thoroughly must local officials investigate the need for, and ramifications of, what has been called "erogenous zoning"? In City of Renton v. Playtime Theatres, 475 U.S. 41 (1986), the majority approved the Seattle suburb's (population 32,000) plan "that prohibits adult motion picture theaters from locating within 1,000 feet of any residential zone, single- or multiple-family dwelling, church, park, or school." The effect of the ordinance was to leave 520 acres available for such restricted uses. According to the majority, "The appropriate inquiry in this case, then, is whether the Renton ordinance is designed to serve a substantial governmental interest and allows for reasonable alternative avenues of communication."

The Court relied primarily on *Young* in upholding the ordinance, despite the fact that Renton did not engage in its own study before settling on the plan, instead utilizing studies prepared by the city of Seattle. (The Supreme Court of Washington had approved that city's Combat Zone approach in Northend Cinema v. City of Seattle, 90 Wash. 2d 709, 585 P.2d 1153 (1978)):

> The First Amendment does not require a city, before enacting such an ordinance, to conduct new studies or produce evidence independent of that already generated by other cities, so long as whatever evidence the city relies upon is reasonably believed to be relevant to the problem the city addresses. That was the case here. Nor is our holding affected by the fact that Seattle ultimately chose a different method . . . than that chosen by Renton, since Seattle's choice of a different remedy to combat the secondary effects of adult theaters does not call into question either Seattle's identification of those secondary effects or the relevance of Seattle's experience to Renton.

City of Renton, 475 U.S. at 51-52. Has the Court now invited any municipality (regardless of size or location) merely to review studies prepared by Detroit or Seattle (or the summaries provided by the Supreme Court) before embarking on its own plan for restricting less desirable uses?

4. The Justices questioned counsel in the *City of Renton* case concerning the suitability of the acreage left available to Playtime and other theater owners:

> *Mr. Prettyman* [counsel for Renton]: These adult theaters are prolifer-

A. Exclusion 483

ating. They are moving into areas unlike what they used to, sort of out on the edges or perhaps right in the middle of downtown. They're going all over now.

And we have made a good faith attempt that was not directed toward a single theater, which sometimes is the case. A theater moves in and we say, we're going to get that theater. We didn't do that.

We, we, we wanted to deal with the problem in advance, and we submit to you it was a good faith attempt, and we have left plenty room, room that's more than commodious enough for these theaters to come into. It's easily accessible.

And I submit to you that if this effort fails, that it will really prevent small cities and towns across the country from dealing in an intelligent fashion ahead of time with this very serious problem. . . .

Mr. Burns [counsel for Playtime]: In *Young*, the Court made its decision based upon the fact that there were a myriad of locations available, that there were locations available in all kinds of zones, all commercial zones.

The Renton ordinance specifically removes adult theaters from all commercial zones of the City of Renton. They simply are not allowed in the commercial zones.

I think in that respect a look at the map is useful. If you would look at the last page of the jurisdictional statement, which is page 142a, Appendix V, you can see where these theaters have been relegated to. It's essentially an industrial wasteland. . . .

The essential difference between this case and *Young* is that there is an intolerable burden on speech that exists as a result of this ordinance, and that's problem of access.

If government makes no rule about access and does not limit access to speech, then there's no intrusion that can be blamed on the government and no violation of the First Amendment.

On the other hand, if government does make the rule and government does limit access, then I think government has the duty to establish that not only are there permissible locations, but that somebody can actually go there, because otherwise they've precluded them through a de facto zoning scheme from going anywhere, and they've created what they've perhaps set out to do, was censor the material and remove it entirely from the City.

In this respect, I believe that the zone that I described and as depicted on that map is a substantial burden on speech. The alternative locations are unsatisfactory. As this Court has said before, an individual is not to have his right of free speech circumscribed on the argument that he can exercise it somewhere else.

The court of appeals, and dissenting Justices Brennan and Marshall, were skeptical concerning the availability and suitability of the unrestricted sites.

5. As for the Boston neighborhood identified with the cluster approach, see the Associated Press wire story that appeared in June 1984:

Ten years after city planners created the "Combat Zone" — Boston's officially designated sanctum of sleaze — the garish array of peep shows, erotic book stores and strip joints lining lower Washington Street still draws thrill-seekers and derelicts.

But behind its brazen front, the Combat Zone is dying of respectability.

At lunch hour, city workers in three-piece suits clog sidewalks once lined with prostitutes. On a side street, stores and movie houses that used to traffic in sex are boarded up....

The spread of respectable uses into the Combat Zone has been nurtured by Boston officialdom.

Tax breaks and other incentives have been extended to businesses that locate near the zone.

6. For a case testing the limits of good taste, see Pensack v. City and County of Denver, 630 F. Supp. 177, 177-178 (D. Colo. 1986):

> The plaintiff, Laurie Pensack, is the sole proprietor of a bakery business which she operates under the name Le Bakery Sensual ... in Aurora, Colorado. Le Bakery is different from other bakeries in that it specializes in "theme" cakes made to meet customers' requests.... Le Bakery's advertising emphasizes that it is an "outlet for erotic edible and custom baked goods beyond your wildest dreams!"...
>
> ...On March 12, 1984, the Zoning Administrator of the City and County of Denver issued a cease and desist order to Le Bakery, contending that the retail bakery use which had been approved had been converted "into an adult bookstore and a sexually-oriented commercial enterprise" in violation of that provision of the Denver Zoning Ordinance which requires that certain uses in a B-4 zone must be located more than 500 feet from any residential district, and that not more than two such uses may be located within 1,000 feet of each other. The uses subject to that separation requirement include adult amusement or entertainment centers, adult bookstores, sexually-oriented commercial enterprises, and adult theaters.

The trial court held that, despite defendants' *Young* argument, the ordinance as applied violated the baker's first amendment rights.

■ SCHAD v. BOROUGH OF MOUNT EPHRAIM
452 U.S. 61 (1981)

Justice WHITE delivered the opinion of the Court.

In 1973, appellants began operating an adult bookstore in the commercial zone in the Borough of Mount Ephraim in Camden County, N. J. The store sold adult books, magazines, and films. Amusement licenses shortly issued permitting the store to install coin-operated devices by virtue of which a customer could sit in a booth, insert a coin,

A. Exclusion

and watch an adult film. In 1976, the store introduced an additional coin-operated mechanism permitting the customer to watch a live dancer, usually nude, performing behind a glass panel. Complaints were soon filed against appellants charging that the bookstore's exhibition of live dancing violated §99-15B of Mount Ephraim's zoning ordinance, which described the permitted uses in a commercial zone, in which the store was located, as follows:

> B. Principal permitted uses on the land and in buildings.
> (1) Offices and banks; taverns; restaurants and luncheonettes for sit-down dinners only and with no drive-in facilities; automobile sales; retail stores, such as but not limited to food, wearing apparel, millinery, fabrics, hardware, lumber, jewelry, paint, wallpaper, appliances, flowers, gifts, books, stationery, pharmacy, liquors, cleaners, novelties, hobbies and toys; repair shops for shoes, jewels, clothes and appliances; barbershops and beauty salons; cleaners and laundries; pet stores; and nurseries. Offices may, in addition, be permitted to a group of four (4) stores or more without additional parking, provided the offices do not exceed the equivalent of twenty percent (20%) of the gross floor area of the stores.
> (2) Motels. Mount Ephraim Code §99-15B(1), (2) (1979).

Section 99-4 of the Borough's code provided that "[a]ll uses not expressly permitted in this chapter are prohibited."

Appellants were found guilty in the Municipal Court and fines were imposed. Appeal was taken to the Camden County Court, where a trial de novo was held on the record made in the Municipal Court and appellants were again found guilty. The County Court first rejected appellants' claim that the ordinance was being selectively and improperly enforced against them because other establishments offering live entertainment were permitted in the commercial zones.[3] Those establishments, the court held, were permitted, nonconforming uses that had existed prior to the passage of the ordinance. In response to appellants' defense based on the First and Fourteenth Amendments, the court recognized that "live nude dancing is protected by the First Amendment" but was of the view that "First Amendment guarantees are not involved" since the case "involves solely a zoning ordinance" under which "[l]ive entertainment is simply not a permitted use in any establishment" whether the entertainment is a nude dance or some other form of live presentation. . . . The Appellate Division of the Superior Court of New

---

3. The building inspector, who is responsible for enforcing the zoning ordinance, testified that three establishments located in commercial zones of the Borough offered live music. However, he stated that they were permitted to do so only because this use of the premises preceded the enactment of the zoning ordinance and thus qualified as a "nonconforming" use under the ordinance. Munic. Ct. Tr. 21-25, 35-36, 55-59.

The Police Chief also testified. He stated that he knew of no live entertainment in the commercial zones other than that offered by appellants and by the three establishments mentioned by the building inspector. Id., at 67.

Jersey affirmed appellants' convictions in a per curiam opinion "essentially for the reasons" given by the County Court. App. to Juris. Statement 14a. The Supreme Court of New Jersey denied further review. Id., at 17a, 18a.

Appellants appealed to this Court. Their principal claim is that the imposition of criminal penalties under an ordinance prohibiting all live entertainment, including nonobscene, nude dancing, violated their rights of free expression guaranteed by the First and Fourteenth Amendments of the United States Constitution. . . .

The power of local governments to zone and control land use is undoubtedly broad and its proper exercise is an essential aspect of achieving a satisfactory quality of life in both urban and rural communities. But the zoning power is not infinite and unchallengeable; it "must be exercised within constitutional limits." Moore v. East Cleveland, 431 U.S. 494, 514 (1977) (STEVENS, J., concurring in judgment). Accordingly, it is subject to judicial review; and as is most often the case, the standard of review is determined by the nature of the right assertedly threatened or violated rather than by the power being exercised or the specific limitation imposed.

Where property interests are adversely affected by zoning, the courts generally have emphasized the breadth of municipal power to control land use and have sustained the regulation if it is rationally related to legitimate state concerns and does not deprive the owner of economically viable use of his property. Agins v. City of Tiburon, 447 U.S. 255, 260 (1980); Village of Belle Terre v. Boraas, 416 U.S. 1 (1974); Euclid v. Ambler Realty Co., 272 U.S. 365, 395 (1926). But an ordinance may fail even under that limited standard of review. Moore v. East Cleveland, supra, at 520 (STEVENS, J., concurring in judgment); Nectow v. Cambridge, 277 U.S. 183 (1928).

Beyond that, as is true of other ordinances, when a zoning law infringes upon a protected liberty it must be narrowly drawn and must further a sufficiently substantial government interest. . . .

As an initial matter, this case is not controlled by Young v. American Mini Theatres, Inc., the decision relied upon by the Camden County Court. Although the Court there stated that a zoning ordinance is not invalid merely because it regulates activity protected under the First Amendment, it emphasized that the challenged restriction on the location of adult movie theaters imposed a minimal burden on protected speech. . . .

In this case, however, Mount Ephraim has not adequately justified its substantial restriction of protected activity. None of the justifications asserted in this Court was articulated by the state courts and none of them withstands scrutiny. First, the Borough contends that permitting live entertainment would conflict with its plan to create a commercial area that caters only to the "immediate needs" of its residents and that

A. Exclusion

would enable them to purchase at local stores the few items they occasionally forgot to buy outside the Borough. No evidence was introduced below to support this assertion, and it is difficult to reconcile this characterization of the Borough's commercial zones with the provisions of the ordinance. Section 99-15A expressly states that the purpose of creating commercial zones was to provide areas for "local and *regional* commercial operations." (Emphasis added.) The range of permitted uses goes far beyond providing for the "immediate needs" of the residents. Motels, hardware stores, lumber stores, banks, offices, and car showrooms are permitted in commercial zones. The list of permitted "retail stores" is nonexclusive, and it includes such services as beauty salons, barbershops, cleaners, and restaurants. Virtually the only item or service that may not be sold in a commercial zone is entertainment, or at least live entertainment. The Borough's first justification is patently insufficient.

Second, Mount Ephraim contends that it may selectively exclude commercial live entertainment from the broad range of commercial uses permitted in the Borough for reasons normally associated with zoning in commercial districts, that is, to avoid the problems that may be associated with live entertainment, such as parking, trash, police protection, and medical facilities. The Borough has presented no evidence, and it is not immediately apparent as a matter of experience, that live entertainment poses problems of this nature more significant than those associated with various permitted uses; nor does it appear that the Borough's zoning authority has arrived at a defensible conclusion that unusual problems are presented by live entertainment. . . .

. . . [N]o evidence has been presented to establish that live entertainment is incompatible with the uses presently permitted by the Borough. Mount Ephraim asserts that it could have chosen to eliminate all commercial uses within its boundaries. Yet we must assess the exclusion of live entertainment in light of the commercial uses Mount Ephraim allows, not in light of what the Borough might have done.[18]

To be reasonable, time, place, and manner restrictions not only must serve significant state interests but also must leave open adequate alternative channels of communication. . . .

The Borough nevertheless contends that live entertainment in general and nude dancing in particular are amply available in close-by areas outside the limits of the Borough. Its position suggests the argument that if there were countywide zoning, it would be quite legal to allow live entertainment in only selected areas of the county and to exclude it from primarily residential communities, such as the Borough

18. Thus, our decision today does not establish that every unit of local government entrusted with zoning responsibilities must provide a commercial zone in which live entertainment is permitted.

of Mount Ephraim. This may very well be true, but the Borough cannot avail itself of that argument in this case. There is no countywide zoning in Camden County, and Mount Ephraim is free under state law to impose its own zoning restrictions, within constitutional limits. Furthermore, there is no evidence in this record to support the proposition that the kind of entertainment appellants wish to provide is available in reasonably nearby areas. The courts below made no such findings; and at least in their absence, the ordinance excluding live entertainment from the commercial zone cannot constitutionally be applied to appellants so as to criminalize the activities for which they have been fined. "[O]ne is not to have the exercise of his liberty of expression in appropriate places abridged on the plea that it may be exercised in some other place." Schneider v. State, 308 U.S., at 163.

Accordingly, the convictions of these appellants are infirm, and the judgment of the Appellate Division of the Superior Court of New Jersey is reversed and the case is remanded for further proceedings not inconsistent with this opinion. . . .

Chief Justice BURGER, with whom Justice REHNQUIST joins, dissenting. . . .

The residents of this small enclave chose to maintain their town as a placid, "bedroom" community of a few thousand people. To that end, they passed an admittedly broad regulation prohibiting certain forms of entertainment. Because I believe that a community of people are — within limits — masters of their own environment, I would hold that, as applied, the ordinance is valid.

At issue here is the right of a small community to ban an activity incompatible with a quiet, residential atmosphere. The Borough of Mount Ephraim did nothing more than employ traditional police power to provide a setting of tranquility. This Court has often upheld the power of a community "to determine that the community should be beautiful as well as healthy, spacious as well as clean, well-balanced as well as carefully patrolled." Berman v. Parker, 348 U.S. 26, 33 (1954). Justice Douglas, speaking for the Court, sustained the power to zone as "ample to lay out zones where family values, youth values, and the blessings of quiet seclusion and clean air make the area a sanctuary for people." Village of Belle Terre v. Boraas, 416 U.S. 1, 9 (1979). Here we have nothing more than a variation on that theme.

Notes

1. The oral argument reveals that the Justices wanted to be certain that they were indeed reviewing a total ban of a form of protected speech:

A. Exclusion

Question: But, do you agree, or don't you, that the ordinance bans all live entertainment?

Mr. Fishman [counsel for Mount Ephraim]: I agree that the ordinance prohibits the utilization of land and structures in the commercial zone —

Question: For any live entertainment?

Mr. Fishman: — for any live entertainment, Shakespeare —

Question: And, of course, I take it that live entertainment is not permitted in any other zone — ?

Mr. Fishman: That's correct.

Question: So there is no live entertainment in the Borough?

Mr. Fishman: That's incorrect. If a person — a lot of examples have been raised as to whether or not you can have Christmas carols at the office Christmas party. The answer to that is yes.

Question: But there is no commercial live entertainment?

Mr. Fishman: That's correct.

Question: In the city?

Mr. Fishman: That's correct.

Question: And so it would ban a play, any kind of a play, for example?

Mr. Fishman: It would ban a theater. It would not necessarily ban a play.

Question: Well, it would ban a commercial theater.

Mr. Fishman: Correct.

Question: Or a circus.

Mr. Fishman: Correct.

Question: And it would ban any kind of commercial live entertainment, any kind of live entertainment for which a fee is charged for profit, profit-making — ?

Mr. Fishman: At the point that the structure or land ceases to be an office or a home and becomes either a theater or an opera house or a concert hall or a sports arena or whatever, at that point it offends the zoning ordinance because this ordinance is created as a retail sales zone to satisfy the immediate needs —

Question: Now, what's your justification for saying that the ordinance is valid even though it forbids any, although it forbids among other things a commercial theater with a live cast? . . .

Mr. Fishman: Well, I think there are several justifications. One is that zoning in and of itself is a compelling state interest. I think that the combining of compatible uses into zones and the blending of compatible zones into a comprehensive zoning ordinance is as has been held by this Court the most essential function performed by local government because it's in that way that the quality of life in these communities can be preserved.

Officially, the devotion of the limited amount of commercial space that a town like the Borough of Mount Ephraim has to the satisfaction of immediate needs of the residents of a borough is certainly a compelling state interest. The avoidance of those problems inherent in the omitted uses of live entertainment, like traffic, crowds, parking, trash, demands for medical and police facilities, the avoidance of these things for a Borough like Mount Ephraim is a compelling state interest. So at each of these levels I think a compelling state interest has been shown.

2. Sensing a weakness in the fortress protecting land-use decisions from judicial second-guessing, landowners and their often creative attorneys entered the breach. Sometimes the setting for the assertion of fundamental rights appeared silly, even when compared to the live nude dancing in Mount Ephraim. There are, for example, a number of reported opinions concerning the protections afforded owners and operators of video games.

In America's Best Family Showplace Corp. v. City of New York, 536 F. Supp. 171, 173-174 (E.D.N.Y. 1982), District Judge McLaughlin turned down a restaurateur who asserted that the city's limit of four game machines (installing the fifth machine would require an arcade license) presented a *Schad*-type unconstitutional restriction of protected speech:

> This Court . . . is not persuaded that plaintiff's video games, unlike the nude dancing in *Schad*, are a form of speech protected by the First Amendment. . . .
>
> In no sense can it be said that video games are meant to inform. Rather, a video game, like a pinball game, a game of chess, or a game of baseball, is pure entertainment with no informational element. That some games "talk" to the participant, play music, or have written instructions does not provide the missing element of "information." I find, therefore, that although video game programs may be copyrighted, they "contain so little in the way of particularized form of expression" that video games cannot be fairly characterized as a form of speech protected by the First Amendment. . . .
>
> Since video games do not implicate First Amendment problems, the validity of the City's regulatory scheme must be measured against the less rigorous standards of due process and equal protection under the Fourteenth Amendment.

See also Caswell v. Licensing Commission, 387 Mass. 864, 444 N.E.2d 922 (1983) (appellant "failed to demonstrate that video games import sufficient communicative, expressive, or informative elements to constitute expression protected under the First Amendment"); Marshfield Family Skateland v. Town of Marshfield, 389 Mass. 436, 450 N.E.2d 605 (1983) (total prohibition of commercial operation of coin-activated amusement devices not invalid). Can you think of any other constitutionally protected rights that might be at risk? Do law-abiding teenagers have the right to congregate in a game parlor? Can you distinguish the *America's Best* case if the machines in question are designed to test the participant's knowledge of trivia? See Ziegler, Trouble in Outer Galactica: The Police Power, Zoning, and Coin-Operated Video-Games, 34

A. Exclusion 491

Syracuse L. Rev. 453 (1983); Note, First Amendment Protection of Artistic Entertainment: Toward Reasonable Municipal Regulation of Video Games, 36 Vand. L. Rev. 1223 (1983).

3. If dancing, why not "swinging"? Defendants, who were charged with conducting a health club without a license, contended that the operation of their business was specially protected. The appellate court described the club as "a variant of the concept popularly known as 'Plato's Retreat,' a business in which patrons are provided with a series of connecting rooms so that they might assemble to promote, discuss and practice an activity commonly known as 'swinging'"; and concluded that "'free heterosexual activity' . . . does not per se qualify for First Amendment protection." The conviction stood. People v. Morone, 150 Cal. App. 3d 18, 19, Cal. Rptr. 316, 317-318 (Dept. Super. Ct. 1983).

4. The perceived evils targeted by the City of Roseburg Municipal Code included the practice of occult arts for profit. Plaintiffs leased premises in the Oregon city and intended to engage in palmistry, only to be informed by city officials that their chosen pursuit was illegal. Because the city attempted to "restrict the right to speak and write on the basis of the content of the communication that is within the protection of Article I, section 8" of the Oregon Constitution, the court of appeals invalidated the ordinance. Marks v. City of Roseburg, 65 Or. App. 102, 670 P.2d 201 (Ct. App. 1983), review denied, 678 P.2d 738 (1984). See also Spiritual Psychic Science Church of Truth v. City of Azusa, 154 Cal. App. 3d 1187, 201 Cal. Rptr. 852 (Ct. App. 1984) (fortune-telling and prophecy, even for profit, are protected speech; municipal ordinance violated California Constitution).

5. The Massachusetts Supreme Judicial Court, relying on a woman's fundamental privacy rights as articulated in Roe v. Wade, 410 U.S. 113 (1973), invalidated a local bylaw amendment that classified an "abortion clinic" as a "prohibited use" throughout the town of Southborough. Framingham Clinic, Inc. v. Board of Selectmen, 373 Mass. 279, 367 N.E.2d 606, 611-612 (1977):

> The Southborough regulation . . . is a serious abridgment of constitutional rights. The desires of members of the community to disfavor an "abortion clinic" — desires which, reflexively, may cause these persons to see an economic detriment to themselves in the existence of the clinic — cannot extenuate such a violation. The report of the Southborough planning board about public sentiment was thus an irrelevancy, and a dangerous one, for that way would lie the extinction of many liberties which are, indeed, constitutionally guaranteed against invasion by a majority. . . .
> Neither could Southborough justify its own exclusionary rule by saying that a woman might overcome it by going elsewhere in the Commonwealth. . . . The picture of one community attempting to throw off on others would not be a happy one.

The clinic's troubles with the town continued, leading to a subsequent decision by the high court. See Framingham Clinic, Inc. v. Zoning Board of Appeals, 382 Mass. 333, 415 N.E.2d 840 (1981) (plaintiffs entitled to building permit, despite building commissioner's "view that an abortion could not 'promote life'"). See also West Side Women's Services, Inc. v. City of Cleveland, 573 F. Supp. 504 (N.D. Ohio 1983) (city ordinance prohibiting licensing of abortion services in retail business zones failed strict scrutiny, per Judge Battisti).

■ LARKIN v. GRENDEL'S DEN, INC.
459 U.S. 116 (1982)

Chief Justice BURGER delivered the opinion of the Court. . . .

Appellee operates a restaurant located in the Harvard Square area of Cambridge, Mass. The Holy Cross Armenian Catholic Parish is located adjacent to the restaurant; the back walls of the two buildings are 10 feet apart. In 1977, appellee applied to the Cambridge License Commission for approval of an alcoholic beverages license for the restaurant.

Section 16C of Chapter 138 of the Massachusetts General Laws provides: "Premises . . . located within a radius of five hundred feet of a church or school shall not be licensed for the sale of alcoholic beverages if the governing body of such church or school files written objection thereto."[1]

Holy Cross Church objected to appellee's application, expressing concern over "having so many licenses *so* near" (emphasis in original).[2] The License Commission voted to deny the application, citing only the objection of Holy Cross Church and noting that the church "is within 10 feet of the proposed location."

On appeal, the Massachusetts Alcoholic Beverages Control Commission upheld the License Commission's action. The Beverages Control

---

1. Section 16C defines "church" as "a church or synagogue building dedicated to divine worship and in regular use for that purpose, but not a chapel occupying a minor portion of a building primarily devoted to other uses." "School" is defined as "an elementary or secondary school, public or private, giving not less than the minimum instruction and training required by [state law] to children of compulsory school age." Mass. Gen. Laws. Ann., ch. 138, §16C (1974).

Section 16C originally was enacted in 1954 as an absolute ban on liquor licenses within 500 feet of a church or school, 1954 Mass. Acts, ch. 569, §1. A 1968 amendment modified the absolute prohibition, permitting licenses within the 500-foot radius "if the governing body of such church assents in writing," 1968 Mass. Acts, ch. 435. In 1970, the statute was amended to its present form, 1970 Mass. Acts, ch. 192.

2. In 1979, there were 26 liquor licensees in Harvard Square and within a 500-foot radius of Holy Cross Church; 25 of these were in existence at the time Holy Cross Church objected to appellee's application.

A. Exclusion

Commission found that "the church's objection under Section 16C was the only basis on which the [license] was denied."

Appellee then sued the License Commission and the Beverages Control Commission in United States District Court. Relief was sought on the grounds that §16C, on its face and as applied, violated the Equal Protection and Due Process Clauses of the Fourteenth Amendment, the Establishment Clause of the First Amendment, and the Sherman Act. . . .

Appellants contend that the State may, without impinging on the Establishment Clause of the First Amendment, enforce what it describes as a "zoning" law in order to shield schools and places of divine worship from the presence nearby of liquor-dispensing establishments. It is also contended that a zone of protection around churches and schools is essential to protect diverse centers of spiritual, educational, and cultural enrichment. It is to that end that the State has vested in the governing bodies of all schools, public or private, and all churches, the power to prevent the issuance of liquor licenses for any premises within 500 feet of their institutions.

Plainly schools and churches have a valid interest in being insulated from certain kinds of commercial establishments, including those dispensing liquor. Zoning laws have long been employed to this end, and there can be little doubt about the power of a state to regulate the environment in the vicinity of schools, churches, hospitals, and the like by exercise of reasonable zoning laws. . . .

The zoning function is traditionally a governmental task requiring the "balancing [of] numerous competing considerations," and courts should properly "refrain from reviewing the merits of [such] decisions, absent a showing of arbitrariness or irrationality." Arlington Heights v. Metropolitan Housing Dev. Corp., 429 U.S. 252, 265 (1977). Given the broad powers of states under the Twenty-first Amendment, judicial deference to the legislative exercise of zoning powers by a city council or other legislative zoning body is especially appropriate in the area of liquor regulation.

However, §16C is not simply a legislative exercise of zoning power. As the Massachusetts Supreme Judicial Court concluded, §16C delegates to private, nongovernmental entities power to veto certain liquor license applications, Arno v. Alcoholic Beverages Control Comm'n, 377 Mass., at 89, 384 N.E.2d, at 1227. This is a power ordinarily vested in agencies of government. . . . We need not decide whether, or upon what conditions, such power may ever be delegated to nongovernmental entities; here, of two classes of institutions to which the legislature has delegated this important decisionmaking power, one is secular, but one is religious. Under these circumstances, the deference normally due a legislative zoning judgment is not merited. . . .

This Court has consistently held that a statute must satisfy three criteria to pass muster under the Establishment Clause:

> First, the statute must have a secular legislative purpose; second, its principal or primary effect must be one that neither advances nor inhibits religion . . . ; finally, the statute must not foster "an excessive government entanglement with religion." Lemon v. Kurtzman, [403 U.S. 602] at 612-613 [(1971)], quoting Waltz v. Tax Comm'n, [397 U.S.] at 674.

Independent of the first of those criteria, the statute, by delegating a governmental power to religious institutions, inescapably implicates the Establishment Clause.

The purpose of §16C, as described by the District Court, is to "protec[t] spiritual, cultural, and educational centers from the 'hurly-burly' associated with liquor outlets." 495 F. Supp., at 766. There can be little doubt that this embraces valid secular legislative purposes. However, these valid secular objectives can be readily accomplished by other means — either through an absolute legislative ban on liquor outlets within reasonable prescribed distances from churches, schools, hospitals, and like institutions,[7] or by ensuring a hearing for the views of affected institutions at licensing proceedings where, without question, such views would be entitled to substantial weight.[8] . . .

The churches' power under the statute is standardless, calling for no reasons, findings, or reasoned conclusions. That power may therefore be used by churches to promote goals beyond insulating the church from undesirable neighbors; it could be employed for explicitly religious goals, for example, favoring liquor licenses for members of that congregation or adherents of that faith. . . . In addition, the mere appearance of a joint exercise of legislative authority by Church and State provides a significant symbolic benefit to religion in the minds of some by reason of the power conferred. It does not strain our prior holdings to say that the statute can be seen as having a "primary" and "principal" effect of advancing religion.

Turning to the third phase of the inquiry called for by Lemon v. Kurtzman, we see that we have not previously had occasion to consider the entanglement implications of a statute vesting significant governmental authority in churches. This statute enmeshes churches in the

---

7. . . . Section 16C, as originally enacted, consisted of an absolute ban on liquor licenses within 500 feet of a church or school, see n. 1, supra; and 27 States continue to prohibit liquor outlets within a prescribed distance of various categories of protected institutions, with certain exceptions and variations. . . . The Court does not express an opinion as to the constitutionality of any statute other than that of Massachusetts.

8. Eleven States have statutes or regulations directing the licensing authority to consider the proximity of the proposed liquor outlet to schools or other institutions in deciding whether to grant a liquor license. . . .

exercise of substantial governmental powers contrary to our consistent interpretation of the Establishment Clause; . . .

. . . [T]he core rationale underlying the Establishment Clause is preventing "a fusion of governmental and religious functions," Abington School District v. Schempp, 374 U.S. 203, 222 (1963). See, e.g., Walz v. Tax Comm'n, 397 U.S., at 674-675; Everson v. Board of Education, 330 U.S. 1, 8-13 (1947).[10] The Framers did not set up a system of government in which important, discretionary governmental powers would be delegated to or shared with religious institutions.

Section 16C substitutes the unilateral and absolute power of a church for the reasoned decisionmaking of a public legislative body acting on evidence and guided by standards, on issues with significant economic and political implications. The challenged statute thus enmeshes churches in the processes of government and creates the danger of "[p]olitical fragmentation and divisiveness on religious lines," Lemon v. Kurtzman, supra, at 623. Ordinary human experience and a long line of cases teach that few entanglements could be more offensive to the spirit of the Constitution.

The judgment of the Court of Appeals is affirmed.

So ordered.

Justice REHNQUIST, dissenting.

Dissenting opinions in previous cases have commented that "great" cases, like "hard" cases, make bad law. Northern Securities Co. v. United States, 193 U.S. 197, 400-401 (1904) (Holmes, J., dissenting); Nixon v. Administrator of General Services, 433 U.S. 425, 505 (1977) (Burger, C. J., dissenting). Today's opinion suggests that a third class of cases — silly cases — also make bad law. The Court wrenches from the decision of the Massachusetts Supreme Judicial Court the word "veto," and rests its conclusions on this single term. The aim of this effort is to prove that a quite sensible Massachusetts liquor zoning law is apparently some sort of sinister religious attack on secular government reminiscent of St. Bartholemew's Night. Being unpersuaded, I dissent.

Notes

1. It was clear from the argument before the Court that the Massachusetts ordinance in question was not the run-of-the-mill plan

---

10. At the time of the Revolution, Americans feared not only a denial of religious freedom, but also the danger of political oppression through a union of civil and ecclesiastical control. B. Bailyn, Ideological Origins of the American Revolution 98-99, n. 3 (1967). See McDaniel v. Paty, 435 U.S. 618, 622-623 (1978). In 18th-century England, such a union of civil and ecclesiastical power was reflected in legal arrangements granting church officials substantial control over various occupations, including the liquor trade. See, e.g., 26 Geo. 2, ch. 31, §2 (1753) (church officials given authority to grant certificate of character, a prerequisite for an alehouse license); S. Webb & B. Webb, The History of Liquor Licensing in England, Principally from 1700 to 1830, pp. 8, n. 1, 62-67, 102-103 (1903).

for separating favored uses from potentially sinful ones. Even the spirit of Justice Brandeis was invoked to instruct his modern counterparts as to the abuse engendered in the delegation scheme:

> *Question:* Mr. Tribe, I'm still worried about the original proposition of alleging that some dealers will pay off somebody and get permission. Couldn't you just as easily say that the Alcoholic Beverage Control Board itself might take a little money and throw the act on that basis?
>
> *Mr. Tribe* [counsel for Grendel's Den]: But happily, Justice Marshall, there are laws against bribery. There are no laws against making contributions to a church in order to show that one is good-spirited and that one is not going to be a problematic neighbor. And the line between a payoff and a contribution —
>
> *Question:* It could be that you've never heard of anything like it before.
>
> *Mr. Tribe:* Justice Brandeis feared that exactly this would happen.
>
> *Question:* In 18 — what?
>
> *Mr. Tribe:* In 1891.[43]
>
> *Question:* Well, this is 1982.
>
> *Mr. Tribe:* But the problem is an enduring one. It was his point that, although he was an ardent prohibitionist and believed in local zoning power, it was his belief that the temptation to shade things a little and make decisions on impermissible bases would be irresistible, but difficult to prove in particular cases. And he was talking about a veto power wielded by all neighbors, not a veto power wielded by one neighbor that happens to be a church dedicated to divine worship.
>
> So that the abuse that led him, despite his belief about temperance and despite his belief about the importance of local zoning, the abuse that would inhere in this kind of governmental power being delegated to private parties was something that ought to be prevented by not giving this kind of veto power.
>
> *Question:* I agree, but I don't see the necessity for saying the reason is because they'll take money illegally.
>
> *Mr. Tribe:* Well, Justice Marshall, that is the necessity to which we would be placed if Justice Rehnquist's suggestion that there ought to be an antitrust trial —
>
> *Question:* Well, count me out of that.
>
> *Mr. Tribe:* That is not, Justice Marshall, by any means indispensable to our prevailing. What we are saying is that giving a property owner that happens to be a church a power of life and death over nearby establishments violates the Constitution.
>
> It is the sort of power that in England they had for hundreds of years, finally got rid of in the Beer Act of 1830; the kind of power that the American colonies refused to give their established churches. It is the kind of power that Massachusetts didn't delegate when it had a flat ban on liquor in 1954.

---

43. Counsel for Grendel's Den quoted a statement made by Brandeis in 1891, in testimony before the Massachusetts legislature, concerning a ban similar to that imposed by Section 16C. See appellee's brief at 33 n.31. — EDS.

A. Exclusion

Note also how in its brief each party framed the question that the case presented to the Court:

> Appellants: Whether a state may, within the limits imposed by the Establishment Clause of the First Amendment, accommodate the diverse interests of its citizens through a zoning statute which shields objecting schools and churches from the disturbances associated with the distribution and consumption of liquor within their immediate vicinity.
>
> Appellee: May a state delegate to each "church or synagogue . . . dedicated to divine worship" an unfettered governmental power to decide which restaurants, liquor stores, and bars may be licensed to serve or sell alcoholic beverages within a 500-foot radius of the religious body's premises?

What question(s) did the Justices decide were worthy of their consideration and resolution?

2. Did counsel for Grendel's Den go overboard in its use of 1891 Brandeis quotes and English and colonial statutes? Apparently so, according to a three-judge panel of the First Circuit. In Grendel's Den v. Larkin, 749 F.2d 945 (1st Cir. 1984), an appeal of the district court's assessment of attorney's fees and costs under 42 U.S.C. §1988, Judge Coffin wrote:

> When we look at the First Amendment portion of plaintiff's brief, we note that seven of the fourteen pages are devoted to a historical analysis, largely in four footnotes, summarizing anti-"establishment" attitudes of seventeenth and eighteenth century Americans, and of lessons to be learned from sixteenth, and seventeenth century England. While this analysis may be fresh and interesting, it was only briefly reflected in a footnote in the Supreme Court's opinion.

749 F.2d at 954. There are other interpretations. For example, one wonders — given Chief Justice Burger's strong record of supporting local decision-making generally, and his specific approval of popular participation in City of Eastlake v. Forest City Enterprises, infra page 1078 — whether Professor Tribe's argument could have carried the day without this evidence of original intent?

The court was also concerned about the "failure to keep accurate and contemporaneous time records," and even criticized counsel for being too enthusiastic: "the early economy of effort and careful focus upon only what was necessary was lost in the heat and excitement of litigating an interesting First Amendment case." Id. at 951-952, 953. Based on these and other findings (even Tribe's lodging at the Watergate Hotel was judged too extravagant), the court reduced Professor Tribe's fees from $176,137.50 to $81,987.50. Id. at 960.

Who foots the bill for such high-priced services (in this case, up to $175 per hour)? While the district court split the fees and costs down the middle between the Cambridge License Commission and the Massachusetts Alcoholic Beverage Control Commission, the court of appeals reduced the city agency's share to 25 percent. Id. at 960. While the fight over fees raged on, Grendel's Den, over the objection of the Holy Cross Church, was issued a license and began serving alcoholic beverages on April Fool's Day, 1983. Id. at 948.

3. Given the possibility of striking a deep governmental pocket at the end of a successful civil rights claim, there should be no surprise at either the proliferation of §1983 cases, or at Justice Department-sponsored efforts to curb "excessive" fees. See Lawyers Enrichment Act, Wall St. J., Oct. 24, 1985: "Taking fee setting partly out of the hands of judges by setting limits and correcting the imbalance between plaintiffs and defendants would restore fairness and logic, improve the quality of justice and, not least, remove yet another unreasonable burden from the taxpayer."

Is there an alternative way to "chill" abusive use of civil rights statutes? See Raskiewicz v. Town of New Boston, 754 F.2d 38 (1st Cir. 1985), in which a landowner's §1983 action based on failures to secure a permit to remove gravel was labeled "'totally frivolous and unwarranted'" by a district court judge who granted summary judgment for the town, and awarded the defendant attorney's fees and costs. Id. at 45-46. The court of appeals did not warmly receive the landowner's "frivolous" appeal; it "order[ed] that Raskiewicz be taxed with double costs." Id. at 46.

4. In further support of the reduction in fees and costs in the *Grendel's Den* follow-up, Judge Coffin noted: "Although in an important and topical area of the law, the legal point that the case made is so fact-specific and, as the subsequent events have illustrated, so easily avoided by legislation [see Mass. Gen. Laws Ann. ch. 138, §16C (West Supp. 1987)], that it is not likely to be of much precedential value." 749 F.2d at 956. The next case, and the decisions discussed in the notes that follow, suggest otherwise. See also Welch v. Clairborne County Beer Board, 678 S.W.2d 52 (Tenn. 1984), appeal dismissed, 471 U.S. 1010 (1985) (court upheld ordinance allowing nearby private residential landowners right to protest, not veto, award of liquor license).

■ GROSZ v. CITY OF MIAMI BEACH
721 F.2d 729 (11th Cir. 1983), cert. denied, 469 U.S. 827 (1984)

GOLDBERG, Senior Circuit Judge: . . .

[In 1977, the plaintiffs — an Orthodox rabbi and his wife — applied for city permits to remodel their garage/recreation room "for 'playroom use.'" Instead, "the plaintiffs specifically stocked the inside of the building for religious services," despite the fact that city officials "specifically informed" the Groszes "that the structure [located in a single-family residential zone] could not be remodeled as a religious institution." In 1981, owing to citizen complaints, the plaintiffs received a "notice of violation" threatening criminal prosecution for violation of the zoning ordinance. The district court rejected plaintiffs' assertions that the ordinance on its face was either vague or overbroad. However, the trial court concluded that the ordinance was unconstitutional as applied, because of the city's failure to offer a compelling state interest for imposing a burden on free exercise rights.]

Before a court balances competing governmental and religious interests, the challenged government action must pass two threshold tests. The first test distinguishes government regulation of religious beliefs and opinions from restrictions affecting religious conduct. The government may never regulate religious beliefs; but, the Constitution does not prohibit absolutely government regulation of religious conduct. Given a regulation's focus on conduct, government action passes this first threshold. Braunfeld v. Brown, 366 U.S. 599, 603 (1961); Cantwell v. Connecticut, 310 U.S. 296, 303-304 (1940).

The second threshold principle requires that a law have both a secular purpose and a secular effect to pass constitutional muster. . . .

If a government action challenged under the free exercise clause survives passage through the belief/conduct and secular purpose and effect thresholds, the court then faces the difficult task of balancing government interests against the impugned religious interest. This constitutional balancing is not a simple process. We gain some sense of direction, however, from one basic principle: the balance depends upon the cost to the government of altering its activity to allow the religious practice to continue unimpeded versus the cost to the religious interest imposed by the government activity. . . .

In this case, the thresholds pass quickly beneath our feet. The City's zoning law affects prayer and religious services, and so involves conduct. Therefore, balancing not absolutism is appropriate. That the law has both secular purpose and effect is noncontroversial. No one contends that zoning laws are based upon disagreement with religious tenets or are aimed at impeding religion. Similarly, given zoning's historical function in protecting public health and welfare, see Village of Belle Terre v. Boraas, 416 U.S. 1 (1974), and the incidental nature of the asserted burden on religion, the essential effect of zoning laws is clearly secular.

The City of Miami Beach asserts a governmental interest in enforcing its zoning laws so as to preserve the residential quality of its RS-4 zones. By so doing the City protects the zones' inhabitants from problems of traffic, noise and litter, avoids spot zoning, and preserves a coherent land use zoning plan. . . .

Doctrine also requires that we consider the impact of a religious based exemption to zoning enforcement. In that regard we find that granting an exception would defeat City zoning policy in all neighborhoods where that exception was asserted. Maintenance of the residential quality of a neighborhood requires zoning law enforcement whenever that quality is threatened. Moreover, no principled way exists to limit an exception's costs just to the harm it would create in this case. Crowds of 500 would be as permissible as crowds of 50. Problems of administering the exception such as distinguishing valid religious claims from feigned ones, therefore, need not even be considered. A religion based exception would clearly and substantially impair the City's policy objectives. Together, the important objectives underlying zoning and the degree of infringement of those objectives caused by allowing the religious conduct to continue place a heavy weight on the government's side of the balancing scale.

In calculating the burden on religion, we first determine whether the conduct interfered with constitutes religious practice. The religion of Appellee, Naftali Grosz, requires him to conduct religious services twice daily in the company of at least ten adult males. Solicitation of neighborhood residents to attend and the participation of congregations larger than ten, the conduct on which the City based its notice of violation, are not integral to Appellees' faith. However, the trial judge made no findings, and the record is not clear regarding the extent to which, if any, these objectionable but nonessential practices aid Appellees in gathering ten men and conducting the required services. We assume therefore, that the nonessential practices further the religious conduct. We must also assume, then, that Appellees suffer some degree of burden on their free exercise rights.

Turning to the significance of that burden, we note that Miami Beach does not prohibit religious conduct per se. Rather, the City prohibits acts in furtherance of this conduct in certain geographical areas. The relevant question is to what degree does the City's exclusion of Appellees' activities from RS-4 zoned areas burden religious conduct. The City's zoning regulations permit organized, publicly attended religious activities in all zoning districts except the RS-4 single family districts. The zones that allow religious institutions to operate constitute one half of the City's territory. Appellees' home lies within four blocks of such a district. Appellees do not confront the limited choice of ceasing their conduct or incurring criminal liability. Alternatively, they may conduct the required services in suitably zoned areas, either by securing another site away from their current house or by making their home elsewhere in the city. We cannot know the exact impact upon Appellees, in terms of convenience, dollars or aesthetics, that a location

A. Exclusion

change would entail. The burden imposed, though, plainly does not rise to the level of criminal liability, loss of livelihood, or denial of a basic income sustaining public welfare benefit. In comparison to the religious infringements analyzed in previous free exercise cases the burden here stands towards the lower end of the spectrum.

In discussing the process for reaching a final balance we noted earlier that courts are frequently forced to undertake an ad hoc balancing when existing free exercise doctrine does not command a specific result. But, such ad hoc balancings need not always be based only on appeals to a court's basic intuitive sense. Fortunately, the instant case arises in a factual context in which substantial, relevant case precedent exists to guide our balancing. This case is not the first to involve balancing government's interest in restricting the location of religious conduct. . . .

. . . In [Lakewood Congregation of Jehovah's Witnesses v. City of Lakewood, 699 F.2d 303 (6th Cir.1983)], a church congregation challenged a zoning ordinance that prohibited their building a church on a lot they had previously purchased. The Sixth Circuit characterized the infringement on religious freedom as an "inconvenient economic burden" and a "subjective aesthetic burden." The City of Lakewood's interest in creating residential districts to promote its citizens' health and well being was held to outweigh the congregation's religious interests. We think *Lakewood*'s balancing process reached the correct result in a case very similar to this one. The Sixth Circuit faced, if anything, a closer balance than the one called for today — as opposed to the one half of Miami Beach territory where Appellees may conduct their religious services, the City of Lakewood permits church buildings on only around ten percent of its land. . . .

The judges who have precedentially performed balancings on the free exercise trapeze have encountered great difficulty with the weights and measures involved. Balancings must avoid constitutionalizing secularity or sectarianizing the Constitution. In this area, where religious guarantees of the Constitution compete with the rights of government to perform its function in the modern era, certitude is difficult to attain. All should understand that we have not written today for every situation in which these issues might arise — only that we have done our best as amateur performers in solving this very, very delicate problem. We who perform on this flying trapeze may not always be daring and young, but we must avoid that slip that could take us into the doctrinal confusion below.

We find that the burden upon government to allow Appellees' conduct outweighs the burden upon the Appellees' free exercise interest. Therefore, we reverse the trial court judgment as to the Ordinance's unconstitutionality as applied. We remand to the district court with instructions to enter judgment in favor of the City.

Notes

1. As in the free speech realm of the first amendment (see Metromedia, Inc. v. City of San Diego, infra page 547), the Supreme Court's guidance for lower federal courts attempting to decide on the proper approach in religion cases has been problematic. Balancing, inquiring as to less restrictive means, and demanding compelling state interests have each been employed in recent Supreme Court cases, depending on the directness of the confrontation with protected rights, the choices remaining with the burdened plaintiff, and the existence of a countervailing fundamental interest. See Gunther, Constitutional Law 1512-1527 (11th ed. 1985); 3 Rotunda, Nowak & Young, Treatise on Constitutional Law: Substance and Procedure §§21.6, 21.8 (1986). See also Reynolds, Zoning the Church: The Police Power Versus the First Amendment, 64 B.U.L. Rev. 767 (1985); Pearlman, Zoning Religious Uses: Emerging Judicial Patterns, Land Use L. & Zoning Dig., June 1985, at 3; Note, Zoning Ordinances Affecting Churches: A Proposal for Expanded Free Exercise Protection, 132 U. Pa. L. Rev. 1131 (1984); Comment, Justice Douglas' Sanctuary: May Churches Be Excluded from Suburban Residential Areas?, 45 Ohio St. L.J. 1017 (1984); Note, Land Use Regulation and the Free Exercise Clause, 84 Colum. L. Rev. 1562 (1984).

2. Compare the court's scrutiny in *Grosz* to the more reverent posture in Westchester Reform Temple v. Brown, 22 N.Y.2d 488, 239 N.E.2d 891, 293 N.Y.S.2d 297 (1968), a dispute centering on the synagogue's expansion plans:

> First, the Temple's plan provides for a setback of 62 feet from the building line on Mamaroneck Road while the Planning Commission insists that the setback be no less than 130 feet (5 times the height of the building as remodeled) and, second, the Temple plans to allow 29 feet to the adjoining lot on the north for a short distance while the Planning Commission insists that at least 40 feet be allowed to the adjoining side lot.

While the zoning ordinance withstood a constitutional challenge on its face — as under the ordinance the Planning Commission was to "consider . . . whether the expansion is for educational, religious, or benevolent purposes" — the court affirmed a holding that as applied to the petitioner, the ordinance "bore no substantial relationship to the health, safety, welfare or morals of the community and violated the guarantees of religious freedom of the Federal and State Constitutions":

> To sustain the Planning Commission's decision, it must be convincingly shown that the Temple's proposed expansion will have a direct and

A. Exclusion

immediate adverse effect upon the health, safety or welfare of the community. This has not been done. . . .

Religious structures enjoy a constitutionally protected status which severely curtails the permissible extent of governmental regulation in the name of the police powers, but the power of regulation has not been altogether obliterated. . . . [W]here an irreconcilable conflict exists between the right to erect a religious structure and the potential hazards of traffic or diminution in value, the latter must yield to the former. . . .

What has occurred here is that the Planning Commission, under the guise of reasonable regulation, has unconstitutionally abridged religious freedom.

3. See also Jewish Reconstructionist Synagogue v. Incorporated Village of Roslyn, 38 N.Y.2d 283, 342 N.E.2d 534 (1975):

> Unlike the ordinances which we upheld in the *Westchester* case, . . . the special use ordinance before us directs authorities to *deny* the use permit if they find that the religious use will have *any* detrimental effect on public safety, health, or welfare, including effects on traffic, on fire safety, and on the character of the neighborhood. It contains no substantial requirement that efforts to accommodate or mitigate these effects be made. . . .
>
> The variance ordinance falls to the same analysis. While residents may apply for variances from setback requirements and the board may grant them, religious uses are subject to an invariable requirement of 100 feet. . . . [T]he invariability of the ordinance offends against the requirement that efforts to accommodate religious uses be made.

But see Holy Spirit Association for the Unification of World Christianity v. Rosenfeld, 91 A.2d 190, 458 N.Y.S.2d 920 (1983):

> Generally, municipalities should make efforts to accommodate proposed religious uses, subject to conditions reasonably related to land use. . . . In the instant case, however, the Unification Church's misrepresentations to the zoning board, and its conceded violations of provisions of the zoning ordinance while its application was pending, fully justified the zoning board's denial of a special use permit.

Can the Euclid case be cited for the proposition that churches may be excluded from residential districts? See Lakewood, Ohio Congregation of Jehovah's Witnesses, Inc. v. City of Lakewood, 699 F.2d 303 (6th Cir. 1983) (discussed in *Grosz*, supra page 501).

4. What impact does the Supreme Court's opinion in Larkin v. Grendel's Den have on ordinances like that in *Westchester* that treat religious institutions favorably? Stated otherwise, at some point could a municipality's efforts to accommodate religious uses amount to an unconstitutional establishment of religion?

5. Consider the types of church organizations, and how they should be handled by counsel on either side. In Board of Zoning Appeals of Indianapolis v. Wheaton, 118 Ind. App. 38, 76 N.E.2d 597 (1948), the variance requested would have allowed construction of a church, priest's mansion, a convent or sisters' home, a school, and off-street parking facilities; in State ex rel. Anshe Chesed Congregation v. Bruggemeier, 97 Ohio App. 67, 115 N.E.2d 65 (1953), a main temple, social hall, junior temple, library, executive offices, religious school, residence for a caretaker, and a parking lot.

6. In Roman Catholic Archbishop of Detroit v. Village of Orchard Lake, 333 Mich. 389, 394, 53 N.W.2d 308, 310 (1952), an ordinance allowing churches under special permit in three zones comprising about 10 percent of the village's area was held contrary to the spirit of the Northwest Ordinance of 1787: "Religion, morality, and knowledge being necessary to good government and the happiness of mankind, schools and the means of education shall forever be encouraged."

7. For recent decisions in this troublesome area of confrontation between the police power and the first amendment, see State v. Cameron, 100 N.J. 586, 498 A.2d 1217 (1985) (ordinance excluding churches from residential zone held unconstitutionally vague as applied to minister using home one hour each week for services); Islamic Center of Mississippi v. City of Starkville, 840 F.2d 293 (5th Cir. 1988) ("The burden on relatively impecunious Muslim students... is more than incidental, and the ordinance leaves no practical alternative for establishing a mosque in the city limits."); and Fahri v. Commissioners of Borough of Deal, 204 N.J. Super. 575, 499 A.2d 559 (Super. Ct. App. Div. 1985) (borough failed to use least restrictive means in categorizing churches and other places of worship as conditional uses). But see First Assembly of God v. City of Alexandria, 739 F.2d 942 (4th Cir.), cert. denied, 469 U.S. 1019 (1984) (court rejected first amendment challenge to city's imposition of conditions on grant of permit for church's operation of private day school); Fountain Gate Ministries, Inc. v. City of Plano, 654 S.W.2d 841 (Tex. Ct. App. 1983) (court affirmed injunction prohibiting church from operating college in single-family residential zone).

B. ANTICOMPETITIVENESS

It is specifically averred ... that prospective buyers of land for industrial, commercial and residential uses in the metropolitan district of Cleveland are deterred from buying any part of this land ... ; that the ordinance ... has the effect of diverting the normal industrial, commercial and residential development thereof to other and less favorable locations.
— *Euclid v. Ambler*, 272 U.S. at 384-385

B. Anticompetitiveness

The relatively unrestrained market in industrial and commercial sites in metropolitan Cleveland was one of the first victims of Euclid's comprehensive zoning ordinance — at least according to the Ambler Realty Company. Not only was Ambler's piece of real estate, nestled between Euclid Avenue and the Nickel Plate Railroad, severely devalued, but also certain unnamed parties would have virtual monopolies on the most intensive (and potentially lucrative) uses permitted on selected, choice lots in the newly planned suburb, at least for the foreseeable future.

This second seed planted in *Euclid* — the use of regulatory power to control or eliminate competition — has blossomed into two sets of challenges to Euclidean zoning. First, as revealed in Chapter III, in the decades following the Court's approval of zoning in theory, many jurisdictions wrestled with a practical problem left unresolved in early ordinances — the nonconforming use. The preexisting gas station, repair shop, or laundry surrounded by block after block of residential and recreational buildings could monopolize business within its captive market. The government officials who in their wisdom isolated the nonconforming use with a fervent prayer that it would just disappear, actually freed the owner from the burdens of competition he or she would have experienced in a zone set aside for similar pursuits. Thus, the judiciary's often tortured attempts to validate plans for amortizing, purchasing, or severely restricting modifications of nonconforming uses were determined attempts in part to rid zoning of its inherent anticompetitive nature.

The second set of challenges was prompted chiefly by two controversial Supreme Court antitrust cases — City of Lafayette v. Louisiana Power & Light,[44] and Community Communications v. City of Boulder, infra page 513. In attempting to define the limits of the Parker v. Brown[45] umbrella that shields states from the devastating torrent of Sherman and Clayton Act antitrust challenges, the Court's rulings on alleged utilities (*Lafayette Power*) and cable franchise (*Boulder*) abuses suggested the possibility of litigation involving a conspiracy to restrain trade between a municipality's zoning authorities and a favored property owner. For example, Justice Potter Stewart, in his dissent in *Lafayette Power*, voiced the fears of many a local legislator:

---

44. 435 U.S. 389 (1978). The company's counterclaim alleged that the petitioners (cities) had engaged in such illegal activities as conditioning the provision of gas and water service on the customer's agreement to purchase electricity from the city (known as a "tie-in") and conspiring "to engage in sham and frivolous litigation against LP&L before various federal agencies and federal courts for the purpose, and with the effect, of delaying approval and construction of LP&L's proposed nuclear electric generating plant." Id. at 405 (plurality opinion). Five justices held that the cities were not beyond the reach of the Sherman Act.

For one early reaction to the decision, see Bosselman, Does the *Lafayette* Case Bring Zoning Under the Antitrust Laws?, Land Use L. & Zoning Dig., Feb. 1979, at 4-6.

45. 317 U.S. 341 (1943) (articulating state action exemption from Sherman Act).

Each time a city grants an exclusive franchise, or chooses to provide a service itself on a monopoly basis, *or refuses to grant a zoning variance to a business* . . . state legislative action will be necessary to ensure that a federal court will not subsequently decide that the activity was not "contemplated" by the legislature.[46]

The cases, statutes, and commentary included in this section were largely inspired by this and other suggestions of potential governmental liability. These readings suggest that this Euclidean legacy, like exclusion, retains its controversial nature. More importantly, even after congressional tampering with the regulatory market,[47] the anticompetitive seed remains a genuine concern for attorneys challenging or defending officials who may be engaged in making land-use decisions upon which ride millions of dollars in invested capital as well as the demographic and economic make-up of the affected area.

It might seem ironic that a program with Progressive roots has such a strong anticompetitive flavor, given the rich trust-busting image of late nineteenth and early twentieth century reformers. What is often forgotten is that before the First World War public monopolies were often considered the solution to many private sector abuses. So, for example, Frederic Howe proffered municipal ownership of lucrative utilities to avoid the corruption that plagued the awarding of franchises by urban machines.[48] It is helpful to understand zoning as a variation on this municipal ownership theme, for local governments, particularly in the new suburbs not yet swallowed by annexation, in effect retained control of land development rights through comprehensive land-use planning and the restriction of uses. That neither public ownership nor zoning was able to overcome the graft and corruption that infested franchise awards and the unfettered real estate market is yet another example of an ultimately unsatisfying public/private distinction.

The anticompetitive component of zoning also suggests that the reformers who advanced urban planning theory were not solely re-

---

46. 435 U.S. at 438 (Stewart, J., dissenting) (emphasis added). — Eds.

47. See the discussion of the Local Government Antitrust Act of 1984, infra page 515.

48. See Howe, supra note 13, at 62:

In city and state is the greed for franchise grants and special privileges that explains the worst of the conditions. This is the universal cause of municipal shame. By privilege, democracy has been drugged.

An examination of the conditions in city after city discloses one sleepless influence that is common to them all. Under the surface phenomena the activity of privilege appears, the privileges of the street railways, the gas, the water, the telephone, and electric-lighting companies. The connection of those industries with politics explains most of the corruption; it explains the power of the boss and the machine; it suggests the explanation of the indifference of the "best" citizen and his hostility to democratic reform.

That municipal ownership would greatly diminish, if not wholly correct, most of the abuses of municipal administration I am firmly convinced.

sponsible for the popularity of height, area, and use zoning. One does not have to be an unstinting adherent to Gabriel Kolko's capture thesis[49] to acknowledge that vested real estate interests, such as the Fifth Avenue merchants in New York City, played an important role in the alliance that ensured a future for American zoning. In other words, the attraction and enhanced value of an area set aside as the only available industrial or commercial property were probably hard to overcome in the minds of many influential conservative property owners (or judges) otherwise predisposed to oppose government regulation of land ownership. The readings that follow concern the propriety of using federal and state antitrust sanctions to correct or discourage the unfortunate by-product of even the most well-considered planning and zoning scheme — conspiratorial behavior motivated by the financial impact of public land-use decisions and nondecisions.

■ SCOTT v. CITY OF SIOUX CITY
736 F.2d 1207 (8th Cir. 1984), cert. denied, 471 U.S. 1003 (1985)

HEANEY, Circuit Judge. . . .

Sioux City officials and businesses have been increasingly concerned with downtown development since the mid-1960's. In 1964, a committee of downtown businesses and community leaders submitted a plan to the city council evaluating alternatives for maintaining a viable business climate in the city. The city council appointed a Central City Committee to formulate recommendations for orderly development of the central business district. The city applied for funds from the federal government to prepare a General Neighborhood Renewal Plan encompassing 215 acres and to plan a three-block total clearance project known as Central Business District-East (CBD-E). Eventually, the city acquired real estate in the CBD-E, offered it for redevelopment to private parties, and issued bonds for the construction of parking garages and other improvements. Meanwhile, an eleven-block area adjacent to the CBD-E was also targeted for redevelopment and designated the Central Business District-West (CBD-W). The city applied for federal assistance to survey and plan this area in 1966 but did not receive the funds until 1971. The city thereafter proceeded with active redevelopment of the CBD-W and entered into redevelopment agreements with a private developer, Metro Center, Inc., in February of 1974.

---

49. Kolko, The Triumph of Conservatism: A Reinterpretation of American History, 1900-1916, at 3 (1963): "It is business control over politics (and by 'business' I mean the major economic interests) rather than political regulation of the economy that is the significant phenomenon of the Progressive Era."

At the time the city council contracted with Metro Center, its president was Howard Weiner who had been a member of the Sioux City Council from January of 1973 to November 7, 1973. Weiner lost his bid for re-election to the city council and became president of Metro Center three weeks later. Metro Center submitted the sole bid to redevelop three parcels in the CBD-W. Its proposal included plans for a major hotel, department stores, a convention center and related commercial development. Under the redevelopment contract, the city was obligated to obtain federal grants for the CBD-W area, secure real estate, clear the property for redevelopment, and provide streets, sidewalks, street lights and other urban utilities. In return, Metro Center was obligated to purchase the property from the city, build the commercial facilities it had proposed, procure financing and secure tenants.

The appellants acquired their property along the southern limits of Sioux City in 1962. In 1966, the city annexed the property and apparently zoned it to permit commercial development. In May of 1974, soon after the city entered into the contract with Metro Center, the appellants sold 19 acres of this land to General Growth Properties, a real estate development company, for the development of a regional shopping center. The appellants retained approximately 70 acres of adjoining land which they allege they planned to develop commercially to take advantage of business drawn to the regional shopping center. As part of the purchase agreement, the appellants agreed to construct roads to facilitate the area development. When the transaction was complete, the parties publicly announced General Growth's plans to develop a regional shopping center.

The prospect of a regional shopping center competing for commercial tenants with the downtown project concerned Weiner, the president of Metro Center. Weiner states in his deposition that he talked to council members about the importance of limiting commercial development outside the downtown and specifically about the threat posed by General Growth's plan for a regional shopping center. On July 22, 1974, the city council enacted the Interim Development Ordinance which temporarily suspended unplanned development within the city pending the completion of the Plan and Zoning Commission's comprehensive review of the general plan and zoning ordinance. The interim ordinance did not change any zoning classifications, but it restricted the issuance of building permits, approval of site plans in designated areas, and certain types of residential and commercial development.

In November, 1975, appellant Gene Scott requested a "preplat" conference with the planning department and an informal review of the proposed development of his property under the Interim Development Ordinance. The Community Development Director advised the council that the request was in conflict with the provisions and policy

B. Anticompetitiveness

of the interim ordinance. On February 17, 1976, the city council granted a conditional variance for preparation of a grading plan only. Scott never applied for a building permit or variance under either the interim ordinance or the permanent ordinance enacted by the city council on August 2, 1976. The permanent ordinance also left appellants' property with a zoning classification that does not allow for the development of a regional shopping center and other retail commercial developments.

The appellants filed their original complaint on January 19, 1979. The complaint alleged violations of the Sherman Act, 15 U.S.C. §§1 and 2, and was amended December 3, 1981 to allege a violation of the Civil Rights Act, 42 U.S.C. §1983. The appellants contended that the city and its council members conspired with Weiner and Metro Center to prevent the appellants from developing their land around General Growth's planned regional shopping center. On December 15, 1982, the district court rejected the defendants' first motion for summary judgment holding that the state action immunity doctrine of Parker v. Brown, 317 U.S. 341 (1943), did not shield the municipal defendants and that, in view of this Court's decision in Westborough Mall v. City of Cape Girardeau, 693 F.2d 733 (8th Cir. 1982), cert. denied, 461 U.S. 945, (1983), appellants' civil rights claim presented a question for the jury. On May 3, 1983, the court also denied a renewed motion for summary judgment in which the defendants contended that the Iowa Urban Renewal Law provided state authorization sufficient to trigger state action immunity. The court subsequently reconsidered that denial in light of our then-recent opinion, Gold Cross Ambulance & Transfer v. City of Kansas City, 705 F.2d 1005 (8th Cir. 1983), cert. filed, 52 U.S.L.W. 3039 (1983), and granted the defendants' summary judgment motion on June 17, 1983. This appeal followed.

The initial issue in this case is whether the state action doctrine shields the municipal defendants from liability for violations of the federal antitrust laws. . . .

These [8th Circuit] cases analyzed the state action immunity issue in two steps: First, the state legislature must have authorized the challenged municipal activity. Second, the legislature must have intended to displace competition. . . .

To determine whether the state authorized the acts complained of we must first determine what those acts are. The appellants specifically challenge the council's passage of the ordinances which prevented them from commercially developing their land. They also challenge the council's dealings with Metro Center prior to the passage of the ordinances. Thus, the first question is whether the Iowa Urban Renewal Law authorized both zoning in furtherance of urban renewal goals and the relationship between the city and Metro Center complained of here.

The Iowa Urban Renewal Law gives both general and specific

authorization for a municipality's use of zoning power to further the policy of urban renewal. . . .

The more difficult question is whether the Iowa Legislature intended to sanction the specific zoning ordinances complained of here. . . .

We agree with the district court that the importance the Iowa Legislature placed on urban renewal, and the broad powers it gave to municipalities to address the problem, support a finding that the legislature contemplated the type of zoning ordinances passed by Sioux City. The Iowa Legislature considered the decay of its urban areas a serious threat to the economic, social and physical welfare of state residents. It noted that the existence of slum and blighted areas contributes to the spread of disease and crime, reduces tax revenues, impairs the growth of municipalities and retards the provision of housing accommodations. To combat this "growing menace," the legislature empowered municipalities not only to zone, inspect, and regulate private real estate, but to do all things necessary to assure the success of their urban renewal projects. The legislature's deep concern and broad delegation of power contributes to our finding that it contemplated the challenged zoning.

A more compelling reason to find the necessary legislative intent, however, is that the legislature has put municipalities in the position of partially financing commercial development. The Iowa Urban Renewal Law allows cities to raise a substantial amount of money for their urban renewal ventures through federal and local government loans, tax levies and the issuance of bonds. The district court found Sioux City had raised approximately $30 million in public financing to support its urban renewal project. . . .

. . . [T]he state legislature must have anticipated that once a municipality became financially and legally committed to commercial development in urban areas, it would use its delegated powers, including the power to zone and rezone, to protect that commitment. Consultants to the Sioux City Council advised discouraging shopping centers in favor of the downtown because dispersing major retailing facilities among several locations in a market of Sioux City's scale would reduce the chances of success for the downtown project. The challenged ordinances were thus a reasonable and necessary consequence of the city's role in implementing state urban renewal goals. . . .

Our holding that the Iowa Urban Renewal Law provides a clear and affirmative expression of a state policy favoring Sioux City's action does not end our inquiry. The appellants assert the city council acted outside the state authorization and thus its actions cannot be shielded from antitrust liability. They allege that the city's zoning decision was the product of an anticompetitive "conspiracy" between the city and Metro Center rather than urban renewal policy. They further allege that because the city council did not follow the procedures outlined in the urban renewal statute for amending the plan when it passed the challenged ordinances, it forfeited state authorization.

A city council could conceivably violate the antitrust laws by entering into an agreement with a private developer to restrain trade. . . .

. . . [W]e do not believe a material issue of fact exists as to whether the city acted outside the state's authorization for antitrust purposes either in its dealings with Metro Center prior to passing the challenged ordinances or in the procedures followed to enact them. We therefore affirm the district court's grant of summary judgment to the municipal defendants on appellants' antitrust claims. . . .

[The court of appeals also affirmed the district court's rejection of appellants' §1983 claims.]

Notes

1. Shopping centers are veritable magnets for antitrust challenges. See, for example, Ensign Bickford Realty Corp. v. City Council, 68 Cal. App. 3d 467, 137 Cal. Rptr. 304 (1977), in which the plaintiff challenged the Livermore City Council's decision to restrict commercial uses to the Springtown area:

> Bickford contends that the purpose of the City Council in making the above decision was to restrict competition, and that inasmuch as the restriction on competition or the protection of monopolies is an impermissible zoning objective, the City Council's decision cannot stand. . . .
>
> Despite the principle that cities may not directly restrict competition under the guise of the zoning power, it must be recognized that land use and planning decisions cannot be made in a vacuum, and all such decisions must necessarily have some impact on the economy of the community. . . .
>
> . . . There is no evidence, nor can it be inferred, that the City Council was attempting to permit commercial development on one parcel and deny it as to another for the purpose of creating a business monopoly or to unreasonably regulate the commercial development of the City.

See also Weaver and Dyersen, Central Business District Planning and the Control of Outlying Shopping Centers, 14 Urb. L. Ann. 57 (1977); Levin, The Antitrust Challenge to Local Government Protection of the Central Business District, 55 U. Colo. L. Rev. 21 (1983).

In Mason City Center Associates v. City of Mason City, 468 F. Supp. 737 (N.D. Iowa 1979), the court denied the city's motion to dismiss for failure to state a claim. The complaint alleged that a developer had agreed with the City to organize a Downtown Center on condition that the city prevent any regional shopping center that would compete with the Center. The plaintiff's request for a rezoning of its 35-acre tract from an Agriculture and Mining District to Business was denied. "Although zoning statutes assumedly sometimes have anticompetitive effects, it is somewhat fatuous to contend that they inevitably reflect a state's clear and affirmative intent to displace competition with regulation or monopoly public service." Id. at 742. Undaunted, the city filed a counterclaim alleging that the plaintiffs' actions amounted to tortious interference with business relationships. A jury awarded the city $250,000 on the counterclaim, but an appellate court reversed, calling the damages highly speculative. Mason City Center Associates v. City of Mason City, 671 F.2d 1146 (8th Cir. 1982).

2. See Statement in Favor of the Hartz Mountain Rezoning Application (July, 1978):

> The monopoly within the Meadowlands would be a strong and coercive one — a monopoly for an as yet unconstructed regional shopping center is far more pervasive than one given to help avoid the decline of an existing central business area, as in Tenafly. Furthermore, while there the zoning did limit the location of retail stores in the downtown area, it did not go so far as to create an absolute monopoly. Anybody can choose to locate downtown — there are many sites and potential landlords. One can build more, higher, and thereby produce more space; sites are open for bidding and the air is full of competitive spirit and activity. But a single shopping center, with its unified leases, selection of types of tenants, covenants not to compete, and control over use of space, results in far more restrictions of basic commercial freedoms than those engendered by many landlords and buildings.

See also Mandelker, Control of Competition as a Proper Purpose in Zoning, 14 Zoning Digest 33, 40-41 (1962).

Given the strong public policy against restraints on competition that is embedded in the Sherman Antitrust Act (15 U.S.C. §§1, 2), should courts allow excluded parties to attack lease covenants permitting "snobby" shopping mall tenants to veto prospective "discount" neighbors? See Dalmo Sales Co. v. Tysons Corner Regional Shopping Center, 429 F.2d 206 (D.C. Cir. 1970), in which the court of appeals affirmed the trial court's decision not to interfere by means of a preliminary injunction.

3. The question of monopoly shield can be seen in yet another context. What if the New York City Planning Commission decided to ban all further construction of office buildings in Manhattan, not on grounds of inadequacy of infrastructure, but simply because it agrees with existing office building owners that there is an oversupply of office space? Would this action be permissible in light of the Supreme Court's decision in City of Lafayette v. Louisiana Power and Light Co.?

4. By the time the court of appeals rendered its decision in *Mason*

B. Anticompetitiveness 513

City, the Supreme Court had heightened the fears of local land-use officials even further. The case, Community Communications Co. v. City of Boulder, 455 U.S. 40 (1981), involved a home-rule municipality and the implications of awarding the newest franchise plum — cable television. Boulder passed an ordinance prohibiting Community Communications from expanding its existing cable service for three months, during which time the city council planned to draft a model ordinance and to invite other cable television companies to enter the city market. The petitioner sought, and was granted, a preliminary injunction by the district court, based on allegations of Sherman Act violations; the court of appeals reversed, distinguishing the *Lafayette* case.

Justice Brennan, for the Court (at 55), denied the city's claim that home-rule status itself provided the state-action shield:

> [P]lainly the requirement of "clear articulation and affirmative expression" is not satisifed when the State's position is one of mere *neutrality* respecting the municipal actions challenged as anticompetitive. A State that allows its municipalities to do as they please can hardly be said to have "contemplated" the specific anticompetitive actions for which municipal liability is sought.

Justice Rehnquist (dissenting, at 71) was displeased with the potential impact of the majority's holding on intergovernmental relationships:

> In order to defend itself from Sherman Act attacks, the home rule municipality will have to cede its authority back to the State. It is unfortunate enough that the Court today holds that our federalism is not implicated when municipal legislation is invalidated by a federal statute. It is nothing less than a novel and egregious error when this Court uses the Sherman Act to regulate the relationship between the States and their political subdivisions.

5. The antitrust claims brought by Westborough Mall, Inc., against a city and competing shopping center developer warranted a reversal of the trial court's grant of summary judgment in Westborough Mall v. City of Cape Girardeau, 693 F.2d 733 (8th Cir. 1982), cert. denied, 461 U.S. 945 (1983). Westborough alleged that public officials and the rival developer conspired to cause a reversion of plaintiffs' zoning for the shopping center site from commercial to residential, despite a provision in the original rezoning that exempted the site from "automatic reversion." The appellate court rejected *Noerr-Pennington* (exempting lobbying and other efforts to secure governmental action) and Parker v. Brown defenses (citing *Lafayette* and *Boulder*), and allowed plaintiffs to proceed with their attempts to

> prove at trial that there was an agreement between the city officials and

the [rival] developers which was intended to harm or unreasonably restrain trade; that as a direct result plaintiffs have been injured; and that the damages sustained are capable of reasonable ascertainment and are not speculative or conjectural.

Id. at 745. On remand, the jury rejected the antitrust count. See 794 F.2d 330, 335 (8th Cir. 1986) (plaintiff abandoned antitrust claim but successfully appealed rejection of §1983 due process claim).

6. In light of *Boulder*'s language concerning express state authorization for local anticompetitive activities, some state lawmakers responded with protective legislation. See, for example, N.D. Cent. Code §40-01-22 (1983):

> All immunity of the state from the provisions of the Sherman Antitrust Act . . . is hereby extended to any city governing body acting within the scope of the grants of authority contained in sections 40-05-01, 40-05-02, and 40-05.1-06. When acting within the scope of the grants of authority contained in [these] sections . . . , a city or city governing body shall be presumed to be acting in furtherance of state policy.

See also Maryland's clear articulation of the anticompetitive nature of land-use controls in Md. Ann. Code art. 23A, §2(b) (36) (1987):

> (i) It has been and shall continue to be the policy of this State that the orderly development and use of land and structures requires comprehensive regulation through implementation of planning and zoning controls.
> (ii) It has been and shall continue to be the policy of this State that planning and zoning controls shall be implemented by local government.
> (iii) To achieve the public purposes of this regulatory scheme, the General Assembly recognizes that local government action will displace or limit economic competition by owners and users of property.
> (iv) It is the policy of the General Assembly and of this State that competition and enterprise shall be so displaced or limited for the attainment of the purposes of the State policy for implementing planning and zoning controls as set forth in this article and elsewhere in the public local and public general law. . . .

7. The *Boulder* Court's extension of *Lafayette* also inspired a flurry of antitrust challenges to a wide range of local government functions, an extensive lobbying effort by local officials seeking congressional protection, and a rash of articles that, for the most part, attempted to correct different components of the Court's analysis. See Lee, Local Government Practices and the Antitrust Merits, 1985 S. Ill. U. L. Rev. 455 (law review editors should consult the first footnote); Hovenkamp and Mackerron, Municipal Regulation and Federal Antitrust Policy, 32 UCLA L. Rev. 719 (1985) (see notes 129 and 130, at 738-739, for an

B. Anticompetitiveness

impressive list of post-*Boulder* cases); Brennan, Local Government and Antitrust Policy: An Economic Analysis, 12 Fordham Urb. L.J. 405 (1984); Deutsch, Antitrust Challenges to Local Zoning and Other Land Use Controls, 60 Chi. Kent L. Rev. 63 (1984); Jacobs, Antitrust and the Public Defendant: Application of the Antitrust Laws to Governmental Entities, 9 U. Dayton L. Rev. 451 (1984); Freilich, Donovan, and Ralls, Antitrust Liability and Preemption of Authority, 15 Urb. Law. 705 (1983); and Witt, Antitrust Law and the *Boulder* Case: New Threat to the Planning and Zoning Process, 1983 Inst. on Plan. Zoning & Eminent Domain 75.

Lobbying by officials of cities, counties, and other political subdivisions (primarily through their trade organizations) intensified after a federal district court in Illinois entered judgment against local government defendants in the amount of $28,500,000 (trebling plaintiffs' $9,500,000 claim). Unity Ventures v. County of Lake, No. 81C 2745 (N.D. Ill. Jan. 12, 1984). See Developer's Suit Against Localities Nets $28.5 Million Treble Damage Award, 46 Antitrust & Trade Reg. Rep. (BNA) 595 (No. 1157, Mar. 22, 1984). In testimony before the Senate Judiciary Committee, for example, William J. Althaus, Mayor of York, Pennsylvania (on behalf of the United States Conference of Mayors), observed: "Local governments throughout the United States are trembling in fear and uncertainty over this issue. The *Unity Ventures, Grayslake* case has served to move local officials up a notch or two on the Richter Scale."

Congress responded just before adjourning for the 1984 elections with the Local Government Antitrust Act of 1984, Pub. L. No. 98-544, 98 Stat. 2750 (1984) (codified at 15 U.S.C.A. §§35, 36 (West Supp. 1987)). The Act shields "any local government, official or employee thereof acting in an official capacity" from "damages, interest on damages, costs, or attorney's fees" recoverable under the treble damages provisions of the Clayton Act (15 U.S.C. §§15, 15a, 15c). Nor can such relief be recovered "against a person based on any official action directed by a local government, or official or employee thereof acting in an official capacity." While the major financial threat was thus lifted, Congress left undisturbed injunctive relief (and corresponding attorney's fees for prevailing parties), as well as the right to proceed against government officials not acting in their official capacities.

8. Meanwhile, the case responsible for much of the panic preceding this congressional rescue was still before the judge on motions for j.n.o.v. and a new trial. On March 19, 1986, District Judge Bua announced an opinion that addressed two key issues that had arisen since the alarming jury verdict in 1984: the retroactive effect of the Local Government Antitrust Act and the implications of the Supreme Court's decision in Town of Hallie v. City of Eau Claire, 471 U.S. 34

(1985), in which the Justices considered the meaning of "clearly articulated state policy," as used in *Lafayette* and *Boulder*:

> In this case, which has progressed beyond a jury verdict, Congress has placed the burden of proof on the defendants to show "compelling equities." The defendants must rebut the prima facie evidence that the Act shall not apply. They have failed to meet this burden. . . .
>
> The jury verdict for this case was rendered in January 1984, long before this Act was passed. The verdict will stand because the defendants have failed to meet their burden of proving that compelling equities necessitate the retroactive application of the Act. . . .
>
> In *Town of Hallie*, four towns surrounding the City of Eau Claire alleged that the City conditioned the provision of sewage treatment, over which it had a monopoly, upon a property owner's agreement to annex his property to the City. The towns alleged that this condition constituted a tying arrangement in violation of the Sherman Act. The Supreme Court affirmed the dismissal of the towns' claim, holding that the City of Eau Claire's actions reflected a "clearly articulated and affirmatively expressed" state policy to permit municipalities to condition the provision of sewage treatment upon an agreement to annex.
>
> *Town of Hallie* established that, to pass the "clear articulation" test, a state statute must "clearly contemplate that a city may engage in anticompetitive conduct." The legislature, however, need not expressly have stated in either a statute or its legislative history that it intended for the action to have anticompetitive effects. . . .
>
> . . . [T]he agreement here was entered into for the purpose of allocating sewage connections between individual municipalities in Lake County and the County itself. The municipalities stopped using their individual treatment plants and agreed to have all of their sewage treated by the County through a series of Interceptors to be built by the County. The goal of these agreements was to provide uniform sewage treatment for the entire County. In exchange, the municipalities received a right to determine which users outside of their boundaries would receive sewage treatment service under the new County-wide system. . . .
>
> . . . [T]he Illinois legislature intended that the cooperative agreement between Grayslake and Lake County not be the subject of federal antitrust suits since anticompetitive effects are clearly foreseeable under the legislative scheme for sewage treatment. Accordingly, the Court holds that the doctrine of state action immunity under the antitrust laws applies here to the local government's alleged violative conduct. Since the state action doctrine under Parker v. Brown, 317 U.S. 341 (1943) applies, the jury's verdict and award for the federal antitrust action must be vacated and the action dismissed.

Unity Ventures v. County of Lake, 631 F. Supp. 181 (N.D. Ill. 1986), aff'd, 841 F.2d 770 (7th Cir. 1988).

9. The Supreme Court's most recent offering, a rebuff to a challenge brought against Berkeley, California's stringent rent control ordinance, demonstrated the Justices' difficulty in designing a frame-

B. Anticompetitiveness

work for applying rules designed to redress private conspiracy and monopoly to public entities engaged in an expanding range of activities. In Fisher v. City of Berkeley, 475 U.S. 260 (1986), Justice Marshall, writing for the majority, never reached the immunity issue, "find[ing] traditional antitrust analysis adequate to resolve the issue presented here." The Court found that the rent control scheme constituted unilateral action beyond the scope of §1 of the Sherman Act, noting that "owners of residential property in Berkeley have no more freedom to resist the city's rent controls than they do to violate any other local ordinance enforced by substantial sanctions." How would this logic affect a claim brought by a disgruntled landowner denied development rights by local decision-makers? Note, however, that evidence of corruption — for example, competing developers making rezoning decisions rubber-stamped by government officials — might warrant antitrust protection ("there may be cases in which what appears to be a state- or municipality-administered price stabilization scheme is really a private price-fixing conspiracy").

Justice Brennan dissented: "Ultimately, the Court is holding that a municipality's authority to protect the public welfare should not be constrained by the Sherman Act. That holding excludes a broad range of local government anticompetitive activities from the reach of antitrust laws. This flies in the face of the fact that Congress has not enacted such a broad antitrust exemption for municipalities" (citing *Boulder*, *Lafayette*, and the Local Government Antitrust Act). One commentator has labeled Brennan "profoundly skeptical of the legitimacy of municipal decision-making," citing his reiteration from *Boulder* that the American system of government "'has no place for sovereign cities.'" Payne, Supreme Court Narrows Municipal Antitrust Liability, 15 Real Est. L.J. 161, 163-164 (1986). For a fuller exploration of Justice Brennan's views in the crucial area of local governance, see Haar & Kayden, Landmark Justice (1989).

10. Because the Court and Congress have not completely sheltered municipalities from antitrust actions, we will continue to see claims of conspiracy and monopoly joined with allegations of due process and civil rights violations in the briefs prepared for plaintiffs negatively affected by governmental decisions concerning the use and enjoyment of land. For discussions of the appropriateness of antitrust sanctions for otherwise-protected public regulation, see Hovekamp and Mackerron, Municipal Regulation and Federal Antitrust Policy, 32 UCLA L. Rev. 719, 782-783 (1985) ("'state action' exemption subverts federal antitrust policy by permitting states to determine where and how much they want to regulate"; "'state action' doctrine demeans the municipality by ignoring the established division of regulatory power between each state and its own governmental subdivisions"); Deutsch, Antitrust Challenges to Local Zoning and Other Land Use Controls, 60 Chi. Kent L. Rev. 63, 87-88 (1984) (antitrust laws should apply only when "local

governments act as developers, or at least as partners of developers," and in the event of "corruption, improper influence for the benefit of private individuals, and official's self-dealing").

C. URBAN DESIGN

> [T]he coming of one apartment house is followed by others, interfering by their height and bulk with the free circulation of air and monopolizing the rays of the sun which otherwise would fall upon the smaller homes, and bringing, as their necessary accompaniments, the disturbing noises incident to increased traffic and business, and the occupation, by means of moving and parked automobiles, of larger portions of the streets, thus detracting from their safety and depriving children of the privilege of quiet and open spaces for play, enjoyed by those in more favored localities, — until, finally, the residential character of the neighborhood and its desirability as a place of detached residences are utterly destroyed.
>
> — *Euclid v. Ambler*, 272 U.S. at 394

One of the most striking departures from "established principles" that land-use law has taken of late is the patent acknowledgment of aesthetics as a legitimate goal of the state's police power, either independently or as part of the amorphous concept labeled "general welfare." While some earlier federal and state court decisions had allowed aesthetic regulation in through the back door — for example, by acknowledging the traffic hazards of disturbing signs[50] or the economic benefit of preserving natural beauty[51] — more recent jurists have taken Justice William Douglas's language in Berman v. Parker, infra page 788, as authority for justifying regulations solely on the basis of such subjective qualities as beauty and historical worth: "It is within the power of the legislature to determine that the community should be beautiful as well as healthy, spacious as well as clean." In the spirit of *Berman*, New York City's landmark preservation program was approved in *Penn Central*, infra page 537, and Detroit's anti-combat zone ordinance passed constitutional muster in Young v. American Mini Theatres, Inc., supra page 478.

Precedent for such an expansive understanding of the breadth of the police power can be located in the lines from *Euclid* that introduce

---

50. See, e.g., Railway Express Agency v. New York, 336 U.S. 106 (1949) (state regulation of advertising vehicles survived equal protection challenge).
51. See, e.g., City of Miami Beach v. Ocean & Inland Co., 147 Fla. 549, 3 So. 2d 364 (1941) (resort city's restrictive zoning ordinance upheld).

C. Urban Design

this section. Sutherland's language is sprinkled with the buzzwords of 1980s litigation and legislation. The preservation of open space mandated by statute in California[52] and the judicial acceptance of subdivision exactions in the form of parks and other recreational facilities[53] are not too far removed from "the privilege of quiet and open spaces to play" recognized in *Euclid*. The enhanced appreciation of sunlight as an important energy source in the Wisconsin suburb in Prah v. Maretti, supra page 130, and as a precious urban amenity in the nation's crowded downtowns (whose planners are seeking to avoid the dark canyons of Manhattan), are 1980s efforts to combat "monopolizing the rays of the sun."

Some official denials to the contrary, aesthetic sensibility was an important component of height, area, and use zoning. For every planner who attempted to promote his or her profession on the basis of "The Sheer Cost of Ugliness" (the title of an address to the Sixteenth National Conference on City Planning, in 1924),[54] there was the simple assertion that beauty was good in and of itself:

> The object of the City Planning Conference [of 1926], as I understand it, is not only to promote cities and towns which shall be more convenient for business and for traffic, but also to promote cities and towns which shall be more beautiful places in which to live. . . . We must consider for our children not only plenty of air and plenty of light and playgrounds, but we must consider also beautiful surroundings in which they shall grow up.[55]

The speaker was Mrs. W. L. Lawton of Glens Falls, New York, in 1926 the Chairman of the National Committee for Restriction of Outdoor Advertising.

Ambler counsel Newton D. Baker summarized the point in an argument designed to contrast such unsupportable subjectivity with the mighty demands made by the due process clause, as expansively interpreted by the Four Horsemen: "Even if the world could agree by unanimous consent upon what is beautiful and desirable, it could not, under our constitutional theory, enforce its decision by prohibiting a land owner, who refuses to accept the world's view of beauty, from making otherwise safe and innocent uses of his land."[56] This carefully

---

52. Cal. Govt. Code §§65560-65570 (West 1983).
53. See, e.g., Associated Home Builders of the Greater East Bay, Inc. v. City of Walnut Creek, 4 Cal. 3d 633, 484 P.2d 606, 94 Cal. Rptr. 630 (1971).
54. Crawford, The Sheer Cost of Ugliness, in Proceedings of the Sixteenth National Conference on City Planning 141 (1924).
55. Lawton, Regulation of Outdoor Advertising, in Planning Problems of Town, City and Region: Papers and Discussions at the Eighteenth National Conference on City Planning 86, 86 (1926). — Eds.
56. *Euclid v. Ambler*, 272 U.S. at 376 (argument for appellee).

crafted appeal, complete with references to Justice Thomas M. Cooley (one of the important influences on Sutherland's jurisprudence),[57] missed the mark, although Baker's specific reference to the inherent subjectivity of aesthetic regulation remained a popular objection for decades to come.

The past few years have witnessed a new appreciation of the potential benefit and harm, in economic and psychological terms, posed by the appearance of the urban and suburban landscape. This appreciation, coupled with the judiciary's acceptance of the findings and recommendations of experts in architecture and historic preservation, has led in some cases to the patent abandonment of common law rules outlawing regulation based on arbitrary and subjective tastes. Consider whether this belief in expertise is well founded. Are the takings clause and the limits on the police power enough to check the most zealous architectural board? Is it likely that one day we will point with pride to the flowering of aesthetics as a symbol of the new cultural awareness of our generation, and to the acceptance, without a grimace, of beauty and urban design in legislation and judicial opinions?

■ SCENIC HUDSON PRESERVATION CONFERENCE v. FEDERAL POWER COMMISSION
354 F.2d 608 (2d Cir. 1965), cert. denied, 384 U.S. 941 (1966)

HAYS, C. J.: In this proceeding the petitioners are the Scenic Hudson Preservation Conference, an unincorporated association consisting of a number of nonprofit, conservationist organizations, and the Towns of Cortlandt, Putnam Valley and Yorktown. Petitioners ask us, pursuant to 313(b) of the Federal Power Act, 16 U.S.C. 825*l* (b), to set aside three orders of the respondent, the Federal Power Commission. . . .

A pumped storage plant generates electric energy for use during peak load periods, using hydroelectric units driven by water from a headwater pool or reservoir. The contemplated Storm King project would be the largest of its kind in the world. Consolidated Edison has estimated its cost, including transmission facilities, at $162,000,000. The project would consist of three major components, a storage reservoir, a powerhouse, and transmission lines. The storage reservoir, located over a thousand feet above the powerhouse, is to be connected to the powerhouse, located on the river front, by a tunnel 40 feet in diameter. The powerhouse, which is both a pumping and generating station, would be 800 feet long and contain eight pump generators.

---

57. See Paschal, Mr. Justice Sutherland: A Man Against the State 16-20 (1951).

C. Urban Design

Transmission lines would run under the Hudson to the east bank and then underground for 1.6 miles to a switching station. . . . Thereafter, overhead transmission lines would be placed on towers 100 to 150 feet high and these would require a path up to 125 feet wide through Westchester and Putnam Counties for a distance of some 25 miles until they reached Consolidated Edison's main connection with New York City. . . .

Section 10(a) of the Federal Power Act, 16 U.S.C. 803(a), reads:

Section 803. Conditions of license generally.

All licenses issued under sections 792, 793, 795-818, and 820-823 of this title shall be on the following conditions: . . .

(a) That the project adopted, . . . shall be such as in the judgment of the Commission *will be best adapted to a comprehensive plan for improving or developing a waterway or waterways for the use or benefit of interstate or foreign commerce, for the improvement and utilization of water-power development, and for other beneficial public uses, including recreational purposes*; and if necessary in order to secure such plan the Commission shall have authority to require the modification of any project and of the plans and specifications of the project works before approval. (Emphasis added.)

"Recreational purposes" are expressly included among the beneficial public uses to which the statute refers. The phrase undoubtedly encompasses the conservation of historic sites. . . .

In recent years the Commission has placed increasing emphasis on the right of the public to "out-door recreational resources." 1964 F.P.C. Report 69. Regulations issued in 1963, for the first time, required the inclusion of a recreation plan as part of a license application. F.P.C. Order No. 260-A, amending Sec. 4.41 of Regulations under Federal Power Act, issued April 18, 1963, 29 F.P.C. 777, 28 Fed. Reg. 4092. The Commission has recognized generally that members of the public have rights in our recreational, historic and scenic resources under the Federal Power Act. Namekagon Hydro Co., 12 F.P.C. 203, 206 (1954) ("the Commission realizes that in many cases where unique and most special types of recreation are encountered a dollar evaluation is inadequate as the public interest must be considered and it cannot be evaluated adequately in dollars and cents"). In affirming Namekagon the Seventh Circuit upheld the Commission's denial of a license, to an otherwise economically feasible project, because fishing, canoeing and the scenic attraction of a "beautiful stretch of water" were threatened. Namekagon Hydro Co. v. Federal Power Comm'n, 216 F.2d 509, 511-512 (7th Cir. 1954). . . .

The Federal Power Commission argues that having intervened "petitioners cannot impose an affirmative burden on the Commission."

But, as we have pointed out, Congress gave the Federal Power Commission a specific planning responsibility. See Federal Power Act Section 10(a), 16 U.S.C. 803(a). The totality of a project's immediate and long-range effects, and not merely the engineering and navigation aspects, are to be considered in a licensing proceeding. . . .

In this case, as in many others, the Commission has claimed to be the representative of the public interest. This role does not permit it to act as an umpire blandly calling balls and strikes for adversaries appearing before it; the right of the public must receive active and affirmative protection at the hands of the Commission. . . .

The Commission should reexamine all questions on which we have found the record insufficient and all related matters. The Commission's renewed proceedings must include as a basic concern the preservation of natural beauty and of national historic shrines, keeping in mind that, in our affluent society, the cost of a project is only one of several factors to be considered. The record as it comes to us fails markedly to make out a case for the Storm King project on, among other matters, costs, public convenience and necessity, and absence of reasonable alternatives. Of course, the Commission should make every effort to expedite the new proceedings.

Petitioners' application, pursuant to Federal Power Act 313(b), 16 U.S.C. 825*l* (b), to adduce additional evidence concerning alternatives to the Storm King project and the cost and practicality of underground transmission facilities is granted.

The licensing order of March 9 and the two orders of May 6 are set aside, and the case remanded for further proceedings.[58]

■ SCENIC HUDSON PRESERVATION CONFERENCE v. FEDERAL POWER COMMISSION
453 F.2d 463 (2d Cir. 1971)

OAKES, C. J. (dissenting). . . .

The final matters which, to my mind, tip the scales for a reversal

---

58. Testifying as to the existence and measurement of natural beauty and bouncing it against other considerations (aside from introducing these ephemeral subjects to a harassed trial court) raises the issue of admissibility of expert testimony on the matter directly in question, much as does the problem of whether a zoning ordinance is in accordance with a comprehensive plan. There is also the barrier of the traditional rule concerning expert evidence on matters of common knowledge. Special considerations in the preparation of the testimony of experts in environmental litigation are discussed by Sive, Securing, Examining and Cross-examining Expert Witnesses in Environmental Cases, Law and the Environment 48 (Baldwin & Page eds. 1970). He describes one interesting response to a question put to a planner of the Storm King project. "Q: Have you ever in your experience found an area which you decided was so beautiful that you didn't think that you could improve it? A: Personally I think practically anything can be improved. In my past experience I have not had any area which wasn't improved or something like that." See also Sive, Some Thoughts of an Environmental Lawyer in the Wilderness of Administrative Law, 70 Colum. L. Rev. 612 (1970). — EDS.

C. Urban Design

rather than simply a reversal and remand are two. The first concerns what may broadly be called aesthetics, impairment by the project of the mountain's scenic grandeur. The commission's Finding 148 refers to the mountain "swallow[ing]" the "scar of the highway, the intrusive railroad structure and fills and tolerat[ing] both the barges and scows which pass by it and the thoughtless humans [sic] who visit it without seeing it...." The finding goes on to say that just as the mountain swallows present day intrusions, "it will swallow the structures which will serve the needs of people for electric power." This argument borders on the outrageous; it can be used to justify every intrusion on nature from strip mining to ocean oil spills, viz., "the Santa Barbara coastline already has an ocean-side highway, numerous offshore oil rigs, and a lot of flotsam and jetsam comes on to the beaches, etc...." Two scenic wrongs do not necessarily make a right. On the basis of the commission's thesis, wherever you have one billboard you can put two, wherever you have one overhead transmission line you can put another, you can add blight to blight to blight. That a responsible federal agency should advance that proposition in the form of a finding and in the teeth of the NEPA seems to me shocking. The commission's finding overlooks the fact that we are considering here a power station which above ground will consist of a concrete tailrace with abutments 32 feet high and 685 feet long, cutting back existing shore line from 195 to 260 feet, exclusive of any access road. This location, as the commission concedes, is on a small riverbottom foothill which "is visually a part of Storm King Mountain...." The mountain may "swallow" the project, but the concrete tailrace and abutments, as long as a good-sized football stadium — over an eighth of a mile — and three stories high, will surely be stuck in its craw.[59]

59. Examples are increasing of far-reaching state legislation to protect the recreational and aesthetic values of very large areas, such as the Adirondack Park Agency Act, ch. 348 of Laws of New York 1973. See Leighty, Aesthetics as a Legal Basis for Environmental Control, 17 Wayne L. Rev. 1347 (1971), and Horn, Questions Concerning the Proposed Private Land Use and Development Plan for the Adirondack Park, 24 Syracuse L. Rev. 989 (1973). A striking concatenation of legal powers for environmental ends is analyzed in Gifford, An Islands Trust: Leading Edges in Land Use Laws, 11 Harv. J. Legis. 417 (1974). State scenic rivers legislation has been passed in response to the Wild and Scenic Rivers Act of 1968, 16 U.S.C. §§1271-1287. Additions to the federal system must either be approved by Congress or requested by the governor of a state and approved by the Secretary of the Interior, and the amount of riparian land which may be acquired in fee by the federal government is limited. Once a river is designated a scenic river, however, all agencies of the United States are forbidden to assist by "loan, grant, license, or otherwise in the construction of any water resources project that would have a direct and adverse effect on the values for which said river was established, as determined by the Secretary charged with its administration" (§1278). How effectively will such a prohibition inhibit development? Is it necessary for the state to acquire an "easement" from the owner to prevent development, considering the impact of this provision? Does denial of a "loan, grant, license" constitute a taking without just compensation if it effectively prevents development of an owner's riparian land for other than agricultural uses? The Tennessee Scenic Rivers Act provides in §11-13-103 that Class III river areas shall be "subject to public control by zoning, tax incentives, acquisition of easements of fee title

Notes

1. See Talbot, Settling Things: Six Case Studies in Environmental Mediation 8-11, 24 (1983):

> In subsequent years, as the FPC reconsidered Consolidated Edison's licensing bid, the issues surrounding Storm King came to involve more than the scenic impact of an immense power station constructed at the base of the mountain. And, among all of the legal, economic, and environmental questions raised by opponents, none proved to be as complicated and as intriguing as the impact of the plant on the fish in the Hudson River. The opponents' charge that the plant would kill striped bass and other species attracted attention, at least in part, because many people had been previously unaware that there were still fish in the river. . . .
>
> Less obvious, but in the view of many fish biologists far more serious, was the entrainment of young fish and of fish eggs into plant cooling systems. Opponents of the Indian Point nuclear units likened the cooling systems to giant predators that, over time, would drain, mash, and suffocate all aquatic life from the Hudson River. . . .
>
> After reviewing the existing fish studies and retaining its own experts, the EPA staff concluded that cooling towers were the only way to assure that the plants would not do irreparable damage to the Hudson River. . . .
>
> . . . Environmental groups had a mixed reaction to the EPA decision. Some saw the EPA's call for cooling towers as a victory, assuming that their cost might make at least some of the plants unprofitable and thus not worth building. Others began wondering what scenic impact the cooling towers would have should EPA prevail and the utilities be forced to build them. Cooling towers, the environmental groups knew, are immense structures that can measure 550 feet in diameter and 600 feet in height. One cooling tower would rival the scenic intrusion of the proposed Storm King powerhouse that had first provoked environmental concern on the Hudson River in 1964. Now, in 1975, EPA was requiring that six cooling towers be constructed within one 25-mile stretch of the river. Thus, the prospect of cooling towers was not welcomed by Scenic Hudson's original supporters. But sport fishermen, who had previously supported the Scenic Hudson's campaign, now seemed ready to support the towers if that were the only way to protect the fish.
>
> Between the spring of 1975 and early 1977 the great cooling tower controversy disappeared from public view as the utilities and the EPA prepared their respective cases for a hearing examiner. . . .

---

and other means sufficient to realize the purpose for which such river is designated a state scenic river." Distinguish regulating land uses under the police power to protect aesthetic values in a wilderness area with such regulation along an urban highway. Along a river? An entire forest or a single lot? Suppose all government agencies were required to deny "loans, grants, licenses" to businesses which use advertising signs above a specified size; would this be as effective as zoning? — Eds.

C. Urban Design 525

[From 1977 through 1980 the utility companies, EPA, environmental groups, state agencies, and others fought in court, in administrative hearings, and in the press. After nearly fourteen years of adversarial struggles, the parties moved toward a negotiated settlement in 1979, and settled on Russell Train, former EPA Administrator, as a mediator. The mediation sessions that followed were drawn out and highly technical.]

The war on the Hudson ended with Consolidated Edison's agreement to forfeit its Storm King license and to turn the site over to the Palisades Interstate Park Commission. Consolidated Edison and the other utilities promised that they would reduce their plants' water withdrawals through plant outages from May to July for a period of 10 years. They also promised a fish hatchery, new water intakes at Indian Point, a $12 million endowment for a research organization, the reimbursement of legal costs to the environmental groups, and a 25-year moratorium on any new power plants without cooling towers north of the George Washington Bridge. In return, the cooling tower requirements at Indian Point, Roseton, and Bowline were dropped; all litigation and administrative proceedings among the parties ceased; and the environmental groups actively supported the agreement, and its costs, before regulatory agencies.

2. In 1969, the Congress passed the National Environmental Policy Act (see supra page 33), a combination of statement of national environmental policy and statutory scheme to ensure implementation of that policy by all agencies of the federal government. The congressional recognition of the impact of human activity in producing "population growth, high density urbanization, industrial expansion, resource exploitation" obviously has significant implications for the land-use planner. *All* agencies of the federal government are brought under the sweeping mandate of the act. A "systematic, interdisciplinary approach" is directed in the planning and decision-making process. Note particularly the requirement of §102(2)(C) for a "detailed statement by the responsible official," the so-called environmental impact statement (EIS).

What does, or should, the term "environmental impact" include? Clearly air, water, and noise pollution, and probably the effects on plant and animal life, but what about the social, economic, aesthetic, and cultural effects on the residents of a city in the vicinity of a proposed high-rise office building? Or the various effects of the construction of a penal facility in a suburban community? Are "quality of life" effects environmental impacts of the kind contemplated by NEPA? If environmental amenities and values are "presently unquantified," is there an implication that the federal agencies should set about the quantification process? If environmental amenities are not, or cannot be, quantified, how then is the planner supposed to give them "appropriate consideration" in decision-making? See Hagman, NEPA's Progeny Inhabit the States — Were the Genes Defective?, 7 Urb. L. Ann. 3 (1974).

In Ely v. Velde, 451 F.2d 1130 (4th Cir. 1971), an action was brought by residents of a rural community of alleged historical and architectural significance to enjoin construction of a penal facility in the area. The court borrowed a description of the community from the opinion of the district court:

> Green Springs is an area of land consisting of approximately 10,000 acres located in the Western part of Louisa County. It is a uniquely historical and architecturally significant rural community in that almost all of the homes were built in the nineteenth century and have been maintained in substantially the same condition ever since. Three of the homes, Boswell's Tavern, Hawkwood and Westend, are on the National Register for Historic Places, as provided in [NHPA].

451 F.2d at 1133-1134. The court noted that not only were the soil and water requirements of the project not taken into account, but neither were the environmental or cultural factors, and then went on to hold that an EIS would have to be prepared before the project could proceed. Here again the court carefully refused to reach the merits of the issue of the placement of the facility. And if the procedural requirements of NEPA are met — in this case the preparation of a sufficient EIS by the agency involved — it appears that the merits of this land-use decision would never be reached in federal court.

In Hanley v. Mitchell, 460 F.2d 640 (2d Cir. 1972), the federal agency argued that the construction of a prison facility and an adjacent federal office building in lower Manhattan would not significantly affect the quality of the human environment. The thrust of the government case was that since the area already contained many government buildings, including several courthouses, further construction of the same type would not adversely affect the 50,000 people who lived in the area and in adjacent Chinatown. The court, after echoing the now-familiar disclaimer that only the issue of compliance with the procedural aspects of NEPA was before them, took the agency to task for not considering the environmental impact of constructing a jail across the street from two large apartment houses. The neighborhood fears of "riots and disturbances" as well as the possible traffic and parking problems generated were among the factors the court said should have been considered:

> [NEPA] contains no exhaustive list of so-called "environmental considerations," but without question its aims extend beyond sewage and water and even beyond air pollution. The Act must be construed to include protection of the quality of life for city residents. Noise, traffic, overburdened mass transportation systems, crime, congestion and even availability of drugs all affect the urban "environment" and are surely results of the

C. Urban Design

"profound influences of . . . high-density urbanization [and] industrial expansion" [citing §101(a) of NEPA].

460 F.2d at 646-647.

■ LUTHERAN CHURCH IN AMERICA v. CITY OF NEW YORK
35 N.Y.2d 121, 316 N.E.2d 305, 359 N.Y.S.2d 7 (1974)

GABRIELLI, Judge. . . .

. . . By amendment to the New York City Charter and Administrative Code (ch. 8-A) the Landmarks Preservation Commission was created and given the power to designate historic districts and also to designate individual properties as historic landmarks. We are here concerned with the latter aspect. Based on the statutory scheme, designations can be made after notice and a public hearing (Administrative Code of City of New York, ch. 8-A, §207-2.0, subds. a, c; §207-12.0), but in determining whether or not to make the contemplated designation "the commission . . . shall not be confined to consideration of the facts, views, testimony or evidence submitted at such hearing." (§207-12.0, subd. b.) Should the owner of a building which has been designated a landmark desire to alter or demolish it, application may be made to the commission for such permission (§207-5.0, subd. a) which quite probably would not be forthcoming in cases where demolition is sought. It is further provided that the owner is expected to realize at least a 6% return on his property (§207-1.0, subd. q) and if he proves economic hardship by the fact of a lesser return the commission is given discretion to ease the hardship by effectuating a real estate tax rebate (§207-8.0, subd. c), or the commission is afforded the additional right of producing a buyer or lessee who could profitably utilize the premises without the sought-for alteration or demolition (§207-8.0, subd. a, par. [2]; subd. i); and then, should these remedies prove unrealistic or unobtainable the city, if it desires the preservation of the property enough, is given the power to condemn (§207-8.0, subd. g, par. [2]).

Plaintiff, a religious corporation, not subject to the ameliorative provisions of section 207-8.0 just noted, alleged in its complaint that it is the owner of certain land at the corner of Madison Avenue and 37th Street in New York City, improved with a residential building which had been previously converted to use for offices for plaintiff's corporate-religious purposes. The property was purchased in 1942 by plaintiff's predecessor, The United Lutheran Church in America, it having been used since its construction in 1853 until that time as a residence. In November, 1965 the commission designated plaintiff's building a "landmark", the consequence of which is that by reason of the Landmarks

Law plaintiff could not alter or destroy the structure without the commission's approval. The structure involved, not included as a part of any landmark district, is situated in midtown Manhattan surrounded by a variety of structures including modern multistory office, apartment and other commercial structures. It appears undisputed that plaintiff's office space requirements increased to such an extent that, even with the addition of a brick wing in 1958, the building became totally inadequate. In addition, prior to the enactment of the Landmarks Law plaintiff had engaged an architect who had prepared sketches of a new building to be erected upon demolition of the existing building and these sketches had been presented to plaintiff during the summer of 1965. ...

In response to these causes of action, the answer submitted by the city and the commission states generally a lack of knowledge or information sufficient to form a belief concerning most of plaintiff's factual allegations. Then, as a "defense", it is alleged that the subject property is zoned residential; that an exhaustive study was made of the subject building which had been the home of J. P. Morgan, Jr.; that a public hearing was held on the question in September, 1965 notice of which was received by plaintiff which, in fact, appeared through counsel who spoke against the designation; and that the commission, after considering all the evidence, found that the property has importance "because it was the residence of J. P. Morgan, Jr. during the first half of the twentieth century, that the house is significant as an early example of Anglo-Italianate architecture, that it is one of the few free standing Brownstones remaining in the City, that it displays an impressive amount of fine architectural detail and that it is a handsome building of great dignity." ...

What do we have in the case before us where title remains in private hands and where the government regulation which severely restricts the use to which the property may be put is neither in pursuance of a general zoning plan, nor invoked to curtail noxious use?

A zoning ordinance in order to be validly applied cannot, for one thing, serve to prohibit use to which the property is devoted at the time of the enactment of the ordinance (see 1 Anderson, New York Zoning Law and Practice [2 ed.], §6.01 et seq.). Here, plaintiff has submitted ample proof not seriously contested, that the use to which the property has been put for over 20 years would have to cease because of the inability under the designation to replace the building. Also, and of chief importance, zoning is void if confiscatory. ...

In the instant case it could ... be well argued that the commission has added the Morgan house to the resources of the city by the designation (it being argued, inter alia, that the house, as a tourist attraction because of its designation, aids the city generally), and that while such designations might not wreak confiscatory results in all

C. Urban Design

situations (as where business might well be promoted by the designation) it does have that effect here where plaintiff is deprived of the reasonable use of its land. . . .

The decision in Matter of Trustees of Sailors' Snug Harbor v. Platt, 29 A.D.2d 376, 288 N.Y.S.2d 314, although inconclusive on the question of confiscation since further facts had to be developed, is correct in refusing to declare the entire law unconstitutional on its face. The question posed there was whether in that instance regulation went too far. The buildings there sought to be preserved had become inadequate for their charitable purpose and were to be replaced. The Appellate Division ruled that where designation would prevent or seriously interfere with the carrying out of the charitable purpose it would be invalid. That is a simple enough concept and ought to apply here. . . .

As noted in the dissent, the statutory scheme (virtually all of §207-8.0), providing for alternate proposals and perhaps ultimate condemnations in cases where economic return is insufficient or where there is no wish by the owner to sell or lease the property, is not applicable here. Plaintiff is a charitable organization and not otherwise subject to the various administrative alternatives set up in section 207-8.0 which could result in condemnation of the property sought to be altered or demolished. We save for another day consideration of those provisions where sought to be applied. What has occurred here, however, where the commission is attempting to force plaintiff to retain its property as is, without any sort of relief or adequate compensation, is nothing short of a naked taking. As in [Morris County Land Improvement Co. v. Township of Parsippany-Troy Hills] (40 N.J. 539, 193, A.2d 232), the commission, without any move toward invoking the power of eminent domain, is attempting to add this property to the public use by purely and simply invading the owner's right to own and manage. Legitimate zoning stops far short of this because it does not appropriate to public use. Where the owner can make a case for alteration or demolition the municipality would have to relinquish the designation, provide agreeable alternatives or condemn the premises.

Such a case has been alleged and proved here, contrary to assertions in the dissent, and stands substantially unrebutted by the defendants. It is uncontested that the existing building is totally inadequate for the plaintiff's legitimate needs and must be replaced if plaintiff is to be able freely and economically to use the premises especially as it appears that adjoining structures have been integrated with plaintiff's operation. The power given the municipality to force termination of plaintiff's free use of the premises short of condemnation (which would provide compensation for plaintiff's complete loss) directly violates plaintiff's rights under the Fifth and Fourteenth Amendments to the United States Constitution, and sections 6 and 7 of article I of the New York Constitution. As in Vernon Park Realty v. City of Mount Vernon, 307

N.Y. 493, 121 N.E.2d 517, we find a situation exceeding the permissible limits of the zoning power.

The order appealed from should be modified, with costs, to the extent that the landmark designation as here applied is declared to be confiscatory.

JASEN, Judge (dissenting).

I dissent and vote to reverse the order of the Appellate Division and to uphold the designation of the Morgan Mansion as a city landmark. . . .

The historic preservation movement in the United States began in 1850 when the State of New York acquired the Hasbrouck House, General Washington's Revolutionary War headquarters at Newburgh. Since then, however, many cherished buildings, essential parts of the Nation's architectural and cultural heritage, have fallen before the wrecker's ball. Indeed, more than 50% of the 12,000 buildings listed in the Historic American Building Survey, commenced in 1933 by the Federal Government, have since been razed. (See Conti, Preserving the Past, Wall St. J., Aug. 8, 1970, p. 1, col. 1.) As is well illustrated here, the situation is most critical in urban areas where the forces that produce physical change are most dynamic. Urban landmarks typically do not exhaust the building potential of their location and may be designed for uses different from neighboring buildings. As urban concentration increases, the demands for additional housing and commercial space become all the more incessant and sharpen the debate whether the value of historic preservation counterbalances whatever limitation may thereby be imposed on urban growth. For many reasons, widespread public ownership of historic property is simply not feasible. Historic property may be expensive to acquire and maintain and in public ownership would quite likely be removed from economically productive uses, thereby reducing the community tax base. Economic considerations alone suggest the desirability of providing standards, controls and incentives to encourage private owners to preserve their historic properties for use in economically productive enterprises.

The City of New York has responded to this challenge with a thoughtful and comprehensive statutory scheme. Enacted in 1965 pursuant to the State enabling legislation (New York State Historic Preservation Act of 1956 [former General City Law, §20(25-a), Consol. Laws, ch. 21, L. 1956, ch. 216]), the Landmarks Preservation Law seeks to preserve improvements and districts of especial historical, cultural or architectural significance of the life of the city.[4] . . . However, there

---

4. Typically, this law leans heavily on economic reasons for its justification as a valid exercise of the police power. But while economics is perhaps inextricably intertwined with such legislation, in the main the purposes sought to be achieved are aesthetic. Historic preservation promotes aesthetic values by adding to the variety, the beauty and the quality

C. Urban Design

is no express provision governing the instant situation where the charitable owner does not wish to sell or lease his property, but claims it is unsuited for his purposes and cannot obtain commission approval for his proposal to alter or demolish the structure. Before undertaking adjudication of the constitutionality of the Landmarks Preservation Law as applied to this type of situation, we should have the benefit of a full exposition of all factual issues with express findings made in the courts below. . . .

BREITEL, C.J., concurs in the dissent.[60]

Notes

1. The traditional formula is that while aesthetic goals will count as an additional legislative purpose, if health, safety, morals, or other ends traditionally associated with "public welfare" are being served, they cannot be the only purpose of regulation. See, e.g., Baltimore v. Swartz, Inc., 268 Md. 79, 299 A.2d 828 (1973). In other words, that the ordinance reflects a desire to attain aesthetic ends does not invalidate an otherwise valid ordinance. E.g., Naegele Outdoor Advertising Co. v. Minnetonka, 281 Minn. 492, 162 N.W.2d 206 (1968). With the desire to eliminate visual pollution, some jurisdictions began to uphold regulatory schemes primarily or solely aesthetic in purpose. E.g., Stone v. City of Maitland, 446 F.2d 83 (5th Cir. 1971). People v. Goodman, 31 N.Y.2d 262, 267, 290 N.E.2d 140, 144, 338 N.Y.S.2d 97, 101 (1972), dealt with a drugstore sign within the Fire Island National Seashore: "To be sure, not every artistic conformity or non-conformity is within

---

of life. Perhaps it is time that aesthetics took its place as a zoning end *independently* cognizable under the police power for "a high civilization must . . . give full value and support to the . . . great branches of man's scholarly and cultural activity in order to achieve a better understanding of the past, a better analysis of the present, and a better view of the future". (National Foundation on the Arts and Humanities Act of 1965, U.S. Code, tit. 20, §951.) Indeed, under our cases that would be but a moderate analogical extension. . . .

60. But see Society for Ethical Culture v. Spatt, 51 N.Y.2d 449, 415 N.E.2d 922 (1980), in which the New York Court of Appeals allowed the city to block the demolition of the Society's Meeting House, a building "deemed worthy of landmark status due to its exemplification as the first building facade of the art nouveau style pioneered in this country by the noted architect Robert D. Kohn, who was also president of the Society." 51 N.Y.2d at 452. The court distinguished the *Lutheran Church* case in the following manner:

> [B]y no means are we assured that the only feasible solution to this problem would entail the demolition of the now protected building facade. . . . There is no genuine complaint that eleemosynary activities within the landmark are wrongfully disrupted, but rather the complaint is instead that the landmark stands as an effective bar against putting the property to its most lucrative use.

Id. at 455-456. See Comment, First Amendment Challenges to Landmark Preservation Statutes, 11 Fordham Urb. L.J. 115 (1982). — EDS.

the regulatory ambit of the police power. Indeed, regulation in the name of aesthetics must bear *substantially* on the economic, social and cultural patterns of the community or district."

State v. Diamond Motors, Inc., 50 Haw. 33, 429 P.2d 825 (1967), upheld a comprehensive sign ordinance which prohibited, among other things, the erection and maintenance in industrial districts of ground signs exceeding 75 square feet in area or exceeding 16 feet in height from the ground:

> Appellee's answering brief admittedly "does not extend to supporting the proposition that aesthetics alone is a proper objective for the exercise of the City's police power." Perhaps, the "weight of authority" in other jurisdictions persuaded the City to present the more traditional arguments because it felt that it was safer to do so. However, the brief of The Outdoor Circle as amicus curiae presents, as we think, a more modern and forthright position.
>
> We accept beauty as a proper community objective, attainable through the use of the police power. We are mindful of the reasoning of most courts that have upheld the validity of ordinances regulating outdoor advertising and of the need felt by them to find some basis in economics, health, safety, or even morality. . . . We do not feel so constrained.
>
> Hawaii's constitution provides:
>
> "The State shall have power to conserve and develop its natural beauty, objects and places of historic or cultural interest, sightliness and physical good order, and for that purpose private property shall be subject to reasonable regulation." (Article VIII, Section 5 [now Article IX, Section 7, slightly amended].)
>
> Appellants argue that this constitutional provision has no application to this case because the offending sign is located in an industrial area. We do not agree. The natural beauty of the Hawaiian Islands is not confined to mountain areas and beaches. The term "sightliness and physical good order" does not refer only to junk yards, slaughter houses, sanitation, cleanliness, or incongruous business activities in residential areas, as appellants argue.

2. "Just what is meant by the use of the term aesthetic is not entirely clear; but apparently it is intended to designate thereby matters which are evident to sight only, as distinguished from those discerned through smell and hearing." Sundeen v. Rogers, 83 N.H. 253, 258, 141 A. 142, 144 (1928). "[I]t may be that in the development of a higher civilization, the culture and refinement of the people has reached the point where the educational values of the Fine Arts, as expressed and embodied in architectural symmetry and harmony, is so well recognized as to give sanction, under some circumstances, to the exercise of this power even for such purposes." Cochran v. Preston, 108 Md. 220, 229, 70 A. 113, 114 (1908). "It is obvious that matters of taste cannot be crystallized in quantitative terms, but the desire for beauty is a funda-

C. Urban Design

mental urge whose satisfaction is essential to healthy living in the full sense of the term." American Public Health Association, Housing for Health 205 (1941). "[T]he public view as to what is necessary for aesthetic progress greatly varies. Certain Legislatures might consider that it was more important to cultivate a taste for jazz than for Beethoven, for posters than for Rembrandt, and for limericks than for Keats." City of Youngstown v. Kahn Bros. Building Co., 112 Ohio St. 654, 661, 662, 148 N.E. 842, 844 (1925); an early egalitarian court phrased it, "The law can know no distinction between citizens because of the superior cultivation of the one over the other." Quintini v. Bay St. Louis, 64 Miss. 483, 1 So. 625, 628 (1887). "The word *aesthetic*, in the Latin form *aesthetica*, was first used . . . to designate the science of sensuous knowledge, whose goal is beauty, in contrast with logic whose goal is truth." Webster's New International Dictionary (2d ed. 1956). "*Informal.* In accordance with accepted notions of good taste." American Heritage Dictionary (1978).

The American Institute of Architects' choice of the best builder's house of 1950 was refused mortgage insurance by the FHA. Again, the VA imposed a $1000 design penalty on an architect-designed house in Tulsa, Oklahoma, that House and Home had displayed on its 1954 cover. The Pruitt-Igoe public housing project, which starred in a TV vehicle when HUD Secretary George Romney had it blown up, had won an architectural award in its day.

How does the "legal syntax" fit with the realities of the urban environment? Are the doctrinal statements concerning aesthetics — even within one reported decision — consistently adhered to by the court? At this point review the earlier types of zoning controls — are there any, although the term is not used, which are nevertheless understandable primarily in terms of aesthetic values? See Weismantel, Legislating the Urban Design Process, 1970 Urb. L. Ann. 196, proposing an innovative design code.

3. Preservation of historically or architecturally significant areas plays a special role. The "Old San Diego Planning District," some 230 acres, was viewed tolerantly in Bohannan v. City of San Diego, 30 Cal. App. 3d 416, 106 Cal. Rptr. 338 (4th Dist. 1973); the ordinances prescribed the use of materials and styles "in general accord with the appearance of the structures built . . . prior to 1871." Williamsburg, Virginia provides that any building erected or altered in any zone of the city "shall have such design and character as not to detract from the value and general harmony of design of buildings already existing in the surrounding area in which the building is located or is to be located." Williamsburg City Code §30-80 (1979). See Vieux Carre Property Owners and Associates, Inc. v. City of New Orleans, 167 So. 2d 367 (La. 1964). For the Vieux Carre Ordinance, and the New York City Landmark Preservation Law, see 4 Anderson, American Law of

Zoning §§26.93, 26.95 (1968). A review of the legal tools for historical preservation is contained in Comment, 19 Buffalo L. Rev. 611 (1970). See also Davis, State Tax Incentives for Historic Preservation (1985) (funded by National Trust for Historic Preservation's State Legislation Project), a state by state guide to the tax relief offered to owners of historic properties: exemptions, credit or abatement, special assessment, income tax deductions, sales tax relief, tax levies. Id. at 2. Compare the English system, Town and Country Planning Act of 1968, ch. 72, pt. v. What about the approach taken in the National Conference of Commissioners on Uniform State Laws, Uniform Conservation Easement Act (1982)?

4. At least one court, while recognizing that the value of the use of land abutting on a highway for the location of a billboard is entirely dependent on its visibility from the highway, has held that though the abutting owner has a right in the nature of an easement appurtenant to have that condition continued, the right is restricted to the display of advertising related to business conducted on the premises.[61] See Kelbro, Inc. v. Myrick, 113 Vt. 64, 30 A.2d 527 (1943), and Wilson, Billboards and the Right to Be Seen from the Highway, 30 Geo. L.J. 723 (1942); contra, Murphy, Inc. v. Town of Westport, 131 Conn. 292, 40 A.2d 177 (1944).

5. The subject of aesthetics and regulation of land-use is a popular one in the periodical literature. See Agnore, Beauty Begins a Comeback, 11 J. Pub. L. 260 (1962); Anderson, Regulation of Land Use for Aesthetic Purposes, 15 Syracuse L. Rev. 33 (1963); Note, Zoning, Aesthetics & the First Amendment, 64 Colum. L. Rev. 81 (1964); Police Power & Design of Buildings, 5 National Resources J. 122 (1965); Williams, Legal Techniques to Protect and Promote Aesthetics Along Transportation Corridors, 17 Buffalo L. Rev. 701 (1968); Masotte, Aesthetic Zoning and the Police Power, 46 J. Urb. L. 773 (1969); Symposium, 15 Prac. Law. 17 (1969); Note, 48 J. Urb. L. 740 (1971); Wilson and Winkler, The Response of State Legislation to Historic Preservation, 36 Law & Contemp. Probs. 329 (1971). See also the report of the President's Conference on Beauty: Beauty for America, Proceedings of the White House Conference on Natural Beauty (1965); Rose, Preservation and Community: New Direction in the Law of Historic Preservation, 33 Stan. L. Rev. 473 (1981); Netherton, The Due Process Issue in Zoning for Historic Preservation, 19 Urb. Law. 77 (1987).

6. In People v. Stover, 12 N.Y.2d 462, 191 N.E.2d 272, 240 N.Y.S.2d 734 (1963), Van Voorhis, J. (dissenting), stated:

---

61. A fascinating account of a run-in between the aesthetic authority and an individualist who wished to display a sign supporting world government can be found in the November 29, 1952, issue of The New Yorker Magazine. Compare the dissenting opinion in Landau Advertising Co. v. Zoning Board of Adjustment, 387 Pa. 552, 559, 128 A.2d 559, 563 (1957). See Lynch, What Time Is This Place? (1972).

C. Urban Design 535

The ordinance whose validity is now being upheld prohibits the erection and maintenance of clotheslines in a front or side yard abutting a street.... What has happened here is that these defendants conceived the unusual idea of hanging what the majority opinion describes as "tattered clothing, old uniforms, underwear, rags and scarecrows" across their yard as a form of protest against the amount of their taxes....

This ordinance is unrelated to the public safety, health, morals or welfare except insofar as it compels conformity to what the neighbors like to look at. Zoning, important as it is within limits, is too rapidly becoming a legalized device to prevent property owners from doing whatever their neighbors dislike. Protection of minority rights is as essential to democracy as majority vote. In our age of conformity it is still not possible for all to be exactly alike, nor is it the instinct of our law to compel uniformity wherever diversity may offend the sensibilities of those who cast the largest numbers of votes in municipal elections. The right to be different has its place in this country. The United States has drawn strength from differences among its people in taste, experience, temperament, ideas, and ambitions as well as from differences in race, national or religious background. Even where the use of property is bizarre, unsuitable or obstreperous it is not to be curtailed in the absence of overriding reasons of public policy. The security and repose which come from protection of the right to be different in matters of aesthetics, taste, thought, expression and within limits in conduct are not to be cast aside without violating constitutional privileges and immunities. This is not merely a matter of legislative policy, at whatever level. In my view, this pertains to individual rights protected by the Constitution.

12 N.Y.2d at 470-472, 191 N.E.2d at 277-278.

7. Cleveland Heights, Ohio, had used the zoning power to prevent Donna S. Reid from building a one-story modern house in a neighborhood of multi-story traditional structures. The city's action was upheld against the charge that it invalidly restricted Ms. Reid's right to freedom of expression. Reid v. Architectural Board of Review, 119 Ohio App. 67, 192 N.E.2d 74 (1963). The architectural board had said that the proposed house "does not maintain the high character of community development in that it does not conform to the character of the houses in the area." The court said that other houses nearby "are, in the main, dignified, stately and conventional structures, two and one-half stories high." The proposed house was "a flat-roofed complex of twenty modules, each of which is ten feet high, twelve feet square and arranged in a loosely formed 'U' which winds its way through a grove of trees." See Poole, Architectural Appearance Review Regulations and the First Amendment: The Good, The Bad, and The Consensus Ugly, 19 Urb. Law. 287 (1987).

8. In January 1982, the Paradise Valley Board of Adjustment denied a variance to a landowner who desired approval to build a "Triptych," according to preliminary plans prepared by Frank Lloyd

Wright and presented to a prior owner of the property one week before Wright's death in 1959. The Court of Appeals of Arizona rejected the plaintiff's vested rights theory, noting that she had "failed to show any substantial expenditures of money in reliance upon approval of her building plans." Neither were the Board's actions deemed arbitrary or capricious. Burroughs v. Town of Paradise Valley, 724 P.2d 1239 (Ariz. Ct. App. 1986).

9. What do Sylvester Stallone and 13-year old Jeffrey Kisor have in common? Both are victims of aesthetic strong-arming. Stallone's neighbors instituted suit for damages and injunctive relief, seeking to have the actor lower the red brick, spiked wall surrounding his Pacific Palisades property: "'It's no beauty,' says [one neighbor]. 'It takes away from the community.'" According to another neighbor, "'When you're walking around you want to see yard and house. We all feel the same way. It's too high.'" Wall St. J., July 23, 1986.

The Lakeside Park, Kentucky, City Council decided that Jeffrey's treehouse violated the zoning ordinance prohibiting detached structures. The illegal structure "has 42 square feet of space, including a porch, and even has an attached milk-crate pulley system for deliveries. Sometimes Jeffrey takes a radio there to play rock music, sometimes he invites friends over and sometimes he imagines he is Rambo under seige." The Council subsequently rejected a zoning change to allow treehouses, leaving Jeffrey's father somewhat frustrated: "'They're looking at the esthetics of the property rather than at the people who live on it,' he said. 'But that's what your own property is for — so you and your children can enjoy it and play on it.'" N.Y. Times, July 20, 1986.

10. Private land-use regimes present equally provocative questions of aesthetic control. Consider the following provisions taken from the "DEED, AGREEMENT AND DECLARATION . . . by and between THE HOWARD RESEARCH AND DEVELOPMENT CORPORATION [HRD, the developer of Columbia, Maryland] . . . , and [a residential purchaser], Grantee, and THE COLUMBIA PARK AND RECREATION ASSOCIATION, INC. [CPRA] . . .":

> Section 7.02. No Structures shall be commenced, erected, placed, moved on to or permitted to remain on any Lot, nor shall any existing Structure upon any Lot be altered in any way which materially changes the exterior appearance thereof, nor shall any new use be commenced on any Lot, unless plans and specifications (including a description of any proposed new use) therefor shall have been submitted to and approved in writing by the Architectural Committee.
>
> Section 7.03. The Architectural Committee shall have the right to disapprove any plans and specifications submitted hereunder because of any of the following:

C. Urban Design

(a) the failure of such plans or specifications to comply with any of the Wilde Lake Restrictions:

(b) failure to include information in such plans and specifications as may have been reasonably requested;

(c) objection to the exterior design, appearance or materials of any proposed Structure;

(d) incompatibility of any proposed Structure or use with existing Structures or uses upon other Lots in the vicinity;

(e) objection to the location of any proposed Structure upon any Lot or with reference to other Lots in the vicinity;

(f) objection to the grading plan for any Lot;

(g) objection to the color scheme, finish, proportions, style of architecture, height, bulk or appropriateness of any proposed Structure;

(h) objection to parking areas proposed for any Lot on the grounds of (i) incompatibility to proposed uses and Structures on such Lot or (ii) the insufficiency of the size of parking areas in relation to the proposed use of the Lot; or

(i) any other matter which, in the judgment of the Architectural Committee, would render the proposed Structure, Structures or uses inharmonious with the general plan of improvement of the Property or with Structures or uses located upon other Lots in the vicinity....

Do these provisions, especially 7.03 (d) through (i), provide sufficient guidance to the architectural committee? Would they be effective if they were any more specific? Is the committee exercising a governmental function that might subject it to due process requirements? See LeBlanc v. Webster, 483 S.W.2d 647 (Mo. App. 1972). See also Rhue v. Cheyenne Homes, Inc., 168 Colo. 6, 449 P.2d 361 (1969) (architectural committee's refusal to approve plans to move Spanish style home into modern ranch and split level development reasonable and in good faith); Davis v. Huey, 620 S.W.2d 561 (Tex. 1981) (refusal of developer to approve building plans exceeded authority under restrictive covenants).

■ PENN CENTRAL TRANSPORTATION CO. v. NEW YORK CITY
438 U.S. 104 (1978)

Mr. Justice BRENNAN delivered the opinion of the Court....

This case involves the application of New York City's Landmarks Preservation Law to Grand Central Terminal. The Terminal, which is owned by the Penn Central Transportation Co. and its affiliates, is one of New York City's most famous buildings. Opened in 1913, it is regarded not only as providing an ingenious engineering solution to the problems presented by urban railroad stations, but also as a magnificent example of the French beaux-arts style....

On August 2, 1967, following a public hearing, the Commission designated the Terminal a "landmark" and designated the "city tax block" it occupies a "landmark site." . . .

On January 22, 1968, appellant Penn Central, to increase its income, entered into a renewable 50-year lease and sublease agreement with appellant UGP Properties, Inc. (UGP), a wholly owned subsidiary of Union General Properties, Ltd., a United Kingdom corporation. Under the terms of the agreement, UGP was to construct a multistory office building above the Terminal. UGP promised to pay Penn Central $1 million annually during construction and at least $3 million annually thereafter. The rentals would be offset in part by loss of some $700,000 to $1 million in net rentals presently received from concessionaires displaced by the new building.

Appellants UGP and Penn Central then applied to the Commission for permission to construct an office building atop the Terminal. Two separate plans, both designed by architect Marcel Breuer and both apparently satisfying the terms of the applicable zoning ordinance, were submitted to the Commission for approval. The first, Breuer I, provided for the construction of a 55-story office building, to be cantilevered above the existing facade and to rest on the roof of the Terminal. The second, Breuer II Revised, called for tearing down a portion of the Terminal that included the 42d Street facade, stripping off some of the remaining features of the Terminal's facade, and constructing a 53-story office building. The Commission denied a certificate of no exterior effect on September 20, 1968. Appellants then applied for a certificate of "appropriateness" as to both proposals. After four days of hearings at which over 80 witnesses testified, the Commission denied this application as to both proposals. . . .

[A]ppellants filed suit in New York Supreme Court, Trial Term, claiming, inter alia, that the application of the Landmarks Preservation Law had "taken" their property without just compensation in violation of the Fifth and Fourteenth Amendments and arbitrarily deprived them of their property without due process of law in violation of the Fourteenth Amendment. Appellants sought a declaratory judgment, injunctive relief barring the city from using the Landmarks Law to impede the construction of any structure that might otherwise lawfully be constructed on the Terminal site, and damages for the "temporary taking" that occurred between August 2, 1967, the designation date, and the date when the restrictions arising from the Landmarks Law would be lifted. . . .

. . . The question of what constitutes a "taking" for purposes of the Fifth Amendment has proved to be a problem of considerable difficulty. While this Court has recognized that the "Fifth Amendment's guarantee [is] designed to bar Government from forcing some people alone to bear public burdens which, in all fairness and justice, should be borne

C. Urban Design 539

by the public as a whole," Armstrong v. United States, 364 U.S. 40, 49 (1960), this Court, quite simply, has been unable to develop any "set formula" for determining when "justice and fairness" require that economic injuries caused by public action be compensated by the Government, rather than remain disproportionately concentrated on a few persons. See Goldblatt v. Hempstead, 369 U.S. 590, 594 (1962). Indeed, we have frequently observed that whether a particular restriction will be rendered invalid by the Government's failure to pay for any losses proximately caused by it depends largely "upon the particular circumstances [in that] case." United States v. Central Eureka Mining Co., 357 U.S. 155, 168 (1958); see United States v. Caltex, Inc., 344 U.S. 149 (1952).

In engaging in these essentially ad hoc, factual inquiries, the Court's decisions have identified several factors that have particular significance. The economic impact of the regulation on the claimant and, particularly, the extent to which the regulation has interfered with distinct investment backed expectations are of course relevant considerations. So too is the character of the governmental action. A "taking" may more readily be found when the interference with property can be characterized as a physical invasion by Government, see e.g., United States v. Causby, 328 U.S. 256 (1946), than when interference arises from some public program adjusting the benefits and burdens of economic life to promote the common good.

"Government could hardly go on if to some extent values incident to property could not be diminished without paying for every such change in the general law," Pennsylvania Coal Co. v. Mahon, 260 U.S. 393, 413 (1922), and this Court has accordingly recognized, in a wide variety of contexts, that Government may execute laws or programs that adversely affect recognized economic values. Exercises of the taxing power are one obvious example. A second are the decisions in which this Court has dismissed "taking" challenges on the ground that, while the challenged Government action caused economic harm, it did not interfere with interests that were sufficiently bound up with the reasonable expectations of the claimant to constitute "property" for Fifth Amendment purposes.

More importantly for the present case, in instances in which a state tribunal reasonably concluded that "the health, safety, morals or general welfare" would be promoted by prohibiting particular contemplated uses of land, this Court has upheld land use regulations that destroyed or adversely affected recognized real property interests. See Nectow v. City of Cambridge, 277 U.S. 183, 188 (1928). Zoning laws are of course the classic example, see Euclid v. Ambler Realty Co., 272 U.S. 365 (1926), . . . which have been viewed as permissible governmental action even when prohibiting the most beneficial use of the property. . . .

. . . Because this Court has recognized, in a number of settings, that States and cities may enact land use restrictions or controls to enhance the quality of life by preserving the character and desirable aesthetic features of a city, appellants do not contest that New York City's objective of preserving structures and areas with special historic, architectural, or cultural significance is an entirely permissible governmental goal. . . .

. . . [A]ppellants, focusing on the character and impact of the New York City law, argue that it effects a "taking" because its operation has significantly diminished the value of the Terminal site. Appellants concede that the decisions sustaining other land use regulations, which, like the New York law, are reasonably related to the promotion of the general welfare, uniformly reject the proposition that diminution in property value, standing alone, can establish a taking, see Euclid v. Ambler Realty Co., (75% diminution in value caused by zoning law); Hadacheck v. Sebastian, [239 U.S. 394 (1915)] (87½% diminution in value); . . . and that the taking issue in these contexts is resolved by focusing on the uses the regulations permit. Appellants, moreover, also do not dispute that a showing of diminution in property value would not establish a "taking" if the restriction had been imposed as a result of historic district legislation, see generally Maher v. City of New Orleans, 516 F.2d 1051 (CA5 1975), but appellants argue that New York City's regulation of individual landmarks is fundamentally different from zoning or from historic district legislation because the controls imposed by New York City's law apply only to individuals who own selected properties.

Stated baldly, appellants' position appears to be that the only means of ensuring that selected owners are not singled out to endure financial hardship for no reason is to hold that any restriction imposed on individual landmarks pursuant to the New York scheme is a "taking" requiring the payment of "just compensation." Agreement with this argument would of course invalidate not just New York City's law, but all comparable landmark legislation in the Nation. We find no merit in it.

It is true, as appellants emphasize, that both historic district legislation and zoning laws regulate all properties within given physical communities whereas landmark laws apply only to selected parcels. But, contrary to appellants' suggestions, landmark laws are not like discriminatory, or "reverse spot," zoning: that is, a land use decision which arbitrarily singles out a particular parcel for different, less favorable treatment than the neighboring ones. In contrast to discriminatory zoning, which is the antithesis of land-use control as part of some comprehensive plan, the New York City law embodies a comprehensive plan to preserve structures of historic or aesthetic interest wherever they might be found in the city, and as noted, over 400 landmarks and 31 historic districts have been designated pursuant to this plan.

C. Urban Design

Equally without merit is the related argument that the decision to designate a structure as a landmark "is inevitably arbitrary or at least subjective, because it is basically a matter of taste," Reply Brief for Appellants 22, thus unavoidably singling out individual landowners for disparate and unfair treatment. . . . [A] landmark owner has a right to judicial review of any commission decision, and, quite simply, there is no basis whatsoever for a conclusion that courts will have any greater difficulty identifying arbitrary or discriminatory action in the context of landmark regulation than in the context of classic zoning or indeed any other context.

Next, appellants observe that New York City's law differs from zoning laws and historic district ordinances in that the Landmarks Law does not impose identical or similar restrictions on all structures located in particular physical communities. It follows, they argue, that New York City's law is inherently incapable of producing the fair and equitable distribution of benefits and burdens of governmental action which is characteristic of zoning laws and historic district legislation and which they maintain is a constitutional requirement if "just compensation" is not to be afforded. It is of course true that the Landmarks Law has a more severe impact on some landowners than on others, but that in itself does not mean that the law effects a "taking." Legislation designed to promote the general welfare commonly burdens some more than others. The owners of the brickyard in *Hadacheck*, of the cedar trees in Miller v. Schoene, and of the gravel and sand mine in Goldblatt v. Hempstead, were uniquely burdened by the legislation sustained in those cases.[30] Similarly, zoning laws often impact more severely on some property owners than others but have not been held to be invalid on that account. For example, the property owner in *Euclid* who wished to use his property for industrial purposes was affected far more severely by the ordinance than his neighbors who wished to use their land for residences. . . .

Appellants' final broad-based attack would have us treat the law as

---

30. Appellants attempt to distinguish these cases on the ground that, in each, Government was prohibiting a "noxious" use of land and that in the present case, in contrast, appellants' proposed construction above the Terminal would be beneficial. We observe that the uses in issue in *Hadacheck, Miller,* and *Goldblatt* were perfectly lawful in themselves. They involved no "blameworthiness, . . . moral wrongdoing, or conscious act of dangerous risk-taking which induce[d society] to shift the cost to a particular individual." Sax, 74 Yale L.J. 36, 50 (1964). These cases are better understood as resting not on any supposed "noxious" quality of the prohibited uses but rather on the ground that the restrictions were reasonably related to the implementation of a policy — not unlike historic preservation — expected to produce a widespread public benefit and applicable to all similarly situated property.

Nor, correlatively, can it be asserted that the destruction or fundamental alteration of a historic landmark is not harmful. The suggestion that the beneficial quality of appellants' proposed construction is established by the fact the construction would have been consistent with applicable zoning laws ignores the development in sensibilities and ideals reflected in landmark legislation like New York City's.

an instance, like that in United States v. Causby, [328 U.S. 256 (1946)] in which Government, acting in an enterprise capacity, has appropriated part of their property for some strictly governmental purpose. Apart from the fact that *Causby* was a case of invasion of airspace that destroyed the use of the farm beneath and this New York City law has in no wise impaired the present use of the Terminal, the Landmarks Law neither exploits appellants' parcel for city purposes nor facilitates nor arises from any entrepreneurial operations of the city. The situation is not remotely like that in *Causby* where the airspace above the property was in the flight pattern for military aircraft. The Landmarks Law's effect is simply to prohibit appellants or anyone else from occupying portions of the airspace above the Terminal, while permitting appellants to use the remainder of the parcel in a gainful fashion. This is no more an appropriation of property by Government for its own uses than is a zoning law prohibiting, for "aesthetic" reasons, two or more adult theatres within a specified area, see Young v. American Mini Theatres, Inc., or a safety regulation prohibiting excavations below a certain level. See Goldblatt v. City of Hempstead [369 U.S. 590 (1962)]. . . .

Rejection of appellants' broad arguments is not however the end of our inquiry, for all we thus far have established is that the New York law is not rendered invalid by its failure to provide "just compensation" whenever a landmark owner is restricted in the exploitation of property interests, such as air rights, to a greater extent than provided for under applicable zoning laws. We now must consider whether the interference with appellants' property is of such a magnitude that "there must be an exercise of eminent domain and compensation to sustain [it]." Pennsylvania Coal Co. v. Mahon, 260 U.S., at 413. . . .

Unlike the governmental acts in *Goldblatt*, *Miller*, *Causby*, *Griggs*, and *Hadacheck*, the New York City law does not interfere in any way with the present uses of the Terminal. Its designation as a landmark not only permits but contemplates that appellants may continue to use the property precisely as it has for the past 65 years, as a railroad terminal containing office space and concessions. So the law does not interfere with what must be regarded as Penn Central's primary expectation concerning the use of the parcel. More importantly, on this record, we must regard the New York City law as permitting Penn Central not only to profit from the Terminal but to obtain a "reasonable return" on its investment.

Appellants, moreover, exaggerate the effect of the Act on its ability to make use of the air rights above the Terminal . . .

Their ability to use these rights has not been abrogated; they are made transferable to at least eight parcels in the vicinity of the Terminal, one or two of which have been found suitable for the construction of new office buildings. Although appellants and others have argued that New York City's transferable development rights program is far from

C. Urban Design 543

ideal, the New York courts here supportably found that, at least in the case of the Terminal, the rights afforded are valuable. While these rights may well not have constituted "just compensation'" if a "taking" had occurred, the rights nevertheless undoubtedly mitigate whatever financial burdens the law has imposed on appellants and, for that reason, are to be taken into account in considering the impact of regulation. . . .

On this record, we conclude that the application of New York City's Landmarks Preservation Law has not effected a "taking" of appellants' property. The restrictions imposed are substantially related to the promotion of the general welfare and not only permit reasonable beneficial use of the landmark site but afford appellants opportunities further to enhance not only the Terminal site proper but also other properties.[36]

Affirmed.

Mr. Justice REHNQUIST, with whom THE CHIEF JUSTICE and Mr. Justice STEVENS join, dissenting. . . .

. . . The question in this case is whether the cost associated with the city of New York's desire to preserve a limited number of "landmarks" within its borders must be borne by all of its taxpayers or whether it can instead be imposed entirely on the owners of the individual properties. . . .

Even where the government prohibits a noninjurious use, the Court has ruled that a taking does not take place if the prohibition applies over a broad cross section of land and thereby "secure[s] an average reciprocity of advantage." Pennsylvania Coal Co. v. Mahon, 260 U.S. 393, 415 (1922). It is for this reason that zoning does not constitute a "taking." While zoning at times reduces *individual* property values, the burden is shared relatively evenly and it is reasonable to conclude that on a whole an individual who is harmed by one aspect of the zoning will be benefited by another.

Here, however, a multimillion dollar loss has been imposed on appellants; it is uniquely felt and is not offset by any benefits flowing from the preservation of some 500 other "Landmarks" in New York. Appellees have imposed a substantial cost on less than one one-tenth of one percent of the buildings in New York for the general benefit of all its people. It is exactly this imposition of general costs on a few individuals at which the "taking" protection is directed. The Fifth Amendment "prevents the public from loading upon one individual

---

36. We emphasize that our holding today is on the present record which in turn is based on Penn Central's present ability to use the Terminal for its intended purpose and in a gainful fashion. The city conceded at oral argument that if appellants can demonstrate at some point in the future that circumstances have changed such that the Terminal ceases to be, in the city's counsel's words, "economically viable," appellants may obtain relief. See Tr. of Oral Arg. 42-43.

more than his just share of the burdens of government, and says that when he surrenders to the public something more and different from that which is exacted from other members of the public, a full and just equivalent shall be returned to him." Monongahela Navigation Co. v. United States, 148 U.S. 312, 325 (1893). . . .

Appellees, apparently recognizing that the constraints imposed on a Landmark site constitute a taking for Fifth Amendment purposes, do not leave the property owner empty handed. As the Court notes, the property owner may theoretically "transfer" his previous right to develop the Landmark property to adjacent properties if they are under his control. Appellees have coined this system "Transfer Development Rights," or TDR's.

Of all the terms used in the Taking Clause, "just compensation" has the strictest meaning. The Fifth Amendment does not allow simply an approximate compensation but requires "a full and perfect equivalent for the property taken." . . .

. . . Because the record on appeal is relatively slim, I would remand to the Court of Appeals for a determination of whether TDR's constitute a "full and perfect equivalent for the property taken."

Notes

1. Judge Breitel held for the New York Court of Appeals that it is only "the privately created and privately managed ingredient which is the property on which the reasonable return is to be based." 42 N.Y. 2d 324, 366 N.E. 2d 1271, 397 N.Y.S.2d 914 (1977). Does this holding survive the Supreme Court opinion? Suppose an expressway is built along the boundary of property A, bringing with it commercial development and doubling the value of the property. If the government later regulates the use of property A, is the owner entitled to a reasonable return only on the value of his property before the expressway was built? Can it be argued that *all* increase in the value of land is in some sense publicly created? See Comment, Grand Central Terminal and the New York Court of Appeals: "Pure" Due Process, Reasonable Return, and Betterment Recovery, 78 Colum. L. Rev. 134, 157-160 (1978).

2. Judge Breitel argued that the compensation "need not be the 'just' compensation required in eminent domain, for there has been no attempt to take property." This is a response to what has come to be known as the "disparity issue." Government regulation that leaves the owner a reasonable return requires no compensation. Yet if the regulation goes only slightly farther, leaving something less than a reasonable return, there must be compensation all the way up to the highest and

C. Urban Design 545

best use. Judge Breitel's response was that "just" compensation is required only for exercises of eminent domain. A regulation that goes too far is not an exercise of eminent domain, but simply an invalid regulation. Such a regulation can be saved by granting compensation merely to the level of "reasonable return." This position has also been advocated in Costonis, The Disparity Issue: A Context for the Grand Central Terminal Decision, 91 Harv. L. Rev. 402 (1977) and Costonis, "Fair" Compensation and the Accommodation Power: Antidotes for the Taking Impasse in Land Use Controversies, 75 Colum. L. Rev. 1021 (1975).

Consider the last paragraph of the excerpt from Justice Brennan's opinion, along with his footnote 30. Is this the same as the Breitel approach? For more on regulatory takings, see infra page 875.

3. The Supreme Court in *Penn Central* applied principles taken from zoning cases and cases involving regulations protecting the public health and safety to a case involving preservation of a single historic landmark. Should the importance of the public purpose affect the amount of damage that may be inflicted without compensation? Consider the statement of one commentator that "courts have required compensation more readily when . . . the regulation is aimed at providing amenities such as historic preservation rather than protecting the public health or safety; when the prohibited use bears no resemblance whatever to common law nuisance; and when the law benefits a much larger group than it burdens." The Supreme Court — 1977 Term, 92 Harv. L. Rev. 57, 230 (1978).

4. What is an owner's property interest in inchoate uses? The Court in *Penn Central* spoke of protecting "investment backed expectations." See also HFH, Ltd. v. Superior Ct., 15 Cal. 3d 508, 542 P.2d 237, 125 Cal. Rptr. 365 (1975), cert. denied, 425 U.S. 904 (1976); Hotel Coamo Springs, Inc. v. Hernandez Colon, 426 F. Supp. 664 (D.P.R. 1976). When does an expectation become "investment backed"? When the owner hires the architects to plan new construction? Presumably the purchase price of a parcel of land reflects all of the available potential uses. Is the expectation of pursuing one of those uses therefore "investment backed" from the time the property is purchased? Could it be argued that Penn Central's expectation of building a tower over Grand Central Terminal was investment backed?

5. Before the *Penn Central* decision, New York's Landmarks Preservation Commission had been "circumspect in its designation of privately owned structures." After *Penn Central,* however, the commission became bolder and more active; as of early 1984, it had designated 44 historic districts containing more than 16,000 buildings, 690 individual landmarks, and 45 interior or scenic landmarks. Of late, the commission has been charged with "overstepp[ing] its role by becoming involved in land use matters that should properly be addressed by the

City Planning Commission," and with assisting "community activists" in "neighborhood preservation and the obstruction of unwanted development." A critic of the commission points to the 1981 "historic district" designation of a large portion of Manhattan's Upper East Side as

> [t]he most egregious example of trespass on planning and zoning matters.... In one vote the Commission gave blanket protection to 60 city blocks containing 1,044 buildings on some of New York's most valuable real estate, thereby freezing development in one of the city's most vital areas.... Even Beverly Moss Spatt, a former LPC chairman known for her aggressive preservationist views, voted against the designation because she felt the Commission was "usurping the City Planning Commission's powers to prevent demolition, to prevent development and change" in an area that was not "a unified historic district in terms of architectural style or historicity."

Rose, Landmarks Preservation in New York, The Public Interest No. 74, at 132 (1984). See Babcock & Siemon, Grand Central Station: Beware the Establishment Aroused, in The Zoning Game Revisited 59-75 (1985).

6. See N.Y. Times, Sept. 21, 1986:

> Such is the nature of New York City real estate that even the thin air above it can fetch a price if the location is right. For example, First Boston Corporation, the investment company, agreed a few years ago to pay $55 a foot for 1.5 million square feet of "air rights" over Grand Central Terminal. Last week, it was reported that the company wanted to use about half of the rights to build a 74-story tower on a Madison Avenue site zoned for a far smaller building....
>
> But the First Boston proposal involves moving the terminal's air rights several blocks, to a site between 46th and 47th Streets. First Boston argues that there is a "chain of ownership" since the terminal's owner, the Penn Central Corporation, still holds "subsurface" rights to land around Grand Central, including railroad tracks. Edward N. Costikyan, a lawyer for First Boston, argued that land ownership is "three-dimensional."

7. St. Bartholomew's Episcopal Church is a Romanesque stone structure built in 1918 on midtown Manhattan's Park Avenue. The architect was Bertram Goodhue. The church's proposal to construct a fifty-nine-story office building on the site of its adjacent community house sparked a challenge under New York's Landmarks Preservation Law. A sharp debate over the constitutionality of the law, the role of the first amendment, and the architectural, aesthetic, and historic merits of the proposal created what has been called "one of the most important landmarks struggles of the decade." The view of the church is that it has a right, protected under the first amendment, to use its land as it

C. Urban Design

sees fit; and that the millions of dollars in office rents will finance charitable work that is an essential obligation of the congregation. The rector said, "There are many people in this city who could care less, but the commitment to theology is at the heart of this matter." A lawyer for opponents of the plan replied: "There is no first amendment right to construct office buildings. I know of no faith whose major tenet is to construct office buildings." See N.Y. Times, Dec. 21, 1984.

8. After *Penn Central*, the Supreme Court's next stab at the elusive goal of beauty in our cities came in Metromedia, Inc. v. City of San Diego, 453 U.S. 490 (1981). This case confounds students of the first amendment with a confusing array of opinions regarding the constitutionality of a San Diego ordinance that severely restricted outdoor advertising displays. Justice White, for a plurality, analyzed the city's aesthetic justification for the billboard ban:

> ... There is no suggestion that the commercial advertising at issue here involves unlawful activity or is misleading. Nor can there be substantial doubt that the twin goals that the ordinance seeks to further — traffic safety and the appearance of the city — are substantial governmental goals. It is far too late to contend otherwise with respect to either traffic safety, Railway Express Agency, Inc. v. New York, 336 U.S. 106 (1949), or esthetics, see Penn Central Transportation Co. v. New York City, 438 U.S. 104 (1978); Village of Belle Terre v. Boraas, 416 U.S. 1 (1974); Berman v. Parker, 348 U.S. 26, 33 (1954)....
>
> ... It is not speculative to recognize that billboards by their very nature, wherever located and however constructed, can be perceived as an "esthetic harm." San Diego, like many States and other municipalities, has chosen to minimize the presence of such structures.[16] Such esthetic judgments are necessarily subjective, defying objective evaluation, and for that reason must be carefully scrutinized to determine if they are only a public rationalization of an impermissible purpose. But there is no claim in this case that San Diego has as an ulterior motive the suppression of speech, and the judgment involved here is not so unusual as to raise suspicions in itself....
>
> The constitutional problem in this area requires resolution of the conflict between the city's land-use interests and the commercial interests of those seeking to purvey goods and services within the city. In light of the above analysis, we cannot conclude that the city has drawn an ordinance broader than is necessary to meet its interests, or that it fails directly to advance substantial government interests.

---

16. The federal Highway Beautification Act of 1965, Pub. L. 89-285, 79 Stat. 1028, as amended, 23 U.S.C. §131 (1976 ed. and Supp. III), requires that States eliminate billboards from areas adjacent to certain highways constructed with federal funds. The Federal Government also prohibits billboards on federal lands. 43 CFR §2921.0-6(a) (1980). Three States have enacted statewide bans on billboards. Maine, Me. Rev. Stat. Ann., Tit. 23 §1901 et seq. (1980); Hawaii, Haw. Rev. Stat. §264-71 et seq., §445-111 et seq. (1976); Vermont, Vt. Stat. Ann., Tit. 10, §488 et seq. (1973).

Still, the plurality viewed the ordinance as encompassing invalid time, place, and manner restrictions.

Though concurring in the judgment, Justice Brennan analogized what he perceived as a total billboard ban to the prohibition on live entertainment outlawed in *Schad*:

> I think that the city has failed to show that its asserted interest in aesthetics is sufficiently substantial in the commercial and industrial areas of San Diego. I do not doubt that "[i]t is within the power of the [city] to determine that the community should be beautiful," Berman v. Parker, 348 U.S. 26, 33 (1954), but that power may not be exercised in contravention of the First Amendment.... A billboard is not *necessarily* inconsistent with oil storage tanks, blighted areas, or strip development. Of course, it is not for a court to impose its own notion of beauty on San Diego. But before deferring to a city's judgment, a court must be convinced that the city is seriously and comprehensively addressing aesthetic concerns with respect to its environment. Here, San Diego has failed to demonstrate a comprehensive coordinated effort in its commercial and industrial areas to address other obvious contributors to an unattractive environment....

9. The division on the Court in the area of protection for commercial and noncommercial speech continued in Members of the City Council of Los Angeles v. Taxpayers for Vincent, 466 U.S. 789 (1984), holding that a city ordinance prohibiting the posting of signs on public property did not violate the first amendment rights of a group of supporters for a political candidate. The city proffered aesthetic, economic, and safety interests to support the reasonableness of its ban. The majority, this time by Justice Stevens, accepted

> the City's position that it may decide that the esthetic interest in avoiding "visual clutter" justifies a removal of signs creating or increasing that clutter.... As is true of billboards, the esthetic interests that are implicated by temporary signs are presumptively at work in all parts of the city ... and there is no basis in the record in this case upon which to rebut that presumption. These interests are both psychological and economic.

466 U.S. at 816-817.

In dissent, Justice Brennan, joined by Marshall and Blackmun, stated:

> the Court's lenient approach towards the restriction of speech for reasons of aesthetics threatens seriously to undermine the protections of the First Amendment.... In my view, the City of Los Angeles has not shown that its interest in eliminating "visual clutter" justifies its restriction of appellees' ability to communicate with the local electorate.

Id. at 818 (Brennan, J., dissenting).

C. Urban Design

Has the Court trapped itself within the complex analytical matrix it has devised to evaluate governmental impact on various forms of speech — some more protected than others? Does the majority in *Taxpayers for Vincent* sacrifice the protections offered "core political speech" by rewarding the city's consistent, absolutist approach? Is the dissent's "harder look" at the city's rationale a bad precedent, a surreptitious bit of Lochnerizing? See Mandelker, The Free Speech Revolution in Land Use Control, 60 Chi. Kent L. Rev. 51 (1984); Pearlman, Zoning and the First Amendment, 16 Urb. Law. 217 (1984); Weinstein, Billboards, Aesthetics, and the First Amendment: Municipal Sign Regulation After *Metromedia,* Land Use L. & Zoning Dig., Aug. 1984, at 3.

10. In communities across the country, portable signs — a simple, inexpensive solution to temporary (and sometimes permanent) advertising needs — have fallen victim to regulatory attacks. For decisions in which *Metromedia* and *Taxpayers for Vincent* have been successfully invoked by restrictive city governments, see Don's Porta Signs, Inc. v. City of Clearwater, 829 F.2d 1051 (11th Cir. 1987); Lindsay v. City of San Antonio, 821 F.2d 1103 (5th Cir. 1987), cert. denied, 108 S. Ct. 707 (1988). Do the smaller size, portability, and blandness of such signs — in contrast with giant billboards and garish neon spectacles — somehow make justifications like aesthetics and safety less convincing?

11. Notice the three cases cited by Justice White for the proposition that it is too late to contend that aesthetics is not a substantial governmental goal: *Penn Central,* Village of Belle Terre v. Boraas, supra page 248, and Berman v. Parker, infra page 788. Are there not other rationales upon which the holdings in these cases are based? Do three "aesthetics-plus" cases equal the conclusion that "aesthetics alone" meets due process requirements? Or does there remain something inherently subjective about this regulatory goal that should give the court pause before either enshrining it with health, safety, and morals, or including it within that catch-all — general welfare? See Dukeminier, Zoning for Aesthetic Objectives: A Reappraisal, 20 Law & Contemp. Probs. 218 (1955); Costonis, Law and Aesthetics: A Critique and a Reformulation of Policy, 80 Mich. L. Rev. 355 (1980); Williams, Subjectivity, Expression, and Privacy: Problems of Aesthetic Regulation, 62 Minn. L. Rev. 1 (1977); Rowlett, Aesthetic Regulation Under the Police Power: The New General Welfare and the Presumption of Constitutionality, 34 Vand. L. Rev. 603 (1981).

In 1982, North Carolina became, according to the supreme court's reckoning, the eighteenth member of the "new majority" of jurisdictions "authorizing regulation based on aesthetics alone." In sixteen states, "purely aesthetic regulation was an open question"; ten states had "no reported cases on aesthetic regulation." The court cited Bufford, Beyond the Eye of the Beholder: A New Majority of Jurisdictions

Authorize Aesthetic Regulation, 48 UMKC L. Rev. 125 (1980). See State v. Jones, 305 N.C. 520, 290 S.E.2d 675 (1982): "We do not grant blanket approval of all regulatory schemes based upon aesthetic considerations. Rather, we adopt the test . . . that the diminution in value of an individual's property should be balanced against the corresponding gain to the public from such regulation." According to the new calculus, Buncombe County Ordinance 16401, under which the defendant was required to enclose his junkyard, was deemed valid.

The shape of the city, the variety of physical forms that urban development might conceivably take, requires exploration by researchers in many fields. You have examined the court's struggle with the beautiful. Here are discussions by a national government department entrusted with vast powers over the character of the physical environment, and by a roundtable of city planning experts. Consider the sensitive interplay necessary between their policy aims and the relationship among government, the entrepreneur, and the individual.

■ MINISTER OF HOUSING AND LOCAL GOVERNMENT, DESIGN
3 Encyclopedia of Planning 4535 (1974)

1. One of the objects of development control is to prevent bad design and encourage good. Planning is concerned with the environment in which people live and work, and this necessarily entails consideration of aesthetic qualities — those that make an environment visually pleasing or the reverse, as well as questions of practical convenience, health and safety. But there are obvious difficulties, and some dangers, in exercising control of design. One cannot lay down rules defining what is good and what is bad, for aesthetic judgments are largely subjective and opinions, including expert opinions, often differ. Taste varies from person to person; and it also changes from generation to generation. Control must therefore be applied with restraint and with great discrimination.

2. It is particularly important that it should not be used to stifle initiative and experiment in design, or to favour the familiar merely because it is familiar. A design is not bad because it is new and different; it may be very good. Control should prevent design which is clearly bad; but it must also allow freedom for the creative processes that make good architecture.

3. The design of buildings is the business of the professional architect, and developers usually find it advisable to employ an architect when the appearance of the proposed development is likely to be

C. Urban Design

important. Planning authorities are also usually guided by professional architectural advice in considering such proposals in order to ensure that the architectural aspects are properly appreciated. Clear and definite criticisms of a design on grounds that can be explained carry more weight than vague objections about it being "inappropriate" or "out of keeping with adjoining development."

4. There may be two questions about the design of a building. The first is whether the design is bad in itself; fussy, or ill-proportioned, or downright ugly. The second is whether, even if the design is not bad in itself, it would be bad on the particular site: out of scale with close neighbours, an urban design in a rural setting or a jarring design in a harmonious scene. The latter point is often overlooked: too many buildings are designed as separate entities, apparently without reference to their surroundings. The relationship between new development and its context is almost always important, and sometimes crucial. This is not to say that new development need always conform to the character of the existing development around it, for unless the place has some special architectural or other qualities that are worth preserving, there is often no reason why the new development should not be different in character. It may, indeed, be better if it is. But the setting should always be studied and taken into account, for it may well influence the design of the new.

5. This is particularly true of buildings in rural surroundings, where landscape and natural features may largely determine the design; and in conservation areas and other places of distinct architectural or historic character. In some of these, for example the Georgian square or Regency terrace, consistency of architectural style is the dominant feature and any new development will be expected to conform to it. Others comprise less formal groupings of buildings of different ages and styles and allow more scope for new development and greater freedom of design; but every new building should nevertheless be designed as part of the larger whole, with due regard to its special characteristics.[62]

■ URBAN DESIGN
37 Progressive Architecture 97 (Aug. 1956)

Sert: We know more about the problems of our cities than we ever did before the methods of research and analysis were adopted in

---

62. In addition to design control, planning authorities in Britain have many specific powers directly related to amenity. For example, they have the power to prohibit the felling, lopping, or destruction of a single tree, group of trees, or substantial woodland (Town and Country Planning Act, 1971, ch. 78, §60); they can control all outdoor advertisements (§63); and they can require any owner of any "garden, vacant site or open land" to abate any injury to the amenity of the area caused by the use or condition of his or her land (§65). — EDS.

this field. In fact, in late years, the scientific phase has been more emphasized than the artistic one. This may be due to a natural reaction against past practice, when city planning was based on the superficial "city beautiful" approach, which ignored the roots of the problems and attempted only window-dressing effects. Urban design is that part of city planning which deals with the physical form of the city. This is the most creative phase of city planning and that in which imagination and artistic capacities can play a more important part. It may also be in some respects the most difficult and controversial phase; and because of all these factors it has been less explored than other aspects. With the new approach to architecture, landscape architecture, road engineering and city planning, accepted formulas had to be thrown overboard. . . . I do believe that now, after many years of individual, isolated work, we are logically coming to an era of synthesis. Like the instruments in an orchestra, these elements of urban design all have their parts to play in the total performance. The result must be harmonious and cannot be reached by individual competition. I believe we are conscious that city planners, landscape architects and architects can be only part of a larger team of specialists required to solve urban problems; but I also believe that our three professions are already very close and that it may be easier first to come to an agreement among ourselves and then, later on, discuss the participation and relationship of the other specialists who should complete the team. The urban designer must first of all believe in cities, their importance and their value to human progress and culture. We must be urban minded. . . .

Segoe: The simile of an orchestra with city planning is an intriguing one. There are always some players in an orchestra who feel that the role of the conductor is rather superfluous, but those of us who listen, feel that the conductor has an important part to play. But before he can conduct, someone must have provided a score, and the problem remains who should be the composer and who should be the conductor?

Sert: It is true that someone has to write the score. There is a program that has to be written, after a very careful analytical study of the conditions of a community. This program has to be written not only by the people who have done the analysis but also with the help of those who are going to do the synthesis. This program — this score — would have to remain flexible, contrary to that for an orchestra, because we operate within a considerable period of time, and with a living organism — the city — where conditions are constantly being modified. But if everything is once assembled in correct proportion in a score, the work allowing for all modifications — will benefit. There will have to be a conductor also, or rather

C. Urban Design 553

conductors, who will take different parts of the work as their presence is more useful to its progress. . . .

Abrams: Legislative architecture, financial tyrannies, and social and political taboos design our houses, locate our industries, and harden our traffic arteries. If anyone challenges this, I ask him how much ingenuity the architect has under the FHA manual. Can Frank Lloyd Wright build a public housing project on land costing $5 a square foot at $2,500 per room cost that will not look like a housing project? With the economics of the elevator dictating nothing else but a six- or a thirteen-story project and the legislative limitation on per-room cost (which means using only a certain-size brick and a certain-size room) will Wright's project in New York look different from Neutra's and Neutra's look different from Sert's? . . . Was Stuyvesant Town the architect's fault or the natural result of Metropolitan Life's calculation that, since New York City gave tax exemption on the building, the greater the building coverage, the more the tax exemption? Is the private developer expected to build monuments to civilization or to maximum milkability? Will the entrepreneur, tooled for profit, retool for prestige? . . . The political revolution has released all the constitutional powers we need to do anything the designer wants to achieve. . . . All that is needed are the funds and the simple legislation and that's a function of political pressures. The problem today is mainly one of know-how in the art of political pressures — to get the thing done.

Kepes: Our knowledge about legal, political, or technical issues in the action pattern are basically defined for us by the value scale that we develop for ourselves. And this value scale, on the other hand, is certainly defined by the images that we create about ourselves and about our relation to the world around us. If we cannot find a real understanding, a real image of our role in the universe, I think all these wonderful tools and this wonderful equipment cannot come to full use. We are all speaking today about being out-of-scale with the world around us — things are moving faster than we can grasp, things are becoming bigger and more complex, and we can't understand and organize them. Somehow the old structure principle, the old images, the old way of seeing are not adequate to handle these large dimensions. How can we get away from our inherited and evidently limited values? What we call the esthetic experience — the experience of the sensibilities, the ability to perceive the total in an ordered form — must be channelized to the broad scale of experience that we are here talking about. . . . One of the more important aspects of creating a better urban environment is to open the eyes of the man who is involved in design to these values which have been gradually and in a very stuttering way developed in the work of the painters, the sculptors, and those other people who have been perhaps more frustrated, perhaps more sensitive in responding to the difficulties of the surroundings.

Sasaki: I should like to dwell on one significant force instrumental in shaping the city, which I think needs mentioning: and this force is that of the *designers*. I maintain that since the visual aspect of a city is only that which is created, it is obvious that to a large degree the individuals mentioned are most responsible for the ultimate expression of the urban environment. . . . The chief faults in design may be: 1. *Eclecticism without meaning.* Often under the guise of architectural harmony, stylistic conformity of present periods as well as the past is willingly, or sometimes unwillingly, practiced. 2. *Monumentality without meaning; or lack of scale.* The so-called modern buildings clad in steel and glass too often lack any sense of being related to human beings. While it is true that in our times we have developed a technological scale, which may express a dimension never witnessed before, it is still true, none the less, that it is the human animal who must live in and understand this creation. 3. *Lack of relationship with surroundings; or emphasis on the spectacular.* If we take an attitude of awareness of the situation in which a creation is to be placed, we may choose to be humble on the one hand, or on the other we may choose to be quite bold and daring. But the notion that each and every building must be different than anything ever done before is, to me, an abhorrent design notion. . . .

Jacobs: Planners and architects are apt to think, in an orderly way, of stores as a straight-forward matter of supplies and services — commercial space. But stores in city neighborhoods are much more complicated creatures which have evolved a much more complicated function. They are a big portion of the glue that makes an urban neighborhood a community instead of a dormitory. A store is also a storekeeper. One supermarket can replace 30 neighborhood delicatessens, fruit stands, groceries, and butchers, as a Housing Authority planner explains. But it cannot replace 30 storekeepers, or even one. The stores themselves are social centers — especially the bars, candy stores, and diners. A store is also often an empty store *front*. Into these fronts go all manner of churches, clubs and mutual uplift societies. The storefront activities are enormously valuable. They are the institutions that people create, themselves. If you are a nobody, and you don't know anybody who isn't a nobody, the only way you can make yourself heard in a large city is through certain well defined channels. These channels all begin in holes-in-the-wall. They start in Mike's barbershop or the hole-in-the-wall office of a man called "Judge," and they go on to the Thomas Jefferson Democratic Club where Councilman Favini holds court, and now you are started on up. It all takes an incredible number of confabs. The physical provision for this kind of process cannot conceivably be formalized.... Some very important sides of city life, much of the charm, the creative social activity and the vitality shift over to the old vestigial areas because there is literally no place for them in the new scheme of things. This is a ludicrous situation, and it ought to give planners the shivers. ...

Bacon: When we look at our preparation for urban design both in terms of concepts and people, we must pause with some concern. We have the three principals: planning, architecture, and administration. What we lack is the capacity to function as a whole.... The kind of design approach discussed here must be recognized in the beginning of administrative directives. Unless these are formulated or directly influenced by a designer they cannot possibly take into account the primary design relationships. The concept of a firm position of leadership in the formulation of public policy and the assumption of an important administration role where policy is formed is almost foreign to the thinking of the architectural profession. The planners have traditionally considered the design of physical structures as a detail. Administrators almost invariably think in terms of specific projects and procedures rather than the underlying correlative relationships. What we need is the architect-planner-administrator, and if we ever get it we will then really have an urban designer.

Sert: ... If we want to get an element of life into the city we have to have the formal and the informal, the intimate and the monumental. If every little space wants to be monumental then, finally, when we come to the center of the city there is no monumentality at all.... So, in reply to "where do we go from here?" I would suggest that we adopt a positive attitude. We shouldn't wait too long, for the cities may move faster than we do and when we discover new and better design formulas we will find the work has already been carried out by other hands. When we ask how cities should be designed, I think it important to bear in mind that we are not designing for the mayor, or for the planning commission, or for the traffic expert — but only for the people and with the people. Without this we shall never get ahead.

D. PAROCHIALISM

It is said that the Village of Euclid is a mere suburb of the City of Cleveland.... But the village, though physically a suburb of Cleveland, is politically a separate municipality, with powers of its own and authority to govern itself as it sees fit within the limits of the organic law of its creation and the State and Federal Constitutions.

— *Euclid v. Ambler*, 272 U.S. at 389

One could easily substitute "City of Petaluma" and "Town of Ramapo" — two municipalities in the vicinity of large central cities (San Francisco and New York City) that have attempted to resist the pressures of growth — for the reference to "the Village of Euclid" in the paragraph above. In many ways, the Court's 1926 decision cleared the way for similarly situated communities to limit population and to ward off the evils of urbanization despite the fact that the municipality in question stood in the way of residential development for central city residents hoping to escape the physical confinement and other problems of inner-city life.

The use of public and private land-use controls was closely connected to the growth of politically distinct suburbs. In the words of one suburban Chicago critic of annexation: "Under local government we can absolutely control every objectionable thing that may try to enter our limits — but once annexed we are at the mercy of city hall."[63] Boston's experience was not atypical:

> It was already apparent in the 1880's that to join Boston was to assume all the burdens and conflicts of a modern industrial metropolis. To remain apart was to escape, at least for a time, some of these problems. In the face of this choice the metropolitan middle class abandoned their central city. . . .
>
> . . . Beyond Boston the special suburban form of popularly managed local government continued to flourish. In suburbs of substantial income and limited class structure, high standards of education and public service were often achieved. Each town, however, now managed its affairs as best it could surrounded by forces largely beyond its control.[64]

Zoning out, or segregating, the city's most distasteful uses could help ensure that the escape to the suburbs would not mean replicating the problems left behind.

Euclid itself, sixteen square miles of predominantly agricultural land when it was incorporated in 1903, was a relatively new governmental unit when its officials began studying zoning in 1922.[65] Through the village ran Euclid Avenue, the continuation of a street in Cleveland that boasted one of the nation's grandest, mansion-lined streets. In addition, there was the Cleveland Tractor Company plant located near

---

63. Jackson, Crabgrass Frontier: The Suburbanization of the United States 151 (1985) (quoting March 9, 1907, editorial from Morgan Park Post).

64. Warner, Streetcar Suburbs: The Process of Growth in Boston (1870-1900) 164-165 (2d ed. 1978). — Eds.

65. Toll, supra note 16, at 214, 216.

D. Parochialism

the Nickel Plate Railroad. But zoning, even in the village immortalized in the term Euclidean, could not keep metropolitan Cleveland away for long: today Euclid boasts a population of 60,000 (many of whom are of eastern European descent)[66] and a General Motors plant on Ambler Realty's former site.

Because of zoning's contribution to the continued isolation of middle-class communities, courts and legislatures in some states have mandated regional responsibility for suburban areas, while in other areas planning and zoning controls have been recaptured by state officials.[67] These shifts in the nature and operation of zoning law are not necessarily timely reactions to late-twentieth century socioeconomic and governance realities. They can be appreciated as well as inevitable, if sorely delayed, responses to the suburban movement given credence and support by the Court in *Euclid*.

Judges throughout the country, with the encouragement and assistance of generations of commentators, continue to seek an instructive meaning for the most equivocal adjective in the land-use planning glossary: "comprehensive." Must all uses be provided for in every community's "comprehensive" plan? If instead a neighboring town "specializes" in commerce or light industry, does this satisfy the needs of the community broadly defined? Where do the obligations of the municipality end — at the town limits, within certain radii extending out from the town's central attraction (a large employer, shopping center, or affluent neighborhood)? If lawmakers and courts approve of parochial behavior by suburbs or exurbs, can and should the central city respond with unfavorable tax, regulatory, or public employment treatment of nonresidents?[68] Or is the refusal to accept regional responsibilities a defensible expression of competent, decentralized government, a Jeffersonian goal we lose sight of in our quest for state, even national, uniformity?

1. The Puzzle of Comprehensiveness

Consider how the following judicial attempts at definition compare with common parlance, expectations of planners and developers, and the ideas and aspirations of the framers of the model act, infra page 564:

66. 1980 Census data reveal a high percentage of persons of Slavic origin.
67. See infra page 743.
68. For opinions discussing possible commerce and privilege and immunities clause violations involved in favoring local residents, see White v. Massachusetts Council of Constr. Employers, Inc., 460 U.S. 204 (1983); United Bldg. & Constr. Trades Council v. Mayor & Council of Camden, 465 U.S. 208 (1984). See also Wolf, Potential Legal Pitfalls Facing State and Local Enterprise Zones, 8 Urb. L. & Poly. 77, 85-89 (1986).

Borough of Cresskill v. Borough of Dumont, 15 N.J. 238, 104 A.2d 441 (1954), VANDERBILT, C. J.: "The first complaint in effect charges that the amendatory ordinance is not in accordance with the comprehensive zoning plans in effect in the boroughs of Cresskill, Demarest, Dumont and Haworth in that it fails to take into consideration the physical, economic, and social conditions prevailing throughout the entire area of those four municipalities and the use to which the land in that region can and may be put most advantageously, and that regard was given solely to the political boundaries of the Borough of Dumont in utter disregard of the contiguous residential areas of the plaintiff boroughs. . . .

"The appellant spells out from the language of . . . constitutional and statutory provisions that the responsibility of a municipality for zoning halts at the municipal boundary lines without regard to the effect of its zoning ordinances on adjoining and nearby land outside the municipality. Such a view might prevail where there are large undeveloped areas at the borders of two contiguous towns, but it cannot be tolerated where, as here, the area is built up and one cannot tell when one is passing from one borough to another. Knickerbocker Road and Massachusetts Avenue are not Chinese walls separating Dumont from the adjoining boroughs. At the very least Dumont owes a duty to hear any residents and taxpayers of adjoining municipalities who may be adversely affected by proposed zoning changes and to give as much consideration to their rights as they would to those of residents and taxpayers of Dumont. To do less would be to make a fetish out of invisible municipal boundary lines and a mockery of the principles of zoning. . . .

"The vital problem here, and that upon which our decision necessarily rests, is whether, as charged by the respondents, the ordinance constitutes 'spot zoning.' R.S. 40:55-32, N.J.S.A. provides that zoning regulations 'shall be in accordance with a comprehensive plan' to promote the specified statutory purposes. The test is whether the zoning change in question is made with the purpose or effect of establishing or furthering a comprehensive zoning scheme calculated to achieve the statutory objectives or whether it is 'designed merely to relieve the lot of the burden of the restriction of the general regulation by reason of conditions alleged to cause such regulation to bear with particular harshness upon it.' Conlon v. Board of Public Works of City of Paterson, 11 N.J. 363, 366, 94 A.2d 660, 662 (1953). . . . Our inquiry therefore has been directed to ascertaining whether in view of the purposes of the zoning act the action of the borough in rezoning Block 197 represents sound judgment based on the policy of the statute 'to advance the common good and welfare' or whether it is arbitrary and unreasonable and furthers 'purely private interests.' Schmidt v. Board of Adjustment of City of Newark, 9 N.J. 405, 422, 88 A.2d 607, 615 (1952).

"The Borough of Dumont, as we have seen, is predominantly a

D. Parochialism 559

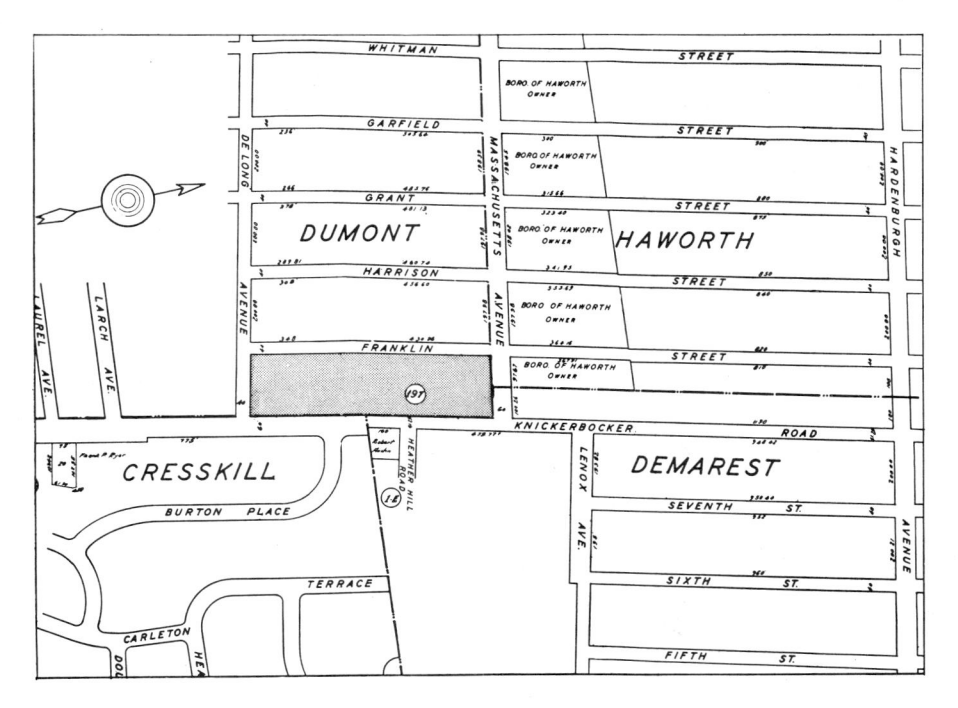

residential community composed largely of one-family dwellings, as are the contiguous boroughs. The area surrounding Block 197 is, of course, residential and has been so zoned for years. The mayor testified that 200 to 220 one-family dwellings are to be constructed on the property adjoining Block 197 on the west. There is not the slightest indication that the character of the neighborhood is changing. The only exception to residential use in Dumont within one-half mile of the block in question is a small corner lot which the trial court properly characterized as a case of spot zoning at its worst. The business zone of Dumont, at which there is a fine shopping center, is one-half mile away. The comprehensive zoning plan of the borough reveals an intention to maintain this whole area as a residential one and the testimony clearly shows that the block is suitable for the construction of residences. There is no reason why it should not and cannot be used profitably for that purpose."[69]

---

69. In 1960, the town of Houghton adopts a comprehensive plan and passes a zoning ordinance that zones a sizable area of land R-2 (permitted uses include high-rise, multiple-family apartments). Within three years a state highway is constructed, severing a portion of this area from the rest of Houghton. The sole remaining means of access to this strip is through the neighboring municipalities of Bellevue and Clyde Hill which, in 1960, have

Fairlawns Cemetery Association v. Zoning Commission of Bethel, 138 Conn. 434, 440, 86 A.2d 74, 77 (1952). INGLIS, J.: "The validity of the zoning regulations in question depends very largely upon whether they meet the requirements of the enabling act.... The gist of this [act] is that zoning regulations enacted pursuant thereto must possess two characteristics. First, they must be expressive of a plan which is comprehensive. Second, they must promote the public welfare, which is another way of saying that they must be within the police power.

"The word 'comprehensive' as used in the statute means '[i]ncluding much; comprising many things; having a wide scope.' Webster's New International Dictionary (2d ed.). Accordingly, to be valid, a zoning ordinance must be one which is designed to further a plan which relates to a substantial area of the municipality enacting it and to the reasonable needs of the community, both at present and in the foreseeable future. There must be a plan and that plan must be comprehensive as to territory, public needs and time. Bartram v. Zoning Commission, 136 Conn. 89, 93, 68 A.2d 308; Kuehne v. Town Council, 136 Conn. 452, 460, 72 A.2d 474. The zoning regulations in question are clearly expressive of a plan to maintain the predominantly residential character of the town but still permit the less objectionable forms of business. The plan is not applied to a narrowly restricted area or for a limited time. In terms, the regulations cover nearly the whole town of Bethel and are in effect for an indefinite time. They leave some districts of the town open for use other than business and residential. They therefore satisfy the requirement of the statute that such regulations be in accordance with a comprehensive plan."

Connor v. Township of Chanhassen, 249 Minn. 205, 212-213, 81 N.W.2d 789, 795-796 (1957). MURPHY, J.: "In support of the contention that the ordinance as adopted is unconstitutional, the plaintiffs assert that the regulations do not conform to §366.14 which provides that the regulation 'shall be made in accordance with the comprehensive plan.' It is contended that the zoning of sections as commercial or business

---

zoned and developed the land adjacent to the now severed strip for single-family homes. Residents of this neighboring land file suit when they discover that a property owner in the strip is planning to build a high-rise apartment. Upon what grounds? What result? See Bishop v. Town of Houghton, 69 Wash. 2d 786, 420 P.2d 368 (1966) (neighboring landowners claimed changed conditions since 1960; town's refusal to rezone to prevent apartment construction not arbitrary or capricious); Town of River Vale v. Town of Orangetown, 403 F.2d 684 (2d Cir. 1968) (New Jersey township has standing to challenge rezoning of contiguous area in neighboring New York town), noted in 83 Harv. L. Rev. 679 (1970); Note, 71 Yale L.J. 720 (1972); Miller v. Upper Allen Tp. Zoning Hearing Bd., 535 A.2d 1195 (Pa. Commw. Ct. 1987) (contiguous landowners in neighboring community had standing as "persons aggrieved" to intervene in zoning appeal, overruling contrary dictum in prior case).

D. Parochialism 561

districts is necessary to establish comprehensive zoning. The plaintiffs point out that the industrial district established by the amended ordinance created an area in the southern tier of sections not suitably located for business available to the use of residents in the township area.

"The comprehensive plan, as far as the record in the case before us is concerned, is found in the zoning regulations themselves in light of the purpose of the regulations as expressed in §366.14 which provides that the regulations shall promote the 'health, morals, convenience, order, prosperity, or welfare of the present and future inhabitants of any such town, including . . . lessening congestion in streets or roads . . . ; securing safety from fire and other dangers; . . . preventing, on the one hand, excessive concentration of population and, on the other hand, excessive and wasteful scattering of population or settlement'; with a view to facilitating and conserving 'provisions for transportation, water flowage, water supply, drainage, sanitation, educational opportunities, recreation, soil fertility . . . and protection of both urban and non-urban development.' . . .

"It appears from an examination of the authorities as well as the language used in §366.14 that the term 'comprehensive zoning' does not necessarily mean a plan which makes allowances for the establishment of districts to be set aside for various commercial and professional purposes which provide a defined area with complete business and professional service. The term comprehends that the ordinance shall take the place of and include within its provisions the numerous ordinances which were formerly enacted independently and included such subjects as 'Tenement House Codes,' 'Sanitary Codes,' 'Fire Zone' provisions, and parts of 'Building Codes,' as well as provisions with reference to codes relating to restrictions with reference to height, proportion of parcels that must be kept open, and unbuilt yard lines, etc. 1 Metzenbaum, Law of Zoning (2d ed.) p. 15."

Udell v. Haas, 21 N.Y.2d 463, 235 N.E.2d 897, 288 N.Y.S.2d 888 (1968). KEATING, J.: "Zoning is not just an expansion of the common law of nuisance. It seeks to achieve much more than the removal of obnoxious gases and unsightly uses. Underlying the entire concept of zoning is the assumption that zoning can be a vital tool for maintaining a civilized form of existence only if we employ the insights and the learning of the philosopher, the city planner, the economist, the sociologist, the public health expert and all the other professions concerned with urban problems.

"The fundamental conception of zoning has been present from its inception. The almost universal statutory requirement that zoning conform to a 'well-considered plan' or 'comprehensive plan' is a reflection of that view. (See Standard State Zoning Enabling Act, U.S. Dept. of Commerce [1926].) The thought behind the requirement is that consideration must be given to the needs of the community as a whole. In exercising their zoning powers, the local authorities must act for the benefit of the community as a whole following a calm and deliberate consideration of the alternatives, and not because of the whims of either an articulate minority or even majority of the community. (De Sena v. Gulde, 24 A.D.2d 165 [2d Dept., 1965].) Thus, the mandate of the Village Law (§177) [that zoning be "in accordance with a comprehensive plan"] is not a mere technicality which serves only as an obstacle course for public officials to overcome in carrying out their duties. Rather, the comprehensive plan is the essence of zoning. Without it, there can be no rational allocation of land use. It is the insurance that the public welfare is being served and that zoning does not become nothing more than just a Gallup poll.

"No New York case has defined the term 'comprehensive plan.' Nor have our courts equated the term with any particular document. We have found the 'comprehensive plan' by examining all relevant evidence. As the trial court noted, generally New York cases 'have analyzed the ordinance ... in terms of consistency and rationality.' While these elements are important, the 'comprehensive plan' requires that the rezoning should not conflict with the fundamental land use policies and development plans of the community. These policies may be garnered from any available source, most especially the master plan of the community, if any has been adopted, the zoning law itself and the zoning map."[70]

Baker v. City of Milwaukie, 520 P.2d 479 (Or. App. 1974). FOLEY, J.: "The Oregon requirement that zoning be in accord with a well-considered plan was added by Oregon Laws 1919, ch. 300, §2. There was no requirement that a city prepare a comprehensive plan either at the time of passage of ch. 300 or at the time this petition was filed. In fact, the

---

70. In Town of Bedford v. Mount Kisco, 33 N.Y.2d 178, 187, 306 N.E.2d 155, 159, 351 N.Y.S.2d 129, 135 (1973), this gloss was added:

> The trial court appeared to conclude that the Village Board had no authority to adopt a zoning change which did not conform to the comprehensive zoning plan which had been adopted 10 years previously, notwithstanding intervening changes in property use, in the absence of some formal amendment of the plan. We have held that zoning changes must indeed be consonant with a total planning strategy, reflecting consideration of the needs of the community (Udell v. Haas, 21 N.Y.2d 463, 288 N.Y.S.2d 888, 235 N.E.2d 897). What is mandated is that there be comprehensiveness of planning, rather than special interest, irrational *ad hocery.* The obligation is support of comprehensive planning, not slavish servitude to any particular comprehensive plan. Indeed sound planning inherently calls for recognition of the dynamics of change.

D. Parochialism

first reference to a comprehensive plan in the statutes arose in the area of county planning where Oregon Laws 1947, ch. 537, provided that the county must prepare a comprehensive plan. We cannot impute a legislative intent to ORS 227.240 requiring a city to prepare a separate document that controls the provisions of a zoning ordinance or placing a statutory duty upon the city council to amend its zoning ordinance to conform to its comprehensive plan. . . .

"Petitioner correctly points out that the Supreme Court in Fasano v. Washington Co. Comm., 96 Or. Adv. Sh. 1059, 507 P.2d 23 (1973), indicated that the comprehensive plan is the basic instrument for county or municipal land-use planning. However, we cannot read into Fasano a requirement that cities adopt comprehensive plans or that zoning ordinances be amended to conform to later adopted comprehensive plans. Fasano dealt generally with county zoning and planning and specifically with ORS ch. 215 which mandates that a county zoning ordinance implement the county comprehensive plan. No such requirement existed for cities at the time of this proceeding. See ORS ch. 227.

"Our determination that the zoning ordinance is the controlling document in the city of Milwaukie zoning scheme negates petitioner's contentions dealing with the alleged lack of conformity of the comprehensive plan and the zoning ordinance. . . ."

Baker v. City of Milwaukie, 533 P.2d 772 (Or. 1975). HOWELL, J.: "In summary, we conclude that a comprehensive plan is the controlling land use planning instrument for a city. Upon passage of a comprehensive plan a city assumes a responsibility to effectuate that plan and conform prior conflicting zoning ordinances to it. We further hold that the zoning decisions of a city must be in accord with that plan and a zoning ordinance which allows a more intensive use than that prescribed in the plan must fail."[71]

Bell v. City of Elkhorn, 122 Wis. 2d 558, 364 N.W.2d 144 (1985). CALLOW, J.: "The question of whether a zoning ordinance may constitute a comprehensive plan is a matter of first impression in Wisconsin. . . .

---

71. See Sullivan and Kressel, Twenty Years After — Renewed Significance of the Comprehensive Plan Requirement, 9 Urb. L. Ann. 33 (1975). See also Or. Rev. Stat. Ann. §197.015(5) (1985):

> "Comprehensive plan" means a generalized, coordinated land use map and policy statement of the governing body of a local government that interrelates all functional and natural systems and activities relating to the use of lands, including, but not limited to, sewer and water systems, transportation systems, educational facilities, recreational facilities, and natural resources and air and water quality management programs. "Comprehensive" means all-inclusive, both in terms of the geographic area covered and functional and natural activities and systems occurring in the area covered by the plan.

"Several courts have held that planning legislation requires the preparation and adoption of a separate comprehensive plan document and that the adoption of a formal comprehensive plan is a condition precedent to the enactment of a zoning ordinance. However, none of those cases involved the interpretation of a statute containing the language that ordinances must be 'in accordance with a comprehensive plan.'

"We find the majority view to be persuasive on this issue. While sec. 62.23(7)(c) requires that zoning regulations be made 'in accordance with a comprehensive plan,' the statute contains no requirement that a comprehensive plan must be a formal document separate from the zoning ordinance nor does it require that a comprehensive plan be adopted prior to the enactment of a zoning ordinance. The purpose of a comprehensive plan is to provide an orderly method of land use regulation for the community. That purpose can be accomplished by the zoning ordinance itself without the need of a separate document labeled 'Comprehensive Plan.' The clear intent of the legislature in enacting sec. 62.23, Stats., was to have cities design a general plan to control the use of property in the community. This can be accomplished with or without the advice of a plan commission because the creation of a plan commission is at the discretion of the governing body of the community. The power to zone is exclusively vested in the city council.

". . . Elkhorn's zoning ordinance serves as a general plan to control and direct the use and development of property in the city and serves as a guide to future community development. As such, we hold that the ordinance itself is a comprehensive plan as required by sec. 62.23(7)(c), Stats. No separate comprehensive plan document need be adopted by a city as a condition precedent to enacting a zoning ordinance."

■ UNITED STATES DEPARTMENT OF COMMERCE, A STANDARD CITY PLANNING ENABLING ACT
(1928)

Sec. 6. *General Powers and Duties.*[31] — It shall be the function and

---

31. *"Powers and duties":* The general function of a planning commission is to prepare a general design of the city's development, so that development may take place in a systematic, coordinated, and intelligently controlled manner. The matters to be covered by the design may be broadly classified as dealing with (a) streets, (b) other types of public grounds, (c) public buildings, (d) public utilities, (e) development of private property (zoning). [The original draft read: "The matters to be covered by the design may be broadly classified as dealing with (a) streets, (b) other types of public grounds, (c) buildings, (d) utilities."]

This act is based on the theory that a planning commission should view all these phases of a city's development in a broad and comprehensive fashion and should not concern itself with detailed administrative duties which rightfully belong to other branches

D. Parochialism   565

duty of the commission to make and adopt[72] a master plan[32] for the physical development[33] of the municipality, including any areas[73] outside of its boundaries[34] which, in the commission's judgment, bear relation to the planning of such municipality. Such plan, with the accompanying maps,[74] plats, charts, and descriptive matter, shall show the commission's recommendations for the development of said territory, including, among other things, the general location, character, and extent[36] of streets, viaducts, subways, bridges, waterways, water

---

of the government. It should not, for example, be required to pass on details of street elevations or details of installation and construction which the city engineer is best equipped to determine.

The planning commission's function in such matters is to make a general design as to location, which it is especially competent to do in view of its knowledge of the needs of the city and the probable trend of the city's future growth. The regular city department or board concerned should ordinarily decide the advantages and disadvantages of specific lots within a given range of area. It may consult the planning commission during the negotiations and should, in any event, submit its final decision as to location to the commission. . . .

72. Originally "to make a master plan for. . . ." — EDS.

32. *"A master plan"*: By this expression is meant a comprehensive scheme of development of the general fundamentals of a municipal plan. An express definition has not been thought desirable or necessary. What is implied in it is best expressed by the provisions of this section which illustrate the subject matter that a master plan should consider.

33. *"Physical development"*: The word "physical" is used so as to make it plain that the planning commission should limit its activities to those problems of city life which are to be worked out through influencing the physical development of the territory.

73. Originally "land." — EDS.

34. *"Areas outside of its boundaries"*: No city planning commission can make an effective or adequate plan for its own municipality unless it takes into consideration present conditions and future growth of the territory outside its boundaries. This might seem like giving to a municipality the power to interfere with the administrative or legislative freedom of other municipalities, but the mere making of a plan by a city contains no such interference. There can be, therefore, no harm, but, on the contrary, great benefits will result from permitting one municipality to cover in its plan as much of surrounding country as it may please, and the educational and moral effect of so doing may be of very great importance. The making of a plan is merely the making of a plan. It is a design which may or may not be carried out. In the process of making a city plan which covers territory outside the city limits the planning commission and its technical men will, of course, consult with planning commissions of neighboring municipalities, if there be any such commissions, and with the officials and civic organizations of these neighboring municipalities. The making of the city plan may well be the beginning of cooperation which will do away with any mutual jealousies or fears which may exist in the relations of neighboring municipalities, and may ultimately lead to regional planning movements. Annexation of the smaller municipalities with the larger is often difficult or impossible to bring about, and the fear of being annexed is one of the causes of the difficulties in the way of cooperative action by the municipalities of a region. . . .

74. Originally "such plan, including maps, plats. . . ." — EDS.

36. *"General location, character, and extent"*: These words have very great importance. They indicate the demarcation of the commission's functions. As pointed out in the general discussion of the commission's powers and duties, it is not intended that the planning commission shall include in the master plan such exact details of location or

fronts, boulevards, parkways, playgrounds, squares, parks, aviation fields, and other public ways, grounds and open spaces, the general location of public buildings and other public property, and the general location and extent of public utilities and terminals, whether publicly or privately owned or operated, for water, light, sanitation, transportation, communication, power, and other purposes; also the removal, relocation, widening, narrowing, vacating, abandonment, change of use or extension of any of the foregoing ways, grounds, open spaces, buildings, property, utilities, or terminals; as well as a zoning plan[38] for the control of the height, area, bulk, location, and use of buildings and premises. As the work of making the whole master plan progresses, the commission may from time to time adopt and publish a part or parts thereof, any such part to cover one or more major sections or divisions of the municipality or one or more of the aforesaid or other functional matters to be included in the plan.[75] The commission may from time to time amend, extend, or add to the plan.

Sec. 7. *Purposes in view.*[40] — In the preparation of such plan the commission shall make careful and comprehensive surveys and studies of present conditions and future growth of the municipality and with due regard to its relation to neighboring territory. The plan shall be made with the general purpose of guiding and accomplishing a coordinated, adjusted, and harmonious development of the municipality and its environs which will, in accordance with present and future needs, best promote health, safety, morals, order, convenience, prosperity, and general welfare, as well as efficiency and economy in the process of development; including, among other things, adequate provision for traffic, the promotion of safety from fire and other dangers, adequate provision for light and air, the promotion of the healthful and convenient distribution of population, the promotion of good civic design and arrangement, wise and efficient expenditure of public funds, and the adequate provision of public utilities and other public requirements.

---

engineering plans and specifications as will come to be needed when the public improvement or building is to be actually constructed.

38. *"Zoning plan":* Where no zoning plan has been made and no zoning commission exists, the preparation of a zoning plan should be undertaken by the city planning commission, as zoning is simply one phase of city planning. This section assumes that a zoning enabling act is in force in the State where it is proposed to adopt the present act. If there is no such law in force, then a proper zoning enabling act should be secured and should be incorporated into and made a part of this general planning act.

75. This whole sentence is not included in the original draft. — Eds.

40. *"Purposes in view":* The purposes underlying the making of the plan are stated here to aid the members of a city planning commission in understanding the nature of their task and in making sure that the plan developed will be a comprehensive one and not a piecemeal one, and will be the result of careful study both of present conditions and future growth, and that it will consider the needs and development, not only of the municipality, but of its environs as well.

2. Community Growth Policies

■ MEIER, PLANNING FOR TOMORROW'S WORLD
Planning 16, 17, 23 (1956)

First let us establish the crude dimensions of city growth in North America. Population projections indicate that it is not unlikely that 100 million or so souls will be added between now and the end of the century. Places must be found for them. Their earnings and financial resources should be substantially higher than those we see around us now, so that the decisions as to where and how to live will be made by individuals. Their private conceptions of what is a decent place to live will set the demand; and the housing and services, in our political system, tend naturally to adapt to meet this demand. . . .

Still more disturbing is another paradox. Planners find that the redevelopment of cities in America is frustrated by the political boundaries that separate the city itself from its suburbs and so have strongly advocated measures that would make the metropolitan region the basic planning and administrative unit. Perhaps, in a few instances at least, this may be achieved in the course of several decades by employing a step by step approach. But by then, it appears, the metropolitan unit will itself be obsolete. It may stand in the way of future progress as effectively as the gerrymandering of the last generations blocks our effort today.

Can we cope with a web of urbanism hundreds of miles in extent? Should it ever be permitted to come into being? Or is this still much too oversimplified a picture? These are some of the questions brought to mind as a result of the extrapolations.[76]

■ MINISTRY OF HOUSING AND LOCAL GOVERNMENT, CIRCULAR NO. 42/55
August 3, 1955

1. Following upon his statement in the House of Commons . . . I am directed by the Minister of Housing and Local Government to draw

---

[76]. There are no private rooms or green spaces in the world described by John Hersey in his novel My Petition for More Space (1974). It is so crowded that its people stand in line for everything and everything has its allotted time: a twenty-minute wait for six minutes in the toilet; thirty minutes for fifteen at the breakfast table; hours at the Bureau of Petitions to request a change (nearly always refused) in one's life — a different job, permission to have a child. There is one unpaved area in the city — "the Green," a glass-walled lawn with trees; the longest lines in the city form every day to look in at it. "And just as one who too often handles hard things gets calluses on his hands, so the many who see all the sweet and sad things in all the lives around them get scales on their eyes — with the dulling of sight comes a deadening of feeling." — EDS.

Community Direct Cost Analysis* [10,000 units]

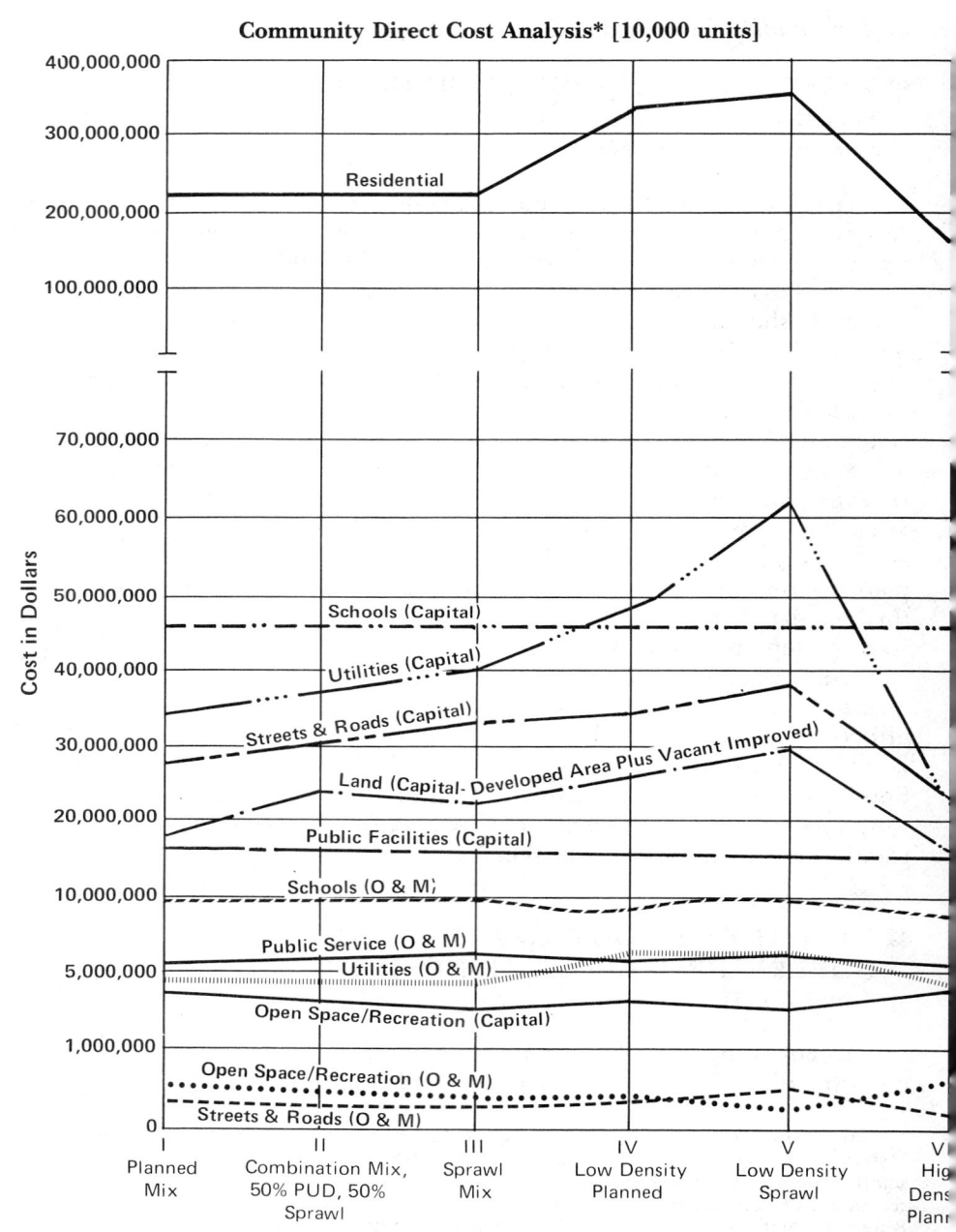

	I	II	III	IV	V	VI
	Planned Mix	Combination Mix, 50% PUD, 50% Sprawl	Sprawl Mix	Low Density Planned	Low Density Sprawl	High Density Planned

Cost in Dollars

- Residential
- Schools (Capital)
- Utilities (Capital)
- Streets & Roads (Capital)
- Land (Capital- Developed Area Plus Vacant Improved)
- Public Facilities (Capital)
- Schools (O & M)
- Public Service (O & M)
- Utilities (O & M)
- Open Space/Recreation (Capital)
- Open Space/Recreation (O & M)
- Streets & Roads (O & M)

Source: Environmental Protection Agency, The Costs of Sprawl: Detailed Cost Analysis 10 (1974).

568

Neighborhood Direct Cost Analysis* [1,000 Housing Units]

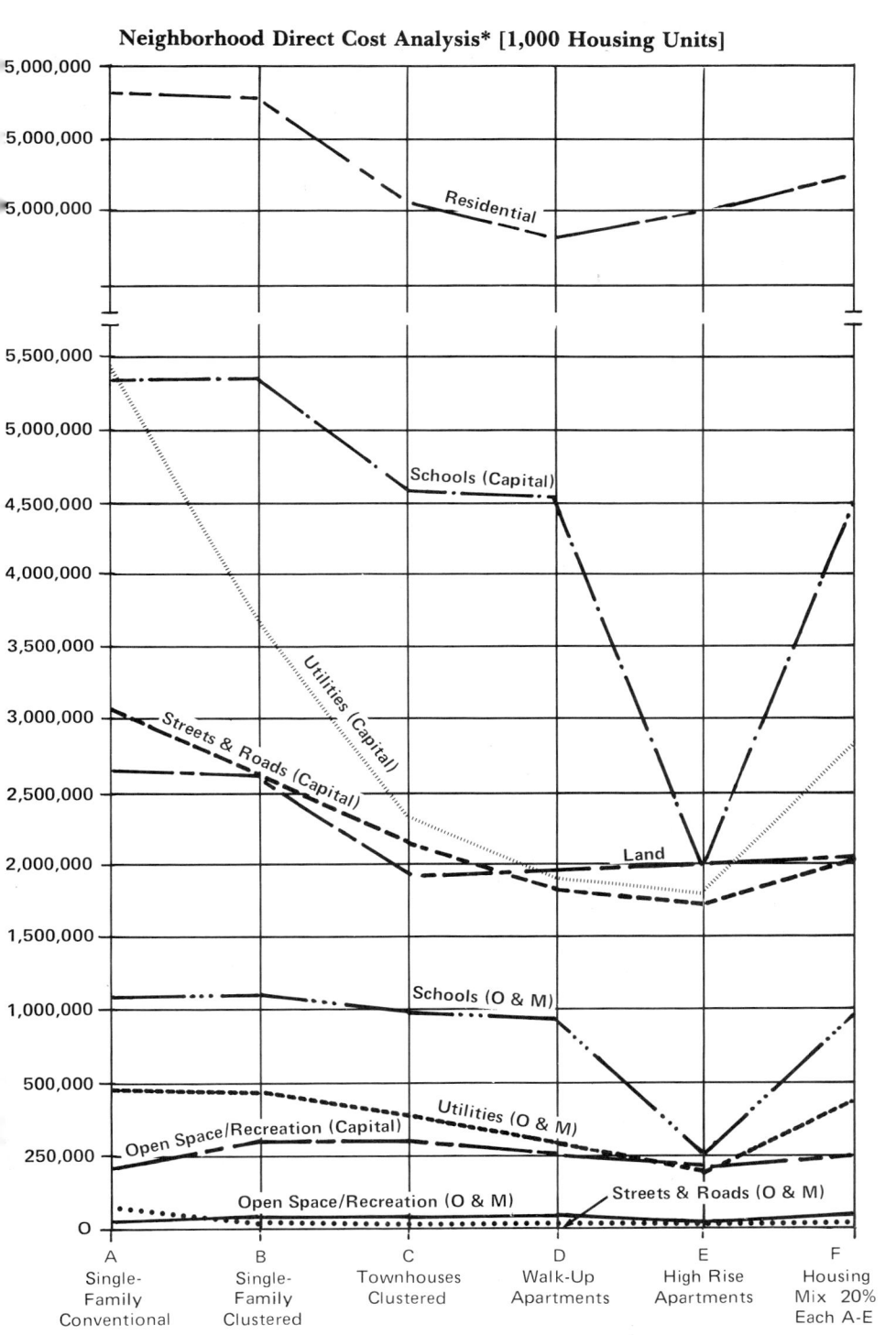

	A Single- Family Conventional	B Single- Family Clustered	C Townhouses Clustered	D Walk-Up Apartments	E High Rise Apartments	F Housing Mix 20% Each A-E

* *Source*: Environmental Protection Agency, The Costs of Sprawl: Detailed Cost Analysis 17 (1974).

your attention to the importance of checking the unrestricted sprawl of the built-up areas, and of safeguarding the surrounding countryside against further encroachment.

2. He is satisfied that the only really effective way to achieve this object is by the formal designation of clearly defined Green Belts around the areas concerned.

3. The Minister accordingly recommends Planning Authorities to consider establishing a Green Belt wherever this is desirable in order:

(a) to check the further growth of a large built-up area;

(b) to prevent neighbouring towns from merging into one another; or

(c) to preserve the special character of a town.

4. Wherever practicable, a Green Belt should be several miles wide, so as to ensure an appreciable rural zone all round the built-up area concerned.

5. Inside a Green Belt, approval should not be given, except in very special circumstances, for the construction of new buildings or for the change of use of existing buildings for purposes other than agriculture, sport, cemeteries, institutions standing in extensive grounds, or other uses appropriate to a rural area. . . .

Consider the flood plain regulations and wetland legislation (infra page 702) as the foundation of an open space plan or "green belt." How does the idea of a "green belt" relate to the concept of capacity of the land? See Whyte, The Last Landscape 182-184 (1970); Note, 27 U. Fla. L. Rev. 142 (1974). Is the "green belt" as envisioned by English planners primarily an aesthetic visual amenity for the community? Could such an amenity be created by exercise of the police power? What lessons can be derived from the English experience that are applicable to the problems of growth policy? Compare the approaches to growth taken by the communities in the following cases.

■ GOLDEN v. PLANNING BOARD OF TOWN OF RAMAPO[77]
30 N.Y.2d 359, 285 N.E.2d 291, 334 N.Y.S.2d 138, appeal dismissed, 409 U.S. 1003 (1972)

SCILEPPI, Judge. . . .

Experiencing the pressures of an increase in population and the

---

[77]. Decided together with Rockland County Builders Assn. v. Planning Board of Town of Ramapo.

D. Parochialism 571

ancillary problem of providing municipal facilities and services,[1] the Town of Ramapo, as early as 1964, made application for grant under section 801 of the Housing Act of 1964 (78 U.S. Stat. 769) to develop a master plan. The plan's preparation included a four-volume study of the existing land uses, public facilities, transportation, industry and commerce, housing needs and projected population trends. The proposals appearing in the studies were subsequently adopted pursuant to section 272-a of the Town Law, Consol. Laws, c. 62, in July, 1966 and implemented by way of a master plan. The master plan was followed by the adoption of a comprehensive zoning ordinance. Additional sewage district and drainage studies were undertaken which culminated in the adoption of a capital budget, providing for the development of the improvements specified in the master plan within the next six years. Pursuant to section 271 of the Town Law, authorizing comprehensive planning, and as a supplement to the capital budget, the Town Board adopted a capital program which provides for the location and sequence of additional capital improvements for the 12 years following the life of the capital budget. The two plans, covering a period of 18 years, detail the capital improvements projected for maximum development and conform to the specifications set forth in the master plan, the official map and drainage plan.

Based upon these criteria, the Town subsequently adopted the subject amendments for the alleged purpose of eliminating premature subdivision and urban sprawl. Residential development is to proceed according to the provision of adequate municipal facilities and services, with the assurance that any concomitant restraint upon property use is to be of a "temporary" nature and that other private uses, including the construction of individual housing, are authorized.

The amendments did not rezone or reclassify any land into different residential or use districts,[2] but, for the purposes of implementing the

---

1. The Town's allegations that present facilities are inadequate to service increasing demands goes uncontested. We must assume, therefore, that the proposed improvements, both as to their nature and extent, reflect legitimate community needs and are not veiled efforts at exclusion (see National Land & Inv. Co. v. Easttown Twp. Bd. of Adj., 419 Pa. 504, 215 A.2d 597). In the period 1940-1968 population in the unincorporated areas of the Town increased 285.9%. Between the years of 1950-1960 the increase, again in unincorporated areas, was 130.8%; from 1960-1966 some 78.5%; and from the years 1966-1969 20.4%. In terms of real numbers, population figures compare at 58,626 as of 1966 with the largest increment of growth since the decennial census occurring in the undeveloped areas. Projected figures, assuming current land use and zoning trends, approximate a total Town population of 120,000 by 1985. Growth is expected to be heaviest in the currently undeveloped western and northern tiers of the Town, predominantly in the form of subdivision development with some apartment construction. A growth rate of some 1,000 residential units per annum has been experienced in the unincorporated areas of the Town.

2. As of July, 1966, the only available figures, six residential zoning districts with varying lot size and density requirements accounted for in excess of nine tenths of the Town's unincorporated land area. Of these the RR classification (80,000 square feet

proposals appearing in the comprehensive plan, consist, in the main, of additions to the definitional sections of the ordinance, section 46-3, and the adoption of a new class of "Special Permit Uses," designated "Residential Development Use." "Residential Development Use" is defined as "The erection or construction of dwellings on any vacant plots, lots or parcels of land" (§46-3, as amd.); and, any person who acts so as to come within that definition, "shall be deemed to be engaged in residential development which shall be a separate use classification under this ordinance and subject to the requirement of obtaining a special permit from the Town Board" (§46-3, as amd.).

The standards for the issuance of special permits are framed in terms of the availability to the proposed subdivision plat of five essential facilities or services: specifically (1) public sanitary sewers or approved substitutes; (2) drainage facilities; (3) improved public parks or recreation facilities, including public schools; (4) State, county or town roads — major, secondary or collector; and, (5) firehouses. No special permit shall issue unless the proposed residential development has accumulated 15 development points, to be computed on a sliding scale of values assigned to the specified improvements under the statute. Subdivision is thus a function of immediate availability to the proposed plat of certain municipal improvements; the avowed purpose of the amendments being to phase residential development to the Town's ability to provide the above facilities or services.

Certain savings and remedial provisions are designed to relieve of potentially unreasonable restrictions. Thus, the board may issue special permits vesting a present right to proceed with residential development in such year as the development meets the required point minimum, but in no event later than the final year of the 18-year capital plan. The approved special use permit is fully assignable, and improvements scheduled for completion within one year from the date of an application

---

minimum lot area) plus R-35 zone (35,000 square feet minimum lot area) comprise over one half of all zoned areas. The subject sites are presently zoned RR-50 (50,000 square feet minimum lot area). The reasonableness of these minimum lot requirements are not presently controverted, though we are referred to no compelling need in their behalf (see Salamar Bldrs. Corp. v. Tuttle, 29 N.Y.2d 221, 325 N.Y.S.2d 933, 275 N.E.2d 585; see also, National Land & Inv. Co. v. Easttown Twp. Bd. of Adj., 419 Pa. 504, 215 A.2d 597, supra; Concord Twp. Appeal, 439 Pa. 466, 268 A.2d 765). Under present zoning regulations, the population of the unincorporated areas could be increased by about 14,600 families (3.5 people) when all suitable vacant land is occupied. Housing values as of 1960 in the unincorporated areas range from a modest $15,000 (approx. 30%) to higher than $25,000 (25%), with the undeveloped western tier of Town showing the highest percentage of values in excess of $25,000 (41%). Significantly, for the same year only about one half of one percent of all housing units were occupied by nonwhite families. Efforts at adjusting this disparity are reflected in the creation of a public housing authority and the authority's proposal to construct biracial low-income family housing (see Fletcher v. Romney, 323 F. Supp. 189 [S.D.N.Y.]; Matter of Greenwald v. Town of Ramapo, 35 A.D.2d 958, 317 N.Y.S.2d 839; Matter of Farrelly v. Town of Ramapo, 35 A.D.2d 957, 317 N.Y.S.2d 837).

D. Parochialism 573

are to be credited as though existing on the date of the application. A prospective developer may advance the date of subdivision approval by agreeing to provide those improvements which will bring the proposed plat within the number of development points required by the amendments. And applications are authorized to the "Development Easement Acquisition Commission" for a reduction of the assessed valuation. Finally, upon application to the Town Board, the development point requirements may be varied should the board determine that such a variance or modification is consistent with the on-going development plan.

The undisputed effect of these integrated efforts in land use planning and development is to provide an over-all program of orderly growth and adequate facilities through a sequential development policy commensurate with progressing availability and capacity of public facilities. While its goals are clear and its purposes undisputably laudatory, serious questions are raised as to the manner in which these ends are to be effected, not the least of which relates to their legal viability under present zoning enabling legislation, particularly sections 261 and 263 of the Town Law. The owners of the subject premises argue, and the Appellate Division has sustained the proposition, that the primary purpose of the amending ordinance is to control or regulate population growth within the Town and as such is not within the authorized objectives of the zoning enabling legislation. We disagree.

In enacting the challenged amendments, the Town Board has sought to control subdivision in all residential districts, pending the provision (public or private) at some future date of various services and facilities. A reading of the relevant statutory provisions reveals that there is no specific authorization for the "sequential" and "timing" controls adopted here. That, of course, cannot be said to end the matter, for the additional inquiry remains as to whether the challenged amendments find their basis within the perimeters of the devices authorized and purposes sanctioned under current enabling legislation. Our concern is, as it should be, with the effects of the statutory scheme taken as a whole and its role in the propagation of a viable policy of land use and planning.

... In the end, zoning properly effects, and only in the manner prescribed, those purposes detailed under section 263 of the Town Law. It may not be invoked to further the general police powers of a municipality (see, e.g., Westwood Forest Estates v. Village of South Nyack, 23 N.Y.2d 424, 297 N.Y.S.2d 129, 244 N.E.2d 700).[5]

Even so, considering the activities enumerated by section 261 of

---

5. This distinction, though often unarticulated, is elemental and we have in the past held the exercise of the zoning power ultra vires and void where the end sought to be accomplished was not peculiar to the locality's basic land use scheme, but rather related to some general problem, incidental to the community at large. ...

the Town Law, and relating those powers to the authorized purposes detailed in section 263, the challenged amendments are proper zoning techniques, exercised for legitimate zoning purposes. The power to restrict and regulate conferred under section 261 includes within its grant, by way of necessary implication, the authority to direct the growth of population for the purposes indicated, within the confines of the township. It is the matrix of land use restrictions, common to each of the enumerated powers and sanctioned goals, a necessary concomitant to the municipalities' recognized authority to determine the lines along which local development shall proceed, though it may divert it from its natural course. . . .

Experience, over the last quarter century, however, with greater technological integration and drastic shifts in population distribution has pointed up serious defects and community autonomy in land use controls has come under increasing attack by legal commentators, and students of urban problems alike, because of its pronounced insularism and its correlative role in producing distortions in metropolitan growth patterns, and perhaps more importantly, in crippling efforts toward regional and State-wide problem solving, be it pollution, decent housing, or public transportation.

Recognition of communal and regional interdependence, in turn, has resulted in proposals for schemes of regional and State-wide planning, in the hope that decisions would then correspond roughly to their level of impact. Yet, as salutary as such proposals may be, the power to zone under current law is vested in local municipalities, and we are constrained to resolve the issues accordingly. What does become more apparent in treating with the problem, however, is that though the issues are framed in terms of the developer's due process rights, those rights cannot, realistically speaking, be viewed separately and apart from the rights of others "'in search of a [more] comfortable place to live.'"

There is, then, something inherently suspect in a scheme which, apart from its professed purposes, effects a restriction upon the free mobility of a people until sometime in the future when projected facilities are available to meet increased demands. Although zoning must include schemes designed to allow municipalities to more effectively contend with the increased demands of evolving and growing communities, under its guise, townships have been wont to try their hand at an array of exclusionary devices in the hope of avoiding the very burden which growth must inevitably bring. Though the conflict engendered by such tactics is certainly real, and its implications vast, accumulated evidence, scientific and social, points circumspectly at the hazards of undirected growth and the naive, somewhat nostalgic imperative that egalitarianism is a function of growth.

Of course, these problems cannot be solved by Ramapo or any

D. Parochialism 575

single municipality, but depend upon the accommodation of widely disparate interests for their ultimate resolution. To that end, State-wide or regional control of planning would insure that interests broader than that of the municipality underlie various land use policies. Nevertheless, that should not be the only context in which growth devices such as these, aimed at population assimilation, not exclusion, will be sustained; especially where, as here, we would have no alternative but to strike the provision down in the wistful hope that the efforts of the State Office of Planning Coordination and the American Law Institute will soon bear fruit.

Hence, unless we are to ignore the plain meaning of the statutory delegation, this much is clear: phased growth is well within the ambit of existing enabling legislation. And, of course, it is no answer to point to emergent problems to buttress the conclusion that such innovative schemes are beyond the perimeters of statutory authorization. These considerations, admittedly real, to the extent which they are relevant, bear solely upon the continued viability of "localism" in land use regulation; obviously, they can neither add nor detract from the initial grant of authority, obsolescent though it may be. The answer which Ramapo has posed can by no means be termed definitive; it is, however, a first practical step toward controlled growth achieved without forsaking broader social purposes. . . .

It is the nature of all land use and development regulations to circumscribe the course of growth within a particular town or district and to that extent such restrictions invariably impede the forces of natural growth. Where those restrictions upon the beneficial use and enjoyment of land are necessary to promote the ultimate good of the community and are within the bounds of reason, they have been sustained. "Zoning [, however,] is a means by which a governmental body can plan for the future — it may not be used as a means to deny the future" (National Land & Inv. Co. v. Easttown Twp. Bd. of Adj., 419 Pa. 504, 528, 215 A.2d 597, 610, supra). Its exercise assumes that development shall not stop at the community's threshold, but only that whatever growth there may be shall proceed along a predetermined course. It is inextricably bound to the dynamics of community life and its function is to guide, not to isolate or facilitate efforts at avoiding the ordinary incidents of growth. What segregates permissible from impermissible restrictions, depends in the final analysis upon the purpose of the restrictions and their impact in terms of both the community and general public interest. The line of delineation between the two is not a constant, but will be found to vary with prevailing circumstances and conditions.

What we will not countenance, then, under any guise, [are] community efforts at immunization or exclusion. But, far from being exclusionary, the present amendments merely seek, by the implementation of sequential development and timed growth, to provide a balanced cohesive community dedicated to the efficient utilization of land. The restrictions conform to the community's considered land use policies as expressed in its comprehensive plan and represent a bona fide effort to maximize population density consistent with orderly growth. True other alternatives, such as requiring off-site improvements as a prerequisite to subdivision, may be available, but the choice as how best to proceed, in view of the difficulties attending such exactions . . . cannot be faulted.

Perhaps even more importantly, timed growth, unlike the minimum lot requirements recently struck down by the Pennsylvania Supreme Court as exclusionary, does not impose permanent restrictions upon land use. Its obvious purpose is to prevent premature subdivision absent essential municipal facilities and to insure continuous development commensurate with the Town's obligation to provide such facilities. They seek, not to freeze population at present levels but to maximize growth by the efficient use of land, and in so doing testify to this community's continuing role in population assimilation. In sum, Ramapo asks not that it be left alone, but only that it be allowed to prevent the kind of deterioration that has transformed well-ordered and thriving residential communities into blighted ghettos with attendant hazards to health, security and social stability — a danger not without substantial basis in fact.

We only require that communities confront the challenge of population growth with open doors. Where in grappling with that problem, the community undertakes, by imposing temporary restrictions upon development, to provide required municipal services in a rational manner, courts are rightfully reluctant to strike down such schemes. The timing controls challenged here parallel recent proposals put forth by various study groups and have their genesis in certain of the pronouncements of this and the courts of sister States. While these controls are typically proposed as an adjunct of regional planning, the preeminent protection against their abuse resides in the mandatory ongoing planning and development requirement, present here, which attends their implementation and use.

We may assume, therefore, that the present amendments are the product of foresighted planning calculated to promote the welfare of the township. The Town has imposed temporary restrictions upon land use in residential areas while committing itself to a program of development. It has utilized its comprehensive plan to implement its timing controls and has coupled with these restrictions provisions for low and moderate income housing on a large scale. Considered as a whole, it represents both in its inception and implementation a reasonable attempt to provide for the sequential, orderly development of land in conjunction with the needs of the community, as well as individual

D. Parochialism

parcels of land, while simultaneously obviating the blighted aftermath which the initial failure to provide needed facilities so often brings.

The proposed amendments have the effect of restricting development for onwards to 18 years in certain areas. Whether the subject parcels will be so restricted for the full term is not clear, for it is equally probable that the proposed facilities will be brought into these areas well before that time. Assuming, however, that the restrictions will remain outstanding for the life of the program, they still fall short of a confiscation within the meaning of the Constitution....

In sum, where it is clear that the existing physical and financial resources of the community are inadequate to furnish the essential services and facilities which a substantial increase in population requires, there is a rational basis for "phased growth" and hence, the challenged ordinance is not violative of the Federal and State Constitutions. Accordingly, the order appealed from should be reversed and the actions remitted to Special Term for entry of a judgment declaring section 46-13.1 of the Town Ordinance constitutional.

BREITEL, Judge (dissenting).

The limited powers of district zoning and subdivision regulation delegated to a municipality do not include the power to impose a moratorium on land development. Such conclusion is dictated by settled doctrine that a municipality has only those powers, and especially land use powers, delegated or necessarily implied.

But there is more involved in these cases than the arrogation of undelegated powers. Raised are vital constitutional issues, and, most important, policy issues trenching on grave domestic problems of our time, without the benefit of a legislative determination which would reflect the interests of the entire State. The policy issues relate to needed housing, planned land development under government control, and the exclusion in effect or by motive, of walled-in urban populations of the middle class and the poor....

A glance at history suggests that Ramapo's plan to have public services installed in advance of development is unrealistic. Richard Babcock, the distinguished practitioner in land development law, some years ago addressed himself to the natural desire of communities to stay development while they caught up with the inexorable thrust of population growth and movement. He observed eloquently that this country was built and is still being built by people who moved about, innovated, pioneered, and created industry and employment, and thereby provided both the need and the means for the public services and facilities that followed (Babcock, The Zoning Game, at pp. 149-150). Thus, the movement has not been in the other direction, first the provision of public and utility services and then the building of homes, farms, and businesses. This court has said as much, in effect, in Westwood Forest Estates v. Village of South Nyack, 23 N.Y.2d 424, 297

N.Y.S.2d 129, 244 N.E.2d 700,[78] unanimously and in reliance on commonplace authority and precedent.

As said earlier, when the problem arose outside the State the judicial response has been the same, frustrating communities, intent on walling themselves from the mainstream of development, namely, that the effort was invalid under existing enabling acts or unconstitutional. The response may not be charged to judicial conservatism or self-restraint. In short, it has not been illiberal. It has indeed reflected the larger understanding that American society is at a critical crossroads in the accommodation of urbanization and suburban living, with effects that are no longer confined, bad as they are, to ethnic exclusion or "snob" zoning. Ramapo would preserve its nature, delightful as that may be, but the supervening question is whether it alone may decide this or whether it must be decided by the larger community represented by the Legislature. Legally, politically, economically, and sociologically, the base for determination must be larger than that provided by the town fathers.

Accordingly, I dissent and vote to affirm the orders in both cases.[79]

Notes

1. Ramapo is about 35 miles from midtown Manhattan. It became more accessible because of the construction of the New York State Thruway, the Tappan Zee Bridge, and the extension of the Garden State Parkway to the Thruway. The town borders New Jersey's Bergen County, and is very close to Mahwah, New Jersey, which is the location of a large Ford Motor Company assembly plant. Only the unincorporated area of the town is subject to the controlled-growth ordinance. Statistics from the 1970 census show that Ramapo Township, including the incorporated villages, had 71,739 white residents and 4563 black residents; of the black residents, 4147 lived in the incorporated village of Spring Valley. Of all vacant land set aside for residential use, fully 65 percent was limited to what may fairly be described as "large lot" zoning, the minimum required lot areas ranging from 25,000 to 80,000 square feet. The lawsuit arose in connection with the proposed development of 50,000-square-foot lots. There was no district in the town of Ramapo that was set aside for multifamily housing. Multifamily

---

78. This was an opinion by Judge Breitel that invalidated an ordinance lowering the density for apartments in order to reduce the burden on the sewage treatment plant. Cf. Belle Harbor Realty Corp. v. Kerr, 43 App. Div. 2d 727, 350 N.Y.S.2d 698 (1973). — Eds.

79. Sections 2-101 and 2-102 of the Model Land Development Code would require that zoning and subdivision regulations be combined into a single "development ordinance" administered by a single "land development agency." — Eds.

D. Parochialism

housing was limited to the incorporated areas, such as Suffern and Spring Valley, which already contained most of such housing.

To what extent do you think the court was influenced by the town's fight (including litigation against some town residents) to build "biracial low-income family housing"? See footnote 2 in the opinion. This housing consisted of approximately 200 units, 75 percent of which were designed for and occupied by the elderly, all of whom were white. About fifty units were occupied by low-income families, five or ten of whom were black. See Bosselman, Can the Town of Ramapo Pass a Law to Bind the Rights of the Whole World?, 1 Fla. St. U.L. Rev. 234 (1973), and the Raleigh-Marlowe-like response in Landman, No, Mr. Bosselman, the Town of Ramapo Cannot Pass a Law to Bind the Rights of the Whole World: A Reply, 10 Tulsa L.J. 169 (1974).

2. The attorney for the Town of Ramapo wrote that this was "not an exclusionary zoning case":

> The confusion of many attorneys in the battle against exclusionary zoning is unfortunate. There is a tendency to view all zoning as intrinsically evil simply because some communities utilize these tools in an exclusionary manner. This problem has been around for a long time. Should we go back to no zoning at all, to unlimited urban sprawl and development chaos in suburban areas merely because some of the tools are essentially neutral? They can be used correctly or incorrectly, depending upon the motivation of the regulators. Our efforts must be to eliminate the abuses, while simultaneously developing stronger efforts to preserve the quality of our communities and of the environment. We must assure economic and racial equality in planning, not without planning.

Freilich, Ramapo Township: Comments of Attorney Who Drafted the Ordinance, 24 Zoning Dig. 72, 73-74 (1972). Cf. Notes, 57 Cornell L. Rev. 827 (1972); 47 N.Y.U. L. Rev. 723 (1972); and 26 Stan. L. Rev. 585 (1974).

Do you agree? If it is not exclusionary, why do the planning devices control only housing, not industrial and commercial development? Should the court have compared Ramapo's resulting tax effort with that of other communities in the region? If so, what standard should it have applied and why?

3. Under the ordinance, development, as a matter of right, required the accumulation of fifteen points according to the system in the table on page 580. What changes in the point system would you propose for your community? Should the town in this plan be able to restrict development until the installation of services over which it has little or no control?

How can a long-range capital budget plan take into account changing circumstances suggesting revised local priorities, inflation, unpredictable construction costs, delays in related state or county

Development Point System*

	Points
Sewers	
Public sewers available	5
Package sewer plants	3
County-approved septic system (in one Zoning District)	3
All others	0
Drainage	
(Percentage of required drainage capacity available)	
100% or more	5
90% to 99.9%	4
80% to 89.9%	3
65% to 79.9%	2
50% to 64.9%	1
Less than 50%	0
Improved public park or recreation facility	
(Including public school site)	
Within 1/4 mile	5
Within 1/2 mile	3
Within 1 mile	1
Further than 1 mile	0
Improved roads	
(State, county or town major, secondary or collector roads improved with curbs and sidewalks)	
Direct access	5
Within 1/2 mile	3
Within 1 mile	1
Further than 1 mile	0
Firehouse	
Within 1 mile	3
Within 2 miles	1
Further than 2 miles	0

* *Source:* Record of Appeal, Golden v. Planning Board of Town of Ramapo, appeal dismissed, 409 U.S. 1003 (1972).

projects, and delays or moratoria on state and federal aid affecting projects essential to the plan? Ramapo encountered some difficulty completing its capital budget programs. Two severe hurricanes, Doria in August 1971 and Agnes in June 1972, caused serious flood damage. The town was forced to appropriate $1.5 million to mop up. Much of the work scheduled for those years in the 1971 capital budget was deferred and, as a consequence, no formal capital budgets were adopted for 1972 and 1973. The adopted 1974 capital budget differed significantly from the 1971 budget; the major emphasis in the later budget was directed toward road improvements believed necessary because of state road projects, including a new state Thruway interchange, moving more traffic onto roads in the town.

4. Prior to institution of the plan, the town grew at an average of

D. Parochialism 581

about 620 dwelling units per year. In the first five years of the plan (through June 1974), Ramapo granted special permits for development meeting the fifteen-point test on 71 applications involving 1084 acres and 991 lots. It granted variances for development not passing the point test on 146 applications involving 488 acres and 648 lots, and denied variances on 12 applications involving 100 acres and 113 lots. The total approved special permits and variances involved 1639 lots and 1714 dwelling units over the five-year period, or approval for an average of 367 dwelling units per year. Generally, approved development was located near prior development. The approvals were not spread evenly over the years; the first year had a particularly high number of variances, while activity in the last year declined along with the nationwide slump in the home-building industry. And it should be clear that the granting of a special permit or variance does not mean actual construction.

As you will recall, developers whose property does not have adequate municipal services may bear the cost of installation of those services and proceed with development. In twenty-one instances, a developer increased its point total by providing improvements at its own expense. Usually, the developer provided drainage improvements, improved roads, or recreational facilities. No developer completed sewer construction, nor had any ever proposed the construction of a firehouse.

5. See Charles v. Diamond, 41 N.Y.2d 318, 360 N.E.2d 1265 (1977), in which the court held that a municipality cannot use its own delay, otherwise unjustified, in providing public services as the basis for refusing approval to new development. "Temporary restraints necessary to promote the overall public intent are permissible. Permanent interference with the reasonable use of private property for the purposes for which it is suited is not." Id. at 1300. Immediately after citing the eighteen-year period upheld in *Ramapo*, the court said:

> However, the crucial factor, perhaps even the decisive one, is whether the ultimate economic cost of the benefits is being shared by the members of the community at large, or, rather, is being hidden from the public by the placement of the entire burden upon particular property owners. . . .
>
> Petitioner has alleged sufficient facts to create a triable issue as to whether the village sewer ordinance is being applied to his property unconstitutionally. Ultimate constitutionality hinges upon several important and diverse, yet not exclusive, factors. At the trial, it will be relevant to establish the exact nature of the village sewage disposal problem. Only when the problem has been specifically identified can it be determined what steps are necessary to correct the difficulty and at what cost, in terms both of expense and time. (Cf. Berenson v. Town of New Castle, 38 N.Y.2d 102, 378 N.Y.S.2d 672, 341 N.E.2d 236.) . . . Although reasonable excuse may justify delay, the village must be committed firmly

to the construction and installation of the necessary improvements. (See Matter of Golden v. Planning Bd. of Town of Ramapo, 30 N.Y.2d 359, 382, 334 N.Y.S.2d 138, 155, 285 N.E.2d 291, 304.) Absent the constraints imposed by law or contract, governmental officials may conduct affairs of government at their own pace. However, where the municipality has affirmatively barred substantially all use of private property pending remedial municipal improvements, unreasonable and dilatory tactics, targeted really to frustrate all private use of property, are not justified. The municipality may not, by withholding the improvements that the municipality has made the necessary prerequisites for development, achieve the result of barring development, a goal that would perhaps be otherwise unreachable.

Regarding the withholding of municipal services as a means of growth control, see also Okemo Trailside Condominiums v. Blais, 380 A.2d 84 (Vt. 1977); Robinson v. City of Boulder, infra page 670; Associated Home Builders v. City of Livermore, 135 Cal. Rptr. 41, 557 P.2d 473 (1976).

6. "On March 14, 1983, the town board of Ramapo, New York, drastically revised its famous growth control program by dropping its point system allocation for subdivision approval. The program achieved high visibility and was widely copied after New York's highest court upheld it as a valid timing technique for controlling new development. Now the growth control program is perceived as having discouraged needed economic development and growth." Reconsidering Innovative Land Use Controls, Land Use L. & Zoning Dig., May 1983, at 3. The Wall Street Journal reported, in an article dated August 31, 1983, "Ramapo's problem now is too little growth. Fred Rella, township supervisor, says, 'We want more growth, but growth that's compatible with our country-like atmosphere.'" Should the court now feel foolish for its assumption that the abandoned plan was "the product of foresighted planning calculated to promote the welfare of the community"?

7. A tight economy can often change the most carefully crafted planning schemes. In some financially pressed communities anxious to increase their revenue base, officials have resorted to privatizing what are traditionally governmental services and amenities:

> What Hartz has done over the last decade would make any good-sized municipality feel a sense of civic accomplishment. In 1978, the company spent $400,000 to build a new commuter railroad platform and parking area to enhance its Harmon Cove project in Secaucus, and convinced N.J. Transit to schedule stops there for its trains.
>
> A few years later, in another Secaucus project, Hartz built a bridge over the New Jersey Turnpike's eastern spur that joins two sections of its Harmon Meadow mixed-use project. The company also built an access

D. Parochialism

bridge over Route 3 to bring traffic from the Turnpike into the complex....

Hartz did not approach the local government for assistance. "We didn't even consider asking them," said Mr. Gold. "The township of Weehawken has been financially pressed for many years. There's no way they could do that."

Stanley D. Iacono, the mayor of Weehawken, agreed. "If they want to move on the project," he said, "they've got to help themselves."

N.Y. Times (Real Estate section), Aug. 3, 1986.

For a critical evaluation of private sector initiatives, complete with a helpful introduction to the growing body of literature in this area, see Bendick, Privatization of Public Services: Recent Experience, in Public-Private Partnership: New Opportunities for Meeting Social Needs 153 (Brooks, Liebman & Schelling eds. 1984). Communities considering contracting out or deferring to private entities must consider potential gains and losses in terms of accountability, efficiency, and performance. How similar are such large-scale private infrastructure efforts to the developer's assumption of the local planner's functions in immensely popular cluster development devices like PUDs? Is the deference accorded public officials appropriate for their corporate counterparts? Should liability (and immunity) depend on function or on sources of funds?

■ CONSTRUCTION INDUSTRY ASSOCIATION v. CITY OF PETALUMA
522 F.2d 897 (9th Cir.), cert. denied, 424 U.S. 934 (1975)

CHOY, Circuit Judge. The City of Petaluma (the City) appeals from a district court decision voiding as unconstitutional certain aspects of its five-year housing and zoning plan. We reverse.

The City is located in southern Sonoma County, about 40 miles north of San Francisco. In the 1950's and 1960's, Petaluma was a relatively self-sufficient town. It experienced a steady population growth from 10,315 in 1950 to 24,870 in 1970. Eventually, the City was drawn into the Bay Area metropolitan housing market as people working in San Francisco and San Rafael became willing to commute longer distances to secure relatively inexpensive housing available there. By November 1972, according to unofficial figures, Petaluma's population was at 30,500, a dramatic increase of almost 25 percent in little over two years.

The increase in the City's population, not surprisingly, is reflected in the increase in the number of its housing units. From 1964 to 1971, the following number of residential housing units were completed:

1964	270
1965	440
1966	321
1967	234
1968	379
1969	358
1970	591
1971	891

In 1970 and 1971, the years of the most rapid growth, demand for housing in the City was even greater than above indicated. Taking 1970 and 1971 together, builders won approval of a total of 2000 permits although only 1482 were actually completed by the end of 1971.

Alarmed by the accelerated rate of growth in 1970 and 1971, the demand for even more housing, and the sprawl of the City eastward, the City adopted a temporary freeze on development in early 1971. The construction and zoning change moratorium was intended to give the City Council and the City planners an opportunity to study the housing and zoning situation and to develop short and long range plans. The Council made specific findings with respect to housing patterns and availability in Petaluma, including the following: That from 1960-1970 housing had been in almost unvarying 6000 square-foot lots laid out in regular grid patterns; that there was a density of approximately 4.5 housing units per acre in the single-family home areas; that during 1960-1970, 88 percent of housing permits issued were for single-family detached homes; that in 1970, 83 percent of Petaluma's housing was single-family dwellings; that the bulk of recent development (largely single-family homes) occurred in the eastern portion of the City, causing a large deficiency in moderately priced multi-family and apartment units on the east side.

To correct the imbalance between single-family and multi-family dwellings, curb the sprawl of the City on the east, and retard the accelerating growth of the City, the Council in 1972 adopted several resolutions, which collectively are called the "Petaluma Plan" (the Plan).

The Plan, on its face limited to a five-year period (1972-1977), fixes a housing development growth rate not to exceed 500 dwelling units per year. Each dwelling unit represents approximately three people. The 500-unit figure is somewhat misleading, however, because it applies only to housing units (hereinafter referred to as "development-units") that are part of projects involving five units or more. Thus, the 500-unit figure does not reflect any housing and population growth due to construction of single-family homes or even four-unit apartment buildings not part of any larger project.

The Plan also positions a 200 foot wide "greenbelt" around the City, to serve as a boundary for urban expansion for at least five years,

D. Parochialism 585

and with respect to the east and north sides of the City, for perhaps ten to fifteen years. One of the most innovative features of the Plan is the Residential Development Control System which provides procedures and criteria for the award of the annual 500 development-unit permits. At the heart of the allocation procedure is an intricate point system, whereby a builder accumulates points for conformity by his projects with the City's general plan and environmental design plans, for good architectural design, and for providing low and moderate income dwelling units and various recreational facilities. The Plan further directs that allocations of building permits are to be divided as evenly as feasible between the west and east sections of the City and between single-family dwellings and multiple residential units (including rental units), that the sections of the City closest to the center are to be developed first in order to cause "infilling" of vacant area, and that 8 to 12 percent of the housing units approved be for low and moderate income persons.

In a provision of the Plan, intended to maintain the close-in rural space outside and surrounding Petaluma, the City solicited Sonoma County to establish stringent subdivision and appropriate acreage parcel controls for the areas outside the urban extension line of the City and to limit severely further residential infilling.

The purpose of the Plan is much disputed in this case. According to general statements in the Plan itself, the Plan was devised to ensure that "development in the next five years, will take place in a reasonable, orderly, attractive manner, rather than in a completely haphazard and unattractive manner." The controversial 500-unit limitation on residential development-units was adopted by the City "[i]n order to protect its small town character and surrounding open space." The other features of the Plan were designed to encourage an east-west balance in development, to provide for variety in densities and building types and wide ranges in prices and rents, to ensure infilling of close-in vacant areas, and to prevent the sprawl of the city to the east and north. The Construction Industry Association of Sonoma County (the Association) argues and the district court found, however, that the Plan was primarily enacted "to limit Petaluma's demographic and market growth rate in housing and in the immigration of new residents." . . .

According to undisputed expert testimony at trial, if the Plan (limiting housing starts to approximately 6 percent of existing housing stock each year) were to be adopted by municipalities throughout the region, the impact on the housing market would be substantial. For the decade 1970 to 1980, the shortfall in needed housing in the region would be about 105,000 units (or 25 percent of the units needed). Further, the aggregate effect of a proliferation of the Plan throughout the San Francisco region would be a decline in regional housing stock quality, a loss of the mobility of current and prospective residents and a deterioration in the quality and choice of housing available to income earners with real incomes of $14,000 per year or less. If, however, the Plan were considered by itself and with respect to Petaluma only, there is no evidence to suggest that there would be a deterioration in the quality and choice of housing available there to persons in the lower and middle income brackets. Actually, the Plan increases the availability of multi-family units (owner-occupied and rental units) and low-income units which were rarely constructed in the pre-Plan days. . . .

The City also challenges the standing of the Association and the Landowners to maintain the suit. The standing requirement raises the threshold question in every federal case whether plaintiff has made out a "case or controversy" between himself and the defendant within the meaning of Article III of the Constitution. In order to satisfy the constitutional requirement that courts decide only cases or controversies and to ensure the requisite concreteness of facts and adverseness of parties, plaintiff must show that he has a "personal stake in the outcome of the controversy," or that he has suffered "some threatened or actual injury resulting from the putatively illegal action." Further, the plaintiff must satisfy the additional court-imposed standing requirement that the "interest sought to be protected by the complainant is arguably within the zone of interests to be protected or regulated by the statute or constitutional guarantee in question." A corollary to the "zone of interest" requirement is the well-recognized general rule that "even when the plaintiff has alleged injury sufficient to meet the 'case or controversy' requirement, . . . the plaintiff generally must assert his own legal rights and interests, and cannot rest his claim to relief on the legal rights or interests of third parties." Warth v. Seldin, 422 U.S. 490, 499 (1975). Appellees easily satisfy the "injury in fact" standing requirement. The Association alleges it has suffered in its own right monetary damages due to lost revenues. Sonoma County builders contribute dues to the Association in a sum proportionate to the amount of business the builders do in the area. Thus, in a very real sense a restriction on building in Petaluma causes economic injury to the Association.

The two Landowners also have already suffered or are threatened with a direct injury. It is their position that the Petaluma Plan operated, of itself, to adversely affect the value and marketability of their land for residential uses, and such an allegation is sufficient to show that they have a personal stake in the outcome of the controversy.

Although appellees have suffered or are threatened with direct personal injury, the "zone of interest" requirement poses a huge stumbling block to their attempt to show standing. The primary federal claim upon which this suit is based — the right to travel or migrate — is a claim asserted not on the appellees' own behalf, but on behalf of a group of unknown third parties allegedly excluded from living in Petaluma. Although individual builders, the Association, and the Land-

D. Parochialism 587

owners are admittedly adversely affected by the Petaluma Plan, their economic interests are undisputedly outside the zone of interest to be protected by any purported constitutional right to travel. Accordingly, appellees' right to travel claim "falls squarely within the prudential standing rule that normally bars litigants from asserting the rights or legal interests of others in order to obtain relief from injury to themselves." Warth v. Seldin, 422 U.S. at 509. . . .

Although we conclude that appellees lack standing to assert the rights of third parties, they nonetheless have standing to maintain claims based on violations of rights personal to them. Accordingly, appellees have standing to challenge the Petaluma Plan on the grounds asserted in their complaint that the Plan is arbitrary and thus violative of their due process rights guaranteed by the Fourteenth Amendment and that the Plan poses an unreasonable burden on interstate commerce. . . .

Although we assume that some persons desirous of living in Petaluma will be excluded under the housing permit limitation and that, thus, the Plan may frustrate some legitimate regional housing needs, the Plan is not arbitrary or unreasonable. We agree with appellees that unlike the situation in the past most municipalities today are neither isolated nor wholly independent from neighboring municipalities and that, consequently, unilateral land use decisions by one local entity affect the needs and resources of an entire region. It does not necessarily follow, however, that the *due process* rights of builders and landowners are violated merely because a local entity exercises in its own self-interest the police power lawfully delegated to it by the state. If the present system of delegated zoning power does not effectively serve the state interest in furthering the general welfare of the region or entire state, it is the state legislature's and not the federal courts' role to intervene and adjust the system. As stated supra, the federal court is not a super zoning board and should not be called on to mark the point at which legitimate local interests in promoting the welfare of the community are outweighed by legitimate regional interests. . . .

. . . [T]he public welfare is sufficiently broad to uphold Petaluma's desire to preserve its small town character, its open spaces and low density of population, and to grow at an orderly and deliberate pace.

The district court found that housing in Petaluma and the surrounding areas is produced substantially through goods and services in interstate commerce and that curtailment of residential growth in Petaluma will cause serious dislocation to commerce. 375 F. Supp. at 577, 579. Our ruling today, however, that the Petaluma Plan represents a reasonable and legitimate exercise of the police power obviates the necessity of remanding the case for consideration of appellees' claim that the Plan unreasonably burdens interstate commerce.

It is well settled that a state regulation validly based on the police power does not impermissibly burden interstate commerce where the regulation neither discriminates against interstate commerce nor operates to disrupt its required uniformity. As stated by the Supreme Court almost 25 years ago:

> When there is a reasonable basis for legislation to protect the social, as distinguished from the economic, welfare of a community, it is not for this Court because of the Commerce Clause to deny the exercise locally of the sovereign power of the [state].

Breard v. Alexandria, 341 U.S. 622, 640 (1951). It is wholly beyond a court's limited authority under the Commerce Clause to review state legislation by balancing reasonable social welfare legislation against its incidental burden on commerce.

Consequently, since the local regulation here is rationally related to the social and environmental welfare of the community and does not discriminate against interstate commerce or operate to disrupt its required uniformity, appellees' claim that the plan unreasonably burdens commerce must fail.

Notes

1. Consider the following criteria used to review development proposals in Petaluma:

> Applications are reviewed by the Residential Development Evaluation Board. In general, the board considers the extent to which the proposal is in conformity with the general plan and the environmental design plan. In addition, the resolution establishes two broad categories of review criteria, which are quantified by the use of a numerical rating system. The following are the factors in the section on availability of public facilities and services on a scale of zero to five points:
> 1. the capacity of the water system to provide for the needs of the proposed development without system extensions beyond those normally installed by the developer;
> 2. the capacity of the sanitary sewers to dispose of the wastes of the proposed development without system extensions beyond those normally installed by the developer;
> 3. the capacity of the drainage facilities to adequately dispose of the surface runoff of the proposed development without system extensions beyond those normally installed by the developer;
> 4. the ability of the Fire Department of the city to provide fire protection according to the established response standards of the city without the necessity of establishing a new station or requiring addition of major equipment to an existing station;

D. Parochialism 589

5. the capacity of the appropriate school to absorb the children expected to inhabit a proposed development without necessitating adding double sessions or other unusual scheduling or classroom overcrowding;

6. the capacity of major street linkage to provide for the needs of the proposed development without substantially altering existing traffic patterns or overloading the existing street system, and the availability of other public facilities (such as parks and playgrounds) to meet the additional demands for vital public services without extension of services beyond those provided by the developer.

The second category of review is on the quality of design and contribution of public welfare and amenity, each item of which is assigned from 0 to 10 points on each of the following:

1. site and architectural design quality which may be indicated by the harmony of the proposed buildings in terms of size, height, color, and location with respect to existing neighboring development;

2. site and architectural design quality which may be indicated by the amount and character of landscaping and screening;

3. site and architectural design quality which may be indicated by the arrangement of the site for efficiency of circulation, on- and off-site traffic safety, privacy, etc.;

4. the provision of public and/or private usable open space and/or pathways along the Petaluma River or any creek;

5. contributions to and extensions of existing systems of foot or bicycle paths, equestrian trails, and the greenbelt provided for in the Environmental Design Plan;

6. the provision of needed public facilities such as critical linkages in the major street system, school rooms, or other vital public facilities;

7. the extent to which the proposed development accomplishes an orderly and contiguous extension of existing development as against "leap frog" development;

8. the provision of units to meet the city's policy goal of 8 per cent to 12 per cent low- and moderate-income dwelling units annually.

McGivern, Putting a Speed Limit on Growth, 38 Planning 263 (1972). (McGivern was the Petaluma Director of Planning.)

2. For a recent update of the Petaluma Plan, prepared by the city's current Director of Community Development and Planning, see Salmons, Petaluma's Experiment in Growth Management, Urb. Land, Sept. 1986, at 7:

> In 1977, a second environmental design plan, or short-range general plan, was adopted that ran largely along the lines of the first (1972) plan. . . .
>
> The ordinance called for an annual maximum of 5 percent population growth, which, at the time, in 1978, equalled about 500 new units per

year. Because of increased population growth in the intervening years, the cap is now around 700 units per year. Since 1977, housing production has rarely approached the 5 percent limit.

Other features of the 1977 system included exemptions: for housing for low-income persons, the elderly, and the handicapped; for developments with fewer than 10 units; and for infill projects under five acres. The ordinance also introduced the new concept of reservations for future-year allocations. This feature applied particularly to larger projects of more than 100 units. This move was indicative of a changed development community, in which fewer developers chose to work in Petaluma, but those who did, tended to undertake larger projects. . . .

In 1981, additional revisions were made to the evaluation criteria of the residential development control system, to focus more heavily on design features. Also, the composition of the evaluation board was modified to include only the appointed planning commission and the city's architectural review committee. This gave the appointed commissioners an advantage when they later had to rule officially on the projects. Exemption from review now applies to projects having fewer than 15 units, rather than the earlier 10 units. Projects are rated all year long, instead of only once a year, on a competitive basis, and environmental review has to occur before project evaluation. . . .

. . . In spite of Petaluma's 500-unit limit, and its later 5 percent limit, its average population growth has actually been about 2 percent, and its housing unit production has remained around 2.5 percent. There has not been the demand for as many units as are now available through the system.

3. In order to conclude that the Petaluma plan violates the right to travel, must the court find that there is an identifiable class of persons whose rights have been violated? What is the classification in Petaluma? If the right extends to intrastate travel, do all zoning ordinances violate the right to travel? If the right is limited to interstate travel, could California pass a Petaluma-type plan for the entire state? Can California delegate to every community in the state the power to pass a Petaluma-type plan? Would such a delegation violate the right to travel from state to state? On *Petaluma* and the right to travel, see also Carmichael, Land Use Controls and the Right to Travel, 6 Cumb. L. Rev. 541 (1976); and Note, Land Use — Can An "Inclusionary" Land Use Plan Withstand a Right to Travel Challenge?, 10 Suffolk L. Rev. 623 (1976).

4. How should courts react to phased growth controls mandated not by localities but by regional or state agencies as part of a larger plan to encourage growth in areas better able to accommodate it at different points in time? See Norbeck Village Joint Venture v. Montgomery Council, 254 Md. 59, 254 A.2d 700 (1969) (restrictive zoning within a "green wedge" of a radial corridor in Year 2000 Plan for the Washington, D.C., region).

5. On March 22, 1974, the St. Petersburg, Florida, City Council

D. Parochialism 591

took the first step to approve an ordinance to limit the city's population to 235,000. Tampa Tribune, Mar. 23, 1974. The proposed population "cap" would require all persons who moved in after January 1, 1973, to register with the city — because it was estimated that the limit was exceeded in July of the previous year! All who arrived after the population reached 235,000 would be required to move within six months. City planning department records indicated that housing already built or under construction since July 1973 would, when occupied, increase the population to 267,000. The city council did not take the additional steps necessary to pass the proposal; some of the proponents conceded the proposal was unconstitutional, but acted in order to demonstrate dramatically the need for controlled growth. St. Petersburg Times, Mar. 23, 1974.

6. In 1972, the voters of Boca Raton, Florida, passed the following charter amendment: "The total number of dwelling units within the existing boundaries of the City is hereby limited to forty thousand (40,000). No building permit shall be issued for the construction of a dwelling unit within the City which would permit the total number of dwelling units within the City to exceed forty thousand (40,000)." In accordance with this cap, densities were cut in half for multi-family zoning classifications. The changes were successfully challenged by landowners in two separate actions. See City of Boca Raton v. Boca Villas Corp., 371 So. 2d 154 (Fla.), cert. denied, 381 So. 2d 765 (1979), cert. denied, 449 U.S. 824 (1980); City of Boca Raton v. Arvida Corp., 371 So. 2d 160 (Fla.), cert. denied, 381 So. 2d 765 (1979), cert. denied, 449 U.S. 824 (1980). The court of appeals affirmed the trial court's holding that "the cap lacks any rational relationship to a permissible objection." 371 So. 2d at 156.

7. Another response to growth has been enactment of a temporary regulation to prevent further development pending further planning and the adoption of permanent controls. Judicial review has focused on legislative authorization to impose such restrictions and on the reasonableness of the regulations. Reasonable limitations as to time and area are important, and there should be a variance procedure for those suffering unnecessary hardship.

Is Steel Hill Development, Inc. v. Town of Sanbornton, supra page 390, an interim zoning case? Compare New Jersey Shore Builders' Association v. Township of Ocean, 128 N.J. Super. 135, 319 A.2d 255 (App. Div. 1974) (upheld six-month moratorium on major subdivisions and industrial developments pending preparation of a comprehensive zoning revision), and Meadowland Regional Development Agency v. Hackensack Meadowlands Development Commission, 119 N.J. Super. 572, 293 A.2d 192 (App. Div. 1972), aff'd, 62 N.J. 72, 299 A.2d 69 (1972) (upheld two-year moratorium for comprehensive planning of 10,000 acres of reclaimed land) with Board of Supervisors of Fairfax

County v. Horne, 216 Va. 113, 215 S.E.2d 453 (1975) (no express or implied authority for county enactment of Interim Development Ordinance moratorium). See Rivkin, Growth Control via Sewer Moratoria, 33 Urb. Land 10 (1974).

More recent cases concerning moratoria and temporary ordinances include: Anderson v. Pima County, 27 Ariz. App. 786, 558 P.2d 981 (Ariz. App. 1976) (interim ordinances constitutionally permissible in general but overturned particular ordinance unauthorized by state legislation); Frisco Land and Mining Co. v. State of California, 74 Cal. App. 3d 736, 141 Cal. Rptr. 820, (1977), cert. denied, 436 U.S. 918 (1978) (developer not entitled to damages for losses resulting from delay between adoption of California Coastal Zone Act in November, 1972 and organization of regional commission in March 1973); and Matthews v. Greene County Board of Appeals, 273 S.E.2d 128 (Va. 1977) (interim ordinance arbitrary and unreasonable). Compare Arnold Bernhard & Co. v. Planning & Zoning Commission of Town of Westport, 194 Conn. 152, 479 A.2d 801 (1984) (nine-month moratorium on accepting and granting development applications in business district authorized by state statute), with Harlow v. Planning & Zoning Commission of Town of Westport, 194 Conn. 187, 479 A.2d 808 (1984) (same nine-month moratorium not applicable to landowners who filed application for site plan approval one week before moratorium adopted).

8. An increasing number of towns, particularly in Massachusetts, have tried to manage growth through impact zoning. Drawing on NEPA and the lawyer's continuing faith in procedural solutions, these towns have amended their zoning bylaws to require a statement of the impact of proposed subdivisions on town services and the local environment. See Stimson, Impact Zoning, House & Home, Aug. 1972, at 58-67; Geraldi, The Town That Said No to No-Growth, House & Home, Dec. 1973, at 62 (Dec. 1973). The amendment to the zoning bylaw may take the following form:

> In order to evaluate the impact of the proposed development on Town services and the welfare of the community, there shall be submitted an Impact Statement which describes the impact of the proposed development on (1) all applicable Town services, including but not limited to schools, sewer system, protection; (2) the projected generation of traffic on the roads of and in the vicinity of the proposed development; (3) the subterranean water table, including the effect of proposed septic systems; and (4) the ecology of the vicinity of the proposed development. The Impact Statement shall also indicate the means by which Town or private services required by the proposed development will be provided, such as by private contract, extension of municipal services by a warrant approved at Town Meeting, recorded covenant, or by contract with homeowner's association.

D. Parochialism

What effect would this requirement have on development in a given community? Consider a proposal to add to the impact statement requirement the following provision:

> The Planning Board shall disapprove with detailed reasons any subdivision plan for which the submitted Impact Statement does not indicate reasonably adequate Town or other services available to the proposed subdivision prior to the submission of the said subdivision plan, or for which the Impact Statement does not indicate that damage to the ecology in the vicinity of the proposed subdivision will be minimized to the extent reasonably possible by the land owner.

As town counsel, would you recommend such an addition and do you think it can withstand challenge in court? Would you prefer such an approach to a *Ramapo*-type plan? Cf. Board of Appeals of Maynard v. Housing Appeals Committee of Department of Community Affairs, 370 Mass. 64, 345 N.E.2d 382 (1976), an interesting confrontation between a city asserting environmental harm and the Committee granted preemptive powers by the Anti-Snob Zoning Act (supra page 392). The court upheld the Committee's decision to issue a permit for construction of low- and moderate-income housing; the developer agreed to pay for and construct a 2,000-foot sewer line extension, among other conditions.

See also Conway v. Town of Stratham, 120 N.H. 257, 414 A.2d 539 (1980):

> To require a comprehensive plan prior to implementation of temporary growth controls would allow uncontrolled growth to flourish during the period of the plan's formation. A slow-growth ordinance, therefore, may be valid as a temporary measure to allow a town reasonable time to develop a master or comprehensive plan and to provide for phasing in growth.

■ CALIFORNIA GOVERNMENT CODE
§65863.6 (West 1983)

In carrying out the provisions of this [zoning] chapter, each county and city shall consider the effect of ordinances adopted pursuant to this chapter on the housing needs of the region in which the local jurisdiction is situated and balance these needs against the public service needs of its residents and available fiscal and environmental resources. Any ordinance adopted pursuant to this chapter which, by its terms, limits the number of housing units which may be constructed on an annual basis shall contain findings as to the public health, safety, and welfare of the city or county to be promoted by the adoption of the ordinance which justify reducing the housing opportunities of the region.

■ CALIFORNIA EVIDENCE CODE
§669.5 (West Supp. 1988)

(a) Any ordinance enacted by the governing body of a city, county, or city and county which directly limits, by number, (1) the building permits that may be issued for residential construction or (2) the buildable lots which may be developed for residential purposes, is presumed to have an impact on the supply of residential units available in an area which includes territory outside the jurisdiction of such city, county, or city and county.

(b) With respect to any action which challenges the validity of such an ordinance, the city, county, or city and county enacting such ordinance shall bear the burden of proof that such ordinance is necessary for the protection of the public health, safety, or welfare of the population of such city, county, or city and county.

(c) This section does not apply to ordinances which (1) impose a moratorium, to protect the public health and safety, on residential construction for a specified period of time, if, under the terms of the ordinance, the moratorium will cease when the public health or safety is no longer jeopardized by such construction, or (2) create agricultural preserves . . . , or (3) restrict the number of buildable parcels by limiting the minimum size of buildable parcels within a zone or by designating lands within a zone for nonresidential uses.

Notes

1. In Building Industry Association of Southern California v. City of Camarillo, 41 Cal. 3d 810, 718 P.2d 68, 226 Cal. Rptr. 81 (1986), the court considered the appropriateness of §65863.6 to a growth-control ordinance ("Measure A") adopted by initiative, and the constitutionality of §669.5 in light of the California constitution's protection of voter-generated legislation. According to Measure A, between 1982 and 1985, up to 400 "dwelling units" could be constructed, not including "[s]ingle family homes, subsidized low income and senior citizen housing, remodeling of existing dwellings, and fourplexes or lesser numbered multiple dwellings on a single lot."

The plaintiffs who challenged the ordinance would receive the benefit of the shift in burden, for 669.5 did not "'effectively bar[ ]' initiative action." The majority opinion noted that the information

D. Parochialism

produced during the campaign to adopt Measure A "can serve as data for the local government to use in defending the ordinance." However, the consideration and balancing demanded in §65863.6 would not apply: "How can one prove that the voters weighed and balanced the regional housing needs against the public service, fiscal, and environmental needs? ... It is simply not logical or feasible to place this balancing requirement on the voters."[80]

2. How effective does the initiative remain as an end run around legislative efforts to restrict local growth controls? Should there be limits to such "plebiscitary democracy"? See Sager, Insular Minorities Unabated: Warth v. Seldin and City of Eastlake v. Forest City Enterprises, Inc., 91 Harv. L. Rev. 1373, 1425 (1978): "the cases reflect the equation of the local zoning process with the joint exercise of the prerogatives of private ownership; the municipality is a club, which enjoys the mandatory and exclusive membership of its residents and landowners. And majority will — however insular, unjust, or irrational — prevails."

3. To this point, our focus has been on the actions, criticisms, and handwringing by courts, legislators, voters, and commentators. What can those in the private sector who are active in the development process add to our understanding of the problems posed by metropolitan growth and parochial control, and, more importantly, to the search for effective solutions? See, e.g., Leinberger, Curbing Growth Controls, Wall St. J., Jan. 22, 1987:

> Why has the long-simmering no-growth/slow-growth movement suddenly become a powerful nationwide force for business to contend with? It is primarily because millions of jobs are now being created at the outskirts of our metropolitan areas, and politically savvy middle-class suburbanites don't want office buildings and business parks rising near their neighborhoods and attracting traffic to their once-tranquil streets. ...
>
> ... [B]usiness and developers must formulate a more satisfying vision

---

80. In light of the majority's stance, consider whether the following observation remains accurate: "The Supreme Court of California ... generally has deferred to municipal development controls, apparently in the Pollyannish view that giving suburbs a free hand at planning will lead to a better future." Ellickson, Suburban Growth Controls: An Economic and Legal Analysis, 86 Yale L.J. 385, 511 (1977).

On the limitations of judicial solutions in socioeconomic zoning and related areas, see Inman and Rubinfield, The Judicial Pursuit of Local Fiscal Equity, 92 Harv. L. Rev. 1662, 1749 (1979):

> When [legislative] efforts proved ineffective in extending public resources to the poor, the strategy of judicial reform to alter the rules of local financing seemed an attractive option. But now it seems apparent that this option is also limited, and for essentially the same reason which blocked the legislative route — the key causes of fiscal inequality, income disparities and decentralized financing, are left undisturbed.

For more on referendum zoning, see infra page 1078. — EDS.

of what the newly created urban village cores should be. Who can blame suburban residents for fighting nearby commercial construction when they see that many urban village cores are little more than could-be-anywhere tall buildings surrounded by surface parking lots?

Wouldn't nearby residents feel differently about the urban village cores if their proximity offered cultural benefits or a genuine pedestrian-oriented center, much like the traditional downtowns? To create that urban excitement, business and developers should attract high-density shopping, entertainment and housing to the office-dominated urban village cores. . . .

. . . [T]he business community must act as a catalyst in defining and designing our 21st-century metropolitan areas. Either business takes the lead or slow-growth/no-growth citizens' revolts will be the only thing growing rapidly in our metropolitan areas.

The complicated land-use scheme for a 1980s suburb — complete with computer-generated maps and diagrams and detailed printouts of census and ecological data — may little resemble the Village of Euclid's basic height, area, and use ordinance prepared in 1922. Indeed, the makeup and expectations of society have changed greatly in the interim. A careful evaluation of more than a half-century of experience in the courts, in legislative chambers, and in planners' offices instructs us that although Sutherland's words and phrases in *Euclid* may have suggested the course of legal and political struggles for years to come, he and his fellow Justices did not anticipate the diverse modifications that have been designed to make zoning more adaptable to demographic, economic, and technological change, and more responsive to social needs within and without the borders of the community.

Sometimes courts and lawmakers have recognized that land-use decisions — made by fallible humans and thus subject to mistakes and worse — are not necessarily entitled to great deference. On occasion, regional responsibilities have been mandated to correct imbalances, or local officials have been instructed to consider the environmental or aesthetic ramifications of their acts. At other times economic forces have served to correct extreme controls, forcing local officials to abandon even the most carefully prepared plans.

After some seventy years of application, zoning should now be of age. But technological advances, drastic changes in the interpretation of property rights and constitutional law, and novel problems of urban land use have had their effect on the Euclid type of ordinance. Zoning is undergoing an evolution as fundamental in its nature and in its effect upon property rights as marked the emergence of comprehensive zoning in 1913 from the fragmentary regulations that preceded it. In the midst of this fermentation the basic purposes of zoning may at

D. Parochialism

times be overlooked. Clarifying the theory of land planning and translating it into legislation and administration is the pressing job. Can premises and goals be sifted out and related to new devices in order to achieve rational land law policies and to work out an organization of society both efficient and fair in dealing with property concepts?

V

Regulating the Tempo and Sequence of Growth

The postwar building boom swept into the undeveloped land surrounding the larger cities. The low annual rate of residential construction during the thirties and the war years gave way — thanks to the high level of economic prosperity and increased marriage and birth rates — to an unprecedented expansion in home building in the metropolitan areas. Within these areas, the highest rate of growth occurred at the periphery. In an irregular series of leaps and bounds, farms, private estates, and vacant tracts of land on the outskirts of population clusters were absorbed into the surging city. The 1950 census showed that while the central cities gained 5.7 million (13 percent) over the preceding decade, the outlying suburbs increased by 9 million (35 percent).[1] And this is a continuing trend: the 1970 census figures show that while the twenty-five largest cities gained 710,000 over their populations in 1960, the twenty-five largest metropolitan areas gained 8.9 million.[2] In the 1980s, most suburban rings became predominant over the central cities that spawned them.[3] The major finding of the 1980 census was the general dispersal of population away from urban centers. Although Manhattan, for example, gained 23.5

1. See supra page 8.
2. N.Y. Times, Sept. 6, 1970; cf. N.Y. Times, Oct. 21, 1985.
3. Leinberger and Lockwood, How Business Is Reshaping America, Atlantic Monthly, Oct. 1986, at 43.

599

million square feet of office space from 1982 to 1985, its share of the metropolitan area's office space fell from 62 percent to 60 percent.[4] We are, in short, no longer an urban, but a suburban nation.

Subdivisions are entered into for profit. They occur where the growth of population, or some other indicium of land demand, indicates a sufficiently profitable market. Sometimes they are carried out by the original owners of the land, more frequently by professionals engaged in the business of real estate development. Within this process, more is involved than a private bargain between vendor and purchaser. For subdividers are dealing in the permanent assets of the community: subdividers do not merely sell land; in all but the smallest developments, they have to lay out roads and provide access to the lots. And in so doing they are determining the main outlines and future character of the community. Thus the street system and the arrangement of lots of the growing cities are in effect planned, designed, and constructed piecemeal by a number of private real estate developers. Often these independent operations are poorly designed, uncoordinated both with each other and with the layout of the central city, and totally inadequate to cope with the consequent load of automobile, truck, and pedestrian traffic.

Farsighted developers were and are aware of these dangers. But many subdivisions are constructed without regard to the convenience or well-being of the resulting community, and in the course of time sink inevitably into the status of a slum; the poor location of new subdivisions "where street systems and housing were not conformed to topography" is listed as the "first slum-inducing factor."[5]

How does land-use law view this problem of regulating the pattern of urban expansion? The New Jersey court summed up as follows:

> We are surrounded with the problems of planless growth. The baneful consequences of haphazard development are everywhere apparent. There are evils affecting the health, safety and prosperity of our citizens that are well-nigh insurmountable because of the prohibitive corrective cost. To challenge the power to give proper direction to community growth and development . . . is to deny the vitality of a principle that has brought men together in organized society for their mutual advantage.[6]

Small wonder then that all states (with a long-time holdout by green-hilled Vermont) have enacted legislation regulating the subdivisions of land for purposes of sale and development. A priori one would conclude

---

4. See Peirce and Guskind, The Mid-Atlantic's Suburban Growth Boom: At What Cost?, 3 Bell-Atlantic Q. 9 (1986).

5. Ford, Slums and Housing 444 (1936).

6. Mansfield and Swett, Inc. v. Town of West Orange, 120 N.J.L. 145, 150, 151, 198 A. 225, 229 (1938).

that physical planning makes its greatest advances where land is vacant and the forces of investment and vested interest are muted.[7] And the range and intensity of subdivision control and direction found in American legislation do not belie this assumption.

The character of the nation, sociologically and economically, has been changed by a new form of urban environment. How shall this transition of acreage into new urban uses be effected so as to assure desirable results? Again the lawyer's role becomes more complex: land use involves far more than physical control. For better or worse the lawyer has become involved in the making and remaking of the social environment, and to this end the findings of economists, sociologists, and psychologists must be incorporated into the traditional framework of legislation and judicial opinion.[8] The social problems of today differ from those envisaged in the debates of Hamilton and Jefferson, and in many fields their treatment must depend primarily on legal regulation and definition.[9]

A. CONFLICT AT THE RURAL-URBAN FRINGE: THE DEVELOPER'S "OWN SWEET WILL"[10]

1. Enabling Legislation for Subdivision Control

Early legislation dealt with subdivision maps as a part of the recording system — facilitating transfer of ownership and demarcating

---

7. Furthermore, that perennial Banquo of city planning controls — how accurate are the anticipatory estimates of the course of future development? — is (to some extent) eliminated in this area: development is more imminent, and the planned design is not threatened so immediately with obsolescence. But see the results of failures to anticipate described in Antiquated Subdivisions: Beyond Lot Mergers and Vested Rights (Glickfeld ed. 1984).
8. See the perceptive article by Dunham, The Lawyer's Role in Developing an Area, 28 Rocky Mt. L. Rev. 453 (1956), and the view from the planner's world in Perrin, With Man in Mind (1970).
9. For a tantalizing glimpse into this process, see Kalish and Sutton, A Lawyer's Role in the Construction of a New City, 24 Pa. B.A.Q. 216 (1953), 25 id. 299 (1954), McAuslan, The Plan, the Planners and the Lawyers, 1971 J. Pub. L. 247; The Lawyer in Housing, Urban Development, 4 J. Urb. Law. 221 (1972).
10. To use the court's words: "Town planning is a new field of legislation, comparable with the recent development of zoning laws and regulations. Its purpose is to preserve through a governmental agency a uniform and harmonious development of the growth of a village and to prevent the individual owner from laying out streets according to his own sweet will without official approval." Village of Lynbrook v. Cadoo, 252 N.Y. 308, 314, 169 N.E. 394, 396-397 (1929).
Until quite recently the American subdivider had a comparatively free hand. You will recall the types of restraints imposed by congressional legislation on the western town sites and their relative paucity and ineffectiveness. See supra page 25. See also Gates, History of Public Land Law Development (1968).

municipal from private lands. But their primary concern was to avoid confusion in the registry of deeds; they dealt with the accuracy and uniformity of survey methods, boundary and monument descriptions, and the like (sometimes going to the extreme of prescribing the use of black India ink).[11] A few statutes[12] required approval of the plat by a public officer, but again the range of inquiry was highly limited.

Encouragement of land subdivision was a natural policy during the period when most communities beheld the future as one of indefinite and rewarding expansion. The creation of streets and the extension of utilities and services were charged against the public treasury, with the expectation of early recovery in taxes from the resulting property development. Several booms and busts in the past foretold possible embarrassments. But it was not until the decline in the building industry, preceding the general business depression of 1929 by several years, that the full extent of that problem was understood. The more recent crisis of the 1960s, 1970s, and 1980s, on the other hand, concerns the rate of development; public facilities are threatened with inundation by a new wave of building; the character of a community may be changed overnight.[13] How can growth be paced at a rate the community can absorb?

These different crises spawn new controls. An important contribution was made in 1928 by that national draftsman, the United States Department of Commerce, in the form of its model law for subdivision control. However, unlike the success achieved by its model zoning act, which blitzed through one state legislature after another, the model subdivision law has not become, by common adoption, a national law. By and large the states have tended to go their individual ways. Hence the bewildering variety of legislation and regulations, which certainly testifies to the flexibility of American legislatures in coping with the problem of subdivision control. (In a sense, too, this complexity is a tribute to the ingenuity of American developers and their attorneys.)

The practicing lawyer must work within the framework of pertinent state law and the regulations of the local community. Often attorneys

11. An interesting and by no means unusual problem is the determination of which state has the honor of claiming Andrew Jackson as its son; owing to the inaccuracy of surveys, it is not clear in which of nine counties the log cabin was located.
12. E.g., Mich. Pub. Act 1885, No. 111. See the annotation in Iowa Code Ann. §409.1 (1949); State ex rel. Strother v. Chase, 42 Mo. App. 343 (1890). For a discussion of the Act of 1809, 2 Stat. 511, permitting subdivision in the District of Columbia if the "dimensions correspond with the original lots," see Bauman v. Ross, 167 U.S. 548, 550 (1897). Magnolia Development Co. v. Coles, 10 N.J. 223, 227, 89 A.2d 664, 666 (1952), contains a description of the narrow control powers conferred by such a statute.
13. In Beach v. Planning & Zoning Commission of Milford, 141 Conn. 79, 103 A.2d 814 (1954), the planning commission was held not to have authority (under the state enabling act) to deny a subdivision because it would cause an "unbearable financial burden" to the town in providing schools, roads, and police and fire protection. But cf. Smith v. Morris Township, 101 N.J. Super. 271, 244 A.2d 145 (App. Div. 1968).

A. Conflict at the Rural-Urban Fringe

will find the legislation and supplementary regulations difficult to grasp, ambiguous, and incomplete. Then he or she may consider whether an argument can be developed from the presence or absence of a comparable provision in the law of another state. Most important, this variety (which may suggest to the cynic that it is simpler to obtain change in legislation than to litigate via judicial machinery or to secure a change in the way people act) serves as a warning: affairs must be so arranged that at some future date new acts or regulations will not frustrate the client's purpose. An awareness, on the part of the lawyer, of the thinking of the local officials and planners, and of community goals, may prove to be the best way to represent a client.

The following battery of enabling acts suggests the range of devices and stratagems employed to battle with this intractable problem. Its variety offers scope for what is, in effect, a comparative law study: What are the origins and purposes of the different subdivision acts? What physical and economic considerations cause differences in state laws aiming at the same evil? What political considerations are involved? What can be learned in this area from the attempts of law in the books to catch up with law in action? Are the procedures designed to achieve the purported ends? What are the various agencies — from recorder of deeds, local planning or building commissions, county and state departments, to the FHA of the national government — that must be coordinated and integrated? And what is the job of the lawyer who has to run this gamut of approval?

An attempt is here made to assemble the different legislative approaches, and to highlight similarities and contrasts by grouping analogous provisions.

a. Definitions

■ UNITED STATES DEPARTMENT OF COMMERCE, A STANDARD CITY PLANNING ENABLING ACT
§1 (1928)

"Subdivision" means the division of a lot, tract, or parcel of land into two or more lots, plats, sites, or other divisions of land for the purpose, whether immediate or future, of sale or of building development.

■ WISCONSIN STATUTES ANNOTATED
§236.02 (West Supp. 1986)

(12) "Subdivision" is a division of a lot, parcel or tract of land by the owner thereof or the owner's agent for the purpose of sale or of building development, where:

(a) The act of division creates 5 or more parcels or building sites of 1½ acres each or less in area; or

(b) Five or more parcels or building sites of 1½ acres each or less in area are created by successive divisions within a period of 5 years.

■ MASSACHUSETTS GENERAL LAWS ANNOTATED
Ch. 41, §81L (West 1979)

"Subdivision" shall mean the division of a tract of land into two or more lots and shall include resubdivision, and, when appropriate to the context, shall relate to the process of subdivision or the land or territory subdivided; provided, however, that the division of a tract of land into two or more lots shall not be deemed to constitute a subdivision within the meaning of the subdivision control law if, at the time when it is made, every lot within the tract so divided has frontage on (*a*) a public way or a way which the clerk of the city or town certifies is maintained and used as a public way, or (*b*) a way shown on a plan theretofore approved and endorsed in accordance with the subdivision control law, or (*c*) a way in existence when the subdivision control law became effective in the city or town in which the land lies, having, in the opinion of the planning board, sufficient width, suitable grades and adequate construction to provide for the needs of vehicular traffic in relation to the proposed use of the land abutting thereon or served thereby, and for the installation of municipal services to serve such land and the buildings erected or to be erected thereon. Such frontage shall be of at least such distance as is then required by zoning or other ordinance or by-law, if any, of said city or town for erection of a building on such lot, and if no distance is so required, such frontage shall be of at least twenty feet. Conveyances or other instruments adding to, taking away from, or changing the size and shape of, lots in such a manner as not to leave any lot so affected without the frontage above set forth, or the division of a tract of land on which two or more buildings were standing when the subdivision control law went into effect in the city or town in which the land lies into separate lots on each of which one of such buildings remains standing, shall not constitute a subdivision.[14]

14. What is a "way"? A paper street? A driveway on what was formerly a large estate? See Rettig v. Planning Board of Rowley, 332 Mass. 476, 126 N.E.2d 104 (1955). Perry v. Planning Board of Nantucket, 15 Mass. App. 144, 444 N.E.2d 389 (1983), held that "public way" did not include streets depicted on town plans and for which easements had been taken, unless they in fact existed on the ground. — Eds.

b. Governmental Organization

■ **NEW JERSEY STATUTES ANNOTATED**
(West Supp. 1986)

§40:55D-37

a. The governing body may by ordinance require approval of subdivision plats by resolution of the planning board as a condition for the filing of such plats with the county recording officer and approval of site plans by resolution of the planning board as a condition for the issuance of a permit for any development, except that subdivision or individual lot applications for detached one or two dwelling-unit buildings shall be exempt from such site plan review and approval. . . .

c. Each application for subdivision approval . . . and each application for site plan approval . . . shall be submitted by the applicant to the county planning board for review or approval . . . and the municipal planning board shall condition any approval that it grants upon timely receipt of a favorable report on the application by the county planning board or approval by the county planning board by its failure to report thereon within the required time period.

§40:55D-46

a. An ordinance requiring site plan review and approval shall require that the developer submit to the administrative officer a site plan and such other information as is reasonably necessary to make an informed decision as to whether the requirements necessary for preliminary site plan approval have been met. The site plan and any engineering documents to be submitted shall be required in tentative form for discussion purposes for preliminary approval. If any architectural plans are required to be submitted for site plan approval, the preliminary plans and elevations shall be sufficient.

b. If the planning board required any substantial amendment in the layout of improvements proposed by the developer that have been the subject of a hearing, an amended application for development shall be submitted and proceeded upon, as in the case of the original application for development. The planning board shall, if the proposed development complies with the ordinance and this act, grant preliminary site plan approval.

c. Upon the submission to the administrative officer of a complete application for a site plan which involves 10 acres of land or less, and 10 dwelling units or less, the planning board shall grant or deny preliminary approval within 45 days of the date of such submission or within such further time as may be consented to by the developer.

REQUESTING SUBDIVISION APPROVAL IN HENRICO COUNTY, VIRGINIA*

- A conditional request is submitted to the Planning Office by the applicant with the following information:
  — Application form with check list completely filled out.
  — Eight (8) prints of the proposed subdivision plats.
  — Filing fee (amount determined by the number of lots submitted).
- The Conditional request is then reviewed by members of the County staff for compliance with County standards and regulations. The applicant and/or his representative meet with the County staff to discuss any comments, after which the Planning Office staff prepares a report and recommendations for transmittal to the Planning Commission.
- The Planning Commission reviews the request at a public hearing at which time the Planning staff presents each proposal. After hearing information concerning the proposal, the Planning Commission may take action in one of four ways: grant approval of the request, grant approval of the request with recommended changes or conditions, deny approval of request, or defer hearing of the request for further review.
- If the request is approved, the applicant has a period of six months in which to apply for final approval.
- A request for final approval is submitted to the Planning Office by the applicant with the following information:
  — Letter of transmittal requesting final approval.
  — Eight (8) prints of the final plats.
  — Four (4) sets of detailed construction plans prepared by a professional engineer or certified surveyor detailing the construction of required improvements.
  — Filing fee (amount determined by the number of lots submitted).
- The Final request is reviewed by the Staff and heard at a public hearing by the Planning Commission in the same manner as a Conditional request. If the Final request is approved, the applicant has a period of ninety days in which to record the subdivision.
- Should the applicant be unable to request final approval or record the subdivision plats within the required time period, a written request for an extension of conditional or final approval may be submitted to the Planning Office for consideration by the Planning Commission.

In order to record the subdivision, the applicant must submit two (2) linen prints and one (1) transparency (polyester film) to the Planning Office for a final review prior to its recordation in the Clerk's Office of the County.

After the subdivision plats are recorded, the developer may submit plans for building permit approval.

*Source: . . . so, you need to subdivide your property?, Planning Office, County of Henrico, Virginia (pamphlet).

A. Conflict at the Rural-Urban Fringe

Upon the submission of a complete application for a site plan which involves more than 10 acres, or more than 10 dwelling units, the planning board shall grant or deny preliminary approval within 95 days of the date of such submission or within such further time as may be consented to by the developer. Otherwise, the planning board shall be deemed to have granted preliminary approval of the site plan.

§40:55D-50

a. The planning board shall grant final approval if the detailed drawings, specifications and estimates of the application for final approval conform to the standards established by ordinance for final approval, the conditions of preliminary approval and, in the case of a major subdivision, the standards prescribed by the "Map Filing Law," P.L. 1960, c. 141 (C. 46:23-9.9 et seq.); provided that in the case of a planned unit development, planned unit residential development or residential cluster, the planning board may permit minimal deviations from the conditions of preliminary approval necessitated by change of conditions beyond the control of the developer since the date of preliminary approval without the developer being required to submit another application for development for preliminary approval.

b. Final approval shall be granted or denied within 45 days after submission of a complete application to the administrative officer, or within such further time as may be consented to by the applicant. Failure of the planning board to act within the period prescribed shall constitute final approval and a certificate of the administrative officer as to the failure of the planning board to act shall be issued on request of the applicant, and it shall be sufficient in lieu of the written endorsement or other evidence of approval, herein required, and shall be so accepted by the county recording officer for purposes of filing subdivision plats. . . . [15]

■ TEXAS PROPERTY CODE ANNOTATED
§12.002 (Vernon Supp. 1988)

(a) The county clerk may not record a plat or replat of a subdivision of real property unless it is approved as provided by law by the appropriate county or municipal authority. . . .

---

15. In Dunkin' Donuts of New Jersey v. Township of North Brunswick Planning Board, 193 N.J. Super. 513, 475 A.2d 71 (App. Div. 1984), the defendant planning board's denial of plaintiff's application for site approval was based solely upon the anticipated detrimental impact of the proposed use on traffic congestion and safety. The court held that

> [a] planning board should consider off-site traffic flow and safety in reviewing proposals for vehicular ingress to and egress from a site. Pursuant to ordinance it may condition site plan approval upon a contribution to necessary off-site street improvements. But the authority to prohibit or limit uses generating traffic into already congested streets or streets with a high rate of accidents is an exercise of the zoning power vested in the municipal governing body. — EDS.

(d) A county clerk commits an offense if the clerk violates Subsection (a).... An offense under this subsection is a misdemeanor punishable by fine of not less than $50 or more than $200.[16]

■ MARYLAND ANNOTATED CODE
Art. 66B, §5.03 (1983)

(a) ... [T]he planning commission shall prepare regulations governing the subdivision of land within its jurisdiction. Those regulations may provide for the adequate control of shore erosion; the control of sediment and the protection from flooding; the proper arrangement of streets in relation to other existing planned streets and to the master plan; the adequate and convenient placement of public school sites and of open spaces for traffic, utilities, access of fire-fighting apparatus, recreation, light and air and the avoidance of congestion of population, including minimum width and area of lots....

(c) Before any regulations shall be submitted to the local legislative body for adoption a public hearing shall be held thereon and all such regulations, or if in the opinion of the commission it is best, a brief synopsis of such regulations, sufficient to inform a person of ordinary intelligence of the nature and contents of such regulations, together with the time and place of such public hearing, shall be published once or more, if the commission deems best, in a weekly or daily newspaper of general circulation in such county or municipal corporation. When such regulations are adopted by the local legislative body, a copy thereof shall be certified by the commission to the clerk of the circuit court in which the jurisdiction is located for record.

c. Jurisdiction

■ UNITED STATES DEPARTMENT OF COMMERCE, A STANDARD CITY PLANNING ENABLING ACT
§12 (1928)

The territorial jurisdiction of any municipal planning commission over the subdivision of land shall include all land located in the

---

16. The plaintiff seeks a mandamus requiring acceptance of a plat of sixty acres for cemetery purposes. The plot had been approved by the city planning commission, but subsequently disapproved by the city council. The Fort Worth ordinance requires a submittal of a plat to the city planning commission and the council. See Hollis v. Parkland Corp., 120 Tex. 531, 40 S.W.2d 53 (1931) (all that 1927 Texas statute required was commission approval; city council's action irrelevant); cf. Sparks v. Bolton, 335 S.W.2d 780 (Tex. Civ. App. 1960). — Eds.

A. Conflict at the Rural-Urban Fringe

municipality and all land lying within 5 miles of the corporate limits of the municipality and not located in any other municipality, except that, in the case of any such nonmunicipal land lying within 5 miles of more than one municipality having a planning commission, the jurisdiction of each such municipal planning commission shall terminate at a boundary line equidistant from the respective corporate limits of such municipalities.

■ INDIANA CODE ANNOTATED
(West 1983)

§36-7-4-205

A municipal plan commission shall adopt a comprehensive plan . . . for the development of the municipality and of the contiguous unincorporated area, designated by the commission, that is outside the corporate boundaries of the municipality, and that, in the judgment of the commission, bears reasonable relation to the development of the municipality.[17]

(b) Except as limited by the boundaries of unincorporated areas subject to the jurisdiction of other municipal plan commissions, an area designated under this section may include any part of the contiguous unincorporated area within two (2) miles from the corporate boundaries of the municipality. If, however, the corporate boundaries of the municipality or the boundaries of that contiguous unincorporated area include any part of the public waters or shoreline of a lake (which lies wholly within Indiana), the designated area may also include:

(1) any part of those public waters and shoreline of the lake; and

(2) any land area within two thousand five hundred (2,500) feet from that shoreline. . . .

§36-7-4-70

(c) The municipal plan commission has exclusive control over the approval of plats and replats involving unincorporated land within its jurisdiction, unless the legislative body of the county has adopted a subdivision control ordinance covering those lands. In this case, the county plan commission has exclusive control over the approval. . . .

(e) The plan commission may appoint a plat committee to hold hearings on and approve plats and replats on behalf of the commission. The plat committee consists of three (3) or five (5) persons, with at

---

17. Not having a master plan or a comprehensive zoning ordinance, a city was precluded from extending its jurisdictional area in Hundt v. Costello, 480 N.E.2d 284 (Ind. 1985). — Eds.

least one (1) of the members being a member of the commission. Each appointment of a member of the plat committee is for a term of one (1) year, but the commission may remove a member from the committee. The commission must mail notice of the removal, along with written reasons, if any, for the removal, to the member at his residence address. A member who is removed may not appeal the removal to a court or otherwise. The plat committee may take action only by a majority vote. . . .

d. Standards and Requirements

■ REVISED STATUTES OF ONTARIO
Ch. 379, §36 (1980)

(4) In considering a draft plan of subdivision, regard shall be had, among other matters, to the health, safety, convenience and welfare of the future inhabitants and to the following,

(a) whether the plan conforms to the official plan and adjacent plans of subdivision, if any;

(b) whether the proposed subdivision is premature or necessary in the public interest;

(c) the suitability of the land for the purposes for which it is to be subdivided;

(d) the number, width, location and proposed grades and elevations of highways, and the adequacy thereof, and the highways linking the highways in the proposed subdivision with the established highway system in the vicinity, and the adequacy thereof;

(e) the dimensions and shape of the lots;

(f) the restrictions or proposed restrictions, if any, on the land, buildings and structures proposed to be erected thereon and the restrictions, if any, on adjoining lands;

(g) conservation of natural resources and flood control;

(h) the adequacy of utilities and municipal services;

(i) adequacy of school sites;

(j) the area of land, if any, within the subdivision that, exclusive of highways, is to be conveyed or dedicated for public purposes.

(5) The Minister may impose such conditions to the approval of a plan of subdivision as in his opinion are advisable and, in particular but without restricting in any way whatsoever the generality of the foregoing, he may impose as a condition,

(a) that land to an amount determined by the Minister but not exceeding 5 percent of the land included in the plan shall be conveyed to the municipality for park purposes or, if the land is not in a municipality, shall be dedicated for park purposes;

(b) that such highways shall be dedicated as the Minister considers necessary;

(c) when the subdivision abuts on an existing highway that sufficient land, other than land occupied by buildings or structures, shall be dedicated to provide for the widening of the highway to such width as the Minister considers necessary; and

(d) that the owner of the land enter into one or more agreements with the municipality, or, where the land is not in a municipality, with the Minister, dealing with such matters as the Minister may consider necessary, including the provision of municipal services.

■ WASHINGTON REVISED CODE ANNOTATED
§58.17.110 (Supp. 1987)

The city, town, or county legislative body shall inquire into the public use and interest proposed to be served by the establishment of the subdivision and dedication. It shall determine if appropriate provisions are made for, but not limited to, the public health, safety, and general welfare, for open spaces, drainage ways, streets, alleys, other public ways, water supplies, sanitary wastes, parks, playgrounds, sites for schools and schoolgrounds, and shall consider all other relevant facts and determine whether the public interest will be served by the subdivision and dedication. If it finds that the proposed plat makes appropriate provisions for the public health, safety, and general welfare and for such open spaces, drainage ways, streets, alleys, other public ways, water supplies, sanitary wastes, parks, playgrounds, sites for schools and schoolgrounds and that the public use and interest will be served by the platting of such subdivision, then it shall be approved. If it finds that the proposed plat does not make such appropriate provisions or that the public use and interest will not be served, then the legislative body may disapprove the proposed plat. Dedication of land to any public body, may be required as a condition of subdivision approval and shall be clearly shown on the final plat. The legislative body shall not as a condition to the approval of any plat require a release from damages to be procured from other property owners.[18]

---

18. "But in those areas where we find there is sluggish sale rather than very great overhang we are instructing our offices that if a man may come in and ask for fifty units, we say, 'Don't issue the master for the fifty units. Have him go out there and start twenty. Get those firmly sold, and if they are sold we will give another twenty for the balance.' So what we are trying to do is not to create any surpluses in any area." A response of Mr. Sweeney, Assistant Deputy Administrator of the Veterans Administration, in Subcommittee of the Senate Committee on Banking and Currency, Hearings, 84th Cong., 1st Sess. 32 (1955). Cf. Greenlawn Memorial Park v. Neenah, 270 Wis. 378, 71 N.W.2d 403 (1955). — Eds.

e. Sanctions

■ NEW JERSEY STATUTES ANNOTATED
§40:55D-55 (West Supp. 1986)

If, before final subdivision approval has been granted, any person transfers or sells or agrees to transfer or sell, except pursuant to an agreement expressly conditioned on final subdivision approval, as owner or agent, any land which forms a part of a subdivision for which municipal approval is required by ordinance pursuant to this act, such person shall be subject to a penalty not to exceed $1,000.00, and each lot disposition so made may be deemed a separate violation.

In addition to the foregoing, the municipality may institute and maintain a civil action:

    a. For injunctive relief; and

    b. To set aside and invalidate any conveyance made pursuant to such a contract of sale if a certificate of compliance has not been issued in accordance with section 44 of this act, but only if the municipality (1) has a planning board and (2) has adopted by ordinance standards and procedures in accordance with section 29 of this act.

In any such action, the transferee, purchaser or grantee shall be entitled to a lien upon the portion of the land, from which the subdivision was made that remains in the possession of the developer or his assigns or successors, to secure the return of any deposits made or purchase price paid, and also, a reasonable search fee, survey expense and title closing expense, if any. Any such action must be brought within 2 years after the date of the recording of the instrument of transfer, sale or conveyance of said land or within 6 years, if unrecorded.

■ WASHINGTON REVISED CODE ANNOTATED
(Supp. 1987)

§58.17.210

No building permit, septic tank permit, or other development permit, shall be issued for any lot, tract, or parcel of land divided in violation of this chapter or local regulations adopted pursuant thereto unless the authority authorized to issue such permit finds that the public interest will not be adversely affected thereby. The prohibition contained in this section shall not apply to an innocent purchaser for value without actual notice. All purchasers' or transferees' property shall comply with provision of this chapter and each purchaser or

A. Conflict at the Rural-Urban Fringe

transferee may recover his damages from any person, firm, corporation, or agent selling or transferring land in violation of this chapter or local regulations adopted pursuant thereto, including any amount reasonably spent as a result of inability to obtain any development permit and spent to conform to the requirements of this chapter as well as cost of investigation, suit, and reasonable attorneys' fees occasioned thereby. Such purchaser or transferee may as an alternative to conforming his property to these requirements, rescind the sale or transfer and recover costs of investigation, suit, and reasonable attorneys' fees occasioned thereby.[19]

§58.17.300

Any person, firm, corporation, or association or any agent of any person, firm, corporation, or association who violates any provision of this chapter or any local regulations adopted pursuant thereto relating to the sale, offer for sale, lease, or transfer of any lot, tract or parcel of land, shall be guilty of a gross misdemeanor and each sale, offer for sale, lease or transfer of each separate lot, tract, or parcel of land in violation of any provision of this chapter or any local regulation adopted pursuant thereto, shall be deemed a separate and distinct offense.

■ PENNSYLVANIA STATUTES ANNOTATED
Ch. 53, §22773 (Supp. 1986)

A county recorder who records a plat of a subdivision without the approval of the same, as herein provided, shall be deemed guilty of a misdemeanor and shall be fined not to exceed five hundred dollars,

---

19. Does the third sentence of this section contradict the first two sentences? See Crown Cascade, Inc. v. O'Neal, 100 Wash. 2d 256, 668 P.2d 585 (1983).

The invasion of the sacred precinct of marketable title gave rise to violent reactions in New Jersey, Massachusetts, and Wisconsin. See Report Submitted to Committee on Mercantile Affairs of the Massachusetts Legislature, Mass. L.Q., May 1951, at 27; Mass. L.Q., Apr. 1952, at 23. See repeal of chapter 351 of Wisconsin Laws 1953 by chapter 624 of that year. The explosions in three of the more planning-conscious states provide a source for many sermons. What lessons do you derive? How did skillful and meticulous conveyancers and judges of the land court overlook the existence of a law affecting realty for more than ten years after its passage? What curative legislation would you suggest for relieving the confusion? As to similar problems under a Torrens system, such as Australia's, again owing to the absence of the concept of integrating the subdivision into the general city plan, see Re Nelson and Tammer's Contract, [1952] V.L.R. 391, and Note, Plans of Subdivision, 28 L. Inst. J. 216 (1954). See City of Newark v. Padula, 26 N.J. Super. 251, 97 A.2d 735 (App. Div. 1953); Salvatore v. Trace, 109 N.J. Super. 83, 262 A.2d 409, aff'd, 262 A.2d 485 (App. Div. 1970) (title is not marketable without subdivision approval). — Eds.

and the plat of subdivision so recorded shall be null and void and so marked.[20]

f. Exactions

■ CALIFORNIA GOVERNMENT CODE
§66477 (West 1983 & Supp. 1987)

The legislative body of a city or county may, by ordinance, require the dedication of land or impose a requirement of the payment of fees in lieu thereof, or a combination of both, for park or recreational purposes as a condition to the approval of a tentative map or parcel map, provided that:

(a) The ordinance has been in effect for a period of 30 days prior to the filing of the tentative map of the subdivision or parcel map.

(b) The ordinance includes definite standards for determining the proportion of a subdivision to be dedicated and the amount of any fee to be paid in lieu thereof. The amount of land dedicated or fees paid shall be based upon the residential density, which shall be determined on the basis of the approved or conditionally approved tentative map or parcel map and the average number of persons per household. . . . [T]he dedication of land, or the payment of fees, or both, shall not exceed the proportionate amount necessary to provide three acres of park area per 1,000 persons residing within a subdivision subject to this section, unless the amount of existing neighborhood and community park area, as calculated pursuant to this subdivision, exceeds that limit, in which case the legislative body may adopt the calculated amount as a higher standard not to exceed five acres per 1,000 persons residing within a subdivision subject to this section.

20. Compare Brous v. Smith, 304 N.Y. 164, 106 N.E.2d 503 (1952), with State ex rel. Webber v. Vajner, 92 Ohio App. 233, 108 N.E.2d 569 (1952). See Huber v. Village of Richmond Heights, 121 N.E.2d 457 (Ohio App. 1954) ("No person . . . shall lay out or use any private road . . . for access to more than one dwelling house, or sell . . . more than one lot . . . fronting on any private road . . . unless such private road has been improved in accordance with . . . specifications attached hereto").

Not atypical is the Massachusetts protection for developers that when a plan is submitted under the subdivision control law, it is to be governed by laws in effect at the time of submission, and, once approved, the law cannot be changed for a stated period of time. Mass. Gen. Laws ch. 40A, §7 (1979) (7 years). Cf. Conn. Gen. Stat. Ann. §8-26a (Supp. 1975); N.J. Stat. Ann. 40:55-1:18 (Supp. 1974); N.Y. Village Law §7-708 (McKinney 1973). As to the effects of a "perimeter plan," see Bellows Farm, Inc. v. Building Inspector of Acton, 364 Mass. 253, 303 N.E.2d 728 (1973). — Eds.

A. Conflict at the Rural-Urban Fringe 615

(1) The park area per 1,000 members of the population of the city, county, or local public agency shall be derived from the ratio that the amount of neighborhood and community park acreage bears to the total population of the city, or local public agency as shown in the most recent available federal census. The amount of neighborhood and community park acreage shall be the actual acreage of existing neighborhood and community parks of the city, county, or local public agency as shown on its records, plans, recreational element, maps, or reports as of the date of the most recent available federal census. . . .

(c) The land, fees, or combination thereof are to be used only for the purpose of developing new or rehabilitating existing neighborhood or community park or recreational facilities to serve the subdivision.

(d) The legislative body has adopted a general plan or specific plan containing policies and standards for parks and recreation facilities, and the park and recreational facilities are in accordance with definite principles and standards.

(e) The amount and location of land to be dedicated or the fees to be paid shall bear a reasonable relationship to the use of the park and recreational facilities by the future inhabitants of the subdivision.

(f) The city, county, or other local public agency to which the land or fees are conveyed or paid shall develop a schedule specifying how, when, and where it will use the land or fees, or both, to develop park or recreational facilities to serve the residents of the subdivision. Any fees collected under the ordinance shall be committed within five years after the payment of such fees or the issuance of building permits on one-half of the lots created by the subdivision, whichever occurs later. If the fees are not committed, they, without any deductions, shall be distributed and paid to the then record owners of the subdivision in the same proportion that the size of their lot bears to the total area of all lots within the subdivision.

(g) Only the payment of fees may be required in subdivisions containing 50 parcels or less, except that when a condominium project, stock cooperative, or community apartment project exceeds 50 dwelling units, dedication of land may be required notwithstanding that the number of parcels may be less than 50.

(h) Subdivisions containing less than five parcels and not used for residential purposes shall be exempted from the requirements of this section. However a condition may be placed on the approval of such parcel map that if a building permit is requested for construction of a residential structure or structures on one or more of the parcels within four years the fee may be required to be paid by the owner of each such parcel as a condition to the issuance of such permit.

(i) If the subdivider provides park and recreational improvements to the dedicated land, the value of the improvements together with any equipment located thereon shall be a credit against the payment of fees or dedication of land required by the ordinance.

Problems

You are counsel for *A* in the following situations. Considering the application of the foregoing statutes, how would you advise *A*? Will it make any difference if the purchaser demands sale from a plat?

a. *A*, a builder, proposes to hold title to a tract of land in the name of her development company, erect eight residences, and rent them. Any difference if she wishes to lease apartments or stores in a multiunit project? In Gerard v. San Juan County, 715 P.2d 149 (Wash. App. 1986), a related sequence of conveyances and subdivisions constructed so as to use short plat exemptions to create an eighteen-parcel long platting was held to be an effort to circumvent the purposes of the platting ordinance and therefore illegal. Cf. Mount Laurel Township v. Barbieri, 151 N.J. Super. 27, 376 A.2d 541 (1977) (subdivision effected through "contrived" partition judgment ineffective).

b. Upon reading the definition in the state statute, similar to that of Wisconsin, *A*, a builder, suggests that he sell four parcels each year. Compare N.Y. Atty. Gen., Ann. Rep. 161 (Leg. Doc. No. 80, 1951) with 36 Ops. Wis. Atty. Gen. 185 (1947). See also Wis. Stat. Ann. §236.45(2) (1987).

c. *A*, whose ninety-acre farm fronts on a public road, wishes to convey the rear half of his farm to his son as a wedding present. Cf. Loechner v. Campoli, 49 N.J. 504, 231 A.2d 553 (1967).

d. There are two houses on the farm — the "new house" and the "old home." *A* wishes to convey the old home to his son.

e. After years of bickering, *A* and her immediate neighbor have agreed to change the boundary line of their adjoining properties by moving it back a few feet. See N.J. Stat. Ann. §40:55D-7 (West Supp. 1987).

f. The town in which *A*'s land is located has adopted no ordinances affecting subdivisions. *A* wishes to begin selling lots. Cf. Pratt v. Adams, 229 Cal. App. 2d 879, 40 Cal. Rptr. 505 (1964).

g. *A*'s proposed subdivision has been refused approval by the local planning commission on the ground that it is located too far from the center of the city to be developed at the present time. Another plat has been refused permission on the ground that it is "in an inappropriate region, to wit, near a railroad."

h. The planning commission approves *A*'s plan of subdivision. However, when the map is presented to the county surveyor, she refuses

A. Conflict at the Rural-Urban Fringe 617

to approve it on the ground that certain improvements, such as an adequate water supply, have not been provided. See Shorb v. Barkley, 108 Cal. App. 2d 873, 240 P.2d 337 (1952). As to the special role of planning commissions, see Kane v. Zoning Board of Greenwich, 97 R.I. 152, 196 A.2d 421 (1964). In general, see Yokley, The Law of Subdivisions ch. 8 (2d ed. 1981). In Grand Land Co. v. Township of Bethlehem, 196 N.J. Super. 547, 483 A.2d 818 (1984), it was held that township approval for subdivision of a lot for residential use could not be conditioned on reserving adjoining land for continued agricultural use.

i. The refusal of subdivision permission reads as follows: "Permission denied inasmuch as applicant's land is located in the valley and should be kept agricultural, it being the policy of this board to confine residential developments to the less fertile hills."

j. Prior to 1968, *A* made a layout of his tract of land for the purpose of developing it, and filed a map, which had been approved by the town plan commission, in the town clerk's office. Most of the lots were 25 by 100 feet. In 1968, subdivision regulations were passed requiring lot sizes of at least 6000 square feet for each family housed thereon. Owing to the higher standards now deemed a prerequisite by consumers, *A* wishes to combine two of the original lots into a single lot for the purpose of sale. See State ex rel. LaVoie v. Building Commission of Trumbull, 135 Conn. 415, 65 A.2d 165 (1949); Clauss v. Postma, 32 N.J. Super. 147, 108 A.2d 34 (Law Div. 1954). Would the result be different if the requirement of 6000 square feet were embodied in a zoning ordinance?

k. *A* sells a one-acre parcel out of a thirty-two-acre estate to *B*, and delivers the deed without the subdivision first having been approved by the planning board of the governing body. The municipality files a complaint seeking to enjoin the conveyance. City of Newark v. Padula, 26 N.J. Super. 251, 97 A.2d 735 (App. Div. 1953).

l. *A* proposes to convert an existing apartment house, containing more than five dwelling units, into a stock cooperative. See California Coastal Commission v. Quanta Investment, 113 Cal. App. 3d 579, 170 Cal. Rptr. 263 (1980).

2. *Authorizing Dealmaking: Development Agreements*

Entering into public-private agreements about development, as crucial as they are in the real world, raises serious questions regarding the bargaining away of the police power, as well as the capacity to assure the satisfactory discharge of conditions imposed upon the developer, and the ability to limit the actions of future legislative bodies.

Summary of Santa Monica Development Agreements* (excerpts)

Deviations from planning standards	Public benefits	Time limits	Subsequent approvals needed	Level of environmental review	Status
Colorado Place — 900,000-sq.-ft. mixed use (office-hotel-restaurants)					
"Average building height" measurement; "Useable area" definition vs. gross building area; Hotel use in General Industrial Zone.	100 deed-restricted affordable rental units; 150,000-sq.-ft. park area; Day care center; 1.5% arts and social services fee; Traffic control measures; Energy conservation measures; Specified infrastructure improvements; Affirmative action.	Phase I to start in 120 days of agreement execution; Phase II to start by date certain; Total project to be completed in eight years; Certain public benefits tied to phases; Contract term, 55 years	Park area design; Day care center lease; Traffic and emission abatement plan; Phase I landscape design; Phase II architectural and landscape design; Affirmative action plan; Phase II building permit.	Negative declaration.	Phase I completed; Amendments for subordination, reduced parking, and phasing time limits extension approved; Amendments for Phase II design changes pending.
1034-1050 Fourth St. — 50-unit condominium and rental unit project on two separate sites					
Increased lot coverage; Certain encroachments into yards permitted; Reduced parking requirements; Exemptions from certain condo design requirements; Waiver of certain fees and assessments.	23 deed-restricted, affordable rental units; Relocation benefits and first rights to existing site tenants; Affordable units remain under rental control law.	Site 1 — start within 18 months of demolition; Site 2 — start within 24 months of date building at Site 1 starts; Contract term, 40 years.	Parking variance (Site 2); Final subdivision map; Architectural and landscaping; Coastal Commission approval; Building permit.	Negative declaration.	Project amendments pending — no construction to date.

Bayview Plaza Holiday Inn — 134-room hotel addition and remodeling

Ten-story hotel addition in high-density residential zone.	Landscape improvements of existing street median; Street improvements; Minimum exterior improvements to existing building; Targeted hiring program; Job training program; Shuttle bus system or in lieu payment; Fee to Civic Center Fund; Public art and craft displays; Room vouchers for emergency lodging; Free parking; Prevailing construction wages; Relocate two existing buildings and construct six new rental units on site.	Start within 18 months of building permit; Complete within 24 months of starting date; Contract term, 39 years; Certain obligations terminate 25 years from Certificate of Occupancy, others in 40 years from Certificate of Occupancy.	Architectural, signage, landscaping; Subdivision maps; Coastal Commission approval; Building permit.	Environmental impact report; Various mitigation measures, required through development agreement — related to noise, design, parking, circulation, public safety, and energy conservation.	Project completed.

* *Source*: Silvern, Negotiating the Public Interest: California's Development Agreement Statute, Land Use L. & Zoning Dig., Oct. 1985, at 3, 7-8.

California's Statute on Development Agreements is the best known effort to authorize agreements on a state-wide basis:

§65864. The Legislature finds and declares that:

(a) The lack of certainty in the approval of development projects can result in a waste of resources, escalate the cost of housing and other development to the consumer, and discourage investment in and commitment to comprehensive planning which would make maximum efficient utilization of resources at the least economic cost to the public.

(b) Assurance to the applicant for a development project that upon approval of the project, the applicant may proceed with the project in accordance with existing policies, rules and regulations, and subject to conditions of approval, will strengthen the public planning process, encourage private participation in comprehensive planning, and reduce the economic costs of development.

(c) The lack of public facilities, including, but not limited to, streets, sewerage, transportation, drinking water, school, and utility facilities, is a serious impediment to the development of new housing. Whenever possible, applicants and local governments may include provisions in agreements whereby applicants are reimbursed over time for financing public facilities.

§65865. (a) Any city, county, or city and county, may enter into a development agreement with any person having a legal or equitable interest in real property for the development of the property as provided in this article.

(b) Any city may enter into a development agreement with any person having a legal or equitable interest in real property in unincorporated territory within that city's sphere of influence for the development of the property as provided in this article. However, the agreement shall not become operative unless annexation proceedings annexing the property to the city are completed within the period of time specified by the agreement. If the annexation is not completed within the time specified in the agreement or any extension of the agreement, the agreement is null and void.

(c) Every city, county, or city and county, shall, upon request of an applicant, by resolution or ordinance, establish procedures and requirements for the consideration of development agreements upon application by, or on behalf of, the property owner or other person having a legal or equitable interest in the property.

(d) A city, county, or city and county may recover from applicants the direct costs associated with adopting a resolution or ordinance to establish procedures and requirements for the consideration of development agreements.

§65865.2. A development agreement shall specify the duration of the agreement, the permitted uses of the property, the density or intensity of use, the maximum height and size of proposed buildings, and provisions for reservation or dedication of land for public purposes. The development agreement may include conditions, terms, restrictions, and requirements for subsequent discretionary actions, provided that such conditions, terms, restrictions, and requirements for subsequent discretionary actions shall not prevent development of the land for the uses and to the density or intensity of development set forth in the agreement. The agreement may provide that construction shall be commenced within a specified time and that the project or any phase thereof be completed within a specified time.

The agreement may also include terms and conditions relating to applicant financing of necessary public facilities and subsequent reimbursement over time.

§65865.4. Unless amended or canceled . . . a development agreement shall be enforceable by any party thereto notwithstanding any change in any applicable general or specific plan, zoning, subdivision, or building regulation adopted by the city, county, or city and county entering the agreement. . . .

Cal. Govt. Code (West Supp. 1987). Compare Florida's approach in Fla. Stat. Ann. §§163.3220-.3243 (West Supp. 1988). See Rhodes, The Florida Local Government Development Agreement Act, Fla. B.J., Oct. 1988, at 81 ("Unlike its California counterpart, the Florida Act was not a business community driven response to 'late vesting' caselaw."). See also Wegner, Moving Toward the Bargaining Table, 65 N.C.L. Rev. 957, 994-1038 (1987).

B. THE ATTITUDE OF THE JUDICIARY

1. Scrutinizing the Dealmaking Process

■ AYRES v. CITY COUNCIL OF LOS ANGELES
34 Cal. 2d 31, 207 P.2d 1 (1949)

SHENK, Justice. This appeal is by the petitioner from a judgment denying relief in a mandamus proceeding brought to compel the respondent city council to approve a proposed subdivision map without certain imposed conditions.

A tentative map for the subdivision of thirteen acres owned by the petitioner in what is commonly known as the Westchester District in the city of Los Angeles was submitted in October 1944 to the city planning commission pursuant to the Subdivision Map Act, Stats. 1937, p. 1874, as amended, now Sec. 11500 et seq. Business & Professions Code. The planning commission attached four conditions to which the petitioner objected, whereupon he appealed to the city council. The matter was noticed for a hearing before that body, after which an order was made sustaining each of the conditions. The petitioner thereupon commenced the present proceeding in the superior court. . . . Findings were made and judgment entered upholding the lawfulness and reasonableness of the imposed conditions. The appeal involves the sufficiency of the evidence to support the findings and judgment.

The area known as Westchester District of which the proposed thirteen acre subdivision forms a part consists of 3023 acres. It is bisected in a northerly and southerly direction by Sepulveda Boulevard, and easterly and westerly by Manchester Boulevard. It extends one mile to the south of Manchester and a mile and a half to the north; and one mile on either side of Sepulveda. Before subdivision the land in the district was owned by Los Angeles Extension Company, Security-First National Bank of Los Angeles, and Superior Oil Company. The petitioner represented the latter as subdivider and selling agent. In 1940 the formation of a general plan of development of the district was commenced. The plan fixed the business area on Sepulveda Boulevard immediately south of Manchester Boulevard and the petitioner was placed in charge of development by the subdividers. The so-called cellular design of residence lot subdivision was employed so that the rear of residential lots abuts the principal thoroughfares, thus prohibiting access to the lots therefrom. Another purpose of this type of subdivision was to minimize the amount of land required for street purposes. This general plan had been followed in the Westchester district. Requirements insuring uniformity were imposed, among which were the dedication of a ten foot strip in the residence areas and a thirteen foot strip on each side in the business section for the widening of Sepulveda Boulevard, and the setting aside of a strip for planting purposes varying in width at the rear of lots in the residence sections bordering the principal thoroughfares.

The petitioner's thirteen acre tract, the last of the subdivisions in the district, is a long narrow triangle. Its northerly boundary is less than 500 feet in length, and the southerly point of the triangle about 2400 feet from the northerly line. Arizona Avenue runs along the westerly line. Sepulveda Boulevard, the principal thoroughfare and heavily trafficked artery, borders the easterly line. These highways converge and form the southerly point of the triangle. Sepulveda Boulevard, from a point a short distance north of the convergence to the north line of the tract, is 100 feet wide but south of that point is 110 feet wide. Seventy-Seventh Street enters Arizona Avenue from the west approximately opposite the center of the tract, and the proposed subdivision map shows the extension of that street through the tract. Seventy-Ninth Street enters Arizona Avenue from the west a short distance north of the southerly point of the tract. An extension of that street through the subdivision would leave a triangular tip of land about $12\frac{1}{2}$ feet wide by 75 feet to the southerly point. The proposed subdivision would include ten residence lots north of the Seventy-Seventh Street extension fronting on Arizona Avenue with 80 foot frontages and

B. The Attitude of the Judiciary 623

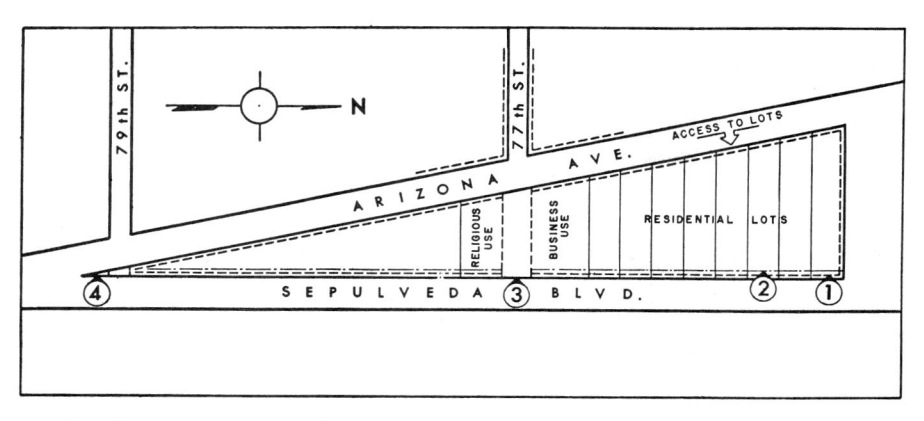

1. Ten-foot strip for street widening.
2. Ten-foot strip for planting.
3. Widening of street to 80 feet.
4. Dedication of triangle.

depths to Sepulveda Boulevard varying from 312 to 462 feet. Entrance to the residence lots would be from Arizona Avenue exclusively. The lot immediately north of and adjoining the Seventy-Seventh Street extension is proposed to be used for business drive-in and the lot south of Seventy-Seventh Street for religious purposes.

The four conditions imposed by the planning commission and approved by the city council and the trial court are:

1. That a ten foot strip abutting Sepulveda Boulevard be dedicated for the widening of that highway.
2. That an additional ten foot strip along the rear of the lots be restricted to the planting of trees and shrubbery for the purpose of preventing direct ingress and egress between the lots and Sepulveda Boulevard.
3. That the extension of Seventy-Seventh Street be dedicated to a width of eighty instead of sixty feet.
4. That the area which would be covered by an extension of Seventy-Ninth Street and south to the point of the triangle be dedicated for street use for the purpose of eliminating it as a traffic hazard.

The petitioner objected to the foregoing conditions on the ground that they were not expressly provided for by the Subdivision Map Act nor by city ordinance; that conditions 1, 2 and 4, and condition 3 in so far as it required dedication in excess of 60 feet in width, bear no reasonable relationship to the protection of the public health, safety or general welfare, and amount to a taking of private property for public use without compensation. . . .

Section 11525 of the Subdivision Map Act vests control of the design and improvement of subdivisions in the governing bodies of cities and counties, subject to review as to reasonableness by the superior court in and for the county in which the land is situated. . . .

Section 11551 states that if there is a local ordinance regulating the design and improvement of subdivisions the subdivider shall comply with its provisions before the map may be approved; but if there is no such ordinance the governing body as a condition precedent to approval may require streets and drainage ways properly located and of adequate width but may make no other requirements.

The words "Design" and "Improvement" as used in the act are defined. Section 11510 provides that "Design" refers to street alignment, grades and widths, alignment and widths of easements and right of ways for drainage and sanitary sewers and minimum lot area and width. Section 11511 defines "Improvement" as only such street work and utilities to be installed, or agreed to be installed, by the subdivider on the land to be dedicated for streets, highways, etc., as are necessary for the general use of the lot owners in the subdivision and local neighborhood traffic and drainage needs. . . .

It appears to be the petitioner's contention that no condition may be exacted which is not expressly provided for by the Subdivision Map Act or the ordinance provisions not in conflict therewith; that at all events the requirements may deal only with streets to be laid out by the subdivider within the confines of the subdivision to take care of traffic needs therein, and that no dedication may be exacted for additions to existing streets or highways.

It must be obvious at the outset that this effect may not be drawn from the statute or from the city's organic law or ordinances. The foregoing review of those provisions does not indicate that the authority of the city planners is so circumscribed. . . . Where as here no specific restriction or limitation on the city's power is contained in the Charter, and none forbidding the particular conditions is included either in the Subdivision Map Act or the city ordinances, it is proper to conclude that conditions are lawful which are not inconsistent with the Map Act and the ordinances and are reasonably required by the subdivision type and use as related to the character of local and neighborhood planning and traffic conditions.

The petitioner relies on section 11551 of the act which purports to limit authority to impose conditions in the absence of local ordinances, and on the definition of the word "Improvement" in section 11511. But here the applicable provisions of the ordinances and of the act do not restrict reasonable conditions to provide streets and highways in relation to the local and neighborhood traffic needs. The word "Im-

B. The Attitude of the Judiciary 625

provement" as used in the act refers only to such improvements as are *to be installed by the subdivider* on the land to be dedicated to those needs. Implicit therein is the recognition that reasonable conditions may be imposed for the dedication of land for necessary purposes which is not to be improved by the subdivider. The provisions of the act do not impose the restrictions or limitations on the land which may be dedicated as invoked by the petitioner, but merely constitute a definition of the word "improvement" as used in the act. If the dedications for the widening of Sepulveda Boulevard and for the elimination of the southern tip of the triangle are otherwise lawfully required it can be no source of complaint to the petitioner that he is not required to make the improvement as well as the dedication. The trial court correctly determined that the conditions imposed were not precluded by the act.

The Subdivision Map Act, Sec. 11552, and the city ordinances indicate that the matters for consideration in relation to the reasonableness of imposed conditions contemplate the character of the neighborhood, the kinds, nature and extent of improvements, the quality or kinds of development to which the area is best adapted, the traffic needs, and other phases, including the size, use, physical or other conditions of the property, and the type of subdivision.

As to condition 1, that a ten foot widening strip be dedicated, the finding is that the widening of Sepulveda Boulevard had been in contemplation by the authorities whether or not the petitioner intended to subdivide; but that the creation and the proposed uses of the subdivision would give rise to traffic and other conditions necessitating the widening of the boulevard; that the widening was necessary for and would benefit the lot owners, and that the requirement was reasonably related to the protection of the public health, safety and general welfare.

With regard to condition 2, that an additional ten feet be reserved for a planting strip, the court found that such a strip was already in contemplation, but that the creation of the subdivision necessitated the restricted use to confine ingress and egress to and from the lots away from Sepulveda Boulevard; to screen the lot owners from the traffic noises, fumes and views of the fast-moving traffic on the boulevard; to provide safety islands for residents crossing the boulevard on foot and waiting lanes for vehicular traffic, and that the imposition of the condition was reasonably related to the protection of the public health, safety and general welfare.

It was found that the foregoing pattern of subdivision, including the widening and planting strips in the development of Sepulveda Boulevard frontage, was in conformity with neighborhood plan and design, and had been carried out without objection by the petitioner and others in the district until the filing by petitioner of the tentative map for subdivision of his thirteen acres. Variations in some requirements, changes in or abandonment of others, delays in making improvements, incompleteness of the master plans or failure to indicate thereon the precise details, the court found to be minor, not unauthorized, and without adverse bearing on the lawfulness or reasonableness of the conditions imposed.

The finding as to condition 3, respecting the required eighty foot width of the Seventy-Seventh Street extension through the tract, was covered by the trial court's general conclusion that there was no unreasonable application of the Subdivision Map Act as to any of the conditions objected to by the petitioner.

Specifically as to condition 4, the dedication to eliminate the southerly tip of the triangle, it was found that without regard to the subdivision it had been the intention to project Seventy-Ninth Street either across the petitioner's tract or below it; also that the subdivision would give rise to and create traffic conditions and hazards necessitating the elimination of the tip for the proper control of traffic in the locality, would benefit the lot owners in the proposed subdivision, and was reasonably related to the protection of the public health, safety and general welfare. . . .

The contentions respecting the required width of the Seventy-Seventh Street extension will not be further discussed except to note that the proposed business and religious uses of the respective abutting lots and the fact that Seventy-Seventh is the only street to transverse the tract between Sepulveda Boulevard and Arizona Avenue, sufficiently support the conclusion that the required width is reasonably related to the potential traffic needs.

The petitioner does not quarrel with the conclusion that the other conditions are desirable and that their fulfillment will accomplish the ends stated. His more specific complaint is that the city contemplated taking the property for the purposes indicated in any event, that the benefit to the lot owners and the tract will be relatively small compared to the beneficial return to the city at large; therefore that the requirements amount to an exercise of the power of eminent domain under the guise of pursuing the authority of subdivision map proceedings, and that the exercise thereof is unconstitutional unless compensation be paid.

In his arguments the petitioner appears to have lost sight of the particular type of lot subdivision and uniformity of neighborhood design and plan theretofore applied in the locality, including the requirement for strip dedication for widening purposes and strip restriction to planting use without dedication. As stated, consideration of these matters is not precluded by the provisions of the Subdivision Map Act, but on the contrary both the statutory provisions and the local law indicate that the subdivision design and use should conform to neighborhood planning and zoning requirements. Here the greater than average depth of the lots minimizes the land loss and street

B. The Attitude of the Judiciary 627

improvement cost. In fact it may be said that the petitioner's position would seem to be greatly improved by this type of subdivision and its related requirements in conformity with neighborhood planning and zoning. The regular design of subdivision, with ingress and egress to and from Sepulveda Boulevard, would have been out of harmony with the neighborhood plan and traffic needs. It would have required dedication and improvement by the petitioner of lateral service roads and lanes for diversion of the local traffic to and from the main artery which the evidence shows would have used more land than for the widening and planting strips, and would have increased the cost of the improvements to be installed by the petitioner. The record indicates that the so-called cellular design was generally adopted because it interfered less with the free flow of traffic, minimized the hazards on the main thoroughfares, and reduced land dedication and improvement expense. The petitioner and the lot owners in the subdivision will participate in these benefits and savings by the selection of and adherence to the particular design. In fact the petitioner makes no objection to that design as such. It is to be assumed that he prefers it with the resulting savings in land and cost. But he seeks in addition compensation for the fulfillment of the conditions which make this type of lot subdivision feasible. . . .

Questions of reasonableness and necessity depend on matters of fact. They are not abstract ideas or theories. In a growing metropolitan area each additional subdivision adds to the traffic burden. It is no defense to the conditions imposed in a subdivision map proceeding that their fulfillment will incidentally also benefit the city as a whole. Nor is it a valid objection to say that the conditions contemplate future as well as more immediate needs. Potential as well as present population factors affecting the subdivision and the neighborhood generally are appropriate for consideration. Nor does the fact that master plans are incomplete, or that the specific details are not shown thereon, affect the result. It was in evidence that the city had been working toward the formulation of a complete and entire master plan, although all the elements or parts thereof were not as yet in the final stage of completion. The contention that the requirements for a master plan or some overall plan must be approved and adopted before authority vests in relation to the conditions here imposed is without merit since in any event the charter contemplates that portions thereof may be adopted. It is inconceivable that a master plan including all essential factors for a growing city could be completed in a short period of time. The trial court correctly concluded that delay in the adoption of the final master plan or plans had no material bearing on the controversial issues in this proceeding. The reasonableness of the conditions and the authority to impose them do not necessarily depend upon their inclusion in the official master plan for the district. As noted, subdivision design and improvement obviously include conformance to neighborhood planning and zoning, and it may properly be said that the formulation and acceptance of the uniform conditions in the development of the district constitute the practical adoption of a master plan and zoning requirements therefor. Nor is there merit in the petitioner's contention that a uniform plan is lacking because of some discrepancies in uniformity or delays in enforcement or fulfillment of the conditions. Time, funds and manpower are requisites to execution, and lack of speed in accomplishment, or some changes because of differing circumstances as to use or otherwise, cannot defeat the otherwise uniform and reasonable application of the imposed conditions in a growing community.

The petitioner may not prevail in his contention that, since the use of the land for the purposes stated was contemplated in any event, the dedication and use reservation requirements in this proceeding are unconstitutional as an exercise of the power of eminent domain. A sufficient answer is that the proceeding here involved is not one in eminent domain nor is the city seeking to exercise that power. It is the petitioner who is seeking to acquire the advantages of lot subdivision and upon him rests the duty of compliance with reasonable conditions for design, dedication, improvement and restrictive use of the land so as to conform to the safety and general welfare of the lot owners in the subdivision and of the public. . . .

The judgment is affirmed.

GIBSON, C. J., and EDMONDS, TRAYNOR, and SPENCE, JJ., concur.

CARTER, Justice (dissenting). I dissent. If the Subdivision Map Act is construed to mean that the City Planning Commission may require a dedication of land *to improve streets already in existence* from one who proposes to subdivide before his tentative map may be approved and recorded, regardless of the fact that there is no ordinance requiring such dedication, then it is my position that such a procedure is nothing more than a taking of appellant's property without making compensation therefor. . . .

The construction placed upon the Subdivision Map Act by the majority has the effect of telling the subdivider that he may dedicate land to the city for the privilege of recording and selling—a matter which is not a privilege, but a *right*, in other situations, or let the land go idle, or sell it and go to jail, pay a fine, or both. This, it appears to me, amounts to a form of duress that is reminiscent of the type of practice which prevailed in another country prior to the last great war.

It is true that in Archer v. City of Los Angeles, 19 Cal. 2d 19, 23, 24, 119 P.2d 1, 4, a majority of this Court said:

> The state or its subdivisions may take or damage private property without compensation if such action is essential to safeguard public health, safety,

or morals. In certain circumstances, however, the taking or damaging of private property for such a purpose is not prompted by so great a necessity as to be justified without proper compensation to the owner. The liability of the state under article I, section 14 of the California Constitution arises when the taking or damaging of private property is not so essential to the general welfare as to be sanctioned under the "police power," and the injury is one that would give rise to a cause of action on the part of the owner independently of the constitutional provision.

This is a doctrine of statism with which I positively disagree as appears from my dissenting opinion in that case.[21]

■ HOME BUILDERS AND CONTRACTORS ASSOCIATION OF PALM BEACH COUNTY v. BOARD OF COUNTY COMMISSIONERS
446 So. 2d 140 (Fla. Dist. Ct. App. 1983), review denied, 451 So. 2d 848, appeal dismissed, 469 U.S. 976 (1984)

DOWNEY, Judge. . . .

Appellants, Home Builders and Contractors Association of Palm Beach County, Inc. (hereafter Home Builders), and Ted Satter Enterprises, Inc., filed suit against the Board of County Commissioners of Palm Beach County for declaratory and injunctive relief to invalidate Palm Beach County ordinance 79-7, as amended, denominated the "Fair Share Contribution for Road Improvements Ordinance." From a final judgment upholding the validity of the ordinance, Home Builders has perfected this appeal.

The Palm Beach 1980 County Comprehensive Plan recognized that in view of the unusual growth rate being experienced in the county and in order to maintain a consistent level of road service and quality of life, extensive road improvements would be necessary, requiring regulation of new development activity which generates additional automobile traffic. The County Commission therefore enacted Ordi-

---

21. See Reps and Smith, Control of Urban Land Subdivision, 14 Syracuse L. Rev. 405 (1963); Heyman and Gilhool, The Constitutionality of Imposing Increased Community Costs on New Suburban Residents Through Subdivision Exactions, 73 Yale L.J. 1119 (1964); Johnston, Constitutionality of Subdivision Control Exactions, 52 Conn. L.Q. 871 (1967); Bosselman and Stroud, Mandatory Tithes: The Legality of Land Development Linkage, 9 Nova L.J. 381 (1985); Symposium: Exactions: A Controversial New Source for Municipal Funds, 50 Law & Contemp. Probs. 1 (1987). Cf. Krieger v. Planning Commission of Howard County, 224 Md. 320, 167 A.2d 885 (1961).

In Cupp v. Board of Supervisors of Fairfax County, 318 S.E.2d 407 (Va. 1984), the court held that a county board could not require the owner of a nursery, as a prerequisite to its expansion, to dedicate a portion of his land and to construct a roadway in light of evidence that construction was not needed to provide access to the nursery, but was needed to relieve congestion on the highway running by the nursery. — EDS.

nance 79-7 in order to finance the necessary road capital improvements and to regulate increases in traffic levels. The ordinance would require any new land development activity generating road traffic to pay its "fair share" of the reasonably anticipated cost of expansion of new roads attributable to the new development.

The ordinance has a formula which takes into consideration the costs of road construction and the number of motor vehicle trips generated by different types of land use. It provides for a fee of $300 per unit for single family homes, $200 per unit for multi-family, $175 per unit for mobile homes with other amounts for commercial or other development, all subject to annual review. The fee is to be paid upon commencement of any new land development activity generating traffic. The ordinance divides the county into forty zones, indicated on a map incorporated by reference into the ordinance, and establishes a trust fund for each zone. Funds collected from building activity in a particular zone may only be spent in that zone, and must be spent within a reasonable time after collection (not later than six years) or returned to the present owner of the property....

Home Builders contends the ordinance is invalid because of the disparity between the people who benefit and the people who pay. As stated in its brief:

> Our position is that since anyone can drive a vehicle over any of these roads, regardless of whether he lives in the zone or has paid the impact fee, there is too great a disparity between those who pay and those who receive the benefit, making the charge in reality a tax, which the county does not have the power to impose.

If by that argument it is Home Builders' position that the benefits accruing from roads constructed with the impact fees collected must be used exclusively or overwhelmingly for the subdivision residents in question, we would have to differ. It is difficult to envision any capital improvement for parts, sewers, drainage, roads, or whatever, which would not in some measure benefit members of the community who do not reside in or utilize the new development. For example, landowners abutting a subdivision may well derive substantial benefit from intrasubdivision drainage facilities. Parks within subdivisions are not restricted to subdivision residents only. Furthermore, intrasubdivision streets and roads may be extensively used by persons not residents thereof.

A resume of the decisions in this and other jurisdictions demonstrates that those attacking impact fees often rely upon this same argument; it is one frequently found and generally rejected.... Our recent decision in Hollywood, Inc. v. Broward County, 431 So. 2d 606 (Fla. 4th DCA 1983), also supports a holding that benefit accruing to

B. The Attitude of the Judiciary 631

the community generally does not adversely affect the validity of a development regulation ordinance as long as the fee does not exceed the cost of the improvements required by the new development and the improvements adequately benefit the development which is the source of the fee.

Next Home Builders contends that the fair share ordinance is arbitrary and discriminatory and thus violates the equal protection provisions of the Federal and State Constitutions. The thrust of the argument is that since municipalities may "opt out" of the ordinance under Article VIII, Section 1(f) of the Florida Constitution, and thirty-three of the thirty-seven municipalities in the county have opted out, equal protection is denied to those subject to the ordinance.

We disagree. Using the rational basis test articulated in In re Estate of Greenberg, 390 So. 2d 40 (Fla. 1980), we believe the evidence demonstrates that the ordinance bears a reasonable relationship to a legitimate state purpose. . . .

Furthermore, the fact that an impact fee is payable on land located in the county whereas it would not be payable on nearby land in a municipality which has opted out does not offend equal protection. Unequal or different charges or fees assessed in incorporated and unincorporated areas, like different hours for retail liquor sales and other areas of regulation which may lack uniformity, are not improper where such legislation is otherwise a valid exercise of governmental power.

In addition, we would observe that for aught we know any of these municipalities which have opted out may themselves one day enact impact fees, which will tend to lessen the ostensible unequal treatment of land development in different areas.

Finally, appellants maintain that the ordinance is a tax rather than a regulatory fee and thus in violation of Article VII, Section 1(a) of the Florida Constitution. In all candor we concede this is the most difficult point raised in this appeal. As one reads the various cases involving the dichotomy between a fee and a tax the distinction almost seems to become more amorphous rather than less. In any event, some years ago this court decided Broward County v. Janis Development Corp., 311 So. 2d 371 (Fla. 4th DCA 1975), and held that a county ordinance imposing an impact fee for roads was in reality a tax rather than a fee. Appellants naturally rely heavily upon *Janis* to support their argument that this ordinance is a tax in sheep's clothing and that impact fees and roads are simply not compatible. However, the problem with the *Janis* ordinance was not that it involved an impact fee for roads (as opposed to parks or drainage, etc.) but rather that the legislation had several inherent defects. For example, the money generated by the ordinance far exceeded the cost of meeting the needs brought about by the new development. In addition, the ordinance was lacking in specific restrictions regarding the use of revenue received. These are the features which required this court to hold it was not dealing with a regulatory fee. The amount and use of the funds simply did not jibe with the concept of regulation; it smacked more of revenue raising which is descriptive of a tax. . . .

The present ordinance recognizes that the rapid rate of new development will require a substantial increase in the capacity of the county road system. The evidence shows that the cost of construction of additional roads will far exceed the fair share fees imposed by the ordinance. In fact the county suggests that under the ordinance the cost will exceed the revenue produced by eighty-five percent. The formula for calculating the amount of the fee is not rigid and inflexible, but rather allows the person improving the land to determine his fair share by furnishing his own independent study of traffic and economic data in order to demonstrate that his share is less than the amount under the formula set forth in the ordinance. Lastly, expenditure of the funds collected is localized by virtue of the zone system. . . .

For the foregoing reasons, we affirm the judgment appealed from.

Notes

1. The Texas Supreme Court considered a challenge to an in lieu cash payments plan in City of College Station v. Turtle Rock Corp., 680 S.W.2d 802 (Tex. 1984):

> The ordinance contains provisions to the following effect:
>
> (1) that a developer must grant to the city a fee simple dedication of one acre of land for each 133 proposed dwelling units;
> (2) that a developer must pay cash in lieu of land if fewer than 133 units are proposed;
> (3) that the city may decide whether to accept the dedication or to require cash payment if between one and five acres of land are to be dedicated;
> (4) that the developer may elect to pay cash, subject to a city council veto, in lieu of any dedication required.
>
> The ordinance further requires that the city establish a special fund for the deposit of all sums paid in lieu of land dedication. These sums must be expended within two years for the acquisition or development of a neighborhood park; otherwise the owners of property in the subdivision are entitled to a refund.

While the court of appeals had held all park dedication ordinances per se invalid, "'not[ing] that parks are not necessarily beneficial to a community or neighborhood,'" the high court reasoned:

B. The Attitude of the Judiciary 633

The issue in this appeal is not whether parks are always and necessarily a benefit to the community; the issue is whether Turtle Rock met its burden for summary judgment of showing that College Station's ordinance is invalid as a matter of law....

College Station's ordinance requires that only a small portion of a developer's subdivision tract be dedicated to serve park needs. It does not render the developer's entire property "wholly useless" nor does it cause a "total destruction" of the entire tract's economic value. It is a regulatory response to the needs created by the developer's use of the land.

Cf. Berg Development Co. v. City of Missouri City, 603 S.W.2d 273 (Tex. Civ. App. 1980) (park dedication ordinance that did not prevent city from using in lieu funds for purposes other than parks unconstitutional).

2. In Banberry Development Corp. v. South Jordan City, 631 P.2d 899 (Utah 1981), after stating that an order to comply with the reasonableness standard as to a municipal fee for services should not require newly developed properties to bear more than their equitable share of capital costs, the court listed the factors that the municipality should consider:

(1) the cost of existing capital facilities; (2) the manner of financing existing capital facilities (such as user charges, special assessments, bonded indebtedness, general taxes, or federal grants); (3) the relative extent to which the newly developed properties and the other properties in the municipality have already contributed to the cost of existing capital facilities (by such means as user charges, special assessments, or payment from the proceeds of general taxes); (4) the relative extent to which the newly developed properties and the other properties in the municipality will contribute to the cost of existing capital facilities in the future; (5) the extent to which the newly developed properties are entitled to a credit because the municipality is requiring their developers or owners (by contractual arrangement or otherwise) to provide common facilities (inside or outside the proposed development) that have been provided by the municipality and financed through general taxation or other means (apart from user charges) in other parts of the municipality; (6) extraordinary costs, if any, in servicing the newly developed properties; and (7) the time-price differential inherent in fair comparisons of amounts paid at different times.

See also §2-103 of the Model Land Development Code (Permits Subject to Conditions).

3. The California Supreme Court in Associated Home Builders of Greater East Bay, Inc. v. City of Walnut Creek, 4 Cal. 3d 633, 484 P.2d 606, 94 Cal. Rptr. 630, appeal dismissed, 404 U.S. 878 (1971), provides the leading explanation of the rationale behind the reasonable relationship test. The court explained:

> We see no persuasive reason in the face of these urgent needs caused by present and anticipated future population growth on the one hand and the disappearance of open land on the other to hold that a statute requiring the dedication of land by a subdivider may be justified only upon the ground that the particular subdivider upon whom an exaction has been imposed will, solely by the development of his subdivision, increase the need for recreational facilities to such an extent that additional land for such facilities will be required. . . . [Therefore] the amount and location of land or fees shall bear a reasonable relationship to the use of the facilities by the future inhabitants of the subdivision.

The impact on home prices by the new route of development charges and fees is examined in Peterson and Muller, Housing Cost Reduction Through the Tax-Exempt Market, in Housing and the New Financial Markets 408 (Florida ed. 1986). Other approaches to reduce up-front capital costs include the formation of special utility districts (formed by petitions by developers) authorized to issue tax-exempt bonds or community-wide financing through the issuance of general obligation bonds. See The Changing Structure of Infrastructure Finance (Nicholas ed. 1986).

4. In Hillis Homes, Inc. v. Snohomish County, 650 P.2d 193 (Wash. 1982), although characterized as "fees," the payment demand was held to be a tax and therefore invalid. The court stated:

> The record is replete with evidence of the increased costs imposed on counties by new residential developments. We are sympathetic to the plight of counties faced with the obligation of providing services to a rapidly growing population and hampered by lack of revenue. However, no matter how desperate the needs of the counties, they remain creatures of the constitution and the legislature. Const. art. 11, §4. Their powers are limited to those granted them by the constitution and legislature, expressly or by implication. Our review of the validity of counties' actions must therefore be an inquiry into whether those actions are authorized. If the legislature has not authorized the action in question, it is invalid no matter how necessary it might be.

In Miller v. City of Port Angeles, 38 Wash. App. 904, 691 P.2d 229 (1984), the court held that not all requirements for payment by a government body are taxes:

> Where fees are intended primarily to regulate the development of a specific subdivision and not simply to raise revenue, they will not be considered taxes. . . . Widening streets and installing controls for the safety of pedestrians and vehicle traffic are regulatory measures within the proper exercise of the City's police power, and it can require that the cost of these measures be borne by those who created the need.

B. The Attitude of the Judiciary

The condition pertaining to contributing to the Golf Course Road Arterial Improvement Fund was not unconstitutionally vague, merely because the completion of the improvements and the ultimate cost remained uncertain. Id. at 234. See also Diamond, The Death and Transfiguration of Benefit Taxation: Special Assessments in Nineteenth-Century America, 12 J. Legal Stud. 201 (1983); Diamond, Constitutional Limits on the Growth of Special Assessments, 6 Urb. L. & Poly., 311 (1984).

5. It is stated in Planning Rules and Regulations for Puerto Rico, art. 55 (1952): "Due consideration shall be given to the allocation of suitable areas for schools, parks and playgrounds. At least five per cent . . . of the total area of every proposed subdivision, involving the establishment of a new street, or streets, shall be reserved and dedicated for recreational purposes." Is this a codification of the *Ayres* decision? See Zayas v. Planning Board, 69 P.R.R. 27 (1948); Segarra v. Planning Board, 71 P.R.R. 139 (1950). A Massachusetts law provides that the planning board cannot "impose, as a condition for the approval of a plan of a subdivision, that any of the land . . . be dedicated to the public use . . . as a public way . . . without just compensation." Mass. Gen. Laws Ann. ch. 41, §81Q (Supp. 1979).

6. On another point in *Associated Home Builders of Greater East Bay*, supra page 633, the Sierra Club, as amicus curiae, urged that the dedication or fee was justified even if the recreational facilities were not used for the specific benefit of the future residents of the subdivision. While not ruling on it directly, the court stated, "Parenthetically, however, we perceive merit in the position of amicus curiae. It is difficult to see why, in the light of the need for recreational facilities . . . and the increasing mobility of our population, a subdivider's fee in lieu of dedication may not be used to purchase or develop land some distance from the subdivision residents." 484 P.2d at 612 n.6. What of fire and police protection? What of an apartment house built on land that is not subdivided? What of development on high density land?

7. Alfred Marshall "suggested . . . 'that every person putting up a house in a district that has got as closely populated as is good should be compelled to contribute towards providing free playgrounds.'" Pigou, Economics of Welfare 192 (4th ed. 1932). A considerable number of jurisdictions in the United States are attempting to do just this, some requiring dedications of up to 10 or 12 percent of the total area of the subdivision for public purposes.

8. In Grupe v. California Coastal Commission, 166 Cal. App. 3d 148, 212 Cal. Rptr. 578 (1985), the court upheld a condition, imposed in a new development permit, requiring the dedication of an easement affecting two-thirds of respondent's parcel, that would provide access to a beach on the property. The lot owner had applied for a building permit for a single-family home on a 15,200 square foot beachfront

lot. The permit required a dedication of between 8000 and 10,000 square feet parallel to the shoreline for public access and passive recreation. Previously developed properties in the surrounding area had not been similarly burdened so that the land would not be accessible from anywhere other than the shoreline below the high tide mark. Additionally, the easement did not provide access to the beach from any public road as the parcel is located in a "private 'locked gate' residential community."

The court upheld the mandatory dedication in the face of the landowner's challenge that it was not reasonably related to needs created by the construction of the dwelling. The court held that only an "indirect relationship" between the exaction and a need attributable to development is required.[22]

But two years after the *Grupe* decision, the Supreme Court delivered a blow to local governing bodies, particularly those in California, that tied development exactions seemingly only indirectly to the planned development. Justice Scalia took the opportunity of his first Supreme Court land-use opinion to reconsider the lack of respect given private property as opposed to other personal rights, and to question the broad discretion given local decision-makers. As you read the majority's disapproval of the condition required of the beachfront owner, consider how the Court's new search for something beyond mere rationality endangers the holdings in many of the exaction cases we have studied thus far.

■ NOLLAN v. CALIFORNIA COASTAL COMMISSION
107 S. Ct. 3141 (1987)

Justice SCALIA delivered the opinion of the Court. . . .

The Nollans own a beachfront lot in Ventura County, California. A quarter-mile north of their property is Faria County Park, an oceanside public park with a public beach and recreation area. Another public beach area, known locally as "the Cove," lies 1,800 feet south of their lot. A concrete seawall approximately eight feet high separates the beach portion of the Nollans' property from the rest of the lot. The historic mean high tide line determines the lot's oceanside boundary.

---

22. See also Bauman and Ethier, Development Exactions and Impact Fees: A Survey of American Practices, 50 Law & Contemp. Probs. 51 (1987); Delaney, Gordon, and Hess, The Needs-Nexus Analysis: A Unified Test for Validating Subdivision Exactions, User Impact Fees and Linkage, 50 id. 139 (1987).

B. The Attitude of the Judiciary

The Nollans originally leased their property with an option to buy. The building on the lot was a small bungalow, totalling 504 square feet, which for a time they rented to summer vacationers. After years of rental use, however, the building had fallen into disrepair, and could no longer be rented out.

The Nollans' option to purchase was conditioned on their promise to demolish the bungalow and replace it. In order to do so, under California Public Resources Code §§30106, 30212, and 30600 (West 1986), they were required to obtain a coastal development permit from the California Coastal Commission. On February 25, 1982, they submitted a permit application to the Commission in which they proposed to demolish the existing structure and replace it with a three-bedroom house in keeping with the rest of the neighborhood.

The Nollans were informed that their application had been placed on the administrative calendar, and that the Commission staff had recommended that the permit be granted subject to the condition that they allow the public an easement to pass across a portion of their property bounded by the mean high tide line on one side, and their seawall on the other side. This would make it easier for the public to get to Faria County Park and the Cove. The Nollans protested imposition of the condition, but the Commission overruled their objections and granted the permit subject to their recordation of a deed restriction granting the easement.

On June 3, 1982, the Nollans filed a petition for writ of administrative mandamus asking the Ventura County Superior Court to invalidate the access condition. They argued that the condition could not be imposed absent evidence that their proposed development would have a direct adverse impact on public access to the beach. The court agreed, and remanded the case to the Commission for a full evidentiary hearing on that issue.

On remand, the Commission held a public hearing, after which it made further factual findings and reaffirmed its imposition of the condition. . . .

The Nollans filed a supplemental petition for a writ of administrative mandamus with the Superior Court, in which they argued that imposition of the access condition violated the Takings Clause of the Fifth Amendment, as incorporated against the States by the Fourteenth Amendment. The Superior Court ruled in their favor on statutory grounds. . . .

The Commission appealed to the California Court of Appeal. While that appeal was pending, the Nollans satisfied the condition on their option to purchase by tearing down the bungalow and building the new house, and bought the property. They did not notify the Commission that they were taking that action.

The Court of Appeal reversed the Superior Court. 177 Cal. App.

3d 719, 223 Cal. Rptr. 28 (1986). It disagreed with the Superior Court's interpretation of the Coastal Act, finding that it required that a coastal permit for the construction of a new house whose floor area, height or bulk was more than 10% larger than that of the house it was replacing be conditioned on a grant of access. It also ruled that that requirement did not violate the Constitution under the reasoning of an earlier case of the Court of Appeal, Grupe v. California Coastal Comm'n, 166 Cal. App. 3d 148, 212 Cal. Rptr. 578 (1985).... It ruled that the Nollans' taking claim also failed because, although the condition diminished the value of the Nollans' lot, it did not deprive them of all reasonable use of their property....

Had California simply required the Nollans to make an easement across their beachfront available to the public on a permanent basis in order to increase public access to the beach, rather than conditioning their permit to rebuild their house on their agreeing to do so, we have no doubt there would have been a taking....

Given, then, that requiring uncompensated conveyance of the easement outright would violate the Fourteenth Amendment, the question becomes whether requiring it to be conveyed as a condition for issuing a land use permit alters the outcome. We have long recognized that land use regulation does not effect a taking if it "substantially advance[s] legitimate state interests" and does not "den[y] an owner economically viable use of his land," Agins v. Tiburon, 447 U.S. 255, 260 (1980). See also Penn Central Transportation Co. v. New York City, 438 U.S. 104, 127 (1978) ("a use restriction may constitute a 'taking' if not reasonably necessary to the effectuation of a substantial government purpose"). Our cases have not elaborated on the standards for determining what constitutes a "legitimate state interest" or what type of connection between the regulation and the state interest satisfies the requirement that the former "substantially advance" the latter.[3] They have made clear, however, that a broad range of governmental

---

3. Contrary to Justice Brennan's claim, our opinions do not establish that these standards are the same as those applied to due process or equal-protection claims. To the contrary, our verbal formulations in the takings field have generally been quite different. We have required that the regulation "substantially advance" the "legitimate state interest" sought to be achieved, Agins v. Tiburon, 447 U.S. 255, 260 (1980), not that "the State 'could rationally have decided' the measure adopted might achieve the State's objective." Post, quoting Minnesota v. Clover Leaf Creamery Co., 449 U.S. 456, 466 (1981). Justice Brennan relies principally on an equal protection case, Minnesota v. Clover Leaf Creamery Co., supra, and two substantive due process cases, Williamson v. Lee Optical of Oklahoma, Inc., 348 U.S. 483, 487-488 (1955) and Day-Brite Lighting, Inc. v. Missouri, 342 U.S. 421, 423 (1952), in support of the standards he would adopt. But there is no reason to believe (and the language of our cases gives some reason to disbelieve) that so long as the regulation of property is at issue the standards for takings challenges, due process challenges, and equal protection challenges are identical; any more than there is any reason to believe that so long as the regulation of speech is at issue the standards for due process challenges, equal protection challenges, and First Amendment challenges are identical....

B. The Attitude of the Judiciary

purposes and regulations satisfies these requirements. See Agins v. Tiburon, supra, at 260-262 (scenic zoning); Penn Central Transportation Co. v. New York City, supra (landmark preservation); Euclid v. Ambler Realty Co., 272 U.S. 365 (1926) (residential zoning); Laitos and Westfall, Government Interference with Private Interests in Public Resources, 11 Harv. Envtl. L. Rev. 1, 66 (1987). The Commission argues that among these permissible purposes are protecting the public's ability to see the beach, assisting the public in overcoming the "psychological barrier" to using the beach created by a developed shorefront, and preventing congestion on the public beaches. We assume, without deciding, that this is so — in which case the Commission unquestionably would be able to deny the Nollans their permit outright if their new house (alone, or by reason of the cumulative impact produced in conjunction with other construction) would substantially impede these purposes, unless the denial would interfere so drastically with the Nollans' use of their property as to constitute a taking.

The Commission argues that a permit condition that serves the same legitimate police-power purpose as a refusal to issue the permit should not be found to be a taking if the refusal to issue the permit would not constitute a taking. We agree. Thus, if the Commission attached to the permit some condition that would have protected the public's ability to see the beach notwithstanding construction of the new house — for example, a height limitation, a width restriction, or a ban on fences — so long as the Commission could have exercised its police power (as we have assumed it could) to forbid construction of the house altogether, imposition of the condition would also be constitutional. Moreover (and here we come closer to the facts of the present case), the condition would be constitutional even if it consisted of the requirement that the Nollans provide a viewing spot on their property for passersby with whose sighting of the ocean their new house would interfere. Although such a requirement, constituting a permanent grant of continuous access to the property, would have to be considered a taking if it were not attached to a development permit, the Commission's assumed power to forbid construction of the house in order to protect the public's view of the beach must surely include the power to condition construction upon some concession by the owner, even a concession of property rights, that serves the same end. If a prohibition designed to accomplish that purpose would be a legitimate exercise of the police power rather than a taking, it would be strange to conclude that providing the owner an alternative to that prohibition which accomplishes the same purpose is not.

The evident constitutional propriety disappears, however, if the condition substituted for the prohibition utterly fails to further the end advanced as the justification for the prohibition. When that essential nexus is eliminated, the situation becomes the same as if California law forbade shouting fire in a crowded theater, but granted dispensations to those willing to contribute $100 to the state treasury. While a ban on shouting fire can be a core exercise of the State's police power to protect the public safety, and can thus meet even our stringent standards for regulation of speech, adding the unrelated condition alters the purpose to one which, while it may be legitimate, is inadequate to sustain the ban. Therefore, even though, in a sense, requiring a $100 tax contribution in order to shout fire is a lesser restriction on speech than an outright ban, it would not pass constitutional muster. Similarly here, the lack of nexus between the condition and the original purpose of the building restriction converts that purpose to something other than what it was. The purpose then becomes, quite simply, the obtaining of an easement to serve some valid governmental purpose, but without payment of compensation. Whatever may be the outer limits of "legitimate state interests" in the takings and land use context, this is not one of them. In short, unless the permit condition serves the same governmental purpose as the development ban, the building restriction is not a valid regulation of land use but "an out-and-out plan of extortion." J. E. D. Associates, Inc. v. Atkinson, 121 N.H. 581, 584, 432 A.2d 12, 14-15 (1981). See also Loretto v. Teleprompter Manhattan CATV Corp., 458 U.S., at 439, n. 17.[5]

The Commission claims that it concedes as much, and that we may sustain the condition at issue here by finding that it is reasonably related to the public need or burden that the Nollans' new house creates or to which it contributes. We can accept, for purposes of discussion, the Commission's proposed test as to how close a "fit" between the condition and the burden is required, because we find that this case does not meet even the most untailored standards. The Commission's principal contention to the contrary essentially turns on a play on the word "access." The Nollans' new house, the Commission found, will interfere with "visual access" to the beach. That in turn (along with other shorefront development) will interfere with the desire of people who drive past the Nollans' house to use the beach, thus creating a "psychological barrier" to "access." The Nollans' new house will also, by a process not altogether clear from the Commission's opinion but presumably potent enough to more than offset the effects of the psychological barrier, increase the use of the public beaches, thus creating the need for more "access." These burdens on "access" would be alleviated by a requirement that the Nollans provide "lateral access" to the beach.

---

5. One would expect that a regime in which this kind of leveraging of the police power is allowed would produce stringent land-use regulation which the State then waives to accomplish other purposes, leading to lesser realization of the land-use goals purportedly sought to be served than would result from more lenient (but nontradeable) development restrictions. Thus, the importance of the purpose underlying the prohibition not only does not *justify* the imposition of unrelated conditions for eliminating the prohibition, but positively militates against the practice.

B. The Attitude of the Judiciary 641

Rewriting the argument to eliminate the play on words makes clear that there is nothing to it. It is quite impossible to understand how a requirement that people already on the public beaches be able to walk across the Nollans' property reduces any obstacles to viewing the beach created by the new house. It is also impossible to understand how it lowers any "psychological barrier" to using the public beaches, or how it helps to remedy any additional congestion on them caused by construction of the Nollans' new house. We therefore find that the Commission's imposition of the permit condition cannot be treated as an exercise of its land use power for any of these purposes. Our conclusion on this point is consistent with the approach taken by every other court that has considered the question, with the exception of the California state courts....

... We do not share Justice Brennan's confidence that the Commission "should have little difficulty in the future in utilizing its expertise to demonstrate a specific connection between provisions for access and burdens on access" that will avoid the effect of today's decision. We view the Fifth Amendment's property clause to be more than a pleading requirement, and compliance with it to be more than an exercise in cleverness and imagination. As indicated earlier, our cases describe the condition for abridgement of property rights through the police power as a "substantial advanc[ing]" of a legitimate State interest. We are inclined to be particularly careful about the adjective where the actual conveyance of property is made a condition to the lifting of a land use restriction, since in that context there is heightened risk that the purpose is avoidance of the compensation requirement, rather than the stated police power objective.

We are left, then, with the Commission's justification for the access requirement unrelated to land use regulation:

> Finally, the Commission notes that there are several existing provisions of pass and repass lateral access benefits already given by past Faria Beach Tract applicants as a result of prior coastal permit decisions. The access required as a condition of this permit is part of a comprehensive program to provide continuous public access along Faria Beach as the lots undergo development or redevelopment. App. 68.

That is simply an expression of the Commission's belief that the public interest will be served by a continuous strip of publicly accessible beach along the coast. The Commission may well be right that it is a good idea, but that does not establish that the Nollans (and other coastal residents) alone can be compelled to contribute to its realization. Rather, California is free to advance its "comprehensive program," if it wishes, by using its power of eminent domain for this "public purpose," see U.S. Const., Amdt. V; but if it wants an easement across the Nollans' property, it must pay for it.

Reversed.

Justice BRENNAN, with whom Justice MARSHALL joins, dissenting. . . .

The first problem . . . is that the Court imposes a standard of precision for the exercise of a State's police power that has been discredited for the better part of this century. Furthermore, even under the Court's cramped standard, the permit condition imposed in this case directly responds to the specific type of burden on access created by appellants' development. Finally, a review of those factors deemed most significant in takings analysis makes clear that the Commission's action implicates none of the concerns underlying the Takings Clause. The Court has thus struck down the Commission's reasonable effort to respond to intensified development along the California coast, on behalf of landowners who can make no claim that their reasonable expectations have been disrupted. The Court has, in short, given appellants a windfall at the expense of the public. . . .

. . . In this case, California has employed its police power in order to condition development upon preservation of public access to the ocean and tidelands. The Coastal Commission, if it had so chosen, could have denied the Nollans' request for a development permit, since the property would have remained economically viable without the requested new development. Instead, the State sought to accommodate the Nollans' desire for new development, on the condition that the development not diminish the overall amount of public access to the coastline. . . .

The Court finds fault with this measure because it regards the condition as insufficiently tailored to address the precise type of reduction in access produced by the new development. The Nollans' development blocks visual access, the Court tells us, while the Commission seeks to preserve lateral access along the coastline. Thus, it concludes, the State acted irrationally. Such a narrow conception of rationality, however, has long since been discredited as a judicial arrogation of legislative authority. . . .

The Commission is charged by both the state constitution and legislature to preserve overall public access to the California coastline. Furthermore, by virtue of its participation in the Coastal Zone Management Act program, the State must "exercise effectively [its] responsibilities in the coastal zone through the development and implementation of management programs to achieve wise use of the land and water resources of the coastal zone," 16 U.S.C. §1452(2), so as to provide for, inter alia, "public access to the coas[t] for recreation purposes." §1452(2)(D). The Commission has sought to discharge its responsibilities in a flexible manner. . . . The Court's insistence on a precise fit between the forms of burden and condition on each individual parcel along the California coast would penalize the Commission for its flexibility, hampering the ability to fulfill its public trust mandate. . . .

B. The Attitude of the Judiciary 643

... The Commission's determination that certain types of development jeopardize public access to the ocean, and that such development should be conditioned on preservation of access, is the essence of responsible land use planning. The Court's use of an unreasonably demanding standard for determining the rationality of state regulation in this area thus could hamper innovative efforts to preserve an increasingly fragile national resource....

With respect to the permit condition program in general, the Commission should have little difficulty in the future in utilizing its expertise to demonstrate a specific connection between provisions for access and burdens on access produced by new development. Neither the Commission in its report nor the State in its briefs and at argument highlighted the particular threat to lateral access created by appellants' development project. In defending its action, the State emphasized the general point that *overall* access to the beach had been preserved, since the diminution of access created by the project had been offset by the gain in lateral access. This approach is understandable, given that the State relied on the reasonable assumption that its action was justified under the normal standard of review for determining legitimate exercises of a State's police power. In the future, alerted to the Court's apparently more demanding requirement, it need only make clear that a provision for public access directly responds to a particular type of burden on access created by a new development....

Nonetheless it is important to point out that the Court's insistence on a precise accounting system in this case is insensitive to the fact that increasing intensity of development in many areas calls for far-sighted, comprehensive planning that takes into account both the interdependence of land uses and the cumulative impact of development.[13]...

... State agencies ... require considerable flexibility in responding to private desires for development in a way that guarantees the preservation of public access to the coast. They should be encouraged to regulate development in the context of the overall balance of competing uses of the shoreline. The Court today does precisely the opposite, overruling an eminently reasonable exercise of an expert state agency's judgment, substituting its own narrow view of how this balance should be struck. Its reasoning is hardly suited to the complex reality of natural resource protection in the twentieth century. I can only hope

---

13. As the California Court of Appeals noted in 1985, "Since 1972, permission has been granted to construct more than 42,000 building units within the land jurisdiction of the Coastal Commission. In addition, pressure for development along the coast is expected to increase since approximately 85% of California's population lives within 30 miles of the coast." Grupe v. California Coastal Comm'n 166 Cal. App. 3d 148, 167, n. 12, 212 Cal. Rptr. 578, 589, n. 12 (1985). See also Coastal Zone Management Act, 16 U.S.C. §1451(c) (increasing demands on coastal zones "have resulted in the loss of living marine resources, wildlife, nutrient-rich areas, permanent and adverse changes to ecological systems, decreasing open space for public use, and shoreline erosion").

that today's decision is an aberration, and that a broader vision ultimately prevails. . . .

Notes

1. Has the majority raised the ghost of *Lochner* or just restored private property to a respectable position? Will the five-member bloc hold in other land-use contexts, such as inclusionary zoning, rent control, and conditional zoning, even special use permitting? Are we on the threshold of wholesale revision or, similar to the suggestion of the dissenters in *Warth* (supra page 448), is the holding explainable by the majority's underlying dissatisfaction with the regulatory scheme? Compare Scalia, Economic Affairs as Human Affairs, 4 Cato J. 703, 705-706 (1985) (Supreme Court's rejection of economic substantive due process "is good—or at least . . . the suggestion that it change its position is even worse") with Epstein, Judicial Review: Reckoning on Two Kinds of Error, 4 Cato J. 711, 717-718 (1985) (Supreme Court opinions on economic liberties and property rights "intellectually incoherent"— "some movement in the direction of judicial activism is clearly indicated").

2. Is the majority's dictum concerning "substantially advancing" legitimate state interests a satisfactory substitute for the "vital and pressing standard" called for by the President's Commission, supra page 368?

3. With the withdrawal of federal funds, local communities have looked to other sources for the provision of municipal services and, above all, for affordable housing. Devices such as inclusionary zoning, incentive zoning, and TDR are manifestations of this search. Most recently attention has concentrated on linkage programs and how these would fare, both constitutionally and statutorily, under the evolving tests for subdivision exactions.

Boston sought to shift to private land developers the cost of housing that the local government believed it could no longer afford. By ordinance, it set up "Developmental Impact Project Contributions" (Boston Zoning Code Article 26A, 1986) requiring any office developer proposing to build in excess of 100,000 square feet (Article 26A also applies to enlargement or substantial rehabilitation of more than 100,000 square feet in existing buildings) and seeking a variance, conditional use permit, exception, zoning map change, or text amendment to contribute to a housing trust fund or to build low- and moderate-income housing. The payment option, known as the "housing contribution grant," is six dollars for each square foot of office space over 100,000 square feet, payable over a seven-year period in equal installments. Under the linkage ordinance, the city has obtained over $35

B. The Attitude of the Judiciary

million. The language of the Boston ordinance is ambiguous as to whether housing contribution grants must be spent for low- and moderate-income housing; the only explicit restriction on use of grant money is the requirement that 10 percent be spent on housing in neighborhoods immediately adjacent to the office development paying the linkage amount. See Article 26A, §2(3) (C).[23]

The ordinance came under oblique attack in Bonan v. General Hospital Corp., No. 76438 (Mass. Super. Ct. Apr. 11, 1985). Asserting jurisdiction over matters not argued by council, Judge Greenberg found that the linkage provision was not expressly or impliedly authorized by either city or state zoning legislation, and noted that the fees were more in the nature of a tax that had not been expressly provided for by state law.

Upon appeal, the Supreme Judicial Court of Massachusetts in Bonan v. City of Boston, 398 Mass. 315, 496 N.E.2d 640 (1986), reversed judgment as to the city defendants, stating that the plaintiffs had not properly demonstrated that they were entitled to a ruling as to the validity of Article 26. The court did not reach the merits of Judge Greenberg's conclusions concerning statutory authority to impose development impact project exactions. At the close of the opinion, the justices offered the following unsolicited advice to Massachusetts General Hospital (MGH):

> The other unresolved question is what, if anything, should happen to the judgment as it applies to MGH, which has not appealed. The plaintiffs appear to have lacked standing to obtain declaratory relief against MGH to the same extent that they lacked standing to obtain relief against the city defendants. MGH has taken the position that it prevailed in the trial court on all issues that directly affected the subject zoning change. This conclusion may not be correct. The judgment, in addition to declaring art. 26 a nullity, stated "that so long as the zoning change secured by [MGH] is contingent upon the housing payment exaction, it cannot stand." At the very least, that language casts a shadow over MGH's authorization to proceed with its project. MGH may be well advised to seek relief from judgment by filing a motion under Mass. R. Civ. P. 60 (b), 365 Mass. 828 (1974).

In any regulation of activity, it is essential to know and understand the nature of the regulatee. Who is in the subdivision business? Is it a one-shot affair, a profession, a "responsible" industry? Is the developer only interested in quick turnover and quick profits? Is she the "magician

---

23. See Kayden and Pollard, Linkage Ordinances and Traditional Exactions Analysis: The Connection Between Office Development and Housing, 50 Law & Contemp. Probs. 127 (1987). See also the discussion of San Francisco's Office/Housing Production Program, supra page 268.

of modern times . . . the advance guard of civic progress . . . the unsung and romantic hero of modern times"?[24] Is this an industry that leads to self-regulation? What sanctions can be used? What carrots? How must controls be shaped in view of the highly cyclical nature of the business? Is the group so divergent — ranging from a Levitt to a farmer dealing with his own land — that no uniform type of regulation or administration is conceivable? Is the postwar trend of selling a complete home-cum-lot, instead of retail merchandising of vacant lots, taken into account in the emerging controls?[25] What of the subdivision of land for commercial or industrial purposes, or for integrated uses? What is the role of mortgage lenders, and of government credit agencies?

Theoretically the best control is education. If the profit motive can be preserved or even enhanced, while promoting the community interest, the ideal would be attained. Some subdividers have conceded that regulation "is not only necessary but also desirable."[26] Does the trend of modern residential construction and financing offer any hopes along these lines? What has been the educational influence of the FHA through its publications and firsthand counsel?

Are the statutory financial requirements too burdensome? Are they in conflict with the national policy of encouraging low-cost housing? Does the additional risk they thrust on the developer encourage monopoly and the large operator? Does the statutory set-up affect a large subdivider more, or less, adversely than a small one?

At the other extreme from education as a means of control is public land ownership. Does the fact that the community can easily enforce its wishes if it holds title to the land resolve subdivision problems? Or is this simply an interim solution? Or only an answer to some problems, and if so, which? Should a program be adopted with respect to tax-delinquent properties in depressed subdivisions that return to the city? This last possibility suggests the use of betterment assessments and other tax controls. Are these instruments too blunt for control of design? How can planning controls be integrated with the system of real property assessment and taxation? The condemnation of development rights under the British system[27] may be suggestive of other alternatives.

It has been suggested that the subdivision of land be regulated in the manner of a public utility. The theory underlying this suggestion must be that, like light and power, land should be controlled because

---

24. These words in the Economist for August 22, 1925 (at 25), were thrown back in 1939 — in a different phase of the business cycle — by Monchow, Seventy Years of Real Estate Subdividing 159 (1939). On the whole, the subdivider has not had to be content with mute Miltons.

25. See McMichael, Real Estate Subdivisions 1 (1949).

26. The Code of Ethics of the National Association of Home Builders provides: "(f) Members shall comply both in spirit and letter with rules and regulations prescribed by law and government agencies for the health, safety and progress of the community."

27. See page 869 infra.

B. The Attitude of the Judiciary

leaving it to the forces of economic competition might prove disastrous.[28] Is the Washington statute, supra page 611, constitutional? Do you think it an effective statute? Is it possible that it permits the planning commission less leeway in controlling subdivisions than do the other statutes? What kinds of information and what degree of precision would be needed before a planning board would be able to support in court the refusal of a certificate of convenience and necessity to a developer on the sole ground of economic prematurity? Should there be a quota system along OPA lines for existing subdividers or for ordinary homeowners who wish to resell their houses?[29] Consider again the impact of the national government on local land development through the FHA; before approving the subdivision for mortgage insurance, the FHA is required to make an analysis of the market demand for the property.[30]

Before we decide to rely completely on uniform acts and federal regulations, let us consider the potential for courts to accommodate evolving social needs, changing technologies, and moral demands. The following Case Study comprises a lesson in the lasting value of common law adjudication, even in what has been called our "age of statutes." See Calabresi, A Common Law for the Age of Statutes (1982).

CASE STUDY #2

2. Mandating the Provision of Services

a. *Hawkins* and Hope

■ HAWKINS v. TOWN OF SHAW
303 F. Supp. 1162 (N.D. Miss. 1969)

KEADY, D. J. In this suit plaintiffs, who bring a class action for Negro citizens of the Town of Shaw, Mississippi, seek injunctive relief

---

28. The premature subdivision, accompanied by costs of useless streets and weed-choked utilities, has threatened the economic stability of communities. Cornick, in his classic study, showed that 62.2 percent of a total outstanding debt of $61,853,910 consisted of special district debt incurred principally for the improvement and servicing of new subdivisions. Premature Subdivision of Urban Lands 129 (1938). In four townships in the Detroit region, in 1938, 66.5 percent of all subdivided lots were for sale as tax-delinquent property. Segoe, Local Planning Administration 514 (1941). In Chicago, in 1946, 25,000 parcels of land were delinquent, largely attributable to excessive subdivision, according to Aschman, Dead Land, 25 Land Econ. 240 (1949). Rough and rocky legal topography proves fully as unbuildable as its physical counterpart. In their recent study of the situation, the authors conclude that: "[P]remature subdivisions may constitute a land-use time bomb for local governments who are lulled into believing that premature subdivision is a precursor of economic development." Shultz & Groy, The Premature Subdivision of Land in Colorado 8 (1986).

29. What possibilities does such a system offer as an alternative to the zoning route for preventing premature residential development in a tract suited primarily for industry?

30. As to the effectiveness of the potential control, see Melli, Subdivision Control in Wisconsin, 1953 Wis. L. Rev. 389.

against defendants, the Town's Mayor, Clerk and five Aldermen, under 42 U.S.C. §1983, to restrain defendants from discriminating because of race and poverty in providing the inhabitants with certain municipal services, namely: street paving and street lighting, sanitary sewers, water mains and fire hydrants, and surface water drainage. Defendants entered a denial to the charge that disparity of municipal services afforded to the town's inhabitants was the result of racial or economic discrimination. Following the adoption of a pre-trial order, a three day evidentiary hearing was conducted.

Incorporated in 1886, the Town of Shaw consisted originally of one square mile located in Bolivar County, Mississippi. Its territorial limits were not changed until 1965 when new subdivisions were added to the south and east of the original town extending into Sunflower County. The municipality is largely surrounded by Delta farms and plantations and its economy is almost wholly oriented to agriculture. The town's present population is estimated to be approximately 2500 persons, of which 1500 are Negroes and 1000 whites. There are approximately as many Negro citizens who are qualified to vote as there are white voters. The town's population was for years relatively static, showing little gain for the twenty year period, 1940-1960.[3]

Operating under a Code charter adopted pursuant to §§3374-34 et seq. of the Miss. Code of 1942, the town elects its Mayor, Clerk and Board of Aldermen to serve for terms of four years. Because of deaths and resignation, only two of defendant Aldermen have remained in office since the inception of their terms in July, 1965.

There are various patterns of residential neighborhoods in the town. In some instances white and Negro residents live on the same streets, yet in other instances, particularly in the oldest and newest subdivisions, there are separate white and Negro neighborhoods. A significant portion of the Negro population resides in the town's peripheral or outer area, with substantial numbers of white people residing near the town's business or commercial center. Prior to 1965, many years had elapsed since the dedication of any new residential subdivisions for either race. Some of the older Negro neighborhoods were in subdivisions laid out many years ago, without zoning regulations, which resulted in houses being erected on exceedingly small lots abutting upon dedicated streets and alleys of inadequate narrow width. To some extent, the older white neighborhoods suffer from the same planning deficiency.

The town has sought to provide its inhabitants certain services, such as street paving and street lighting, a system of surface water drainage, water mains with fire hydrant protection, and since 1963 a

---

3. The official 1960 census counted 2062 residents of Shaw, consisting of 1327 Negroes, 724 whites and 11 others.

B. The Attitude of the Judiciary 649

sanitary sewerage system. The town's services and facilities are paid from revenues derived by imposition of ad valorem taxes and the sale of water and electricity to its citizens. There are no bonds outstanding, and the town has a $145,000 operating surplus.

Street paving. Six different paving projects, financed solely out of general revenues and without special assessments, have occurred at irregular intervals during the past 23 years. Of the approximately 11.8 miles of residential streets in the town, about one-half traverse white neighborhoods and one-half serve Negro neighborhoods. Some streets in both types of neighborhoods are not hard surfaced, but almost all those are graveled. The streets yet remaining unpaved are largely those in the peripheral or outer areas of the town furthest removed from the central or business section. Initially, concrete paving was afforded to those streets serving commercial and industrial interests and to the areas nearest the town's center. In some cases this resulted in more street paving in white than Negro neighborhoods, but the paving actually done in the municipality was on the basis of general usage, traffic needs and other objective criteria. Residential neighborhoods not facing principal streets or thoroughfares long remained unpaved, regardless of their character as white or black neighborhoods. Also, these heavily traveled streets were later repaired and resurfaced in subsequent asphalt paving programs. . . .[5]

Street lights. The evidence shows that the town has ample lighting provided for the streets; that for the commercial streets and principal thoroughfares such lighting is provided by high intensity mercury vapor fixtures; that in some areas largely occupied by white residents the lighting fixtures house medium intensity mercury vapor lamps, while in the outlying and largely Negro neighborhoods bare bulb lighting is predominantly used. The brighter lights are provided for those streets forming either a state highway, or serving commercial, industrial or special school needs, or otherwise carrying the heaviest traffic load. While the more powerful equipment, only recently installed, does provide superior lighting, there is no showing that the lighting provided by bare bulbs is practically inadequate or that an insufficient number of such lights has been erected, or that detriment of any kind has been sustained by the town's inhabitants, white or Negro, as the result of inferior or inadequate street lighting.

---

5. The three Negro neighborhoods of greatest size with yet unpaved streets are: (1) Promised Land Addition in the southwest section, whose streets have not been paved because of the necessity of first installing new water mains on the rights of way; (2) Reeder Addition located in the northwest quadrant of the town (Bryant Street, Dorsey Street and other nearby unnamed streets) whose dedicated streets are too narrow to permit surfacing without acquiring additional right of way from abutting property owners; and (3) the approximate west half of Johnson Addition (northeast quadrant) dedicated in 1891 in small lots abutting extremely narrow streets, again rendering asphalt paving undesirable without additional right of way. Substandard housing exists throughout the entire area.

Sanitary sewers. Prior to 1963 the town had no municipal sanitary sewerage system, and its more prosperous inhabitants relied upon septic tanks and privately installed facilities. The greater portion of the Negro families were without indoor plumbing and open ditch sewage existed, to a large degree, throughout the town. In 1963 a modern system complete with lagoon was constructed with drainage lines routed to practically all of the white residential areas as well as the more recent Negro subdivisions having better housing and indoor toilet facilities. Since 1965 the central sewerage system has been extended into various additional Negro neighborhoods. The only "Negro" areas presently remaining unserved by sanitary sewers are sections described generally as the Reeder Addition (Bryant and Dorsey Streets), Canal Street from Gale to the railroad, South Elm extended (1000 feet) and Rogers Street east of Highway 61. Part of the problem in reaching all older unserved areas has been the necessity for bringing this service into newer subdivisions developed for both races and brought into the town, as it is the town's firm policy to make sewer installations for all such new areas. The great majority of the town's Negro residents is afforded sewerage facilities although many such residences actually continue without indoor plumbing, not yet required by local law. The town's policy is to make additions to the sewerage system for extension of the service to all desiring to take advantage of it.

Surface water drainage. Having flat, nonporous soil with slow run-off conditions, Shaw suffers from drainage problems common to the Delta area. . . .

Water mains and fire hydrants. Water is supplied from several deep wells to all town inhabitants. A flat consumer's charge is made; there are no water meters, nor any effective control for possible water waste. No inhabitant is without water brought to his residence. . . .

None of the plaintiffs, or other Negro citizens of the community, ever requested the town's governing authority to provide additional municipal services in their neighborhoods. However, plaintiffs' counsel contend that the court should require defendants to complete by a specific date, namely, September 30, 1971, the construction of specific facilities "to equalize the black neighborhoods with their white counterparts" at an estimated cost of $250,000, as below detailed,[8] by directing

---

8. Plaintiffs' counsel suggest the following definite improvements:
   (1) Street paving costs of $146,000 for asphalting 8000 feet of 50-foot wide streets and 11,000 feet of 30-foot wide streets.
   (2) Sanitary sewer costs of $10,000 for laying 4000 additional feet of line in Reeder Addition and along Elm and Canal Streets.
   (3) Street light costs of $3,100 for replacing every existing street light in the black neighborhoods with mercury vapor fixtures.
   (4) Water main costs of $50,000 (in excess of the 50% local contribution, $55,000, for the HUD project) to install new water mains and new fire hydrants in certain Negro neighborhoods.

B. The Attitude of the Judiciary 651

the use of $145,000 presently in the town treasury and by devoting two years' general revenues, and proceeds from a bond issue, if necessary, to complete the work.[9]

We begin with the familiar rule that the "exercise of the powers of the municipality with respect to the making of public improvements, the establishment of public utilities, and the furnishing of public services, rests in the discretion of the governing municipal authorities, insofar as the matter is not controlled by positive law, and the courts will not undertake to control or interfere with the exercise of such discretion in the absence of bad faith or abuse." 38 Am. Jur. Municipal Corporations, §560, p. 248. Nor is it a valid objection that a public improvement by a municipal corporation "incidentally benefits some individuals more than others, or that from the place of residence, or for other reasons, every inhabitant of the municipality cannot use it, if every inhabitant who is so situated that he can use it has the same right to use it as the other inhabitants." Ibid. Thus, it would seem that determination of the necessity and character of public improvements, the matter of their construction and the priority of accomplishment, ordinarily, are questions to be resolved by officials, usually elected, who constitute the governing authority of the municipality. "Normally, the widest discretion is allowed the legislative judgment in determining whether to attack some rather than all of the manifestations of the evil aimed at; and normally that judgment is given the benefit of every conceivable circumstance which might suffice to characterize the classification as reasonable rather than arbitrary and invidious." McLaughlin v. Florida, 379 U.S. 184, 191 (1964).

Furthermore, a presumption exists that public officials will discharge their official duties in accordance with law, exercising an honest judgment, and this presumption will be given effect in the absence of clear evidence to the contrary.

Plaintiffs would avoid the application of these well settled legal principles by claiming that they have been denied the equal protection of the laws as guaranteed by the Fourteenth Amendment, that they have made out a prima facie case of racial and economic discrimination by showing long-continued statistical disparities between white and black neighborhoods in the services provided by the town,[10] and that

---

9. Defendants' counsel advise that since the trial of the case the town has established a bi-racial planning commission in accordance with §2890.5 Miss. Code 1942. A commission organized under that statute would have authority to prepare and propose (1) a master plan of physical development of the municipality; (2) proposed zoning ordinances and maps; (3) regulations governing subdivision of land; (4) building or setback lines on roads; and (5) recommendations to the town's governing authorities with respect to the aforesaid items.

10. Plaintiffs analogize their case to situations involving voting, school desegregation and jury discrimination, in which federal courts have held that disparity based on statistical information alone may establish a prima facie case of racial discrimination. Gomillion v.

defendants have failed to explain such disparities upon rational grounds unrelated to race or poverty. While plaintiffs cite no case making that formula generally applicable to all municipal services, yet it is not to be doubted that "[t]he Equal Protection Clause reaches the exercise of state power *however manifested,* whether exercised directly or through subdivisions of the State." (Emphasis added.) Avery v. Midland County, 390 U.S. 474, 479.

It is equally true that, since the central purpose of the Fourteenth Amendment was to eliminate racial discrimination emanating from a state's official sources, "racial classifications are constitutionally suspect," subject to the "most rigid scrutiny," and they are "in most circumstances irrelevant to any constitutionally acceptable legislative purpose." McLaughlin v. Florida, supra, 379 U.S. at 192. Where racial classifications are involved, the Equal Protection and Due Process Clauses of the Fourteenth Amendment "command a more stringent standard" in reviewing discretionary acts of state or local officers. Jackson v. Godwin, 400 F.2d 529, 537 (5 Cir. 1968).

Plaintiffs have compiled certain statistics which they claim support a charge that defendants and their predecessors in office have racially classified the black and white neighborhoods by providing better or more complete facilities to the latter neighborhoods, but they would ignore all legitimate deductions to be made from the evidence running counter to statistical racial disparity. But we do not understand that a court may adopt that manner of reasoning. If actions of public officials are shown to have rested upon rational considerations, irrespective of race or poverty, they are not within the condemnation of the Fourteenth Amendment, and may not be properly condemned upon judicial review. Persons or groups who are treated differently must be shown to be similarly situated and their unequal treatment demonstrated to be without any rational basis or based upon an invidious factor such as race. Davis v. Georgia State Board of Education, 408 F.2d 1014 (5 Cir. 1969).

In this case, the fundamental fact emerging from the evidence is that, historically, the town's municipal officers, whether due to an almost static population, limited finances, or adverse economic factors, have long followed a policy of slowly providing basic municipal services to the town's inhabitants. Until the recent past, the municipal policy might be characterized by some as conservative and unprogressive, with no more than $50,000 public improvement bonds having ever been issued.

Lightfoot, 364 U.S. 339 (1960) (racial statistics of persons denied right to municipal vote); United States ex rel. Seals v. Wiman, 304 F.2d 53 (5th Cir. 1962) (racial statistics of jurors); Whitus v. Georgia, 385 U.S. 545 (1967) (racial statistics of jurors); Green v. School Board of New Kent County, Va., 391 U.S. 430 (1968) (racial statistics of public school students); United States v. Board of Education of Bessemer, 396 F.2d 44 (5th Cir. 1968) (racial statistics of school teachers).

B. The Attitude of the Judiciary 653

The town, operating on a pay-as-you-go management, has simply not made improvements of the size and character that might be expected under more liberal minded government. That was, apparently, the kind of local government preferred by Shaw's citizens. In any case, cautious fiscal policy dominated the town until recent times, beginning not earlier than 1955. Consequently, some needed facilities were not enjoyed by anyone; they simply did not exist. . . . Also, lack of zoning regulations and haphazard subdivision dedications have hampered the town in its ability to pave all streets; the necessity for acquiring rights of way and easements in order first to properly lay sewers and then adequate street surfacing has accounted for some delay in project fulfillment. Modern sanitary sewers, by any standard certainly considered a necessity, were not installed in any part of the town until 1963. While the complaint about less than 100% sanitary sewerage for all residences is certainly a real one, that condition arises basically from the fact that local law does not yet require indoor plumbing. The lack of sanitary sewers in certain areas of the town is not the result of racial discrimination in withholding a vital service; rather it is a consequence of not requiring, through a proper housing code, certain minimal conditions for inhabited housing. Assuredly, a federal court is not called upon to order the adoption of a housing code by a municipality for the forcing of usage by all of a central sewerage system, and yet the lack of precisely that is a fundamental problem confronting plaintiffs.

. . . Defendants' assertions that they have not discriminated because of race or poverty are supported by substantial, rational considerations explaining the quality and quantity of presently available town's services. These facts negative plaintiffs' assertions of racial and economic discrimination. Marshall v. Mayor and Board of Selectmen of McComb, Mississippi, 251 Miss. 750, 171 So. 2d 347 (1965).

Finally, the nature of the relief sought by plaintiffs in their class action directly involves the exercise of administrative judgment in diverse areas of local government. This is a field in which courts should be reluctant to enter because of their incompetence, generally, to bring about a better result than officials chosen by the local inhabitants. This observation is particularly appropriate as to the Town of Shaw, where Negro citizens have voting power approximately equal to that of white citizens. Such problems as plaintiffs have disclosed by the evidence, and which, in our opinion, do not constitute an abridgment of their constitutional rights, are to be resolved at the ballot box. It is that remedy and not injunctive relief which plaintiffs must seek.

An order dismissing the complaint will be entered.[31]

---

31. The index to the amicus curiae brief, Joint Center for Urban Studies of M.I.T. and Harvard University, in appealing the case to the Fifth Circuit, reads as follows:

Argument. I. The Plaintiff-Appellants in This Municipal Services Equalization

■ HAWKINS v. TOWN OF SHAW
437 F.2d 1286 (5th Cir. 1971)

TUTTLE, Circuit Judge:

Referring to a portion of town or a segment of society as being "on the other side of the tracks" has for too long been a familiar expression to most Americans. Such a phrase immediately conjures up an area characterized by poor housing, overcrowded conditions and, in short, overall deterioration. While there may be many reasons why such areas exist in nearly all of our cities, one reason that cannot be accepted is the discriminatory provision of municipal services based on race. It is such a reason that is alleged as the basis of this action.

Appellants are Negro citizens of the Town of Shaw, Mississippi. They alleged that the town has provided various municipal services including street paving and street lighting, sanitary sewers, surface water drainage as well as water mains and fire hydrants in a discriminatory manner based on race. Appellants brought a class action seeking injunctive relief under 42 U.S.C. §1983 against the town, the town's mayor, clerk and five aldermen. After a three-day trial, the trial court applied the traditional equal protection standard despite the presence of appellants' undisputed statistical evidence which we feel clearly showed a substantial qualitative and quantitative inequity in the level and nature of services accorded "white" and "black" neighborhoods in Shaw....

Because this court has long adhered to the theory that "figures speak and when they do, Courts listen," Brooks v. Beto, 366 F.2d 1, 9

Suit Having Made Out a Prima Facie Case of Racial Discrimination Through the Introduction of Uncontroverted Statistical Evidence of Substantial Racial Disparity in the Provision of Existing Designated Services, the Trial Court Erred in Failing to Require of the Defendants Positive Evidence of a Rationale of These Statistics Which Would Overcome the Established Inference of Constitutionally Forbidden Discrimination.

  A. In The Presence of A Prima Facie Case of Racial Discrimination, A Trial Court Engaged In The Task Of Selecting The Judicial Standard For Equal Protection Review Cannot Indulge Presumptions Of Regularity Concerning The Defendants' Official Discharge Of Their Local Governmental Offices; Propound Speculative Deductions Of Alternative Rationale; Or, Rely Upon The Defendants' Professions Of An Absence Of Discriminatory Intent Or Purpose So As To Defeat The Plaintiffs' Bid For The Rigorous Standard Of Equal Protection Scrutiny....

  B. When The Plaintiffs' Statistical Evidence Of Racial Disparity Was Accompanied By An Allegation That The Entire Existing Pattern Was Typical Of A History Of Unequal Provision, The Trial Court Erred In Failing To Recognize An Independent Ground For Judicial Concern Which Ought To Intensify The Defendants' Affirmative Obligation To Adduce Positive Evidence In Support Of A Persuasive Alternative Rationale.

  II. Since the Plaintiffs' Case Below Rested Explicitly Upon a Charge of a Denial of Equal Protection as Guaranteed by the Fourteenth Amendment, it is the Responsibility of this Court to Independently Appraise the Evidence As It Relates to the Alleged Constitutional Right. — EDS.

B. The Attitude of the Judiciary 655

(1966), . . . we feel that appellants clearly made out a prima facie case of racial discrimination. The trial court thus erred in applying the traditional equal protection standard, for as this Court and the Supreme Court have held: "Where racial classifications are involved, the Equal Protection and Due Process Clauses of the Fourteenth Amendment 'command a more stringent standard' in reviewing discretionary acts of state or local officers. Jackson v. Godwin, 400 F.2d 529, 537 (5th Cir., 1968)." In applying this test, defendants' actions may be justified only if they show a compelling state interest. Loving v. Virginia, 388 U.S. (1967). We have thoroughly examined the evidence and conclude that no such compelling interests could possibly justify the gross disparities in services between black and white areas of town that this record reveals. . . .

Notes

1. Judge Tuttle noted:

> Appellants also alleged the discriminatory provision of municipal services based on wealth. This claim was dropped on appeal. It is interesting to note, however, that the Supreme Court has stated that wealth as well as race renders a classification highly suspect and thus demanding of a more exacting judicial scrutiny. McDonald v. Board of Election Commissioners of Chicago, 394 U.S. 802, 807 (1969).

437 F.2d at 1287.

This promising avenue of constitutional challenge was blocked significantly in the following few years. See San Antonio Independent School District v. Rodriguez, 411 U.S. 1 (1973).

2. In 1972, the Fifth Circuit reviewed the *Hawkins* case en banc, issuing a per curiam opinion upholding the findings of the original panel:

> In judging human conduct, intent, motive and purpose are elusive subjective concepts, and their existence usually can be inferred only from proven facts. As stated in the original opinion, the record before us does not contain direct evidence which establishes bad faith, ill will or any evil motive on the part of the town of Shaw and its public officials. However, the record proof does clearly establish conduct which cannot be judicially approved.
>
> In order to prevail in a case of this type it is not necessary to prove intent, motive or purpose to discriminate on the part of city officials. We feel that the law on this point is clear, for "'equal protection of the laws' means more than merely the absence of governmental action designed to discriminate; . . . 'we now firmly recognize that the *arbitrary quality of*

thoughtlessness can be as disastrous and unfair to private rights and to public interest as the perversity of a willful scheme.'" (Emphasis supplied.) Norwalk CORE v. Norwalk Redevelopment Agency, 2 Cir. 1968, 395 F.2d 920, 931.

... Moreover, in our judgment the facts before us squarely and certainly support the reasonable and logical inference that there was here neglect involving clear overtones of racial discrimination in the administration of governmental affairs of the town of Shaw resulting in the same evils which characterize an intentional and purposeful disregard of the principle of equal protection of the laws.

Federal Courts are reluctant to enter the field of local government operations. The conduct of municipal affairs is "an extremely awkward vehicle to manage." It is apparent from our original opinion, and we repeat here, that we do not imply or suggest that every disparity of services between citizens of a town or city creates a right of access to the federal courts for redress. We deal only with the town of Shaw, Mississippi, and the facts as developed in this record.

Hawkins v. Town of Shaw, 461 F.2d 1171, 1172-1173 (1972).

3. Consider the dissent of Judge Clark:

> The en banc court's reaffirmance of the original panel opinion embarks this circuit on what must surely become another weary journey to an inefficient and insufficient remedy for a problem that cannot find a solution in the courts. Judge Wisdom is right when he observes in concurring that the Town of Shaw does not present a unique case. Rather, Shaw is typical of thousands of towns and hundreds of cities in this nation. An examination of any urban gathering of people will highlight the inequalities among the places where they live. The degree of affluence or poverty of each family in the community is almost uniformly reflected in its home. Whether one counts it good or bad, such variance in living standards is a hallmark of our American liberty. It inheres in every free society. Only in some egalitarian Utopia do all families live in equal surroundings. A failure to recognize this fact is at the heart of the mistake the court makes in choosing the course it launches today. . . .
>
> · . . . [T]here is absolutely no way to escape the conclusion that this is purely a property rights case. It is a property right which requires the municipal service in nearly every instance brought out by this record and, interestingly enough, we have no information as to the race of the owner of the properties involved, only the race of the occupants. A novel situation indeed would exist if our plan required the city to furnish municipal services to a parcel of property that the property owner did not want and could not afford to utilize. Yet this result is not only possible, it is probable here.

461 F.2d at 1183, 1186 (Clark, J., dissenting).

What if the record had shown that 85 percent of the properties involved were owned by absentee white landlords? Are not the same

B. The Attitude of the Judiciary

hardships being imposed on the same class of citizens? Is the right to electric power or municipal water a "property right" that belongs only to the landlord? Who actually pays the property tax — the landlord, or the tenant in his monthly rent? Do the rights of services change if they are financed through a property tax rather than through income or sales taxes? Has Judge Clark "forgotten" that in the Town of Shaw paving, sewerage, and other city improvements are "paid out of general funds derived from ad valorem taxes and revenues from the operation of municipal electrical and water systems" (437 F.2d at 1294)?

4. The Urban Institute was asked to devise a methodology for measuring recreation equality in a suit by residents of a predominantly black section of the District of Columbia. Their study — what should be the yardsticks: capital or operating expenditures, quantity of opportunities, quality of facilities? — concluded that a "prima facie showing of discrimination . . . is not clear; such a judgment depends on which measure of service is chosen" (1975). "Study Defends Services to Anacostia" was the way the Washington Post carried the story. Mar. 3, 1975.

5. In an editorial on February 7, 1971, the New York Times asked: "If the town of Shaw can be compelled to deal out its public services with an even hand, why should the city of New York be exempt from, let us say, having to pick up garbage as thoroughly and frequently on upper Park Avenue as on lower? . . . Would a gigantic investment in Harlem evoke a lawsuit on grounds of neglect from the residents of Astoria? Should Bensonhurst go to court for the same ratio of patrolmen as Bedford-Stuyvesant?" It would not take long for other federal courts to limit the *Hawkins* mandate, as the next section shows.

b. Federal Bars

■ BEAL v. LINDSAY
468 F.2d 287 (2d Cir. 1972)

FRIENDLY, Chief Judge: . . .

Crotona Park is the smallest of four multi-community parks maintained by New York City in the Borough of the Bronx. The complaint brought against New York City officials by individual black and Puerto Rican residents of areas surrounding the park and an association called Bronx Citizens for a Cleaner Park alleged that, of the four Community Planning Districts directly serviced by the park, the black and Puerto Rican population equals or exceeds 70% in three, and the percentage receiving public assistance in the four districts ranges from 22.1% to 42.2%. For the Bronx as a whole, the percentage of black and Puerto Rican residents is 32.5%, and approximately 13% receive public assistance. The proportions of black and Puerto Rican residents and persons receiving public assistance for the Community Planning Districts surrounding the other three parks in the Borough — Van Cortlandt, Pelham Bay, and Bronx — are significantly lower than in the districts surrounding Crotona Park and generally lower than for the Borough as a whole. The complaint alleged that:

> The maintenance of Crotona Park is almost nonexistent. What was once one of the major parks in the city is now a mass of broken glass and litter strewn about. Most of the benches and fencing are broken and nonusable. Numerous abandoned automobiles often litter the roads running through the park for days. Little or no attempt has been made to clean up the park despite numerous requests by residents of the community.
> On the contrary, Van Courtland [sic] Park, Pelham Bay Park and Bronx Park are kept in near spotless condition. During warm weather seasons, numerous park personnel can be seen removing the litter created by weekend crowds. Within a couple of days, these parks are spotless.

It went on to claim that proportionally fewer recreational, maintenance and supervisory personnel were assigned to Crotona than to the three other parks. It sought injunctive and declaratory relief against the City's failing to equalize the equipment, facilities, services and repairs in Crotona with that in the three other parks. . . .

Implicit in plaintiffs' case is the proposition that the equal protection clause not merely prohibits less state effort on behalf of minority racial groups but demands the attainment of equal results. We very much doubt this, when, as here, the factor requiring added effort is not the result of past illegal action. Nothing in Hawkins v. Town of Shaw suggests that if the town had installed modern street lamps in the black quarter and these were repeatedly vandalized, the town must go on and on, even though this would mean a greater unit expenditure than in other areas. In a case like this, the City has satisfied its constitutional obligations by equal input even though, because of conditions for which it is not responsible, it has not achieved the equal results it desires. Cf. Fessler and Haar, Beyond the Wrong Side of the Tracks: Municipal Services in the Interstices of Procedure, 6 Harv. Civ. Rights-Civ. Lib. L. Rev. 441, 461-463 (1971).[4] How much further to go beyond equal effort in order to redeem Crotona Park is a matter of municipal policy, not of constitutional command. We add that, in determining whether there has been equality of effort, federal courts must not hold municipalities to standards of precision that are unattainable in the process of government. . . .

4. . . . In these early days of developing the implications of *Town of Shaw*, it seems wiser, particularly in view of the difficult problems with respect to remedy, generally not to go beyond requiring equality of input, except where something more is needed to remedy the effect of past unlawful conduct.

B. The Attitude of the Judiciary

We do not minimize the gravity of plaintiffs' grievances. But, in view of the level of the City's efforts, the problem resulting from the inefficacy of its expenditures to keep Crotona Park in its previous satisfactory state is one to be resolved through cooperative efforts by the City and the community surrounding the park, which also has its responsibilities, not by interposition on the part of a federal court.[32]

Notes

1. While the anticipated deluge of *Hawkins*-type suits was effectively dammed by *Beal* and other decisions, a few "unequally served" citizens — aided by particularly persevering public interest lawyers — have achieved court victories. Federal judges from the Middle District of Florida have been receptive to such challenges, especially when the requisite intent to discriminate leaps out from the historical and statistical evidence, and when constitutional claims are bolstered by supportable allegations of violations of Title VI of the Civil Rights Act of 1964, 42 U.S.C. §2000d (1982):

> No person in the United States shall, on the ground of race, color, or national origin, be excluded from participation in, be denied the benefits of, or be subjected to discrimination under any program or activity receiving Federal financial assistance.

See Ammons v. Dade City, 594 F. Supp. 1274 (M.D. Fla. 1984), aff'd, 783 F.2d 982 (11th Cir. 1986); Dowdell v. Apopka, 511 F. Supp. 1375 (M.D. Fla. 1981), aff'd in part, 698 F.2d 1181 (11th Cir. 1983); Johnson v. City of Arcadia, 450 F. Supp. 1363 (M.D. Fla. 1978). For a good summary of the advantages and shortcomings of Title VI litigation in the equal services setting, see Jaffe, Municipal Service Disparities: Liability Under Title VI of the Civil Rights Act of 1964, Land Use L. & Zoning Dig., Feb. 1987, at 3.

2. Race- and wealth-based discrimination in the provision of essential services is by no means only a rural southern or urban northeastern problem. For example, the city of Los Angeles has been involved in a political and socioeconomic imbroglio concerning efforts of local residents to beef up police protection in high-crime areas of the city. See Los Angeles District to Vote on Hiring More Police, N.Y. Times, Feb.

---

32. Cf. Pasadena City Board of Education v. Spangler, 427 U.S. 424, 436-437 (1976) ("having once implemented a racially neutral [public school] attendance pattern in order to remedy the perceived constitutional violations on the part of the defendants, the District Court had fully performed its function of providing the appropriate remedy for previous racially discriminatory attendance patterns"). — EDS.

25, 1987; Voters Decline to Pay for Police in Inner-City Area of Los Angeles, N.Y. Times, June 4, 1987.

3. Despite these occasional victories, there remain four substantial bars to federal relief: (1) the need to demonstrate discriminatory intent (Washington v. Davis, 426 U.S. 229 (1976); Village of Arlington Heights v. MHDC, supra page 450); (2) the nonfundamentality of the right to decent housing (Lindsey v. Normet, 405 U.S. 56 (1972); (3) the failure of the Supreme Court to characterize wealth a suspect characterization (San Antonio Independent School District v. Rodriguez, 411 U.S. 1 (1973)); and (4) the use of equality of input to satisfy constitutional obligations (Beal v. Lindsay). Can evidence be found for a pre-constitutional, common law duty to provide equal (and adequate) municipal services?

c. Tracing the Common Law Duty to Serve

■ BRACTON, "DE ADQUIRENDO RERUM DOMINIO" (OF ACQUIRING THE DOMINION OF THINGS)
2 *De Legibus et Consuetudinibus Angliae (On the Laws and Customs of England)* 166-167 (S. Thorne trans. 1968)[33]

Of liberties and who may grant liberties and which belong to the king.
We have explained above how rights and incorporeal things are transferred and *quasi*-transferred, how they are possessed or *quasi*-possessed, and how retained by actual use. Now we must turn to liberties [and see] who can grant liberties, and to whom, and how they are transferred, how possessed or *quasi*-possessed, and how they are retained by use. Who then? It is clear that the lord king [has all] dignities, [It is

---

33. See Haar & Fessler, The Wrong Side of the Tracks, 60, 62 (1986):

While Bracton's portrayals of the legal order and relative position of the Crown versus unchecked private advantage have been assailed by some as fiction on a grand scale, his prescription for a revised royal order was both superb propaganda and sound statesmanship. In fact, the title that Bracton assigned to his text was unrivaled as a revealing, if cryptic, summation of his concern: "*De Adquirendo Rerum Dominio*" ("Of Acquiring the Dominion of Things").

The major premise of the Bractonian case was that by virtue of his ultimate responsibility as a font of justice and guarantor of civil order, the King was vested with all dignities and possessed of an "ordinary jurisdiction and power over all who are within his realm." Bracton was not espousing an order in which the government actively cultivated ownership of all wealth so as to orchestrate every economic decision. Instead, he found it necessary to distinguish, by some neutral principle, those privileges or liberties that could be held in private hands from those that could not be alienated from the Crown. His irreducible proposal was that those activities connected with "justice and the peace belong to no one save the crown alone and the royal dignity, nor can they be separated from the crown, since they constitute the crown . . . without which it can neither subsist nor endure."

the lord king] himself who has ordinary jurisdiction and power over all who are within his realm. For he has in his hand all the rights belonging to the crown and the secular power and the material sword pertaining to the governance of the realm. . . .

. . . [P]rivileges, . . . though they belong to the crown, may nevertheless be separated from it and transferred to private persons, but only by special grace of the king himself; if his grace and special grant do not appear time does not bar the king from his action. Time does not run against him here since there is no need for proof. For it ought to be apparent to all that such things belong to the crown unless the contrary can be shown by a special grant. In other matters, however, where proof is needed, time runs against him just as against all others. When such liberties have been granted by the king they are at once *quasi*-transferred and *quasi*-possessed, and he to whom they are granted at once has *quasi*-use, though a case in which he ought to use does not at once arise. When one does arise and he uses he at once retains possession through use, [but] whether there is actual use or not he will always be in possession or *quasi*-possession of the delegated jurisdiction or the thing until he loses it by abuse or non-use.

■ TRESPASS ON THE CASE IN REGARD TO CERTAIN MILLS
Y.B. 22 Hen. 6, fo. 14 (C.P. 1444)

[See opinion, supra page 91.]

■ HAAR AND FESSLER, THE WRONG SIDE OF THE TRACKS
21-23 (1986)

Over a period of centuries the Bractonian calipers of abuse and misuse measured the forward movement of the judicial assault upon glaring oppression within the social order. The demise of feudalism was hastened by a curious combination of judicial action and inaction. . . . Local monopolies over the grinding of grain, the baking of bread, and the brewing of ale were the economic props of a system that taxed the many for the support of the few; when newly liberated citizens sought to ply the trade of miller, baker, or brewer, the threat of competition shook the feudal manor. A conditional judicial willingness to extend protection to the lord's monopolies turned the sword of privilege into the plowshare of the "duty to serve." The courts allowed competition to be suppressed, as the ruling groups demanded, but only if the monopolist could demonstrate that his facilities were sufficient to serve the needs of each and every member of the claimed populace in an equal, adequate, and nondiscriminatory manner, and at a reasonable price.

Monopolies in transportation proved as important to the rise of commerce in England as they were to the expansion of the settlements in North America. . . . [T]he common law courts conditioned their recognition of royally granted monopolies upon the duty to serve. The most fascinating and instructive example of the relation of privilege to obligation was the ferry monopoly, the cause for much judicial comment that is of special interest in our day.

The founding of the American Republic coincided with a second great upheaval, . . . the Industrial Revolution. The energy harnessed by Watt transformed the law as it remade the industrial world. Turnpike interests may have doomed the steam coaches, or "teakettles," which sought to traverse conventional road surfaces, but this triumph stamped upon them new obligations to the public. The railroads then emerged as the focus of legal and ideological struggles concerning the duty to serve, much as even now their tracks often divide the more from the less desirable parts of town. While the economic and demographic significance of this technological advance posed many problems, two abuses provided especially menacing challenges to the equality norm and its judicial proponents. For forty years rate discrimination and exclusive contracts defied legislative redress, leaving the field to the deliberative processes of the common law. Judges therefore faced the new task of reweaving the tapestry of the duty to serve. If royal writs had outlawed rate discrimination by the crown's monopolies (of ferries, bridges, markets, and the like) and had decreed that all should be served at a "reasonable charge," what was to be the fate of a transportation mogul who stood ready to favor certain customers or regions with less than reasonable charges? Building upon the English duty to serve, which had tamed the transportation monopolies in the formative years of independence, the judiciaries of the several states struggled to redefine the concept of the "reasonable" rate to include the requirement of a uniform or "common" rate. This doctrine became a powerful tool for the opponents of rate discrimination.

And how were the courts to deal with the swift completion of a regional, and then national, rail transportation system encompassing a myriad of auxiliary services, ranging from express forwarding to livestock feeding to grain elevators? If the railroads could contract to recognize a single purveyor as the exclusive source of an auxiliary service, the natural monopoly could be effectively extended to unnatural frontiers. Judicial intervention also met this second challenge — albeit through more indirect means. The emergence of legislative action, and even dominance in railway affairs, did not undercut the doctrine of the

B. The Attitude of the Judiciary

duty to serve. The courts remained the prophets of the equality norm. In fact, the appearance of state and, with the 1887 Interstate Commerce Act, federal regulatory legislation meant the enhancement — not eclipse — of the common law duty to serve, as the new branch of government drew on common law precedents for its regulatory activities. Clearly, the presence of such legislation reflected not so much a disaffection with the common law effort to advance the equality norm, but a recognition that the authority of judicial tribunals ended at the borders of the forum state. Moreover, state tribunals in those years were reluctant to move too radically in creating out-of-the-ordinary remedies for the railroads' novel abuses.

However persuasive the evidence of the judiciary's goals and attainments in advancing the equality norm against the excesses of the railroads, this legal approach applies most directly to the issue of municipal services. . . . As early common law courts consolidated their understanding of an increasingly complex economy, they became attached to the concept of the "public calling." The first gas and electric companies likewise found their operations identified as "affected with a public interest"; the intensity of the public need for such services occasioned the imposition of the duty to serve. Telephone and telegraph companies, like the railroads before them, found that they had purchased judicial recognition of their monopoly status at a price — the imposition of the duty to serve. In this sense the courts provided a pragmatic definition for monopoly: a service or product entrenched in a market that effectively renders competition impracticable. But, in turn, such recognition entailed a quid pro quo of automatically requiring the monopoly to serve the public interest. Thus even in the heyday of laissez-faire capitalism, many state courts advanced the proposition that while partiality and discriminatory or unreasonable charges might be permitted in private enterprises, such tactics were impermissible in the cases of public callings and municipal monopolies.

Although the drama detailing the development of municipal utilities introduced a new major character — the regulatory commission — the state courts were clearly not written out of the script. In fact, not much time passed before the quasi-judicial administrative bodies turned to the common law for guidance and support.

■ WHITE AND SNOAK AND HIS WIFE v. PORTER
Hardres 176, 145 Eng. Rep. 439 (Ex. 1672)

Upon English bill the case appeared to be that there was a custom within a manor held of the King in fee-farm, that all the copyhold tenants of the said manor should grind all their corn and grain baked and brewed within their antient copyhold messuages at a copyhold mill within the manor, and not elsewhere, of which copyhold mill the plaintiff Snoak in the right of his wife was tenant for life, and the plaintiff White had purchased the freehold and inheritance: and another person had erected another mill within the said manor, at which divers of the copyhold tenants ground their corn.

And it was held by the court that the purchase of the freehold and inheritance of the copyhold mill had not destroyed the copyhold during the life for which it was held; and that the reversioner of the freehold of the copyhold is subject to the King's fee-farm rent, but not the copyhold during the wife's life. And that therefore the copyholder for life should have no benefit as fee-farmer.

But Tr. 11 Car. Rot. 41, in this court, *Sir John Trevor* contra *Powel*. It was held by the court that a covenant on the King's part is equivalent to a fee-farm to entitle the patentee to the privilege of this court.

And Mich. 3 Car. in this court *Seintley* contra *Bendel*, held by the court that a new erected house is within the custom, and that none may grind elsewhere, but in case of excessive toll, or that the grist cannot be ground in convenient time.

And it was also held in this case, that to compel all the tenants within the King's mannor to grind at the King's mill, is a personal prerogative of the Kings, which no other lord can have without tenure, custom or prescription. But it will extend to a fee-farm, because it is for the King's advantage. And that the custom in this case does not go to the estate, but to the thing itself, and runs along with the mill, into whose hands soever it comes. And that the suit here must be as debtor and accountant only, because the copyhold for life is not liable to the fee-farm. And if two join, as they do here, where one of them is, and the other is not liable to the fee-farm, that is irregular, unless that other be a privileged person. It was decreed against Potter who had erected the new mill, that he should not withdraw or take away any grist from the other mill; but his mill was not decreed to be demolished; for that can be done in the King's own case only, or in the case of his patentee.

■ MESSENGER v. PENNSYLVANIA RAILROAD
37 N.J.L. 531 (1874)

The opinion of the court was delivered by BEDLE, J. The first count of this declaration alleges that in consideration that the plaintiffs were large shippers of live hogs over the lines of the defendants' railways

B. The Attitude of the Judiciary

from Pittsburg to Jersey City, the defendants agreed to transport such stock over their railways between those termini, at the regular rates, which were fifty cents per one hundred pounds, subject to a drawback to the plaintiffs of ten cents on the one hundred pounds; also, that if the defendants transported for any other parties than the plaintiffs and seven others named, the same kind of freight from Pittsburg to Jersey City, for less than the regular rates stated, or allowed a drawback from said rates to any others than the plaintiffs and the seven named, that they would allow such further drawback to the plaintiffs as would reduce the cost of shipment to ten cents per hundred pounds less than that of any other person or persons, except the parties mentioned. . . .

The business of the common carrier is for the public, and it is his duty to serve the public indifferently. He is entitled to a reasonable compensation, but on payment of that he is bound to carry for whoever will employ him, to the extent of his ability. A private carrier can make what contract he pleases. The public have no interest in that, but a service for the public necessarily implies equal treatment in its performance, when the right to the service is common. Because the institution, so to speak, is public, every member of the community stands on an equality as to the right to its benefit, and, therefore, the carrier cannot discriminate between individuals for whom he will render the service. In the very nature, then, of his duty and the public right, his conduct should be equal and just to all. So, also, there is involved in the *reasonableness* of his compensation the same principle. A want of uniformity in price for the same kind of service under like circumstances is most unreasonable and unjust, when the right to demand it is common. It would be strange if, when the object of the employment is the public benefit, and the law allows no discrimination as to individual customers, but requires all to be accommodated alike as individuals, and for a reasonable rate, that by the indirect means of unequal prices some could lawfully get the advantage of the accommodation and others not. A direct refusal to carry for a reasonable rate would involve the carrier in damages, and a refusal, in effect, could be accomplished by unfair and unequal charges, or if not to that extent, the public right to the convenience and usefulness of the means of carriage could be greatly impaired. Besides, the injury is not only to the individual affected, but it reaches out, disturbing trade most seriously. Competition in trade is encouraged by the law, and to allow any one to use means, established and intended for the public good, to promote unfair advantages amongst the people and foster monopolies, is against public policy, and should not be permitted. . . .

. . . This public good is common, and unequal and unjust favors are entirely inconsistent with the common right. So far as their duty to serve the public is concerned, they are not only common carriers, but public agents, and in their very constitution and relation to the public, there is necessarily implied a duty on their part, and a right in the public, to have fair treatment and immunity from unjust discrimination. The right of the public is equal in every citizen, and the trust must be performed so as to secure and protect it.

■ STATE EX REL. WEBSTER v. NEBRASKA TELEPHONE CO.
17 Neb. 126, 22 N.W. 237 (1885)

REESE, J. This is an original application for a *mandamus* to compel the respondent to place and maintain in the office of the relator a telephone and transmitter, such as are usually furnished to the subscribers of the respondent. . . .

The pleadings and proofs show that the relator is an attorney at law in Lincoln, Nebraska; that he is somewhat extensively engaged in the business of his profession, and which extends to Lincoln and Omaha, and surrounding cities and county seats, including quite a number of the principal towns in south-eastern Nebraska; that this territory is occupied by respondent exclusively, together with a large portion of south-western Iowa, including in all about 1,500 different instruments. By the testimony of one of the principal witnesses for respondent, we learn that the company is incorporated for the purpose of furnishing individual subscribers telephone connection with each other under the patents owned by the American Telephone Company; instruments to be furnished by said company and sublet by the Nebraska Telephone Company to the subscribers to it. This is clearly the purpose of the organization. While it is true, as claimed by respondent, that it has been organized under the general corporation laws of the state, and in some matters has no higher or greater rights than an ordinary corporation; yet it is also true that it has assumed to act in a capacity which is to a great extent public, and has, in the large territory covered by it, undertaken to satisfy a public want or necessity. This public demand can only be supplied by complying with the necessity which has sprung into existence by the introduction of the instrument known as the telephone, and which new demand or necessity in commerce the respondent proposes satisfying. . . .

. . . The principles established and declared by the courts, and which were and are demanded by the highest material interests of the country, are not confined to the instrumentalities of commerce, nor to the particular kind of service known or in use at the time when these principles were enunciated, "but they keep pace with the progress of the country, and adapt themselves to the new developments of time and circumstances. They extend from the horse with its rider to the stage coach, from the sailing vessel to the steam-boat, from the coach and the steam-boat to the railroad, and from the railroad to the telegraph," and from the telegraph to the telephone, "as these new agencies are successfully brought into use to meet the demands of increasing population and wealth. They were intended for the goverment of the business to which they related, at all times and under all circumstances." Pensacola Tel. Co. v. W. U. Tel. Co. 96 U.S. 9. . . .

. . . Respondent is a common carrier of news, the same as a telegraph company. The duty of common carriers is one of law, growing out of their office, and not of contract. The remedy by mandamus is the appropriate one. The duty is of a public character, and there is no other adequate mode of relief.

Questions

1. Are you satisfied with the court's reasons for refusing to tear down the competing mill in *White and Snoak*? Is this a subtle (though physical) reminder to the franchisees that their victory was less than absolute?

2. Is the incremental judicial activism in cases like *Messenger* justified in the face of substantial private sector abuse, or is more harm done by the justices' failure to await a market or legislative correction?

3. How helpful is the common law formulation of quasi-public pursuits? Is public duty just another form of regulation; are the courts coming dangerously close to a confiscatory taking?

■ REID DEVELOPMENT CORP. v. PARSIPPANY-TROY HILLS TOWNSHIP
10 N.J. 229, 89 A.2d 667 (1952)

HEHER, J.

By this civil action in lieu of mandamus, plaintiff seeks to compel the defendant township to extend its water mains laid in Intervale Road through an intersecting street known as Fairway Place, for a distance of 600 feet, "under the usual terms and conditions," to provide water for lands of plaintiff on either side of Fairway Place in process of development for residential uses.

Plaintiff applied for the extension on April 26, 1950, and again on May 31 ensuing; and not long thereafter, on June 14, it was advised in writing by the local governing body that the township then had "a more than ample supply of lots" having a frontage of less than 100 feet; that the Intervale Lake area, which includes plaintiff's lands, "deserves lots of 100 feet frontage," and "In order to benefit the township by having your development built up in 100 foot lots, . . . we are willing to reduce your improvement costs by supplying all the labor for installing whatever mains, hydrants, fittings, etc. are needed on your land for a water system, and by rebating to you over a period of years out of water rental received from your parcels fronting on the said water system thus installed on your land the cost of the materials needed in such system — providing you revise your map in 100 foot frontage lots approved by the Planning Board." Reference was made to "sad cesspool and septic tank experiences in several parts of the Township where, before the adoption of a Zoning Law, lots smaller than 100 foot frontage have been built on." Plaintiff rejected the condition and thereupon brought this proceeding. The Superior Court ruled that "the extension of a water main by a municipality is a governmental function" calling for "the exercise of a degree of discretion on the part of the municipality," and there was no abuse of discretion here. . . .

The action taken by the local authority was arbitrary and unreasonable. The water facility is a municipally-owned public utility established under legislative authority. The provision of water for the public and private uses of the municipality and its inhabitants is the exclusive province of the local agency; and it is elementary that the exercise of the power must be in all respects fair and reasonable and free from oppression. There can be no invidious discrimination in the extension of the service thus undertaken by the municipality as a public responsibility. Equal justice is of the very essence of the power. Impartial administration is the controlling principle. The rule of action must apply equally to all persons similarly circumstanced. There is a denial of the equal protection of the laws unless the water service be available to all in like circumstances upon the same terms and conditions, although the rule of equality may have a pragmatic application. Persons situated alike shall be treated alike. . . .

A public water company is under a duty as a public utility to supply water to all inhabitants of the community who apply for the service and tender the usual rates. The obligation includes the establishment of a distributive plant adequate to serve the needs of the municipality and the enlargement of the system to meet the reasonable demands of the growing community. The utility is under a duty to serve all within the area who comply with fair and just rules and regulations applicable to all alike. The obligation is enforceable by mandamus. While it has been held that a municipality so engaged exercises a governmental discretion as to the extension of the water mains, governed largely by the extent of the need and economic considerations, the discretionary authority must be fairly and reasonably used; and the remedial process of

B. The Attitude of the Judiciary

mandamus may be invoked for an abuse of discretion if the extension be arbitrarily refused. Lawrence v. Richards, 111 Me. 92, 88 A. 92, 47 L.R.A., N.S., 654 (Sup. Jud. Ct. 1913); City of Greenwood v. Provine, 143 Miss. 42, 108 So. 284, 45 A.L.R. 824 (Sup. Ct. 1926); Lukrawka v. Spring Valley Water Co., 169 Cal. 318, 146 P. 640 (Sup. Ct. 1915).[34] It would seem that no sound distinction can be made, in respect of the extension of the service, between a municipality which has undertaken to provide water to the community and a water company performing the function of a public utility. . . .

Here, the provision of water to the plaintiff landowner was conditioned not by a circumstance of action or being reasonably bearing upon the exercise of the function, but rather by wholly alien considerations related to planning and zoning; and this was not within the province of the governing body. There was then no suggestion that the enlargement of the service was indefensible on economic grounds. The need was not denied; nor was it asserted that the cost would be prohibitive or greatly disproportionate to the return. Indeed, the municipality offered to "reduce the landowner's improvement costs" by supplying labor at the outset and by rebating over a period of years out of water rentals accruing from the extension the cost of materials required for the installation of a water system on plaintiff's lands. And no question is made now as to the need.

---

34. See Haar & Fessler, supra note 33, at 183:

> A more direct attack on the public/private distinction emerged in other cases. Its earliest strategies were encoded in a 1926 Mississippi case, City of Greenwood v. Provine. Although the state high court refused to order the city to extend a water main by only two blocks in order to provide service to a new customer, Justice Holden suggested that this was not a closed subject. In this specific instance, the court ostensibly relied on the rule that such matters should be left to the discretion of local officials. The judges did not order the requested extensions to Greenwood's "Boulevard," an area outside the corporate limits at the time the water mains were laid. Nonetheless, although some later courts have cited the *Greenwood* opinion as authority for the traditional discretionary rule, a close reading reveals that Justice Holden and his brethren were unwilling to leave matters entirely in local hands:
>
> > It is our judgment that the discretion to be exercised by the city authorities in the extension of its water system may be said to be limited to a refusal to extend where to do so would be unreasonable under the conditions and circumstances presented in the particular case; but, as we have said, unless the discretion is abused by municipal authorities, their decision will be determinative.
>
> This call for reasonable and temperate action was buttressed by the court's citing of the *Lukrawka* decision, the California case that had held that *privately* owned utilities were obligated to make all reasonable extensions. Thus, although the Mississippi tribunal failed to order the short extension, it served notice that local autonomy and its attendant public/private distinction were not unassailable barriers to judicial intervention in the event of abuse of discretion. The Progressive marriage of judicial deference to municipal expertise was beginning to sour. — EDS.

The stipulation of facts and the proofs reveal that it has been the practice of the municipality to provide extensions of the water system under the same or similar circumstances. While not a formula common to all cases, the enlargement was usually granted on terms that the land developer would bear the initial cost of the installation and be reimbursed to the extent of 75% of the outlay from the water revenues collected for taps on the added water line during a given period, the remaining 25% to be retained by the township for "its maintenance and pumping charges for furnishing water" to the new facility. . . .

. . . [T]he regulation is ultra vires. It purports to vest in the governing body a naked and arbitrary power to grant or withhold consent to the expansion of the service. The discretion is absolute. The extension may be at the expense of the landowner in the one case and the township in another, depending upon the mere will of the governing body. There is no standard to insure impartial action. Access to water facilities is not a matter of grace. Rights of persons and of property cannot by legislative fiat be made subject to the will or unregulated discretion of another. It matters not whether the facility is in the hands of the municipality or a privately-owned public utility. Arbitrary use of the power contravenes fundamental law and is not within the legislative province. . . .

It is vigorously urged that the extension of water mains by a municipality involves the exercise of a legislative or governmental discretion which precludes the remedy of mandamus.

Where, as here, there was a plain abuse of authority, mandamus will lie to command performance of what under the clearly established or admitted facts constitutes a peremptory duty. . . .

Here, wholly extraneous considerations governed the exercise of the discretionary authority. On the admitted facts, the extension of the water facilities was plaintiff's right; and it was an abuse of discretion to use the grant as a means of coercing the landowner into acceptance of the minimum lot-size restriction upon his lands, however serviceable to the common good. Such benefits are to be had through the channels prescribed by the law. There is no statutory authority for this condition. Planning and zoning powers may not be exerted by indirection; the exercise of these functions must needs be in keeping with the principles of the enabling statutes.

Notes

1. In Robinson v. City of Boulder, 190 Colo. 357, 547 P.2d 228 (1976), the court considered whether the city, in operating a water and sewer system that exclusively served an area beyond the city limits,

B. The Attitude of the Judiciary

could refuse to supply essential services "on the grounds that the landowners' proposal was inconsistent with the Boulder Valley Comprehensive Plan and various aspects of the city's interim growth policy." The city denied that it was operating as a public utility, a position the trial and appellate courts rejected, the latter concluding:

> [W]e hold that inasmuch as Boulder is the sole and exclusive provider of water and sewer services in the area surrounding the subject property, it is a public utility. As such, it holds itself out as ready and able to serve those in the territory who require the service. There is no utility related reason, such as insufficient water, preventing it from extending these services to the landowners. Unless such reasons exist, Boulder cannot refuse to serve the people in the subject area.

As for Boulder's inconsistency argument, the state supreme court ruled that "in matters pertaining to land use in unincorporated areas . . . a city is given only an advisory role."

2. See Gillette, Equality and Variety in the Delivery of Municipal Services, 100 Harv. L. Rev. 946, 955-957 (1987):

> There is certainly a respectable literature in public finance and public choice theory that envisions local government primarily as a provider of the services that constituents prefer. . . . For instance, the inequitable distribution [of municipal services] . . . would not exist if we lived in the world hypothesized by Charles Tiebout's classic work.[29] In such a world, individuals would enjoy perfect mobility, and enough communities would exist so that each individual could gravitate to the locality offering a package of services that satisfied personal preferences. Individuals in this world would possess information about the differences between communities, and the public services provided by any one locality would have no external effects. "Equality of services" would be irrelevant, for the political market would correct any allocation of services that failed to coincide with constituents' (consumer-voters') desires. Those whose preferences were no longer reflected in the communal choice would costlessly move. In such a world, judicial intervention to reorder the package of services offered would necessarily produce a decrease in personal welfare, at least if welfare were measured by individual preferences. A judicial role in the structuring of municipal functions could be justified only by reference to paternalism or irrational individual choices.
>
> Examination of the need for Tiebout's assumptions, however, reveals

---

29. See Tiebout, A Pure Theory of Local Expenditures, 64 J. Pol. Econ. 416 (1956); Note, Equalization of Municipal Services: The Economics of *Serrano* and *Shaw*, 82 Yale L. J. 89 (1972). Refinements of Tiebout's initial models constitute a major academic industry. See, e.g., W. Oates, Fiscal Federalism (1972); Epple & Zelenitz, The Implications of Competition Among Jurisdictions: Does Tiebout Need Politics?, 89 J. Pol. Econ. 1197 (1981); Henderson, The Tiebout Model; Bring Back the Entrepreneurs, 93 J. Pol. Econ. 248 (1985); Williams, The Optimal Provision of Public Goods in a System of Local Government, 74 J. Pol. Econ. 18 (1966).

that the goods allocated by government have properties that may simultaneously impose judicially enforceable obligations in the non-Tiebout world. The Tiebout model assumes unconstrained mobility for the residents of any locality so that individuals who are dissatisfied with the package of services offered by their particular local government can move to a more congenial supplier. The model implicitly assumes that the failure of a local government to provide specific services can be remedied primarily, if not solely, by another local government. Unlike the case of most goods and services in our market economy, in the Tiebout model the private sector is not the presumptive remedy for a governmental failure to supply a good or service. Residents of a locality who are dissatisfied with the supplied goods and services do not purchase the goods from a private supplier or go into business for themselves to produce the goods. This presumption suggests that the private market cannot be relied on for efficient production of the goods at issue, and that they must instead be provided collectively.

3. Professor Wood supplies a political model alternative:

Given this general characteristic of the governmental process, we should acknowledge three specific differences between the political economy and the private economy in the way resources are used and activities undertaken. First, in the political economy the basic unit of decision-making is not the individual producer or consumer; it is the group, formally or informally organized. Second, the mechanism through which resources are obtained and expenditures made is not the price mechanism of the marketplace, but the budgetary process. Finally, the "products" provided by government are public products; that is, theoretically they are always indivisible among persons, and practically, they are frequently so.

... In explaining the behavior of the Region's political economy, then, we must do what some writers on municipal affairs have not done — abandon the assumptions of the Age of Reason. One cannot show how governments in fact behave by assuming the existence of the conscientious citizen rationally striving to do his duty, or the divisibility of public goods and services on a unit basis, or full knowledge on the part of each citizen of the character of his government's expenditures and receipts. The guidelines are in fact not very precise nor easily quantifiable.

So at rockbottom the significance of the Service State becomes this: as more and more resources pass from the private sector to the public sector, the process which determines their use changes from that of the marketplace to the uncertain world of politics.

1400 Governments: The Political Economy of the New York Metropolitan Region 17-22 (1961).

Questions

1. At first, the crown's franchisees were obligated to act in the interest of the common weal because they "looked public." By the mid-

twentieth century, public providers of essential services were made to serve equally based on the fact that they "looked private." Have the courts come full circle in rationalizing the duty to provide equality in the provision of essential services?

2. Would the Mississippi court have been dismayed or complimented by the New Jersey court's citation of *Greenwood* to support their mandate in *Reid Development*?

3. Does the ultimate goal of "zoning by indirection" differ from the purpose of exclusionary zoning by referendum? Do the courts focus too much (or too little) on the means employed by local officials?

4. Is the common law system of decision-making up to the task of filling the gaps left by newly hesitant federal courts? Is this just the judicial version of New Federalism? Why has the common law approach survived, even thrived, despite the impressive growth of administrative law? How does the availability of state legislation merely abrogating undesirable common law principles affect our appreciation of the centuries-old duty to serve?

3. Private Subdivision Controls: The Lawyer as Urban (and Suburban) Planner

One of the themes traced in this book is the erosion of traditional barriers between "private" and "public" law. Plunged into the new settings of urban expansion and redevelopment, an ancient branch of the common law — conditions, easements, covenants, and servitudes — reflects how thin is the line between what are deemed private arrangements and what is considered the social interest.

Feudal land law was not greatly worried by this public-private distinction. Indeed, to feudal eyes private rights were a privilege in exchange for which the state could exact the means for discharging functions today unhesitantly assumed to be the responsibility of government. The tenant held land — but in return he was expected to supply knights for the defense of the realm and for adventures abroad; to contribute funds to the national coffers; and even to administer justice. "If we examine our notion of feudalism," asks Maitland, "does it not seem this, that land law is not private law, that public law is land law, that public and political rights and duties of all sorts and kinds are intimately and quite inextricably blended with rights in land?"[35] To the medieval lawyer, apparently, private and public law merged into each other.

However, the revolutions of the seventeenth and eighteenth centuries lent a new importance to private sovereignty in land. Blackstone's

---

35. The Constitutional History of England 155 (1913).

viewpoint is typical of the period.[36] But, even then, questions like the potency of private law agreements to bind future generations of landowners had to be resolved by the emphasis of selected social values. Familiar examples are the continuing policy struggles underlying disentailing, or the rule against perpetuities.[37]

The real estate developer may scoff at the "starry-eyed planner," but inadvertently, like Molière's Bourgeois Gentilhomme, he is poking fun at himself as well. Owners, with the aid of the courts, have in effect always planned land uses. Since the beginnings of urban civilization there has been a continuous effort, by means of private restrictions, to discipline, thwart, and regulate the changes in the physical environment inevitably wrought by time and technology. Strong is the desire to perpetuate selected land arrangements. The large-scale subdivision is an attempt to stabilize land uses; privately planned to attain specified objectives, new towns, such as the aluminum city at Kitimat, have sprung up where formerly only eagles soared over waterfalls.

The legal issues relating to the private planning of neighborhood environment arise chiefly at one of two junctures. A landowner embarking on development may desire a scheme of restrictions to bind the future. Alternatively, a private investor or a public authority may find designs threatened by a restriction imposed by a prior generation that knew not, for instance, that a crooked swamp would someday evolve into Gramercy Park, in New York City.[38] The lawyer, drafting an estate plan for the disposition of property, or formulating corporate organizations, is accustomed to thinking in terms of the question marks that shroud the future. But in land-use decisions the time factor is even more in the foreground, and the consequences, in terms of large areas of land and great numbers of people, are both more widely felt and more difficult to predict. In this legal planning the impact of public controls on private land-use arrangements needs increasingly to be taken into account. The concern of government with proper standards of housing and land use has introduced a mixed set of considerations for landowners — limitations on permissible private arrangement; direct and often competitive public developments; and the disposal of publicly acquired land to private enterprise for use according to a plan. At the same time, for the developer (and this is underlined by the urban renewal programs), private restrictions are necessary supplements to public controls.

How does the process of private planning compare with public

---

36. See infra page 780.
37. See Aigler, The Dead Hand (1956); Fratcher, Perpetuities and Other Restraints (1954); American Law Institute Proceedings 1978, at 222-278, 280-307 (1979); id. 1979, at 424-481 (1980).
38. See Ascher, Private Covenants in Urban Redevelopment, in Urban Redevelopment: Problems and Practices 223 (Woodbury ed. 1953).

B. The Attitude of the Judiciary

planning? How does the building scheme differ from zoning and subdivision control in planning area, detail, duration, flexibility, effect on property rights? Which is easier to administer? How does the court's role differ from the one it plays in zoning or in the "interpretive" process of private nuisance? When, in the role of draftsman, would you select one technique rather than another?

In view of accepted social policies and the interdependence of urban land, how far should private arrangements between the interested parties be honored? To what extent should decision-making be left to the individual property owner? For what purposes can private parties invoke the force of the state to supplement private agreement? What if the two forms of regulation conflict? As city planning grows to maturity, what need is there for private restrictions? Truly, Maitland's dictum of constitutional law secreted in the interstices of property law may yet have to be reversed as "fixed" real property concepts yield to amorphous constitutional policy.[39]

Many devices are available to the draftsman for imposing long-range controls and for achieving land-planning ends. Restrictions may be created by conveyances on special limitation or on condition subsequent.[40] If desired, an easement may be reserved; again, a negative

---

39. Owing to its history (perhaps even to the nature of the problem) many have complained over the lack of coherency in this field of law. Lord Justice Romer has observed that "the established rules concerning it are purely arbitrary, and the distinctions, for the most part, quite illogical." Grant v. Edmondson, [1931] 1 Ch. 1, 28. More recently, others have stressed the inadequacy of these long-hallowed real property concepts in coping with the problems of urbanism. Judge Clark, who strove mightily with the Restater of Servitudes for the American Law Institute, concluded that many of the debates are "ancient battles of property law, little calculated to help in the attack upon slum clearance, problems of blighted urban areas, or the development of low-cost housing."

40. The use of the land may also be controlled by executory limitations. See also Jost, The Defeasible Fee and the Birth of the Modern Residential Subdivision, 49 Mo. L. Rev. 695, 708-709, 728, 735 (1984):

> While the law of real covenants, negative easements, and equitable servitudes was still in a formative stage until late in the nineteenth century, the drafter of deed restrictions of that period had ready access to an elaborate law of defeasible fees developed in closely related contexts, such as charitable or public donations, industrial development, family settlements, and support arrangements. It was natural for many developers to turn first to this body of law for models for drafting residential subdivision restrictions. It is not surprising, therefore, that use of defeasible fees for deed restrictions was widespread during the period from 1870 until 1920, appearing before other forms of restriction in many jurisdictions and becoming nearly universal in some areas....
>
> The popularity of the defeasible fee as a land use planning device was relatively brief. It is not difficult to understand its demise. From the start, the courts were hostile to the use of forfeiture as a tool for land use planning. Traditional abhorrence of forfeitures disposed the courts against enforcing deed restrictions written in conditional language through defeasance. Judges found numerous ways of avoiding forfeiture. The simplest approach was to construe a condition strictly to avoid finding a violation. Other approaches attacked the use of defeasible fees more directly....
>
> Ultimately, the defeasible fee gave way to the equitable servitude as the

easement may enable the grantee to insist that the grantor shall not engage in certain acts on the grantor's retained land. Or a grantor may exact promises from his grantees that they will use their parcels in a prescribed fashion. Alternatively, the choice may be that of retaining a fee and controlling through the terms of a lease.[41] The questions always are: Have the parties chosen the proper method for reaching the objective they desire? Does the language unambiguously define the intention? Whatever the choice, have the formalities been observed so that it can be attained?

The modern subdivision brings the heavenly world of concepts down to the functional level of clients' problems. Today, the building scheme for the development of a land tract provides a striking example of persons subject to the rights and duties of a plan they never drafted, an agreement they never made. Carried to an extreme, the private arrangement may govern so many relations as to constitute local legislation and taxation promulgated by private government.

■ HARROD v. RIGELHAUPT
1 Mass. App. 376, 298 N.E.2d 872 (1973)

GRANT, Justice.

This is a bill in equity brought in the Land Court for declaratory and injunctive relief with respect to a restriction on the height of buildings in an alleged scheme of common development of land in Wellfleet....

The common grantor was one Henderson, who was not a commercial developer but a practicing lawyer in New York City who (or whose wife) owned a summer home in Wellfleet several miles to the south of and out of sight from the development in question. In 1949 Henderson's title to the entire area shown on the accompanying sketch plan was confirmed and registered under the provisions of G.L. c. 185. In December of that year Henderson conveyed Lots B and C to his wife by a deed which contained no restrictions. The deeds out from Henderson of Lots J-1 through J-10 and J-12 through J-17 range in

---

restrictive device of choice. For a host of reasons, conditions enforced by forfeiture were inferior to servitudes enforced by injunction for assuring compliance with deed restrictions. Perhaps the most important development contributing to the ascendancy of the equitable servitude was the maturation by the end of the nineteenth century of the doctrine of the equitable servitude common scheme, which permitted developers to impose restrictions on all properties in a subdivision for the benefit of all others.

41. English lawyers prefer to exercise land-use controls through clauses in a long-term lease. However, the traditions and usages of American real estate market probably foreclose its availability.

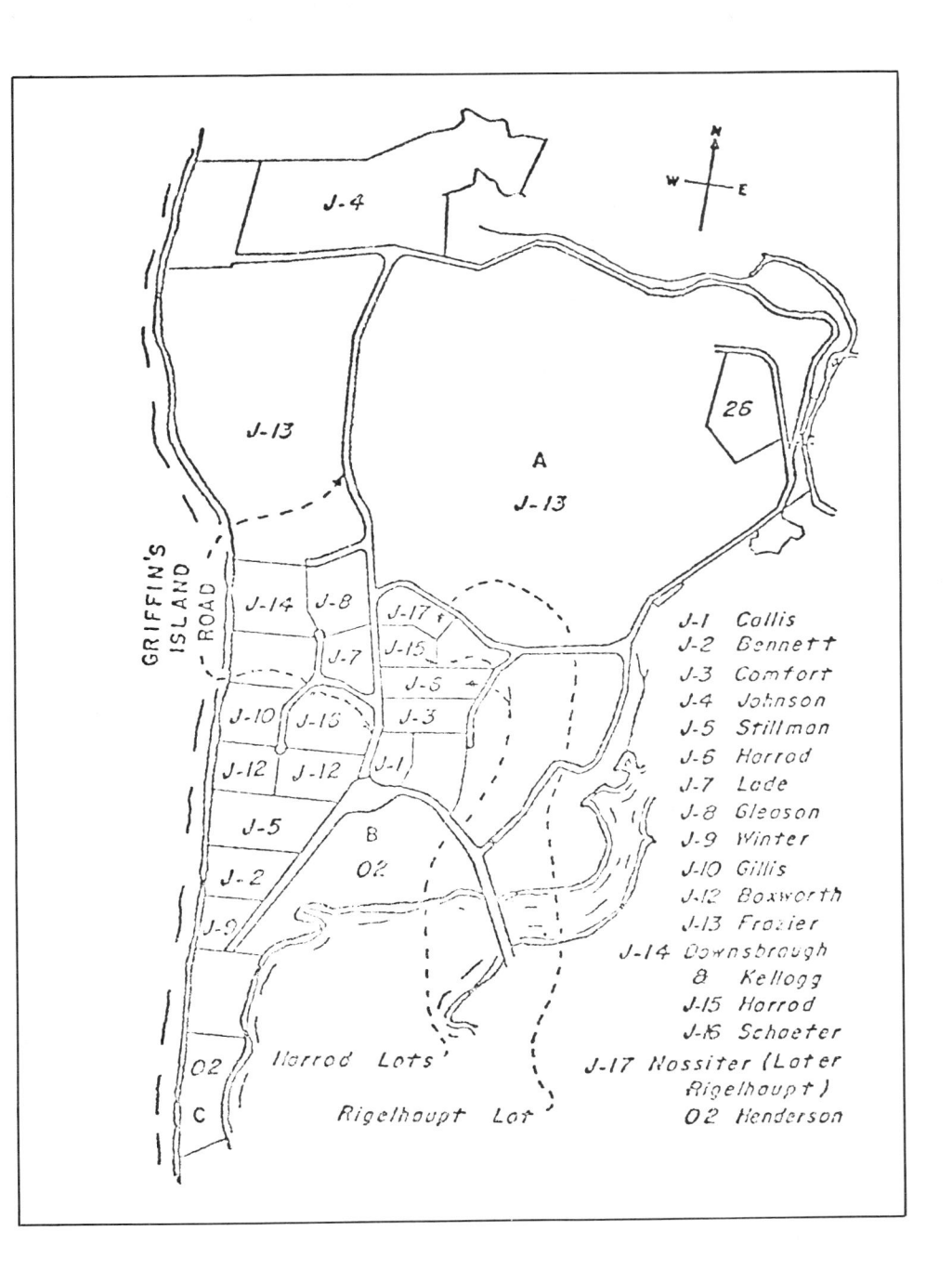

J-1   Callis
J-2   Bennett
J-3   Comfort
J-4   Johnson
J-5   Stillman
J-6   Harrod
J-7   Lade
J-8   Gleason
J-9   Winter
J-10 Gillis
J-12 Boxworth
J-13 Frazier
J-14 Downsbrough
      & Kellogg
J-15 Harrod
J-16 Schaefer
J-17 Nossiter (Later
      Rigelhaupt)
O2   Henderson

date from November of 1952 through January of 1959 and contain the provisions presently to be discussed. All the lots comprised portions of the original Lot A, which appears to have contained more than 400 acres of land prior to any subdivision. The lots lying to the southerly of Lot J-13 (which contained 315.95 acres) range in size (where disclosed) from 3.66 to 9.10 acres. By the time of Henderson's conveyance out of Lot J-17 nine separate subdivision plans of portions of Lot A had been registered in the Land Court on dates ranging from May of 1952 to May of 1957. Henderson died in 1961. On his death the unsold portions of Lot A passed to his wife, who in 1965 conveyed them to the United States of America to become parts of the Cape Cod National Seashore established in 1961 under Pub. L. 87-126, 75 Stat. 284.

Except as otherwise indicated, the following language appears in the original deeds out of all the lots lying to the southerly of Lot J-13, and the defendants' transfer certificate of title recites that their lot "is subject to and has the benefit of the restrictions set forth" in such language: "Said premises are hereby conveyed subject to and with the benefit of the following provisions which shall be binding upon and inure to the benefit of the Grantor and Grantee and their respective heirs and assigns, except as hereinafter limited. " Seven specific provisions follow, many of which resemble common provisions of zoning by-laws and appear to reflect the fact that no part of Lot A was subject to any zoning by-law of the town of Wellfleet during Henderson's lifetime.

The third provision, critical in this case, reads in pertinent part as follows:

> During the life of the Grantor no building shall be erected on the granted premises except in accordance with plans and specifications which shall have been approved in writing by the Grantor. . . . After the death of the Grantor, (a) no building shall be erected on the granted premises (i) unless the design is suitable to the area and will not unduly obstruct the view from adjoining plots, (ii) which shall consist of more than two stories, cellar and attic, and, if it is located upon a hilltop, or if the roof line will rise above adjacent hilltops, which shall exceed 15' in height, from the lowest point of the grade adjacent to the building to the highest point of the roof or of any projection other than chimneys, or aerials, extending above the roof. . . .

. . . At the conclusion of the foregoing provisions there appears the following:

> 9. The restrictions established by the preceding paragraphs . . . shall remain in force until January 1, 2050 . . . and all said restrictions are imposed for the benefit of the remaining land of the Grantor . . . [in Lot A] but no owner shall be liable except for breaches occurring during such owner's ownership.

B. The Attitude of the Judiciary 679

The plaintiffs purchased Lot J-6 by a deed dated August 18, 1954, and thereafter proceeded to construct the original portion of the house in which they now live. They purchased Lot J-15, which remains vacant, by a deed dated August 19, 1957. Lot J-17 was purchased by the defendants' immediate predecessor in title by a deed dated January 16, 1959, and she thereafter proceeded to construct the original portion of the house which is now in dispute. The defendants purchased Lot J-17 and the original house thereon on November 16, 1966. In March of 1970, under circumstances which will appear more fully in a later portion of this opinion, the defendants commenced the construction of an addition to their house which, it is agreed, is approximately twenty-six feet in overall height measured from the lowest point of the grade adjacent to the building.

The parties are in agreement that the existence or not of a common scheme of development is to be determined by the intent of Henderson, the common grantor, in the light of all the attendant circumstances. See Snow v. Van Dam, 291 Mass. 477, 481, 197 N.E. 224 (1935), and cases cited.

The defendants point to the absence of any recorded (registered) plan of subdivision of all of Lot A at the time Henderson commenced the sale of the J lots as indicative of a lack of intention on his part to create and impose a common scheme. It is true that there was no such overall plan here. However, two subdivision plans of portions of Lot A had already been registered in the Land Court by the time of the sale of Lot J-1, and these were followed by an orderly progression of seven other subdivision plans as further sales were made. Such a pattern of subdivision plans and ensuing sales undoubtedly reflected the considerable time and expense involved in securing the necessary authorizations from the Land Court for the issuance of separate certificates of title to the various portions of Lot A and, in our opinion, does not stand in the way of a determination that Henderson had a common scheme of development in mind at the time he commenced his sales. See Snow v. Van Dam, 291 Mass. 477, 478-479, 480, 485-486, 194 N.E. 224 (1935)....

The defendants' principal arguments against the existence of such a scheme are ones concerning the proper construction of the language of the various provisions previously summarized or quoted. In essence the arguments are that all restrictions were personal to Henderson, whose intention went no further than to benefit such remaining portions of Lot A as he might continue to own at the time of his death, which did not include the plaintiffs' lots. We cannot accede to such arguments. Henderson himself owned no home or other structure located in Lot A which he might have been desirous of protecting. The preface to the restrictions recites that "[s]aid premises are ... conveyed *subject to and with the benefit of* the following provisions which shall be *binding upon and inure to the benefit of the* Grantor and *Grantee and* their respective *heirs and* assigns . . ." (emphasis supplied). The year 2050, when the restrictions were to expire, was almost one hundred years distant at the time of the 1952 sale of Lot- J-1[13] and well beyond Henderson's own life expectancy.

The restriction on the height of building was but one of numerous restrictions on the general uses which could be made of the lots which were being conveyed out of Lot A. There was no zoning by-law of the town of Wellfleet then applicable to any part of Lot A, and we have already noted Henderson's concern with the general lack of public controls over the use of that land. We perceive a general intention on his part to create by express restrictions a system of private zoning for the benefit of and of general application to all of Lot A. Henderson would personally supervise and approve the design and suitability of the houses which might be constructed to the southerly of Lot J-13 during his lifetime, but his own personal (and otherwise unworkable) standards were to be replaced, after his death, by the objective standards specifically set out in the restrictions, and in particular by the fifteen (earlier twenty)-foot height restriction set out in paragraph 3(a)(ii) thereof.[14]

We hold that there was here a common scheme of development within the meaning of and the rules laid down in Snow v. Van Dam, 291 Mass. 477, 481-486, 197 N.E. 224 (1935), and that there is appurtenant to the plaintiffs' Lots J-6 and J-15 a right to specific enforcement of the fifteen-foot height restriction against the building located on the defendants' Lot J-17 unless such enforcement should be precluded by one or more of the factors set out in G.L. c. 184, §30.

The Factors Set Forth in G.L. c. 184, §30[15]

The judge of the Land Court, following the remand from this court, took a view of the premises of the parties in the company of

---

13. See G. L. c. 184, §23, which provides in pertinent part that "[c]onditions or restrictions, *unlimited as to time*, by which the . . . use of real property is affected, shall be limited to the term of thirty years after the date of the deed . . . creating them . . ." (emphasis supplied).

14. We do not believe Henderson's general intention was negatived by the provision in paragraph two of the restrictions, previously noted, to the general effect that after his death only the immediate abutters need to be consulted for permission to erect prefabricated, metal, sectional or portable buildings. The sizes of the various lots were such that buildings of those types would be of legitimate concern only to those persons whose properties should abut on a particular lot.

15. The first paragraph of §30, inserted by St. 1961, c. 448, §1, reads as follows:

No restriction shall in any proceeding be enforced or declared to be enforceable, . . . unless it is determined that the restriction is at the time of the proceeding of actual and substantial benefit to a person claiming rights of enforcement. No restriction determined to be of such benefit shall be enforced or declared to be

B. The Attitude of the Judiciary

their counsel. Following the view and the taking of evidence the judge found that the fifteen-foot height restriction is of actual and substantial benefit to the plaintiffs and that none of the factors listed in §30 precludes the enforcement of that restriction in equity.

1. We summarize the subsidiary findings, all of them warranted by the evidence, made by the judge under the first sentence of §30. Lot J-6 slopes from Griffin's Island Road to the top of a hill. The plaintiffs were originally attracted to the lot by its gorgeous view, its size and its seclusion. After purchasing the lot in 1954 they proceeded to construct a house thereon (which did not exceed twelve feet in height) which they moved into in the summer of 1955. They purchased Lot J-15 in 1957. For approximately fifteen years, until the construction of the twenty-six foot high addition to the defendants' house, the plaintiffs could see no house from their property except the defendants' original house (roughly 600 feet distant from the plaintiffs' house), of which they could see only the chimney and a television antenna. The defendants' two-story addition is clearly visible from part of the plaintiffs' house and from other parts of the plaintiffs' property, particularly from Lot J-15. Their view (as determined by the judge's view) has been impaired by the addition. The plaintiffs' privacy has been invaded and lessened by the construction of the addition, and the amenities of their property have been impaired. The judge's ultimate finding was that the restriction is of "actual and substantial benefit" to the plaintiffs. After careful consideration we find ourselves unable to pronounce that finding plainly wrong, either as matter of fact or as matter of law.

2. We concur with the judge's findings that changes in applicable public controls have not reduced materially the need for the height restriction or the likelihood of its accomplishing its original purpose,

---

enforceable, except in appropriate cases by award of money damages, if (1) changes in the character of the properties affected or their neighborhood, in available construction materials or techniques, in access, services or facilities, in applicable public controls of land use or construction, or in any other conditions or circumstances, reduce materially the need for the restriction or the likelihood of the restriction accomplishing its original purposes or render it obsolete or inequitable to enforce except by award of money damages, or (2) conduct of persons from time to time entitled to enforce the restriction has rendered it inequitable to enforce except by award of money damages, or (3) in case of a common scheme the land of the person claiming rights of enforcement is for any reason no longer subject to the restriction or the parcel against which rights of enforcement are claimed is not in a group of parcels still subject to the restriction and appropriate for accomplishment of its purposes, or (4) continuation of the restriction on the parcel against which enforcement is claimed or on parcels remaining in a common scheme with it or subject to like restrictions would impede reasonable use of land for purposes for which it is most suitable, and would tend to impair the growth of the neighborhood or municipality in a manner inconsistent with the public interest or to contribute to deterioration of properties or to result in decadent or substandard areas or blighted open areas, or (5) enforcement, except by award of money damages, is for any other reason inequitable or not in the public interest.

or rendered the restriction obsolete. The combined effects of §§4(b) and (d) and 5(b) of Pub. L. 87-126, 75 Stat. 284, 289-291, and of §§2.3.1(I) and 2.3.4 of the zoning by-law belatedly adopted by the town of Wellfleet in 1966 did not prevent the local authorities (after notice to the Secretary of the Interior) from granting a building permit to the defendants for the construction of the twenty-six foot addition.

3. In 1969 the plaintiffs commenced the construction of an addition to their house, no part of which exceeded fifteen feet in height. Construction of the addition to the defendants' house commenced on or about March 10, 1970. By May 11 it became obvious from the framing and otherwise that a second story was contemplated. On that day one of the plaintiffs orally advised the defendants that their addition might be in violation of certain restrictions. The defendants immediately consulted counsel, who advised them to suspend construction pending a determination of the applicability of any restrictions to the proposed addition. Construction was resumed on or about May 22. On June 16, 1970, the present bill was filed, and a temporary restraining order against further construction was issued on the same day. If the defendants had ceased all construction at that point, the addition could have been closed in and protected from the elements at an approximate total cost of $3,500. Following the filing by the plaintiffs of a petition for contempt for violation of the court's order, some form of agreement (presumably without prejudice) was negotiated between counsel under which the defendants have proceeded to complete the exterior of the addition, which the judge found from his view is now complete except for some interior plastering. It is agreed that it would now cost the defendants approximately $15,000 to alter the addition in such fashion as to comply with the fifteen-foot height restriction. We agree with the judge's findings that the defendants chose to proceed with the addition knowing of the risks involved and that it would not be inequitable to grant specific performance of the restriction.

Notes

1. See Clark, Real Covenants and Other Interests Which "Run with Land" 5 (2d ed. 1947).

> Confusion results from the fact that essentially the same interest may be treated under some circumstances as any one of these things. Thus a formal agreement not to build a store upon Blackacre might be in effect an easement, or a covenant, or an equitable servitude. If, however, it is claimed by prescription it must be treated as an easement; if it is couched in terms of formal promise it cannot, under some authorities, be an easement; and if it is contained in a general neighborhood plan for

B. The Attitude of the Judiciary 683

residential development, it can only be made fully effective as an equitable restriction. It is clear, therefore, that the various interests overlap each other, and that the distinctions between them often break down.

See Norman and Losey, Covenants Running with the Land and Equitable Servitudes: Two Concepts or One?, 21 Hastings L.J. 1319 (1970). See Red Canyon Sheep Co. v. Ickes, 98 F.2d 308, 315 (D.C. Cir. 1938) (difficulty of characterizing rights under the Taylor Grazing Act, cited supra page 33. See Browder, Running Covenants and Public Policy, 77 Mich. L. Rev. 12 (1978); Reichman, Towards a Unified Concept of Servitudes, 55 S. Cal. L. Rev. 1175 (1982); French, Towards a Modern Law of Servitudes, 55 S. Cal. L. Rev. 1261 (1982); Berger, Some Reflections on a Unified Law of Servitudes, 55 S. Cal. L. Rev. 1323 (1982).

2. X owned land on which were located an oak flooring plant and a sawmill power plant from which came steam to heat kilns in the oak flooring plant. In 1947, X executed a mortgage to M, conveying as security the oak flooring plant only. The mortgage contained a covenant by X, his heirs and assigns that in the event of foreclosure, he would furnish at cost sufficient steam power to operate the plant. Subsequently X defaulted, and M foreclosed. The adjacent tract on which the sawmill was situated was mortgaged to Y; Y foreclosed, and leased the property to T.

M now demands that steam power be furnished in accordance with the agreement. Argue the case for T. See Nordin v. May, 188 F.2d 411 (8th Cir. 1951); 208 F.2d 131 (8th Cir. 1953). See also Baker v. Lunde, 96 Conn. 530, 114 A. 673 (1921).

3. While adopting the Development Agreements statute (supra page 618), California lawmakers added article 2.7 in 1985, ch. 996 (codified at Cal. Govt. Code §§65870-75 (West 1987 Supp.)). Section 65871 reads in part:

> (a) In addition to any other method for the creation of an easement, an easement may be created pursuant to an ordinance adopted implementing this article, by a recorded covenant of easement made by an owner of real property to the city or county. An easement created pursuant to this article may be for parking, ingress, egress, emergency access, light and air access, landscaping, or open-space purposes.
>
> (b) At the time of recording of the covenant of easement, all the real property benefited or burdened by the covenant shall be in common ownership. . . .
>
> (c) A covenant of easement recorded pursuant to this section shall describe the real property to be subject to the easement and the real property to be benefited thereby. The covenant of easement shall also identify the approval, permit, or designation granted which relied upon or required the covenant.

(d) A covenant executed pursuant to this section shall be enforceable by the successors in interest to the real property benefited by the covenant.

4. London County Council v. Allen, [1914] 3 K.B. 642, 673: "I regard it as very regrettable that a public body should be prevented from enforcing a restriction on the use of property . . . by the apparently immaterial circumstance that the public body does not own any land in the immediate neighbourhood." Parliament agreed. Housing Act, 1925, 15 Geo. 5, ch. 14, §110. See Jennings, Courts and Administrative Law — The Experience of English Housing Legislation, 49 Harv. L. Rev. 426 (1936). Cf. Kelly v. Barrett, [1942] 2 Ch. 379 (benefit annexed to easement of way); Van Sant v. Rose, 260 Ill. 401, 407, 103 N.E. 194, 196 (1913) ("It would seem inconsistent . . . to say, as the covenantees had no other land in the neighborhood, they had no interest in the performance of the covenants. The only purpose their having other land in the vicinity could serve would be to show that they would be injuriously affected."). For other views of "easements in gross," see Loch Sheldrake Associates v. Evans, 306 N.Y. 297, 118 N.E.2d 444 (1954); Pratte v. Balatsos, 99 N.H. 430, 113 A.2d 492 (1955).

Notes on Enforcement and Administration

1. Who, in the case of a large subdivision, should be appropriately entrusted with the administration of the common plan? Increasingly the choice has turned toward the community association. This raises questions of enforcement by a person who does not have an interest in the land, and the preemption by the association of all enforcement rights so as to foreclose individual suits. Operations of the association should be compared with those of a city council, for in effect it frequently becomes government by contract. Do some kinds of private property rights become the equivalent of the right to govern — and, therefore, subject to constitutional limitations? Are there any remedies or coercive techniques unique to a governmental land development agency? The method of enforcement of decision may be the key that distinguishes public from private decision-making.

Neighborhood opinion, local good feeling, and moral suasion are all part of the enforcement of plans; much can be done short of legal proceedings. The Declaration of Restrictions for the Diamond Heights Redevelopment provides that in the event of a breach "it shall be the duty of the Redevelopment Agency to endeavor immediately to remedy such breach by conference, consultation, and persuasion." See also Note, 1950 Wis. L. Rev. 709, 710-711.

In the first twenty years of architectural control at Radburn, only one restriction resulted in a lawsuit. Ascher, Private Covenants in Urban

B. The Attitude of the Judiciary

Redevelopment, in Urban Redevelopment: Problems and Practices 294 (Woodbury ed. 1953). Should there be a division of function between plan approval and enforcement?

2. In Van Deusen v. Ruth, 343 Mo. 1096, 1100, 125 S.W.2d 1, 2 (1938), the agreement provided that "all or any of the foregoing . . . restrictions may be modified, amended, released or extinguished" by owners of 75 percent of the frontage involved. An attempt to exclude apartment houses, originally allowed in the subdivision, was held not within this language. Cf. Lehmann v. Revell, 354 Ill. 262, 188 N.E. 531 (1933). See Bessette v. Guarino, 128 A.2d 839 (R.I. 1957) (restrictions to remain in effect for eleven and one-half years, then subject to change but only with consent of two-thirds of lot owners).

3. In 1925, Block 148, which includes the parcels of property owned by plaintiffs and defendants, was developed according to a declared scheme. Restrictions provided that a portion in the rear of each lot be dedicated to the common use of all the property owners on the block, thereby forming a central court. Fences were prohibited. The declaration recites that the pertinent covenants, restrictions, and easements expire on January 1, 1965; it contains no provision for an extension. In March 1965, 62 out of 73 of the then owners of parcels on the block executed an agreement, duly recorded, providing for an extension of the covenants, restrictions, and easements contained in the 1925 declaration. Defendant has erected a fence upon his parcel, obstructing the central court and its use in common, and insists that he need not abide by the 1965 agreement, which he refused to sign. What result? The court in Brandwein v. Serrano, 72 Misc. 2d 95, 338 N.Y.S.2d 192 (1972), held that landowners who did not consent to the imposition of the restrictions are not bound by them and cannot be enjoined.

4. Under article XV of the Palos Verdes Restrictions, a member has as many votes as building sites he holds. Is this a wise provision? See Green Gables Home Owners Association v. Sunlite Homes, Inc., 202 P.2d 143 (Cal. App. 1949). What should be the method of computation of assessments by the community association? Suppose it is an unincorporated association? The restriction reads: "Such monthly assessment for all lots can be raised from the then current assessment by a majority vote of the owners of any and all lots in Japanese Gardens at a meeting of lot owners." Owners seek an injunction against a raise in their assessments because the developer has retained the majority of lots and thus can raise their assessments by "the plenary power of his sole vote." What result? In Japanese Gardens Mobile Estates v. Hunt, 261 So. 2d 193 (Fla. 1972), the court held that under deed restrictions recorded by the developer of a mobile home park, which provided for monthly assessments to defray costs of maintenance, such assessments could be raised by a majority vote of the owners of any and all lots. See also infra page 1075.

5. "Paragraph 17 of the instruments imposing restrictions provides, with minor variations among the several instruments, as follows: 'The Van Sweringen Company reserves the right to waive, change or cancel any and all of the restrictions contained in this instrument or in any other instrument given by the Van Sweringen Company in respect to lots or parcels within the Van Sweringen Company's subdivisions, or elsewhere *if, in its judgment, the development or lack of development warrants the same or if, in its judgment, the ends or purposes of said subdivisions would be better served. . . .*' (Emphasis added.)

"Paragraph 18 of those instruments provides: 'The herein enumerated restrictions, rights, reservations, limitations, agreements, covenants and conditions shall be deemed as covenants and not as conditions hereof, and shall run with the land, and shall bind the owner until the first day of May, 2026, in any event, and continuously thereafter, unless and until any proposed change shall have been approved in writing by *the owners of the legal title to all the land on both sides of the highway within the block in which is located the property,* the use of which is sought to be altered by said proposed change.' (Emphasis added.)"

The developer proposes to build a shopping center on an eighty-acre parcel within the originally restricted residential neighborhood where homes are valued at from $40,000 and $90,000. Plaintiffs, adjacent landowners, bring suit seeking a permanent injunction. See Berger v. The Van Sweringen Co., 6 Ohio St. 2d 100, 216 N.E.2d 54 (1966), in which the court held for the plaintiffs. The development company's reservation of the right to waive, change, or cancel restrictions under certain circumstances in permitting use of land for shopping center was an abuse of discretion.

6. Evaluate the following statement: "[Deed restrictions] are an individualistic approach to the problem of preserving a desired condition for a limited time in a limited area. They lack the compulsion of a public law enforced by public officials who may impose a rigid pattern of integrated supervision upon everyone concerned." Reeve, Recent Developments in the Law of Property, The Metropolis in Modern Life 188 (Fisher ed. 1955). For a defense of the value of restrictive covenants as compared to public zoning, see Siegan, Land Use Without Zoning (1972), and Ellickson, Alternatives to Zoning: Covenants, Nuisance Rules and Fines as Land Use Controls, 40 U. Chi. L. Rev. 681 (1973), both excerpted supra. For a discussion of the use of covenants in urban planning in France and Belgium, see McCarthy, The Enforcement of Restrictive Covenants in France and Belgium: Judicial Discretion and Urban Planning, 73 Colum. L. Rev. 1 (1973).

7. Consider the following statute, assigning certain local governments the power to enforce ostensibly private restrictions:

> Section 1. This Act applies to incorporated cities, towns, or villages

C. The Official Map Technique

if the incorporated city, town, or village does not have zoning ordinances and provided the city, town, or village passes an ordinance that requires uniform application and enforcement of this statute to all property and citizens.

Section 2. (a) An incorporated city, town, or village may sue in any court of competent jurisdiction to enjoin or abate violation of a restriction contained or incorporated by reference in a duly recorded plan, plat, replat, or other instrument affecting a subdivision inside its boundaries.

(b) As used in this Act, "restriction" means a limitation which affects the use to which real property may be put, fixes the distance buildings or structures must be set back from property lines, street lines, or lot lines, or affects the size of a lot or the size, type, and number of buildings or structures which may be built on the property.

Tex. Rev. Civ. Stat. Ann. art. 974a-1 (Vernon Supp. 1987). "In enacting this law the state was acting as a neutral governmental arbitrator to resolve conflicts between citizens. It provides a method for orderly settlement of potential disputes between its citizens by court action." City of Houston v. Walker, 615 S.W.2d 831, 835 (Tex. Civ. App. 1981). See also City of Houston v. Waggoner, 666 S.W.2d 602 (Tex. Ct. App. 1984) (statute does not authorize city to defend deed restriction, or represent lot owners, against legal attack). The current version of this statute, slightly revised, appears at Tex. Local Govt. Code Ann. §§230.001-.004 (Vernon 1988).

Does this statutory scheme present a more effective mode of enforcement, or do you perceive constitutional (improper delegation of public power), political (selective enforcement), and practical (drain on public coffers) problems? See Elliott, Municipal Enforcement of Private Restrictive Covenants, Land Use L. & Zoning Dig., June 1986, at 3, 5-8.

C. THE OFFICIAL MAP TECHNIQUE: THE "DEAD HAND" OF THE FUTURE

■ HEADLEY v. CITY OF ROCHESTER
272 N.Y. 197, 5 N.E.2d 198 (1936)

LEHMAN, Judge. The plaintiff since 1918 has been the owner of premises in the city of Rochester which are bounded on the south by East avenue and on the west by North Goodman street. East avenue and North Goodman street have been, for more than 20 years, public streets or highways. In 1931, pursuant to article 3 of the General City Law (Consol. Laws, c. 21), the council of the city of Rochester passed an ordinance which amended, changed, and added to an official map or plan previously adopted by the council "so as to correct and revise said established Official Map or Plan and to lay out new streets and highways and to widen existing highways." In that map or plan the southerly 25 feet of plaintiff's said premises are included in East avenue, as widened, and a strip of plaintiff's premises extending along its westerly edge is included in North Goodman street, as widened. The plaintiff has brought an action to obtain a judgment declaring "that the ordinance and map and plan adopted by the said City of Rochester as aforesaid is unconstitutional and void." At Special Term the complaint was dismissed. The Appellate Division reversed and granted judgment "declaring that the ordinance, map and plan herein involved, are void and ineffectual to create any limitations or restrictions upon the use or conveyance of plaintiff's property."

By chapter 690 of the Laws of 1926, the Legislature added article 3, entitled "Official Maps and Planning Boards," to the General City Law. That article empowers the legislative body of every city to establish an official map or plan of the city showing the streets, highways, and parts theretofore laid out and established by law. Section 26. It empowers such legislative body "whenever and as often as it may deem it for the public interest, to change or add to the official map or plan of the city so as to lay out new streets, highways or parks, or to widen or close existing streets, highways, or parks." Section 29. It further empowers the legislative body of the city to create a planning board of five members, and it requires that, before making any addition or change in an official map in accordance with section 29 "the matter shall be referred to the planning board for report thereon." The planning board is given "power and authority to make such investigations, maps and reports and recommendations in connection therewith relating to the planning and development of the city as to it seems desirable." Section 31.

The adoption or revision of a general map pursuant to the provisions of the General City Law does not have the effect of divesting the title of the owner of land in the bed of a street as shown on the map; it does not have the effect of placing upon the city a duty to begin, presently, condemnation proceedings to acquire such land. Article 3 of the statute provides the machinery for intelligent planning in advance for the needs of the city as the city is expected to grow in the future. Only time can prove whether the city has wisely gauged the future, and the city is under no compulsion to open any street shown on the map unless and until the legislative body of the city decides that it is actually needed.

The mere adoption of a general plan or map showing streets and parks to be laid out or widened in the future, without acquisition by the city of title to the land in the bed of the street, can be of little

C. The Official Map Technique 689

benefit to the public if the development of the land abutting upon and in the bed of the proposed streets proceeds in a haphazard way, without taking into account the general plan adopted and, especially, if permanent buildings are erected on the land in the bed of the proposed street which would hamper its acquisition or use for its intended purpose. So long as the owners of parcels of land which lie partly in the bed of streets shown on such a map are free to place permanent buildings in the bed of a proposed street and to provide private ways and approaches which have no relation to the proposed system of public streets, the integrity of the plan may be destroyed by the haphazard or even malicious development of one parcel or tract to the injury of other owners who may have developed their own tracts in a manner which conforms to the general map or plan.

A statutory requirement that a city must acquire title to the land in the bed of the streets shown on the general map or plan, and provide compensation for the land taken, would create practical difficulties which would drastically limit, if, indeed, they did not render illusory, any power conferred upon the city to adopt a general map or plan which will make provision for streets which will be needed only if present anticipations of the future development of the city are realized. On the other hand, to leave the land in private ownership, and, without compensation to the owner, incumber it with restrictions upon its use which would result in diminution in its value, might be inequitable and perhaps even beyond the power of the state. To meet the difficulty, the Legislature has provided in section 35 of the General City Law that,

> for the purpose of preserving the integrity of such official map or plan no permit shall hereafter be issued for any building in the bed of any street or highway shown or laid out on such map or plan, provided, however, that if the land within such mapped street or highway is not yielding a fair return on its value to the owner, the board of appeals or other similar board in any city which has established such a board having power to make variances or exception in zoning regulations shall have power in a specific case . . . to grant a permit for a building in such street or highway which will as little as practicable increase the cost of opening such street or highway, or tend to cause a change of such official map or plan, and such board may impose reasonable requirements as a condition of granting such permit, which requirements shall inure to the benefit of the city.

The sole complaint of the plaintiff is that, so long as that section remains in force, the effect of the ordinance adopted by the city is to restrict the use to which the plaintiff may put his land in the bed of the street, and to that extent constitutes a taking of his property, and that, since the city is not required to pay any compensation to him unless or until at some time in the indefinite future it may choose to take title to the land, the effect of the ordinance is to deprive him of his property without due process of law....

... Though the section has been on the statute books since 1926, its validity has not been challenged in any other case in this court. It is perhaps not without significance that during these years no owner has claimed that the statute has actually interfered with his enjoyment of the land, or has prevented him from obtaining a permit to improve the land in a manner which he deemed desirable.

The plaintiff in this case, too, makes no such claim. The complaint alleges only the conclusion of the pleader that, by reason of the filing of the ordinance and map or plan, "the plaintiff has been, and is, deprived of his property without the payment of compensation therefor." The complaint is silent as to how the plaintiff is injured by the ordinance and the map. The stipulation of facts upon which the case was submitted for decision again fails to indicate in what manner the ordinance has caused damage to the plaintiff or interferes with any use to which the plaintiff desires to put the land. On the contrary, it appears from the stipulated facts that "the plaintiff has at present no plans for the use of said premises nor any particular desire as to the purposes for which he expects to use the same" and "that the plaintiff, because of the claim of the defendant under said ordinance and map, is undecided as to whether he shall endeavor to build upon said premises or endeavor to sell the same."...

... If without building upon the strips of his land which may in the future be included in the widened streets, the plaintiff's property cannot be developed in the manner which the plaintiff desires or which would best conduce to the enjoyment or profit which an owner might derive from his land, and, if it were shown that the statute, if valid, would require or even justify a denial of a permit for such development, the adoption of the map might constitute a grievance. In the absence of proof of such facts, it is difficult to see how the plaintiff has been deprived in any manner of the use of his property. Before the court should even consider the question of whether the Legislature could under the police power restrict, without compensation, the use of land in private ownership, there should be proof at least that the statute is in some manner interfering with or diminishing the value of the present property rights of the person complaining. Compare in this respect the allegations contained in the complaint upon which the Supreme Court of the United States based its jurisdiction to consider such question in Village of Euclid, Ohio, v. Ambler Realty Co., 272 U.S. 365, 368, 374....

The opinion of the Appellate Division leans heavily upon Forster v. Scott, 136 N.Y. 577, 32 N.E. 976, as authority for its decision. The analogy between the cases is quite illusory and the principles here involved are not touched by that case. There the city of New York, in

C. The Official Map Technique 691

accordance with the provisions of chapter 681 of the Laws of 1886, filed a map of a proposed street or avenue which as the court pointed out "covers the entire lot" of the plaintiff. The statute provided that "no compensation shall be allowed for any building, erection or construction which at any time, subsequent to the filing of the maps, plans, or profiles mentioned in section six hundred and seventy-two of the act, may be built, erected or placed in part or in whole upon or through any street, avenue, road, public square or place exhibited upon such maps, plans or profiles." 136 N.Y. 577, at page 582, 32 N.E. 976. The plaintiff made a contract to sell his land to the defendant. He agreed to convey a good title to the land "in fee simple, free from any lien or incumbrance." The defendant refused the title, claiming that the filing of the map created an incumbrance upon the property. The validity of the title was submitted to the court upon stipulated facts. It appeared from them that no building was erected on the plaintiff's land and

> the same is a vacant lot which derives almost its entire value from the possibility of being used for building purposes. If the lot cannot now be built upon without the house being destroyed, without compensation in the event of the street being opened as prescribed by the statutes above set forth, the lot is not worth what defendant agreed to pay, whereas if it can be used for building purposes it is worth at least $5,000.

In other words, the statute purported to give the city the right at some indefinite time in the future to appropriate the land of the plaintiff shown on the map without paying for it the value it would then have if, pending such appropriation, its owner chose to improve it for the only purpose for which it had substantial value.

The court there said: "An incumbrance is said to import every right to or interest in the land, which may subsist in another, to the diminution of the value of the land, but consistent with the power to pass the fee by a conveyance." 136 N.Y. 577, at page 582, 32 N.E. 976, 977. . . . If the statute was valid, the land "could not be used for building purposes, except at the risk to the owner of losing the cost of the building at some time in the future." 136 N.Y. 577, at page 583, 32 N.E. 976, 977. . . . The value of the land was derived from its availability for building purposes, and that value would be drastically reduced if the owner could not obtain compensation for the improvements put upon the land. Since these facts were stipulated, it could hardly be doubted that the statute attempted to create a public right or interest in the land which diminished its value and would, therefore, constitute an incumbrance as defined by the court. Then, in an action between vendor and vendee under a contract of sale, the court was bound to pass upon the validity of the statute.

Every element which led the court to find in the case that the filing of the map, in accordance with the statute there challenged, created, if the statute were valid, an incumbrance upon the property, is wanting in the case now under review. The statute here does not purport to give to the city the right to appropriate the plaintiff's land or any part of it for less than the full value of the lands with the improvements thereon erected at the time of such appropriation. The only restrictions upon the use of any part of the plaintiff's land while title thereto remains in the plaintiff result indirectly from the conditions which the statute attaches to the grant thereafter of a permit to erect a building upon the small portion of plaintiff's land, which, as shown on the map, will lie in the bed of the street on which the plaintiff's land abuts, if or when at some time in the future the city may desire to carry out its intention to widen the street. Since it is affirmatively shown that the plaintiff has no plans at present for the use of the premises, it seems plain that what this court said and decided in the case of Forster v. Scott, supra, cannot possibly be regarded as any precedent for the grant of a judgment declaring the statute invalid, unless from the facts here presented the court as matter of law would be constrained to draw the inference that the conditions which the Legislature has sought to impose upon the grant of a permit for the use of a small part of plaintiff's land creates a limitation upon its use "to the diminution of the value of the land."

No inference of law, indeed no inference of fact, that the attempted condition has affected or will affect the use to which the plaintiff's land will be put or has diminished the value of the land, may be drawn from the stipulated facts. There is no suggestion that a plot of 19,000 square feet cannot be suitably improved and put to the most profitable use by the erection of a building which does not encroach upon the small portions which may be used hereafter to widen the street. Sometimes landowners in a particular district assume mutual obligations to set back buildings some distance from the streets. Sometimes such obligations are imposed by zoning ordinance. Sometimes an owner does so voluntarily because he believes that such a setback is the best use for the land immediately abutting on the street. The plaintiff or any successor in title to the property could use the land within the bed of the widened street for such purpose even without a permit. It may be the best use to which that land could be put, even if no map had been adopted, and there were no probability that the city would in time widen the street. Certainly it cannot be said that owners of property do not receive any benefit from the adoption of general maps or plans for the development of city streets, if they can develop their land with some assurance that other owners will not be permitted to frustrate the plan, maliciously or unreasonably. Whether the state may impose conditions for the issuance of permits in order to protect the integrity of the plan of a city where it appears that such conditions interfere with a reasonable use to which the land would otherwise be put or diminishes the value of the land should not now be decided. Without proof that the imposition of such conditions has deprived an owner of land of some benefit he would otherwise derive from the land, there can be no deprivation of property for which compensation should be made.

Solicitude for the protection of the rights of private property against encroachment by government for a supposed public benefit does not justify the courts in declaring invalid a public law which serves a public purpose, because 10 years after it has been on the statute books a single owner, without proof, or even claim, of actual injury, asserts that he has been deprived of his property.

The judgment of the Appellate Division should be reversed and that of the Special Term affirmed, with costs in this court and in the Appellate Division.[42]

Notes

1. Is Judge Lehman's reasoning consistent with his opinion in the *Arverne Bay* case, supra page 195?

2. See §9 of the Restriction of Ribbon Development Act, 1935, 25 & 26 Geo. 5, ch. 47 (preventing owner from making an improvement, "which is immediately practicable and for which there is a demand"). Is there any difference in the treatment of an owner when his land is regarded as a source of annual income, rather than a salable item in the commercial land market? Cf. Platt v. City of New York, 196 Misc. 360, 92 N.Y.S.2d 138 (Sup. Ct. 1949). See also Collier, Compensation and the County of Cumberland Plan §160 (permitting claim for compensation for prohibiting building in beds of proposed new roads), and ch. 6 (parks, recreation, and foreshore reserves) (1952).

3. In a concurring memorandum in Petterson v. Radspi Realty and Coal Corp., 265 App. Div. 824, 37 N.Y.S.2d 841, 842 (2d Dept. 1942), Lazansky, P. J., stated, "Section 35 is unconstitutional." The *Headley* case "is not to the contrary, although it casts a shadow in that direction." Do you agree? And for a later case holding unconstitutional an application of the official map procedures of §35, see Roer Construction Corp. v. City of New Rochelle, 207 Misc. 46, 136 N.Y.S.2d 414 (Sup. Ct. 1954). In Rand v. City of New York, 3 Misc. 2d 769, 155

---

42. Cf. Grosso v. Board of Adjustment of Millburn Township, 137 N.J.L. 630, 633, 61 A.2d 167, 169 (1948) ("It was plainly not open to the defendant municipality, in the exercise of the planning power, to dedicate the locus to highway uses on the 'official map' and thereby deprive the landowner of all use thereof, without making compensation, until the municipality was prepared to lay out the street. That would constitute a palpable deprivation of the property without due process of law"). But see N.J. Stat. Ann. §40:55-1.38 (Supp. 1957), which was repealed in L.1975, ch. 291, §800, eff. Aug. 1, 1976. — EDS.

N.Y.S.2d 753 (Sup. Ct. 1956), the board of appeals granted the plaintiff a permit to build a garage in the bed of a proposed street, on condition that the cost be amortized over ten years, in the event of future condemnation. The useful life of the garage is fifty years. Without instituting certiorari to review this determination, the plaintiff successfully brought an action for declaratory relief. Cf. Vangellow v. City of Rochester, 190 Misc. 128, 71 N.Y.S.2d 672 (Sup. Ct. 1947) (official map not void; board of appeals retains jurisdiction over some issues).[43]

4. In Jensen v. City of New York, 42 N.Y.2d 1079, 369 N.E.2d 1179, 399 N.Y.S.2d 645 (1977), plaintiff, an aged widow, complained that her property was included in the city's official street map and that she was therefore prohibited from obtaining a building permit. As a matter of fact, she had no reason to seek such a permit, desiring only to sell the premises or to make badly needed repairs. The court held that the inclusion deprived her of the use of her property without due process of law and declared the official map void. Judge Cooke, dissenting, argued that mere plotting in anticipation of a public improvement does not constitute a taking, citing the *Headley* case:

> The net result would be no different if a municipality envisioned plans on a wider scale, not to encompass a major portion of a single parcel or even a few parcels, but to envelop an entire neighborhood. Surely, the vagaries of changing needs, public attitudes and economic conditions could visit substantial delay upon the proposed project, but even the impending impact of the cloud cast upon the neighborhood's future would not in itself entitle a single owner to a declaration of the plan's unconstitutionality as to him.

---

43. See also State ex rel. Miller v. Manders, 2 Wis. 2d 365, 86 N.W.2d 469 (1957); Kucirek and Beuscher, Wisconsin's Official Map Law, 1957 Wis. L. Rev. 176.

Interestingly, the preservation of street sites was a factor in the planning of Washington in the 1790s. L'Enfant tore down a house built by a Mr. Carroll on a site proposed for "five grand fountains" with "constant spout of water." The demolition was completed just prior to the issuing of an injunction. A legal opinion by Jefferson apparently sealed the fate of L'Enfant, who soon thereafter resigned his job as planner for Washington. Jefferson wrote:

> The plan of the city has not yet been definitely determined by the President. . . . A deed with the whole plan annexed, executed by the President, and recorded, will ultimately fix it. But till a sale, or partition, or deed, it is open to alteration. Consequently, there is as yet no such thing as a street, except adjacent to the lots actually sold or divided; the erection of a house in any part of the ground cannot as yet be a nuisance in law. Mr. Carroll is tenant in common of the soil with the public, and the erection of a house by a tenant in common on the common property, is no nuisance. Mr. Carroll has acted imprudently, intemperately, foolishly; but he has not acted illegally. There must be an establishment of the streets, before his house can become a nuisance in the eye of the law. Therefore, till that establishment, neither Major L'Enfant, nor the commissioners, would have had a right to demolish his house, without his consent.

Thomas Jefferson and the National Capital 82 (Padover ed. 1946).

C. The Official Map Technique

See also Howard County v. JJM, Inc., 301 Md. 256, 482 A.2d 908 (1984) (statute requiring reservation of state road right-of-way in subdivision unconstitutional); Ventures in Property I v. City of Wichita, 225 Kan. 698, 594 P.2d 671 (1979) (inverse condemnation found for developer that was declined flat plat approval owing to contemplated highway).

5. In Miller v. City of Beaver Falls, 368 Pa. 189, 82 A.2d 34 (1951), Justice Bell expounded:

> The question raised is a very important one. Planning the future development or the building of a City Utilitarian and Beautiful, for present and future generations, has become the fashion of the day. There is no doubt that parks have a beneficial effect on public health and public welfare and their establishment and maintenance is certainly desirable. . . .
>
> Shall this principle relating to streets, which are narrow, well defined and absolutely necessary, be extended to parks and playgrounds which may be very large and very desirable but not necessary? The injustice to property owners of permitting a municipal body to tie up an owner's property for three years must be apparent to every one. The city can change its mind and abandon or refuse to take the property at the end of three years; but in the meantime the owner has been, to all intents and purposes, deprived of his property and its use and the land is practically unsalable. He cannot build thereon because if he does the law is clear that he cannot recover damages for the loss of any building erected within the plotted line.
>
> The action of the City of Beaver Falls in plotting this ground for a park or playground and freezing it for three years is, in reality, a taking of property by possibility, contingency, blockade and subterfuge, in violation of the clear mandate of our Constitution that property cannot be taken or injured or applied to public use without just compensation having been first made and secured. The contention of the City in this case, if adopted, would make a travesty of the constitutional provisions protecting rights of property.

6. It is curious to note that the Pennsylvania court in Forbes Street, 70 Pa. 125 (1871), relied on the New York case of In re Furman Street, 17 Wend. 649 (N.Y. 1836), for validating mapped street legislation. It did so without noticing the ground on which the New York court based its decision (no provision in the New York Constitution requiring that just compensation be given for property taken from a private owner) nor the subsequent New York decisions (e.g., Forster v. Scott, 136 N.Y. 577, 32 N.E. 976 (1893)) coming to a different conclusion under the later New York Constitution.

The engineer for the Philadelphia Board of Surveyors stated that not once during his service did he observe a case of uncompensated damage or hardship to property because of the mapped street laws. Black, Building Lines and Reservations for Future Streets 123-124 (1935).

D. LIMITATIONS ON LOCAL DISCRETION

The great American selling of the continent has long been a feature of land law.[44] In the past decades, there have been several national scandals involving fraudulent promotions and sales of land, scandals so dramatic that state legislative activity in this area has increased dramatically. Buyers for properties located in such attractive locales as Arizona, California, Colorado, Florida, and New Mexico, for example, are lured from across the country and over the seas.[45]

The sales pitch utilized in raw land promotions is questionable at best, immoral and illegal at worst. Government officials have responded primarily along two lines: more stringent control over the subdivision of property, and full disclosure requirements under state or federal law. Currently, the majority of the states have legislation establishing guidelines for the promotional sale of real estate. However, the degree of regulation and the substantive laws themselves vary greatly from state to state.

The Uniform Law Commissioners offered a Model Land Sales Practice Act, seeking to place individual purchasers of large-scale promotional land offerings on an equal bargaining basis with the

---

44. See Schnidman, So You Think You Have Problems? Antiquated Subdivisions in Florida, in Antiquated Subdivisions: Beyond Lot Mergers and Vested Rights 63, 65 (Glickfeld ed. 1984) (Lincoln Institute of Land Policy Conference Proceedings):

In California, there are almost one million lots in 1,557 subdivisions on file with the U.S. Department of Housing and Urban Development's Office of Interstate Land Sales Registration (OILSR). These subdivisions total 695,000 acres. In contrast, Florida has almost two million lots in 2,063 subdivisions, covering close to 1.5 million acres. Further, Florida has 145 active subdivisions of over 1,000 acres, while California has only 75. And seven of Florida's subdivisions are over 50,000 acres.

A further problem for Florida is that laws aimed at consumer protection prevented the California-type "paper subdivision." Roads and drainage canals were required by the state before property could be registered for sale. The result . . . is massive acreage committed to development prior to any home building:

Subdivisions

State	All Types	O-Types	O-Types Over 1,000 Acres	Lots	Acres
Florida	2,063	704	145	1,981,133	1,438,943
California	1,557	455	75	951,593	694,339

The figures used are based on the OILSR Catalogue Report. O-Type subdivisions are defined as "active projects offering 25 lots or more for sale on the interstate market which must submit a full statement of record and property report to OILSR."

45. The mood of the real estate boom — this time the Florida bubble of the early twenties — was captured most graphically by Alva Johnston, who defined "vision" as "a gift that enabled an observer to mistake spots before the eyes for magnificent cities." He describes how "experienced hell-fire preachers were found to be among the best sales-talk artists, and the Bible Belt was combed for them," and tells of lawyers working all night long "and drinking gallons of black coffee in an effort to keep up with their real-estate business." The Legendary Mizners 274, 276-277 (1953).

D. Limitations on Local Discretion

promoter-seller. This is achieved by the imposition of stringent examination requirements on the promotional offering to ensure full and fair disclosure, so that unencumbered legal title is conveyed to the purchaser and sufficient safeguards are provided to assure that the seller will complete promised offsite improvements of the land. Thus far, the Model Act has been adopted in ten states.

The looming federal presence[46] became an actuality in 1971. The problem of interstate sales of land had become so blatant that the Federal Trade Commission initiated action against GAC Corporation. The full implications of the FTC action began to emerge in the Interstate Land Sales Full Disclosure Act, passed by Congress in 1968 to deal with the problem which the FTC finally confronted in 1971 with its complaint against GAC. The original draft of the act placed responsibility for administration and enforcement with the Securities and Exchange Commission; however, industry pressures succeeded in moving this responsibility to HUD.

■ INTERSTATE LAND SALES FULL DISCLOSURE ACT
15 U.S.C. §1701 et seq. (1982)

§1703. (a) It shall be unlawful for any developer or agent, directly or indirectly, to make use of any means or instruments of transportation or communication in interstate commerce, or of the mails —

(1) with respect to the sale or lease of any lot not exempt under section 1702 of this title —

(A) to sell or lease any lot unless a statement of record with respect to such lot is in effect in accordance with section 1706 of this title;

(B) to sell or lease any lot unless a printed property report, meeting the requirements of section 1707 of this title, has been furnished to the purchaser or lessee in advance of the signing of any contract or agreement by such purchaser or lessee;

(C) to sell or lease any lot where any part of the statement of record or the property report contained an untrue statement of a material fact or omitted to state a material fact required to be stated therein pursuant to sections 1704 through 1707 of this title or any regulations thereunder; or

---

46. There had been foreshadowings in FTC v. R. F. Keppel & Bros. Inc., 291 U.S. 304 (1934): "It is unnecessary to attempt comprehensive definition of the unfair methods which are banned . . . New or different practices must be considered as they arise in the light of the circumstances in which they are employed." See also FTC v. Sperry and Hutchinson Co., 405 U.S. 232 (1972); Whitney, Standing and Remedies Available to the Department of HUD under the ILSFDA, 6 Geo. Mason U.L. Rev. 171 (1983).

(D) to display or deliver to prospective purchasers or lessees advertising and promotional material which is inconsistent with information required to be disclosed in the property report; or

(2) with respect to the sale or lease, or offer to sell or lease, any lot not exempt under section 1702(a) of this title —

(A) to employ any device, scheme, or artifice to defraud;

(B) to obtain money or property by means of any untrue statement of a material fact, or any omission to state a material fact necessary in order to make the statements made (in light of the circumstances in which they were made and within the context of the overall offer and sale or lease) not misleading, with respect to any information pertinent to the lot or subdivision;

(C) to engage in any transaction, practice, or course of business which operates or would operate as a fraud or deceit upon a purchaser; or

(D) to represent that roads, sewers, water, gas, or electric service, or recreational amenities will be provided or completed by the developer without stipulating in the contract of sale or lease that such services or amenities will be provided or completed.

The day after the FTC-GAC consent agreement was made public, the Office of Interstate Land Sales Regulation (OILSR) announced that GAC had agreed to amend its filings to meet the disclosure requirements established by the agreement, and to notify and offer refunds to purchasers prior to completion of amended filings. Is HUD's role only to assure a full disclosure of the facts to the prospective buyer? Is the FTC's role broader, despite the brevity of §5 of the Federal Trade Commission Act, because it is charged with the responsibility to assure that the acts and practices are not "unfair or deceptive"? Using their combined authority, HUD and FTC have a clear mandate to protect the consumer in transactions involving the interstate sale of raw land, but does this responsibility extend to protection of the environment itself? Consider the position taken by HUD on just that issue in Flint Ridge Dev. Co. v. Scenic Rivers Association of Oklahoma, 426 U.S. 776 (1976) (preparation of environmental impact statement inconsistent with HUD Secretary's duties under Disclosure Act).

Notes

1. Professor Paulson suggests that "when we talk about protecting consumers, we are talking about a lot of people other than land buyers: taxpayers, commuters, legitimate developers, and anybody who values

or benefits from an attractive, orderly environment."[47] How should this broad class be protected? Compare mandatory subdivision regulation requirements (as in Colorado), the state land-use requirements presented infra page 743, §5 of the FTC Act, the Interstate Land Sales Full Disclosure Act, and the National Environmental Protection Act as applied by the court in the *Scenic Rivers* case. Which consumer group does each protect? Which most effectively protects the environment? With which of these must the Sharp Development Company comply if it intends to market a thirty-acre parcel for a shopping center? The same thirty acres for one hundred condominiums and townhouses? As half-acre lots for recreational homes? As an industrial park?

2. Would a legal duty such as a warranty of "merchantability" or "fitness for particular purpose," similar to that which the Uniform Commercial Code established in connection with the sale of goods (§§2-314 to 2-318), provide better protection for the buyer than full disclosure alone does? If a lot is sold as a site for a recreational home should not the lot be "fit for the particular purpose" for which it was purchased? Cf. Schipper v. Levitt & Sons, Inc., 44 N.J. 70, 207 A.2d 314 (1965). See also the FHA warranty requirements, which must be included in the mortgage. 12 U.S.C. §1701j-1(a).

■ FULLER, FREEDOM — A SUGGESTED ANALYSIS
68 Harv. L. Rev. 1305, 1324-1325 (1955)

The great advantage of systems of social order that are built up by the fitting together of many individual decisions is that those decisions have been reached with reference to specific situations of fact. The words of a language, for example, have come into existence because in some particular context people wanted to say something and needed a word to say it with. Words are not created by someone who thinks they might come in handy on some later occasion. . . .

Imagine a newly settled rural community in which it is apparent that sooner or later a path will be worn through a particular woodland. Suppose the community decides to plan the path in advance. There would be definite advantages in this course. Experts could be brought in. A general view of the whole situation could be obtained that would not be available to any individual wayfarer. What would be lacking would be the contribution of countless small decisions by people actually using the path, the decision, for example, of those whose footprints pulled the path slightly to the east so that they might look at a field of

---

47. Paulson, What Should Be Done to Improve Consumer Protection, 33 Urb. Land, July-Aug. 1974, at 24. See also Malloy, The ILSFDA, 24 B.C.L. Rev. 1187 (1983).

daisies, or of those who detoured around a spot generally dry, but unaccountably wet in August.

I hope the figure of the path will not be taken with more seriousness than it is offered. Lest I be accused of romanticizing the problem, I should like to close by relating an actual incident that seems in point.

Through the foresight of the city fathers the Cambridge Common is provided with an elaborate network of paved sidewalks, carefully planned to serve the convenience of any person wishing to traverse the Common from any angle. It was found, however, that at certain points people perversely insisted on walking across the grass. The usual countermeasures were tried, but failed. Now the city is taking down its barriers and its "keep-off-the-grass" signs and is busily engaged in paving the paths cut by trespassing feet. Those who have had experience with the problem of designing forms for the life of the human animal will see here, I believe, a pattern of events that has repeated itself many, many times.

The pressures of growth have heightened our consciousness with respect to the natural landscape, environmental and consumer protection, and diminishing resources. The inevitable result has been legislation on the federal level, mimicked and reshaped by the states. Indeed, beginning in the 1970s, land-use planning law entered another regulatory plane; in contrast to the spirit of deregulation noted supra page 363, calls for "super-regulation" were heard and increasingly heeded in the federal and state capitols.

One of the themes raised by the readings in the next chapter is the centralization of power and responsibility, a far cry from the local controls detailed in Chapter III. Is this Dillon's rule run rampant? Do the constituencies for the environmental movement have different motivations from other growth control advocates? Comprehensive planning has made for strange bedfellows and enemies, politically and judicially. Land-use disputes cause interest groups on the "left" and "right" to reshape their alliances. Environmentalists and planning advocates are often pitted against minority groups eager to share in the American dream of suburban homeownership, as in the debate over locating desperately needed affordable housing within a stone's throw of Thoreau's cherished Walden Pond. Too, large-scale developers and the true believers in the sanctity of private property square off against middle-class suburban whites who are anxious about high-density intrusions. Have such realignments, and the compromises they engender, resulted in coherent, or ineffective, law? Have lawmakers adequately addressed the down side of centralized control — the resentment of local officials, and the inability to relate to the unique concerns and needs of specific towns, cities, or counties?

VI

Protecting the Environment: The "No Choice" Doctrine

In the past two decades, the environmental movement has swept the nation, raising the consciousness of the American public and altering the laws of the land. Congress has acted to regulate air, water, and noise pollution, solid waste management, and the use of herbicides and pesticides; Congress has also moved to protect federal lands, to preserve wildlife, and to protect the seacoast. States have followed with their counterpart environmental statutes. Legislation is voluminous and complex, but the basic thrust is to control the use of resources that economists describe as public goods because of two characteristics: they can be jointly consumed in a manner in which one person's enjoyment does not interfere with another's; and it is difficult to exclude from consumption. See Musgrave & Musgrave, Public Finance in Theory and Practice 51-82 (1973). Traditionally, land has not been considered such a resource; the private property aspects of land use have been paramount. But environmental concerns are altering the public's view; in response, the law itself is changing rapidly as the relationship of land use to the environment becomes increasingly clear.

A. PRESERVING THE HYDROLOGIC CYCLE ("ONLY PRESERVING NATURE FROM DESPOILAGE")

■ FLOOD PLAIN CONSERVATION AND PROTECTION
Zoning Ordinance-Resolution, Fayette Co., Kentucky (1984)

21.4 ESTABLISHMENT OF FLOOD PLAIN ZONING DISTRICTS — The flood hazard areas of Fayette County shall be delineated either as a General Flood Plain District under Section 21.5 or as a Floodway District, and Flood-Fringe District under Section 21.6 and 21.7 depending on the technical information available to define the boundaries of the District. Further all districts are overlay districts, and the requirements of each are in addition to those contained in the underlying zone, such as single-family residential R-1C, or highway business zone B-3.

21.41 Methods Used to Define Flood Hazard Areas

21.411 Soil Survey Method — The Fayette County Soil Survey, conducted by the Soil Conservation Service, U.S. Department of Agriculture, in 1968, is used to define the flood hazard area in terms of a General Flood Plain District. This survey will be utilized primarily for the rural areas outside the Urban Service Area. Since in these rural areas the natural flood plains have not been seriously altered by high intensity development, and since the policy of the County is to prevent intense residential, commercial or industrial development in this area, this survey defines the flood hazard area with sufficient accuracy to protect the flood plains from minor encroachment, and to prevent the location of structures within these areas without unduly restricting the use of such land. This soil survey will also be utilized to define the flood hazard areas within the Urban Service Area until the hydrologic calculations necessary to define these flood hazard areas in terms of a Floodway and Flood-Fringe District are obtained.

21.412 Hydrologic Calculation Method — Hydrologic calculations of the flood hazard area, which will separate the flood hazard area into Floodway and Flood Fringe Districts, are to be used as they become available to regulate development. In calculating the boundaries of the Floodway and Flood-Fringe Districts, the regulatory flood shall be a 100-year frequency flood, and it shall be assumed that the entire drainage area contributing storm water runoff which is deposited in the channel location in question will be developed as the Generalized Land Use Plan suggests. It is intended that hydrologic calculations shall be made as quickly as local and federal funds can be obtained for the necessary engineering surveys, and priorities established for surveys of the major streams in Lexington determined....

21.5 GENERAL FLOOD PLAIN DISTRICT (GFP) — The General Flood Plain District is that portion of the flood hazard area subject to periodic

A. Preserving the Hydrologic Cycle

flooding and delineated by the location of alluvial soils as listed below and defined on the maps and associated data comprising the Soil Survey of Fayette County, 1968. . . .

21.51 Permitted Uses — The following uses having a low flood-damage potential and low obstructive effect upon flood flows shall be permitted within the General Flood Plain District to the extent that they are not prohibited by any other ordinance and provided they do not require structures, fill, obstructive features, or storage of materials or equipment. But no use shall adversely affect the capacity of the channels or floodways or any tributary to the main stream, drainage ditch, or any other drainage facility or system. . . .

[The permitted uses include "[a]gricultural uses," "[u]ses accessory to industrial-commercial uses," "[u]ses accessory to private and public recreational uses," and "[u]ses accessory to residential uses."]

21.52 Special Permit Uses — All uses other than those specified in Section 21.51 are permitted only after issuance of a special permit as provided under Section 21.8, Special Permit Uses. . . .

21.6 FLOODWAY DISTRICT (FW) — The Floodway District is that portion of the flood hazard area determined by the hydraulic calculations as the stream channel and overbank areas which are capable of conveying the regulatory flood discharge, keeping it within designated heights and velocities. The floodway is intended to carry the deeper fast-moving water, and serves as the primary drainageway for conveyance of floodwater.

21.61 Permitted Uses — The uses permitted as a matter of right shall be the same as listed in Section 21.51 for the General Flood Plain District. . . .

21.7 FLOOD-FRINGE DISTRICT (FF) — The Flood-Fringe District is that portion of the flood hazard area beyond the limits of the Floodway District determined by hydrologic calculations to be subject to inundation by the regulatory flood discharge. Floodwaters in this district are usually shallow and slow-moving.

Development in the flood-fringe area tends to remove natural valley storage for floodwaters and increases the flood heights. But these undesirable effects are weighed against the economic losses to landowners and the community if development is prohibited altogether.

As the floodway lines are shifted closer to the channel, flood heights increase and regulatory-flood-fringe limits move outward. The flood-fringe district serves primarily to store floodwaters.

21.71 Permitted Uses — The following uses shall be permitted uses within the Flood-Fringe District to the extent that they are not prohibited by any other ordinance:

21.711 Any use permitted in Section 21.51.

21.712 Structures constructed on fill so that the lowest floor is above the regulatory flood-protection elevation. The fill shall come up to a point no lower than one (1) foot below the regulatory flood-protection elevation for the particular area and shall extend at such elevation at least 15 feet beyond the limits of any structure or building erected thereon. However, no use shall be constructed which will adversely affect the capacity of channels or floodways of any main stream or tributary to the main stream, drainage ditch, or any other drainage facility or system, or will increase the regulatory flood-protection elevation.

■ DOOLEY v. TOWN OF FAIRFIELD
151 Conn. 304, 197 A.2d 770 (1964)

SHEA, Associate Justice.

In February, 1961, the defendant, after notice and hearing, amended the zoning regulations of Fairfield by creating a new zone called flood plain district.* Thereafter, the defendant changed the zonal classification of an area of about 404 acres from residence B to flood plain district. In the first case, the plaintiff, Frank J. Dooley, both owns and is under a contract of May, 1960, to purchase from Catherine A. Nemesky land which is within the area covered by this change of zone. In the second case, the plaintiffs, Thomas J. Carroll, Patrick L. Carroll, Jr., and Frank W. Carroll, are the owners of land included in the same area. Separate appeals from the action of the defendant in changing the zone were taken to the Court of Common Pleas. Subsequently, in May, 1961, the defendant amended the zoning regulations to forbid the excavation, filling and removal of soil, earth or gravel within the flood plain district except under a special exception. Fairfield Zoning Regs. §22.3. Separate appeals from the adoption of this amendment were also taken to the Court of Common Pleas and constitute the third and fourth cases. By agreement, all of these appeals to the Court of Common Pleas were tried together. The court rendered judgments dismissing all of the appeals, and from the judgments the plaintiffs have appealed to us. On stipulation of the parties, the appeals to us have been combined.

All of the land included in the change of zone is in the Pine Creek

---

* [Fairfield Zoning Regs. (1960, as amended)].

Sec. 22.2 PERMITTED USES: In Flood Plain District the following uses only shall be permitted:
Parks, playgrounds, marinas, boat houses, landings and docks, clubhouses and necessary uses.
Wildlife sanctuaries operated by governmental units or non-profit organizations.
Farming, truck and nursery gardening.
Motor vehicle parking as an accessory to a permitted use in this district or an adjacent district.

A. Preserving the Hydrologic Cycle

area of Fairfield. Of the 404 acres in the new flood plain district, the town owns 206 acres, the United States government owns 28 acres, and private parties own the remaining 170 acres. South Pine Creek, a tidal stream with an opening about 100 feet wide on Long Island Sound, runs irregularly inland through a part of the area, and water from the creek has overflowed the surrounding land during abnormally high tides.

In September, 1960, the Fairfield flood and erosion control board, which had been created under authority of what is now §25-84 of the General Statutes, declared the 404 acres a flood plain area. A record of the action of that board, including a map and legal description of the property, was sent to the defendant together with a proposal that the zone of the property be changed to a flood plain district. Thereafter, the defendant took the action of which the plaintiffs now complain.

Prior to the change of zone, the defendant, acting as a planning commission, had denied not less than two applications for approval of a subdivision of the Dooley property. The defendant, as a zoning commission, itself had proposed, in 1960, to upgrade the area which is now in the new flood plain district to R-3 residence. This proposal was opposed by the flood and erosion control board and the health department. From the reasons given by the defendant for changing the zone of the plaintiffs' property, it is evident that the report of the flood and erosion control board had a strong influence in the decision.

The plaintiffs claim that the application of the regulations to their property constitutes the taking of property without compensation and without due process of law in violation of the fifth and fourteenth amendments to the constitution of the United States and in violation of §11 of article first of the Connecticut constitution. . . .

An analysis of the uses permitted under §22.2 of the zoning regulations in a flood plain district clearly demonstrates that the use of the plaintiffs' land has been, for all practical purposes, rendered impossible. First, to restrict the use of privately owned property to parks and playgrounds bars the development of the land for residential or business purposes and raises serious questions as to the constitutionality of the restriction. See Dunham, Flood Control via The Police Power, 107 U. Pa. L. Rev., 1098, 1108. The practical effect of this limitation on use is to restrict potential buyers of the property to town or governmental uses, thus depreciating the value of the property. Second, the property of the plaintiffs is about half a mile from Long Island Sound, and consequently, the property could not be used for a marina, a boathouse or a landing and dock. Third, the Fairfield zoning regulations contain no definition of a clubhouse. Generally, a clubhouse is defined as a house occupied by a club or commonly used for club activities. Webster, Third New International Dictionary. The definition includes fraternity houses, sorority houses and houses of secret societies and social clubs generally. Although the term "clubhouse" may be construed broadly, the presence of one on the plaintiffs' land, considering the acreage involved, would have little effect in preventing a substantial diminution in the value of the land. Fourth, paragraph 2 of §22.2 of the regulations permits the use of the property for wildlife sanctuaries operated by governmental units or nonprofit organizations. Obviously, such a use does not provide the landowner with any reasonable or practical means of obtaining income or a return from his property. Again, this use contemplates a diminution in land value and subsequent acquisition by some governmental agency, either by purchase or by condemnation. Fifth, the regulations also permit farming, truck and nursery gardening. At the public hearing, a real estate expert testified that farming has long since been ruled out in this area. Finally, the regulations also permit motor vehicle parking as an accessory to a permitted use in the flood plain district or an adjacent district. But under §22.3 of the regulations, the land cannot be filled or paved except by special exception granted by the defendant under stringent conditions, and then only for a limited time.

From this analysis of the regulations, it cannot be questioned that the testimony of the plaintiffs' real estate expert is based on sound observation. He stated that these regulations had a very substantial effect on the value of the property, causing a depreciation in value of at least 75 percent.

The plaintiff Dooley is under contract to purchase the Nemesky property for $80,000. Much of that property is on good high ground and was not under water in the 1938 hurricane. The land could be used for houses which would be readily salable in the price range of $15,000 to $17,000 per unit. Some burrowing and filling might be necessary to develop the property for building purposes; such work could be done under the original zonal classification, which permitted the building of one- and two-family residences.

So far as the Carroll land is concerned, a real estate expert stated that it could be used as residential property. Some time before the defendant changed the zone of the Carroll property to flood plain district, the town levied a sewer assessment of over $11,000 against the property. Since the present regulations prohibit any building whatever on the land other than those included within the permitted uses, the sewer system can be utilized for no practical purpose so long as the property is privately owned. Arverne Bay Construction Co. v. Thatcher, 278 N.Y. 222, 232, 15 N.E.2d 587.

There can be no doubt that, from the standpoint of private ownership, the change of zone to flood plain district froze the area into a practically unusable state. The uses which are presently permitted in the new zone place such limitations on the area that the enforcement of the regulation amounts, in effect, to a practical confiscation of the land. Further, although the objective of the Fairfield flood and erosion control board is a laudable one and although we have no reason to doubt the high purpose of their action, these factors cannot overcome constitutional principles. The plaintiffs have been deprived by the change of zone of any worthwhile rights or benefits in their land. Where most of the value of a person's property has to be sacrificed so that community welfare may be served, and where the owner does not directly benefit from the evil avoided (see, e.g., the old smoke nuisance cases such as State v. Hillman, 110 Conn. 92, 147 A. 294), the occasion is appropriate for the exercise of eminent domain. Our statutes empower the flood and erosion control board to purchase or condemn property if it is needed for flood control. General Statutes, §25-86. . . .

We hold that the action of the defendant in changing the zone, so far as it affects the properties of the plaintiffs as described in their complaints, is unreasonable and confiscatory and therefore, as to these properties, is in violation of the fourteenth amendment to the United States constitution and §11 of article first of the constitution of Connecticut. In consequence, the regulations pertaining to the flood plain district can have no application to the plaintiffs' properties. All four appeals should be sustained.

There is error, the judgments are set aside and the cases are remanded with direction to sustain the appeals.[1]

Notes

1. Responding to the growing national problem, Congress passed the National Flood Insurance Act of 1968, based on a philosophy of voluntary participation. Pub. L. No. 90-448, Title XIII, 82 Stat. 572. Any community that took steps to prevent development in the flood hazard areas was eligible for federally subsidized insurance. However, in 1973 Congress amended the Act, giving the Secretary of HUD power to designate Flood Prone Communities, which will be required either to participate in the flood insurance program or to demonstrate that they are not flood hazard areas. 42 U.S.C. §4105(b) (in 1983, the HUD Secretary's functions under the Act were transferred to the Director of the Federal Emergency Management Agency). To participate in the program the community must adopt an adequate flood plain ordinance "with effective enforcement provisions." 42 U.S.C. §4022. The reason

---

1. For further discussion of these issues see Dunham, Flood Control Via the Police Power, 107 U. Pa. L. Rev. 1098 (1959); Buechert, Recent Natural Resource Cases, 4 Nat. Resources J. 445 (1965); Plater, The Taking Issue in a Natural Setting: Floodlines and the Police Power, 52 Tex. L. Rev. 201 (1974); and Tierney, The National Flood Insurance Program, 8 Urb. Law. 279 (1976). — EDS.

for these mandatory requirements was that since 1936 the federal government had spent an estimated $9 billion on flood protection works, in addition to massive amounts for disaster relief, and that despite this expenditure, annual losses from floods continued to increase.

If a court holds that "adequate protection of the flood plain" is a taking, but the Director finds that the level of encroachment — which the courts would require a community to permit in order to avoid the "taking" issue — is not adequate protection, how can the community respond?

2. Why should the state delegate to local government the responsibility for regulation of a problem that has no relationship to jurisdictional boundaries? What recourse does the downstream community have if the upstream community fails to protect the flood plain from encroachment? Why did Congress place the responsibility on the local community and not the states?

3. Are the uses permitted in the Fayette County ordinance, supra, sufficient to avoid classification as a taking as defined by the Connecticut court? Does separation of the flood plain into a floodway and floodfringe based on hydrologic calculations make the regulation more "reasonable"? Is the General Flood Plain District dependent on the subsequent shift to a hydrologic method of distinguishing between the flood-fringe and the floodway to avoid the constitutional challenge raised in *Dooley*?

4. Under the "reasonableness" test, is there a valid distinction between the impact of such a regulation on urban and rural land that would necessitate the use of hydrologic calculation in the urban areas, whereas soil surveys would be adequate in rural areas? If the ordinance is applied to rural farmland, has the property been diminished in value by such a regulation? What activities of the farmer would be inhibited by the ordinance?

5. In limiting the power of the state to regulate the encroachment of private uses into the flood plain, has the court failed to take into account the principle behind the common law doctrine that held a person liable for alteration of the natural flow of surface water from his own land in a manner which harmed his neighbor? Is there a "right" on the part of a riparian owner to alter the flow of water to the detriment of the downstream owners? If a flood plain regulation only protects the natural capacity of the flood plain to safely convey floodwaters downstream, what right is being "taken"?

6. Why does the court in *Dooley* grant relief to the plaintiff when it believes that the board of zoning appeals probably could not legally grant such relief because it "would seriously undermine the legislative purpose of the ordinance"? Does not the court's decision have a much more devastating effect on the policy?

■ DELAWARE WETLANDS ACT
Tit. 7, Ch. 66 (1983)

Sec. 6602. *Purpose.*

It is declared that much of the wetlands of this State have been lost or despoiled by unregulated dredging, filling and like activities and that the remaining wetlands of this State are in jeopardy of being lost or despoiled by these and other activities; that such loss or despoliation will adversely affect, if not entirely eliminate, the value of such wetlands as sources of nutrients to finfish, crustacea and shellfish of significant economic value; that such loss or despoliation will destroy such wetlands as habitats for plants and animals of significant economic and ecological value and will eliminate or substantially reduce marine commerce, recreation and aesthetic enjoyment; and that such loss or despoliation will, in most cases, disturb the natural ability of wetlands to reduce flood damage and adversely affect the public health and welfare; that such loss or despoliation will substantially reduce the capacity of such wetlands to absorb silt and will thus result in the increased silting of channels and harbor areas to the detriment of free navigation. It is hereby determined that the coastal areas of Delaware are the most critical areas for the present and future quality of life in the State and that the preservation of the coastal wetlands is crucial to the protection of the natural environment of these coastal areas. Therefore, it is declared to be the public policy of this State to preserve and protect the productive public and private wetlands and to prevent their despoliation and destruction consistent with the historic right of private ownership of lands.

Sec. 6603. *Definitions.*

"Wetlands" shall mean those lands above the mean low water elevation including any bank, marsh, swamp, meadow, float or other low land subject to tidal action in the State of Delaware along the Delaware Bay and Delaware River, Indian River Bay, Rehoboth Bay, Little and Big Assawoman Bays, the coastal inland waterways, or along any inlet, estuary or tributary waterway or any portion thereof, including those areas which are now or in this century have been connected to tidal waters, whose surface is at or below an elevation of two feet above local mean high water, and upon which may grow or is capable of growing any but not necessarily all of the following plants:

Eelgrass (*Zoxtera marina*), Wedgeon Grass (*Ruppia maritima*), Sago Pondweed (*Potamogeton pectinatus*), Saltmarsh Cordgrass (*Spartina alterniflora*), Saltmarsh Grass (*Spartina cynosuroides*),[2] . . . and those lands not currently used for agricultural purposes containing two hundred acres or more of contiguous non-tidal swamp, bog, muck, or marsh exclusive

---

2. Twenty-one more plants are listed. — EDS.

of narrow stream valleys where fresh water stands most, if not all, of the time due to high water table, which contribute significantly to ground water recharge, and which would require intensive artificial drainage using equipment such as pumping stations, drain fields or ditches for the production of agricultural crops.

Sec. 6604. *Permit Required.*

(a) Any activity in the wetlands requires a permit from the Department except the activity or activities exempted by this Chapter and no permit may be granted unless the county or municipality having jurisdiction has first approved the activity in question by zoning procedures provided by law.

(b) The Secretary shall consider the following factors prior to issuance of any permit: (1) Environmental impact, including but not limited to, likely destruction of wetlands and flora and fauna; impact of the site preparation on tidal ebb and flow and the otherwise normal drainage of the area in question, especially as it relates to flood control; impact of the site preparation and proposed activity on land erosion; effect of site preparation and proposed activity on the quality and quantity of tidal waters, surface, ground and subsurface water resources and other resources; (2) Aesthetic effect, such as the impact on scenic beauty of the surrounding area; (3) The number and type of public and private supporting facilities required and the impact of such facilities on all factors listed in this subsection; (4) Effect on neighboring land uses, including but not limited to, public access to tidal waters, recreational areas and effect on adjacent residential and agricultural areas; (5) State, county and municipal comprehensive plans for the development and/or conservation of their areas of jurisidiction. . . .

(c) The Secretary may require a bond in an amount and with surety and conditions sufficient to secure compliance with the conditions and limitations, if any, set forth in the permit. . . .

Sec. 6607. *Procedures, Regulations and Application Fees.* . . .

(b) The Secretary shall inventory, as promptly as he is able, all wetlands within the State and prepare suitable maps. . . .

(c) The Secretary shall adopt a wetlands designation or any other regulation only after holding a public hearing in accordance with Sec. 6609.

(d) The Secretary shall, in furtherance of the purpose of this Chapter, adopt regulations

(i) setting forth procedures, including provisions for fees, which shall govern the processing of permit applications and the conduct of hearings;

(ii) elaborating standards consistent with Section 6604 by which each permit application will be reviewed and acted upon;

(iii) controlling or prohibiting activities on lands designated or proposed for designation as wetlands, which regulations may vary from area to area according to the ecological value of the subject wetlands and the threat to the health and welfare of the people of this State which their alteration would pose. . . .

Sec. 6612. *Appeal from Board's Decision.*

(a) Any person or persons, jointly or severally affected by any decision or non-decision of the Board, or any taxpayer, or any officer, department, board or bureau of the State, may appeal to the Superior Court in and for the county in which the use in question is wholly or principally located by filing a petition, duly verified, setting forth that such decision is illegal, in whole or in part, specifying the grounds of the illegality. . . .

Sec. 6613. *Taking.*

If the Superior Court finds that the action appealed from constitutes a taking without just compensation, it shall invalidate the order and grant appropriate relief, unless the Secretary at this stage, consents to the reversal or modification of his decision. However, the Secretary may, through negotiation or condemnation proceedings under 10 Del. C., Chapter 61, acquire the fee simple or any lesser interest, including but not limited to, a perpetual negative easement or other interest which assures that the affected land shall not thereafter be altered, dredged, dumped upon, filled or otherwise altered subject to any reasonable reservations to the land owner as the Secretary may have stipulated to prior to assessment of damages. A decision of the Superior Court that the action appealed from constitutes a taking without just compensation shall not become effective for three (3) years [from] the date of decision and shall not become effective at all if within that period the Secretary has initiated action to acquire fee simple or any lesser interest in the wetlands in question. A finding of the Superior Court that the denial of a permit or the restrictions imposed by a granted permit constitutes a taking without just compensation shall not affect any land other than that of the petitioning land owner. If the Secretary has not initiated action to acquire fee simple or any lesser interest in the wetlands in question within three (3) years from the date of a final court ruling, the permit must be granted as applied.

Notes

1. The Delaware Wetlands Act holds up a decision of the superior court for three years. Why was such a provision included in the statute? What impact will it have on the property owner who applies for a permit that is denied by the secretary but permitted by the superior court? If the original project for which the permit was sought becomes

financially unfeasible during the three-year delay, would a new permit be required if a subsequent project were significantly different from the original proposal? Could the secretary again refuse the permit? How would the New York court view such a provision in light of its decisions in *Arverne Bay* and *Ramapo* (supra pages 195 and 570)?

2. Compare the definition of "wetlands" in the Delaware statute with the following language from Maine's statute: "any swamp, marsh, bog, beach, flat or other contiguous lowland which is subject to tidal action or normal storm flowage at any time excepting periods of maximum storm activity." 38 Me. Rev. Stat. Ann. §472 (West Supp. 1987). Is the Maine definition sufficiently specific to give notice to a property owner that her property is subject to the requirements of the act? Could a deficiency be remedied by the wetlands control board through an administrative definition along the lines of the Delaware statute?

3. What are the differences between regulating the use of wetlands or flood plains or coastal areas under a permit system rather than by zoning district classification?

4. Compare wetlands regulation and flood plain regulation. How does construction in a flood plain differ from construction in a wetland area? Distinguish the impact of construction on the environment, on adjacent landowners, on the property owner, and on society in each case. Can you discern sufficient difference to justify regulation of the flood plain under the police power without calling it a taking, while not allowing such regulation of wetlands? For further discussion, see Notes, 52 B.U.L. Rev. 724 (1972), 56 Minn. L. Rev. 869 (1972), and Healy & Rosenberg, Land Use and the States (2d ed. 1979).

■ JUST v. MARINETTE COUNTY
56 Wis. 2d 7, 201 N.W.2d 761 (1972)

HALLOWS, Chief Justice.

Marinette county's Shoreland Zoning Ordinance Number 24.... was designed to meet standards and criteria for shoreland regulation which the legislature required to be promulgated by the department of natural resources....

Shorelands for the purpose of ordinances are defined ... as lands within 1,000 feet of the normal high-water elevation of navigable lakes, ponds, or flowages and 300 feet from a navigable river or stream or to the landward side of the flood plain, whichever distance is greater. The state shoreland program is unique. All county shoreland zoning ordinances must be approved by the department of natural resources prior to their becoming effective.... If a county does not enact a shoreland zoning ordinance which complies with the state's standards, the de-

A. Preserving the Hydrologic Cycle

partment of natural resources may enact such an ordinance for the county. . . .

There can be no disagreement over the public purpose sought to be obtained by the ordinance. Its basic purpose is to protect navigable waters and the public rights therein from the degradation and deterioration which results from uncontrolled use and development of shorelands. In the Navigable Waters Protection Act, sec. 144.26, the purpose of the state's shoreland regulation program is stated as being to "aid in the fulfillment of the state's role as trustee of its navigable waters and to promote public health, safety, convenience and general welfare." In sec. 59.971(1), which grants authority for shoreland zoning to counties, the same purposes are reaffirmed. The Marinette county shoreland zoning ordinance in secs. 1.2 and 1.3 states the uncontrolled use of shorelands and pollution of navigable waters of Marinette county adversely affect public health, safety, convenience, and general welfare and impair the tax base.

The shoreland zoning ordinance divides the shorelands of Marinette county into general purpose districts, general recreation districts, and conservancy districts. A "conservancy" district is required by the statutory minimum standards and is defined in Sec. 3.4 of the ordinance to include "all shorelands designated as swamps or marshes on the United States Geological Survey maps which have been designated as the Shoreland Zoning Map of Marinette County, Wisconsin or on the detailed Insert Shoreland Zoning Maps." The ordinance provides for permitted uses and conditional uses. One of the conditional uses requiring a permit under Sec. 3.42(4) is the filling, drainage or dredging of wetlands according to the provisions of sec. 5 of the ordinance. "Wetlands" are defined in sec. 2.29 as "(a)reas where ground water is at or near the surface much of the year or where any segment of plant cover is deemed an aquatic according to N. C. Fassett's "Manual of Aquatic Plants." Section 5.42(2) of the ordinance requires a conditional-use permit for any filling or grading "Of any area which is within three hundred feet horizontal distance of a navigable water and which has surface drainage toward the water and on which there is: (a) Filling of more than five hundred square feet of any wetland which is contiguous to the water . . . (d) Filling or grading of more than 2,000 square feet on slopes of twelve per cent or less."

In April of 1961, several years prior to the passage of this ordinance, the Justs purchased 36.4 acres of land in the town of Lake along the south shore of Lake Noquebay, a navigable lake in Marinette county. This land had a frontage of 1,266.7 feet on the lake and was purchased partially for personal use and partially for resale. During the years 1964, 1966, and 1967, the Justs made five sales of parcels having frontage and extending back from the lake some 600 feet, leaving the property involved in these suits. This property has a frontage of 366.7

feet and the south one half contains a stand of cedar, pine, various hard woods, birch and red maple. The north one half, closer to the lake, is barren of trees except immediately along the shore. The south three fourths of this north one half is populated with various plant grasses and vegetation including some plants which N. C. Fassett in his manual of aquatic plants has classified as "aquatic." There are also non-aquatic plants which grow upon the land. Along the shoreline there is a belt of trees. The shoreline is from one foot to 3.2 feet higher than the lake level and there is a narrow belt of higher land along the shore known as a "pressure ridge" or "ice heave," varying in width from one to three feet. South of this point, the natural level of the land ranges one to two feet above lake level. The land slopes generally toward the lake but has a slope less than twelve per cent. No water flows onto the land from the lake, but there is some surface water which collects on land and stands in pools.

The land owned by the Justs is designated as swamps or marshes on the United States Geological Survey Map and is located within 1,000 feet of the normal high-water elevation of the lake. Thus, the property is included in a conservancy district and, by sec. 2.29 of the ordinance, classified as "wetlands." Consequently, in order to place more than 500 square feet of fill on this property, the Justs were required to obtain a conditional-use permit from the zoning administrator of the county and pay a fee of $20 or incur a forfeiture of $10 to $200 for each day of violation.

In February and March of 1968, six months after the ordinance became effective, Ronald Just, without securing a conditional-use permit, hauled 1,040 square yards of sand onto this property and filled an area approximately 20-feet wide commencing at the southwest corner and extending almost 600 feet north to the northwest corner near the shoreline, then easterly along the shoreline almost to the lot line. He stayed back from the pressure ridge about 20 feet. More than 500 square feet of this fill was upon wetlands located contiguous to the water and which had surface drainage toward the lake. The fill within 300 feet of the lake also was more than 2,000 square feet on a slope less than 12 percent. It is not seriously contended that the Justs did not violate the ordinance and the trial court correctly found a violation.

The real issue is whether the conservancy district provisions and the wetlands-filling restrictions are unconstitutional because they amount to a constructive taking of the Justs' land without compensation. Marinette county and the state of Wisconsin argue the restrictions of the conservancy district and wetlands provisions constitute a proper exercise of the police power of the state and do not so severely limit the use or depreciate the value of the land as to constitute a taking without compensation.

. . . Whether a taking has occurred depends upon whether "the

A. Preserving the Hydrologic Cycle

restriction practically or substantially renders the land useless for all reasonable purposes." Buhler v. Racine County, [33 Wis. 2d 137, 146 N.W.2d 403 (1966)]. The loss caused the individual must be weighed to determine if it is more than he should bear. As this court stated in *Stefan* [Auto Body v. State Highway Commission, 21 Wis. 2d 363, 369-370, 124 N.W.2d 319, 323 (1963)],

> . . . if the damage is such as to be suffered by many similarly situated and is in the nature of a restriction on the use to which land may be put and ought to be borne by the individual as a member of society for the good of the public safety, health or general welfare, it is said to be a reasonable exercise of the police power, but if the damage is so great to the individual that he ought not to bear it under contemporary standards, then courts are inclined to treat it as a "taking" of the property or an unreasonable exercise of the police power. . . .

This case causes us to reexamine the concepts of public benefit in contrast to public harm and the scope of an owner's right to use of his property. In the instant case we have a restriction on the use of a citizen's property, not to secure a benefit for the public, but to prevent a harm from the change in the natural character of the citizen's property. We start with the premise that lakes and rivers in their natural state are unpolluted and the pollution which now exists is man made. The state of Wisconsin under the trust doctrine has a duty to eradicate the present pollution and to prevent further pollution in its navigable waters. This is not, in a legal sense, a gain or a securing of a benefit by the maintaining of the natural status quo of the environment. What makes this case different from most condemnation or police power zoning cases is the interrelationship of the wetlands, the swamps and the natural environment of shorelands to the purity of the water and to such natural resources as navigation, fishing, and scenic beauty. Swamps and wetlands were once considered wasteland, undesirable, and not picturesque. But as the people became more sophisticated, an appreciation was acquired that swamps and wetlands serve a vital role in nature, are part of the balance of nature and are essential to the purity of the water in our lakes and streams. Swamps and wetlands are a necessary part of the ecological creation and now, even to the uninitiated, possess their own beauty in nature.

Is the ownership of a parcel of land so absolute that man can change its nature to suit any of his purposes? The great forests of our state were stripped on the theory man's ownership was unlimited. But in forestry, the land at least was used naturally, only the natural fruit of the land (the trees) were taken. The despoilage was in the failure to look to the future and provide for the reforestation of the land. An owner of land has no absolute and unlimited right to change the essential natural character of his land so as to use it for a purpose for which it was unsuited in its natural state and which injures the rights of others. The exercise of the police power in zoning must be reasonable and we think it is not an unreasonable exercise of that power to prevent harm to public rights by limiting the use of private property to its natural uses.

This is not a case where an owner is prevented from using his land for natural and indigenous uses. The uses consistent with the nature of the land are allowed and other uses recognized and still others permitted by special permit. The shoreland zoning ordinance prevents to some extent the changing of the natural character of the land within 1,000 feet of a navigable lake and 300 feet of a navigable river because of such land's interrelation to the contiguous water. The changing of wetlands and swamps to the damage of the general public by upsetting the natural environment and the natural relationship is not a reasonable use of that land which is protected from police power regulation. Changes and filling to some extent are permitted because the extent of such changes and fillings does not cause harm. We realize no case in Wisconsin has yet dealt with shoreland regulations and there are several cases in other states which seem to hold such regulations unconstitutional; but nothing this court has said or held in prior cases indicates that destroying the natural character of a swamp or a wetland so as to make that location available for human habitation is a reasonable use of that land when the new use, although of a more economical value to the owner, causes a harm to the general public.

Wisconsin has long held that laws and regulations to prevent pollution and to protect the waters of this state from degradation are valid police-power enactments. The active public trust duty of the state of Wisconsin in respect to navigable waters requires the state not only to promote navigation but also to protect and preserve those waters for fishing, recreation, and scenic beauty.

The Justs rely on several cases from other jurisdictions which have held zoning regulations involving flood plain districts, flood basins and wetlands to be so confiscatory as to amount to a taking because the owners of the land were prevented from improving such property for residential or commercial purposes. While some of these cases may be distinguished on their facts, it is doubtful whether these differences go to the basic rationale which permeates the decision that an owner has a right to use his property in any way and for any purpose he sees fit. . . .

In State v. Johnson (1970), Me., 265 A.2d 711, the Wetlands Act restricted the alteration and use of certain wetlands without permission. The act was a conservation measure enacted under the police power to protect the ecology of areas bordering the coastal waters. The plaintiff owned a small tract of a salt-water marsh which was flooded at high

A. Preserving the Hydrologic Cycle

tide. By filling, the land would be adapted for building purposes. The court held the restrictions against filling constituted a deprivation of a reasonable use of the owner's property and, thus, an unreasonable exercise of the police power.[3] In MacGibbon v. Board of Appeals of Duxbury (1970), 356 Mass. 635, 255 N.E.2d 347, the plaintiff owned seven acres of land which were under water about twice a month in a shoreland area. He was denied a permit to excavate and fill part of his property. The purpose of the ordinance was to preserve from despoilage natural features and resources such as salt marshes, wetlands, and ponds. The court took the view the preservation of privately owned land in its natural, unspoiled state for the enjoyment and benefit of the public by preventing the owner from using it for any practical purpose was not within the limit and scope of the police power and the special permits.

It seems to us that filling a swamp not otherwise commercially usable is not in and of itself an existing use, which is prevented, but rather is the preparation for some future use which is not indigenous to a swamp. Too much stress is laid on the right of an owner to change commercially valueless land when that change does damage to the rights of the public. It is observed that a use of special permits is a means of control and accomplishing the purpose of the zoning ordinance as distinguished from the old concept of providing for variances. The special permit technique is now common practice and has met with judicial approval, and we think it is of some significance in considering whether or not a particular zoning ordinance is reasonable.

A recent case sustaining the validity of a zoning ordinance establishing a flood plain district is Turnpike Realty Company v. Town of Dedham (June, 1972), 72 Mass. 1303, 284 N.E.2d 891. The court held the validity of the ordinance was supported by valid considerations of public welfare, the conservation of "natural conditions, wildlife and open spaces." The ordinance provided that lands which were subject to seasonal or periodic flooding could not be used for residences or other purposes in such a manner as to endanger the health, safety or occupancy thereof and prohibited the erection of structures or buildings which required land to be filled. This case is analogous to the instant facts. The ordinance had a public purpose to preserve the natural condition of the area. No change was allowed which would injure the purposes sought to be preserved and through the special-permit technique, particular land within the zoning district could be excepted from the restrictions.

The Justs argue their property has been severely depreciated in value. But this depreciation of value is not based on the use of the land in its natural state but on what the land would be worth if it could be

---

3. But see In re Spring Valley Development, 300 A.2d 736 (Me. 1973). — EDS.

filled and used for the location of a dwelling. While loss of value is to be considered in determining whether a restriction is a constructive taking, value based upon changing the character of the land at the expense of harm to public rights is not an essential factor or controlling. . . .

The Judgment in case number 106, dismissing the Justs' action, is modified to set forth the declaratory adjudication that the shoreland zoning ordinance of respondent Marinette County is constitutional; that the Justs' property constitutes wetlands and that particularly the prohibition in the ordinance against the filling of wetlands is constitutional; and the judgment, as so modified, is affirmed. The judgment in case number 107, declaring a forfeiture, is affirmed.

Notes

1. See Bryden, A Phantom Doctrine: The Origins and Effects of Just v. Marinette County, 1978 Am. B. Found. Res. J. 397, 434-437:

> Given the availability of conditional use permits, landowners appear to have no great incentive to disobey the law; this may be why, by all accounts, very little illegal filling occurs in Marinette County. The Justs, however, were not ordinary landowners. Although it is fatuous to try to summarize a human personality in a sentence or two, the reader must know something about the Justs or their case will be difficult to understand. Outwardly, they did not differ greatly from ordinary, hospitable people of comfortable but modest means — he, a self-described "laborer," she, a bookkeeper — who have invested in land. The difference was that the Justs were not merely mildly skeptical about government, in the robust but amiable and pragmatic fashion of some rural individualists; they were darkly, intensely hostile to the dominant forces in America, in the manner of the John Birch Society which they eventually joined. Confronted by rules that they perceived as a sinister threat to their portion of the American Dream, they fought back with a single-minded tenacity that was fueled more by ideological passion than by acquisitive cunning, chasing the white whale of regulation all the way to the Supreme Court of Wisconsin.
>
> The Justs chose to fill without applying for a permit because they believed that the ordinance was unconstitutional: "It was a matter of principle. . . . We intended to break the ordinance, but we didn't intend to break the law of the land." Ronald Just began filling around the beginning of February 1968; and before long the zoning administrator, having detected the violation, warned the Justs that filling without a permit was illegal. Disregarding this warning, Just continued filling. . . .
>
> The Justs' attorney recalls that before the trial the corporation counsel offered a settlement: The Justs would be granted a conditional use permit if they applied for one and desisted from litigation. They rejected this

A. Preserving the Hydrologic Cycle

proposal because they "wanted to face the constitutional issue four-square."

2. The Wisconsin court views the "public trust doctrine" as creating a duty "to eradicate the present pollution and to prevent further pollution in its navigable waters." Could the Sierra Club sue Wisconsin for breach of the "public trust" if pollution is allowed to continue unabated? How pure does the "public trust" doctrine require the water to be? Why is this doctrine limited to navigable waters? Does pollution impair navigability? Compare the arguments for abating pollution under the public trust doctrine with the concept of a "public" nuisance. Which provides the better rationale for judicial decisions?

3. What are the "natural uses" of land? Distinguish filling wetlands from grading a steep slope. Is one a more natural use than the other? Could the court hold that to limit the use of land to activity which is reasonable in view of the natural capacity of the land is a proper exercise of the police power, and that the hardship to the individual is not unreasonable because she could clearly perceive the limited capacity of the land in its natural state when she purchased it? Reconsider the "large lot" zoning cases, supra page 386. Does the concept of capacity provide a more workable justification for the use of large lots, as well as for defining the "point on the spectrum" where the public interest in lot size ceases? Can the state limit use to "natural capacity"? Or is there a right to alter the capacity of land to obtain the highest economic yield? Does a definition of capacity, to be enforceable under the police power, have to relate to the external effects of altering the natural environment or to increasing the intensity of its use?

4. In State v. Johnson, cited in *Just*, the court reasoned as follows: (a) The usual exercise of the police power is not a taking because if the owner is injured, he is compensated "by sharing in the general benefits which the regulations intended." (b) But where the regulation "unreasonably" deprives the owner of one of the "essential attributes" of his property, or "destroys its value, restricts or interrupts its common necessary, or profitable use, . . . and thereby seriously impairs its value," then a taking of property has occurred. (c) The extent of diminution is then compared to the purpose of the regulation to determine if it is unreasonable. If the regulation attempts to provide a public benefit rather than prevent public harm, then the degree of diminution in value allowed is reduced.

In appraising the facts of *Johnson*, the Maine court found that

> [a]s distinguished from conventional zoning for town protection, the area of Wetlands representing a "valuable natural resource of the State," of which appellants' holdings are but a minute part, is of state-wide concern. The benefits from its preservation extend beyond town limits and are

As soon as things pick up a little we're going to have it landscaped.

A. Preserving the Hydrologic Cycle

state-wide. The cost of its preservation should be publicly borne. To leave appellants with commercially valueless land in upholding the restriction presently imposed, is to charge them with more than their just share of the cost of this state-wide conservation program, granting fully its commendable purpose. In the phrasing of [State v. Robb, 100 Me. 180, 60 A.2d 874], their compensation by sharing in the benefits which this restriction is intended to secure is so disproportionate to their deprivation of reasonable use that such exercise of the State's police power is unreasonable.

State v. Johnson, 265 A.2d 711, 716 (Me. 1970).

How does this analysis differ from that in *Just*? Are the courts simply reading the facts differently, or is there a distinct difference in legal theory? What is the "common, necessary, or profitable use" of wetland? Clearly, when a community zones as a park land suitable for a single-family home without substantial improvement of the lot, it is "creating a public benefit." Is preventing the development of a wetland the same sort of "creation of a public benefit"?

5. The court distinguishes between filling wetlands and polluting wetlands. If dredging and filling or other physical alterations of the wetlands upset the ecological balance, how is this different from polluting them with sewage? Why is there a difference between imposing costs on the landowner, such as sewage treatment, and preventing use?

6. See Robin Lewis Makes His Living Creating Marshes and Swamps, Wall St. J., Sept. 2, 1987:

> The continental U.S. once had 215 million acres of wetlands. But the land was cheap, and developers and farmers bought, drained and filled it. By the mid-1970s, when environmental laws slowed wetland destruction, just 99 million acres remained, an area roughly the size of California. . . .
> To save wetlands without prohibiting development, regulators devised a policy known as "mitigation." It allows landowners who show that they don't have any alternative sites to build on marshes — as long as they replace them. For each marsh they destroy, developers must typically restore a dilapidated marsh or build an entirely new one.
> Enter the marsh builders. They evaluate, repair and custom-build marshes — or swamps, which are basically marshes dominated by trees — to satisfy rules administered by a slew of local, state and federal regulators. Their clients range from public agencies planning highways through swamplands, to shopping-mall developers building on marshes, to homeowners looking to replace back-yard bogs with tennis courts.

7. Provisions of the Clean Water Act mandate that "any discharge of dredged or fill materials into 'navigable waters' . . . is forbidden unless authorized by a permit issued by the Corps of Engineers." In United States v. Riverside Bayview Homes, Inc., 474 U.S. 121 (1985), the Corps insisted, and the Court agreed, that "the Act cover[ed] all

'freshwater wetlands' that were adjacent to other covered waters." The respondent insisted that Corps permission need not be secured in order to fill its eighty acres of marshland in Macomb County, Michigan in preparation for construction of a housing development.

Justice White noted that the language and history of 33 C.F.R. §323.2(c) (1985) made clear that the wetlands need not be periodically inundated to fall within the Act. While upholding the Corps' interpretation, he observed (at 132):

> In determining the limits of its power to regulate discharges under the Act, the Corps must necessarily choose some point at which water ends and land begins. Our common experience tells us that this is often no easy task: the transition from water to solid ground is not necessarily or even typically an abrupt one. Rather, between open waters and dry land may lie shallows, marshes, mudflats, swamps, bogs — in short, a huge array of areas that are not wholly aquatic but nevertheless fall far short of being dry land. Where on this continuum to find the limit of "waters" is far from obvious.

Is there any sense to this hydrologic search for determinative distinctions? Why should we require the presence of moisture to invoke the sovereign's protection? Doesn't society have the same historical and ecological stake in deserts, mountains, and unbroken plains?

What impact do private and public land-use planning devices have on the shape of the nonurban environment? The materials that follow suggest the influence the tax code can have on our quality of life in places ecologically or historically sensitive, and the need to modify rules of law fashioned in the city setting in order to meet rural needs.

■ INTERNAL REVENUE CODE §170(h)
(1986)

(1) In general. — For purposes of subsection (f)(3)(b)(iii), the term "qualified conservation contribution" means a contribution —
    (A) of a qualified real property interest,
    (B) to a qualified organization,
    (C) exclusively for conservation purposes.

(2) Qualified property interest. — For purposes of this subsection, the term "qualified real property interest" means any of the following interests in real property:

(A) the entire interest of the donor other than a qualified mineral interest,

(B) a remainder interest, and

(C) a restriction (granted in perpetuity) on the use which may be made of the real property. . . .

(4) Conservation purpose defined. —

(A) In general. — For purposes of this subsection, the term "conservation purpose" means —

(i) the preservation of land areas for outdoor recreation by, or the education of the general public,

(ii) the protection of relatively natural habitat of fish, wildlife, or plants, or similar ecosystem,

(iii) the preservation of open space (including farmland and forest land) where such preservation is —

(I) for the scenic enjoyment of the general public, or

(II) pursuant to a clearly delineated Federal, State, or local governmental conservation policy, and will yield a significant public benefit, or

(iv) the preservation of an historically important land area or a certified historic structure.

■ TREASURY REGULATIONS §1.170A-14
(1986)

(4) Preservation of open space — . . . An open space easement donated on or after December 18, 1980, must meet the requirements of section 170(h) in order to be deductible.

(ii) Scenic enjoyment — (A) Factors. A contribution made for the preservation of open space may be for the scenic enjoyment of the general public. Preservation of land may be for the scenic enjoyment of the general public if development of the property would impair the scenic character of the local rural or urban landscape or would interfere with a scenic panorama that can be enjoyed from a park, nature preserve, road, waterbody, trail, or historic structure or land area, and such area or transportation way is open to, or utilized by, the public. "Scenic enjoyment" will be evaluated by considering all pertinent facts and circumstances germane to the contribution. Regional variations in topography, geology, biology, and cultural and economic conditions require flexibility in the application of this test, but do not lessen the burden on the taxpayer to demonstrate the scenic characteristics of a donation under this paragraph. The application of a particular objective factor to help define a view as "scenic" in one setting may in fact be entirely inappropriate in another setting. Among the factors to be considered are:

(1) The compatibility of the land use with other land in the vicinity;

(2) The degree of contrast and variety provided by the visual scene;

(3) The openness of the land (which would be a more significant factor in an urban or densely populated setting or in a heavily wooded area);

(4) Relief from urban closeness;

(5) The harmonious variety of shapes and textures;

(6) The degree to which the land use maintains the scale and character of the urban landscape to preserve open space, visual enjoyment, and sunlight for the surrounding area;

(7) The consistency of the proposed scenic view and a methodical state scenic identification program, such as a state landscape inventory; and

(8) The consistency of the proposed scenic view with a regional or local landscape inventory made pursuant to a sufficiently rigorous review process, especially if the donation is endorsed by an appropriate state or local governmental agency.

(B) Access. To satisfy the requirement of scenic enjoyment by the general public, visual (rather than physical) access to or across the property by the general public is sufficient. Under the terms of an open space easement on scenic property, the entire property need not be visible to the public for a donation to qualify under this section, although the public benefit from the donation may be insufficient to qualify for a deduction if only a small portion of the property is visible to the public.

Notes

1. Akers v. Commissioner, 799 F.2d 243 (6th Cir. 1986), is a welcome rarity — a humorous tax case. The judges were asked to determine the accuracy of the appraisal of the fair market value of a scenic easement that was donated to the Tennessee Conservation League by Mr. and Mrs. Akers. The easement burdened 1340 acres in Cheatham County, Tennessee, and provided "that only one family dwelling unit can be erected for each 200 acres, and that there can be no excavation, topographical changes, or removal of trees without permission of the Conservation League." The court chose the Tax Court's $114,000 estimate over the $772,000 figure offered by the Akerses:

A. Preserving the Hydrologic Cycle

The difference between the two valuations thus boils down to a difference between the worth of the Treanor Tract prior to subdivision and the worth of the land at some point afterwards. It is rather like the difference between the worth of a gravid or potentially gravid sow and the postpartum worth of a sow-cum-shoats.

... It is indisputable that the Treanor Tract was a single property immediately prior to the grant of the easement, and the regulatory definition does suggest that the appropriate question is what a hypothetical Malcolm Forbes would have paid for it as one tract, rather than what two dozen hypothetical yuppies would have paid for it as 24 "Ranchettes."

2. In a recent case concerning the correct valuation of a corporation's charitable donation of a conservation easement, the Tax Court held the value to be $7 million less than the taxpayer's estimate, resulting in a substantial deficiency judgment as well as the added insult of an increased rate of interest on the underpayment related to the corporation's "tax-motivated transaction." Stanley Works v. Commissioner, 87 T.C. 389 (1986). See also Roddewig, Preservation Easement Law: An Overview of Recent Development, 18 Urb. Law 229 (1986).

3. Notice that §170(h)(4)(A)(iii) of the Internal Revenue Code includes the preservation of farmland as a "conservation purpose." How can zoning devices complement this tax policy? See, for example, Codorus Township v. Rodgers, 89 Pa. Commw. 79, 492 A.2d 73 (1985):

The present content of the MPC in Pennsylvania reflects a nationwide legislative trend toward using zoning as one of the tools for the preservation of agricultural land. As noted four years ago in Coughlin and Keene, The Protection of Farm Land: An Analysis of Various State and Local Approaches, 33 Land Use Law & Zoning Digest 5, 6-8 (1981), there were then 270 local (county and municipal) agricultural zoning efforts which the authors had identified. Their survey showed that, in addition to rather simplistic ordinances requiring only a substantial minimum lot size (ranging from as little as ten acres to as much as 640 acres), local legislative patterns employed exclusive agricultural use districts and also area-based allocation ordinances — similar to the one before us here — which allow owners to build additional dwellings for each unit of land of a specified area that they own. . . .

The most recent decision on point, nationally speaking, is Wilson v. County of McHenry, 92 Ill. App.3d 997, 48 Ill. Dec. 395, 416 N.E.2d 426 (1981), in which the Illinois Appellate Court upheld the validity of agricultural zoning, in a county zoning ordinance which set a 160-acre lot area minimum in the agricultural district for the declared objective of promoting the public interest by preserving prime farmland and channeling residential development toward existing urban centers. . . .

The township [Codorus] offered the testimony of Joseph Hoheneder, the assistant director of the York County Planning Commission, who testified about a statistical study indicating the significant loss in farmland in the county in recent years, and a concurrent increase in population.

The township also presented the testimony of John Smith, the York County agricultural agent, who testified that, in his opinion, although small tracts are possible for certain types of farms, it is more economically feasible to operate a farm in York County on tracts in excess of 50 acres, because a greater amount of land is required to use modern farming equipment and methods appropriate to the region's characteristics. . . .

The ordinance provisions here involved are rationally related to the legitimate goal of preserving agricultural land in Codorus Township. However, we emphasize that a fifty-acre lot area minimum is not necessarily valid in every situation, whether required for agricultural preservation purposes or otherwise, but must be scrutinized, as here, under a substantive due process analysis in the context in which it is presented.

The legal literature on farmland preservation is voluminous. See, for example, Roberts, The Law and the Preservation of Agricultural Land (1982); Juergensmeyer & Wadley, 1 Agricultural Law ch. 4 (1982 & Supp. 1985); Rose, Farmland Preservation Policy and Programs, 24 Nat. Resources J. 592 (1984); Thompson, "Right to Farm" Laws, 1983 Zoning & Plan. L. Handbook 207; Urban Land Institute, Has the "Farmland Crisis" Been Overstated?: Recommendations for Balancing Urban and Agricultural Land Needs, 1983 Zoning & Plan. L. Handbook 235 (questioning findings of National Agricultural Lands Study (NALS), Final Report (1981)); Keene, Agricultural Land Preservation: Legal and Constitutional Issues, 15 Gonz. L. Rev. 621 (1980).

How suitable is the transfer of development rights technique to the goal of agricultural land protection? See Juergensmeyer & Wadley, supra, at §4.11 n.8:

> Examples of TDRs include Collier County, Florida, which in 1974 adopted a TDR plan for its cypress swamp and designated 84 percent of the county's land as a special treatment (SP) zone requiring special permission prior to development. New Jersey has had the most activity with its TDR plan. The 1976 legislature approved $5 million for an agricultural preserve demonstration project. An estimated 10,000 acres will be preserved which, calculated at $500 a preservation acre, is relatively cheap. . . .
>
> . . . The Buckingham Township [Pennsylvania] plan, designed with agricultural preservation in mind, gave each landowner in the agricultural district one development certificate per acre owned. Each owner could sell his rights to landowners in three higher density residential districts. "Conveyance of development rights requires the seller to restrictively covenant his land and rezone the land into an agricultural preservation district permitting only one residence in every twenty-five acres." Twelve development rights have been sold at $1,800 each. Their experience, however, does not have a happy ending, since "a Bucks County, Pennsylvania, court has declared the Buckingham zoning ordinance invalid" based upon exclusionary principles.

B. ENVIRONMENTAL POLICY ACTS: CONTROLLING THE "DESTRUCTIVE ENGINE OF MATERIAL 'PROGRESS'"

Recall the requirement for the filing of an environmental impact statement set forth by §102(2)(C) of NEPA. Private-developer activity subject to federal regulation or funding is directly affected by the EIS requirement, as can be seen by the original HUD guidelines for the implementation of NEPA.[4] The project is then considered through a series of environmental clearance procedures in HUD that will result in either nonapproval, or a clearance (and federal funding) that may or may not have required the preparation of an EIS, depending upon the significance of the proposed project.[5] Other federal agencies have similar requirements and procedures.

The ability of the private developer to pursue a project that requires any measure of federal assistance or control without regard to environmental consequences has thus been sharply curtailed — at least on paper. Do you think that NEPA has been given this effect by the federal agencies? Is it possible that some of the applicants' statements received by a regional office of HUD are given but a cursory review and then promptly reissued by HUD as the EIS? Passing this obvious circumnavigation of NEPA, would you suppose that each regional HUD office has the required expertise or manpower to discharge the statutory responsibility?

The seminal interpretation of NEPA came in J. Skelly Wright's opinion in Calvert Cliffs' Coordinating Committee v. Atomic Energy Commission, 449 F.2d 1109 (D.C. Cir. 1971), a decision that has spawned hundreds of citations in fewer than three decades. In judicially reviewing a number of AEC rules for compliance with federal environmental strictures, Wright set the ground rules for NEPA interpretation:

---

4. 38 Fed. Reg. 19182-19195 (1973), Department of Housing and Urban Development Regulations Governing Departmental Policies, Responsibilities, and Procedures under NEPA.

5. The applicable HUD form, as devised in 1973, requires the applicant to furnish a description of the existing physical, social, and aesthetic environment; to state how the environment will affect the project and, more important, how the project will affect the environment; to describe the quality of the environment created by the project and its impact upon the expected residents or users of the project; to list the alternatives to the project that were considered and the reasons for their rejection; to set forth additional alternatives that would avoid adverse environmental impacts; and to describe the provisions of the proposal which were specifically designed to reduce adverse environmental impact or to enhance environmental quality. The only exemption from the clearance procedures are projects which have been determined not to be "major federal actions significantly affecting the quality of the human environment": individual actions on one- to four-family dwellings, training grants, or rehabilitation and modernization projects which do not extend the life of the project twenty years or more. 38 Fed. Reg. 19,191-19,195 (1973). For current HUD regulations and forms, see 24 C.F.R. pt. 50 (Protection and Enhancement of Environmental Quality).

NEPA, first of all, makes environmental protection a part of the mandate of every federal agency and department. The Atomic Energy Commission, for example, had continually asserted, prior to NEPA, that it had no statutory authority to concern itself with the adverse environmental effects of its actions. Now, however, its hands are no longer tied. It is not only permitted, but compelled, to take environmental values into account. Perhaps the greatest importance of NEPA is to require the Atomic Energy Commission and other agencies to *consider* environmental issues just as they consider other matters within their mandates. . . .

The sort of consideration of environmental values which NEPA compels is clarified in Section 102(2)(A) and (B). In general, all agencies must use a "systematic, interdisciplinary approach" to environmental planning and evaluation "in decisionmaking which may have an impact on man's environment." In order to include all possible environmental factors in the decisional equation, agencies must "identify and develop methods and procedures . . . which will insure that presently unquantified environmental amenities and values may be given appropriate consideration in decisionmaking along with economic and technical considerations." "Environmental amenities" will often be in conflict with "economic and technical considerations." To "consider" the former "along with" the latter must involve a balancing process. In some instances environmental costs may outweigh economic and technical benefits and in other instances they may not. But NEPA mandates a rather finely tuned and "systematic" balancing analysis in each instance.

To ensure that the balancing analysis is carried out and given full effect, Section 102(2)(C) requires that responsible officials of all agencies prepare a "detailed statement" covering the impact of particular actions on the environment, the environmental costs which might be avoided, and alternative measures which might alter the cost-benefit equation. The apparent purpose of the "detailed statement" is to aid in the agencies' own decision making process and to advise other interested agencies and the public of the environmental consequences of planned federal action. Beyond the "detailed statement," Section 102(2)(D) requires all agencies specifically to "study, develop, and describe appropriate alternatives to recommended courses of action in any proposal which involves unresolved conflicts concerning alternative uses of available resources." This requirement, like the "detailed statement" requirement, seeks to ensure that each agency decision maker has before him and takes into proper account all possible approaches to a particular project (including total abandonment of the project) which would alter the environmental impact and the cost-benefit balance. Only in that fashion is it likely that the most intelligent, optimally beneficial decision will ultimately be made. Moreover, by compelling a formal "detailed statement" and a description of alternatives, NEPA provides evidence that the mandated decision making process has in fact taken place and, most importantly, allows those removed from the initial process to evaluate and balance the factors on their own.

Of course, all of these Section 102 duties are qualified by the phrase "to the fullest extent possible." We must stress as forcefully as possible that this language does not provide an escape hatch for footdragging

B. Environmental Policy Acts

agencies; it does not make NEPA's procedural requirements somehow "discretionary." Congress did not intend the Act to be such a paper tiger. Indeed, the requirement of environmental consideration "to the fullest extent possible" sets a high standard for the agencies, a standard which must be rigorously enforced by the reviewing courts.

Deeply influencing the momentum of the "quiet revolution" in national habits concerning the environment has been the attitude of the judiciary. They have insisted upon strict procedural compliance with NEPA. Perhaps this is an interpretation necessarily arising out of the statute, perhaps a recognition of the basic human condition that requires incentive to action — a generalization many would consider particularly applicable to the federal bureaucracy. Through the simple procedural device — the impact statement — environmental policy statutes have been given substantive bite.

■ COALITION FOR LOS ANGELES COUNTY PLANNING IN THE PUBLIC INTEREST v. BOARD OF SUPERVISORS
8 E.R.C. 1249 (L.A. Co. Super. Ct. Civil No. 63218, 1975; not officially reported)

THOMAS, J.: . . .

2. The adoption by the Board of Supervisors of its 1973 General Plan is a "project" for which an EIR is required, if it "may have a significant effect on the environment."

3. In determining whether a project "may have a significant effect on the environment," the courts properly interpret that phrase to impose a low threshold requirement for preparation of an EIR.

4. The adoption by the Board of Supervisors of the 1973 General Plan was a project which "may have a significant effect on the environment," and thus required preparation of an EIR.

5. EIRs prepared pursuant to CEQA [California Environmental Quality Act] are subject to judicial review to determine their sufficiency and adequacy as informational documents. This court has confined its review in this case to determining whether the Board of Supervisors prejudicially abused its discretion (a) by failing to proceed in the manner required by law, or (b) by failing to have substantial evidentiary support for its determination.

6. In determining the adequacy of an EIR on a general plan, the court properly considers the general plan itself to be a part of the EIR.

7. When a court determines the adequacy of an EIR, the court must weigh the significance of the report made against that which reasonably could be expected. Thus, a project of large import deserves

the expenditure of more time and money in the preparation of an EIR than does one of small import.

8. An EIR prepared for a general plan cannot be less than an adequate and sufficient informational document under CEQA simply because the public officials preparing the EIR felt pressed for time or because the general plan was proposed to be amended periodically in the future.

9. The subjective belief of a public agency that an adequate discussion of alternatives to a proposed project is "too big to handle" cannot excuse the agency's failure to disclose the reasons for adopting the proposed project and rejecting the alternatives.

10. The EIR on a project must itself be an adequate informational document, and it is impermissible for the EIR simply to refer to material "in the [public agency's] offices" in an attempt to incorporate such material into the EIR by reference.

11. To be a legally adequate informational document under the procedural requirements of CEQA, an EIR must be a "detailed statement" informing the public and the decisionmakers of the required alternatives. It cannot contain "mere aphorisms or generalities" or "naked conclusions," but must contain factual, detailed information supporting the conclusions expressed in the EIR. It must set out bona fide opposition to the project and the agency's comments thereon, and must contain sound reasons for the recommended course of action and the rejection of alternatives.

12. In order for an EIR on a general plan to be legally adequate under the procedural requirements of CEQA, the EIR must provide sufficient facts and data regarding the project as proposed and alternatives to it to enable the decisionmakers and the public to make a reasoned choice of alternatives. In particular, an EIR on a proposed general plan must not simply mention alternatives to the general plan as proposed, but also must describe those alternatives and describe their environmental impacts. It may not simply state conclusions regarding the environmental and growth-inducing impact of the general plan as proposed, but must provide supporting facts and data which indicate the basis for those conclusions. And it must be accurate and free of misstatements regarding factual matters relating to the environmental and growth-inducing impact of the general plan as proposed and of alternatives thereto.

13. In order for an EIR on a general plan to be legally adequate, the EIR must disclose the public agency's analysis of the environmental and growth-inducing impacts of the general plan as proposed and of alternatives thereto, and the reasons for the choice recommended therein. The EIR must disclose all relevant data in the public agency's possession relating to a proposed project's adverse environmental and

B. Environmental Policy Acts 731

growth-inducing impacts, preferable alternatives to the project, and necessary mitigation measures....

16. Respondents failed to comply with their duty under CEQA to prepare and consider an adequate EIR prior to adopting the 1973 General Plan, in that the EIR prepared for the County's 1973 General Plan is woefully inadequate to constitute a sufficient informational document under CEQA. The Board of Supervisors and the public were not given an EIR which could be used as an informational document complete with an adequate and accurate discussion of the factual basis for the proposed 1973 General Plan, of the alternatives thereto which were considered and the reasons for their rejection, and the Staff's reasoned and factual response to the many criticisms and comments made by the public to the EIR and the proposed 1973 General Plan.

17. Specific inadequacies in the EIR on the 1973 General Plan, each of which is sufficiently substantial and fundamental to render it legally inadequate, include:

(a) the failure to describe any factual basis for the added 178 square miles of urban expansion;
(b) the failure to include the data and analysis within the staff-prepared "conflicts" study and the Malibu/Calabasas study;
(c) the failure to describe accurately the urban development policy upon which the 1990 Land Use Maps were prepared, and the alternative urban development policies studied, and to evaluate the environmental and growth-inducing impacts of the proposed policy and of each alternative, with supporting facts and data;
(d) the failure to discuss all reasonable alternatives, including the alternatives of using a smaller "excess population capacity," of using the basic land use allocations of the *Guide* as refined over a two year period (without adding the additional 178 square miles of urban expansion), and of guiding the added urban expansion areas to the areas most suitable for urban development;
(e) the failure to describe mitigation measures beyond the implementing power or authority of the County; and
(f) the failure to describe and evaluate with supporting facts and data the environmental and growth-inducing impacts of the proposed general plan, particularly as they relate to agriculture, open space lands and transportation....

19. Respondents failed to comply with CEQA by preparing the 1973 General Plan without adequate environmental information and data, without adequate relationship to comprehensive goals and policies, without adequate relation to current projections of expected future

population growth, and without appropriate evaluation of alternative proposals. Rather, the 1973 General Plan, particularly the 1990 Land Use Maps, were developed largely to conform to pre-existing zoning and individual requests of property owners for particular treatment of specific parcels. The information and criteria used and the manner by which the 1990 Land Use Maps were developed were inadequately disclosed in the EIR and in the 1973 General Plan. . . .

32. Ordinance No. 10710 is a zoning ordinance, and therefore falls within the CEQA definition of a "project" for which an EIR is required if its adoption "may have a significant effect on the environment" or for which a Negative Declaration is required if it will not have such an effect, unless its adoption was within the defined list of categorical exemptions.

33. Respondents failed to prepare either an EIR or Negative Declaration as to Ordinance No. 10710, and there is no evidence before the court that it falls within any categorical exemption.

Let judgment be entered accordingly.[6]

■ H.O.M.E.S. v. NEW YORK STATE URBAN DEVELOPMENT CORP.
69 A.D.2d 222, 418 N.Y.S.2d 827 (1979)

WITMER, Justice.

Appellants are landowners in the City of Syracuse and reside therein in close proximity to the former Archbold Stadium on the campus of Syracuse University. They seek reversal of a judgment at Special Term which dismissed their petition and supplemental petition in a CPLR Article 78 proceeding for the review and annulment of determinations by several respondents herein which gave Syracuse University approval for the destruction of Archbold Stadium and the construction on its site of a new year-around sports facility, referred to as a domed stadium. The basic ground for the objection to the project and for instituting the Article 78 proceeding is the alleged failure of

---

6. In 1978, the Court of Appeals (Second District, Division I), in an identically captioned decision, upheld Judge Thomas's award of $170,000 in attorney's fees to the successful plaintiffs. The court noted that

> the fact that nonresidents of Los Angeles County, for example those in adjoining counties or visitors to this county, will enjoy the environmental benefits resulting from the main action does not mean that it is unfair for only the taxpayers of the county to pay plaintiffs' attorneys' fees. Especially in the case of environmental litigation is it possible to argue that more than those persons represented in the action will benefit from its success. Indeed, one might plausibly argue, taking the large view, that significant protection of the environment in any one part of the world inures to the benefit of the whole.

76 Cal. App. 3d 241, 249-250, 142 Cal. Rptr. 766, 772 (1978). — EDS.

B. Environmental Policy Acts

respondent to comply with the legal requirements with respect to the environmental impact which the new facility will have on the area....

In enacting Article 8 of the Environmental Conservation Law (L. 1975, Ch. 612) the New York State Legislature declared a State policy to promote efforts which will prevent or eliminate damage to the environment and enhance human and community resources (ECL, §8-0101) and its intent that all regulatory agencies conduct their affairs with an awareness that they are stewards of the air, water, land and living resources, and that they have an obligation to protect the environment for the use and enjoyment of this and all future generations (ECL, §§8-0103, ¶8; 8-0109, ¶1). Environment is defined in the statute as "the physical conditions which will be affected by a proposed action, including land, air, ... noise, ... and existing community or neighborhood character" (ECL, §8-0105, ¶6). The primary method of achieving the intended surveillance and protection is the requirement of the preparation and submission of an environmental impact statement for any action, including that requiring agency approval if it may have a significant effect on the environment (ECL, §8-0109, ¶2, et seq.). The New York State Urban Development Corporation (UDC), designated by the Legislature to supervise the State's partial funding of the stadium, and the City Planning Commission are agencies governed by this law (ECL, §8-0105, ¶4(i)) and the regulations adopted thereunder (6 NYCRR, Pt. 617), and the construction of the domed facility herein is an "action" subject to such law and regulations (id., 617.2(b))....

Respondents acknowledge that had the University's application contained provision for parking a substantial number of automobiles of patrons of the new facility, an EIS would be required (see 6 NYCRR 617.-[e] Type I(b)(1), since Nov. 1, 1978, 617.12(b)(6)(iii)). They concluded, however, that because no cognizance was given by the University to parking, the plans did not fall within the Environmental Conservation Law. Like the proverbial ostrich, respondents have incredibly put out of sight and mind a clear environmental problem. By any assessment, the stadium is a major project, that is, a Type I action (6 NYCRR 617.15; since Nov. 1, 1978, 617.12). It is estimated to attract from five to ten times as many patrons per year as did Archbold Stadium. The record shows that the traffic and parking problems have heretofore been serious on days when the stadium was used. With the new stadium, they will be much worse in the absence of comprehensive plans and actions to avoid them. Without such, not only will the residents in the area have extreme difficulty entering and leaving their homes and enjoying the use thereof but, more importantly, even fire fighting equipment and other emergency vehicles will be unable to get through to serve the public.

Whether the UDC properly issued its negative declaration that the project will have no significant impact on the environment and hence there is no need for an EIS depends upon whether it made a thorough investigation of the problems involved and reasonably exercised its discretion (ECL, §8-0109, ¶4; 21 NYCRR 4200.5, ¶¶(a) and (c); 4200.6). Since the State law was modeled after the Federal law in this respect (see Governor's memorandum, 1975 McKinney's Session Laws, p. 1761), for construction of the State law we look to the cases which have construed the National Environmental Policy Act (42 U.S.C.A. §4321, et seq.). . . .

The record shows that UDC did not meet the legal requirements in arriving at its determination that the planned domed facility had no environmental significance on the area. Clearly UDC failed to take a "hard look" at the problems and adverse potential effects of the project on traffic stoppage, parking, air pollution or noise level damage. Not only did it fail to analyze the traffic and parking problems entailed, but it vaguely recognized their existence and relied upon general assurances that after the problems developed the University and City of Syracuse would adequately mitigate them by some unspecified appropriate action. It gave no consideration to the effect on the neighborhood of the operation of this facility nor to the consequences of unplanned "subsequent action" which the contemplated new parking facilities would have on the area. It is inconceivable that the Legislature envisioned or intended that its EIS requirements could be avoided by an applicant and agency which both declined to recognize egregious environmental problems. In Alice-In-Wonderland manner, respondents separated and put aside the realities of the traffic and parking problems from the totality of this project. . . .

During the five or six months that this proceeding has been pending, action under the determinations by the UDC and the City Planning Commission was not stayed, because of respondents' assurances to the court, and their insistence on the urgency of continuing the construction of the facility. We are advised that Archbold Stadium has now been demolished and the foundations for the new facility have been laid and the steel installed. Millions of dollars have been expended on the project. The court, of course, is sympathetic with the objectives of respondents and recognizes that in this practical world it is very likely that some means can be found to solve the environmental problems. The court is mindful that over six months ago respondent University gave assurance that within six months acceptable traffic and parking plans would be completed. Indeed, it was on the strength of such assurances that respondents UDC, City Planning Commission and the Onondaga County Planning Board acted favorably on the University's application.

The Environmental Conservation Law may not be flouted, and the court must uphold it. The determinations of UDC and Syracuse City Planning Commission must, therefore, be held arbitrary and capricious

B. Environmental Policy Acts

and subject to being vacated. Respondents should be stayed, therefore, from proceeding with the authorization, funding and construction of the domed facility.

In recognition of and in reliance upon the various representations made in November and December 1978 that within six months suitable traffic and parking plans could and would be developed, the injunction to be contained in the judgment to be entered on this decision should be stayed for a period of four months from the entry of the judgment, in order to afford respondents an opportunity to comply with the provisions of the State Environmental Quality Review Act and the City Zoning Ordinance.

Notes

1. Twenty states have passed environmental statutes — "baby NEPAs" — requiring the filing of environmental impact statements and the systematic review of state projects. Six more states have acted through executive direction. See 2 Grad, Treatise on Environmental Law §9.08 (1987). Which level of government is better able to protect the environment, the state or the federal government? Are both needed? How should the two bureaucracies coordinate their requirements to avoid duplication of effort, in both filing and assessing environmental impact statements? See the California environmental quality statute, which allows submission of the federal impact report in lieu of the state report if certain conditions are met. Cal. Pub. Res. Code §21083.5 (West 1986).

2. In the Maryland Environmental Policy Act, the General Assembly declares that "[e]ach person has a fundamental and inalienable right to a healthful environment, and each person has a responsibility to contribute to the protection, preservation and enhancement of the environment." Md. Nat. Res. Code Ann. §1-302(d) (1983).

Interpreting NEPA, the courts have held that the congressional policy that declares that "each person should enjoy a healthful environment" does not create any new substantive rights. Does the Maryland statute create new substantive rights for which a citizen could bring suit?[7]

3. Minnesota has established an environmental quality board, similar to that under NEPA:

---

7. Compare Hoffman and Plantico, Toward a Theory of Land Use: Planning Lessons from Oregon, 14 Land & Water L. Rev. 1 (1979) with Morgan and Shonkwiler, State Land Use Planning in Oregon with Special Emphasis on Housing Issues, 11 Urb. Law 1 (1979). In general, see Pelham, State Land Use Planning and Regulation: Florida, the Model Code and Beyond (1979). On the issue of one-step permit processing, see Jarrett & Hicks, Untangling the Permit Web (1978).

The members of the board are the director of the state planning agency, the director of public service, the director of the pollution control agency, the commissioner of natural resources, the commissioner of agriculture, the commissioner of health, the commissioner of transportation, the chair of the board of water and soil resources, and a representative of the governor's office designated by the governor. The governor shall appoint five members from the general public to the board . . . At least two of the five public members shall have knowledge of and be conversant in water management issues in the state.

Minn. Stat. Ann. §116C.03 (West Supp. 1988). Does the council structure help to ensure that state agencies comply with the statute? Or does this provide the commissioners and department heads an opportunity to limit the scope of the statute's application?

4. Intelligent decision-making can be accomplished only through an analytical process — impact statement or whatever its name. But the process itself has to be scrubbed of the real and substantial taint of conflict of interest. For example, the consulting firm compiling the EIS for a proposed highway in Pennsylvania, under contract with a state agency, was itself a subsidiary of the construction company that had already been awarded the contract to build the road! Little more need be said, except to ask, regardless of who compiles the EIS for the Federal Highway Admistration or a state highway department, if either of those agencies can be truly objective about the basic decision to build or not to build the highway. Can the same questions be asked of HUD? Of the Nuclear Regulatory Commission?

In Illinois Railroad v. Illinois, 146 U.S. 387, 453 (1892), the Supreme Court held that the "state can no more abdicate its trust over property in which the whole people are interested, like navigable waters and soils under them, so as to leave them entirely under the use and control of private parties . . . than it can abdicate its police powers in the administration of government and the preservation of the peace." How far can the public trust doctrine be carried in relation to the environment and to growth policies? See Matthews v. Bay Head Improvement Association, 95 N.J. 306, 471 A.2d 355, cert. denied, 469 U.S. 821 (1984); Summa Corp. v. California ex rel. State Lands Commission, 466 U.S. 198 (1984); National Audubon Society v. Superior Court, 33 Cal. 3d 419, 658 P.2d 709, 189 Cal. Reptr. 346 (1983).

■ KEYSTONE BITUMINOUS COAL ASSOCIATION v. DeBENEDICTUS
480 U.S. 470 (1987)

Justice STEVENS delivered the opinion of the Court.

In Pennsylvania Coal Co. v. Mahon, 260 U.S. 393, (1922), the Court reviewed the constitutionality of a Pennsylvania statute that admittedly destroyed "previously existing rights of property and contract." Id., at 413. . . . In that case the "particular facts" led the Court to hold that

B. Environmental Policy Acts

the Pennsylvania Legislature had gone beyond its constitutional powers when it enacted a statute prohibiting the mining of anthracite coal in a manner that would cause the subsidence of land on which certain structures were located.

Now, 65 years later, we address a different set of "particular facts," involving the Pennsylvania Legislature's 1966 conclusion that the Commonwealth's existing mine subsidence legislation had failed to protect the public interest in safety, land conservation, preservation of affected municipalities' tax bases, and land development in the Commonwealth. Based on detailed findings, the legislature enacted the Bituminous Mine Subsidence and Land Conservation Act (the "Subsidence Act" or the "Act"), Pa. Stat. Ann., Tit. 52, §1406.1 et seq. (Purdon Supp. 1986). Petitioners contend, relying heavily on our decision in *Pennsylvania Coal*, that §4 and §6 of the Subsidence Act and certain implementing regulations violate the Takings Clause, and that §6 of the Act violates the Contracts Clause of the Federal Constitution. The District Court and the Court of Appeals concluded that *Pennsylvania Coal* does not control for several reasons and that our subsequent cases make it clear that neither §4 nor §6 is unconstitutional on its face. . . .

Coal mine subsidence is the lowering of strata overlying a coal mine, including the land surface, caused by the extraction of underground coal. This lowering of the strata can have devastating effects. It often causes substantial damage to foundations, walls, other structural members, and the integrity of houses and buildings. Subsidence frequently causes sinkholes or troughs in land which make the land difficult or impossible to develop. Its effect on farming has been well documented — many subsided areas cannot be plowed or properly prepared. Subsidence can also cause the loss of groundwater and surface ponds. In short, it presents the type of environmental concern that has been the focus of so much federal, state, and local regulation in recent decades. . . .

Pennsylvania's Subsidence Act authorizes the Pennsylvania Department of Environmental Resources (DER) to implement and enforce a comprehensive program to prevent or minimize subsidence and to regulate its consequences. Section 4 of the Subsidence Act, Pa. Stat. Ann., Tit. 52, §1406.4 (Purdon Supp. 1986), prohibits mining that causes subsidence damage to three categories of structures that were in place on April 17, 1966: public buildings and noncommercial buildings generally used by the public; dwellings used for human habitation; and cemeteries.[6] Since 1966 the DER has applied a formula that generally

---

6. Section 4 provides:

Protection of surface structures against damage from cave-in, collapse, or subsidence

In order to guard the health, safety and general welfare of the public, no owner, operator, lessor, lessee, or general manager, superintendent or other person in charge of or having supervision over any bituminous coal mine shall mine

requires 50% of the coal beneath structures protected by §4 to be kept in place as a means of providing surface support. Section 6 of the Subsidence Act, 52 Pa. Stat. Ann., Tit. 52, §1406.6 (Purdon Supp. 1986), authorizes the DER to revoke a mining permit if the removal of coal causes damage to a structure or area protected by §4 and the operator has not within six months either repaired the damage, satisfied any claim arising therefrom, or deposited a sum equal to the reasonable cost of repair with the DER as security.

In 1982, petitioners filed a civil rights action in the United States District Court for the Western District of Pennsylvania seeking to enjoin officials of the DER from enforcing the Subsidence Act and its implementing regulations. The petitioners are an association of coal mine operators, and four corporations that are engaged, either directly or through affiliates, in underground mining of bituminous coal in western Pennsylvania. The members of the association and the corporate petitioners own, lease, or otherwise control substantial coal reserves beneath the surface of property affected by the Subsidence Act. The defendants in the action, respondents here, are the Secretary of the Commonwealth of Pennsylvania, the Chief of DER's Division of Mine Subsidence, and the Chief of DER's Section on Mine Subsidence Regulation.

The complaint alleges that Pennsylvania recognizes three separate estates in land: The mineral estate; the surface estate; and the "support estate." Beginning well over 100 years ago, land owners began severing title to underground coal and the right of surface support while

---

bituminous coal so as to cause damage as a result of the caving-in, collapse or subsidence of the following surface structures in place on April 27, 1966, overlying or in the proximity of the mine:

 (1) Any public building or any noncommercial structure customarily used by the public, including but not being limited to churches, schools, hospitals, and municipal utilities or municipal public service operations;
 (2) Any dwelling used for human habitation;.and
 (3) Any cemetery or public burial ground; unless the current owner of the structure consents and the resulting damage is fully repaired or compensated.

In response to the enactment in 1977 of the Federal Surface Mining Control and Reclamation Act, 91 Stat. 445, 30 U.S.C. §1201, et seq., and regulations promulgated by the Secretary of the Interior in 1979, 44 Fed. Reg. 14902, the Pennsylvania DER adopted new regulations extending the statutory protection to additional classes of buildings and surface features. Particularly:

 (a)(1) public buildings and non-commercial buildings customarily used by the public [after April 27, 1966], including churches, schools, hospitals, courthouses, and government offices; . . .
 (4) perennial streams and impoundments of water with the storage volume of 20 acre feet;
 (5) aquifers which serve as a significant source of water supply to any public water system; and
 (6) coal refuse disposa[l] areas.

25 Pa. Code §89.145(a) and §89.146(b) (1983).

B. Environmental Policy Acts

retaining or conveying away ownership of the surface estate. It is stipulated that approximately 90% of the coal that is or will be mined by petitioners in western Pennsylvania was severed from the surface in the period between 1890 and 1920. When acquiring or retaining the mineral estate, petitioners or their predecessors typically acquired or retained certain additional rights that would enable them to extract and remove the coal. Thus, they acquired the right to deposit wastes, to provide for drainage and ventilation, and to erect facilities such as tipples, roads, or railroads, on the surface. Additionally, they typically acquired a waiver of any claims for damages that might result from the removal of the coal.

. . . [P]etitioners alleged that both §4 of the Subsidence Act, as implemented by the 50% rule, and §6 of the Subsidence Act, constitute a taking of their private property without compensation in violation of the Fifth and Fourteenth Amendments. They also alleged that §6 impairs their contractual agreements in violation of Article I, §10 of the Constitution. . . .

In *Pennsylvania Coal,* the Pennsylvania Coal Company had served notice on Mr. and Mrs. Mahon that the company's mining operations beneath their premises would soon reach a point that would cause subsidence to the surface. The Mahons filed a bill in equity seeking to enjoin the coal company from removing any coal that would cause "the caving in, collapse or subsidence" of their dwelling. The bill acknowledged that the Mahons owned only "the surface or right of soil" in the lot, and that the Coal Company had reserved the right to remove the coal without any liability to the owner of the surface estate. Nonetheless, the Mahons asserted that Pennsylvania's then recently enacted Kohler Act of 1921, P.L. 1198, 52 Pa. Stat. Ann. 661 et seq. (Purdon 1954), which prohibited mining that caused subsidence under certain structures, entitled them to an injunction. . . .

Unlike the Kohler Act, which was passed upon in *Pennsylvania Coal,* the Subsidence Act does not merely involve a balancing of the private economic interests of coal companies against the private interests of the surface owners. The Pennsylvania Legislature specifically found that important public interests are served by enforcing a policy that is designed to minimize subsidence in certain areas. Section 2 of the Subsidence Act provides:

> This act shall be deemed to be an exercise of the police powers of the Commonwealth for the protection of the health, safety and general welfare of the people of the Commonwealth, by providing for the conservation of surface land areas which may be affected in the mining of bituminous coal by methods other than "open pit" or "strip" mining, to aid in the protection of the safety of the public, to enhance the value of such lands for taxation, to aid in the preservation of surface water

drainage and public water supplies and generally to improve the use and enjoyment of such lands and to maintain primary jurisdiction over surface coal mining in Pennsylvania. Pa. Ann. Stat., Tit. 52, §1406.2 (Purdon Supp. 1986).

The District Court and the Court of Appeals were both convinced that the legislative purposes set forth in the statute were genuine, substantial, and legitimate, and we have no reason to conclude otherwise.

None of the indicia of a statute enacted solely for the benefit of private parties identified in Justice Holmes' opinion are present here. First, Justice Holmes explained that the Kohler Act was a "private benefit" statute since it "ordinarily does not apply to land when the surface is owned by the owner of the coal." 260 U.S., at 414. The Subsidence Act, by contrast, has no such exception. The current surface owner may only waive the protection of the Act if the DER consents. Moreover, the Court was forced to reject the Commonwealth's safety justification for the Kohler Act because it found that the Commonwealth's interest in safety could as easily have been accomplished through a notice requirement to landowners. The Subsidence Act, by contrast, is designed to accomplish a number of widely varying interests, with reference to which petitioners have not suggested alternative methods through which the Commonwealth could proceed. . . .

Thus, the Subsidence Act differs from the Kohler Act in critical and dispositive respects. With regard to the Kohler Act, the Court believed that the Commonwealth had acted only to ensure against damage to some private landowners' homes. Justice Holmes stated that if the private individuals needed support for their structures, they should not have "take[n] the risk of acquiring only surface rights." 260 U.S., at 416. Here, by contrast, the Commonwealth is acting to protect the public interest in health, the environment, and the fiscal integrity of the area. That private individuals erred in taking a risk cannot estop the State from exercising its police power to abate activity akin to a public nuisance. The Subsidence Act is a prime example that "circumstances may so change in time . . . as to clothe with such a [public] interest what at other times . . . would be a matter of purely private concern." Block v. Hirsh, 256 U.S. 135, 155, (1921). . . .

The second factor that distinguishes this case from *Pennsylvania Coal* is the finding in that case that the Kohler Act made mining of "certain coal" commercially impracticable. In this case, by contrast, petitioners have not shown any deprivation significant enough to satisfy the heavy burden placed upon one alleging a regulatory taking. For this reason, their takings claim must fail. . . .

Instead, petitioners have sought to narrowly define certain segments of their property and assert that, when so defined, the Subsidence Act denies them economically viable use. They advance two alternative

B. Environmental Policy Acts

ways of carving their property in order to reach this conclusion. First, they focus on the specific tons of coal that they must leave in the ground under the Subsidence Act, and argue that the Commonwealth has effectively appropriated this coal since it has no other useful purpose if not mined. Second, they contend that the Commonwealth has taken their separate legal interest in property — the "support estate." . . .

The parties have stipulated that enforcement of the DER's 50% rule will require petitioners to leave approximately 27 million tons of coal in place. Because they own that coal but cannot mine it, they contend that Pennsylvania has appropriated it for the public purposes described in the Subsidence Act.

This argument fails for the reason explained in *Penn Central* and *Andrus* [v. Allard, 444 U.S. 51 (1979)]. The 27 million tons of coal do not constitute a separate segment of property for takings law purposes. Many zoning ordinances place limits on the property owner's right to make profitable use of some segments of his property. A requirement that a building occupy no more than a specified percentage of the lot on which it is located could be characterized as a taking of the vacant area as readily as the requirement that coal pillars be left in place. Similarly, under petitioners' theory one could always argue that a set-back ordinance requiring that no structure be built within a certain distance from the property line constitutes a taking because the footage represents a distinct segment of property for takings law purposes. Cf. Gorieb v. Fox, 274 U.S. 603 (1927) (upholding validity of set-back ordinance) (per Holmes, J.). There is no basis for treating the less than 2% of petitioners' coal as a separate parcel of property. . . .

Pennsylvania property law is apparently unique in regarding the support estate as a separate interest in land that can be conveyed apart from either the mineral estate or the surface estate. Petitioners therefore argue that even if comparable legislation in another State would not constitute a taking, the Subsidence Act has that consequence because it entirely destroys the value of their unique support estate. It is clear, however, that our takings jurisprudence forecloses reliance on such legalistic distinctions within a bundle of property rights. . . .

The Court of Appeals, which is more familiar with Pennsylvania law than we are, concluded that as a practical matter the support estate is always owned by either the owner of the surface or the owner of the minerals. . . .

Thus, in practical terms, the support estate has value only insofar as it protects or enhances the value of the estate with which it is associated. Its value is merely a part of the entire bundle of rights possessed by the owner of either the coal or the surface. Because petitioners retain the right to mine virtually all of the coal in their mineral estates, the burden the Act places on the support estate does not constitute a taking. Petitioners may continue to mine coal profitably even if they may not destroy or damage surface structures at will in the process. . . .

The judgment of the Court of Appeals is *Affirmed.*

Chief Justice REHNQUIST, with whom Justice POWELL, Justice O'CONNOR, and Justice SCALIA join, dissenting. . . .

Notes

1. Did the majority's unwillingness to find a regulatory taking (despite the apparent similarities to the act that failed Justice Holmes's "too far" test in *Pennsylvania Coal*) signal that some of the Justices were having second thoughts about cases like *Penn Central,* in which the Court said regulation might indeed amount to a violation of the fifth amendment's just compensation clause? Apparently not, given the Court's decisions near the end of the same term in *First English,* infra page 913, and *Nollan,* supra page 636.

Chief Justice Rehnquist was unpersuaded by the majority's attempt to distinguish the undistinguishable (470 U.S. at 513): "The central purposes of the Act, though including public safety, reflect a concern for preservation of buildings, economic development, and maintenance of property values to sustain the Commonwealth's tax base. We should hesitate to allow a regulation based on essentially economic concerns to be insulated from the dictates of the Fifth Amendment by labeling it nuisance regulation."

Has the majority vindicated Justice Brandeis's fifty-five-year-old dissent? See *Pennsylvania Coal,* 260 U.S. at 417: "[R]estriction imposed to protect the public health, safety or morals from dangers threatened is not a taking. The restriction here in question is merely the prohibition of a noxious use." As for the Court's dismissal of the "27 million tons of coal in place," consider Professor Epstein's position: "[N]o amount of precedent can render coherent a position that is not. The general principle of eminent domain law has always been, and logically must be, this: What has the state taken, and not what has the owner retained." Takings: Descent and Resurrection, 1987 Sup. Ct. Rev. 1, 17.

2. In 1981, the Court rejected another takings challenge to a coal mining statute, this time the Surface Mining Control and Reclamation Act of 1977, 30 U.S.C. §1201 et seq. Hodel v. Virginia Surface Mining & Reclamation Association, Inc., 452 U.S. 264 (1981). The Act was found not to violate the commerce clause, the tenth amendment's limitation on congressional power to interfere with the states' traditional right to regulate land use, or the fifth amendment, for the mere enactment of the legislation did not present the Court with a concrete controversy ripe for judicial resolution.

3. See Laitos and Westfall, Government Interference with Private Interests in Public Resources, 11 Harv. Envtl. L. Rev. 1, 4-5, 74-75 (1987):

> As the federal government has moved to a conservation and environmental ethic in managing public lands and resources, many congressional and executive actions have also limited and sometimes even prevented acquisition or retention of less-than-fee interests in public property. Examples include: the executive creation of federal reservations, the passage of the Federal Land Policy and Management Act of 1976 ("FLPMA"); the enactment of statehood acts; the passage of the Alaska Native Claims Settlement Act of 1971 ("ANCSA"); the administrative application of the 1920 Mineral Leasing Act; the passage of the Outer Continental Shelf Lands Act of 1953 ("OCSLA"); administrative imposition of a moratorium on federal coal leasing by the Secretary of Interior; the passage of the Federal Coal Leasing Amendments Act of 1975 ("FCLAA"); the passage of the Surface Mining Control and Reclamation Act of 1977 ("SMCRA"); executive issuance of Public Land Orders withdrawing certain lands from mineral entry; and the passage of the Federal Water Pollution Control Act Amendments of 1972. . . .
>
> All these federal executive, administrative, and congressional actions can potentially defeat private expectations in the creation of a legal interest in federal lands or resources; or they may burden an established, preexisting private interest in federal lands or resources with unanticipated, and often costly, subsequently imposed federal requirements. . . .
>
> A party seeking to acquire a property interest from the United States or wishing to protect a previously acquired interest risks interference with, or abolishment of, the application/interest by the imposition of subsequent law. Parties facing retroactive application of burdensome new law may counter the effect of the law by demonstrating that the interest threatened is a legitimate "protectible property interest." Such parties may also claim that the interest is a valid existing right or, alternatively, a property right specifically noted in a grandfather clause. Interests falling within these classifications may be immunized entirely from the operation of subsequent law, protected from fifth amendment takings, or shielded from the new law "unreasonably interfering" with the interest. Despite these potential safeguards, the considerable power of the federal government over public lands and resources allows it to impose reasonable, but costly, conditions on interests previously acquired from the United States. Private interests obtained under state law may similarly be subject to unexpected, even harsh limitations, pursuant to the state's police power. A warning of "grantee beware" should therefore be considered by all would-be interest holders of public property.

C. TAKEOVER BY THE STATES?

Most states delegate land-use controls to the local governments along the lines of the Standard State Zoning Enabling Act. Accordingly, a few communities have adopted policies aimed at both distributional and numerical control of growth. For example, Petaluma set a limit on new building permits to be issued each year; Ramapo decided to control the location and timing of municipal services; Aurora, Colorado, drew a blue line around the community and decided to provide municipal services inside that line only; Lexington, Kentucky, set population guidelines for neighborhood areas and adopted an urban service boundary; and Loudoun County, Virginia, adopted fiscal and environmental criteria for determining whether to approve development permits. These local policies should be examined in light of their enabling laws. In analyzing the following statutes, examine the legislative goals and standards for land-use planning, the structure chosen for policy refinement and preparation of the state comprehensive plan, the location of power to implement the policies and plans, and the criteria for state intervention in land-use decisions. What can be implied about the state view of such issues as regionalism, home rule, metropolitanism, environmentalism, centralization, public participation, and planning?

1. Goals and Purposes

The external effects of growth have provided the impetus for states to adopt land-use legislation. However, "growth" subsumes a tremendous number of values and actions. Thus, one must ask what aspect of growth concerns the state? Growth in critical areas? Growth of a particular magnitude? Is the concern with growth stated expressly in the statute? If growth is to be regulated, what is being protected? The environment? The financial capability of the community or state to provide services? The character of the community? Is the statute focused on the amount of growth or on its location? Is such a distinction misleading? Is the legislation intended to preempt the regulations of local governments?

See DeGrove and Stroud, State Land Planning and Regulation: Innovative Roles in the 1980s and Beyond, Land Use L. & Zoning Dig., March 1987, at 3:

> The state programs that emerged in the 1970s reallocated land use planning and permitting responsibility from the local government to the state government. The state authority could be exercised directly by an existing state agency, but was more often exercised by a newly created arm of the state with either statewide or regional jurisdiction. The major state approaches vary, however, according to the scope of the program created. We believe the approaches can be described most meaningfully in four categories. The first approach is a comprehensive/selective one, illustrated by the state programs adopted in Florida and Vermont. This

C. Takeover by the States?

approach is comprehensive in that it may be applied throughout the state; it is selective in its application to particular types of development or geographic areas.

A second approach is comprehensive/general. The programs, for example, in Oregon and Hawaii are statewide in scope and, by their nature, apply generally to all land use activities. A third approach is the coastal program, illustrated in California and North Carolina. In this approach, a significant area of the state — the coast — is planned and regulated across a number of general land use activities. Finally, certain states have selected a particular geographic area to plan and regulate, as characterized in the New Jersey Pinelands program. Although the last two approaches are essentially similar, the coastal approach deserves special attention because it has been developed to a much greater extent than the selective programs applying to noncoastal areas. These approaches illustrate various ways in which states have reasserted their land planning and regulatory authority.

See also the text and commentary for Article 7 of the Model Land Development Code (State Land Development Regulation).

■ MAINE SITE LOCATION OF DEVELOPMENT LAW
Me. Rev. Stat. Ann. tit. 38, §481 (Supp. 1987)

The Legislature finds that the economic and social well-being of the citizens of the State of Maine depend upon the location of state, municipal, quasi-municipal, educational, charitable, commercial and industrial developments with respect to the natural environment of the State; that many developments because of their size and nature are capable of causing irreparable damage to the people and the environment on the development sites and in their surroundings; that the location of such developments is too important to be left only to the determination of the owners of such developments; and that discretion must be vested in state authority to regulate the location of developments which may substantially affect environment. . . .

The purpose of this subchapter is to provide a flexible and practical means by which the State, acting through the Board of Environmental Protection, in consultation with appropriate state agencies, may exercise the police power of the State to control the location of those developments substantially affecting local environment in order to insure that such developments will be located in a manner which will have a minimal adverse impact on the natural environment within the development sites and of their surroundings and protect the health, safety and general welfare of the people.[8]

■ FLORIDA ENVIRONMENTAL LAND AND WATER MANAGEMENT ACT OF 1972[9]
Fla. Stat. Ann. §380.021 (West 1988)

It is the legislative intent that, in order to protect the natural resources and environment of this state as provided in §7, Art. II of the state constitution, insure a water management system that will reverse the deterioration of water quality and provide optimum utilization of our limited water resources, facilitate orderly and well-planned development, and protect the health, welfare, safety, and quality of life of the residents of this state, it is necessary adequately to plan for and guide growth and development within this state. In order to accomplish these purposes, it is necessary that the state establish land and water management policies to guide and coordinate local decisions relating to growth and development; that such state land and water management policies should, to the maximum possible extent, be implemented by local governments through existing processes for the guidance of growth and development; and that all the existing rights of private property be preserved in accord with the constitution of this state and of the United States.

■ HAWAII QUALITY GROWTH ACT OF 1972
Haw. Rev. Stat. (1985)

[§223-1] The purpose of this chapter is to provide for the development of a policy for the State of Hawaii to halt urban sprawl with its attendant need for costly urban services, to preserve and conserve open space areas, to enhance and protect the environment of Hawaii, and to

---

8. Not all potentially harmful uses are state-controlled, however. The final paragraph of §481, added in 1987, states "that noise generated at development sites has primarily a geographically restricted and frequently transient impact which is best regulated at the municipal level pursuant to a municipality's economic development and land use plans." Is performance zoning, supra page 276, a useful local tool? — Eds.

9. In its story of builders and ecologists clashing over the future of Key Largo, the New York Times reports that the ramshackle old Caribbean Club remains, with the cinematic ghosts of Bogart, Bacall, and Robinson drifting around its interior; just about everything else is gone under the onslaught of the Florida boom. Feb. 23, 1975. See Carter, The Florida Experience (1975). For a discussion of Florida's approach and its reaction to Askew v. Cross Key Waterways, 372 So. 2d 913 (Fla. 1978), see Pelham, Regulating Areas of Critical State Concern: Florida and the Model Code, 18 Urb. L. Ann. 3 (1980); cf. Finnell, Coastal Land Management in Florida, 1980 Am. B. Found. Res. J. 303.

C. Takeover by the States?

uplift the quality of life for all its citizens and to provide for implementation of such policy.

[§223-2] The office of the governor shall develop a quality growth policy for the State of Hawaii to effectuate the purpose of this chapter, based upon criteria which shall include the following considerations:

(1) an examination of the environmental impact of proposed urban development;
(2) the relationship between short-term and long-term environmental quality;
(3) any irretrievable commitment of resources through urban development; and
(4) alternatives available to minimize adverse environmental effects as balanced against economic development of the State.

The quality growth policy shall include a comprehensive policy framework for directing growth and land use and shall identify State growth objectives and specific operational constraints to further such objectives.

■ OREGON LAND USE LAW
Or. Rev. Stat. Ann. §197.005 (1985)

The Legislative Assembly finds that:

(1) Uncoordinated uses of lands within this state threaten the orderly development, the environment of this state and the health, safety, order, convenience, prosperity and welfare of the people of this state.

(2) To promote coordinated administration of land uses consistent with comprehensive plans adopted throughout the state, it is necessary to establish a process for the review of state agency, city, county and special district land conservation and development plans for compliance with goals.

(3) Except as otherwise provided in subsection (4) of this section, cities and counties should remain as the agencies to consider, promote and manage the local aspects of land conservation and development for the best interests of the people within their jurisdictions.

(4) The promotion of coordinated state-wide land conservation and development requires the creation of a state-wide planning agency to prescribe planning goals and objectives to be applied by state agencies, cities, counties and special districts throughout the state.

2. Definitions

■ MAINE SITE LOCATION OF DEVELOPMENT LAW
Me. Rev. Stat. Ann. tit. 38, §482 (Supp. 1986)

2. . . . "Development which may substantially affect the environment," in this Article called "development," means any state, municipal, quasi-municipal, educational, charitable, commercial or industrial development, including subdivisions, which occupies a land or water area in excess of 20 acres, or which contemplates drilling for or excavating natural resources, on land or under water where the area affected is in excess of 60,000 square feet, or which is a mining activity, or which is a hazardous activity, or which is a structure; but excluding state highways, state aid highways, borrow pits for sand, fill or gravel, of less than 5 acres or when regulated by the Department of Transportation, and such borrow pits entirely within the jurisdiction of the Maine Land Use Regulation Commission . . . and those activities regulated by the Department of Marine Resources. . . .[10]

■ FLORIDA ENVIRONMENTAL LAND AND WATER MANAGEMENT ACT OF 1972
Fla. Stat. Ann. §380.04 (West 1988)

(1) The term "development" means the carrying out of any building activity or mining operation, the making of any material change in the use or appearance of any structure or land, or the dividing of land into three or more parcels. . . .

(3) The following operations or uses shall not be taken for the purpose of this chapter to involve development as defined in this section:

(a) Work by a highway or road agency or railroad company for the maintenance or improvement of a road or railroad track, if the work is carried out on land within the boundaries of the right-of-way.

(b) Work by any utility and other persons engaged in the distribution or transmission of gas or water, for the purpose of inspecting, repairing, renewing, or constructing on established rights-

---

10. This section was held to apply "to a subdivision consisting entirely of lots located on an island except for a single piece of land located on the mainland. The sole purpose of the mainland portion of the development [was] to provide parking space and water access for the owners of subdivision lots located on the island." See Op. Me. Atty. Gen. No. 84-14, Mar. 30, 1984. — Eds.

C. Takeover by the States?

of-way any sewers, mains, pipes, cables, utility tunnels, power lines, towers, poles, tracks, or the like.

(c) Work for the maintenance, renewal, improvement, or alteration of any structure, if the work affects only the interior or the color of the structure or the decoration of the exterior of the structure.

(d) The use of any structure or land devoted to dwelling uses for any purpose customarily incidental to enjoyment of the dwelling.

(e) The use of any land for the purpose of growing plants, crops, trees, and other agricultural or forestry products; raising livestock; or for other agricultural purposes.

(f) A change in use of land or structure from a use within a class specified in an ordinance or rule to another use in the same class.

(g) A change in the ownership or form of ownership of any parcel or structure.

(h) The creation or termination of rights of access, riparian rights, easements, covenants concerning development of land, or other rights in land.

■ FLORIDA ENVIRONMENTAL LAND AND WATER MANAGEMENT ACT OF 1972
Fla. Stat. Ann. §380.06 (West 1988)

(1) The term "development of regional impact," as used in this section, means any development which, because of its character, magnitude, or location, would have a substantial effect upon the health, safety, or welfare of citizens of more than one county.

■ OREGON LAND USE LAW
Or. Rev. Stat. Ann. §197.015 (1985)

(10) "Land use decision":
  (a) Includes:
    (A) A final decision or determination made by a local government or special district that concerns the adoption, amendment or application of:
      (i) The goals;
      (ii) A comprehensive plan provision;
      (iii) A land use regulation; or
      (iv) A new land use regulation; or
    (B) A final decision or determination of a state agency other than the commission with respect to which the agency is required to apply the goals. . . .

(11) "Land use regulation" means any local government zoning ordinance, land division ordinance ... or similar general ordinance establishing standards for implementing a comprehensive plan. "Land use regulation" does not include small tract zoning map amendments, conditional use permits, individual subdivision, partitioning or planned unit development approvals or denials, annexations, variances, building permits and similar administrative-type decisions.

■ FLORIDA ENVIRONMENTAL LAND AND WATER MANAGEMENT ACT OF 1972
Fla. Stat. Ann. §380.05 (West 1988)

(2) An area of critical state concern may be designated only for:

(a) An area containing, or having a significant impact upon, environmental or natural resources of regional or statewide importance, including, but not limited to, state or federal parks, forests, wildlife refuges, wilderness areas, aquatic preserves, major rivers and estuaries, state environmentally endangered lands, Outstanding Florida Waters, and aquifer recharge areas, the uncontrolled private or public development of which would cause substantial deterioration of such resources. Specific criteria which shall be considered in designating an area under this paragraph include:

1. Whether the economic value of the area, as determined by the type, variety, distribution, relative scarcity, and condition of the environmental or natural resources within the area, is of substantial regional or statewide importance.

2. Whether the ecological value of the area, as determined by the physical and biological components of the environmental system, is of substantial regional or statewide importance.

3. Whether the area is a designated critical habitat of any state or federally designated threatened or endangered plant or animal species.

4. Whether the area is inherently susceptible to substantial development due to its geographic location or natural aesthetics.

5. Whether any existing or planned substantial development within the area will directly, significantly, and deleteriously affect any or all of the environmental or natural resources of the area which are of regional or statewide importance.

(b) An area containing, or having a significant impact upon, historical or archaeological resources, sites, or statutorily defined historical or archaeological districts, the private or public development of which would cause substantial deterioration or complete loss of such resources, sites, or districts. . . .

(c) An area having a significant impact upon, or being significantly impacted by, an existing or proposed major public facility or other area of major public investment including, but not limited to, highways, ports, airports, energy facilities, and water management projects.

3. Standards

■ FLORIDA ENVIRONMENTAL LAND AND WATER MANAGEMENT ACT OF 1972
Fla. Stat. Ann. §380.06 (West 1988)

(12) (a) Within 50 days after receipt of the notice of public hearing . . . the regional planning agency, if one has been designated for the area including the local government, shall prepare and submit to the local government a report and recommendations on the regional impact of the proposed development. In preparing its report and recommendations, the regional planning agency shall identify regional issues based upon the following review criteria and make recommendations to the local government on these regional issues, specifically considering whether, and the extent to which:

1. The development will have a favorable or unfavorable impact on the environment and natural and historical resources of the region.

2. The development will have a favorable or unfavorable impact on the economy of the region.

3. The development will efficiently use or unduly burden water, sewer, solid waste disposal, or other necessary public facilities.

4. The development will efficiently use or unduly burden public transportation facilities.

5. The development will favorably or adversely affect the ability of people to find adequate housing reasonably accessible to their places of employment.

6. The development complies with such other criteria for determining regional impact as the regional planning agency deems appropriate, including, but not limited to, the extent to which the development would create an additional demand for, or additional use of, energy. . . .[11]

---

11. Compare Finnell, Saving Paradise: The Florida Environmental Land and Water Management Act of 1972, 1973 Urb. L. Ann. 1035 with O'Connell, Growth Management in Florida: Will State and Local Governments Get Their Acts Together?, Fla. Envtl. & Urb. Issues, Apr. 1984, at 1. For developments leading to a dramatic revamping of the Florida statutory scheme, see Pelham, Hyde, and Banks, Managing Florida's Growth, 13 Fla. St. U.L. Rev. 515 (1985). — EDS.

■ MAINE SITE LOCATION OF DEVELOPMENT LAW
Me. Rev. Stat. Ann. tit. 38, §484 (1978 & Supp. 1987)

The board shall approve a developmental proposal whenever it finds that:

(1) Financial capacity. The developer has the financial capacity and technical ability to meet state air and water pollution control standards, and has made adequate provision for solid waste disposal, the control of offensive odors, and the securing and maintenance of sufficient and healthful water supplies.

(2) Traffic movement. The developer has made adequate provision for traffic movement of all types into, out of, or within the development area.

(3) No adverse effect on the natural environment. The developer has made adequate provision for fitting the development harmoniously into the existing natural environment and that the development will not adversely affect existing uses, scenic character, or natural resources in the municipality or in neighboring municipalities.

(4) Soil types. The proposed development will be built on soil types which are suitable to the nature of the undertaking.

(5) Ground water. The proposed development will not pose an unreasonable risk that a discharge to a significant ground water aquifer will occur. . . .

At hearings held under this section the burden shall be upon the person proposing the development to affirmatively demonstrate to the board that each of the criteria for approval listed in the preceding paragraphs has been met, and that the public's health, safety and general welfare will be adequately protected.

4. State Land-Use Districts

■ HAWAII LAND USE LAW
Haw. Rev. Stat. §205-2 (Supp. 1987)

There shall be four major land use districts in which all lands in the State shall be placed: urban, rural, agricultural, and conservation. The land use commission shall group contiguous land areas suitable for inclusion in one of these four major districts. . . .

In establishing the boundaries of the districts in each county, the commission shall give consideration to the master plan or general plan of the county.

Urban districts shall include activities or uses as provided by ordinances or regulations of the county within which the urban district is situated.

Rural districts shall include activities or uses as characterized by low density residential lots of not more than one dwelling house per one-half acre in areas where "city-like" concentration of people, structures, streets, and urban level of services are absent, and where small farms are intermixed with the low density residential lots *except that within a subdivision, as defined in section 484-1, the commission for good cause may allow one lot of less than one-half acre, but not less than 18,500 square feet, or an equivalent residential density, within a rural subdivision and permit the construction of one dwelling on such lot, provided that all other dwellings in the subdivision shall have a minimum lot size of one-half acre or 21,780 square feet. Such petition for variance may be processed under the special permit procedure.* These districts may include contiguous areas which are not suited to low density residential lots or small farms by reason of topography, soils, and other related characteristics.

Agricultural districts shall include activities or uses as characterized by the cultivation of crops, orchards, forage, and forestry; farming activities or uses related to animal husbandry, *aquaculture,* game and fish propagation; *aquaculture, which means the production of aquatic plant and animal life for food and fiber within ponds and other bodies of water; wind generated energy production for public, private and commercial use;* services and uses accessory to the above activities including but not limited to living quarters or dwellings, mills, storage facilities, processing facilities, and roadside stands for the sale of products grown on the premises; *wind machines and wind farms; agricultural parks;* and open area recreational facilities, including golf courses and golf driving ranges, provided that they are not located within agricultural district lands with soil classified by the land study bureau's detailed land classification as overall (master) productivity rating class A or B. . . .

Conservation districts shall include areas necessary for protecting watersheds and water sources; preserving scenic and historic areas; providing park lands, wilderness, and beach *reserves;* conserving *indigenous or* endemic plants, fish, and wildlife; preventing floods and soil erosion; forestry; open space areas whose existing openness, natural condition, or present state of use, if retained, would enhance the present or potential value of abutting or surrounding communities, or would maintain or enhance the conservation of natural or scenic resources; areas of value for recreational purposes; and other related activities; and other permitted uses not detrimental to a multiple use conservation concept.[12]

12. All italicized sections added since 1974. See Callies, Regulating Paradise: Land Use Controls in Hawaii (1984); Keith, The Hawaii State Plan Revisited, 7 U. Haw. L. Rev. 29 (1985). — EDS.

Notes

1. In Neighborhood Board No. 24 v. State Land Use Commission, 639 P.2d 1097 (Haw. 1982), the court stated:

> We believe that allowance of a special permit for the development of a recreational theme park covering 103 acres of agricultural land, a major commercial undertaking which developers estimate will attract approximately 1.5 million people annually to the Waianae Coast, accordingly frustrates the objectives and effectiveness of Hawaii's land use scheme. By enacting HRS ch. 205 in 1961, the legislature intended, inter alia, to "[s]tage the allocation of land for development in an orderly plan," H. Stand. Comm. Rep. No. 395, 1st Haw. Leg., 2d Sess., reprinted in 1961 House Journal 855-56, and to redress the problem of "[i]nadequate controls [which] have caused many of Hawaii's limited and valuable lands to be used for purposes that may have a short-term gain to a few but result in a long-term loss to the income and growth potential of our economy." Act 187, 1961 Haw. Sess. Laws 299. The interim statewide land use guidance policies enumerated in HRS §205-16.1 (1976 & Supp. 1981) and the Hawaii state plan, HRS ch. 226, themselves articulate as planning objectives the avoidance of scattered urban development and the accommodation of urban growth in existing urban areas. See HRS §§205-16.1(3), (4), 226-104, -105. We do not believe that the legislature envisioned the special use technique to be used as a method of circumventing district boundary amendment procedures to allow the ad hoc infusion of major urban uses into agricultural districts.
>
> ... We therefore conclude that Oahu's Kahe Point proposal is not an "unusual and reasonable use" which would qualify for a special permit under HRS §205-6, and that the planning commission and LUC abused their discretion in approving Oahu's application. The proposed recreational theme park is more properly the subject of a district boundary amendment petition, which would be considered in accordance with the requirements of procedure and proof set forth in HRS §205-4.

See also Healy & Rosenberg, Land Use and the States 185-186 (2d ed. 1979).

2. In Committee to Save the Bishop's House, Inc. v. Medical Center Hospital of Vermont, Inc., 137 Vt. 142, 400 A.2d 1015 (1979), an action was begun to enjoin merged hospitals from demolishing the Bishop's House and constructing a parking lot to serve the smaller unit. In construing the Vermont statute, the court held that though the two hospitals were separated by only one-half mile, the lot was not "incident to the use" of the larger hospital. The opinion went on:

> [A] careful reading of the statute as a whole, and of section 6001(3) in particular, convinces us that it was the Legislature's intent to involve the state in land use decisions in cases where a permanent mechanism exists

C. Takeover by the States?

for their review at the municipal level only where activity on a very major scale is planned. . . . The implication is clear that the Legislature sought to mandate a second layer of review of proposed land use decisions, imposing substantial additional administrative and financial burdens on an applicant, and possibly interfering to some extent with local control of land use decisions, only where values of state concern are implicated through large-scale changes in land utilization. . . . We will not presume an intention on the part of the Legislature in enacting Act 250 to dilute the authority delegated to the municipalities to regulate land use decisions.

In In re Baptist Fellowship of Randolph, Inc., 481 A.2d 1274 (Vt. 1984), the court found that a church's construction of a meetinghouse was a "development" subject to the plan review requirements of Act 250 (Title 10 of Vermont Statutes Annotated). The church argued that the phrase "in exchange for" — contained in Environmental Board Rule 2(L) (defining the "commercial purpose" aspect of "development") — did not include church activities, since the church did not require its users to make any payment of any kind. "Act 250," the court stated, "speaks to land use and not to the particular institutional activity associated with that land use; to exclude a church from the provisions of Act 250 simply because of its evangelical services could not be justified on environmental grounds."

3. On the unanticipated hazards of statewide planning, see 1000 Friends of Oregon v. Wasco County Court, 299 Or. 344, 703 P.2d 207, 213 (1985): "This case involves a question of whether the Statewide Land Use Planning Goals, and particularly the Urbanization Goal . . . apply to a county's decision to approve a petition for the incorporation of a new city (Rajneeshpuram) and to authorize an incorporation election." The dispute centered on the notorious Chivaldis Rajneesh Meditation Center, located on a 64,000-acre ranch in Wasco and Jefferson Counties.

4. Which is more important, the size or the impact of the development? Isn't the concept behind the planned unit development, new towns, and urban renewal that better planning occurs when done on a larger scale? Aren't innovative design concepts easier to implement in large-scale developments? Shouldn't the statutes encourage large-scale development outside critical environmental areas? Or is the problem that large-scale development generates more and more development? What is an area of "natural growth" or a "growth pole"? Aren't they partially the result of such growth generators as intersections between major transportation facilities?

5. The Model Land Development Code was drafted on the premise, as Babcock explained, that "to the extent that there should be a voice in some decisions that can speak for a constituency greater than the municipality, the state is the appropriate authority. This implies a

rejection of at least two alternatives, the national government and metropolitanism of some sort." 1972 Urb. L. Ann. 59.

He goes on to say that "planning without the attributes of sovereignty . . . is nothing." Is this a fair appraisal of the potential of regional agencies? Certainly it is descriptive of much of their past performance; this being the case, why would states propose the creation of new regional agencies? Compare the approaches in Florida, Oregon, and Hawaii.

For two neighboring states' differing approaches to protecting the same precious resource, see Md. Nat. Res. Code Ann. §§8-1801 to -1816 (Supp. 1988) (Chesapeake Bay Coastal Area Protection Program); Va. Code Ann. §§10.1-2100 to -2115 (Supp. 1988) (Chesapeake Bay Preservation Act). Potentially, how sweeping is the Virginia Act, given §10.1-2115: "The provisions of this chapter shall not affect vested rights of any landowner under existing law"?

D. POLITICS, ECONOMICS, AND THE LIMITS OF LEGALISM

1. Coastal New Federalism

■ NOLLAN v. CALIFORNIA COASTAL COMMISSION
107 S. Ct. 3141 (1987)

[See supra page 636 for opinion.[13]]

■ WOLF, ACCOMMODATING TENSIONS IN THE COASTAL ZONE: AN INTRODUCTION AND OVERVIEW
25 Nat. Resources J. 7, 7-10, 14-19 (1985)

From the time of our earliest settlements, coastal land has been considered the most desirable for aesthetic, economic, and recreational

---

13. For a case explaining the origins and operation of California's coastal zone planning scheme, see City of Chula Vista v. Superior Court of the County of San Diego, 133 Cal. App. 3d 472, 183 Cal. Rptr. 909 (1982) (substantial evidence supported decision of California Coastal Commission to disapprove city's Local Coastal Program). Recall also that the New Jersey Supreme Court approved that state's coastal program's use of inclusionary zoning in the *Egg Harbor* case, supra page 433. Would such a holding pass the Supreme Court's *Nollan* test?

D. POLITICS, ECONOMICS, AND THE LIMITS OF LEGALISM 757

reasons. As America matured, even as the population began to inhabit the great center of the continent, the coast retained its magnetism.

In recent decades, two new movements — attendant with profound social, economic, and political ramifications — have been identified with the coast: efforts to conserve the country's natural treasures and the race for energy independence. The tensions and demands occasioned by these key developments proved too much for the state and local mechanisms that had been established to plan and manage activities within and affecting coastal areas.[5] Cries for a national mediatory presence culminated in the passage of the Coastal Zone Management Act of 1972 (CZMA),[6] a controversial legislative scheme that has since been refined three times (in 1976, 1978, and 1980).

The promulgation and implementation of the CZMA signified a dramatic break with federal legislative and administrative schemes created in the late 1960s and early 1970s. The familiar "sticks" — threatened cut-offs of desperately needed funds, new and expanded causes of action in federal courts, and detailed regulatory and statutory orders — were replaced by two attractive "carrots": substantial direct financial assistance in the form of matching grants, and a provision mandating that federal coastal activities must be consistent with approved state programs. . . .

Unlike "pure" environmental or "pure" energy development interest legislation, the CZMA's chief focus is on the planning side, as suggested by the term "management." In fact, it is this planning element — the refusal to take a substantive stand on either side of the struggle between conservation and resource development — that has led to the most heated debates over the purpose and implementation of the decade-old program. . . .

In many ways CZMA presents an archetypal New Federalism blueprint, for it attempts to restructure local, state, and federal relationships, often placing the concerns and demands of the former two levels of government over and above the usually ascendant third. With its declared emphasis on management and planning,[16] as opposed to specific action and results, the federal CZM structure fits well with the Reagan Administration's view of the most beneficial role of the central government. Still, because CZM funds are budget line items, the program has been subjected to severe economic constraints, a fate shared by other promising federal cooperative projects. . . .

---

5. The disastrous Santa Barbara oil spill in 1969 is perhaps the most familiar symbol of the risks involved in failing to meet the demands of competing coastal uses.
6. Pub. L. No. 92-583, 86 Stat. 1280 (codified as amended at 16 U.S.C. §§1451-1464 (1982)).
16. E.g., 16 U.S.C. §1452(2)(I) (1982) (state management programs to provide for "assistance to support comprehensive planning, conservation, and management . . .").

... In the absence of specific federal orders and specifications, a wide range of programs has been prodded and nurtured through CZM:

> [C]oastal programs range from stringent regulation in California, where a coastal property owner may be forbidden to build on his own land, to permissive overseeing in Louisiana, where some conservationists complain that oil companies are allowed to mangle the fragile shoreline at will.
>   In South Carolina, helicopter crews on regular patrol look for landowners illegally diking marsh lands. In Massachusetts, no fewer than 315 community conservation commissions coordinate with the state in carrying out 27 coastal conservation policies.[27] ...

As with any other program grounded in law and regulation, CZM has as its ultimate arbiter the judiciary. While there have been some exceptions, generally the courts, as in the land-use field as a whole, have been quite deferential to states and localities in their efforts to plan and manage coastal regions in accordance with the tone and substance of the CZMA. For example, a federal district court upheld the right of the California Coastal Commission, in accordance with the consistency provision of the CZMA, to review the Interstate Commerce Commission's approval of plans to remove nearly seven miles of railroad tracks on the Monterey Peninsula.[37] Similarly, the U.S. Court of Appeals, Third Circuit, ruled that the Environmental Protection Agency acted arbitrarily and contrary to the CZMA by insisting on grant conditions that, if enforced, would have run contrary to state and local coastal planning decisions.[38]

It was left to five Justices of the United States Supreme Court, in a decision announced January 11, 1984, to provide the most significant (and controversial) interpretation of the statutory foundation of CZM.[39] Secretary of the Interior v. California arose from the Interior Department's plans to sell oil and gas leases on the OCS [Outer Continental Shelf] off the California coast. The California Coastal Commission viewed these activities as "directly affecting" the coastal zone and demanded a consistency review in accordance with §307(c)(1) of the CZMA.[40] The demand was rejected by Interior. The state, along with the Natural Resources Defense Council, Inc., the Sierra Club, Friends of the Earth, Friends of the Sea Otter, and the Environmental Coalition

---

27. Hill, Federal Law on Coastal Land Use, After 12 Years, Is Having Wide Impact, N.Y. Times, Sept. 16, 1984, at 36, col. 1.
37. Southern Pac. Transp. Co. v. California Coastal Comm'n, 520 F. Supp. 800 (N.D. Cal. 1981).
38. Cape May Greene, Inc. v. Warren, 698 F.2d 179 (3d Cir. 1983).
39. Secretary of the Interior v. California, [464] U.S. [312], 104 S. Ct. 656 (1984).
40. "Each Federal agency conducting or supporting activities directly affecting the coastal zone shall conduct or support those activities in a manner which is, to the maximum extent practicable, consistent with approved state management programs." 16 U.S.C. §1456(c)(1) (1982).

© Walt Kelly. Courtesy of Publishers-Hall Syndicate.

on Lease Sale No. 53, instituted litigation against the Interior Department, Secretary Watt and two other department officials, and the Bureau of Land Management, seeking declaratory and injunctive relief. . . .

Justice Sandra Day O'Connor's majority opinion first noted the ambiguity of the phrase "directly affecting" and then turned to the

759

legislative history in an effort to clarify the meaning of the two words. She concluded that the language was added to the CZMA as a compromise between a broad House and a restrictive Senate interpretation: "The [House-Senate] Conference accepted the Senate's narrower definition of the 'coastal zone,' but then expanded §307(c)(1) to cover activities on federal lands not 'in' but nevertheless 'directly affecting' the zone." Further study of the 1972 CZMA Conference Report led the majority to a dramatic (and nearly determinative) assertion: "[W]e are impelled to conclude that the 1972 Congress did not intend §307(c)(1) to reach OCS lease sales."

Justice O'Connor did not stop there, however; she proceeded to make the following findings: (1) §307(c)(1) is "irrelevant to OCS lease sales," an activity covered by §307(c)(3), a section that "definitely does *not* require consistency review of OCS lease sales." (2) The 1970 amendments to the Outer Continental Shelf Lands Act of 1953 (OCSLA) confirm that a lease sale is a distinct statutory stage that gives the lessee "only a priority in submitting plans to conduct those activities" (i.e., exploration, development, and production) that *will* trigger the consistency requirements of §307(c)(3)(B). (3) Even if §307(c)(1) were applicable, a lease sale "grants the lessee the right to conduct only very limited, 'preliminary activities' on the OCS." Granted, that right might come at a high price;[49] still, because federal approval may be denied at several points down the line, "the possible effects on the coastal zone that may eventually result from the sale of a lease cannot be termed 'direct.'"

It would be difficult to craft an opinion that focused more narrowly on statutory language *qua* language. The majority declared that Congress, not the Court, had made the policy choice and that the plaintiffs' (and dissent's) contrary construction of the CZMA was "superficially plausible but ultimately unsupportable." Justice O'Connor did pay lip service to the benefits of collaboration between state and federal agencies. Ultimately, however, she and her colleagues paved the way for the ascendancy of the latter's policies and goals over those of the former in the setting — OCS energy development — that has become the central focus of the CZM movement.[55]

49. In his dissent, Justice John Paul Stevens noted, "In the lease sale at issue in this case, $220,000,000 was bid on the disputed tracts."
55. See, e.g., Berger & Saurenman, The Role of Coastal States in Outer Continental Shelf Oil and Gas Leasing: A Litigation Perspective, 3 Va. J. of Nat. Resource L. 35 (1983); Harvey, Federal Consistency and OCS Oil and Gas Development: A Review and Assessment of the "Directly Affecting" Controversy, 13 Ocean Dev. & Int'l L. J. 481 (1984); Miller, Offshore Federalism: Evolving Federal-State Relations in Offshore Oil and Gas Development, 11 Ecology L. Q. 401 (1984); Note, The Seaweed Rebellion: Federal-State Conflicts Over Offshore Oil and Gas Development, 18 Willamette L. Rev. 535 (1982); Comment, The Seaweed Rebellion Revisited: Continuing Federal-State Conflict in OCS Oil and Gas Leasing, 20 Willamette L. Rev. 83 (1984).

D. Politics, Economics, and the Limits of Legalism

Notes

1. See Hildreth and Johnson, CZM in California, Oregon, and Washington, 25 Nat. Resources J. 103, 113-114 (1985):

> All four programs — BCDC [San Francisco Bay], California, Washington, and Oregon — were spurred by strong feelings of distrust of local government and dissatisfaction with past performance on land use control in the coastal zone. Proponents of coastal zone programs leveled sharp criticisms at local governments. Local governments, for example, were seen as pushovers for developers. Often these governments provided no special protection to beaches, views, access ways, or other valuable coastal resources. Instead, local officials seemed overly interested in enhancing tax bases. These governments had no institutional responsibility to consider regional, statewide, or national public interests. Their limited jurisdictional base created disincentives for coordinated planning and zoning programs with neighboring jurisdictions. . . .
>
> In all three states, local governments actively opposed legislation creating coastal zone programs — a predictable reaction because each was designed to invade the traditional turf of local governments. Local governments correctly viewed such programs as attacks on their past performance and as undisguised attempts to force change in the way coastal resources were managed. Local officials who wanted to protect their power base provided some of the most intense lobbying against the coastal programs during the legislative process. In addition, they wanted to assure (and were reasonably successful in doing so) that any loss of local governmental power would be temporary.

See also Hildreth & Johnson, Ocean and Coastal Law chs. 11-12 (1983); California Coastal Commission v. Granite Rock Co., 107 S. Ct. 1419 (1987) (CZMA did not preempt Commission's permit requirement for mining of unpatented claim in national forest).

2. Turf battles and petty jealousies are, unfortunately, not confined to the multilevel planning and management scheme encompassed in CZM. The case study that follows shows the real dangers involved in intergovernmental disputes, particularly when the subject matter is our rich and fragile environment.

CASE STUDY #3

2. The Judicial Role in Complex Environmental Disputes: The Case of Boston Harbor

The shorthand we use to describe our governmental structures and how they interact has always been a little misleading. We find comfort in phrases like "separation of powers," but reality routinely seems to blur the neat delineation of tasks and responsibilities that such catchphrases bring to mind.

Perhaps nowhere is this more the case than in the sphere of environmental problems. Perplexing as these issues seem in their scientific dimension, they also send complex reverberations through our political, legal, and economic institutions. Political communities are confronted with questions of allocations and trade-offs, and interjurisdictional and regional conflicts for which new rules and new attitudes have to be devised. In the courthouse, judges ponder whether the nature of environmental litigation demands innovative approaches that might strain traditional conceptions of the judicial role. New relationships among institutions are required where tradition may have dictated that each decision-making entity operate within its own well-defined sphere of influence.

This case study looks at one manifestation of this phenomenon. The focus is on the effort to clean up the long-polluted waters of Boston Harbor, an issue destined to capture headlines and sound bites during the 1988 presidential campaign. The material centers on a three-year period in the history of this ongoing dispute — from 1982 to 1984, when the question of harbor pollution came before a Massachusetts state judge in the form of the City of Quincy v. Metropolitan District Commission litigation. While the configuration of forces and main players obviously varies from case to case, the Boston Harbor litigation is typical to the extent that it highlights the tensions inherent in, as well as the potential benefits of, innovative judicial intervention in complex environmental litigation.

■ GRIFFIN, THE POLITICS AND LITIGATION OF BOSTON HARBOR: FROM SUPERIOR COURT TO BEACON HILL
Harvard Law School Program on the Legal Profession (1985)

Boston Harbor is the vital nerve for commercial and recreational activity in Massachusetts and for much of New England. As the largest seaport in New England, the Harbor provides a base for the important shipping and shipbuilding industries. The Harbor, encompassing an area of 47 square miles, also serves as a home for a large shellfish industry. In recent years, the Boston waterfront has attracted numerous commercial and residential investors and developers, representing the enormous economic potential of the area. In addition, the Harbor offers numerous recreational activities including: swimming, boating, fishing, and exploration and use of the Harbor's 30 islands.

Despite its economic and recreational importance, Boston Harbor

D. Politics, Economics, and the Limits of Legalism

is seriously polluted from discharges of human and industrial wastes into its waters. "Each and every day some 450 million gallons of wastewater and 100,000 pounds of sludge enter the Harbor," from discharges of the Metropolitan Sewerage System and the municipal systems which are joined to it. These discharges lead to serious pollution problems such as visual and olfactory pollution, organic pollution, eutrophication, accumulation of toxic substances, and concentrations of disease producing bacteria.

SEWERAGE SYSTEM

Before the Quincy suit in 1982, the Boston Metropolitan Sewerage District, which serves 43 communities, was under the control of the MDC [Metropolitan District Commission], one of five agencies within the state Executive Office of Environmental Affairs (EOEA). Each of the 43 communities maintained an independent local sewer collection system and the MDC through its Metropolitan Sewerage Division operated pumping stations to lift local wastewater into the 228 miles of MDC interceptor sewers. The MDC facilities were designed to screen out large debris and to remove grit from the incoming sewage before it entered the treatment system. After this process, the influent was moved to either the Deer Island treatment plant, which services 22 northern metropolitan communities, or the Nut Island plant, which services the southern section of the system. At the treatment plants, the waste went through primary treatment which includes a process of screening, sedimentation, and skimming designed to remove settable solids and to reduce the concentration of suspended solids. Next the effluent was chlorinated to kill bacteria before it was discharged into the Harbor via submerged outfalls, ranging only 480 feet to 6,000 feet from shore at the Nut Island plant.

Even this minimal treatment process suffered from serious flaws, which led to the discharge of raw or partially treated sewage into Boston Harbor and its adjacent waters. For example, overflows occurred during rainstorms since infiltration (seepage of ground water into sewer pipes) and inflow (water and sewage from local pipe connections, often illegal, to storm drains) placed tremendous strains on the limited capacity of the sewerage plants. When Deer Island capacities were exceeded from this infiltration/inflow (I/I) problem, or even if there was an operational failure, the sewage was diverted to Moon Island, where a backup facility is located. This facility does not have a primary treatment process and thus raw sewerage was dumped into Boston Harbor from Moon Island, even regardless of the tides. Also during rainstorms, the combined sewer systems, designed to carry both storm water and sewage, deposited raw sewage mixed with rainwater along the shores of the Harbor and its tributaries. Combined sewers are utilized by 50% of the population served by the MDC. Additionally, Deer and Nut Island capacity problems were exacerbated by design flaws, operational difficulties, and mechanical breakdowns. . . .

These deficiencies . . . led to significant amounts of dry and wet weather overflows of raw sewage into Harbor waters. In 1981, Nut and Moon Island facilities alone were responsible for the discharges of a combined total of 6.1 billion gallons of raw or partially treated sewage into Harbor waters.

QUINCY LITIGATION

The residents of Quincy, a city on the south shore of the Harbor, know too well of the pollution. In recent years on numerous occasions, public health officials have closed Quincy beaches, because Quincy waters posed serious health dangers to bathers due to high levels of bacteria. Officials also closed clam flats over concerns of shellfish contamination from the poor water quality. "For the solicitor of the City of Quincy, . . . the final insult came one morning when the young lawyer went down to run along the shore. It was low tide, and in the pale dawn he saw what he took to be scattered gleaming jellyfish, all down the beach. To his revulsion, William B. Golden discovered that 'they weren't jellyfish. They were little patties of human waste, and patties of grease.'"

The city of Quincy filed suit in Norfolk Superior Court in December 1982, against the MDC and the Boston Water and Sewer Commission (BWSC), the agencies that owned and were responsible for the operation of the Nut and Moon Island facilities. Quincy Bay is located between these two facilities and according to the plaintiff, the discharges and overflows of sewage and pollutants from these plants seriously contaminated surrounding waters and adversely affected commercial and recreational uses of the beaches in and around the city of Quincy. Quincy sought injunctive, remedial, and declaratory relief from the chronic pollution.

Quincy asserted five causes of action under violations of Massachusetts environmental and clean water statutes and under the common law violation of nuisance. The MDC, in turn, filed a counterclaim together with its answer on April 20, 1983. It asserted that the pollution at Wollaston Beach in Quincy was actually caused by Quincy-operated storm drains, which empty into the beach waters.

Following the initiation of the suit, Peter Koff, an experienced environmental attorney retained by Quincy, recalled that the parties engaged in discussions for several months while they attempted to strike a compromise. According to Koff, when he realized that the defendants would not seriously consider entering a consent decree, he took steps to move the case along. In May 1983, he filed motions for a preliminary injunction, for reference to a master, and for an order requiring notice of Nut Island discharges, all of which were marked for hearing in June.

D. Politics, Economics, and the Limits of Legalism

Before the hearings, the plaintiff also amended its complaint, in which these additional defendants were joined in the suit — Thomas C. McMahon, Anthony D. Cortese, and James S. Hoyte, all state environmental agency heads.

Hoyte, Secretary of EOEA, suspected that the plaintiff waited until May to file its motions since Massachusetts Superior Court Judge Paul Garrity was due to sit in Norfolk Superior Court, where Quincy brought the suit, for the month of June. In Massachusetts, Superior Court judges circulate from county to county, and Judge Garrity was assigned to Norfolk County for June. The plaintiff's strategy to have Judge Garrity hear its motions was well calculated, because Garrity is widely known as a court activist. The Judge strongly believes that when the political system is willing to duck an important issue, the courts must step in and address the problem when necessary, even if it is political in nature. Garrity also had a reputation of being very tough and bold, evidenced by the fact he took the unusual and extraordinary remedial measure of placing the Boston Housing Authority in receivership in the 1975 case of Perez v. BHA. [379 Mass. 703, 400 N.E.2d 1231 (1980).]

On June 15, Judge Garrity held hearings on the motions filed by the plaintiff. Twelve days later, Garrity issued his findings, rulings and orders on Quincy's application for preliminary injunctive relief which requested a moratorium on all new sewer connections or, in the alternative, a two gallon reduction of existing waste water flow for every new gallon added to the system. Garrity, in applying the standard under Rule 65 (Massachusetts Rules of Civil Procedure), declined to grant the preliminary injunction. However, he did find that the balancing of the harms of the two parties was closely related to the public interest, which, in turn, was "inextricably intertwined with what is most appropriate by way of remedy." In calculating appropriate remedies, Garrity considered the case enormously complex in technical and political terms, as well as in fiscal responsibility. He therefore indicated his desire to appoint a special master "to come up with the most effective remedy and to prepare a comprehensive order with provisions for oversight and fine-tuning. . . ."

Following a hearing on July 6, Judge Garrity appointed Harvard Law School Professor Charles M. Haar special master pursuant to Rule 53 of the Massachusetts Rules of Civil Procedure. Haar was primarily charged by the court to make findings of fact as to all issues raised in the complaint and to make recommendations for remedial relief. Most importantly, Judge Garrity requested that Professor Haar report back to the court within 30 days, which expressed the court's urgency to address the problems of Boston Harbor.

Garrity appointed a special master despite objections from the defendants' attorney. . . . [State Assistant Attorney General] Sloman strongly believed that this process was not the proper way to conduct a lawsuit of such importance. In his brief opposing the appointment of a special master, Sloman argued that it was inappropriate for judges to refer cases to a special master if the underlying controversy was of widespread public interest involving the official acts of elected officials. He argued:

> The complexity of the matter is not, as the city might suggest, sufficient to offset the public interest impediments to a reference to a master. The Court's citation in *Shell Oil* [Co. v. City of Revere, 383 Mass. 682, 421 N.E.2d 1181 (1981)] of Bartlett-Collins Co. v. Surinam Navigation Co., supra, [381 F.2d 546 (10th Cir. 1967)] is particularly telling given that decision's castigation of the reference: "That the case involves complex issues of fact and law is no justification for reference to a Master, but rather is an impelling reason for a trial before an experienced judge." 381 F.2d at 551....

PROCESS OF THE SPECIAL MASTER

PROCEDURE AND SCHEDULE

Several days following his appointment, Professor Haar and his deputy master, Steven Horowitz, an associate at the Boston law firm of Hill and Barlow, held a meeting with all the participants in the suit. At that meeting, all sides agreed on the record to allow ex parte contacts by the special master. The parties agreed to the ex parte contacts in light of the 30 day deadline, but the special master was required to base the findings of fact in his report on evidence and documents in the public record. Under the tight time frame imposed by the court, Haar felt that this was the best way to proceed because, "unless . . . ex parte contacts were agreed to by the parties, a chance for doing anything about this case was limited." He believed that there was simply too much information and data that had to be collected in such a short time to use traditional fact finding procedures.

Also in order to save time, the parties also agreed to a "hearing on the record" process in which direct testimony would be submitted to the special master by affidavit simultaneously by both parties. After the testimony was exchanged, witnesses were to be cross-examined in person at hearings, which were initially scheduled for July 21-22.

Following the two weeks of this intense preparation, Professor Haar presided over the formal hearings on July 21, 22, and 27. On the first day, Sloman and Koff raised all sorts of evidentiary objections to the affidavits. Horowitz describes Haar's response:

> [Haar] took a very tough position. . . . [H]e thought the lawyers were being excessively technical and he was not interested in listening to a lot of technical objections. He felt that they missed the point — that we were

D. Politics, Economics, and the Limits of Legalism 767

working on a very expedited basis, and he essentially rejected all the objections that had been raised. And [he] made everyone back down . . .

Professor Haar was willing to push the parties in the direction he wanted. Hoyte explains:

> They [Haar and Horowitz] . . . I think probably had an appropriate mix of being cooperative and ready to work hand in hand, at the same time be[ing] prepared to raise a little Cain if they didn't feel they were moving in the direction they wanted or moving as quickly as possible.

Also on the first day of the hearings, Koff wanted to file a motion to join the Environmental Protection Agency (EPA) as a defendant. In a parallel action in Federal District Court, EPA had been sued jointly with MDC by the Conservation Law Foundation in June 1983. Because Quincy initiated its action first, the District Court stayed the federal suit. EPA still cooperated with the special master in state court by providing valuable technical information. It also was a potential financial resource. However, Koff sought EPA's direct involvement in the state suit.

Horowitz realized that this strategy was plagued by a serious problem: EPA would invoke its absolute right of removal and thus end state court jurisdiction. Horowitz met with Koff and the other Quincy lawyers before they filed the motion. After they discussed the probable outcome, Horowitz convinced them not to join EPA.

Surrounding the hearings, Haar conducted tours of the sewerage facilities on July 20 and 23. He was joined by the other participants and members from the media.

According to the established procedures, Haar and Horowitz held ex parte meetings before and after the hearings. They met with the lawyers, the parties and their witnesses, as well as with Judge Garrity, the court-retained experts, and several peripheral actors including the Conservation Law Foundation lawyers, EPA representatives, and public finance experts. Haar felt that these meetings were particularly instructive in helping them understand the technical dimensions of the case.

Haar believed that the procedure with the ex parte contacts and the formal hearings was designed to facilitate a compromise, as well as adjudicate the suit. Haar viewed the mastership as:

> . . . a mediating, arbitrating process as well as a litigating process. Courts are also trying to settle and mediate, but I think the emphasis is far more on the mediation, compromise side in the case of a master suit than it is when you have a traditional judge.

The state defendants, distinct from the position of their attorneys, made their intentions clear in the beginning that they wanted to resolve this suit. According to Secretary Hoyte, who coordinated the defense for the state agencies:

> ... from day one, we as an administration had determined that we were going to cooperate with the City of Quincy to find a way of solving the Boston Harbor pollution problem.

Assistant Attorney General Sloman, however, took the position that the case should be treated as a tort "slip and fall" case. In other words, Sloman was only concerned with whether the plaintiff stated a violation of law upon which it was entitled to relief. In his straightforward approach, he felt the procedure, namely the ex parte meetings, had serious flaws. For instance, Sloman felt that:

> The proceedings were replete with ethical considerations. This is not how you conduct a trial. The ex parte communications were definitely a problem. The master knew things that I didn't know, and I don't know how he knew them. The master relied upon ex parte communications, upon evidence that was untested in the adversary process. The opportunity for us to respond to that was again catch-up ball. He knew things before I did; I then had to find out what it is that he knew through those witnesses, and so I was always catching up. Contacts between the master and the judge, which apparently were taking place — it shows up later on that these experts were hired with the court's assent, and I didn't know about that — those strike me as ethical considerations. Nonetheless, the exigencies of the circumstances dictated them. I can only identify them, without making judgments that they were good, bad or indifferent. It was a problem in the conduct of the case.

Haar and Horowitz were sensitive to the ethical problems that ex parte contacts might create. They made sure that every finding of fact in the report was supported by evidence in the public record. However, Haar also felt that the theoretical and ethical concerns were somewhat exaggerated. Haar believes that even a traditional judge does not compartmentalize his mind to rely only on the evidence in the record. And while he did realize that ex parte contacts is tricky business because of a tendency "to trust your own judgment more than you should," he also felt "it's the only way to extract certain information; it's the only way people will talk to you and tell you what they really mean."

DRAFTING REMEDIES

After the hearings, Haar and Horowitz, as well as the research assistants, directed their full attention toward producing a final draft of the report. In this process, they refined their proposals for remedies. In formulating the proposed remedies, Haar and Horowitz largely

D. Politics, Economics, and the Limits of Legalism 769

depended on the recommendations in the parties' memoranda and on the experts' suggestions. They also were extremely conscious of the political complexities involved in the case.

Haar wanted to capture Governor Dukakis's attention:

> I thought that the Governor was very important to us and that he ought to have been fully alerted (and I don't think he was) to the great advantages that he would gain with the environmental community, and with the conservationists, and to the political clout that the Boston Harbor has. I think that is one of the things that the Judge is very aware of, and I became more and more aware that Boston Harbor is a winner, that Boston Harbor was something that the people cared about, that a public official who acted to address the situation could come out as a white knight. That's what I was trying to get the Governor to see.

Haar was also aware that some immediate results were necessary to foster public support. He believed that:

> ... [Y]ou've got to show some immediate results.... [Y]ou can't say to people, "Well, in 10 years from now, we'll have this shiny new plant and everything will be hunky-dory." I agree you need long-range goals and it does take time to achieve them, but you must also include intermediate short range steps as well and that's what the remedies were trying to do....

In taking these diffuse interests into consideration, Haar and his staff primarily proposed remedies which required the defendants to submit various plans to upgrade the quality of the sewerage system according to a specific timetable.

Haar encountered a particularly difficult problem in drafting remedies. Although everyone agreed that MDC facilities caused substantial pollution in Boston Harbor, it was not clear that discharge from Nut and Moon Islands polluted Quincy Bay. In fact, Eric Adams, one of the court-appointed experts and an MIT professor in the field of hydrodynamics, believed that:

> As a whole, I'm sure that they [MDC] were contributing to pollution on the beach. But I guess it's still my opinion that the major source was probably the storm drains or, at least, there wasn't enough evidence, ... very good direct evidence that MDC was to blame in that local problem.

As a remedy, Haar and Horowitz recommended that the parties conduct a test jointly to evaluate the volume of the pollutants coming out of the Quincy storm drains.

Haar and Horowitz also rejected Quincy's suggestion to place a moratorium on all new sewer connections. They felt that the economic consequences of a moratorium would be catastrophic by essentially precluding any further construction and development in the Boston metropolitan area.

Perhaps the most important suggested remedy, according to Professor Haar, was the requirement that the state defendants submit a financial plan to the court. The plan was to include a discussion of the feasibility of establishing an independent sewerage authority capable of issuing revenue bonds. Haar, who had been a member of the Commonwealth's Finance Advisory Board, developed the idea of a financial plan independent of any of the parties' suggestions. Haar felt that the financing of the sewerage system was "too bifurcated. The person responsible didn't pay, the budgeteer didn't have the question of hiring." Haar therefore felt that a new impetus was needed and he hoped that the financial plan would lead to a new authority to run and finance the sewerage system.

THE POLITICAL STRUGGLE INTENSIFIES

On August 3, Haar and Horowitz met Hoyte for breakfast at the Wursthaus in Harvard Square. During their meeting, Haar told Hoyte that he was at this point indignant at the defendants and their lawyers for the conflicting signals he was receiving from them. The defendants repeatedly assured Haar that they were willing to cooperate and strike a compromise. They indicated to Haar that they wanted to settle the case and accept the special master's report.

However, Sloman resisted compromise. For example, he had challenged the role of the master and made evidentiary objections at the hearings. Sloman also thought that the remedies outlined in the report alone would not lead to a clean harbor and indicated that he might challenge the report.

Despite Sloman's position, Haar found the state defendants cooperative for the most part throughout the proceedings. Hoyte points out that:

> ... all [of the state agencies] cooperated quite fully with Special Master Haar and I suspect that one of the reasons why he was able to get things done quickly as he was is that we were all trying to facilitate that analysis.

Nevertheless, Professor Haar had the impression that Sloman was pushing the case further than his clients wanted to go. The state defendants were quite satisfied with the report, as Hoyte explains:

> We did have a situation where the agencies involved, including this office [EOEA], felt that the Master's Report had captured quite well the essence of the situation and indeed, as I said, we worked very closely with Professor Haar, so it would have been anomalous, to say the least, if we

D. Politics, Economics, and the Limits of Legalism 771

said the Master's Report didn't capture it, because we provided a lot of input into that Report.

Despite Hoyte's positive reponse to the report, Sloman was quite adamant against sacrificing his legal position by entering a consent decree. Professor Haar realized the Attorney General's Office felt that:

The judges have been pushed by the political system into too large a role in these delicate social problems that ought to be handled by the political process rather than by the judicial process.

Haar realized that this position was developed, in part, by the history of the mental retardation cases in Massachusetts, in which the state entered into several consent decrees which have proven to be a thorn in its side.

Hoyte adds:

I think that the Attorney General's Office felt that there were larger issues at play here with respect to when it's appropriate to have the state, regardless of what the agency is, regardless of who the administration might be, but when it's appropriate for the state to enter into consent judgments on the one hand or to say things or do things which compromise the possibility of later positions in the course of legal proceedings....

RESPONSES TO THE REPORT

When the special master's report was filed on August 9, Professor Haar held a press conference to explain the report and its significance. The subsequent media response was overwhelmingly supportive. Haar had been, however, very careful to nurture a relationship with the media. For example, he invited the press to join the tour of the MDC treatment facilities and made himself available for interviews. Additionally, he organized the report so that reporters could extract information from it easily. Furthermore, he had several meetings with the Boston Globe editorial staff during the month.

All the participants in the process understood the importance that the media played. Sloman suggests:

This is a public case. It's a public law case; it's a public issue case. For that reason, the media is entitled, and should be involved in the process.

However, Sloman was not completely satisfied with the way the media was used:

My only complaint would be that, not infrequently, the litigation was being played out not for litigation purposes, but for media purposes.... [T]he media played a substantial role in the unfolding of the development of the case.

The state defendants openly supported the report in the papers. An MDC official, Stephen Burgay, indicated in the Boston Globe on August 9 that the MDC was willing to accept and implement the suggested remedies in the report since the agency considered the remedies to be realistic.

Meanwhile, Sloman maintained his same position and was quoted in the same article:

> Our position to date has been that, in view of the willingness of [the] administration as a whole to address the question of pollution of the harbor, why do you also need a court order? . . .

SETTLEMENT OF THE SUIT?

. . . Judge Garrity opened hearings on the objections to the special master's report at the end of August. These hearings were abruptly ended, however, when a settlement suddenly was agreed upon by the state agency defendants and the city of Quincy. This settlement evolved into a procedural order which was implemented by the court on September 7.

The main provisions of the order were:

- The litigation was to be suspended and the remedies proposed by the special master were to be adopted with the specific timetables suggested in the report. The last provision of the order was left open-ended, allowing the parties to later agree on specific measures not within the scope of the litigation, such as industrial wastes and sludge management.
- The defendants gave their moral commitment to comply with the procedural order.
- Judge Garrity was to maintain jurisdiction over the case with the power to reopen the litigation.
- Professor Haar was appointed to assess the progress of the defendants.

Sloman seemingly was forced to succumb to the political pressures; however, Horowitz feels that Sloman agreed to a political solution without giving up any legal rights of his clients. According to Horowitz:

> . . . he [Sloman] preserved his legal position throughout. What happened was that collectively the group found a way to give enough of what the Judge wanted and what the plaintiff wanted without Sloman giving up the essence of his legal position which really has to do with legal principles

as distinct from policies. What he didn't want was to give up his legal principles for the sake of policy when he found a way, or we all found a way, . . . to maintain that there was no consent decree, there was no court order to require any of these elements of the procedural order that ultimately came to pass, and that he was just agreeing to suspend the case. That's all he was doing, and he made an express moral commitment and not a legal one. So, I don't think that he gave up what he was insisting on all along.

Sloman concurs and characterizes the procedural order as:

. . . a stay, a suspension of judicial activity while the state does its business consistent with what the Master recommended. If the state fails in that regard, or the City of Quincy is unhappy with the results of what the state does, then Quincy's remedy is to go back to court and start up the preliminary injunction hearings again. . . . I view the procedural order as the remedy I had been articulating since December of 1982—let the state do its business as it feels best.

Notes

1. Shortly after the events described above, Judge Garrity's dissatisfaction with the pace of Harbor cleanup and compliance with the procedural order precipitated a dramatic confrontation between the court and the Massachusetts legislature. At a hearing in October 1984, the judge stated that he would consider taking drastic steps if the legislature did not move expeditiously to enact the reforms called for in the Master's report — in particular, the creation of a new authority with sufficient financial and institutional strength to tackle the job. In November, in the face of continued legislative inaction, he carried through on this threat, placing a moratorium on all development in communities served by the MDC, and beginning hearings on the question of whether the MDC should be placed in receivership.

The response to this move was loud and dramatic and was not significantly tempered by a decision a week later by the Massachusetts Supreme Judicial Court overturning Garrity's order. (Garrity, in any event, indicated that he would continue fashioning such troublesome orders until he found one that passed muster.) Whatever the legal merits of this approach, it proved successful as a method for calling legislative inertia to task. Developers, frantic at the thought of losing valuable time in the completion of various projects, became vociferous lobbyists on behalf of legislation creating the authority. The media and community groups joined in the fray more vigorously than they had in the past. The legislature, despite bridling at what some considered excessive interference by the judiciary in legislative functions — "I have a belief about court orders," Representative Michael Creedon told the Boston Globe, "I ignore them" — ultimately passed the bill in the final days of the legislative sessions, and within a few days of Garrity's retirement from the bench. 1984 Mass. Acts ch. 372, §§1-29 (establishing Massachusetts Water Resources Authority).

For related developments in federal court, see United States v. Metropolitan District Commission, 847 F.2d 12 (1st Cir. 1988) (affirming fee award for Conservation Law Foundation attorneys in federal case). See also Connerty v. MDC, 398 Mass. 140, 495 N.E.2d 840 (1986) (licensed master clam digger, unable to harvest shellfish following MDC's discharge of raw sewage into Boston Harbor, not entitled to recover under environmental statutes or common law nuisance).

2. Brazil, Special Masters in Complex Cases, 53 U. Chi. L. Rev. 394, 414, 416, 422 (1986):

> One other innovative role played recently by special masters seems especially noteworthy: helping a court and parties flesh out an equitable decree in a complex public lawsuit. Masters have long been used to monitor compliance with injunctions or to administer funds. But employing a master to help a court decide the content of an injunction is more controversial.
>
> A fascinating recent example of this kind of assignment occurred in City of Quincy v. Metropolitan District Commission, a case filed in Massachusetts state court in late 1982....
>
> An unusual dimension of Professor Haar's work in *City of Quincy* is that he viewed his role as partly political. He decided that feasible long-range solutions would require the support of the public and of the many governmental agencies operating and regulating the sewage system....
>
> Masters' apparent successes as quasi-judicial politicians raise many perplexing questions about masters' roles in these cases. Given that judges issue orders affecting complex institutional relationships and having significant political and economic implications, should we consider expanding or changing the processes by which courts reach their decisions? These decisions may impinge on all of society, but who should be allowed to participate in the decisionmaking processes? Should courts be explicitly permitted to take into account political considerations, for example, in selecting feasible remedies? Should courts attempt to influence public opinion in order to facilitate implementation of legal rulings? Should the judiciary's capacity to perform administrative functions be expanded so that it could implement its own orders or step in to fill legally mandated but unmet administrative needs? Changes along these lines might rob the judiciary of the appearance of neutrality and objectivity arguably essential to perceptions of its legitimacy and authority.

See also Little, Court-Appointed Special Masters in Complex En-

D. Politics, Economics, and the Limits of Legalism

vironmental Litigation: City of Quincy v. Metropolitan District Commission, 8 Harv. Envtl. L. Rev. 435 (1984).

3. Certainly a major theme in the Boston Harbor case concerns the strengths and limitations of mediation and consensus building within the framework of complex cases. For discussions of the potential of mediation and negotiation in other environmental and land-use contexts, see supra page 154; Bacow & Wheeler, Environmental Dispute Resolution (1984), and Levitt & Kerlin, Managing Development Through Public-Private Negotiations (1985).

Growth policy and environmental protection present the courts with complex, emotional questions. Costs and benefits are difficult, if not impossible, to quantify; short-term benefits are frequently achieved at the expense of future generations. In resolving such intricate issues the courts frequently resort to definitional analysis rather than complicated economic, social, or scientific analysis. Has the same sort of definitional approach used in water law been applied to the legal questions involved in the growth policy cases? Are the ways courts phrase the questions as unrelated to the economic and social problems of growth as categories of water are to the hydrologic cycle? As you examine the materials in Chapter VII, keep in mind the insights developed regarding "capacity of land," and probe how this idea relates to the questions of "highest and best use."

VII

Government as Landowner and Redistributor: Comprehensive Planning as the Public Use

Master plans and the implementation of urban design call forth the full panoply of government power. Regulatory measures affect rights in land, leaving property in private ownership; this chapter deals with a more dramatic application of state power — the outright acquisition of interests in land by government through its power of eminent domain.[1]

Evidence of the land requirements of public enterprises abounds in the form of government offices, hospitals, schools, port facilities, parks, civic centers — and, not least, in military testing grounds and nuclear power plants. The cost simply for the rights of way on the 41,000-mile interstate highway system has been conservatively estimated at $9 billion. But compulsory acquisition can do more than secure sites for government functions; public ownership of land, either alone or in conjunction with other forms of land-use control, opens new vistas in directing the development of urban land. Exercised at strategic places and at crucial times, it can influence land development far beyond the limits of the property held. A new highway directly affects the sur-

---

1. Other land acquisition techniques must be kept in mind as well: gift, open market purchase, exchange, tax delinquency. In a sense, this material deals with the other side of the coin with which Western land disposal policies contended. See page 12, supra.

rounding environment.[2] Slum clearance may set off the economic renewal of an entire community and eliminate past errors — albeit, perhaps, to foster new ones. Obstinate or greedy private property owners who stand in the way of the common weal may be required to yield to the people's sovereign right of acquisition. In addition, there is the holy grail — still in the offing — of recapturing the value created through planning and public development.

To ensure proper planning, to discourage land speculation, and to meet the complications engendered by large-scale migration to cities, major changes have occurred throughout the world in urban land tenures, land patterns, and land policies.[3] Increasingly, land acquisition is relied upon as a catalyst of public policies. New techniques of land assembly and of compensation have developed. Large-scale nationalization of land has been seriously considered and sometimes enacted. Beginning in 1947,[4] the British produced statutes of overwhelming significance for property law and, with the nationalization of development values, a potential revolution in land law as drastic as that of Quia Emptores in 1290. The implications and effects of large-scale acquisition — including the purchase of reserve land for future needs — are crucial for the lawyer.

Judicial, legislative, and popular attitudes toward the exercise of eminent domain have been influenced by the demands and exigencies of sweeping nonlegal developments. A rule of law developed to accommodate the needs of a cart-and-horse society was adapted to facilitate the construction of railroads, superhighways, and airports. A restriction of the sovereign's power was transformed into a positive, effective tool for economic and social progress. In recent years, following the surge of case law interpreting and generally upholding urban renewal programs, state and local governments have asked courts to bestow their blessings (or withhold sanctions) on the employment of eminent domain to counter private sector investment and location decisions, or even to facilitate the transfer of fee title from one nonpublic owner to another. Our current appreciation of the power of eminent domain is such that perhaps no category of property — real and personal, corporeal and incorporeal, private and public — is out of reach. Nor does it appear that the judiciary will require much beyond lip service in order to justify a taking, as long as the requisites of due process are followed and compensation is duly granted.

While eminent domain resembles the police and tax powers in many aspects, there are crucial differences. In coping with the variegated city planning problems, consider which of the techniques is more

2. For example, the national system of interstate highways will affect more than 90 percent of all cities having a population of 50,000 or more.
3. See Abrams, Man's Struggle for Shelter (1964); Rodwin, Nations and Cities (1970).
4. 10 & 11 Geo. 6, ch. 51.

efficient in particular situations. Should there be different standards of judicial review? Does compensation avoid all dangers in the use of eminent domain? What different types of legislative, administrative, or other restraints are available for avoiding the arbitrary imposition of compulsory purchase? How can the various methods of control and inducement be combined most effectively? Have the cases really reached the point of merger of the police and eminent domain powers? If so, how and why did such a merger occur? Is this instead a distinction that does require differences, given the requirement of compensation only in the event a taking has occurred? How helpful has the commentary of "experts" such as law professors been in resolving hard questions regarding explicit and implicit confiscation of vested property rights? Is it time we returned to the original intent of those responsible for drafting the fifth amendment and state analogues in order to arrive at a rationalization for severe limitations on takings and police powers run amok?[5] Or, as Justice Stevens has recently suggested, should we write off the "temporary harms" that owners suffer owing to governmental decision-making as "an inevitable cost of doing business in a highly regulated society"?[6]

In elaborating the rights protected and determining where compensation must be paid, particularly within the contexts of urban renewal and economic development, it is no exaggeration to state that a definition and redefinition of the institution of private property is always at stake. Existing "rights" are abrogated or modified; individual expectations, including ties to home and neighborhood, are disrupted; and novel property interests are created. The language of the fifth amendment — "nor shall private property be taken for public use, without just compensation" — suggests the key questions in balancing private rights and the social interest: What does the term "property" mean? When is property "taken"? Is the taking for a "public use"? What constitutes "just compensation"?

---

5. See Note, The Origins and Original Significance of the Just Compensation Clause of the Fifth Amendment, 94 Yale L.J. 694, 708 (1985):

> The just compensation clause of the Fifth Amendment reflected the liberalism of its author, James Madison, who in synthesizing revolutionary era trends gave them substance and coherence. Madison intended the clause to have narrow legal consequences: It was to apply only to the federal government and only to physical takings. But he meant it to have broad moral implications as a statement of national commitment to the preservation of property rights. The ideology underlying the clause ran counter to the republicanism espoused by the Anti-Federalists, the opponents of the Constitution. In the years after ratification of the Constitution, however, Madisonian liberalism came to dominate American legal and political thought.

6. Williamson County Regional Planning Commn. v. Hamilton Bank, 473 U.S. 172, 204 (1985) (Stevens, J., concurring in the judgment).

A. FROM BLACKSTONE TO *BERMAN*'S PROGENY: REDEFINING THE PUBLIC USE REQUIREMENT

■ BLACKSTONE, COMMENTARIES
*139

So great moreover is the regard of the law for private property, that it will not authorize the least violation of it; no, not even for the general good of the whole community. If a new road, for instance, were to be made through the grounds of a private person, it might perhaps be extensively beneficial to the public; but the law permits no man, or set of men, to do this without consent of the owner of the land. In vain may it be urged, that the good of the individual ought to yield to that of the community; for it would be dangerous to allow any private man, or even any public tribunal, to be the judge of this common good, and to decide whether it be expedient or no. Besides, the public good is in nothing more essentially interested, than in the protection of every individual's private rights, as modelled by the municipal law.[7]

■ SCHLESINGER, SOVIET LEGAL THEORY
93, 94 (2d Ed. 1951)

In contrast with capitalist states, State enterprise is regarded as the normal state of affairs. Private enterprise exists not by any original

---

7. See Miller, The Life of the Mind in America 224-225 (1965):

> In the inspired phrasing of the Declaration of Independence the conventional trilogy of the English eighteenth century — "life, liberty, and property" — was changed into "life, liberty, and the pursuit of happiness." Thomas Jefferson left to posterity a conundrum, but the mass of American lawyers never doubted that his happiness was a polite genteelism for the acquisition of wealth. In the agrarian days of 1790 this would have been too obvious to need stressing, but with the dizzy rush of the economy after 1815 an apprehension arose lest Jefferson's words might become a real threat. The lawyers rallied once more to the figure who had so often provided their strength and consolation: Blackstone. Here he was of tremendous help, for he freed them from allegiance to the notion that property rights derived from the Lockean social compact or that they were in any sense dependent on the society's recognition that the owner had made something his own by mixing his labor in it. Not at all, said Blackstone: the concept of property exists even before there is any society at all; to protect the individual in the enjoyment of this absolute right, vested in him by the immutable law of nature, governments are created. . . . Thus the absolute right of property was prior to the Constitution of the United States, to the constitutions of the states, to all enumerated bills of rights, to Jefferson's dangerous verbiage, but above all prior to and supreme over any of the political trickeries associated with the name of Andrew Jackson. . . .

See also Burns, Blackstone's Theory of the "Absolute" Rights of Property, 54 U. Cinn. L. Rev. 67 (1985).

A. Redefining the Public Use Requirement 781

right of its own, but because and in so far as it is permitted in the public interest.... Thus, private property, in Soviet Law, is always to be regarded as an institution secondary to public property, and admitted only in the latter's interest. In doubtful cases the assumption, in the U.S.S.R., is always in favor of public property.

■ CHIEF JOSEPH
McLuhan, Touch the Earth 54 (1972)

The earth was created by the assistance of the sun, and it should be left as it was.... The country was made without lines of demarcation, and it is no man's business to divide it.... I never said the land was mine to do with as I choose. The one who has the right to dispose of it is the one who created it. I claim a right to live on my land, and accord you the privilege to live on yours.

■ STATE CONSTITUTIONAL PROVISIONS

"Whenever an attempt is made to take private property for a use alleged to be public, the question whether the contemplated use be really public shall be a judicial question, and determined as such without regard to any legislative assertion that the use is public." Arizona Const. art. 2, §17 (1910).

"The necessary use of lands for the construction of reservoirs or storage basins, for the purpose of irrigation, or for rights of way for the construction of canals, ditches, flumes or pipes, to convey water to the place of use for any useful, beneficial or necessary purpose, or for drainage; or for the drainage of mines, or the working thereof, by means of roads, railroads, tramways, cuts, tunnels, shafts, hoisting works, dumps, or other necessary means to their complete development, or any other use necessary to the complete development of the material resources of the state, or the preservation of the health of its inhabitants, is hereby declared to be a public use, and subject to the regulation and control of the state." Idaho Const. art. 1, §14 (1890).

"Private property ought and shall ever be held inviolate, but always subservient to the public welfare, provided a compensation in money be made to the owner." Ohio Const. art. 8, §4 (1802).

The usual formula is that the power of eminent domain is an "inherent attribute of sovereignty." As a more sonorous age put it, the "power is a universal one, and is as old as political society."[8] However, the federal constitution, establishing a government of delegated powers, contains no express grant of eminent domain, and it was not until 1875 that it was finally settled that the United States could condemn in its own name in its own courts.[9] The courts found eminent domain to be an implied power, "necessary and appropriate" for the execution of powers expressly conferred.[10] Prior to that time, the state would condemn property and turn it over to the federal government.[11] The fifth amendment is now construed as a recognition of a preexisting power, rather than a grant of a power.[12]

State constitutions prohibiting the taking of property for a private use are codifications of a doctrine evolved by many American courts as natural law.[13] At first, the breadth of the accepted view as to what constituted a "public use" and the rare instances calling for condemnation of land rendered the public use requirement an insignificant limitation. But in the 1850s, it was narrowed down to mean use by the public.[14]

The Mill Act Cases — which in more than a poetic sense are forerunners of modern urban renewal statutes — tested and stretched this narrow view. Lewis stated: "[T]hey cannot be justified upon principle without virtually expunging the words public use from the constitution."[15] Consider how they were accepted in the following passage from an opinion of Chief Justice Shaw of the Supreme Judicial Court of Massachusetts, later characterized as "a very ingenious and perhaps flawless evasion":[16]

> The relative rights of land-owners and mill-owners are founded on the established rule of the common law, that every proprietor, through whose territory a current of water flows, in its course towards the sea, has an equal right to the use of it, for all reasonable and beneficial purposes, including the power of such stream for driving mills, subject

---

8. Thayer, Constitutional Law 945 (1895).

9. Kohl v. United States, 91 U.S. 367 (1875).

10. United States v. Gettysburg Ry., 160 U.S. 668 (1896); cf. United States v. 2271.29 Acres of Land, 31 F.2d 617 (W.D. Wis. 1928).

11. 1 Nichols, Eminent Domain §34 (2d ed. 1917); and 1 Nichols' The Law of Eminent Domain §1.24 (rev. 3d ed. 1988).

12. United States v. Carmack, 329 U.S. 230, 241-242 (1946); Note, Land Taking and Nineteenth Century America, 40 U. Chi. L. Rev. 854 (1973); Stoebuck, A General Theory of Eminent Domain, 47 Wash. L. Rev. 553 (1972).

13. See Grant, The "Higher Law" Background of the Law of Eminent Domain, 6 Wis. L. Rev. 67 (1931).

14. See Nichols, The Meaning of Public Use in the Law of Eminent Domain, 20 B.U.L. Rev. 615 (1940); Bosselman, Callies & Banta, The Taking Issue: An Analysis of the Constitutional Limits of Land Use Control (1973).

15. 1 Lewis, Eminent Domain 559-560 (3d ed. 1909); see also Horwitz, The Transformation of American Law, 1780-1860, at 47-53 (1977).

16. 1 Nichols, Eminent Domain §84, at 233 (2d ed. 1917).

A. Redefining the Public Use Requirement

to a like reasonable and beneficial use, by the proprietors above him and below him, on the same stream. Consequently, no one can deprive another of his equal right and beneficial use, by corrupting the stream, by wholly diverting it, or stopping it from the proprietor below him, or raise it artificially, so as to cause it to flow back on the land of the proprietor above. This rule, in this Commonwealth, is slightly modified by the mill acts, by the well-known provision, that when a proprietor erects a dam on his own land, and the effect is, by the necessary operation of natural laws, that the water sets back upon some land of the proprietor above, a consequence which he may not propose as a distinct purpose, but cannot prevent, he shall not thereby be regarded as committing a tort, and obliged to prostrate his dam, but may keep up his dam, paying annual or gross damages, the equitable assessment of which is provided for by the acts. It is not a right to take and use the land of the proprietor above, against his will, but it is an authority to use his own land and water privilege to his own advantage and for the benefit of the community. It is a provision by law, for regulating the rights of proprietors, on one and the same stream, from its rise to its outlet, in a manner best calculated, on the whole, to promote and secure their common rights in it.[17]

The frontier problems in the United States, which have strained and refined the concept of eminent domain, have arisen in connection with public housing and redevelopment. Establishing a humane physical environment, creating functional cities, clearing slums and forestalling blighted areas — all are increasingly recognized as crucial challenges to the American system and resources. Federal and state legislation is primarily aimed at utilizing private initiative and establishing a broad framework within which private energies can be effectively released. It is this uneasy combination[18] that has raised constitutional and practical problems of a unique type: urban redevelopment and renewal, like Tennyson's flower, present in concentrated focus the whole range of questions evoked by eminent domain.

The "housing project" emphasis of the United States Housing Act of 1937, 50 Stat. 888, 42 U.S.C. §1401, which made substantial federal aid available to authorities undertaking slum clearance and the provision of low-rent housing, reflected the earlier approach to possible remedies.[19] By contrast, the redevelopment philosophy underlying the

---

17. Bates v. Weymouth Iron Co., 8 Cush 548, 552, 553 (Mass. 1851). On more recent efforts to allocate the burden of proof, see Note, 56 Cornell L. Rev. 651 (1971). — Eds.

18. The legislative philosophy encourages private enterprise to play the major role of investment and initiative. Stress is laid upon extensive industry campaigns and the support of citizens' associations — as witness the activities of the American Council to Improve Our Neighborhoods — to make the program succeed. See Meyerson, Urban Renewal, in Planning 169 (1955). Even enforcement of various aspects of the program is delegated to private groups. See Keyes, The Boston Rehabilitation Program (1970).

19. See Robinson and Weinstein, The Federal Government and Housing, 1952 Wis. L. Rev. 581; Riesenfeld & Maxwell, Modern Social Legislation 823-885 (1950); Friedman, Government and Slum Housing (1968). See infra page 1007.

Housing Act of 1949, 63 Stat. 413, 42 U.S.C. §1441, aimed at subsidizing the gap between the market value for existing land uses and the re-use value of the land if cleared and developed for the purpose indicated by a redevelopment plan.[20] In 1954, the 1949 act was amended (68 Stat. 622, 42 U.S.C. §§1451-1460) to make explicit provision for slum prevention as well as elimination, and the summary term "urban renewal" injected into the already overburdened vocabulary of the city planner. Urban renewal — which encompasses rehabilitation and conservation of deteriorating areas as well as redevelopment — became the focus of hopes for a new face for American cities.[21] The block grant approach initiated by the Housing and Community Development Act of 1974, Pub. L. No. 93-383, officially brought to an end the era of federal urban renewal, although the New Federalism approach was more an evolution than a dramatic scuttling of past programs.[22] Still, the most important legal by-product of renewal — our expansive understanding of "public use" — remained intact.

Time and critics have not been kind to federal, state, and local officials who fought the good fight from the 1940s through the 1970s to rebuild America's most neglected neighborhoods.[23] As you study Justice Douglas's jurisprudential legerdemain in Berman v. Parker, and the cases that followed his blending of police power goals and eminent domain justifications, consider whether the liberation (or demise) of public use is yet another negative legacy of urban renewal, to go along with former shopping areas devoid of people on the weekends; unbroken strings of bland "modern" architectural hulks; and the demolition of ethnic urban villages. Or, have we allowed a few extreme examples of both — of bulldozers and government officials out of control — to skew our appreciation of ambitious urban programs and our appraisal of judicial deference to public/private endeavors that would most likely have failed to survive eminent domain scrutiny before 1954?

■ KASKEL v. IMPELLITTERI
306 N.Y. 73, 115 N.E.2d 659 (1953), cert. denied, 347 U.S. 934 (1954)

DESMOND, Judge.... [P]laintiff, as a taxpayer, disputes the conclusion of various qualified public bodies and officers that the area, in

---

20. See Guandolo, Housing Codes in Urban Renewal, 25 Geo. Wash. L. Rev. 1 (1956); Report of the President's Committee on Urban Housing (1968).

21. See Colean, Renewing Our Cities (1953); President's Advisory Committee on Government Housing Policies and Programs, Recommendations and Programs 119 (1953); Siegel & Brooks, Slum Prevention Through Conservation and Rehabilitation (1953); and Notes, 21 U. Chi. L. Rev. 489 (1954); 29 Ind. L.J. 109 (1953); 63 Mich. L. Rev. 892 (1965).

22. For more details on this and other post-urban-renewal federal and state programs, see Chapter VIII.

23. See, e.g., Anderson, The Federal Bulldozer: A Critical Analysis of Urban Renewal, 1949-1962 (1964); Jacobs, The Death and Life of Great American Cities (1961).

A. Redefining the Public Use Requirement 785

Manhattan, bounded by Columbus Circle, Broadway, Eighth Avenue, Ninth Avenue, West 58th and West 59th Street, is "substandard and insanitary." Plaintiff says it is not, and demands that the courts hold a trial to settle this allegedly justiciable issue of fact. But there is no dispute as to the physical facts. In rounded figures, 20% of the land proposed to be taken is occupied by dwellings all but one of which are more than sixty years old, 7% of the site is covered by hotels and rooming houses, 34% is in parking lots where once there were outmoded buildings, and 39% is occupied by nonresidential structures. Of course, none of the buildings are as noisome or dilapidated as those described in Dickens' novels or Thomas Burke's "Limehouse" stories of the London slums of other days, but there is ample in this record to justify the determination of the city planning commission that a substantial part of the area is "substandard and insanitary" by modern tests, and that the whole 6.32 acres, taken together, may reasonably be considered a single "area" for clearance and redevelopment purposes. Power to make that determination has been lodged by the Constitution, N.Y. Const. XVIII, §1, and, the statute, General Municipal Law, McK. Consol. Laws, c. 24, §72-k, in the city planning commission and the board of estimate, and when those bodies have made their finding, not corruptly or irrationally or baselessly, there is nothing for the courts to do about it, unless every act and decision of other departments of government is subject to revision by the courts....

... One can conceive of a hypothetical case where the physical conditions of an area might be such that it would be irrational and baseless to call it substandard or insanitary, in which case, probably, the conditions for the exercise of the power would not be present. However, the situation here actually displayed is one of those as to which the Legislature has authorized the city officials, including elected officials, to make a determination, and so the making thereof is simply an act of government, that is, an exercise of governmental power, legislative in fundamental character, which, whether wise or unwise, cannot be overhauled by the courts. If there were to be a trial here and the courts below should decide in favor of plaintiff, there would be effected a transfer of power from the appropriate public officials to the courts. The question is simply not a justiciable one....

The judgment should be affirmed, with costs.

VAN VOORHIS, Judge (dissenting).... There is no rational basis, according to plaintiff, for linking the Columbus Circle portion of the site area to the Ninth Avenue section in order to eliminate tenements on or in the immediate vicinity of Ninth Avenue. The contention is that redevelopment of the Ninth Avenue section, where some substandard and insanitary tenements are located, is unrelated to the more valuable property to be acquired in the vicinity of Columbus Circle, where there are no tenements, that these are really two separate areas, and that the small amount of slum dwellings on and near Ninth Avenue could easily be eliminated separately, and would not have been undertaken jointly except for the coliseum. If that be true, plaintiff is entitled to enjoin the expenditure by the city of its share in the cost as a waste of public funds, regardless of however desirable a coliseum might be or however advantageous it might be to the city to have two thirds of its land cost paid from the Treasury of the United States. If the main purpose of combining these two areas is not slum clearance, but merely to lend color to the acquisition of land for a coliseum under the guise of a slum clearance project, then the combined project is not authorized by statute, and a taxpayer's action can be maintained to restrain it under section 51 of the General Municipal Law, Denihan Enterprises v. O'Dwyer, 302 N.Y. 451, 99 N.E.2d 235. In that event, the courts would not be invading the administrative province, but performing their duty in limiting administrative officials, capable and public spirited as they may be, to spending public money for purposes authorized by law. . . .

. . . [Dickens and Burke] have nothing to do with condemning the Manufacturers Trust Building in this "slum" area, assessed at $1,500,000, in order to make way for a coliseum — a laudable object, to be sure, but not one whose connection with slum clearance is so clear as to be taken for granted without trial. . . .

. . . In this case the controversial question is simply whether public funds are to be spent for one public purpose which is authorized by statute or for another and different public purpose which is not authorized by statute. . . .

LEWIS, C. J., and CONWAY, DYE and FROESSEL, J. J., concur with DESMOND, J. VAN VOORHIS, J., dissents in opinion in which FULD, J., concurs.[24]

---

24. Virginia Housing Authorities Law, Va. Code §36-3(h), defines a "slum" as "any area where dwellings predominate which, by reason of dilapidation, overcrowding, lack of ventilation, light or sanitary facilities, or any combination of these factors, are detrimental to safety, health or morals." Cf. Greenfield and Lewis, An Alternative to a Density Function Definition of Overcrowding, in Land Economics 282 (1967).

In Bristol Redevelopment and Housing Authority v. Dentow, 198 Va. 171, 93 S.E.2d 288 (1956), the court concluded that since "the area as a whole does not meet the statutory definition, it necessarily follows that the action of the local Authority . . . and . . . of the council . . . were devoid of legal authority, arbitrary and unwarranted." See Green Street Assn. v. Daley, 373 F.2d 1 (7th Cir. 1967), cert. denied, 387 U.S. 932 (1967) (complaint of "a deliberate plan to create a no-Negro buffer zone" between a shopping area and surrounding residential property). See also Norwalk CORE v. Norwalk Redevelopment Agency, 395 F.2d 920 (2d Cir. 1968) (claim for denial of equal protection made out when defendants "did not assure, or even attempt to assure, relocation for Negro and Puerto Rican displacees in compliance with a contract to a same extent as they did for whites"). See also Allen v. City Council, 215 Ga. 778, 113 S.E.2d 621 (1960) (court sustained demurrer to allegation that designated site was not a slum area but "the best colored business and residential area" in Augusta). — EDS.

■ JACOBS, THE DEATH AND LIFE OF GREAT AMERICAN CITIES
9-10 (1961)

The general street atmosphere of buoyancy, friendliness and good health was so infectious that I began asking directions of people just for the fun of getting in on some talk. I had seen a lot of Boston in the past couple of days, most of it sorely distressing, and this struck me, with relief, as the healthiest place in the city. But I could not imagine where the money had come from for the rehabilitation, because it is almost impossible today to get any appreciable mortgage money in districts of American cities that are not either high-rent, or else imitations of suburbs. To find out, I went into a bar and restaurant (where an animated conversation about fishing was in progress) and called a Boston planner I know.

"Why in the world are you down in the North End?" he said. "Money? Why, no money or work has gone into the North End. Nothing's going on down there. Eventually, yes, but not yet. That's a slum!"

"It doesn't seem like a slum to me," I said.

"Why, that's the worst slum in the city. It has two hundred and seventy-five dwelling units to the net acre! I hate to admit we have anything like that in Boston, but it's a fact."

"Do you have any other figures on it?" I asked.

"Yes, funny thing. It has among the lowest delinquency, disease and infant mortality rates in the city. It also has the lowest ratio of rent to income in the city. Boy, are those people getting bargains. Let's see ... the child population is just about average for the city, on the nose. The death rate is low, 8.8 per thousand, against the average city rate of 11.2. The TB death rate is very low, less than 1 per ten thousand, can't understand it, it's lower even than Brookline's. In the old days the North End used to be the city's worst spot for tuberculosis, but all that has changed. Well, they must be strong people. Of course it's a terrible slum."

"You should have more slums like this," I said. "Don't tell me there are plans to wipe this out. You ought to be down here learning as much as you can from it."

"I know how you feel," he said. "I often go down there myself just to walk around the streets and feel that wonderful, cheerful street life. Say, what you ought to do, you ought to come back and go down in the summer if you think it's fun now. You'd be crazy about it in summer. But of course we have to rebuild it eventually. We've got to get those people off the streets."[25]

---

25. See Frieden, Policies for Rebuilding, in Urban Renewal 585, 621-623 (Wilson

■ BERMAN v. PARKER
348 U.S. 26 (1954)

Mr. Justice DOUGLAS delivered the opinion of the Court.

This is an appeal (28 U.S.C. §1253) from the judgment of a three-judge District Court which dismissed a complaint seeking to enjoin the condemnation of appellants' property under the District of Columbia Redevelopment Act of 1945, 60 Stat. 790, D.C. Code, 1951, §§5-701-5-719. The challenge was to the constitutionality of the Act, particularly as applied to the taking of appellants' property. The District Court sustained the constitutionality of the Act.

By §2 of the Act, Congress made a "legislative determination" that "owing to technological and sociological changes, obsolete lay-out, and other factors, conditions existing in the District of Columbia with respect to substandard housing and blighted areas, including the use of buildings in alleys as dwellings for human habitation, are injurious to the public health, safety, morals, and welfare; and it is hereby declared to be the policy of the United States to protect and promote the welfare of the inhabitants of the seat of the Government by eliminating all such injurious conditions by employing all means necessary and appropriate for the purpose."*

Section 2 goes on to declare that acquisition of property is necessary to eliminate these housing conditions.

Congress further finds in §2 that these ends cannot be attained "by the ordinary operations of private enterprise alone without public participation"... and that "the acquisition and the assembly of real property and the leasing or sale thereof for redevelopment pursuant to a project area redevelopment plan ... is hereby declared to be a public use."

Section 4 creates the District of Columbia Redevelopment Land Agency (hereinafter called the Agency), composed of five members, which is granted power by §5 (a) to acquire and assemble, by eminent domain and otherwise, real property for "the redevelopment of blighted

---

ed. 1966); Urban Analysis 389 (Page & Seyfried eds. 1970); Marris, Grieving (1974). Professionals were undaunted by the rising criticisms; e.g., see Editorial, 27 J. Housing 468 (1970) ("urban renewal is a wanted program.... So, in the San Francisco story on the four preceding pages and in the stories of the 20 cities that follow, the Journal presents evidence of the versatility and flexibility of the renewal process"). — EDS.

* The Act does not define either "slums" or "blighted areas." Section 3 (r), however, states:

> "Substandard housing conditions" means the conditions obtaining in connection with the existence of any dwelling, or dwellings, or housing accommodations for human beings, which because of lack of sanitary facilities, ventilation, or light, or because of dilapidation, overcrowding, faulty interior arrangement, or any combination of these factors, is in the opinion of the Commissioners detrimental to the safety, health, morals, or welfare of the inhabitants of the District of Columbia.

A. Redefining the Public Use Requirement 789

territory in the District of Columbia and the prevention, reduction, or elimination of blighting factors or causes of blight." . . .

. . . Section 6(b) authorizes the Planning Commission to adopt redevelopment plans for specific project areas. These plans are subject to the approval of the District Commissioners after a public hearing; and they prescribe the various public and private land uses for the respective areas, the "standards of population density and building intensity," and "the amount or character or class of any low-rent housing." §6(b).

Once the Planning Commission adopts a plan and that plan is approved by the Commissioners, the Planning Commission certifies it to the Agency. §6 (d). At that point, the Agency is authorized to acquire and assemble the real property in the area. Id.

After the real estate has been assembled, the Agency is authorized to transfer to public agencies the land to be devoted to such public purposes as streets, utilities, recreational facilities, and schools, §7 (a), and to lease or sell the remainder as an entirety or in parts to a redevelopment company, individual, or partnership. §7 (b), (f). The leases or sales must provide that the lessees or purchasers will carry out the redevelopment plan and that "no use shall be made of any land or real property included in the lease or sale nor any building or structure erected thereon" which does not conform to the plan, §§7 (d), 11. Preference is to be given to private enterprise over public agencies in executing the redevelopment plan. §7 (g).

The first project undertaken under the Act relates to Project Area B in Southwest Washington, D.C. In 1950 the Planning Commission prepared and published a comprehensive plan for the District. Surveys revealed that in Area B, 64.3% of the dwellings were beyond repair, 18.4% needed major repairs, only 17.3% were satisfactory; 57.8% of the dwellings had outside toilets, 60.3% had no baths, 29.3% lacked electricity, 82.2% had no wash basins or laundry tubs, 83.8% lacked central heating. In the judgment of the District's Director of Health it was necessary to redevelop Area B in the interests of public health. The population of Area B amounted to 5,012 persons, of whom 97.5% were Negroes.

The plan for Area B specifies the boundaries and allocates the use of the land for various purposes. It makes detailed provisions for types of dwelling units and provides that at least one-third of them are to be low-rent housing with a maximum rental of $17 per room per month.

After a public hearing, the Commissioners approved the plan and the Planning Commission certified it to the Agency for execution. The Agency undertook the preliminary steps for redevelopment of the area when this suit was brought.

Appellants own property in Area B at 712 Fourth Street, S. W. It is not used as a dwelling or place of habitation. A department store is located on it. Appellants object to the appropriation of this property for the purposes of the project. They claim that their property may not be taken constitutionally for this project. It is commercial, not residential property; it is not slum housing; it will be put into the project under the management of a private, not a public, agency and redeveloped for private, not public, use. That is the argument; and the contention is that appellants' private property is being taken contrary to two mandates of the Fifth Amendment — (1) "No person shall . . . be deprived of . . . property, without due process of law"; (2) "nor shall private property be taken for public use, without just compensation." To take for the purpose of ridding the area of slums is one thing; it is quite another, the argument goes, to take a man's property merely to develop a better balanced, more attractive community. The District Court, while agreeing in general with that argument, saved the Act by construing it to mean that the Agency could condemn property only for the reasonable necessities of slum clearance and prevention, its concept of "slum" being the existence of conditions "injurious to the public health, safety, morals and welfare." 117 F. Supp. 705, 724-725.

The power of Congress over the District of Columbia includes all the legislative powers which a state may exercise over its affairs. We deal, in other words, with what traditionally has been known as the police power. An attempt to define its reach or trace its outer limits is fruitless, for each case must turn on its own facts. The definition is essentially the product of legislative determinations addressed to the purposes of government, purposes neither abstractly nor historically capable of complete definition. Subject to specific constitutional limitations, when the legislature has spoken, the public interest has been declared in terms well-nigh conclusive. In such cases the legislature, not the judiciary, is the main guardian of the public needs to be served by social legislation . . . This principle admits of no exception merely because the power of eminent domain is involved. The role of the judiciary in determining whether that power is being exercised for a public purpose is an extremely narrow one.

Public safety, public health, morality, peace and quiet, law and order — these are some of the more conspicuous examples of the traditional application of the police power to municipal affairs. Yet they merely illustrate the scope of the power and do not delimit it. See Noble State Bank v. Haskell, 219 U.S. 104, 111. Miserable and disreputable housing conditions may do more than spread disease and crime and immorality. They may also suffocate the spirit by reducing the people who live there to the status of cattle. They may indeed make living an almost insufferable burden. They may also be an ugly sore, a blight on the community which robs it of charm, which makes it a place from which men turn. The misery of housing may despoil a community as an open sewer may ruin a river.

A nefarious urban-demolition scheme by the evil "Aim" challenges "Captain America's" new sidekick, a black man called the Falcon who lives in Harlem with his winged namesake.

    We do not sit to determine whether a particular housing project is or is not desirable. The concept of the public welfare is broad and inclusive. See Day-Brite Lighting, Inc. v. Missouri, 342 U.S. 421, 424. The values it represents are spiritual as well as physical, aesthetic as well as monetary. It is within the power of the legislature to determine that the community should be beautiful as well as healthy, spacious as well as clean, well-balanced as well as carefully patrolled. In the present case, the Congress and its authorized agencies have made determinations that take into account a wide variety of values. It is not for us to reappraise them. If those who govern the District of Columbia decide that the nation's Capital should be beautiful as well as sanitary, there is nothing in the Fifth Amendment that stands in the way.
    Once the object is within the authority of Congress, the right to realize it through the exercise of eminent domain is clear. For the power of eminent domain is merely the means to the end. See Luxton v. North River Bridge Co., 153 U.S. 525, 529-530; United States v. Gettysburg Electric R. Co., 160 U.S. 668, 679. Once the object is within the authority of Congress, the means by which it will be attained is also for Congress to determine. Here one of the means chosen is the use of

private enterprise for redevelopment of the area. Appellants argue that this makes the project a taking from one businessman for the benefit of another businessman. But the means of executing the project are for Congress and Congress alone to determine, once the public purpose has been established. See Luxton v. North River Bridge Co., supra; cf. Highland v. Russell Car Co., 279 U.S. 253. The public end may be as well or better served through an agency of private enterprise than through a department of government — or so the Congress might conclude. We cannot say that public ownership is the sole method of promoting the public purposes of community redevelopment projects. What we have said also disposes of any contention concerning the fact that certain property owners in the area may be permitted to repurchase their properties for redevelopment in harmony with the over-all plan. That, too, is a legitimate means which Congress and its agencies may adopt, if they choose.

In the present case, Congress and its authorized agencies attack the problem of the blighted parts of the community on an area rather than on a structure-by-structure basis. That, too, is opposed by appellants. They maintain that since their building does not imperil health or safety nor contribute to the making of a slum or a blighted area, it cannot be swept into a redevelopment plan by the mere dictum of the Planning Commission or the Commissioners. The particular uses to be made of the land in the project were determined with regard to the needs of the particular community. The experts concluded that if the community were to be healthy, if it were not to revert again to a blighted or slum area, as though possessed of a congenital disease, the area must be planned as a whole. It was not enough, they believed, to remove existing buildings that were insanitary or unsightly. It was important to redesign the whole area so as to eliminate the conditions that cause slums — the overcrowding of dwellings, the lack of parks, the lack of adequate streets and alleys, the absence of recreational areas, the lack of light and air, the presence of outmoded street patterns. It was believed that the piecemeal approach, the removal of individual structures that were offensive, would be only a palliative. The entire area needed redesigning so that a balanced, integrated plan could be developed for the region, including not only new homes but also schools, churches, parks, streets, and shopping centers. In this way it was hoped that the cycle of decay of the area could be controlled and the birth of future slums prevented. Cf. Gohld Realty Co. v. Hartford, 141 Conn. 135, 141-144, 104 A.2d 365, 368-370; Hunter v. Redevelopment Authority, 195 Va. 326, 338-339, 78 S.E.2d 893, 900-901. Such diversification in future use is plainly relevant to the maintenance of the desired housing standards and therefore within congressional power.

The District Court below suggested that, if such a broad scope

A. Redefining the Public Use Requirement 793

were intended for the statute, the standards contained in the Act would not be sufficiently definite to sustain the delegation of authority. 117 F. Supp. 705, 721. We do not agree. We think the standards prescribed were adequate for executing the plan to eliminate not only slums as narrowly defined by the District Court but also the blighted areas that tend to produce slums. Property may of course be taken for this redevelopment which, standing by itself, is innocuous and unoffending. But we have said enough to indicate that it is the need of the area as a whole which Congress and its agencies are evaluating. If owner after owner were permitted to resist these redevelopment programs on the ground that his particular property was not being used against the public interest, integrated plans for redevelopment would suffer greatly. The argument pressed on us is, indeed, a plea to substitute the landowner's standard of the public need for the standard prescribed by Congress. But as we have already stated, community redevelopment programs need not, by force of the Constitution, be on a piecemeal basis — lot by lot, building by building.

It is not for the courts to oversee the choice of the boundary line nor to sit in review on the size of a particular project area. Once the question of the public purpose has been decided, the amount and character of land to be taken for the project and the need for a particular tract to complete the integrated plan rests in the discretion of the legislative branch.

The District Court indicated grave doubts concerning the Agency's right to take full title to the land as distinguished from the objectionable buildings located on it. 117 F. Supp. 705, 715-719. We do not share those doubts. If the Agency considers it necessary in carrying out the redevelopment project to take full title to the real property involved, it may do so. It is not for the courts to determine whether it is necessary for successful consummation of the project that unsafe, unsightly, or insanitary buildings alone be taken or whether title to the land be included, any more than it is the function of the courts to sort and choose among the various parcels selected for condemnation.

The rights of these property owners are satisfied when they receive that just compensation which the Fifth Amendment exacts as the price of the taking.

The judgment of the District Court, as modified by this opinion is Affirmed.[26]

---

26. How do you in turn evaluate the evaluation of Anderson (later an advisor on urban affairs to President Nixon):

> Court opinions of this nature [Berman v. Parker] do not answer the basic question; they simply evade the question with consummate skill. What they really said is that the reuse of the cleared land by a private person is not the objective of urban renewal, is incidental to the process, and is therefore constitutional. This is an

Notes

1. Circuit Judge Prettyman, in an opinion below, viewed the power of eminent domain more narrowly, and took the limitations of the police power more seriously than Justice Douglas:

> We hold that the taking of title to real estate for the public purpose of eliminating or of preventing slums is within the power of eminent domain, even though the use to which the property is put after seizure is not a public use; provided (1) that the seizure of the title is necessary to the elimination of the slum or (2) that the proposed disposition of the title may reasonably be expected to prevent the otherwise probable development of a slum. . . .
>
> Is a modern apartment house a better breeder of men than is the detached or row house? . . . Even if the line between regulation and seizure, between the power to regulate and the power to seize, is not always etched deeply, it is there. And, even if we progress in our concepts of the "general welfare," we are not at liberty to obliterate the boundary of governmental power fixed by the Constitution. . . .
>
> Of course the plan as pictured in the prospectus is attractive. In all probability it would enhance the beauty and the livability of the area. If undertaken by private persons the project would be most laudable. . . . But as yet the courts have not come to call such pleasant accomplishments a public purpose.

Schneider v. District of Columbia, 117 F. Supp. 705 (D.D.C. 1953).

2. In United States v. Twin City Power Co., 350 U.S. 222 (1956), Justice Douglas stated what he believed to be the appropriate degree of judicial deference as follows: "The decision of Congress that this project will serve the interests of navigation involves engineering and policy considerations for Congress and Congress alone to evaluate. Courts should respect that decision until and unless it is shown 'to involve an impossibility,' as Mr. Justice Holmes expressed it in Old Dominion Co. v. United States, 269 U.S. 55, 66." Can this opinion, or that of Berman v. Parker, be reconciled with United States v. Wunderlich, 342 U.S. 98, 101 (1951), where the same Justice wrote: "Absolute discretion is a ruthless master. It is more destructive of freedom than any of man's other inventions."

3. Bridgewater Township sought to condemn a 120-acre "economic wasteland" to be redeveloped as a regional shopping center. Township

---

illogical argument — the seizure of private property for someone else's private use may be incidental and not the objective of urban renewal, but this does not make it constitutional. What if some renewal official decided to make theft part of the urban renewal process? Would the courts declare that theft is not the objective of urban renewal, is incidental to the process, and is therefore constitutional?

The Federal Bulldozer 189 (1967).

A. Redefining the Public Use Requirement 795

officials cited the definition of "blighted" in N.J.S.A. §40:55-21.1(e) as authority: "A growing or total lack of proper utilization of areas caused by the condition of the title, diverse ownership of real property therein and other conditions, resulting in a stagnant and unproductive condition of land potentially useful and valuable for contributing to and serving the public health, safety and welfare." A majority of the state supreme court agreed that plaintiffs' parcel, "the heart of the triangle," was properly included in the blighted area. Levin v. Township Committee of the Township of Bridgewater, 577 N.J. 506, 274 A.2d 1 (1971).

Justice Haneman disagreed, finding an abuse of discretion because of the township's rejection of a previous offer to develop the property and because

> there is no necessity to proceed by condemnation to remove a cloud upon title. The alleged faulty titles ensuing from municipal tax foreclosures, titles of unknown owners, and any other questionable titles, could have long since been cured and can yet be cured in a normal accepted proceeding, i.e., either suit to quiet title or a new strict or in rem foreclosure.... [T]he municipality has undertaken a proceeding for a blight declaration which is certainly a retardant rather than a stimulant for the expenditure of money for private development.

274 A. 2d at 32-33 (Haneman, J., dissenting).[27]

27. After *Levin*, what limits are left to what government can do by appeal to "public benefit" or the doctrine of "blight"? Would the Socratic midwife pronounce *Levin* a true progeny of *Berman* or merely a "wind child"?

In People ex rel. Gutknecht v. City of Chicago, 3 Ill. 2d 539, 545, 546-547, 121 N.E.2d 791, 795 (1954), the statute defined a "conservation area" as

> an area of not less than 160 acres in which the structures in 50% or more of the area are residential having an average age of thirty-five years or more. Such an area is not yet a slum or blighted area as defined in the Blighted Areas Redevelopment Act of 1947, but such area by reason of dilapidation, obsolescence, deterioration or illegal use of individual structures, overcrowding of structures and community facilities, conversion of residential units into nonresidential use, deleterious land use or layout, decline of physical maintenance, lack of community planning, or any combination of these factors may become such a slum and blighted area.

Among the attacks on this statute was one "that the 'line of demarcation between a public and private use in the employment of eminent domain to eliminate slum areas . . . must be the elimination rather than the prevention of slums.'"

The court responded:

> But we are aware of no constitutional principle which paralyzes the power of government to deal with an evil until it has reached its maximum development. Nor is there force in the argument that if the use of eminent domain in the prevention of slums is permitted "every piece of property within the city or State can be condemned to prevent it from becoming a slum." Legitimate use of governmental power is not prohibited because of the possibility that the power may be abused.

See also Zisook v. Maryland-Drexel Neighborhood Redevelopment Corp., 3 Ill. 2d

4. As a result of United States ex rel. TVA v. Welch, 327 U.S. 546 (1946), the Yale Law Journal published The Public Use Limitation on Eminent Domain: An Advance Requiem, 58 Yale L.J. 599 (1949). Was this, like Mark Twain's obituary, premature? Justice Black, writing for the Court, concluded that there was no right of review of the public use requirement; Justice Frankfurter, in his specially concurring opinion on the extent of the judiciary's reexamination of legislative determinations, wrote: "But the fact that the nature of the subject matter gives the legislative determination nearly immunity from judicial review does not mean that the power to review is wanting." 327 U.S. at 557. But see United States v. New York, 160 F.2d 479 (2d Cir. 1947), cert. denied, 331 U.S. 832 (1947); United States v. 44 Acres of Land, 110 F. Supp. 168 (W.D.N.Y. 1953). "The Supreme Court of the United States has not in this century held a use to be private which a state court has declared to be public. . . . So irrefutably has the 'wondrous elasticity' of the public use limitation been demonstrated that the principle that private property can be condemned only for public purposes can accurately be viewed as having been repudiated. There is only one inconsistency created by the demise of the public use limitation — it expurgates a part of the United States Constitution." King, Rex non Potest Peccare??? The Decline and Fall of the Public Use Limitation on Eminent Domain, 76 Dick. L. Rev. 266-268 (1971).

5. Courtesy Sandwich Shop, Inc. v. Port of New York Authority, 12 N.Y.2d 379, 396-397, 190 N.E.2d 402, 409, 240 N.Y.S.2d 1, 12 (1963), upheld the power of the Port of New York Authority to develop the World Trade Center on a site in lower Manhattan. In dissent, it was pointed out:

> Of course, if the "centralizing" of these private functions of foreign commerce be deemed to be a public purpose, then the rental obtained from the buildings or offices would be of the essence of the project, and not merely "incidental," and so could be utilized to offset the deficits of operating the Hudson & Manhattan Railroad. That means that being engaged in foreign trade, in some capacity, transforms a private entrepreneur into one conducting a public purpose if it is selected by the Port Authority as one from among many to be housed in the project area. On this uncertain principle depends the constitutionality of this whole statute. The Appellate Division was correct in stating that under the powers conferred by this statute the Authority could use nine tenths of the 13 blocks for obtaining revenue to offset the revenue deficits of the Hudson & Manhattan provided only that they were rented to private manufacturers, traders, or other entrepreneurs whose activities were being "cen-

---

570, 121 N.E.2d 804 (1954); Bollens, Special District Governments in the United States (1957); Rabinoff v. District Court, 360 P.2d 1114 (Colo. 1971); Note, 63 Mich. L. Rev. 892 (1965).

A. Redefining the Public Use Requirement

tralized," i.e., to whom the Authority decided to rent space in the project area.

6. Even after Berman v. Parker, some state courts remained hesitant to abandon their review function. See, for example, the court's objections to the Prudential Center mixed-use project in In re Opinion of the Justices, 332 Mass. 769, 126 N.E.2d 795 (1955):

> The difficulty inherent in any attempt to frame a comprehensive definition of public purpose was adverted to in Allydonn Realty Corp. v. Holyoke Housing Authority, 304 Mass. 288, 23 N.E.2d 665, where an attempt was made to suggest some of the considerations that might have weight.[28] However, in dealing with this difficult subject one proposition is thoroughly established practically everywhere, and so far as we are aware without substantial dissent, and that is that public money cannot be used for the primary purpose of acquiring either by eminent domain or by purchase private lands to be turned over or sold to private persons for private use....
>
> We are not unmindful of the proposed "Legislative Declaration of Necessity" in §2 of the act to the effect that the tax structure of the city is threatened; that the yard will be an area of "economic blight" and "a

---

28. See Allydonn Realty Corp. v. Holyoke Housing Authority, 304 Mass. 289, 293, 23 N.E.2d 665, 667 (1939):

> Some of the factors which the cases suggest as proper to be considered are these: Whether the benefit is available on equal terms to the entire public in the locality affected; whether the service or commodity supplied is one needed by all or by a large number of the public; whether the enterprise bears directly and immediately, or only remotely and circumstantially, upon the public welfare; whether the need to be met in its nature requires united effort under unified control, or can be served as well by separate individual competition; whether private enterprise has in the past failed or succeeded in supplying the want or in eradicating the evil; whether, in so far as benefits accrue to individuals, the whole of society has an interest in having those individuals benefited; whether a proposed extension of governmental activity is in line with the historical development of the Commonwealth and with the general purpose of its founders; whether it will be necessary to use public ways or to invoke the power of eminent domain; whether a special emergency exists, such as may be brought about by war or public calamity.

The *Allydonn* opinion distinguished Opinion of the Justices, 211 Mass. 624, 98 N.E. 611 (1912):

> That proposed statute contained no provision for the eradication of sources of disease and danger. It was not a slum clearance law. It did not eliminate unsafe or unsanitary dwellings. The court said, "The substance of it is that the commonwealth is to go into the business of furnishing homes for people who have money enough to pay rent and ultimately to become purchasers." 211 Mass. at page 625, 98 N.E. at page 612. The "dominating design" of that statute was "the furtherance of the advantage of individuals." Any effect that it might have in preserving the public safety, health, and morals was incidental, remote and doubtful. The court further said, "It is the essential character of the direct object of the expenditure which must determine its validity...." 211 Mass. at page 626, 98 N.E. at page 612.

304 Mass. 296, 23 N.E.2d 669. — Eds.

potential breeding place for crime and juvenile delinquency" and will adversely affect values; that the development of the yard in the manner proposed is "necessary to support the economic well-being of the city and the commonwealth"; that private enterprise will not undertake the orderly and integrated development of the yard, with further recitals setting forth the advantages of the plan. Nevertheless there is no suggestion that the area is now a slum. There is only an apprehension lest it become one. There would seem to be other means, perhaps through building and zoning regulations, of preventing that result. The project is not a slum clearance one, and the principle on which rest such cases as . . . Berman v. Parker, 348 U.S. 26, is not applicable. Neither does the area appear as yet to be blighted in any other sense than that high taxes and declining values retard development — a thing that could with equal accuracy be said of a great many tracts of land in Boston and in other cities in the Commonwealth. The main difference between the area we are now considering and such other tracts seems to be that the location of this tract makes it more prominent than many others, and this is hardly a difference in principle. It seems plain that the primary design of the bill is to provide for the acquisition of the area by the use, at the outset at least, of substantial sums of public money and later of comparatively small sums, to formulate a plan for development, including the devoting of some portions of the area to truly public uses, and the return of the remainder to private ownership to be rented or sold for private profit, with the expectation that adjacent areas and the city as a whole will benefit through the increase of taxable property and of values. But this kind of indirect public benefit has never been deemed to render a project one for a public purpose. A careful and sympathetic examination of the proposed act discloses the impossibility of concluding, without flying in the face of long established and well reasoned precedent, that public money spent under its provisions would be spent for a public purpose.

For later developments see Opinion of the Justices, 341 Mass. 768, 167 N.E.2d 858 (1960); Moskow v. BRA, 349 Mass. 553, 210 N.E.2d 699 (1965). As to the case for review by state rather than federal courts, and as to whether different inquiries should be made in supervising city rather than state activities, see Note, 78 Harv. L. Rev. 1596 (1965). The cases that follow indicate that any restrictive state trend was short-lived.

■ POLETOWN NEIGHBORHOOD COUNCIL v. CITY OF DETROIT
410 Mich. 616, 304 N.W.2d 455 (1981)

PER CURIAM. This case arises out of a plan by the Detroit Economic Development Corporation to acquire, by condemnation if necessary, a large tract of land to be conveyed to General Motors Corporation as a site for construction of an assembly plant. . . .

A. Redefining the Public Use Requirement

This case raises a question of paramount importance to the future welfare of this state and its residents: Can a municipality use the power of eminent domain granted to it by the Economic Development Corporations Act to condemn property for transfer to a private corporation to build a plant to promote industry and commerce, thereby adding jobs and taxes to the economic base of the municipality and state?

Const 1963, art 10, §2, states in pertinent part that "[p]rivate property shall not be taken for public use without just compensation therefor being first made or secured in a manner prescribed by law". Art 10, §2 has been interpreted as requiring that the power of eminent domain not be invoked except to further a public use or purpose. Plaintiffs-appellants urge us to distinguish between the terms "use" and "purpose", asserting they are not synonymous and have been distinguished in the law of eminent domain. We are persuaded the terms have been used interchangeably in Michigan statutes and decisions in an effort to describe the protean concept of public benefit. The term "public use" has not received a narrow or inelastic definition by this Court in prior cases. Indeed, this Court has stated that "'[a] public use changes with changing conditions of society'" and that "'[t]he right of the public to receive and enjoy the benefit of the use determines whether the use is public or private'". . . .

Plaintiffs-appellants do not challenge the declaration of the Legislature that programs to alleviate and prevent conditions of unemployment and to preserve and develop industry and commerce are essential public purposes. Nor do they challenge the proposition that legislation to accomplish this purpose falls within the constitutional grant of general legislative power to the Legislature in Const 1963, art 4, §51, which reads as follows:

> The public health and general welfare of the people of the state are hereby declared to be matters of primary public concern. The legislature shall pass suitable laws for the protection and promotion of the public health.

What plaintiffs-appellants do challenge is the constitutionality of using the power of eminent domain to condemn one person's property to convey it to another private person in order to bolster the economy. They argue that whatever incidental benefit may accrue to the public, assembling land to General Motors' specifications for conveyance to General Motors for its uncontrolled use in profit making is really a taking for private use and not a public use because General Motors is the primary beneficiary of the condemnation.

The defendants-appellees contend, on the other hand, that the controlling public purpose in taking this land is to create an industrial site which will be used to alleviate and prevent conditions of unemployment and fiscal distress. The fact that it will be conveyed to and ultimately used by a private manufacturer does not defeat this predominant public purpose.

There is no dispute about the law. All agree that condemnation for a public use or purpose is permitted. All agree that condemnation for a private use or purpose is forbidden. Similarly, condemnation for a private use cannot be authorized whatever its incidental public benefit and condemnation for a public purpose cannot be forbidden whatever the incidental private gain. The heart of this dispute is whether the proposed condemnation is for the primary benefit of the public or the private user.

The Legislature has determined that governmental action of the type contemplated here meets a public need and serves an essential public purpose. The Court's role after such a determination is made is limited. . . .

As Justice Cooley stated over a hundred years ago "the most important consideration in the case of eminent domain is the necessity of accomplishing some public good which is otherwise impracticable, and . . . the law does not so much regard the means as the need". People ex rel Detroit & Howell R Co v Salem Twp Board, 20 Mich 452, 480-481 (1870).

When there is such public need, "[t]he abstract right [of an individual] to make use of his own property in his own way is compelled to yield to the general comfort and protection of community, and to a proper regard to relative rights in others". Id. Eminent domain is an inherent power of the sovereign of the same nature as, albeit more severe than, the power to regulate the use of land through zoning or the prohibition of public nuisances.

In the instant case the benefit to be received by the municipality invoking the power of eminent domain is a clear and significant one and is sufficient to satisfy this Court that such a project was an intended and a legitimate object of the Legislature when it allowed municipalities to exercise condemnation powers even though a private party will also, ultimately, receive a benefit as an incident thereto.

The power of eminent domain is to be used in this instance primarily to accomplish the essential public purposes of alleviating unemployment and revitalizing the economic base of the community. The benefit to a private interest is merely incidental. . . .

. . . The power of eminent domain is restricted to furthering public uses and purposes and is not to be exercised without substantial proof that the public is primarily to be benefited. Where, as here, the condemnation power is exercised in a way that benefits specific and identifiable private interests, a court inspects with heightened scrutiny the claim that the public interest is the predominant interest being advanced. Such public benefit cannot be speculative or marginal but

A. Redefining the Public Use Requirement

must be clear and significant if it is to be within the legitimate purpose as stated by the Legislature. We hold this project is warranted on the basis that its significance for the people of Detroit and the state has been demonstrated. . . .

The decision of the trial court is affirmed. . . .

COLEMAN, C. J., and KAVANAGH, WILLIAMS, LEVIN, and BLAIR MOODY, JR., JJ., concurred.

FITZGERALD, J. (dissenting). . . .

The city places great reliance on a number of slum clearance cases here and elsewhere in which it has been held that the fact that the property taken is eventually transferred to private parties does not defeat a claim that the taking is for a public use. . . . Despite the superficial similarity of these cases to the instant one based on the ultimate disposition of the property, these decisions do not justify the condemnation proposed by the city. The public purpose that has been found to support the slum clearance cases is the benefit to the public health and welfare that arises from the elimination of existing blight, even though the ultimate disposition of the property will benefit private interests.

However, in the present case the transfer of the property to General Motors after the condemnation cannot be considered incidental to the taking. It is only through the acquisition and use of the property by General Motors that the "public purpose" of promoting employment can be achieved. Thus, it is the economic benefits of the project that are incidental to the private use of the property.

The city also points to decisions that have found the objective of economic development to be a sufficient "public purpose" to support the expenditure of public funds in aid of industry. What constitutes a public purpose in a context of governmental taxing and spending power cannot be equated with the use of that term in connection with eminent domain powers. The potential risk of abuse in the use of eminent domain power is clear. Condemnation places the burden of aiding industry on the few, who are likely to have limited power to protect themselves from the excesses of legislative enthusiasm for the promotion of industry. The burden of taxation is distributed on the great majority of the population, leading to a more effective check on improvident use of public funds. . . .

The majority relies on the principle that the concept of public use is an evolving one; however, I cannot believe that this evolution has eroded our historic protection against the taking of private property for private use to the degree sanctioned by this Court's decision today. The decision that the prospect of increased employment, tax revenue, and general economic stimulation makes a taking of private property for transfer to another private party sufficiently "public" to authorize the use of the power of eminent domain means that there is virtually no limit to the use of condemnation to aid private businesses. Any business enterprise produces benefits to society at large. Now that we have authorized local legislative bodies to decide that a different commercial or industrial use of property will produce greater public benefits than its present use, no homeowner's, merchant's or manufacturer's property, however productive or valuable to its owner, is immune from condemnation for the benefit of other private interests that will put it to a "higher" use.[15]...

The condemnation contemplated in the present action goes beyond the scope of the power of eminent domain in that it takes private property for private use. I would reverse the judgment of the circuit court.

RYAN, J., concurred with FITZGERALD, J.

RYAN, J. (dissenting). This is an extraordinary case....

The real controversy which underlies this litigation concerns the propriety of condemning private property for conveyance to another private party because the use of it by the new owner promises greater public "benefit" than the old use. The controversy arises in the context of economic crises. While unemployment is high throughout the nation, it is of calamitous proportions throughout the state of Michigan, and particularly in the City of Detroit, whose economic lifeblood is the now foundering automobile industry. It is difficult to overstate the magnitude of the crisis. Unemployment in the state of Michigan is at 14.2%. In the City of Detroit it is at 18%, and among black citizens it is almost 30%. The high cost of doing business in Michigan generally has driven many manufacturers out of this state and to the so-called sunbelt states on a continuing basis during the past several years. Nowhere is the exodus more steady or more damaging than from the Metropolitan Detroit area. It is appropriate to take judicial notice of the fact that the view is widely held that the Chrysler Corporation, headquartered in Detroit, is "on the ropes", surviving only because of hundreds of millions of dollars of federally insured loans. It is likewise appropriate to note judicially the commonly known and readily verifiable fact that the Ford Motor Company, the American Motors Corporation and the General Motors Corporation have all, within days, reported for the previous year the largest financial losses in their histories.

A new national administration and a reconstituted Congress are struggling to find acceptable means to assist the American automotive

---

15. It would be easy to sustain the proposed project because of its large size and the extent of the claimed benefits to flow from it. The estimate is that approximately 6150 persons would be employed in the factory itself, with the generation of substantial other employment, business activity, and tax revenue as a result. However, it must be remembered that the dislocations and other costs of the project are also massive. The project plan indicates that a total of 3438 persons will be displaced by the project, that it will require the destruction of 1176 structures, and that the cost of the project to the public sector will be nearly $200,000,000.

A. Redefining the Public Use Requirement 803

industry to compete with the overseas automobile manufacturing competition which is largely accountable for domestic automobile industry losses. To meet that competition, domestic manufacturers are finding it necessary to construct new manufacturing facilities in order to build redesigned, lighter and more economical cars. That means new factories and new factory locations. . . .

The evidence then is that what General Motors wanted, General Motors got. The corporation conceived the project, determined the cost, allocated the financial burdens, selected the site, established the mode of financing, imposed specific deadlines for clearance of the property and taking title, and even demanded 12 years of tax concessions.[9] . . .

It is easy to underestimate the overwhelming psychological pressure which was brought to bear upon property owners in the affected area, especially the generally elderly, mostly retired and largely Polish-American residents of the neighborhood which has come to be called Poletown. As the new plant site plans were developed and announced, the property condemnation proceedings under the "quick-take" statute begun and the demolitionist's iron ball razed neighboring commercial properties such as the already abandoned Chrysler Dodge Main plant, a crescendo of supportive applause sustained the city and General Motors and their purpose. . . .

The judiciary, cognizant of General Motors' May 1 deadline for the city's taking title to all of the property, moved at flank speed. The circuit court conducted a trial on defendants' motion to dismiss plaintiffs' complaint from November 17 to December 2, 1980, and the decision to dismiss the complaint was made on December 9, 1980. Application for leave to appeal prior to decision by the Court of Appeals was received in this Court on December 15, 1980. However, the trial transcript was not received by us until January 5, 1981. We promptly convened, conferred, and granted leave to appeal on January 29, 1981. The case was argued on March 3, 1981.

9. What is reported here is not meant to denigrate either the role or the good faith of General Motors Corporation. It is a private, profit-making enterprise. Its managers are answerable to a demanding board of directors who, in turn, have a fiduciary obligation to the corporation's shareholders. It is struggling to compete worldwide in a depressed economy. It is a corporation having a history, especially in recent years, of a responsible, even admirable, "social conscience". In fact, this project may well entail compromises of sound business dictates and concomitant financial sacrifices to avoid the worsening unemployment and economic depression which would result if General Motors were to move from the state of Michigan as other major employers have. The point here is not to criticize General Motors, but to relate accurately the facts which attended the city's decision to condemn private property to enable General Motors to build a new plant in Detroit and to "set the scene" in which, as will be seen hereafter, broad-based support for the project was orchestrated in the state, fostering a sense of inevitability and dire consequence if the plan was not approved by all concerned. General Motors is not the villain of the piece.

In less than two weeks, the lead opinions were filed by this Court and released. It is in such circumstances that we were asked to decide, and did decide, an important constitutional issue having towering implications both for the individual plaintiff property owners and for the City of Detroit and the state alike, to say nothing of the impact upon our jurisprudence. . . .

It is plain, of course, that condemnation of property for transfer to private corporations is not wholly proscribed. For many years, and probably since the date of Michigan's statehood, an exception to the general rule has been recognized. The exception, which for ease of reference might be denominated the instrumentality of commerce exception, has permitted condemnation for the establishment or improvement of the avenues of commerce — highways, railroads, and canals, for example — and can be traced to the common law where it was considered an exception to a general rule. . . .

Examination of the cases involving the instrumentality of commerce exception reveal that three common elements appear in those decisions that go far toward explicating and justifying the use of eminent domain for private corporations: 1) *public* necessity of the extreme sort, 2) continuing accountability to the *public*, and 3) selection of land according to facts of independent *public* significance. . . .

The production of automobiles certainly entails public benefits. Nevertheless, it could hardly be contended that the existence of the automotive industry or the construction of a new General Motors assembly plant requires the use of eminent domain. . . .

. . . [O]nce CIP [Central Industrial Park] is sold to General Motors, there will be no public control whatsoever over the management, or operation, or conduct of the plant to be built there. General Motors will be accountable not to the public, but to its stockholders. Who knows what the automotive industry will look like in 20 years, or even 10? For that matter, who knows what cars will look like then? For all that can be known now, in light of present trends, the plant could be fully automated in 10 years. Amid these uncertainties, however, one thing is certain. The level of employment at the new GM plant will be determined by private corporate managers primarily with reference, not to the rate of regional unemployment, but to profit. . . .

Without belaboring the obvious, the location of CIP is, to say the least, solely a result of conditions laid down by General Motors, which were designed to further its private, pecuniary interest. These are facts of private significance. . . .

From now on "the protean concept of public benefit" will be the sole criterion by which we are to adjudge the constitutionality of employing eminent domain for private corporations. The concept of public benefit is indeed protean. It is also nebulous. The state taking

A. Redefining the Public Use Requirement

clause has now been placed on a spectrum that admits of no principles and therefore no limits. . . .

With this case the Court has subordinated a constitutional right to private corporate interests. As demolition of existing structures on the future plant site goes forward, the best that can be hoped for, jurisprudentially, is that the precedential value of this case will be lost in the accumulating rubble.[29]

Notes

1. Press coverage of Poletown's "demise" was extensive. An article in Time Magazine entitled "The Last Days of Poletown" reported that when Ralph Nader "fired off a letter to General Motors Chairman Roger Smith, demanding that the company find another site 'that does not destroy a community of 3,500 Americans,'" Detroit's Mayor, Coleman Young, called Nader a "carpetbagger." The Village Voice was less than subtle: the July 8, 1981, headline read: "A Neighborhood Dies So GM Can Live."

2. Consider the "bargain" struck in *Poletown*. In exchange for site preparation (costing $200 million) and tax abatements for twelve years at 50 percent, GM promised to implement a "Minority Business Enterprise Participation Program"; to recall former employees in accordance with the Management-Union agreement, while giving priority for new hiring to residents of Detroit and Hamtramck; and to "employ, for the

---

29. See Cannata v. City of New York, 11 N.Y.2d 210, 218-219, 182 N.E.2d 395, 399, 227 N.Y.S.2d 903, 908-909 (1962) (Van Voorhis, J., dissenting):

> It might be thought, perhaps, that in the march of progress there is no limit to the power of the Legislature even short of authorizing municipal officials to determine, through zoning or eminent domain, who shall be permitted to own real estate in cities and to what purpose each separate parcel may be devoted. The sound view is still, however, that due process includes substantive as well as merely procedural limitations and that under the mores of the day there are substantive limits to what municipalities can do with private property, even by means of statutes enacted under the spur of single-minded city planners imbued with evangelistic fervor. At some stage the rights of private property owners become entitled to be respected, even if their use of their properties does not coincide with the ideas, however enlightened, of the avant garde. The fundamental principle of government still applies which the mentor of the young Cyrus tried to implant in him in ancient Persia. When asked whether a ruler should compel a subject whose coat was too large for him to trade it with another whose coat was too small, if one of them objected to the exchange, the young future ruler replied in the affirmative, for the reason that then each would have a coat that fitted him. The mentor told him that he was wrong, since he had confused expediency with justice. The question here, it seems to me, is where to draw the line between supposed expediency and justice.

Will a revitalization of the doctrine of due process prove helpful to complainants in condemnation cases? — EDS.

operation of the Assembly Plant, at least three thousand (3,000) employees within four (4) years from the date hereof, economic conditions permitting." Central Industrial Park Project Development Agreement Between General Motors Corporation as Developer and the Central Industrial Park Joint Venture, April 30, 1981. How would you evaluate this agreement as a Detroit voter/taxpayer, as a GM shareholder, as a competitor located in Detroit, and as a judge considering a cause of action for breach of contract?

3. See Haar, The Joint Venture Approach to Urban Renewal: From Model Cities to Enterprise Zones, in Public-Private Partnership: New Opportunities for Meeting Social Needs 63, 77 (Brooks, Liebman & Schelling eds. 1984):

> It is not surprising . . . that the Supreme Court of Michigan — a state with pockets of unemployment hovering around 20 percent — should find that the jobs and tax revenues resulting from a major plant site of the world's largest automobile company were sufficient to establish a public use. The *Poletown* dissent's jeremiad — "there is virtually no limit to the use of condemnation to aid private businesses" — is spoken against the strong winds of prevailing jurisprudence. In fact, the only exceptions to the trend to find takings for economic growth invulnerable to a public use challenge come from courts in the still-growing Sun Belt. And it is questionable whether even those judges would continue to disapprove of public-private joint ventures "with no assurance of more than negligible advantage to the general public," if their jurisdictions were faced with double-digit unemployment and severe budgetary straits.
>
> As a replacement for, or in conjunction with, the weighing of interests, other courts have inquired as to the nature and extent of legal controls retained and guarantees secured by the governmental parties in the joint venture. Assurances of continued regulation and the setting aside in perpetuity of public areas are two common elements of public control that have found judicial favor. In the case before the Michigan Supreme Court, the majority deemed itself satisfied with the "promises" of increased employment and revenues from the GM-Detroit joint venture, promises the critics found insubstantial indeed.

See also Michelman, Property as a Constitutional Right, 38 Wash. & Lee L. Rev. 1097 (1981); Ross, Transferring Land to Private Entities by the Power of Eminent Domain, 51 Geo. Wash. L. Rev. 355 (1983); Bennett, Eminent Domain and Redevelopment: The Return of Engine Charlie, 31 De Paul L. Rev. 115 (1981).

4. When the Otis Elevator Company closed its Yonkers, New York plant in 1982, owing to technological and economic factors, the city sued, claiming that the company had breached an implied agreement to remain in operation "for a reasonable time to be set by law, . . . alleged to be at least sixty years." The court in City of Yonkers v. Otis Elevator Co., 844 F.2d 42 (2d Cir. 1988), rejected the city's implied

A. Redefining the Public Use Requirement

promise, quasi-contract, and equitable estoppel theories, holding that the company matched the public urban renewal commitment with a mere "goal" (ultimately unrealized) to remain in Yonkers.

Can the community claim a property right to a continued presence by a key employer? During pretrial hearings in a union's lawsuit growing out of U.S. Steel's decision to close two steel plants in Youngstown, Ohio, Judge Thomas Lambros pondered:

> [I]t seems to me that a property right has arisen from this lengthy, long-established relationship between United States Steel, the steel industry as an institution, the community in Youngstown, the people in Mahoning County and the Mahoning Valley in having given and devoted their lives to this industry. Perhaps not a property right to the extent that can be remedied by compelling U.S. Steel to remain in Youngstown. But I think the law can recognize the property right to the extent that U.S. Steel cannot leave that Mahoning Valley and the Youngstown area in a state of waste, that it cannot completely abandon its obligation to that community, because certain vested rights have arisen out of this long relationship and institution.

On reconsideration, the judge concluded that such a right did not exist, a position affirmed by the Sixth Circuit in Local 1330, United Steel Workers v. United States Steel Corp., 631 F.2d 1264 (6th Cir. 1980). One commentator has regretted Judge Lambros's about-face, positing an elaborate theory of reliance interests and common enterprises. Singer, The Reliance Interest in Property, 40 Stan. L. Rev. 611 (1988) (the Lambros quotation is found at 619).

5. The Supreme Court of Washington remains a bulwark against the expanse of "public use." In 1981, the Court disapproved of the city of Seattle's condemnation of property for the Westlake Project, a public-private venture that was to include a public park and other open spaces, monorail terminal, public garage, art museum, and over 186,000 square feet of private retail and cinema space: "where the purpose of a proposed acquisition is to acquire property and devote only a portion of it to truly public uses, the remainder to be rented or sold for private use, the project does not constitute public use." In re City of Seattle, 96 Wash. 2d 616, 638 P.2d 549, 556 (1981).

Subsequently, the city changed its strategy, first selling previously acquired property to a private developer with conditions regarding architectural plans. The city then attempted to condemn adjacent property, held by Mall, Inc., for the public park component of the Project. This time, the court found that the original "constitutional infirmities" had been eliminated, for "Seattle is now condemning property for only one purpose — to establish a city park." City of Seattle v. Mall, Inc., 104 Wash. 2d 621, 707 P.2d 1348, 1350 (1985). Justice Utter, who had dissented from the majority's narrow holding four years earlier, noted that "it is regrettable that, at considerable expense, the City of Seattle has had to reshape its form and alter its means to achieve the substance of its long-recognized ends." 707 P.2d at 1351 (Utter, J., concurring). Can you offer any reasons why such a distinction should make a difference, in constitutional terms?

6. Michigan authorities used a "quick-take" statute to acquire the Poletown properties in a swift manner. Consider the due process protections afforded by the current version of the statute that reads, in pertinent part:

> Sec. 5. (1) Except as provided in section 25(4), before initiating negotiations for the purchase of property, the agency shall establish an amount which it believes to be just compensation for the property and promptly shall submit to the owner a good faith offer to acquire the property for the full amount so established. The amount shall not be less than the agency's appraisal of just compensation for the property. The agency shall provide the owner of the property and the owner's attorney with an opportunity to review the written appraisal, if an appraisal has been prepared, or if an appraisal has not been prepared, the agency shall provide the owner or the owner's attorney with a written statement and summary, showing the basis for the amount the agency established as just compensation for the property. If an agency is unable to agree with the owner for the purchase of the property, after making a good faith written offer to purchase the property, the agency may file a complaint for the acquisition of the property in the circuit court in the county in which the property is located. . . .
>
> (3) At the time the complaint is filed, the agency shall deposit the amount estimated to be just compensation with a bank, trust company, or title company in the business of handling real estate escrows, or with the state treasurer, municipal treasurer, or county treasurer. The deposit shall be set aside and held for the benefit of the owners, to be disbursed upon order of the court as provided in section 8. . . .

Mich. Comp. Laws Ann. §213.55 (1986).

> Sec. 9. (1) Upon filing of a complaint and making the deposit as provided in section 5 and after opportunity is given for a person to file a motion for review under section 6 or, if motion for review is filed, upon final determination of the motion, the court shall fix the time and terms for surrender of possession of the property to the agency and enforce surrender by appropriate order or other process. The court also may require surrender of possession of the property after the motion for review filed under section 6 has been heard, determined and denied by the circuit court, but before a final determination on appeal, if the agency demonstrates a reasonable need.

Mich. Comp. Laws Ann. §213.59 (1986). See Ackerman and Yanich,

Eminent Domain: The Constitutionality of Condemnation Quick-Take Statutes, 60 U. Det. J. Urb. L. 1 (1982).[30]

■ CITY OF OAKLAND v. OAKLAND RAIDERS
32 Cal. 3d 60, 646 P.2d 835, 183 Cal. Rptr. 673 (1982)

RICHARDSON, J. — The City of Oakland (City) appeals from a summary judgment dismissing with prejudice its action to acquire by eminent domain the property rights associated with respondent Oakland Raiders' (the Raiders) ownership of a professional football team as a franchise member of the National Football League (NFL). . . .

The Raiders limited partnership is comprised of two general partners, Allen Davis and Edward W. McGah, and several limited partners, all of whom are individual respondents herein. In 1966 the Raiders and the Oakland-Alameda County Coliseum, Inc., a nonprofit corporation, entered into a five-year licensing agreement for use of the

---

30. See Joiner v. City of Dallas, 380 F. Supp. 754 (N.D. Tex.), aff'd, 419 U.S. 1042 (1974):

> Plaintiffs' basic complaint is that the Texas eminent domain statutes have not been brought into the Twentieth Century. We are thoroughly sympathetic with this indictment, for surely this case presents a telling example of the basically unsatisfactory consequences of attempting to fit a statutory scheme designed for a rural, frontier society to the realities of modern, urban civilization. Unfortunately, antiquarianism is no guarantee of unconstitutionality, and outmoded statutes are not invalid per se. In the absence of some other perceived constitutional defects, it is not for the judiciary to engine old laws into modernity.
>
> Measured against the accumulated wisdom of economists, sociologists, city planners, psychologists, and other persons of both scholarship and practical experience, we have no doubt that the Texas eminent domain statutes fall far short of perfection. It might well be, for example, that given the realities of modern civilization, the condemning authority ought to ask for, listen to, and cautiously weigh the opinions of affected property owners before commencing condemnation proceedings. Moreover, today's property owners as a class are better able to participate intelligently in the decision-making process. Not only do they have access to government assistance programs which will help them to propose and articulate viable alternatives to a suggested project, but they also have the ability to present a new dimension to a discussion that has far too long been dominated by panjandrums representing a select elite. It might also be that in defining "just compensation" the condemnor should consider the economic realities of displacement, the practical limitations of relocation, and the modification of life styles resulting from the creation of a "public project," and voluntarily adjust the compensation standard to recompense property owners more completely.
>
> Even if we had the ability to do so, however, which we do not, we could not accept plaintiffs' invitation to write a model eminent domain code. Our job is adjudicative and judicial, not legislative or programmatic. And in performing this role the standard against which we must measure the Texas statutes here challenged is not that supplied by legislative reformers, but that provided by the United States Constitution.

For a British perspective on matters of notice and timing for valuation, see Hanily v. Minister of Local Government & Planning, [1952] 1 All E.R. 1293 (Q.B.).

Oakland Coliseum by the Raiders. Having been given five three-year renewal options, the Raiders exercised the first three, and failed to do so for the football season commencing in 1980 when contract negotiations for renewal terminated without agreement. When the Raiders announced its intention to move the football team to Los Angeles, City commenced this action in eminent domain. . . .

. . . City insists that what it seeks to condemn is "property" which is subject to established eminent domain law. City contends that whether it can establish a valid "public use" must await a determination of the court after a full trial at which all relevant facts may be adduced. In answer, respondents argue that the law of eminent domain does not permit the taking of "intangible property not connected with realty," thereby rendering impossible City's condemnation of the football franchise which respondents describe as a "network of intangible contractual rights." Further, respondents claim that the taking contemplated by City cannot as a matter of law be for any "public use" within City's authority. . . .

. . . [T]he power which is statutorily extended to cities is not limited to certain types of property. In discussing the broad scope of property rights which are subject to a public taking under the new law, the Law Revision Commission comment notes that "Section 1235.170 is intended to provide the broadest possible definition of property and to include any type of right, title or interest in property that may be required for public use." To that end the commission eliminated the "duplicative listings of property types and interests subject to condemnation" which had appeared in the earlier eminent domain statutes.

Despite the apparent lack of any constitutional or statutory restrictions, respondents nonetheless assert that "intangible property" such as the contractual and other rights involved in the instant action never before has been taken by condemnation, and that such taking should not be santioned now. . . .

Following the reasoning of *Kimball* [Laundry Co. v. U.S. (1949)] 338 U.S. 1, numerous other decisions both federal and state have expressly acknowledged that intangible assets are subject to condemnation. . . .

For eminent domain purposes, neither the federal nor the state Constitution distinguishes between property which is real or personal, tangible or intangible. Nor did the 1975 statutory revision do so. . . .

While broad, the eminent domain power is not unlimited. Section 1240.010 cautions: "The power of eminent domain may be exercised to acquire property only for a public use." Further, a public entity's taking may be challenged on the grounds that it (1) reflects a "gross abuse of discretion" (§1245.255, subd. (b)); (2) is arbitrary, capricious, totally lacking in evidentiary support, or in violation of the procedural requirements of the eminent domain law (§1245.255, subd. (a); or (3)

A. Redefining the Public Use Requirement

was the result of bribery (Code Civ. Proc., §1245.270). On the other hand, the statutory authorization to utilize the power of eminent domain for a given "use, purpose, object, or function" constitutes a legislative declaration that the exercise is for a "public use." (§1240.010.)

Is it possible for City to prove that its attempt to take and operate the Raiders' football franchise is for a valid public use? We have defined "public use" as "a use which concerns the whole community or promotes the general interest in its relation to any legitimate object of government." On the other hand, "It is not essential that the entire community, or even any considerable portion thereof, shall directly enjoy or participate in an improvement in order to constitute a public use." (Fallbrook Irrigation District v. Bradley (1896) 164 U.S. 112, 161-162.) Further, while the Legislature may statutorily declare a given "use, purpose, object or function" to be a "public use" (§1240.010), such statutory declarations do not purport to be exclusive....

No case anywhere of which we are aware has held that a municipality can acquire and operate a professional football team, although we are informed that the City of Visalia owns and operates a professional class A baseball franchise in the California League; apparently, its right to do so never has been challenged in court. In our view, several decisions concerning recreation appear germane. In City of Los Angeles v. Superior Court (1959) 51 Cal. 2d 423, 434 [333 P.2d 745], we noted that a city's acquisition of a baseball field, with recreational facilities to be constructed thereon to be used by the city, was "obviously for proper public purposes." Similarly, in County of Alameda v. Meadowlark Dairy Corp. (1964) 227 Cal. App. 2d 80, 84 [38 Cal. Rptr. 474, 48 A.L.R.3d 332], the court upheld a county's acquisition by eminent domain of lands to be used for a county fair, reasoning that "Activities which promote recreation of the public constitute a public purpose." (Id., at p. 85.) Considerably earlier, in Egan v. San Francisco (1913) 165 Cal. 576, 582 [133 P. 294], in sustaining a city's power to build an opera house, we declared: "Generally speaking, anything calculated to promote the education, the recreation or the pleasure of the public is to be included within the legitimate domain of public purposes."

The examples of Candlestick Park in San Francisco and Anaheim Stadium in Anaheim, both owned and operated by municipalities, further suggest the acceptance of the general principle that providing access to recreation to its residents in the form of spectator sports is an appropriate function of city government....

From the foregoing we conclude only that the acquisition and, indeed, the operation of a sports franchise may be an appropriate municipal function. If such valid public use can be demonstrated, the statutes discussed herein afford City the power to acquire by eminent domain any property necessary to accomplish that use.

We caution that we are not concerned with the economic or

governmental wisdom of City's acquisition or management of the Raiders' franchise, but only with the legal propriety of the condemnation action. In this period of fiscal constraints, if the city fathers of Oakland in their collective wisdom elect to seek the ownership of a professional football franchise are we to say them nay? And, if so, on what legal ground? Constitutional? Both federal and state Constitutions permit condemnation requiring only compensation and a public use. Statutory? The applicable statutes authorize a city to take "any property," real or personal, to carry out appropriate municipal functions. Decisional? Courts have consistently expanded the eminent domain remedy permitting property to be taken for recreational purposes. . . .

Respondents urge, further, that because the NFL constitution bars a city from holding a franchise and being a member, the expenditure of any public monies for acquisition of the Raiders' franchise cannot be deemed in the public interest. On the other hand, an affidavit filed by the NFL commissioner avers that "a brief interim ownership" by City "would not be inconsistent with the NFL Constitution. . . ." (7) We, of course, are not bound by such an interpretation. Assuming its validity, however, respondents answer that if City contemplates the prompt transfer to private parties of the property interests which it seeks to condemn, after such brief ownership, that transfer would vitiate any legitimate "public use" which is a prerequisite to condemnation in the first place. In turn, City points to the statute which, as previously noted, expressly authorizes that to which respondents object: "[A] person may acquire property under subdivision (a) with the intent to sell, lease, exchange or otherwise dispose of the property or an interest therein," provided such retransfer is made "subject to such reservations or restrictions as are necessary to protect or preserve the attractiveness, safety, and usefulness of the project." (§1240.120, subd. (b).) So long as adequate controls are imposed upon any retransfer of the condemned property, there is no reason why the "public purpose" which justifies a taking may not be so served and protected. We envision that the adequacy of any such controls can only be determined within the factual context of a specific retransfer agreement. . . .

We reverse and remand the case to the trial court for further proceedings not inconsistent with this opinion.

Mosk, J., Newman, J., Kaus, J., and Reynoso, J., concurred.

Feinberg, J. — I concur in the judgment; I also agree with much of the Chief Justice's concurring and dissenting opinion.

Bird, C. J., Concurring and Dissenting. — The power of eminent domain claimed by the City in this case is not only novel but virtually without limit. This is troubling because the potential for abuse of such a great power is boundless. Although I am forced by the current state of the law to agree with the result reached by the majority, I have not signed their opinion because it endorses this unprecedented application

A. Redefining the Public Use Requirement

of eminent domain law without even pausing to consider the ultimate consequences of their expansive decision. It should be noted that research both by the parties and by this court has failed to disclose a single case in which the legal propositions relied on here have been combined to reach a result such as that adopted by the majority.

There are two particularly disturbing questions in this case. First, does a city have the power to condemn a viable, ongoing business and sell it to another private party merely because the original owner has announced his intention to move his business to another city? For example, if a rock concert impresario, after some years of producing concerts in a municipal stadium, decides to move his productions to another city, may the city condemn his business, including his contracts with the rock stars, in order to keep the concerts at the stadium? . . .

Second, even if a city were legally able to do so, is it proper for a municipality to drastically invade personal property rights to further the policy interests asserted here?

The rights both of the owners of the Raiders and of its employees are threatened by the City's action. Thus, one unexplored aspect of the majority's decision is the ruling that contract rights can be taken by eminent domain. The cases relied on by the majority in support of this holding chiefly concerned inverse condemnations suits. Those cases essentially held that when a state condemns a business, the government is obligated to compensate the business owner for the value of the contract rights destroyed by the taking. In this case, the City seeks to condemn employment contracts between the Raiders and dozens of its employees. Can the City acquire personal employment contracts as simply as it can acquire a tract of land? Are an employee's rights violated by this nonconsensual taking of an employment contract or personal services agreement?

At what point in the varied and complex business relationships involved herein would this power to condemn end? In my view, this court should proceed most cautiously before placing a constitutional imprimatur upon this aspect of creeping statism. These difficult questions are deserving of more thorough attention than they have yet received in this litigation.

Notes

1. On June 30, 1986, the Supreme Court closed the books on the city's eminent domain litigation: the Justices denied certiorari in the city's challenge to the finding of the California Court of Appeal, First District, that the taking of the team franchise would unduly burden

interstate commerce. City of Oakland v. Oakland Raiders, 174 Cal. App. 3d 414, 220 Cal. Rptr. 153 (Ct. App. 1985), cert. denied, 478 U.S. 300 (1986). The appellate court's summary (at 416-418) reads like the most nightmarish fact pattern imaginable from a law school civil procedure examination:

> Plaintiffs sued in 1980 to acquire by eminent domain the property of defendants Oakland Raiders (Raiders), a National Football League (NFL or League) franchise. The Alameda County Superior Court issued a preliminary injunction prohibiting transfer of the franchise from Oakland, the case was transferred to Monterey County (Code Civ. Proc., §394), and summary judgment was entered for defendants. On appeal the Supreme Court reversed, holding our eminent domain statute allowed condemnation of intangible property and that plaintiff had a right to show whether its attempted exercise of eminent domain over the Raiders franchise would be a valid public use. (City of Oakland v. Oakland Raiders (1982) 32 Cal. 3d 60, 183 Cal. Rpt. 673, 646 P.2d 835 [*Raiders I*].) We subsequently granted a peremptory writ of mandate directing the trial court to hold a hearing on plaintiff's application for reinstatement of the preliminary injunction against transfer of the franchise from Oakland. (City of Oakland v. Superior Court (1982) 136 Cal. App. 3d 565, 186 Cal. Rptr. 326 [*Raiders II*].) In the meantime, however, Raiders home games were played in Los Angeles. In early 1983 the trial court reinstated and modified the injunction against transfer, providing that all 1983 Raiders home games for the *1983* season would be played in Oakland "unless and until judgment after trial is entered in favor of [d]efendants before the beginning of the 1983 season." After trial in May 1983 the court entered judgment against plaintiff. Following various procedural maneuvers by plaintiff we issued an alternative writ of mandate, denied plaintiff's requested stay of judgment, and eventually issued a writ of mandate ordering the trial court to (i) vacate its judgment and (ii) proceed to determine those remaining objections to plaintiff's eminent domain action that it had not previously ruled on. (City of Oakland v. Superior Court (1983) 150 Cal. App. 3d 267, 279-280, 197 Cal. Rptr. 729 [*Raiders III*].)
>
> On remand the court again entered judgment for defendants. Its decision is based primarily on three independent grounds: (1) that plaintiff's stated purpose is not a public use; (2) that plaintiff's action is invalid under federal antitrust law; and (3) that plaintiff's action is invalid under the commerce clause of the federal constitution.

2. The team's battles (on and off the field) continued, although in different forms. In a recent decision concerning antitrust causes of action brought by the Raiders and the Los Angeles Coliseum (the Raiders' new home) against the NFL and its member teams, the Ninth Circuit "(1) affirm[ed] the trebled damages injury verdict in favor of the Coliseum [over $14 million]; (2) vacate[ed] the Raiders' antitrust damage recovery [over $34 million], and remand[ed] for further

A. Redefining the Public Use Requirement

proceedings; and (3) reverse[d] the judgment of liability and damages on the claim for breach of the implied promise of good faith and fair dealings [over $11 million]." Los Angeles Memorial Coliseum Commn. v. National Football League, 791 F.2d 1356 (9th Cir. 1986), cert. denied, 108 S. Ct. 92 (1987). See Kurlantzick, Thoughts on Professional Sports and the Antitrust Laws, 15 Conn. L. Rev. 183 (1983).

Finally (?), there was this item in the New York Times Sports People column for December 11, 1986:

> A Superior Court jury in San Diego decided yesterday that Al Davis, managing general partner of the Los Angeles Raiders, was responsible for a heart attack suffered in 1981 by Eugene V. Klein, former owner of the San Diego Chargers.
>
> The jury awarded $5 million in compensatory damages and $48,606.82 in medical expenses after deliberating for two days in Klein's malicious prosecution suit against Davis. Lawyers for Klein said that he suffered a near-fatal heart attack while testifying in Davis's antitrust suit against the National Football League.
>
> The lawyers said that during the final arguments Davis sought to inflict emotional and physical damage because of his dislike for Klein, a bitter Davis rival on and off the field.

3. One might think, upon reading Chief Justice Rose Bird's articulation of concern for private property rights being trampled by "creeping statism," and her refusal to engage in judicial activism in the face of a distasteful legislative act, that she was a conservative, restrained jurist. Of course, such was not the popular conception of the chief justice, who fell from the voters' grace and failed to stand for approval in statewide elections in November 1986.

4. On the night of March 28-29, 1984, office and athletic equipment of the Baltimore Colts NFL team was loaded onto Aero-Mayflower Co. moving vans bound for the Colts' new home in Indianapolis. The next day, March 30, the Maryland legislature passed Emergency Bill 1042, 1984 Md. Laws ch. 6, and the Baltimore City Council enacted Emergency Ordinance No. 32, authorizing the city of Baltimore to "condemn sports franchises." The issue before the federal district court in Mayor of Baltimore v. Baltimore Football Club, 624 F. Supp. 278, 289 (D. Md. 1985), was whether the team was located in Maryland by the time the city attempted to take the Colts. In granting the team's motion for summary judgment, the court noted:

> The team's principal place of business and its tangible property were both outside Maryland on that date [March 30, 1984], and it is clear that the owner's intention was to relocate outside of Maryland. Under any of the workable tests for determining the situs of the franchise, the Court concludes that the Colts were "gone" on March 30, 1984.

What kind of preventive legislation would you propose for states and localities concerned about losing their cherished (and profit-generating) sports teams?[31]

5. Other communities have contemplated using their eminent domain power to prevent the loss or escape of a business. In a move the Wall Street Journal (June 8, 1984) labeled "Eminent Nonsense," New Bedford, Massachusetts considered acquiring a cutting-tool factory fallen on hard times. Not to be outdone by their neighbors to the south, "Boston's city fathers, all shook up over the imminent closing of the Colonial Provision Co. packing plant that supplies hot dogs to Fenway Park, wanted to exercise eminent domain, take over the plant and keep the hot dogs coming." The City's legal counsel cautioned against such a move, however. Parting Sorrows, Wall St. J., Feb. 13, 1986. In light of *Poletown, Oakland Raiders,* and the *Midkiff* case that follows, how would you have advised the city in these instances? What would you want to know about pertinent state (common, constitutional, and statutory) law, the financial status of the community and of the targeted business, and the terms of the proposed acquisition? See Bluestone & Harrison, The Deindustrialization of America: Plant Closings, Community Abandonment, and the Dismantling of Basic Industry (1982); Comment, Eminent Domain as a Tool to Set Up Employee-Owned Businesses in the Face of Shutdowns, 4 Antioch L.J. 271 (1986); Comment, Eminent Domain: The Ability of a Community to Retain an Industry in the Face of an Attempted Shut Down or Relocation, 12 Ohio N.U.L. Rev. 231 (1985).

■ HAWAII HOUSING AUTHORITY v. MIDKIFF
467 U.S. 229 (1984)

JUSTICE O'CONNOR delivered the opinion of the Court. . . .

The Hawaiian Islands were originally settled by Polynesian immigrants from the western Pacific. These settlers developed an economy around a feudal land tenure system in which one island high chief, the ali'i nui, controlled the land and assigned it for development to certain subchiefs. The subchiefs would then reassign the land to other lower ranking chiefs, who would administer the land and govern the farmers

---

31. On January 9, 1981, California Congressmen Stark and Edwards introduced H.R. 823, the Sports Franchise Relocation Act. The Act would have prevented team owners from changing their assigned territory except in the event of noncompliance with a material provision of a stadium lease agreement, inadequacy of the existing stadium, or three years of losses of net income preceding notice of intent to move. Consider the efficacy and wisdom of the bill, one of several unsuccessful legislative efforts to provide special rules for the movement of professional sports teams.

A. Redefining the Public Use Requirement

and other tenants working it. All land was held at the will of the ali'i nui and eventually had to be returned to his trust. There was no private ownership of land.

... In the mid-1960's, after extensive hearings, the Hawaii Legislature discovered that, while the State and Federal Governments owned almost 49% of the State's land, another 47% was in the hands of only 72 private landowners. The legislature further found that 18 landholders, with tracts of 21,000 acres or more, owned more than 40% of this land and that on Oahu, the most urbanized of the islands, 22 landowners owned 72.5% of the fee simple titles. The legislature concluded that concentrated land ownership was responsible for skewing the State's residential fee simple market, inflating land prices, and injuring the public tranquility and welfare.

To redress these problems, the legislature decided to compel the large landowners to break up their estates.... [T]he Hawaii Legislature enacted the Land Reform Act of 1967 (Act), Haw. Rev. Stat., ch. 516, which created a mechanism for condemning residential tracts and for transferring ownership of the condemned fees simple to existing lessees. By condemning the land in question, the Hawaii legislature intended to make the land sales involuntary, thereby making the federal tax consequences less severe while still facilitating the redistribution of fees simple.

Under the Act's condemnation scheme, tenants living on single-family residential lots within developmental tracts at least five acres in size are entitled to ask the Hawaii Housing Authority (HHA) to condemn the property on which they live. Haw. Rev. Stat. §§516-1(2), (11), 516-22(1977). When 25 eligible tenants,[1] or tenants on half the lots in the tract, whichever is less, file appropriate applications, the Act authorizes HHA to hold a public hearing to determine whether acquisition by the State of all or part of the tract will "effectuate the public purposes" of the Act. §516-22....

After compensation has been set, HHA may sell the land titles to tenants who have applied for fee simple ownership. HHA is authorized to lend these tenants up to 90% of the purchase price, and it may condition final transfer on a right of first refusal for the first 10 years following sale. §§516-30, 516-34, 516-35. If HHA does not sell the lot to the tenant residing there, it may lease the lot or sell it to someone else, provided that public notice has been given. §516-18. However, HHA may not sell to any one purchaser, or lease to any one tenant, more than one lot, and it may not operate for profit. §§516-28, 516-32. In practice, funds to satisfy the condemnation awards have been

---

1. An eligible tenant is one who, among other things, owns a house on the lot, has a bona fide intent to live on the lot or be a resident of the State, shows proof of ability to pay for a fee interest in it, and does not own residential land elsewhere nearby. Haw. Rev. Stat. §§516-33(3), (4), (7) (1977).

supplied entirely by lessees. While the Act authorizes HHA to issue bonds and appropriate funds for acquisition, no bonds have issued and HHA has not supplied any funds for condemned lots. . . .

The starting point for our analysis of the Act's constitutionality is the Court's decision in Berman v. Parker, 348 U.S. 26 (1954). . . .

. . . The Court explicitly recognized the breadth of the principle it was announcing, noting:

> Once the object is within the authority of Congress, the right to realize it through the exercise of eminent domain is clear. For the power of eminent domain is merely the means to the end. . . . Once the object is within the authority of Congress, the means by which it will be attained is also for Congress to determine. Here one of the means chosen is the use of private enterprise for redevelopment of the areas. Appellants argue that this makes the project a taking from one businessman for the benefit of another businessman. But the means of executing the project are for Congress and Congress alone to determine, once the public purpose has been established. Id., at 33.

The "public use" requirement is thus coterminous with the scope of a sovereign's police powers.

There is, of course, a role for courts to play in reviewing a legislature's judgment of what constitutes a public use, even when the eminent domain power is equated with the police power. But the Court in *Berman* made clear that it is "an extremely narrow" one. Id., at 32. . . .

. . . [T]he Court has made clear that it will not substitute its judgment for a legislature's judgment as to what constitutes a public use "unless the use be palpably without reasonable foundation." United States v. Gettysburg Electric R. Co., 160 U.S. 668, 680 (1896).

To be sure, the Court's cases have repeatedly stated that "one person's property may not be taken for the benefit of another private person without a justifying public purpose, even though compensation be paid." Thompson v. Consolidated Gas Corp., 300 U.S. 55, 80 (1937). Thus, in Missouri Pacific R. Co. v. Nebraska, 164 U.S. 403 (1896), where the "order in question was not, *and was not claimed to be,* . . . a taking of private property for a public use under the right of eminent domain," id., at 416 (emphasis added), the Court invalidated a compensated taking of property for lack of a justifying public purpose. But where the exercise of the eminent domain power is rationally related to a conceivable public purpose, the Court has never held a compensated taking to be proscribed by the Public Use Clause.

On this basis, we have no trouble concluding that the Hawaii Act is constitutional. The people of Hawaii have attempted, much as the settlers of the original 13 Colonies did, to reduce the perceived social and economic evils of a land oligopoly traceable to their monarchs. The

A. Redefining the Public Use Requirement 819

land oligopoly has, according to the Hawaii Legislature, created artificial deterrents to the normal function of the State's residential land market and forced thousands of individual homeowners to lease, rather than buy, the land underneath their homes. Regulating oligopoly and the evils associated with it is a classic exercise of a State's police powers. We cannot disapprove of Hawaii's exercise of this power.

Nor can we condemn as irrational the Act's approach to correcting the land oligopoly problem. The Act presumes that when a sufficiently large number of persons declare that they are willing but unable to buy lots at fair prices the land market is malfunctioning. When such a malfunction is signalled, the Act authorizes HHA to condemn lots in the relevant tract. The Act limits the number of lots any one tenant can purchase and authorizes HHA to use public funds to ensure that the market dilution goals will be achieved. This is a comprehensive and rational approach to identifying and correcting market failure.

Of course, this Act, like any other, may not be successful in achieving its intended goals. But "whether *in fact* the provision will accomplish its objectives is not the question: the [constitutional requirement] is satisfied if . . . the . . . [state] Legislature *rationally could have believed* that the [Act] would promote its objective." Western & Southern Life Ins. Co. v. State Bd. of Equalization, 451 U.S. 648, 671-672 (1981). When the legislature's purpose is legitimate and its means are not irrational, our cases make clear that empirical debates over the wisdom of takings — no less than debates over the wisdom of other kinds of socioeconomic legislation — are not to be carried out in the federal courts. Redistribution of fees simple to correct deficiencies in the market determined by the state legislature to be attributable to land oligopoly is a rational exercise of the eminent domain power. Therefore, the Hawaii statute must pass the scrutiny of the Public Use Clause. . . .

The mere fact that property taken outright by eminent domain is transferred in the first instance to private beneficiaries does not condemn that taking as having only a private purpose. The Court long ago rejected any literal requirement that condemned property be put into use for the general public. "It is not essential that the entire community, nor even any considerable portion, . . . directly enjoy or participate in any improvement in order [for it] to constitute a public use." Rindge Co. v. Los Angeles, 262 U.S., at 707. "[W]hat in its immediate aspect [is] only a private transaction may . . . be raised by its class or character to a public affair." Block v. Hirsh, 256 U.S., at 155. As the unique way titles were held in Hawaii skewed the land market, exercise of the power of eminent domain was justified. The Act advances its purposes without the State's taking actual possession of the land. In such cases, government does not itself have to use property to legitimate the taking; it is only the taking's purpose, and not its mechanics, that must pass scrutiny under the Public Use Clause.

Similarly, the fact that a state legislature, and not the Congress, made the public use determination does not mean that judicial deference is less appropriate.[7] Judicial deference is required because, in our system of government, legislatures are better able to assess what public purposes should be advanced by an exercise of the taking power. State legislatures are as capable as Congress of making such determinations within their respective spheres of authority. Thus, if a legislature, state or federal, determines there are substantial reasons for an exercise of the taking power, courts must defer to its determination that the taking will serve a public use.

. . . Accordingly, we reverse the judgment of the Court of Appeals, and remand these cases for further proceedings in conformity with this opinion.

Notes

1. The Hawaii Land Reform Act survived state constitutional scrutiny as well, as the state supreme court found a valid public use and just compensation under article I, section 20 of the Hawaii Constitution. The court noted:

> The Hawaii provision differs [from the fifth amendment to the United States Constitution] only insofar as it provides that "property shall not be taken or damaged. . . ." The "or damaged language" was added by the Hawaii Constitutional Convention of 1968 to bring our eminent domain provision in line with that of twenty-five other states.

Hawaii Housing Authority v. Lyman, 704 P.2d 888, 896 n.12 (Hawaii 1985). Yet the court in *Lyman* chose not to "embrace the Court's broader ruling in [*Midkiff*], equating the public use requirement of eminent domain with the state's police power," instead limiting its state constitutional review "to an examination of the Act's constitutionality under the minimum rationality standard, which we adopt as appropriate for judicial evaluation of the legislature's public use determinations." Id. at 896-897. How could the *Midkiff* Court have been *more* deferential? Since a disgruntled loser will still recover just compensation in the event of a valid taking, does (and should) the Supreme Court require anything more than mere rationality or a "conceivable public purpose"? See

---

7. It is worth noting that the Fourteenth Amendment does not itself contain an independent "public use" requirement. Rather, that requirement is made binding on the States only by incorporation of the Fifth Amendment's Eminent Domain Clause through the Fourteenth Amendment's Due Process Clause. See Chicago, B. & Q. R. Co. v. Chicago, 166 U.S. 226 (1897). It would be ironic to find that state legislation is subject to greater scrutiny under the incorporated "public use" requirement than is congressional legislation under the express mandate of the Fifth Amendment.

A. Redefining the Public Use Requirement

Durham, Efficient Just Compensation as a Limit on Eminent Domain, 69 Minn. L. Rev. 1277 (1985); Note, Containing the Effect of Hawaii Housing Authority v. Midkiff on Takings for Private Industry, 71 Cornell L. Rev. 428 (1986); Note, Hawaii Housing Authority v. Midkiff: A Final Requiem for the Public Use Limitation on Eminent Domain?, 60 Notre Dame L. Rev. 388 (1985).

2. The plaintiffs claim that the enabling act is unconstitutional because it provides that the commission authorized to build and lease off-street parking facilities shall have no power to determine the charges made by the private operators to the public for services. What result? See Foltz v. City of Indianapolis, 234 Ind. 656, 130 N.E.2d 650 (1955); Omaha Parking Authority v. City of Omaha, 163 Neb. 97, 77 N.W.2d 862 (1956); Larsen v. City and County of San Francisco, 152 Cal. App. 2d 355, 313 P.2d 959 (1st Dist. 1957); cf. Nichols, Real Property Taxation of Divided Interests in Land, 11 Kan. L. Rev. 309 (1963).

3. A limited dividend housing company, organized to condemn land for low-rent housing, is sponsored by a trade union; 30 percent of the tenant-stockholders are members of the union. Is the proposed taking for a public use? See Amalgamated Housing Corp. v. Kelly, 193 Misc. 961, 82 N.Y.S.2d 577 (Sup. Ct. 1948) (yes — purpose of law permitting taking by Amalgamated "is to protect and safeguard the entire public from the menace of the slums"); State Highway Commissioner v. Buck, 226 A.2d 840, 842 (N.J. 1967).

4. Before its repeal in 1975, §1001 of the California Civil Code provided: "Any person may, without further legislative action, acquire private property for any use specified . . . by proceedings had under [eminent domain]; and any person seeking to acquire property for any of the uses . . . is 'an agent of the State.'" Connecting a residence with the mains of an established sewer system is declared to be such a public use. When an apartment owner sought to condemn a right of way over adjoining land for a new sewer line, the neighbor objected. The California Supreme Court, in Linggi v. Garovotti, 45 Cal. 2d 20, 286 P.2d 15 (1955), reversed the trial court's grant of a demurrer, but found that "[a] somewhat stronger showing of ["right and justification for the proposed condemnation"] is necessary than if the condemnor were a public or quasi public entity." 286 P.2d at 20. The legislature enacted a modified private condemnation provision in 1976. See Cal. Civ. Code §1001 (West 1982) and the accompanying "Law Revision Committee Comment."

5. The first excerpt that follows describes private acquisition efforts necessitated by the absence of the use of eminent domain. In a post-*Midkiff* world, should the state play the lead role in assembling property for a new theme park that promises untold wealth in the form of tax revenues, employment, and general revitalization? Or, is there a legal, financial, or moral limit to the extent of direct public participation?

How do the methods, motives, and attitudes of the private taker/purchaser differ from those of master condemnor Robert Moses, the subject of the second excerpt?

■ MOSLEY, DISNEY'S WORLD
280-283 (1985)

In the summer of 1964, mysterious strangers from out of state began buying up large tracts of land on the outskirts of the small central Florida city of Orlando. All efforts to track down the identity of the buyers were unsuccessful. The outsiders, who obviously had plenty of money and were willing to pay cash, made it a condition of the sales that they effected that landowners not divulge the identities of the buyers — who were using phony names, in any case — and swore them to secrecy over the price and other details of the transactions.

Local gossip soon had it that the U.S. Government was behind the purchases, and the wiseacres prophesied that Washington, already beginning operations on its space program at nearby Cape Canaveral, would soon be moving into the Orlando neighborhood and building a vast new complex to manufacture everything from intercontinental missiles to hydrogen bombs.

Then someone let slip the fact that the famous Walt Disney had flown into the area twice recently from Hollywood on his private Beechcraft plane, and that a woman believed to be his wife had even been heard to remark, over a hamburger in a junk-food restaurant in Kissimmee, "But it's just swamp, Walt! How could you possibly want anything here?"

Was it just a coincidence? It seemed so — especially when it was pointed out that Disney's father and mother had been married near Kissimmee, and it was plausible to suppose that their celebrated son was simply making a sentimental pilgrimage. But the mysterious sales went on, and soon thirty thousand acres of central Florida land, citrus groves, forests and swamps, plus some choice farmland, had passed into the hands of the secret buyers.

It was at this moment that Emily Bavar, a reporter who edited the Sunday magazine of the Orlando Sentinel, quite fortuitously accepted a promotional trip to California to attend the tenth anniversary celebration of the opening of Disneyland. Mrs. Bavar, intrigued by what was going on in her own state, asked Walt Disney if he was buying up land in Florida to build another Disneyland. He did not bat an eyelid at her question but replied, "Who would ever want to build a theme park in Florida — with the sort of climate, rivers, and landscape you have over there?"...

"In essence his reply was, 'I couldn't tell you even if I knew because [Walt's brother] Roy is in charge.' But," Emily Bavar said, "though I

A. Redefining the Public Use Requirement 823

could just as well have been wrong, I just knew Walt was being evasive. But what made me particularly suspicious was the fact that he knew so much about Florida, its problems about rain, humidity, and transportation. I didn't believe him when he denied my instinctive feeling. I decided to take a chance."....

From Walt's point of view, all the secrecy was needed because he wished to avoid the mistakes he had made in Anaheim, and he was determined to buy enough land not to be hemmed in by honky-tonk rivals. Once it was known that a vast Disney theme park was in the making, outside hotel, restaurant, and fairground interests would have moved in to snap up adjacent land, sending prices through the roof, as well as ruining the nature of the enterprise.

Not only that. He had sent emissaries from Burbank to Tallahassee, the Florida capital, headed by the shrewd marketing man Card Walker, to make a deal with the local government before signing the final papers. In return for bringing such an enormous tourist attraction into the state, Walker asked for a quid pro quo on behalf of his boss, and the governor gave it to him. For the first time in Florida's history, control over all the territory to be included in the future Disney World was ceded to the owners. The new park would become what amounted to a self-governing community, with its own laws and police services, hospitals, health and all necessary maintenance departments, plus a special tax rate; and no outside authority would be able to enter its territory without an invitation from the owners nor would its finances or affairs be subject to control by the state.[32]

---

32. See Disney's Plan to Build Cities on Florida Tract Could Shape Its Future, Wall St. J., July 9, 1985:

... Disney planners have started work on a proposal to transform the Disney World acreage into fully developed recreation-oriented communities. The new cities, which could take shape in as little as 15 years, are expected to include industry, commerce and residential neighborhoods, at a cost reckoned in billions of dollars....

In 1967, the Florida legislature, in a series of five acts, obligingly endowed Disney with powers normally reserved for county governments. Through the new, but unpopulated, municipalities of Bay Lake and Lake Buena Vista, and through the specially established Reedy Creek Improvement District, the company was authorized to float tax-exempt bonds, to establish its own zoning and to exercise police and eminent-domain powers. The legislature also gave the district specific authority, so far unexploited, to build an airport and even to generate power by nuclear fission....

So far, Disney hasn't taken full advantage of its authority, partly for fear of killing the golden goose.... Permanent residents ... have been strictly taboo because of what [Disney chairman Charles] Cobb terms "the one man, one vote problem": Full-fledged citizens, once enfranchised, might detract from Disney's self-governing authority and vote down Disney corporate proposals....

The problem was inherent in Mr. Disney's original plan. But he himself never had to find a practical way to balance individual rights against the engineering of a new society. — EDS.

The champion eminent domainer of all times is probably Robert Moses. For his public works, he dispossessed close to half a million people. The following incident describes his first use of the power of appropriation.

■ CARO, THE POWER BROKER: ROBERT MOSES AND THE FALL OF NEW YORK
184-185 (1974)

The Timber Pointers were shocked when they learned that Moses planned to turn the adjoining estate into a public park. Pointing to the spot where the proposed park would run alongside the club's golf course, old Horace Havemeyer, "the Sultan of Sugar," growled to his young brother-in-law, stockbrocker W. Kingsland Macy: "I tell you, Macy, if they get a park over there, there'll be so much screwing you won't be able to tee up a ball." Havemeyer, Macy and Wall Street trader Buell Hollister had even more reason to be disturbed than the other ninety-seven Timber Point members. Anxious to attract more of "the right kind of people" to East Islip, the trio had recently decided to purchase the Taylor Estate themselves, divide its 1,486 acres into thirty building lots and sell them, at prices ranging from $50,000 on up, to thirty persons so right that they would even be invited to join, on purchase of a lot, the Timber Point Club. The proposition promised to be highly rewarding financially as well as socially.... Learning of these machinations, Moses asked Macy to drop around to his office. When the stockbroker arrived, Moses bluntly ordered him not to consummate the deal. Macy indignantly refused to agree. Then, as he was later to testify under oath, "Mr. Moses told me they were going to take that place away from us and nothing we could do would stop it.... Mr. Moses informed me that he had the arbitrary power to seize this property, which was owned by myself and my associates, even though the state did not have one cent to pay for it.... Mr. Moses told me that he could take my home away from me. He told me personally that his power was such that he could seize my house, put me out of it and arrest me for trespass if I tried to get into it again.... Mr. Moses told me not only that he possessed this arbitrary power, but that he was able to control the press of New York City, so as to hold me up to such obloquy that I would not be able to stand it." And Moses was as good as his word. No sooner had Havemeyer, Hollister and Macy actually purchased the Taylor Estate than, without even a pretense of negotiating with them as the law required, he directed Park Commission attorneys to draw up a Notice of Entry and Appropriation and serve it on the

A. Redefining the Public Use Requirement

three men — and while it was being served he stationed armed state troopers on the property and instructed them not to allow the three men to enter it even to remove personal property they had left there....

To Macy, the idealist, the case represented something that was more important than money. When Havemeyer wrote, "This . . . is my limit," Macy replied that he would carry on alone. Appeals attorneys told him that if he was willing to press the fight vigorously, he would probably win, although the victory might not come until the case had been transferred out of the state courts and into the United States Supreme Court, which would focus on the basic constitutionality of the use by a state agency of one individual's money to seize the property of another. Macy authorized them to proceed. But Moses' attorneys continued to make motions and file briefs, and when Macy's appeal from Dunne's decision finally reached the Appellate Division in February 1928, his legal costs had mounted to $43,192.61 — a burden beyond his financial resources. By April 1928, his attorneys were dunning him for payment of a $1,100 bill. Although the case would eventually be brought before the Court of Appeals, which upheld Dunne's decision, and an attempt was made to bring it to the United States Supreme Court — Justice Louis Brandeis brought the legal fight to an end on January 21, 1929, four years after the Biltmore hearing, by refusing to issue a writ of certiorari which would have enabled the Court to hear the case — it was obviously not pressed vigorously in these last stages, as though the case were really over already.

And, in fact, it was. Moses had never stopped developing the Taylor Estate — as if its acquisition were a fait accompli. By the spring of 1927, he had laid concrete for access roads and parking fields, set out scores of stone fireplaces and picnic tables, erected wooden bathhouses with showers and lockers and finished renovating the mansion and outbuildings, at a total cost of hundreds of thousands of dollars. During the summer of 1927, it had hundreds of thousands of visitors. By the time the higher courts came to rule on the question of whether the Taylor Estate was a park, it *was* a park. What was a judge to do? Tell the state to tear up the roads and tear down the buildings, to destroy what hundreds of thousands of dollars of the public's money had been spent to build? Tell the people who had visited the Taylor Estate that they could visit it no more? In theory, of course, judges should not be influenced by such considerations. But judges are human. And their susceptibility to such considerations was undoubtedly increased by Moses' willingness to attack publicly those of them who ruled against him, as he had done to the "local judge," thereby letting the public know exactly who it was who was closing the park to them....

. . . The final hearing before the State Court of Appeals was the twenty-fifth separate appellate proceeding in the Taylor Estate case.

The case was, the Herald Tribune said, "a landmark of eminent domain."

Are there realistic, workable, and efficient alternatives to secretive private land assemblage and to public-private confrontations over land that stands in the way of the common good? The next section offers one provocative option.

B. LAND BANKS

The more specialized purposes sought for by the land bank are:

1. *Advance acquisition of land for public purposes.* — Many government services, roads, schools, hospitals, recreation to name but a few, require substantial amounts of land. Land assembly, as we are continuing to find out, is complicated, legally vexatious, costly, uncertain and time-consuming. And this is a continuing process, so long as government endures. Therefore, for purposes of convenience, so that the necessary land is available in an appropriate amount when the time comes to provide the government service, and also for considerations of cost, advance acquisition would be an important function of a land bank.

2. *Avoiding the expenses of urban sprawl.* — The ragged process of subdivision development, including leapfrogging, is often dictated by the price of land as well as by its availability. Consequently, urban infrastructure, paid for by government, has to follow — however reluctantly and expensively — this path of growth. This means that land relatively close to developed centers often remains idle or unoccupied, while land further from the center is being freshly developed and occupied. Vacant lots and empty buildings are not only a waste of resources in themselves but they contribute to a further waste of resources in transportation; they cause more roads and rails and cars and fuel to be used than would be needed were development more compact, and they oblige travelers to spend more time in transit through these dead spaces that increase the distance from center to periphery.

3. *An instrument for perfecting the land market* — Land banks are well adapted to correct the errors and scars of the past. Scattered throughout many of our older suburbs are pockets of underdevelopment, dotted with small lots of odd sizes or occupied by vacant buildings. This collection of sites frequently adds up to an impressive total of developable land, but its present form is uninviting to developers. These odd bits and remnants can be assembled into parcels suitable for building. Furthermore, there are often pockets of legal blight, where

B. Land Banks

the land has been rendered undevelopable because of problems over the estate or title. A public agency could assemble these odd pieces of land into economic plots and make them available by sale or lease to developers.

This function emphasizes a most appropriate role for government activity and support — perfecting the market for urban land. This land market is one of the more laggard sectors of the economy. It performs its jobs — setting prices and allocating resources — poorly. Many reasons have been given for this condition, most notably the nature of the land commodity, which is nonhomogeneous: in the terms of the lawyer, every piece of land is unique and therefore appropriate for specific performance. It is also "lumpy" or discontinuous and costly relative to the financial capacities of the participants in the market. There is also a poor flow of information, aggravated by political boundaries and fragmentations of the market. Holdouts have monopoly power. Indeed, it can be said that in the urban land market relative prices do not correspond to real economic scarcities, and resources are therefore not allocated to their most efficient uses. By acquiring such land, and making it available in a planned pattern that imparted more order to the whole process of urban growth, the bank would reduce uncertainty and confusion in the land market. This would mean a stabilization of the market for land — much in the same way as a central bank, such as the Federal Reserve Bank, stabilizes the money market.

Last, not only in its dealing with the knowledge and supply side of the equation, but in its other activities, the land bank, guided by considerations of urban development, and having a clearly discernible basis for its decisions on price and the rate of release of land from its inventories, would be acting to moderate fluctuations in the price of land. In a way, many of the complaints about speculators in metropolitan lands could be alleviated. The functioning of the private land market could be improved, while development decisions could still be left to private persons acting, as always, subject to the controls over land use. In other words, the land bank would perform the holding function and the supply function on precisely the same basis as private holders, by selling or leasing to the highest bidder, but it need not interfere with or encroach on the development function.

4. *A key tool for orderly urban development.* — The overwhelming difficulty with metropolitan plans is that few tools exist to realize affirmatively the goals and objectives enunciated in them. Through the techniques of the land bank it should be possible to control the pace at which demand for government services will increase by controlling the speed and direction of urban growth itself.

5. *Recapturing land values created by government activities.* — Land values are enhanced when new government services are provided.

These increments, reflecting the activities of society, nonetheless inure to particular individuals who held the land before that progress took place and who, though they may have anticipated such increments and even invested for that very reason, have done little to bring them about. It is fitting that such increments return to the public purse, thereby permitting lower property taxes than otherwise prevail. Moreover, since public expenditures and regulations have such a profound effect on land values, there are constant pressures toward graft, dishonesty, and subornation of public officials; with a bank, increments in land values should automatically revert to it, and pressures to extend government services to outlying areas would be moderated.

What does emerge as the overall rationale of the program is the relation of metropolitan land reserve policies to comprehensive metropolitan planning and land-use control. It is a flexible and powerful tool for guiding the future growth of the community.

Tentative Draft No. 5 of the ALI Model Land Development Code (March 30, 1973) did not include authorization for land banking — "because of the Reporters' own ambivalence on this issue." The Council of ALI reversed, asking for a draft statute. (See Article 6 of the 1975 Code.)

Advocates of the proposal include National Committee on Urban Growth Policy, The New City (1969); American Institute of Architects, First Report of the National Policy Task Force (1972); Reps, The Future of American Planning: Requiem or Renaissance?, 1967 Planning 47; Note, 23 Case W. Res. L. Rev. 897 (1972). Foreign experience is said to make a strong case for land banking. See Passow, Land Reserves and Teamwork in Planning Stockholm, 36 J. Am. Inst. Planners 179 (1970).

There are conflicting immediate precedents, but only for small-scale operations. One proposed technique is acquiring land in advance of need — particularly in connection with highways. On the basis of origin and destination studies, engineers can conclude with some degree of certainty whether a new highway is required within the foreseeable future. If unimproved land is immediately acquired to meet anticipated need, right-of-way costs can be reduced substantially, and ribbon residential or commercial development avoided. Airports are also being planned to accommodate expansion.[33]

Another pertinent technique — although seemingly doomed by the nomenclature it bears — is "excess condemnation." Where upheld, it has been justified on three theories: removal and replatting of odd-shaped remnants of land; taking of abutting land so that planning

---

33. A big buffer area rings Montreal's new airport covering 138 square miles (Kennedy International is less than 8 square miles). "To assure a fully integrated and balanced approach to planning," the government explains, "planners of the Montreal airport concluded that a large land mass should be put under the control of the airport authority." N.Y. Times, Jan. 6, 1975.

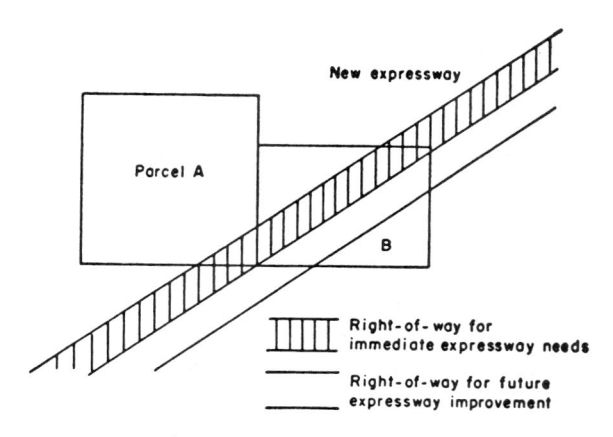

Source: Highway Research Board, Special Report 26, at 5 (1957).

restrictions may be imposed to protect the public improvement from inharmonious environment; and the taking of surplus land so that a profit may be obtained upon resale after the value is enhanced by the completion of the project. The occasional decision outlawing this device led in many states to constitutional amendments expressly authorizing excess condemnation. (Incidentally, how do these decisions avoid the rule that public necessity is nonreviewable?) Some provisions so emphasize the right to impose restrictions upon resale that the intention is apparently to protect the improvement rather than to provide a means of paying for it.[34] An interesting situation in which the excess-taking problem arises under a different label is Vilbig v. Housing Authority of Dallas, 287 S.W.2d 323 (Tex. 1955) (whether adequate development of housing project required land which at time of resolution of necessity of taking was unbuildable and was subsequently

---

34. In Missouri it is provided:

[T]he state, or any county or city may acquire by eminent domain such property. . . . in excess of that actually to be occupied by the public improvement or use in connection therewith, as may be reasonably necessary to effectuate the purposes intended. . . . and may sell such excess property with such restrictions as shall be appropriate to preserve the improvements made.

Mo. Const. art. 1, §27. On the other hand, the New York amendment read, until 1963:

The legislature may authorize cities . . . to take more land and property than is needed for actual construction in the laying out, widening, extending or relocating parks, public places, highways or streets; provided, however, that the additional land and property so authorized to be taken shall be no more than sufficient to form suitable building sites abutting on such park, public place, highway or street. After so much of the land and property has been appropriated for such park, public place, highway or street as is needed therefor, the remainder may be sold or leased.

N.Y. Const. art. 1, §7(e) (1938).

resold for commercial purposes).[35] More recently, a fourth theory — "substitute condemnation" — has emerged.[36]

Note

In 1984, in an effort to control rampant construction on Nantucket, town officials established a land bank to preserve open land. A 2 percent tax on property sales is collected that is used to purchase land to be preserved for public use. In 1986, the bank collected $5.1 million. Approximately one-third of the island is now publicly held, and officials look forward to preserving half of the island through the land bank.

The impact on the private land market has been substantial: "The more land the town holds, the more the remaining lots increase in value. Building lots that in 1980 sold for $27,000 cost $87,000 in 1986. In the same period, the average price of a house climbed from $171,000 to $345,000." N.Y. Times, May 23, 1987.

For a discussion of the use of the land banking concept to promote farm ownership, see 1 Juergensmeyer & Wadley, Agricultural Law §4.14 (1982).

Problem

Governor Frugal has been exploring a program to stimulate the state housing construction industry. Frugal's commitment is to large-scale projects that are conscientiously planned so as to accommodate environmental demands, provide for personal amenities, and respond to the social challenge of balanced housing. The governor has become increasingly concerned over the pivotal problem of large land assembly — and the prohibitive costs created by the "holdouts." Frugal hesitates, however, to create a land banking bureaucracy and believes that the power of outright condemnation is too blunt a tool in the hands of a private developer.

When Frugal described this problem at a recent governor's conference, a governor from an oil-producing state asked: "Why don't you unitize your land the way we do our oil fields? It's obvious that planned production gets the most out of a scarce resource and keeps down the long-run costs for everyone. It makes no sense to let a driller come in and make a fast buck by skimming off the cream. And you can't let

---

35. See Opinion of the Justices, 330 Mass. 713, 113 N.E.2d 452 (1953) (sites along a turnpike for gas stations, restaurants, and other auxiliary services).
36. K.J.C. Realty Inc. v. State, 69 Misc. 2d 99, 329 N.Y.S.2d 252 (Sup. Ct. Erie Co. 1972).

freeloaders drill right next to the best wells or cash in on a neighbor's pressurized secondary recovery system. So we unitize the whole oil field, regulate the distance between wells, determine rates of optimum production, and oversee the pooling agreements. Sure, it's coercive, but at least it keeps things in the private marketplace and it lets the landowner in on a piece of the action rather than letting the oil companies condemn property and reap windfall profits."

Governor Frugal is intrigued by this suggestion and wants you, as general counsel, to investigate it. What would such a system look like? How would it differ from the standard urban renewal approach or that of a land bank? Can we get the same results with the tools we already have? How valid is the oil/land analogy? Are there any constitutional problems? See Huie, Woodward & Smith, Oil and Gas, Cases and Materials 122 (1972); Hemingway, The Law of Oil and Gas (2d ed. 1983); Smith, The Kansas Unitization Statute, 16 Kan. L. Rev. 567 (1968).

C. THE RIDDLE OF JUST COMPENSATION

■ BLACKSTONE, COMMENTARIES
139

In this and similar cases the legislature alone can, and indeed frequently does, interpose, and compel the individual to acquiesce. But how does it interpose and compel? Not by absolutely stripping the subject of his property in an arbitrary manner; but by giving him a full indemnification and equivalent for the injury thereby sustained. The public is now considered as an individual, treating with an individual for an exchange. All that the legislature does, is to oblige the owner to alienate his possessions for a reasonable price; and even this is an exertion of power, which the legislature indulges with caution, and which nothing but the legislature can perform.

■ HORWITZ, THE TRANSFORMATION OF AMERICAN LAW, 1780-1860
63-64 (1977)

[T]he principle that the state should compensate individuals for property taken for public use was not widely established in America at the time of the Revolution. Only colonial Massachusetts seems rigidly to have followed the principle of just compensation in road building. New York, by contrast, usually limited the right of compensation to land already improved or enclosed or else it provided that compensation should be paid by those who benefited from land taken to build private roads. Despite the efforts of Thomas Jefferson to establish the principle of just compensation in postrevolutionary Virginia, no law providing compensation for land taken for roads was enacted until 1785, although the state had regularly compensated slave owners for slaves killed as a result of unlawful or rebellious activities. Until the nineteenth century, Pennsylvania and New Jersey still denied compensation on the ground that the original proprietary land grants had expressly reserved a portion of real property for the building of roads.

Not only was eighteenth century practice strongly weighted against compensation but so was its constitutional theory. Of the first postrevolutionary state constitutions, only those of Vermont and Massachusetts contained provisions requiring compensation. By 1800 only one additional state — Pennsylvania — constitutionally provided for compensation for takings under the power of eminent domain. Even by 1820 a majority of the original states had not yet enacted constitutional clauses providing for compensation for land taken. Yet, under the influence of Blackstone's strict views about the necessity of providing compensation, reinforced by the antistatist bias of prevailing natural law thinking, by this time statutory provisions for compensation had become standard practice in every state except South Carolina, whose courts continued to uphold uncompensated takings of property. And even without the benefit of a constitutional or statutory provision, some judges were remarkably quick to hold, in Chancellor Kent's words, that "provision for compensation — in a statute — is an indispensable attendant on the due and constitutional exercise of the power of depriving an individual of his property." He established a practice of enjoining public officials from undertaking any activity for which there was no advance provision for compensation.

■ STATE CONSTITUTIONAL PROVISIONS

"The right of property is before and higher than any constitutional sanction; and private property shall not be taken, appropriated or damaged for public use, without just compensation therefor." Ark. Const. art. 2, §22 (1874).

"No property, nor right of way, shall be appropriated to the use of any corporation until full compensation therefor shall be first made to the owner, in money, or first secured to him by a deposit of money, which compensation, irrespective of any benefit from any improvement proposed by such corporation; shall be ascertained by a jury of twelve men, in a court of competent jurisdiction, as shall be prescribed by law." Id. art. 12, §9.

C. The Riddle of Just Compensation

"And whenever the public exigencies require that the property of any individual should be appropriated to public uses, he shall receive a reasonable compensation therefor." Mass. Const. pt. 1, art. 10 (1780).

The constitutions of most of the thirteen original states did not require compensation upon the condemnation of land. The seemingly unending supply of raw land in America — much of it not even privately owned and of little value in its unimproved state — made it appear unnecessary to limit land takings in any significant way. Indeed, it was the practice in several of the states, even after the Revolution, to acquire land without compensation.[37] But with the establishment of roads, limitations began to appear.[38] Today all states but New Hampshire[39] and North Carolina[40] have inserted requirements for compensation in their constitutions.

---

37. 3 Nichols' Eminent Domain §8.1[1] n. 10 (rev. 3d ed. 1985). See State v. Dawson, 3 Hill 99 (S.C. 1836). And as late as 1868 five of the original states were without this guarantee. Grant, The "Higher Law" Background of the Law of Eminent Domain, 6 Wis. L. Rev. 67 (1931).

38. For example, the colony of Massachusetts Bay in 1639 provided, upon the laying out of a highway:

> That if any man be thereby damaged in his improved ground, the town shall make him reasonable satisfaction, by estimation of those that laid out the same . . . and if any person find himself justly grieved with any act or thing, done by the persons deputed aforesaid, he may appeal to the county court aforesaid, but if he be found to complain without cause, he shall surely pay all charges of the parties, and court, during that action, and also be fined to the county as the court shall adjudge.

The Charters and General Laws of the Colony and Province of Massachusetts Bay 127 (1814).

39. New Hampshire's constitution addresses the issue without dealing explicitly with compensation:

> Every member of the community has a right to be protected by it, in the enjoyment of his life, liberty, and property; he is therefore bound to contribute his share in the expense of such protection, and to yield his personal service when necessary. But no part of a man's property shall be taken from him, or applied to public uses, without his own consent, or that of the representative body of the people. Nor are the inhabitants of this state controllable by any other laws than those to which they, or their representative body, have given their consent.

Pt. 1 art. 12. Compensation was read into the constitution as "one of the first principles of natural justice." 1 N.H.B.J. 12 (1959); and see Sibson v. State 111 N.H. 305, 282 A.2d 664 (1971); Burrows v. City of Keene, 121 N.H. 590, 432 A.2d 15 (1981).

Montana grants to private corporations the power to "purchase, take, receive, lease, or otherwise acquire, own, hold, improve, use, and otherwise deal in and with real or personal property or any interest therein, wherever situated, and to acquire property by proceedings in eminent domain." Mont. Code Ann. §35-1-108(7) (1987). Does this create any federal constitutional problems? What are its implications as Montana's mining companies focus less on precious metals and more on fossil fuels? See Montana Power Co. v. Bokma, 153 Mont. 390, 457 P.2d 769 (1969); Note, 35 Mont. L. Rev. 279 (1974).

40. Here compensation has been required under natural law principles. Staton v.

A standard of compensation for federal takings was set by the fifth amendment to the federal constitution; its requirement of "just compensation" is deemed incorporated within the meaning of "due process" under the fourteenth amendment[41] and therefore binding upon the states. As the law stands today, therefore, every condemnor must pay at least "just compensation"; a state constitution or a state or federal statute may require more than the minimum.[42]

1. Fair Market Value

■ RILEY v. DISTRICT OF COLUMBIA REDEVELOPMENT LAND AGENCY
246 F.2d 641 (D.C. Cir. 1957)

FAHY, Circuit Judge. The case is before the full Court now on reconsideration of an unreported decision of a division of the Court of May 17, 1956. In that decision, by a divided Court, a judgment of the District Court for appellant in the sum of $7,000.00, awarded to her by a jury as compensation for her home, which had been taken in condemnation proceedings by the District of Columbia Redevelopment Land Agency, was set aside. The case was remanded for further proceedings including a new trial if necessary. A majority of the full Court now reach the same conclusion for the reasons herein stated.

The property had been bought by appellant as a home in 1951. She undertook to pay $9,950.00, of which some $300.00 was paid in cash and $9,655.00 was represented by three notes secured by trusts on the property. The notes called for monthly payments, including principal and interest, of $72.50. Appellant installed a new furnace and gas and did some roofing, guttering and other work at a total cost of $877.00. The home thus represented obligations and expenditures of some $10,800.00. In March, 1955, the jury awarded appellant $7,000.00 as just compensation, that is, as the fair market value of the property. This was $3,800.00 less than she had paid for it, plus the improvements

---

Norfolk and Carolina Ry., 111 N.C. 278, 16 S.E. 181 (1892). The recent decisions claim to find a constitutional backing in the "due process" and "law of the land" clauses. See State v. Core Banks Club Properties, Inc., 275 N.C. 328, 167 S.E.2d 385 (1969); Long v. City of Charlotte, 306 N.C. 187, 293 S.E.2d 101 (1982).

41. Fallbrook Irrigation District v. Bradley, 164 U.S. 112 (1896); Missouri Pacific Ry. v. Nebraska, 164 U.S. 403, 417 (1896). A similar interpretation of due process had appeared in many of the early state constitutions. See Corwin, The Doctrine of Due Process of Law Before the Civil War, 24 Harv. L. Rev. 366, 478 (1911).

42. As to the federal requirement that a state recognize certain incidents of property as compensable property rights, see Sauer v. City of New York, 206 U.S. 536 (1907). Compare Pumpelly v. Green Bay and Mississippi Canal Co., 80 U.S. (13 Wall.) 166 (1872) with Northern Transportation Co. v. Chicago, 99 U.S. 635 (1879).

C. The Riddle of Just Compensation

referred to, and would leave her without the property and still owing some $1,900.00 on the deferred purchase price notes.

The jury was properly instructed that the property at the time of the taking,

> ... is to be appraised at its fair market value as of June 21, 1954, the date of the taking by the Land Agency, with reference to the most advantageous, highest or best use or uses to which it can be put. By fair market value is meant what the property would sell for in cash or terms equivalent to cash, when offered for sale by one who is willing but is not obliged to sell, to one who desires but is not obliged to buy.

It has long been recognized that the fair market value may be either what the property would sell for in cash or on terms equivalent to cash. Kerr v. South Park Commissioners, 117 U.S. 379, 386-387; Shoemaker v. United States, 147 U.S. 282, 304. These are alternative criteria for establishing the fair market value.

The terms are equivalent to cash if the deferred purchase money notes are such that under normal conditions the notes can be turned into cash at their face amount. Thus, the principal of the notes is not increased by the addition thereto of a charge for credit. The rate of interest earned by the notes and their underlying security are factors to be considered in determining their cash value.

We think in this case the jury should have been given such an explanation of the expression "terms equivalent to cash." The chief evidence as to the fair market value of the house was the 1951 sale to appellant for $9,950.00 on terms, prior to her expenditure of $877.00 for improvements, and the 1954 valuations of the two Agency appraisers, neither of which exceeded $7,000.00. The proper determination of the fair market value of the property, in face of this divergent evidence, required an understanding of what terms are "equivalent to cash." Without it the jury could not reach a reasoned conclusion as to the relationship between the 1951 credit sale to appellant and the fair market value of the property. A credit sale is indicative of the fair market value of the property only to the extent to which the notes can be turned into cash, that is, are "equivalent to cash."

The circumstances of this case made it especially necessary that such an explanation be given. Unjustified doubt was cast on the relation of the 1951 sale to the 1954 fair market value by a factual error of the two Agency appraisers. One of these appraisers testified that in reaching his valuation he gave little weight to the sale to appellant "because the third trust would run at perpetuity.... The monthly payment was not enough to pay even the interest on the property." The other appraiser made a similar statement. Yet the contract of sale and appellant's receipt book, both of which are in the record, reveal that the monthly payments of $72.50 covered all interest and were reducing the principal each month. At the time of the trial $752.70 had already been paid on the principal, in addition to the $295.00 down payment. These erroneous statements could not fail to influence the jury toward the view of the Agency appraisers that the 1951 purchase by appellant was at a price grossly in excess of the fair market value of the property.

The erroneous statements weakening the $9,950.00 figure become more serious when considered with the foundation for the much lower valuations of the Agency appraisers. They relied largely upon reproduction costs calculated on a rule of thumb cubic footage basis, less depreciation. The testimony of one appraiser, especially, would have led the jury to believe that this is a formula for arriving at the fair market value. This is not so. While the jury could be informed by the witness of these calculations in explanation of the process by which he arrived at his opinion of fair market value, the calculations were not themselves evidence of fair market value for this type of property. There is no necessary relationship between reproduction cost and market value. Cost of reproduction is a method of valuation usually resorted to "where the character of the property is such as not to be susceptible to the application of the market value doctrine." 4 Nichols, On Eminent Domain, §12.313 (3rd ed. 1951). There is no indication that this is the case here. Furthermore, the rule of thumb basis for estimating cost of reproduction, used by the Agency appraisers, has been described as being "not even approximately accurate, except for a few highly standardized types of structures." 2 Orgel, Valuation Under Eminent Domain §193 (1953). There is no showing that this was such a standardized structure. Accordingly, if such testimony is repeated on a new trial the jury should be cautioned that it is before them only in explanation of the process by which the witness arrives at his opinion of fair market value, not as independent evidence of such value, and, further, that the cubic foot cost method of computing reproduction cost is not entitled to great weight in such a case as this even in arriving at reproduction cost.

The wide divergence between the recent credit sale of the house and the evaluations of the Agency appraisers, plus the serious factual error made by the appraisers, and the uncertain method used by them in making their evaluations, made it necessary that the jury be instructed as to the meaning of a sale on terms equivalent to cash, so as to be able to relate the 1951 sale to fair market value. Such an instruction is not required in every case. There have been innumerable condemnation proceedings throughout the country, including now the cases affecting other parcels of land which were tried with this one in our District Court, which we do not draw in question. Those cases are not before us for decision. We have pointed out the special circumstances which lead us to hold that the failure to explain the meaning of "terms

C. The Riddle of Just Compensation 837

equivalent to cash" impairs this particular judgment. We shall set it aside and remand the case for further proceedings not inconsistent with this decision, which may include a new trial.

It is so ordered.[43]

WASHINGTON, Circuit Judge (concurring). A majority of the court has decided to set aside the judgment in this case on the ground that the jury was not adequately instructed as to how they should use the evidence of a recent credit sale of the property in arriving at their determination of the property's fair market value in cash. I concur in the court's opinion,[1] on the understanding that what the court wishes a condemnation jury to be told in this regard is substantially along the following lines: The standard to be applied is fair market value. This standard can be represented by cash or terms *equivalent* to cash. When notes are given as part of the purchase price in a credit sale, their discounted or estimated value in cash may be deemed equivalent to cash. The way in which the jury should decide what cash value the notes have must depend on what evidence of value is in the record.[44] Thus, if the evidence includes only the terms of the notes, then the

---

43. Consider Judge Prettyman's valuation rationale in the circuit court panel's previous (unreported) opinion:

> Of course a sale is not attack-proof. Every and any sale is not conclusive as to value. A sale may be forced. Or a purchase may be so necessitous as not to be fair. Or terms may be involved. The cash price, which is the yardstick of value, may differ from a price upon terms. Or a particular sale may be out of line with the market. And the condition of the property or the condition of the market may change between the date of the sale and the valuation date.
>
> In the case at bar we have a sale of the identical property on an open market within three years of the valuation date. The starting point in a case such as this must be the sale. . . .
>
> The Government appraisers relied upon a reproduction cost less depreciation. Some confusion occurs in this field by reason of confusion between replacement cost and reproduction cost. Replacement cost may well be the cost of a similar article or property on the open market. It is usually accepted as the top limit of a fair value, because no willing buyer will pay more for one article than he has to pay for an identical article. Reproduction cost is another concept altogether. It is the amount required to reproduce the article by manufacturing or building it. It may or may not have a relationship to market value. Buyers in a given market may pay more for a completed house, ready to use, than they will pay for a house to be planned, built and furnished. Time, energy and worry are invoked in the latter. The question is the mood of the market at the moment.

Riley v. District of Columbia Redevelopment Land Agency, No. 12782, D.C. Cir., May 17, 1956. — EDS.

1. When this case was previously heard by a panel of the court, I voted to affirm. Since a majority of the full court, after consideration en banc, has now concluded that a reversal is appropriate in the interests of justice and good judicial administration, and since no change in the substantive law of eminent domain is being effected, I am willing to join the majority's effort to clarify a portion of the charge to the jury.

44. In an unreported opinion (see supra note 43), a dissenting Judge Washington opined: "A jury is far better equipped to deal with matters of this sort than an appellate court. Here it has acted well within the scope of its authority and responsibility. Its verdict should not be disturbed." — EDS.

jury should consider those terms, including the amount of the down payment and the interest rates, along with all known factors relevant to the sale, in deciding in the light of their own familiarity with prevailing credit conditions in the community, for how much real value the property was actually sold. If there is evidence as to what the notes could in fact be discounted for, then the jury should of course consider such evidence. The total received by the seller in a credit sale — namely, the discount price of the notes plus any down payment — is, of course, not a conclusive indication of the value of the property, but is simply one factor to be considered along with all the other evidence.

I am authorized to say that Chief Judge EDGERTON and Circuit Judge BAZELON join in the foregoing analysis.

BURGER, Circuit Judge, dissenting, with whom BASTIAN, Circuit Judge, concurs. . . .

An earlier opinion of a panel of this court reversed the District Court's judgment by a two-to-one vote on the general ground that appellant's "pertinent and direct evidence of value," namely the credit sale to her in 1951, "was not dispelled and no contrary evidence was satisfactorily presented.". . .

That opinion reaches a conclusion which both as to result and reason is plainly against the overwhelming weight of authority and would require by way of instructions more than called for in any condemnation case previously decided in this country. In so doing, that opinion ignores the warning that "hard cases make bad law." Mrs. Riley's situation presents one of those "hard cases."

Judge Fahy's opinion sets forth the charge which was given and a glance shows it is the conventional, traditional and correct charge which has been approved over the years. If it is not fair of course it should be changed. Whenever existing rules of law cannot meet newly developed conditions affecting important rights of substantial numbers we should not be fearful of a new solution merely because it is new. But that is not the case here; no new or unusual situation not previously considered by the courts is shown to exist. Indeed, the present opinions admit the jury "was properly instructed.". . .

It is because the problem is simple that the basic charge which has long been approved should not be tampered with. Judge Washington's restrictive interpretation of what should be given by way of explanation is less likely to cause confusion but neither explanation is necessary.

The several proposals for additional instructions start from the premise that the jury needed some explanation of the phrase "terms equivalent to cash." I would agree that a jury is entitled to know the meaning of terms used in a charge but I question that any new explanation is called for now any more than it has been in the past. It would never occur to me that a definition of this phrase was required for any jury, and least of all in a condemnation case where jurors are so-called "blue-ribbon" jurors, selected only from freeholders. This case

C. The Riddle of Just Compensation 839

was tried with the cases of a number of other landowners and involved over 40 parcels of land in all. The same jury heard all evidence in all the cases. Fourteen lawyers sat in the courtroom representing the various claimants *and not one of them thought to raise the point now regarded as crucial.* . . .

A purchase on "terms equivalent to cash" has always meant and means today terms of deferred payments, the aggregate of which (exclusive of interest) is the same price at which the property can be purchased for all cash.[5] Economic conditions of the country generally and of the real estate market particularly are of course not rigid. Today such deferred terms may require at least 40% cash down to keep the price "equivalent to cash"; a year or two from now it might be down to 35% or up to 45%. When a purchaser is lacking cash and cannot meet the prevailing "down payment" requirements of the market, he must bear the burden of a premium for longer credit terms in the form of a higher price. But this is not the *market* price; it is the market price *plus* the premium he must pay the seller or other lender for his lack of cash and the consequent need for long credit. This is not the *market price*, it is *his* price in his particular and peculiar circumstances.[6] . . .

I next come to what seems to be one of the important grounds obliquely relied upon as a ground for reversal in an effort to strengthen obviously weak grounds for remand. This ground is simply a criticism of the *testimony* of the experts called by the Government because they cast "[u]njustified doubt" on the evidence of appellant. . . . Of course that was the *tendency* of the Agency's evidence, just as Mrs. Riley's evidence was intended and directed toward the view that the government experts were low in their figures. But the very essence and purpose of an adversary proceeding is to do just what each litigant did here and it had never occurred to me that errors *in the testimony* constitute grounds for reversal. The adverse party, not the appellate court, must bear the burden of showing that the expert for one litigant has been inaccurate, or has exaggerated or even that he testified falsely. It is indeed novel to imply that it is reversible error for expert witnesses in an adversary civil proceeding to give testimony which influences the jury in one direction! . . .

This case is a reversal without an appellate holding that any error occurred in the trial. It is a manifestation of the unspoken doctrine of the second chance, by which this court, in a case which arouses sympathy, gives a litigant another trial. Where we see an obvious miscarriage of

---

5. Judge Washington's concurring opinion states this long accepted and basic proposition but in another way.
6. In its en banc consideration of this case some members of the court called for briefs from amici curiae, as well as from the litigants, on whether there are not *two* fair market values of a house, one its value in *cash* and another its value on deferred payments, i.e., *credit*. This dissent assumes that no member of the court now intends to suggest that there are *two* values for a parcel of real estate.

justice this would be warranted, but not when, as here, there is neither error nor injustice.[45]

Note on Valuation Formulas

Conducting a land damage case challenges the ingenuity of the attorney. That a jury is usually involved[46] complicates the matter even

---

45. "After three years of this kind of thing you don't worry yourself. You just go on as if nothing had happened and hope something does.... If I knew it was going to be like this to get the price I paid for the house I would have given up long ago. It just isn't worth it — not this way." — An interview with Mamie Riley, April 23, 1957. See Grutzner, Housing Projects Make Bitter D.P.'s, N.Y. Times, Mar. 18, 1957; Berger and Rohan, The Nassau County Study: An Empirical Look into the Practice of Condemnation, 67 Colum. L. Rev. 430 (1967). Mrs. Riley owed $1900 as the result of a deficiency judgment obtained against her by the third trust holder (who eventually settled for $850, pursuant to a stipulation reached with the United States and Mrs. Riley). In the Washington area, second trust notes were bought and sold frequently at 60 percent or less of the total obligation, and third trust notes could sell for 30 percent or less. Would compensation for the full face value of such a note have been just? To Mrs. Riley? To the note holder? To the taxpayers? Are there any conceivable alternatives which might achieve greater equity for all parties? See Select Subcommittee on Real Property Acquisition, House Committee on Public Works, 88th Cong., 2d Sess. (1964).

Administrator Cole of the Housing and Home Finance Agency had this to say of the *Riley* case:

> Since the case is in process of appeal, I do not propose here to discuss the legal aspects. They are for the courts to deal with, and we may expect that the case will be settled with justice and equity.
> But underneath this particular case are problems of justice and equity that no court of law can solve. Only the community itself, with the cooperation of the housing industry and appropriate Government agencies, can settle or correct them. It is for us — for you, for me, and many others — to deal with the existing inequity and injustice.
> Most specifically, I am talking about the conditions underlying the nation-wide state of affairs that can produce a *Riley* case. They are economic and social. And they thrive in slums.
> The *Riley* case happens to be well publicized. But it is only a single symptom of a serious ailment. Persons of low income — especially those who are Negroes or members of other minority groups — are most susceptible to it. Limited not only financially but by prejudice and custom to certain areas of community — that is, largely to slums and blighted sections — they are exploited by speculators in substandard dwellings. The high demand forces them to pay in many cases well in excess of what, in terms of quality and utility, is a fair market price—Eds.

46. Notice and opportunity to be heard before a competent tribunal are considered basic to due process under both federal and state constitutions. On the other hand, there is no right to trial by jury; if a jury is required for determining compensation, it is only by virtue of a statute or a state constitution. See Bauman v. Ross, 167 U.S. 548, 593 (1897); Dohany v. Rogers, 281 U.S. 362, 369 (1929). The states have created a great variety of tribunals, with varying procedures and composition, for the determination of compensation of eminent domain cases. About half require the use of a common law jury; of these, a distinction is sometimes made between the state as condemnor and other condemning bodies, with a jury required only in the latter instance.

It is provided by Fed. R. Civ. P. 71A(h):

> If the action involves the exercise of the power of eminent domain under the law of the United States, any tribunal specially constituted by an Act of Congress governing the case for the trial of the issue of just compensation shall be the

C. The Riddle of Just Compensation 841

further: when valuation formulas are difficult for the lawyer to grasp, a jury is even more bewildered.[47] Even Congress can be befuddled by modes, theories, and amounts of compensation. See Conference Report, Statement of the Managers, Technical and Miscellaneous Revenue Act of 1988 (H.R. 4333) (Oct. 24, 1988):

> tribunal for the determination of that issue; but if there is no such specially constituted tribunal any party may have a trial by jury of the issue of just compensation by filing a demand therefor within the time allowed for answer or within such further time as the court may fix, unless the court in its discretion orders that, because of the character, location, or quantity of the property to be condemned, or for other reasons in the interest of justice, the issue of compensation shall be determined by a commission of three persons appointed by it.

See Fed. R. Civ. P. 71A advisory committee's note; 81 A.B.A. Rep. 137-139 (1956). Whether the task of valuation may be adequately performed by nonprofessionals confronting conflicting estimates of value remains a weighty problem not unfamiliar to other aspects of the judicial process.

The well-known tendency of the plaintiff's experts to stretch high, and defendant's experts to crouch low (with the jury dividing by two) has led to suggestions for the use of testimony by a disinterested appraiser — whose fee is taxed as costs.

Section 828 of the New York Executive Law "expressly empowers the [State Commission on Cable Television] to determine the reasonable amount to be paid by a cable television company to a property owner in exchange for permitting cable television service on his property." The New York Court of Appeals, on remand from a Supreme Court decision holding that a cable company's permanent physical occupation amounted to a compensable taking (see infra page 887), rejected the plaintiff's argument that §828 was "unconstitutional because it violates the separation of powers doctrine": "Neither the Federal nor the State Constitution proscribes determination of compensation for the taking by a commission rather than a court." Loretto v. Teleprompter Manhattan CATV, 58 N.Y.2d 143, 446 N.E.2d 428, 431, 434 (1983). Cf. FCC v. Florida Power Corp., 480 U.S. 245 (1987) (limiting private utility company charges for cable attachments to utility poles).

If a commission can decide this issue, why not an arbitrator? In Thomas v. Union Carbide Agricultural Products, 473 U.S. 568 (1985), the Supreme Court upheld a statutory scheme "requiring arbitration of disputes of registrants concerning compensation under FIFRA [Federal Insecticide, Fungicide, and Rodenticide Act]," despite the company's assertion that Congress's selection of binding arbitration with limited judicial review violated Article III of the Constitution.

"Always ask for a jury," is the advice given property owners by Fade, Trial Tactics to Make the Compensation Just for the Owner, 1973 Inst. on Plan. Zoning & Eminent Domain, 261, 262. See United States v. Reynolds, 397 U. S. 14 (1970). In Florida, where the condemnor is required to pay all costs of the condemnee, settlements by negotiation dropped from 90 percent to 20 percent in Dade County. See Britton, Effect in Florida of Requiring Condemnor to Pay Condemnee's Entire Litigation Expense, 10 Right of Way 15 (Oct. 1963). Professor Ayer refers to a "litigation avoidance payment," whereby the condemnor subtracts from the fair market value the amount it would cost the condemnee to pursue his or her remedy in court. Allocating the Costs of Determining Just Compensation, 21 Stan. L. Rev. 693 (1969).

"Attorneys who specialized in condemnation cases have advised the Commission that normally they must decline to accept a case where the difference between the condemnor's offer and the probable award if the case is tried is less than $3000-$5000. The reason is that the unrecoverable costs of defending such a case will equal or exceed the potential increment between the offer and the award." 1969 Cal. Law Revision Commission Reports, 128 n.10. See Fait, Arbitration—A Third Alternative, 2 Pacific L. J. 245 (1971).

By the way, are appraisal and attorney fees part of just compensation? See Note, 77 Dick. L. Rev. 316 (1972-73).

47. See Corrado v. Providence Redevelopment Agency, 294 A.2d 387 (R.I. 1972). Trial lawyers stress the effect of visual evidence on the mind of jurors. The jury is often

Manassas National Battlefield Park (the Park) . . . incorporates the battlefield where two significant Civil War battles were fought — First Manassas and Second Manassas. However, much of the battlefield of Second Manassas . . . has not been acquired as part of the Park. No major development occurred on the area, until a recent proposal was approved by the Prince William County Virginia Board of Supervisors to construct a mixed residential/nonresidential development on the William Center Tract. The proposed development would include a 1.2 million square foot shopping mall, major office space, and residential area.

In an editorial titled "Veto the Land Grab," the Richmond Times-Dispatch (Oct. 28, 1988) noted:

Recent sales data on land in the vicinity of the 542-acre tract sought by Congress indicate that the value of the land itself, exclusive of improvements, ranges anywhere from $58 million to more than $155 million.

To those totals must be added compensation for: land improvements such as houses, roads, curbs and gutters; eviction of up to six families from the tract; relocation of existing electrical power easements there; contractual commitments made by the developer in exchange for rezoning, such as $2 million in cash for an interchange and a recreational complex; restoration of the 542 acres to pre-development status; interest payments to the property owner and more.

The legislative taking became law on November 10, 1988. Pub. L. No. 100-647. Payment of just compensation, when determined, would come from the Claims and Judgments Fund under 31 U.S.C. §1304.

Since eminent domain cases are characterized as a battle of wits between experts, the real estate appraiser, in addition to having the usual qualifications prized in a witness, should be one with experience in the area in dispute.[48] The appraiser will talk in the terms of her profession, and it becomes necessary for the lawyer to understand her. "Fair market value" is the conclusion sought by courts, but there are different ways of reaching that result.

In determining fair market value, the fact-finding body (jury, judge, or administrative tribunal) is not bound to any specific figure in evidence or to any amount based on any specific formula, so long as the finding is not inconsistent with the evidence.

---

taken to the site but there is a question of the value of the view where the structure has been demolished. See Bishop, Keep the Jury's Interest, 1972 Inst. on Plan. Zoning & Eminent Domain 273, 295. Engineering plans, photographs, and models should be selected with care; there is the story of the attorney who, in the course of praising the sturdy construction of his client's building, pounded on the table—whereupon the scale model of the structure collapsed.

48. See Friedmann, Selection of Appraisers for Condemnation, 23 Appraisal J. 363 (1955); Cook County v. Holland, 3 Ill. 2d 36, 119 N.E.2d 760 (1954) (requiring more than categorical statements that witness is familiar with the property).

C. The Riddle of Just Compensation 843

1. *Sales of similar properties.* Under certain circumstances (such as those discussed in the *Riley* case) sales of the same property or of similar property in the locality, within a reasonable period before or after the time in issue, have great evidentiary value. In most states, evidence of sales of comparable property is now admitted on direct examination.[49]

2. *Capitalization of income.* This approach aims at arriving at the sum that would be paid in order to receive the income thrown off by the property. Business profits are generally avoided as evidence of value. The difficulty arises in allocating profits between those inhering in the real estate itself, or in the business aside from the physical property. Courts generally permit a jury to be told whether a business is profitable; also, they have a tendency to treat with liberality the capitalization of profits approach in the hands of an expert witness. And where no other evidence is available, a court may be constrained to permit its use.

Where rentals are the profits concerned, an exception to this rule exists. Evidently the extra stability and predictability attributed to rental income and expense, in contradistinction to the ordinary business venture, suggest special treatment to the minds of judges. The net rental value of a building takes into account present rentals in the building, rentals from similar property, the terms of existing leases, and due discount for vacancies or rental losses. Expenses, including interest, taxes, and depreciation, are subtracted from the discounted rental income value to arrive at the net figure.[50] Frequently, land is separated from the buildings in order to avoid the problem of nondepreciation of land, and also to take into account investors' expectations as to different yields of land and buildings.

Next, the appraiser must capitalize net rentals to arrive at a principal sum. Applying a hypothetical state of return to the property, she will come out with what she calls the fair market value.[51] It is not proper to select a capitalization rate which is, for example, the going savings bank rate, or the legal rate of interest, as this would not take into consideration

---

49. See American Society of Appraisers, The Applicable Method for Valuation of Underdeveloped Land 5-6 (1972), attacking "the legal dictum that 'comparable sales are the best evidence of value' in the case of marketable noninvestment property"; cf. Roblas v. City of Tucson, 16 Ariz. App. 100, 491 P.2d 489 (1971); Scavo v. Commonwealth Department of Highways, 439 Pa. 233, 266 A.2d 759 (1970).

50. Often the question arises as to the actual property taxes to be used in the formula, as distinguished from the hypothetical taxes at the actual tax rate applied to the final capitalization figure which is the subject of the trial. To avoid this dilemma, appraisers will frequently add the tax rate, the expected percentage yield, and the depreciation rate, and use this total percentage applied to the income determining the final capitalization figure.

51. Where "I" represents net income, "R" the rate of return, and "C" the capital sum, the equation is $C = \frac{100I}{R}$. Cf. United States v. Eden Memorial Park Assn., 350 F.2d 933 (9th Cir. 1965).

the varied risks of different pieces of property. A multiple factor is sometimes used on the gross rental. This type of appraisal is used with most success in areas with infrequent current sales but where rentals are fairly well established. Where property is not being put to its best and highest use, it is to the owner's disadvantage to introduce evidence of current rentals. A word of warning is in order here: the application of a rule of thumb in determining the rate of capitalization to both a modern office building and a tenement in a slum area reveals the margin of potential error in this kind of appraisal. And the effect of changes in the money market on the rate of return should always be considered.[52]

3. *Replacement cost less depreciation.* The cost of reproducing a structure may be highly relevant in determining just compensation. It is certainly appropriate in case of a building designed or constructed for a particular use, such as a church or a plant for a specialized manufacturing process.[53] And it is generally admissible provided the improvements are fairly adapted to the site.

In speaking of replacement cost it is necessary to distinguish between replacement by an exact replica and replacement by premises of equal utility. While the cases are not entirely consistent, the latter concept is used more frequently. This requires an appraiser to compute the cost of the property and then to depreciate it for wear and tear and for functional obsolescence. One of the major battles over the reproduction or replacement valuation concerns the amount of depreciation to be deducted in arriving at an estimate of the fair market value of the property. The usual manner of determining depreciation — an expert estimates depreciation by making a physical examination of the property — makes cross-examination of the witness difficult.[54]

The accounting methods of depreciation — straight line, declining charges, sinking fund, and so forth — are also used. Another method

52. Income derived from farming and ranching is allowed as evidence to determine just compensation, because, like rent, this income is considered resulting from the property itself, not as business income. For example, in Board of County Commissioners v. Delaney, 592 P.2d 1338, 1340 (Colo. App. 1978), a case involving the partial taking of plaintiff's land for the construction of an interstate highway, the appellate court held admissible evidence of reduced income attributable to "a decrease in the cattle carrying capacity of the properties [as] an indication of a decrease in the productivity of the land itself."

53. See Chiloway Charcoal, Inc. v. State of New York, 26 N.Y.2d 162, 304 N.Y.S.2d 968 (1969). There are difficult qualifications for admitting evidence of this kind. See Tigar v. Mystic River Bridge Authority, 329 Mass. 514, 518, 109 N.E.2d 148, 150, 151 (1952). See also Note, 37 B.U.L. Rev. 495 (1957).

54. Professor Bonbright has said that outside the field of public utility valuation "where the only plausible defense of replacement cost is that it constitutes a desirable rate base in its own right, quite without reference to value in any accurate sense, the sharpest disputes as to the relevance of this type of evidence arise with respect to business properties that are yielding disappointing income." 1 The Valuation of Property 150 (1937). See also McMichael, Appraising Manual (4th ed. 1970).

sometimes employed is depreciating the property at a slower or more rapid rate at the beginning of its useful life. There are other techniques of determining depreciation,[55] but those mentioned are the ones encountered most often. Whatever may be appropriate for rate regulation purposes, the method most relied on for the condemnation process is that of "observed depreciation." It is the only depreciation method that is not aimed at apportioning the cost of a physical asset on a periodic basis, but that is directed toward establishing the present value of the property — the aim of the court in condemnation cases.[56]

4. *Combination of methods.* In many jurisdictions, combinations of methods are permitted and used. For example, in Massachusetts, assessed valuations for the past three years are admissible. Original cost less depreciation is frequently admissible. But the most common combination is capitalization of income and replacement cost less depreciation. A slight variation is the scaling down of reproduction cost less depreciation to a level where it is supported by the earnings.[57]

Notes and Problems

1. On January 16, 1973, the Supreme Court announced two sets of opinions concerning the amount of compensation required when the value of the condemned property is affected in a significant way by governmental activity. In Almota Farmers Elevator & Warehouse Co. v. United States, 408 U.S. 470 (1973), a badly divided Court (there were two concurring and four dissenting Justices), answered the following question in the affirmative:

Whether, upon condemnation of a leasehold, a lessee with no right of

---

55. Another method which is used for public utilities, but which has rarely made its way into the reported cases, is an actuarial study of the life of assets and their depreciation on that basis.

56. In In re Site for School Industrial Arts, 2 Misc. 2d 403, 407, 154 N.Y.S.2d 402, 407 (Sup. Ct. 1956), the court said:

Those who would endeavor to extend this principle so as to limit "value" to the original cost of construction or the current cost of reconstruction less depreciation are adopting an economic theory which derives from Adam Smith's classic doctrine that the value of an article equals the cost of its production. The modern appraiser has learned that the law of supply and demand will furnish a more correct index of value and that "market value," the standard in condemnation, is determined not so much by cost as by the relative desirability, abundance and utility of the particular property in the community.

57. Cf. Boston Gas Co. v. Assessors of Boston, 334 Mass. 549, 137 N.E.2d 462 (1956), in which the court allowed such evidence in determining the tax base, saying that otherwise the company would be deprived of an opportunity to prove value. "The search for 'fair market value,'" Bigham reminds us, "is a snipe hunt carried out at midnight on a moonless landscape." Fair Market Value, Just Compensation, and the Constitution: A Critical View, 24 Vand. L. Rev. 63 (1970-71).

renewal is entitled to receive as compensation the market value of its improvements without regard to the remaining term of its lease, because of the expectancy that the lease would have been renewed.

Justice Stewart reasoned:

> At the time of that "taking" Almota had an expectancy of continued occupancy of its grain elevator facilities. The Government must pay just compensation for those interests "probably within the scope of the project from the time the Government was committed to it." United States v. Miller, 317 U.S., at 377. It may not take advantage of any depreciation in the property taken that is attributable to the project itself. At the time of the taking in this case, there was an expectancy that the improvements would be used beyond the lease term. But the Government has sought to pay compensation on the theory that at that time there was no possibility that the lease would be renewed and the improvements used beyond the lease term. It has asked that the improvements be valued as though there were no possibility of continued use. That is not how the market would have valued such improvements; it is not what a private buyer would have paid Almota.
>
> The constitutional requirement of just compensation derives as much content from the basic equitable principles of fairness, United States v. Commodities Trading Corp., 339 U.S. 121, 124 (1950), as it does from technical concepts of property law. United States v. Fuller, [409 U.S.] at 490. It is, of course, true that Almota should be in no better position than if it had sold its leasehold to a private buyer. But its position should surely be no worse.

What if government activity has enhanced the value of the condemned tract? In United States v. Fuller, 409 U.S. 488 (1973), Justice Rehnquist, for a five-member majority, denied compensation to the operators of a large Arizona ranch for "value accruing to the fee [simple] lands as a result of their actual or potential use in combination with the Taylor Grazing Act 'permit lands' [43 U.S.C. §513b]":

> [W]e believe that there is a significant difference between the value added to property by a completed public works project, for which the Government must pay, and the value added to fee lands by a revocable permit authorizing the use of neighboring lands that the Government owns. The Government may not demand that a jury be arbitrarily precluded from considering as an element of value the proximity of a parcel to a post office building, simply because the Government at one time built the post office. But here respondents rely on no mere proximity to a public building or to public lands dedicated to, and open to, the public at large. Their theory of valuation aggregates their parcel with land owned by the Government to form a privately controlled unit from which the public would be excluded.... We hold that the Fifth Amendment does not require the Government to pay for that element of value based on the

C. The Riddle of Just Compensation

use of respondents' fee lands in combination with the Government's permit lands.

Justice Powell, dissenting, did not believe that "basic equitable principles of fairness" justified this departure from the market-value rule. Can you otherwise defend the majority's "working rule" (the first sentence of the immediately preceding blocked quotation)?

2. Justice Powell also attempted to distinguish the government's role as a private property owner (when the government simply decides to put its own property to a new use, the devaluation of an adjacent riparian landowner's property is noncompensable) from the government's role as a condemnor (government action that devaluates land adjacent to a completed government project is a compensable loss). But can the government be considered as just another private property owner when, as under the Taylor Grazing Act, permits are granted at a rate lower than that which a rational private owner would offer? Should the withdrawal of such a subsidy be counted as a compensable loss — assuming that the withdrawal is motivated by the decision that another use of these resources is most beneficial to the public in general? See The Supreme Court, 1972 Term, 87 Harv. L. Rev. 189 (1973); Note, 27 Sw. L.J. 692 (1973).

"The value of land, and of most other objects of value, is based almost entirely upon unenforceable expectations in regard to the conduct of other persons. When the courts, in any connection, arbitrarily refuse to consider such expectations, they are closing their eyes to the most important facts of economic existence." Is this criticism of a half century ago still applicable today? See Cormack, Legal Concepts in Cases of Eminent Domain, 41 Yale L.J. 221, 254 (1931).

3. In United States v. 50 Acres of Land, 469 U.S. 24 (1986), the city of Duncanville, Texas claimed that the United States owed more than $1.2 million in compensation for the condemnation of a sanitary landfill, that figure being the cost of acquiring and developing a substitute site. The petitioner (and the Court) disagreed, determining that $199,950, the fair market value of the condemned facility, amounted to just compensation. While the Constitution's command to the federal government includes compensation for the taking of public land, despite the apparent limitation to "private property" (see United States v. Carmack, 329 U.S. 230 (1946)), "[t]he text of the Fifth Amendment does not mandate a more favorable rule of compensation for public condemnees than from private parties." 469 U.S. at 31.

4. United States v. Cors, 337 U.S. 325 (1949), involved a suit in the Court of Claims to recover just compensation for requisitioning a steam tug. The tug was built in 1895, and used until March 1942, when the Coast Guard advertised it for sale to the highest bidder. It was sold to the plaintiff for $2875. Expending labor and materials in repairing

and improving the vessel, he used it as a towing steam vessel until it was requisitioned by the War Shipping Administration in October 1942 to be used by the Navy as a steam heating plant for naval combat vessels. Its original cost was estimated to be $45,000, its replacement cost $56,000; the United States offered $9000 as its present value. The case pivoted about the clause in the Merchant Marine Act that states, "but in no case shall the value of the property taken or used be deemed enhanced by the causes necessitating the taking or use." The Court of Claims found that the demand for tugs was due in part at least to the government's need for vessels in the prosecution of the war. In his dissenting opinion, Justice Frankfurter believed that the core of the problem could be perceived in this colloquy in the court below:

> *Judge Hand:* It comes to this, that a society which foresees a shortage, a consequent shortage in one kind of supply, must either proceed at once to seize, or must subject itself and society at large to the disadvantage which comes from the shortage. But when the shortage comes, it may not say "So far, and no farther. We leave the property in your hands for use, but we are helpless to prevent your further exploitation of society by your special interest."
> Is that your position?
>
> *Mr. McInnis:* I think, your Honor, that this is the logical implication of my argument.
>
> *Judge Hand:* It does seem to me, if it is all perfectly clearly known in advance, to put a society in a rather helpless position as against a small group that has control of all of one vital commodity. You can imagine cases where that would work a result that no one would support. You can imagine the destruction of a large part of food in a community where there was no immediate relief, and, as I understand your argument, they either have to take it now, or when they would find it more convenient to take it they should have to submit to the increase in value, however clearly the owners were advised at a given point, "This marks the end of that kind of profit — scarcity profit."
>
> *Mr. McInnis:* I think that is correct, Judge. But I would agree —
>
> *Judge Hand* (interposing): It might be that the Constitution protects that kind of profit. I won't say now.

5. In United States v. Twin City Power Co., 350 U.S. 222 (1956), the Court said:

> The holding of the *Chandler-Dunbar* case [United States v. Chandler-Dunbar Water Power Co., 229 U.S. 53 (1913)] that water power in a navigable stream is not by force of the Fifth Amendment a compensable interest when the United States asserts its easement of navigation is in

C. The Riddle of Just Compensation

harmony with another rule of law expressed in United States v. Miller, 317 U.S. 369, 375.

Since the owner is to receive no more than indemnity for his loss, his award cannot be enhanced by any given gain to the taker. Thus, although the market value of the property is to be fixed with due consideration of all its available uses, its special value to the condemnor as distinguished from others who may or may not possess the power to condemn, must be excluded as an element of market value.

The Court in the *Chandler-Dunbar* case emphasized that it was only loss to the owner, not gain to the taker, that is compensable. 229 U.S., at 76. If the owner of the fast lands can demand water-power value as part of his compensation, he gets the value of a right that the Government in the exercise of its dominant servitude can grant or withhold as it chooses. The right has value or is an empty one dependent solely on the Government. What the Government can grant or withhold and exploit for its own benefit has a value that is peculiar to it and that no other user enjoys. Cf. United States ex rel. T.V.A. v. Powelson, 319 U.S. 266, 273 et seq. To require the United States to pay for this water-power value would be to create private claims in the public domain.

The holding evoked sharp reactions: "Said ruling [United States v. Twin City Power Co.] by said Justices constitutes a precedent of such magnitude as to render all property rights precarious, and the goal of socialized property both inexpensive and convenient and hence nearer attainment. Said ruling by said Justices constitutes misconduct, misbehavior and a 'misdemeanor' within the meaning of the impeachment provisions of the Constitution." A Resolution Requesting Impeachment of Certain United States Supreme Court Justices, Ga. Act 1957, No. 100, at 553, 565.

A public utility acquired land and received a license from the Federal Power Commission to use the tract as a dam site. Is evidence of value as a dam site admissible? Grand River Dam Authority v. Grand-Hydro, 335 U.S. 359 (1948); United States v. 531.13 Acres of Land, 366 F.2d 915 (4th Cir. 1966). See Hale, Value to the Taker in Condemnation Cases, 31 Colum. L. Rev. 1 (1931); Powell, Just Compensation and the Navigation Power, 31 Wash. L. Rev. 271 (1956). Justice Rehnquist's opinion in *Fuller* relied upon the Court's decision in *Twin City*. How do you explain the fact that Justice Douglas, author of the *Twin City* opinion, dissented in *Fuller*?

See United States v. Willow River Power Co., 324 U.S. 499, 502-503, 510 (1945):

It is clear, of course, that a head of water has value and that the Company has an economic interest in keeping the St. Croix at the lower level. But not all economic interests are "property rights"; only those economic advantages are "rights" which have the law back of them, and only when they are so recognized may courts compel others to forbear from interfering with them or to compensate for their invasion. The law long has recognized that the right of ownership in land may carry with it a legal right to enjoy some benefits from adjacent waters. But that a closed catalogue of abstract and absolute "property rights" in water hovers over a given piece of shore land, good against all the world, is not in this day a permissible assumption. We cannot start the process of decision by calling such a claim as we have here a "property right"; whether it is a property right is really the question to be answered. Such economic uses are rights only when they are legally protected interests. Whether they are such interests may depend on the claimant's rights in the land to which he claims the water rights to be appurtenant or incidental; on the navigable or non-navigable nature of the waters from which he advantages; on the substance of the enjoyment thereof for which he claims legal protection; on the legal relations of the adversary claimed to be under a duty to observe or compensate his interests; and on whether the conflict is with another private riparian interest or with a public interest in navigation....

Rights, property or otherwise, which are absolute against all the world are certainly rare, and water rights are not among them. Whatever rights may be as between equals such as riparian owners, they are not the measure of riparian rights on a navigable stream relative to the function of the Government in improving navigation. Where these interests conflict they are not to be reconciled as between equals, but the private interest must give way to a superior right, or perhaps it would be more accurate to say that as against the Government such private interest is not a right at all.

Compare the *Willow River* Court's reluctance to recognize a protected private property right with the majority opinion in Kaiser-Aetna v. United States, 444 U.S. 164 (1979), in which Justice Rehnquist found that only through a taking would the government be able to compel a company, which had dredged and deepened a nonnavigable pond, to allow the public to enjoy the recreational benefits of the resulting navigable body of water.

6. Both *Fuller* and *Almota* involve the condemnee's reasonable expectations for his property interest. This question arises frequently with regard to possible zoning changes.

A's sixteen-acre tract, containing a small residence and truck garden, was zoned residential. The whole tract was taken by the city for a school and playground site. May an expert for *A* testify as to the market value under each of the following conditions:

a. If there were no zoning.
b. If the property were zoned commercial (*A* arguing that the location made the site a "naturally" commercial one, the zoning map notwithstanding).
c. Conceding present residential zoning, but taking into account

C. The Riddle of Just Compensation

the possibility of a change in zoning from residential to industrial or commercial. H. & R. Corp. v. District of Columbia, 351 F.2d 740 (D.C. Cir. 1965); Note, 46 Mich. L. Rev. 988 (1948).

d. Conceding present residential zoning, but including the value of the land as a potential subdivision for single-family residences. See In re Inwood Hill Park, 230 App. Div. 41, 243 N.Y. Supp. 63 (1st Dept. 1930); 4 Nichols, Eminent Domain §12.3142[1] (3d ed. 1950).

e. Would the fact that a nonconforming machine shop occupied the site change the measure of damages? It was ignored in Long Beach City High School District v. Stewart, 30 Cal. 2d 763, 185 P.2d 585 (1947). Cf. Note, 14 U. Chi. L. Rev. 232 (1947).

A high standard was set in Masten v. State, 11 App. Div. 2d 370, 206 N.Y.S.2d 672, 674 (1960) ("condition and continuing trend that rendered early rezoning very nearly inevitable"); Renewal Authority v. Lorince, 499 P.2d 925 (Okla. 1972); Passaretti v. State, 27 App. Div. 2d 1021, 325 N.Y.S.2d 707 (1971); State Department of Highways v. Monsur, 258 So. 2d 162 (La. 1972). In Utah Road Commission v. Hopkins, 29 Utah 2d 162, 165, 506 P.2d 57, 60 (1973), Justice Henriod, in dissent, said:

> [W]ith respect to evidence of platted undeveloped property, where someone who owns property or where maybe the city fathers a half century before simply drew a plat and admits that without the plat, he could get, say $1,000 on the market, but with his platted scheme he could get $100,000, *if* — and this "iffy" business is important, — he sold it in conjecturally individual, sidewalked, curb-and-guttered lots with sewer, electric service, gas service, garbage service, free of earthquakes, free from pollution problems, dysentery, no fire protection, a bad mayor, a worse city council, a commune next door, or what have you, — all of which just as conjecturally could make the land more valuable to raise carrots, to raise rabbits, to raise Cain.

7. The highway commission of the state of Ames desired to build an express highway from one end of the state to the other. The highway started in Boomtown and terminated in Textown. *X* owned some land in Boomtown that Ames condemned for highway purposes. Because of the building and operation of a Corporal Electric plant in Boomtown, real estate values in that area were at an all-time high. Appraisers for the government and for *X* agreed that the current fair market value of *X*'s land was $4000. The highway commissioners agreed that when Corporal Electric settled into routine operations, *X*'s land might be worth $500 more than its normal value of $1000. It was further

admitted into evidence, over *X*'s objection, that neighboring landowners with similar tracts had accepted $2000 from Ames as full compensation for their land.

In Textown the situation was quite different: all the cotton mills had been shut down owing to the development of synthetic fibers. *Y*'s land at current market in Ames was worth about $500. In normal times, the land was worth $1000. It has been rumored that Eastinghouse Electric is planning to build a plant in Textown. If this occurs, land values in Textown are expected to skyrocket, and *Y*'s land should fetch about $3000. Adjoining landowners to *Y*, with similar tracts of land, had agreed to a figure of $750 as full compensation.

What issues are raised and how should they be resolved? See Alishausky v. MacDonald, 117 Conn. 138, 167 A. 96 (1933); Chicago, K. & W. R. R. v. Parsons, 51 Kan. 408, 32 P. 1083 (1893); Howell v. State Highway Department, 167 S.C. 217, 166 S.E. 129 (1932); 55 Am. City, Mar. 1940, at 35-36.

8. In order to prevent tasteless, commercial exploitation of the assassination of President Kennedy, the United States acquired items of evidence considered by the Warren Commission — Lee Harvey Oswald's personal papers, the contents of his wallet, and photographs. A special master determined their market value as $17,729.37. The district court awarded $3000, the sum stipulated to be the "market value of personal property similar in kind." On appeal, in Porter v. United States, 473 F. 2d 1329 (5th Cir. 1973), Oswald's widow won an increased award based on the additional value attributable to collectors' demand.

9. Consider the following:

> The plaintiffs in each action claim to be owners or parties in interest to real property situated within a 101 block area within the City of Syracuse and known as the Syracuse Hill Neighborhood Development Program. This is a designated urban renewal area and contains over 1600 individual parcels of land. . . .
>
> It is plaintiffs' contention in both actions, and, as appears by the complaints, that as a result of the actions of the defendants, the vicinity of the plaintiffs' property has suffered a "condemnation blight." This, they allege, has transformed the area into one which is highly undesirable for either residential or commercial purposes; it has become a high crime rate area where vandalism is rampant and where it is not safe to live or work. Plaintiffs further allege that tenants have moved from the area, resulting in loss of rental income. Further, plaintiffs claim that they have been forced to pay excessive insurance premiums and that they have been compelled to expend monies for the protection of their property from vandalism and that the properties have been reduced in value. . . .
>
> Although the Court is sympathetic to the plight of the plaintiffs in these cases, it finds no constitutional or case authority in support of the

C. The Riddle of Just Compensation

causes of action alleged in the complaints. As harsh as it may be, the principle of damnum absque injuria prevails, and the complaints in each of the above entitled actions are, accordingly, dismissed on the ground that they fail to state a cause of action.

Fisher v. City of Syracuse, 78 Misc. 2d 124, 355 N.Y.S.2d 239 (Sup. Ct.), aff'd, 46 A.D.2d 216, 361 N.Y.S.2d 773 (1974), cert. denied, 423 U.S. 833 (1975). Should the same result obtain in a jurisdiction with a constitutional provision requiring compensation for property "taken or damaged"? Had you been the lawyer for Fisher, could you have provided a theory on which the plaintiffs might have stated a cause of action? What would you have appealed to as "constitutional or case authority in support of the causes of action alleged"? See Klopping v. City of Whittier, 8 Cal. 3d 39, 500 P.2d 1345, 104 Cal. Rptr. 1 (1972); Note, 25 Hastings L.J. 786 (1974); McGee, Urban Renewal in the Crucible of Judicial Review, 56 Va. L. Rev. 826 (1970); Dillon, Condemnation Blight, 3 Pac. L. Rev. 571 (1972).

10. Plaintiff owns a 13,150-acre ranch in a remote region. By 1963, state plans for a lake project that would provide recreational facilities, power, and domestic water became known to the public. Condemnor appraisal witness testifies that cattle grazing is the highest and best use of plaintiff's land and that its normal market value is $125 an acre (the highest price for which land had ever been sold in the region before announcement of the project). Owner's expert witness testifies that "development" is the land's highest and best use and that the land is worth $600 an acre, on the basis of 1965-1966 sales of neighboring parcels as "comparable sales." Condemnor objects to introduction of these sales on grounds that the sales prices reflect an enhancement in value attributable to benefits created by the very project for which condemnation was sought and therefore are not a proper element of "just compensation." What decision? See Merced Irrigation District v. Woolstenhulme, 4 Cal. 3d 478, 483 P.2d 1, 93 Cal. Rptr. 833 (1971).

11. Suppose the court had held that damages resulting from the announcement of plans for urban renewal give rise to a cause of action for compensation. What effect would you expect such a ruling to have on urban renewal officials? See City of Buffalo v. Clement Co., 28 N.Y.2d 241, 269 N.E.2d 895, 321 N.Y.S.2d 345 (1971) (after company, printer of Time, Life, and Reader's Digest, had moved, following a nine-year "pattern of continuous agitation," redevelopment officials decided they were not ready to acquire the property); see Note, 72 Colum. L. Rev. 772 (1972). But see Kanner, Condemnation Blight: Just How Just Is Just Compensation?, 48 Notre Dame Law. 765 (1973): "The *Clement* decision constitutes a broad wink to condemning agencies to sock it to owners by way of blighting activities falling short of *physical* interference and legislative enactments." See also Hagman, Planning

(Condemnation) Blight, Participation and Just Compensation: Anglo-American Comparisons, 4 Urban Law. 434 (1972).

12. "This Court found that a de facto appropriation occurred on April 23, 1968 [after] the State through its contractors entered upon claimant's property.... On April 23, 1968, while excavating a portion of subject property, the contractor unearthed the skeleton of a mastodon which had met its demise at this spot untold thousands of years ago. The State contends that by reason of the de facto appropriation, now settled to have occurred on April 23, 1968 (the date the bones were unearthed), the State has title to the fossil skeleton." Under what theories might this contention be attacked? See Hunterfly Realty Corp. v. State, 74 Misc. 2d 345, 346 N.Y.S.2d 455 (Ct. Cl. 1973) (personal property remains Hunterfly's because title not yet vested in state).

13. The redevelopment authority complains that it is being denied equal protection of the laws because in all other kinds of condemnations, the valuation is fixed as of the date of filing the complaint in the proceedings. "Condemnors of blighted property, however, are arbitrarily singled out for subjection to the rule of valuation as of the date of declaration of blight — a date which may be years earlier than the filing of the complaint or the taking of possession of the property." The court was unsympathetic in Jersey City Redevelopment Agency v. Kugler, 57 N.J. 374, 277 A.2d 873 (1971). See how Congress has reacted to the problem in the Uniform Relocation Assistance and Real Property Acquisition Policies Act, 84 Stat. 1894, Pub. L. No. 91-646 (1971).

14. "The proposition that an increase in market value occasioned by the announcement of a condemnation project is to be disregarded" has as its logical corollary the proposition that "evidence on any decrease in value caused by the announcement must likewise be disallowed." How "logical" is the corollary? See Klopping v. City of Whittier, supra.

15. In one of his classic pronouncements, Justice Holmes stated: "The Constitution does not require a disregard of the mode of ownership — of the state of the title. It does not require a parcel of land to be valued as an unencumbered whole.... It merely requires that an owner of property taken should be paid for what is taken from him." Boston Chamber of Commerce v. Boston, 217 U.S. 189 (1910).

A, owner in fee, leases Blackacre to *B* for ten years at a rental of $5000 per year. The rent is fixed on the basis of 5 percent of the fair market value of Blackacre, the current selling price of which is $100,000. At the end of five years, the fair market value of Blackacre has declined to $50,000. Assume the property is then taken by eminent domain proceedings. How are the interests of *A* and *B* to be valued? Suppose the value had increased to $150,000. See Note, 21 Buffalo L. Rev. 174 (1971); Niehuss & Fisher, Problems of Long-term Leases 35 (1930). Cf. State Highway Commission v. Burk, 200 Or. 211, 265 P.2d 783 (1954); Sowers v. Schaeffer, 155 Ohio 454, 99 N.E.2d 313 (1951).

C. The Riddle of Just Compensation

Should the method of determining the compensation awarded to a lessee depend on the length of the term? A Tennessee appellate court applied the same rule (known as "bonus value") to long- and short-term leases: "the total fair market value of the taken property is apportioned by first determining the lessee's interest, which is the fair market value of the leasehold of that property minus rent actually called for under the lease, with the remainder of the property's fair market value going to the lessor." State ex rel. Department of Transportation v. Gee, 565 S.W. 2d 498, 502 (Tenn. Ct. App.), reh'g denied, 567 S.W.2d 470 (1977). The court felt compelled by prevailing state law to reject the approach of several jurisdictions that "apportion the award when a long-term lease is involved by first valuing the lessor's present interest in the estate in the reversion and in future rental payments."

16. Cities grow rapidly, the law more slowly. Eminent domain may be a clumsy instrument — costly and time-consuming to both condemnor and private owner. It took the Chicago Housing Authority fully fifteen months after filing the original petition for condemnation of land for the Frances Cabrini Homes before it could enter on some of the parcels. The average length of time of the first stage of urban renewal (survey and planning) was 544 days; the next stage (passing on loans and grants) took an average of 706 days; and the final stage, 337 days — an average of over four and one-third years to put into contract form. But this was only the beginning! Acquisition, demolition, disposition, and construction still had to take place. The Douglas Commission found that consumed time was between six and nine years.

17. When must an owner mitigate damages because of an imminent condemnation? Should a farmer, who is scheduled to have his or her property taken on August 31, plant a crop in the spring that will not mature until the fall? United States v. Brinks, 413 F.2d 733 (10th Cir. 1969). At times, quick taking may not be desirable from the condemnor's perspective; in Piz v. Housing Authority of Denver, 132 Colo. 457, 389 P.2d 905 (1955), the authority had offered $27,500 for a bakery, and was held not entitled to abandon the proceedings after a jury had awarded $42,000 for it.

2. Injurious Affection: Incidental, Consequential, and Severance Damages

■ IN RE WATER FRONT IN CITY OF NEW YORK
190 N.Y. 350, 83 N.E. 299 (1907)

CULLEN, C.J. Under the provisions of chapter 16 of the Greater New York charter (Laws 1901, p. 351, c. 466) the dock commissioner of the city was empowered to acquire such lands, wharves, piers, easements, and other property rights as might be necessary for the execution of the plans for the improvement of the water front of the city of New York theretofore adopted or that might thereafter be adopted by the department of docks and the commissioners of the sinking fund. These proceedings were instituted under said charter to acquire several pieces of land owned by the appellant, the Consolidated Gas Company of New York. The award of the commissioners as to such pieces was confirmed by an order of the Special Term, and that order was affirmed by the Appellate Division by a divided court. Both parties have appealed to this court, each complaining of the award of the commissioners in many respects. Of the conflicting contentions made by the parties it is sufficient to say that in our opinion they are, with one exception, without merit and need no discussion. The exception referred to, however, presents a question of great importance, and of much conflict in the decisions of the various states. As to two pieces of the company's land, parts only of such pieces or tracts were sought to be acquired by the city. While the commissioners found that such parts were of substantial value, they also found that the benefit which would accrue from the improvement to the remainder of such tracts was greater than the value of the lands taken, and hence they made the company no award therefor.

The authority for the rule of compensation thus adopted by the commissioners is based on section 822 of the charter, which enacts as to land taken for water front improvement:

> If all of the property of such owner is taken, the compensation awarded shall be the fair and just value of the said property. If the property of the riparian proprietor has been built upon or improved, and if such buildings or improvements are upon a single tract contiguous to or adjoining lands under water, or which were originally under water, and used in connection therewith, and part only of such property is proposed to be taken, the fair and just value of the entire premises shall first be ascertained, and then there shall be ascertained the like value of the premises in the condition in which they will be after the part is taken, and the difference in value, be it more or less than the separate value of the part taken, shall constitute the measure of compensation.

Despite the strenuous argument of the counsel for the gas company, we are clear that this provision is applicable to the lands taken from the company, and that the action of the commissioners was in accordance with the rule laid down by the statute. Therefore there is but a single question before us. That is, whether the statutory rule of compensation conforms to the requirement of the Constitution that private property shall not be taken for public use without just compensation. Article 1, §6. . . . The question before us has been the subject of many diverse

C. The Riddle of Just Compensation 857

views in the courts of the various states. Mr. Lewis, in his work on Eminent Domain, thus states the condition of the authorities, dividing them into five classes: (1) States holding that benefits cannot be set off at all (Mississippi), (2) Holding that special benefits may be set off against the remainder, but not against the part taken (Maryland, Nebraska, Tennessee, Virginia, West Virginia, Wisconsin). (3) Holding that benefits both general and special may be set off against the remainder, but not against the part taken (Georgia, Louisiana, Kentucky, Texas). (4) Holding that special benefits may be set off against the part taken and the remainder (Connecticut, Kansas, Maine, Minnesota, Missouri, New Hampshire, North Carolina, Oregon, Pennsylvania, Virginia, District of Columbia). (5) Holding that benefits, both general and special, may be set off against the part taken and the value of the remainder (Alabama, California, Delaware, Illinois, Indiana, New York, Ohio, Oregon, South Carolina). It would be impossible, within the limits of an opinion, to discuss the various decisions cited by the learned author, or to examine in every case the accuracy of his classification. It may be observed, however, that Illinois, whatever may have been the earlier decisions in that state, cannot now be placed in the fifth class, because the later cases hold that the owner must be paid the full value of the land taken in money alone without regard to the benefits he may receive. With reference to this state also, I think the author has fallen into error, and that with us the question is still an open one. In the several cases cited by the Supreme Court of the United States in Bauman v. Ross, 167 U.S. 548, and by Mr. Lewis . . . with the single exception of Rexford v. Knight, [15 Barb. 627], the proceedings, the validity of which were attacked, were dual, involving not only an award of compensation for land taken, but an assessment on adjacent property for the cost of the improvement. I cannot find that in any of those cases the owner was awarded anything less than the full value of his land; the attack being made on the provision for setting off the assessment against the award. It is the blending of the two powers, that of eminent domain and that of taxation, which has led to the confusion as to the effect of the decisions of this state. . . .

We will first consider the proceedings as solely in the exercise of the power of eminent domain. It is the settled law of this state that the character and quantity of the estate in lands to be acquired for public use rests wholly in the determination of the Legislature. It may, as in this case it has, authorize the acquisition of the fee in which case there is no right of reversion left in the original owner. . . . It [has often been] held that the acquisition having been made by the city in good faith for a public purpose, on the abandonment of that purpose, the city could sell the lands for private use, and that no right or interest remained in the original owner. . . . If, then, under the settled law of this state, land acquired in fee for a public use can be forever diverted from the owner, and there is no obligation to continue the public use for which it was appropriated and no cause of action arises in favor of the landowner for the abandonment of the improvement, how is it possible to assert that the benefits that result from such an improvement can be considered as compensation for deprivation of the land? With the utmost deference to the opinions of the learned courts of other states and of the United States, it seems to me that the question admits of but one answer.... That benefits may not be set off against consequential damages to the part of the land not taken I do not assert. On the contrary, this would generally accomplish an equitable result . . . but this much we can hold, and I think we should hold, that in no case should an award be made for less than the value of the property actually taken by condemnation. In that position the courts of this state will not stand alone, but will have the support of those in the states already enumerated in the first three of Mr. Lewis' classes, and, in addition thereto, the courts of Illinois.

It remains to be considered whether the charter provisions under discussion can be supported as an exercise of the power of taxation; for, although the Legislature has not labeled the set off of benefits against an award as a tax or local assessment, still, if it had the power to impose such a tax, a failure to properly denominate it could not affect the validity of the statute. It is unquestionable that the Legislature might defray the cost of the improvement either in whole or in part, by special tax or assessment on the adjacent property, and it also might have empowered the local authorities to do the same thing. At an early period in this state it was assumed, both by courts and the profession, that the power of taxation possessed by the Legislature was practically unqualified and unlimited. Such probably was the case. That, however, is not the law as it exists to-day. The change has not been effected by any new provision in the Constitution of this state, but by the adoption of the fourteenth amendment to the federal Constitution, and the doctrine to which we are about to give effect has been declared by that court whose decisions on federal questions are controlling.... Treated as an exercise of the power of taxation, it would be difficult to imagine a selection for taxation, both as to persons to be taxed and the amount of the tax, more arbitrary and capricious than the statutory provision before us. Liability to and amount of tax is left to pure accident, which can have no just relation to the subject. It is true that an owner a part of whose land is taken cannot be made to contribute to the expense of the improvement more than the benefit that accrues to his remaining land, but his neighbor, the situation of whose land may be exactly the same as that of the remaining land's first owner, if none of his land is taken, pays nothing. So, also, in the case of two landowners from each of whom land is taken, the one from whom the least land is taken may have the greater benefit to his remaining land. While it may be just

C. The Riddle of Just Compensation 859

and equitable in a certain sense as between the owner and the public that the owner should contribute towards the cost of the improvement, it is certainly most inequitable as between him and other owners. In such a case equity requires equality, and, while doubtless the state might, under the power of taxation, impose the cost of the improvement in whole or in part on the owners of property specially benefited thereby, it cannot arbitrarily select one or more and exempt the others, depending on accidental circumstances which have no just relation to the liability or immunity of the parties. . . .

In conclusion a word should be said as to the case of Bauman v. Ross, 167 U.S. 548, decided by the Supreme Court of the United States. In that case the act of Congress, the validity of which was upheld, directed the laying out and construction of highways in the District of Columbia, and authorized the acquisition of lands for such purpose by condemnation. It provided that in estimating damages for the taking of any land the jury should take into consideration the benefit to the owner by enhancing the value of the remainder of his land, and the court was authorized to require that the damages and benefits should be stated separately. The validity of this provision was upheld, and it must be conceded that the opinion of the court deals principally with the question of whether such rule of compensation is a compliance with the provision of the Constitution. But the statute also provided for an assessment of one-half the cost of any improvement upon the adjacent property, and directed that, in case any sum had been deducted for benefits from the award for land taken, allowance for such deduction should be made in determining the amount of the assessment. The proceeding was therefore of the dual nature already alluded to, being not only an exercise of the power of eminent domain but also of the taxing power. I feel by no means confident the court would have upheld the statute had it not provided for the allowance referred to on the assessment, and, even despite that provision, it seems to me that cases might arise under the statute where one owner would pay his share of the whole cost of the improvement, while other owners would only be subjected to one-half of such cost.

The orders of the Appellate Division and of the Special Term so far as they relate to parcels 16 and 33, should be reversed, and the proceedings remitted to the commissioners for further report in accordance with this opinion. In all other respects the order of the Appellate Division is affirmed, without costs in this court to either party.[58]

---

58. See In re City of New York, 256 N.Y. 643, 177 N.E. 175 (1931); 1 Orgel, Valuation Under Eminent Domain §§7, 48 (2d ed. 1953). Another theory for the treatment of benefits is set forth in Haar and Hering, The Determination of Benefits in Land Acquisition, 51 Cal. L. Rev. 833, 878-880 (1963). — EDS.

Notes

1. In Rand v. City of Boston, 164 Mass. 354, 41 N.E. 484 (1895), members of the Supreme Judicial Court split over the question "whether damages can be recovered . . . for diminishing the market value of the plaintiffs' land, obstructing its light and air, and occasioning dust to be blown upon it, by building an embankment and bridge upon land taken from a third person, on the opposite side of the street from the plaintiffs' land." Justice Holmes, for the majority, offered a negative answer, based on a narrow reading of the statute allowing compensation for "'damages sustained by any person in his property by the taking of land for . . . a public way.'"

Justice Knowlton, dissenting along with Justice Morton, observed: "I know no good reason why the distance of a few feet between the property of the petitioners and the embankment should affect their rights otherwise than to diminish the amount that should be allowed them."[59]

2. "§12. The damages for property taken . . . shall be fixed at the value thereof before the taking, and in case only part of a parcel of land is taken there shall be included damages for all injury to the part not taken caused by the taking or by the public improvement for which the taking is made. . . . In determining the damages to a parcel of land injured when no part of it has been taken, regard shall be had only to such injury as is special and peculiar to such parcel." Mass. Gen. Laws Ann. ch. 79, §12. Compare Sullivan v. Commonwealth, 335 Mass. 619, 142 N.E.2d 347 (1957) with Webster Thomas Co. v. Commonwealth, 336 Mass. 130, 143 N.E.2d 216 (1957).

3. A landowner had two tracts of land in the city of Providence.

---

59. In Lincoln v. Commonwealth, 164 Mass. 368, 375, 41 N.E. 489, 490 (1895), the court said:

> Statutes like the present, which contemplate a taking of land, generally do not provide for compensation unless there is a taking; and therefore, in proceedings under the act, some of the plaintiff's land must have been taken, in order to give him a standing in court. Whether this is just or not, so long as it is within the limits of the constitution, is not for us to consider. It is enough for us that this condition generally is found in the words of the act. See Rand v. City of Boston (decided this day). If, however, a part of the plaintiff's land has been taken, his locus standi is established, and the question of construction just referred to arises, — as to what, if any, damages shall be allowed for the harm to his adjoining land. Assuming that none of the damages claimed could be recovered under the act, but for the taking, one naturally asks, why should the taking of adjoining land make a difference? The question has been asked a great many times, and the difficulty will be found forcibly stated by Lord Esher in Reg. v. Essex, 17 Q.B. Div. 447, 452. If such a difference is to be made, the foundation for it must be found in the words of the statute. It may be said, to be sure, that the plaintiff gets no more than justice, even if others get less . . . ; and that when he is compelled to sell the land, we ought to consider all that he naturally would consider in fixing the price for a voluntary sale.

C. The Riddle of Just Compensation

They were separated by a street open to the public. The owner often used both tracts for storing heavy equipment used in his business; he testified that one tract would be insufficient to store the equipment. On a taking of one of the tracts, is the owner entitled to damages for the tract not taken? See Sasso v. Housing Authority of the City of Providence, 82 R.I. 451, 111 A.2d 226 (1955) (owner loses — taking of one parcel did not "necessarily" and "permanently" injure the other); compare International Paper Co. v. United States, 227 F.2d 201 (5th Cir. 1955) (timber-bearing land and noncontiguous paper mill) with Baetjer v. United States, 143 F.2d 391 (1st Cir. 1944) (separation of processing plant from sugar fields by two-mile-wide body of water). See People v. Dickinson, 230 Cal. App. 932, 41 Cal. Rptr. 427 (1st Dist. 1964). Suppose that the two tracts had once been one parcel, and that a portion of one tract had previously been condemned for the street which now separates the two?

See also State v. Silver, 92 N.J. 507, 457 A.2d 463, 467 (1983):

> The diminished value of the remaining property constitutes the severance damages visited upon that property as a result of the taking. New Jersey cases have expressed the computation in either of two ways.
>
> In one group of cases it has been held that the measure of damages is the market value of the land taken plus the difference before and after the taking in market value of the remainder area. This concept of the measure of damages may be graphically illustrated by the following equation:
>
> Value of land taken + (value of remainder area before taking − value of remainder area after taking) = just compensation.
>
> The second rule enunciated by some courts is the so-called "before and after rule," wherein the damages to the condemnee are computed as the difference between the value of the entire tract before the taking and the value of the remainder area after the taking. This approach is embodied in the following formula:
>
> Value of entire parcel before taking − value of remainder area after taking = just compensation.
>
> In this State either formula may be employed.

Is there any difference between the two formulas? See 7A Nichols' The Law of Eminent Domain §12.02[3] (rev. 3d ed. 1988) (first method presents "particular difficulty" of determining value of part taken).

What are the criteria for deciding whether the property is part of a single parcel, or is itself a distinct parcel? Would it differ from the zoning and subdivision classifications of lots? See Public Water Supply District No. 2 v. Alex Bascom County, 370 S.W.2d 281 (Mo. 1963) (three undeveloped lots in platted subdivision treated as single parcel).

Typical Expressway problems*

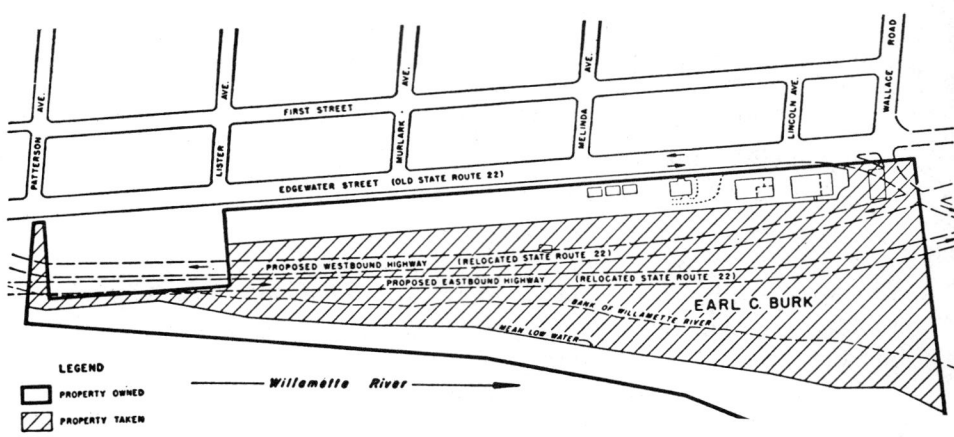

*The first six illustrations are taken from Highway Research Board, Special Report 26 (1957). Cf. Bacich v. Board of Control of California, 23 Cal. 2d 343, 144 P.2d 818 (1944); Schnider v. California, 38 Cal. 2d 439, 241 P.2d 1 (1952); Carazalla v. Wisconsin, 269 Wis. 593, 71 N.W.2d 276 (1955); State, By and Through State Highway Commission v. Burk, 200 Or. 211, 265 P.2d 783 (1954).

C. The Riddle of Just Compensation

4. The United States condemned sixteen acres of appellant's eighty-two-acre farm as part of the site for an air base. The district court awarded damages for the taking and severance. The appellants sought additional compensation for the diminution in value of the remaining land caused by the particular use to which the land taken was put. The court of appeals held that there could be no additional recovery, since the land taken was only on the periphery of the air base and was put to no specific use. Boyd v. United States, 222 F.2d 493 (8th Cir. 1955).

5. The United States condemned the plant of a laundry for a temporary term, extendable from year to year. During the army's three and a half years' possession, the laundry was forced to suspend operations. Rejecting the laundry's claim for loss due to destruction of its "trade routes," compensation was awarded only for rental value plus an allowance to restore the plant to its original condition. In reversing, the Supreme Court held that the trade routes were property for which compensation was required under the fifth amendment.

> The only distinction to be made, therefore, between the attitudes which generate going-concern value and those of which tangible property is compounded is as to the tenacity of the past's hold upon the future: in the case of the latter a forecast of future demand can usually be made with greater certainty, for it is more probable on the whole that people will continue to want particular goods or services than that they will continue to look to a particular supplier of them. It is more likely, in other words, that people will persist in wanting to have their laundry done than that they will keep on sending it to a particular laundry. But as the probability of continued patronage gains strength, this distinction becomes obliterated, and the intangible acquires a value to a potential purchaser no different from the value of the business' physical property. Since the Fifth Amendment requires compensation for the latter, the former, if shown to be present and to have been "taken," should also be compensable.

Kimball Laundry Co. v. United States, 338 U.S. 1, 10-11 (1949) (five-to-four decision), noted, 63 Harv. L. Rev. 352 (1949).

6. Congress authorized taking "any real property, temporary use thereof or other interest therein." The United States condemned land and buildings for use by the army for an initial term of six months, with a right to renew for additional year periods during the war emergency. Lessee of a warehouse with two years remaining of its term, in order to comply with the court's order of immediate possession, incurred expenses for the removal of its personal property. Should removal expenses be included in the measure of just compensation? United States v. Westinghouse Electric and Manufacturing Co., 339 U.S. 261 (1950); see United States v. 967,905 Acres of Land, 447 F.2d

764 (8th Cir. 1971), cert. denied, 405 U.S. 974 (1972). Of what other governmental technique does this remind you?

7. "It is well established that reasonable restriction of access, rerouting of public highways and circuity of travel occasioned thereby are legally not compensable." Commonwealth Department of Highways v. Diuguid, 469 S.W.2d 707, 708 (Ky. 1971). "Property owners possess the right to direct access to the through highway; and while damages are not predicated upon diversion of traffic from the highway, it is proper to allow damages to be based on the diversion of the highway from direct access to property of the owners." State Highway Commission v. Peters, 416 P.2d 390, 395-396 (Wyo. 1966). "If the facts established at the trial of a claim show that the access involved is more than merely circuitous so that it can be characterized as 'unsuitable,' compensability follows." Priestly v. State, 295 N.Y.S.2d 659, 662-663, 23 N.Y.2d 152 (1968). Which of the above formulas would you find easiest to defend? Are they mutually exclusive? See Kuehn, Comment: Loss of Access — A Right to be Compensated, 60 Ky. L.J. (1971-72); Palmore, Damages Recoverable in a Partial Taking, 21 Sw. L. Rev. 740 (1967).

Notes on Goodwill and Relocation

1. Professor Zimmer has written of the personal disasters suffered by small businesspeople:

> The programs for rebuilding cities are effectively eliminating the small marginal businesses. For such units, relocation is frequently not feasible. These businesses tend to be owned by older persons and those with very limited financial resources. Displacement in such cases has the effect of depriving the owners of their usual livelihood, meager as it may have been prior to the disruption. For the most part, the owner received no compensation for his loss, even though he had been forced to vacate his site. In some instances where they happened to own the building that they occupied, some minor adjustments may have been made in the price paid for the property which would make the loss less severe. But no such even token adjustments were possible in the case of renters.

Urban Renewal: The Record and the Controversy 380, 401 (Wilson ed. 1966).

2. Arthur Abrams has been a pharmacist for forty years; for the past twenty-eight years he had operated a pharmacy in the area embraced by the Watts Redevelopment Project. At the time of condemnation, he was 64 years of age and suffering from rheumatoid arthritis. In addition to compensation for loss of real estate and fixtures, he

C. The Riddle of Just Compensation

claims damages of $25,000 for loss of the value of the business or "goodwill," and $10,000 for his inventory of drugs. State law does not provide for such damages. The trial court found that (1) by reason of his age and physical condition, Abrams is unemployable, and must rely for a livelihood on his own business, his only present and potential source of livelihood and his sole asset; (2) Abrams is incapable of starting a new business located in a new area; and (3) the value of the drugs has been reduced to zero since state law prohibits sale of prescription drugs without a certification of purity — the cost of which would exceed the value of the drugs. What result? See Community Redevelopment Agency of Los Angeles v. Abrams, 41 Cal. App. 3d 608, 116 Cal. Rptr. 308 (2d Dist. 1974) (both sums recoverable). See also Kanner, Damages in Condemnation, in Real Estate Valuation in Condemnation 203-209 (PLI 1973).

3. Noyes, The Institution of Property 441 (1936):

> Some of these protected processes owe their legal status as objects of property wholly to legally created monopoly. Others are based on a temporary factual monopoly which the law merely recognizes. The latter kind of monopoly arises when a process is to some extent inimitable. Public service franchises, patents and copyrights belong to the former class exclusively, since the act of granting them involves their being made immediately inimitable. But goodwill, memberships in marketing organizations, etc., owe their monopolistic position not to grant but to the fact that they are relatively and temporarily inimitable except by false pretense.

As to whether goodwill constitutes "property" in a constitutional sense, consider how helpful the following definitions are in solving the problem:

> Property, which is the subject of ownership, is the exclusive right of dominion, possession, use, and power of disposition. . . . [The] word . . . is used to indicate rights, privileges, powers, and immunities, or any varying aggregate of them.
> . . . The fundamental attribute of wealth, in its economic sense, is its usefulness — the benefits that are to be derived from it. One who possesses wealth possesses certain rights, which are simply rights of use and enjoyment. It is the possession of these rights that constitutes property.

Schmutz, Condemnation Appraisal Handbook 20, 21 (1949). "To have a property interest in a benefit, a person clearly must have more than an abstract need or desire for it. He must have more than a unilateral expectation of it. He must, instead, have a legitimate claim of entitlement to it." Board of Regents of State Colleges v. Roth, 408 U.S. 564, 577 (1972).

4. Typically, the court's inquiry is limited to a determination of

just compensation in market, rather than moral, terms. Complaints over the costs and psychological impact of relocating going concerns and neighborhood residents have led to legislative intervention, though even this extra-judicial relief is sometimes unsatisfactory. For example, in Auraria Businessmen against Confiscation, Inc. v. Denver Urban Renewal Authority, 183 Colo. 441, 517 P.2d 845 (1974), the court upheld the relocation payment provisions of the state urban renewal and relocation assistance acts in the face of the following challenge:

> It is appellants' position . . . that by denying compensation for loss of goodwill or profit associated with dislocation, the statute deprives them of property without due process of law and without just compensation, and discriminates against them as a class in violation of the Equal Protection clauses of the federal and state constitutions.

In Norfolk Redevelopment and Housing Authority v. Chesapeake & Potomac Telephone, 464 U.S. 30 (1983), the Court denied C&P's claim for compensation based on provisions of the Uniform Relocation Assistance and Real Property Acquisition Policies Act of 1970, 84 Stat. 1894, 42 U.S.C. §4601 et seq. The term "displaced person" under the Act includes "[b]usinesses as well as natural persons," thus making a company eligible for relocation benefits. However, C&P's assertion that it was "'displaced' within the meaning of the Act when it relocate[d] telephone lines because an urban renewal project call[ed] for realignment of existing street patterns" ran contrary to the traditional common law requirement that utility companies "bear the entire cost of relocating from a public right-of-way." Moreover, there was nothing in the legislative history of the Act to suggest a contrary rule.

5. The Model Eminent Domain Code tracks closely with the federal act. The Preliminary Comment states that Article XIV of the Model Code ("Relocation Assistance") "is intended to extend the same benefits and requirements to all projects or programs conducted or directed by both public and private condemnors, whether or not federal financial assistance is being provided. This broader approach is believed not only to be more consonant with an equitable and even-handed state policy, but should eliminate special legislation and equal protection problems under the state and federal constitutions that could attend a statutory scheme of more selective scope." 13 U.L.A. 130 (1986).

6. See Fox v. HUD, 468 F. Supp. 907, 909-911, 916 (E.D. Pa. 1979), aff'd, 680 F.2d 315 (3d Cir. 1982):

> This case has a long, but fascinating, pretrial history set in a bed of tensions generated by the nature of the parties and disputes involved. In December 1969, the original Washington Square West Project Area Committee filed an action (Civil Action No. 69-2972) against the United

C. The Riddle of Just Compensation 867

States Department of Housing and Urban Development (HUD) and the Redevelopment Authority of the City of Philadelphia (RDA) seeking to enjoin urban renewal activities in the Area due to an alleged lack of adequate citizen participation.

The newly filed class action was brought on behalf of present and former residents of the Area who alleged that defendants' urban renewal activities drove low and moderate income persons, predominantly non-whites, out of the Area and transformed a formerly racially and economically integrated community into a predominantly white, affluent one. . . .

The settlement provides for the construction or rehabilitation of 131 units of subsidized housing on certain properties within the Area that RDA presently owns; 111 units will be substantially rehabilitated and 20 units will be new construction. HUD will seek private developers of the units, and prepare a Developer's Packet consistent with the terms of the settlement which provides that consideration will be given to a developer's proposal if it suggests scattering the subsidized housing on various preapproved sites throughout the Area instead of concentrating the subsidized units in one or two locations. . . .

. . . Three hundred units of subsidized housing in the Postal Workers Union Building also will be available to the elderly and the handicapped. Although these additional units are not reserved for persons displaced from the Area, it is reasonable to assume that some dislocatees will be housed there. But even if the 300 units were added to the units made available pursuant to the settlement, a substantial likelihood remains (given just the number of non-whites displaced) that if the case proceeded to trial on the merits, plaintiffs would achieve more housing units within the Area than they do under the settlement.

Nevertheless, the Court is convinced that other factors render this settlement reasonable and fair to subclasses II, III and IV, the most important being that it allows this case to proceed to a speedy resolution. This lawsuit was commenced in 1969 and plaintiffs have been without relief since before that time. If the case went to trial, undoubtedly, it would take several months to be presented. Although securing as speedy relief as possible is crucial given the nature of the claims involved, relief would be indefinitely prolonged if the case went to trial.

Commons, Institutional Economics, 820 (1934): "[T]he American distinction between the taxing power and the police power is, to a great extent, a legal fiction growing out of our system of government, and is unnecessary from the economic and fiscal standpoint. . . . Taxation, then, is the pervasive and privileged exercise of the police power. . . ."

New York City Housing Authority v. Muller, 270 N.Y. 333, 340-341, 1 N.E.2d 153, 155 (1936): "The fundamental purpose of government is to protect the health, safety, and general welfare of the public.... Its power plant for the purpose consists of the power of taxation, the police power, and the power of eminent domain.... [I]t seems to be constitutionally immaterial whether one or another of the sovereign powers is employed."

■ EPSTEIN, TAKINGS: PRIVATE PROPERTY AND THE POWER OF EMINENT DOMAIN
196-198 (1985)

In principle, the demand of just compensation is satisfied when two conditions occur simultaneously: (1) the total size of the pie — the sum of the value of all ownership and personal rights — is maintained or increased: and (2) the size of each individual slice of the pie is maintained or increased as well.

Where (2) is satisfied, (1) will necessarily be satisfied as well. However, (1) may be satisfied where (2) is not. In these cases the inquiry must focus on the way (if there is one) in which payments of explicit compensation can bring about a social arrangement satisfying both (1) and (2), taking into account the administrative costs of the move. Standing alone, propositions (1) and (2) do not uniquely distribute any net social surplus, but this surplus has already been accounted for in my treatment of public use, which also mandates pro rata distribution.

The theme of implicit in-kind compensation is recurrent in the law of eminent domain. Holmes hinted at this theme in one of his many propositions in Pennsylvania Coal Co. v. Mahon, when he wrote that government action may be sustained where it secures the "average reciprocity of advantage" of all interested parties. It lies at the root of the assertion in Armstrong v. United States that explicit compensation is required where burdens are placed upon a few which "in fairness and justice" should be placed upon the public at large....

There are instances in which a government action has an enormous disproportionate economic impact without a corresponding duty of state compensation. For example, in cases of *damnum absque injuria*, an individual owner is left worse off by government action that falls short of a taking. Suppose the government erects a large office building that blocks the view of a lake from a large luxury apartment complex, sharply cutting market rents. The economic impact is surely disproportionate, but the government is not obligated to compensate, because the owners of the complex would have no claim for damages, let alone for injunctive relief, against a private neighbor not previously bound by a restrictive covenant. Similarly, there is no cause for compensation if the government terminates the privileges of a single individual in accordance with its reserved powers under grant, as with the grazing rights in Fuller v. United States. The harm is concentrated on one person, but compensation is not required because the plaintiff as a licensee at will cannot show that his economic loss was triggered by any violation of his rights.

In addition, some admitted takings, such as the seizure of contaminated dump sites, are justified in full under the police power. The impact in such a case may be massively disproportionate, but the antinuisance rationale may completely justify the government restrictions. Yet compensation is not required, even with the loss clearly established. . . .

D. AN EXPERIMENT IN FINANCE: THE BRITISH TOWN AND COUNTRY PLANNING ACTS[60]

Effective and comprehensive land-use planning is bound up — both in ethical and financial terms — with the problem of compensation. Fear of incurring a heavy compensation bill may distort planning activities. Either the amplitude of planning has to be limited to reduce costs, or the level of compensation has to be skimped so that effective planning can be achieved.

The financial issue led British administrators to compose a new strategy. The same public planning that depreciates some land values (thereby creating the right to compensation) also enhances others. Hence, from the bill for compensation there would be excluded items whose value exceeded any "real" loss suffered by the landowner —

---

60. In general, see Cullingworth, Town and Country Planning in Britain (10th ed. 1988); Heap, An Outline of Planning Law (9th ed. 1987); Telling, Planning Law and Procedure (7th ed. 1986); Leach, Disturbance on Compulsory Purchase (3d ed. 1975). The Journal of Planning and Environment Law and the Encyclopedia of Planning are valuable guides. On the economic concepts, see Turvey, Development Charges and the Compensation-Betterment Problem, 63 Econ. J. 299 (1953); Parker, The Financial Aspects of Town and Country Planning Legislation, 64 id. 72 (1954); Munby, Development Charges and the Compensation-Betterment, 64 id. 87; Turvey, A Rejoinder, 64 id. 358 (1954); Self, Cities in Flood 147-164 (1957). See also Windfalls for Wipeouts: Land Value Capture and Compensation (Hagman & Misczynski eds. 1978). For a Gilbert & Sullivanesque view of the topic, see Mynors, The Town and Country Planning (Compensation) Act 1985 — An Afterthought, 1985 J. Plan. & Envt. L. 536, 537: "I know the mythic history, from Uthwatt down to Heseltine, / Each time the Commons interfere, it seems that less and less is mine."

Under the front-page headline, "U.N. Meeting Urges Curb on Private Land Holding," N.Y. Times, June 12, 1976, the story quoted from the Conference resolution that "[p]rivate land ownership also is a principal instrument of accumulation and concentration of wealth and therefore contributes to social injustice; if unchecked it may become a major obstacle in the planning and implementation of development schemes."

"floating" value. Second, betterment assessments would be collected from the owner who gained by planning — "shifting" value. Finally, a resolution of the twin problems of payment of compensation and recovery of betterment paves the way for inexpensive exercise of the power of compulsory acquisition. What makes these bold measures so interesting is their seeking to achieve these goals without impairing the efficient operation of the private land market.[61]

■ REPORT OF THE EXPERT COMMITTEE ON COMPENSATION AND BETTERMENT
CMD. No. 6386, at 14, 16, 22-23, 27-29 (1942)

23. Potential development value is by nature speculative. The hoped-for building may take place on the particular piece of land in question, or it may take place elsewhere; it may come within five years, or it may be twenty-five years or more before the turn of the particular piece of land to be built upon arrives. . . .

24. Potential value is necessarily a "floating value," and it is impossible to predict with certainty where the "float" will settle as sites are actually required for purposes of development. When a piece of undeveloped land is compulsorily acquired, or development upon it is prohibited, the owner receives compensation for the loss of the value of a probability of the floating demand settling upon his piece of land. The probability is not capable of arithmetical quantification. In practice where this process is repeated indefinitely over a large area the sum of the probabilities as estimated greatly exceeds the actual possibilities, because the "float," limited as it is to actually occurring demands, can only settle on a proportion of the whole area. There is therefore overvaluation. . . .

27. In theory, in view of these considerations, it should be possible to compensate all owners whose land is decreased in value by restrictions on development out of a "betterment" fund levied from owners the value of whose land is thereby increased. No scheme has, however, yet

---

61. See Davidson, Planning and Compensation in Victoria, Econ. Record, May 1955, at 44, 45:

[T]here will be injustice, the breach of an implied promise by society, only if limitations are imposed maliciously or otherwise in bad faith. Even this speculativeness should be largely eliminated if the planning authority is working to a scheme which is well known to the public. As for the period during which the tradition against compensation is being built up, injustice can be alleviated — though hardly removed except probably at excessive sacrifice of planning aims — by reducing limitations on the development of land which is now "ripe" and which has therefore already gone to a big premium. . . . The question of distributive justice is only part of the problem of planning compensation: perhaps the more important part is the question of allocation of resources.

been devised under which in actual practice compensation and betterment can be equated in this way. In ascertaining the betterment there immediately arises the difficulty of establishing the amount by which a particular parcel of land has increased in value as the direct consequence of the restriction imposed on the other land and not from other causes....

28. These, in outline, are the factors which, as regards undeveloped land in particular, constitute the key to the difficulties of compensation and betterment which have hampered planning. If land with potential development value is purchased by a public authority or is restricted against development or certain forms of development, compensation has to be paid for individual loss of land values which have not in fact been destroyed but which have only shifted to other land. In addition, where the land belongs to a number of owners, the aggregate of values claimable by individual owners when separately assessed, owing to the factor of "floating value," greatly exceeds the real loss of the claimants taken as a group. On the other hand betterment cannot be collected to any substantial degree in respect of the shifted values because it is impossible to say with certainty whether, and to what extent, a given land value is attributable to a given cause.

37. ... [T]he compensation difficulty exists because planning, which is directed to securing the best social use of land, tries to operate within a system of land ownership under which there is attached to land a development value depending on the prospects of its profitable use. If there is to be a completely satisfactory basis for planning which gets rid of the difficulty, that system itself must be revised....

■ HAAR, LAND PLANNING LAW IN A FREE SOCIETY
100-101 (1951)

The White Paper of 1944* issued by the Coalition Government accepted the analysis of the Uthwatt Committee[62] as "substantially correct." Indeed it called the Committee's final report a "masterly analysis of the abstruse problems lying at the root of any effective system of town and country planning." Nevertheless, it calmly proceeded to outline an entirely new system for balancing compensation and betterment.

A global system of compensation was felt to present great difficulties because of the varying magnitude and large number of individual land

---

* The Control of Land Use, Cmd. No. 6537 (1944).
62. This is the Expert Committee on Compensation and Betterment. An extract from its report appears supra page 870. — EDS.

interests, the lack of data on which to base valuations, and the uncertainties of future development and future values. The White Paper proposed to continue the old system of compensation, with the exception that "excessive float" would be eliminated. The method advanced for achieving this objective was to determine potential development values as of March 31, 1939. This would fix the right to compensation for deprivation of any such value. But no money was to be paid until the landowner was actually deprived of the development potential previously valued.

So far as betterment was concerned, the Uthwatt periodic levy on site-value increase was rejected by the White Paper. It was described as unfair since it fell on a potential, as distinct from a realized, increase of value, and on increases which might have been paid for by the owner. The Coalition Government, therefore, proposed in its stead that whenever permission was granted to develop or redevelop for a different use, a betterment charge should be imposed at the rate of 80 percent of the difference between the value of land with benefit of permission and its value had permission been refused.

Finally, the view of the White Paper as to the proper relation between compensation and betterment was a modest one. It suggested that "the payments received in betterment should, over a reasonable period of years and over the country as a whole, provide a fund adequate to pay fair compensation. The processes of planning and development in all their aspects will, therefore, be so managed as ultimately to secure such a balance."

■ TOWN AND COUNTRY PLANNING ACT, 1947
10 & 11 Geo. 6, ch. 51

58. — (1) . . . [P]ayments shall be made in accordance with a scheme to be made by the Treasury . . . in respect of interests in land which are depreciated in value by virtue of the provisions of this Act.

(2) The aggregate amount of the payments to be made shall be the sum of three hundred million pounds. . . .

60. — (1) Any claim for a payment . . . shall be made to the Central Land Board in such manner, within such period, and accompanied by such particulars and verified by such evidence, as may be prescribed by regulations. . . .

61. — (1) . . . [A]n interest in land shall be deemed to be depreciated in value by virtue of the provisions of this Act if the restricted value of that interest on the appointed day,[63] calculated in

---

63. July 1, 1948. — Eds.

D. The British Town and Country Planning Acts 873

accordance with the provisions of this and the next following section, is less than the unrestricted value of that interest on that day as so calculated; and references . . . to the development value of an interest in land shall be construed as references to the difference between those values.

(2) Subject to the following provisions of this section —

(a) the restricted value of an interest in land on the appointed day shall be taken to be the value of that interest as it subsists on that day, calculated on the assumption that planning permission would be granted . . . for development of any class specified in the Third Schedule[64] to this Act, but would not be so granted for any other development; and

(b) the unrestricted value of an interest in land on the appointed day shall be taken to be the value which that interest would have had as it subsists on that day if the provisions of this Act (other than this . . . section) had not passed.

69. — (1) . . . [T]here shall be paid to the Central Land Board in respect of the carrying out of any operations . . . and in respect of any use of land . . . a development charge of such amount (if any) as the Board may determine, and accordingly no such operations shall be carried out, and no such use shall be instituted or continued, except with the consent in writing of the Central Land Board, until the amount of the charge (if any) to be paid in respect of those operations or that use has been determined by the Board in accordance with the provisions of this Part of this Act, and the Board have certified that the amount so determined has been paid or secured to their satisfaction in accordance with those provisions.

(2) This . . . applies to all operations for the carrying out of which planning permission under Part III of this Act is required, and to all uses of land for the institution or continuance of which such permission is so required. . . .[65]

70. — (2) In determining whether any and if so what development charge is to be paid . . . the Board shall have regard to the amount by which the value of the land with the benefit of planning permission for those operations or that use (calculated without regard to any charge payable in respect thereof under this Part of this Act . . .) exceeds the value which it would have without the benefit of such permission, and shall not give any undue or unreasonable preference or advantage to one applicant over another.

(3) . . . [S]uch regulations may in particular provide for securing that the amount of the said charge shall be determined on different

---

64. This exempts eight classes of development, such as rebuilding if the cubic content is not exceeded by one tenth, or conversion into two or more dwelling houses. — EDS.

65. Naturally the charge did not apply to Third Schedule operations. — EDS.

principles in relation to operations or uses of different classes, or in relation to operations or uses carried out or begun at different periods.

■ McAUSLAN, COMPENSATION AND BETTERMENT
Cities, Law, and Social Policy 77-90 (Haar ed. 1984)

What general conclusions can be drawn from forty years of grappling with the compensation-betterment problem, from the time of the Uthwatt report to the present day? On compensation, since the reintroduction of market value for compulsory acquisition of land in 1959, there has been little dispute on matters of principle, apart from variants of policies on quasi-land nationalization at existing-use value introduced for brief periods in the late 1960s and mid-1970s. There is remarkably little objection to the firm policy of no general right to compensation for planning restrictions, and the operation of the provision that a local planning authority may be required to purchase land rendered incapable of reasonably beneficial use by virtue of the refusal of planning permission, while not without its imperfections, equally does not generate noticeable pressure for change. In the late 1960s, a significant body of opinion existed that compensation for losses and depreciation caused by public works was grossly inadequate and unfair. The Land Compensation Act of 1973 met most of those criticisms of the law as it then stood, although administration of the law still leaves a good deal to be desired. One might say that compensation is, in a market economy, the expression of the principle that one has to pay for what one wants to do with respect to land, and so it is not surprising that, where there is widespread, almost unthinking, acceptance of private rights in land, and a market for those rights, the principle of compensation at market value (whether in respect to acquisition of or loss of value of those private rights) should not generate much critical comment and that discussion should be confined to alleged inequities in the implementation of the principle.

Betterment, on the other hand, is entirely different. It is not part of the assumptions about private rights in land and the market for those rights. As was suggested earlier, a particular approach to or philosophy about land-use planning must be adopted before one can concede that public collection of betterment is acceptable, even equitable. Adoption of a different philosophy leads one to believe that collection of betterment is unreasonable, even iniquitous. While betterment is seen in these terms, frontal assaults on the problem are likely to be repelled completely as soon as electoral fortunes allow. Developments over the last decade have shown, however, that, if the problem can be presented in a different way, or in a different light, or acted upon without specific reference to its existence, then progress toward a solution can be made, almost by stealth. Matters that, when confronted head on, are seen as issues of principle to be fought over without compromise are accepted without much fuss when presented as part and parcel of some eminently sensible, nonideological practice or reform. In a word, incrementalism appears to be a better way forward for proponents of betterment collection than is major high-profile, radical-looking reform, whatever the political propaganda benefits the latter approach might be thought to give. It must be admitted that incrementalism has disadvantages: it is slow, piecemeal change that can be reversed easily; it is difficult to sell to political activists because it smacks of compromise and lack of political moral fiber; it is, at present, somewhat unfashionable in Britain, and, in this area at any rate, it would allow opponents of the policy (that is, commercial developers and their professional advisers) to always be one step ahead of change and so never seriously affected by it. Against all these admitted disadvantages, incrementalism seems to have one advantage: it has produced results — not dramatic or radical, and vulnerable to reversal as the current arguments over planning gain indicate, but results nonetheless. With regard to an issue that has defied major and radical reforms again and again over the past four decades, this would seem to be a significant advantage, and the principle lesson to be learned from this survey of the subject.

E. REGULATION VERSUS TAKING

Achieving the goals of comprehensive city planning must constantly take into account potential constitutional challenges. To what extent, in the name of solving a land-use problem, may government regulate private property without running afoul of the prohibition against taking without just compensation? The attempt to distinguish "regulation" from "taking" is the most haunting jurisprudential problem in the field of contemporary land-use law — one that we have encountered many times already, one that may be the lawyer's equivalent of the physicist's hunt for the quark. Chapter II deals with nuisance law and the private limits put upon use of one's property, with damages taking the form, often, of an inverse taking. Subsequent chapters deal with the distinctively public regulations: the government's right to restrict uses to designated districts and to promote aesthetics, growth, and the more intangible social values; the consequences of forcing developers of subdivisions to internalize costs previously foisted upon the community, balancing severe private detriment with widely shared public benefits; lastly, in this chapter, the issue of the meaning of "taking" within the eminent domain process itself. Perhaps you have been able to synthesize the various decisions and the different subject areas of land-use planning, or are ready to subscribe to Professor Van Alstyne's plague-on-both-your-houses: "judicial opinions rejecting constitutional attacks . . . seldom provide reliable guides to the relevant substantive standards," while "decisions invalidating land use controls are often equally devoid of helpful explanatory data." Taking or Damaging by Police Power: The Search for Inverse Condemnation Criteria, 44 S. Cal. L. Rev. 1, 14 (1971). See Kanner, Inverse Condemnation Remedies in an Era of Uncertainty, 1980 Inst. on Plan. Zoning & Eminent Domain 177. The problems have vexed the commentators into explorations radiating many and diverse philosophical perspectives.

The question of regulation versus taking is basically one of the manner in and extent to which governmental power affects the rights of the individual. Neither the quotation from Blackstone nor that from Schlesinger (supra page 780) portrays the kind of political system within which our problem can arise. The first depicts a society in which an individual's land may never be taken, regardless of how necessary the regulation; the second, a society in which the individual may never question the necessity of governmental regulation, regardless of how totally his or her land has been taken.

The case for a minimal government has found its most articulate proponent in recent years in Nozick's Anarchy, State, and Utopia (1974), which argues (at 63-64) that rights belong to individuals, "and there are things no person or group may do to them [without violating their rights]":

> [W]hy not allow any boundary crossing provided full compensation is paid? Full compensation keeps the victim on as high an indifference curve as he would occupy if the other person hadn't crossed. Therefore a system that allows all boundary impingements provided that full compensation is paid is equivalent to a system requiring that all prior agreements about the right to cross a border be reached at that point on the contract curve most favorable to the *buyer* of the right. If you would be willing to pay as much as $\$n$ for the right to do something to me, and $\$m$ is the least I would accept (receiving less than $\$m$ places me on a lower indifference curve), then there is the possibility of our striking a mutually advantageous bargain if $n \geq m$. Within the range between $\$n$ and $\$m$, where should the price be set? One cannot say, lacking any acceptable theory of a just or fair price (witness the various attempts to construct *arbitration* models for two-person, nonconstant sum games). Certainly, no reason has even been produced to think that all exchanges should take place at that point on the contract curve one of the parties most favors, to make the benefits of the exchange redound solely to that party. Allowing boundary crossing

E. Regulation Versus Taking

provided only that full compensation is paid "solves" the problem of distributing the benefits of voluntary exchange in an unfair and arbitrary manner.

The classic expression for maximum government is Hobbes, Leviathan, Part II, ch. 24, which captures the issue this way:

> [T]he Introduction of *Propriety* is an effect of Common-wealth; which can do nothing but by the Person that Represents it, it is the act onley of the Soveraign; and consisteth in the Lawes, which none can make that have not the Soveraign Power. And this they well knew of old, who called that *Nomos*, (that is to say, *Distribution*,) which we call Law; and defined Justice, by *distributing* to every man *his own*.
>
> In this Distribution, the First Law, is for Division of the Land it selfe: wherein the Soveraign assigneth to every man a portion, according as he, and not according as any Subject, or any number of them, shall judge agreeable to Equity, and the Common Good....
>
> From whence we may collect, that the Propriety which a subject hath in his lands, consisteth in a right to exclude all other subjects from the use of them; and not to exclude their Soveraign, be it an Assembly, or a Monarch. For seeing the Soveraign, that is to say, the Common-wealth (whose Person he representeth,) is understood to do nothing but in order to the common Peace and Security, this Distribution of lands, is to be understood as done in order to the same: And consequently, whatsoever Distribution he shall make in prejudice thereof, is contrary to the will of every subject, that committed his Peace, and safety to his discretion, and conscience; and therefore by the will of every one of them, is to be reputed voyd. It is true, that a Soveraign Monarch, or the greater part of a Soveraign Assembly, may ordain the doing of many things in pursuit of their Passions, contrary to their own consciences, which is a breach of trust, and of the Law of Nature; but this is not enough to authorise any subject, either to make warre upon, or so much as to accuse of Injustice, or any way to speak evil of their Soveraign; because they have authorised all his actions, and in bestowing the Soveraign Power, made them their own.

Professor Michelman, in what is perhaps the most perceptive treatment of this subject, offers the world view of utilitarianism as a third alternative.[66] Since utilitarianism deifies neither the individual

---

66. Hegel, of course, also sought to transcend the sterile thesis/antithesis of individualism and totalitarianism:

> This interest [private choice and particular interest] invokes freedom of trade and commerce against control from above; but the more blindly it sinks into self-seeking aims, the more it requires such controls to bring it back to the universal. Control is also necessary to diminish the danger of upheavals arising from clashing interests and to abbreviate the period in which their tension should be eased through the working of a necessity of which they themselves know nothing.
>
> The oversight and care exercised by the public authority aims at being a

nor the state, it is well adapted to an appreciation and resolution of the tensions presented in the regulation-versus-taking context.

> We . . . receive from Bentham a theory of social utility which can explain why collective allocational decision making, deemed unobjectionable in and of itself, *might* be deemed impermissible if attended by capricious redistributions. And we may be encouraged to try to derive from that theory some criteria for determining which collective allocational decisions, attended by what particular distributional impacts, should be deemed impermissible unless those impacts are offset by compensation payments. . . .
>
> The problem . . . is to show that utilitarian property theory, applied with utmost consistency, does *not* require payment of compensation in every case of social action which is disappointing to justified, investment-backed expectations. There is no difficulty as long as our utilitarians will agree with us that productivity cannot be measured except in terms of individual satisfactions; that maximizing such satisfactions depends not only on the volume of the inputs of labor, land, and capital, but on the direction in which those inputs are steered, in other words, on sound allocating; that, because of human interdependence and the external

---

middle term between an individual and the universal possibility, afforded by society, of attaining individual ends. It has to undertake street-lighting, bridge-building, the pricing of daily necessaries, and the care of public health. In this connexion, two main views predominate at the present time. One asserts that the superintendence of everything properly belongs to the public authority, the other that the public authority has nothing at all to settle here because everyone will direct his conduct according to the needs of others. The individual must have a right to work for his bread as he pleases, but the public also has a right to insist that essential tasks shall be properly done. Both points of view must be satisfied, and freedom of trade should not be such as to jeopardize the general good.

Philosophy of Right §236.

Rousseau likewise saw that the tension must be kept alive, with its resolution sought in a higher synthesis, not in a dissolution of either of the human impulses that gives rise to the dilemma:

> It is certain that the right of property is the most sacred of all the rights of citizenship, and even more important in some respects than liberty itself: either because it more nearly affects the preservation of life, or because, property being more easily usurped and more difficult to defend than life, the law ought to pay a greater attention to what is most easily taken away; or finally, because property is the true foundation of civil society, and the real guarantee of the undertakings of citizens: for if property were not answerable for personal actions, nothing would be easier than to evade duties and laugh at the laws. On the other hand, it is no less certain that the maintenance of the State and the government involves costs and outgoings; and as every one who agrees to the end must acquiesce in the means, it follows that the members of a society ought to contribute from their property to its support. Besides, it is difficult to secure the property of individuals on one side, without attacking it on another; and it is impossible that all regulations which govern the order of succession, will, contracts & c. should not lay individuals under some constraint as to the disposition of their goods, and should not consequently restrict the right of property.

Rousseau, On Political Economy 377.

E. Regulation Versus Taking

effects inevitably associated with economic activity, the soundest allocations cannot be reached without some collective control; and that the necessary collective adjustments of market-determined activity are bound to occasion disappointment to justified expectations, under circumstances in which it would be practically impossible to arrive at a comprehensive set of apparently "correct" compensation settlements. . . .

. . . [W]e must remember that the utilitarian's solicitude for security is instrumental and subordinate to his goal of maximizing the output of satisfactions. Security of expectation is cherished, not for its own sake, but only as a shield for morale. Once admit that not all capricious redistributive effects are totally demoralizing, and utilitarian theory can tell us where to draw the line between compensable and noncompensable collective impositions. An imposition is compensable if not to compensate would be critically demoralizing; otherwise, not.

Property, Utility and Fairness: Comments on the Ethical Foundations of "Just Compensation" Law, 80 Harv. L. Rev. 1165, 1212-1213 (1967).

1. The Supreme Court's Decisional Labyrinth: A Conversation among the Justices

Granting then that we live in a society that recognizes both the right of government to regulate and the right of individuals to own and enjoy private property, the question remains: How is one to know (or tell) when regulation leaves off and when taking begins? This way of formulating the question (which is charged by some to be a rewriting of the Constitution) is due in no small part to Justice Holmes's oft-quoted ruling in Pennsylvania Coal Co. v. Mahon, 260 U.S. 393, 415-416: "[I]f regulation goes too far it will be recognized as a taking. . . . This is a question of degree — and therefore cannot be disposed of by general propositions."

After a century of judicial attention, have we come any closer to a solution? What have we gained from the process of exploration, besides the realization that the police power and eminent domain — concepts the Court has conjoined for purposes of "public use" analysis — remain painfully (even hopelessly) at odds in the constant struggle between the right to hold property and the obligation to protect society? The confusion that permeates the Court's most recent efforts (see section E.3 infra) makes quite attractive the *Mugler* Court's simple declaration that eminent domain is not involved or the *Block* dissenters' assertion of absolute rights to control one's property. Still, we are moved by complainants like Mr. Hadacheck, whose property has been severely depreciated in value because of regulations promulgated by officials unafraid of a judicial slap on the wrist.[67]

Do the cases that repeat Holmes's famous "too far" incantation in *Mahon* merely reify the takings myth, giving constitutional and practical effect to a metaphorical tale first spun by the "Yankee from Olympus"?[68] Or is Holmes's concept of a continuum consonant with the needs of a society faced with a growing governmental presence? Is the bundle of rights analogy, employed in *Allard*, and cases like *Kaiser-Aetna* that focus on the right to exclude, helpful or further evidence of avoidance behavior, like the Court's recent fixation on "investment-backed expectations"?

As you read the words of the opinions, note the cumulative pattern of legal precedent and judicial gloss, the way in which dictum becomes elevated into holding, the flow of phrases and formulas, and the manner in which succeeding generations of Justices have incorporated and reacted to the academic discourse excerpted in the next section.[69]

Justice Harlan:[70]   Undoubtedly the State, when providing, by legislation, for the protection of the public health, the public morals, or the public safety, is subject to the paramount authority of the Constitution of the United States, and may not violate rights secured or guaranteed by that instrument, or interfere with the execution of the powers confided to the general government.

Upon this ground — if we do not misapprehend the position of defendants — it is contended that, as the primary and principal use of beer is as a beverage; as their respective breweries were erected when it was lawful to engage in the manufacture of beer for every purpose; as such establishments will become of no value as property, or, at least, will be materially diminished in value, if not employed in the manufacture of beer for every purpose; the prohibition upon their being so employed is, in effect, a taking of

---

67. The plaintiffs in HFH, Ltd. v. Superior Court, 15 Cal 3d. 508, 542 P.2d 237, 125 Cal. Rptr. 365 (1975) cert. denied, 425 U.S. 904 (1976), asserted that, as a result of the city's general plan, "their land, which they purchased for some $388,000 and hoped to sell for $400,000, suffered a decline in market value to $75,000." The California Supreme Court's finding that inverse condemnation did not amount to a taking made *HFH* a cause célèbre among advocates of compensation for regulatory takings.

68. See, e.g., Siemon, Of Regulatory Takings and Other Myths, 1 J. Land Use & Envtl. L. 105 (1985). As for the popularity of Holmes's contribution, see Carlisle, The Section 1983 Land Use Case: Justice Stevens and the Hunt for the Taking Quark, 16 Stetson L. Rev. 565, 565 n. 1: "*Pennsylvania Coal* has been cited in the state and federal courts 99,732 times from 1922 through 1986."!

69. The "Conversation" is by no means intended as a complete compendium. Recall, for example, the important contributions to the regulatory takings debate made by Justice Sutherland in *Euclid* (supra page 178), Justice Brennan in *Penn Central* (supra page 537), and Justice Stevens in *Keystone* (supra page 736).

70. Mugler v. Kansas, 123 U.S. 623 (1887).

E. Regulation Versus Taking 881

property for public use without compensation, and depriving the citizen of his property without due process of law....

... [T]he present case must be governed by principles that do not involve the power of eminent domain, in the exercise of which property may not be taken for public use without compensation. A prohibition simply upon the use of property for purposes that are declared, by valid legislation, to be injurious to the health, morals, or safety of the community, cannot, in any just sense, be deemed a taking or an appropriation of property for the public benefit.... The power which the States have of prohibiting such use by individuals of their property as will be prejudicial to the health, the morals, or the safety of the public, is not — and, consistently with the existence and safety of organized society, cannot be — burdened with the condition that the State must compensate such individual owners for pecuniary losses they may sustain, by reason of their not being permitted, by a noxious use of their property, to inflict injury upon the community. The exercise of the police power by the destruction of property which is itself a public nuisance, or the prohibition of its use in a particular way, whereby its value becomes depreciated, is very different from taking property for public use, or from depriving a person of his property without due process of law. In the one case, a nuisance only is abated; in the other, unoffending property is taken away from an innocent owner.

Justice McKenna:[71] The petition sets forth ... that petitioner is the owner of a tract of land within the limits described in the ordinance upon which tract of land there is a very valuable bed of clay, of great value for the manufacture of brick of a fine quality, worth to him not less than $100,000 per acre or about $800,000 for the entire tract for brick-making purposes, and not exceeding $60,000 for residential purposes or for any purpose other than the manufacture of brick. That he has made excavations of considerable depth and covering a very large area of the property and that on account thereof the land cannot be utilized for residential purposes or any purpose other than that for which it is now used....

That if the ordinance be declared valid he will be compelled to entirely abandon his business and will be deprived of the use of his property....

... It is to be remembered that we are dealing with one of the most essential powers of government, one that is the least limitable. It may, indeed, seem harsh in its exercise, usually is on some individual, but the imperative necessity for its existence precludes any limitation upon it when not exerted arbitrarily. A vested interest

---

71. Hadacheck v. Sebastian, 239 U.S. 394 (1915).

cannot be asserted against it because of conditions once obtaining. To so hold would preclude development and fix a city forever in its primitive conditions. There must be progress, and if in its march private interests are in the way they must yield to the good of the community. The logical result of petitioner's contention would seem to be that a city could not be formed or enlarged against the resistance of an occupant of the ground and that if it grows at all it can only grow as the environment of the occupations that are usually banished to the purlieus.

Justice Holmes:[72]   The fact that tangible property is also visible tends to give a rigidity to our conception of our rights in it that we do not attach to others less concretely clothed. But the notion that the former are exempt from the legislative modification required from time to time in civilized life is contradicted not only by the doctrine of eminent domain, under which what is taken is paid for, but by that of the police power in its proper sense, under which property rights may be cut down, and to that extent taken, without pay. . . . Congress has stated the unquestionable embarrassment of Government and danger to the public health in the existing condition of things. The space in Washington is necessarily monopolized in comparatively few hands, and letting portions of it is as much a business as any other. Housing is a necessary of life. All the elements of a public interest justifying some degree of public control are present. The only matter that seems to us open to debate is whether the statute goes too far. For just as there comes a point at which the police power ceases and leaves only that of eminent domain, it may be conceded that regulations of the present sort pressed to a certain height might amount to a taking without due process of law. . . .

Assuming that the end in view otherwise justified the means adopted by Congress, we have no concern of course with the question whether those means were the wisest, whether they may not cost more than they come to, or will effect the result desired. It is enough that we are not warranted in saying that legislation that has been resorted to for the same purpose all over the world, is futile or has no reasonable relation to the relief sought.

Justice McKenna:[73]   The police power has some pretense for its invocation. Regarding alone the words of its definition, it embraces power over everything under the sun, and the line that separates its legal from its illegal operation can not be easily drawn. But it must be drawn. To borrow the illustration of another, the line that separates day from night can not be easily discerned or traced, yet

---

72. Block v. Hirsh, 256 U.S. 135 (1921).
73. Block v. Hirsh, 256 U.S. 158 (1921) (McKenna, J., dissenting).

E. Regulation Versus Taking

the light of day and the darkness of night are very distinct things. And as distinct in our judgment is the puissance of the Constitution over all other ordinances of power, and as distinct are the cited cases from this case; and if they can bear the extent put upon them, what extent can be put upon the case at bar or upon the limit of the principle it declares? It is based upon the insistency of the public interest and its power. As we understand, the assertion is, that legislation can regard a private transaction as a matter of public interest. It is not possible to express the possession or exercise of more unbounded or irresponsible power.

Justice Holmes:[74]   The statute forbids the mining of anthracite coal in such way as to cause the subsidence of, among other things, any structure used as a human habitation, with certain exceptions, including among them land where the surface is owned by the owner of the underlying coal and is distant more than one hundred and fifty feet from any improved property belonging to any other person. As applied to this case the statute is admitted to destroy previously existing rights of property and contract. The question is whether the police power can be stretched so far.

Government hardly could go on if to some extent values incident to property could not be diminished without paying for every such change in the general law. As long recognized, some values are enjoyed under an implied limitation and must yield to the police power. But obviously the implied limitation must have its limits, or the contract and due process clauses are gone. One fact for consideration in determining such limits is the extent of the diminution. When it reaches a certain magnitude, in most if not in all cases there must be an exercise of eminent domain and compensation to sustain the act. So the question depends upon the particular facts. The greatest weight is given to the judgment of the legislature, but it always is open to interested parties to contend that the legislature has gone beyond its constitutional power.

The general rule at least is, that while property may be regulated to a certain extent, if regulation goes too far it will be recognized as a taking. It may be doubted how far exceptional cases, like the blowing up of a house to stop a conflagration, go — and if they go beyond the general rule, whether they do not stand as much upon tradition as upon principle. In general it is not plain that a man's misfortunes or necessities will justify his shifting the damages to his neighbor's shoulders. We are in danger of forgetting that a strong public desire to improve the public condition is not enough to warrant achieving the desire by a shorter cut than the constitutional way of paying for the change. As we already have

---

74. Pennsylvania Coal Co v. Mahon, 260 U.S. 393 (1922).

said, this is a question of degree — and therefore cannot be disposed of by general propositions. But we regard this as going beyond any of the cases decided by this Court. . . .

We assume, of course, that the statute was passed upon the conviction that an exigency existed that would warrant it, and we assume that an exigency exists that would warrant the exercise of eminent domain. But the question at bottom is upon whom the loss of the changes desired should fall. So far as private persons or communities have seen fit to take the risk of acquiring only surface rights, we cannot see that the fact that their risk has become a danger warrants the giving to them greater rights than they bought.[75]

Justice Brandeis:[76] Every restriction upon the use of property imposed in the exercise of the police power deprives the owner of some right theretofore enjoyed, and is, in that sense, an abridgment by the State of rights in property without making compensation. But restriction imposed to protect the public health, safety or morals from dangers threatened is not a taking. The restriction here in question is merely the prohibition of a noxious use. The property so restricted remains in the possession of its owner. The State does not appropriate it or make any use of it. The State merely prevents the owner from making a use which interferes with paramount rights of the public. Whenever the use prohibited ceases to be noxious, — as it may because of further change in local or social conditions, — the restriction will have to be removed and the owner will again be free to enjoy his property as heretofore.

Justice Stone:[77] Acting under the Cedar Rust Act of Virginia, defendant in error, the state entomologist, ordered the plaintiffs in error to cut down a large number of ornamental red cedar trees growing on their property, as a means of preventing the communication of a rust or plant disease with which they were infected to the apple orchards in the vicinity. . . .

. . . [T]he state was under the necessity of making a choice

---

75. In a letter to Laski, Holmes-Laski Letters 346 (Howe ed. 1963), Holmes worried:

> I fear I am out of accord for the moment with my public minded friends in another way. Frankfurter generally writes to me about any important opinions of mine and he has been silent as to the one I sent you in which Brandeis dissented [*Pennsylvania Coal*]; probably feeling an unnecessary delicacy about saying that he disagrees. Of course I understand the possibility of thinking otherwise — I could not fail to, even if Brandeis had agreed. But nevertheless when the premises are a little more emphasized, as they should have been by me, I confess to feeling as much confidence as I often do. I have always thought old Harlan's decision in Mugler v. Kansas was pretty fishy.

See also Roberts, Mining with Mr. Justice Holmes, 39 Vand. L. Rev. 287 (1986) — Eds.
76. Pennsylvania Coal Co. v. Mahon, 260 U.S. 416 (1922) (Brandeis, J., dissenting).
77. Miller v. Schoene, 276 U.S. 272 (1928).

E. Regulation versus Taking

between the preservation of one class of property and that of the other wherever both existed in dangerous proximity.... When forced to such a choice the state does not exceed its constitutional powers by deciding upon the destruction of one class of property in order to save another which, in the judgment of the legislature, is of greater value to the public. It will not do to say that the case is merely one of a conflict of two private interests and that the misfortune of apple growers may not be shifted to cedar owners by ordering the destruction of their property; for it is obvious that there may be, and that here there is, a preponderant public concern in the preservation of the one interest over the other. And where the public interest is involved preferment of that interest over the property interest of the individual, to the extent even of its destruction, is one of the distinguishing characteristics of every exercise of the police power which affects property.

Justice Clark:[78] The Town of Hempstead has enacted an ordinance regulating dredging and pit excavating on property within its limits. Appellants, who engaged in such operations prior to the enactment of the ordinance, claim that it in effect prevents them from continuing their business and therefore takes their property without due process of law in violation of the Fourteenth Amendment....

Concededly the ordinance completely prohibits a beneficial use to which the property has previously been devoted. However, such a characterization does not tell us whether or not the ordinance is unconstitutional. It is an oft-repeated truism that every regulation necessarily speaks as a prohibition. If this ordinance is otherwise a valid exercise of the town's police powers, the fact that it deprives the property of its most beneficial use does not render it unconstitutional.

Justice Brennan:[79] Appellees are engaged in the trade of Indian artifacts: several own commercial enterprises, one is employed by such an enterprise, and one is a professional appraiser. A number of the artifacts are partly composed of the feathers of currently protected birds, but these artifacts existed before the statutory protections came into force....

The regulations challenged here do not compel the surrender of the artifacts, and there is no physical invasion or restraint upon them. Rather, a significant restriction has been imposed on one means of disposing of the artifacts. But the denial of one traditional property right does not always amount to a taking. At least where an owner possesses a full "bundle" of property rights, the destruc-

---

78. Goldblatt v. Town of Hempstead, 369 U.S. 590 (1962). Counsel for the Town of Hempstead in the New York courts included one Mario Matthew Cuomo of Brooklyn, a lawyer destined for more extensive public service.
79. Andrus v. Allard, 444 U.S. 51 (1979).

tion of one "strand" of the bundle is not a taking, because the aggregate must be viewed in its entirety.

Justice Rehnquist:[80] The Hawaii Kai Marina was developed by the dredging and filling of Kuapa Pond, which was a shallow lagoon separated from Maunalua Bay and the Pacific Ocean by a barrier beach. Although under Hawaii law Kuapa Pond was private property, the Court of Appeals for the Ninth Circuit held that when petitioners converted the pond into a marina and thereby connected it to the bay, it became subject to the "navigational servitude" of the Federal Government. Thus, the public acquired a right of access to what was once petitioners' private pond....

Here, the Government's attempt to create a public right of access to the improved pond goes so far beyond ordinary regulation or improvement for navigation as to amount to a taking under the logic of Pennsylvania Coal Co. v. Mahon....

... While the consent of individual officials representing the United States cannot "estop" the United States, it can lead to the fruition of a number of expectancies embodied in the concept of "property" — expectancies that, if sufficiently important, the Government must condemn and pay for before it takes over the management of the landowner's property. In this case, we hold that the "right to exclude," so universally held to be a fundamental element of the property right, falls within this category of interests that the Government cannot take without compensation.[81]

Justice Rehnquist:[82] Here the requirement that appellants permit appellees to exercise state-protected rights of free expression and petition on shopping center property clearly does not amount to an unconstitutional infringement of appellants' property rights under the Taking Clause. There is nothing to suggest that preventing appellants from prohibiting this sort of activity will unreasonably impair the value or use of their property as a shopping center. The PruneYard is a large commercial complex that covers several city blocks, contains numerous separate business establishments, and is open to the public at large.... Appellees were orderly, and they limited their activity to the common areas of the shopping center. In these circumstances, the fact that they may have "physically invaded" appellants' property cannot be viewed as determinative.

---

80. Kaiser-Aetna v. United States, 444 U.S. 164 (1979).
81. In a dissent from the appeal dismissal of a Massachusetts case that deflected a challenge to Cambridge's rent control ordinance, Justice Rehnquist reemphasized the importance of the right to exclude. Fresh Pond Shopping Center v. Callahan, 464 U.S. 875 (1983) (Rehnquist, J., dissenting from dismissal of appeal). — Eds.
82. Pruneyard Shopping Center v. Robins, 447 U.S. 74 (1980).

E. Regulation versus Taking

Justice Powell:[83] The application of a general zoning law to particular property effects a taking if the ordinance does not substantially advance legitimate state interests, or denies an owner economically viable use of his land. The determination that governmental action constitutes a taking is, in essence, a determination that the public at large, rather than a single owner, must bear the burden of an exercise of state power in the public interest. Although no precise rule determines when property has been taken, the question necessarily requires a weighing of private and public interests....

In this case, the zoning ordinances substantially advance legitimate governmental goals. The State of California has determined that the development of local open-space plans will discourage the "premature and unnecessary conversion of open-space land to urban uses." Cal. Govt. Code Ann. §65561(b) (West Supp. 1979). The specific zoning regulations at issue are exercises of the city's police power to protect the residents of Tiburon from the ill effects of urbanization. Such governmental purposes long have been recognized as legitimate.

... The zoning ordinances benefit the appellants as well as the public by serving the city's interest in assuring careful and orderly development of residential property with provision for open-space areas. There is no indication that the appellants' 5-acre tract is the only property affected by the ordinances. Appellants therefore will share with other owners the benefits and burdens of the city's exercise of its police power. In assessing the fairness of the zoning ordinances, these benefits must be considered along with any diminution in market value that the appellants might suffer.

Justice Marshall:[84] New York law provides that a landlord must permit a cable television company to install its cable facilities upon his property. N.Y. Exec. Law §828(1) (McKinney Supp. 1981-1982). In this case, the cable installation occupied portions of appellant's roof and the side of her building....

... [W]e have long considered a physical intrusion by government to be a property restriction of an unusually serious character for purposes of the Takings Clause. Our cases further establish that when the physical intrusion reaches the extreme form of a permanent physical occupation, a taking has occurred. In such a case, "the character of the government action" not only is an important factor in resolving whether the action works a taking but also is determinative....

... [A]n owner suffers a special kind of injury when a *stranger* directly invades and occupies the owner's property.... [P]roperty

---

83. Agins v. City of Tiburon, 447 U.S. 255 (1980).
84. Loretto v. Teleprompter Manhattan CATV Corp., 458 U.S. 419 (1982).

law has long protected an owner's expectation that he will be relatively undisturbed at least in the possession of his property. To require, as well, that the owner permit another to exercise complete dominion literally adds insult to injury. Furthermore, such an occupation is qualitatively more severe than a regulation of the *use* of property, even a regulation that imposes affirmative duties on the owner, since the owner may have no control over the timing, extent, or nature of the invasion.

Justice Blackmun:[85] The right to exclude others is generally "one of the most essential sticks in the bundle of rights that are commonly characterized as property." With respect to a trade secret, the right to exclude others is central to the very definition of the property interest. Once the data that constitutes a trade secret is disclosed to others, or others are allowed to use that data, the holder of the trade secret has lost his property interest in the data. That the data retain usefulness for Monsanto even after they are disclosed — for example, as bases from which to develop new products or refine old products, as marketing and advertising tools, or as information necessary to obtain registration in foreign countries — is irrelevant to the determination of the economic impact of the EPA action on Monsanto's property right. The economic value of that property right lies in the competitive advantage over others that Monsanto enjoys by virtue of its exclusive access to the data, and disclosure or use by others of the data would destroy that competitive edge.

2. Of Bright Lines and Balancing: The Commentators Respond

In contrast to the Justices' reluctance to draw sharp distinctions, to define the boundaries of permissible regulation, generations of commentators have stepped forward to supply Holmes's "general propositions" without which particular cases could scarcely be decided at all. The dialogue that follows encompasses a spectrum of positions along, and beyond, the continuum first drawn in *Pennsylvania Coal*.

Some commentators look to the government's action and conclude that if the regulation is reasonably related to the public welfare then (short of actual physical invasion and taking) it never gives rise to a compensable taking, regardless of the extent of the property owner's loss;[86] others look to the extent of the diminution in value and conclude

---

85. Ruckelshaus v. Monsanto Co., 467 U.S. 986 (1984).
86. This position carried the day, for example, in two nineteenth-century cases. In Commonwealth v. Tewksbury, 11 Met. 55 (Mass. 1846), defendant was convicted of a misdemeanor for carrying away a quantity of gravel and sand from his own beach (the statute prohibited such conduct so as to prevent natural embankments from being broken

E. Regulation versus Taking

that if the loss is real and substantial, then it gives rise to a claim of compensable taking, regardless of the desirability of the regulation in question; still other writers posit a balancing test, a utilitarian calculus that includes all but absolutizes none of the variables, insists that each be weighed in the particular equation, but leaves the quantification to be worked out case by case.

Other commentators are not content with balancing a valid governmental regulation against the declared expectations of property owners. They insist on probing further. Granted that the governmental regulation is valid, does it matter whether the government is functioning in its role as an impartial arbitrator, or as a competing individual property owner? Does it matter whether the government is proscribing harmful activity or exacting affirmative benefits from the property owner? Are some "expectations" more worthy of recognition than others? Are some "public purposes" more public than others? These are questions that cannot be resolved on their face. The wisdom of regulations will rarely be open to judicial scrutiny; and property "expectations" are not self-validating, depending upon how fervently they are expected. If one is to go behind the mere calculus of regulations and expectations, one will need to consider other factors.[87]

---

up). Similarly, in Commonwealth v. Alger, 7 Cush. 53 (Mass. 1851), defendant was convicted for building a wharf beyond the statutory harbor lines on flats of which he was the owner. Chief Justice Shaw wrote the opinion in both cases, upholding the statutes in question as being valid police regulations, not a taking. In the latter case, he wrote:

> We think it is a settled principle, growing out of the nature of well ordered civil society, that every holder of property, however absolute and unqualified may be his title, holds it under the implied liability that his use of it may be so regulated, that it shall not be injurious to the equal enjoyment of others having an equal right to the enjoyment of their property, nor injurious to the rights of the community. . . . Rights of property, like all other social and conventional rights, are subject to such reasonable limitations in their enjoyment, as shall prevent them from being injurious, and to such reasonable restraints and regulations established by law, as the legislature, under the governing and controlling power vested in them by the constitution, may think necessary and expedient.
>
> This is very different from the right of eminent domain, the right of a government to take and appropriate private property to public use, whenever the public exigency requires it; which can be done only on condition of providing a reasonable compensation therefor. . . . [The owner] is restrained; not because the public have occasion to make the like use, or to make any use of the property, or to take any benefit or profit to themselves from it; but because it would be a noxious use, contrary to the maxim sic utere tuo, ut alienum non laedas. It is not an appropriation of the property to a public use, but the restraint of an injurious private use by the owner, and is therefore not within the principle of property taken under the right of eminent domain.

7 Cush. at 84-86.
  87. See Montesquieu, The Spirit of Laws, ch. 15:

> That we should not regulate by the principles of political law those things which depend on the principles of civil law.
>
> As men have given up their natural independence to live under political laws,

Once the threshold has been set and crossed, hard questions are raised concerning the appropriate remedy for costly regulatory improprieties. To some observers, an injunction is sufficient relief. To others, nothing short of full monetary compensation will make up for the constitutional affront. The middle positions are filled by offers of "fair" compensation and "temporary" damages.

Finally, the thorniest question of all. One may opt for the simplest of approaches (all losses are to be spread, or all valid regulations are to be enforced, come what may). Or one may see a difference in kind between regulation and taking and seek out a bright line between them (harm is controlled by regulation, whereas benefits must be sought only by a compensable taking; or, when government functions as an arbitrator, it regulates, whereas when it functions as a competitor, it must compensate). Or one may see the difference as merely one of degree and go to a balancing approach (with more or less of relevance depending on the factors one considers important). But when all is said and done, the final question remains: Is the outcome fair to the parties involved?[88]

Imagine the commentators settled around a table, each articulating in turn his or her appraisal of the takings/regulation puzzle, and bravely proffering a solution. Are the "experts" any more successful or logical than their juristic counterparts? Are the pragmatists or ideologues more convincing? Is it too late to abandon *Pennsylvania Coal* as one camp demands, given the fact that the cases that precede and follow this

---

they have given up the natural community of goods to live under the civil laws.

By the first, they acquired liberty; by the second, property. We should not decide by the laws of liberty, which, as we have already said, is only the government of the community, what ought to be decided by the laws concerning property. It is a paralogism to say that the good of the individual should give way to that of the public; this can never take place, except when the government of the community, or, in other words, the liberty of the subject is concerned; this does not affect such cases as relate to private property, because the public good consists in every one's having his property, which was given him by the civil laws, invariably preserved.

Let us, therefore, lay down a certain maxim, that whenever the public good happens to be the matter in question, it is not for the advantage of the public to deprive an individual of his property, or even to retrench the least part of it by a law, or a political regulation. In this case we should follow the rigour of the civil law, which is the Palladium of property.

Thus when the public has occasion for the estate of an individual, it ought never to act by the rigour of political law; it is here that the civil law ought to triumph, which, with the eyes of a mother, regards every individual as the whole community.

If the political magistrate would erect a public edifice, or make a new road, he must indemnify those who are injured by it; the public is in this respect like an individual who treats with an individual. It is fully enough that it can oblige a citizen to sell his inheritance, and that it can strip him of this great privilege which he holds from the civil law, . . . not being forced to alienate his possessions.

88. For more on Rawls, Michelman, and fairness, see Note, 59 Va. L. Rev. 1049-1052, 1060-1064, 1067-1068 (1973).

E. Regulation versus Taking

debate are a house of cards built on Holmes's foundation? Or would the proposed modifications of the "too far" test cause the house to topple anyway, under the weight of abstract mathematical and jurisprudential formulas? Once you complete the "transcript" of the debate, you will be in a better position to consider whether judicial allusions to these and other academic contributions help or unduly complicate the decision-making process.

a. Can We Meaningfully Distinguish between the Police Power and Eminent Domain?

Freund:[89] If we differentiate eminent domain and police power as distinct powers of government, the difference lies neither in the form nor in the purpose of taking, but in the relation which the property affected bears to the danger or evil which is to be provided against.

Under the police power, rights of property are impaired not because they become useful or necessary to the public, or because some public advantage can be gained by disregarding them, but because their free exercise is believed to be detrimental to public interest; it may be said that the state takes property by eminent domain because it is useful to the public, and under the police power because it is harmful, or as Justice Bradley put it, because "the property itself is the cause of the public detriment."

From this results the difference between the power of eminent domain and the police power, that the former recognises a right to compensation, while the latter on principle does not.

Stoebuck:[90] ... A police power regulation on land use is an eminent domain taking only when its effect is specially directed toward benefitting a governmental entity in the use of land in which that entity holds incidents of ownership. "Specially directed" ordinarily signifies that the governmental land is singled out as the sole beneficiary, or one of a select group of beneficiaries, but it does not imply that governmental officials need have actual intent to produce the benefit. Use of the phrase "holds incidents of ownership" instead of the word "owner" allows for the possibility that there might be a benefit to the government as holder of interests in land less than the fee, such as an easement or a leasehold. ...

Under the test or doctrine stated not many land-use regulations amount to takings. Most building codes, fire codes, health regula-

---

89. The Police Power, Public Policy and Constitutional Rights 546-547 (1904).
90. Police Power, Takings, and Due Process, 37 Wash. & Lee L. Rev. 1057, 1093 (1980).

tions, zoning restrictions, and environmental regulations, which together must comprise the bulk of land-use regulations, would not. Their beneficial effects are ordinarily spread widely and faintly throughout the community with some increased impact in and around the immediate area in which they are in effect. It is not the intent of the test, for example, to make governmental land an eminent domain transferee simply by its lying within or adjacent to the boundaries of a zoning district. Rather, the intent is to suggest that a regulation, to cause a taking, must have some feature or features that single out governmental ownership for benefits that do not accrue to the ownership interests of others. This eliminates the test from operating on the vast majority of regulations.

Beuscher:[91] ... It may be that the courts will identify as controlling against use of inverse condemnation, the fact that the governmental action in question was taken in a setting in which the governmental body was thinking solely in terms of regulation and had no public improvement or other activity in mind that could possibly lead to inverse liability for "takings." The courts, in short, might conclude that it is undesirable public policy to permit the purchase of compliance with unauthorized regulations and in such cases they may continue to insist that the landowner's sole remedy is an injunction against enforcement premised on a judicial finding of invalidity.

In this connection the courts may give understandable emphasis to the scope of enabling statutes, so far as concerns administrative agencies and local units of government. If the governmental "regulation" is beyond the scope of the delegated power, it should be fairly easy to refuse inverse condemnation, unless, of course, the same governmental body has clear eminent domain authority over the subject matter. Again, where delegated regulatory authority is present in the enabling act, but where the governmental body has been granted no eminent domain power for the type of interest involved, courts may find an easy out. They may conclude in this situation that the landowner's only recourse is to have the regulation declared invalid, eminent domain is not available. But the difficulty with the latter position is that most inverse condemnation holdings are *not* premised on statutory delegations of eminent domain authority but directly on the constitutional assurance of just compensation.

Sax:[92] Government as enterpriser operates in a host of areas, requiring

---

91. Some Tentative Notes on the Integration of Police Power and the Eminent Domain By the Courts: So-Called Inverse or Reverse Condemnation, 1 Urb. L. Ann. 1, 14 (1968).

92. Takings and the Police Power, 74 Yale L.J. 36, 62-63 (1964).

E. Regulation versus Taking 893

money, equipment and real estate. It maintains an army which must be fed and clothed and supplied; it builds and maintains bridges and roads and buildings, and for these it must have land and other economic resources; it operates schools and offices and must have money to staff and equip them. Unrelated to ancient and disreputable notions about governmental and proprietary functions, the concept of government in its enterprise capacity as used here describes the economic function of providing for and maintaining the material plant, whether that be the state capitol or a retail liquor store. In this capacity, government must acquire economic resources, which, by one means or another, it must get from the citizenry. It is to be noted that in the performance of this enterprise capacity, government is very much like those who function in the private sector of the economy, and indeed is in its resource-acquiring job a competitor with private enterprisers; it is a consumer of land, machines, clothing, and the like.

In addition to its enterprise capacity, in which government acquires resources for its own account, government also plays another and quite different role. It "governs." That is, it mediates the disputes of various citizens and groups within the society, and it resolves the conflict among competing and conflicting alternatives. Typically in this function it says, as between neighbors, that one fellow must cease keeping pigs in his backyard or must cease making bricks at a certain location; as between management and labor it imposes a duty of collective bargaining; as between tenant and landlord it may adjust prices or impose certain standards for health and safety. The essence of this function is that government serves only as an arbiter, defining standards to reconcile differences among the private interests in the community.

While quite different in design and function, the impact and ultimate purpose of government acting in its roles are quite similar. The impact on individual property-owners, whether the government is acting in its enterprise capacity or in its role as mediator, is the same kind of impairment of legally acquired, established economic values. And in performing both functions the government imposes upon private property for the ultimate purpose of furthering the public interest. Certainly, then, it is not urged that these functions are so sharply distinct as to present a perfect theoretical dichotomy. But it is urged that as a practical matter the distinction is real and clear enough to provide the basis for a workable rule of law.

The rule proposed here is that when economic loss is incurred as a result of government enhancement of its resource position in its enterprise capacity, then compensation is constitutionally required; it is that result which is to be characterized as a taking. But losses, however severe, incurred as a consequence of government acting merely in its arbitral capacity are to be viewed as a noncompensable exercise of the police power.

Costonis:[93] Refashioning the jurisprudential mosaic . . . leads to a four-element decisional model for the takings issue. The model's dominant element is the proposition that *a governmental incursion, physical or regulatory, under which property is taken is a presumptive, not a per se, taking.* The remaining three elements address how a reviewing court should evaluate government's efforts to overcome that presumption. The object of the model's second element, termed here the "due process-takings phase," is to determine whether government has established that the redistribution effected by the measure is fair in principle. Two questions are asked: What are the competing values advanced by the measure and by the property that it seeks to redistribute? Does the measure accommodate these values in a way that fairly mediates between the broader welfare and indemnity concerns embodied in these values? The central concern at this phase is whether government can establish a link between the use to which the affected property is devoted and the measure's purposes that qualifies the incursion as fair. If the link is not established, analysis ends because a taking will be found. Otherwise, reasoning moves to the model's third element, termed here its "pure takings phase," which considers the measure's fairness in operation: Does the measure infringe more severely upon the property taken than is required to achieve its intended goals? Shaping the analysis under both the due process-takings phase and the pure takings phase is the model's fourth element: the character of the showing that government must make to satisfy the inquiries posed in both these phases. The severity of this graduated burden depends principally upon the relative weight assigned to the specific welfare and indemnity values identified in the model's due process-takings phase.

b. When (If Ever) Is Compensation Appropriate?

Michelman:[94] A strictly utilitarian argument leading to the specific identification of "compensable" occasions would have a quasi-mathematical structure. Let us define three quantities to be known as "efficiency gains," "demoralization costs," and "settlement costs."

---

93. Presumptive and Per Se Takings: A Decisional Model for the Taking Issue, 58 N.Y.U. L. Rev. 465, 468-469 (1983). See Ross, Modeling and Formalism in Takings Jurisprudence, 61 Notre Dame L. Rev. 372 (1986).

94. Property, Utility and Fairness: Comments on the Ethical Foundations of "Just Compensation" Law, 80 Harv. L. Rev. 1165, 1214-1215 (1967).

E. Regulation versus Taking

"Efficiency gains" we define as the excess of benefits produced by a measure over losses inflicted by it, where benefits are measured by the total number of dollars which prospective gainers would be willing to pay to secure adoption, and losses are measured by the total number of dollars which prospective losers would insist on as the price of agreeing to adoption. "Demoralization costs" are defined as the total of (1) the dollar value necessary to offset disutilities which accrue to losers and their sympathizers specifically from the realization that no compensation is offered, and (2) the present capitalized dollar value of lost future production (reflecting either impaired incentives or social unrest) caused by demoralization of uncompensated losers, their sympathizers, and other observers disturbed by the thought that they themselves may be subjected to similar treatment on some other occasion. "Settlement costs" are measured by the dollar value of the time, effort, and resources which would be required in order to reach compensation settlements adequate to avoid demoralization costs. Included are the costs of settling not only the particular compensation claims presented, but also those of all persons so affected by the measure in question or similar measures as to have claims not obviously distinguishable by the available settlement apparatus.

A measure attended by positive efficiency gains is, under utilitarian ethics, prima facie desirable. But felicific calculation under the definition given for efficiency gains is imperfect because it takes no account of demoralization costs caused by a capricious redistribution, or alternatively, of the settlement costs necessary to avoid such demoralization costs. When pursuit of efficiency gains entails capricious redistribution, either demoralization costs or settlement costs must be incurred. It follows that if, for any measure, both demoralization costs and settlement costs (whichever were chosen) would exceed efficiency gains, the measure is to be rejected; but that otherwise, since either demoralization costs or settlement costs must be paid, it is the lower of these two costs which should be paid. The compensation rule which then clearly emerges is that compensation is to be paid whenever settlement costs are lower than both demoralization costs and efficiency gains. But if settlement costs, while lower than demoralization costs, exceed efficiency gains, then the measure is improper regardless of whether compensation is paid. The correct utilitarian statement, then, insofar as *the issue of compensability* is concerned, is that compensation is due whenever demoralization costs exceed settlement costs, and not otherwise.

Sax:[95] The purpose of the analysis . . . is not to permit a redistribution

---

95. Takings, Private Property and Public Rights, 81 Yale L.J. 149, 161-162, 164 (1971).

of land to achieve the most socially beneficial use, but only to put competing resource-users in a position of equality when each of them seeks to make a use that involves some imposition (spillover) on his neighbors, and those demands are in conflict. . . .

It thus becomes necessary to explain what is meant by a use of property that has a spillover or inextricable effect on other property. The first and most obvious example of this situation is that in which my use of my land results in a physical restriction of the uses that may be made of other land, such as the mining of coal which results in drainage on lower-lying land.

A second type of spillover effect is the use of a common to which another landowner has an equal right, such as the dumping of water from industrial use into a stream upon which a landowner downstream depends for water supply. . . .

There is yet a third, less physical, kind of spillover effect. It is a use of property that affects the health or well-being of others, such as the treatment of land with toxic substances that results in the death of wildlife, or a use of property that imposes an affirmative obligation on the community, such as residential development in a remote area that would require the furnishing of police protection.

Any demand of a right to use property that has spillover effects in any of the three senses described above may constitutionally be restrained, however severe the economic loss on the property owner, without any compensation being required; for each of the competing interests that would be adversely affected by such uses has, a priori, an equal right to be free of such burdens.

. . . [A]ny uses of property that do not involve such spillover effects *are* constitutionally entitled to protection, and may not be restricted without the payment of compensation. Notably, this distinction prevents a use of property from being restricted without compensation simply because a neighboring demand would provide a greater net benefit to the society. . . .

. . . The only appropriate question in determining whether or not compensation is due is whether an owner is being prohibited from making a use of his land that has no conflict-creating spillover effects. If the answer is affirmative, compensation is due for the value of land for that use.

Hagman and Misczynski:[96] Several leading commentators have concluded that if a regulation is so harsh as to constitute a taking, then the government should be given an opportunity to validate the regulation by paying compensation at the difference between the value of the property as regulated and as it could be regulated

---

96. Executive Summary, in Windfalls for Wipeouts: Land Value, Capture, and Compensation xxxiv, xxxv, xliii (1978).

E. Regulation versus Taking

constitutionally. For that compensation, the government acquires a property interest equivalent to the right to develop in excess of the regulation.

Because such an approach appears to be acquisitory, the authors take the position that the proposal might be unconstitutional, as would a holding of property by regulatory acquisition unless full compensation is paid. Moreover, if there is a distinction between these mere regulations such as downzonings (no compensation) and the regulatory acquisitions (compensation), the government will tend to clothe its regulatory acquisitions as mere regulations in order to acquire land cheaply. Therefore, in either case, the rule should be the same — namely, compensation should be paid in the form of damages and not as payment for a purchase of an interest.

The rule is particularly feasible if accompanied by windfall recapture. The absence of such recapture is a leading reason why the American Law Institute (ALI) proposal calls for acquisition of an interest. Without windfall recapture, if a landowner were paid damages and if the regulation were later removed and the development right restored, the landowner in effect would be paid twice. . . .

That any windfall for wipeout scheme will be adopted in America is problematical. The authors initially had hoped that logic would carry the day. Planners, environmentalists, do-gooders, socialists, and the like are relatively easily persuaded that windfall recapture is desirable, but not if wipeout mitigation also is provided. On the other hand, landowners, developers, private entrepreneurs, and the like all favor wipeout mitigation, but not if it is funded by windfall recapture.

Because support or opposition depends on whose ox is being gored or fed, logic may not carry the day. Those who favor windfalls for wipeouts likely will earn the distrust of both sides.

Williams, Smith, Siemon, Mandelker, and Babcock:[97] We are appalled at the marvel we are witnessing. . . . [T]he spread of "temporary taking" idea threatens to reach epidemic proportions. . . .

We have all remained comparatively silent too long. . . . We now state without equivocation that as a general proposition neither the Constitution, constitutional jurisprudence nor any decision of the United States Supreme Court commands or justifies the payment of compensation as a remedy when a land use regulation is found to be a constitutionally impermissible taking and is declared

---

97. White River Junction Manifesto, 9 Vt. L. Rev. 193, 194 (1984). See Berger and Kanner, Thoughts on The White River Junction Manifesto: A Reply to the "Gang of Five's" View on Just Compensation for Regulatory Taking of Property, 19 Loyola L.A.L. Rev. 685 (1986).

invalid as applied to a specific tract of land — even though the regulation does not involve a physical invasion or appropriation of private property.

c. How Much Compensation?

Costonis:[98] . . . [B]y casting the police and eminent domain powers as correlatives, the phrase "taking issue" is a misnomer that accords neither with logic, legal doctrine nor sound policy. With rare exception, regulatory measures said to be takings are simply measures which exceed the allowable limits of the police power. Nor does it follow that the cure to this problem lies exclusively in eminent domain, which requires, in most states, that dollar compensation be fixed by a condemnation jury according to a "highest and best use" standard. Instead, government may take one of three paths. Eminent domain is, of course, one solution, but government will seldom opt for it because it is often both fiscally impracticable and too drastic for the modest regulatory purposes at hand. It can retrench to the police power by liberalizing the overly restrictive measure, often at the cost, however, of compromising the measure's intended planning result. Or, . . . it may avoid that result by predicating the measure on the accommodation power and affording the landowner fair compensation. Less demanding than just compensation, fair compensation may be secured by dollars or by some non-dollar but market-worthy alternative; it may bypass the jury trial and other procedural complexities prescribed for eminent domain actions by state statutes and constitutions; and it is not keyed to the restricted parcel's highest and best use but to a standard based on a lesser economic return, designated in this article as the Reasonable Beneficial Use standard. . . .

Fair compensation under the accommodation power differs from the eminent domain power's just compensation in three basic respects. First, its measure is the difference between the parcel's economic return under the challenged restriction and under the Reasonable Beneficial Use standard; for just compensation, the relevant measure would be the difference between the return under the regulation and the return possible under the Allowable Use category or — through manipulation of the "reasonable probability" exception — under an even higher level. Second, fair compensation may take the form of any marketworthy alternative, whether or not monetary; just compensation, on the other hand,

---

98. "Fair" Compensation and the Accommodation Power: Antidotes for the Taking Impasse in Land Use Controversies, 75 Colum. L. Rev. 1021, 1022-1023, 1052 (1975).

E. Regulation versus Taking

would probably have to be in dollars. Finally, procedures for the award of fair compensation can be streamlined by eliminating such features as the condemnation jury and the bifurcated system, currently existing, that requires an initial declaratory action to determine whether a regulatory measure is a "taking" and then a formal eminent domain proceeding to fix the requisite compensation.

Bosselman, Callies, and Banta:[99] ... [I]n the long run the strategy that would contribute most to a more equitable resolution of the taking cases would be simply to spend more time in the drafting of regulations and the presentation of facts supporting — or opposing — them. Too often these regulations take the form of sweeping prohibitions and blanket indictments of all development simply because no one has taken the time to study the problem in depth and work out a reasonable compromise between the needs of the environment and the rights of the individuals.

Finally, state and local governments should undertake experiments with new methods to provide compensation to landowners. The system of compensable regulations proposed for the American Law Institute's Model Land Development Code is an example of such a system. Density transfer systems such as those proposed by Professor Costonis also may provide a way of furnishing landowners the equivalent of compensation.

We doubt that any of these strategies will provide an answer for all situations. It will be necessary to pick and choose a strategy or combination of strategies to deal with each set of problems as they arise. Only an approach that rejects the two extremes — stop-growth and full-speed-ahead — will provide a long range solution to the problems posed by the taking issue.

Calabresi:[100] The justification for allocation of losses on a nonfault basis which is found most often among legal writers is that if losses are broadly spread — among people and over time — they are least harmful. First, the theory runs, the real burden of a loss is smaller the more people share it. Second, the theory argues, the longer the time over which the total money burden of a loss is borne, the smaller its real burden will be.

Analogues to these views can be found in economic theory. The advantages of interpersonal loss spreading would probably be stated in terms of two propositions; (a) that taking a large sum of money from one person is more likely to result in economic dislocation, and therefore in secondary or avoidable losses, than

---

99. The Taking Issue 326-328 (1973).
100. Some Thoughts on Risk Distribution and the Law of Torts, 70 Yale L.J. 499, 517-518 (1961).

taking a series of small sums from many people, and (b) that even if the total economic dislocation is the same, many small losses are preferable to one large one, simply because people feel they suffer less if 10,000 of them lost $1 than if one loses $10,000.

While the first of these propositions is an empirical generalization not too difficult to accept, the second is in its precise terms a variant of the economist's theory of the diminishing marginal utility of money. This theory has been in substantial disfavor among modern economists. The reason for this disfavor is illustrated by recent studies which have indicated, for example, that a loss of a relatively small amount of money, if it results in a change in social status, may be nearly as significant to an individual as a much larger loss which causes an approximately equal change in his social position. On the other hand, a relatively small loss, if it can be borne without giving up certain symbols of social status — be they the house on the right street or the television set — feels infinitely smaller to people than an only slightly larger loss which does involve a change in status. While this indicates the weaknesses of such a strict utilitarian pain-pleasure analysis as the marginal utility of money theory, with its implication that a loss of $5 divided among five people necessarily hurts less than $5 on one person, it does not detract much from the basic justification for loss spreading. We need merely take an additional step and recognize that social dislocations, like economic dislocations, will occur more frequently if one person bears a heavy loss than if many people bear light ones. One can, of course, conceive of situations where the extra $1 charged to one thousand people would be one thousand straws which would break one thousand backs and ruin one thousand homes or businesses, while $1,000 charged to one person would only ruin him, albeit thoroughly. But such situations seem mildly unlikely.

The economic bases of inter-*temporal* loss spreading are not dissimilar. There is less danger of economic dislocation, and hence of secondary losses, if losses are spread over time. Social dislocations are also less likely if individuals can buy their risk-of-loss burden on a long term credit plan.

Thus, there are substantial reasons for allocating losses in ways which spread the burden over as many people and over as long a time as is possible.

d. Are We Asking the Right Questions?

Epstein:[101] [T]he dominant line of opinion — one that can again be traced to Justice Holmes in *Mahon* — is that regulation, far from

---

101. Takings: Private Property and the Power of Eminent Domain 102-104 (1985).

E. Regulation versus Taking

being a subclass of takings, is outside the scope of the eminent domain clause unless it is taken "too far." This general proposition necessarily provokes disputes at the margin. But the task here is not to determine which, if any, of those cases are wrongly decided under prevailing doctrine. Instead it is to insist that today's powerful presumption in favor of regulation has set the margin in the wrong place. The conclusive presumption should be that all regulation, whether or not compensable, falls within the eminent domain clause. . . .

. . . Where regulation of use and disposition is permitted as a matter of course, then the individuals who control the levers of government power can get what they want at reduced expenditure of their own wealth. Therefore, their willingness to take and pay for land for public use will be lessened as close substitutes are made available to them at virtually no charge. The current relaxed approach to regulation skews the incentives for political groups by making one form of state action subject to powerful constitutional control while leaving its close substitutes wholly unregulated. Once taxation, regulation, and modification of liability rules are recognized as interchangeable techniques for social control, then the full panoply of government controls over the possession, use, and disposition of property must be scrutinized under the clause. In short steps we have moved a long way from taking land for the post office.

Rose:[102] Takings jurisprudence uses two quite divergent vocabularies, each reflecting one of the two divergent concepts of property. The takings dilemma is thus not simply a confusion over legal terms, to be solved by adopting scientific policy. Like the dilemma over state action, the takings dilemma is a legal manifestation of a much deeper cultural and political argument about the civic nature of what Holmes would have called the "human animal."

This impasse is particularly unfortunate because both views of property have considerable commonsensible appeal. The argument for protecting acquisitiveness rests on the intuitive propositions that human beings act to further their own material well-being, that it is fruitless to attempt to suppress this characteristic entirely, and that the ability of individuals to act in their own best interest may have substantial social benefits. The civic argument rests on the equally intuitive propositions that any community — including one that protects private property — must rely on some moral qualities of public spiritedness and mutual forbearance in its individual members to bond the community together, and that a

---

102. *Mahon* Reconstructed: Why the Taking Issue Is Still a Muddle, 57 S. Cal. L. Rev. 561, 596-599 (1984).

democracy may be particularly dependent on these qualities because it relies not on force, but on voluntary compliance with the norms of the community....

With all due respect for Holmes, ... the author submits that there are more promising approaches to takings issues. First, takings jurisprudence could turn to ordinary language as a guide for what constitutes a taking of property. While ordinary language might not yield a principled reconciliation of the various concepts incorporated in our ideas of property, ordinary understandings do take into account the different elements we want, including the wish to protect industriousness as well as the wish to foster civic responsibility. A takings jurisprudence based on ordinary understanding can protect the expectations that most people have about their property (since, by definition, most people are aware of or share the ordinary understanding), including expectations about the risk of regulation. Ordinary understanding can simultaneously accommodate the need for civic responsibility in dealing with property, since that need is also part of ordinary understanding.

Second, takings jurisprudence should not assume that all governments are identical in takings questions and should therefore look more closely at the governmental entity doing the taking. Citizens may be protected against federal legislative takings by the Madisonian safeguards accompanying a large and diverse legislature; there may be other types of protections against takings available at the local level. A sensible jurisprudence should not assume that what constitutes a taking of property at the federal level is necessarily a taking at the local level, or vice versa.

Third, in order to deepen our jurisprudence about property and takings, we need to reassess our own traditions with respect to property.... A reassessment of past practices can help delineate the contents of ordinary understanding by revealing both the continuities and the changes in assumptions about the rights and duties entailed in property ownership. Moreover, a deeper historical understanding can also help liberate us from outmoded past practices by putting some distance between the past and the present. Ordinary practice is part of a tradition and cannot be entirely reinvented. But if some of our views about property are dysfunctional remnants, historical inquiry will help to identify them, and it will also highlight those traditional property concepts that are still valid for us.

3. Ending the Procedural Tango

From 1980 to 1986, in a series of four cases that made their way ultimately to a decision by the Supreme Court,[103] the Justices disap-

---

103. Agins v. City of Tiburon, 447 U.S. 255 (1980); San Diego Gas & Electric Co. v.

E. Regulation versus Taking

pointed an ever-growing audience of practitioners, jurists, and academics awaiting a definitive answer to the regulatory takings puzzle — that is, whether and when governmental regulation can amount to a taking that requires compensation under the fifth amendment.

The refusal, or inability, of the Court to end this stalemate resulted in more than the inevitable disagreements between federal and state courts — even within the same state.[104] More than the reputation of the Court was at issue, given the high stakes and serious politics involved in land development, particularly in states such as California and Florida, with volatile economic, demographic, and ecological environments. A curious alliance of developers, minority group advocates, libertarians, and champions of private property talked of frustrated investment-backed expectations and of exclusionary policies resulting from a refusal to compensate regulatory wrongs. To this group, Justice Brennan's attempt, in his *San Diego Gas* dissent, to compensate for regulation run amok was considered an inevitable remedy.[105] The opponents of compensation — environmentalists, planners, established homeowners, and state and local governments — raised the spectre of haphazard, rampant development and the chilling effect on protective legislation.

■ SAN DIEGO GAS & ELECTRIC CO. v. CITY OF SAN DIEGO
450 U.S. 621 (1981)

Justice BRENNAN, with whom Justice STEWART, Justice MARSHALL, and Justice POWELL join, dissenting. . . .

In 1966, appellant assembled a 412-acre parcel of land as a potential site for a nuclear power plant. At that time, approximately 116 acres of the property were zoned for industrial use, with most of the balance

---

City of San Diego, 450 U.S. 621 (1981); Williamson County Regional Planning Commission v. Hamilton Bank, 473 U.S. 172 (1985); MacDonald, Sommer & Frates v. Yolo County, 477 U.S. 340 (1986). See Justice Rehnquist's rendition of the procedural tango in First English Evangelical Lutheran Church v. County of Los Angeles, infra page 914. In defense of the Court, it should be pointed out that, while avoiding until 1987 a head-on confrontation with Holmes's "too far" language, the Justices in each case were in effect following Justice Brandeis's fourth rule of constitutional decision-making: "The Court will not pass upon a constitutional question although properly presented by the record, if there is also present some other ground upon which the case may be disposed of." Ashwander v. Tennessee Valley Authority, 297 U.S. 288, 347 (1936) (Brandeis, J., concurring).

104. Compare Martino v. Santa Clara Valley Water District, 703 F.2d 1141 (9th Cir.), cert. denied, 464 U.S. 847 (1983) (approving damages for regulatory taking) with Agins v. City of Tiburon, 25 Cal. 3d 266, 598 P.2d 25, 157 Cal. Rptr. 372 (1979), aff'd on other grounds, 447 U.S. 255 (1980) (refusing to recognize damages for taking by regulation).

105. See, e.g., Bauman, The Supreme Court, Inverse Condemnation and the Fifth Amendment: Justice Brennan Confronts the Inevitable in Land Use Controls, 15 Rutgers L.J. 15 (1983).

zoned in an agricultural holding category. In 1967, appellee city of San Diego adopted its general plan designating most of appellant's property for industrial use. In 1973, the city took three critical actions which together form the predicate of the instant litigation: it down-zoned some of appellant's property from industrial to agricultural; it incorporated a new open-space element in its plan that designated about 233 acres of appellant's land for open-space use;[1] and it prepared a report mapping appellant's property for purchase by the city for open space use, contingent on passage of a bond issue. App. 49.

Appellant filed suit in California Superior Court alleging, inter alia, a "taking" of its property by "inverse condemnation" in violation of the United States and California Constitutions,[2] and seeking compensation of over $6 million. After a nonjury trial on liability, the court held that appellee city had taken a portion of appellant's property without just compensation, thereby violating the United States and California Constitutions. A subsequent jury trial on damages resulted in a judgment of over $3 million, plus interest as of the date of the "taking," and appraisal, engineering, and attorney's fees.

The California Court of Appeal, Fourth District, affirmed, holding that there was "substantial evidence to support the court's conclusion [that] there was inverse condemnation." The California Supreme Court granted the city's petition for a hearing, but later transferred the case back to the Court of Appeal for reconsideration in light of Agins v. City of Tiburon, 24 Cal. 3d 266, 598 P. 2d 25 (1979), aff'd, 447 U.S. 255 (1980). Expressly relying on *Agins*, the Court of Appeal this time reversed the Superior Court, holding:

Unlike the person whose property is taken in eminent domain, the

---

1. The city's plan defined "open space" as "any urban land or water surface that is essentially open or natural in character, and which has appreciable utility for park and recreation purposes, conservation of land, water or other natural resources or historic or scenic purposes." App. 52, n. 3.

2. The phrase "inverse condemnation" generally describes a cause of action against a government defendant in which a landowner may recover just compensation for a "taking" of his property under the Fifth Amendment, even though formal condemnation proceedings in exercise of the sovereign's power of eminent domain have not been instituted by the government entity. Agins v. City of Tiburon, 447 U.S. 255, 258, n. 2 (1980); United States v. Clarke, 445 U.S. 253, 257 (1980). See, e.g., Cal. Civ. Proc. Code Ann. §1245.260 (West Supp. 1981). In the typical condemnation proceeding, the government brings a judicial or administrative action against the property owner to "take" the fee simple or an interest in his property; the judicial or administrative body enters a decree of condemnation and just compensation is awarded. See ibid. See generally 6 J. Sackman, Nichols' Law of Eminent Domain §24.1 (rev. 3d ed. 1980). In an "inverse condemnation" action, the condemnation is "inverse" because it is the landowner, not the government entity, who institutes the proceeding.

"Eminent domain" is the "power of the sovereign to take property for public use without the owner's consent." Id., §1.11, at 1-7. Formal proceedings initiated by the government are loosely referred to as either "eminent domain" or "condemnation" proceedings. See Agins v. City of Tiburon, supra, at 258, n. 2.

E. Regulation versus Taking

individual who is deprived of his property due to the state's exercise of its police power is not entitled to compensation.... A local entity's arbitrary unconstitutional exercise of the police power which deprives the owner of the beneficial use of his land does not require compensation; rather the party's remedy is administrative mandamus.... App. 65-66.

The California Supreme Court denied further review.

The Court today holds that the judgment below is not "final" within the meaning of 28 U.S.C. §1257 because, although the California Court of Appeal "has decided that monetary compensation is not an appropriate remedy for any taking of appellant's property that may have occurred, ... it has not decided whether any other remedy is available because *it has not decided whether any taking in fact has occurred.*" Ante, at 633 (emphasis added). With all due respect, this conclusion misreads the holding of the Court of Appeal. In faithful compliance with the instructions of the California Supreme Court's opinion in Agins v. City of Tiburon, supra, the Court of Appeal held that the city's exercise of its police power, however arbitrary or excessive, could not *as a matter of federal constitutional law* constitute a "taking" under the Fifth and Fourteenth Amendments, and therefore that there was no "taking" without just compensation in the instant case....

Since the Court of Appeal held that no Fifth Amendment "taking" had occurred, no just compensation was required. This is a classic final judgment. I therefore dissent from the dismissal of this appeal, and address the merits of the question presented.

The Just Compensation Clause of the Fifth Amendment, made applicable to the States through the Fourteenth Amendment, Webb's Fabulous Pharmacies, Inc. v. Beckwith, 449 U.S. 155, 160 (1980); see Chicago, B. & Q. R. Co. v. Chicago, 166 U.S. 226, 239, 241 (1897), states in clear and unequivocal terms: "[N]or shall private property be taken for public use, without just compensation." The question presented on the merits in this case is whether a government entity must pay just compensation when a police power regulation has effected a "taking" of "private property" for "public use" within the meaning of that constitutional provision. Implicit in this question is the corollary issue whether a government entity's exercise of its regulatory police power can ever effect a "taking" within the meaning of the Just Compensation Clause....

The principle applied in [earlier] cases has its source in Justice Holmes' opinion for the Court in Pennsylvania Coal Co. v. Mahon, 260 U.S. 393, 415 (1922), in which he stated: "The general rule at least is, that while property may be regulated to a certain extent, if regulation goes too far it will be recognized as a taking."[14] The determination of

---

14. One interpretation of the *Pennsylvania Coal* opinion insists that the word "taking"

a "taking" is "a question of degree — and therefore cannot be disposed of by general propositions." Id., at 416.[15] . . .

Police power regulations such as zoning ordinances and other land-use restrictions can destroy the use and enjoyment of property in order to promote the public good just as effectively as formal condemnation or physical invasion of property. From the property owner's point of view, it may matter little whether his land is condemned or flooded, or whether it is restricted by regulation to use in its natural state, if the effect in both cases is to deprive him of all beneficial use of it. From the government's point of view, the benefits flowing to the public from preservation of open space through regulation may be equally great as from creating a wildlife refuge through formal condemnation or increasing electricity production through a dam project that floods private property. Appellees implicitly posit the distinction that the government *intends* to take property through condemnation or physical invasion whereas it does not through police power regulations. But "the Constitution measures a taking of property not by what a State says, or by what it intends, but by what it *does*." Hughes v. Washington, 389 U.S. 290, 298 (1967) (Stewart, J., concurring) (emphasis in original); see Davis v. Newton Coal Co., 267 U.S. 292, 301 (1925). It is only logical, then, that government action other than acquisition of title, occupancy, or physical invasion can be a "taking," and therefore a *de facto* exercise of the power of eminent domain, where the effects

---

was used "metaphorically," and that the "gravamen of the constitutional challenge to the regulatory measure was that it was an invalid exercise of the police power under the due process clause, and the [case was] decided under that rubric." Fred F. French Investing Co. v. City of New York, 39 N.Y.2d, at 594, 350 N.E.2d, at 385; see also Brief for Appellees 37-38. In addition to tampering with the express language of the opinion, this view ignores the coal company's repeated claim before the Court that the Pennsylvania statute took its property without just compensation. Brief for Pennsylvania Coal Company, at 7-8, 16, 19-20, 24, 28-33; Brief for the Mahons, at 73.

15. More recent Supreme Court cases have emphasized this aspect of "taking" analysis, commenting that the Court has been unable to develop any "set formula to determine where regulation ends and taking begins," Goldblatt v. Town of Hempstead, 369 U.S. 590, 594 (1962), and that "[it] calls as much for the exercise of judgment as for the application of logic," Andrus v. Allard, 444 U.S. 51, 65 (1979). See Penn Central Transp. Co. v. New York City, 438 U.S., at 124 ("ad hoc, factual inquiries"); United States v. Central Eureka Mining Co., 357 U.S. 155, 168 (1958) ("question properly turning upon the particular circumstances of each case").

One distinguished commentator has characterized the attempt to differentiate "regulation" from "taking" as "the most haunting jurisprudential problem in the field of contemporary land-use law . . . one that may be the lawyer's equivalent of the physicist's hunt for the quark." C. Haar, Land-Use Planning 766 (3d ed. 1976). See generally id., at 766-777; Berger, A Policy Analysis of the Taking Problem, 49 N.Y.U.L. Rev. 165 (1974); Michelman, Property, Utility, and Fairness: Comments on the Ethical Foundations of "Just Compensation" Law, 80 Harv. L. Rev. 1165 (1967); Sax, Takings and the Police Power, 74 Yale L.J. 36 (1964). Another has described a 30-year series of Court opinions resulting from this case-by-case approach as a "crazy-quilt pattern." Dunham, Griggs v. Allegheny County in Perspective: Thirty Years of Supreme Court Expropriation Law, 1962 S. Ct. Rev. 63.

E. Regulation versus Taking 907

completely deprive the owner of all or most of his interest in the property.

Having determined that property may be "taken for the public use" by police power regulation within the meaning of the Just Compensation Clause of the Fifth Amendment, the question remains whether a government entity may constitutionally deny payment of just compensation to the property owner and limit his remedy to mere invalidation of the regulation instead. Appellant argues that it is entitled to the full fair market value of the property. Appellees argue that invalidation of the regulation is sufficient without payment of monetary compensation. In my view, once a court establishes that there was a regulatory "taking," the Constitution demands that the government entity pay just compensation for the period commencing on the date the regulation first effected the "taking," and ending on the date the government entity chooses to rescind or otherwise amend[19] the regulation. This interpretation, I believe, is supported by the express words and purpose of the Just Compensation Clause, as well as by cases of this Court construing it.

The language of the Fifth Amendment prohibits the "tak[ing]" of private property for "public use" without payment of "just compensation." As soon as private property has been taken, whether through formal condemnation proceedings, occupancy, physical invasion, or regulation, the landowner has *already* suffered a constitutional violation, and "'the self-executing character of the constitutional provision with respect to compensation.'" United States v. Clarke, 445 U.S. 253, 257 (1980), quoting 6 J. Sackman, Nichols' Law of Eminent Domain §25.41 (rev. 3d ed. 1980), is triggered. This Court has consistently recognized that the just compensation requirement in the Fifth Amendment is not precatory: once there is a "taking," compensation *must* be awarded....

... Invalidation unaccompanied by payment of damages would hardly compensate the landowner for any economic loss suffered during the time his property was taken.[22]

---

19. Under this rule, a government entity is entitled to amend the offending regulation so that it no longer effects a "taking." It may also choose formally to condemn the property.

22. The instant litigation is a good case in point. The trial court, on April 9, 1976, found that the city's actions effected a "taking" of appellant's property on June 19, 1973. If true, then appellant has been deprived of all beneficial use of its property in violation of the Just Compensation Clause for the past seven years.

Invalidation hardly prevents enactment of subsequent unconstitutional regulations by the government entity. At the 1974 annual conference of the National Institute of Municipal Law Officers in California, a California City Attorney gave fellow City Attorneys the following advice:

IF ALL ELSE FAILS, MERELY AMEND THE REGULATION AND START OVER AGAIN.

If legal preventive maintenance does not work, and you still receive a claim attacking the land use regulation, or if you try the case and lose, don't worry about

Moreover, mere invalidation would fall far short of fulfilling the fundamental purpose of the Just Compensation Clause. That guarantee was designed to bar the government from forcing some individuals to bear burdens which, in all fairness, should be borne by the public as a whole. When one person is asked to assume more than a fair share of the public burden, the payment of just compensation operates to redistribute that economic cost from the individual to the public at large. Because police power regulations must be substantially related to the advancement of the public health, safety, morals, or general welfare, see Village of Euclid v. Ambler Realty Co., 272 U.S. 365, 395 (1926), it is axiomatic that the public receives a benefit while the offending regulation is in effect.[23] If the regulation denies the private property owner the use and enjoyment of his land and is found to effect a "taking," it is only fair that the public bear the cost of benefits received during the interim period between application of the regulation and the government entity's rescission of it. The payment of just compensation serves to place the landowner in the same position monetarily as he would have occupied if his property had not been taken.

The fact that a regulatory "taking" may be temporary, by virtue of the government's power to rescind or amend the regulation, does not make it any less of a constitutional "taking." Nothing in the Just Compensation Clause suggests that "takings" must be permanent and irrevocable. Nor does the temporary reversible quality of a regulatory "taking" render compensation for the time of the "taking" any less obligatory. This Court more than once has recognized that temporary reversible "takings" should be analyzed according to the same constitutional framework applied to permanent irreversible "takings." For example, in United States v. Causby, at 258-259, the United States had executed a lease to use an airport for a one-year term "ending June 30, 1942, with a provision for renewals until June 30, 1967, or six

---

it. All is not lost. One of the extra "goodies" contained in the recent [California] Supreme Court case of Selby v. City of San Buenaventura, 10 C.3d 110, appears to allow the City to change the regulation in question, even after trial and judgment, make it more reasonable, more restrictive, or whatever, and everybody starts over again. . . .

See how easy it is to be a City Attorney. Sometimes you can lose the battle and still win the war. Good luck.

Longtin, Avoiding and Defending Constitutional Attacks on Land Use Regulations (Including Inverse Condemnation), in 38B NIMLO Municipal Law Review 192-193 (1975) (emphasis in original).

23. A different case may arise where a police power regulation is not enacted in furtherance of the public health, safety, morals, or general welfare so that there may be no "public use." Although the government entity may not be forced to pay just compensation under the Fifth Amendment, the landowner may nevertheless have a damages cause of action under 42 U. S. C. §1983 for a Fourteenth Amendment due process violation.

E. Regulation versus Taking

months after the end of the national emergency, whichever [was] the earlier." The Court held that the frequent low-level flights of Army and Navy airplanes over respondents' chicken farm, located near the airport, effected a "taking" of an easement on respondents' property. 328 U.S., at 266-267. However, because the flights could be discontinued by the Government at any time, the Court remanded the case to the Court of Claims: "Since on this record *it is not clear whether the easement taken is a permanent or a temporary one*, it would be premature for us to consider whether the amount of the award made by the Court of Claims was proper." Id., at 268 (emphasis added). In other cases where the Government has taken only temporary use of a building, land, or equipment, the Court has not hesitated to determine the appropriate measure of just compensation.

But contrary to appellant's claim that San Diego must formally condemn its property and pay full fair market value, nothing in the Just Compensation Clause empowers a court to order a government entity to condemn the property and pay its full fair market value, where the "taking" already effected is temporary and reversible and the government wants to halt the "taking." Just as the government may cancel condemnation proceedings before passage of title, see 6 J. Sackman, Nichols' Law of Eminent Domain §24.113, p. 24-21 (rev. 3d ed. 1980), or abandon property it has temporarily occupied or invaded, see United States v. Dow, 357 U.S. 17, 26 (1958), it must have the same power to rescind a regulatory "taking." . . .

The constitutional rule I propose requires that, once a court finds that a police power regulation has effected a "taking," the government entity must pay just compensation for the period commencing on the date the regulation first effected the "taking," and ending on the date the government entity chooses to rescind or otherwise amend the regulation. Ordinary principles determining the proper measure of just compensation, regularly applied in cases of permanent and temporary "takings" involving formal condemnation proceedings, occupations, and physical invasions, should provide guidance to the courts in the award of compensation for a regulatory "taking." As a starting point, the value of the property taken may be ascertained as of the date of the "taking." The government must inform the court of its intentions vis-à-vis the regulation with sufficient clarity to guarantee a correct assessment of the just compensation award. Should the government decide immediately to revoke or otherwise amend the regulation, it would be liable for payment of compensation only for the interim during which the regulation effected a "taking." Rules of valuation already developed for temporary "takings" may be particularly useful to the courts in their quest for assessing the proper measure of monetary relief in cases of revocation or amendment, although additional rules may need to be developed. Alternatively the government may choose formally to condemn the property, or otherwise to continue the offending regulation: in either case the action must be sustained by proper measures of just compensation.

It should be noted that the Constitution does not embody any specific procedure or form of remedy that the States must adopt.... The States should be free to experiment in the implementation of this rule, provided that their chosen procedures and remedies comport with the fundamental constitutional command. The only constitutional requirement is that the landowner must be able meaningfully to challenge a regulation that allegedly effects a "taking," and recover just compensation if it does so. He may not be forced to resort to piecemeal litigation or otherwise unfair procedures in order to receive his due....

In Agins v. City of Tiburon, 24 Cal. 3d, at 275, 598 P.2d, at 29, the California Supreme Court was "persuaded by various policy considerations to the view that inverse condemnation is an inappropriate and undesirable remedy in cases in which unconstitutional regulation is alleged." In particular, the court cited "the need for preserving a degree of freedom in land-use planning function, and the inhibiting financial force which inheres in the inverse condemnation remedy," in reaching its conclusion. Id., at 276, 598 P.2d, at 31. But the applicability of express constitutional guarantees is not a matter to be determined on the basis of policy judgments made by the legislative, executive, or judicial branches.[26] Nor can the vindication of those rights depend on the expense in doing so....

Notes

1. See Corrigan v. City of Scottsdale, 149 Ariz. 538, 720 P.2d 513, 515-517 (1986):

Article 2 §17 of the Arizona Constitution provides in part:

No private property shall be taken or damaged for public or private use

---

26. Even if I were to concede a role for policy considerations, I am not so sure that they would militate against requiring payment of just compensation. Indeed, land-use planning commentators have suggested that the threat of financial liability for unconstitutional police power regulations would help to produce a more rational basis of decisionmaking that weighs the costs of restrictions against their benefits. Dunham, From Rural Enclosure to Re-Enclosure of Urban Land, 35 N.Y.U. L. Rev. 1238, 1253-1254 (1960). Such liability might also encourage municipalities to err on the constitutional side of police power regulations, and to develop internal rules and operating procedures to minimize overzealous regulatory attempts. Cf. Owen v. City of Independence, 445 U.S. 622, 651-652 (1980). After all, if a policeman must know the Constitution, then why not a planner? In any event, one may wonder as an empirical matter whether the threat of just compensation will greatly impede the efforts of planners. Cf. id., at 656.

E. Regulation versus Taking

without just compensation having first been made . . . [and] until full compensation therefor be first made in money, or ascertained and paid into court for the owner, irrespective of any benefit from any improvement 'proposed by such corporation, which compensation shall be ascertained by a jury. . . .

This provision, like the Fifth Amendment, prohibits a taking of property without just compensation but unlike the Fifth Amendment, specifically requires compensation for a taking to be made by a payment of money in a judicially determined amount. In the instant case, the court of appeals held and we agree that the Hillside Ordinance does "constitute a taking of property for which just compensation must be made." Corrigan v. City of Scottsdale, 149 Ariz. at 565, 720 P.2d at 540. . . . We believe that once a taking is found, the Arizona Constitution mandates the payment of money as damages for any injury suffered. We agree with the simple logic expressed by Justice Brennan in his San Diego Gas & Electric v. City of San Diego dissent. . . .

We are not alone in holding that a landowner may recover damages for a temporary taking by zoning. In a case where the plaintiff-landowner's Waterway Development Permit application was denied because the city "sought to impose a servitude upon the property to preserve 'the natural and traditional character of the land and waterway'", the Texas Supreme Court stated, "[t]here was no suggestion that government may take or hold another's property without paying for it, just because the land is pretty. Our conclusion is that the City of Austin was liable in damages to the plaintiffs." City of Austin v. Teague, 570 S.W.2d 389, 394 (Tx. 1978).

In New Jersey, it has been flatly held that "[t]emporary takings are compensable." Sheerr v. Township of Evesham, 184 N.J. Super. 11, 445 A.2d 46, 73 (1982). . . .

More significantly, in a case very similar to the one before us the New Hampshire Supreme Court not only allowed damages for a temporary taking but also reasonable attorneys' fees and double costs. Burrows v. City of Keene, 121 N.H. at 601-602, 432 A.2d at 22. In *Burrows,* the city not only failed to approve the plaintiff's subdivision plans but further, as in this case, zoned 109 acres of the plaintiff's land into a conservation area. . . .

2. See Fulton, A New Era for Private Property Rights, Cal. Law., Nov. 1987, at 27.

Over the past few years, several state courts — including those in Texas, New Hampshire, Wisconsin, North Dakota, Oregon and Arizona — have . . . ordered trials where landowners have alleged a permanent or temporary taking by regulation.

The ultimate outcome of these legal disputes has varied widely. In some cases, compensation has been paid for a temporary taking, even though the regulation was subsequently changed. But because of the short duration of these takings, the amounts have been small, in the range of

$30,000 to $50,000. In one Oregon case, the state Supreme Court ordered a trial on the taking issue (Suess Builders Co. v. Beaverton (Or 1982) 656 P.2d 306), but the landowner went home empty-handed because he failed to prove a taking had occurred.

More common, however, is a . . . settlement, in which the city chooses to buy the land rather than risk damages at a trial. Since buying land is costly, a coalition of environmental groups is trying to get on next year's ballot a $770 million bond issue that would help California communities buy environmentally sensitive land. Some environmental advocates say the money could be used to handle — or even avert — takings claims, particularly along the coast.

3. Unless the disconcerting dance around the issues was to continue, the Court seemed to have three options: (1) decide that regulation, perhaps even temporary decision-making, may under certain circumstances amount to a fifth amendment taking that requires compensation; (2) decide that regulation, a police power function, can never amount to a taking in the eminent domain sense, but might, under due process analysis, be invalidated; or (3) decide not to decide this issue, until the Justices have had the chance to observe a significant amount of state experimentation with options (1) and (2).

The Court's next two attempts were equally unsatisfactory to those awaiting a firm answer. In MacDonald, Sommer & Frates v. Yolo County, 447 U.S. 340, 344, 350-351 (1986), appellant's tentative subdivision map was rejected by the Yolo County Planning Commission owing to concerns over public access, sewer service, police protection, and water service. Appellant's actions for declaratory judgment and monetary relief alleged that "'none of the beneficial uses' allowed even for agricultural land would be suitable."

The Court was not ready to hear the takings claim:

[A] court cannot determine whether a municipality has failed to provide "just compensation" until it knows what, if any, compensation the responsible administrative body intends to provide. . . .

. . . Our cases uniformly reflect an insistence on knowing the nature and extent of permitted development before adjudicating the constitutionality of the regulations that purport to limit it. . . . Most recently, in Williamson Planning Comm'n v. Hamilton Bank [, 473 U.S. 172 (1985)], we held that the developer's failure either to seek variances that would have allowed it to develop the property in accordance with its proposed plat, or to avail itself of an available and facially adequate state procedure by which it might obtain "just compensation," meant that its regulatory taking claim was premature.

Here, in comparison to the situations of the property owners in [*Agins, San Diego Gas,* and *Hamilton Bank*], appellant has submitted one subdivision proposal and has received the Board's response thereto. Nevertheless, appellant still has yet to receive the Board's "final, definitive

E. Regulation versus Taking 913

position regarding how it will apply the regulation at issue to the particular land in question." Williamson Planning Comm'n v. Hamilton Bank, 473 U.S., at 191.

Given the financial, social, and jurisprudential implications — and the court's unsatisfactory record up to and beyond *San Diego Gas* — the burden was on the Court either to render a substantive decision or to state once and for all that, contrary to previous assertions and implications, the Justices would not address this central question of American land-use law. In 1987, six Justices finally settled on the first option.

■ FIRST ENGLISH EVANGELICAL LUTHERAN CHURCH OF GLENDALE v. COUNTY OF LOS ANGELES
107 S. Ct. 2378 (1987)

Chief Justice REHNQUIST delivered the opinion of the Court. . . .

In 1957, appellant First English Evangelical Lutheran Church purchased a 21-acre parcel of land in a canyon along the banks of the Middle Fork of Mill Creek in the Angeles National Forest. The Middle Fork is the natural drainage channel for a watershed area owned by the National Forest Service. Twelve of the acres owned by the church are flat land, and contained a dining hall, two bunkhouses, a caretaker's lodge, an outdoor chapel, and a footbridge across the creek. The church operated on the site a campground, known as "Lutherglen," as a retreat center and a recreational area for handicapped children.

In July 1977, a forest fire denuded the hills upstream from Lutherglen, destroying approximately 3,860 acres of the watershed area and creating a serious flood hazard. Such flooding occurred on February 9 and 10, 1978, when a storm dropped 11 inches of rain in the watershed. The runoff from the storm overflowed the banks of the Mill Creek, flooding Lutherglen and destroying its buildings.

In response to the flooding of the canyon, appellee County of Los Angeles adopted Interim Ordinance No. 11,855 in January 1979. The ordinance provided that "[a] person shall not construct, reconstruct, place or enlarge any building or structure, any portion of which is, or will be, located within the outer boundary lines of the interim flood protection area located in Mill Creek Canyon. . . ." The ordinance was effective immediately because the county determined that it was "required for the immediate preservation of the public health and safety. . . ." The interim flood protection area described by the ordinance included the flat areas on either side of Mill Creek on which Lutherglen had stood.

The church filed a complaint in the Superior Court of California a little more than a month after the ordinance was adopted. As subsequently amended, the complaint alleged two claims against the county and the Los Angeles County Flood Control District. The first alleged that the defendants were liable under Cal. Gov't Code Ann. §835 (West 1980) for dangerous conditions on their upstream properties that contributed to the flooding of Lutherglen. As a part of this claim, appellant also alleged that "Ordinance No. 11,855 denies [appellant] all use of Lutherglen." The second claim sought to recover from the Flood District in inverse condemnation and in tort for engaging in cloud seeding during the storm that flooded Lutherglen. Appellant sought damages under each count for loss of use of Lutherglen. The defendants moved to strike the portions of the complaint alleging that the county's ordinance denied all use of Lutherglen, on the view that the California Supreme Court's decision in Agins v. Tiburon, 24 Cal. 3d 266, 157 Cal. Rptr. 372, 598 P.2d 25 (1979), aff'd on other grounds, 447 U.S. 255 (1980), rendered the allegation "entirely immaterial and irrelevant[, with] no bearing upon any conceivable cause of action herein." See Cal. Civ. Proc. Code Ann. §436 (West Supp. 1987) ("The court may . . . strike out any irrelevant, false, or improper matter inserted in any pleading").

In Agins v. Tiburon, supra, the Supreme Court of California decided that a landowner may not maintain an inverse condemnation suit in the courts of that State based upon a "regulatory" taking. 24 Cal. 3d, at 275-277, 157 Cal. Rptr., at 376-378, 598 P.2d, at 29-31. In the court's view, maintenance of such a suit would allow a landowner to force the legislature to exercise its power of eminent domain. Under this decision, then, compensation is not required until the challenged regulation or ordinance has been held excessive in an action for declaratory relief or a writ of mandamus and the government has nevertheless decided to continue the regulation in effect. Based on this decision, the trial court in the present case granted the motion to strike the allegation that the church had been denied all use of Lutherglen. It explained that "a careful re-reading of the *Agins* case persuades the Court that when an ordinance, even a non-zoning ordinance, deprives a person of the total use of his lands, his challenge to the ordinance is by way of declaratory relief or possibly mandamus." Because the appellant alleged a regulatory taking and sought only damages, the allegation that the ordinance denied all use of Lutherglen was deemed irrelevant.

On appeal, the California Court of Appeal read the complaint as one seeking "damages for the uncompensated taking of all of Lutherglen by County Ordinance No. 11,855. . . ." It too relied on the California Supreme Court's decision on *Agins* in rejecting the cause of action, declining appellant's invitation to reevaluate *Agins* in light of this Court's opinions in San Diego Gas & Electric Co. v. San Diego, 450 U.S. 621 (1981). The court found itself obligated to follow *Agins* "because the

E. Regulation versus Taking 915

United States Supreme Court has not yet ruled on the question of whether a state may constitutionally limit the remedy for a taking to nonmonetary relief. . . ." It accordingly affirmed the trial court's decision to strike the allegations concerning appellee's ordinance. The Supreme Court of California denied review. . . .

. . . Appellant asks us to hold that the Supreme Court of California erred in Agins v. Tiburon in determining that the Fifth Amendment, as made applicable to the States through the Fourteenth Amendment, does not require compensation as a remedy for "temporary" regulatory takings — those regulatory takings which are ultimately invalidated by the courts. Four times this decade, we have considered similar claims and have found ourselves for one reason or another unable to consider the merits of the *Agins* rule. See MacDonald, Sommer & Frates v. Yolo County, 447 U.S. 340 (1986); Williamson County Regional Planning Comm'n v. Hamilton Bank, 473 U.S. 172 (1985); San Diego Gas & Electric Co., supra; Agins v. Tiburon, supra. For the reasons explained below, however, we find the constitutional claim properly presented in this case, and hold that on these facts the California courts have decided the compensation question inconsistently with the requirements of the Fifth Amendment.

I

Concerns with finality left us unable to reach the remedial question in the earlier cases where we have been asked to consider the rule of *Agins*. In each of these cases, we concluded either that regulations considered to be in issue by the state court did not effect a taking, Agins v. Tiburon, supra, 24 Cal. 3d, at 263, 157 Cal. Rptr. 372, 598 P.2d 25, or that the factual disputes yet to be resolved by state authorities might still lead to the conclusion that no taking had occurred. *MacDonald, Sommer & Frates; Williamson County; San Diego Gas & Electric Co.* Consideration of the remedial question in those circumstances, we concluded, would be premature.

The posture of the present case is quite different. Appellant's complaint alleged that "Ordinance No. 11,855 denies [it] all use of Lutherglen," and sought damages for this deprivation. In affirming the decision to strike this allegation, the Court of Appeal assumed that the complaint sought "damages for the uncompensated *taking* of all use of Lutherglen by County Ordinance No. 11,855." It relied on the California Supreme Court's *Agins* decision for the conclusion that "the remedy for a *taking* [is limited] to nonmonetary relief. . . ." The disposition of the case on these grounds isolates the remedial question for our consideration. . . . The constitutional question pretermitted in our earlier cases is therefore squarely presented here.[6]

---

6. Our cases have also required that one seeking compensation must "seek compen-

We reject appellee's suggestion that, regardless of the state court's treatment of the question, we must independently evaluate the adequacy of the complaint and resolve the takings claim on the merits before we can reach the remedial question. However "cryptic" — to use appellee's description — the allegations with respect to the taking were, the California courts deemed them sufficient to present the issue. We accordingly have no occasion to decide whether the ordinance at issue actually denied appellant all use of its property or whether the county might avoid the conclusion that a compensable taking had occurred by establishing that the denial of all use was insulated as a part of the State's authority to enact safety regulations. These questions, of course, remain open for decision on the remand we direct today. We now turn to the question of whether the Just Compensation Clause requires the government to pay for "temporary" regulatory takings.

II . . .

. . . [A] governmental body may acquiesce in a judicial declaration that one of its ordinances has effected an unconstitutional taking of property; the landowner has no right under the Just Compensation Clause to insist that a "temporary" taking be deemed a permanent taking. But we have not resolved whether abandonment by the government requires payment of compensation for the period of time during which regulations deny a landowner all use of his land.

In considering this question, we find substantial guidance in cases where the government has only temporarily exercised its right to use private property. . . .

These cases reflect the fact that "temporary" takings which, as here, deny a landowner all use of his property, are not different in kind from permanent takings, for which the Constitution clearly requires compensation. Cf. *San Diego Gas & Electric Co.*, 450 U.S., at 657 (Brennan, J., dissenting) ("Nothing in the Just Compensation Clause suggests that 'takings' must be permanent and irrevocable"). It is axiomatic that the Fifth Amendment's just compensation provision is "designed to bar Government from forcing some people alone to bear public burdens which, in all fairness and justice, should be borne by the public as a whole." Armstrong v. United States, 364 U.S., at 49. In the present case the interim ordinance was adopted by the county of Los Angeles in January 1979, and became effective immediately. Appellant filed

---

sation through the procedures the State has provided for doing so" before the claim is ripe for review. Williamson County Regional Planning Comm'n v. Hamilton Bank, 473 U.S. 172, 194 (1985). It is clear that appellant met this requirement. Having assumed that a taking occurred, the California court's dismissal of the action establishes that "the inverse condemnation procedure is unavailable. . . ." Id., at 197. The compensation claim is accordingly ripe for our consideration.

E. Regulation versus Taking

suit within a month after the effective date of the ordinance and yet when the Supreme Court of California denied a hearing in the case on October 17, 1985, the merits of appellant's claim had yet to be determined. The United States has been required to pay compensation for leasehold interests in shorter duration than this. The value of a leasehold interest in property for a period of years may be substantial, and the burden on the property owner in extinguishing such an interest for a period of years may be great indeed. Where this burden results from governmental action that amounted to a taking, the Just Compensation Clause of the Fifth Amendment requires that the government pay the landowner for the value of the use of the land during this period. Cf. United States v. Causby, 328 U.S., at 261. ("It is the owner's loss, not the taker's gain, which is the measure of the value of the property taken"). Invalidation of the ordinance or its successor ordinance after this period of time, though converting the taking into a "temporary" one, is not a sufficient remedy to meet the demands of the Just Compensation Clause. . . .

Nothing we say today is intended to abrogate the principle that the decision to exercise the power of eminent domain is a legislative function, "'for Congress and Congress alone to determine.'" Hawaii Housing Authority v. Midkiff, 467 U.S. 229, 240 (1984), quoting Berman v. Parker, 348 U.S. 26, 33 (1954). Once a court determines that a taking has occurred, the government retains the whole range of options already available — amendment of the regulation, withdrawal of the invalidated regulation, or exercise of eminent domain. . . . We merely hold that where the government's activities have already worked a taking of all use of property, no subsequent action by the government can relieve it of the duty to provide compensation for the period during which the taking was effective.

We also point out that the allegation of the complaint which we treat as true for purposes of our decision was that the ordinance in question denied appellant all use of its property. We limit our holding to the facts presented, and of course do not deal with the quite different questions that would arise in the case of normal delays in obtaining building permits, changes in zoning ordinances, variances, and the like which are not before us. We realize that even our present holding will undoubtedly lessen to some extent the freedom and flexibility of land-use planners and governing bodies of municipal corporations when enacting land-use regulations. But such consequences necessarily flow from any decision upholding a claim of constitutional right; many of the provisions of the Constitution are designed to limit the flexibility and freedom of governmental authorities and the Just Compensation Clause of the Fifth Amendment is one of them. As Justice Holmes aptly noted more than 50 years ago, "a strong public desire to improve the public condition is not enough to warrant achieving the desire by a shorter cut than the constitutional way of paying for the change." Pennsylvania Coal Co. v. Mahon, 260 U.S., at 416.

Here we must assume that the Los Angeles County ordinances have denied appellant all use of its property for a considerable period of years, and we hold that invalidation of the ordinance without payment of fair value for the use of the property during this period of time would be a constitutionally insufficient remedy. The judgment of the California Court of Appeals is therefore reversed, and the case is remanded for further proceedings not inconsistent with this opinion.

It is so ordered.

Justice STEVENS, . . . dissenting.

One thing is certain. The Court's decision today will generate a great deal of litigation. Most of it, I believe, will be unproductive. But the mere duty to defend the actions that today's decision will spawn will undoubtedly have a significant adverse impact on the land-use regulatory process. The Court has reached out to address an issue not actually presented in this case, and has then answered that self-imposed question in a superficial and, I believe, dangerous way.

Four flaws in the Court's analysis merit special comment. First, the Court unnecessarily and imprudently assumes that appellant's complaint alleges an unconstitutional taking of Lutherglen. Second, the Court distorts our precedents in the area of regulatory takings when it concludes that all ordinances which would constitute takings if allowed to remain in effect permanently, necessarily also constitute takings if they are in effect for only a limited period of time. Third, the Court incorrectly assumes that the California Supreme Court has already decided that it will never allow a state court to grant monetary relief for a temporary regulatory taking, and then uses that conclusion to reverse a judgment which is correct under the Court's own theories. Finally, the Court errs in concluding that it is the Takings Clause, rather than the Due Process Clause, which is the primary constraint on the use of unfair and dilatory procedures in the land-use area. . . .

There is no dispute about the proposition that a regulation which goes "too far" must be deemed a taking. See Pennsylvania Coal Co. v. Mahon, 260 U.S. 393, 415 (1922). When that happens, the Government has a choice: it may abandon the regulation or it may continue to regulate and compensate those whose property it takes. In the usual case, either of these options is wholly satisfactory. Paying compensation for the property is, of course, a constitutional prerogative of the sovereign. Alternatively, if the sovereign chooses not to retain the regulation, repeal will, in virtually all cases, mitigate the overall effect of the regulation so substantially that the slight diminution in value that the regulation caused while in effect cannot be classified as a taking of property. We may assume, however, that this may not always be the case. There may be some situations in which even the temporary

E. Regulation versus Taking

existence of a regulation has such severe consequences that invalidation or repeal will not mitigate the damage enough to remove the "taking" label. This hypothetical situation is what the Court calls a "temporary taking." But, contrary to the Court's implications, the fact that a regulation would constitute a taking if allowed to remain in effect permanently is by no means dispositive of the question whether the effect that the regulation has already had on the property is so severe that a taking occurred during the period before the regulation was invalidated. . . .

In my opinion, the question whether a "temporary taking" has occurred should not be answered by simply looking at the reason a temporary interference with an owner's use of his property is terminated. Litigation challenging the validity of a land-use restriction gives rise to a delay that is just as "normal" as an administrative procedure seeking a variance or an approval of a controversial plan.[12] Just because a plaintiff can prove that a land-use restriction would constitute a taking if allowed to remain in effect permanently does not mean that he or she can also prove that its temporary application rose to the level of a constitutional taking. . . .

There is, of course, a possibility that land-use planning, like other forms of regulation, will unfairly deprive a citizen of the right to develop his property at the time and in the manner that will best serve his economic interests. The "regulatory taking" doctrine announced in *Pennsylvania Coal* places a limit on the permissible scope of land-use restrictions. In my opinion, however, it is the Due Process Clause rather than that doctrine that protects the property owner from improperly motivated, unfairly conducted, or unnecessarily protracted governmental decisionmaking. Violation of the procedural safeguards mandated by the Due Process Clause will give rise to actions for damages under 42 U.S.C. §1983, but I am not persuaded that delays in the development of property that are occasioned by fairly conducted administrative or judicial proceedings are compensable, except perhaps in the most unusual circumstances. On the contrary, I am convinced that the public interest in having important governmental decisions made in an orderly, fully informed way amply justifies the temporary burden on the citizen that is the inevitable by-product of democratic government. . . .

The policy implications of today's decision are obvious and, I fear, far reaching. Cautious local officials and land-use planners may avoid taking any action that might later be challenged and thus give rise to a

---

12. States may surely provide a forum in their courts for review of general challenges to zoning ordinances and other regulations. Such a procedure then becomes part of the "normal" process. Indeed, when States have set up such procedures in their courts, we have required resort to those processes before considering takings claims. See Williamson, Planning Comm'n v. Hamilton Bank, 473 U.S. 172 (1985).

damage action. Much important regulation will never be enacted,[17] even perhaps in the health and safety area. Were this result mandated by the Constitution, these serious implications would have to be ignored. But the loose cannon the Court fires today is not only unattached to the Constitution, but it also takes aim at a long line of precedents in the regulatory takings area. It would be the better part of valor simply to decide the case at hand instead of igniting the kind of litigation explosion that this decision will undoubtedly touch off.

I respectfully dissent.[106]

---

17. It is no answer to say that "[a]fter all, if a policeman must know the Constitution, then why not a planner?" San Diego Gas & Electric Co. v. San Diego, 450 U.S. 621, 661, n. 26 (1981) (Brennan, J., dissenting). To begin with, the Court has repeatedly recognized that it itself cannot establish any objective rules to assess when a regulation becomes a taking. See Hodel v. Irving, 107 S. Ct. 2076 (1987); Andrus v. Allard, 444 U.S. 51, 65 (1979); *Penn Central*, 438 U.S., at 123-124. How then can it demand that land planners do any better? However confusing some of our criminal procedure cases may be, I do not believe they have been as open-ended and standardless as our regulatory takings cases are. As one commentator concluded: "The chaotic state of taking law makes it especially likely that availability of the damages remedy will induce land-use planning officials to stay well back of the invisible line that they dare not cross." Johnson, Compensation for Invalid Land-Use Regulations, 15 Ga. L. Rev. 559, 594 (1981); see also Sallet, The Problem of Municipal Liability for Zoning and Land-Use Regulation, 31 Cath. U.L. Rev. 465, 478 (1982); Charles v. Diamond, 41 N.Y.2d 318, 331-332, 392 N.Y.S.2d 594, 604, 360 N.E.2d 1295, 1305 (1977); Allen v. City and County of Honolulu, 58 Haw. 432, 439, 571 P.2d 328, 331 (1977).

Another critical distinction between police activity and land-use planning is that not every missed call by a policeman gives rise to civil liability; police officers enjoy individual immunity for actions taken in good faith. See Harlow v. Fitzgerald, 457 U.S. 800 (1982); Davis v. Scherer, 468 U.S. 183 (1984). Moreover, municipalities are not subject to civil liability for police officers' routine judgment errors. See Monell v. New York City Dept. of Social Services, 436 U.S. 658 (1978). In the land regulation context, however, I am afraid that any decision by a competent regulatory body may establish a "policy or custom" and give rise to liability after today.

106. Consider these immediate responses to the decision:

> The justices of the Supreme Court got up the courage to stick their toes in the waters of private property rights, and came up grinning. It wasn't too hot for comfort after all to use the Constitution to rescue a property owner from a government edict. . . .
>
> Ownership in America is not a privilege, but a right. It has made possible the growth from agrarian poverty to industrial predominance. The Third World is only now learning that broad-based economic development is impossible without a rule of law that limits government expropriation.
>
> The takings clause is where political philosophy and pragmatism merge. The country not only does good by protecting private property, it also does well.

Wall St. J., June 11, 1987.

> The Supreme Court's decision yesterday on controls on land use may have a dampening effect on zoning, planning, landmarks preservation and environmental conservation in New York City.
>
> Indeed, by late afternoon a group of Staten Island property owners were planning to demand compensation for any parcels that are designated as freshwater wetlands by the New York State Department of Environmental Conservation. . . .
>
> Property owners in the Adirondack Park were celebrating yesterday, in their belief that the Supreme Court case would result in enormous compensation for

E. Regulation versus Taking

Notes

1. According to Michael Berger, the landowner's council in *First English*, one and one-half years after the Justices' holding, the case was still in the brief-argument-rebrief stages before the California Court of Appeal. See also Berger, Happy Birthday, Constitution: The Supreme Court Establishes New Ground Rules for Land-Use Planning, 20 Urb. Law. 735 (1988).

2. In an early post-*First English* holding, the court in Wheeler v. City of Pleasant Grove, 833 F.2d 267 (11th Cir. 1987), utilized the following calculus for determining damages to landowners and developers injured by a referendum outlawing construction of an apartment complex for which a building permit had already been secured:

> In the case of a temporary regulatory taking, the landowner's loss takes the form of an injury to the property's potential for producing income or an expected profit. The landowner's compensable interest, therefore, is the return on the portion of the fair market value that is lost as a result of the regulatory restriction. Accordingly, the landowner should be awarded the market rate return computed over the period of the temporary taking on the difference between the property's fair market value without the regulatory restriction and its fair market value with the restriction. See Nemmers v. City of Dubuque, 764 F.2d 502, 505 (8th Cir. 1985). Under this approach, the landowner recovers what he lost. To award any affected party additional compensation for lost profits or increased costs of development would be to award double recovery: the relevant fair market values by definition reflect a market estimation of future profits and development costs with respect to the particular property at issue.

What do you make of this formula contrasted with the district court's finding that, because the value of the property after the invalid regulation was lifted exceeded the value before the referendum, the landowners "had suffered no compensable loss"?

---

zoning measures that the state enacted in 1973.

"It means the state owes us hundreds of millions of dollars, perhaps more than a billion," said Anthony D'Elia, executive director of the Local Government Review Board, which represents county legislatures and towns within the park.

But Robert Glennon, counsel for the Adirondack Park Agency, said, "All it means is that their claims will go to trial."

James Fischer, president of the National Association of Homebuilders, said: "It is the most important land-use decision in the United States since 1926, when the Court first declared zoning constitutional. And it is recognition by our nation's highest Court that under the Constitution landowners are entitled to compensation when their land is made useless by zoning, planning, environmental and other land-use restrictions."

N.Y. Times, June 10, 1987. — EDS.

Consider Professor Epstein's position:

> Landowners may urge that the damages for interim zoning be determined by the difference in the interim period between the present discounted rental value of the unregulated land and the discounted rental value of the land under regulation. In fact the correct measure would seem to be the present discounted value of the land subject to the most extensive *permissible* regulation and its present discounted value under the interim system in place.

Takings: Descent and Resurrection, 1987 Sup. Ct. Rev. 1, 31 n.83. See also Mixon, Compensation Claims Against Local Governments for Excessive Land-Use Regulations, 20 Urb. Law. 675 (1988).

3. Do the significant (and time-consuming) procedural barriers posed by the Court's earlier tries at the takings puzzle mean that ripe, suitable cases will be few and far between? Is it prudent or paranoid for the city attorney to view every denial of a rezoning as a potential fifth amendment case waiting to be filed? What safeguards would you recommend for local planners and decision-makers in light of *First English* and Justice Scalia's heightened scrutiny in *Nollan*? In other words, how can planners (and attorneys) get to "know the Constitution" in this area?[107] For the response of the federal government, see Governmental Actions and Interference with Constitutionally Protected Property Rights, Exec. Order No. 12,630, 53 Fed. Reg. 8859 (1988): "The purpose of this Order is to assist Federal departments and agencies in undertaking . . . reviews and in proposing, planning, and implementing actions with due regard for the constitutional protections provided by the Fifth Amendment and to reduce the risk of undue or inadvertant burdens on the public fisc resulting from lawful governmental action."

For early commentary on *First English*, see Siemon and Larson, The Taking Clause Trilogy: The Beginning of the End?, 33 Wash. U.J. Urb. & Contemp. Law 169 (1988); Peterson, Land Use Regulatory "Takings" Revisited, 39 Hastings L.J. 335 (1988).

4. Though certainly less notorious than the "Big Three" regulatory takings cases from the October 1986 Term — *Keystone, Nollan*, and *First English* — a fourth case, Hodel v. Irving, 107 S. Ct. 2076 (1987), presents a much more intricate (even obscure) set of facts. The Court's opinion, penned by Justice O'Connor, invalidated §207 of the Indian Land Consolidation Act of 1983, for that provision substituted admin-

---

107. There's always the seminar taught by "leading land use planning and development law experts." One workshop, entitled The New Realities of Land Use and the Constitution: Staying out of Court, Winning in Court (Winter 1989), features sessions on "Which Land Use Regulatory Techniques Are Constitutional?," "The New Pillars of Constitutional Takings Law," and "Calculating Monetary Damages for Temporary Takings."

E. Regulation versus Taking

istratively convenient escheat for constitutionally protected descent and devise of certain undivided fractional interests in allotted Native American lands.

5. The Rehnquist Court passed up an opportunity to invalidate an elaborate rent-control scheme in Pennell v. City of San Jose, 108 S. Ct. 849 (1988). Writing for a majority of six, the Chief Justice rejected a facial challenge to the ordinance and deemed the regulatory takings assertion premature:

> [T]he mere fact that a Hearing Officer is enjoined to consider hardship to the tenant in fixing a landlord's rent, without any showing in a particular case as to the consequences of that injunction in the ultimate determination of the rent, does not present a sufficiently concrete factual setting for the adjudication of the takings claim appellants raise here.

Reagan appointees Scalia and O'Connor, in dissent, were more anxious to wield the fifth amendment axe against the redistributive scheme, noting "the unfairness of making one citizen pay, in some fashion other than taxes, to remedy a social problem that is none of his creation."

Only the foolhardy would aver that *First English* will quiet the regulatory takings debate; the Court solidified the position taken in *Pennsylvania Coal* but left to later decisions the task of filling in the details on this complex constitutional canvas.

Still, the topic of inquiry has shifted a bit. The Court — in recognizing a monetary remedy for temporary regulatory takings — will force counsel and clients to consider seriously what makes up just compensation. Governmental bodies will need to structure their plans and regulations more carefully and creatively, to use incentives in place of bald assertions of police power. As the next chapter suggests, officials in all strata of governance have a great deal of experience to draw on in crafting these post-*First English* programs and policies.

VIII

Government as Joint Venturer: Evolution and Evaluation of Public/Private Partnerships

Laissez-faire myths to the contrary, government involvement in the formation and operation of private business has a history as old as the Republic. The process of incorporation, the awarding of exclusive franchises, the provision of tax incentives, and the delegation of the power of eminent domain are all pre-Civil War attributes of the American polity.[1] As discussed in Chapter VII, the eminent domain clause often facilitated economic development, particularly when that development was tied to technological innovations such as steam power and railroad and airline transportation. Moreover, as is often the case

---

1. See, e.g., Handlin & Handlin, Commonwealth: A Study of the Role of Government in the American Economy: Massachusetts, 1774-1861 at 79 (rev. ed. 1969):

> [The state] freed from taxation the Boston glasshouses and cotton factories in Worcester and Rehoboth and elsewhere for periods of from five to ten years. Breweries which turned out one hundred barrels annually received the identical concession to encourage the production of the healthful beverage, create a product for export, and supply a market for farmers. Salt and sugar works had the same advantage held out to them for a time. Sometimes either the state or the town extended the exemption to employees of the new venture. Thus the foremen of a factory in Beverly were relieved of the poll tax and the laborers at the Boston glass factory released from militia duty.

See also Scheiber, The Road to *Munn*: Eminent Domain and the Concept of Public Purpose in the State Courts, in Law in American History 365 (Fleming & Bailyn eds. 1971).

after years of excess, complainants called upon the court to restore the balance between the public and private spheres.

Over the past few decades, government has taken an active role in promoting urban economic development partnerships of various shapes, reflecting different perceptions of needs, responsibilities, and goals. In a curious and significant progression, for each generation since the Second World War, a program to revitalize American cities has gained prominence, symbolizing the prevailing economic and political milieu. We have already studied urban renewal, the domestic counterpart to post-war reconstruction. In the mid-1960s, Model Cities were the watchwords. In the push toward a Great Society, the ever-burgeoning central government attempted to foster urban revitalization through a dosage of federal funds and a concomitant mass of regulations.[2] Yet central to the "Demonstration" program was the effort to involve the private sector in the formulation and implementation of plans for reviving distressed neighborhoods. Responsibility for the program — what President Johnson referred to as the "diamond in his crown" — was delegated to a new cabinet agency: the Department of Housing and Urban Development (HUD), itself a symbol of the administration's concern with the quality of life in the nation's population centers.

As the nation moved rightward on the political spectrum, there was talk of a New Federalism, of delegation of responsibility to state and local officials.[3] While the New Communities program was enhanced, older cities were far from ignored. In the mid-1970s, Community Development Block Grants (CDBG) were the embodiment of the revenue-sharing philosophy to the planning commissions, neighborhood groups, and developers and lenders in the inner city. The Carter Administration's Creative Federalism translated into Urban Development Action Grants (UDAG), a detailed system for leveraging private capital with a limited commitment of federal dollars.

In the 1980s, at least in the federal arena, we witnessed a shift away from active governmental solutions to the problems of our troubled metropolitan areas. The new paradigm was the public/private joint venture; the shibboleth again was New Federalism. Both were epitomized by the enterprise zone (EZ) concept — the use of tax, regulatory,

---

2. See Frieden & Kaplan, The Politics of Neglect: Urban Aid from Model Cities to Revenue Sharing (1975).

3. Although Ronald Reagan labeled his administration's agenda the New Beginning, there were distinct echoes of Richard Nixon's New Federalism. See, e.g., Inaugural Address, 1981 Pub. Papers 1, 2 (Jan. 20, 1981):

> It is my intention to curb the size and influence of the Federal establishment and to demand recognition of the distinction between the powers granted to the Federal Government and those reserved to the States or to the people. All of us need to be reminded that the Federal Government did not create the States; the States created the Federal Government.

Cf. Mollenkopf, The Contested City 127-135 (1983) (discussing Nixon's New Federalism).

VIII ■ Evolution and Evaluation of Public/Private Partnerships

and financing incentives to attract private investment to the most neglected areas of the nation's cities and towns. EZs are just one ingredient in the new alphabet soup of state and local finance and development tools, programs that would have profoundly impressed Justice Brandeis, the champion of social and economic experimentation.[4]

What follows is not the usual casebook fare, and so much the better. Judicial inquiries and intrusions have been few and far between in this realm; the hesitation of the courts has been even more extreme than in "traditional" land-use areas. What we are left to study is an ever-growing mountain of legislative and administrative guidelines: amendments piled on top of original enactments, revised rules appended to modifications of regulations past, new forms supplementing or superseding existing ones. Yours will be a view from but a small climb up this summit, with notes, edited passages, and the occasional case as your guides. Though you have been spared exposure to reams of minutiae, you should still be left with a useful impression of the authorization, rationalization, and administration of modern urban programs.

These statutes, regulations, and forms comprise the record of the public/private partnerships conceived by legislators and special interest groups as the (often complicated) means toward a simple, though profound, end: the revitalization of the nation's most depressed regions. The most familiar term used to describe these arrangements — a term used in fact to label this chapter — is joint venture. Is this more than just a handy catchword for the wide range of cooperative efforts sampled in this chapter? What do you make of the following consideration of "joint venture," as something much more substantive and instructive?

> While joint ventures of public and private enterprises are much deliberated, even verbally embraced, the form of this arrangement is still clouded and evolving. Analogies from the world of private land developers are illuminating in structuring an appropriate public role. . . . One helpful precursor is the form of business organization used to combine different interest groups — lenders, builders, developers, packagers — in the private sector itself: the traditional joint venture in real estate syndications. In many ways the joint venture of government and business is most

---

4. New State Ice Co. v. Liebmann, 285 U.S. 262, 311 (1932) (Brandeis, J., dissenting):

There must be power in the states and the nation to remould, through experimentation, our economic practices and institutions to meet changing social and economic needs. . . .

. . . It is one of the happy incidents of the federal system that a single courageous state may, if its citizens choose, serve as a laboratory; and try novel social and economic experiments without risk to the rest of the country.

analogous to a limited partnership, a form of organization popular in the world of property development.

In a . . . partnership, the parties can demand the maximum from each other. Each general and limited partner contributes what it is best at providing: money, marketing, management, or other specialized skills. In return, each party retains defined powers, rights, and remedies for breach. No one participates unless a potential profit is seen.

In the public-private venture, the private interests can be said to fill the role of general partner: they are responsible for construction of the project (after site clearing) and day-to-day management of the completed structures, and also remain accountable for business losses and liabilities incurred. The public sector serves as a sort of limited partner, a "money person" who provides the funds for site clearance and advances the "costs" of foregone revenues, in anticipation of increased employment, a revitalized urban area, and the possibility of future tax revenue. Like any other limited partner, the public needs to retain two basic rights: (1) the right to keep informed as to progress on the project, and (2) the right to an accounting of the return which it is due. These private and public rights and responsibilities should be articulated through negotiation and recorded in a written agreement for each redevelopment project.

Further, if a joint venture is to address the structural problems underlying the urban crisis, the need for overall evaluation becomes pressing. Equity considerations demand that this evaluation reflect all viewpoints, something missing, for example, from Detroit's decision to provide GM with a site in Poletown.[5] Goals of the program should be delineated, target populations defined and measured, and before-and-after conditions of [targeted] areas compared. As a consequence, there will be increasing pressure on the public sector to seek creative solutions to the difficulties of public cost-benefit analyses. Ways will need to be found to assign — indeed, to quantify — newly emergent values, as, for example, the social benefits of integrated neighborhoods. . . .

Thus the public sector should prepare an urban impact or public benefit statement that attempts to describe the net benefit to the public springing from the proposed urban redevelopment project. Such a document, prepared prior to the signing of the formal agreement, can force all parties to consider the costs and benefits to those not officially a party to the deal but whose interests are ultimately at its core. Significantly, rigorous cost-benefit analysis can place the city in a strong negotiating stance to demand the maximum contribution from the private sector.

The outcome of these two documents — a written contract defining public and private rights and responsibilities and an impact statement — may be seen together as a form of constitution, setting out rules for the exercise of powers by the public and private sectors within the confines of the joint venture. The ambiguous nature of public benefit can be dispelled in the negotiation process, highlighted by cost-benefit analysis

---

5. See Poletown Neighborhood Council v. City of Detroit, supra page 798. — Eds.

and public participation, and formalized by written documents. At a minimum, the procedure could endow the term "public use" with more depth and reasonableness (and, ultimately, acceptability) than it has been accorded in recent eminent domain judicial cases.... For the private sector, such a process is common; for the public sector, such an explicit costing is somewhat less usual....

[The *Poletown*] result suggests the proper role of the court in evaluating a "public" use. It should verify that the local government secures a good deal, one in which a balance of responsibility evolves from the negotiation process.... Courts are traditionally concerned, in challenges to police power regulations, that a city is regulating a private interest too heavily, hovering at the unconstitutional brink of a taking. When considering joint ventures, the courts should be concerned with the converse: whether the city is helping an individual business too much, failing to obtain a balance of responsibility.

... Casting the arrangements for urban revitalization in the form of private market limited partnership agreements, which will be specifically enforced, can be significant in formulating public policy, and writing the rules for power sharing can be equally important in implementing the joint venture society that is fast becoming the dominant form of twentieth-century capitalism.[6]

Keep this proposal and the following questions in mind as you survey the legislative and administrative framework for the modern public/private partnership. Are the lessons you learn in studying partnership and corporation law translatable in the context of urban development? Is there a role for the court beyond occasional whistleblowing? Do the compromise, gamesmanship, and need to "sell" voters on the idea — three inescapable elements of any political struggle — spell doom for all well-meaning, ambitious programs? Are private market mechanisms for developing property subject to (and worthy of) replication? What should the next major initiative look like and how would you have its framers balance public and private needs and contributions?

---

6. Haar, The Joint Venture Approach to Urban Renewal: From Model Cities to Enterprise Zones, in Public-Private Partnership: New Opportunities for Meeting Social Needs 63, 81-84 (Brooks, Liebman & Schelling eds. 1984). — Eds.

A. VARIATIONS ON A THEME: FEDERAL ATTEMPTS TO SPUR ECONOMIC REDEVELOPMENT AND NEIGHBORHOOD REVITALIZATION

1. Model Cities

■ DEMONSTRATION CITIES AND METROPOLITAN DEVELOPMENT ACT OF 1966
Pub. L. No. 89-754, 80 Stat. 1255, 1255-1258, 1260 (1966)

Sec. 101. The Congress hereby finds and declares that improving the quality of urban life is the most critical domestic problem facing the United States. The persistence of widespread urban slums and blight, the concentration of persons of low income in older urban areas, and the unmet needs for additional housing and community facilities and services arising from rapid expansion of our urban population have resulted in a marked deterioration in the quality of the environment and the lives of large numbers of our people while the Nation as a whole prospers.

The Congress further finds and declares that cities, of all sizes, do not have adequate resources to deal effectively with the critical problems facing them, and that Federal assistance in addition to that now authorized by the urban renewal program and other existing Federal grant-in-aid programs is essential to enable cities to plan, develop, and conduct programs to improve their physical environment, increase their supply of adequate housing for low- and moderate-income people, and provide educational and social services vital to health and welfare.

The purposes of this title are to provide additional financial and technical assistance to enable cities of all sizes (with equal regard to the problems of small as well as large cities) to plan, develop, and carry out locally prepared and scheduled comprehensive city demonstration programs containing new and imaginative proposals to rebuild or revitalize large slum and blighted areas; to expand housing, job, and income opportunities; to reduce dependence on welfare payments; to improve educational facilities and programs; to combat disease and ill health; to reduce the incidence of crime and delinquency; to enhance recreational and cultural opportunities; to establish better access between homes and jobs; and generally to improve living conditions for the people who live in such areas, and to accomplish these objectives through the most effective and economical concentration and coordination of Federal, State, and local public and private efforts to improve the quality of urban life. . . .

A. Federal Attempts to Spur Redevelopment and Revitalization

Sec. 103. (a) A comprehensive city demonstration program is eligible for assistance . . . only if —

(1) physical and social problems in the area of the city covered by the program are such that a comprehensive city demonstration program is necessary to carry out the policy of the Congress as expressed in section 101;

(2) the program is of sufficient magnitude to make a substantial impact on the physical and social problems and to remove or arrest blight and decay in entire sections or neighborhoods; to contribute to the sound development of the entire city; to make marked progress in reducing social and educational disadvantages, ill health, under-employment, and enforced idleness; and to provide educational, health, and social services necessary to serve the poor and disadvantaged in the area, widespread citizen participation in the program, maximum opportunities for employing residents of the area in all phases of the program, and enlarged opportunities for work and training;

(3) the program, including rebuilding or restoration, will contribute to a well-balanced city with a substantial increase in the supply of standard housing of low and moderate cost, maximum opportunities in the choice of housing accommodations for all citizens of all income levels, adequate public facilities (including those needed for education, health and social services, transportation, and recreation), commercial facilities adequate to serve the residential areas, and ease of access between the residential areas and centers of employment; . . .

Sec. 104. (a) The Secretary is authorized to make grants to, and to contract with, city demonstration agencies to pay 80 per centum of the costs of planning and developing comprehensive city demonstration programs.

(b) Financial assistance will be provided under this section only if (1) the application for such assistance has been approved by the local governing body of the city, and (2) the Secretary has determined that there exist (A) administrative machinery through which coordination of all related planning activities of local agencies can be achieved, and (B) evidence that necessary cooperation of agencies engaged in related local planning can be obtained.

Sec. 105. . . . (c) To assist the city to carry out the projects or activities included within an approved comprehensive city demonstration program, the Secretary is authorized to make grants to the city demonstration agency of not to exceed 80 per centum of the aggregate amount of non-Federal contributions otherwise required to be made to all projects or activities assisted by Federal grant-in-aid programs . . . which are carried out in connection with such demonstration program. . . .

Sec. 111. (a) There are authorized to be appropriated, for the purpose of financial assistance and administrative expenses under sections 104 and 106, not to exceed $12,000,000 for the fiscal year ending June 30, 1967, and not to exceed $12,000,000 for the fiscal year ending June 30, 1968.

(b) There are authorized to be appropriated, for the purpose of financial assistance and administrative expenses under sections 105, 106, and 107, not to exceed $400,000,000 for the fiscal year ending June 30, 1968, and not to exceed $500,000,000 for the fiscal year ending June 30, 1969.

(c) Appropriations authorized under this section shall remain available until expended.[7]

Notes

1. Along with emphasizing the need to utilize government resources to solve urban problems, those who crafted and implemented Model Cities stressed from the beginning the importance of private sector contributions and community participation. For example, President Johnson, in his January 26, 1966, message to Congress concerning past and potential urban programs, stated:

> From the experience of three decades, it is clear to me that American cities require a program that will . . . [m]obilize local leadership and private initiative so that local citizens will determine the shape of their

---

7. House Report (Banking and Currency Committee) No. 1931, issued September 1, 1966, to accompany S. 3708, painted a dismal portrait of the nation's cities and of localized efforts to combat urban distress:

> Slums and blight are widespread. There are over 7 million homes in urban areas that are run down or deteriorated. More than 3 million do not have adequate plumbing or hot and cold running water. In many of our central cities entire sections and neighborhoods are in need of major surgery to overcome decay.
> Increasingly the old, the poor, and the underprivileged are concentrated in these slum and blighted areas of the central city. As slums and blight spread, crime, delinquency, want and disease follow. While the need for city services grows, the city's ability to provide these services is impaired by the very blight that creates the demand.
> More blight, greater demand for city services, decreasing revenues to meet the demand — that is the descending spiral confronting many American cities.
> Significantly, the independent efforts of cities to help themselves are in large measure self-defeating. The more determined the city's effort to raise funds to meet the need for increased services, the more likely the effort drives its affluent citizens to the nearby suburbs. Similarly, the greater tax burden the city places on industry within its borders, the less its opportunity to attract and hold the industry and commerce its economy requires. So the city becomes, increasingly, a home for the economically deprived, those least able to bear the cost of municipal services. . . .
> . . . We must bring to bear national resources. The city plays a critical role in American life. The success of the city in providing the physical and social framework through which millions of poor and disadvantaged Americans are prepared to participate fully in the Nation's life is a vital national concern. — Eds.

A. Federal Attempts to Spur Redevelopment and Revitalization

new city — free from the constraints that have handicapped their past efforts and inflated their costs.

Legislators, administrators, and bureaucrats for the ensuing two decades continued to explore effective ways of including these two key elements in the revitalization package.

2. A number of reasons have been proffered for the failure of Model Cities to reach its ambitious goals: lack of strong congressional commitment (in contrast to the strong support of the Johnson, then Nixon, White Houses), the unfortunate proliferation in the number of targeted areas and the paperwork required of local participants, the inevitable shortcomings of a new federal bureaucracy, and the inability of local governments to expend allocated funds. See Haar, Between the Idea and the Reality (1975).

The movement in Washington to revenue sharing and devolution to state and local officials left Model Cities in its wake. Section 116(a) of the Housing and Community Act of 1974 (Public Law 93-383) halted new grants or loans, "[e]xcept with respect to projects and programs for which funds have been previously committed."

2. New Communities

■ HOUSING AND URBAN DEVELOPMENT ACT OF 1970
Pub. L. No. 91-609, 84 Stat. 1770, 1793-1798 (1970)

Sec. 710. (a) The Congress finds that this Nation is likely to experience during the remaining years of this century a population increase of about seventy-five million persons.

(b) The Congress further finds that continuation of established patterns of urban development, together with the anticipated increase in population, will result in (1) inefficient and wasteful use of land resources which are of national economic and environmental importance; (2) destruction of irreplaceable natural and recreational resources and increasing pollution of air and water; (3) diminished opportunity for the private homebuilding industry to operate at its highest potential capacity in providing good housing needed to serve the expanding population and to replace substandard housing; (4) costly and inefficient public facilities and services at all levels of government; (5) unduly limited options for many of our people as to where they may live, and the types of housing and environment in which they may live; (6) failure to make the most economic use of present and potential resources of many of the Nation's smaller cities and towns, including those in rural and economically depressed areas, and decreasing employment and business opportunities for their residents; (7) further lessening of employment and business opportunities for the residents of central cities and of the ability of such cities to retain a tax base adequate to support vital services for all their citizens, particularly the poor and disadvantaged; (8) further separation of people within metropolitan areas by income and by race; (9) further increases in the distances between the places where people live and where they work and find recreation; and (10) increased cost and decreased effectiveness of public and private facilities for urban transportation. . . .

(e) The Congress further finds that desirable new community development on a significant national scale has been prevented by difficulties in (1) obtaining adequate financing at moderate cost for enterprises which involve large initial capital investment, extensive periods before investment can be returned, and irregular patterns of return; (2) the timely assembly of sufficiently large sites in economically favorable locations at reasonable cost; and (3) making necessary arrangements, among all private and public organizations involved, for providing site and related improvements (including streets, sewer and water facilities, and other public and community facilities) in a timely and coordinated manner.

(f) It is, therefore, the purpose of this part to provide private developers and State and local public bodies and agencies (including regional or metropolitan public bodies and agencies) with financial and other assistance necessary for encouraging the orderly development of well-planned, diversified, and economically sound new communities, including major additions to existing communities, and to do so in a manner which will rely to the maximum extent on private enterprise; strengthen the capacity of State and local governments to deal with local problems; preserve and enhance both the natural and urban environment; increase for all persons, particularly members of minority groups, the available choices of locations for living and working, thereby providing a more just economic and social environment; encourage the fullest utilization of the economic potential of older central cities, smaller towns, and rural communities; assist in the efficient production of a steady supply of residential, commercial, and industrial building sites at reasonable cost; increase the capability of all segments of the home-building industry, including both small and large producers, to utilize improved technology in producing the large volume of well-designed, inexpensive housing needed to accommodate population growth; help create neighborhoods designed for easier access between the places where people live and the places where they work and find recreation; and encourage desirable innovation in meeting domestic problems whether physical, economic, or social. It is also the purpose of this part to improve the organizational capacity of the Federal

A. Federal Attempts to Spur Redevelopment and Revitalization

Government to carry out programs of assistance for the development of new communities and the revitalization of the Nation's urban areas.

Sec. 711.... (f) The term "land development" means the process of clearing and grading land, making, installing, or constructing waterlines and water supply installations, sewerlines and sewage disposal installations, steam, gas, and electric lines and installations, roads, streets, curbs, gutters, sidewalks, storm drainage facilities, and other installations or work, whether on or off the site, which the Secretary deems necessary or desirable to prepare land for residential, commercial, industrial, or other uses, or to provide facilities for public or common use....

Sec. 713. (a) The Secretary (acting through the Community Development Corporation) is authorized to guarantee, and enter into commitments to guarantee, the bonds, debentures, notes, and other obligations issued by or on behalf of private new community developers and State land development agencies for the purpose of financing real property acquisition and land development and to compensate for the use of real property or the removal of liens or encumbrances on such property, pursuant to the new community development programs approved by the Secretary....

(b) The full faith and credit of the United States is pledged to the payment of all guarantees made under this section with respect to principal, interest, and any redemption premiums....

(d) The outstanding principal obligations guaranteed under this section with respect to a single new community development program shall at no time exceed $50,000,000.

(e) The aggregate of the outstanding principal obligations guaranteed under this section shall at no time exceed $500,000,000....[8]

---

8. The new community guaranty program was originally authorized in Title VII of the Housing and Urban Development Act of 1968, and incorporated in the more ambitious legislation two years later. In their "Minority Views," dated December 17, 1970, Republican members of the House Banking and Currency Committee objected to the funding, philosophy, and bureaucracy presented by H.R. 19436:

> The minority takes the position that it would like to approve another housing bill in 1970. It has accordingly extended its ideas, its recommendations, and its cooperation to that end. Unfortunately, the majority have preferred a bill which in the terms of the younger generation could be well characterized as "too much." In so doing it has chosen to ignore, we hope only for the present, a long-needed codification of present housing law, recommended by the minority and the present administration, and by a number of dignitaries in the previous administration as well.
>
> In its stead, the majority have approved a bill which asks approval of authorizations totaling in excess of $7 billion. In so doing it whets the appetite of various concerned pressure groups for even larger sums with their resulting taxpayer and higher price impact....
>
> Section 130 of the bill would authorize a direct Federal program for the development of new communities on federally owned lands. The developer would be a Federal corporation within the Department of Housing and Urban Develop-

Notes

1. Planning, of course, is not a new idea; that is what municipal, state, and regional planning agencies are all about. But even if those agencies have the power to promulgate a master plan, they are still limited to telling people what they cannot do; rarely do they force anyone to do anything. The new community developer — part social dreamer, part businessperson — acts positively, taking a piece of virgin land (or recycled urban real estate) and putting everything together into one neat package.

This sounds great — but there are serious problems. Three major ones are land acquisition, finance, and fitting the new community into a larger plan, be it a regional or a national urban growth policy. These trouble areas (and others) are interrelated, and running through all the problems and all the possible solutions is the question of the mix of public and private involvement which, on the one hand, is unavoidable, and on the other, is necessary.

2. The great majority of new communities built in the United States have been located in or on the fringe of urban areas. This is largely a matter of economics; private developers, even with a federal guarantee, are out to make a profit, and the market for large-scale housing, commercial, and industrial construction is in urban areas. This creates serious acquisition problems, since the necessary land has already been subject to suburban speculation, or consists of relatively small farm tracts ripe for speculation. A "new-town-in-town" may require the assembly of literally thousands of separate parcels, and in that way is similar to an urban renewal project.

The legal and practical ramifications of large-scale acquisitions received the attention of the drafters of the Model Land Development Code:

Section 5-201. Public Purpose

The assembly of land for large scale development is a public purpose for which the State Land Planning Agency may acquire land subject to

---

ment. Funds for the entire capital investment would be provided by the Congress, rather than by utilizing the approach of Federal guarantees plus loans to cover interest payments. . . .

This provision would unwisely and unnecessarily inject a Washington-based Federal corporation into local development; the corporation would be unqualified to handle something that can be done far better by private enterprise and State and local public bodies. A new community is not something which can be designed and built to exact and unchanging specifications. In England, you cannot tell Harlow from Stevenage, on first glance, and having them so alike is a mistake. A new community is developed over a period of many years. It requires sensitivity to changing local conditions and close attention to market and financial considerations. This is a task for private industry working with local government, and not one for the Federal bureaucracy. The Federal corporation proposed is far more likely to undertake projects that only "serve as models" of how not to do the job.

Garden City*

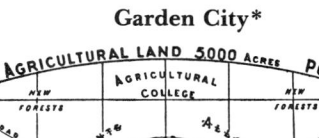

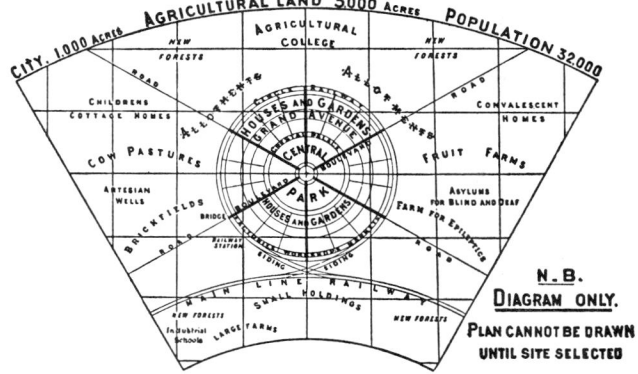

Stevenage New Town†

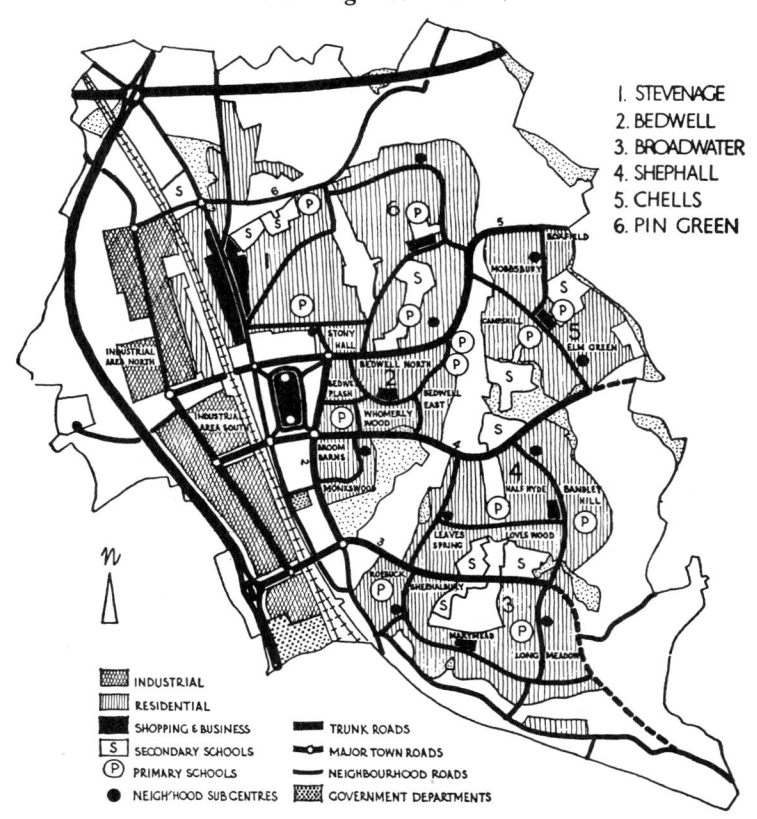

1. STEVENAGE
2. BEDWELL
3. BROADWATER
4. SHEPHALL
5. CHELLS
6. PIN GREEN

INDUSTRIAL
RESIDENTIAL
SHOPPING & BUSINESS
S SECONDARY SCHOOLS
P PRIMARY SCHOOLS
● NEIGH'HOOD SUB CENTRES
TRUNK ROADS
MAJOR TOWN ROADS
NEIGHBOURHOOD ROADS
GOVERNMENT DEPARTMENTS

*Drawing by Ebenezer Howard.
†*Source*: Building the New Town of Stevenage (1954).

the provisions of this Part. Before exercising the power of condemnation the State Land Planning Agency shall adopt a rule, identifying the categories of large scale development that should be encouraged in order to accomplish improved patterns of land development, and for which the Agency intends to acquire land pursuant to this Part.

Section 5-202. Eligibility of Applicants

The State Land Planning Agency may acquire an interest in land within a development site in accordance with this Part if such acquisition is requested by

(1) a private developer who has already acquired control by purchase, option, agreement with a governmental agency or otherwise of over [60] percent of a development site for development meeting the standards of rules adopted under §5-201; or

(2) a developer that is a governmental agency having the authority under other law to undertake development meeting the standards of rules adopted under §5-201. . . .

Section 5-204. Order Directing Land Acquisition

(1) The State Land Planning Agency shall issue an order directing the acquisition of land under this Part only if it finds that

(a) the proposed development will be large scale development meeting the standards of rules adopted under §5-201;

(b) the developer is an eligible developer under §5-202 and there is reasonable assurance that he is capable of completing the project according to his plan;

(c) the development is not inconsistent with any state or local Land Development Plan;

(d) the development will contribute to better patterns of growth for the area than would be likely to result in the absence of the development;

(e) there is reasonable assurance that the public facilities necessary to serve the development will be constructed at the appropriate time.

3. Any governmental commitment to new communities should be made in the context of an urban growth strategy. This seems to have been the intent of Congress in linking together in Title VII the beginnings of a growth policy and the new communities program. But to proclaim the link is only to begin; the real issues are in translating the plan into a reality through the vehicle of new communities.

First comes the question of who will plan. Would state legislation be as adaptable as private controls? At what point should residents assume control of their new community? Residents of Columbia would achieve a majority in the "private government" (the Columbia Park and Recreation Association) when the town is one-half complete; however, their lots are sold subject to fifty-year restrictions limiting uses substan-

A. Federal Attempts to Spur Redevelopment and Revitalization 939

tially to the developer's plan. In general, see Eichler & Kaplan, The Community Builders (1967).

Not only is the impact of a new community region-wide, but it also cuts through important social, political, and economic questions. In Columbia, developer James Rouse made all these decisions himself: he established panels of experts to make recommendations on schools, libraries, medical care, recreation, even religion. He established the Columbia Association, which owned all public facilities and was in effect a quasi-government, complete with taxing power (through assessments). And, most obviously, he determined Columbia's location.

Should these matters be left to the developer, or should there be public involvement? If the latter, by whom? Most of these decisions must be made before the first resident moves in. But if the new community is truly regional in nature, should its framework be established by the municipalities within whose borders it happens to fall?

Planning realities raise another issue. There is an obvious reluctance to establish a strong, active planning force, especially on a regional level. Should new communities be permitted without such a planning agency, or should the federal or state government use its money as a tool to force (or entice) a plan, or at least establish a strong pattern for one through the placement of new communities? Is such an approach feasible?

And then there is national planning — moving jobs and people to underdeveloped or depressed areas. Can new communities do this absent direct government intervention? Will anyone build such a community? If not, is the new community essentially a tool for controlling suburban growth? What is needed to make it an effective tool? Consider the resources needed to build any new community, and how readily each is available in the suburban setting.

4. The court in Sierra Club v. Lynn, 502 F.2d 43, 52-54 (5th Cir. 1974) — an unsuccessful challenge, based on alleged environmental harm, to HUD's decision to grant federal assistance to the developers of the San Antonio Ranch New Town — summarized the origins and operation of the New Communities program. See also Murray, New Communities: In Search of Cibola — Some Legislative Trials, 12 Urb. L. Ann. 177, 196 n. 105 (1976): "Final federal commitment [for San Antonio Ranch] was never given. Development has progressed with private financing. The irony is that the area was already under growth pressure and 'uncontrolled' development may be more serious than growth by a project such as the new community."

5. "In order to provide for the management and orderly liquidation of assets, and discharge of liabilities, acquired or incurred in connection with the new communities program ... the liquidation of the ... program shall be carried out pursuant to the provisions of law applicable

to the revolving fund." Act of November 30, 1983, Pub. L. No. 98-181, §474, 97 Stat. 1253, 1258 (1983).

On April 13, 1983, in testimony before the House Appropriations Subcommittee on HUD-Independent Agencies, Warren T. Lindquist, General Manager of the New Community Development Corporation, and Representative Edward P. Boland (Massachusetts) participated in the following exchange:

> *Mr. Boland* . . . I do not know whether or not this program has been a total failure. I suppose it is another example of programs generated by the Congress that have not met with complete success. Maybe they got started at the wrong time. I think that maybe one of the reasons for the failures in some of these areas and perhaps the locations developed were not the right areas. . . . [W]hy have they all, with the exception of one, resulted in what one would call failures?
>
> *Mr. Lindquist* . . . [M]y own opinion is that the program was not correctly conceived in the first place. I have no quarrel with the objectives of the program, of course, but I think it was unreasonable to assume that the Government in a very short time would be able to develop the underwriting capacity necessary to underwrite these very big very complicated long-term real estate transactions when some of the biggest insurance companies in the world, who have been doing this for years and years, were not able to do so without considerable discomfort to themselves. So that was the first problem that was wrong with it — to think the Government would be able to develop the underwriting expertise.
>
> Next, I think it was conceptually unsound to believe that, even if this underwriting expertise were developed given the circumstances and the climate of the times, the experts would have been able to apply that expertise objectively and on the merits. It should have been anticipated that those evaluating projects would be subjected to considerable social and political pressure to produce results, pressures which in ordinary financial institutions would not be a factor. This contributed to the fact that several of the new communities' debt was guaranteed which should not have been guaranteed.
>
> It takes three things to make a real estate venture successful, and I am not doing the old chestnut about location, location, location. But location is certainly, as you suggested in your opening remarks, Mr. Chairman, a key factor. Another absolute essential requirement is good management, experienced capable management with enough depth and continuity. The third thing is adequate capital. If any one of those three is inadequate, the venture cannot succeed. In all but one of these projects, all three elements were not there. The only one in which all three elements were present was Woodlands, the only successful project.[11] Some of the others did have management

---

11. See Department of Housing and Urban Development-Independent Agencies Appropriations for 1984: Hearings Before a Subcommittee of the Committee on Appro-

and location, but their pockets were not deep enough to withstand the crunch of 1974 and the more recent one. But it was not really those two crunches in my view that put the other new communities against the wall. Those, other than Woodlands, that had good management and good location, I think, were unsoundly underwritten. I think the financial planning was unsound in that the debt service was so great and they were leveraged so highly that the generation of an adequate cash flow to meet the debt service and provide for operation and development required such a sales pace that there was just no way that it could be done. This is why we had the unfortunate financial experience that we did.

6. The British, despite some setbacks, have been far more successful with their New Towns program:

There are twenty-eight new towns in Britain, plus four in Northern Ireland. For the twenty-eight British new towns, total population prior to designation was 946,000, an average of about 33,000 per town. Few were built on largely virgin sites. In March 1981, total population was 2,049,000 — equal to about 4 percent of the British population and representing an influx of 1,103,000. Employment in these new towns (at 954,000) was in satisfactory balance with their residential populations. Most of the earlier new towns had population targets of around 50,000, targets often increased subsequently by up to 50 percent. A few of the later new towns (for example, Milton Keynes) are much larger. About half of the new towns' planned development is virtually completed now. Of course, further

---

priations, 99th Cong., 1st Sess. 732 (1983):

The Woodlands, Texas. The Woodlands consists of 32,000 acres located on Interstate 45 in the southern edge of Montgomery County in the Houston metropolitan area. The current population is estimated to be 16,000. There are 6,597 dwelling units, including 1,034 units for low- and moderate-income households. About 6,000 jobs are located onsite. Over 2.9 million square feet of commercial/industrial space are developed. An integrated pedestrian/bikeway system, which serves the dual purpose of recreation and the provision of an energy-conserving alternative means of internal circulation, is being constructed in tandem with other development. The developer has redeemed $14.5 million of the $50 million it borrowed under the Title VII loan guarantee, bringing the outstanding loan guarantee down to $33.5 million. NCDC and the developer negotiated an agreement that substituted a major bank letter of credit for land as HUD's security for the HUD-guaranteed debt and established a simplified, enforceable affirmative action program. . . .

Other projects with guarantees outstanding were Harbison, South Carolina; Maumelle, Arkansas; and St. Charles, Maryland. Other HUD-related new communities were Shenandoah, Georgia; Cedar-Riverside, Minnesota; Flower Mound, Texas; Park Forest, South, Illinois; Soul City, North Carolina; Grananda, New York; Jonathan, Minnesota; Sycamore Woods, Ohio; Riverton, New York; Park Central, Texas; Radisson, New York; and Roosevelt Island, New York. Id. at 732-734. HUD estimated "the cumulative net cost to the Federal Government through the end of fiscal year 1983 to be approximately $590 million, including $168 million in grants and net recovery of fees and the sale of assets of $92 million." Id. at 361-362. — Eds.

growth does (and will continue to) occur, producing problems of adaptation for towns designed for a limited size.

Self, The British Planning Experience and New Towns, 1945-1983, in Cities, Law, and Social Policy 141, 144 (Haar ed. 1984).

3. Community Development Block Grants (CDBG)

■ HOUSING AND COMMUNITY DEVELOPMENT ACT OF 1974
Pub. L. No. 93-383, 88 Stat. 633, 633-635, 637-640 (1974)

Sec. 101. (a) The Congress finds and declares that the Nation's cities, towns, and smaller urban communities face critical social, economic, and environmental problems arising in significant measure from —

(1) the growth of population in metropolitan and other urban areas, and the concentration of persons of lower income in central cities; and

(2) inadequate public and private investment and reinvestment in housing and other physical facilities, and related public and social services, resulting in the growth and persistence of urban slums and blight and the marked deterioration of the quality of the urban environment. . . .

(c) the primary objective of this title is the development of viable urban communities, by providing decent housing and a suitable living environment and expanding economic opportunities, principally for persons of low and moderate income. Consistent with this primary objective, the Federal assistance provided in this title is for the support of community development activities which are directed toward the following specific objectives —

(1) the elimination of slums and blight and the prevention of blighting influences and the deterioration of property and neighborhood and community facilities of importance to the welfare of the community, principally persons of low and moderate income;

(2) the elimination of conditions which are detrimental to health, safety, and public welfare, through code enforcement, demolition, interim rehabilitation assistance, and related activities;

(3) the conservation and expansion of the Nation's housing stock in order to provide a decent home and a suitable living environment for all persons, but principally those of low and moderate income;

(4) the expansion and improvement of the quantity and quality of community services, principally for persons of low and moderate income, which are essential for sound community development and for the development of viable urban communities;

A. Federal Attempts to Spur Redevelopment and Revitalization 943

(5) a more rational utilization of land and other natural resources and the better arrangement of residential, commercial, industrial, recreational, and other needed activity centers;

(6) the reduction of the isolation of income groups within communities and geographical areas and the promotion of an increase in the diversity and vitality of neighborhoods through the spatial deconcentration of housing opportunities for persons of lower income and the revitalization of deteriorating or deteriorated neighborhoods to attract persons of higher income; and

(7) the restoration and preservation of properties of special value for historic, architectural, or esthetic reasons.

It is the intent of Congress that the Federal assistance made available under this title not be utilized to reduce substantially the amount of local financial support for community development activities below the level of such support prior to the availability of such assistance.

(d) It is also the purpose of this title to further the development of a national urban growth policy by consolidating a number of complex and overlapping programs of financial assistance to communities of varying sizes and needs into a consistent system of Federal aid....

Sec. 103. (a)(1) The Secretary is authorized to make grants to States and units of general local government to help finance Community Development Programs approved in accordance with the provisions of this title. The Secretary is authorized to incur obligations on behalf of the United States in the form of grant agreements or otherwise in amounts aggregating such sum, not to exceed $8,400,000,000 as may be approved in an appropriation Act....

Sec. 104. (a) No grant may be made ... unless an application shall have been submitted to the Secretary in which the applicant —

(1) sets forth a summary of a three-year community development plan which identifies community development needs, demonstrates a comprehensive strategy for meeting those needs, and specifies both short- and long-term community development objectives which have been developed in accordance with area-wide development planning and national urban growth policies;

(2) formulates a program which (A) includes the activities to be undertaken to meet its community development needs and objectives, together with the estimated costs and general location of such activities, (B) indicates resources other than those provided under this title which are expected to be made available toward meeting its identified needs and objectives, and (C) takes into account appropriate environmental factors;

(3) describes a program designed to —

(A) eliminate or prevent slums, blight, and deterioration where such conditions or needs exist; and

(B) provide improved community facilities and public improvements, including the provision of supporting health, social, and similar services where necessary and appropriate;

(4) submits a housing assistance plan . . .

(6) provides satisfactory assurances that, prior to submission of its application, it has (A) provided citizens with adequate information concerning the amount of funds available for proposed community development and housing activities, the range of activities that may be undertaken, and other important program requirements, (B) held public hearings to obtain the views of citizens on community development and housing needs, and (C) provided citizens an adequate opportunity to participate in the development of the application; but no part of this paragraph shall be construed to restrict the responsibility and authority of the applicant for the development of the application and the execution of its Community Development Program. . . .

(b) . . .

(2) Any grant under this title shall be made only on condition that the applicant certify to the satisfaction of the Secretary that its Community Development Program has been developed so as to give maximum feasible priority to activities which will benefit low- or moderate-income families or aid in the prevention or elimination of slums or blight. . . .[12]

12. See Senate Report No. 93-693 to accompany S. 3066 (February 27, 1974):

The Committee bill reported herewith is an omnibus bill of 8 chapters covering a broad range of Federal housing and urban development programs. Although the main thrust of the proposed legislation is to consolidate and simplify existing programs, it contains authority for the development of several new programs, the most important of which is a new and far-reaching block grant community development program. . . .

The most significant feature of the bill is the new block grant program to provide Federal assistance to localities for community development. This is brought about by consolidating and simplifying ten categorical urban development grant programs and replacing them with a single, more comprehensive, flexible and soundly financed community development block grant program. . . . The Committee adopted the block grant approach primarily to insure that Federal funds would be used with a priority to eliminate slums and blight and to upgrade and make the Nation's cities more livable, attractive and viable places in which to live. One of the most important provisions of the Committee bill is the development of a 2-year Federal funding cycle at an assured and adequate level so that localities are always working with a known level of Federal grants for the next year as well as the current year subject only to the meeting of minimum Federal performance standards.

In approving alternative provisions to the Administration-supported special revenue sharing proposals, the Committee followed the Administration's plan calling for an overhaul and consolidation of existing urban renewal and related programs, but disagreed with the proposed plan for distributing Federal funds automatically to the Nation's cities without proper regard to the use of such funds in carrying out national objectives specified in the Act. The Committee bill outlines specific objectives of the program and contains procedures to insure that the Federal funds are used to meet these objectives to the maximum extent feasible. — Eds.

A. Federal Attempts to Spur Redevelopment and Revitalization

Notes

1. In 1977, an additional goal was added by Congress: "(8) the alleviation of physical and economic distress through the stimulation of private investment and community revitalization in areas with population outmigration or a stagnating or declining tax base." Housing and Community Development Act of 1977, Pub. L. No. 95-128, §104(a), 91 Stat. 1111, 1111 (1977). House Report No. 95-236 to accompany H.R. 6655 (May 2, 1977) noted:

> [W]ithout a broader approach which integrates economic development activities at both the neighborhood and citywide levels, much of the block grant's long-term impact may be negated. The provision of more standard, livable housing in more attractive urban neighborhoods will not be enough: residents of these neighborhoods need jobs which result in incomes adequate to support that housing and the related public infrastructure.

Block grant recipients have responded quite creatively to this modification. See, for example, Urban Counties Using CDBG, Other Funds for Economic Development Projects, Study Says, [14 Current Developments] Hous. & Dev. Rep. (WG&L) 806, 806-807 (Feb. 23, 1987):

> Urban counties are actively using community development block grant funds for economic development, particularly for commercial redevelopment and industrial land development purposes, according to a study by the National Association of Counties (NACo)....
> Many counties have used CDBG funds in conjunction with the Small Business Administration Section 503 state and local development company program. Twenty counties issued about $35 million in SBA 503 debentures in fiscal 1985, according to the study. Fourteen counties used $9.3 million in urban development action grant funds for economic development activities. Almost $7 million in Economic Development Administration loans and grants were also used by respondent counties for economic development efforts....
> State, local, and private funds are other sources of revenue for economic development projects, according to the study. Almost a quarter of the respondent counties spent $12 million of their own general revenue funds in fiscal 1985 for economic development projects.
> The study cited the following as examples of innovative financing programs:
> - Allegheny County, Pa.'s linked-deposit program, which invests pension fund assets in local banks as a compensating balance to generate fixed-interest business loans for job creation;
> - Volusia County, Fla.'s public-private partnership to provide financing support for county economic development, which uses county

general revenue funds, per capita shares from municipalities, and donations from private firms;

- Anoka County, Minn.'s private non-profit economic development partnership, which provides funding for a small staff and for promotional/technical assistance activities; and
- Clackamas County, Ore.'s use of state lottery proceeds for economic development purposes.

As indicated in the NACo study, Small Business Administration (SBA) and Economic Development Administration (EDA) programs complement CDBG economic development efforts. The SBA, an independent federal agency created in 1958, administers several loan programs that provide fixed asset financing and venture capital loans for private concerns (the §7(a) and Small Business Investment Company (SBIC) programs), as well as funding for state and local development companies (Section 501, 502, and 503 programs). See 15 U.S.C. §631 et seq.

A successor to the Area Redevelopment Administration (1961), EDA was created by the Public Works and Economic Development Act of 1965, Pub. L. No. 89-136, codified at 42 U.S.C. §3121 et seq. (1982). EDA funds (administered by the Secretary of Commerce), though originally targeted to employment and development efforts in rural areas, have been made available to a great number of large and small city redevelopment areas over the past decade. EDA programs include §302 state and local economic development planning grants and §304 state supplemental grants. Funding authorization for EDA grew from $25 million in FY 1966 to $189.9 million in FY 1987.

2. The South Wright View Heights Action Committee instituted suit in 1982 against HUD Secretary Samuel Pierce and other federal and local officials, alleging that, among other violations, in seeking CDBG funds "[t]he City failed to provide for citizen participation and failed to discuss the resources available to Plaintiffs in a timely fashion." Nickols v. Pierce, 556 F. Supp. 1280, 1281 (S.D. Ohio 1982). The court, in denying injunctive relief to restrain construction of an improved gutter and sewer system for the city, provided (at 1283-1284) a helpful summary of the Small Cities component of the CDBG program:

> The Small Cities Community Development Block Grant Program (hereinafter the Program) was established by the Housing and Community Development Act of 1977. The Program was designed to assist cities and communities with a population of less than 50,000, and with a high concentration of impoverished citizens and substandard housing, to expand housing opportunities for low and moderate income families and to meet community development needs.
>
> Among the objectives of the Program is the correction of deficiencies in public facilities. Community development activities eligible for funding

A. Federal Attempts to Spur Redevelopment and Revitalization

under the Program to achieve this objective include the construction of streets, sewers and drainage systems. . . .

. . . Comprehensive grants are available for community development projects that involve two or more activities that are related to each other and that will be carried out in a coordinated manner. Single purpose grants are designed to address and resolve a specific community development need. The grant competition in each of the four competition areas is separate and distinct. . . .

The first step in the application process for a grant under the Program is the submission of a formal preapplication. In this document, each applicant describes, in quantifiable terms, its community needs and problems and the effect which its proposed community development program is expected to have on the community.

Each preapplication is reviewed by the appropriate Area Office of HUD. Because the demand for grants exceeds the availability of funds, a National Rating System has been devised to ensure that grants are awarded fairly and equitably.

Preapplicants receiving a satisfactory score are invited to submit a full application. HUD reviews each application in order to ascertain that all of the requirements for funding under the Community Development Block Grant Program have been met.

Each grant applicant under the Program is required to provide its citizens with an adequate opportunity for meaningful involvement and participation in the planning, implementation and assessment of the proposed community development program. In order to achieve this goal, Federal regulations require applicants to develop and follow a written citizen participation plan.

3. Congressional concern for adequate citizen participation has led to changes in the original §104(a)(6). What do you think were the motivations behind, and goals of, each of these subtle modifications?

> (6) provides satisfactory assurances that, prior to submission of its application, it has (A) prepared and followed a written citizen participation plan which provides citizens an opportunity to participate in the development of the application, encourages the submission of views and proposals, particularly by residents of blighted neighborhoods and citizens of low- and moderate-income, provides for timely responses to the proposals submitted, and schedules hearings at times and locations which permit broad participation;

Housing and Community Development Act of 1977, Pub. L. No. 95-128, §104(a), 91 Stat. 1111, 1115 (1977).

> (2) In order to permit public examination and appraisal of such statements, to enhance the public accountability of grantees, and to facilitate coordination of activities with different levels of government, the grantee shall —

U.S. DEPARTMENT OF HOUSING AND URBAN DEVELOPMENT
COMMUNITY DEVELOPMENT BLOCK GRANT PROGRAM
ENTITLEMENT PROGRAM

HOUSING ASSISTANCE PLAN

Form Approved OMB No. 2506-0063

1. NAME OF COMMUNITY
2. GRANT NUMBER: B – – – –
3. PERIOD OF APPLICABILITY — FROM: TO:
4. DATE OF SUBMISSION — 4a. ☐ Original ☐ Revision ☐ Amendment
5. HUD APPROVAL — (Signature of Authorized Official) (Date)

PART I - HOUSING ASSISTANCE NEEDS

TABLE I - HOUSING STOCK CONDITIONS

	TENURE TYPE	STANDARD UNITS — OCCUPIED UNITS (A)	STANDARD UNITS — VACANT UNITS (B)	SUBSTANDARD UNITS — OCCUPIED UNITS (C)	SUBSTANDARD UNITS — VACANT UNITS (D)	SUBSTANDARD UNITS SUITABLE FOR REHAB — OCCUPIED UNITS Total (E)	OCCUPIED UNITS Lower Income (F)	VACANT UNITS (G)
6	Owner							
7	Renter							

TABLE II - RENTAL SUBSIDY NEEDS OF LOWER INCOME HOUSEHOLDS

		ELDERLY (H)	SMALL FAMILY (I)	LARGE FAMILY (J)	TOTAL (K)
8	Very Low Income				
9	Percent	%	%	%	100%
10	Other Lower Income				
11	ETR				
12	To be Displaced				
13	Total				
14	Percent	%	%	%	100%

PART II - THREE YEAR GOAL

TABLE I - UNITS TO BE ASSISTED

		REHABILITATION OF SUBSTANDARD UNITS (L)	NEW CONSTRUCTION (M)	CONVERSION TO STANDARD UNITS (N)	HOME IMPROVEMENTS (O)
15	Owner				
16	Renter				

(UNITS EXPECTED TO ASSIST LOWER INCOME HOUSEHOLDS)

17	Owner				
18	Renter				

TABLE II - LOWER INCOME HOUSEHOLDS TO RECEIVE RENTAL SUBSIDIES

		ELDERLY (P)	SMALL FAMILY (Q)	LARGE FAMILY (R)	TOTAL (S)
19	Households to be Assisted				
20	Percent		%	%	%	100%

TABLE III - GOALS FOR HUD RESOURCES: SUBJECT TO LOCAL REVIEW AND COMMENT

		ELDERLY (T)	SMALL FAMILY (U)	LARGE FAMILY (V)	TOTAL (W)
21	Households to be Assisted				

HOUSING TYPE PREFERENCE (Maximum Number of Units that will be Accepted)

22 | NEW | REHAB | EXISTING

23 ☐ Check this box if the applicant wishes to review State Housing Agency proposals within its jurisdiction.

PART III - GENERAL LOCATIONS

24 Attach map identifying the general locations of proposed assisted housing.

HUD-7091.1 (10-82)
(24 CFR 570.306)

948

Form Approved
OMB No. 2506-0082

**U.S. DEPARTMENT OF HOUSING AND URBAN DEVELOPMENT
COMMUNITY DEVELOPMENT BLOCK GRANT PROGRAM**

NAME OF GRANTEE

GRANT NUMBER

GRANTEE PERFORMANCE REPORT

STATUS OF FUNDS—PARTS I AND II

PERIOD COVERED

_____ TO _____

PART I: SUMMARY OF RESOURCES AND EXPENDITURES

CDBG FUNDS
(Thousands of $)

1. UNEXPENDED CDBG FUNDS AT END OF PREVIOUS REPORTING PERIOD $ _____

2. ADDITIONAL CDBG FUNDS RECEIVED
   a. ENTITLEMENT GRANT
      (HUD-7082, line 9e) $ _____
   b. SURPLUS FROM URBAN RENEWAL/NDP SETTLEMENT
      (HUD-7082, line 10b) $ _____
   c. PROCEEDS FROM LOANS GUARANTEED UNDER SECTION 108 $ _____
   d. PROGRAM INCOME RECEIVED DURING THE PROGRAM YEAR,
      EXCEPT REVOLVING FUND INCOME. $ _____

   SOURCE   **AMOUNT**

   e. REVOLVING FUND PROGRAM INCOME RECEIVED DURING THE
      PROGRAM YEAR (enter the sum of all amounts reported on the status
      of Funds Part III, Column (f)) $ _____
   f. TOTAL ADDITIONAL CDBG FUNDS RECEIVED (sum of lines 2a-e) $ _____

3. TOTAL CDBG FUNDS AVAILABLE FOR USE DURING THIS REPORTING
   PERIOD (sum of lines 1 and 2f) $ _____

4. CDBG FUNDS EXPENDED DURING THIS REPORTING PERIOD
   (as shown in Activity Summary Forms, column (g)) $ _____

5. UNEXPENDED BALANCE OF CDBG FUNDS AT END OF THIS
   REPORTING PERIOD (line 3 minus line 4) $ _____

PART II: OVERALL BENEFIT TO LOW AND MODERATE INCOME PERSONS

6. EXPENDITURES SUBJECT TO PROGRAM BENEFIT RULES THIS REPORTING PERIOD
   a. TOTAL CDBG FUNDS EXPENDED DURING THIS REPORTING PERIOD (from line 4 above) $ _____
   b. LESS: PLANNING AND GENERAL ADMINISTRATIVE COSTS
      (as shown in Activity Summary forms, column (g)) $ _____
   c. TOTAL EXPENDITURES SUBJECT TO PROGRAM BENEFIT RULES
      (line a minus line b) $ _____

7. EXPENDITURES PRINCIPALLY BENEFITTING LOW AND MODERATE INCOME
   PERSONS DURING THIS REPORTING PERIOD (as shown in Activity Summary forms, column (g)) $ _____

8. PERCENT BENEFIT TO LOW AND MODERATE INCOME PERSONS
   (line 7 as a percent of line 6(c)) _____ %

HUD-4949.3 (3-83)
(24 CFR Part 570 & HB 6510.2)

(A) furnish citizens information concerning the amount of funds available for proposed community development and housing activities and the range of activities that may be undertaken;

(B) publish a proposed statement in such manner to afford affected citizens or, as appropriate, units of general local government an opportunity to examine its content and to submit comments on the proposed statement and on the community development performance of the grantee; and

(C) hold one or more public hearings to obtain the views of citizens on community development and housing needs.

In preparing the final statement, the grantee shall consider any such comments and views and may, if deemed appropriate by the grantee, modify the proposed statement. The final statement shall be made available to the public, and a copy shall be furnished to the Secretary together with the certifications required . . .

Housing and Community Development Amendments of 1981, Pub. L. No. 97-35, §302(a), 95 Stat. 384, 384-385 (1981).

(A) furnish citizens or, as appropriate, units of general local government information concerning the amount of funds available for proposed community development and housing activities and the range of activities that may be undertaken, including the estimated amount proposed to be used for activities that will benefit persons of low and moderate income and the plans of the grantee for minimizing displacement of persons as a result of activities assisted with such funds and to assist persons actually displaced as a result of such activities; . . .

42 U.S.C. §5304(a)(2) (Supp. 1986) (reflecting changes made by Housing and Urban-Rural Recovery Act of 1983, Pub. L. No. 98-181, §104(a), 97 Stat. 1155, 1161 (1983)).

4. Congress has also shifted on the issue of gentrification resulting from CDBG-funded activities. In the 1977 amendments, an encouraging note was sounded, as the goals of the program were augmented to include "foster[ing] neighborhood development in order to induce higher-income persons to remain in, or return to, the community." Pub. L. No. 95-128, §104(a), 91 Stat. 1111, 1114 (1977). By 1981, however, caution was in the air, as Congress required of block grant recipients a "housing assistance plan" that

indicates the general locations of proposed housing for lower income persons, with the objective of (i) furthering the revitalization of the community, including the restoration and rehabilitation of stable neighborhoods to the maximum extent possible, and the reclamation of the housing stock where feasible through the use of a broad range of techniques for housing restoration by local government, the private sector, or community organizations, including provision of a reasonable oppor-

A. Federal Attempts to Spur Redevelopment and Revitalization 951

tunity for tenants displaced as a result of such activities to relocate in their immediate neighborhood, (ii) promoting greater choice of housing opportunities and avoiding undue concentrations of assisted persons in areas containing a high proportion of low-income persons, and (iii) assuring the availability of public facilities and services adequate to serve proposed housing projects.

Pub. L. No. 97-35, §302(a), 95 Stat. 384, 386 (1981).

■ **24 C.F.R. §570.424**
(1988)

§507.424 SELECTION SYSTEM FOR COMPREHENSIVE GRANTS

Applications are rated and scored against each of the following factors. All points for each factor are rounded to the nearest whole number. The maximum score possible is 615.

		Points
(1)	Need — absolute number of poverty persons	75
(2)	Need — percent of poverty persons	75
(3)	Program impact	400
(4)	Outstanding performance:	
	Fair Housing	40
	Local equal opportunity efforts	25 . . .

(d) *Performance in fair housing and equal opportunity (50 points)* — (1) *Fair Housing efforts (40 points)* — (i) *Twenty points* are awarded to applicant providing assisted housing for low and moderate income families located in a manner which provides housing choice either in areas outside of minority and low and moderate income concentrations; or in a neighborhood which is experiencing revitalization and substantial displacement as a result of private reinvestment, by enabling low and moderate income persons to remain in their neighborhood. However, if the community is predominantly inhabited by persons who are members of minority and/or low income groups, HUD shall assess the extent to which assisted housing is distributed throughout the community. . . .[13]

---

13. You will recall that Parma, Ohio officials were directed to "take required steps for submitting an acceptable application for CDBG funds," following HUD's rejection of the city's application because of the failure to include an adequate housing assistance plan. See United States v. City of Parma, supra page 457.
   Yet another "string" attached to the receipt of block grant funds is the requirement that workers on CDBG- and UDAG-funded projects be paid at "prevailing wage" rates

(2) *Local Equal Employment and Entrepreneurial Efforts (25 points).* (i) *Fifteen points* are awarded to each applicant which demonstrates that at least five percent of all its contracts based on dollar value have been awarded within the past two years to minority owned and controlled businesses, providing the applicable percentage of minority population is five percent or less. If the applicable percentage of minority population exceeds five percent, then the applicant must have a corresponding percentage of its contracts awarded to minority businesses; however, twenty percent of the total dollar value of its contracts awarded to minority business enterprise will be sufficient for award of points for any applicant. The applicable percentage of minority population is the percentage of minorities in the applicant's jurisdiction, or in the county, whichever is higher.

(ii) *Ten points* are awarded to each applicant which demonstrates that its percentage of minority permanent, full-time employment is greater than the percentage of minorities within the county, unless the percentage of minority population in the community itself exceeds that of the county, in which case minority employment must reflect the minority population of the community.

4. *Urban Development Action Grants (UDAG)*

■ HOUSING AND COMMUNITY DEVELOPMENT ACT OF 1977
Pub. L. No. 95-128, 91 Stat. 1111, 1125-1127 (1977)

Sec. 119. (a) In order to promote the primary objective of this title of the development of viable urban communities, . . . the Secretary is authorized to make urban development action grants to severely distressed cities and urban counties to help alleviate physical and economic deterioration through reclamation of neighborhoods having excessive housing abandonment or deterioration, and through community revitalization in areas with population outmigration or a stagnating or declining tax base. Grants made under this section shall be for the support of severely distressed cities and urban counties that require increased public and private assistance in addition to the assistance

---

"in accordance with the Davis-Bacon Act, as amended (40 U.S.C. §§276a to 276a-5). 42 U.S.C. §5310 (1982). HUD and the Department of Labor have taken conflicting positions regarding the application of this prerequisite. See Pierce Requests Help from Meese in Resolving Davis-Bacon Dispute, [14 Current Developments] Hous. & Dev. Rep. (BNA) 495 (Nov. 3, 1986). Public and private sector participants in economic development and their legal advisors must decide at what point such requirements, as well as the inevitable paperwork and red tape associated with any governmental program, outweigh the advantages of federal funding. — EDS.

A. Federal Attempts to Spur Redevelopment and Revitalization 953

otherwise made available under this title and other forms of Federal assistance.

(b) Urban development action grants shall be made only to cities and urban counties that have, in the determination of the Secretary, demonstrated results in providing housing for persons of low- and moderate-income and in providing equal opportunity in housing and employment for low- and moderate-income persons and members of minority groups. The Secretary shall issue regulations establishing criteria in accordance with the preceding sentence and setting forth minimum standards for determining the level of physical and economic distress of cities and urban counties for eligibility for such grants, which standards shall take into account factors such as the age and condition of housing stock, including residential abandonment; average income; population outmigration; and stagnating or declining tax base.

(c) Applications for assistance under this section shall —

(1) include documentation of eligibility for grants in accordance with the standards described in subsection (b);

(2) describe a concentrated urban development action program setting forth a comprehensive action plan and strategy to alleviate physical and economic distress through systematic change.... Such program shall be developed as to take advantage of unique opportunities to attract private investment, stimulate investment in restoration of deteriorated or abandoned housing stock, or solve critical problems resulting from population outmigration or a stagnating or declining tax base;

(3) include the activities to be undertaken in the urban development action program, together with the estimated costs and general locations of such activities;

(4) indicate public and private resources which are expected to be made available toward achieving the action plan and strategy described in paragraph (2); and

(5) provide satisfactory assurances that, prior to submission of its application, it has (A) prepared and followed a written citizen participation plan, which plan provides the opportunity for citizens to participate in the development of the application, with special attention to measures to encourage the statement of views and the submission of proposals by low- and moderate-income people and residents of blighted neighborhoods, and to scheduling hearings at times and locations which are convenient to all citizens, (B) provided citizens with adequate information concerning the amount of funds available for proposed activities under this section, the range of activities that may be undertaken, and other important program requirements, and (C) held public hearings to obtain the views of citizens on needs which may be dealt with under this section....

(i) No assistance may be provided under this section for projects intended to facilitate the relocation of industrial or commercial plants or facilities from one area to another, unless the Secretary finds that such relocation does not significantly and adversely affect the unemployment or economic base of the area from which such industrial or commercial plant or facility is to be relocated.

(j) The Secretary shall allocate the amounts available for grants under this section in a manner which achieves a reasonable balance among programs that are designed primarily (1) to restore seriously deteriorated neighborhoods, (2) to reclaim for industrial purposes underutilized real property, and (3) to renew commercial employment centers.

(k) Not less than 25 per centum of the funds made available for grants under this section shall be used for cities under fifty thousand population which are not central cities of a standard metropolitan statistical area.[14]

Notes

1. Section 104(a) of the Housing and Community Development Amendments of 1979, Pub. L. No. 96-153, 93 Stat. 1101, 1102-1104,

---

14. House Report No. 95-236 to accompany H.R. 6655 (May 2, 1977) reads in part:

> Congressional concern over the fragmentation and diffusion of purposes inherent in the categorical grant-in-aid structure led to the community development block grant program in 1974. Although this program has ameliorated significant problems and inequities in the Federal response to community development needs, the committee recognizes the need for a new initiative to respond effectively to the pressing needs of cities and urban counties most distressed by excessive housing and economic deterioration.
>
> Community development block grant funding provides severely distressed cities with insufficient resources to respond to new problems or to take advantage of new opportunities in housing or economic development. Current funding levels allow such distressed localities to undertake maintenance programs and complete current projects, but are not sufficient to allow the launching of major new undertakings.
>
> Localities have no means of funding special or unique development opportunities. This is particularly true in the area of economic development opportunities, which require heavy front-end investments. . . .
>
> The action grant program which the committee is recommending would differ dramatically from previous efforts, because the commitment of private-sector financial participation would occur at the front end. Projects would not be funded that have only the hope of private investment. The committee believes that guaranteed participation of private-sector resources is essential to the success of the urban development action grant program.
>
> Only the showing of a significant influx (or reinvestment) of private capital can counter the image of decline. Recent experience in a number of cities has shown that such influx in the form of a critical project or set of activities can turn around the perception of the private sector about the desirability of the investment climate. When this perception changes, the private sector chooses to invest substantial amounts of funds in the city rebuilding process without additional public subsidy. — Eds.

A. Federal Attempts to Spur Redevelopment and Revitalization

set aside UDAG support for "pockets of poverty" located in communities not otherwise qualified for federal assistance under §119(e) and 24 C.F.R. §570.452. According to 24 C.F.R. §570.466(a), for cities with populations over 50,000, the following criteria must be met:

> (i) *Area.* The Pocket of Poverty must be an area composed of contiguous census tracts, enumeration districts or block groups. The defined geographic area must contain at least 10,000 persons or 10 percent of the jurisdiction's population.... Enumeration districts and block groups with median income levels greater than 120 percent of the median income of the jurisdiction must be excluded in defining the Pocket of Poverty.
> (ii) *Income.* At least 70 percent of the families and unrelated individuals residing in the Pocket of Poverty must have incomes below 80 percent of the jurisdiction's median income.
> (iii) *Poverty.* At least 30 percent of the residents residing in the Pocket of Poverty must have incomes below the national poverty level pursuant to criteria provided by the Office of Management and Budget.

For smaller cities, the pocket "must contain at least 2,500 persons or 10 percent of the jurisdiction's population, whichever is more."

2. From the beginning, critics of CDBG and UDAG have claimed that allocation formulas and distress criteria for community development funding reflect a clear bias in favor of older cities in the Northeast and Midwest. See, for example, Additional Views of Representative Mark Hannaford on H.R. 6655, reprinted in 1977 U.S. Code Cong. & Admin. News 2949, 2950-2951:

> [T]his bill takes $750 million in increased authorizations for fiscal year 1978 from the country at large and shifts nearly all of that amount to the cities of the Midwest and Northeast; $400 million is earmarked for the new urban action grant program, which was created specifically to help those older cities of the Midwest and East which are deteriorating economically. The remaining $350 million is primarily used for increased entitlements under the new formula, with those newer and growing cities of the South and West required to use an old formula and get only what amounts to an inflationary increase over last year's funds. For example, the community development entitlement for Los Angeles in 1977 was $17 per capita, and for Detroit it was $20 per capita, an acceptable inequity. Next year under the new formula, Los Angeles will improve slightly to just under $19 per capita, while the per capita allowance for Detroit jumps to $42.49, well over two to one. This is an absolutely unacceptable inequity....
> The new formula is heavily biased against the West. It is heavily biased against the South, and it is heavily biased against the suburbs. If one represents a district largely comprised of suburbs in the West, he is going to have a hard time explaining this legislation to his constituents.

> I can support the principle upon which the original community development legislation was based, that the Nation at large should support the revitalization of the cities of the Nation rather uniformly. The countryside and the suburbs draw important cultural, educational, recreational, and commercial benefits from the cities that serve them. But I cannot accept that the suburbs in my district in Los Angeles and Orange Counties, Calif., some of them with many low-income people, should be taxed to support the revitalization of Detroit or Newark.
>
> Further, let me point out one more fact to my colleagues. By concentrating our community development efforts in the older and deteriorating cities, we run the risk of allowing the still financially viable newer cities and suburbs to deteriorate. Would not a little preventive attention now be cheaper in the long run than curative support in the years ahead? I firmly believe this to be true.

Are there not other federal spending and tax incentive programs that demonstrate an equally obvious preference for geographical and demographic areas "excluded" from CDBG and UDAG? In the 1987 Act, Congress implemented a two-pot allocation system, basing selection for 35 percent of UDAG funding solely on project merit. See §515 of the Housing and Community Development Act of 1987, codified at 42 U.S.C. §5318.

3. Nor has UDAG been immune from cries that the program fosters dislocation of local residents and gentrification of (often-ethnic) "urban villages." Recall, for example, the plaintiffs' claims in Munoz-Mendoza v. Pierce, supra page 76. Apparently as a result of these and other criticisms of the program, in the summer of 1988 the full House and Senate Appropriations Committee voted to provide no additional UDAG funding for fiscal year 1989. Pub. L. No. 100-404 (1988).

4. The original §119(i), amended as codified at 42 U.S.C. §5318(h) (1982), sought to prevent the use of UDAG support for "job piracy" — luring an employer in state A to state B. In 1985, undoubtedly influenced by a lawsuit brought by New York City to block a UDAG grant to Jersey City, the HUD Assistant Secretary for Community Planning and Development issued an Anti-Pirating Policy (50 Fed. Reg. 1505 (1985)). According to the Policy, a rebuttable presumption of an illegal relocation would arise in specified instances of development that "will significantly and adversely affect the level of unemployment and the economic base of the area from which the facility is presumed to be relocated." Congress included other restrictions in §516 of the Housing and Urban Development Act of 1987, 100 Stat. 1934-1936. The Jersey City grant was ultimately canceled by HUD Secretary Pierce. See 132 Cong. Rec. H3603-07 (daily ed. June 12, 1986) (debate over proposed amendment to 42 U.S.C. §5318(h)).

5. The heart of UDAG is the use of federal money to attract private dollars that would not otherwise make their way to distressed

A. Federal Attempts to Spur Redevelopment and Revitalization

areas. De Rosa v. HUD, 787 F.2d 840 (2d Cir. 1986), involved a challenge brought by low- and moderate-income residents, and by a local community action agency, to a $12.8 million hotel construction project. The court was called upon to interpret the private-to-public funds leveraging ratio designed for UDAG projects. Judge Oakes wrote for the court (at 844-846):

> UDAG grants may be made "only where the Secretary determines that there is a strong probability that (1) the non-Federal investment in the project would not be made without the grant, and (2) the grant would not substitute for non-Federal funds which are otherwise available to the project." 42 U.S.C. §5318(j) (1982). Thus, among other criteria to be considered in determining which communities will receive UDAGs, the Secretary should consider "the extent to which the grant will stimulate economic recovery by leveraging private investment." In furtherance of these policies, 24 C.F.R. §570.459(b)(2) (1982) requires that "[e]ach project considered for selection for [UDAG] funding must have a leveraging ratio of at least 2.5 to 1.0." 24 C.F.R. §570.451(l) defines "leveraging ratio" as "the total amount of firm private commitment generated by the project divided by the amount of action grant funds awarded to the project." Under 24 C.F.R. §570.451(i) (1982), "firm private commitment" means that "agreement by which the private participating party in the action grant program agrees to perform an activity specified in the application and demonstrates the financial capacity to deliver the resources necessary to carry out the activity, and commits the resources to the project."
>
> Appellants argue that the Section 108 loan funds[15] are public funds that cannot be considered "firm private commitment," and that the use of those funds in connection with the financing of the hotel project leaves the project short of the requirement that every dollar of public funds

---

15. See 787 F.2d at 842:

Also involved is a $7.3 million federal loan guarantee to the City under the Community Development Block Grant (CDBG) program authorized under Section 108 of the Housing and Community Development Act of 1974, as amended, 42 U.S.C. §5308 (1982); 24 C.F.R. §§570.700-570.705 (1982). Under section 108 and the corresponding regulations, the Federal Financing Bank loans funds to a municipality and the United States Department of Housing and Urban Development (HUD) guarantees that repayment will be made. The developer obtained from a local bank $7.3 million in construction financing and personally guaranteed repayment. Initially, the plan called for the City to purchase the hotel from the developer and convey it back to the same developer, taking back a purchase money mortgage, but as the project evolved the City is to purchase the completed hotel and lease it to a limited partnership in which the developer is a general partner. The Section 108 loan will be used by the City to acquire the hotel and land from the developer. In the original plan, the developer pledged the proceeds to be received from the City on sale as collateral for the loan, but we were advised by the City's brief that the construction loan as ultimately obtained was not conditioned, as initially envisaged, upon the developer's pledge of sale proceeds (including the City's Section 108 funds) as collateral. — EDS.

generate at least 2.5 dollars of private investment, in violation of HUD's own rules and regulations. . . .

But we agree with the appellees that the regulations contemplate that funds to be repaid by a private developer are "private commitment"; whether those funds are loans from a private or public institution is immaterial. The definition of "firm private commitment" does not depend on whether funds that may reach the private developer originated from a public source. . . . [I]t is the developer's obligation to repay that makes funds "firm private commitment." The construction loan in this case thus was "firm private commitment" even though there was an agreement that if the project were carried through to completion the City would use its Section 108 loan to purchase it.

We do not comment on the wisdom of this method of obtaining the "front end" private sector financial participation envisioned by Congress when it created the UDAG program. All we hold here is that, when calculating the leveraging ratio, HUD's own regulations view as "firm private commitment" any funds, regardless of source, that private investors are ultimately liable to repay. The private party need only demonstrate the capacity to deliver the necessary funding to the specific project regardless of source and commit itself to do so.

5. Federal Enterprise Zones (EZ)

■ HOUSING AND COMMUNITY DEVELOPMENT ACT OF 1987
Pub. L. No. 100-242, 101 Stat. 1815, 1957-1963 (1988)

Sec. 701. (a) (1) For purposes of this section, the term "enterprise zone" means any area that —

(A) is nominated by one or more local governments and the State or States in which it is located for designation as an enterprise zone (in this section referred to as a "nominated area"); and

(B) the Secretary of Housing and Urban Development designates as an enterprise zone, after consultation with —

(i) the Secretaries of Agriculture, Commerce, Labor, and the Treasury, the Director of the Office of Management and Budget, and the Administrator of the Small Business Administration; and

(ii) in the case of an area on an Indian reservation, the Secretary of the Interior.

(2) (A) The Secretary of Housing and Urban Development may designate not more than 100 nominated areas as enterprise zones.

(B) Of the areas designated under clause (i), not less than $\frac{1}{3}$ shall be areas that —

A. Federal Attempts to Spur Redevelopment and Revitalization

(i) are within a local government jurisdiction or jurisdictions with a population of less than 50,000 (as determined under the most recent census data available);

(ii) are outside of a metropolitan statistical area (as designated by the Director of the Office of Management and Budget); or

(iii) that are determined by the Secretary, after consultation with the Secretary of Commerce, to be rural areas.

(3) (A) Except as provided in subparagraph (B), the Secretary shall designate the nominated areas with the highest average ranking with respect to the criteria set forth in subparagraphs (C), (D), and (E) of subsection (c)(3). For purposes of the preceding sentence, an area shall be ranked within each such criterion on the basis of the amount by which the area exceeds such criterion, with the area that exceeds such criterion by the greatest amount given the highest ranking.

(B) An area shall not be designated under subparagraph (A) if the Secretary determines that the course of action with respect to such area is inadequate.

(C) Subparagraph (A) shall be applied separately with respect to areas described in paragraph (2)(B) and to other areas. . . .

(c) . . . (3) For purposes of paragraph (1), a nominated area meets the requirements of this paragraph if the State and local governments in which it is located certify and the Secretary, after such review of supporting data as he deems appropriate, accepts such certification, that —

(A) the area is one of pervasive poverty, unemployment, and general distress;

(B) the area is located wholly within the jurisdiction of a local government that is eligible for Federal assistance under section 119 of the Housing and Community Development Act of 1974, as in effect on the date of the enactment of this Act;

(C) the unemployment rate, as determined by the appropriate available data, was not less than 1.5 times the national unemployment rate for that period;

(D) the poverty rate (as determined by the most recent census data available) for each populous census tract (or where not tracted, the equivalent county division as defined by the Bureau of the Census for the purpose of defining poverty areas) within the area was not less than 20 percent for the period to which such data relate; and

(E) the area meets at least one of the following criteria:

(i) Not less than 70 percent of the households living in the area have incomes below 80 percent of the median income of households of the local government (determined in the same manner as under section 119(b)(2) of the Housing and Community Development Act of 1974).

(ii) The population of the area decreased by 20 percent or more between 1970 and 1980 (as determined from the most recent census available). . . .

(d) (1) No nominated area shall be designated as an enterprise zone unless the local government and the State in which it is located agree in writing that, during any period during which the area is an enterprise zone, such governments will follow a specified course of action designated to reduce the various burdens borne by employers or employees in such area. A course of action shall not be treated as meeting the requirements of this paragraph unless the course of action include provisions described in not less than 4 of the subparagraphs of paragraph (2).

(2) The course of action under paragraph (1) may be implemented by both such governments and private nongovernmental entities, . . . may include, but is not limited to —

(A) a reduction of tax rates or fees applying within the enterprise zone;

(B) an increase in the level of public services, or in the efficiency of the delivery of public services, within the enterprise zone;

(C) actions to reduce, remove, simplify, or streamline paperwork requirements within the enterprise zone;

(D) involvement in the program by public authorities or private entities, organizations, neighborhood associations, and community groups, particularly those within the nominated area, including a written commitment to provide jobs and job training for, and technical, financial, or other assistance to, employers, employees, and residents of the nominated area;

(E) the giving of special preference to contractors owned and operated by members of any minority; and

(F) the gift (or sale at below fair market value) of surplus land in the enterprise zone to neighborhood organizations agreeing to operate a business on the land.

(3) In evaluating courses of action agreed to by any State or local government, the Secretary shall take into account the past efforts of such State or local government in reducing the various burdens borne by employers and employees in the area involved.

(4) (A) The course of action implemented under paragraph (1) may not include any action to assist —

(i) any establishment relocating from one area to another area; or

(ii) any subcontractor whose purpose is to divest, or whose economic success is dependent upon divesting, any other contractor or subcontractor of any contract customarily performed by such other contractor or subcontractor. . . .

A. Federal Attempts to Spur Redevelopment and Revitalization

SEC. 704. (a) Upon the written request of the governments that designated and approved an area that has been designated as an enterprise zone under section 701, the Secretary of Housing and Urban Development (or, with respect to any rule issued under title V of the Housing Act of 1949, the Secretary of Agriculture) may, in order to further the job creation, community development, or economic revitalization objectives of the zone, waive or modify all or part of any rule that the Secretary has authority to promulgate, as such rule pertains to the carrying out of projects, activities, or undertakings within the zone.

(b) No provision of this section may be construed to authorize the Secretary to waive or modify any rule adopted to carry out a statute or Executive order that prohibits, or the purpose of which is to protect persons against, discrimination on the basis of race, color, religion, sex, marital status, national origin, age, or handicap. . . .

SEC. 705. Section 3 of the Department of Housing and Urban Development Act is amended by adding at the end the following new subsection:

"(d) The Secretary shall —

"(1) promote the coordination of all programs under the jurisdiction of the Secretary that are carried on within an enterprise zone designated pursuant to section 701 of the Housing and Community Development Act of 1987;

"(2) expedite, to the greatest extent possible, the consideration of applications for programs referred to in paragraph (1) through the consolidation of forms or otherwise; and

"(3) provide, whenever possible, for the consolidation of periodic reports required under programs referred to in paragraph (1) into one summary report submitted at such intervals as may be designated by the Secretary."[16]

---

16. House Report No. 100-122(I) to accompany H.R. 4 (June 2, 1987) reads in part:

> This proposed Enterprise Zone legislation is one part of the larger Administration proposal which falls within the jurisdiction of the Committee on Ways and Means. Since the basic structure of this federal Enterprise Zone proposal requires major tax legislation, approval by this Committee of the proposal contained in this bill would not create the Enterprise Zone program that the Administration has been recommending for the past few years.
>
> The Committee has approved several initiatives as part of this year's housing authorization bill, and in approving this proposal has recognized the initiatives contained in the Enterprise Zone proposal that seek to address the economic distress and unemployment in both large and small urban communities. The Committee clearly recognized that there will be no enterprise zones created without the enactment of that part of the legislation currently pending before the Committee on Ways and Means.

HUD, apparently viewing the legislation differently, has begun the implementation process. See Enterprise Zone Development, 53 Fed. Reg. 30,944 (1988) (to be codified at 24 C.F.R. pt. 596) — EDS.

Notes

1. With the enactment of Title VII of the Housing and Community Development Act of 1987, Ronald Reagan technically realized the one articulated urban policy goal of his first successful presidential campaign. At best Title VII was a strong endorsement of enterprise zones (EZs) with the promise of future complementary action. At worst, the Act was a symbolic offering to a lame-duck President who once had grand dreams of "freeing enterprise" through EZs.[17]

The waivers and modifications of HUD rules and the program coordination specified in §705 are a far cry from the tax and financing incentives featured in earlier federal zone proposals. See, for example, S. 2298, sponsored by the Reagan Administration in 1982, with its elimination of capital gains taxes, 10 and 5 percent income tax credits for EZ employers and employees, and the continued availability of cherished industrial development bonds. See Haar, Wolf, Sheon & Friedlander, Urban Enterprise Zones: Inner City Panacea or Supply-Side Showpiece?, Lincoln Institute of Land Policy, Basic Concept Series No. 105 (1982); Boeck, The Enterprise Zone Debate, 16 Urb. Law. 71 (1984).

2. The major impetus for zones in the United States was the "freeport" idea espoused in 1977 by Peter Hall, a professor of geography at Reading University. Impressed with the economic vitality of Hong Kong and Singapore, Hall (a former chairman of the Fabian Society) proposed a U.K. adaptation: "'Small, selected areas of inner cities would be simply thrown open to all kinds of initiative, with minimal control. In other words, we would aim to recreate the Hong Kong of the 1950s and 1960s inside inner Liverpool or inner Glasgow.'" See Butler, Enterprise Zones: Greenlining the Inner Cities 96-97 (1981) (quoting Hall).

The next year, in a move illustrating the curious closeness of far

---

17. In his February 26, 1982, State of the Union Address, President Reagan took the opportunity to make the following challenge to Congress:

> Hand in hand with this program to strengthen the discretion and flexibility of state and local governments, we're proposing legislation for an experimental effort to improve and develop our depressed urban areas in the 1980s and 1990s. This legislation will permit states and localities to apply to the Federal Government for designation as urban enterprise zones. A broad range of special economic incentives in the zones will help attract new business, new jobs, new opportunity to America's inner cities and rural towns. Some will say our mission is to save free enterprise. Well, I say we must free enterprise so that, together, we can save America.

A few weeks later, on March 23, 1982, the President offered the following observation: "In its basic thrust, enterprise zones are the direct opposite of the model cities programs of the 1960s." Review the early part of this chapter and consider whether "mirror image" or "skewed reflection" would constitute a more accurate description.

left and far right, Sir Geoffrey Howe (destined to be Chancellor of the Exchequer and Foreign Secretary in the Thatcher government) presented a plan for "Enterprise Zones" to the Bow Group of the Conservative Party in London's depressed Isle of Dogs dockland region (today an EZ). The British zone program as eventually implemented by the Conservatives, with its tax exemptions and deregulation, along with outright government aid (a far cry from the original visions of both Hall and Howe), stands as the first true incarnation of EZs. Although critics and supporters have voiced their "I told you so," the jury is still out on British zones. See, for example, Lloyd and Botham, The Ideology and Implementation of Enterprise Zones in Britain, 7 Urb. L. & Poly. 33 (1985).

There are foreign cousins occupying the branches of the EZ family tree as well. As a preliminary experimentation with capitalism, China in 1980 created four Special Economic Zones offering reduced income taxation and some infrastructure expense. Belgium's Young Liberals, a libertarian group aligned with the Christian Democrats, are responsible for the establishment in 1982 of six T-zones (the "T" is for tewerkstelling, meaning "employment"). T-zones are industrial parks offering tax relief and regulatory simplification. Even France's Socialist government, early in 1984, approved a tax incentive package designed to attract manufacturing businesses into twelve depressed zones.

3. The key proponents of a federal zone program in the United States included Stuart Butler of the Heritage Foundation (an influential Washington, D.C. think-tank), Members of Congress Jack Kemp and Robert Garcia (sponsors of the Urban Jobs and Enterprise Act of 1980), and the Reagan Administration. See Callies and Tamashiro, Enterprise Zones: The Redevelopment Sweepstakes Begins, 15 Urb. Law. 231 (1983); Williams, State and Local Development Incentives for Successful Enterprise Zone Initiatives, 14 Rut. L.J. 41 (1982). Despite (or, perhaps, because of) President Reagan's recurrent rhetoric in support of the concept, it was not until late 1983 that the House Ways and Means Committee conducted a hearing to explore the zone concept. At that forum, legislators, representatives of the executive branch, and a long list of experts debated the merits of the administration's proposal and of tax-incentive targeting bills sponsored by Members of Congress from both parties and from across the political spectrum. Tax Incentives Targeted to Distressed Areas: Hearing Before the Committee on Ways and Means, House of Representatives, 98th Cong., 1st Sess. (1984). Ultimately, EZs remained on the conference floor when the 98th Congress passed its last revenue package.

4. In an apparent reversal of American political trends for the past few decades, many states have taken up the EZ gauntlet from a hesitant central government, promulgating and implementing an impressive array of zone programs. A few states produced zone legislation

merely in order to posture themselves to receive one or more federal designations in the event a national bill were enacted. See, e.g., R.I. Gen. Laws §42-64.3-5 (1984). A few other states developed symbolic zone packages of existing tax and other incentives with no indication of any significant activity within the near future.

Roughly thirty states have "taken the plunge," preparing and instituting a new package of geographically targeted tax, financing, and/or regulatory incentives designed for economic redevelopment and, in most cases, neighborhood revitalization. Although it is still too early to make sweeping claims for the success or failure of such programs, initial observations and data from zones in Connecticut, Maryland, Missouri, Kentucky, Virginia, and Pennsylvania (among others) indicate that progress, in terms of increased capital and employment, and in more symbolic terms, has been made in the state EZ laboratory. See Jones, Marshall & Weisbrod, Business Impacts of State Enterprise Zones (1985) (study prepared for United States Small Business Administration); United States Department of HUD, State-Designated Enterprise Zones: Ten Case Studies (1986); Wolf, Potential Legal Pitfalls Facing State and Local Enterprise Zones, 8 Urb. L. & Poly. 77 (1986). Case Study #4, infra page 992, provides a detailed look at one state's EZ program.

B. REPLICATION AND INNOVATION: THE STATE AND LOCAL EXPERIENCE

State and local governments, particularly over the past two decades, have become much more than passive observers of the succeeding waves of federal redevelopment efforts discussed in part A of this chapter. Increasingly, the responsibility for the packaging and promotion of public-private partnerships for economic development and area revitalization has fallen to state and local bureaucracies, a phenomenon necessitated by New Federalism policies, escalating budget deficits, and political battling (urban vs. suburban, East vs. West).

While the focus of each program discussed in this section is much narrower in geography, and the monies expended (or revenues forgone) less impressive than those sporting a Washington, D.C. return address, in many key cases the impact on local investment, employment, and property-use patterns has been quite profound. For example, the ripple effects of a large plant relocation can reach beyond the immediate confines of the factory site, having an impact on service and support industries, and on the transportation, taxation, educational, and housing needs of the community.

B. The State and Local Experience

The tools employed to spur redevelopment match in diversity the social and economic ramifications of large- (and, often, even smaller-) scale investment and employment decisions. As you study the materials that follow — your introduction to this rapidly adapting area of state law and governance theory regarding economic development and revitalization — recall the questions of accountability, targeting, and fairness that were raised in the context of federal programs. Are these issues more immediate when the policymakers, particularly elected officials, meet close by in city hall, the county building, or in the state capitol? How, if at all, is the potential for abuse affected by this decentralization? Is the consideration afforded traditional land-use decision-making more, or less, appropriate when the immediate legal agenda includes the law of taxation, finance, and general state and municipal regulation?

1. The New Urban Alphabet Soup: IRB, TIF, UDC, EDC, and the Like[18]

Stimulating investment through tax incentives. Many states and municipalities offer various forms of property tax relief as a means to stimulate economic growth within their borders. In several instances, relief has taken the form of declining abatements in the property tax for businesses or individuals meeting express legislative prerequisites. A typical abatement scheme might work as follows: in the first year of eligibility, an industrial or commercial venture, or a new residential structure within the targeted area, receives a 100 percent exemption on all property taxes, decreasing by 20 percent in each subsequent year, until the sixth year, when the abatement has been exhausted.[19] Although this form of property tax relief does provide a substantial incentive to qualified businesses or individuals, it still requires that an enterprise pay a substantial portion of its property tax bill in the early years of operation. Because the rate of business failure is particularly high during the first five years of operation, this form of abatement imposes a heavy tax liability upon a business or individual at perhaps the most critical period of a concern's early life, thus compromising the utility of declining tax abatement.

In recognition of this high small business mortality rate, several state and local governments have provided a more attractive property tax subsidy to encourage development or other designated activities

---

18. The editors thank Professor Robert A. Williams, Jr. of the University of Arizona for allowing us to include this edited and updated version of sections of his fine article, State and Local Government Incentives for Successful Enterprise Zone Initiatives, 14 Rutgers L.J. 41 (1982).

19. See, e.g., N.J. Stat. Ann. §54:4-3.101 (West 1986).

within a targeted area: property tax deferral. Essentially, this technique seeks to stimulate new construction and rehabilitation activity by deferring property tax reassessment on new or improved structures; the low initial assessment on property in the targeted area is maintained even after the property has been improved. Later, during theoretically more profitable years when the owner is better able to pay, the property is assessed at its "proper" value and the owner is taxed accordingly. When a business has been allowed time to mature and stabilize to the point where it can "pay its own way," the taxing authority demands its full share of that business's profits. In effect, the taxing authority simply makes the decision not to tax activity occurring in places where, in all likelihood, it would not have occurred absent the tax incentive. In this sense, property tax deferral can be viewed not as a permanent subsidy (which is how a taxing entity would view any permanent property tax reduction or elimination) but rather as a long-term investment which must be "carried" by the taxing authority for an extended period before "payout" in the form of increased taxable economic activity actually occurs.

One of the more controversial programs utilizing the tax deferral mechanism is New York City's J-51 program of tax incentives for property owners who affirmatively provide new dwelling units through rehabilitating and converting the city's decaying residential and commercial structures. As a complement to annual tax abatements, property owners receive tax exemptions of 12 or 32 years for the increased value resulting from qualifying improvements.[20]

More recently site value taxation has been successfully implemented in a number of cities. This *ad valorem* form of taxation taxes only the value of land, disregarding the value of improvements. Since it does not penalize development or rehabilitation by higher assessments, construction and site improvement are encouraged, rather than burdened.[21] Site value taxation should ideally have the effect of encouraging new construction and improvements, while at the same time

---

20. See New York City's J-51 Program: A Redefinition of Housing Objectives, Lincoln Institute of Land Policy, Policy Analysis Series No. 209 (Haar ed. 1983); Griffith, Revitalization of Inner City Housing Through Property Tax Exemptions and Abatement: New York City's J-51 to the Rescue, 18 Urb. L. Ann. 153 (1980).

21. On site value taxation and its variant forms, see Harris, Local Responsibility and Land Taxation: Lessons from the United States Experience (1976); Due, Universality and Neutrality of the Value Added Tax Reexamined, 55 Taxes 469 (1977); Lackman, Value and Added Tax vs. Property Tax: A Case Study, 8 Real Est. L.J. 34 (1979); McCalmont, Differential Taxation of Site Values and Structure, 43 S. Econ. J. 924 (1976); Parker, Compliance Costs of the Value-Added Tax, 54 Taxes 369 (1976); Pollock and Sharp, The Effect of Shifting the Property Tax Base from Improvement Value to Land Value: An Empirical Estimate, 53 Land Econ. 67 (1977). See also Note, Site Value Taxation: Economic Incentives and Land Use Planning, 9 Harv. J. on Legis. 115 (1971).

These, of course, are but the most recent echoes of Henry George's single tax proposals of the 1880s.

B. The State and Local Experience

reducing the amount of vacant land within a targeted redevelopment area held solely for speculative investment purposes. As original site valuations in the distressed area are likely to be relatively low, those establishing new ventures will have low property tax payments. Furthermore, the absence of an "assessment penalty" encourages these businesses to invest in capital improvements on the site. As the area and its businesses become more successful, site valuation increases, imposing a heavy tax on the speculative landholder receiving no income from a nonproductive asset.

Financing capital investment and infrastructure. Industrial revenue bonds (IRBs), first used in Mississippi in 1936, have since been embraced in nearly every state as a primary economic tool.[22] Also known as industrial development bonds, these tax-exempt government obligations are secured neither by the state's full faith and credit nor by a governing entity's general tax revenues, but by revenues paid by the industry receiving the bond proceeds. Because the interest payments of IRBs are tax-exempt, the interest rates are lower than those for other conventional private market obligations, making them an attractive source of start-up capital. A city or state utilizing IRBs can finance industrial development projects with capital costing less than the market rate — frequently 2 to 4 percent below current private market interest charges. The interest rate is generally higher, however, than that attached to government bonds backed by the state's "full faith and credit" or "moral obligation," which makes IRBs an attractive investment for mutual funds and individuals.

Usually, IRB programs are operated by a legislatively created development authority, empowered to incur tax-exempt debt and make low-interest loans to businesses seeking to expand, locate, or move into the authority's jurisdiction. Georgia operates a fairly typical industrial revenue bond program.[23] In 1969, the state legislature created local

---

22. Cong. Budget Office, Small Issue Industrial Revenue Bonds xii (study issued Apr. 1981). Federal legislation governing the tax treatment of IRB issues is found at §103(b) of the Internal Revenue Code. The literature on IRBs is extensive. See generally Price, ABC's of Industrial Development Bonds (1981). Criticism of the use of IRBs by state and local governments for low-cost financing of fast food chains, retail outlets, and other commercial enterprises is likewise extensive. An outline of the critics' arguments can be found in Note, Small Issue Industrial Development Bonds: The Growing Abuse, 39 Wash. & Lee L. Rev. 223 (1982). The IRS and Congress have frequently sought to curtail the use of IRBs in response to the argument that IRB tax-exempt financing for commercial projects results in fiscal drain on the United States Treasury. See Note, The Limited Tax-Exempt Status of Interest on Industrial Development Bonds Under Subsection 103(c) of the Internal Revenue Code, 85 Harv. L. Rev. 1649 (1972); Proposed Legislation Relating to Amendment of Internal Revenue Code: Hearings on H.R. 15414 Before the Senate Comm. on Finance, 90th Cong., 2d Sess. 82 (1968). For recent changes made by Congress in IRB financing, see Staff of Joint Comm. on Taxation, 99th Cong., 2d Sess., General Explanation of the Tax Reform Act of 1986, at 1128-1242 (Comm. Print 1987).

23. See Ga. Code Ann. §69-1507(b) (Supp. 1986). See generally Hester, Industrial

development authorities designed to develop commerce, industry, and employment revenue bonds to finance acquisition, construction, or expansion of industrial facilities. The list of eligible projects authorized by the state legislature basically duplicates the list of exempt facilities stated in the Internal Revenue Code, such as airports, docks, wharves, mass transit facilities, and parking lots. Projects also include convention centers with accompanying hotels and restaurants. Essentially, the Georgia authority lends its right to issue tax-exempt bonds to the business, in return for the promise that the business will locate or expand within the authority's jurisdiction; the authority then finances the project and the business pays the principal, redemption premium, and interest payments on the bonds as they come due.

Perhaps the most critical component of a successful redevelopment plan will be the level, amount, and quality of public services and infrastructure available within the targeted area. Tax Increment Financing (TIF) is a local government borrowing technique that is used successfully in a growing number of states to help finance the infrastructure needed to commence and maintain large redevelopment projects. Under the TIF program, redevelopment improvements are financed by issuing low-cost, federally tax-exempt bonds and devoting the proceeds to streets, parks, sewers, and other public facilities.[24] As business activity increases in the well-planned, successful redevelopment area, property values and property tax revenues increase. This increase is then used to retire the debt on the TIF bonds. This flexible financing tool can be used to fund any of the site improvements that an increase in economic activity will demand, even to pay for additional essential services such as adequate police and fire protection; proceeds from TIF have even been used to finance low-interest loans for the rehabilitation of existing structures and to provide start-up capital for small businesses.

Creating the appropriate (and effective) public-private redevelopment vehicle. State and local governments employ a wide range of public agency vehicles to promote economic growth, particularly in distressed areas. One such vehicle is the state-created independent development authority. This entity typically assumes a corporate structure, and is usually managed by an independent board of directors appointed by the state's governor. Outside the state civil service system, these authorities have the ability and resources to attract top-flight managers from the private sector and are able to adopt the efficient practices and techniques of corporate business to manage publicly created revenue producing activities such as toll bridges, roads, seaports, and airports. Typically, a

---

Development Bond Financing Under the Georgia Development Authorities Law, 14 Ga. St. B.J. 10 (1977).

24. On TIF, see generally Davidson, Tax-Related Development Strategies for Local Government, 13 Real Est. L.J. 121 (1984); Davidson, Tax Incentive Financing as a Tool for Community Redevelopment, 56 U. Det. J. Urb. L. 405 (1979).

B. The State and Local Experience

state development authority raises capital by utilizing the tax-exempt status of the state to issue tax-free bonds in the private financial money markets; proceeds of the bonds are then used to construct the revenue-raising enterprise.

New York's Urban Development Corporation (UDC) is the initial and most famous example of the several different types of corporate development authorities created to promote development specifically in distressed urban areas. The 1968 legislation creating the UDC, the New York State Urban Development Act,[25] was debated and passed in the wake of the assassination of Dr. Martin Luther King, Jr., owing in large part to the enormous pressure exerted by then-Governor Nelson Rockefeller (including threats not to sign any private bills of legislators).[26] The legislative findings accompanying the bill stated its public purpose to be

> to attract and house new industries and thereby to reduce the hazards of unemployment. The unaided efforts of private enterprise have not met and cannot meet the needs of providing such facilities due to problems encountered in assembling suitable building sites, lack of adequate public services, the unavailability of private capital for development in such urban areas, and the inability of private enterprise alone to plan, finance and coordinate industrial and commercial development with residential developments for persons and families of low income and with public services and mass transportation.

The UDC's enabling legislation empowers it to undertake a wide array of activities promoting urban redevelopment, including the financing and/or construction of low- and moderate-income housing, industrial and commercial facilities, public buildings and infrastructure, and new communities.[27]

The State Industrial Finance Authority (SIFA) provides another model for the development of a public agency to promote and manage economic growth in targeted areas. More than thirty states have passed legislation creating SIFAs (sometimes called State Industrial Development Authorities) for the purpose of inducing industry to locate or remain in the state.[28] Like state development authorities, SIFAs are created as public agencies. They provide loans, loan guarantees, interest rate subsidies, and second and third mortgages to businesses, either

---

25. N.Y. Unconsol. Law §§6251-85 (McKinney 1979 & Supp. 1987).
26. See Reilly and Schulman, The State Urban Development Corporation: New York's Innovation, 1 Urb. Law. 129, 131-132 (1969).
27. N.Y. Unconsol. Law §6252 (McKinney 1979 & Supp. 1987).
28. See Williams, supra note 18, at 103 n. 189. SIFAs differ from the UDC-type model in that the SIFA's legislative mandates are more narrowly drawn. See, e.g., Mass. Gen. Laws Ann. ch. 40E, §§1-21, ch. 40F, §§1-5, ch. 40G, §§1-9 (West 1979 & Supp. 1986).

directly or through local industrial development authorities. SIFAs can also issue industrial revenue bonds to finance business ventures. Many SIFAs target assistance to businesses located in areas characterized by high unemployment or a large percentage of low-income residents. Funding for SIFAs is obtained through state appropriations, bond issues, or revenues from assisted projects.[29]

At least twenty states have passed legislation establishing Business Development Corporations (BDCs) (also called Development Credit Corporations), private for-profit financial institutions designed to make private capital more available to business and industry.[30] Like SIFAs, BDCs provide a significant portion of the funding for new and developing businesses in the community. The similarities end there, however, as BDCs frequently focus their resources on high-risk businesses unable to obtain conventional assistance. Furthermore, financing is obtained primarily from private sources.[31]

Getting the community involved. In the past, Community Development Corporations have operated satisfactorily by permitting neighborhood residents to control and direct economic development within their neighborhoods. To be truly effective in carrying out their operations, however, such corporations require both technical and financial support from outside sources. One vehicle used to assist locally based community development corporations is the State Public Development Corporation (SPDC), established in several states to provide technical assistance and funding to local community development corporations for project planning, physical infrastructure costs, and venture capital.

Unlike the BDC, the SPDC is not funded privately, but instead receives appropriations from the state. Furthermore, an SPDC provides direct assistance only to locally based and controlled community development corporations rather than to individual businesses; such a policy helps to guarantee community input and control over the business and industrial development of an area.[32]

29. There are a number of examples of successful SIFAs. The Pennsylvania Industrial Development Authority (PIDA) provides long-term, low-interest financing for businesses locating or expanding in the state. In recent years, PIDA has specifically targeted a large percentage of its loans to small businesses and to areas of high unemployment. See Pa. Stat. Ann. tit. 73, §§301-314 (Purdon 1971 & Supp. 1987).

30. See. e.g., N.J. Stat. Ann. §§17:52-1 to -27 (West 1985). See also Thomas and Roye, Regulation of Business Development Companies Under the Investment Company Act, 55 S. Cal. L. Rev. 895 (1982).

31. The Kansas Development Credit Corporation (KDCC) serves as an example of an innovative approach to BDC financing of new and expanding business ventures. The KDCC makes short- and long-term loans to businesses, provides management services for its borrowers, and has developed a program for selling SBA-guaranteed loans, written by Kansas banks, to private investors. The original lender bank thus has more capital available to reloan to Kansas businesses. KDCC itself has also received money from a consortium of banks in a pooled risk lending program. See Kan. Stat. Ann. §§17-2328 to -2335 (1981).

32. See, for example, the enabling legislation for the Massachusetts Company Development Finance Corporation, Mass. Gen. Laws Ann. ch. 40F, §§1-5 (West 1979).

B. The State and Local Experience

The Economic Development Corporation (EDC) is perhaps the most frequently encountered type of local development entity. Typically private, non-profit organizations authorized by state and local legislation, EDCs are often headed by a board composed of public and private sector directors, and staffed by technical personnel paid from public and private sources. EDCs may enter into city contracts to perform such activities as land acquisition and clearance, site improvements, and new construction or rehabilitation; they also may serve as packagers of federal, state, and local assistance for private developers, providing technical and managerial assistance at no cost. EDC funding usually derives from city appropriations, private contributions, and revenues from profit-making ventures.[33]

2. Public Purpose Redux: Tax Incentives before the Bench

In an 1875 Supreme Court opinion, notable more for its invocation of the principle of implied limitations on government than for its precedential value in the area of judicial review of state taxation,[35] Justice Samuel F. Miller found invalid a Kansas bond program employed to aid a Topeka "manufactory of iron bridges." Loan Association v. City of Topeka, 87 U.S. (20 Wall.) 655, 656 (1875). Notwithstanding his rhetoric concerning legislative power, Miller's words foreshadow the substantive due process that lurked but a few decades off:

> We have established, we think, beyond cavil, that there can be no lawful tax which is not laid for a public purpose. It may not be easy to draw the line in all cases so as to decide what is a public purpose in this sense and what is not.
> It is undoubtedly the duty of the Legislature which imposes or authorizes municipalities to impose a tax, to see that it is not to be used for purposes of private interest instead of a public use, and the courts can only be justified in interposing when a violation of this principle is clear and the reason for interference cogent. And in deciding whether, in the given case, the object for which the taxes are assessed falls upon the one side or the other of this line, they must be governed mainly by the course and usage of the government, the objects for which taxes have

---

33. The state of Michigan has encouraged the formation of EDCs since 1974. Once established by local government pursuant to state legislative authorization, Michigan's EDCs may acquire, rehabilitate, improve, construct, maintain, lease, or sell project land or properties. EDCs may also lend or invest public funds for private development projects. Local governments may condemn land using their eminent domain powers and then sell it to the Corporation, which, in turn, may lease to businesses at below-market prices. Michigan's EDCs receive financing through loans and grants from local, state, and federal government sources. See Mich. Comp. Laws Ann. §§125.1601 to .1636 (West 1986).

35. See Tribe, American Constitutional Law 563-565 (2d ed. 1988).

been customarily and by long course of legislation levied, what objects or purposes have been considered necessary to the support and for the proper use of the government, whether State or municipal. Whatever lawfully pertains to this and is sanctioned by time and the acquiescence of the people may well be held to belong to the public use, and proper for the maintenance of good government, though this may not be the only criterion of rightful taxation.

But in the case before us, in which the towns are authorized to contribute aid by way of taxation to any class of manufacturers, there is no difficulty in holding that this is not such a public purpose as we have been considering. If it be said that a benefit results to the local public of a town by establishing manufactures, the same may be said of any other business or pursuit which employs capital or labor. The merchant, the mechanic, the inn-keeper, the banker, the builder, the steamboat owner are equally promoters of the public good, and equally deserving the aid of the citizens by forced contributions. No line can be drawn in favor of the manufacturer which would not open the coffers of the public treasury to the importunities of two thirds of the business men of the city or town.[36]

Although much has changed — in jurisprudence, economics, and politics — since the warning shot fired by Justice Miller and his colleagues, the debate over the proper role in evaluating state and local tax provisions remains heated. Questions of uniformity, equal protection, and the impact on interstate commerce continue to plague the Justices.[37] Indeed, in a recent decision reversing the nearly century-old precedent of Pollock v. Farmer's Loan & Trust Co., 157 U.S. 429

---

36. Justice Clifford, dissenting, was concerned not only with the majority's activism ("Courts cannot nullify an Act of the State Legislature on the vague ground that they think it opposed to a general latent spirit supposed to pervade or underlie the Constitution . . ."), but also with the effects of the decision: "[T]here is much more to be dreaded from judicial decisions which may have the effect to sanction the fraudulent repudiation of honest debts, than from any statutes passed by the State to enable municipal corporations to meet and discharge their just pecuniary obligations." 87 U.S. at 669-670 (Clifford, J., dissenting).

For an account of the evolving (and more indulgent) state and federal court positions post-*Loan Association*, see Gold, Economic Development Projects: A Perspective, 19 Urb. Law. 193, 204-209 (1987).

37. See Gunther, Constitutional Law 332 (11th ed. 1985):

The cases have been what Justices have called a "tangled underbrush" and a "quagmire" because in the area of state taxation the variables are even more numerous and complex and the tools of analysis even more uncertain than in the field of state regulation of commerce. Types of taxes and types of taxed activities vary widely. The most commonly litigated taxes have been property taxes, sales and use taxes, net and gross receipts taxes, and license and franchise taxes. The typical subjects of taxation have been interstate transportation and interstate sales, and various segments thereof. Moreover, far more than in the state regulatory area, the Court has had great difficulty in assessing the validity of particular tax schemes: in the search for legitimate interests, the need for revenue can always be set forth.

B. The State and Local Experience

(1895), five Justices observed that "the owners of state bonds have no constitutional entitlement not to pay taxes on income they earn from state bonds, and States have no constitutional entitlement to issue bonds paying lower interest rates than other issuers." South Carolina v. Baker, 108 S. Ct. 1355 (1988).

Given this less than stable state of the law, it would be foolish to attempt to summarize any hard-and-fast rules concerning the legitimacy of the range of tax and financing schemes utilized to attract and retain investment, employment, and development. What is more instructive is to isolate selected decisions from one jurisdiction in order to observe the shifts in governmental and juridical techniques and rationales. Our focus thus moves to one state court — the Supreme Court of Florida — and, of necessity, to a body of law distinct in many ways from federal constitutional, statutory, and common law. Therefore we have included as an introduction to this "tutorial," selections from the Florida Constitution (past and present) — the starting point for the judicial exploration that follows.

■ FLORIDA CONSTITUTION (1885)
Art. IX, §10 (superseded)

The credit of the State shall not be pledged or loaned to any individual, company, corporation or association; nor shall the State become a joint owner or stock-holder in any company, association or corporation. The Legislature shall not authorize any county, city, borough, township or incorporated district to become a stock holder in any company, association or corporation, or to obtain or appropriate money for, or to loan its credit to, any corporation, association, institution or individual.

■ FLORIDA CONSTITUTION (1968)
Art. VII, §10

Neither the state nor any county, school district, municipality, special district, or agency of any of them, shall become a joint owner with, or stockholder of, or give, lend or use its taxing power or credit to aid any corporation, association, partnership or person; but this shall not prohibit laws authorizing: . . .

(c) the issuance and sale by any county, municipality, special district or other local governmental body of (1) revenue bonds to finance or refinance the cost of capital projects for airports or port facilities, or (2) revenue bonds to finance or refinance the cost of capital projects for industrial or manufacturing plants to the extent that the interest thereon is exempt from income taxes under the then existing laws of the United States, when, in either case, the revenue bonds are payable solely from revenue derived from the sale, operation or leasing of the projects. If any project so financed, or any part thereof, is occupied or operated by any private corporation, association, partnership or person pursuant to contract or lease with the issuing body, the property interest created by such contract or lease shall be subject to taxation to the same extent as other privately owned property.

■ FLORIDA CONSTITUTION (1984)
Art. VII, §11

(a) State bonds pledging the full faith and credit of the state may be issued only to finance or refinance the cost of state fixed capital outlay projects authorized by law, and purposes incidental thereto, upon approval by a vote of the electors; provided state bonds issued pursuant to this subsection may be refunded without a vote of the electors at a lower net average interest cost rate. The total outstanding principal of state bonds issued pursuant to this subsection shall never exceed fifty percent of the total tax revenues of the state for the two preceding fiscal years, excluding any tax revenues held in trust under the provisions of this constitution.

■ FLORIDA CONSTITUTION (1968)
Art. VII, §12

Counties, school districts, municipalities, special districts and local governmental bodies with taxing powers may issue bonds, certificates of indebtedness or any form of tax anticipation certificates, payable from ad valorem taxation and maturing more than twelve months after issuance only:
    (a) to finance or refinance capital projects authorized by law and only when approved by vote of the electors who are owners of freeholds therein not wholly exempt from taxation; or
    (b) to refund outstanding bonds and interest and redemption premium thereon at a lower net average interest cost rate.

■ FLORIDA CONSTITUTION (1980)
Art. V, §3

    (b) The Supreme court: . . .
    (2) When provided by general law, shall hear appeals from final

B. The State and Local Experience

judgments entered in proceedings for the validation of bonds or certificates of indebtedness and shall review action of statewide agencies relating to rates or services of utilities providing electric, gas, or telephone service.

■ FLORIDA CONSTITUTION (1968)
Art. VIII, §2

(b) Municipalities shall have governmental, corporate and proprietary powers to enable them to conduct municipal government, perform municipal functions and render municipal services, and may exercise any power for municipal purposes except as otherwise provided by law. Each municipal legislative body shall be elective.

■ FLORIDA CONSTITUTION (1968)
Art. X, §6

(a) No private property shall be taken except for a public purpose and with full compensation therefor paid to each owner or secured by deposit in the registry of the court and available to the owner.

■ STATE v. CLAY COUNTY DEVELOPMENT AUTHORITY
140 So. 2d 576 (Fla. 1962)

DREW, Justice. . . .

In 1958, the Authority acquired a surplus airfield consisting of approximately 1300 acres of land located in Clay County and known as Fleming's Island Satellite Field. . . . While the legislative act contemplated the development of these lands primarily for public purposes, the only use made of the Fleming's Island Satellite Field property since its acquisition by the Authority is for occasional drag strip racing operated by a private corporation under a contractual arrangement with the Authority. . . .

In July, 1961, the Authority entered into a lease agreement with Eclipse Plastic Industries, Inc., a private corporation, whereby the Authority agreed to construct, erect, install and equip an industrial plant on a described portion of Fleming's Island Satellite Field and thereafter to lease such tract, as improved, to the private corporation for a term of sixteen years, with an option to the company to renew said lease at the expiration of said period for an additional term of ten years. In such agreement it was provided that the Authority would finance the cost of building and equipping said plant through the issuance and sale by the Authority of revenue certificates payable solely from the sums to be paid by the company to the Authority over the initial sixteen year term of the lease.[2] It was further provided that the total cost of building and constructing said plant and equipping the same would not exceed the sum of $500,000, and that any sums in excess thereof should be supplied by the lessee. The agreement contained in detail the provisions to be incorporated into the definitive lease including the provisions that the company would have the exclusive use and exclusive control of said premises and property during the entire term of the indenture and any renewals thereof and that the premises would be used in the operation of the business of manufacturing plastic containers and other plastic products, subject only to the restrictions and limitations of the definitive lease. . . .

. . . [I]t is crystal clear that the primary purpose to be served by the issuance of these obligations is the financing of a private enterprise contrary to the express provisions of Section 10 of Article IX of the Constitution of this State, F.S.A. The public obligation is to be incurred for the sole purpose of building and equipping this industrial plant. The fact that such building and structures will occupy only a small portion of the 1300 acres of land of the Authority is of no consequence in determining whether the purpose of improvement is incidental and falls within the ambit of our holdings in the *Gate City Garage* [,Inc. v. City of Jacksonville, 66 So. 2d 653 (Fla. 1953)] and *Panama City* [v. State, 93 So. 2d 608 (Fla. 1957)] cases. The dominant and paramount purpose is to lend the credit of the county to a private corporation to finance a private enterprise for private profit which will be under the exclusive control and in the exclusive possession of such enterprise for more than twenty-five years. The only possible public purpose which it serves is to promote the general development of the area by furnishing employment to the residents of Clay County. This is the factor which prompted the project. If we approve the issuance of bonds by the public authorities of this State to build and finance private enterprises and put such enterprises in the exclusive possession and control of such leases as is proposed to be done here, in order to alleviate unemployment and to promote the economic development of the area, then there is no limit to the extent to which the credit of the State and its authorities may be extended to private interests. In such event the constitutional provision above quoted will become meaningless. . . .

---

2. The total annual income to the Authority from the lease was the identical amount required to pay principal and interest on the bonds for that year. At the expiration of the sixteen year term, the total anticipated income from such rentals would then have fully paid off the original issue of certificates.

We have carefully considered the argument of the Authority that the validation of these bonds is warranted by the rationale of this Court in a number of our previous decisions. We have carefully examined each of these cases and find no similarity between the questions there presented and the one now under consideration. Each of those cases involved the issuance of governmental obligations for what had been long determined by this Court in previous cases to be public purposes. *State v. Daytona Beach* [Racing and Recreational Facilities District, 89 So. 2d 34 (Fla. 1956)], for example, involved the issuance of certificates to construct racing and recreational facilities. In that case we again referred to the fact that, while the facilities were proposed to be leased to private corporations for a portion of the year, such leases were *incidental to the public purpose of providing recreational facilities.* . . . We find in none of these cases comfort to the Authority. On the contrary, each of these cases supports the conclusion which we reach that the certificates proposed to be issued for the construction of the proposed project are condemned by Article IX, Section 10, of the Constitution and that the decree of the trial court must be and the same is hereby,

Reversed.

■ STATE v. HOUSING FINANCE AUTHORITY
376 So. 2d 1158 (Fla. 1979)

ADKINS, Justice.

This is a direct appeal from the final judgment of the circuit court in Polk County, Florida, validating certain revenue bonds.

The revenue bonds were authorized under the provisions of chapter 78-89, Laws of Florida; section 159.601, Florida Statutes (1978) et seq., known as the "Florida Housing Finance Authority Law" (hereinafter referred to as the Florida Housing Law).

When this law was enacted, the legislature made a finding that there was a shortage of housing and capital for investment in housing in this state; that this shortage was a threat to the "health, safety, morals, and welfare" of the residents of the state; that such shortage could not be relieved except through the encouragement of investment by a private enterprise; and, that:

> The financing, acquisition, construction, reconstruction, and rehabilitation of housing and of the real and personal property and other facilities necessary, incidental, and appurtenant thereto are exclusively public uses and purposes for which public money may be spent, advanced, loaned, or granted and are governmental functions of public concern.

These findings contained in section 159.602, Florida Statutes

(1978), were sufficient to show an express determination by the legislature that the housing authority law related to a matter of public concern and related to a proper governmental function. . . .

The state says that the issuance of the bonds and the use of the proceeds to purchase mortgages of private residences is not a proper public purpose, relying upon State v. Washington County Development Authority, 178 So. 2d 573 (Fla. 1965). The Washington case held that the financing of a single private construction project by the issuance of revenue bonds by a public agency was, under the facts of that case, not constitutionally permissible because in violation of art. IX, section 10, Florida Constitution of 1885. The purpose sought to be achieved by the *Washington* bonds was the improvement of the general economy of the county. In *Washington,* there was no legislative determination of public purpose and this Court found that the proposed housing development was not related to the public health, safety, morals, or welfare, but was only for the convenience of a fragment of the public.

In the case *sub judice,* there existed a specific finding by the legislature, the Board of County Commissioners, and the Authority that the project is related to the health, safety, morals, and welfare of the residents of Polk County. What constitutes a public purpose is, in the first instance, a question for the legislature to determine, and its opinion should be given great weight. A legislative declaration of public purpose is presumed to be valid, and should be deemed correct unless so clearly erroneous as to be beyond the power of the legislature.

The findings by the legislature contained in section 159.602, Florida Statutes (1978), should not be disturbed. We find that the issuance of the Authority's revenue bonds is adequately supported by a proper public purpose.

Also, the constitution has been revised since the *Washington* case was decided. The prohibition against the lending of public credit was materially changed by the constitution of 1968. We have pointed out that the lending of credit means the assumption by the public body of some degree of direct or indirect obligation to pay a debt of the third party. Where there is no direct or indirect undertaking by the public body to pay the obligation from public funds, and no public property is placed in jeopardy by a default of the third party, there is no lending of public credit.

Under the constitution of 1968, it is immaterial that the primary beneficiary of a project be a private party, if the public interest, even though indirect, is present and sufficiently strong. Of course, public bodies cannot appropriate public funds indiscriminately, or for the benefit of private parties, where there is not a reasonable and adequate public interest. An indirect public benefit may be adequate to support the public participation in a project which imposes no obligation on the

B. The State and Local Experience   979

public, and the qualification of the direct beneficiary complies with the
principles of due process and equal protection.[38]

■ STATE v. CITY OF MIAMI
379 So. 2d 651 (Fla. 1980)

OVERTON, Justice. . . .
. . . In 1964, the City Commission of Miami adopted a resolution
providing for the issuance of $4,500,000 in convention center bonds.
These bonds were sold in 1969, but construction of the convention
center was delayed indefinitely due to increased costs. In 1977, the City
of Miami (City) entered into an agreement with an architectural firm

---

38. See The Report of the President's Commission on Housing 169-170 (1982):

The first use of tax-exempt financing for housing involved general obligation
bonds issued to fund home loans for veterans. The "Cal-Vet" program was begun
in California during the 1920s, and similar programs have been used in other
States since then. During 1981, veterans' programs were active in California,
Oregon, and Wisconsin, and $0.9 billion in such bonds were issued.

State housing finance agencies (HFAs) traditionally have been the major
providers of tax-exempt funds for housing. Forty-six States and the District of
Columbia currently have HFAs that raise funds with revenue bonds to originate
or purchase residential mortgages, or to finance programs that involve below-
market rate lending to private mortgage lending institutions (loan-to-lender programs). State HFAs often have interacted with Federal rental housing programs
(such as HUD's Section 8 program) to link tax-exempt financing with Federal
subsidies, thereby lowering the cost of rental housing for low- and moderate-
income families. Until 1975, in fact, virtually all State HFA activity focused on
multifamily housing. During the 1975-80 period, however, State agencies issued
large amounts of single-family mortgage revenue bonds.

Local use of tax-exempt financing for housing traditionally has been quite
limited, consisting primarily of issues by local housing authorities to provide low-
rate interim and permanent financing of public housing projects whose debt service
payments are provided by HUD. Since 1978, however, local government entities
have issued mortgage revenue bonds to provide below-market rate funds for home
loans, in some cases for middle-income families in suburban areas. By 1980, local
mortgage revenue bond programs were active in more than 20 States, and the
volume of single-family issues exceeded $5 billion.

The rapid growth of single-family revenue bond financing at both the State
and local levels increased total tax-exempt financing of housing to nearly $14
billion by 1980, accounting for roughly 30 percent of all municipal bonds sold —
the largest single use of tax-exempt financing. In response to both mounting costs
to the Treasury (in terms of forgone tax revenues) and use by some municipalities
of tax-exempt funds to support neighborhoods and borrowers other than those
most in need, the Federal government set limits and conditions on the issuance of
single-family mortgage revenue bonds at the end of 1980. The Mortgage Subsidy
Bond Tax Act of 1980 sets limits on the volume of tax-exempt financing of single-
family housing that can occur within any State during the 1981-83 period, and
forbids new issues of such bonds after the end of 1983.

The Tax Reform Act of 1986 extended restricted authority to issue tax-exempt "mortgage
revenue bonds" through December 31, 1988. In 1988, the program was again extended
through 1989. See §143 of the Internal Revenue Code. — EDS.

to prepare a master plan of the entire convention center site. Later that year, in an agreement between the City and the University of Miami (University), the City agreed to construct a convention center with a parking garage and further agreed to cause to be constructed a hotel and retail area. The City also agreed to provide the University with adequate parking in the parking garage. The University, in return, agreed to rent a conference center area for a term of thirty years with two thirty-year renewal options. In 1979, the City entered a development agreement in which the City agreed to lease to the developer certain properties for the purpose of constructing and operating a hotel and other facilities at its own expense for a term of forty-five years with a forty-five-year renewal option. The City agreed to construct a water plant to service the needs of the convention center and the hotel and further agreed to give the developer priority to reserve a share of the spaces in the parking garage. The City Commission approved the execution of the development agreement and adopted an ordinance authorizing the issuance of revenue bonds of the City in an amount not exceeding $60,000,000. The bonds were secured by a pledge of the net revenues derived by the City from or in connection with the convention center-garage and other revenues of the City exclusive of ad valorem tax revenues. . . .

Article VII, section 10, of the Florida Constitution prohibits a municipality from lending or using its credit to any private enterprise. When public revenue bonds are used to finance a project other than those described in section 10(c), the particular circumstances must be considered in determining whether the lending or use of public credit for the project is contemplated. The validity of the proposed public revenue bond financing project depends on whether the bond issuance serves a paramount public purpose. . . .

In the instant case, it is our view that the convention center-garage does serve a valid public purpose. As noted by the trial court, this facility will provide a forum for educational, civic, and commercial activities and organizations. Further testimony at the bond validation proceeding indicated that this facility will also increase tourism and international trade. We have previously held that these interests serve a public purpose. This Court has also recognized that the redevelopment of downtown areas with the aid of improved parking facilities serves a valid public purpose.

The incidental benefits accruing to the developer and the University are not so substantial as to tarnish the public character of this convention center-garage. . . .

The function of this Court in a bond validation proceeding is to determine whether the authorizing body has the power to act and whether it exercises that power in accordance with the purpose and intent of the law.

We find that the trial judge was correct in holding that the proposed

B. The State and Local Experience 981

issuance of bonds was authorized by law, and his final judgment validating the bonds is affirmed.

It is so ordered.[39]

STATE v. MIAMI BEACH REDEVELOPMENT AGENCY
392 So. 2d 875 (Fla. 1980)

Per Curiam. . . .

The Miami Beach Redevelopment Agency was created by the commission of the city of Miami Beach pursuant to the Community

---

39. Not surprisingly, given the heated controversy over abuses in the use of tax-exempt IDBs, the Tax Reform Act of 1986 placed further restrictions on exempt activities, particularly private activity bonds governed by §141 of the Internal Revenue Code. See Staff of Joint Comm. on Taxation, 99th Cong., 2d Sess., General Explanation of the Tax Reform Act of 1986, at 1151-1154 (Comm. Print 1987):

> Congress was concerned with the large and increasing volume of tax-exempt bonds being issued under prior law. The effects of this increasing volume included an inefficient allocation of capital; an increase in the cost of financing traditional governmental activities; the ability of higher-income persons to avoid taxes by means of tax-exempt investments; and mounting revenue losses.
>
> At the same time, Congress recognized the important cost savings that tax-exempt financing could provide for State and local governments, in a period marked by reductions in direct Federal expenditures for such purposes. To the extent possible, Congress desired to restrict tax-exempt financing for private activities without affecting the ability of State and local governments to issue bonds for traditional governmental purposes.
>
> Between 1975 and 1985, the volume of long-term tax-exempt obligations for private activities (including tax-exempt IDBs, student loan bonds, mortgage revenue bonds, and bonds for use by certain nonprofit charitable organizations) increased from $8.9 billion to $116.4 billion. As a share of total State and local government borrowing, financing for these activities increased from 29 percent to 53 percent. Essentially, these bonds provided an indirect Federal subsidy to private activities. . . .
>
> The Act retains the ability of qualified governmental units to issue tax-exempt debt for the financing of traditional governmental activities. These include general government operations and the construction and operation of such governmental facilities as schools, roads, government buildings, and governmentally owned and operated sewage, solid waste, water, and electric facilities.
>
> While retaining the ability to issue bonds for governmental purposes, Congress was concerned that, under prior law, a significant amount of bond proceeds from governmental issues was being used to finance private activities not specifically authorized to receive tax-exempt financing. . . .
>
> While continuing tax-exempt financing for certain activities of nongovernmental persons, Congress believed it important to control the total volume of tax-exempt bonds issued for such activities. To accomplish this, the Act provides a limitation on the aggregate annual amount of private activity bonds that each State (including local governments therein) may issue. Congress believed that this new private activity bond volume limitation will ensure that the activities for which private activity bonds are issued will be scrutinized more closely by governmental units, and that such bonds will be targeted better to serve those persons and activities for which the exceptions are intended. Imposition of a single volume limitation, in place of the separate limitations imposed under prior law, was intended to allow State and local governments flexibility in allocating this limited Federal subsidy among qualifying activities.

Redevelopment Act of 1969, chapter 69-305, Laws of Florida, codified as chapter 163, part III, Florida Statutes (1975). The act was amended in 1977 to authorize "tax increment financing" of community redevelopment projects without referendum. Ch. 77-391, Laws of Fla.; see ch. 163, pt. III, Fla. Stat. (1977). . . .

Section 163.335(1), Florida Statutes (1977), declares that slums and blighted areas in the state are "a serious and growing menace, injurious to the public health, safety, morals, and welfare. . . ." It states further that the existence of slums and blighted areas contributes to "the spread of disease and crime. . . ." Such areas are "an economic and social liability imposing onerous burdens which decrease the tax base and reduce tax revenues," and their existence "impairs or arrests sound growth, retards the provision of housing accommodations, aggravates traffic problems and substantially hampers the elimination of traffic hazards and the improvement of traffic facilities;" . . .

Section 163.385 provides the authority for the issuance of bonds to finance redevelopment projects. It provides in part that, "[t]he security for such bonds may be based upon the anticipated assessed valuation of the completed community redevelopment project and such other revenues as may be legally available." Subsection (2) provides:

> Bonds issued under this section shall not constitute an indebtedness within the meaning of any constitutional or statutory debt limitation or restriction, and shall not be subject to the provisions of any other law or charter relating to the authorization, issuance, or sale of bonds. Bonds issued under the provisions of this part are declared to be issued for an essential public and governmental purpose and, together with interest thereon and income therefrom, shall be exempted from all taxes, except those taxes imposed by chapter 220 on interest, income, or profits on debt obligations owned by corporations.

The act provides as the mechanism for the financing of projects that each redevelopment agency shall establish a redevelopment trust fund. The governing body of the local government unit must, before the exercise of any redevelopment powers, provide by ordinance for the funding of the trust fund. §163.387(1), Fla. Stat. (1977).

This subsection provides further:

> The annual funding of the redevelopment trust fund shall be an amount not less than that increment in the income, proceeds, revenues, and funds of the county or municipality derived from or held in connection with its undertaking and carrying out of community redevelopment projects under this part. Such increment shall be determined annually and shall be that amount equal to the difference between:
> (a) The amount of ad valorem taxes levied each year by all taxing

B. The State and Local Experience

authorities except school districts on taxable real property contained within the geographic boundaries of a community redevelopment project; and

(b) The amount of ad valorem taxes which would have been produced by the rate upon which the tax is levied each year by or for all taxing authorities except school districts upon the total of the assessed value of the taxable property in the community redevelopment project as shown upon the [most recent] assessment roll used in connection with the taxation of such property by each taxing authority [prior] to the effective date of the ordinance approving the community redevelopment plan. . . .

Section 163.387 contains a final disclaimer:

Revenue bonds issued under the provision of this part shall not be deemed to constitute a debt, liability, or obligation of the local governing body or the state or any political subdivision thereof, or a pledge of the faith and credit of the local governing body or the state or any political subdivision thereof, but shall be payable solely from the revenues provided therefor. All such revenue bonds shall contain on the face thereof a statement to the effect that the agency shall not be obligated to pay the same or the interest thereon except from the revenues of the community redevelopment agency held for that purpose and that neither the faith and credit nor the taxing power of the local governing body or of the state or of any political subdivision thereof is pledged to the payment of the principal of, or the interest on, such bonds.

Id. §163.387(5).

The Miami Beach Redevelopment Agency's complaint sought validation of $80 million in bonds to finance land acquisition and $300 million in bonds to finance improvements. . . .

The State Attorney of the Eleventh Judicial Circuit, on behalf of the appellant the State of Florida, argues five issues in her brief. She contends that the Miami Beach Redevelopment Agency has no authority to bring an action for validation of bonds; that the agency is not a legally constituted entity; that the city commission was without authority to exercise the redevelopment powers provided for by the act; that the redevelopment project involves the use of eminent domain for purposes not public, in violation of article X, section 6, Florida Constitution; and that the bonds to be issued will be payable from ad valorem tax revenues but have not been approved by referendum as required by article VII, section 12, Florida Constitution. . . .

[The Court rejected the first four contentions.]

Two preliminary observations are in order. First, we observe that the recitals in the statute and in the bond resolutions, to the effect that the bonds shall not be deemed a pledge of the ad valorem taxing power and therefore do not require a referendum, are not conclusive of the issue in this proceeding. The legislative finding of constitutionality is presumptively correct, but this Court must disapprove it if it is clearly erroneous. The Court looks at the substance and not the form of the proposed bonds. However, once bonds are validated, and if appealed, the validation is affirmed, then recitations of constitutionality and satisfaction of conditions precedent are binding on the issuing authority, which will not be heard to question such matters in actions brought for the enforcement of bondholders' rights. Where bonds are unconstitutional and void *ab initio,* and the purchaser takes them with knowledge of their potential invalidity, the recitals of constitutionality will not be held binding on the issuer, but after validation, the courts will protect even the purchasers of unconstitutional bonds.

Second, when a government agency with taxing power is authorized by statute to levy a tax and to appropriate the proceeds thereof to the repayment of bonds, the statutory authority to levy the tax "may be regarded as mandatory and not merely permissive." State ex rel. Babson v. City of Sebring, 115 Fla. 176, 181, 155 So. 669, 672 (1934). After bonds have been issued, validated, and sold, the statutory authority to devote governmental revenues to the retirement of bonds becomes a contractual duty to do so. . . .

This Court very early held that article IX, section 6 of the Constitution of 1885 did not require a referendum when bonds were proposed to be sold to finance construction of a public works project that would be self-liquidating, that is, would generate revenue sufficient to repay the bonds without any supplemental allocations of tax revenues to that purpose. The Court later expanded this rule to allow the pledging of various sources of local government revenue other than ad valorem taxes. . . .

On the other hand, when a project is financed by the sale of bonds to be repaid with revenues produced by the project supplemented by governmental funds derived from ad valorem taxation, an approving vote of the electorate is required. . . .

. . . [T]he constitution was revised in 1968 to alter the language of the referendum requirement for local bonds. That part of the revision which added the words "certificates of indebtedness" and "any form of tax anticipation certificates" was found by the Court to have expressly rejected the judicial distinction among categories of public obligations. Most significantly here, there was added to the provision the qualifying words "payable from ad valorem taxation." Art. VII, §12, Fla. Const. This limitation on the scope of the referendum requirement seems to have been a ratification of prior judicial interpretation, and the law has continued to say that local revenue sources other than ad valorem taxation may be pledged without referendum.

The bonds in the instant case are payable from a trust fund, and the fund will receive revenue from two sources. One source is the money the Agency receives from sales, leases, and charges for the use of, redeveloped property. This source is analogous to revenues generated by a utility or facility. The other source is the money to be contributed each year by the county and city, measured by the tax increment. The source of this revenue is not limited to any specific governmental revenue. That the statutory duty to make the annual contributions would become a contractual duty, part of the obligation of the bonds, does not mean, however, that these bonds are payable from ad valorem taxation, in the constitutional sense of the term.

. . . [T]here is nothing in the constitution to prevent a county or city from using ad valorem tax revenues where they are required to compute and set aside a prescribed amount, when available, for a discrete purpose. The purpose of the constitutional limitation is unaffected by the legal commitment; the taxing power of the governmental units is unimpaired. What is critical to the constitutionality of the bonds is that, after the sale of bonds, a bondholder would have no right, if the redevelopment trust fund were insufficient to meet the bond obligations and the available resources of the county or city were insufficient to allow for the promised contributions, to compel by judicial action the levy of ad valorem taxation. Under the statute authorizing this bond financing the governing bodies are not obliged nor can they be compelled to levy any ad valorem taxes in any year. The only obligation is to appropriate a sum equal to any tax increment generated in a particular year from the ordinary, general levy of ad valorem taxes otherwise made in the city and county that year. Issuance of these bonds without approval of the voters of Dade County and the City of Miami Beach, consequently, does not transgress article VII, section 12.

All of the objections raised by the state have been considered. We hold that these bonds pass legal muster on all counts, and we therefore affirm the judgment of validation.[40]

---

40. There are exceptions to the general trend of judicial approval of TIF. For example, in Miller v. Covington Dev. Auth., 539 S.W.2d 1 (Ky. 1976), the Kentucky Supreme Court invalidated the state's program, finding an unconstitutional delegation of legislative power to the Local Development Authority, the agency that would have used the increased revenues attributable to redevelopment projects. Additionally, the court was troubled because, despite the benefits of TIF, "[t]he stubborn fact remains that school taxes can be raised only for school purposes, and there is neither jot nor tittle . . . that suggests the improvement of the schools or the improvement of education as being among [the legislation's] objectives." Id. at 5. In 1986, Kentucky lawmakers revitalized TIF by replacing the invalidated provisions. Ky. Rev. Stat. Ann. §§99.756 to .771 (Michie Bobbs-Merrill Supp. 1986).

See §144(c) of the Internal Revenue Code (part of the TRA of 1986), detailing criteria for granting tax-exempt status to a "qualified redevelopment bond," defined as "any bond issued as part of an issue 95 percent or more of the net proceeds of which are to be used for 1 or more redevelopment purposes in any designated blighted area." See

Notes

1. Recall the pattern of judicial acceptance of an expanded notion of public use in eminent domain law, as detailed in Chapter 7. Is there an even greater justification for this "liberalization" in the area of taxation?

Consider the position of dissenting Justice Fitzgerald in *Poletown*, supra page 798: "Condemnation places the burden of aiding industry on the few, who are likely to have limited power to protect themselves from the excesses of legislative enthusiasm for the promotion of industry. The burden of taxation is distributed on the great majority of the population, leading to a more effective check on improvident use of public funds." How effective *is* the "check on improvident use"? Is a "tax expenditure" — less obvious than a budget line item — not only easier to get through the legislative process, but also more prone to widespread abuse? See Surrey & McDaniel, Tax Expenditures (1985). On efforts to monitor use and effectiveness, see Bradford, Untangling the Income Tax 239-242 (1986); Staff of the Joint Committee on Taxation, 99th Cong., 2d Sess., Estimates of Federal Tax Expenditures for Fiscal Years 1988-1992 (Comm. Print 1987).

2. If Congress, given the Court's blessing in South Carolina v. Baker, 108 S. Ct. 1355 (1988), were to consider eliminating the state and local bond interest exclusion, what arguments would you make in opposition? From which interest groups would you seek lobbying support? How would you promote your position to the electorate?

3. On the Impact of Redevelopment Partnerships

■ JACKSON v. NEW YORK STATE URBAN
DEVELOPMENT CORPORATION
67 N.Y.2d 400, 494 N.E.2d 429, 503 N.Y.S.2d 298 (1986)

KAYE, Judge.

These cases, involving the State Environmental Quality Review Act (SEQRA) and the Eminent Domain Procedure Law (EDPL), challenge the plan of the New York State Urban Development Corporation (UDC) and its subsidiary (Times Square Redevelopment Corporation) to redevelop the Times Square area of Manhattan. According to UDC, the project represents an attempt to eliminate the persistent blight that has characterized the area and return it to productive use. Petitioners, who work or own buildings in the area or reside nearby, contend that UDC,

---

also Comment, Tax Increment Financing: Municipalities Avoiding Voter Accountability, 1987 Det. C.L. Rev. 89. — EDS.

B. The State and Local Experience

in its eagerness to get underway, has violated State law in several respects....

The project had its formal inception nearly six years ago with a Memorandum of Understanding, signed June 27, 1980, in which UDC and the city agreed to cooperate in a plan, with private participation, to redevelop the Times Square area. In February 1981, UDC and the city's Department of City Planning and Public Development Corporation issued a 100-page discussion document, identifying among its goals elimination of blight, revitalization of the area as an entertainment center, development of commercial potential, and strengthening of nearby areas. To these ends, the document proposed a mix of office towers, hotel space, theaters and retail space; presented options for the development of eight sites within the tentatively designated project area; and solicited public comment....

These four proceedings were commenced in December 1984 and early 1985 by two groups of petitioners.[1] The first group — the *Jackson* petitioners — consists of Fannie Mae Jackson and Larry Flower, elderly, disabled residents of Clinton, a neighborhood abutting the project area to the northwest, and designated a secondary impact area. One proceeding alleges violations of SEQRA, the second violations of EDPL. The thrust of both is that UDC and the FEIS [Final Environmental Impact Statement] did not adequately address the project's impact on the elderly, who will be forced out of their apartments by rising rents and unscrupulous landlords taking advantage of the gentrification of Clinton caused by the project. The *Jackson* petitioners claim that mitigation measures set forth in the FEIS are illusory and inadequate....

The *Jackson* petitioners urge that the FEIS was deficient in not giving sufficient attention to the impact of the project on the elderly citizens of Clinton, and in not adopting effective measures to mitigate their anticipated displacement by gentrification.

In a discussion that was greatly expanded between the DEIS [Draft Environmental Impact Statement] and the FEIS, UDC considered the effects of the project on Clinton, which the FEIS described as "a working class neighborhood" composed primarily of "[f]ive-story, walk-up residential buildings" with "light industrial, institutional and other public uses, and retail and commercial uses ... scattered throughout." The FEIS reviewed Clinton's history and characteristics, and presented

---

1. Additionally, the project has been the subject of several Federal actions: Cine 42nd St. Theatre Corp. v. Nederlander Org., 609 F. Supp. 113; Rosenthal & Rosenthal v. New York State Urban Dev. Corp., 605 F. Supp. 612, affd. Per Curiam 771 F.2d 44, cert. denied, 106 S. Ct. 1204; G. & A. Books v. Stern, 604 F. Supp. 898, affd. 770 F.2d 288, cert. denied sub nom. M.J.M. Exhibitors v. Stern, 106 S. Ct. 1195. (See also, Matter of Waybro Corp. v. Board of Estimate, 67 N.Y.2d 349, 502 N.Y.S.2d 707, 493 N.E.2d 931 [decided herewith].)

statistics on its population, income, rents and real estate values. As noted, since 1970 pressures on real estate values had increased in Clinton, and the city had already taken measures, including establishing a Clinton special district, to preserve and strengthen the residential character of that neighborhood. Nonetheless, since 1980 warehousing of rental apartments had increased and the resale value of some residential buildings has increased dramatically.

The FEIS recognized that the project would exacerbate these problems and identified measures available to the city to mitigate this impact, including strengthening antiharassment provisions and expanding city agencies charged with enforcement of such laws. At the same time, the FEIS considered other mitigation measures suggested by the public, including proposals that UDC establish a fund, derived from a portion of developers' profits, to provide low- and moderate-income housing in Clinton or to provide help to displaced Clinton residents. The FEIS rejected these suggestions, primarily because "to the extent that the project will generate funds for public amenities, such funds are committed to the acquisition and renovation of theatres on 42nd Street, and to subway improvements, both of which are major project goals. It is unlikely that surplus funds will become available which could be used to mitigate secondary impacts."

Finally, in approving the project plan UDC indorsed a number of mitigation measures, including the following specifically addressed to Clinton:

> (c) the Department of City Planning's intent to propose modifications to the Clinton Special District regulations in order to: (1) strengthen antiharassment provisions to protect current tenants; (2) prevent improper eviction and relocation practices; (3) revise zoning bonus provisions; and (4) make minor changes in the Clinton Special District sub-area boundaries;
>
> (d) the expansion of the Office of Midtown Enforcement's Clinton Enforcement Initiative to prevent tenant harassment, code violations and street nuisances in Clinton, all symptoms of illegal efforts to induce residential vacancies when land values increase, or to avoid the requirements of the Clinton Special District when renovation or conversion take place;
>
> (e) the Department of Housing Preservation and Development's commitment to the Clinton Special District to preserve the present character of the Clinton community, during both the construction and operation of the Project.

Even assuming that Clinton is "the locality" of the project within the meaning of EDPL 204(B)(3) — a question we need not decide — UDC plainly specified the general effect of the proposed project on the environment and residents of that neighborhood. The FEIS set

B. The State and Local Experience 989

forth the environmental impact of the proposed action on the Clinton community as a whole. Moreover, UDC recognized that many of Clinton's residents were of low to moderate income, and discussed their potential displacement due to rising real estate values. Having done so, UDC had no duty to give separate consideration to elderly residents of Clinton. Petitioners emphasize that eviction is particularly traumatic and difficult for the elderly. As the Appellate Division pointed out, "the elderly poor may have problems associated with displacement which are unique from the problems of other groups. However, the same can be said of other groups, such as children, who may be uprooted from familiar schools and moved from safe living quarters to inadequate living quarters, or of racial minorities, who face additional problems of racism in seeking new living quarters. The bottom line is that displacement from one's home is a serious threat with harsh ramifications for any poor person and the FEIS did not ignore this" (110 A.D.2d 304, 313, 494 N.Y.S.2d 700)....

The *Jackson* petitioners contend that they are given "less protection than birds or fish," pointing to Action for Rational Tr. v. West Side Highway Project, 536 F. Supp. 1225, affd. in part revd. in part sub nom. Sierra Club v. United States Army Corps of Engrs., 701 F.2d 1011 and Badura v. Guelli, 94 A.D.2d 972, 464 N.Y.S.2d 98, but those cases do not stand for a proposition that an EIS must separately consider every conceivable subgroup....

It may well have been wiser to earmark developers' profits for housing displaced persons in a secondary impact area than for subway and other improvements in the project area. But the Legislature has pointedly left such choices for the agency, not the courts. Dissatisfaction with an agency's proposed mitigation measures is not redressable by the courts so long as those measures have a rational basis in the record. The statutory goals of EDPL are fulfilled once there has been adequate disclosure and the agency has concluded, based upon sufficient evidence, that a public purpose would be served. That threshold has been met here.... Just as an agency must take a hard look at alternatives and consider a reasonable range of alternatives so, too, must an agency, employing a rule of reason, take a hard look at and consider potential mitigation measures. Here, there is substantial evidence that UDC has done so, and its choices cannot be upset by us.

Thus, we conclude that Special Term and the Appellate Division properly rejected the claims of the *Jackson* petitioners....

Notes

1. The third edition of this casebook painted a bleak picture of UDC's future:

In February 1975, UDC startled the investment world by doing the unthinkable — it defaulted on $135 million worth of debt to the big New York banks. Earlier, six nearly uninterrupted days of talks failed to get the banks to bail out UDC on $104.5 million in bond anticipation notes. Governor Carey reiterated his forecast that the failure of the corporation could lead to the collapse of bond markets across the country. N.Y. Times, Feb. 25, 1975. The state's first offer involved spending $270 million raised by selling mortgages on completed UDC projects to a new state agency. "No one seems to have a lien on anything," a legislative lawyer was quoted. On March 27, the eleven major New York commercial banks tentatively agreed to lend UDC $140 million to help it finish its projects — a day before an expected flood of lawsuits that would have forced it to declare itself bankrupt. "One unanswered question today was why the commercial bankers had agreed to participate even to this extent, after weeks during which some powerful members of the group had refused to offer the UDC any credit." N.Y. Times, Mar. 27, 1975.

UDC president Edward Logue, a few weeks before his February 6, 1975 resignation, spoke candidly of financial problems before the New York Senate Committee on Housing and Urban Development: "UDC's current financing problem can be summarized as an apparent inability to raise sufficient capital, through sale of its bonds, to complete its current construction program." He went on to list the reasons behind the loss of institution and investor confidence in UDC's securities: the moratorium on federal housing subsidies; inability to produce cash flow projections; the general deterioration of the bond market coupled with staggering capital funding needs for 1974-1975 of close to $1 billion. In his farewell message to the staff, he added: "One major source of trouble was the Nixon Administration's utter mismanagement of the economy, so badly handled that a whole new word 'stagflation' had to be created to express the somewhat bewildering phenomenon of deepening recession and rampant inflation."

As the *Jackson* case indicates, however, the UDC phoenix rose from the ashes. Following a reorganization, the UDC reentered the redevelopment arena in 1977, this time forgoing the bond route. The ambitious Times Square Project symbolizes the renewed strength of New York's innovative public-private project vehicle. See Osborn, New York's Urban Development Corporation: A Study in the Unchecked Power of Public Authority, 43 Brooklyn L. Rev. 237 (1977).

2. The arguments of the Clinton residents in the *Jackson* case strongly suggest that even the most innovative relocation scheme leaves much to be desired, particularly when one focuses on the specific needs of an identifiable group of displaced people. For an especially complicated relocation scheme, see Fox v. HUD, supra page 866.

For a helpful introduction to the growing body of literature on the causes and implications of gentrification, see Montgomery, Interpreting Gentrification Case Studies: A Perspective, 28 Wash. U. J. Urb. &

DOONESBURY
by Garry Trudeau
DR. DAN, I WONDER IF YOU COULD EXPLAIN TO OUR LISTENERS WHAT "GENTRIFICATION" MEANS..
FOR SURE. IT WORKS LIKE THIS: A DEVELOPER BUYS A DILAPIDATED HOUSE IN A DEPRESSED NEIGHBORHOOD..
HE FIXES IT UP AND RESELLS IT TO A YOUNG, MIDDLE-CLASS COUPLE. THIS ENCOURAGES OTHER "GENTRY" TO BUY INTO THE NEIGHBORHOOD, AND BEFORE LONG, A FANTASTIC REAL ESTATE MARKET BOOMS WHERE NONE EXISTED BEFORE!
AND WHAT HAPPENS TO THE LOW INCOME TENANTS WHO ARE DISPLACED? DOES ANYONE CARE?
SURE, WE DO. THESE PEOPLE ARE VERY IMPORTANT TO THE WHOLE PROCESS!
THEY ARE?
OF COURSE. THEY MOVE ON TO DEVALUE OTHER PROPERTIES. WITHOUT THEM, THE WHOLE SYSTEM FALLS APART.
11-13
G B Trudeau

Contemp. L. 241 (1985). Also see the Model Anti-Displacement Zoning Ordinance included in Marcuse, To Control Gentrification: Anti-Displacement Zoning and Planning for Stable Residential Districts, 13 N.Y.U. Rev. L. and Soc. Change 931 (1984-1985). For additional proposed remedies, see Bryant and McGee, Gentrification and the Law: Combatting Urban Displacement, 25 Wash. U. J. Urb. & Contemp. L. 43 (1983).

CASE STUDY #4

4. Maryland Enterprise Zones

■ GREATER BALTIMORE COMMITTEE, INC., REPORT OF THE ENTERPRISE ZONE SUBCOMMITTEE
1-3, 8, 10, 20-22 (July 10, 1981)

The Greater Baltimore Committee is a business organization with a membership of over eight hundred Baltimore area firms and is the Chamber of Commerce of Metropolitan Baltimore. . . .

Perhaps more than any other City, Baltimore has given great attention and consideration to the enterprise zone concept. Baltimore City first expressed an interest in the concept over a year ago when the Department of Housing and Community Development invited Dr. Stuart M. Butler to come to Baltimore and explain the enterprise zone concept in detail to the Department's staff.

Since that time, an inter-departmental working group has been actively studying enterprise zones and Baltimore City officials have presented their views and support of enterprise zones in several forums nationwide. In an appearance before the Subcommittee, Baltimore City officials revealed that they have had four areas under study as possible sites for enterprise zones for some time.

Among the sites under study is the Park Heights area of Baltimore City. Park Heights seems to be well suited to the enterprise zone concept. Park Heights is a depressed area with high unemployment and is somewhat unique in that it is a residential area with good quantities of open land available for capital investments. Baltimore City has moved ahead with an aggressive business development program which has been substantially aided by federal programs which may be discontinued as well as being enhanced by private sector commitments to the area. . . .

In addition, enterprise zone law has been enacted by the Maryland State Legislature with the support of the City. This enabling legislation

B. The State and Local Experience

was passed to ensure that Maryland law will not conflict with Federal enterprise zone legislation. . . .[41]

With these cautions, and with the hope that the enterprise zones concept and legislation can be refined and improved, *the Enterprise Zone Subcommittee believes that the enactment of enterprise zone legislation may be of some help to the difficult process of making the urban centers of our nation more effective economically in terms of new business and new jobs.*

It appears to the Subcommittee that while existing urban programs have positively aided in urban revitalization, they have not made significantly satisfactory inroads in widespread unemployment or economic development. Once again, it is urged that the adoption of the enterprise zone concept be tempered by the realization of its possible limitations.

We believe the Legislation's final form should be simple in terms of comprehension so that the incentives may be clearly understood and evaluated. The enterprise zone law should not be so loaded with benefits and reporting requirements that it becomes a Christmas tree, meaning all things to all people, rather than a simple experiment. *We also urge that enterprise zone law and administration not be saddled with onerous or burdensome bureaucracy and paperwork that has bedevilled so many other programs.* If entrepreneurs are to be encouraged to take a chance on enterprise zones, so should the government. Flexibility should not be sacrificed to some mythical accounting of public dollars. . . .

The Subcommittee feels the establishment of ten to twenty-five zones per year for three years extends the enterprise zone concept beyond the realm of experimentation into the inventory of proven, operational public policy. The Subcommittee suggests that the refined enterprise zone be established in a limited number of sites not to exceed ten. . . .

The Subcommittee is quite familiar with what Baltimore has done in terms of economic development and what remains to be done to cope with its problems of unemployment and underdevelopment. The Subcommittee is also familiar with the City's pioneering in what is in effect an enterprise zone in its Park Heights development, and the City's desire to continue its tradition of aggressive experimentation by becoming an enterprise zone test city. *The Enterprise Zone Subcommittee believes that Baltimore should, for these reasons, make an excellent site for the experiment and so recommends.* With all of the tools for economic and social

---

41. In 1981, in (unrealized) anticipation of a federal act, the Maryland legislature passed its first EZ statute, H.B. 1588. An EZ was defined as an area "officially designated" by the federal government. This EZ program, providing for a reduction in state workers' compensation premiums and unemployment insurance fund contributions and for an exemption from state income tax, was repealed when S.B. 811 was enacted in 1982. The federally triggered designation was carried over to the current legislation. However, state incentives to businesses located in any federal EZ would not be automatic. Md. Ann. Code art. 41, §12-302(f) (1986). — EDS.

development and support in use in Baltimore, the enterprise zone may add still another dimension that may contribute, within the limits set by its proponents.

■ FUNKHOUSER AND SAQUELLA, ESTABLISHING ENTERPRISE ZONES IN MARYLAND
3-7 Lincoln Institute of Land Policy, Basic Concepts Series No. 106 (1984)

In early February, 1982, a representative of the Baltimore City administration contacted the Governor's office to ask about his sponsoring or backing for enterprise zone legislation being prepared by Baltimore City. A meeting was held soon thereafter to review the proposed legislation. Although many changes were eventually made, the enacted bill resembled this first version in many respects.

The meeting involved Baltimore City representatives from the Mayor's Office and the Baltimore Economic Development Corporation and state officials from the Governor's office and the Department of Economic and Community Development. After some preliminary discussion and suggested changes by state officials, Baltimore City officials urged state officials to sponsor the legislation. Baltimore City believed that state sponsorship would enhance the legislation's changes for enactment and prevent it from being labeled a "City bill."

Initially, state officials were reluctant to sponsor the bill for two reasons. First, they did not believe that they had sufficient knowledge of the bill or the subject matter. Although state officials had visited enterprise zones in the United Kingdom the previous summer, they had many concerns about duplicating the British concept in Maryland and were aware of the General Assembly's traditional reluctance to use the tax system, a key aspect of the bill, to influence certain kinds of economic activity. Second, they had not done the prior political consultation usually involved in sponsoring legislation, especially a bill embodying such a new concept. In addition, the filing deadline for legislation was just a few days away.

Despite these doubts, state officials changed their position, and it was decided that the Department of Economic and Community Development (DECD) rather than the Governor would sponsor the legislation. . . .

With DECD now sponsoring the legislation, state officials began a closer examination of the bill, and a concentrated effort was made over the next few days to arrive at a mutually acceptable draft and meet the closely approaching filing deadline. . . .

Throughout work on the legislation, there was philosophical dis-

B. The State and Local Experience

cussion as to just what an enterprise zone should attempt to do. A consensus formed that the primary purpose of the zone was to create jobs, especially jobs for chronically unemployed individuals. This consensus was reflected in the requirement added to the legislation that a business had to create jobs to earn any of the incentives offered. This emphasis by state officials on job creation was also a result of the visits to Great Britain and Ireland. The decisions on size and job creation placed a strong emphasis in the Maryland program toward economic activity and job creation rather than community revitalization. . . .

The initial proposal provided for a direct loan program for businesses in an enterprise zone. State officials did not want to operate another direct loan program and also believed that the authorized amount was insufficient to conduct a direct loan program if it were approved. The result was that the loan program was changed to a program to provide for loan guarantees of up to 100%. . . .

The enterprise zone legislation was introduced as HB 1775 and SB 811. Both bills received joint referrals: HB 1775 to the Ways and Means and the Economic Matters Committees; SB 811 to the Economic Affairs and the Budget and Taxation Committees. Ways and Means and Economic Affairs were the primary bodies in the respective chambers. . . .

On March 30, 1982, the Senate Economic Affairs Committee voted to give SB 811 a favorable report. The Senate Budget and Taxation Committee would have to do the same before the bill could reach the full Senate. The latter committee was initially skeptical about the bill and was the first body to raise seriously the issue of fiscal cost. However, after it considered the favorable arguments made by committee chairmen and the major effort already made by the Economic Affairs Committee, the Senate Budget and Taxation Committee put aside its hesitancy and favorably voted the bill.

After an explanation of the bill and the more than sixty amendments, the Senate voted preliminary approval on April 2nd. SB 811 received final Senate approval on April 6th. Although some twenty-five hours were spent discussing the bill in various committees, it went through the Senate floor with no debate.

The House received SB 811 on April 6th, just six days before final adjournment scheduled for April 12th. The House subcommittee — realizing the enormous amount of work already done on the Senate side to develop a solid piece of legislation, and the growing momentum for the bill — moved quickly to recommend it to the full committee. The subcommittee could not refer to "all the problems" in the bill because they had all been corrected in the Senate. Also, because of their involvement with the Senate subcommittee, the members better understood and felt more confident about the legislation. The full Ways and Means Committee voted favorably on April 8th. The Committee

Incentives Available in Existing State and Local EZ Programs*

A. Statutory authority

Alabama (AL)	Ala. Code §11-40-16
Arkansas (AR)	Ark. Stat. Ann. §§9-1701 to -1710
California (CA)	Cal. Gov't Code §§7070-7077, 7080-7099
Colorado (CO)	Colo. Rev. Stat. §§39-30-101 to -109
Connecticut (CT)	Conn. Gen. Stat. §§32-70 to -75
Florida (FL)	Fla. Stat. §§290.001-290.015
Georgia (GA)	H.B. No. 629 (1982)
Hawaii (HI)	Haw. Rev. Stat. §§209E-1 to -13
Illinois (IL)	Ill. Ann. Stat. Ch. 67 1/2, §§601-617
Indiana (IN)	Ind. Code Ann. §§4-4-6.1-1 to -8
Kansas (KS)	Kan. Stat. Ann. §§12-17,107 to 17,111
Kentucky (KY)	Ky. Rev. Stat. §§154.650-.700
Louisiana (LA)	La. Rev. Stat. Ann. §§51:1781-1790
Maryland (MD)	Md. Ann. Code art. 41, §§12-301 to -305
Michigan (MI)	Mich. Comp. Laws Ann. §§125.2101-.2122
Minnesota (MN)	Minn. Stat. Ann. §§273.1312-.1314
Mississippi (MS)	Miss. Code Ann. §§57-51-1 to -15
Missouri (MO)	Mo. Ann. Stat. §§135.200-.255
Nevada (NV)	Nev. Rev. Stat. §§274.010-.300
New Jersey (NJ)	NJ Stat. Ann. §§52:27H-60 to -89
New York (NY)	N.Y. Gen. Mun. Law §§955-969
Ohio (OH)	Ohio Rev. Code Ann. §§5709.61-.66
Oklahoma (OK)	Okla. Stat. tit. 62, §§690.1-.17
Oregon (OR)	Or. Rev. Stat. §§284.110-.260
Pennsylvania (PA)	16 Pa. Code Ch. 23 (1983)
Rhode Island (RI)	R.I. Gen. Laws §§42-64.3-1 to -11
Tennessee (TN)	Tenn. Code Ann. §§13-28-101 to -114
Texas (TX)	Tex. Rev. Civ. Stat. Ann. art. 5190.7
Vermont (VT)	Vt. Stat. Ann. tit. 10, §§691-698
Virginia (VA)	Va. Code §§59.1-270 to -284
West Virginia (WV)	W.Va. Code §§5B-2B-1 to -9

B. The State and Local Experience

Incentives Available in Existing State and Local EZ Programs
(continued)

B. Tax incentives

Property tax reduction or exemption	CT, GA, HI, IL, IN, KY, MD, MI, MN, MO, NY, OH, OR, PA, RI, TX
Franchise tax deferral	LA, NV, NJ, OH, TX, VA
Sales tax exemption on zone purchases and/or sales	AR, CO, CT, FL, HI, IL, KS, KY, LA, MN, MS, NJ, NY, OK, TX, VA, WV
Investment tax credits for real improvements	CO, FL, IL, KS, MN, MO, NY, OK
Employee training expense credit	CT, IL, MO, NV, OH
Employer credit for selective hiring	AR, CA, CO, FL, HI, IN, KS, LA, MD, MO, NJ, NY, OH, RI, VT, WV
New job tax credit	AR, CO, CT, FL, IN, LA, MD, MS, MO, NJ, NY, OH, RI, VT
Income tax credit-employer	AR, CA, CO, CT, FL, HI, IL, IN, KS, LA, MD, MN, MS, MO, NJ, NY, OH, RI, VT, WV
Income tax deduction/credit-employee	CA, IN, RI
Community investment tax credits	FL, IL, PA, TN
Miscellaneous tax credits/reductions	AL, CA, HI, IN, KY, MN, NV, NJ, NY, OH, PA, TN, TX, VA, WV

C. Capital financing

Capital investment fund	CT, FL, IL, IN, MD, MS, NY, OK, PA
Bond support	CA, CT, FL, IL, KS, LA, MS, NV, NY, OK, TX, VT
Public/private support mix	CA, IL, IN, LA, MD, MN, MS, NV, OH, PA, VT
Tax increment financing	FL, IN, KS, MI, NV, NY, TX

D. Miscellaneous incentives

Insurance for zone businesses	IL, NV
Regulatory relief	AL, AR, CA, HI, IL, IN, KY, LA, MI, MO, NV, NJ, NY, OH, OR, PA, RI, TN, TX, VA, WV
Public corp. created to provide services	CA, IL, IN, KY, NV, NJ, NY, PA, TN, TX

* *Source:* Wolf, Potential Legal Pitfalls Facing State and Local Enterprise Zones, 8 Urban Law & Poly. 77, 119-20 (1986-1987). Arizona, Delaware, the District of Columbia, Maine, Utah, and Wisconsin have since joined the EZ fold.

members raised few questions, relying mostly on the recommendation of the subcommittee. Also, in contrast to the Senate, the rural delegates had now become strong advocates of the bill.

On April 9th, the House of Delegates gave preliminary approval to the bill. The floor leader for the bill expected extensive questioning and debate, but there was no debate on the preliminary approval and no amendments were offered.

State officials discovered two technical defects in the bill after it had passed the Senate, but rather than correct the bill in the House and possibly lose it in the chaos of the day of adjournment, it was decided to leave the bill alone and to correct it the next year. It was important to have no amendments, as this would have necessitated sending the bill back to the Senate and raised the threat of final action not occurring before adjournment on April 12th.

On April 10th, the House of Delegates gave final legislative enactment of SB 811 by vote of 121-0. The Governor signed the bill on May 20th, and it became law on July 1, 1982.

■ MARYLAND ANNOTATED CODE
Art. 41 (1986)[42]

§12-302.

(a) *Application by political subdivision.* — Any political subdivision may apply to the Secretary for designation of an area within that political subdivision as an enterprise zone, but if a county seeks to designate an area within a municipal corporation as an enterprise zone, then the governing body of the municipal corporation must first consent.

(b) *Application by county on behalf of municipal corporation.* — Any county may apply to the Secretary on behalf of a municipal corporation, with the consent of such municipal corporation, for designation of any area within that municipal corporation as an enterprise zone.

(c) *Joint applications by political subdivisions.* — Two or more political

---

42. These statutes reflect changes made in the original state EZ program. Subsequent amendments have excluded owners of residential property from receiving tax credits, allowed for joint applications by two or more political subdivisions, clarified the terms under which a business could receive tax credits, defined "economically disadvantaged," and redefined "qualified employees."

In 1985, H.B. 1715 was passed, allowing an exemption from the ban on out-of-state banks locating in Maryland. The statute provides that a non-Maryland bank may locate in an EZ if it can meet stringent criteria, including the employment of "at least 500 persons full time at the facility." The same legislation allows the banking commissioner to waive the EZ requirement, but only if the facility employs 750 persons. See Md. Fin. Inst. Code Ann. §5-903(c) (1986). This bill was apparently passed to allow Citicorp to locate on a particular site in the Hagerstown zone. However, Citicorp gave up the EZ incentives in favor of a location just outside the zone that was more visible from an adjacent highway.

Enterprise Zones in Maryland

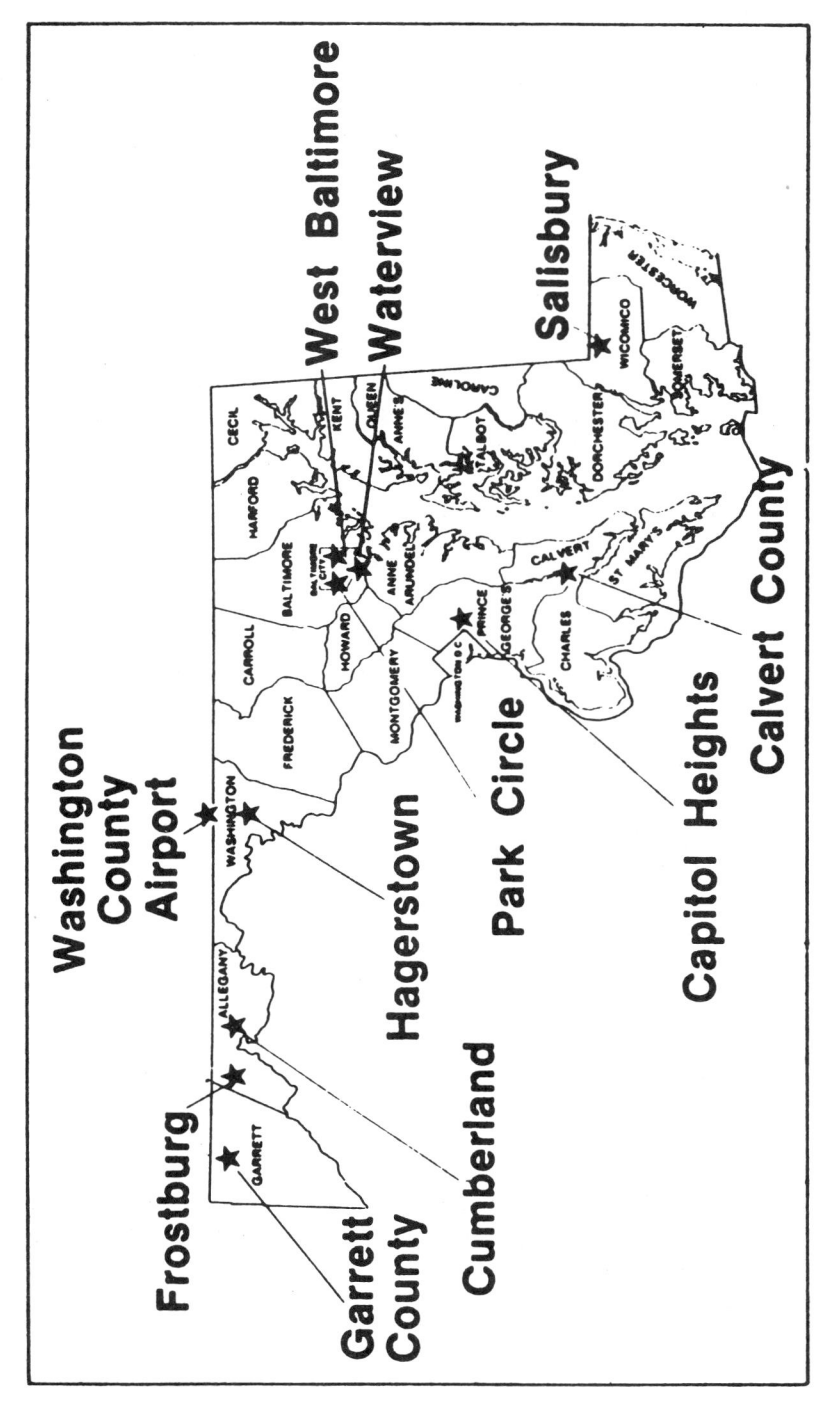

Source: Maryland Department of Economic and Community Development.

subdivisions may apply jointly to the Secretary for designation of an area as an enterprise zone which may be located astride their common boundaries. . . .

(e) *Restrictions on designations by Secretary.* — Within 60 days following any submission date, the Secretary may designate one or more enterprise zones from among the applications submitted to the Secretary on or before that submission date, provided, however, that the Secretary may not designate more than 6 enterprise zones in any 12 month period and no county may receive more than 1 area designated as an enterprise zone in any calendar year. The determination of the Secretary as to the areas designated enterprise zones shall be final, except that, for any area not designated an enterprise zone, a political subdivision may reapply at any time to the Secretary for designation of that area as an enterprise zone. . . .

§12-303.

(a) *In general.* — The Secretary may not designate any area an enterprise zone unless that area satisfies at least one of the following requirements:

(1) The average rate of unemployment in the area, or within a reasonable proximity within that county to that area, for the most recent 18 month period for which data are available must be at least 150 percent of the average rate of unemployment in either the State of Maryland or the United States, whichever average rate is greater, during the same period;

(2) The population in the area or within a reasonable proximity within that county to that area is a low-income poverty area on the basis of the most recent census;

(3) At least 70 percent of the families living in the area or within a reasonable proximity within that county to that area have incomes that are less than an amount equal to 80 percent of the median family income within the political subdivision in which the area is located; or

(4) Population in the area or within a reasonable proximity within that county to that area decreased by 10 percent between the date of the most recent census and the date of the immediately preceding census, and the political subdivision can demonstrate to the Secretary's satisfaction that either chronic abandonment or demolition of property is occurring in that area or substantial property tax arrearages exist within that area. . . .

§12-304.

(a) *In general.* — The following incentives and initiatives shall be available to business entities to the extent provided for in this section:

(1) The special property tax credit set forth in §9-103 of the Tax-Property Article.[43]

(2) The income tax credits set forth in Article 81, §291A of the Code.

(3) The consideration for loans under the Maryland Industrial Land Act. . . .[44]

(4) The consideration for grants and loans from the Maryland Industrial and Commercial Redevelopment Fund. . . .

(5) Insurance by the Enterprise Zone Venture Capital Guarantee Fund. . . .

■ BALTIMORE ECONOMIC DEVELOPMENT CORP. (BEDCO), ENTERPRISE ZONE ANNUAL REPORT
1-4 (1984)

The Park Circle Industrial Park was designated a State enterprise zone by the Secretary of the Department of Economic and Community Development in December 1982. At that time, the Park was undergoing

---

43. In the first five years of operation, the tax credit is equal to 80 percent of the property tax imposed on the EZ property, declining 10 percent per year in the sixth through tenth years (from 70 to 30 percent). — EDS.

44. This credit may amount to up to $1500 per qualified employee, depending on the wages paid that employee, whether the employee is an "economically disadvantaged individual," and whether the employee has been rehired after having been laid off for longer than six months by the qualified zone employer. For pertinent definitions, see Md. Ann. Code art. 81, §291A (Supp. 1986):

(3) "Qualified employee" means an individual who:
  (i) Is a new employee or an employee rehired after being laid off for more than 6 months by the business entity;
  (ii) Is employed at least 25 hours per week by a business entity for at least 6 months before or during that business entity's taxable year for which a credit is claimed;
  (iii) Spends at least one-half of the hours under subparagraph (ii) of this paragraph, either in the enterprise zone or on activities of the business entity resulting directly from its location in the enterprise zone; and
  (iv) Is hired by the business entity after the later of:
    1. The date on which the enterprise zone is designated; or
    2. The date on which the business entity locates in the enterprise zone;
(4) "Economically disadvantaged individual" means an individual who is certified by provisions adopted by the Department of Employment and Training as an individual who, before becoming employed by a business entity in an enterprise zone:
  (i) Was qualified to participate in training activities for the economically disadvantaged under Title II, Part B of the Federal Comprehensive Employment and Training Act or its successor and was unemployed for at least 30 consecutive days before becoming employed by the business entity; or
  (ii) In the absence of an applicable federal act, met the criteria for an economically disadvantaged individual established by the Secretary of Economic and Community Development. — EDS.

significant physical changes.... Today, these changes are, for the most part, completed and job creation activities are well underway. There are numerous businesses which have either located in the Park or with whom the City is currently negotiating a commitment....

The cornerstone of the Park is Control Data's Business and Technology Center which is located on a 5.9 acre site on Druid Park Drive. The BTC serves as an incubator for small and new businesses and in this case many of the businesses are minority owned and operated. In addition to providing office and industrial space, the BTC provides a set of shared services such as financial, legal, secretarial, and accounting. These services are important to new businesses but are often unaffordable except through the economies of scale available at a BTC. The facility was developed in a vacant surplus City-owned school which Control Data leased. In addition, they constructed a shell building behind the school, utilizing a $1.5M MILA [Maryland Industrial Loan Act] loan.

The facility is currently 60% occupied, housing 57 tenants. Of these, over 85% are minority owned. In total, these firms have created 220 jobs. All of the jobs are new to Park Circle and all employers have given priority consideration to Park Heights residents in hiring. The facility represents an investment by Control Data of approximately $3.5M. The major tenant in the facility is the Commercial Credit Company which has opened a bindery. The bindery was visited by President Reagan in 1981. The bindery employs 59 people and represents an investment by Commercial Credit of about $750,000.

The availability of enterprise zone benefits, particularly the property tax credits, were extremely important with regard to the development of the BTC. The BTC was certified by the City as eligible for the property tax credits and received the credit by the State....

The City of Baltimore is quite pleased with the status of the Park Circle Industrial Park Enterprise Zone and considers the availability of enterprise zone benefits pivotal to the successful completion of the Industrial Park. When one reviews the companies located within the Park, the significance of the benefits becomes apparent.[45]

45. See McReynolds, Enterprise Zones: Are They Working?, Baltimore Bus. J., Apr. 2-8, 1984, at 12:

> It's been just over a year now since the state legislature decided to work a little magic and breathe life back into Maryland's dying areas by using an old Oriental trick called enterprise zones. And the jury is still out on how well this sleight of hand is working, with wide variations in the results experienced by the zones.
>
> The detractors cry that there have been little or no significant turnabouts in the economically stricken parts of the state as a result of all the financial incentives. But leaders in the enterprise movement point proudly to the $18 million in private and public investments in these areas that is to serve as the foundation on which the 10-year program will be built.... [T]hese zones have spawned 330 new jobs in the state. They also have generated $12.5 million in private investment for new

MARYLAND FORM 500Z

(Revised 1987)

ATTACH TO: Maryland Form 500, 502, or 505

ENTERPRISE ZONE TAX CREDIT

FOR TAXABLE YEAR BEGINNING _____ , 19 _____
ENDING _____ , 19 _____

19 ___

DO NOT WRITE IN THIS SPACE

Name as shown on Form 500, 502, or 505

Federal Employer Identification No. (or Social Security No.) | Maryland Central Registration No.

SEE INSTRUCTIONS ON REVERSE SIDE
ATTACH A COPY OF THE LOCAL ZONE ADMINISTRATOR'S CERTIFICATION

PART A — CREDIT FOR ECONOMICALLY DISADVANTAGED EMPLOYEES

1. Number of employees eligible for first year credit ....
2. Number of employees eligible for second year credit ....
3. Number of employees eligible for third year credit ....
4. Credit for first year (limited to $1,500 of wages paid to each employee) ....
5. Credit for second year (limited to $1,000 of wages paid to each employee) ....
6. Credit for third year (limited to $500 of wages paid to each employee) ....
7. Total (Add Lines 4, 5, and 6) ....

PART B — CREDIT FOR REHIRED EMPLOYEES

8. Number of employees eligible for first year credit ....
9. Number of employees eligible for second year credit ....
10. Credit for first year (limited to $1,000 of wages paid to each employee) ....
11. Credit for second year (limited to $750 of wages paid to each employee) ....
12. Total (Add Lines 10 and 11) ....

PART C — CREDIT FOR OTHER QUALIFIED EMPLOYEES

13. Number of employees eligible for credit not included in PART A or B ....
14. Credit (limited to $500 of wages paid to each employee) ....

PART D — SUMMARY

15. Enter amount from Line 7 ....
16. Enter amount from Line 12 ....
17. Enter amount from Line 14 ....
18. Carry over of excess credit from prior tax years (Attach computation) ....
19. Tentative Credit (Add Lines 15 through 18) ....
20. Enter tax from Form 500-line 9, Form 502-line 62, or Form 505-line 62 ....
21. Allowable Credit (Line 19 or Line 20, **whichever is less**) (Enter on Form 500-lines 2c and 10c, Form 502-lines 21 and 68, or 505-lines 19 and 68) ....
22. Excess Credit Carry Forward (Subtract Line 20 from Line 21) ....

1003

■ MARYLAND DIVISION OF LOCAL GOVERNMENT ASSISTANCE, MARYLAND'S ENTERPRISE ZONE PROGRAM: A THIRD YEAR REPORT
9-10 (June 13, 1986)

The Enterprise Zone Program has been in operation three years, time enough to generate data sufficient to provide a tentative evaluation of its effectiveness as an economic and community development tool, but not long enough to allow for a definitive program evaluation. Based on our analysis of the data now available, it appears that utilization of the program is growing and that it is increasingly meeting the objectives established for it. . . .

An examination of the program to date provides us with reason to be optimistic about its future. During the three years of program operation there has been a net increase of 78 new business ventures in the zones. Increased activity in the zones is reflected in recent rapid increases in the utilization of the property tax credits and the income tax credit.

Zone administrators report that during 1985 firms within the zones invested $21.8 million in capital improvements, machinery and new construction. Since the beginning of the program, zone administrators report a total investment of $62.1 million.

Data provided by businesses in the zones indicate that well over 2,000 new jobs have been created, many of them for disadvantaged workers. These records indicate that over $24 million in wages have been paid to workers employed since the various zones were established. The data available to us does not allow an estimation of the number of pre-zone existing jobs that have been retained as a result of the program.

According to state records, the cost of the program to the state has been modest. Direct costs to date for the income tax incentive and the property tax incentive total just over $618,000. The total cost to the state is just over $429,000 and, to local jurisdictions, slightly over $189,000.

---

construction, rehabilitation, machinery and equipment. Public investment in the areas total $5.5 million.

But unfortunately for areas such as Allegany County and Capitol Heights, these numbers don't divide up evenly among the different zones. And the effect of the state's new classifications is just as varied and difficult to categorize as the locations themselves.

Probably the most successful enterprise zone in the state — in terms of capital improvements and new jobs created — is the Park Circle enterprise zone in northwest Baltimore.

For a less flattering view of results in the Park Circle EZ, see Weiss, Enterprise Zones Are Just Part of the Answer for Reviving an Urban Economy, Governing, Aug. 1988, at 57, 61. — EDS.

C. Housing the Deserving and Undeserving Poor 1005

... [U]tilization of the tax incentives is growing. This is generally a positive sign that the Enterprise Zone program is becoming a viable economic and community development tool in Maryland. Careful monitoring of the program to ensure its effectiveness will now become increasingly important.

Questions

1. Given the difficulty of ascertaining the reasons businesses locate, invest, or expand in a particular area, how would you recommend state and local officials monitor the success or failure of an EZ program?

2. What answer should officials give to nonzone businesses that complain about unfair competition? After all, those companies that receive zone incentives can lower the cost to the consumer of (and the profit to the business from) goods and services.

3. Maryland's decision to use zones solely for economic development distinguishes the program from most of the other state EZs, whose sponsors paid at least lip service to the goal of neighborhood revitalization. Can the trickle down from a healthy business climate to area residents effectively take the place of a direct infusion of state and local funds?

4. Do you perceive any problems, particularly state and federal constitutional ones, with state EZ schemes? See Wolf, Potential Legal Pitfalls Facing State and Local Enterprise Zones, 8 Urb. L. & Poly. 77, 78 (1986): "The potential pitfalls include: unconstitutional taxation and financing schemes, questionable preferential hiring requirements, anticompetitive decision-making, equal protection violations, deregulatory complications, and eminent domain problems."

C. HOUSING THE DESERVING AND UNDESERVING POOR

Providing decent housing — what Justice Holmes characterized as "a necessary of life"[46] — has been the goal of public/private partnerships for the past five decades. While governmental programs often have complemented the redevelopment efforts discussed in Part A of this chapter, there have been conflicts as well — over the efficacy and wisdom of publicly financed or subsidized housing, the demographic and political implications of selecting low- to moderate-income housing

46. Block v. Hirsh, 256 U.S. 135, 156 (1921).

sites, and the equity and economic efficacy of incentives made available to builders, lenders, and investors active in the housing field.

As in the parallel history of urban redevelopment programs, the nation has also experienced the same devolution of responsibility from federal to state and local participants, the same evolution and diversification of the public/private partnership. The sources of capital for improving the lot of the homeless and "under-housed" — ranging from grants to loans and loan guarantees, real estate syndications motivated by tax incentives, mortgage revenue and secondary market bond issues, and housing vouchers — have produced an impressive inventory of habitable, even desirable, housing stock, despite the inevitable by-products of scandal, waste, and faulty targeting. The past few years have witnessed significant cutbacks in existing support and incentive programs,[47] reflecting concerns over an increasing budget deficit and the proper role of the federal government in the housing arena. Lacking a crystal ball, we can only guess how future federal and state administrations will respond to new shortfalls in the availability of decent housing stock.

The materials that close this chapter indicate that discrimination in the location, population, and treatment of lower-income neighborhoods and housing projects remains a serious challenge for courts and legislatures. Today, activism in the name of equality has lost much of its appeal, not only for elected officials and lawyers, but also for judges concerned about the proper judicial posture when faced with legislative abdication and bureaucratic morasses. Many have questioned whether judges are adequately trained for the task of overseeing large-scale redistributive efforts.[48] When the people have spoken, by referendum or by clear messages to their elected representatives, is the activist judge a rebel without just cause? Should we rely instead on the marketplace, rather than inefficient land-use controls (or nontraditional tools like inclusionary and incentive zoning), to encourage a healthy income mix?[49]

---

47. For a recent volume of essays evaluating the impact of Reagan Administration budget cuts on the nation's urban centers, see Reagan and the Cities (Peterson & Lewis eds. 1986).

48. The leading treatment remains Chayes, The Role of the Judge in Public Law Litigation, 89 Harv. L. Rev. 281 (1976).

49. On the relationship between the supply of housing and land-use controls, see Fischel, The Economics of Zoning Laws: A Property Rights Approach to American Land Use Controls 125-149 (1985).

C. Housing the Deserving and Undeserving Poor

1. *Alternative Paths to Affordable Housing*

■ MITCHELL, THE HISTORICAL CONTEXT FOR HOUSING POLICY
Federal Housing Policy and Programs 3-17 (1985)

Direct involvement by the federal government in housing really began a half century ago, during the 1930s. Since then every Congress has enacted legislation designed to remedy some shortcomings in the nation's housing delivery system, including defects in previous legislation. A simple chronology summarizing major housing legislation and executive actions, prepared for the U.S. Congress in 1975, devoted one-half page to four entries from 1892 to 1931, and 222 pages to those 1931 through 1974....

The trial and error attacks of the past half-century have led to a bewildering variety of housing-related programs. In their broadest outlines these have included:

1. a federally regulated mortgage finance system;
2. mortgage insurance;
3. interest rate subsidies to home owners, developers, and landlords;
4. tax deductions for mortgage interest;
5. special depreciation allowances for rental housing;
6. low-rent public housing;
7. rent supplements for low-income households;
8. subsidy packages for central city redevelopment; and
9. anti-discrimination measures....

The activism of the 1960s spawned a host of highly visible study commissions and reports. The National Advisory Commission on Civil Disorders, chaired by Illinois Governor Otto Kerner, produced its famous "Kerner Report" in early 1969. The report warned that "Our Nation is moving toward two societies, one black, one white — separate and unequal." Two other commissions appointed in 1967 issued reports on successive days in December, 1968, which were particularly relevant to housing policies. The National Commission on Urban Problems, chaired by Senator Paul Douglas, produced Building the American City, a classic review of urban problems, with summaries and recommendations about housing and urban-related programs. The President's Committee on Urban Housing, chaired by industrialist Edgar F. Kaiser, produced A Decent Home, which focused especially on how the private enterprise system could be harnessed to provide more and better housing for the urban masses. It was the Kaiser Commission which first recommended that a production goal of 26 million new and rehabilitated housing units be established as national policy and that 6 million of those units be targeted for low-income families.

The Housing Act of 1968 did, in fact, officially establish that 26-million-unit, 10-year production goal. Among the new programs aimed at achieving that objective was the Section 235 interest-rate subsidy, designed to make homeownership more accessible to low-income families by lowering monthly mortgage payments. From 1971 through 1973 housing starts exceeded 2 million annually, thanks in large part to the provisions of the Housing Act of 1968.

By 1973 federal housing programs abounded. The cost was rising, and future subsidy payments already committed reached levels that were disturbing to the administration. Between 1968 and 1973 some 375,000 public housing units had been made available for occupancy, whereas only 470,000 had been added in the 18 years since 1949. Changes in public housing rentals made by a series of amendments proposed by Senator Edward Brooke in 1969 and 1970 linked payments to tenants' ability to pay rather than to operating costs. But public housing tenants by that time were no longer primarily the working poor temporarily down on their luck and upwardly mobile. They were, increasingly, members of a semi-permanent dependent class whose incomes, often from public sources, were low and whose chances of upward mobility were dim. Public housing authorities throughout the country were faced with overwhelming cash flow problems and dismal financial outlooks. When scandals began to surface, especially involving the new interest-subsidy programs, President Nixon had had enough. As public criticism mounted, he ordered HUD to conduct an extensive national housing policy review. As expected, the review recommended that current programs be suspended until the federal government's role could be assessed and redefined. The 1973 moratorium was accordingly declared and new authorizations were suspended....[50]

50. See Pennsylvania v. Lynn, 501 F.2d 848, 849-852 (D.C. Cir. 1974), in which the court refused to order the Secretary of HUD "to resume accepting, processing, and, where appropriate, approving applications for federal subsidy under three different housing programs." Judge McGowan supplied the following summary of the programs suspended by President Nixon's moratorium:

1. Section 101 is a rent supplement program under which the federal government agrees to make monthly rental payments on behalf of qualified tenants in housing erected under other government programs, such as 236 and 221(d)(3) projects. The government's contract with the developer, which may run for up to forty years, provides for HUD supervision of rent charges and tenant eligibility. Tenants, who must have incomes and assets below the applicable area maxima for public housing eligibility and be drawn from one of six specially targeted groups, pay rent equal to 25% of their income, and HUD pays the rest.
2. Section 235 is aimed at "assisting lower income families in acquiring homeownership" by subsidizing construction of single-family units for their

C. Housing the Deserving and Undeserving Poor

Public housing had by the early 1970s come under attack from nearly all directions, not just its traditional realtor enemies. Friends of government housing subsidy now questioned the efficiency of public housing; enormous capital outlays for new projects seemed to be disproportionate to the number of clients served. And on the related grounds of horizontal equity, public housing was woefully inadequate; approximately 3 million people living in about 1 million public housing units in 1971 constituted less than 5 percent of the eligible households....

... The [Housing and Community Development A]ct, under its Section 8, created three separate programs: one for existing housing units, one for units requiring substantial rehabilitation, and one for new rental housing construction. Under each, qualified low-income tenants would find suitable and affordable housing in the local market and pay one-fourth of their income as rent, the deficit to be made up by Section 8 allotments, usually to the local housing authority. This system of housing subsidy was intended to achieve the final feature of the act noted here: the scattering of low-income housing. If tenants found their own housing with private landlords, there would be no clearly visible subsidized housing projects and, hopefully, no inordinate concentration of low-income tenants in slums....

Notes

1. Just as legal controls over physical style and permitted use have a decided effect on the value of development, so can fiscal policy in its turn determine the location, type, and rate of development.[51] The degree to which credit is available influences the investment programs of financial institutions, the nature of the building industry, the volume

---

purchase. The builder/sponsor enters into an agreement whereby the government insures the mortgage, and then subsidizes its repayment to the extent that principal, interest, taxes, and insurance exceed 20% of the qualified vendee's income, with a subsidy ceiling so that the effective interest rate is not reduced below one per cent.

3. Section 236 follows a similar pattern for the purpose of "reducing rentals for lower income families" in housing owned by non-profit or "limited dividend" sponsors. HUD and the sponsors enter into an agreement for government regulation of rents and tenant eligibility, in return for which the government insures the mortgage and undertakes to pay the mortgage interest in excess of one per cent. Tenants pay rent calculated on the basis of operating expenses and mortgage interest at one per cent, or twenty-five per cent of their income, whichever is greater. — Eds.

51. Section 220, 68 Stat. 596, codified as amended at 12 U.S.C. §1715k (1982), providing generous terms for insured mortgages in urban renewal areas, and §221, 68 Stat. 599, codified as amended at 12 U.S.C. §1715*l* (1982), doing the same for relocation areas, are examples of this understanding of the need to spur private investment in order to achieve public land goals.

of construction, the standards of quality and design — and may even sway the basic pattern of land tenure.

The single most important form of private investment in the American economy is residential real estate. At the same time, this "castle" is the sector of the economy subject to most intensive and extensive regulation. In fact, so vital today is the risk-bearing role of government, by means of its insurance and guarantee function and its secondary market purchases, that the distinction between "public" and "private" housing is far less significant than is generally assumed.[52] The turbulent history of HUD's relations with private investors illustrates the problems arising where government attempts to influence, by a combination of carrots and sticks, the marketing and operation of property it neither owns nor manages. The housing industry has assumed many of the characteristics of a public utility — without the judicial and administrative framework common to that sector of the economy.

The effectiveness of credit control and taxation should be contrasted with the other weapons of direction at the sovereign's command. What are their potentials and limitations? Can more drastic conditions be attached to the granting of credit than to a police power regulation or to an eminent domain taking? Which form of government intervention has the greater impact on the land market? How can credit policies be employed to advance chosen land policies? How can the mortgage and other credit instruments be adapted to the requirements of finance in a mobile, federal society?[53]

---

52. See Straus, Two-Thirds of a Nation (1952); Wendt, The Role of the Federal Government in Housing (1956); Abrams, The City Is the Frontier (1965). The scheme for the development of Washington is an interesting early example of the joint venture approach. Land for the capital was donated to the federal government by the proprietors, and in return they were ceded back every other lot after the site plan had been prepared and approved. See Morris v. United States, 174 U.S. 196, 202-203 (1899).

53. Suggestions for improving the housing situation have gone so far as to advocate a Uniform Mortgage Act, and the Uniform Commissioners did propose such a model law in the 1920s. More recently, traditional and nontraditional lenders — particularly during highly inflationary times — have sought protection through a wide and ever-expanding range of alternative mortgage instruments. Despite the occasional outcry by consumer groups or isolated members of Congress, so far the rule has been congressional and federal regulatory support for innovative mortgage devices. See, for example, 12 U.S.C. §3801 (1982) (initial section of Alternative Mortgage Transaction Parity Act of 1982):

(a) The Congress hereby finds that —
(1) increasingly volatile and dynamic changes in interest rates have seriously impaired the ability of housing creditors to provide consumers with fixed-term, fixed-rate credit secured by interests in real property, cooperative housing, manufactured homes, and other dwellings;
(2) alternative mortgage transactions are essential to the provision of an adequate supply of credit secured by residential property necessary to meet the demand expected during the 1980's; and
(3) the Comptroller of the Currency, the National Credit Union Adminis-

Federal Role in Residential Mortgage Markets
(Amounts outstanding at end of period, in billions of dollars)

Type of Involvement	1969	1970	1971	1972	1973	1974	1975	1976	1977	1978	1979	1980	1981
Mortgage Assets Held													
1. Total Federal agencies	$8.9	$9.3	$9.1	$8.8	$8.3	$9.8	$15.8	$14.9	$17.6	$21.0	$24.1	$28.4	$31.5
2. GNMA	4.9	5.2	5.3	5.1	4.0	4.8	7.4	4.2	3.7	3.5	3.9	4.6	4.8
3. FHA	0.7	0.8	1.0	1.3	1.7	2.2	3.1	3.6	3.7	3.8	3.8	3.9	4.3
4. VA	2.7	2.7	2.4	2.1	1.8	1.9	1.9	1.6	1.5	1.5	1.7	1.7	1.9
5. FmHA	0.6	0.6	0.4	0.3	0.8	0.9	0.4	0.7	0.9	0.6	0.5	1.5	2.2
6. FFB[a]	n.a.	n.a.	n.a.	n.a.	n.a.	n.a.	3.0	4.8	7.8	11.6	14.2	16.6	19.3
7. Total federally related agencies	11.0	15.9	18.8	21.6	26.9	34.6	37.4	37.8	38.3	47.3	56.7	64.5	69.5
8. FNMA	11.0	15.5	17.8	19.8	24.2	29.6	31.8	32.9	34.4	43.3	51.1	57.3	61.4
9. FHLMC	n.a.	0.4	1.0	1.8	2.6	4.6	5.0	4.3	3.3	3.1	4.0	5.1	5.3
10. Federal Land Banks	n.a.	n.a.	n.a.	n.a.	0.1	0.4	0.6	0.6	0.7	0.9	1.6	2.1	2.8
11. Total agency holdings	19.9	25.2	27.9	30.4	35.2	44.4	53.2	52.7	55.9	68.4	74.0	92.9	101.0
12. Percent of total mortgages outstanding	6.0%	7.0%	7.0%	6.7%	6.9%	8.1%	9.0%	7.2%	7.3%	7.7%	7.3%	8.5%	8.7%
Insurance and Guarantees													
13. Total Mortgage loans	$100.2	$109.2	$120.7	$131.1	$135.0	$140.2	$147.0	$154.1	$161.8	$176.4	$199.1	$225.1	$239.5
14. FHA	64.5	71.9	31.2	86.4	85.0	84.0	85.4	87.1	88.2	94.4	107.1	123.5	133.3
15. VA	35.7	37.3	39.5	44.7	50.0	56.2	61.6	67.0	73.6	82.0	92.0	101.6	106.2
16. Total mortgage pass-through securities	1.4	2.6	6.8	11.1	14.3	19.4	29.4	44.1	63.7	80.7	108.7	130.0	147.4
17. GNMA	n.a.	0.3	3.1	5.5	7.9	11.8	18.3	30.6	44.9	54.3	76.4	93.9	105.8
18. FHLMC	n.a.	n.a.	0.1	0.4	0.8	0.8	1.6	2.7	6.6	11.9	15.2	16.9	19.8
19. FmHA	1.4	2.2	3.7	5.1	5.6	6.9	9.5	10.8	12.2	14.5	17.1	19.3	21.8
20. Total credit underwritten	101.6	111.4	124.5	136.6	141.4	147.9	158.1	167.6	180.6	202.8	231.4	261.3	281.1
21. Percent of total mortgages outstanding	30.3%	31.1%	31.3%	30.0%	27.8%	26.9%	26.8%	25.4%	23.5%	22.9%	23.0%	23.8%	24.1%
Underwritten Credit Held by Agencies													
22. Total amount held	$15.8	$21.0	$23.9	$26.3	$29.1	$34.2	$39.5	$38.2	$40.5	$48.1	$54.1	$61.2	$65.0
23. Percent of agency mortgage holdings	79.4%	83.3%	85.7%	86.5%	82.7%	77.0%	74.2%	72.5%	72.5%	70.4%	73.1%	65.9%	64.4%
24. Percent of total credit underwritten	15.6%	18.9%	19.2%	19.2%	20.6%	23.1%	25.0%	22.8%	22.4%	23.7%	23.4%	23.4%	23.1%

[a] Federal Financing Bank (FFB) holdings of Certificates of Beneficial Ownership issued by the FmHA.

Source: The Report of the President's Commission on Housing 160-161 (1982).

To the average American the purchase of a house represents his or her largest item of capital expenditure, and is usually achieved only through the extensive use of borrowed money. Apartment construction has traditionally been even more dependent on mortgage capital. The size and quality of the selected dwelling, the decision whether to buy or to rent, all hinge on the amount of the down payment and the severity of the monthly debt service incurred. Thus the power to manipulate the supply of mortgage funds and to specify the terms of the mortgage is decisive (within certain economic limits) in determining how much housing will be made available to what groups of the population, and where, within the metropolitan area, it will be sited.

The Federal Housing Administration is a child of the depression of the thirties. Created under the terms of the National Housing Act of 1934, 48 Stat. 1246, codified as amended at 17 U.S.C. §1701 et seq. (1982), it represented an emergency measure to inject life into the construction industry and the real estate market. By insuring qualified lenders against loss, it facilitates investment in the traditionally risky field of real estate. This function, combined with new mortgage maturity, amortization, and loan-to-value terms, constitutes the unique contribution of FHA.[54]

2. Interest rates may seem incidental to city planning, but if they are set too high, architects will look for jobs, plans will molder on the drawing boards, and grass will grow on project sites. An attack on the rate of interest has been the instrument chosen by Congress for pushing through different measures of housing reform and building programs. This mode and extent of intervention explains some of the paradoxes in our efforts to provide adequate housing.

The Federal National Mortgage Association (FNMA), a federally chartered corporation, provides a secondary market for mortgage obligations. Originally it was charged with three principal functions:

---

tration, and the Federal Home Loan Bank Board have recognized the importance of alternative mortgage transactions and have adopted regulations authorizing federally chartered depository institutions to engage in alternative mortgage financing.

(b) It is the purpose of this chapter to eliminate the discriminatory impact that those regulations have upon nonfederally chartered housing creditors and provide them with parity with federally chartered institutions by authorizing all housing creditors to make, purchase, and enforce alternative mortgage transactions so long as the transactions are in conformity with the regulations issued by the Federal agencies.

54. See Colean, The Impact of Government on Real Estate Finance in the United States (1950); Fisher & Rapkin, The Mutual Mortgage Insurance Fund (1956); Morton, Urban Mortgage Lending: Comparative Markets and Experience (1956); Haar, Federal Credit and Private Housing (1960); Grigsby, Housing Markets and Public Policy (1963). A helpful introduction to the mortgage insurance programs operated by the FHA, VA, and by the growing number of private mortgage insurers (PMIs) can be found at §11.2 of Nelson & Whitman, Real Estate Finance Law (2d ed. 1985).

management and liquidation, to dispose of the then-existing portfolio; special assistance functions, to help in the financing of special housing programs and to ameliorate the effects of unfavorable economic conditions on the housing market; and the secondary market operations, which became the present FNMA. The Housing and Urban Development Act of 1968 partitioned FNMA into two separate and distinct corporations. One, dubbed the Government National Mortgage Association (GNMA), remained in HUD and retained the management and liquidation and special assistance functions. The other corporation, which retained the name FNMA along with the assets and capital structure of the secondary market operations, became a government-sponsored corporation subject to regulation by the Secretary of HUD.

The Federal Home Loan Mortgage Corporation (FHLMC) was created two years later (1970) as part of the Federal Home Loan Bank System. "Freddie Mac" purchases FHA, VA, and conventional residential loans primarily from savings and loan associations. The success of "Fannie Mae," "Ginnie Mae," and "Freddie Mac" in purchasing and packaging mortgages for investors led several private entities into the secondary mortgage market in the 1980s. See Malloy, The Secondary Mortgage Market — A Catalyst for Change in Real Estate Transactions, 39 Sw. L.J. 991, 994 n. 23 (1986):

> Private participants include Sears Roebuck, Merrill Lynch, MGIC, Ticor Mortgage Insurance Company, Residential Funding Corporation, G.E. Credit Corp., HOMAC-The Home Mortgage Access Corp., and Salomon Brothers, among others. Additional private participants in this market include Morgan Stanley & Co., Drexel Burnham Lambert, Inc., Dean Witter Reynolds, Inc. and Donaldson, Lufkin & Jenrette, Inc. The Wall Street investment banking firm of Salomon Brothers made $200 million, or 40% of its total 1983 profit, on mortgages.

3. Section 8 constituted the key housing assistance program of the 1974 housing act. It modified and replaced a proposed revision of the public housing leasing program (§23 of the Housing Act of 1937); it was also designed as a substitute for the §236 rental housing assistance program and for rent supplements.

> Sec. 8. (a) For the purpose of aiding lower-income families in obtaining a decent place to live and of promoting economically mixed housing, assistance payments may be made with respect to existing, newly constructed, and substantially rehabilitated housing in accordance with the provisions of this section.
> (b)(1) The Secretary is authorized to enter into annual contributions contracts with public housing agencies pursuant to which such agencies may enter into contracts to make assistance payments to owners of existing dwelling units in accordance with this section. In areas where no public

housing agency has been organized or where the Secretary determines that a public housing agency is unable to implement the provisions of this section, the Secretary is authorized to enter into such contracts and to perform the other functions assigned to a public housing agency by this section.

Despite success in stimulating new construction and rehabilitation of lower income rental units,[55] mounting budget deficits translated into extensive modifications of the Section 8 program. Congress, in the Housing and Urban-Rural Recovery Act of 1983, Pub. L. No. 98-101, §209, 97 Stat. 1153, 1183, eliminated Section 8 assistance for new construction and substantial rehabilitation (except for the §220 programs for elderly or handicapped housing), targeting remaining funds for existing housing stock.

4. Two replacement programs were instituted under the 1983 initiative. First, Congress implemented the Section 8 Housing Voucher Program authorized by §8(o) of the United States Housing Act of 1937, §207, 97 Stat. 1181-1182:

> (o)(1) In connection with the rental rehabilitation and development program . . . the Secretary is authorized to conduct a demonstration program using a payment standard in accordance with this subsection. The payment standard shall be used to determine the monthly assistance which may be paid for any family, as provided in paragraph (2) of this subsection. . . .
>
> (2) The monthly assistance payment for any family shall be the amount by which the payment standard for the area exceeds 30 per centum of the family's monthly adjusted income, except that such monthly

---

55. Of course, there are those whose evaluations are less flattering. See, for example, Additional Views of Senator William L. Armstrong, S. Rep. No. 98-142, 98th Cong., 1st Sess. 109, reprinted in 1983 U.S. Code Cong. & Admin. News 1867, 1879-1880:

> [F]rom the start, Section 8 proved ill-conceived, poorly managed, and scandalously costly. Its initial appropriation was modest — only $42 million. But in eight short years Congress committed to Section 8 more than $145 billion. Some one million units were built or leased, and 200,000 are awaiting occupancy. The Congressional Budget Office at one point estimated that a newly constructed Section 8 unit could have a lifetime cost of more than $500,000. Eligibility was so broad that 30 million Americans — a GAO figure — were eligible for the subsidy. Abuses abound. Published reports documented that Section 8 was a program for the "greedy, not the needy." Elaborate housing was built that lined the pockets of the developers at the expense of the poor. Other scandalous practices were reported:
>
> Section 8 contracts were given to developers who, coincidentally, contributed significant campaign sums to reigning politicians.
>
> Illegal aliens were housed in subsidized units.
>
> Those with incomes exceeding Section 8's already broad eligibility standards lived in units built for the poor.
>
> Newspaper and magazine headlines screamed "Billion Dollar Nightmare at HUD," "Very Poor Last in Line to Receive Federal Housing Assistance," "Taj Mahal in New York: Symptoms of Rent Subsidy Headaches," "Housing and Politics: The Way It Works."

C. Housing the Deserving and Undeserving Poor

assistance payment shall not exceed the amount by which the rent for the dwelling unit (including the amount allowed for utilities in the case of a unit with separate utility metering) exceeds 10 per centum of the family's monthly income.

(3) Assistance payments may be made only for (A) a family determined to be a very low-income family at the time it initially receives assistance, or (B) a family previously assisted under this Act. In selecting families to be assisted, preference shall be given to families which, at the time they are seeking assistance, occupy substandard housing, are involuntarily displaced, or are paying more than 50 per centum of family income for rent....

(6) A contract with a public housing agency for annual contributions under this subsection shall be for an initial term of sixty months. The Secretary shall require (with respect to any unit) that (A) the public housing agency inspect the unit before any assistance payment may be made to determine that it meets housing quality standards for decent, safe, and sanitary housing established by the Secretary for the purpose of this section, and (B) the public housing agency make annual or more frequent inspections during the contract term. No assistance payment may be made for a dwelling unit which fails to meet such quality standards, unless any such failure is promptly corrected by the owner and the correction verified by the public housing agency.

Many housing analysts have argued that housing allowance, rent certification, and income maintenance schemes offer significant advantages. Although these demand- or consumer-oriented strategies need some form of administrative support and monitoring, virtually every dollar of aid would reach the target group. The idea has a direct and simple appeal — give cash outright to the poor, who can then choose their own housing. But while it is clear that housing problems of low-income families result in part from inability to spend enough for housing, it is also clear that these problems result in part from weaknesses in the housing market itself, including regulatory practices that discourage innovation, high construction and maintenance costs, inadequate information, and discriminatory practices. See Report of the President's Commission on Housing xxii-xxiv (1982).

Stirring issues are raised by the new forms of subsidy. What are the pros and cons of the housing allowance concept? Should recipients be required to live in standard housing? Would this exert too much of an inflationary force on the "decent" housing market? Will racial and economic integration be promoted by the housing allowance? Are there conditions and areas in which housing allowances would be more beneficial than in others? How would you administer a housing allowance program? See Section 8 Housing Vouchers, 52 Fed. Reg. 5250 (1987). What type of housing would be eligible for the subsidy given to the recipients? Are these standards to be related to the existing market in which the recipient lives? Should one expect substantial improvements to be made in a below-code building by the landlord in order to qualify for the program?

To replace the long-term rent subsidy obligations entailed in the Section 8 new construction program, Congress created Housing Development Grants (HoDAGs) in the 1983 Act. §301, 97 Stat. 1196-1206. Similar to the UDAG discussed in Part A of this chapter, HoDAGs are grants, employed to leverage private funds, that are awarded directly to eligible localities on a competitive basis. The grant may "not exceed 50 percent of HUD's determination of the total costs associated with the construction or substantial rehabilitation of the project," while "[t]he number of lower income units . . . equals or exceeds 20 percent of the total units of the projects." Resale of the units (as condominium or cooperative units) is prohibited for 20 years. 24 C.F.R. pt. 850 (1988).

Not surprisingly, given this invitation to developers to create a lower income set-aside in a subsidized middle-income complex, critics decry the extravagance and poor targeting of the program. See, for example, Controversial Federal Program Helps Developer To Build Rental Units, Mostly for Middle Class, Wall St. J., Aug. 20, 1985.

5. On the not-too-distant-horizon lie full-scale programs for tenant purchase of the nation's public housing units. Inspired perhaps by recommendations of the President's Commission on Housing (at page 39 of the 1982 Report), the Reagan Administration in 1985 implemented a homeownership demonstration program limited to eighteen public housing authorities. See Nashville PHA Converting 68 Units into Coops Under HUD Homeownership Demo, [14 Current Developments] Hous. & Dev. Rep. (BNA) 339 (Sept. 8, 1986). Congress responded in 1987 with a demonstration program for purchase of public housing units by "resident management corporations." 42 U.S.C. §1437s. Lower-income purchasers from the corporation (families already renting a unit in the project are given highest priority) may resell the units "only to the resident management corporation, a lower income family residing in or eligible to reside in public housing or housing assisted under section 8, or to the public housing agency." Strict limits are also placed on the resale price that the unit owner may receive. For comparative insights, see Howenstine, Selling Public Housing to Individuals and Cooperatives, 7 Urb. L. & Poly. 1, 7-8 (1985):

> In the United Kingdom, local governments (local authorities) were authorized in 1966 to sell existing public housing to a sitting tenant who had occupied the unit for at least three years. The sale price was based on market value, less a discount of 3% for each year of continuous tenancy subject to a maximum of 30% in built-up areas and 45% elsewhere. In 1980, in an effort to stimulate sales, sitting tenants were given the right to buy their housing unit from the local authority if they had occupied the unit for at least three years. The discount was increased to a basic 33% after three years' residence, with one additional percentage for every

C. Housing the Deserving and Undeserving Poor

extra year up to a maximum of 50%. In the Housing and Building Control Bill introduced on June 23, 1983, the Government proposed a 60% discount for tenants with thirty or more years of tenancy.

Do you foresee any constitutional problems with the legislative redistribution of property rights from public housing entities to private tenants, or with this federal intrusion on state (PHA) territory? Would such a program create a disincentive for public landlords otherwise inclined to repair or rehabilitate older structures?

6. A major source of public/private funding for low-income housing — joint venture syndications based on a wide range of tax incentives — was placed in limbo by the Tax Reform Act of 1986. Pub. L. No. 99-514. What follows is an insiders' explanation of pre-1986 realities and the reasons for Congress's dramatic changes in the rules of the syndication game:

> Congress was concerned that the tax preferences for low-income rental housing available under prior law were not effective in providing affordable housing for low-income individuals. Congress believed a more efficient mechanism for encouraging the production of low-income rental housing could be provided through the low-income rental housing tax credit.
>
> The primary tax preferences provided for low-income housing under prior law were tax-exempt bond financing, accelerated cost recovery deductions, five-year amortization of rehabilitation expenditures, and special deductions for construction period interest and taxes. These preferences operated in an uncoordinated manner, resulted in subsidies unrelated to the number of low-income individuals served, and failed to guarantee that affordable housing would be provided to the most needy low-income individuals.
>
> A major shortcoming of the prior-law tax subsidies was that, beyond a minimum threshold requirement of low-income housing units that were required to be served, the degree of subsidy was not directly linked to the number of units serving low-income persons. As a result, there was no incentive to provide low-income units beyond the minimum required. Under the tax credit, however, the amount of the low-income housing tax credit which an owner may receive is directly related to the number of rental units made available to low-income individuals. By providing tax credits which are based on the number of units serving low-income persons, an incentive exists to provide a greater number of housing units for more low-income individuals.
>
> Another weakness of the Federal tax subsidies available under prior law was that they were not targeted to persons of truly low-income. For example, a study by the General Accounting Office (GAO) of tax-exempt bond financed residential rental projects found that above-average income renters could qualify under prior law as "low" or "moderate" income for two reasons. First, persons with incomes as high as 80 percent of area median income were eligible to occupy units reserved for low- and

moderate-income tenants. This income ceiling was relatively high, particularly when compared with the median income of renters. Second, the Treasury Department did not require household incomes to be adjusted for family size until after 1985. Congress believed that the low-income housing tax credit (as well as tax-exempt bond financing for low-income housing, discussed in Title XIII) should be provided only for households with incomes not exceeding 50 percent or 60 percent of area median income. Congress further believed that these income limits should be adjusted for family size. These provisions better target affordable housing to those persons most in need of assistance.

Staff of Joint Comm. on Taxation, 99th Cong., 2d Sess., General Explanation of the Tax Reform Act of 1986, at 152-153 (Comm. Print 1987).

Congress took a much more direct — though, to syndication packagers, far less attractive — tack: the tax credit for low-income housing included in §42 of the amended Internal Revenue Code. In common with HoDAG prerequisites, certain specific set-aside criteria must be met by projects eligible for the new credit (§42(g)):

> QUALIFIED LOW-INCOME HOUSING PROJECT. — For purposes of this section —
> (1) IN GENERAL. — The term "qualified low-income housing project" means any project for residential rental property if the project meets the requirements of subparagraph (A) or (B) whichever is elected by the taxpayer:
> (A) 20-50 TEST. — The project meets the requirements of this subparagraph if 20 percent or more of the residential units in such project are both rent-restricted and occupied by individuals whose income is 50 percent or less of area median gross income.
> (B) 40-60 TEST. — The project meets the requirements of this subparagraph if 40 percent or more of the residential units in such project are both rent-restricted and occupied by individuals whose income is 60 percent or less of area median gross income.
> Any election under this paragraph, once made, shall be irrevocable. For purposes of this paragraph, any property shall not be treated as failing to be residential rental property merely because part of the building in which such property is located is used for purposes other than residential rental purposes.
> (2) RENT-RESTRICTED UNITS. —
> (A) IN GENERAL. — For purposes of paragraph (1), a residential unit is rent-restricted if the gross rent with respect to such unit does not exceed 30 percent of the income limitation under paragraph (1) applicable to individuals occupying such unit. . . .

On what bases would you evaluate the success of this approach? How would you calculate and then factor in the amount of "tax expenditures"

C. Housing the Deserving and Undeserving Poor

saved by avoiding solely tax-motivated ventures? How dire a housing emergency, and how much reluctance on the part of private investors and public officials, would justify a return to pre-1986 residential housing tax shelters?

7. Congress, inspired by a church-alliance funded plan to build 5000 single-family homes in East Brooklyn, New York, enacted the Nehemiah Housing Opportunity Grants program in Title VI of the Housing and Community Development Act of 1987, 101 Stat. 1951-1956. The plan authorizes the expenditure of federal funds to support programs — run by nonprofit community-based organizations — for construction or substantial rehabilitation of one-to-four family homes in distressed areas. The funds will be used to provide no-interest second mortgage loans, held by the HUD Secretary, of up to $15,000 per home. There is a definite save-the-neighborhood flavor to this program; note, for example, this statement from House Report No. 100-122(I) (June 2, 1987): "[R]edevelopment of these areas must be on a scale large enough to withstand the forces of deterioration that surround them, and to generate the kinds of positive externalities necessary to help turn neighborhoods around." Are the psychological, civic (and political) benefits of homeownership substantial enough to warrant the expense of this public/private venture and of the mortgage programs discussed in the readings that follow?

■ MASSACHUSETTS HOUSING FINANCE AGENCY v. NEW ENGLAND MERCHANTS NATIONAL BANK
356 Mass. 202, 249 N.E.2d 599 (1969)

CUTTER, J. . . . We recognize, of course, that the Act resembles the bill (1966 House Bill No. 3696; see 1965 House Doc. No. 4040) considered by the Justices in Opinion of the Justices, 351 Mass. 716. See 1966 Ann. Surv. Mass. Law, §15.38; Note, 80 Harv. L. Rev. 1811. A majority of the Justices there advised (p. 728) that,

> [S]o far as the purpose of . . . [that] bill is to provide housing for families of moderate income, the bill does not appear to be confined to a public purpose. The possibility that the rents paid by moderate income families, possibly up to seventy-five per cent in a project, will subsidize lower rents paid by low income families is too indirect and uncertain to enable us to say that expenditures of tax money under this bill will be for a public purpose. . . .

The intention of the complex statutory provisions of the Act is to make available mortgage financing at favorable interest rates to housing projects in which, in general, one quarter of the tenants will be in the "low income" category and the other tenants will be of moderate income. The lower interest rates will be achieved (a) by having MHFA borrow on a favorable basis by giving its bonds or notes, which are to be exempt from all Massachusetts property and income taxes and presumably also from current Federal income taxes, thus (b) permitting MHFA to lend to a borrower from it at interest [rates] lower than those which would be charged if the borrower were to obtain funds in the general mortgage market. The saving in interest is to be applied in part (but not entirely) to making possible lower rentals . . .

If the present projects are fair examples of the savings in interest available to a project owner from MHFA financing, most of that saving will be applied to the reduction of rents payable by low income families, although there may be also smaller reduction, below general market levels, of rents for moderate income tenants. The rent for any moderate income tenant, however, will not be allowed, under §7(b) of the Act . . . to fall below one sixth of the tenant's net annual income for the time being (or the fair market rental, whichever is lower). Thus the Act itself provides for upward rent adjustments for moderate income tenants to prevent their receiving any undue part of the benefit of MHFA financing.

Despite the precautions taken in the Act to minimize benefits to tenants of moderate income, the question inevitably arises whether MHFA's lending (at lower than market interest rates) of money borrowed on tax exempt notes is for other than a public purpose because part of the housing and rent savings accrues to persons of moderate income not within the low income group usually regarded as suitable objects of public support. Also, §9A(b) of the Act appropriated to MHFA a sum, repayable by MHFA, to provide for initial expenses and by §9B(c), continuing legislative appropriations to the Capital Reserve Fund are at least contemplated.

It is urged upon us by MHFA, in effect, that the Act is intended . . . to accomplish slum clearance more effectively and more permanently than in earlier subsidized public housing by avoiding undue concentration of low income tenants and by achieving for such tenants "exposure to and close contact in as many areas as possible with more successful members of society." The Legislature, so MHFA contends, has made a "determination to proceed with . . . housing . . . low income families in projects also inhabited by those somewhat more affluent." It is also argued by MHFA that "families with middle class property standards are more likely to . . . assist in maintaining reasonable standards of . . . property upkeep which will . . . instruct low income families . . . in how to take care of housing and . . . insure that the project's basic value will not be radically lowered by tenant abuse."

After stating that the upward adjustment of "rentals . . . on three

C. Housing the Deserving and Undeserving Poor 1021

units . . . to obtain a sufficient 'subsidy' . . . enable[s] the fourth unit to be made available for low income persons," MHFA makes the following contentions:

> To the extent that the higher rental in these units will be below what the free market would charge, a necessary inducement will be provided to families not of low income to live together with low income . . . families in the project. . . . [T]he inducement . . . [may] counteract the fact that people do not normally choose to live in projects or neighborhoods with people of substantially lower incomes . . . [or] to "subsidize" lesser rents charged in other units to make this possible. It is this mixing of families of varied economic means which will provide for the prevention and hence "permanent elimination" of slum conditions in the project, which was expected in . . . [earlier] days . . . to occur simply through the construction of low-rent housing.

Some of these contentions were made in substance in 1965 House Doc. No. 4040, pp. 37-41, upon which was based the bill considered in the 1966 advisory opinion (351 Mass. 716).

It is not for this court to consider whether these contentions are sound as a matter of economics and public policy. That is a legislative matter. Our duty is merely to consider whether the Legislature reasonably could consider them to be valid and could rationally regard the provisions of proper housing for low income families as the fundamental purpose of the Act and any benefits to persons of moderate income as only incidental to the primary objective, although contributing to its achievement. We are of opinion that the Legislature may properly enact legislation which proceeds on the basis of the considerations for which MHFA contends.

We have taken into account the changes in the 1966 bill which were made after our advisory opinion concerning it (351 Mass. 716). Although more precise standards for, and more effective limitation of, MHFA loans appropriately could have been imposed, material improvement of the original 1966 bill has been achieved. We mention some improvements in the margin.[12] The most important change for present

---

12. Among the changes from 1966 House Bill No. 3696 found in the Act are the following: Section 1(d) now contains a reasonably clear and objective definition of the term "low income persons or families," although, as already noted, it is made somewhat indefinite by §1(e) which loosely defines "[a]nnual income." We have been told, however, that MHFA on March 25, 1969, has appropriately determined the amount of "reasonable allowances for dependents" in the light of "allowances granted by various public agencies under comparable . . . programs." MHFA thus recognizes that, in fixing such allowances, it must take into account available and reasonable criteria concerning the size of such allowances. Certain obscure definitions of the 1966 bill have been removed. A less imprecise declaration of public necessity . . . has been substituted in §2. Under a new form of §5(g) MHFA must make specific findings in effect (a) that each project will carry out the objectives of the Act for the benefit of low income families, and (b) that (see new

purposes is the insertion of new §5(g) requiring findings by MHFA.... This provision we interpret as designed to ensure, among other things, that low income families will obtain substantial benefit from each project and that (with stated exceptions) each project will be matched within a reasonable time by public agency elimination of an equal number of substandard units. To this extent slum clearance and elimination is thus added to the other objectives of the Act.

The Act appropriately might have provided specifically that rents for tenants other than low income persons or families should not be fixed below the market rent level for comparable property by more than the minimum amount found by MHFA to be necessary to induce suitable persons of moderate income to occupy apartments in a project where the mixture of tenants may be extremely diverse. We, however, regard such a requirement as reasonably implied in the general provisions and structure of §§5, 6, and 7 of the Act.... The existence of this implied requirement in some degree is confirmed by MHFA's own application of the standards of these sections in approving the four projects for which commitments have been made. We thus conclude that the standards, expressly stated or implied in the Act, effectively require MHFA (a) to restrict loans under the Act to such projects as are of substantial benefit to low income persons and families; and (b) to make sure that any benefit to tenants not within the low income category will be at most incidental to, and no greater than is necessary for, achieving the Act's primary objective of proper housing in appropriate surroundings of persons of low income.

Notes

1. Once the validity of HFAs was established, state and local bond activity took off, aided and abetted by congressional authorization of the §235 homeownership and §236 rent subsidy programs, and later by the Section 8 set-aside program for state agencies. The high inflation rates beginning in the late 1970s created a new market of middle-income borrowers unable to qualify for conventional financing. State and local housing entities responded with tax-free mortgage subsidy bond programs that Congress ultimately found subject to much abuse.

---

form of §5(g)[4]) an equivalent number of substandard housing units in the same general housing area will be eliminated. More adequate provisions governing rental levels and tenant selection have been substituted for unsatisfactory provisions of the original 1966 bill. An unduly broad delegation of power to MHFA contained in old §7 no longer appears. Section 9B(c) of the Act ... is changed from the corresponding provision (see §8A) of the original 1966 bill. The Act does not contain §11 of the original 1966 bill, purporting to impose certain restrictions on future legislative action. See House Bill No. 3985.

C. Housing the Deserving and Undeserving Poor

Lawmakers were disturbed that favorable tax treatment designed to spur lower-income homeownership was working its way up to the higher (less deserving) ranks of the economic ladder.

The result was the new §103A of the Internal Revenue Code, specifying that 90 percent of the loans in the bond issue must be for first-time homebuyers and that 20 percent of the funds be targeted to distressed areas. Modifications were made in the Tax Reform Act of 1984 (the mortgage credit certification program) and, more recently, the prerequisites for qualification as tax-free were tightened further in the Tax Reform Act of 1986. See §143 of the code, raising the 90 percent threshold to 95 percent and implementing income limitations for loan recipients.

2. States by no means limit their housing activities to such bond programs. For example, see Atlantic City Housing Project First to Use Casino Redevelopment Funds, [14 Current Developments] Hous. & Dev. Rep. (BNA) 29 (June 2, 1986):

> A $17.5 million Atlantic City, N.J. housing revitalization project will be the first in the state to be financed with casino reinvestment funds.
>
> The Atlantic County Improvement Authority (ACIA) will use $5.7 million from the Casino Reinvestment Development Authority (CRDA) as well as state and other funds to finance the construction of 47 single family for-sale homes and 110 new garden apartment units, and the rehabilitation of 19 rental units. Of these houses and rental units, 44 will be for low- and moderate-income persons. . . .
>
> Under legislation signed by Gov. Thomas H. Kean in 1985, Atlantic City gambling casinos are required to invest $1.68 billion over 25 years for the development and revitalization of low- and moderate-income housing, public transportation and recreation facilities, and aid to small businesses and enterprises operated by women and minorities. . . .
>
> The housing project, called the Northwest Inlet Revitalization Project, is a nine-block redevelopment effort that consists of three parts. . . .
>
> New three-bedroom townhouses will be sold for $55,000 to eligible families earning between $19,000 and $46,000 annually. The $6 million construction loan will be financed with luxury tax funds. Home mortgages will be provided to individual buyers by CRDA at 7.5 percent for 30 years. Construction has already begun on the townhouses. . . .
>
> In the second phase of the project, 110 garden apartments will be constructed on three sites on the inlet. To provide family-oriented communities, 90 percent of the units are two- and three-bedroom apartments. CRDA will provide financing to the developers, and construction costs will be written down with luxury tax funds and proceeds from a bond issue to build a new convention center in Atlantic City.

See also N. J. Stat. Ann. §5:12-144.1 (West Supp. 1987).

3. Despite these innovative governmental approaches to stimulating low- to moderate-income housing production, the trend, particularly

on the federal level, continues to be withdrawal in favor of purely private efforts. In 1984, Congress responded to the near-monopolization of the secondary mortgage market by the FNMA, GNMA, and FHLMC with the Secondary Mortgage Market Enhancement Act of 1984. Pub. L. No. 440, 98 Stat. 1689.[56]

Owing in large part to these three major participants, the securities market is becoming populated by mortgage-backed securities (MBs, which entitle the investor to an individual share in a pool of mortgages), such as pass-through certificates (by which the holder is paid either a fixed rate of return or a pro rata share of the principal and interest from the underlying loans) and collateralized mortgage obligations (CMOs, which divide payments from the mortgage pool among classes of investors).[57] Mortgage securities totaled $124 billion in 1985. What types of governmental intervention, either carrots or sticks, would you recommend to tap this vast and rapidly expanding source of private funding, in order to help provide housing for the nonaffluent? Review the interstices of an MB prospectus, which you may secure from a local

---

56. See S. Rep. No. 98-293, 98th Cong., 2d Sess. 3, reprinted in 1984 U.S. Code Cong. & Admin. News 2809, 2811:

> This bill is expressly designed to encourage this broadening of the market for mortgage-backed securities by encouraging more extensive involvement of the private sector in the formation of conduits for the flow of mortgage capital from investors to lenders and homebuyers. The bill accomplishes this goal in three ways. First, it continues the process of procedural deregulation which has already markedly improved the operation of the securities market generally. The bill focuses on removal of archaic regulation of mortgage-backed securities which prevent them from functioning in the market as well as other corporate securities, let alone securities sold by Fannie Mae and Freddie Mac.
>
> Second, it seeks to broaden the classes of investors, especially institutional investors, who could purchase mortgage-backed securities but for artificial or archaic regulatory roadblocks.
>
> Third, it changes Fannie Mae's and Freddie Mac's authority only in limited areas. The Committee recognizes the continuing and important role these two agencies will play especially to the market serving lower and middle income homebuyers. But we also believe that a portion of the public market for mortgage-backed securities, namely that for mortgages above $108,300 (jumbo loans as they are called), should be preserved for the private sector.
>
> Fannie Mae and Freddie Mac, along with the Government National Mortgage Association which functions in the FHA and VA insured mortgage market exclusively, together account for 87-92 percent of all public secondary mortgage activity.
>
> These agencies, with their distinct market advantages which can be attributed to their government backing, present insurmountable economic competition to the embryonic private sector.

57. The Tax Reform Act of 1986 provided its own special investment vehicle for the mortgages security market: the real estate mortgage investment conduit (REMIC). See §§860A-G of the Internal Revenue Code. REMICs are similar in structure to CMOs but feature added advantages, such as tax-free treatment at the entity level. See also Richards, "Gradable and Tradable": The Securitization of Commercial Real Estate Mortgages, 16 Real Est. L.J. 99 (1987).

C. Housing the Deserving and Undeserving Poor

investment firm, and consider whether the mortgage securities market is indeed the new frontier for the housing public/private partnership.

2. Site Selection for Federally Subsidized Housing

■ GAUTREAUX v. CHICAGO HOUSING AUTHORITY
296 F. Supp. 907 (N.D. Ill. 1969)

AUSTIN, J. Plaintiffs, Negro tenants in or applicants for public housing, sue on behalf of themselves and all others similarly situated alleging that defendants, the Chicago Housing Authority (CHA), a municipal corporation, and C.E. Humphrey, Executive Director of CHA, have violated their rights under the Fourteenth Amendment of the Constitution of the United States. . . .

. . . Plaintiffs' . . . requests for relief include (1) a declaratory judgment pursuant to 28 U.S.C. Secs. 2201 and 2202 that defendants have selected sites in violation of plaintiffs' constitutional rights, (2) a permanent injunction against the racially discriminatory aspects of the public housing system, (3) an order directing defendants to submit and carry out a plan for selection of future sites to eliminate these discriminatory aspects, and (4) a declaratory judgment that plaintiffs have the right under 42 U.S.C. Sec. 2000d to end the use of federal funds to perpetuate the racially discriminatory aspects of the public housing system and an injunction against such use. Since March 2, 1967 the parties have amassed thousands of pages of depositions, affidavits and exhibits. . . .

Plaintiffs charge that the procedure mainly used by defendants to maintain existing patterns of racial residential separation involved a pre-clearance arrangement under which CHA informally submitted sites for family housing to the City Council Alderman in whose ward the site was located. CHA admits the existence of this procedure. . . . The Alderman to whom White sites were submitted allegedly vetoed these sites because the 90% Negro waiting list and occupancy rate would create a Negro population in the White area. Plaintiffs allege that the few White sites which escaped an Alderman's informal veto were rejected on racial grounds by the City Council when they were formally submitted by CHA for approval.

As of July, 1968, CHA had in operation or development 54 family projects at 64 sites in Chicago consisting of 30,848 units. Exclusive of the four segregated White projects, CHA's family housing tenants are 99% Negroes. Exclusive of the four projects, housing units now located in neighborhoods between 50% and 100% Negro represent 99½% of

	(a) Sites initially selected	(b) White sites initially selected	(c) Percent of units in White sites initially selected	(d) White sites approved	(e) Negro* sites approved
1955 Program	25	4	45%	0	19
1956 Program	11	4	30%	0	5
1958 Program	11	2	31%	0	7
1965 Program	18	9	50%	0	9
1966 Program	38	22	50%	2	9

* The sites classified by Mr. Humphrey as in Negro neighborhoods were primarily in over 95% Negro neighborhoods, but a few sites so classified were in neighborhoods which were one-half White.

the total units operated by CHA; units in neighborhoods between 75% and 100% Negro are 92% of the total; and units in areas over 95% Negro are two-thirds of the total.... A glance at a map depicting Negro areas of residence in Chicago confirms that the 50% to 90% Negro areas are almost without exception contiguous with 90% to 100% Negro areas and that the relatively small numbers of Chicago Negroes not concentrated in the over 90% areas are almost entirely concentrated in the over 50% areas. Therefore, given the trend of Negro population movement, 99½% of CHA family units are located in areas which are or soon will be substantially all Negro.... It is incredible that this dismal prospect of an all Negro public housing system in all Negro areas came about without the persistent application of a deliberate policy to confine public housing to all Negro or immediately adjacent changing areas.

To sustain their burden of proving that defendants' past and present policies have deprived them of their constitutional rights, plaintiffs contend that, during the consideration of each of the five major family housing programs since 1954, White sites meeting all appropriate criteria were rejected for racial reasons....

... One of the two White sites finally approved in 1966 included 400 units and was located on vacant land bounded on one side by a predominantly Negro area and partially occupied by dilapidated Negro shacks. The mere fortuity that this site was included in a 72.8% White census tract does not make it relevant to negate the inference of a policy against choosing sites in White neighborhoods. The other White site approved in 1966 was planned for 36 units. CHA did not proceed formally to submit for City Council approval seven White sites in 1965 because "the Aldermen in whose Wards those sites were located advised of community opposition and indicated they were opposed to such sites in their Wards.".... One White site in the 1965 program was not submitted to the City Council because the City Department of Development and Planning advised against its acquisition, presumably because

C. Housing the Deserving and Undeserving Poor 1027

it conflicted with other urban planning projects. The only White site formally submitted was dropped from consideration by the City Council Committee on Planning and Housing. In 1966 the Department of Development and Planning advised against all 20 of the White sites not formally submitted because it "either (a) disapproved the site, (b) recommended deferment or (c) advised of Aldermanic opposition.". . . Since the Department merely assumed CHA's admitted former role in the pre-clearance procedure, it must be inferred in the absence of a suggestion to the contrary by defendants that only a minimal number of White sites in 1966 were disapproved because they conflicted with other urban development projects. . . .

No criterion, other than race, can plausibly explain the veto of over $99\frac{1}{2}\%$ of the housing units located on the White sites which were initially selected on the basis of CHA's expert judgment and at the same time the rejection of only 10% or so of the units on Negro sites. . . .

On March 2, 1967 this court ruled that "plaintiffs, as present and future users of the system, have the right under the Fourteenth Amendment to have sites selected for public housing projects without regard to the racial composition of either the surrounding neighborhood or of the projects themselves." 265 F. Supp. 582, 583. The statistics on the family housing sites considered during the five major programs show a very high probability, a near certainty, that many sites were vetoed on the basis of the racial composition of the site's neighborhood. In the face of these figures, CHA's failure to present a substantial or even a speculative indication that racial criteria were not used entitles plaintiffs to judgment as a matter of law. Jones v. Georgia, 389 U.S. 24 (1967) (finding of discrimination based entirely on jury selection statistics and absence of explanation); Hernandez v. Texas, 347 U.S. 475 (1954) (same). The additional evidence of intent, composed mostly of uncontradicted admissions by CHA officials, also establishes plaintiffs' right to judgment as a matter of law either considered alone or in combination with the statistics. Cypress v. Newport News General and Nonsectarian Hospital Assn., 375 F. 2d 648 (4th Cir. 1967).

Defendants urge that CHA officials never entertained racist attitudes and that "the racial character of the neighborhood has never been a factor in CHA's selection of a suitable site.". . . In view of CHA's persistent selection of White sites at the initial stage before the pre-clearance procedure and the candor of its officials on deposition, these statements are undoubtedly true. It is also undenied that sites for the projects which have been constructed were chosen primarily to further the praiseworthy and urgent goals of low cost housing and urban renewal. Nevertheless, a deliberate policy to separate the races cannot be justified by the good intentions with which other laudable goals are pursued. Brown v. Board of Education, 347 U.S. 483 (1954). It is also true that there is no evidence that the Aldermen who vetoed White sites were necessarily motivated by racial animus when they followed a policy of keeping Negroes out of White neighborhoods. Most Aldermen apparently talked to their constituents and received unfavorable reactions before exercising their informal vetoes.... But even if the Aldermen's informal surveys were correct in their uniform assessment of public opinion, they cannot acquiesce in the sentiment of their constituents to keep their neighborhoods White and to deny admission to Negroes via the placement of public housing.

CHA finally contends that the impulse originating and sustaining the policy against choosing White sites came from the City Council. But by incorporating as an automatic step in its site selection procedure a practice which resulted in a racial veto before it performed its statutory function of formally presenting the sites to the City Council, CHA made those policies its own and deprived opponents of those policies of the opportunity for public debate. It is no defense that the City Council's power to approve sites may as a matter of practical politics have compelled CHA to adopt the pre-clearance procedure which was known by CHA to incorporate a racial veto. In fact, even if CHA had not participated in the elimination of White sites, its officials were bound by the Constitution not to exercise CHA's discretion to decide to build upon sites which were chosen by some other agency on the basis of race....

Notes

1. No appeal was taken from the district court judgment. The court ordered the Chicago Housing Authority to use "best efforts" to select new housing sites in "general or white" areas of Chicago. Gautreaux v. Chicago Housing Authority, 304 F. Supp. 736, 741, enforcing 296 F. Supp. 907 (N.D. Ill. 1969). The order specified that the next 700 public housing units, and 75 percent of units constructed thereafter, should be located at least one mile from the outer boundary of Cook County census tracts with greater than 30 percent nonwhite population. 304 F. Supp. at 738. See Note, 83 Harv. L. Rev. 1441 (1970).

2. The housing authority delayed in seeking the city's approval for new sites, and the district court, in an unreported decision affirmed by the court of appeals, 436 F.2d 306 (7th Cir. 1970), cert. denied, 402 U.S. 922 (1971), ordered the housing authority to submit sites to the city for approval.

3. Gautreaux v. Romney, 448 F.2d 731 (7th Cir. 1971), reversed a district court ruling that the case against HUD was inadequate and

C. Housing the Deserving and Undeserving Poor

should be severed from the original suit for separate consideration after the decision on the CHA case:

> The Government admits that HUD approved and funded CHA-chosen regular family housing sites between 1950 and 1969, knowing that such sites were not "optimal" and that the reason for their exclusive location in black areas of Chicago was that "sites other than in the south or west side, if proposed for regular family housing, invariably encounter[ed] sufficient opposition in the [Chicago City] Council to preclude Council approval."
>
> Nevertheless, the District Court found that HUD had followed this course only after having made "numerous and consistent efforts . . . to persuade the Chicago Housing Authority to locate low-rent housing projects in white neighborhoods." That finding is not directly challenged on appeal. Moreover, given the acknowledged desperate need for public housing in Chicago, HUD's decision was that it was better to fund a segregated housing system than to deny housing altogether to the thousands of needy Negro families of that city.
>
> On review of the District Court's action, we shall treat all of the above facts as true. The question then becomes whether or not, even granting that "numerous and consistent efforts" were made, HUD's knowing acquiescence in CHA's admitted discriminatory housing program violated either the Due Process Clause of the Fifth Amendment or Section 601 of the Civil Rights Act of 1964.[13] Given a previous court finding of liability against CHA (296 F. Supp. 907), the pertinent case-law compels the conclusion that both of these provisions were violated. . . .
>
> [I]t is apparent that the "dilemma" with which the Secretary no doubt was faced and with which we are fully sympathetic, nevertheless cannot bear upon the question before us. For example, we have been advised that any further HUD pressure on CHA would have meant cutting off funds and thus stopping the flow of new housing altogether. Taking this assertion as true, still the basis of the "dilemma" boils down to community and local governmental resistance to ". . . the only constitutionally permissible state policy. . . ." Green v. Kennedy [309 F. Supp. 1127] at 1137, a factor which, as discussed above, has not yet been accepted as a viable excuse for a segregated result.

448 F.2d at 737-738.

4. In Gautreaux v. Romney, 332 F. Supp. 366 (N.D. Ill. 1971), the district court granted an injunction prohibiting HUD from releasing Model Cities funds until Chicago had approved a minimum number of new public housing units in white areas. On appeal, the Court of Appeals for the Seventh Circuit reversed, holding that it was improper

---

13. "No person in the United States shall, on the ground of race, color, or national origin, be excluded from participation in, be denied the benefits of, or be subjected to discrimination under any program or activity receiving Federal financial assistance." 42 U.S.C. §2000d.

for the district court to threaten termination of federal funds to a program not proven discriminatory in order to remedy discrimination in a different program. Gautreaux v. Romney, 475 F.2d 124 (7th Cir. 1972). See Note, 86 Harv. L. Rev. 427 (1972).

5. Implementation still continued to be delayed, owing to the city's failure to approve sites for new housing. After a supplemental complaint was filed, the district court entered an order suspending operation of the state statute requiring the city's approval before site acquisitions, and ordered the housing authority to begin acquiring sites. 342 F. Supp. 827 (N.D. Ill. 1972), aff'd sub nom. Gautreaux v. Chicago, 480 F.2d 210 (7th Cir. 1973), cert. denied, 414 U.S. 1144 (1974).

6. On December 8, 1972, the Sixth Circuit held that a remedial plan involving suburban school districts in the metropolitan area of Detroit was necessary to redress impermissible segregation in the Detroit school system. Bradley v. Milliken, 484 F.2d 215 (6th Cir. 1972). Counsel for plaintiffs in the Gautreaux litigation then requested a metropolitan remedy in response to the findings on discrimination by the Chicago Housing Authority and HUD. On September 11, 1973, the district court in an unreported opinion denied a metropolitan remedy in *Gautreaux*. Plaintiffs appealed.

7. On July 25, 1974, a divided Supreme Court reversed the Sixth Circuit in Milliken v. Bradley, 418 U.S. 717 (1974), holding that a federal court may not impose a multidistrict, areawide remedy for single-district de jure school segregation violations, where there is no finding that the other included school districts failed to operate unitary school systems or committed acts that effected segregation within the other districts. Concurring in the 5 to 4 majority, Justice Stewart wrote:

> This is not to say, however, that an inter-district remedy of the sort approved by the Court of Appeals would not be proper, or even necessary, in other factual situations. Were it to be shown, for example, that state officials had contributed to the separation of the races by drawing or redrawing school district lines; by transfer of school units between districts; or by purposeful, racially discriminatory use of state housing or zoning laws, then a decree calling for transfer of pupils across district lines or for restructuring of district lines might well be appropriate.

8. On August 26, 1974, the Seventh Circuit reversed the district court and held that a metropolitan remedy was necessary in *Gautreaux*. 503 F.2d 930 (7th Cir. 1974). Writing for the majority, Justice Clark, retired Associate Justice of the Supreme Court sitting by designation, carefully distinguished the Detroit case:

> The equitable factors which prevented metropolitan relief in Milliken

C. Housing the Deserving and Undeserving Poor 1031

v. Bradley are simply not present here. There is no deeply rooted tradition of local control of public housing; rather, public housing is a federally supervised program with early roots in federal statutes. There has been a federal statutory commitment to non-discrimination in housing for more than a century, 42 U.S.C. §1982, and the Secretary of HUD is directed to administer housing programs "in a manner affirmatively to further the policies" of non-discrimination, 42 U.S.C. §3608(d)(5). In short, federal involvement is pervasive.

Similarly, the administrative problems of building public housing outside Chicago are not remotely comparable to the problems of daily bussing thousands of children to schools in other districts run by other local governments. CHA and HUD can build housing much like any other landowner, and whatever problems arise would be insignificant compared to restructuring school systems as proposed in Milliken v. Bradley.[58]

9. The Supreme Court, though affirming the holding of the Seventh Circuit, disagreed with Justice Clark's *Milliken* argument. In Hills v. Gautreaux, 425 U.S. 284 (1976), Justice Stewart wrote for the Court:

Since the *Milliken* decision was based on basic limitations on the exercise of the equity power of the federal courts and not on a balancing of particular considerations presented by school desegregation cases, it is apparent that the Court of Appeals erred in finding *Milliken* inapplicable on that ground to this public housing case. . . .

We reject the contention that, since HUD's constitutional and statutory violations were committed in Chicago, *Milliken* precludes an order against HUD that will affect its conduct in the greater metropolitan area. The critical distinction between HUD and the suburban school districts in *Milliken* is that HUD has been found to have violated the Constitution. That violation provided the necessary predicate for the entry of a remedial order against HUD and, indeed, imposed a duty on the District Court to grant appropriate relief. See 418 U. S., at 744. . . .

Nothing in the *Milliken* decision suggests a per se rule that federal courts lack authority to order parties found to have violated the Consti-

---

58. See Meyerson & Banfield, Politics, Planning and the Public Interest 269 (1955):

The process by which a housing program for Chicago was formulated resembled somewhat the parlor game in which each player adds a word to a sentence which is passed around the circle of players: the player acts *as if* the words that are handed to him express some intention (i.e., as if the sentence that comes to him were *planned*) and he does his part to sustain the illusion. In playing this game the staff of the Authority was bound by the previous moves. The sentence was already largely formed when it was handed to it; Congress had written the first words, the Public Housing Administration had written the next several, and then the Illinois Legislature, the State Housing Board, the Mayor and City Council, and the CHA Board of Commissioners had each in turn written a few. It was up to the staff to finish the sentence in a way that would seem rational, but this may have been an impossibility. — EDS.

tution to undertake remedial efforts beyond the municipal boundaries of the city where the violation occurred. . . .

In this case, it is entirely appropriate and consistent with *Milliken* to order CHA and HUD to attempt to create housing alternatives for the respondents in the Chicago suburbs. Here the wrong committed by HUD confined the respondents to segregated public housing. The relevant geographic area for purposes of the respondents' housing options is the Chicago housing market, not the Chicago city limits. . . .

The more substantial question under *Milliken* is whether an order against HUD affecting its conduct beyond Chicago's boundaries would impermissibly interfere with local governments and suburban housing authorities that have not been implicated in HUD's unconstitutional conduct. . . .

HUD's position, we think, underestimates the ability of a federal court to formulate a decree that will grant the respondents the constitutional relief to which they may be entitled without overstepping the limits of judicial power established in the *Milliken* case. HUD's discretion regarding the selection of housing proposals to assist with funding as well as its authority under a recent statute to contract for low-income housing directly with private owners and developers can clearly be directed towards providing relief to the respondents in the greater Chicago metropolitan area without preempting the power of local governments by undercutting the role of those governments in the federal housing assistance scheme.

Justices Marshall, Brennan and White "join[ed] the Court's opinion except insofar as it appears to reaffirm the decision in *Milliken*."

10. On June 16, 1981, the United States District Court approved a consent decree designed to redress the Chicago public housing legal disputes initiated in 1966 (Gautreaux v. Landrieu, 523 F. Supp. 665 (N.D. Ill. 1981)):

After the Supreme Court's determination that remedial efforts outside Chicago city limits were constitutional, HUD and plaintiffs voluntarily entered into a one year Letter of Understanding in which the parties agreed to investigate the possibilities of metropolitan-wide relief. In connection with its commitments under this Understanding, HUD developed a Section 8 demonstration program for about 400 class members in existing housing throughout the Chicago metropolitan area. The Leadership Council for Metropolitan Open Communities and the Fair Housing Center of the Home Investments Fund also participated in the development of this demonstration program which was extended and expanded under two later Letters of Understanding.

The proposed consent decree is an extension of the agreements under the Letters of Understanding. In sharp contrast to the 1969 judgment order entered against CHA, in which Cook County was divided into Limited and General areas, the proposed decree provides for metropolitan relief by dividing the Chicago Standard Metropolitan Statistical Area (SMSA), composed of six counties including Cook, into three areas:

C. Housing the Deserving and Undeserving Poor

General, Limited and Revitalizing. Thus, under the proposed decree, the Limited Area, with more than 30% minority population, and the General Area, with less than 30% minority concentration, encompasses a much larger geographic area than the Limited and General Areas defined in the 1969 judgment order. In addition, recognizing that total relief to Gautreaux families outside the Limited Area could not be provided in the foreseeable future, the proposed decree introduces the concept of Revitalizing Areas, areas which have substantial minority population and are undergoing sufficient redevelopment to justify the assumption that these areas will become more integrated in a relatively short time. Because these areas are buffer zones between the Limited and General areas with ongoing or planned financial reinvestment by private parties, they are considered the most promising neighborhoods for racial and economic residential integration.

Other significant provisions of the proposed decree provide for: 1) placement of up to 7,100 persons in assisted units in the General and Revitalizing areas; 2) set-asides of Section 8 Contract Authority for a total of 350 new and/or substantially rehabilitated units and 150 Section 8 existing housing certificates for *Gautreaux* plaintiffs; 3) reservation of not less than 6% nor more than 12% of the units in each project for *Gautreaux* plaintiffs; 4) availability of at least $3 million in reallocated Community Development Block Grant Funds for use in the Chicago SMSA; and 5) placement through an outside contractor chosen by HUD and approved by plaintiffs.

The court's refusal to uphold the challenge brought by the Illinois Housing Development Authority (IHDA) and by neighborhood organizations (who objected to descriptions of their areas as "Revitalizing") was affirmed by the Seventh Circuit in Gautreaux v. Pierce, 690 F.2d 616 (7th Cir. 1982). Circuit Judge Pell waxed optimistic about the status of this sixteen-year old lawsuit:

> In 1969, CHA was found to have discriminated on a systemwide basis in the placement of assisted housing. In 1971, HUD was found to have acquiesced knowingly in CHA's discriminatory practices. Having received vindication of their allegations of discrimination, the plaintiff class members proceeded to seek implementation of those determinations. Since 1971, the parties have repeatedly engaged in the Sisyphean task of advancing the issue of an appropriate remedy from the district court, to this court, to the Supreme Court, and to the district court again. The consent decree promises an eventual accomplishment of the original determinations of discrimination practices.

11. Two years later, the case made its way once again to the appellate level. In Gautreaux v. Pierce, 743 F.2d 526 (7th Cir. 1984), the most recent reported opinion, the court upheld the district court's denial of injunctive relief to two intervenors, William Lavicka and

Barbara Piegare. The intervenors challenged the marketing and tenant selection plans for the Assembly Square project, a site selected in accordance with the consent decree approved three years before. Lavicka and Piegare, residents of the same census tract as the project, were concerned about the "tipping" effect the project would have on their neighborhood:

> [Intervenors] claim that their own interest in an integrated community which has not "tipped" racially and become predominantly black will be harmed if the proposed marketing plan is implemented. They claim that the marketing plan will result in an all-black Academy Square project, which would in turn cause their census tract's population to be 57% black, 37% white and 6% other. Appellants' Br. 10. They also claim that the district court has authority under the Fair Housing Act of 1968, 42 U.S.C. §3608(c)-(d), to enjoin this marketing plan and to order implementation of one which imposes racial quotas for Academy Square tenancy.[59]

---

59. In footnote 12 on page 532 of his 1984 opinion, Chief Judge Cummings cited with approval a concurring opinion of Judge Posner from an earlier stage of the *Gautreaux* litigation. Posner, though skeptical about the proffered basis for approving a judicial modification of the consent decree (the "best interests of the community"), had acceded to the majority's holding, as he believed that Lavicka and Piegare lacked standing:

> The appellants' concern is that putting public housing into their neighborhood on the scale contemplated will blight the neighborhood. Such a claim would ordinarily sound in nuisance. But the appellants do not suggest that any state or federal statute or common law principle makes public housing a nuisance either in general or in the specific setting of this case. Their only claim is that the consent decree is being violated. But they are not parties to the decree. The parties are the original plaintiffs — who are black people eligible for public housing — HUD, and the Chicago Housing Authority, none of whom is complaining that the Academy Square project violates the decree. A nonparty has no more rights under a consent decree than he would have under any other contract to which he was not a party.

Gautreaux v. Pierce, 707 F. 2d 265, 272 (7th Cir. 1983) (Posner, J., concurring), aff'g 548 F. Supp. 1284 (N.D. Ill. 1982).

As part of an urban renewal plan for Manhattan's Lower East Side, the New York City Housing Authority arranged for the construction of two apartment buildings containing 360 apartments for low-income tenants. Authority regulations require that former residents of an urban renewal site receive first priority for public housing later built on that site. The community is presently integrated, with a racial balance that is almost equally divided between white and nonwhite residents, and the authority seeks to stem a steady decline in the percentage of the white population in the community. If the regulation is enforced and former residents receive priority, the project would become 80 percent nonwhite to 20 percent white by family, but if the regulation is not enforced and other tenant selection methods are employed, the ratio would be 40 percent nonwhite to 60 percent white by family and closer to 50 percent to 50 percent by population. You are chairman of the authority and your staff has advised you that adherence to the regulation would create a nonwhite "pocket ghetto" that would operate as a racial "tipping factor" causing white residents to take flight and leading eventually to ghettoization of the community. What do you decide to do? If you do not enforce the regulation and employ other tenant selection methods, will your actions be sustained by the courts? See Otero v. New York City Housing Authority, 484 F.2d 1122 (2d Cir. 1973). — Eds.

C. Housing the Deserving and Undeserving Poor 1035

12. See N.Y. Times, Sept. 30, 1984:

> Before 1974, white Chicago aldermen could veto sites proposed for their wards, and no public housing was built in the city until that year, when a court order prohibited aldermanic review.
> The program has crept forward since then.... Only 117 units were completed by 1979, when the original decision was modified to allow construction of half the family units in white areas.
> Soon after the order was modified, Mayor Jane M. Byrne announced that the $100 million scattered-site program would go ahead, but by the summer of 1983 fewer than 400 units had been built or renovated. In July 1983 the housing authority was ordered to acquire at least 390 new units within seven months to prevent the program from going into receivership....
> Authority officials attributed the delays to a lack of funds, difficulty in finding suitable and affordable properties and with contractors, and opposition from white community groups and aldermen. But the authority beat its January deadline and 642 units have been completed, with 173 under way and 1,561 to go. The authority says it will place as many of the remaining 111 projects meant for white areas as possible in the 19 neighborhoods that have no public housing.
> Public opposition, though, continues in many neighborhoods.

However, stirring lessons for all cities with isolated underclass communities are beginning to emerge from this grim struggle. An editorial, Chicago's Housing Pioneers, N.Y.Times, Nov. 1, 1988, reports that under "the *Gautreaux* program," 3500 families (most black and single-parent) moved to private, rent-subsidized suburban apartments. "[N]one of their neighbors know of their public housing backgrounds or their rent subsidies."

13. While Chicago proper was embroiled in the Jarndyce-like *Gautreaux* litigation, one of the Windy City's suburbs settled its court-mandated, low-income housing obligations relatively quickly, painlessly, and creatively. Metropolitan Housing Development Corp. v. Village of Arlington Heights, 616 F.2d 1006 (7th Cir. 1980) — the last proceedings of record in the case found in Chapter IV — raises interesting questions concerning the propriety of following the letter, if not the spirit, of the statutory and decisional laws regarding discrimination:

> After the case reached the district court on remand, the court called the matter for a status report on March 9, 1978, and was advised by the parties that negotiations for settlement were pending and that the case would probably be resolved by a consent decree. After several other status-report hearings the court was advised on June 1, and on June 22, 1978, that a consent decree had been agreed upon by the parties. On June 30, the Village of Mount Prospect moved to intervene as a defendant in order to object to the entry of the proposed consent decree....

The original 15-acre parcel was part of an 80-acre tract just east of the center of Arlington Heights owned by the Clerics of St. Viator, a religious order, whose high school and novitiate building occupied part of the site. . . .

The alternate site provided for in the consent decree consists of 26 acres of vacant property located in an unincorporated area of Cook County between Arlington Heights and the Village of Mount Prospect, presently classified partially C-2 Commercial and partially R-5 Single Family Residence use under the Cook County Zoning Ordinance. Under the terms of the consent decree 14 acres of the property would be developed for commercial use by an independent developer and would include two restaurants.

The remaining 12-acre parcel would be developed to consist of one four-story building with 109 one-bedroom rental apartments available to elderly persons and one two-bedroom apartment available for the apartment manager. Attached townhouses two-stories high would consist of 20 one-bedroom, 40 two-bedroom and 20 three-bedroom units, all available for family use. . . .

In the present posture of this case, there is no longer an issue of the interest of a state or its municipality versus the national interest; the local and national governmental interests are now aligned together against the alleged rights of individual neighboring landowners and of an adjoining village. The changed alignment of interests from that formerly existing requires us to analyze the various interests and the policies they represent in terms of national policies supporting open housing, state and local policies supporting the actions required of Arlington Heights by the consent decree, and the policies supporting the use of consent decrees which effectuate the amalgam of the national and local interests in housing cases such as this. . . .

The trial judge fulfilled his responsibilities in determining that the settlement embodied in the consent decree was fair, adequate, reasonable and appropriate, and his opinion shows how carefully he analyzed the facts of the case in relation to the relevant principles of applicable law.

Dissenting Judge Pell was more skeptical of the Village's motives:

In arguing that this court affirm the district court's approval of the decree, Arlington Heights and the MHDC rely heavily on the strong federal policy, embodied in the Fair Housing Act, which favors and, indeed, mandates the elimination of the effects of racial discrimination in housing, and further upon the policy which favors settlement of litigation. I do not find these policy arguments persuasive because the method chosen by Arlington Heights to effectuate its ever so recently espoused goal of providing a location for the construction of racially integrated housing has involved the selection of a site as far as possible from the center of Arlington Heights and on the doorstep of a neighboring community.

3. "The Best Laid Schemes . . .": Mandating and Enforcing Desegregation

As the facts of Gautreaux illustrate, even when subsidized housing projects are built in white neighborhoods they may be occupied predominantly by whites. When built in black neighborhoods they are occupied predominantly by blacks. Ledbetter, Public Housing — A Social Experiment Seeks Acceptance, 32 Law & Contemp. Prob. 490, 504 (1967), suggests that segregation between projects tends to result wherever prospective tenants are free to choose among projects. Tenant selection, therefore, is an important adjunct to site selection in any effort to combat racial impaction. Does HUD have any special obligations to correct racial imbalance and to redress discrimination when its financial and technical support contributed to the realization of a housing project?

The case that follows serves not only as a helpful review of the history of approaches taken by the federal government (with its state and local allies) to provide housing for the needy, but also as a serious reminder that by assuming the responsibility to support such efforts, government officials may be held to account for the results in human terms. On appeal, by what standards would you assess the involvement (or lack thereof) by HUD? Should one attempt to correct discrimination suffice, as suggested by the court in Beal v. Lindsay, supra page 657? Is the district judge creating a disincentive to well-intended (though already costly and unpopular) programs? Is there an alternative to sanctions on the one hand or judicial indifference on the other?

■ YOUNG v. PIERCE
628 F. Supp. 1037 (E.D. Tex. 1985), modified, 822 F.2d 1368 (5th Cir. 1987)

JUSTICE, Chief Judge.

Plaintiffs in this class action allege that defendant, the United States Department of Housing and Urban Development ("HUD"), has knowingly maintained, and continues to maintain, a system of racially segregated housing in violation of the Constitution and laws of the United States. Specifically, the plaintiff class asserts that HUD, in funding and overseeing this housing, has discriminated against blacks in violation of the Fifth Amendment to the United States Constitution; Title VI of the Civil Rights Act of 1964, 42 U.S.C. §2000d et seq. (prohibiting discrimination in federal programs); Title VIII of the Civil Rights Act of 1968, 42 U.S.C. §3601 et seq. (prohibiting discrimination in the provision of housing); as well as the Civil Rights Act of 1866, 42 U.S.C. §§1981 and 1982. The plaintiff class consists of all black applicants for, and residents of, HUD-assisted housing in thirty-six East Texas counties ("the class action counties"). Defendant HUD is a federal agency which participates in the provision of public housing throughout the nation. Also named as defendants are HUD's Secretary, and the Administrator of HUD's Region VI, which contains the class counties. HUD does not construct, own, or operate any housing itself. Rather, its role is essentially promotional. Through a number of programs, HUD provides significant financial support, technical assistance, and regulatory oversight for the providers of public housing. . . .

This action was filed in 1980. The class was certified by this court's order of July 1, 1982. Young v. Pierce, 544 F. Supp. 1010 (E.D. Tex. 1982). Since that time, the parties have conducted extensive discovery, and have agreed that the issue of liability is ripe for resolution on cross motions for summary judgment. These motions have been extensively briefed, and are accompanied by exhibits and affidavits. . . .

The information produced by HUD indicates that the public housing sites it funds are segregated by race. Blacks live in one set of public housing sites, whites in another. Of 219 sites, made up of low rent sites under management, insured-assisted sites under management, and Section 8 new construction sites under management, 121 — more than half — are completely segregated, one-race projects. An additional sixty-two project sites are 85% or more one-race. In many cases the percentage of non-predominate racial group members is comprised of one or two units in an otherwise one-race project site.

In its standard compliance agreement, defendant defines a race-predominate site as one in which 75% or more of a site is occupied by one race. Using this yardstick, an additional sixteen sites would be added to the list of segregated projects. An additional five sites can be added to this number if black and hispanic residents are treated together. Thus, 199 of the project sites — more than 90% — are either predominantly minority or predominantly white, with the great majority of these being completely segregated.

The pattern of segregation is as striking if projects are grouped according to the form of support they receive from HUD. A measure of the extent of segregation in HUD-assisted housing is that it is simpler to summarize racial occupancy patterns by giving the percentage of *integrated* facilities. Only eleven, or 7%, of the low rent projects are *not* predominately one race. Of thirty-six insured-assisted projects, four, or 11%, are *not* predominately one-race. Of twenty-two Section 8 new construction projects, five, or 23%, are *not* predominately only one race. A close analysis also reveals skewed patterns of participation in these programs. While the races occupy low-rent housing in roughly equal numbers, 77% of all insured-assisted units in the class counties are occupied by blacks. In contrast, 76% of Section 8 new construction units are occupied by whites. Defendants' data also indicates that, in regard

C. Housing the Deserving and Undeserving Poor 1039

to these last two programs, discrimination can be parsed along temporal lines: 84% of projects approved before 1972 are 85 to 100% black. Of those approved after 1972, 48% are 85 to 100% white, 12% are 85 to 100% black, and 39% are at least partially integrated.

The parties agree that there is a rough equivalency of demand for public housing between white and minority groups in the class action counties. According to the 1980 Census, blacks constitute 43% of the persons living below the poverty level in the class action counties, and 66% of those living in housing without plumbing....

The extent of HUD's knowledge of and support for this system of segregated housing is sharply disputed by the parties. In the early stages of this litigation, HUD professed ignorance of segregation in public housing, and now alleges that it has learned of its existence only through this action. HUD also argues that segregation exists in public housing only in spite of its vigorous efforts to eradicate it. Plaintiffs allege that HUD has a duty to acquaint itself with its own functionings, has been in fact aware of the racially identifiable nature of the housing it operates, and has continued to fund and operate this housing while knowing it to be segregated....

The administrative record submitted by HUD contains numerous and compelling indications that HUD was actually aware of the segregated nature of the housing it had created and continued to fund. HUD's own findings, made before the filing of this action, revealed that at least twenty of the public housing authorities in the class action counties were operating in violation of Title VI. For example, ... [t]he Talco PHA operates one all-white site. In 1970, a HUD auditor visited the project. At that time, the PHA was seeking funding for a new site. The auditor wrote that:

> [The PHA chairman] was anxious to discuss the requirements of Title VI and most of all what happens to [a] project in development if the Authority is found not in compliance with the [Methods of Administration]. I told [him] I had seen some projects stopped. All this was brought up because of a young Negro man who was next in line for a unit in the present project. According to [the chairman], the Authority may lose some white tenants, if Negro families move in. I strongly emphasized to both [the chairman] and [the executive officer] that the Authority must comply with its adopted plan. Thus, this young man should be offered a unit.

An occupancy audit of the same PHA in 1978 revealed that it still had not adopted HUD's required methods of administration. In addition, the Executive Director was quoted as saying "there were no blacks in the project, [he] did not want them, and if there was a vacancy available, a white person would be put in right now."...

In each instance set out above, HUD had direct knowledge, reflected in its own administrative records, that conditions in violation of Title

VI existed in the class action counties. Typically, the violations were in the crucial — for the purpose of racial makeup at sites — area of tenant assignment. HUD received, at the very least, indications that twenty of the PHA authorities in the class counties were circumventing HUD regulations and assigning tenants in ways producing segregation. At the most, HUD's response consisted of adoption of a remedial plan. Usually, PHA's were simply admonished to bring their conduct into line with HUD regulations. As long as the proper documents were adopted, and reports filed, HUD approved the PHA's actions. . . .

HUD has intentionally and knowingly continued to promote purposefully segregated housing in the class action counties. It is beyond dispute that the Constitution prohibits the government from funding racial discrimination with the public dollar. Indeed, *any* tangible assistance to segregation is prohibited if it has a "significant tendency to facilitate, reinforce, and support private discrimination." Norwood v. Harrison, 413 U.S. 455, 466 (1973). . . .

HUD's intent to discriminate is established by the combination of HUD's disingenuous assertions of ignorance, its actual knowledge of segregation, and its continuing financial support of each public housing site in the class counties. In those instances where HUD responded at all to its knowledge of discrimination, it has been only through the use of compliance agreements which have been shown by HUD's own data to be ineffective in dealing with discrimination. . . .

Ordered that plaintiffs' motion for summary judgment on the issue of liability shall be, and it is hereby, Granted. It is further

Ordered that defendants' motions for summary judgment, to decertify the class and to modify the class shall be, and they are hereby, Denied.

Notes

1. Shannon v. Department of Housing and Urban Development, 436 F.2d 809, 819, 821-822 (3d Cir. 1970), considered a challenge to HUD's authority to approve changes in a local urban renewal plan without taking into account the impact of project site selection on racial concentration in the community. The original urban renewal plan envisioned a medium-density, home ownership-oriented neighborhood, designed to "create a more stable and racially balanced environment." It was altered to allow construction of a §221(d)(3) project with 100 percent rent supplements, which "from a social standpoint . . . is the functional equivalent of a low-rent public housing project." Challenging this alteration were residents and businesspeople of the area, both black and white, who "claim that in reliance on the original plan, . . . they

C. Housing the Deserving and Undeserving Poor 1041

made substantial investments, commitments, and in some cases home purchases." The area already had a significant concentration of low-income black residents.

Carefully tracing the development and convergence of federal housing and civil rights policy, the court concluded that "[i]ncrease or maintenance of racial concentration is prima facie likely to lead to urban blight and is thus prima facie at variance with national housing policy." While HUD has broad discretion to choose between alternative types of housing, "that discretion must be exercised within the framework of the national policy against discrimination in federally assisted housing.... Here the agency concentrated on land use factors and made no investigation or determination of the social factors involved in the choice of the type of housing which it approved." The court then held that

> [t]he Agency must utilize some institutionalized method whereby, in considering site selection or type selection, it has before it the relevant racial and socioeconomic information necessary for compliance with its duties under the 1964 and 1968 Civil Rights Acts....
>
> ... There will be instances where a pressing case may be made for the rebuilding of a racial ghetto. We hold only that the agency's judgment must be an informed one; one which weighs the alternatives and finds that the need for physical rehabilitation or additional minority housing at the site in question clearly outweighs the disadvantage of increasing or perpetuating racial concentration.

2. The Department of Justice, as part of its effort to eliminate racial quotas, instituted an action against the owners and operators of Starrett City, the nation's largest housing development, with forty-six high-rise buildings containing nearly 6000 apartments. The landlords "sought to maintain a racial distribution by apartment of 64% white, 22% black and 8% hispanic" in the Brooklyn, New York complex, claiming "that these racial quotas are necessary to prevent the loss of white tenants, which would transform Starrett City into a predominantly minority complex."

The government invoked the Fair Housing Act, alleging, among other claims, "that Starrett violated the Act by making apartments unavailable to blacks solely because of race; [and] by forcing black applicants to wait significantly longer for apartments than whites solely because of race." Despite defendants' expert testimony on "tipping" and "white flight," the district court granted summary judgment for the government.

The appellate court affirmed, noting, "Housing practices unlawful under Title VIII [of the Civil Rights Act of 1968] include not only those motivated by a racially discriminatory purpose, but also those that disproportionately affect minorities." The court was concerned that the quotas, already in effect for ten years, "were far from temporary." Nor did Starrett demonstrate that its measures were needed "to remedy past racial discrimination or imbalance within the complex."

The Second Circuit's approval of a plan that favored integration in the *Otero* case, see supra page 1034, was distinguished: "As a one-time measure in response to the special circumstances of the Lower East Side in the early 1970's, the action challenged in *Otero* had an impact on non-whites as a group far less burdensome or discriminatory than Starrett City's continuing practices." United States v. Starrett City Associates, 840 F.2d 1096, 1098-1100, 1102-1103 (2d Cir.), cert. denied, 57 U.S.L.W. 3330 (1988).

Judge Jon O. Newman dissented, disturbed that his colleagues' literal reading of statutory language allowed a violation of the "spirit" of the Act. For support, Newman at 1108, quoted from Dr. Kenneth Clark's affidavit on Starrett's behalf: "'[I]t would be a tragedy if this litigation were to lead to the destruction of one of the model integrated communities in the United States.'"

How do you evaluate the Department's allocation of litigation resources? Can you propose a legislative amendment to the Fair Housing Act that would allow well-intentioned plans to be instituted? Or, given the long history of abuse in social, educational, and professional settings, should all racial and ethnic housing quotas be regarded per se illegal?

3. In Young v. Whiteman, No. P-82-37-CA (E.D. Tex. 1983), an earlier stage of the East Texas litigation, the court ordered a mandatory swap of black and white public housing tenants, declaring that any tenants refusing to transfer would be evicted. In July 1986, Judge Justice, dissatisfied with a HUD plan (submitted in February) to promote integration in East Texas public housing, appointed as special master a University of Alabama law professor. Among other duties, the master was to monitor HUD's compliance with a permanent injunction forbidding the Department from engaging in or promoting racial segregation. Young v. Pierce, 640 F. Supp. 1476 (E.D. Tex. 1986).

HUD appealed, but on April 6, 1987, the parties reached an agreement on several of the disputed issues. On July 20, an appellate panel partially vacated the district court's judgment and remanded the case for a modification of the injunction and of the special master order in accordance with the settlement. 822 F.2d 1368 (5th Cir. 1987).

4. Can HUD discriminate against illegal aliens seeking to live in federally assisted housing? The answer would appear to be "yes," if one reads §214 of the Housing and Community Development Act of 1980, which was amended in 1981 to prohibit the Secretary from making "financial assistance available for the benefit of any [illegal] alien." 42 U.S.C. §1436a (1982). However, HUD's efforts to implement rules in accordance with this policy have been thwarted through several

C. Housing the Deserving and Undeserving Poor

congressional counter-moves, including §164 of the Housing and Community Development Act of 1987, clarifying the lawmakers' desire to avoid dividing families (with members who may not be American citizens) who live in assisted housing.

What impact do these changing policies have on HUD efforts to correct segregation in settings, like East Texas, with large Hispanic populations? Should counsel ask Judge Justice to reconsider the sweeping nature of his court order in the light of the new immigration policy?

5. Given the judicial time and expertise devoted to resolving the problems of those in substandard or segregated housing, it should be no surprise that the plight of the nation's homeless has caught the attention of state and federal judges throughout the country. Is it time to reconsider the Burger Court's rejection of a constitutional right to decent housing (see Lindsey v. Normet, supra page 400), or does state constitutional and common law already provide the necessary foundation for activism in this area? See, for example, McKain v. Koch, 511 N.Y.2d 109, 511 N.E.2d 62 (1987) (court below had power to issue temporary injunction requiring city agencies, "when they have undertaken to provide emergency housing for homeless families with children, to provide housing which satisfies minimum standards of sanitation, safety and decency").

Congress noted among its "findings" for the Housing and Development Act of 1987 that "the tragedy of homelessness in urban and suburban communities across the Nation, involving a record number of people, dramatically demonstrates the lack of affordable residential shelter, and people living on the economic margins of our society (lower income families, the elderly, the working poor, and the deinstitutionalized) have few available alternatives for shelter." 101 Stat. 1819. But are congressional efforts to earmark and increase Section 8 and other "traditional" housing funds enough for those who live on streets and in shelters? Do the special needs of the homeless necessitate a separate legal and administrative strategy? See the Stewart B. McKinney Homeless Assistance Act, Pub. L. No. 100-77, 101 Stat. 482 (1987), codified as amended at 42 U.S.C. §1301 et seq. (establishing Interagency Council on the Homeless); Committee on Housing and Community Development, The Plight of the Homeless, 18 Urb. Law. 925 (1986); Pear, The Need of the Nation's Homeless is Becoming Their Right, N.Y. Times, July 20, 1986.

By their very nature, joint ventures elicit a modern redefinition of private property and the public interest. They raise practical questions concerning the legislative and executive ways of crafting workable plans and beneficial developments. Even the judicial reviews of what constitutes public welfare under the police power, public use under eminent domain, or, of course, public purpose under the spending power, are all subject to reconsideration. As citizens, we have at least a financial interest in whether public-private partnerships directed toward redevelopment and housing for the less fortunate are wisely packaged, administered, and, when their purposes are served or abandoned, liquidated. Although the public sector has been instructed to lessen the active role it assumed most recently in the 1960s, pending ideological and political shifts, the collective citizenry still retains a right to an accounting as would any limited partner in the private setting. Concerned as we are with the fate of our cities, metropolitan areas, and the environment to be bequeathed to future generations, what can we demand of the private sector and of our public officials? What questions should we ask of those responsible for deciding how and where government-subsidized and stimulated funds are spent?

What lessons gleaned from this context can we apply to local and statewide land-use practices and decision-making processes? Is employing the expertise of the private sector the solution to obsolete planning and zoning schemes, much like a developer invited to breathe new life into an abandoned neighborhood or apartment project? Or do the ramifications of public interest goals and the more wide-ranging implications of comprehensive planning decisions require the special training, relative objectivity, and policy insights of the bureaucrat or government consultant? It is to these and other ultimate questions that we turn in our concluding chapter.

IX

Planning for What, How, and by Whom? The Sources of Decision-Making for the Urban Environment

Having examined various urban land problems in the light of city planning policies and their legal implications, you are in a better position to evaluate the complex issues of freedom and planning, tangled and obscured as they may be, that often determine the course of decision.

Does planning achieve a more "rational" allocation and development of land? Which method of planning appears compatible with the tradition of the common law? Is planning "good," "bad," or "indifferent"? Is it worth the effort? Who is to do the planning? Where ultimately are the decisions concerning land use made? Is current land-use planning merely an extension of conventional controls, or does it foreshadow a basic change in the power and function of government? Are the differences between those in favor of planning and those opposed divergencies as to means only, or are the ends themselves in dispute?

This chapter opens with cases, commentary, and legislative provisions that raise questions afresh about the status of the master plan. There follows an exploration—including our fifth case study—of the range of tools and approaches for accommodating interests and harnessing forces. The last section looks more closely at the substitutes for the market mechanism that planners have devised, and goes on to raise, in the form of a dialogue, some of the perplexing issues in planning.

A. THE MASTER PLAN: AN IMPERMANENT CONSTITUTION

Enabling legislation for planning abounds in this country. Planning statutes exist in all but two states.[1] Whatever its other accomplishments, the theory of city planning has at least achieved this first-round victory. From this, one may assume that it is legislative policy to endorse the implications of the master plan. As new concepts of property evolve, special attention must be paid to the role of the master plan in providing a legal framework for the control of land development.[2]

The content of these plans and the procedures for their adoption and implementation vary widely among the states. What are the purposes of city planning? What goals are express or implied? To whom are the plans addressed — the planning commission, other agencies of local government, the citizens of the city, the property owner, the court — or are they simply a letter to the world?

To be more specific, what is the usual content of a master plan? What, as envisioned by the enabling laws, are its uses? Who adopts it? Who maintains or amends it? What is the relationship of the planning commission to other city and state agencies? The lawyer's perspective is necessarily dominated by the question of its impact — what part does the plan play in people's affairs? Does it act as an incentive, or a deterrent to enterprise? How are energies harnessed? Who benefits — and at whose expense? How are public acceptance, interest, and responsibility stimulated? How are property rights affected? What degree of control should the plan exercise over implementing regulations? What criteria should be enumerated for the use of administrators, reviewing courts, and private developers? What is the impact (potential and actual) of the plan on the growth and decay of a city? Are we on the threshold of a new approach to the realization of planning that involves recasting the classic master plan?

Bassett, the draftsman of the Standard Act, has written *the* book on the master plan. Consider how his ideas are exemplified in the model legislation that took shape decades later.

1. See Haar, The Master Plan: An Impermanent Constitution, 20 Law & Contemp. Probs. 353 (1955); 1 Anderson, American Law of Zoning §1.08 (1986).
2. See Excerpts from Paknikar Thesis, New York-Philadelphia Chapter, Am. Inst. Planners (mimeograph, 1954); Kent, The Urban General Plan (1964).
You will want to reexamine the master plans printed supra Chapter I, as well as the statements of goals, to see how far these are carried out by the legislation.

A. The Master Plan: An Impermanent Constitution

■ BASSETT, THE MASTER PLAN[3]
5-6, 16-18, 22-26, 30-31, 50-52, 61-64 (1938)

Governmental units whether towns, villages, cities, counties, or states today realize better than ever before the economy of coordinating improvements connected with the land. Planning commissions are charged with the duty of advising lawmaking bodies regarding this coordination. A master plan is nothing more than the easily changed instrumentality which will show a commission from day to day the progress it has made. Planning with the help of such a plan will prevent clashes between the public improvements made in different years and will serve to avoid duplication and rebuilding. Mistakes in municipal construction cost untold millions of dollars.

Not only is increased attention being given to master plans and to planning commissions throughout the United States, but there is everywhere a desire to know more about the elements of a community plan. Not everything should go into it. What should go in and what should stay out is the burning question. If everything that human ingenuity can devise is made part of a master plan it will become a thing of shreds and patches. . . .

When a community establishes a street it determines the boundary lines of that street. This is the first act of planning. Whatever comes afterward depends upon the locus of these boundary lines. Planning, in the sense used in this book, precedes acquisition and construction. Acquisition, whether by condemnation, cession, or dedication, is not planning. Sometimes ill-prepared laws provide that construction of a street cannot begin until it is approved by a planning commission. This would be too late for such approval because if the boundaries have been fixed and the street acquired, the municipality cannot very well do anything but proceed to construct it. Approval by the commission should be necessary for fixing the boundaries. Construction follows the locating, for locating is the act of planning. Similarly the determination of the locus of boundary lines in all the elements of community planning is the vital act. . . .

In recent years there has been a tendency to place certain sorts of private buildings within the field of planning as, for example, housing. Housing has come to mean the providing of homes for people of small means, built usually by limited dividend corporations or through subsidies from city, state, or nation. Without endeavoring to minimize the importance of such housing, it is not part of planning unless the community owns the site. A school, courthouse, fire house, or city hall is built by a municipality on the site for a public building. Houses for

---

3. Cf. Bassett, Williams, Bettman & Whitten, Model Laws for Planning Cities, Counties, and States (1935); MacAuslan, The Ideologies of Planning Law (1980).

people of small means that are on sites so owned are in the same category, that is, they are built on public land and are operated by and for the community.... They are therefore in the same category as a courthouse or a public school and undoubtedly come within the field of planning.

When, however, such buildings are erected by private corporations, perhaps with the help of subsidies from government and even when perhaps coupled with tax exemption, they are still private. To be sure, all the care that is taken in locating public buildings is required in locating such private buildings, and all the skill and experience of planners should be called in to ascertain the best situation, the size of the plot in proportion to that of the municipality, the supply of light and air, orientation, relation to parks, playgrounds, and streets.

In modern usage municipalities cannot obtain sites for public buildings by dedication. They must either buy or take them by condemnation. This shows, as has been stated, that the legal character of such sites has not such permanency as have streets and parks. Nevertheless from a planning point of view the location, size, and shape of sites for public buildings are of nearly the same importance as the location of streets and parks....

Some critics will say that zoning ought not to be one of the elements of planning because it has to do mainly with private land. No assertion is made that the elements relate to public land in the case of streets, parks, sites for public buildings, and public reservations, although such a statement would be accurate. But this is not so with zoning districts, routes for public utilities, and harbor lines. Zoning districts are land areas, the legal quality of which is impressed on the land by acts of law or the sanction of law.

It is easy to get the wrong impression that zoning relates not to the land but to buildings. To repeat, zoning maps never show buildings, only land. Through regulations applicable to particular districts the community allows certain kinds of buildings and prevents others. If a building burns down the zoning of the particular lot on which it stood does not change. Zoning regulations refer not only to buildings but to uses of vacant land. For instance, an automobile junk yard cannot be placed on vacant land in a residential district....

The writer's view has been that a master plan should not be adopted by any official body except by a planning commission. If finally so adopted copies can well enough be given to the various municipal departments, but if it needs to be adopted by the local legislative body it becomes to a certain extent hardened. Then when the commission desires to alter certain features in it the legislative body must first be persuaded to authorize the change. This is certain to work disastrously because as soon as a plan ceases to be plastic it becomes a quasi-official

A. The Master Plan: An Impermanent Constitution

map which has not been prepared and executed with the care and precision that the law requires in the case of official maps.

There are many advantages in keeping an official map separate from a master plan. An official map must be so precise that surveyors' and builders' stakes can be determined by it. Cities adopt official maps to determine streets, parks, and zoning districts. They are always established by a local legislative body and never by a planning commission. A master plan, however, will show not part but all the elements of the projected features of a city or region.

The need of a master plan arises with the establishment of planning commissions. If we conceive of a commission as an advisory body whose duty is to co-ordinate the various elements of a plan, it becomes apparent that the commission must have the means to denote its latest and best ideas in regard to improvements. This means should not be official because from time to time the master plan should be capable of quick alteration by the commission. The commission itself can of its own accord adopt all or any part of the master plan if an occasion renders this desirable, but if the instrument is its own it is free to make changes. The master plan is for the use of the commission. . . .

A master plan should not be passed by any legislative body. It is a co-ordinated plastic map or plan which a commission can at all times use in its written advice to a legislative body, but to overwork its limited function will result in planning's running wild.[4]

---

4. Legislative intent to protect a comprehensive capital budget of public improvements against subsequent, possibly imprudent, municipal action is examined in City of Chicago v. Central National Bank in Chicago, 5 Ill. 2d 164, 125 N.E.2d 94 (1955). The act required the submission to and the approval of the planning commission before establishing any parking facilities. Defendant argues that giving the commission complete discretion to approve or disapprove a plan submitted by the city council, without any standards or guides prescribed by the statute, is an unlawful delegation of legislative authority. The arguments continue within the profession:

> The reason the TVA Plan is not available is that there is no such document. Nor is there one separate department set off by itself where planners exercise their brains. . . . [T]his does not constitute our idea of planning. . . .
> *Here is the life principle of democratic planning — an awakening in the whole people of a sense of this common moral purpose.* Not one goal, but a direction. Not one plan, once and for all, but the conscious selection by the people of successive plans.

Lilienthal, TVA — Democracy on the March 192, 198 (1944).

> Here in Cincinnati our comprehensive plan was first adopted in 1925, with continuous modification, extension, and other action by the planning organ during the seventeen years since its adoption. In all these years nobody has claimed that it raises any legal question regarding private property or has had any legal effect on private conduct.

Bettman, The Master Plan: Is It an Encumbrance?, 57 Am. City 95 (Oct. 1942). For other opinions on the same subject, by three lawyers and a city planner, see the views of F. B. Williams and R. V. Black, id. 105-107 (Sept. 1942), Blucher, id. 97 (Oct. 1942), and Cram, Mich. St. B. J., Apr. 1956, at 9.

> Let me say at the outset that I believe the term "Master Plan" will eventually

■ AMERICAN LAW INSTITUTE, A MODEL LAND DEVELOPMENT CODE
(1975)

Section 3-102. [See page 58 supra.]

3-105 (1) A Local Land Development Plan shall include a short-term program of specific public actions to be undertaken in stated sequence by specified governmental agencies in order to achieve objectives, policies and standards stated under §3-104.

(2) The short-term program shall cover a period of time to be specified in the Plan, which shall be not less than [one] nor more than [five] years, but the program may indicate the general nature of future actions to be taken after that period.

(3) The Local Land Development Plan may also include

(a) an estimate of the amounts, types, characteristics, and general locations of land to be acquired or reserved, and the transportation, utility and community facilities to be provided or aided, by the local government or other governmental agencies in order to carry out the short-term program;

(b) an estimate of the number of persons and land uses to be displaced by the short-term program, the economic and social consequences of the displacement, and any relocation programs to be undertaken by governmental agencies;

(c) a general description of any development regulations that should be adopted within the period of the short-term program in order to achieve the objectives, policies and standards of the Land Development Plan, and an estimate of the additional trained personnel, if any, required to administer such regulations;

(d) an estimate of the cost of implementing the short-term

---

become obsolete. My reason is that its concept and connotations are unrealistic and inadequate as applied to planning for an area or community.

For one thing, it connotes control or domination of the future growth of the area or community in a manner predetermined by vested authority. To the layman it brings to mind a rigid design or blueprint, such as an architect, or master builder, establishes in building a house or other physical structure.

It further implies that there is one fixed central plan, which must be adhered to rigorously. . . .

On the whole, I believe that the concept and connotation of the term "Master Plan" is too limited, too rigid, and too unrealistic to provide a satisfactory philosophic base for the kind of planning that can and needs to be done by planning agencies in and for the larger urban areas of the United States. Terms, such as "Improvement Plan," "Development Plan," or just plain "City Plan," seem more accurate, more realistic, and more acceptable than the outmoded concept of 'Master Plan."

Stanbery, Is the Term "Master Plan" Obsolete?, 15 ASPO Newsletter 49-50 (1949). See also Monson, An Answer to Stanbery, id. 66 (Aug. 1949); Miles, Stanbery vs. Monson, id. 84 (Oct. 1949), suggesting the term "Organic Plan" as a substitute. In general, see Introduction to Planning History in the United States (Krueckeberg ed. 1983). — EDS.

A. The Master Plan: An Impermanent Constitution

program and a statement of sources of the public funds actually or potentially available;

(e) an estimate of the overall social and economic consequences of the short-term program including the impact on population distribution by characteristics and income, employment, and economic condition within the community and an evaluation, to the extent feasible, of the consequences of alternative short-term programs; and

(f) a statement of the assumptions regarding future private and public development upon which the short-term program is based.[5]

The following collection of opinions documents a diversity of viewpoints on the role of comprehensive planning, a reprise of many of the themes raised in Chapter IV, supra page 557. Taken together, they show the court struggling with the requirement of conforming implementive ordinances with the master plan. This is especially true as we move from mapped locational plans to more open-ended statements of policy plans.[6]

---

5. The note on this section states:

> This Section contains the central planning proposal of the Code. It requires the statement of a specific "short-term" program to be undertaken by the local government to move towards the desired objectives. It also suggests an analysis of the economic feasibility of the recommended undertakings and an estimate of social and economic consequences which will be involved.
>
> The Section is designed to accomplish three primary aims. First, it demands that planners devote major attention to accomplishment of desired objectives rather than simply to formulating them. Second, it gives meaning to the objectives by detailing their costs and consequences. Third, it makes the plan more realistic because the programming time is short enough to be comprehended and action is more likely to flow from the plan's adoption by the governing body. — EDS.

6. Section 9 of A Standard City Planning Act is entitled "Legal Status of Official Plan," but is concerned with the consequences "whenever the commission shall have adopted the master plan." Note that in California, from 1951 to 1953, there was provision for three types of plans: (a) The Master Plan (which could include any or all ten or more minor plans), (b) Official (or Precise) Plans, which could include proposed regulations limiting the uses of land, height, bulk, and open spaces of buildings and limitations with respect to existing or proposed rights of way, and (c) The Plan for Effectuating the Master Plan. Each required hearings and recommendations by the planning commission as well as a hearing and adoption by the local legislative body. Consider the impact of each of these on property affected. In 1953, the California law was changed to eliminate the Plan for Effectuating the Master Plan, and to state merely that

> the planning commission or the planning department shall investigate and make recommendations to the legislative body upon reasonable and practical means for putting into effect the master plan . . . in order that it will serve as a pattern and guide for . . . orderly physical growth and development . . . and as a basis for the efficient expenditure of . . . funds relating to the subjects of the master plan. The measures recommended may include plans, regulations, financial reports, and capital budgets. — EDS.

■ AYRES v. CITY COUNCIL OF LOS ANGELES
34 Cal. 2d 31, 207 P.2d 1 (1949)

[See opinion, supra page 621.]

■ COALITION FOR LOS ANGELES COUNTY PLANNING IN THE PUBLIC INTEREST v. BOARD OF SUPERVISORS
8 E.R.C. 1249 (L.A. County Super. Ct. Civil No. 63218, 1975)

[See opinion, supra page 729.]

■ KOZESNIK v. TOWNSHIP OF MONTGOMERY
24 N.J. 154, 131 A.2d 1 (1957)

WEINTRAUB, J. . . .

No doubt good housekeeping would be served if a zoning ordinance followed and implemented a master plan, Haar, "In Accordance with a Comprehensive Plan," 68 Harv. L. Rev. 1154 (1955), but the history of the subject dictated another course. Initially regulations concerning land use were merely prohibitory or restrictive with respect to specific noxious or dangerous activities. Thereafter a more comprehensive approach developed in the form of zoning, having as its purpose the creation of districts with regulations as to construction and use, including regulations as to height, number of stories, size of buildings, percentage of lot that may be occupied, sizes of yards, courts, etc. R.S. 40:55-30, N.J.S.A. Finally came the Planning Act, which envisions the development of a plan looking to and guiding future development with provision for the location of public improvements, control over subdivisions, and the like. . . .

Thus the historical development did not square with the orderly treatment of the problem which present wisdom would recommend. And doubtless the need for immediate measures led the Legislature to conclude that zoning shall not await the development of a master plan. Accordingly, as of October 15, 1954, while there were 371 zoning ordinances in our State, there were 320 planning boards and but 112 master plans. Professor Haar states that for the most part zoning elsewhere has preceded planning and about one-half of the cities with comprehensive zoning ordinances have not adopted master plans. Haar, "In Accordance with a Comprehensive Plan," supra (68 Harv. L. Rev., at 1157).

A. The Master Plan: An Impermanent Constitution

It is thus clear that the "comprehensive plan" of the zoning statute is not identical with the "master plan" of the Planning Act and need not meet the formal requirements of a master plan. The Zoning Act nowhere provides that the comprehensive plan shall exist in some physical form outside the ordinance itself. The question therefore is whether that requirement inheres in the very nature of a "comprehensive plan."

There has been little judicial consideration of the precise attributes of a comprehensive plan. Haar, "In Accordance with a Comprehensive Plan," supra (68 Harv. L. Rev. 1154). Our own decisions emphasize that its office is to prevent a capricious exercise of the legislative power resulting in haphazard or piecemeal zoning. Without venturing an exact definition, it may be said for present purposes that "plan" connotes an integrated product of a rational process and "comprehensive" requires something beyond a piecemeal approach, both to be revealed by the ordinance considered in relation to the physical facts and the purposes authorized by R.S. 40:55-32, N.J.S.A. Such being the requirements of a comprehensive plan, no reason is perceived why we should infer the Legislature intended by necessary implication that the comprehensive plan be portrayed in some physical form outside the ordinance itself. A plan may readily be revealed in an end-product — here the zoning ordinance — and no more is required by the statute.

The comprehensive plan embraced by an original zoning ordinance is of course mutable. If events should prove that the plan did not fully or correctly meet or anticipate the needs of the total community, amendments may be made, and if the ordinance as thus amended reveals a comprehensive plan, it is of no moment that the new plan so revealed differs from the original one.

■ BOARD OF COUNTY COMMISSIONERS OF CECIL COUNTY v. GASTER
285 Md. 233, 401 A.2d 666 (1979)

SMITH, J.

We granted certiorari in this case in order that we might consider the question of whether a county planning commission acting under subdivision regulations adopted by the county's legislative body might properly disapprove establishment of a proposed subdivision which met all zoning requirements but failed to comply with the master plan, also adopted by the county's legislative body....

Before we get into the legal background for this particular controversy, a word should be said relative to planning and zoning generally. Zoning did not come into Maryland easily.... Prior to the enactment of Chapter 672 of the Acts of 1970, planning and zoning authority for noncharter counties (in the absence of a local law as to a specific county) was found in Maryland Code (1957) Art. 66B, §§10-37, originally enacted by Chapter 599 of the Acts of 1933. It was based on the Standard State Zoning Enabling Act recommended by the U.S. Department of Commerce in the 1920's....

There are three integral parts of adequate land planning, the master plan, zoning, and subdivision regulations. The need for subdivision regulations as a part of that planning is well illustrated by the case here. As it is put in 4 Anderson, American Law of Zoning §23.03 (2d ed. 1977), "[Z]oning ordinances are not calculated to protect the community from the financial loss which may result from imperfect development. Some of these purposes are sought through the imposition of subdivision controls."

The General Assembly certainly contemplated some change from the previously existing scheme of planning and zoning when it decreed that in the counties covered by Art. 66B approval of the master plan by the local legislative body was required and that subdivision regulations should be adopted by such body. How can a county effectively plan for capital expenditures for roads, schools, sewers, and water facilities if, without regard to preexisting plans, a developer, as proposed here, might place a settlement of 1,200 or more people in the middle of a previously undeveloped area, a settlement which would overtax school facilities and which would necessitate improvement of a road whose reconstruction had not been contemplated before 1990? Planning would be futile in such situations.

In those instances the developer, not the constituted authority of the county, is in control of planning for the future of the county. Surely, this was not contemplated by the General Assembly when relative to the master plan it repeatedly used the words "at specified times as far into the future as is reasonable" and then went on to mandate approval of the master plan by the local legislative body and to require the adoption of subdivision regulations.

Notes

1. In Boyds Civic Association v. Montgomery County, 506 A.2d 675 (Md. App. 1986), the court stated:

> [T]he essential distinction between a master plan and comprehensive zoning is that the former merely recommends area development and *proposes* future land use and zoning classifications, while the latter determines *presently permitted* uses for property. See JMC Construction Corp.,

A. The Master Plan: An Impermanent Constitution

Inc. v. Montgomery County, 54 Md. App. 1, 456 A.2d 931 (1983) (citing Howard County v. Dorsey, 292 Md. 351, 438 A.2d 1339 (1982)). Although cases such as *Gaster* and *Coffey* indicate the master plan phase is becoming a more essential step in the zoning process, Maryland's view of master plans still mirrors those of the majority of other states — that it is advisory only. An example is found in Montgomery Co. v. Woodward & Lothrop, Inc., 280 Md. 686, 376 A.2d 483 (1977), where the Court of Appeals, in pertinent part, stated at 704:

> [There is no] requirement, *absent a statute*, that the map amendment must adhere to the recommendations of the General or Master Plan. Such land use planning documents represent only a basic scheme generally outlining planning and zoning objectives in an extensive area, and are in no sense a final plan; they are continually subject to modification in the light of actual land use development and serve as a guide rather than a straitjacket.

Similarly, a defect in the adoption of the Master Plan did not void PUD Regulations. Best v. La Plata Planning Commission, 701 P.2d 91 (Colo. App. 1984).

2. In Roberts v. City of Woonsocket, 575 F.2d 339 (1st Cir. 1978), the court relied on the Supreme Court of Rhode Island's characterization that "§45-24-3 does not require that zoning ordinances conform with the Master Plan adopted by the planning board"; rather, "the meaning of a comprehensive plan for purposes of §45-24-3 is only that the ordinance bear a reasonable relationship to the public health, safety and welfare." In summarizing its holding, an Illinois court concluded:

> [T]he adoption of a comprehensive plan which incorporates valid zoning goals increases the likelihood that the zoning of a particular parcel in conformity therewith is not arbitrary or unrelated to the public interest. The courts in Illinois have increasingly accorded importance to the existence of a comprehensive plan in reviewing zoning cases.

Wilson v. County of McHenry, 92 Ill. App. 3d 997, 416 N.E.2d 426, 429-430 (1981). One court rejected the city's claim that a rezoning was consistent with the comprehensive plan because it brought about a change from a more intensive to a less intensive use. City of Cape Canaveral v. Mosher, 467 So. 2d 468 (Fla. App. 1985).

3. In Las Virgenes Homeowners v. Los Angeles County, 177 Cal. App. 3d 300, 311, 223 Cal. Rptr. 18, 26 (1986), the court reasoned as follows:

> The General Plan consists of two major components: (1) countywide chapters and elements which set countywide policy framework, and (2) areawide and community plans which deal with local issues of unincorporated communities. The areawide plans . . . are extensions or refinements of County-wide policy. The General Plan Land Use Policy Map

identifies general and dominant uses and intensities. The role of the local plan is to identify more specific land uses, determine actual boundaries between land use categories, and establish more specific residential density ranges within the general parameters established by the countywide goals and policies. Because it is necessary to judge proposals in relation to stated policies of the General Plan in addition to the policy map itself, a proposal may be consistent even if not literally supported by the map. The mere examination of land use and other policy maps is insufficient to determine consistency.

See also Siemon, The Paradox of "In Accordance with a Comprehensive Plan" and Post Hoc Rationalizations, 16 Stetson L. Rev. 603, 630 (1987): "In order for there to be a rational and meaningful planning program, the results of the planning effort have to be memorialized in a document of some kind and the instrument must contain discrete statements of policy in regard to land use matters, including compatibility of adjacent uses and the adequacy of public facilities. Whether the document carries the label of plan, or study, or ordinance, so long as the document is written and readily available to affected individuals, this factor can be satisfied."

■ RIDER, TRANSITION FROM LAND USE TO POLICY PLANNING: LESSONS LEARNED
44 J. Am. Inst. Planners 25 (1978)

An unfavorable political environment coupled with a number of misjudgments seriously hampered the intended transition to policy planning. The lessons which may be derived from this experience are important to the evolving practice of planning.

Though both versions of the general plan, the department of general planning's and council's, were much debated, the real issue the community was seeking to cope with was how to manage growth. The failure to isolate this issue from the concept of the general plan not only caused considerable confusion but also resulted in a major diversion of resources which contributed little to a resolution of the city's problems. The focus on the identification of strategic policies became irrevocably lost in the plan's preparation. As a result, the final plan is a collection of miscellaneous thoughts in all subject areas.

Except in the area of growth management, "policies" were arrived at by filtering through long lists of statements until those which seemed generally agreeable remained. Some examples are: "maintain an adequate supply of water," "protect scenic views," "preserve the well-known and widely publicized beauty of Oahu," and "encourage more intensive use of agricultural land." Such statements have the value of setting forth widely held sentiments and, to a large extent, represent a catalogue

A. The Master Plan: An Impermanent Constitution

of wishes rather than a plan. The general plan is a costly illusion rather than a document having operational or strategic value.

It is interesting that, in every area but planning, the city charter provides the executive branch with authority to undertake particular functions but stops short of specifying how those functions should be executed. With planning, the charter commission stated that it wanted to give the city the "tools of policy planning." As a result, the charter goes beyond giving the function of policy planning to the executive branch and specifies what form policy planning should take. Unfortunately, the charter commission was following a long history of city planning in which a general or master plan is a necessary prescription. But the commission and all the professional planners who testified before it failed to realize that the general plan was incompatible with the objective to promote policy analysis.

Policy cannot fit into the formula of the general plan. It is as specific or as general as the problem warrants. Policies cannot be neatly programmed or divided into nine subject areas or, as required by the charter, reviewed at least every five years. They tend to be made in a piecemeal manner and limited to specific issues.

The charter commission made a bold step to transform the general plan into a dynamic planning tool, but a more radical alternative was required. In the author's view, the general plan had to be abandoned as a prerequisite for more effective planning. But this alternative was not defined and would not have been seriously considered, even if identified. The vast struggle to produce a new plan had to take place as the next step in the evolution of the planning process. The question is whether the lesson will prove fruitful.

Other factors contributing to Honolulu's difficulties are the complexities involved in considering a global issue. If the legal requirements were abandoned, planners would be free to shape the analysis in accordance with the best alternative design. The form of development within each region — not just the citywide pattern of growth — might have been considered. This approach would have made the analysis less abstract and permitted planners to evolve a growth management plan that addressed regional or subarea issues which were clamoring for attention. Unfortunately, these issues were regarded as the proper domain of the development plan. The need to preserve the "generality" of the general plan became a major issue. Regional analysis was not necessarily precluded by charter requirements; recall the distinction drawn between the general plan and the development plan. However, available resources and the expectation that the general plan would provide only a broad citywide policy framework, within which regional development plans would be prepared, kept the analysis at a macro level and ruled out the evaluation of specific issues of subareas as part of the preparation of a new general plan.

B. PLANNING PROCESS, MARKET MECHANISM, AND ADMINISTRATIVE CONTROLS

1. The Efficacy and Desirability of Land-Use Controls in Achieving Values

The cases are concerned with the necessity, desirability, and scope of the future planning and control of land development. They raise many issues. Can there be common agreement on goals?[7] When does the enlarging of returns to private operating units conflict with social benefits? Questions arise about the problem of reconciling economic productivity of land with other aims, including the individual's freedom to experiment and diverge from the hive of the community. Can a general theory be developed that will render guidance on particular land-use situations? Are freedom, productivity, and other values more consistent with planning in the case of land than in the case of other factors of production?

■ POLANYI, THE LOGIC OF LIBERTY
134-135 (1951)

At first sight, this looks exactly like a true plan, namely like a comprehensive purpose elaborated in detail through successive stages; the kind of plan, in fact, which can be carried out only by appropriate central direction.

But in reality such an alleged plan is but a meaningless summary of an aggregate of plans, dressed up as a single plan. It is as if the manager of a team of chess-players were to find out from each individual player what his next move was going to be and would then sum up the result by saying: "The plan of my team is to advance 45 pawns by one place, move 20 bishops by an average of three places, 15 castles by an average of four places, etc." He could pretend to have a plan for his team, but actually he would be only announcing a nonsensical summary of an aggregate of plans.

In order to press home this illustration, let us see wherein lies exactly the impossibility of conducting a hundred games of chess by central direction. Why would it be absurd to make one person responsible for the moves of all castles, another for all bishops, etc.? The answer is that the moving of any particular castle or bishop constitutes

---

7. See Krasnowiecki, The Fallacy of the End-State System of Land Use Control, Land Use L. & Zoning Dig., Apr. 1986, at 3. — Eds.

B. Market Mechanism and Administrative Controls 1059

"a move in chess" only in the context of the moves (and possible moves) of the other pieces in the same game. It ceases to be "a move in chess" and is consequently meaningless in the context of the moves of all castles, or of all bishops, in a hundred different games. Such a context is a senseless collocation, falsely described as a purpose; whence the absurdity of entrusting a person with carrying out this fictitious purpose.

■ TUGWELL, THE FOURTH POWER[8]
1-4, 6-9, 16-17, 21-22 (1939)

When historians look back, after several decades, they may be able to see how a directive power offered to range itself alongside the executive, the legislative and the judicial.[1] If, by then, it has developed into a fourth division within our governmental system, there need not

---

8. A later development of essentially the same position (but more diffuse) is found in Tugwell, The Place of Planning in Society (1954), and The Study of Planning as a Scientific Endeavor, 50 Mich. Acad. of Sci., Arts & Letters 34 (1948). Also see Tugwell, Model for a New Constitution, Center Magazine, Sept. 1970. — EDS.

1. It seemed impossible for the purposes of this article to avoid changing a familiar loosely used word into a more precise and technical term. There is some reason for believing that other writers have been approaching this definition in attempting to introduce agreed meaning where before there had been confusion. Perhaps the word "direction" with its two rather subtly different connotations comes as near transferring concepts along with familiar sound as it would ever be possible to do. Others may have burdened the word with less weight than it is made to carry here, and have been less precise, but they have felt the same need. For instance, in this sentence from Mr. Joseph Hudnut's introduction to Werner Hegemann's City Planning: Housing, there is one use: "Neither a collection of buildings nor an aggregation of people makes a city, but rather the form and content of society and *the direction of its march*." But this, obviously, is limited. It is one thing to *point out a direction* which is being taken. It is another thing to *give direction*. Mr. Charles W. Eliot 2nd, has used it in a closer sense — "*the development of order and direction* out of a chaos of rugged individualism"; Mr. George H. Gray (The Planners' Journal, Nov.-Dec. 1938, p. 144) has a sentence which illustrates an equivocal meaning: "*While our economic direction* has always been planned in a fashion (gold standard, tariff schedules, etc.), this planning has for the most part been done in isolation from a general national plan." But Mr. Arthur G. Coons understands the *double entendre*: "Whatever planning is, it is to be seen as *a conscious directive aspect* of the political, social, or economic life of some definite geographical region . . ." ("The Nature of Economic Planning in Democracy," Plan Age, Feb., 1939, p. 43.) Even Sir Henry Bunbury, cautious Britisher that he is, uses the word: "*Social direction and control*, by organs representing the community, of the economic life of a nation — of the conservation, development and utilisation of its varied resources — have become necessary by reason of the immense advances which have taken place in technology, communications, corporate organization, and financial techniques." ("Government Planning Machinery," Public Administration Service publications No. 63, p. 5.) Mr. Soule, perhaps, comes nearer than anyone else to using the word in the full sense intended here: "But how, it is asked, could we retain democracy if authority *to direct all these economic processes* were given to the State?" And in another passage: "It must be remembered, too, that in a free collectivist system government would not own *or direct every activity*." The Future of Liberty, 173, 177. Many others have used the word, sometimes as a kind of synonym for planning, sometimes with a closer approach to the double meaning intended here. Its appropriation may be forgiven, being thus excused as not altogether original.

have been at any time the theatrical recognition which came to the executive out of the administrative futility inherent in parliamentary government during the eighteenth century. The process can be evolutionary and adaptive; it can be, that is, unless it is deliberately so delayed that opposing physical and social forces reduce the American state to relative ineffectiveness. If this last should happen it would be sufficiently dramatic and obvious; but it would not result in the development of a fourth power. For the whole system would either be subjected to a foreign executive or submerged in a chaos out of which anything might emerge — anything, that is, except institutions with fundamental provision for the participation of every citizen after his sort, which is, after all, the democratic sine qua non.

Even if the present trend continues, the process will be one of those which are difficult to see going on; and the constitutional changes which recognize it may lag well behind the fact of its existence.... Americans have been well enough aware of a new precision-created industry in their midst and of a world changed in material and tempo; they have even been aware that planning offered new possibilities of foresight and control. But they have not wanted to learn that all these, from beginning to end, were part of a process which was forcing concomitant changes in government looking toward the modification of conflict and the emphasizing of cooperation.[2] ...

    2. It is difficult to contemplate seriously the planning idea without arriving at some such conclusion. Mr. Charles W. Eliot 2nd, for instance, in 1933 (Planning and National Recovery, National Conference on City Planning, Richmond, p. 32) distinguished several types — "charting" or "economic planning," "budgeting," which describes itself, "purposing" or "projecting," which comprehends physical planning, and so on. "They mean," he said, "quite different things, although they all have a common interest in forethought and organization . . ." These last words show that at that time Mr. Eliot was expecting more than resulted from the New Deal. By 1935 he was fearing, along with others, that planners might be called "regimenters," a term which was satisfactorily opprobrious until attention was recalled to the fact that most of the herding and pushing in our economy is after all done by business for its purposes, rather than by government in the public interest. (Cf. R. G. Tugwell, The Battle for Democracy, p. 193.) "Regimenting" had lost its value as an epithet by 1936. There is a comment, in a recent study by Mr. Rene DeVisme Williamson, which places accurately the source of this fear:

> Much is heard, from the opponents of planning, about the dictatorial power that must regiment every detail if our economy is to be planned. They loudly attack the centralized authority that would jam arbitrary production schedules down the throats of a liberty-loving people, and even interfere with their freedom of consumption. It is contentions such as these which have given planning a bad name in many quarters originally friendly to it. They rest on a very unsound basis and have their source in ignorance. There can be no doubt, of course, that power is necessary for every kind of cooperative action, and planning is no exception. But there lie in the minds of the people who fear planning a number of misconceptions. One of these is that all power must be dictatorial and oppressive. They forget that the ability to convince people by reasonable argument, and to appeal successfully to their emotions, are just as good methods — if not actually much better — of obtaining intelligent and enthusiastic support, as to threaten them with the concentration camp and the firing squad. There are forms of power which a free

B. Market Mechanism and Administrative Controls

The materials and forces of the nation can be arranged to make a pattern; they can produce incredible benefits; but only if they are managed with that objective. It will not happen accidentally. There exists an insistent demand for higher standards which, as things are, makes an almost intolerable drain on upper and middleclass incomes. Between these pressures public officials are made desperate. Politicians divide nicely on issues which involve a little more or less, some favoring more benefits, some striving to reduce expenditures. What pressure is yielded to at the moment is of less importance than the fact of increasing pressure and increasing resistance. The only relief in the long run (aside from explosion) must come from such an increase in benefits and such a diffusion of them as will satisfy those who are presently below standard without reducing everyone to misery. It can only be done by greatly increasing production. And this in turn can only be done by outlawing conflict and enforcing cooperation — just the reverse of the traditional scheme of rewards and punishments. The gradual apprehension of the possibilities in modern technique together with the recurrent sinking spells which disgust people with present forms, customs, morals and leadership, may result in some forcible resolution of the paradox. But assuming that it does not, evolution must necessarily be toward cooperative forms, collective customs, pragmatic morality and technically buttressed leadership; because this is what will give us the greatest product; and also because this is the only door to the future which is available to those who regard the avoidance of force as a necessity....

Planning is quite susceptible of use by autarchies, but it ought not to be identified with them.[7] For, provided it is subject to the right direction, it may be capable of rescuing democratic government from many of its present difficulties.... Planning can preserve a useful kind of democracy; it cannot save all the symbols we like to confuse it with....

Planning is not direction when it is at the service of special interests in society; it becomes direction only when it can affect economic divisiveness; becoming a unifying, cohesive, constructive, and truly

---

people would not do away with were it possible to do so, because they need that kind of power.

Plan Age, Feb. 1939, p. 36....

7. "As for the compatibility of central planning and democracy, planning like any technique is politically neutral. It may be used by any form of politico-economic organization. When employed by totalitarian states, it is dictatorial, militarist, authoritarian. Under a democratically planned collectivism toward which we in America are moving, scientific planning ... will seek social objectives set by bodies representative of the majority and will pursue democratic procedures." Mr. George B. Galloway, Plan Age, Jan. 1939, p. 29.

general force.[8] Its importance in our affairs was certainly gained through sheer effectiveness. The fact that this pervasive smoothness and efficiency accentuates conflicts by making both sides more effective, implies, however, that a point in its growth and extension is reached at which it must be subordinated to general rather than special purposes on penalty of its results becoming destructive to society — and incidentally to itself....

... Until the discovery is made that, although it is possible, through planning, for any interest to gain proportionately over other interests, it can gain more if joined in a general directive movement, the industrial advance, which promised so much a short time ago, cannot be resumed. It may already have been succeeded by decline. For as special interests grow more coherent and better furnished with planning tools, competition among them becomes more effective and therefore more ruinous. It seems not unlikely that the time may already have been reached when social groups must advance together or regress separately.

... Laissez faire, no matter where it seems to lead, has true relationships only with the past. There is no general institution except government. There is no present power within government capable of thus generalizing — certainly none with which recalcitrant industrialists will consent to cooperate....

... A plan for an industry, a city, a nation, is not something which can be experimented with in the old sense. Much more is involved — more people, more property in a wider space and over a longer time. Damage is done by mistakes which may be irreparable. But there is another consideration. The plan or policy cannot be built up from constituent units. It has to grow out of a concept of a functioning whole. An industry cannot place its plants, warehouses, outlets, sources of materials without relation to each other, and it cannot place them without relation to all other related activities: finance, insurance, communication, substitute goods, tariffs and the like. A city cannot provide for schools, fire protection, police, sewers, water and light, and

---

8. It ought not to be implied, of course, that we have more democracy than we actually possess. Authentic American history dictates considerable cautions as to the founders' intentions and as to various shapers' purposes. It is doubtless true that we have much more political democracy than was ever intended. It has increased with the years; technology at least had this effect. Yet vast areas of social life have been withdrawn from the democratic process on the plea of efficiency (which our forefathers did not stress). These areas are more largely economic than governmental. Perhaps the future will show a need for less democracy in government and for more in industry. That would appear to be a reasonable objective if we are to gain efficiency and keep liberty. Number ten of The Federalist represented a point of view which is less characteristic of influential theorists than it once was; but those same fears and cautions concerning popular decision now infect the leaders of industry. There is a whole field of delegation and selection which still remains to be explored in both industry and government; but the dangers in the one are not those which prevail in the other. The dictatorial danger at the moment is industrial and is unlikely to become governmental unless industry succeeds in appropriating its machinery. The danger in government is that of ineffectiveness.

all its other services except through what has come to be called a "Master Plan" implemented by control of the capital budget....

All this reverses many accepted ideas. It is a process unfamiliar, even uncongenial to the American habit.... The individual can no longer exercise his initiative in a matter which affects a large industry or a planned city. The processes of change are reduced to an order in which the individual, except as a member of the cooperating whole, cannot be allowed to function freely, if at all. Others think out problems which affect the individual. Since it is contrary to our habit and since it involves restraints and limitations not envisaged in a view of life shaped in the old individualism, there are many who dissent from it, others who are not clear in their own minds about its processes, and still others who, while using the new devices, appeal to the old ideas, thus seeking to restrain others in matters where they do not themselves accept restraint....

In The Road to Serfdom 48-50 (1956), Professor Hayek argues that, far from being appropriate only for simple conditions, competition is the only way by which coordination can be achieved under a complex state of affairs. He adds:

> The more complicated the whole, the more dependent we become on that division of knowledge between individuals whose separate efforts are coordinated by the impersonal mechanism for transmitting the relevant information known by us as the price system. It is no exaggeration to say that if we had to rely on conscious central planning for the growth of our industrial system, it would never have reached the degree of differentiation, complexity, and flexibility it has attained. [By contrast, the method of central direction] is incredibly clumsy, primitive, and limited in scope.[9]

■ FULLER, FREEDOM — A SUGGESTED ANALYSIS
68 Harv. L. Rev. 1305, 1316, 1319-1320 (1955)

Much discussion of freedom, particularly as it relates to the problem of majority rule, is obscured by a failure to keep in mind a distinction between two fundamental forms of social organization. These are

---

9. See Bell, The Cultural Contradictions of Capitalism (1976); Gaus, Reflections on Public Administration (1947); Mannheim, Freedom, Power and Democratic Planning (1950); Branch, Comprehensive City Planning (1985); Simmie, Beyond the Industrial City?, 60 A.P.A. J. 59 (1983); Offe, Contradictions of the Welfare State (1985); Popper, The Open Society and Its Enemies (3d ed. 1957); Lindsay, The Modern Democratic State (1943); Dahl and Lindblom, Politics and Markets (1977); Clavel, The Progressive City (1986). — EDS.

organization by reciprocity and organization by common ends. Organization by reciprocity occurs in its simplest form when A and B come together in such a way that A gains from B something worth more to him than that which he gives to B, and B makes a similar reciprocal gain. In its crassest and most familiar form, organization by reciprocity is an exchange of economic goods. Organization by common ends occurs in its simplest form when A and B mutually benefit by joining forces to accomplish some objective shared by both but which neither could achieve without the help of the other. . . .

Organization by common ends is truly effective — and, if I may be permitted the expression, most wholesome — where the aims of the association are actively shared, not by a bare majority, but by the great bulk of its membership, and where those aims are meaningful in the sense that they give a fairly clear direction as to the steps necessary for their realization. Hayek is certainly right in saying that the great advantage of the liberal state ("liberal" old style, of course) was that there was an almost universal sharing of its aims: common defense, prevention of fraud and violence, protection of property, enforcement of contracts. Furthermore, those are aims that are readily understood and, when understood, define, in general outlines at least, what ought to be done to effectuate them. The citizen therefore does not need to study the code to learn that he is not supposed to vote twice, welsh on his agreements, or shoot his neighbor through the head.

Contrast with the prosaic aims of the liberal state a national plan for doubling the production of coal. As to such an aim the ordinary citizen cannot know what it implies for his personal interests, and, if he did, he might well be against it. Even if he were willing to accept this aim on faith as a proper governmental objective, it still does not tell him what he should do or refrain from doing to help achieve it; he might, for example, patriotically move from a job in a ball-bearing factory to a coal mine, only to learn later that the greatest block to increased coal production was a shortage of ball bearings for mining machinery. The long and short of it is that he will have to be told what to do, and he will have to take his orders on faith. In such a process freedom, in the sense of a meaningful choice among alternatives, must suffer a serious decline.

This is a very inadequate outline of the problem of freedom as it affects the two fundamental forms of organization. The crucial — and I think neglected — question is: What areas of human activity should be fitted into the one form of organization and what into the other? The mistake of the uncritical "planner" who wants planning for its own sake is to assume that what has been achieved (inadequately, to be sure) through an organization in terms of reciprocity could be more effectively achieved through an organization by common ends. He does not seem to realize that this is like trying to set an intricate ballet to the music of a Sousa march.[10]

■ KELLER, THE PLANNING OF COMMUNITIES: ANTICIPATIONS AND HINDSIGHTS
The Idea of Social Structure 283, 285-286, 290-292 (Coser ed. 1975)

It is by now generally recognized, though not often acted upon, that social and physical planning are interrelated and that one is not likely to be effective without the other. The success of national development plans, for example, ultimately depends on sound local-spatial planning, for in addition to setting national targets for housing, jobs, or education one must also spell out their geographic distribution. Nonetheless, fragmentary and piecemeal planning remains the rule rather than the exception. But if most national plans formulate their objectives too abstractly and without specifying the spatial distribution of their objectives, plans for new communities tend to fall into the opposite error. They often remain unintegrated with the larger national or even regional picture. This lack of coordination between the two levels then results in such well-known disasters as roads that stop in the middle of nowhere, mass facilities without parking places, and tourist hotels cut off from ways to get to or away from them.

Lack of teamwork among disciplines is part of the problem. As is well known, the elephant varies with the discipline examining it, and this partial view limits a full comprehension of its nature.

Selective perception also affects the paradigm of information and explanation utilized. Planners are not typically attuned to the significance of culture pattern and social structure and thus underestimate cultural and structural factors without dispelling their influence. The ensuing gap between intention and result is often filled in by ad hoc and arbitrary decisions.

Examples of the imposition of alien, hence arbitrary, standards and design criteria on groups they are unsuited for are endless. Planners and other experts frequently do not share either the experiences or the aspirations of those they are planning for and substitute the

---

10. See Cross, The Diminishing Fee, 20 Law & Contemp. Probs. 517 (1955); Friedmann, Law and Social Change in Contemporary Britain (1951); Green, Is Zoning by Men Replacing Zoning by Law?, 21 J. Am. Inst. Planners 82 (1955); Stone, The Myths of Planning and Laissez Faire: A Re-Orientation, 18 Geo. Wash. L. Rev. 1 (1949); Cahn and Cahn, The New Sovereign Immunity, 81 Harv. L. Rev. 929 (1968); Fischel, Economics and Zoning Laws, 45 Urb. Land 34 (1986); Solow, Microeconomic Theory, in Economics, the Behavioral and Social Science Survey (Ruggles ed. 1970) — EDS.

Four Policymaking Styles

	Planning for present concerns	Planning for the future			
		Responding to predicted futures		Creating desired future
	Reacting to past problems	*Allocative trend-modifying*	*Exploitive opportunity-seeking*	*Normative goal-oriented*
	Ameliorative problem-solving	*Planning toward the future*	*Planning with the future*	*Planning from the future*
Planning Mode	*Planning for the present* Analyze problems, design interventions, allocate resources accordingly.	Determine and make the *best* of trends and allocate resources in accordance with desires to promote or alter them.	Determine and make the *most* of trends and allocate resources so as to take advantage of what is to come.	Decide on the future *desired* and allocate resources so that trends are changed or created accordingly. Desired future may be based on present, predicted or new values.

	Ameliorate Present Problems	A Sense of Hope	A Sense of Triumphing Over Fate	A Sense of Creating Destiny
"Present" or short range results		New allocations shift activities	New allocations shift activities	New allocations shift activities
"Future" or long range results of actions	*Haphazardly Modify the Future* by reducing the future burden and sequelae of present problems	*Gently Balance and Modify the Future* by avoiding predicted problems and achieving a "balanced" progress to avoid creating major bottlenecks and new problems.	*Unbalance and Modify the Future* by taking advantage of predicted happenings, avoiding some problems and cashing in on others without major concern for emergence of new problems.	*Extensively Modify the Future* by aiming for what could be. "Change the predictions" by changing values or goals, match outcomes to desires, avoid or change problems to ones easier to handle or tolerate.

Source: Berry, The Question of Policy Alternatives (1973).

perspectives they are familiar with — that of middle-class professionals — for those required. This is true not only within but between cultures, as solutions relevant in one setting are automatically transferred to a different one without much regard for whether they will work there. An example is the Neighborhood Unit Idea exported from Britain throughout the world without checking on its viability under different cultural conditions. Both class and cross-cultural paternalism reflect the common, if erroneous, belief that expertise transcends culture and that properly trained outsiders can diagnose and design for insiders.

This is not unrelated to the paternalism that continues to pervade the professions generally. The idea that one can plan *for* people, or that one class or group has a unique claim to truth, or that experts know best is still far from dead, though the results should give us pause. How many new housing projects, for example, are defaced or distorted, partly out of injured pride and partly out of sheer unfamiliarity with a design not suited to the ways of *these* people in *this* place and time? This may be one reason why the ghettoes, shantytowns, and favellas that the new projects are designed to displace keep reemerging. The failure to make the design fit different concepts of privacy, neighborliness, or amenity quickly results in its being perceived as an obstacle to be removed or circumvented. Residents then renounce responsibility for maintenance, illegal services may spring up in the gap left by poorly designed or placed facilities, and residents may practice passive resistance against management.

Despite the accumulated evidence of the past century, planners continue to be reluctant to accept the existence, depth, and power of culture patterns to shape human conduct and desires. They still tend to consider human beings as basically alike and to reduce human needs and wishes to a common biological or economic denominator. . . .

Planning for a world in flux demands a huge effort of the imagination as well as the capacity to invoke new guiding images of what the future may be like. Such images are in short supply in current plans for new communities, most of which bear the imprint of nostalgia rather than anticipation.

A main source of the unanticipated developments in such communities stems from adherence to ideals no longer appropriate to emergent realities. For example, the desire to create comprehensive, self-contained, intimate, face-to-face communities akin to the cozy villages of yesteryear is an illusory quest, I fear, because it misreads the scale of life which is to characterize the twenty-first century. Just as one cannot reduce the scale of an adult by cutting off his legs — at most one impedes his locomotion — so one cannot keep the world of telemobility away from conceptions of modern communities. Still, the pretense persists that these settlements of technicians and professionals

B. Market Mechanism and Administrative Controls 1069

of more than average education and income, in constant contact with the wider world through televiewing, working, vacationing, and visiting, are small, comprehensive, territorially bound villages contentedly turned in upon themselves. In other words, the notion of the local community needs to be reexamined and overhauled. . . .

Currently, people move rather than stay put to pursue jobs, education, romance, adventure. In new towns, in particular, none of the traditional indexes of localism would seem to apply since they tend to be inhabited by transients and strangers, ever in contact with wider and different worlds. Television, that ubiquitous boarder in modern homes, makes sure of that. Both in planning and in sociology, therefore, we need to reconceptualize current notions of community, territoriality, and permanence, as boundaries and distances recede and the world enters our living rooms at the flick of a dial.

It has, of course, long been noted that communities are being transformed in scale and function, but as yet the insufficient operationalization of these notions makes them of little use to planners and builders. In one sense, we are simply witnessing a further extension of a historic process, described by Toennies and other nineteenth-century thinkers, as a movement from *Gemeinschaft* to *Gesellschaft*. *Gesellschaft* referred to the diversified, large-scale, dynamic, social, political, and economic relations of macrosystems called "societies." *Gemeinschaft*, on the other hand, emphasized antithetical traits of local, territorially defined, closed systems and relations marked by common traditions and destinies.

But what was dichotomy, idealized to be sure, in the nineteenth century has become continuum in the twentieth. Today, increasingly, the local community mirrors the very forces with which it was originally contrasted, as diversification and specialization break through its physical form and destroy the unity and uniformity that were its trademark. Accordingly, we must cease to look at community in holistic and dichotomous terms. This is as true of its spatial as of its social characteristics. . . .

The territorial imperative is so entrenched in our perceptions and mind sets, however, that we find it difficult to absorb, not to say plan for, that dramatic possibility. Hence, community planning is not yet geared to nonterritoriality as an emerging concept. This is one reason why this sort of planning is often inadequate and why unanticipated consequences — for good or ill — defeat the loftiest of aims for community cohesion and commitment. This gap between intention and result will not be lessened by more money or time or good will. Needed are new assumptions and better concepts of community, concepts that are closer to the reality and humanity which are after all the ostensible targets and purposes of planning.

■ LOCK, PLANNING: THE FUTURE
Planner, Feb. 1984, at 10

Drawing the threads of this paper together, the major characteristics of planning in the future might best be summarised as follows:

- Planning will survive as an activity in our civilised society because we will want to reconcile conflicting demands for land and resources, to achieve improvements in the quality of life, and to control the ecological balance.
- Planning activity will be focused primarily at the local level, but there will be a strategic function at regional levels.
- Planning will be disengaged from representational democratic institutions such as district and county councils. It will be energised by popular mandate.[11]
- Planners will be wanted as technicians, administrators and arbitrators. A few will be wanted as advocates at the strategic level, and others as managers for particular implementation tasks (notably for intervention in the land and investment market).

---

11. The Constitution of Planners for Equal Opportunity (1970) provides:

Article II. Section I. *Purposes:* Recognizing the positive contribution which planning skills and concepts could offer to the struggle of minority groups for equal opportunity, and realizing the inequities and abuses against those minorities which too often result either by deliberate intent or conscious neglect — from the programs and actions of public and private agencies and institutions, Planners for Equal Opportunity dedicates itself to use its professional competence to safeguard the rights of minorities, to oppose discrimination, to provide equal enjoyment of the fruits of this affluent society, and to support the increase of political influence and independence of minorities. To these aims, purposes and objectives, we hereby adopt the by-laws as hereinafter set forth.

Section 2. *Program:* To carry out its purposes, the organization will engage in the following activities:

a. Develop an action program in which individual members will offer advice and professional aid to local or community groups involved in the struggle for equal opportunity, and assist in bringing planners and such groups together for these purposes.

b. On its own initiative and in response to requests, prepare statements or position papers on general issues within its competence related to the struggle for equal opportunity, and reexamine planning principles and practices where they impair equality of opportunity. . . .

d. Promote the entry of members of minority groups into planning and allied professions and encourage professional schools to recruit minority applicants by making scholarships and other financial aids available to them. . . .

See Harris & Rein, Dilemmas of Social Reform (1967); Titmuss, Essays on the Welfare State (1963); Readings in Community Organization Practice (Kramer & Specht eds. 1969); Confrontation at Ocean Hill-Brownsville (Berube & Gittell eds. 1969); Haefele, Coalitions, Minority Representation and Vote-Trading Possibilities, Public Choice, Spring 1970; Sen, Collective Choice and Social Welfare (1970); Fogelsong, Planning the Capitalist City (1986) is especially pertinent on this issue. — Eds.

B. Market Mechanism and Administrative Controls

2. How Should a Land-Use Decision Be Made?

There is continuous struggle over the respective roles of public and private enterprise in coping with the organization of land use in metropolitan areas. At what point are decisions over land use made, and by whom? How and when do persons affected obtain a right to be heard or record their wishes? To what extent will government superimpose choices differing from the precise wishes of individual owners? Who is the "public" in respect to land-use controls? How does the individual pursuit of "rationality" in the land-use area differ from the public notion of "rationality"? Should some decisions — especially those relating to the siting of uses — be insulated from pressure groups and removed from the political forum? Can the long-term interest be protected by people who do not "own" the land? Indeed, can a democracy, based on majority rule, even plan for the future?[12]

■ CROSS v. BILETT
122 Colo. 278, 221 P.2d 923 (1950)

STONE, Justice. John Rotola applied to the building inspector of Denver for permit to erect a one-story masonry filling station and home appliance store. The application was denied for the reason that it was for a nonconforming use in a residence "B" zone. Appeal was taken to the board of adjustment where both consenting and objecting petitions were filed, and upon hearing . . . the board made finding that the property was more suited for business uses than for residential development and granted the application. Upon certiorari by plaintiffs in error as owners of neighboring property, judgment was entered in the district court dismissing the petition and ordering permit issued for the nonconforming use. . . .

Under the provisions of the Charter Zoning Amendment, section 219A, Charter, Municipal Code of 1927,

> The Council may provide for the appointment of a Board of Adjustment, and in the regulations and restrictions adopted pursuant to the authority of this amendment may provide that the said Board of Adjustment may, in appropriate cases and subject to appropriate conditions and safeguards, make special exceptions to the terms of the ordinance in harmony with

---

12. See Arrow, Social Choice and Individual Values (2d ed. 1963); Churchill, Planning in a Free Society, 20 J. Am. Inst. Planners 189 (1954); Dewey, Planned Use and Democratic Choice, in Planning 12 (1954); Knight, Freedom and Reform (1947); Skinner, Freedom and the Control of Men, 25 Am. Scholar 47 (Winter 1955-1956); Wootton, Freedom Under Planning (1945); Downs, Urban Problems and Prospects (1970); Heymann, The Problem of Coordination, 86 Harv. L. Rev. 797 (1973); Handler, Social Movements and the Legal System (1978); Walzer, Spheres of Justice (1983) — EDS.

its general purpose and intent and in accordance with general or specific rules therein contained.

Thereunder was adopted chapter LXXXI, art. V, section 2190 B, of the Municipal Code of 1927, whereby it is provided that

> When in its judgment the public convenience and welfare will be substantially served or the appropriate use of neighboring property will not be substantially or permanently injured, the board of adjustment may, in a specific case, after public notice and hearing and subject to appropriate conditions and safeguards, determine and vary the application of the regulations herein established in harmony with their general purposes and intent as follows: ... (10) Permit the location ... in any residence district of any use or structure authorized in any other residence district or in any business district. Provided, there shall be on file with the said board the consents, duly signed and acknowledged, of the owners of 80 per cent of all the land within such area as the said board shall have determined to be specially affected by such proposed use or structure, [except certain uses not herein involved].

Reversal is here sought chiefly on the ground that the board of adjustment failed to determine or designate the area specifically affected by such proposed use, and that there were not on file the consents of the owners of 80 per cent of all the land within such area, as required by the ordinance above quoted. . . .

... In the absence of a zoning ordinance, where the right of a municipality is strictly limited to the general police power for protection of the public health and welfare, it is commonly held that only such buildings and occupations may be restricted as are shown to be injurious under such police power; that individuals ought not to be entrusted with the guardianship of their own health, safety or social well being through authority to waive laws or ordinances made for their protection, nor should one individual be permitted to dictate the use of another's property. . . .

With the growth of congested urban populations, containing areas of attractive residential development, with values greatly dependent on conformity, and with the increasing public concern for quiet, safety and beauty, there have been enacted zoning laws under appropriate legislative or constitutional authority in most municipalities in the United States and in many rural areas. The concept of public welfare thereunder has broadened. Under such ordinances uses permitted and legal in one district of the city are prohibited in another. Such prohibition is based not strictly upon the inherent danger to the public health, public morals, the public safety, or the public welfare of the prohibited uses generally, but upon its interference with the appropriate use of property and the maintenance of its value in the zone in which such use is sought. We have repeatedly upheld such restrictions. . . .

B. Market Mechanism and Administrative Controls 1073

Also, with the growth and change of cities, inevitably there come changing use and demand. Areas once residential are found to be in the path of necessary business or other changing use. Properties at the edge of a residential district may, by virtue of change in an adjoining district, necessarily require conversion to nonconforming uses. Failure of adjustment may destroy the value and prevent the proper use which the zoning laws seek to protect. Often such adjustments can be provided for only by granting permission for nonconforming use. Boards of adjustment are created for such purpose. The primary reason for such changing use being the needs and desires of the vicinity, it is a reasonable requirement and primary test of changed condition that the consent of those affected be required before the zoning board may act. Thereby the owner of one property is not dictating the use of his neighbor's property, for the discretion in permitting change of use still lies with the board, yet the board cannot act arbitrarily, but only in cases where the demonstrated need and desire of the community for change so affirmatively appears.

Such situation developed early in New York when inhabitants of some large residential districts, where commercial garages were prohibited, could not obtain storage places for their automobiles. To supply that need, it was provided that in any district the board of appeals had discretion to grant application for the erection of a public garage upon filing the consents of the owners of 80 per cent of the street frontage within the district determined by the board of appeals to be affected by it. Such provisions have been held valid and action of the board without compliance void.... This method of limitation on the action of adjustment boards has been widely followed in other cities (Basset, Zoning, page 126), and has generally been held valid. The question of validity has apparently not heretofore been raised in this jurisdiction.

A line of distinction between such an ordinance and an invalid delegation of authority was laid down by the United States Supreme Court in Eubank v. Richmond, 226 U.S. 137, and Cusack Co. v. City of Chicago, 242 U.S. 526. The former case involved an ordinance providing, "That whenever the owners of two-thirds of property abutting on any street shall, in writing, request the committee on streets to establish a building line on the side of the square on which their property fronts, the said committee shall establish such line," etc. This ordinance was held void for the reason that it left no discretion in the committee as to whether the street line should or should not be established; but delegated full authority to two-thirds of the property owners; that thereby part of the owners fronting on a block determined the extent and kind of use that other owners should make of their lots, and there was no standard by which the power thus given was to be exercised. In the latter case, the involved ordinance required that before any billboard above the size specified might be erected in any block in which one-half of the buildings were used exclusively for residence purposes, the owners of a majority of the frontage of the property on both sides of the street in such block should consent in writing thereto. This ordinance was held valid. The court said that the contention that it constituted a delegation of power to the majority property owners was palpably frivolous, and with reference to Eubank v. Richmond, supra, declared:

> A sufficient distinction between the ordinance there considered and the one at bar is plain. The former left the establishment of the building line untouched until the lot owners should act, and then made the street committee the mere automatic register of that action, and gave to it the effect of law. The ordinance in the case at bar absolutely prohibits the erection of any billboards in the blocks designated, but permits this prohibition to be modified with the consent of the persons who are to be most affected by such modification. The one ordinance permits two-thirds of the lot owners to impose restrictions upon the other property in the block, while the other permits one-half of the lot owners to remove a restriction from the other property owners. This is not a delegation of legislative power, but is, as we have seen, a familiar provision affecting the enforcement of laws and ordinances.

[242 U.S. 526.]

State of Washington ex rel. Seattle Title Trust Co. v. Roberge, 278 U.S. 116, further emphasized the distinction. The zoning ordinance there involved was amended by adding: "A philanthropic home for children or for old people shall be permitted in First Residence District when the written consent shall have been obtained of the owners of two-thirds of the property within four hundred (400) feet of the proposed building." The grant of permission for such building and use was not left in the discretion of the board upon consent of the required percentage of owners, as in the *Cusack* case, but was made mandatory upon such consent, and showed, as the court said, "that the legislative body found that the construction and maintenance of the new home was in harmony with the public interest and with the general scope and plan of the zoning ordinance."

The distinction was noted in Downey v. City of Sioux City, 208 Iowa 1273, 227 N.W. 125, 128, where the court said:

> Generally speaking, it has been held that regulations or ordinances requiring the consent of property owners, or a percentage thereof, in the vicinity for the erection or use of particular kinds of buildings, are invalid on the ground that such is a delegation of governmental power to private citizens . . .
>
> However, a distinction is to be kept in mind in matters of this kind between an ordinance which leaves the enactment of law to individuals,

and an ordinance prohibitory in character. The prohibition may be modified with the consent of the persons most affected by such modifications; hence an ordinance is not invalid by reason of a provision that buildings may be erected or used for particular purposes if the consent of a part or all of the property owners in the vicinity is obtained....

In view of the importance of the question involved, the voluntary construction of the ordinance by the board of adjustment and the unfortunate situation of any who may have acted in reliance on a void permit of the board, we have discussed the authorities on this question at some length. It appears therefrom that the ordinance provision here involved is valid by overwhelming weight of authority and we think also in reason and by test of practical result.

... The power of the board is limited by those rules and any exception made without compliance with those rules is beyond the authority of the board and void. In the case before us the ordinance specifically limits the authority of the board to permit a nonconforming use such as here sought. Before such change may be authorized, the board must determine the area which will be specially affected by such proposed use or structure, and must have on file the consents duly signed and acknowledged of the owners of 80 per cent of all the land within such area. Compliance with those provisions of the ordinance is jurisdictional and the attempted action of the board without such compliance was void.

The judgment of the trial court is reversed.

HOLLAND, J., dissents.[13]

Notes on Private Restrictions

1. Extensive litigation over removal of private restrictions raises important questions as to the degree of stability of the environment, which is either desirable or maintainable. The cases, coping with the change-of-neighborhood doctrine, contain a lore of urban growth and decay. The historian of the city has yet to tap this wealth of social change, the planner to ponder the experiences of this attempt to perpetuate a human aim. Does litigation experience confirm or reject the theses of urban change examined thus far? What does it indicate of limitations of prophecy and of the role of the market mechanism? Should actions for a declaration of unenforceability due to changed circumstances be determined by zoning or planning boards rather than

---

13. See Hale, Freedom Through Law (1952); Fuller, Some Reflections on Legal and Economic Freedoms, 54 Colum. L. Rev. 70 (1954); Note, 67 Harv. L. Rev. 1398 (1954); Reich, The Law of the Planned Society, 75 Yale L.J. 1228 (1966); Dworkin, Taking Rights Seriously (1977) — EDS.

by courts? What weight should be accorded the master plan in determining the desirability of preserving private arrangements? How does legislative action, such as clearing statutes, differ in effect and purpose from judicial doctrines? How can the framework of public controls make private agreement more effective?

2. See Burger v. City of St. Paul, 241 Minn. 285, 64 N.W.2d 73 (1954):

> It appears that between the years 1917 and 1922 the council of the city of St. Paul, pursuant to L. 1915, c. 128, M.S.A. §462.12 et seq., created a restricted residence district along Summit avenue in St. Paul from the intersection of Summit avenue and Selby avenue to the Mississippi River by condemnation proceedings. These proceedings affected and included properties now owned by plaintiff and defendant Jansen. Those who were then the owners of said lots joined in a petition for the creation of the "Restricted Residence District." Assessments for benefits were levied and awards for damages made as provided in condemnation proceedings. The restrictions established were in full force and effect at the time plaintiff and defendant acquired their respective properties.

In 1951, defendant Jansen obtained a permit from the city council to remodel his single-family dwelling unit into a fourplex. The council overruled the unanimous recommendation of the zoning board that the permission be denied. Authorization was sought in a 1923 amendment to the 1915 act, which stipulates that restricted districts created under the 1915 act could be removed by the council in the same manner in which they had been created. The effect of the amendment, according to the trial court, is to empower a city council to authorize remodeling of the restricted residence district without resort to the power of eminent domain through condemnation proceedings or to the police power through zoning and thus to deprive plaintiff (Jansen's neighbor) of his property (a negative easement) without due process of law. The supreme court upheld an injunction forbidding issuance of a building permit and limiting Jansen to a two-family structure.

3. See Cederberg v. City of Rockford, 8 Ill. App. 3d 984, 291 N.E.2d 249 (1972):

> On May 13, 1968, prior to plaintiff's purchase of subdivision lots 16, 17 and 18, an ordinance was passed rezoning lots 17 and 18 from residential to local business. (Lot 16 was rezoned in the same manner on September 3, 1968.) On May 14, 1968, a restrictive covenant, affecting only lots 17 and 18, was executed by the then owner and was thereafter recorded. (Evidence indicates that this was done at the suggestion of the zoning committee, coincidental with, and as a condition to, passage of the committee's report recommending rezoning.) The covenant provided that, notwithstanding the granted local business classification (which, by City's ordinance, permits forty-four types of local businesses), use of the

B. Market Mechanism and Administrative Controls

land in question would be limited to offices. On February 27, 1969, a waiver of the covenant, approved by the mayor, was filed and a replacement covenant was recorded. The latter's terms, stated within the covenant to be in accordance with a report of the City's zoning committee, provided that twenty-six enumerated uses, otherwise permitted in a local business district, would not be allowed on the lots in question. . . .

What is to be thought of a city's attempt to regulate land use by such a combined use of public zoning powers plus private restrictive covenants? If the covenants fall, must the zoning ordinance fall along with them? A later purchaser successfully sought a declaratory judgment to this effect so as to construct a laundry center on the premises. See also Fox v. Miner, 467 P.2d 595 (Wyo. 1970); Perry, Legal and Policy Conflicts Between Deed Covenants and Subsequently Enacted Zoning Ordinances, 24 Vand. L. Rev. 1031 (1971).

4. McDougal, Book Review, 58 Yale L.J. 500, 504-505 (1949), states: "The most effective reform of 'rights in the land of another' might be the administration in the first instance of private agreement, from creation to termination, by the same public officials who are charged with the duty of effecting a rational general plan by public controls." See the Texas arrangement, supra page 686.

5. In an article published in 1976, Professor Reichman envisioned an expansive role for the private associations given strength and substance by enforceable servitudes:

> Could the homeowners' association, which was intended to sail on the waters of conformity, bring about social change? Although the entrepreneurs who created them certainly did not intend to produce such a result, the structure of the homeowners' association could unwittingly provide a mechanism for reversing the anticommunity trends of the last century. Although the days of self-sufficient units are long over, community organization centered around the home, largely independent of general production-consumption lines, still seems feasible. The homeowners' association, focusing on the total residential environment rather than nationwide interests, could provide a vehicle for this type of development. Residents may be expected to participate in the regular and extraordinary meetings of the residential private government out of basic self-interest: the decisions reached in each association meeting may affect each individual owner financially as well as by determining the standard of services to be supplied and the rules of behavior to be enforced.

Reichman, Residential Private Governments: An Introductory Survey, 43 U. Chi. L. Rev. 253, 262-263 (1976).

Eventually, this discussion, like so many others these days, has found a place in the ideological struggles waged by exponents of law and economics, critical legal studies, and their mutual enemy —

liberalism., See, for example, the offerings of Professors Ellickson, Michelman, and Frug in a symposium on "The Public/Private Distinction" (130 U. Pa. L. Rev. 1519-1608), particularly Frug's reaction to Ellickson's defense of "voting by economic stake" rather than "voting by residency": "First, . . . a restriction on the franchise is itself a transfer of wealth, a transfer likely to be from the poor to the rich. Secondly, the restriction on the franchise will prevent all non-property owners . . . from engaging in collective decisionmaking over the future." Cities and Homeowners Associations: A Reply, 130 U. Pa. L. Rev. 1589, 1596 (1982).

■ CITY OF EASTLAKE v. FOREST CITY ENTERPRISES, INC.
426 U.S. 668 (1976)

Mr. Chief Justice BURGER delivered the opinion of the Court. . . .

The city of Eastlake, Ohio, a suburb of Cleveland, has a comprehensive zoning plan codified in a municipal ordinance. Respondent, a real estate developer, acquired an eight-acre parcel of real estate in Eastlake zoned for "light industrial" uses at the time of purchase.

In May 1971, respondent applied to the City Planning Commission for a zoning change to permit construction of a multi-family, high-rise apartment building. The Planning Commission recommended the proposed change to the City Council, which under Eastlake's procedures could either accept or reject the Planning Commission's recommendation. Meanwhile, by popular vote, the voters of Eastlake amended the City Charter to require that any changes in land use agreed to by the Council be approved by a 55 percent vote in a referendum.[1] The City Council approved the Planning Commission's recommendation for reclassification of respondent's property to permit the proposed project. Respondent then applied to the Planning Commission for "parking and yard" approval for the proposed building. The Commission rejected

---

1. As adopted by the voters, Art. VII, §3, of the Eastlake City Charter provides in pertinent part:

> That any change to the existing land uses or any change whatsoever to any ordinance cannot be approved unless and until it shall have been submitted to the Planning Commission, for approval or disapproval. That in the event the city council should approve any of the preceding changes, or enactments, whether approved or disapproved by the Planning Commission it shall not be approved or passed by the declaration of an emergency, and it shall not be effective, but it shall be mandatory that the same be approved by a 55 percent favorable vote of all votes cast of the qualified electors of the City of Eastlake at the next regular municipal election, if one shall occur not less than sixty (60) or more than one hundred and twenty (120) days after its passage, otherwise at a special election falling on the generally established day of the primary election. . . .

the application, on the grounds that the City Council's rezoning action had not yet been submitted to the voters for ratification.

Respondent then filed an action in state court, seeking a judgment declaring the charter provision invalid as an unconstitutional delegation of legislative power to the people.[2] While the case was pending, the City Council's action was submitted to a referendum, but the proposed zoning change was not approved by the requisite 55 percent margin. Following the election, the Court of Common Pleas and the Ohio Court of Appeals sustained the charter provision.[3]

The Ohio Supreme Court reversed. Concluding that enactment of zoning and rezoning provisions is a legislative function, the court held that a popular referendum requirement, lacking standards to guide the decision of the voters, permitted the police power to be exercised in a standardless, hence arbitrary and capricious manner....

The conclusion that Eastlake's procedure violates federal constitutional guarantees rests upon the proposition that a zoning referendum involves a delegation of legislative power. A referendum cannot, however, be characterized as a delegation of power. Under our constitutional assumptions, all power derives from the people, who can delegate it to representative instruments which they create. See, e.g., Federalist Papers, No. 39. In establishing legislative bodies, the people can reserve to themselves power to deal directly with matters which might otherwise be assigned to the legislature.

The reservation of such power is the basis for the town meeting, a tradition which continues to this day in some States as both a practical and symbolic part of our democratic processes. The referendum, similarly, is a means for direct political participation, allowing the people the final decision, amounting to a veto power, over enactments of representative bodies. The practice is designed to "give citizens a voice on questions of public policy."

In framing a state constitution, the people of Ohio specifically reserved the power of referendum to the people of each municipality within the State....

To be subject to Ohio's referendum procedure, the question must be one within the scope of legislative power. The Ohio Supreme Court expressly found that the City Council's action in rezoning respondent's

---

2. Respondent also contended that the charter amendment could not apply to its rezoning application since the application was pending at the time the amendment was adopted. The Court of Common Pleas rejected the argument. Respondent neither appealed this point nor argued it in the Court of Appeals or the Ohio Supreme Court; the issue is therefore not before us.

3. The Court of Common Pleas, however, invalidated the charter provision requiring assessment of election costs against the affected property owner. In affirming, the Court of Appeals also upheld that portion of the trial court's judgment. No appeal was taken to the Ohio Supreme Court on this issue. The question was, accordingly, not passed on by the state supreme court, and is therefore not before us.

eight acres from light industrial to high-density residential use was legislative in nature. Distinguishing between administrative and legislative acts, the court separated the power to zone or rezone, by passage or amendment of a zoning ordinance, from the power to grant relief from unnecessary hardship.[8] The former function was found to be legislative in nature.[9]

The Ohio Supreme Court further concluded that the amendment to the City Charter constituted a "delegation" of power violative of federal constitutional guarantees because the voters were given no standards to guide their decision. Under Eastlake's procedure, the Ohio Supreme Court reasoned, no mechanism existed, nor indeed could exist, to assure that the voters would act rationally in passing upon a proposed zoning change. This meant that "appropriate legislative action [would] be made dependent upon the potentially arbitrary and unreasonable whims of the voting public." The potential for arbitrariness in the process, the court concluded, violated due process.

Courts have frequently held in other contexts that a congressional delegation of power to a regulatory entity must be accompanied by discernible standards, so that the delegate's action can be measured for its fidelity to the legislative will.

Assuming, arguendo, their relevance to state governmental functions, these cases involved a delegation of power by the legislature to regulatory bodies, which are not directly responsible to the people; this doctrine is inapplicable where, as here, rather than a delegation of power, we deal with a power reserved by the people to themselves.[10] . . .

---

8. By its nature, zoning "interferes" significantly with owners' uses of property. It is horn-book law that "[m]ere diminution of market value or interference with the property owner's personal plans and desires relative to his property is insufficient to invalidate a zoning ordinance or to entitle him to a variance or rezoning." There is, of course, no contention in this case that the existing zoning classification renders respondent's property valueless or otherwise diminishes its value below the value when respondent acquired it.

9. The power of initiative or referendum may be reserved or conferred "with respect to any matter, legislative or administrative, within the realm of local affairs. . . ." 5 McQuillan, Municipal Corporations, §16.54, at 208. However, the Ohio Supreme Court concluded that only land use charges granted by the City Council when acting in a *legislative* capacity were subject to the referendum process. Under the court's binding interpretation of state law, a property owner seeking relief from unnecessary hardship occasioned by zoning restrictions would not be subject to Eastlake's referendum procedure. For example, if unforeseeable future changes give rise to hardship on the owner, the holding of the Ohio Supreme Court provides avenues of administrative relief not subject to the referendum process.

10. The Ohio Supreme Court's analysis of the requirements for standards flowing from the Fourteenth Amendment also sweeps too broadly. Except as a legislative history informs an analysis of legislative action, there is no more advance assurance that a legislative body will act by conscientiously applying consistent standards than there is with respect to voters. For example, there is no certainty that the City Council in this case would act on the basis of "standards" explicit or otherwise in Eastlake's comprehensive zoning ordinance. Nor is there any assurance that townspeople assembling in a town meeting, as the people of Eastlake could do, will act according to consistent standards.

B. Market Mechanism and Administrative Controls 1081

Nothing in our cases is inconsistent with this conclusion. Two decisions of this Court were relied on by the Ohio Supreme Court in invalidating Eastlake's procedure. The thread common to both decisions is the delegation of legislative power, originally given by the people to a legislative body, and in turn delegated by the legislature to a *narrow segment* of the community, not to the people at large....

Neither *Eubank* nor *Roberge* involved a referendum procedure such as we have in this case; the standardless delegation of power to a limited group of property owners condemned by the Court in *Eubank* and *Roberge* is not to be equated with decisionmaking by the people through the referendum process. The Court of Appeals for the Ninth Circuit put it this way:

> A referendum, however, is far more than an expression of ambiguously founded neighborhood preference. It is the city itself legislating through its voters — an exercise by the voters of their traditional right through direct legislation to override the views of their elected representatives as to what serves the public interest.

Southern Alameda Spanish Speaking Organization v. City of Union City, California, 424 F.2d 291, 294 (CA9 1970).

Our decision in James v. Valtierra, 402 U.S. 137 (1971), upholding California's mandatory referendum requirement, confirms this view. Mr. Justice Black, speaking for the Court in that case, said:

"This procedure ensures that *all the people* of a community will have a voice in a decision which may lead to large expenditures of local governmental funds for increased public services...."

Mr. Justice Black went on to say that the referendum procedure at issue here is a classic demonstration of "devotion to democracy...." As a basic instrument of democratic government, the referendum process does not, in itself, violate the Due Process Clause of the Fourteenth Amendment when applied to a rezoning ordinance.[13] Since the rezoning decision in this case was properly reserved to the People of Eastlake under the Ohio Constitution, the Ohio Supreme Court

---

The critical constitutional inquiry, rather, is whether the zoning restriction produces arbitrary or capricious results.

13. The fears expressed in dissent rest on the proposition that the procedure at issue here is "fundamentally unfair" to landowners; this fails to take into account the mechanisms for relief potentially available to property owners whose desired land use changes are rejected by the voters. First, if hardship is occasioned by zoning restrictions, *administrative* relief is potentially available. Indeed, the very purpose of "variances" allowed by zoning officials is to avoid "practical difficulties and unnecessary hardship."

The situation presented in this case is not one of a zoning action denigrating the use or depreciating the value of land; instead, it involves an effort to *change* a reasonable zoning restriction. No existing rights are being impaired; new use rights are being sought from the City Council. Thus, this case involves an owner seeking approval of a new use free from the restrictions attached to the land when it was acquired.

erred in holding invalid, on federal constitutional grounds, the charter amendment permitting the voters to decide whether the zoned use of respondent's property could be altered.

The judgment of the Ohio Supreme Court is reversed and the case is remanded for further proceedings not inconsistent with this opinion.

Mr. Justice POWELL, dissenting. There can be no doubt as to the propriety and legality of submitting generally applicable legislative questions, including zoning provisions, to a popular referendum. But here the only issue concerned the status of a single small parcel owned by a single "person." This procedure, affording no realistic opportunity for the affected person to be heard, even by the electorate, is fundamentally unfair. The "spot" referendum technique appears to open disquieting opportunities for local government bodies to by-pass normal protective procedures for resolving issues affecting individual rights.

Mr. Justice STEVENS, with whom Mr. Justice BRENNAN joins, dissenting.

The city's reliance on the town meeting process of decisionmaking tends to obfuscate the two critical issues in this case. These issues are (1) whether the procedure which a city employs in deciding to grant or to deny a property owner's request for a change in the zoning of his property must comply with the Due Process Clause of the Fourteenth Amendment; and (2) if so, whether the procedure employed by the city of Eastlake is fundamentally fair?

Notes

1. California has become the state of ballot-box planning. Arnel Development Co. v. City of Costa Mesa, 28 Cal. 3d 511, 523-524, 620 P.2d 565, 169 Cal. Rptr. 904 (1980), involved a voter-approved initiative that reversed a city zoning amendment of a fifty-acre plot of land. The rezoning would have allowed the construction of 127 single family homes and 539 apartments on that parcel. The California Supreme Court held that any rezoning is a policy decision that may be addressed by the voters in an initiative or referendum election, regardless of the size of the property involved or the significance of the development allowed. "The rezoning of a 'relatively small' parcel, especially when done by initiative, may well signify a fundamental change in city land use policy." As a practical matter, the court stated, the difficulty of gathering signatures to place the measure on the ballot and waging an expensive campaign for voter approval should virtually guarantee that a direct vote will entail an important city policy matter:

> In consequence of these requirements, the initiative can be and is employed to support or oppose major projects which affect hundreds of thousands

B. Market Mechanism and Administrative Controls

of persons and often present questions of policy concerning the quality of life and the future development of the city; it is not likely to be employed in matters which affect only an individual landowner and raise no policy issues.

You will recall from Chapter III that other states view a zoning amendment as a quasi-judicial proceeding, requiring a level of due process to the affected landowner that cannot be provided by a public vote. The Washington Supreme Court, in Leonard v. City of Bothell, 87 Wash. 2d 847, 557 P.2d 1306, 1309 (1976), ruled that a city council action to rezone property could not be subject to a referendum. In that case a landowner requested the city to rezone his 141-acre parcel from its present agricultural zoning to allow construction of a regional shopping center. After the city planning commission had held thirteen public meetings and ten public hearings, and the city council had held twenty-four public meetings and two public hearings on the matter, the property was rezoned. In rejecting a referendum petition which would have put the rezoning to a public vote, the court cited a previous decision that held:

> In amending a zoning code, or reclassifying land thereunder, the same body, in effect, makes an adjudication between the rights sought by the proponents and those claimed by the opponents of the zoning change. The parties whose interests are affected are readily identifiable. Although questions of public policy may permeate a zoning amendment, the decision has a far greater impact on one group of citizens than on the public generally.

2. Shortly after *City of Eastlake* was decided, the California Supreme Court overturned a forty-seven-year-old case that prevented the use of the initiative on zoning measures. The court said that it must "jealously guard" the right of initiative and referendum, which is guaranteed by the state constitution, and must be accommodated by the state zoning enabling statutes. The case upheld a growth control initiative that was passed by the voters of the city of Livermore, a city that experienced a rapid rate of housing construction, moving from a rural town to a bedroom community for San Francisco Bay area commuters. The measure prohibited issuance of building permits until standards were met for the adequacy of school facilities, sewage treatment, and water supply. Associated Home Builders, Inc. v. City of Livermore, 18 Cal. 3d 582, 557 P.2d 473, 135 Cal. Rptr. 41 (1976).

In that case and subsequent decisions, however, California courts have placed a number of restrictions on land-use initiatives. The *Livermore* decision requires growth control initiatives to be related to the regional need for housing. The court later held that growth control initiatives are subject to a statutory requirement establishing a presumption that such ordinances adversely affect regional housing needs and placing the burden of proof upon the locality to show that the ordinance is necessary to promote the public health, safety, and welfare. Building Industry Association v. City of Camarillo, supra page 594. A referendum is invalid if it attempts to enact a zoning change inconsistent with the city's general plan. deBottari v. Norco City Council, 171 Cal. App. 3d 1204, 217 Cal. Rptr. 790 (1985). An initiative must not discriminate against a particular parcel of property. Arnel Development Co. v. City of Costa Mesa (*Arnel II*), 126 Cal. App. 3d 330, 178 Cal. Rptr. 723 (1981). In Margolis v. District Court, 638 P.2d 297 (Colo. 1981), holding that a rezoning is quasi-judicial for purposes of judicial review, though legislative for purposes of referendum and initiative, the court concluded: "We have not been informed, nor are we aware, that subjecting zoning and rezoning decisions to the powers of referendum and initiative has, in and of itself, created significant problems or delays in planning the growth and development of California or Ohio cities."

3. Courts and legislatures continue to debate the wisdom of land-use referenda, particularly when a discriminatory animus is associated with popular participation in the decision-making process. Compare the Supreme Court's approval of referendum zoning in *City of Eastlake* with the straightforward solution presented by the New Jersey legislature: "No zoning ordinance and no amendment or revision to any zoning ordinance shall be submitted to or adopted by initiative or referendum." N.J. Stat. Ann. §40:55D-62(b) (West Supp. 1987). See also Rosenberg, Referendum Zoning: Legal Doctrine and Practice, 53 U. Cin. L. Rev. 381 (1983).

Dean Derrick Bell argues, "Referendum provisions simply repealing fair housing ordinances or laws and upsetting city council or zoning commission approval to build low income housing have become a standard means of barring minorities from suburban, residential communities." Public officials are subject to pressure to vote to protect the civil rights of minorities — even those public officials whose constituents oppose civil rights legislation — because of the public spotlight on voting records and intense lobbying from minority groups. But when the voters take over the legislative process, "few of the concerns that can transform the 'conservative' politician into a 'moderate' public official are likely to affect the individual voter's decision. No political factors counsel restraint on racial passions emanating from long-held and little-considered beliefs and fears." Bell, The Referendum: Democracy's Barrier to Racial Equality, 54 Wash. L. Rev. 1, 8, 14 (1978). See also Sager, Insular Minorities Unabated: Warth v. Seldin and City of Eastlake v. Forest City Enterprises, Inc., 91 Harv. L. Rev. 1373 (1978).

B. Market Mechanism and Administrative Controls

■ CITY OF CLEBURNE v. CLEBURNE LIVING CENTER
473 U.S. 432 (1985)

Justice WHITE delivered the opinion of the Court. . . .
[For the facts in this case, see supra page 357.]

. . .[W]here individuals in the group affected by a law have distinguishing characteristics relevant to interests the state has the authority to implement, the courts have been very reluctant, as they should be in our federal system and with our respect for the separation of powers, to closely scrutinize legislative choices as to whether, how and to what extent those interests should be pursued. In such cases, the Equal Protection Clause requires only a rational means to serve a legitimate end.

Against this background, we conclude for several reasons that the Court of Appeals erred in holding mental retardation a quasi-suspect classification calling for a more exacting standard of judicial review than is normally accorded economic and social legislation. First, it is undeniable, and it is not argued otherwise here, that those who are mentally retarded have a reduced ability to cope with and function in the everyday world. Nor are they all cut from the same pattern: as the testimony in this record indicates, they range from those whose disability is not immediately evident to those who must be constantly cared for. They are thus different, immutably so, in relevant respects, and the states' interest in dealing with and providing for them is plainly a legitimate one. How this large and diversified group is to be treated under the law is a difficult and often a technical matter, very much a task for legislators guided by qualified professionals and not by the perhaps ill-informed opinions of the judiciary. Heightened scrutiny inevitably involves substantive judgments about legislative decisions, and we doubt that the predicate for such judicial oversight is present where the classification deals with mental retardation.

Second, the distinctive legislative response, both national and state, to the plight of those who are mentally retarded demonstrates not only that they have unique problems, but also that the lawmakers have been addressing their difficulties in a manner that belies a continuing antipathy or prejudice and a corresponding need for more intrusive oversight by the judiciary. . . .

Third, the legislative response, which could hardly have occurred and survived without public support, negates any claim that the mentally retarded are politically powerless in the sense that they have no ability to attract the attention of the lawmakers. Any minority can be said to be powerless to assert direct control over the legislature, but if that were a criterion for higher level scrutiny by the courts, much economic and social legislation would now be suspect.

Fourth, if the large and amorphous class of the mentally retarded were deemed quasi-suspect for the reasons given by the Court of Appeals, it would be difficult to find a principled way to distinguish a variety of other groups who have perhaps immutable disabilities setting them off from others, who cannot themselves mandate the desired legislative responses, and who can claim some degree of prejudice from at least part of the public at large. One need mention in this respect only the aging, the disabled, the mentally ill, and the infirm. We are reluctant to set out on that course, and we decline to do so. . . .

We turn to the issue of the validity of the zoning ordinance insofar as it requires a special use permit for homes for the mentally retarded. We inquire first whether requiring a special use permit for the Featherston home in the circumstances here deprives respondents of the equal protection of the laws. If it does, there will be no occasion to decide whether the special use permit provision is facially invalid where the mentally retarded are involved, or to put it another way, whether the city may never insist on a special use permit for a home for the mentally retarded in an R-3 zone. This is the preferred course of adjudication since it enables courts to avoid making unnecessarily broad constitutional judgments.

The constitutional issue is clearly posed. The city does not require a special use permit in an R-3 zone for apartment houses, multiple dwellings, boarding and lodging houses, fraternity or sorority houses, dormitories, apartment hotels, hospitals, sanitariums, nursing homes for convalescents or the aged (other than for the insane or feebleminded or alcoholics or drug addicts), private clubs or fraternal orders, and other specified uses. It does, however, insist on a special permit for the Featherston home and it does so, as the District Court found, because it would be a facility for the mentally retarded. May the city require the permit for this facility when other care and multiple dwelling facilities are freely permitted?

It is true, as already pointed out, that the mentally retarded as a group are indeed different from others not sharing their misfortune, and in this respect they may be different from those who would occupy other facilities that would be permitted in an R-3 zone without a special permit. But this difference is largely irrelevant unless the Featherston home and those who would occupy it would threaten legitimate interests of the city in a way that other permitted uses such as boarding houses and hospitals would not. . . .

The District Court found that the City Council's insistence on the permit rested on several factors. First, the Council was concerned with the negative attitude of the majority of property owners located within 200 feet of the Featherston facility, as well as with the fears of elderly residents of the neighborhood. But mere negative attitudes, or fear, unsubstantiated by factors which are properly cognizable in a zoning

B. Market Mechanism and Administrative Controls 1087

proceeding, are not permissible bases for treating a home for the mentally retarded differently from apartment houses, multiple dwellings, and the like. It is plain that the electorate as a whole, whether by referendum or otherwise, could not order city action violative of the Equal Protection Clause, and the City may not avoid the strictures of that Clause by deferring to the wishes or objections of some fraction of the body politic. . . .

Second, the Council had two objections to the location of the facility. It was concerned that the facility was across the street from a junior high school, and it feared that the students might harass the occupants of the Featherston home. But the school itself is attended by about 30 mentally retarded students, and denying a permit based on such vague, undifferentiated fears is again permitting some portion of the community to validate what would otherwise be an equal protection violation. The other objection to the home's location was that it was located on "a five hundred year flood plain." This concern with the possibility of a flood, however, can hardly be based on a distinction between the Featherston home and, for example, nursing homes, homes for convalescents or the aged, or sanitariums or hospitals, any of which could be located on the Featherston site without obtaining a special use permit. The same may be said of another concern of the Council — doubts about the legal responsibility for actions which the mentally retarded might take. If there is no concern about legal responsibility with respect to other uses that would be permitted in the area, such as boarding and fraternity houses, it is difficult to believe that the groups of mildly or moderately mentally retarded individuals who would live at 201 Featherston would present any different or special hazard.

Fourth, the Council was concerned with the size of the home and the number of people that would occupy it. The District Court found, and the Court of Appeals repeated, that "[i]f the potential residents of the Featherston Street home were not mentally retarded, but the home was the same in all other respects, its use would be permitted under the city's zoning ordinance." App. 93; 726 F.2d, at 200. Given this finding, there would be no restrictions on the number of people who could occupy this home as a boarding house, nursing home, family dwelling, fraternity house, or dormitory. The question is whether it is rational to treat the mentally retarded differently. It is true that they suffer disability not shared by others; but why this difference warrants a density regulation that others need not observe is not at all apparent. At least this record does not clarify how, in this connection, the characteristics of the intended occupants of the Featherston home rationally justify denying to those occupants what would be permitted to groups occupying the same site for different purposes. Those who would live in the Featherston home are the type of individuals who, with supporting staff, satisfy federal and state standards for group housing in the community; and there is no dispute that the home would meet the federal square-footage-per-resident requirement for facilities of this type. See 42 CFR §442.447 (1984). In the words of the Court of Appeals, "The City never justifies its apparent view that other people can live under such 'crowded' conditions when mentally retarded persons cannot." 726 F.2d, at 202.

In the courts below the city also urged that the ordinance is aimed at avoiding concentration of population and at lessening congestion of the streets. These concerns obviously fail to explain why apartment houses, fraternity and sorority houses, hospitals and the like, may freely locate in the area without a permit. So, too, the expressed worry about fire hazards, the serenity of the neighborhood, and the avoidance of danger to other residents fail rationally to justify singling out a home such as 201 Featherston for the special use permit, yet imposing no such restrictions on the many other uses freely permitted in the neighborhood.

The short of it is that requiring the permit in this case appears to us to rest on an irrational prejudice against the mentally retarded, including those who would occupy the Featherston facility and who would live under the closely supervised and highly regulated conditions expressly provided for by state and federal law.

The judgment of the Court of Appeals is affirmed insofar as it invalidates the zoning ordinance as applied to the Featherston home. The judgment is otherwise vacated.

It is so ordered.

Justice STEVENS, with whom THE CHIEF JUSTICE joins, concurring. . . .

. . .[O]ur cases reflect a continuum of judgmental responses to differing classifications which have been explained in opinions by terms ranging from "strict scrutiny" at one extreme to "rational basis" at the other. I have never been persuaded that these so called "standards" adequately explain the decisional process. Cases involving classifications based on alienage, illegal residency, illegitimacy, gender, age, or — as in this case — mental retardation, do not fit well into sharply defined classifications. . . .

. . . I cannot believe that a rational member of this disadvantaged class could ever approve of the discriminatory application of the city's ordinance in this case.[14]

---

14. See Schonfeld, "Not In My Neighborhood": Legal Challenges to the Establishment of Community Residences for the Mentally Disabled in New York State, 13 Fordham Urb. L.J. 281 (1985). For a more extensive discussion of the background, see Minow, When Difference Has Its Home: Group Homes for the Mentally Retarded, Equal Protection and Legal Treatment of Difference, 22 Harv. C.R.-C.L. L. Rev. 111 (1987).

For the most likely candidate for the next NIMBY battleground, see Koch Criticized

■ HENDRICKS AND ALEXANDER, SUBCULTURE CELLS
(1970)

The homogeneous character of cities kills all variety of life styles. A genuine variety of life styles can only grow in a city if the physical environment is constructed to support a vast mosaic of different subcultures.

To understand this conclusion, it is helpful to compare three possible alternative ways in which people with different life styles may be distributed throughout an urban area. In the *heterogeneous city*, people are mixed up, irrespective of their subculture. This seems rich; actually it damps all significant variety, because it tends to reduce all life styles to a common denominator.... What seems heterogeneous, ends up homogeneous and dull.

In a city made of *ghettos* (rich or poor, black or white) people have the support of their own subcultures, but the ghettos are still homogeneous internally — again there is no opportunity for a significant variety of life styles to emerge. And people in a ghetto are isolated from the rest of society, unable to change their ways of life, and often intolerant of ways of life different from their own.

In a *mosaic of subculture cells*, new ways of life can develop, and people can choose which kind of subculture to live in, and can still experience many ways of life different from their own. However, a small subculture is unstable when surrounded by other subcultures, because of harassment or control of land. To be stable, each subculture needs to be separated from neighbouring subcultures by a boundary of non-residential land.

Therefore: Arrange the urban land to form many small cells of residential land, separated from one another by wide swaths of non-residential land — parks, schools, commercial, major roads, etc. — which form the cell boundaries. Make the cells really small, perhaps no

---

on Plan to Open AIDS Shelters, N.Y. Times, Nov. 1, 1988:

> A Koch administration plan to create housing in three boroughs for hundreds of homeless AIDS patients drew mixed reviews yesterday from community boards and local elected officials. Some vehemently opposed the housing, while others said they favored it in principle.
> But the administration ran into a solid wall of criticism for failing to consult community representatives about the politically sensitive plan... It would create beds for 840 patients by 1991 in eight existing buildings in residential areas of Manhattan, Brooklyn and the Bronx. — EDS.

more than a few hundred feet across. Each cell is then free to take on its own life style, and people can intensify their own particular way of life, unharassed by neighbouring cultures.

The cases in this section to the contrary, not all community efforts are designed to exclude. As our final case study illustrates, neighbors — with the prompting of developers — are joining together to make the most out of otherwise bad zoning situations. The DeKalb County episode indicates that when population shifts, infrastructure declines, and old age strikes, homeowners need not sit back and wait for an outmoded plan to be disassembled parcel by parcel, or discarded wholesale.

This new challenge to planners, local legislators — and ultimately to courts — presents in reality the market in zoning rights heretofore only debated in scholarly journals. See supra page 367. How far should lawmakers and judges allow this process to go? Is it helpful to analogize to the referendum cases, or is the special treatment rendered the sovereign public inappropriate for collective action encompassing an area smaller than that defined by the municipality's boundaries? Who stands to lose from these transactions? Should approval of neighborhood buyouts be confined only to those cases in which the master plan is no longer relevant?

CASE STUDY # 5

3. Neighborhood Buyouts of Zoning "Rights"

Albritton v. DeKalb County and the idea of selling state-created land-use rights form a wonderful prism for the ideas presented in this

Drawing by O'Brian; © 1956, 1984. The New Yorker Magazine, Inc.

B. Market Mechanism and Administrative Controls 1091

chapter: What happens when the master (or comprehensive) plan fails to keep pace or is rendered meaningless by exceptions, variances and rezonings? If the relevant community does not object to (or even participates in) a zoning change, does anyone have standing to object? Is the court's role limited to approval or disapproval, or can judges help reshape contracts between developers and residents? The case mediates between strict adherence (such as change/mistake) and letting the market run "free," for it does not seek to reverse the Euclidean revolution — that is, the reassignment of excess development rights from the private owner to the public.

Planners, politicians and the public at large have for years taken it for granted that urban core areas go through periods of socioeconomic transition, often to an extent justifying a thorough revision of prevailing land-use controls. The notion, however, that postwar suburban neighborhoods — the haven of the American dream of single-family detached homes, open space, and *escape* from the urban core — might increasingly be subject to similar pressures has been considerably harder to accept.

The case poses many of these tensions in microcosm, and presents us with the challenge of interpreting traditional relationships of the zoning law to private property in a new context. It involves the proposed buyout by a single developer of 144 suburban homes in the Lake Hearn subdivision of suburban Atlanta. The idea for such a transaction originated among the homeowners themselves. Located near a freeway interchange in one of the fastest growing pockets of commercial and office activity in suburban America, the Lake Hearn residents cited intolerable levels of traffic and a general deterioration in their way of life as the bases for their decision to band together, find a developer (Albritton) to buy their property, and petition the county for a zoning change. Opponents suspected other motives, suggesting that homeowners were willing to abandon a well-maintained, economically stable neighborhood in order to reap a huge windfall. Critics raised the specter of a domino effect — let this neighborhood go, and any number of neighborhoods would simply sell to the highest bidder. Thus were the battle lines formed.

The following material explores many of the issues that arose and strategies that were adopted during the course of the struggle over the rezoning of Lake Hearn. The case, while containing many of the components typical of zoning disputes since *Euclid*, is also representative of a new breed, reflecting changing patterns of growth in American cities, new neighborhood strategies for responding to that growth, and unexplored opportunities for public-private cooperation.

a. The Context: New Forms of Metropolitan Growth and the Buyout Phenomenon

The Lake Hearn controversy took place against the backdrop of a fundamental spatial reorganization of the Atlanta metropolitan area.

Once serving as bedroom communities for the central business district (CBD), Atlanta suburbs are increasingly oriented toward regional subcenters of commercial and office activity. In the 1950s, suburban commercial development was essentially a hodgepodge of gas stations, fast-food restaurants, and grocery stores. Today, suburbs have shed their dependence on the CBD, a shift that involved widespread construction of industrial and office parks, regional shopping centers, and retail outlet stores, typically along an interstate highway. This reshaping of suburban areas is occurring across the country.

■ HAAR AND LINDSAY, BUSINESS AND THE REVOLUTION IN LAND USE PLANNING: NEW PRIVATE SECTOR ROLES AND NEW SUBURBAN FORMS
1-4, Lincoln Institute of Land Policy, Policy Analysis Series No. 213 (1987)

The censuses of 1970 and 1980 confirm statistically what became apparent long ago to urban planners and developers: this is now a nation of suburbs. Americans have long looked away from the central city for fulfillment of their dream of owning a home. The availability of federally insured mortgages, with attendant government-backed secondary market operations, and the rapid development of extensive highway networks, made suburban living — and, later, suburban work — a reality for millions of families.

Today, both in terms of population and economic activity, the metropolitanization of our urban areas continues unabated in changing the face of urban America. This phenomenon is following a distinct pattern throughout much of the United States, characterized by the expansion of a wide variety of land uses in suburban areas, and the clustering of these uses in new centers of economic and demographic concentration. What is occurring is nothing short of a fundamental spatial reorganization of metropolitan areas, a process that planners, community leaders, business people and citizens can ill afford to ignore.

The great expansion of suburban office activity experienced by Atlanta in recent years is part of this national trend. Since 1973, office space has grown 30 percent faster in Atlanta's suburbs than in its downtown area. Most other economically healthy metropolitan areas have witnessed similar trends. Dallas, Tampa, San Francisco and Phoenix, to name a few notable examples, are all experiencing major growth of office and various other higher-density land uses in the suburban portions of their metropolitan areas. Several high-tech office developments in Denver's southeast I-25 corridor have together produced more

B. Market Mechanism and Administrative Controls

office space than all of downtown Denver. Even New York City, then in the throes of a major building boom, watched its share of the metropolitan area's office inventory decline from 75 percent in 1982 to 67 percent in 1984.

Increases in demand for office space reflect "a shift in the economy towards work done at desks and conference tables rather than on work benches and assembly lines." New service and high-tech industries have replaced traditional smokestack industries as the most vigorous sectors of the metropolitan economy. The service sector now accounts for more than 55 percent of all non-agricultural jobs in the United States. Declining employment in the heavy industries has been offset in part by the increase in high-tech employment.

The location of most new office space and employment in the suburbs may be explained by several factors. *First*, technological advances in communications and other fields have given companies new freedom to choose locations outside of the urban core. With businesses more and more reliant upon electronic linkages, the need for physical proximity has diminished in many sectors of the economy. *Second*, the traditional face-to-face communications of central city locations are increasingly available in suburban nodes. *Third*, the financial advantages of moving to a less centrally located site are manifold. Steeply inflated urban land prices, necessitating concomitantly high office rents, have persuaded corporate tenants to seek suburban office space. Office space rents in central business districts are 30 to 50 percent higher than in suburban locations. *Fourth*, noise, congestion and concerns about physical safety in central business districts are contrasted by the physical attractiveness of suburban sites.

In recent years, new growth in suburban areas has organized itself into new physical forms: nodes of higher density mixed-use developments. Old-style, desultory low-rise sprawl and leapfrog development, which characterized the first wave of suburban expansion after World War II — with offices, factories and shopping centers scattered along major arteries — has increasingly been replaced by these new nodes of suburban concentration. Typically, the nodes include *clusters* of office, industrial, retail and housing uses providing many of the advantages that come with urban density without the undesirable side effects. Sometimes, this pattern results in replacement of older suburban areas, through reconcentration of uses in higher densities than customary in the past, and with a greater mixture of complementary uses. As such, it echoes more familiar models of central city urban revitalization efforts.

Changes in city planning theory have encouraged this new metropolitan form. Planners have moved away from strict classification of districts and land uses — the original model for regulating development first upheld in the United States Supreme Court *Euclid* opinion back in 1926 — to flexible design and performance standards embodied in planned unit and cluster development regulations. Developers and lenders favor developments combining office uses and support services required by those who work in the offices and live in surrounding areas. Where earlier suburban office designs tended either toward walkup or storefront offices on major streets, or glamorous but isolated megastructures, the modern suburban mixed-use development represents an attempt "to break the numbing isolation of new suburban office complexes by infusing them with urban essence" — the mixture of sights, sounds and activities that make city streets such stimulating environments, while at the same time still enjoying the amenities of the suburbs.

Today's employees expect a more satisfying and diverse environment for their daily activities. Rising suburban land costs, while not increasing as rapidly as central city costs, nevertheless make inevitable the higher and denser uses of suburban land. Large, unified parcels capture the values of accessibility and proximity for that site.

The pressure that this new form of growth puts on adjacent neighborhoods is often great. In a small but significant number of cases, neighborhoods, discouraged typically after several failed attempts to prevent large-scale commercial and office development on nearby land, have banded together and collectively sought a purchaser for their properties.

■ CLARY AND RASMUSSEN, THE BUYOUT PHENOMENON
Planning, Oct. 1985, at 18, 21-22

[N]eighborhood buyouts, or assemblages in real estate parlance, are happening all over the country, particularly around the burgeoning suburban commercial centers that are beginning to rival, and even outdo, their established downtown counterparts.

Apparently, the idea took hold first in the Atlanta metropolitan area, where Georgia Tech planning professor Anthony Catanese has counted five completed group sales. About five more are underway and some 25 are in the talking stages, many of them north of the city in DeKalb County along Interstate 285, the road that circles the perimeter of the metropolitan area. All of them, says Catanese, are in middle-class, white neighborhoods with 10- to 20-year-old houses, and all are near recent transportation improvements such as an expressway interchange or a rapid transit station.

B. Market Mechanism and Administrative Controls

Those characteristics apply also to the other areas where buyouts have become a noticeable trend: Houston, Dallas, Fairfax County, Virginia, and, of course, Arlington County.

According to Catanese, who has studied buyouts throughout the country, in about half the cases, including Arlington County, the process is initiated by the homeowners, who have concluded that encroaching commercial development has made the area less desirable as a residential neighborhood. The residents are, of course, turned on by the prospect of reaping two to three times the market value of their property — the going price so far in group sales. "What seems to be happening," says Rice University real estate analyst James P. Gaines, quoted in the New York Times, "is that homeowners who once fought development are now banding together and saying, 'Since we can't stop it, let's make some hay out of a bad situation.'"

For help, they can even turn to an article in the August issue of Changing Times magazine — a guide for homeowners on how to market a neighborhood for residential assemblage, including advice on clearing zoning hurdles.

Increasingly, however, developers are approaching homeowners directly, Catanese notes. For what seems like a windfall to the resident adds up to a bargain for the developer, who relishes the prospect of paying far less than the going rate for land that is already commercially zoned. . . .

Once the sale is agreed to by both sides, however, there are still obstacles to surmount — most notably the required rezoning from residential to commercial. Not all residents will go along with the sale. . . . [In an Arlington County example,] some homeowners simply wanted to hold out for more money, others objected to the scale of the development that was proposed, and some didn't want to see a solid, middle-class neighborhood destroyed.

In Houston, the New York Times reported, a group of disgruntled residents went to court to stop the sale of a residential block for expansion of an adjoining shopping center. The objectors lost in state court last December. But in June, in Vienna, Virginia, near Washington D.C., residents of an upper income subdivision were, in fact, successful in blocking a sale by 20 residents of a neighboring subdivision. The developer wanted the parcel for townhouse offices. Vienna is in Fairfax County, where, according to William Keefe, chief of the county's comprehensive planning branch, nine or 10 subdivisions are seeking buyout-related rezonings. Most of them are near Tyson's Corner, the booming office, retail, hotel area that forecasters say will soon be Virginia's biggest "downtown." . . .

Catanese thinks the local governments should have taken the lead on the zoning issue. "What has changed the land use in each case is the transportation facility — the interstate or the transit line — not the developers. When a local or state government puts in a facility, it should reexamine the zoning around it. But governments are reluctant to change zoning unless someone pushes them. And that's bad planning."

The "homeowners," Catanese adds, "are doing the rational thing. Even though it seems un-American to pack up and leave your home, it's actually a sensible decision. The government is often the cause of the change in local land use, so why shouldn't the homeowners be allowed to take advantage of it?"

As the above excerpt notes, the Atlanta area has had a particularly large incidence of this type of activity. A study of this phenomenon by a citizens' panel known as Research Atlanta identified the following characteristics of a typical "buyout community."

1. *Rapid Nonresidential Growth* — Assembled neighborhoods are all located near expanding retail or office activity centers where demand for land is high.
2. *Transportation Accessibility* — The assembled properties are accessible by major roads, interstate interchanges or MARTA Rapid Rail Stations. Road widenings and other improvements as well as new construction make the surrounding area attractive for businesses and, due to traffic congestion and noise, less appealing to homeowners.
3. *Proximity to Nonresidential Development* — All neighborhoods sold to developers are located along major roads. Many assembled neighborhoods, or those in the process, are located at the periphery of office complexes and major retail centers.
4. *Homeowner Frustration* — For years, residents have been fighting approval of nonresidential projects near their homes and have worked extensively with developers to negotiate building height, street setback and buffer restrictions for these projects. At some point, the level of nonresidential development becomes unacceptable. Residents then utilize their knowledge of zoning procedures and development to assemble their properties and seek a buyer.

b. The Lake Hearn Assemblage: Neighborhood Mobilization and County Opposition

Any zoning case can be expected to be laden with emotional issues; however, the homeowners and developer were up against particularly treacherous ones in the Lake Hearn case, which undoubtedly accounts

B. Market Mechanism and Administrative Controls

in part for the county's intransigence.[15] First, homes were going to be destroyed, upper-middle-class homes that at least to the outside observer appeared to be in good shape. Second, the selling homeowners were going to make a lot of money; this may have affected their credibility in the eyes of the county: *anyone* will complain about how unlivable their neighborhood has become if the price is right. For some of the homeowners, the agreement with Albritton meant almost triple the appraised value of their homes. Third, the county claimed to be afraid of a domino effect; it raised the specter of neighborhood after neighborhood selling out to rapacious developers. Indeed, five buyouts had been completed in the Atlanta area, and about thirty more were in some preliminary stage. Finally, the possibility that approval of Albritton's plan would make a rapidly deteriorating traffic situation intolerable hung over the controversy.

While there was a high degree of organization among the Lake Hearn homeowners, the opposition of surrounding neighborhood organizations was also spirited. The following flier was distributed by one such group (Hampton Hall Civic Association) seeking to put pressure on the county to turn down the Albritton/Lake Hearn rezoning request:

STOP LAKE HEARN

1. *Where is Lake Hearn?* The Lake Hearn area is 82 acres of well-maintained single family homes in North DeKalb, conveniently located just northwest of Montgomery Elementary School on Ashford-Dunwoody Road and inside I-285. It contains approximately 143 homes. It is in the Montgomery Elementary and Chamblee High School districts.
2. *Why is Lake Hearn in the news today?* Lake Hearn is in the national news today because commercial development companies have filed to rezone this desirable residential community to office-institutional. Public hearings are scheduled in May 1985 before the DeKalb Planning Commission and the DeKalb County Commission.
3. *Haven't I heard of Lake Hearn before?* Yes. In February 1984 the DeKalb Commission voted unanimously (7-0) to deny an application for rezoning to office-institutional the northern-most 13.5 acres of this tract. At that time, the Commission was well aware that developers were looking closely at the remaining acres comprising this 82 acre tract.

---

15. See Jansak, When the Marketplace "Antiquates" a Built-Out Subdivision, Platted Lands Press, Sept. 1985. — EDS.

4. *What did DeKalb County's professional Planning Department say about the original proposal to rezone just 13.5 acres?* The applicant requested rezoning to permit a 10 story office building containing 522,100 sq. ft. of office space and separate parking for 1775 cars in a four level parking deck and at ground level. The Planning Department concluded that if that development were permitted, the "likely" consequence was that other nearby residential areas would be converted into office-institutional uses. The total impact of this proposal was calculated by the Planning Department. They said 265 homes on 185 acres would be replaced by 7,415,050 sq. ft. of office space, requiring 29,569 parking spaces resulting in a total of 86,758 car trips per day in the area.
5. *Why should I be concerned about the "new" Lake Hearn application?* Simple arithmetic. The current application is for about 82 acres. This is 6.3 times more acreage than the last application. Can you comprehend a development whose impact might be 6.3 times what DeKalb County last estimated?
6. *What would be the impact on Montgomery Elementary School of granting this application?* Almost certain extinction. According to the current school directory, more than 39% of all students attending the school live on or north of West Nancy Creek Drive, the area most likely to be developed if this application is granted.
7. *Why isn't this just another zoning skirmish?* Every conflict has its decisive battle. There are no "natural barriers" to devastation of residential neighborhoods, only principled zoning decisions by our County government officials. It takes guts to make tough decisions. Our county leadership has already shown this courage. It takes vision to stick with it. Neighborhood buyouts are a bad idea whose time will never come!
8. *If I don't live near Lake Hearn, why should I be concerned with this issue?* DeKalb County must send a message to opportunistic developers that well-maintained residential areas are *off limits* for rezoning into office space. This County needs to preserve residential areas, not destroy them. Your neighborhood will be next unless you act now.
9. *What can I do to help our County government in this time of crisis?* Two things: Vote against Lake Hearn rezoning by following the instructions on the reverse side of this sheet. And attend *both* the Planning Commission and County Commissioners' hearings in May. You will be advised of the time and place of these hearings.

Despite the developer's expressed willingness to bear the cost of needed traffic improvements, and to provide buffer space and other amenities, the county planning staff recommended that the rezoning be denied. Some of the bases of the staff's refusal are laid out in the following excerpt.

B. Market Mechanism and Administrative Controls

■ DeKALB COUNTY PLANNING DEPARTMENT RECOMMENDATION, DENIAL JUSTIFICATION
CZ-85043

This proposal of rezoning is inconsistent with recommendations of the Comprehensive Plan and incompatible with area development. The departmental recommendation is based on an analysis of land use and legal considerations, the proposed plan and its intensity, the precedent setting nature of the application and the impact on public services.

Land Use

On January 28, 1977, the Georgia Supreme Court, as a result of the Guhl vs. Holcombe Bridge Road Corporation lawsuit [238 Ga. 322, 282 S.E.2d 830 (1977)], established six (6) criteria to be utilized by local governments when considering rezoning applications. In order to appreciate the land use issues associated with this application, the criteria established by the Court are evaluated below as related to this rezoning request.

1. Existing Uses and Zoning of Nearby Property

The majority of development to the south and east of this land consists of viable, well-maintained single family subdivisions. These residential developments and the subdivisions being considered for rezoning provide needed housing to serve the existing and already zoned Perimeter Center office developments. Adjoining office developments identified as the Cox and Hartford buildings are low intensity uses with maximum floor areas of 9,158 square feet and 12,252 square feet per acre respectively. Although these office uses adjoin the subject properties of this application, they are separated with 80' and 90' heavily wooded buffers which are more than twice the requirement of the Zoning Ordinance. Both structures are a maximum of five stories. These adjoining OI developments are consistent with zoning decisions in the area which reduce height and intensity of land uses next to residential communities. As found in Flournoy vs. Brunswick (12/2/81), "... the fact that there already exist several encroachments into this neighborhood is good reason for the commission to watch and regulate this neighborhood carefully in order to preserve its integrity."

2. Diminution of Property Values by Current Zoning

The property values of these R-100 lots are consistent with other residential values in the neighborhood. In Avera vs. Brunswick (9/6/78), the Court stated "... evidence that property will bring a more profitable return if rezoned is not sufficient to overcome the presumed validity of a zoning ordinance."

3. DESTRUCTION OF PROPERTY VALUES VS. HEALTH, SAFETY AND WELFARE OF PUBLIC

The applicant has not identified a destruction of property values or any injury or loss to the affected property owners based on current zoning. In a 1975 decision, Barrett vs. Hamby (9/16/75), the Court stated ". . . if the zoning regulation results in relatively little gain or benefit to the public while inflicting serious injury or loss to the owner, such regulation is confiscatory and void." The only gain identified by this request is one to the affected owners through sale of rezoned properties. It is not the responsibility of the government to ensure economic gain to property owners through the legislative grant of rezoning.

4. GAIN TO PUBLIC VS. HARDSHIP IMPOSED ON OWNERS

The applicant has not identified hardships imposed upon the owners of these 148 properties. The Court in Guhl vs. Pinkard (1/24/79), said "We ask whether the property owner has carried the burden of showing that the zoning under attack is so detrimental to him and so insubstantially related to the public health, safety, morality and welfare, as to amount to an arbitrary confiscation of his property without compensation by the governing authority." Although it is anticipated that the applicant will file a standard form of constitutional attack, it is not sufficient to show that the current zoning is so detrimental to each of the 148 property owners that it amounts to an unconstitutional taking. The Court places the burden on the property owner to produce sufficient evidence to justify a holding that an ordinance is arbitrary and unreasonable, International Funeral Services vs. DeKalb (11/6/79).

5. SUITABILITY OF PROPERTY FOR ZONED PURPOSES

In the case of DeKalb vs. Chamblee-Dunwoody Hotel (9/8/81), the Court concluded ". . . if the validity of the legislative classification for zoning purposes be fairly debatable, the legislative judgment must be allowed to control." Of the 148 parcels of land affected by this application, 145 are well developed and well maintained subdivision lots. One (1) parcel is developed for recreational purposes and two (2) are remnants of subdivision development which are too small for any independent land use.

As of May 8, 1985, county records identify that 88% of the homes are owner occupied. Whether they are occupied by the owner or leased for residential use, these houses serve as a vital residential part of the community. If any statement is made which would identify a decline of maintenance within the community it cannot be used as justification

B. Market Mechanism and Administrative Controls

for rezoning. Each property owner is independently responsible for the maintenance of his own property regardless of the zoning. Residential sales in the community have been made in the last several years but appear to be consistent with other residential neighborhoods in the county. There have been no reports of failure to market these homes as currently zoned. As the Court found in DeKalb vs. Blalock Machinery (5/26/81), "a genuine effort to sell property as zoned should consist of more than placing a 'for sale' sign on the property and telling several realtor friends that the land is for sale."

6. LENGTH OF TIME PROPERTY HAS BEEN VACANT AS ZONED RELATIVE TO AREA DEVELOPMENT

It is apparent and without doubt that these properties are not vacant. As provided in #5., these lots are developed and well maintained residential properties. Many of these homes are less than ten (10) years old.

While the County Planning Commission subsequently overruled its staff and sided with the petitioners, the Board of County Commissioners of DeKalb County reversed, and Albritton and the homeowners were forced to litigate.

c. The Buyout in Court

■ DeKALB COUNTY v. ALBRITTON PROPERTIES
256 Ga. 103, 344 S.E.2d 653 (1986)

PER CURIAM. . . .
The neighborhood consists of 144 homes, ninety-seven of which are owner occupied, forty-four of which are renter occupied, and three of which are vacant. The average home in the neighborhood was valued by the appellees at $107,000. Each of the homeowners involved in this case has agreed to sell their homes for at least $225,000 to appellee Albritton.

Thirteen neighborhood homes were sold between 1979 and 1984. Ten of the homes, now renter occupied, sold for 18% to 63% over the previous sale price. The three other homes, now owner occupied, sold for 3.24%, 3.77%, and .25% over their previous sale prices. These sales occurred in 1980, 1981, and 1982. No decrease in the value of any home in the neighborhood was shown through appraisal or resale. The rate of appreciation of value for similar homes in DeKalb County averaged ten to twelve percent.

A number of Lake Hearn homeowners testified that the quality of life in the neighborhood had declined as commercial development crept closer to the neighborhood. They stated that traffic had become a problem, that noise from I-285 was intolerable, and that many of the homes in the neighborhood had fallen into disrepair since occupied by renters. They felt that they had lost the battle to preserve the residential character of the neighborhood, and that they should now be allowed to surrender. . . .

An urban planning expert testified for the appellees that the land in question is in the final stages of a "land use succession" from rural to residential to commercial use. He testified that the Perimeter Center is "the most active nodal development in the United States . . ." He asserted that in ten years, Perimeter Center area will have more office and retail space than downtown Atlanta. He stated that the public interest would be harmed by a refusal on the part of the county to allow the land to be used for its natural use. He stated that the increase in land value attributable to rezoning would expand the county tax base, facilitating improvements in the infrastructure. . . .

A planning expert described for the appellants the relationship between land use planning and zoning. He then described the process by which DeKalb County formulated its comprehensive development plan. He testified that he would recommend to DeKalb County that the Lake Hearn neighborhood remain in a low density residential zoning classification. He felt that intensification of land use in the Lake Hearn neighborhood would impact negatively upon the area south of Lake Hearn along Ashford Dunwoody Road. . . .

The appellants differ with the trial court's determination that the county's application of the R-100 zoning classification to the Lake Hearn subdivision deprives the property owners of their constitutional rights.

As the law of zoning has developed in Georgia, the plaintiff, bearing the burden of proof, must first overcome the presumptive validity of the zoning ordinance that he attacks by establishing, by clear and convincing evidence, that the zoning ordinance "is significantly detrimental to him, and is insubstantially related to the public health, safety, morality, and welfare." Flournoy v. City of Brunswick, 248 Ga. 573, 285 S.E.2d 16 (1981). If the plaintiff carries his burden, the defendant must, of course, present evidence overcoming the plaintiff's proof.

(a) First, we address the plaintiffs' assertion that R-100 zoning imposes a significant detriment upon the enjoyment of their property rights.

Residents of Lake Hearn testified that the only access to and from their property led through commercial developments, and that they

B. Market Mechanism and Administrative Controls 1103

now "live[d] in an office park." Taking speculation, acknowledged by the defendant's expert, into account, the appreciation of the value of homes in Lake Hearn lagged seven to nine per cent behind the appreciation in value of similar nearby homes. The value of the entire tract as zoned R-100 amounted to roughly one third, or thirty million dollars, less than the potential value of the tract as zoned O-I.

While evidence conflicted as to the present suitability of the neighborhood for residential use, the appellees' experts established a downturn in viability of the neighborhood as a residential area, and they foresaw a sharper downturn of land value if the land remained under a residential classification. One expert termed the property an inverse spot zone, hemmed in by an interstate highway, some commercial development in DeKalb County, and massive commercial development in Fulton County.

Though the land in question certainly retains some value as zoned, we find that overall, the evidence established the "significant detriment" required to be established under *Flournoy, supra*.[2]

(b) Next, we consider the relationship of that detriment and the present zoning to the public health, safety, morality, and welfare. . . .

A change in the zoning of Lake Hearn from R-100 to O-I would violate the county's comprehensive development plan.[3] Experts for both sides attested to the value of a comprehensive development plan as a land use planning tool. The appellees' experts showed that in allowing commercial development adjacent to Lake Hearn, the county had already violated its plan, and that blind adherence to the plan in this case would only harm the county's citizens by leading to the creation of a blighted neighborhood in Lake Hearn. The appellants' experts testified that the plan was generally designed to preserve the valuable residential character of the Perimeter Center area south of I-285, and that the rezoning of Lake Hearn would frustrate the plan's intent.

As established in the testimony of the many experts, a comprehensive development plan may play an important role in enhancing the public health, safety, morality, and welfare. Two factors in this case, however, combined to render DeKalb County's plan a less effective planning tool.

First, the county sanctioned the violation of its own plan by allowing the construction of three office buildings in the immediate vicinity of Lake Hearn in an area designated for residential development. This alone, however, might not sever the connection between the plan and

---

2. Evidence as to the effect of noise on Lake Hearn, the effect of traffic on Lake Hearn Drive, and the effect of the proximity of I-285 on the neighborhood was evenly matched.

3. Though this may void a rezoning where the jurisdiction has put "teeth" into its zoning ordinance by requiring compatibility between the plan and actual zoning, see Moore v. Maloney, 253 Ga. 504, 321 S.E.2d 335 (1984), this issue was not raised.

the public good in this specific case. Another factor bears upon our determination.

An aerial photograph of the Perimeter Center area reveals that the Fulton-DeKalb County line, which bisects Lake Hearn Drive, may be clearly delineated by the contrast between commercial development in Fulton County and residential development in DeKalb County. The DeKalb County plan of preserving residential development south of I-285 had been outflanked by Fulton County's allowance of commercial development, creating a situation in which land use outside of DeKalb County's control impacts directly upon the property of DeKalb County property owners such as the appellees. This photograph and other evidence produced at trial shows that one price of a failure in cooperation between neighboring jurisdictions may be the unraveling of a comprehensive development plan at its edges.

The intrusion from within DeKalb County upon the development plan and the existence of a radically different land use approach immediately adjacent to Lake Hearn in Fulton County defeat the purpose of the comprehensive development plan for this particular area. This renders the necessity of zoning in compliance with the plan insubstantially related to the public health, safety, morality or welfare. . . .

The appellees showed that they would be willing and able to pay for many improvements necessary to prevent stagnation in traffic patterns. They also showed that the increase in the tax base to the county would be so enormous that improvements in the county infrastructure, including road improvements, would be possible where they were not before. The county showed that the DOT did not plan to allow one of the improvements planned by the appellees, and that, based upon current land use plans, only one improvement in the Lake Hearn area was imminent. Although renewed planning could be mandated by rezoning of Lake Hearn, we find the evidence of the effect of R-100 zoning of Lake Hearn upon traffic in DeKalb County, from physical and financial standpoints, to be equally divided between positive and negative.

The size, topography, and location of the Lake Hearn neighborhood, as well as the nature of surrounding areas and the lack of objection to rezoning by the southern neighbors, lead us to the conclusion that the benefit to the public in applying the R-100 zoning classification to Lake Hearn does not justify the maintenance of that zoning in light of the detriment caused to the property by that zoning. . . .

BELL, Justice, dissenting.

The decision of the majority of this court flies in the face of the substantial evidence which supports the county's decision. In sustaining

B. Market Mechanism and Administrative Controls 1105

the judgment of the superior court, this court has usurped the function of the county commission.

Notes

1. Note that the court does not explicitly address the fact that an entire neighborhood had apparently decided that the applicable land-use designation should be changed. Should such a de facto referendum be given special weight in a zoning decision, or should it be discounted as a factor of the windfall the landowners expect to reap in the event of a rezoning? Consider the following analysis by Nelson, A Breath of Free Markets in Zoning, Wall St. J., May 22, 1985:

> Sales of zoning have in fact been occurring for some time in a de facto way, as when a municipality assesses large fees unrelated to costs as a condition for a zoning change, or requires the donation of parkland or other facilities for general public use....
>
> A further evolution would allow neighborhoods to sell zoning changes directly within the neighborhood. Property owners would have to form an association in order to act collectively. The municipality would then transfer its zoning authorities to the neighborhood association. It would exercise neighborhood use controls as a private property right — in the same way that a condominium association now regulates the "common elements." Like the owner of any other private property, the neighborhood association could sell rights of entry into the neighborhood or enter into other commercial transactions. In effect, a new legal entity — the private neighborhood — would be created.
>
> Such a neighborhood might, for example, allow an existing home to be converted into a small restaurant on payment to the association of an acceptable amount. A larger payment might be needed to gain acceptance for a new multifamily housing unit. In some cases, the neighborhood residents might agree — either unanimously or by some near-unanimous percentage — to sell all their properties to a developer for a new use of the land. The neighborhood association would have to devise a sharing rule for the allocations of sale proceeds among individual property owners.
>
> Rather than selling entry rights, some neighborhoods might reject most or all offers, preferring to avoid any significant changes in neighborhood land use.... Depending on the magnitude of the change, decisions to accept or reject such offers might require a majority or supermajority approval. The current zoning system makes these same decisions, but outside the neighborhood and far less flexibly, because an entire use classification must either be accepted or rejected outright, and no financial payments can legally be made for zoning changes.

2. The court notes that the evidence concerning the traffic effects of rezoning was conflicting, and does not attempt to resolve that conflict.

With the continuing emergence of office and commercial uses in suburban areas, the resulting strain on traffic patterns has emerged as an extremely hot political issue across the United States. Paradoxically, given the apparent inevitability of continued relocation of businesses to the suburbs, the concentration of those businesses in high density nodes of large-scale developments provides one of the few hopes of finding a solution to suburban gridlock:

> Emerging nodal arrangements represent an important step in dealing with the increasing strain put on transportation infrastructure by suburban growth. America's love affair with the automobile continues strong at the same time that its highway systems are showing signs of age. In recent years, as jobs have followed people to the suburbs, traffic patterns have shifted from a radial orientation between central cities and outlying regions to a more dispersed flow within suburban areas themselves. Between 1970 and 1980, the number of work trips to central cities fell by 4.5 percent while those to suburban job locations rose by nearly 15 percent.
>
> This is a continuing trend. According to research reported in the Journal of the American Planning Association, for the foreseeable future, suburban tripmaking in automobiles will increase faster than growth in the population. Older, desultory development, with uses scattered along secondary arteries, and the attendant great distances that commuters must routinely travel every day, contribute to the chaos and confusion of the suburban transportation picture. Forcing people to travel such greater distances to dispersed office jobs adds to traffic problems, wastes time and fuel, and exacerbates pollution. The alternative of channeling the suburban population into the CBD funnel every morning is equally unpalatable. However, older suburban land-use patterns frustrate attempts to deal with the problem through improved transit service. Low-density residential development and dispersed job destinations render unfeasible the design of rational and effective mass transportation systems for intra-suburban travel.
>
> In contrast, relatively high-density developments at metropolitan nodes reduce overall transportation and energy consumption. The concentration of a diversity of uses on one site, particularly in an environment designed to enhance pedestrian flows, minimizes the need for commuting from one daily activity to the next. It also facilitates coordinated efforts to stagger office hours, thereby reducing peak-hour congestion on the highways. Perhaps most importantly, transportation experts have argued convincingly that *increased* employment densities in suburban nodes need to be encouraged in order to rationalize suburban transportation strategies. Only then will sufficient economies of scale exist to promote the expansion of public transport services or to stimulate private sector alternatives.

Haar & Lindsay, Business and the Revolution in Land Use Planning 6-7 (1987).

B. Market Mechanism and Administrative Controls

3. Dallas is one of the few communities in the country to formulate an explicit policy for dealing with buyouts. In a 1985 resolution, the city took note of the fact that "older residential neighborhoods in the City of Dallas have been approached by real estate agents and developers regarding the purchase, rezoning and redevelopment of these neighborhoods." Under the terms of the resolution, if owners of over 65 percent of the property in a neighborhood "delineated by physical barriers such as a railroad, a creek, a designated major thoroughfare, freeway, or identifiable land use barriers," request, the planning commission may (and if over 80 percent, must) "call a public hearing to determine the proper zoning of the property." Certain guidelines are laid out: the planning commission should consider whether the proposed redevelopment is compatible with adjacent land uses and adequately protects the stability of adjoining residential neighborhoods; whether the rezoning should be in the form of a PUD; whether the project will be adequately buffered; and whether the developer should provide an agreement to purchase all of the subject property which will become binding upon the passage of an ordinance rezoning the area.

4. Local opposition is not the only potential obstacle a neighborhood buyout may encounter. The complexities of timing and of holding together a large and fragile coalition of homeowners may result in the unraveling of the agreement between developer and neighborhood. Widely cited as an example of successful and innovative techniques, a buyout initiatied by an association of property owners in the Courtlands neighborhood of Arlington County, Virginia, fell victim to such problems in 1986:

> A year after Arlington County officials approved a daring plan by 22 homeowners to sell their houses in a package for tremendous profits, the deal has dissolved into litigation and the embittered homeowners have been caught in a financial vise.
>
> Homeowners in Arlington's Courtlands neighborhood, capitalizing on rapid development generated by the Court House Metro station two blocks away, had agreed to sell their 50-year-old houses to a Bethesda developer for prices estimated at two to three times the houses' assessed value.
>
> By combining their properties in a 5.2-acre package big enough for dense development, the homeowners seemed assured of receiving an $8.9 million payment from a developer with ambitious ideas.
>
> But the developer, Courchevel Corp., which planned to build a $100 million complex consisting of a 594-unit rental apartment building with adjacent theaters, restaurants and supermarkets, failed to go to settlement last Dec. 31, as it had agreed.
>
> The deal fell through, according to attorneys for Courchevel, when a partner it had hoped to enlist in a joint venture got cold feet because of possible shifts in federal tax laws. The Courtlands homeowners have

now filed suit in Arlington County Circuit Court seeking the $250,000 deposited by Courchevel as earnest money.

According to their lawyers, many of the homeowners had bought new houses late last year, in several cases with the assistance of loans, on the assumption that they would be going to settlement with Courchevel Dec. 31.

When Courchevel defaulted, the lawyers said, some of the homeowners were left in severe financial straits, losing down payments and forced to cancel leases.

Virginia Homeowners Sue After Sale Plan Fails, Washington Post, Feb. 25, 1986.

5. Calvin Trillin's reportage reveals the problems encountered in the assemblage of some of the most precious parcels on the east coast — casino property in Atlantic City. A "real estate man" named Bloom offered $100,000 to each homeowner in a working-class neighborhood, but only if everyone on the block agreed to sell. Some residents claimed that their nicer or bigger houses should bring higher profits than those of their neighbors: "'I tried to explain to them that the new worth of their houses only lies in what the block would become,'" Bloom has said. "'We aren't interested in buying their houses, only the land underneath their houses.'"

Not surprisingly, as the deadline for the offer approached, neighbor-to-neighbor pressure increased. At a neighborhood meeting, signers demanded the names of those who had yet to agree to sell, but were unsuccessful. One hesitant homeowner finally relented: "'If you got all your neighbors working on you, it's tough . . . The first thing they say is "Have you signed yet? No? What's wrong with you?" I'm a stubborn woman, but I had everybody on me.'" Trillin, U.S. Journal: Atlantic City, N.J., Assemblage, New Yorker, Jan. 8, 1979.

C. THE MASTER PLAN: AN INQUIRY IN DIALOGUE FORM

The following dialogue seeks to probe further into the master plan and the land-use planning and control system in the United States. In examining the position taken by Mr. Beauvil, consider where other planners might agree or differ with him. Has he presented an effective case? Had you been Ms. Iffucan's representative, what would your approach have been? Had the case come up under one of the foregoing planning enabling acts, what other arguments would have been available?

C. The Master Plan: An Inquiry in Dialogue Form

Chair: Will the meeting please come to order? This is a hearing before the Committee on Planning and Zoning of the City Council of Lawnfield on Case No. 276. The city council is being asked to overrule the action of the city plan commission on June 21, 1989, which denied the request of a Roberta M. Iffucan to change the zoning of an unplatted tract of five acres from Restricted Dwelling to Light Manufacturing. The plan commission is represented by Mr. Beauvil, Director of Planning for the city. Ms. Iffucan is here represented by her attorney, Mr. Aeucus. Let me say that the committee has familiarized itself with the property involved, and with the relevant materials and records of the plan commission. Accordingly, there is no need to repeat such information. I think it should be known that, because of the special position of the plan commission and the professional competence of its planning staff, this committee has always recognized a strong presumption in favor of the commission's recommendations; hence, the burden is on the appellant to demonstrate that the commission erred. Mr. Beauvil, do you wish to add anything to the recommendation of the commission at this point?

Mr. Beauvil: Mr. Chair, I wish only to reiterate that the commission found that Ms. Iffucan's application was inconsistent with the master plan for the city of Lawnfield, and hence recommended that the appeal be denied.

C: Mr. Aeucus, the floor is yours.

Mr. Aeucus: Thank you, Mr. Chairman. Since this is a legislative, and not a judicial, hearing my burden is extensive. To place the issues in their proper perspective, I must ask Mr. Beauvil if he is willing to submit to my interrogation on matters relating to this appeal?

C: Mr. Beauvil?

B: Certainly. Planning and zoning is my business.

A: Thank you. We understand the ambiguity of your position here, Mr. Beauvil. You are in one sense a defendant to justify the action taken by your commission in this matter; in another sense, you are an expert in the field of city planning. I trust that you will not find these positions in conflict during this hearing, but if you do, this committee and my client must rely upon your testimony as that of the objective professional. Mr. Beauvil, will you repeat for the committee the ground on which the request of Ms. Iffucan was denied?

B: The commission found that it was not consistent with the master plan for Lawnfield.

A: I see mounted on the wall over here a map labeled "Master Plan for Lawnfield, as amended 1-1-82." Is this map the master plan to which you refer?

B: Not exactly. That map is only a graphic summary of the master plan.
A: I have here a map labeled "Zoning Map of the City of Lawnfield, as amended by the City Council 12-15-82." Is this a part of the master plan of Lawnfield?
B: No, not directly.
A: Can you tell us, then, what is the master plan of Lawnfield?
B: Yes. It is the aggregate of all formal decisions made by the city plan commission on matters over which it has specific authority as laid down in the ordinance of April 10, 1951, which established the commission.
A: And what are those matters?
B: Mr. Aeucus, you probably can identify them better than I. The statute empowers the plan commission to create a master plan for the city and environs of Lawnfield. Let me read it: ". . . including, but not limited to, the geographical distribution of systems of transportation and communication, of land uses and population densities, streets, highways, and other facilities for recreation and cultural pursuits, schools, and all other installations for the provision of public services; to determine and recommend proper public measures for the alleviation of slum and blighted conditions and any other circumstances tending to retard the wholesome and efficient development of the city; to determine and recommend any action calculated to improve the economic condition of the community; and to conduct such studies and investigations as are pertinent to any such matters."
A: Very good. Now let's boil that down. If someone walked into your office and wanted to look at the master plan for Lawnfield, what would she be shown?
B: Probably that map on the wall, unless she had some specific question in mind.
A: Maybe I'm just a simple lawyer, but I don't see how you can "map" policies and criteria. Now, what if she wanted to know how this plan would affect a piece of property she owned?
B: Besides that map on the wall we could show her other materials. There are master plan reports adopted by the commission, or amendments specified in the records of the commission. We would locate her property on the map and find all such references relating to it, and then assemble the relevant documents for her.
A: Let's take a concrete case. I see by the papers that the plan commission has scheduled a hearing next Tuesday to consider certain revisions for the major thoroughfare plan for the northwest part of the city. If, after the hearing, the commission moves to adopt these revisions, what will happen to the master plan?
B: The adoption of the revisions will automatically amend the master

C. The Master Plan: An Inquiry in Dialogue Form

plan, and after enough changes accumulate we will redraw the map. I have only one draftsman.

A: Can you tell us what is the nature of these revisions?

B: They relate to a rerouting and change in the scheduling of construction of the extension of Elm Boulevard. The commission had previously scheduled this project for about 2000, but the rapid growth of the city in that direction may justify an earlier recommendation to the city council.

A: Has this master plan or any of its amendments even been approved formally by the city council?

B: No. Approval of the plan by the council is not required.

A: Do you know for a fact that all members of the council are reasonably familiar with the master plan?

B: No.

A: Is it your opinion that they are?

B: Well, no.

A: Is it your impression that the city council generally goes along with the recommendations of the commission?

B: Yes. There have been very few instances in which the council has not acted favorably on a commission recommendation.

A: Do you think that it is a reasonable interpretation of your testimony that the council has been adopting measures to implement a plan with which they are at best only slightly familiar and in whose making they had no part?

B: I suppose that is true.

C: Let me intervene a moment at this point, Mr. Aeucus, to point out that the city council is extremely busy. They may be asked to vote on anything from a change in the building code to relocation of the municipal airport. I do not think that it is a matter of extraordinary significance that the city council does not know all of the circumstances surrounding the recommendations that its agencies make to it.

A: Mr. Chair, it was not my intention to impeach the council for dereliction of duty. No one appreciates more than I the difficulties under which the council labors and the complexity of the problems with which it must deal. I simply wish to indicate that the relationship of the city council to the master plan is one of most peculiar significance. By your own admission at the beginning of these hearings, there is a presumption on the part of the council of the merit of recommendations flowing from the master plan. Under these circumstances the master plan becomes a fundamental document; yet it is left in hands of experts who have no direct responsibility to the community. The very future of this city, its physical improvements, the rights and obligations of its citizens with respect to the conduct of their property interests are controlled by it. Obviously, the master plan and its recommendations cannot be reckoned with in the same light as a recommendation from the sanitation department on the scheduling of garbage trucks.

B: I think you overestimate the policy import of the plan. Policy is only made when the city council enacts a recommendation submitted by the plan commission, and at this time full justification of the recommendation is submitted and a hearing is held so that the recommendation can be openly debated before council action.

A: I am forced to disagree with you. If what you say were true, the plan would have nothing to do with directing the application of human energies in land development. This plan does become the source of expectations upon its enactment by the commission. Aside from its impact on other government departments, private decisions, sometimes expensive ones, are based on the plan, and in this sense, whether formally or not, aren't they the consequences of policy? Under these circumstances, my client is placed in a peculiar position, for if you say that a measure is reasonable or unreasonable by virtue of its consistency with the master plan, she can only attack the plan as it relates to her. Wouldn't you, Mr. Beauvil, agree that it might be a better arrangement if the city council adopted the master plan and amended it in accordance with the procedures for adopting ordinances?

B: No. I think that such a procedure would hamstring planning. The plan is a dynamic thing, and must be so, because the city is dynamic. Small events occurring today cast tremendous shadows over tomorrow. We must be able to accommodate the plan to meet them as we go along, and at the same time, we must be able to improve it as we detect shortcomings.

A: I'm surprised that you're even willing to have the planning commission adopt your plan. Couldn't you keep up with the times by recommending amendments to the council?

B: I don't say that it couldn't be done this way. But we're after a flexible working guide, not a rigid design or blueprint. The real problem is one of perspective. This city council is concerned about the success of its administration; it is natural and proper that immediate criteria be applied to the actions of the political representatives of the citizenry. The criteria relating to the plan, however, must transcend elections. They must be related to the long-range objectives of the community, to the emergent features that are likely to affect the community's future, and to a continuous reevaluation of the effectiveness of the plan.

A: You don't think that a legislative body is competent to apply such criteria?

B: I don't think that they should be so compelled. The value of the

C. The Master Plan: An Inquiry in Dialogue Form

plan to the legislature is in terms of how intelligent and useful the consequences of the policy appear to them.

A: Then you must at least accede to me the right of my client to refuse to recognize the plan as a closed issue in public policy and grant her equal footing with it in this hearing.

B: I would not object to that.

A: Good. I hope that the committee will so note. Mr. Beauvil, a moment ago you made some reference to the long-range objectives of the community embodied in the plan. Did you conduct a poll among the citizens to determine what those objectives should be?

B: No.

A: How then were these objectives determined?

B: Well, in the early studies for the master plan, the commission's staff conducted a number of investigations into such things as the future population growth, the economic base, the character of the land within the city, the uses of land, the channels of movement, and other aspects of the city. The objectives were determined as a result of those studies.

A: Mr. Beauvil, I have had occasion recently to read in the literature of your profession such writers as Mumford, Wright, and Neutra, and these people all had very definite ideas about how people should live — in garden cities, in Broadacre cities, in "biosocial environments." Do you subscribe to such viewpoints?

B: Subscribe is too vigorous a word. I find such views interesting and useful inasmuch as they suggest alternatives for the future of cities.

A: Are there not inherent in such viewpoints some pretty definite ideas about the objectives of city planning?

B: There certainly are.

A: Did you consider any such viewpoints in the determination of your objectives?

B: Are you trying to suggest that the objectives of the master plan are primarily my own creation?

A: Are they not?

B: Only in the sense that there are objectives — orderly change, efficiency of physical relationships, and high levels of public service — on which I think we all agree.

A: Why were the citizens of this community not allowed to voice their own opinions as to these objectives?

B: Because it is very difficult to get cogent or meaningful answers in this situation.

A: Do you mean that the person on the street doesn't have any views on the subject, or can't agree on them?

B: In part, both. The citizen has all the characteristics of a consumer. Few consumers wanted electric frying pans or ball point pens before they were placed on the market. These wants were inert, in a sense; they came to exist only because the product became available. In the same way, if the citizens are asked to think about the future of the community they generally confine their attention to the piecemeal removal of inconveniences and within the framework of the community as it is now.

A: Are you suggesting then that someone must set their objectives for them?

B: I only suggest that this is one of the functions of the planning process: the indication of new and bolder possibilities, and their objectification, if you will, in concrete and dramatic form so that your person in the street will have something concrete to think about.

A: The choice of objectives, however, was determined by yourself or by the commission?

B: True.

A: We lawyers have an expression to cover a case in which a judge states the "facts" in such a way that the outcome becomes "inevitable." Doesn't it seem to you that it would be more in the spirit of the political philosophy of this country if your commission had derived its objectives from what the residents of this city really wanted out of their master plan?

B: No. I have just mentioned one reason why not. If I asked you whether or not you preferred polarized glass in the windshield of your helicopter, you would answer that you don't have a helicopter, and that the inquiry accordingly doesn't make sense. But another question is raised: how relevant are the wants and needs of today to those of tomorrow? Long-range public policy can't confine itself to today's outlook; things are changing too radically and too rapidly. The biggest mistakes we've made in the past have been through giving longer life than they deserved to limited viewpoints of earlier days by encasing them in steel, concrete, and asphalt. This is the story of the modern city: the expensive straining to break out of the straitjackets carefully designed for it by earlier citizens. If the function of planning is to succeed, it can't be restricted to current viewpoints.

A: Come now, how do you square this with democratic policymaking?

B: A very definite program was carried out to tell the public what the plan was all about. Newspapers, radio, and television, talks to civic organizations and schools — we utilized every medium of mass communication to say to the public: "Here is a proposed plan, we want you to know all about it. We're going to hold public hearings so that you can be better informed, object to it, endorse it, suggest changes. It is important to you because the future of your city, of your business, of your home is tied up in it." We held two weeks

C. The Master Plan: An Inquiry in Dialogue Form

of hearings. In the end the plan was changed in a number of respects and finally adopted by the commission.

A: The commission was not bound by any information from the hearings?

B: No.

A: They could ignore them if they wanted?

B: Yes, in the same way that the city council can ignore these hearings. They had to depend on their own judgment as to what was relevant and useful.

A: And you don't think that there were any underlying considerations which influenced you and the commission in the making of this plan?

B: Yes, I'm sure that there were. I think the commission definitely had in mind that a plan should be addressed to improving the quality of living for everyone in the community. I think that they felt strongly about the role of the plan as an instrument to achieve the democratic way of life in our city.

A: I think that this commission must comprise a very unusual collection of people if it develops a plan to further the democratic way of life by the autocratic methods you describe.

B: I'll go along with you that they may be unusual, but I must take exception to your use of the word "autocratic." The commission was very concerned that this plan should promote a richer and more pleasant life for the citizens of this city.

A: You spoke of this plan as a dynamic instrument. I presume that you mean that it is subject to constant modification?

B: Yes.

A: By the same procedures, generally?

B: Yes.

A: Mr. Chair, this has been a most enlightening discussion on the arcane mysteries of the master plan. I would like to point out that Mr. Beauvil's testimony has supported a fundamental contention of my client: that this master plan is a document pregnant with policy implications, that it contains objectives and assumptions arrived at in a fashion incompatible with the democratic control of government. Notwithstanding all of the exceptional efforts made by Mr. Beauvil and his commission to give it an aspect of popular participation, at the heart of the master plan is the fact that an employed expert and an appointed body of citizens made and are making decisions with far-reaching significance for the future of this city. My client, whose property has been most seriously affected in this process, charges that the master plan is unreasonable by virtue of the fashion in which it was engendered and in which it is being changed.

C: We take notice of your position. But I should point out that the

state legislature has apparently decided against you. Does your client wish to raise any further issue in the matter of the recommendation?
A: Yes, Mr. Chair, we wish to probe a little further into the assumptions of the plan as it relates to my client.
C: Proceed.
A: Mr. Beauvil, did it not concern you or your commission that present and real citizens were being asked to give up very real expectations so that some hypothetical future citizens can be provided with some different expectations?
B: Isn't this true of any organized society? Ms. Iffucan's expectations with regard to her proposed industrial property exist only by virtue of the growth and prosperity of the city as a whole, do they not? In the interest of its future as a viable social organism, may not the community drain off some of those expectations where they have adverse consequences for the community's future?
A: Certainly, Mr. Beauvil, but only where such consequences are concrete and demonstrable over time. I submit that there are large areas of pure speculation for which you are trying to assess my client. Can you justify this?
B: From the community's viewpoint it can only be justified in terms of the problem of investment: how much of today's satisfaction in the use of property is the community willing to give up for a more satisfying exploitation of property at a future time?
A: Isn't the real question: how much of *whose* expectations is the community going to confiscate for someone else's future satisfactions?
B: I concede the element of redistribution involved.
A: Let's pursue that. Would you agree that it is a rather unique form of redistribution? The income tax that my client pays is a form of redistribution, but it is in favor of specific groups and through concrete policies. You, on the other hand, ask to redistribute my client's values over a future that is problematic at best and on behalf of nameless and perhaps unborn people who may be citizens of Lawnfield in the future?
B: This is true, but I don't think that it qualifies the wisdom of the redistribution.
A: Mr. Beauvil, would you agree with the following statement: the master plan, like any public policy, should be subjected to the same sort of test that a court would apply to a statute in terms of reasonableness?
B: I would agree so long as you recognize the difference in the meaning of "reasonableness" when applied to such a document.
A: I take "reasonableness" to mean that the measures chosen are logically calculated to achieve ends which are within the power of

C. The Master Plan: An Inquiry in Dialogue Form

the legislature and are so drawn as to avoid the capricious, arbitrary, and discriminatory treatment of any citizen or group of citizens. Do you think this is true of the master plan?

B: Yes, I think so. Although I think the criteria you've stated really apply to those measures arising from the master plan which become officially sanctioned by action of the council.

A: Can you suggest a more relevant criterion for the master plan?

B: I think a more general definition is in order: making certain generally agreed assumptions about the future of the city, and assuming certain objectives relevant thereto, is the plan reasonably calculated to realize the ends endorsed?

A: You would omit any reference to the capriciousness of the impact of the plan?

B: I am not certain that it is relevant to the plan itself. Permit me to qualify my criterion by asserting that it should be consistent with the values that are important to the community, and I think that this will subsume "fairness" and a number of other things.

A: Do you then think that these community values imply the destruction of my client's expectations to use her land for industrial purposes?

B: I don't think they were expectations to which she could lay any special claim. She had previous knowledge of the zoning ordinance. She gambled and lost.

A: She gambled and the plan denied her the right to win, isn't this the case?

B: Has she any right to ask for the rules of the game to be suspended because she drew a full house in a nickel-limit game?

A: I think so, since in this peculiar game her gains from the suspension of the rules would not penalize any of the other players.

B: Let's follow up this game analogy. But let me say first that within the scope of this analogy, I see the master plan and the measures issuing therefrom as having two peculiar functions in this game. It is a general set of rules so conceived that (1) it tends to minimize prospective social losses by charging them to the player where they result from his behavior, and (2) it rationalizes the game by providing an element of predictability in the long-run conduct of public policy.

A: How does this analogy relate to my client's problem?

B: Well, consider land development for a moment to be a three-sided game between X, her competitors, and the public at large. In the unplanned game, X is aware of the fact that she may levy against the public to increase her gains or offset her losses. In consequence, she will select a particular strategy to maximize her economic returns. She may build a grocery store in the middle of a residential neighborhood so that the residents pick up the tab for increased traffic flows through the neighborhood, for the deterioration of the value of adjacent residential property, for the usurpation of curbside parking, and for a multitude of just plain nuisances. The application of a land-use plan limits the game by charging these costs, insofar as measurable, to X. She must meet certain conditions calculated to minimize the negative effects of her operations on abutting properties; she must provide off-street parking in accordance with standards. These costs accrue to her through increased site rents and costs of complying. Under these conditions her alternatives are limited to those with a minimum of social underwriting of her behavior vis-à-vis her competitors. Is this a reasonable interpretation of the game?

A: It ignores a number of relevant points. Is it not possible that strategies may be so limited that the alternatives you talked about become restricted to the point that X can extract the tribute of a monopoly, or partial monopoly position, and isn't this a much more widespread social cost?

B: It is possible, but I don't think very probable.

A: And yet this is exactly what has happened in my client's case. With intelligent foresight she obtained a piece of land a number of years ago which you subsequently zoned for residential purposes. It is a half a mile from the nearest development. She obtains a firm option at $40,000 an acre for the construction of a plant for a NASA contractor and is denied a change of zoning. In the zoned industrial area the owners, aware of their monopoly under the master plan and the zoning ordinance, are sitting back and asking twice as much for less desirable land. Do you think that this is an unreal interpretation?

B: Yes. I can't justify the market behavior of those other owners, but that is the way the market works. It certainly is not perfect, but short of the condemnation of development rights, we must rely on it to order the use of land within the rules of the game.

A: I thought that one of the justifications of planning was to eliminate the imperfections of the land market and permit a more rational utilization of the land within the city.

B: True, but I don't think that you can hold an exception or two against the general principle.

A: You don't think that this element of monopoly cuts through your entire theoretical structure?

B: Not to any considerable extent. I suggest that in most of these cases the monopoly element is weak. In our previous example, there is a narrow limit to the monopoly prices that X may charge, because it's just too easy for a customer to drive a mile farther on to another store. The mobility of urban life is the great equalizer of competitive advantage, and it is certainly a function of the plan to increase

C. The Master Plan: An Inquiry in Dialogue Form

mobility. Some small tribute may be levied by X, but I would consider it a modest payment to avoid the disutilities of having to drive the extra mile.

A: In the second place, your version of the game ignores the landowner. Isn't the landowner on whose property X proposed to locate a substantial loser?

B: How much has he lost? Let's go back to the game analogy. If the neighborhood contained 400 undifferentiated properties, he had one chance in 400 of capitalizing on X's location decision. Assuming that he could make a profit of $10,000, we can value his expectation at $25. Right?

A: Now you're stating a real ivory-tower model, but go ahead.

B: That is what he gives up by covenanting his property or what is levied against him under zoning. There is also the prospect that X will locate next door to him in any one of four locations, which might diminish the value of his property for dwelling use by, say, $5000, in which case the gross value of his expectation of loss is $50. The net value of the planned game to him is actually a gain of $25; he gives up an expectation of gain valued at $25 to avoid an expectation of loss valued at $50.

A: Isn't this a rigged example?

B: I don't think that the principle is unrealistic. In fact, experience has been that real estate boards almost always support exclusive residential zoning in order to protect property values in the way I have just indicated.

A: But my client, Ms. Iffucan, has a signed option, subject to zoning, at $40,000 an acre, and the most it will ever bring for houses is $5000. Don't you think that the value of the unplanned game is substantially greater to her than the planned one?

B: No. The value of the game isn't changed by one player's failing to realize an extreme possibility.

A: This is a rather slender justification.

B: I think you must consider it in conjunction with the second major aspect of the plan: the way in which it changes the rules by altering the element of predictability, and in this sense, rationalizing the game. The plan in its present sense takes cognizance of the future; it explores it to isolate and identify the economic, social, and physical forces at work in the shaping of the community — changes in technology, in resources, in regional and national influences. Having identified these trends and appraised them in terms of impact and probability, the plan is itself a conscious master strategy to optimize the future of the community. It orientates public policy in a predictable way. It endeavors to liquidate the caprice of circumstance and thus provides businessperson X, his or her competitors, the public, and property owners with a rational framework within which each can pursue his or her interests, protected to some extent from the attrition of the unexpected — certainly so far as public policy is concerned.

A: But you have insisted that the master plan must retain its flexibility — the right to change at the slightest whim of a planner, as new facts are uncovered. Is this a definition of predictability? Where is the protection against caprice, against the arbitrary decision of the technician and the professional? Moreover, is there any assurance that the politicians will give it any credence at all?

B: There is no absolute assurance, except the chain of procedure, appraisal, and review that terminates before the city council. I can only suggest that the real assurance is the degree to which the plan and the policy proposals that flow from it commend themselves to the city council. I should point out again, that although recommendations from the commission have been turned down by the council before, through four different administrations the major recommendations of the plan have been put into effect.

A: Would you consider this experience characteristic of most communities throughout the country?

B: No. I know of places where plan commission and city council have not gotten along, with the result that the local plans have been largely ignored. I think these are most unfortunate cases and there are a number of reasons why this situation exists. But such conditions have not obtained here. The importance of planning in the political life of a community is directly related to the acuteness of the land-use problems it faces. To support planning has been good politics in Lawnfield, and I think that this is in part a tribute to the master plan and the commission that has worked on and for it for several years.

A: You would concede, though, that where such enviable relationships do not exist, your arguments in favor of the master plan are subject to some modification?

B: Yes.

C: Understand, Mr. Aeucus, that this city council was elected on a program of making this a better city, a better place for everyone to live in, and that wasn't just platform talk. We think we have a dandy master plan and we're quite interested in letting it do its job.

A: This certainly does you credit, Mr. Chair. But I hope that your enthusiasm will not make you minimize some of the real problems involved, problems such as my client here faces.

C: We most certainly want the plan to be fair to everyone.

A: My point still is that if the plan were only the intellectual exercise of the planning profession, we citizens could remain indifferent to it. But it touches and concerns controls. Mr. Beauvil, how do you

C. The Master Plan: An Inquiry in Dialogue Form

     conceive of the relationship of the zoning ordinance to your master plan?
B: Zoning is the device by which those aspects of the master plan affecting private property are put into effect.
A: The zoning map is the land-use plan, then?
B: No.
A: You mean to say that the zoning map and the land-use plan are different?
B: Yes.
A: How do they differ?
B: Well, perhaps the major difference is one of "ripeness." The zoning map regulates areas in terms of the imminence of certain classes of development. Those which appear to be less imminent in the near future are not expressed by the zoning map, but they do show up on the land-use plan.
A: Can you give me an example?
B: I can give you one of several. In the northeast sector of the city, land is generally undeveloped except for farming and similar agricultural activities. We have reason to believe that it will be several years before there is pressure for development in that area, but we have laid out the general specifications for land use in anticipation of it, including residential, apartment, and retail uses. These are indicated on the land-use plan.
A: But they are not a part of the zoning ordinance?
B: No.
A: What is the area zoned now?
B: It is all in the most restricted residential district, with one-acre minimum lots.
A: In other words, you have zoned it residential and you don't plan for it to develop uniformly for dwellings?
B: That's right.
A: Why doesn't the planned pattern appear on the zoning map?
B: Because the area isn't ripe yet. To downgrade some of the land in the area before it is ripe would probably induce marginal construction of lower-grade uses that might actually impair the best development of the area, when it is ripe.
A: How will you know when it is ripe for development?
B: Well, we'll begin to get submissions for subdivision approval in the area, for one thing. This is a pretty good indication, since a developer has to put up a bond with the city for all public improvements before obtaining approval. We'll begin to note a pronounced rise in the value of the property generally, and this is always a fairly strong signal. And we keep in pretty close touch with the local FHA office, which will probably be asked to approve

any potential development for mortgage purposes before any developer would get out on a limb.

A: What will you do when you decide that the land is ripe for development?

B: We will recommend certain changes in the zoning ordinance to give legal force to the plan for the area.

A: In other words, there are property owners in this area who live under two sets of expectations, one as demonstrated by the master plan, and the other by the current zoning ordinance, is that right?

B: Yes.

A: Do you not consider this a most peculiar circumstance?

B: Why?

A: Suppose that I own a piece of property on a major street in this area. It is now zoned residential, but on inquiring in your office I find that it is slated for commercial development at some time in the future. What would you do if you were in my position?

B: I think I'd hold off doing anything with my land until the area ripened and I could get commercial zoning.

A: Why shouldn't I try to have it rezoned now? Maybe I can put up a fruit stand or lease it for a roadside diner and obtain income from the property while you are waiting for the area to ripen.

B: The commission would probably deny your request.

A: Because the area is not ripe enough? Come now, Mr. Beauvil, how do you think that would stand up in court?

B: I can't see why it shouldn't. It does not seem unreasonable to say that the zoning of a piece of property may be recommended for change under certain conditions necessary to protect the development of the area. In this case one of those conditions is that the area be ripe for development.

A: And *you* will tell *me* when it is ripe? By what standards?

B: By those I mentioned.

A: Don't you think that they are somewhat arbitrary? Especially when the commission would not grant my request as you indicated.

B: Let me modify my statement. The commission would expect you to demonstrate a number of things before they would grant your request. They would expect you to justify such a change in terms of the public interest; that is, to show a need for a change and to show that what you proposed to do was consistent with the proposed development of the area.

A: With the master plan, then?

B: Yes.

A: Don't you think that this is a highly arbitrary way of proceeding? You grant that my property is properly situated for commercial zoning, and yet you capriciously withhold my right to develop it in this way until you think that the time is "ripe"? How do I know you're not treating my client's neighbor more favorably?

C. The Master Plan: An Inquiry in Dialogue Form 1123

B: I don't think that it is capricious. In effect the plan is saying that your property is properly situated for commercial zoning *if* the developments assumed by the plan take place. Since the utility of property depends in a large degree upon its relationship to existing property uses, the nature of the use pattern of an area is a dominant consideration in whether or not the zoning ought to be changed.

A: Don't you think that such a practice unreasonably prejudices my right to use my land in expectation of returns now before the expected pattern develops?

B: No. Your property would prove far more valuable to you when the area develops and provides a sound local basis for your proposed use. If you were permitted to clutter it with marginal improvements in the interim, and perhaps become involved in a long-term lease in so doing, you might actually lose, relative to what your gains would have been. In addition, you may blight the development of the area around you. I don't think this is capricious.

A: Mr. Chair, I think that you must conclude that the manner in which the master plan affects the expectations of private property is an arbitrary exercise of power, a usurpation of your prerogative. There is no ordinance that tells me when I may develop my property, there is only the opinion of your experts as to whether or not "the time is ripe." And to this interpretation of the master plan I must take exception.

C: We note your point, Mr. Aeucus. Mr. Beauvil, you have heard the charge that your use of the master plan is arbitrary, in that it subjects property to legislative determination by an agency enjoying no delegation of legislative powers. Can you justify this?

B: Yes, sir. Ms. Iffucan always has the right to request that the zoning of her property be changed. If the commission responds negatively, she may carry her request to the city council, which can change the action of the commission if it seems to be unreasonable. I can't see where the principle of legislative responsibility has been abridged under this condition.

C: Thank you, Mr. Beauvil. Mr. Aeucus, since your client's property doesn't fall within this case, in what manner do you think that the master plan is unreasonable with respect to her?

A: Mr. Chair, to date I have merely been interested to show from a number of viewpoints that the utilization of the land-use part of the master plan as a kind of extralegislative, superzoning ordinance is unreasonable and certainly not consistent with the common view of governmental responsibility. If this is the case, I am suggesting to you that you should disregard it in coming to a decision about my client's property, and base your conclusions on the simple merits of her application.

C: And what are those?

A: That my client is the owner of a piece of property whose size, shape, and location are felicitous for industry; that this council is on record in supporting industrial development when it is necessary to the future of this city; that my client has entered into an option with a nationally established firm to construct a plant to produce electronic devices under contract to NASA; that the plant in terms of its design, layout, appearance, and landscaping will not impair the development of surrounding property in accordance with the master plan; finally, the plant will substantially benefit the community, not only in terms of the taxable values involved, but also in that it will employ two hundred persons who will spend their payrolls in our city.

C: Mr. Aeucus, do you think we ought to go along with every such request that comes before us, where a person with a new business enterprise who is unwilling to pay the going price for commercial or industrial property finds a piece of property that he or she can purchase for a song in a residential district and then asks us to change the zoning?

A: As a rule, if it makes a wholesome contribution to the prosperity of the community, and does not deprive anyone else of the enjoyment of his or her property, it would seem to me to be unreasonable to deny such uses.

B: May I interject a comment here? I don't think that Mr. Aeucus realizes that one cannot separate so distinctly the land-use plan from other aspects of the master plan. All of these parts are delicately interwoven. For example, last summer, the water and sewerage department undertook to replace an undersized water main from the purification plant. As this area develops, this main will be extended to serve it. They held a series of conferences with us on requirements, and the size of the main was carefully calculated to serve the proposed development of the area according to the master plan. Any substantial departure from the plan that would increase the requirements for water would place them in the position of having to replace this main or to parallel it with another for several miles, a very expensive proposition. Two months ago we worked out with the highway department the specifications for the development of the freeway, including the location of a semidirect interlooping directional interchange that would serve most efficiently the planned development of the area. A substantial change in the type of traffic movement would seriously distort this scheme, which has been approved by the state highway commission. In other words, to impair the plan at this point would result in substantial and expensive changes in the public sector of the development of the area.

A: Mr. Beauvil has just supported my contention about the master plan. There are a vast number of policy decisions being made

C. The Master Plan: An Inquiry in Dialogue Form 1125

about such areas outside of the knowledge of the city council. I can only answer that such procedures most seriously militate against the property rights of my client. Let me sum up my argument briefly. My client has a piece of property admirably suited to the location of a premium grade of industry; she has that industry in hand, an industry that will be a boon to this community and to the area. She is prevented from using this property by the determination of the master plan. The use of the master plan in this fashion is a usurpation of the legislative prerogative to make public policy for this community, and the procedures surrounding it are arbitrary and unreasonable. We request that the council disregard the master plan as a criterion for the reasonableness of this application, and that it be examined on its own merits; if this is done, I think you must agree that the proposal of Ms. Iffucan is not only a reasonable attempt to utilize her property to its best advantage, but would concomitantly serve the interests of this community. Thank you.

C: Mr. Beauvil?

B: I suggest to the council that the master plan is nowhere as arbitrary as suggested. The zoning ordinance, which is what he really complains against, was properly adopted by the city council, representing in its eyes a proper distribution of land uses and specifications throughout the city. The council recognized that the rapid growth of the city and the changing conditions therein might justify changes in the zoning ordinance in the future, and hence provided regulations and procedures for its amendment. With respect to the zoning ordinance, the master plan as it relates to land use is merely a complex guide for such changes. It is the antithesis of arbitrariness to set up objective standards for such changes, and that is all that the land-use plan seeks to do. I reiterate, members of the committee, that Ms. Iffucan's request does not conform with the master plan for the city, and that Ms. Iffucan has submitted neither a reason for departing from this plan, nor an alternative. Under these conditions, I must affirm the recommendation that the request be denied on appeal.

C: Thank you, ladies and gentlemen, I am certain that the committee has been most enlightened by the clear discussion of the master plan and its relation to this case. We will take this request under advisement and submit our findings to the city council at its next scheduled meeting.

Urban land policies of the United States are being increasingly employed to shape land uses to serve social ends in a market economy and in a given historical context. Strong efforts are being made to curb, but to retain, a vigorous group of private entrepreneurs. Even more important, new incentives have been established by government to induce activity in approved channels. Whether such a program as it is, and as it matures, can succeed, is of more than passing interest.

Many of the legal powers for social control and guidance of the urban environment are at hand. New tools are in place, novel strategies unfold for attacking adverse planning and zoning decisions. Responding to critics and court challenges, the laws and regulations affecting the use, development, and preservation of land have undergone changes— both dramatic and subtle. The Euclidean paradigm is thus well suited for the century drawing nigh.

Many problems still remain; intricate issues regarding property rights and welfare abound; fully appropriate legal mechanisms are yet to be devised to implement land policies and to erect the legal structure for city planning. Without underrating the possibilities of radically new techniques and institutional arrangements of land ownership, the older legal instruments need to be understood and imaginatively explored. The novel juxtaposition of familiar concepts and the invention of new types of ordering are today's challenge to the lawyer. Much patience, originality, and ingenuity are required in order to shape appropriate legislative and administrative devices for planning the physical growth of the metropolis. The serious problem is the wise and thoroughly democratic utilization of this increasingly powerful machinery. Will it be used intelligently, with the proper daring and restraint?

— *Would you tell me, please, which way I ought to walk from here?*
— *That depends a good deal on where you want to get to, said the Cat.*
— *I don't much care where, said Alice.*
— *Then it doesn't matter which way you walk, said the Cat.*
— *So long as I get somewhere, Alice added as an explanation.*
— *Oh, you're sure to do that, said the Cat, if you only walk long enough.*

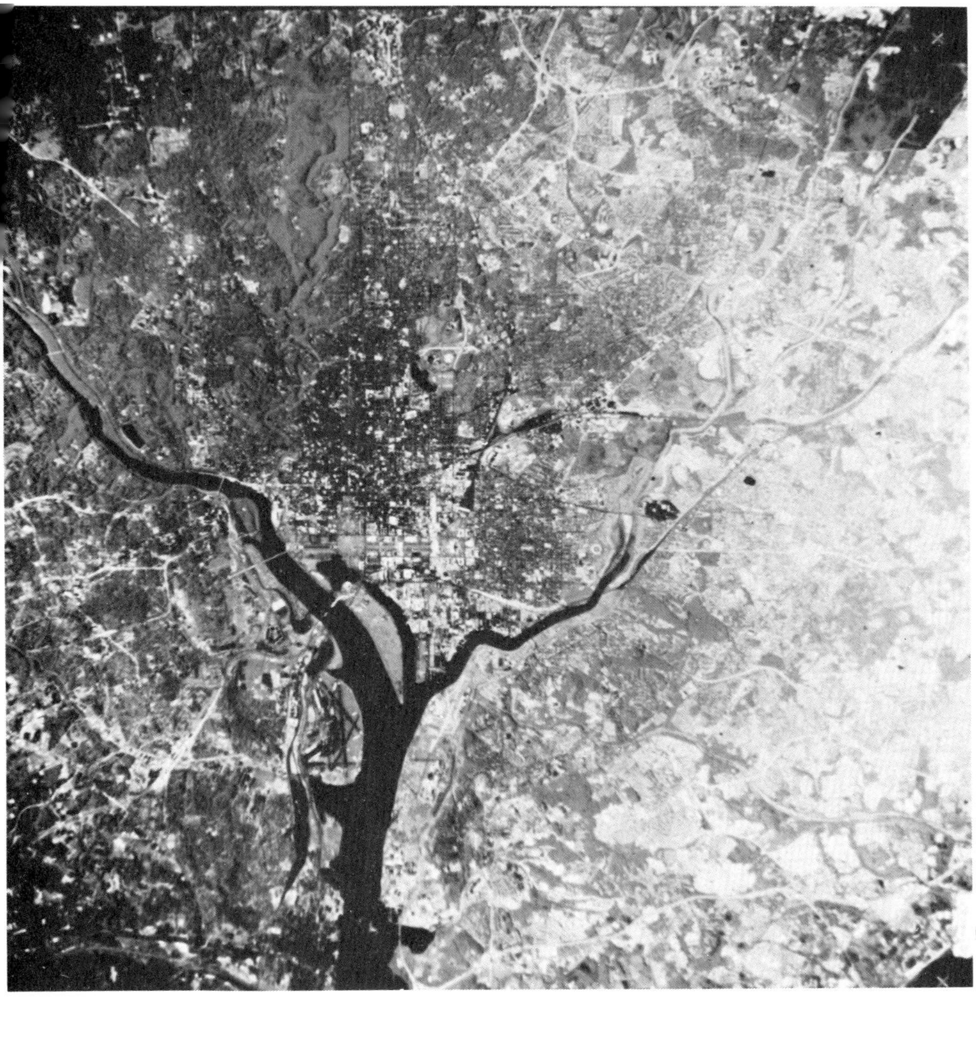

Table of Cases

Principal cases are indicated by italic type.

Abbott v. Zoning Bd. of Review of Warwick, 353
Adams v. Snouffer, 119
Adkins v. Children's Hosp., 189
Agins v. City of Tiburon (Cal. 1979), 903
Agins v. City of Tiburon (U.S. 1980), 887
Ailes v. Decatur County Area Planning Commn., 297
Akers v. Commissioner, 724
Akron v. Chapman, 305
Aldom v. Borough of Roseland, 340
Alevizos v. Metropolitan Airports Commn. of Minneapolis & St. Paul, 104
Alexander v. City of Minneapolis, 481
Allen v. City Council, 786
Allydonn Realty Corp. v. Holyoke Hous. Auth., 797
Almota Farmers Elevator & Warehouse Co. v. United States, 845
Aloe v. Dassler, 353
Amalgamated Hous. Corp. v. Kelly, 821
Ambler Realty Co. v. Village of Euclid, 187, 375
American Smelting & Ref. Co. v. Godfrey, 118
America's Best Family Showplace Corp. v. City of New York, 490

AMG Realty Co. v. Warren Township, 436
Amphitheaters, Inc. v. Portland Meadows, 112
Anderson v. Pima County, 592
Anderson v. Zoning Commn. of Norwalk, 341
Andrus v. Allard, 885
Appeal of _____. *See* name of party
Application of _____. *See* name of party
Applied Chem. Technology, Inc. v. Town of Merrimack, 154
Arcara v. Cloud Books, Inc., 145
Arlington Heights, Village of v. Metropolitan Hous. Dev. Corp. (U.S. 1977), *450*, 660, 1035
Arlington Heights, Village of v. Metropolitan Hous. Dev. Corp. (7th Cir. 1977), 456
Arnel Dev. Co. v. City of Costa Mesa (Cal. 1980), 1082
Arnel Dev. Co. v. City of Costa Mesa (Cal. App. 1981), 1084
Arnold Bernard & Co. v. Planning & Zoning Commn. of Town of Westport, 592

Arverne Bay Constr. Co. v. Thatcher, 195, 693, 712
Ashwander v. TVA, 903
Asian Ams. for Equality v. Koch (N.Y. Sup. Ct. 1985), 438
Asian Ams. for Equality v. Koch (N.Y. App. Div. 1987), 439
Associated Home Builders v. City of Livermore, 411, 582, 1083
Associated Home Builders of Greater East Bay v. City of Walnut Creek, 519, 633, 635
Auraria Businessmen against Confiscation, Inc. v. Denver Urban Renewal Auth., 866
Ayres v. City Council of Los Angeles, 621, 1052

Baetjer v. United States, 861
Baker v. City of Milwaukie (Or. App. 1974), *562*
Baker v. City of Milwaukie (Or. 1975), *563*
Ballstadt v. Pagel, 119
Baltimore v. Swartz, Inc., 531
Banberry Dev. Corp. v. South Jordan City, 633
Banks v. Housing Auth. of San Francisco, 472
Baptist Fellowship of Randolph, Inc., In re, 755
Bates v. Weymouth Iron Co., 783
Bauman v. County of Schuyler, 143
Bauman v. Ross, 602, 840
Beach v. Planning & Zoning Commn. of Milford, 602
Beal v. Lindsay, 657, 660, 1037
Beall v. Montgomery County Council, 327
Bedford, Town of v. Mount Kisco, 562
Bell v. City of Elkhorn, 563
Bellle Terre, Village of v. Borass, 248, 549
Bellows Farm, Inc. v. Building Inspector of Acton, 614
Bennett M. Lifter, Inc. v. Metropolitan Dade County, 241
Berenson v. Town of New Castle, 410
Berg Dev. Co. v. City of Missouri City, 633
Berger v. Van Sweringen Co., 686
Berman v. Parker, 518, 549, 784, *788*
Bessette v. Guarino, 685
Best v. La Plata Planning Commn., 1055
Bishop v. Town of Houghton, 560
Blitz v. Town of New Castle, 411
Block v. Hirsh, 882, 1005
Board of Appeals of Maynard v. Housing Appeals Comm., 593
Board of County Commrs. v. Delaney, 844
Board of County Commrs. of Cecil County v. Gaster, 1053
Board of Regents of State Colleges v. Roth, 865
Board of Supervisors of Fairfax County v. DeGroff Enters., 431
Board of Supervisors of Fairfax County v. Horne, 592
Board of Supervisors v. Snell Constr. Corp., 327
Board of Zoning Appeals of Indianapolis v. Wheaton, 504
Boca Raton, City of v. Arvida Corp., 591
Boca Raton, City of v. Boca Villas Corp., 591
Bohannan v. City of San Diego, 533
Bonan v. City of Boston, 645
Bonan v. General Hosp. Corp., 645
Boomer v. Atlantic Cement Co., 120
Borough of Cresskill v. Borough of Dumont, 558
Borough of Rockleigh v. Astral Indus., Inc., 301
Boston Chamber of Commerce v. Boston, 854
Boston Gas Co. v. Assessors of Boston, 845
Bove v. Donner-Hanna Coke Corp., 119
Boyds Civic Assn. v. Montgomery County, 1054
Boyd v. United States, 863
Brackett v. Board of Appeal, 354
Bradley v. Milliken, 1030
Brandwein v. Serrano, 685
Breed v. Town of Clay, 303
Brennan v. City of Milwaukee, 386
Brett v. Building Commr. of Brookline, 309
Bristol Redev. & Hous. Auth. v. Dentow, 786
Buffalo, City of v. Clement Co., 853
Building Indus. Assn. of S. Cal. v. City of Camarillo, 594, 1084
Burger v. City of St. Paul, 1076
Burroughs v. Town of Paradise Valley, 536

California Coastal Commn. v. Granite Rock Co., 761
Calvert Cliffs' Coordinating Comm. v. Atomic Energy Commn., 727
Cannata v. City of New York, 805
Cape Canaveral, City of v. Mosher, 1055
Cape Resort Hotels v. Alcoholic Licensing Bd. of Falmouth, 300
Carbonara v. Sacca, 243
Cardon Invs. v. Town of New Market, 328

Table of Cases

Carson v. Board of Appeals of Lexington, 290
Caswell v. Licensing Commn., 490
Cederberg v. City of Rockford, 1076
Chappell v. SCA Servs., Inc., 153
Charles v. Diamond, 581
Charlotte Park & Recreation Commn. v. Barringer, 472
Chayt v. Board of Zoning Appeals, 298
Chayt v. Maryland Jockey Club, 328
Cheney v. Village 2 at New Hope, Inc., 279, 392
Chicago, City of v. Central Natl. Bank in Chicago, 1049
Christy v. City of Ann Arbor, 482
Chrobuck v. Snohomish County, 329, 341
Chula Vista, City of v. Superior Court of the County of San Diego, 756
Circle Lounge and Grille, Inc. v. Board of Appeal, 356
City of ――――――――. *See* name of city
Cleburne, City of v. Cleburne Living Center, 253, *357, 1085*
Clemons v. City of Los Angeles, 220
Clifton v. Puente, 472
Coalition for Los Angeles County Planning in the Pub. Interest v. Board of Supervisors (Cal. Super. Ct. 1975), 729, *1052*
Coalition for Los Angeles County Planning in the Pub. Interest v. Board of Supervisors (Cal. App. 1978), 732
Cochran v. Preston, 532
Codorus Township v. Rodgers, 725
Cole v. City of Battle Creek, 301
Collard v. Incorporated Village of Flower Hill, 283, 329
College Station, City of v. Turtle Rock Corp., 632
Colon v. Lisk, 142
Committee to Save the Bishop's House, Inc. v. Medical Center Hosp. of Vt., Inc., 754
Commonwealth v. Alger, 889
Commonwealth Dept. of Highways v. Diuguid, 864
Commonwealth v. Tewksbury, 888
Community Communications Co. v. City of Boulder, 505, 513
Community Redev. Agency of Los Angeles v. Abrams, 865
Connerty v. Metropolitan Dist. Commn., 774
Connor v. Township of Chanhassen, 560
Conservation Law Found. v. Harper, 39
Construction Indus. Assn. v. City of Petaluma, 583
Consumers' Light & Power Co. v. Holland, 113
Conway v. Town of Stratham, 593

Cook County v. Holland, 842
Coral Gables v. Carmichael, 327
Corrado v. Providence Redev. Agency, 841
Correll v. Earley, 471
Corrigan v. Buckley, 471
Corrigan v. City of Scottsdale, 910
Corthouts v. Town of Newington, 244
County of ――――――――. *See* name of county
Courtesy Sandwich Shop, Inc. v. Port of New York Auth., 257, 796
Cross v. Bilett, 1071
Crown Cascade, Inc. v. O'Neal, 613
Cupp v. Board of Supervisors of Fairfax County, 629
Cutting v. Muzzey, 468
C-Y Dev. Co. v. City of Redlands, 470

Dalmo Sales Co. v. Tysons Corner Regional Shopping Center, 512
Dalton v. City and County of Honolulu, 329
Davis v. Huey, 537
Davis v. Sawyer, 149
deBottari v. City Council, 1084
DeKalb County v. Albritton Properties, 1101
De Mars v. Zoning Commn., 385
DeNina v. Bammel Forest Civic Club, Inc., 137
Department of Health v. Ebling Brewing Co., 147
DeRosa v. HUD, 957
DeSimone v. Greater Englewood Hous. Corp. No. 1, 344
Dohany v. Rogers, 840
Don's Porta Signs, Inc. v. City of Clearwater, 549
Dooley v. Town of Fairfield, 704
Duke Power Co. v. Carolina Envtl. Study Group, 154
Dunkin' Donuts of N.J. v. Township of N. Brunswick Planning Bd., 607
Du Page County v. Halkier, 383

Eastlake, City of v. Forest City Enters., Inc., 497, *1078*
Eden v. Zoning Commn. of Bloomfield, 316
Edwards v. Steele, 357
Egg Harbor Assocs., In the Matter of, 433, 756
Elocin, Inc., In re Appeal of, 412
Ely v. Velde, 526
Emmett S. Hickman Co., Application of, 242
Emmi v. Zoning Bd. of Appeals, 356

Ensign Bickford Realty Corp. v. City Council, 511
Erznoznik v. City of Jacksonville, 145
Euclid, Village of v. Ambler Realty Co., 178, 372, 504, 518, 555, 880
Evans v. Abney (Ga. 1968), 472
Evans v. Abney (U.S. 1970), 473
Evans v. Newton, 472
Everett, City of v. Capitol Motor Transp. Co., 195
Eves v. Zoning Bd. of Adjustment of Lower Gwynedd Township, 211, 280

Fahri v. Commissioners of Borough of Deal, 504
Fairlawns Cemetery Assn. v. Zoning Commn. of Bethel, 560
Fallbrook Irrigation Dist. v. Bradley, 834
Fasano v. Board of Commrs. of Wash. County, 330
FCC v. Florida Power Corp., 841
Fernley v. Board of Supervisors of Schuylkill Township, 413
First Assembly of God v. Alexandria, 504
First English Evangelical Lutheran Church of Glendale v. County of Los Angeles, 742, 903, *913*, 923
First Hartford Realty v. Planning and Zoning Commn. of Hartford, 316
Fischer v. Bedminster Township, 383
Fisher v. City of Berkeley, 517
Fisher v. City of Syracuse, 853
Flint Ridge Dev. Co. v. Scenic Rivers Assn. of Okla., 698
Flower Hill Bldg. Corp. v. Village of Flower Hill, 383
Floyd v. New York State UDC, 394
Flynn v. Zoning Bd. of Review of Pawtucket, 353
Foltz v. City of Indianapolis, 821
Fond du Lac, City of v. Department of Natural Resources, 151
Forbes Street, 695
Forster v. Scott, 695
Fountain Gate Ministries, Inc. v. City of Plano, 504
Fox v. HUD, 866, 990
Framingham Clinic, Inc. v. Board of Selectmen, 491
Framingham Clinic, Inc. v. Zoning Bd. of Appeals, 492
Frankland v. City of Lake Oswego, 281
Franklin v. Minister of Town & Country Planning, 81
Franmore Realty Co. v. Le Boeuf, 300
Fred F. French Investing Co. v. City of New York, 269
Fresh Pond Shopping Center v. Callahan, 886

Frisco Land & Mining Co. v. State of California, 592
FTC v. Cement Inst., 150
FTC v. R.F. Keppel & Bros. Inc., 697
Furman Street, In re, 695

Gautreaux v. Chicago Hous. Auth. (N.D. Ill. 1969), *1025*
Gautreaux v. Chicago Hous. Auth. (N.D. Ill. 1969), 1028
Gautreaux v. Chicago Hous. Auth. (7th Cir. 1971), 1028
Gautreaux v. Chicago Hous. Auth. (N.D. Ill. 1972), 1030
Gautreaux v. Chicago Hous. Auth. (7th Cir. 1974), 1030
Gautreaux v. Landrieu, 1032
Gautreaux v. Pierce (7th Cir. 1982), 1033
Gautreaux v. Pierce (7th Cir. 1983), 1034
Gautreaux v. Pierce (7th Cir. 1984), 1033
Gautreaux v. Romney (N.D. Ill. 1971), 1029
Gautreaux v. Romney (7th Cir. 1971), 1028
Gautreaux v. Romney (7th Cir. 1972), 1030
Gerard v. San Juan County, 616
Giles v. Walker, 120
Givner v. Commissioner of Health, 386
Goldblatt v. Town of Hempstead, 307, 885
Golden v. City of Overland Park, 337
Golden v. Planning Bd. of Ramapo, 570, 712
Grand Land Co. v. Township of Bethlehem, 617
Grant v. Edmondson, 675
Grant v. Mayor of Baltimore, 305
Green St. Assn. v. Daley, 786
Greenwood, City of v. Provine, 669, 673
Grendel's Den v. Larkin, 497
Grosso v. Board of Adjustment of Millburn Township, 693
Grosz v. City of Miami Beach, 498
Grupe v. California Coastal Commn., 635

Hadacheck v. Sebastian, 881
Hallie, Town of v. City of Eau Claire, 515
H.&R. Corp. v. District of Columbia, 851
Hang Kie, In re, 164
Hanley v. Mitchell, 526
Hanover v. Housing Appeals Comm., 393
Harlow v. Fitzgerald, 468
Harlow v. Planning & Zoning Commn. of Westport, 592
Harnik v. Levine, 113
Harrison v. Zoning Bd. of Review, 353
Harrod v. Rigelhaupt, 676

Table of Cases

Hartnett v. Austin, 329
Hawaii Hous. Auth. v. Lyman, 820
Hawaii Hous. Auth. v. Midkiff, 816
Hawkins v. Town of Shaw (N.D. Miss. 1969), *647*
Hawkins v. Town of Shaw (5th Cir. 1971), *654*
Hawkins v. Town of Shaw (5th Cir. 1972), 655
Headley v. City of Rochester, 687
Heady v. Zoning Bd. of Appeals for Milford, 352
HFH, Ltd. v. Superior Court, 880
Hillis Homes, Inc. v. Snohomish County, 634
Hills Dev. Co. v. Township of Barnards [Mount Laurel III], 441
Hills v. Gautreaux, 1031
Hills v. Zoning Commn. of Newington, 316
Hitchman v. Township of Oakland, 383
Hodel v. Irving, 922
Hodel v. Virginia Surface Mining & Reclamation Assn., Inc., 742
Hollis v. Parkland Corp., 608
Holman v. Athens Empire Laundry Co., 104
Holy Spirit Assn. for the Unification of World Christianity v. Rosenfeld, 503
Home Builders & Contractors Assn. of Palm Beach County v. Board of County Commrs., 629
Home Builders League of S. Jersey v. Township of Berlin, 415
H.O.M.E.S. v. New York State UDC, 732
HOPE, Inc. v. County of DuPage, 449
Houston, City of v. Waggoner, 687
Houston, City of v. Walker, 687
Howard County v. JJM, Inc., 694
Huber v. Village of Richmond Heights, 614
Huff v. Board of Zoning Appeals, 216
Hulbert v. California Portland Cement Co., 124
Hundt v. Costello, 609
Hunterfly Realty Corp. v. State, 854
Huntington Branch, NAACP v. Town of Huntington, 460
Hurd v. Hodge, 471

Illinois R.R. v. Illinois, 736
Ingram v. City of Ridley, 104
In re, In the Matter of, In re Appeal of ——————. *See* name of party
International Paper Co. v. United States, 861
Iodice v. City of Newton, 432
Islamic Center of Miss. v. Starkville, 504

Jackson v. New York State UDC, 986
Jackson v. Williams, 253
Jantausch v. Borough of Verona, 243
Japanese Gardens Mobile Estates v. Hunt, 685
Javins v. First Natl. Realty Corp., 376
Jefferson Natl. Bank v. Miami Beach, 232
Jenkins v. Missouri, 461
Jensen v. City of New York, 694
Jersey City Redev. Agency v. Kugler, 854
Jewish Reconstructist Synagogue v. Incorporated Village of Roslyn, 503
Joiner v. City of Dallas, 809
Jones v. Alfred H. Mayer Co., 473
Junqua, In re, 147
Just v. Marinette County, 712

Kaiser-Aetna v. United States, 850, 886
Kane v. Board of Appeal, 356
Kane v. Zoning Bd. of Greenwich, 617
Kaskel v. Impellitteri, 784
Kasper v. H.P. Hood & Sons, Inc., 161
Katobimar Realty Co. v. Webster, 236
Kauai, County of v. Pacific Standard Life Ins. Co., 309
Kelbro, Inc. v. Myrick, 534
Kelly v. Barrett, 684
Kensington-Davis Corp. v. Schwab, Matter of, 211
Kentucky-Ohio Gasco v. Bolling, 113
Keystone Bituminous Coal Assn. v. DeBenedictus, 736, 880
Kimball Laundry Co. v. United States, 863
Kirk v. Mabis, 149
Kirk v. Township of Tyrone, 337
Kisil v. City of Sandusky, 349
Kit-Mar Builders, Inc., Appeal of, 389
K.J.C. Realty v. State, 830
Kline v. City of Harrisburg, 168
Klopping v. City of Whittier, 853, 854
Kohl v. United States, 782
Kort v. City of Los Angeles, 242
Kozesnik v. Township of Montgomery, 1052
Krebs v. Hermann, 117
Kropf v. City of Sterling, 343
Kuehne v. Town Council of East Hartford, 313
Kutcher v. Town Planning Commn. of Manchester, 316
K. V. P. Co. v. McKie, 126

Lafayette, County of v. Louisiana Power & Light, 505, 512
Lake Country Estates v. Tahoe Regional Planning Agency, 468
Lakewood, Ohio Congregation of Jehovah's Witnesses, Inc. v. City of Lakewood, 503

La Mesa, City of v. Tweed & Gambrell Planing Mill, 297
Laporte, Application of, 244
Larkin v. Grendel's Den, Inc., 492
Las Virgenes Homeowners v. Los Angeles County, 1055
Lathrop v. Planning & Zoning Commn. of Trumbel, 316
Lawton v. Steele, 141
Lebanon, Town of v. Woods, 316
Leonard v. City of Bothell, 1083
Levin v. Township Comm. of Bridgewater, 794
Life of the Land v. City Council, 283
Lincoln v. Commonwealth, 860
Lindsay v. City of San Diego, 549
Lindsey v. Normet, 400, 660, 1043
Linggi v. Garovotti, 821
Lionshead Lake, Inc. v. Wayne Township, 377
L. M. Pike & Son, Inc. v. Town of Waterford, 355
Loan Assn. v. City of Topeka, 971
Lockhard v. City of Los Angeles, 277
London County Council v. Allen, 684
Long Beach City High School Dist. v. Stewart, 851
Long v. City of Charlotte, 834
Loretto v. Teleprompter Manhattan CATV (U.S. 1982), 109, 887
Loretto v. Teleprompter Manhattan CATV (N.Y. 1983), 841
Los Altos, City of v. Silvey, 244
Los Angeles, City of v. Gage, 290
Los Angeles Memorial Coliseum Commn. v. NFL, 815
Louisville v. Munro, 117
Lukrawka v. Spring Valley Water Co., 669
Lutheran Church in Am. v. City of New York, 527
Lynbrook, Village of v. Cadoo, 601

McCarthy v. City of Manhattan Beach, 205
McCaw v. Harrison, 117
McCombe v. Read, 120
MacDonald v. Board of Commrs., 319
MacDonald, Sommer & Frates v. Yolo County, 912
McKain v. Koch, 1043
McLay v. Maryland Assemblies, Inc., 298
McMinn v. Town of Oyster Bay, 255
Magnolia Dev. Co. v. Coles, 602
M.A. Kravitz Co., In re Appeal of, 412
Mansfield & Swett, Inc. v. Town of West Orange, 600
Margolis v. District Court, 1084

Marinelli v. Board of Appeal, 355
Marks v. City of Roseburg, 491
Marshfield Family Skateland v. Town of Marshfield, 490
Martino v. Santa Clara Valley Water Dist., 903
Martin v. Reynolds Metal Co., 112
Mary Chess, Inc. v. City of Glen Cove, 301
Mason City Center Assocs. v. City of Mason City, 511
Massachusetts Hous. Fin. Agency v. New England Merchants Natl. Bank, 1019
Matthews v. Greene County Bd. of Appeals, 592
Mayers v. Ridley, 474
Mayor of Baltimore v. Baltimore Football Club, 815
Meadowland Regional Dev. Agency v. Hackensack Meadowlands Dev. Commn., 591
Medinger Appeal, 385
Members of the City Council of Los Angeles v. Taxpayers for Vincent, 548
Merced Irrigation Dist. v. Woolstenhulme, 853
Messenger v. Pennsylvania R.R., 664
Metromedia, Inc. v. City of San Diego, 502, 547
Metropolitan Hous. Dev. Corp. v. Village of Arlington Heights (7th Cir. 1977), 456
Metropolitan Hous. Dev. Corp. v. Village of Arlington Heights (7th Cir. 1980), 1035
Miami Beach, City of v. Arthree, 241
Miami Beach, City of v. Ocean & Inland Co., 518
Miami Beach, City of v. Schauer, 340
Middlesex & Boston St. Ry. v. Aldermen of Newton, 433
Miller v. City of Beaver Falls, 695
Miller v. City of Port Angeles, 634
Miller v. Covington Dev. Auth., 985
Miller v. Schoene, 884
Miller v. Upper Allen Township Zoning Hearing Bd., 560
Milliken v. Bradley, 1030
Missouri Pacific Ry. v. Nebraska, 834
Mitchell Land Co. v. Planning & Zoning Bd. of Appeals, 290, 356
Moerder v. City of Moscow, Idaho, 233
Monell v. Department of Social Servs., 467
Moore v. City of East Cleveland, 254
Morris v. City of Los Angeles, 225
Mount Laurel Township v. Barbieri, 616
Mugler v. Kansas, 880
Munoz-Mendoza v. Pierce, 76, 956

Table of Cases

Naegele Outdoor Advertising Co. v. Minnetonka, 531
National Advertising Co. v. County of Monterey, 297
National Land Inv. Co. v. Kohn, 392
Nectow v. City of Cambridge (Mass. 1927), 194
Nectow v. City of Cambridge (U.S. 1928), *190*, 359
Neighborhood Bd. No. 24 v. State Land Use Commn., 754
New Jersey Shore Builders' Assn. v. Township of Ocean, 591
Newport, City of v. Fact Concerts, Inc., 469
New State Ice Co. v. Liebmann, 927
New York City Hous. Auth. v. Muller, 867
Nickols v. Pierce, 946
Nollan v. California Coastal Comm., 206, 269, 433, *636*, 742, *756*, 922
Norbeck Village Joint Venture v. Montgomery Council, 590
Nordin v. May, 683
Norfolk Redev. & Hous. Auth. v. Chesapeake & Potomac Tel., 866
North Carolina Human Relations Council v. Weaver Realty Co., 461
Northend Cinema v. City of Seattle, 482
Norwalk CORE v. Norwalk Redev. Agency, 786
Norway Plains Co. v. Boston & Maine R.R., 130
Norwood Heights Improvement Assn. v. Mayor & City Council of Baltimore, 226

Oakland, City of v. Oakland Raiders (Cal. 1982), *809*
Oakland, City of v. Oakland Raiders (Cal. Ct. App. 1985), 813
Oakwood at Madison, Inc. v. Township of Madison (N.J. Law Div. 1971), *386*, 397
Oakwood at Madison, Inc. v. Township of Madison (N.J. Law Div. 1974), 397
Oakwood at Madison, Inc. v. Township of Madison (N.J. 1977), 410, *414*
O'Connor v. City of Moscow, 302
Okemo Trailside Condominiums v. Blais, 582
Oklahoma City, City of v. Tuttle, 467
1000 Friends of Oregon v. Wasco County Court, 755
Opinion of the Justices (Mass. 1912), 797
Opinion of the Justices (Mass. 1953), 830
Opinion of the Justices, In re, 797
Otero v. New York City Hous. Auth., 1034, 1042

Pacesetter Homes v. Village of Olympia Fields, 281

Parker v. Brown, 505
Parkview Assocs. v. City of New York, 309
Parratt v. Taylor, 467
Parsons v. Board of Zoning Appeals of New Haven, 354
Pasadena City Bd. of Educ. v. Spangler, 659
Pascack Assn., Ltd. v. Township of Washington (N.J. Law Div. 1974), 400
Pascack Assn., Ltd. v. Township of Washington (N.J. 1977), 417
Patterson v. Peabody Coal Co., 104
Peirce Appeal, 298
Pendoley v. Ferreira, 149
Penn Central Transp. Co. v. New York City (N.Y. 1977), 544
Penn Central Transp. Co. v. New York City (U.S. 1978), 518, *537*, 549, 742, 880
Pennell v. City of San Jose, 923
Pennsylvania Coal Co. v. Mahon, 742, 879, 880, 883–884, 888, 923
Pennsylvania v. Lynn, 1, 1008
Penn Township v. Yecko Bros., 175
Pensack v. City & County of Denver, 484
People ex rel. Gutknecht v. City of Chicago, 795
People ex rel. St. Albans-Springfield Corp. v. Connell, 197
People v. Binzley, 244
People v. Goodman, 537
People v. Kasold, 244
People v. Miller, 302
People v. Morone, 491
People v. Stover, 534
Perry v. Planning Bd. of Nantucket, 604
Petterson v. Radspi Realty & Coal Corp., 693
Phillips v. Naff, 471
Pierro v. Baxendale, 241
Piz v. Housing Auth. of Denver, 855
Plumb v. Board of Zoning Appeals of New Haven, 356
Poletown Neighborhood Council v. City of Detroit, 798, 928, 986
Pollack v. Farmers' Loan & Trust Co., 972
Porter v. United States, 852
Powell v. Taylor, 113
Prah v. Maretti, 130
Preble, Town of v. Song Mountain, Inc., 143
Premium Point Park Assn. v. Polar Bar, 242
Priestley v. State, 864
Pruneyard Shopping Center v. Robins, 886
Public Water Supply Dist. No. 2. v. Alex Bascom County, 861
Pure Oil Div. v. Brook Park, 400

1136 Table of Cases

Queenside Hills Realty Co. v. Saxl, 308
Quilici v. Village of Morton Grove, 244
Quincy, City of v. Metropolitan Dist. Commn., 762, 773
Quintini v. Bay St. Louis, 533

Railway Express Agency v. New York, 518
Raising a Covert to the Nuisance, 95
Rand v. City of Boston, 860
Rand v. City of New York, 693
Raskiewicz v. Town of New Boston, 498
Reid v. Architectural Bd. of Review, 535
Reid Dev. Corp. v. Parsippany-Troy Hills Township, 667
Renard v. Dade County, 327
Renton, City of v. Playtime Theatres, 482
Respublica v. Philip Urbin Duquet, 166
Revere v. Riceman, 149
Rex v. White and Ward, 139
Rhue v. Cheyenne Homes, Inc., 537
Rice v. Sioux City Memorial Park Cemetery, 472
Richards's Appeal, 125
Riley v. District of Columbia Redev. Land Agency (D.C. Cir. 1956), 837
Riley v. District of Columbia Redev. Land Agency (D.C. Cir. 1957), *834*
River Vale, Town of v. Town of Orangetown, 560
Roberts v. City of Woonsocket, 1055
Roberts v. Curtis, 471
Robinson Brick Co. v. Luthi, 307
Robinson v. City of Boulder, 582, 670
Robinson v. Indianola Mun. Separate School Dist., 148
Rockhill v. Chesterfield Township, 206
Rodrigue v. Copeland, 109
Roer Constr. Corp. v. City of New Rochelle, 693
Roman Catholic Archbishop of Detroit v. Village of Orchard Lake, 504
Ronda Realty Corp. v. Lawton, 229
Rose v. Chaikin, 136, 278
Rose v. Socony-Vacuum Corp. (R.I. 1934), *95*
Rose v. Socony-Vacuum Corp. (R.I. 1936), 101
Roselle v. Wright, 232
Ruckelshaus v. Monsanto Co., 888
Russell Transp. Ltd. v. Ontario Malleable Iron Co., 113
Rylands v. Fletcher, 126

Sabo v. Monroe Township, 337
St. Louis County v. Pfitzner, 302
Salvatore v. Trace, 613

San Antonio Indep. School Dist. v. Rodriguez, 655, 660
Sanborn v. Wagner, 473
San Diego Gas & Elec. Co. v. City of San Diego, 903
San Francisco, City and County of v. Safeway Stores, 330
Sasso v. Housing Auth. of Providence, 861
Sauer v. City of New York, 834
Save a Valuable Envt. v. City of Bothell, 411
Sawyer v. Davis, 149
Scenic Hudson Preservation Conference v. FPC (2d Cir. 1965), 150, *520*
Scenic Hudson Preservation Conference v. FPC (2d Cir. 1971), *522*
Schad v. Borough of Mount Ephraim, 241, *484*
Schneider v. District of Columbia, 794
Scott v. City of Sioux City, 507
Scott v. Greenville County, 462
Sears, Roebuck & Co. v. Power, 244
Seattle, City of v. Mall, Inc., 807
Seattle, In re City of, 807
Secretary of the Interior v. California, 758
Senefsky v. Lawler, 383
Shannon v. Building Inspector of Woburn, 277
Shannon v. HUD, 1040
Sharon Steel Corp. v. City of Fairmont, 159
Sheffield Masonic Hall Co. v. Sheffield Corp., 234
Shelley v. Kraemer, 375, 470
Sher v. Herbert, 136
Sibson v. State, 833
Sierra Club v. Lynn, 939
Sioux Falls v. Cleveland, 244
Sipperly v. Board of Appeals on Zoning, 356
Site for School Indus. Arts, In re, 845
Slater v. Pacific Am. Oil Co., 104
Smith v. Staso Milling Co., 124
Smith v. Wade, 468
Snyder v. City of Lakewood, 336
Soap Corp. of Am. v. Reynolds, 144
Society for Ethical Culture v. Spatt, 531
Somers, Town of v. Comarco, 303
South Carolina v. Baker, 973, 986
Southern Burlington County NAACP v. Township of Mount Laurel (N.J. Law Div. 1974), *398*
Southern Burlington County NAACP v. Township of Mount Laurel [Mount Laurel I] (N.J. 1975), 376, *402*
Southern Burlington County NAACP v. Township of Mount Laurel (N.J. Law Div. 1978), 418

Table of Cases

Southern Burlington County NAACP v. Township of Mount Laurel [Mount Laurel II] (N.J. 1983), *420*
Spiritual Psychic Science Church of Truth v. City of Azusa, 491
Spur Feeding Co. v. Superior Court of Maricopa County, 129
Spur Industries, Inc. v. Del E. Webb Dev. Co., 128
Stanley Works v. Commissioner, 725
State v. Baker, 253
State v. Cameron, 504
State v. City of Miami, 979
State v. City of Rochester, 337
State v. Clay County Dev. Auth., 975
State v. Core Banks Club Properties, 834
State v. Diamond Motors, Inc., 532
State ex rel. Anshe Chesed Congregation v. Bruggemeier, 504
State ex rel. Dept. of Transp. v. Gee, 855
State ex rel. Lieux v. Village of Westlake, 189
State ex rel. Morehouse v. Hunt, 300
State ex rel. Twin City Bldg. & Inv. Co. v. Houghton, 305
State ex rel. Webster v. Nebraska Tel. Co., 666
State Highway Commn. v. Peters, 864
State v. Housing Fin. Auth., 977
State v. Johnson, 719
State v. Jones, 549
State v. Miami Beach Redev. Agency, 981
State v. Silver, 861
State v. Stark, 145
State v. Zack, 278
Staton v. Norfolk & Carolina Ry., 833
Steel Hill Dev., Inc. v. Town of Sanbornton (1st Cir. 1972), 390, 591
Steel Hill Dev., Inc. v. Town of Sanbornton (D.N.H. 1974), 391
Stevens v. Rockport Granite Co., 118
Stewart v. Humphries, 243
Stone v. City of Maitland, 531
Strachan v. Beacon Oil Co., 161
Suffolk Hous. Servs. v. Town of Brookhaven, 439
Sullivan v. Jones & Laughlin Steel Co. (Pa. 1904), 126
Sullivan v. Jones & Laughlin Steel Co. (Pa. 1908), 126
Sundeen v. Rogers, 532
Surrick v. Zoning Hearing Bd. of Upper Providence Township, 411

Temmink v. Board of Zoning Appeals of Baltimore County, 330
Tenn v. 889 Assocs., 135
Thomas v. Union Carbide Agric. Prods., 841

Thompson v. Kimball, 144
Tortorella v. H. Traiser & Co., 161
Town of _____. *See* name of town
Trafficante v. Metropolitan Life Ins. Co., 473
Tranfaglia v. Building Commr. of Winchester, 355
Trespass on the Case in Regard to Certain Mills, 91, 661
222 East Chestnut St. Corp. v. Board of Appeals of Chicago, 355

Udell v. Haas, 561
Underhill v. Board of Appeals of Oyster Bay, 353
United Advertising Corp. v. Raritan, 304
United Bldg. & Constr. Trades Council v. Mayor & Council of Camden, 557
United States v. Brinks, 855
United States v. Carmack, 782, 847
United States v. City of Birmingham, 460
United States v. City of Black Jack, 460
United States v. City of Parma (N.D. Ohio 1980), 457
United States v. City of Parma (6th Cir. 1981), 457, 951
United States v. Cors, 847
United States ex rel. TVA v. Welch, 796
United States v. 50 Acres of Land, 847
United States v. Fuller, 846
United States v. Gettysburg Ry., 782
United States v. Hunter, 473
United States v. Maryland Bank & Trust Co., 159
United States v. Metropolitan Dist. Commn., 774
United States v. Mirabile, 160
United States v. Riverside Bayview Homes, Inc., 721
United States v. Starrett City Assocs., 1041
United States v. Twin City Power, 794, 848
United States v. Wade, 159
United States v. Westinghouse Elec. & Mfg., 863
United States v. Willow River Power, 849
United States v. Wunderlich, 794
United States v. Yonkers Bd. of Educ., 460
United Steel Workers v. United States Steel, 807
Unity Ventures v. County of Lake (N.D. Ill. 1984), 515
Unity Ventures v. County of Lake (N.D. Ill. 1986), 516
Utah Road Commn. v. Hopkins, 851

Table of Cases

Van Deusen v. Ruth, 685
Vangellow v. City of Rochester, 694
Van Sant v. Rose, 684
Ventures in Property I v. City of Wichita, 695
Vernon Park Realty, Inc. v. City of Mount Vernon, 201
Vickers v. Township Comm. of Gloucester Township, 383
Villbig v. Housing Auth. of Dallas, 829
Village of ——————. *See* name of village

Walling v. City of Fremont, 113
Walters v. McElroy, 125
Ward v. Scott, 349
Warren, Town of v. Hazardous Waste Facility Site Safety Council, 156
Warth v. Seldin, 281, 391, *446*, 644
Washington v. Davis, 660
Water Front in City of New York, In re, 855
Weiss v. Leaon, 471
Welch v. Clairborne County Beer Bd., 498
Welch v. Swasey, 164
Wells v. Pierpont, 327
Welton v. Hamilton, 353
Weltshe v. Graf, 149
Wescott v. Middleton, 116
Westborough Mall v. City of Cape Girardeau, 513
Westchester Reform Temple v. Brown, 502
West Side Women's Servs., Inc. v. City of Cleveland, 492
Westwood Forest Estates v. Village of South Nyack, 577
Weyls v. Zoning Bd. of Appeals, 301

Whalen v. Union Bag & Paper Co., 124
Wheeler v. City of Pleasant Grove, 921
White and Snoak and His Wife v. Porter, 663
White Plains, City of v. Ferrailoli, 253
White v. Massachusetts Council of Constr. Employers, Inc., 557
Whycer v. Urry, 113
Williamson County Regional Planning Commn. v. Hamilton Bank, 469, 779, 913
Wilson v. County of McHenry, 1055
Wilsonville, Village of v. SCA Servs., 153
Windsor Hills Improvement Assn. v. Mayor & City Council of Baltimore, 229
Woodbury v. Zoning Bd. of Review of Warwick, 353
Wood v. Conway Corp., 126
Woodward v. Bowers, 474

Yeager v. Traylor, 117
Yick Wo v. Hopkins, 167
Yonkers, City of v. Otis Elevator Co., 806
Young v. American Mini Theatres, Inc., 478, 518
Young v. Pierce (E.D. Tex. 1985), *1037*
Young v. Pierce (E.D. Tex. 1986), 1042
Young v. Pierce (5th Cir. 1987), 1042
Youngstown, City of v. Kahn Bros. Bldg. Co., 533
Young v. Whiteman, 1042
Young Women's Hebrew Assn. v. Board of Standards & Appeals of the City of New York, In the Matter of, 354

Zahn v. Board of Pub. Works, 194

Index

Abortion Clinics, 491-492
Adult Uses
  erotic bakery, 484
  liquor licensees, 492-497
  live entertainment, 484-492
  nuisances, 145-146
  "swinging," 491
  theaters, 479-484
Aesthetic Regulations, 518-555
  amenity (U.K.), 551
  architectural controls, 535-537
  definitions, 532-533
  historic preservation, 527-531, 533-534, 537-547
  natural beauty, 520-525
  signs and billboards, 518, 531-532, 534, 547-549
Agricultural Lands, 63, 128-129, 390-391, 725-726, 844, 855
Airports, 104-109, 828
Air Rights, 104-109, 269-276, 537-547
Alternative Dispute Resolution (ADR), 152-158, 762-775
Amendments, 313-343
  change-mistake rule, 321-328
  computer study of cases, 317-319
  criteria for deciding upon, 1099-1105
  procedure for securing, 314-316, 329, 332, 336, 1109, 1123-1124
  quasi-judicial (*Fasano* rule), 330-340, 1079, 1083
  referendum and initiative, 309, 593-596, 1078-1084
  spot zoning, 315, 322, 328-329, 558
Amortization. *See* Nonconforming Uses
Anticompetitive Regulations, 504-518
  home rule, 512-513
  Local Government Antitrust Act of 1984, 515-516
  rent control, 516-518
  Sherman Act, 509-514
  state legislative authorization, 514
Antitrust. *See* Anticompetitive Regulations
Architecture. *See* Aesthetic Regulations
Assemblage, 821-823, 936, 1091-1108
Atlanta, 1091-1108
Attorney's Fees, 497-498

Bassett, The Master Plan, 1047-1049
Beuscher, Some Tentative Notes on the Integration of Police Power and the Eminent Domain by the Courts, 892
Blackstone, Commentaries, 780, 831
Bosselman, Callies, and Banta, The Taking Issue, 899
Boston, 76-79, 303, 761-775

1139

1140 Index

Boston Harbor, 761-775
Bracton, *De Adquirendo Rerum Dominio*, 660-661
Building Laws (Pre-Euclidean), 166-168, 183
Building Permits, 175, 301, 308-311, 463-464

Calabresi, Some Thoughts on Risk Distribution and the Law of Torts, 899-900
Caro, The Power Broker, 824-826
Chicago, 51-53, 1025-1035
Chief Joseph, 781
Civil Rights Act of 1964, 659
Civil Rights Act of 1968, 456-462, 473, 475-476
Clean Water Acts, 151
Coastal Regulations, 433, 635-644, 756-761
Coastal Zone Management Act, 642-644, 756-761
Community Development Block Grants (CDBG), 926, 942-952
 citizen participation, 946-947, 950
 economic development, 945-946
 gentrification, 950-951
 selection criteria, 951-952
Comprehensive Environmental Response, Compensation and Liability Act (CERCLA or Superfund), 159-160
Comprehensive Planning, 49, 51-63, 557-567, 729-732, 1047-1056. *See also* Master Plan, Zoning
Contract and Conditional Zoning, 283-289, 329
Conveyancing, 17, 20-21
Corruption and Conflicts of Interest, 326-327, 338-343, 517-518
Costonis, "Fair" Compensation and the Accommodation Power, 898-899
Costonis, Presumptive and Per Se Takings, 894

Daylighting, 234-236, 519
Deregulation and Reregulation, 363-367, 960-961
Descartes, Discourse of the Method of Rightly Conducting the Reason, 63-64
Development Agreements, 617-621
Development Orders (U.K.), 217-220
Downtown Development, 57, 266-268, 507-512
Drinan, Untying the White Noose, 475-476

Due Process Clause, 181-185, 202-203, 254-255, 462-466, 538, 587-588, 693, 805, 908, 1081-1082

Economic Analysis
 alternatives to planning and zoning, 64, 137-139, 363-367
 neighborhood zoning rights, 367-368
 nuisance remedies, 127-130
 regulatory takings, 899-900
Economic Development. *See also* CDBG, EZ, UDC
 eminent domain for, 798-808
 industrial development bonds (IDB), 967-968, 971-977, 979-981, 986
 tax incentives, 956-967
 tax increment financing (TIF), 968, 981-986
Ellickson, Alternatives to Zoning, 137-139
Eminent Domain. *See also* Due Process Clause, Land Banks, Regulatory Takings
 history, 778-784, 831-834
 just compensation
  benefit resulting from taking, 855-860
  betterment and (U.K.), 869-875
  condemnation, effect of announcing, 852-854
  fact-finding bodies, 840-842
  fair market value, 834-840
  goodwill, 863-865
  governmental activity, effect of, 845-849
  implicit-in-kind compensation, 868-869
  leaseholds, 854-855
  relocation, 864-867
  severance damages, 860-861, 863
  TDR and, 544-545, 779
  valuation formulas, 840-845
  zoning, effect of, 850-851
 Mill Act Cases, 783-784
 nonconforming uses, elimination of, 305-308
 private acquisition, contrasted with, 821-823
 private property, 810-811, 849-850
 public use, 788-822
  economic development, 798-808, 816
  judicial scrutiny of, 790-798, 800-801, 807-808, 818-821
  legislation defining, 810-811
  parks, 824-826
  police power, relationship to, 790-793, 818
  private benefit and, 792, 800-803, 819

Index 1141

promoting homeownership, 816-821
public purpose and, 801
sports franchise, operation of, 811-816
urban renewal, 783-798
quick-take procedures, 803, 808-809, 847
taxation and, 801, 867-868, 986
temporary takings, 863-864, 908-909, 917-919
Enterprise Zones (EZ)
    federal program, 958-962
    history, 962-964
    Maryland, 992-1005
    state programs, 963-964, 992-1005
Environmental Controls. *See also* EIS, NEPA
    air pollution, 146-148
    coastal protection, 646-644, 756-761
    critical areas, 750-751
    flood plains, 702-709, 913-914
    hazardous waste, 154-160
    mining, 736-743
    negotiation and mediation, 154-158
    nuclear waste, 158-159
    nuisance remedies and, 154
    preemption, 152-154
    toxic substances, 153-154
    water pollution, 33, 151, 721-722, 761-775
    wetlands, 709-722
Environmental Impact Statements (EIS), 525-527, 727-736, 986-989
Epstein, Takings, 868-869, 900-901
Equalization of Municipal Services, 647-673
    federal constitutional and statutory law, 647-660
    state common law, 661-673
Equal Protection Clause, 249-250, 252, 452-455, 462-466, 651-666, 1085-1088
Exactions. *See* Subdivisions
Exclusionary Zoning, 372-470
    burden of proof, 404-405, 453-456
    California developments, 411, 593-595
    Civil Rights Act of 1968 (Fair Housing Act), 456-462, 473, 475-476
    environmental rationale for, 390, 405-406
    Fair Housing Amendments Act of 1988, 462
    fair share, 407, 414-415, 418-419, 422-425, 435-438
    federal developments, 445-470
    fourteenth amendment violations, 450-456, 460-461
    legislation, 392-397, 440-445
    Massachusetts developments, 392-393
    minimum floor area, 377-385, 415-417
    minimum lot size, 384-392
    mobile homes, 383-384, 428
    New Jersey developments, 376-445
    New York developments, 394-395, 410-411, 438-439, 577-579
    Pennsylvania developments, 392, 411-412
    remedies, 398-401, 408-409, 423-424, 426-430, 443, 458-461, 466-470
    Section 1983, 462-470
Expert Witnesses, 244-248

Fair Housing Act of 1968, 456-462, 473, 475-476
Farmland Preservation, 725-726
Federal Clean Air Act, 147-148
Federal Land and Policy Management Act of 1976, 36-39
Feudal Tenures, 15-17
First Amendment. *See* Free Expression, Religious Uses
Floating Zones, 211-216, 280-281
Floor Area Ratio (FAR), 233-234, 257-259
Free Expression, Regulation of, 145-146, 478-492, 534-535, 547-549
Freund, The Police Power, Public Policy and Constitutional Rights, 891
Frontier, Development of, 12-17, 20-25, 28-29, 31-32
Frug, The City as a Legal Concept, 175-177
Fuller, Freedom — A Suggested Analysis, 699-700, 1063-1065
Funkhouser and Saquella, Establishing Enterprise Zones in Maryland, 994-995, 998

Gentrification, 76-79, 866-867, 950-951, 986-992
Goodman and Kaufman, City Planning in the Sixties, 48, 51
Griffin, The Politics and Litigation of Boston Harbor, 762-773
Group Homes, 248-255, 1085-1089
Growth Controls, 59-61, 567-596, 1083-1084

Haar and Fessler, The Wrong Side of the Tracks, 661-663, 669
Haar and Lindsay, Business and the Revolution in Land-Use Planning, 1092-1094, 1106-1107
Haar, Horowitz, and Katz, Transfer of Development Rights, 273-276
Haar, Sawyer, and Cummings, Computer Power and Legal Reasoning, 317-319

Index

Hagman and Misczynski, Windfalls for Wipeouts, 896-897
Hendricks and Alexander, Subculture Cells, 1089-1090
Historic Preservation, Landmarks, 527-547
Holgate, What is a "Rival Market"?, 94-95
Holznagel, Negotiation and Mediation, 154-156
Horwitz, The Transformation of American Law, 831-832
Housing Codes, 385-386
Housing Programs
  history, 1007-1009
  Housing Development Grants (HoDAG), 1016
  mortgage financing, 977-979, 1010-1013, 1019-1025
  Nehemiah program, 1019
  racial balance, 1037-1043
  Section 8, 1013-1014
  site selection, 450-456, 1025-1036
  tax incentives, 1017-1019
  tenant purchase, 1016-1017
  vouchers, 1014-1016
Houston, 363-365

Immunity, Governmental, 465-466, 467-469, 505-506, 509-516
Incentive Zoning, 256-269
Inclusionary Zoning, 426-428, 431-435
Institutional Litigation, 429-430, 761-775
Interstate Land Sales Full Disclosure Act (ILSFA), 697-698
Inverse Condemnation, 104-109, 904-907. *See also* Eminent Domain, Regulatory Takings

Jacobs, The Death and Life of Great American Cities, 787
Just Compensation. *See* Eminent Domain, Regulatory Takings

Kayden, Incentive Zoning in New York City, 260-265
Keller, The Planning of Communities, 1065, 1068-1069
Kmiec, The Role of the Planner in a Deregulated World, 365-367

Laitos and Westfall, Government Interference with Private Interests in Public Resources, 742-743
Land Banks and Excess Condemnation, 826-831
Linkage, 266-269, 433-434, 644-645

Local Government Antitrust Act of 1984, 515-516. *See also* Anticompetitive Regulations
Lock, Planning: The Future, 1070
Los Angeles, 45, 659-660

Master Plan, 564-566, 1045-1057, 1108-1126. *See also* Comprehensive Planning
Mazziotti, The Underlying Assumptions of Advocacy Planning, 74-76
Meier, Planning for Tomorrow's World, 567
Metropolitan Governance, 3, 5-6, 12
Michelman, Property, Utility, and Fairness, 877-879, 894-895
Mitchell, The Historical Context for Housing Policy, 1007-1009
Mixed-Use Development, 283-284
Mobile Homes, 383-384, 428
Model Cities, 926, 930-933
Model Land Development Code
  Article 4, 298-299
  Section 3-101, 58
  Section 3-102, 58
  Section 3-105, 1050-1051
  Section 5-201, 936, 938
  Section 5-202, 938
  Section 5-204, 938
  Section 7-305, 396
Montgomery County, Md., 59-61
Mosley, Disney's World, 822-823
Moynihan, Urban Conditions, 71-72
Mumford, The Social Foundations of Post-War Building, 67-71
Municipal Services, 571-573, 579-582, 588-589, 647-673, 1083

National Environmental Policy Act of 1969 (NEPA), 33-36, 525-527, 727-729
Neighborhoods
  assemblage, 1091-1092, 1094-1108
  covenants, 470-474, 673-687
  private restrictions, 1075-1078
  zoning decisions by neighbors, 1071-1075, 1081
Nelson, A Property Right Theory of Zoning, 367-368
New Communities, 933-942
New Jersey Fair Housing Act, 440-445
New Towns, 81, 937, 941-942
New York City, 53-56, 256-266, 269-273, 309-311, 374-375, 537-547, 657-659
NIMBY (Not in My Backyard), 1085-1089
Nodes of Development, 1092-1094

Index

Nonconforming Uses, 290-308
  alteration, 298, 300-302
  amortization, 290-297, 299, 304-305
  change of ownership, 302
  eminent domain for elimination of, 305-308
  nuisance, 307
Nuisance. *See also* Environmental Controls
  private nuisance, 91-139
    air pollution, 120-124
    animals, 117-118
    cemeteries, 116-117
    coming to the nuisance, 113, 119
    competing economic interests, 95-101
    definitions, 103-104
    equity jurisprudence and, 124-126
    funeral homes, 113-116
    halfway houses, 117
    interference with sunlight, 130-136
    inverse condemnation through, 104-109
    odors, 117
    overgrowth, 120
    per se, 116
    remedies for, 120-130
    residential neighborhoods and, 118-119
    Restatement of Torts, Second, 103, 133-134
    rival markets, 91-95
    satellite dish, 137
    trespass and, 101-102
    vicinage and, 109-112
    windmill, 136
  public nuisance, 139-151
    air pollution as, 146-148
    definitions, 142-143
    estoppel, 151
    hazardous waste, 15
    licensing, 149
    obstruction of traffic as, 148-149
    piggery as, 149
    police power and, 141-143
    pornography as, 145-146
    remedies for, 143-144
    rock concert as, 143
    standing, 149-150
    zoning and, 149, 184, 307

Official Map, 687-695, 1049
Open Space, 519, 887, 904

Parking. *See* Streets
Parks
  eminent domain, 824-826
  exactions, 632-635
  official map, 695
  unequal provision, 657-659

Parochialism, 555-596
Peattie, Reflections on Advocacy Planning, 73
Performance Zoning, 276-279
Philadelphia, 166-168
Planned Unit Development (PUD), 279-283, 450-452
Planners
  advocates, as, 73-76
  attorneys and, 85-87
  background, 47, 1065, 1068, 1070
  constitutional violations, and, 910, 920, 922
  expert witnesses, 244-248
Planning Commissions, 45-48, 1109-1111
Planning. *See also* Comprehensive Planning, Master Plan, Zoning
  advocacy planning, 73-76
  agencies, 45-50
  computer simulation, 83-85
  criticisms of, 363-368, 1058-1059, 1063-1065, 1068-1069
  enabling legislation, 1046
  neighborhood planning, 56, 76-81
  permission, 217-220, 311-312
  policy planning, 1056-1057
  post-war, 67-71
  process of, 1058-1063, 1066-1067, 1070, 1089-1090
  urban design, 63-68
  zoning and, 210-211, 560-567, 1048-1049, 1052-1056, 1121-1123
Polanyi, The Logic of Liberty, 1058-1059
Police Power. *See* Due Process, Eminent Domain, Nuisance, Regulatory Takings
President's Commission for a National Agenda for the Eighties, 4-5
President's Commission on Housing (1982), Report of, 368-370
Private Restrictions
  architectural controls, 536-537
  covenants, 470-474, 673-687
  defeasible fees, 675-676
  easements, 683-684, 722-726
  enforcement and administration, 684-687, 1077-1078
  homeowners' associations, 1077-1078
  racial restrictions, 470-474
  zoning and, 1075-1077
Public Lands
  disposition, 21-25, 28-29, 31-32
  management, 36-39

Race. *See* Exclusionary Zoning, Housing Programs, Private Restrictions
Referendum and Initiative, 309, 593-596, 1078-1084

1144 Index

Regulatory Takings. *See also* Eminent Domain, Inverse Condemnation
  calculating damages for, 921-922
  compensation for, 894-900, 907-911, 916-17
  distinguish regulation from taking, attempts to, 875-894
  environmental controls and, 711-722, 736-743
  escheat provision as, 922-923
  exactions, 636-645
  investment-backed expectations, 539, 545, 889
  landmark designation, 527-531, 538-544
  official map, 687-695
  ripeness, 469-470, 912-913, 916-917
  state courts on, 198-199, 201-203, 910-911
  "too-far" test, 199-200, 880, 883-884, 891, 900-903, 905-906, 919-920
  United States Supreme Court on, 538-545, 636-644, 736-742, 879-888, 902-910, 912-923
  zoning as, 195-205, 269-273
Religious Uses, Regulation of, 112, 492-504
Rent Control, 516-517, 923
Resource Conservation and Recovery Act (RCRA), 159
Rezoning. *See* Amendments
Rider, Transition from Land Use to Policy Planning, 1056-1057
Rohe and Gates, Planning with Neighborhoods, 80
Rose, *Mahon* Reconstructed, 901-902
Rose, Planning and Dealing, 337-340

Salt Lake County, Utah, 62-63
San Francisco, 266-268
Sax, Takings and the Police Power, 892-894
Sax, Takings, Private Property and Public Rights, 895-896
Schlesinger, Soviet Legal Theory, 780-781
Schools
  desegregation, 429-430, 460-461, 1030-1032
  nuisance, 148-149
  religious, 504
Section 1983, 462-470, 497-498, 647-648, 654, 908
Sewage
  Boston Harbor, 762-773
  duty to extend services, 648-650, 654-655
  exclusionary zoning, 405-406
  growth controls, 580-581, 588

Shopping Centers, 237, 314, 329-330, 507-512
Siegan, Non-Zoning in Houston, 363-365
Signs. *See* Aesthetic Regulations
Solar Energy, 130-136
Special Exceptions, Use Permits, 206-211, 343, 356-362, 1071-1075, 1085-1088
Spot Zoning, 315, 322, 328-329, 558. *See also* Amendments
Standard City Planning Enabling Act, 564, 603, 608
Standing, 356, 391-392, 446-449, 559-560, 586-587
State Land-Use Planning, 48-50, 743-756
  critical area, 750-751
  development of regional impact, 749, 751
  judicial interpretation, 754-755
Statistics
  age, 11, 34
  capital formation, 35
  employment, 17-18
  income, 10, 18
  land area, 2, 27
  local governments, 7
  mobility, 9
  population, 2, 8, 10-11, 13-14, 16, 19, 27
  poverty, 11
  race, 16, 19-20
  real estate value, 2
  retail markets, 18
  rural areas, 2-3, 8
  transportation, 30
  urban land uses, 26-27
Stoebuck, Police Power, Takings, and Due Process, 891-892
Story, Commentaries on the Constitution of the United States, 15-17, 20-21
Streets and Highways
  building on land designated for street, 687-695
  dedication of land for, 621-635
  eminent domain, 829, 851-852, 862, 864, 859
  environmental impact, 147-148, 732-736
  master plan, 53-56, 61-62
  parking, 148-149, 201-203, 732-735, 821
  suburban nodes and, 1106-1107
  unequal provision, 648-649, 654
Subdivisions, 600-657, 671-687, 696-700
  abuses, 696-699
  antiquated, 696
  approval process, 605-610
  buyouts, 1094-1108
  definitions, 603-604
  development agreements, 617-621

Index

exactions
   beach access, 635-644
   impact fees, 629-635
   in lieu payments, 632-633
   legislative provisions, 614-616
   schools and recreation, dedications for, 632-633, 635
   streets, dedications for, 623-628
   validity, 621-645
     improper, 612-614
     legislative provisions, 603-621
     premature, 645-647
     private controls, 470-474, 673-687
     purposes of regulation, 610-611
Suburban Growth, 3, 8, 567-570, 599-601, 1091-1094
Surface Mining and Reclamation Act of 1977 (SMCRA), 742-743

Takings Clause. *See* Eminent Domain, Just Compensation, Regulatory Takings
Taxation
   economic development incentives, 958-986
   eminent domain and, 801, 867-868, 986
   housing incentives, 1017-1019
Town and Country Planning Acts (U.K.), 81, 217-220, 311-312, 551, 872-874
Transferable Development Rights (TDR), 269-276
   operation, 273-276, 542-544
   validity, 271-273
Transportation, 30, 83-84, 777-778. *See also* Streets

Urban Design, 63-67, 518-555. *See also* Aesthetic Regulations
Urban Development Action Grants (UDAG), 76-79, 952-958
Urban Development Corporation (UDC), 394-395, 969, 986-990
Urbanization, 1, 8, 12
Urban Policies, 4-12, 925-964
Urban Renewal, 509-512, 783-798, 926, 1040-1041

Variances, 343-357
   area and use variances, 349-351
   criteria for granting, 344, 347, 354-357
   decision-maker, 215-216, 353, 359-362
   delegation of power, 353
   proliferation, 351-352
Vested Rights, 175, 302-303, 308-311, 463-464
Video Games, 490-491

Washington, D.C., frontispiece, 27, 39-44, 164, 657, 694, 788-794, 1127
Water Pollution Control Act of 1972, 151
Water Quality Act of 1965, 151
Wiles, The Use of Expert Witnesses in Litigation, 246-248
Williams, The Law on Variances, 343-344
Williams, Smith, Siemon, Mandelker, and Babcock, White River Junction Manifesto, 897-898
Williams, State and Local Government Incentives for Successful Enterprise Zone Initiatives, 965-971
Wolf, Accommodating Tensions in the Coastal Zone, 756-760

Zoning
   accessory uses, 242-244
   administration
     board of appeals (or adjustment), 181, 215-216, 359-362
     zoning administrator, 362
   amendments. *See* Amendments
   apartments, 185, 226-229
   arbitrary, 209-210, 230-232
   bulk controls, 227-229, 232-236, 257-259
   city power and, 175-177, 303
   classifications, 178-180, 209-210, 230-231, 236-244, 248-255
   comprehensive plan, in accordance with, 209, 213-215, 286, 315, 324, 333-335, 558-564, 1052-1056
   confiscatory, 202-203
   constitutionality, 178-195
   contract and conditional zoning, 283-289, 329
   critics of, 363-370
   cumulative, 180, 239, 245-246
   delegation to private parties, 492-497, 1071-1075, 1078-1084
   density regulation, 220-229, 279-282
   enabling acts, 166-177, 303
   enforcement, 181
   exclusionary. *See* Exclusionary Zoning
   fiscal zoning, 388-389, 405
   floating zone, 211-216
   height controls, 235-236
   history, 163-165, 187-189, 373-375, 506-507, 518-520, 556
   immigrants and, 167, 374
   impact zoning, 592-593
   incentive zoning, 256-269
   interim and temporary zoning, 168-175, 591-592
   nonconforming uses. *See* Nonconforming Uses
   noncumulative, 236-242, 244-246

nuisance and, 184
performance zoning, 276-279
planning and, 210-211, 560-567, 1048-1049, 1052-1056
popularity of, 163, 189-190
power to, 166-177, 212, 287, 493-495, 1079-1080
retroactivity, 308-311
special exceptions, use permits, 206-211, 216, 343, 356-362, 1071-1075, 1085-1088
spot zoning, 210, 286-287, 315, 322, 328-329
standard of judicial review, 186-187, 193-195, 240-241, 254-255, 331-335, 368-370, 404-405, 453-454, 464-465, 486, 499-500, 636-644
takings and, 199-200
use exclusions, 241, 244, 248-255, 476-504
variances. *See* Variances